Arnold's commentary on Colossians is a landmark work. Written by a lifelong specialist on Colossians, it presents the most detailed and up-to-date information on the religious and cultural background, meticulous if ultimately conservative reflections on authorship and style, and a sensitive interpretation of the text.

***Jörg Frey,*** Professor of New Testament,
University of Zurich, Switzerland

Clinton E. Arnold's *Colossians* is an invaluable resource that enriches both theological and archaeological understandings of this pivotal ancient city. As an archaeologist who has personally surveyed the site and its surroundings, I greatly appreciate the depth with which Arnold engages Colossae's archaeological history, ancient texts, and recent discoveries. His integration of archaeological data with biblical scholarship offers readers a well-rounded exploration of Colossae, providing not only a comprehensive bibliography but also fresh insights from ongoing research. This volume will undoubtedly serve as a critical reference for anyone studying the historical and cultural context of Colossae and its legacy.

***Barış Yener,*** Assistant Professor, Pamukkale University,
Denizli, Turkey

With Clinton Arnold's 1995 monograph, *The Colossian Syncretism*, he became a significant contributor to Colossian scholarship. This commentary is a mature reflection of a lifelong journey with Paul's letter. The journey for Arnold has been an enjoyable one, and it is reflected here. Arnold's work is a fine example of the present emphasis of responsibly incorporating contextual elements, whether literary or cultural, into his exegesis. This commentary combines thorough exegesis with impressive knowledge of both the ancient context and the history of interpretation. His exegesis is thorough and clear throughout. When significant problems arise, space is devoted to various views and a reasoned solution is presented. This commentary will be a standard for many years, providing students of Colossians with an excellent resource to explore this book.

***Joseph D. Fantin,*** Professor of New Testament,
Dallas Theological Seminary

Clint Arnold has written a landmark and magisterial commentary on Colossians, which will remain the standard work for decades to come. His depth of knowledge regarding the local belief systems in the Lycus Valley provides a richness of insight that informs the incisive exegetical comments throughout the volume. This treatment is the culmination of a lifetime of dedicated scholarship on Colossians, and readers will enlarge their understanding of this letter by engaging with Arnold's superb commentary.

***Paul Foster,*** Professor of New Testament and Early Christianity,
University of Edinburgh

This book is an impressive and groundbreaking work, a milestone not only in Paul's research but in the exploration of ancient religious history in general. Aside from all the benefits that come with an exhaustive commentary, Arnold's work is characterized by two enormous impulses: his plea for the authenticity of Colossians (i.e., the authorship of Paul) makes it a central contribution to exegesis, and his thorough analysis of the religious landscape in Colossae, in which the "philosophy" denounced by Paul played an important role, sets completely new accents in religious-historical research on ancient Asia Minor.

***Ulrich Huttner,*** Professor of Greek and Roman History,
Siegen University

Clint Arnold's commitment to historical research, theological exposition, and pastoral explanation gives pastors and scholars alike a commentary on Paul's letter to the believers in the congregation at Colossae that will serve as a North Star of Pauline scholarship in general and research into Colossians in particular for a long time to come.

***Eckhard Schnabel,*** Mary F. Rockefeller Emeritus Distinguished
Professor of New Testament, Gordon-Conwell Theological Seminary

This wonderfully rich and deeply informed commentary is a gift to both scholar and pastor. It is a goldmine, the fruit of a lifetime of research in Pauline literature and decades of work in this letter. Arnold has a keen eye for the political, social, geographical, religious, and literary contexts, as well as the particular challenges of those who first engaged with this letter. His wide-ranging and deeply informed introduction is a model of balanced discussion of magic and local belief, the rival teaching at Colossae, the problem of authorship, the author's situation, and the date and purpose of the text. Every passage of the letter is clarified and enlivened by this magisterial commentary.

***Graham H. Twelftree,*** Professor of New Testament and
Early Christianity, London School of Theology

Destined to become a classic commentary on Paul's letter to the Colossians, Clint Arnold's treatment is deeply and richly informed by the best that biblical scholarship has to offer and is brimming with historical, archaeological, social, linguistic, literary, exegetical, and theological insights on virtually every page.

***Constantine R. Campbell,*** Professor and Research Director,
Sydney College of Divinity

Clinton Arnold's commentary brings to bear his vast knowledge of primary sources to guide the reader with clarity and vibrancy through the labyrinth of various scholarly proposals about this letter to the Colossians. It is a definitive work that not only elucidates the historical situation that led Paul to write it but also expounds on the religious meaning of the text. Therefore, it will be an invaluable resource for academic researchers, ministers, and students.

***David E. Garland,*** Emeritus Professor of Christian Scriptures,
George W. Truett Theological Seminary, Baylor University

Clint Arnold's deep knowledge of the history, cultural context, and inscriptions pertaining to Colossae shine forth in this commentary. The relevant introductory questions are examined with clarity and comprehensiveness. At the same time, his exegesis of the letter is remarkably lucid as he interacts with other scholars, showing wise and mature judgment. This commentary will be a classic for years to come and is the fruit of Arnold's many years of study on Colossians.

***Thomas R. Schreiner,*** James Buchanan Harrison Professor of New
Testament Interpretation, The Southern Baptist Theological Seminary

The most detailed and comprehensive commentary ever written on Colossians! With this excellent work, Clint Arnold has set a new milestone in the interpretation of the epistle.

***Seyoon Kim,*** Senior Professor of New Testament,
Fuller Theological Seminary

In keeping with the excellent reputation of the Word Biblical Commentary series, Clinton Arnold presents a learned commentary on Colossians, rich in sophisticated analysis. Its depth of scholarship means that it may be read with great profit even by those who might sometimes disagree on such issues as authenticity, translation, and interpretation of manuscript evidence. Arnold's research on the historical setting and contribution to our understanding of the Colossian "philosophy" will make it indispensable reading for those working on Colossians for decades to come.

***Margaret Y. MacDonald,*** Professor, Department for the
Study of Religion, Saint Mary's University Halifax

Few scholars have labored over Colossians more extensively or effectively than Clinton E. Arnold. This learned, balanced, expansive commentary on Colossians, which has had a considerable gestation period, is a stunning achievement and will prove be a great gift to both the academy and the church. Arnold's technical, yet accessible, treatment of the letter is an altogether worthy addition to the highly esteemed Word Biblical Commentary series and should be added to the personal libraries of scholars, ministers, and students alike. I know of no better commentary on Colossians.

***Todd D. Still,*** Charles J. and Eleanor McLerran DeLancey Dean
Holder of the William M. Hinson Chair of Christian Scriptures,
Truett Theological Seminary, Baylor University

Clinton Arnold's commentary on Colossians is a high-water mark in the exegetical discipline, a tour de force that will inspire New Testament commentators and readers of the epistle for many years to come. Faced with the absence of any Colossian archaeology and the availability of only a very few inscriptions from the city, Arnold masterfully draws upon a wide selection of epigraphy and archaeology from Hierapolis, Laodicea, and other nearby sites to portray with vivid accuracy the historical and religious background of the Lycus Valley, establishing thereby the Greco-Roman semantic domains and first-century social conventions impacting both on Paul's language and the variegated worldviews of his auditors. This locality-specific investigation of Paul's world is enriched by Arnold's expertise in the Greco-Roman literature, the Greek magical papyri, amulets, and curses, which unveil elements of the syncretistic Colossian error. The Old Testament and the literature of Second Temple Judaism is also exhaustively plumbed in exegetical discussion, alerting readers to the distinctive theological heritage from which Paul's gospel drew. Arnold's meticulous theological exposition of the epistle's message engages the history of scholarship and analyses of literary criticism with rigor and rich insight, opening exciting new vistas for modern readers into the apostle's message to his original auditors. This is aided by excursuses that pursue significant issues of debate in further depth. Challenging scholarly points of contention in many areas (e.g., the epistle's pseudepigraphic authorship), Arnold's landmark commentary is a masterpiece and an exemplum of holistic exegesis for New Testament scholars.

***James R. Harrison,*** Distinguished Professor,
Sydney College of Divinity, Australia

# WORD BIBLICAL COMMENTARY

## Volumes

1 Genesis 1–15 .............. Gordon J. Wenham
2 Genesis 16–50 ............. Gordon J. Wenham
3 Exodus ...................... John I. Durham
4 Leviticus .................... John E. Hartley
5 Numbers** .................... Philip J. Budd
6a Deuteronomy 1:1–21:9, Second Edition ......... Duane L. Christensen
6b Deuteronomy 21:10–34:12 .................. Duane L. Christensen
7a Joshua 1–12, Second Edition .... Trent C. Butler
7b Joshua 13–24, Second Edition ... Trent C. Butler
8 Judges ....................... Trent C. Butler
9 Ruth–Esther ................ Frederic W. Bush
10 1 Samuel, Second Edition ....... Ralph W. Klein
11 2 Samuel .................... A. A. Anderson
12 1 Kings, Second Edition ....... Simon J. DeVries
13 2 Kings ......................... T. R. Hobbs
14 1 Chronicles** .................. Roddy Braun
15 2 Chronicles** ............ Raymond B. Dillard
16 Ezra–Nehemiah** ........ H. G. M. Williamson
17 Job 1–20 .................. David J. A. Clines
18a Job 21–37 ................. David J. A. Clines
18b Job 38–42 ................. David J. A. Clines
19 Psalms 1–50, Second Edition** ............... Peter C. Craigie, with Marvin E. Tate
20 Psalms 51–100** .............. Marvin E. Tate
21 Psalms 101–150, Revised Edition** ............ Leslie C. Allen
22 Proverbs ..................... Roland Murphy
23a Ecclesiastes .................. Roland Murphy
23b Song of Songs/Lamentations ..... Duane Garrett and Paul House
24 Isaiah 1–33, Revised Edition .. John D. W. Watts
25 Isaiah 34–66, Revised Edition .. John D. W. Watts
26 Jeremiah 1–25 .. Peter C. Craigie, Page H. Kelley, and Joel F. Drinkard Jr.
27 Jeremiah 26–52 ............. Gerald L. Keown, Pamela J. Scalise, and Thomas G. Smothers
28 Ezekiel 1–19 .................. Leslie C. Allen
29 Ezekiel 20–48 ................. Leslie C. Allen
30 Daniel, Revised Edition ........ John Goldingay
31 Hosea–Jonah** ................ Douglas Stuart
32 Micah–Malachi** ............. Ralph L. Smith
33a Matthew 1–13** ............ Donald A. Hagner
33b Matthew 14–28** ........... Donald A. Hagner
34a Mark 1–8:26** .............. Robert A. Guelich
34b Mark 8:27–16:20** ............ Craig A. Evans
35a Luke 1–9:20** .................. John Nolland
35b Luke 9:21–18:34** .............. John Nolland
35c Luke 18:35–24:53** ............. John Nolland
36 John, Second Edition** ............. George R. Beasley-Murray
37a Acts 1–9:42 .................... Steve Walton
37b Acts 9:43–19* ................... Steve Walton
37c Acts 20–28* ..................... Steve Walton
38a Romans 1–8** .............. James D. G. Dunn
38b Romans 9–16** ............. James D. G. Dunn
39 1 Corinthians* ......................... TBA
40 2 Corinthians, Second Edition ... Ralph P. Martin
41 Galatians** .......... Richard N. Longenecker
42 Ephesians** ............... Andrew T. Lincoln
43 Philippians ............... Ralph P. Martin and Gerald F. Hawthorne
44a Colossians* ................ Clinton E. Arnold
44b Philemon* ............. Clinton E. Arnold and Daniel K. Darko
45 1 & 2 Thessalonians, Revised Edition .......... Seyoon Kim and F. F. Bruce
46 Pastoral Epistles .......... William D. Mounce
47a Hebrews 1–8** .............. William L. Lane
47b Hebrews 9–13** ............. William L. Lane
48 James ...................... Ralph P. Martin
49 1 Peter** ................ J. Ramsey Michaels
50 Jude, 2 Peter** ........... Richard J. Bauckham
51 1, 2, 3, John, Revised Edition** ...... Stephen S. Smalley
52a Revelation 1–5** ............... David E. Aune
52b Revelation 6–16** .............. David E. Aune
52c Revelation 17–22** ............. David E. Aune

---

**Forthcoming as of 2024*
***Revised/new edition forthcoming as of 2024*

# 44A WORD BIBLICAL COMMENTARY

## Colossians

Second Edition

CLINTON E. ARNOLD

Old Testament Editor: Nancy L. deClaissé-Walford
New Testament Editor: David P. Capes

*To Barbara*

ZONDERVAN ACADEMIC

*Colossians, Volume 44A*


Published in Grand Rapids, Michigan, by Zondervan. Zondervan is a registered trademark of The Zondervan Corporation, L.L.C., a wholly owned subsidiary of HarperCollins Christian Publishing, Inc.

Requests for information should be addressed to customercare@harpercollins.com.

Zondervan titles may be purchased in bulk for educational, business, fundraising, or sales promotional use. For information, please email SpecialMarkets@Zondervan.com.

Library of Congress Cataloging-in-Publication Data

Names: Arnold, Clinton E., author.
Title: Colossians / Clinton E. Arnold.
Description: Second edition. | Grand Rapids, Michigan : Zondervan Academic, [2024] | Series: Word biblical commentary ; 44a | Includes bibliographical references and index.
Identifiers: LCCN 2024024209 (print) | LCCN 2024024210 (ebook) | ISBN 9780310125211 (hardcover) | ISBN 9780310125228 (ebook)
Subjects: LCSH: Bible. Colossians--Commentaries.
Classification: LCC BS2715.53 .A76 2024 (print) | LCC BS2715.53 (ebook) | DDC 227/.707--dc23/eng/20240807
LC record available at https://lccn.loc.gov/2024024209
LC ebook record available at https://lccn.loc.gov/2024024210



*Printed in the United States of America*

25 26 27 28 29 30 31 32 33 34 35 /TRM/ 15 14 13 12 11 10 9 8 7 6 5 4 3 2 1

# Contents



## Introduction



## Text and Commentary

# Editorial Preface

The launching of the Word Biblical Commentary in 1977 brought to fulfillment the dream of a new commentary series on the books of the Bible. The founding editorial board determined to include a number of features in the commentary series that were distinctive at the time and remain essential features of a trustworthy commentary in the twenty-first century.

The original editorial board sought authors from around the world who, while broadly identified as evangelical in its positive, historic sense, represented a rich diversity of denominational allegiances, and who could offer the best in biblical scholarship. It was important for the editors that while these authors were scholars actively engaged in teaching in university and seminary settings, they were also involved in church ministry. That commitment continues today as revisions and updates are undertaken on various volumes in the series.

The board determined that the layout of the commentary series would follow a format consciously designed to assist readers at different levels. First, authors were to use their own *Translations* of the texts as the basis of their comments and exegesis, examining carefully the textual, linguistic, and structural evidence and providing ample explanatory *Notes*. Thus, in the words of the original editorial board, while the series is based on the biblical languages, "it seeks to make the technical and scholarly approach to a theological understanding of Scripture understandable by—and useful to—the fledging student, the working minister, and colleagues in the guild of professional scholars and teachers as well." As revisions and updates are produced, the same careful attention to translation has been maintained. Second, an extensive *Bibliography* at the beginning of each section provided the reader with ample information on the then state of scholarship and an opportunity to dig deeper. That continues in the revisions and updates with only slight changes to the format of the bibliographies. Third, the section titled *Form/Structure/Setting* discussed the redaction, genre, sources, and tradition. They concern the origin of the text, its canonical form, and its relation to the biblical and extrabiblical contexts in order to illuminate the structure and character of the text. And finally, the *Comment* and *Explanation* sections first offered a verse-by-verse interpretation of the text and dialogue with interpreters, engaging with current opinion and scholarly research and then discussing its relevance to the ongoing life of faith communities today. These two important sections are maintained in the revised and updated volumes, and to aid in reading, footnotes are now employed in place of in-text citations. The ongoing revisions and updates also extensively incorporate new scholarship and provide insights into the relevance of the biblical texts for faith communities in the twenty-first century.

The current editorial board, in the spirit of the founding editorial board, pray that "if these aims come anywhere near realization, the intention of the editors will have been met, and the labor of our team of contributors rewarded."

*Old Testament Editor: Nancy L. deClaissé-Walford*
*New Testament Editor: David B. Capes*

# Author's Preface

The letter to the Colossians has been my companion for many years. I first began research on it in 1983 after moving to Aberdeen, Scotland to work on my doctorate under the supervision of I. Howard Marshall. During that time, I benefitted from many conversations about the letter with faculty and student colleagues at the university. These included Robin Barbour, Ruth Edwards, Timothy Geddert, Gary Shogren, Conrad Gempf, Robert Yarbrough, Phil Towner, and many more. My research was also influenced during those years through my trips to Tyndale House, Cambridge, and interaction with Murray Harris, Colin Hemer, and others. I have fond memories of Colin showing me his numerous slides of Asia Minor and many hours of conversation over lunches at Caius College talking about inscriptions and all things Asia Minor. Colossians then became the focus of an intense period of study during eight months of post-doctoral research at the University of Tübingen in 1991 under the mentorship of Peter Stuhlmacher, thanks to an ATS "younger scholars" grant. Tübingen was the place of many fruitful discussions about Colossians not only with Professor Stuhlmacher but also with Martin Hengel and Otto Betz. A trip to Scotland during that time enabled me to spend a day with Robert McL. Wilson, who was in the process of writing his ICC commentary on Colossians. The research from that study leave resulted in my 1995 monograph, *The Colossian Syncretism*.

In 2004, I was approached by Ralph Martin about contributing the replacement volume on Colossians and Philemon for the Word Biblical Commentary series since Peter O'Brien would be unable to revise his work because of his health and other pressing commitments. After an extended conversation with Peter and receiving his blessing to work on this project, I signed the contract and looked forward to immersing myself in writing this commentary after completing some other projects before me. About the time I was beginning to work on the commentary in earnest, I was called by my institution to serve as its academic dean. I was grateful for the opportunity to serve my faculty colleages and students in this way, but I knew that it would slow my progress in completing this volume considerably. Throughout the ten years I served as dean, Colossians was an old friend that gave me enjoyable and refreshing breaks from the rigors of meetings, budgets, assessments, and other administrative responsibilities. Savoring the words of this gem of a letter often refreshed my soul and brought great encouragement.

My service as dean concluded in the summer of 2022, and the senior administration of Biola University graciously granted me a sabbatical leave for the fall semester. This afforded me the opportunity to bring this manuscript to a conclusion.

I have long had an interest in the rise of Christianity in Asia Minor and the overall religious, social, political, and historical context of the challenges facing Christianity in that region. This interest will quickly become apparent to the readers of this commentary. I have made extensive use of the inscriptions found in Asia Minor, as well as archaeological discoveries and historical evidence. So much has been uncovered in recent years in the excavations of Laodicea, Hierapolis, and now Tripolis. The disappointment was that Colossae had never been excavated. But that is happily changing, and the announcement has been made by Pamukkale University that Colossae will be excavated under the direction of Bariş Yener. This is incredibly good news to all of us who have an interest in Colossae and have wondered what remains buried underneath that mound. I have often quipped that I wonder how much I got wrong in my historical descriptions of Colossae and Colossians and how many apologies I will need to issue! Hopefully, excavation will begin soon, and we will all benefit from the discovery of inscriptions, coins, statuary, and public buildings—all of which will shed important light on the letter to the Colossians.

There has been a cascade of important studies on the letter to the Colossians over the last thirty years. Numerous important monographs have been published that have helped bring new and significant insights into the letter. These include in-depth studies by Chris Beetham, Allan Bevere, Alan Cadwallader, Rosemary Canavan, Robert Cavin, Adam Copenhaver, Richard DeMaris, Nicole Frank, Matthew Gordley, John Paul Heil, Ulrich Huttner, Mark Kiley, Harry Maier, Troy Martin, Peter Müller, Tom Sappington, Ian Smith, Angela Standhartinger, Christian Stettler, George van Kooten, Walter Wilson, and others.

Of course, there are numerous essays on Colossians published in the journals during the same time period as well as new commentaries, studies on Pauline theology, and academic publications of various sorts with relevance to Colossians. It is really impossible to give each of these the attention they deserve, but I have endeavored to learn as much as I possibly can from these over the years. Regrettably, two important monographs on Colossians appeared too late to be taken into account for this commentary: Alan Cadwallader's *Colossae, Colossians, Philemon*, and Roy Jeal's *Exploring Colossians*.

I also have a great appreciation for many of the older commentaries. Pride of place goes to J. B. Lightfoot's famous commentary on Colossians, which I have consulted extensively in writing this volume. Many of these older commentaries remain rich, insightful, and helpful, especially with their great attention to fine details of the text. Consequently, you will find references to A. L. Williams, H. Moule, J. Eadie, C. Ellicott, H. A. W. Meyer, A. S. Peake, and others in the pages of this volume.

I am grateful to Mohr Siebeck for permission to use material from my 1995 WUNT monograph, *The Colossian Syncretism*. I am also thankful for permission from the editor of *JETS* to use portions of my 2012 article, "Sceva, Solomon, and Shamanism."

Finally, I dedicate this volume to my wife and dearest friend, Barbara. She has entered deeply into a love of Colossae, Colossians, and western Turkey. Since our first trip there in 1985, she has joined me in chasing down inscriptions at Claros, trudging over every inch of the site of Colossae (and numerous others), spending countless hours in the museums, and dialoguing with me about so many facets of this marvelous letter. I remain deeply grateful for her encouragement and support of my work on this project for so many years.

A commentary is not written for the benefit of the author, but of the readers. It has been and continues to be my prayer that what is written here may prove useful for the teaching and preaching of this incredible and well-loved letter that is part of our Scripture.

*Clinton E. Arnold*
*Talbot School of Theology (Biola University)*
*La Mirada, CA*
*Summer 2024*

# Abbreviations

Abbreviations are according to the *SBL Handbook of Style*. Those not listed in the handbook are given below. I have also listed the abbreviations for many publications of inscriptions and papyri that may not be commonly known by biblical scholars. Abbreviations of all papyri are according to the *Checklist of Editions of Greek, Latin, Demotic and Coptic Papyri, Ostraca and Tablets* (web edition) and are not included in the list below.

| | |
|---|---|
| AB | Anchor Bible |
| *ABD* | *Anchor Bible Dictionary*. Edited by D. N. Freedman. 6 vols. New York: Doubleday, 1992 |
| ACCS | Ancient Christian Commentary on Scripture |
| AJEC | Ancient Judaism and Early Christianity |
| *AJSR* | *Association for Jewish Studies Review* |
| *Alt. v. Hierapolis* | *Altertümer von Hierapolis*. Edited by C. Humann, C. Cichorius, W. Judeich, and F. Winter. Jahrbuch des Kaiserlich Deutschen Archäologischen Instituts, Ergänzungsheft 4. Berlin: Georg Reimer, 1898 |
| AnBib | Analecta Biblica |
| *ANRW* | *Aufstieg und Niedergang der römischen Welt: Geschichte und Kultur Roms im Spiegel der neueren Forschung*. Part 2, *Principat*. Edited by H. Temporini and Wolfgang Haase. Berlin: de Gruyter, 1972– |
| *AnSt* | *Anatolian Studies* |
| ANTC | Abingdon New Testament Commentaries |
| ANTF | Arbeiten zur neutestamentlichen Textforschung |
| *APF* | *Archiv für Papyrusforschung* |
| ATANT | Abhandlungen zur Theologie des Alten und Neuen Testaments |
| AUS | American University Studies |
| *AUSS* | *Andrews University Seminary Studies* |
| AYBRL | Anchor Yale Bible Reference Library |
| *BA* | *Biblical Archaeologist* |
| BBB | Bonner biblische Beiträge |
| BBR | Bulletin for Biblical Research |
| *BCH* | *Bulletin de correspondence hellénique* |
| BECNT | Baker Exegetical Commentary on the New Testament |
| BETL | Bibliotheca Ephemeridum Theologicarum Lovaniensium |
| BGBE | Beiträge zur Geschichte der biblischen Exegese |
| *BGU* | *Aegyptische Urkunden aus den Königlichen Staatlichen Museen zu Berlin, Griechische Urkunden*. 15 vols. Edited by W. Schubart et al. Berlin: Weidmann, 1895–1937 |

| | |
|---|---|
| BibInt | Biblical Interpretation Series |
| BJS | Brown Judaic Studies |
| BNTC | Black's New Testament Commentaries |
| *BSac* | *Bibliotheca Sacra* |
| *BT* | *The Bible Translator* |
| BWANT | Beiträge zur Wissenschaft vom Alten und Neuen Testament |
| *BWK* | *Die Beichtinschriften Westkleinasians*. Edited by G. Petzl. Epigraphica Anatolica 22. Bonn: Habelt, 1994 |
| BZAW | Beihefte zur Zeitschrift für die alttestamentliche Wissenschaft |
| BZNW | Beihefte zur Zeitschrift für die neutestamentliche Wissenschaft |
| CBET | Contributions to Biblical Exegesis and Theology |
| *CBQ* | *Catholic Biblical Quarterly* |
| CEV | Contemporary English Version |
| *CIG* | *Corpus Inscriptionum Graecarum*. Edited by August Boeckh. 4 Vols. Berlin: Reimer, 1828–1877 |
| *CIL* | *Corpus Inscriptionum Latinarum*. Berlin, 1862– |
| ConBNT | Coniectanea Biblica: New Testament Series |
| *CRAI* | *Comptes rendus de l'Académie des inscriptions et belles-lettres* |
| CRINT | Compendia Rerum Iudaicarum ad Novum Testamentum |
| *CTJ* | *Calvin Theological Journal* |
| *CTQ* | *Concordia Theological Quarterly* |
| *CurBR* | *Currents in Biblical Research* |
| *DNTB* | *Dictionary of New Testament Background*. Edited by C. A. Evans and S. E. Porter. Downers Grove, IL: InterVarsity Press, 2000 |
| *DOTP* | *Dictionary of the Old Testament Prophets*. Edited by M. J. Boda and J. G. McConville. Downers Grove, IL: InterVarsity Press, 2012 |
| *DSD* | *Dead Sea Discoveries* |
| *EA* | *Epigraphica Anatolica* |
| *EC* | *Early Christianity* |
| ECAM | Early Christianity in Asia Minor |
| *EDNT* | *Exegetical Dictionary of the New Testament*. Edited by H. Balz and G. Schneider. ET. 3 vols. Grand Rapids: Eerdmans, 1990–1993 |
| EPRO | Etudes préliminaires aux religions orientales dans l'empire romain |
| *ESTJ* | *T&T Clark Encyclopedia of Second Temple Judaism*. 2 vols. Edited by D. Gurtner and L. Stuckenbruck. London: T&T Clark, 2019 |
| *ETL* | *Ephemerides Theologicae Lovanienses* |
| *EvQ* | *Evangelical Quarterly* |
| *EvT* | *Evangelische Theologie* |
| *ExAud* | *Ex Auditu* |

| | |
|---|---|
| *ExpTim* | *Expository Times* |
| FRLANT | Forschungen zur Religion und Literatur des Alten und Neuen Testaments |
| GNT | Grundrisse zum Neuen Testament |
| *GRBS* | *Greek, Roman, and Byzantine Studies* |
| GTA | Göttinger theologischer Arbeiten |
| *GTJ* | *Grace Theological Journal* |
| *HJP* | *The History of the Jewish People in the Age of Jesus Christ.* Emil Schürer. 3 vols. Revised and edited by G. Vermes, F. Millar, and M. Goodman. Edinburgh: T&T Clark, 1973–1986 |
| HNT | Handbuch zum Neuen Testament |
| HThKNT | Herders Theologischer Kommentar zum Neuen Testament |
| *HTR* | *Harvard Theological Review* |
| HTS | Harvard Theological Studies |
| IBC | Interpretation: A Bible Commentary for Teaching and Preaching |
| ICC | International Critical Commentary |
| *IEJ* | *Israel Exploration Journal* |
| *IEph* | *Die Inschriften von Ephesos.* Edited by H. Engelmann, D. Knibbe, and R. Merkelbach. Parts 1–8. IGSK 13. Bonn: Rudolf Habelt, 1980–84 |
| *IErythr* | *Die Inschriften von Erythrai und Klazomenai.* 2 Vols. Edited by H. Engelmann and R. Merkelbach. IGSK 1. Bonn: Rudolf Habelt, 1972 |
| *IG* | *Inscriptiones Graecae* |
| *IG* X.2.1 | *Inscriptiones Thessalonicae et Viciniae.* Part 2, No. 2. Edited by C. Edson. Berlin: de Gruyter, 1972 |
| *IGRR* | *Inscriptiones Graecae ad res Romanas pertinentes.* 4 vols. Edited by R. Cagnat, J. Touvain, P. Jouguet, and G. Lafaye. Paris: Ernest Leroux, 1906–1964 |
| IGSK | Inschriften Griechischer Städte aus Kleinasien |
| *IGUR* | *Inscriptiones Graecae Urbis Romae.* 4 Vols. Edited by L. Moretti. Rome: Istituo Italiono pur la Storia Antica, 1968–1991 |
| *IJO* | *Inscriptiones Judaicae Orientis.* 3 Vols. Edited by D. Noy et al. TSAJ 99, 101, 102. Tübingen: Mohr Siebeck, 2004 |
| *IKibyra* | *Die Inschriften von Kibyra.* Edited by T. Corsten. IGSK 60. Bonn: Rudolf Habelt, 2002 |
| *IKios* | *Die Inschriften von Kios.* Edited by T. Corsten. IGSK 29. Bonn: Rudolf Habelt, 1985 |
| *IKyme* | *Die Inschriften von Kyme.* Edited by H. Engelmann. IGSK 5. Bonn: Rudolf Habelt, 1976 |
| *ILaodikeia* | *Die Inschriften von Laodikeia am Lykos.* IGSK 49. Bonn: Rudolf Habelt, 1997 |

| | |
|---|---|
| *IMagnesia* | *Die Inschriften von Magnesia am Maeander.* Edited by O. Kern. Berlin: Spemann, 1900 |
| *IMilet* | *Milet, Ergebnisse der Ausgrabungen und Untersuchungen seit dem Jahre 1899.* 16 Vols. Edited by T. Wiegend. Berlin: de Gruyter, 1906–1936 |
| *Int* | *Interpretation* |
| *IPerge* | *Die Inschriften von Perge.* 3 Vols. IGSK 46–48. Bonn: Rudolf Habelt, 1992 |
| *IPriene* | *Inschriften von Priene.* Edited by C. J. Fredrich and F. H. von Gaertringen. Berlin: de Gruyter, 1968 |
| *IPrusaOlymp* | *Die Inschriften von Prusa ad Olympum.* 2 Vols. Edited by T. Corsten. IGSK 39–40. Bonn: Rudolf Habelt, 1991, 1993 |
| *ISmyrna* | *Die Inschriften von Smyrna.* Edited by G. Petzl. IGSK 24/1–2. Bonn: Rudolf Habelt, 1982–1990 |
| *IStratonikeia* | *Die Inschriften von Stratonikeia.* 2 Parts. Edited by M. Cetin Sahin. IGSK 21–22. Bonn: Rudolf Habelt, 1981, 1982 |
| *ITQ* | *Irish Theological Quarterly* |
| IVPNTC | IVP New Testament Commentary Series |
| *JANESCU* | *Journal of the Ancient Near Eastern Society of Columbia University* |
| *JBL* | *Journal of Biblical Literature* |
| *JECS* | *Journal of Early Christian Studies* |
| *JETS* | *Journal of the Evangelical Theological Society* |
| *JGRChJ* | *Journal of Greco-Roman Christianity and Judaism* |
| *JHS* | *Journal of Hellenic Studies* |
| *JJS* | *Journal of Jewish Studies* |
| JJTPSup | Supplements to the Journal of Jewish Thought and Philosophy |
| *JLAnt* | *Journal of Late Antiquity* |
| *JÖAI* | *Jahreshefte des Österreichischen archäologischen Instituts* |
| *JRA* | *Journal of Roman Archaeology* |
| JRASup | Journal of Roman Archaeology Supplement |
| *JRS* | *Journal of Roman Studies* |
| JSJSup | Supplements to the Journal for the Study of Judaism |
| *JSNT* | *Journal for the Study of the New Testament* |
| JSNTSup | Journal for the Study of the New Testament Supplement Series |
| *JSP* | *Journal for the Study of the Pseudepigrapha* |
| *JSPL* | *Journal for the Study of Paul and His Letters* |
| JSPSup | Journal for the Study of the Pseudepigrapha Supplement Series |
| *JSS* | *Journal of Semitic Studies* |
| *JTI* | *Journal of Theological Interpretation* |
| *JTS* | *Journal of Theological Studies* |
| KEK | Kritisch-exegetischer Kommentar über das Neue Testament |
| LEC | Library of Early Christianity |

| | |
|---|---|
| LEH | Lust, J., E. Eynikel, and K. Hauspie, eds. *Greek-English Lexicon of the Septuagint*. Rev. ed. Stuttgart: Deutsche Bibelgesellschaft, 2003 |
| LSTS | Library of Second Temple Studies |
| LUÅ | Lunds universitets årsskrift |
| *MAMA* | *Monumenta Asiae Minoris Antiqua*. 11 Vols. Edited by W. M. Calder et al. Manchester and London, 1928–1993 |
| MM | Moulton, J. H., and G. Milligan. *The Vocabulary of the Greek Testament*. London, 1930. Repr., Peabody, MA: Hendrickson, 1997 |
| MNTC | Moffatt New Testament Commentary |
| NAC | New American Commentary |
| NCB | New Century Bible |
| NCCS | New Covenant Commentary Series |
| *Neot* | *Neotestamentica* |
| NETS | New English Translation of the Septuagint |
| *NewDocs* | *New Documents Illustrating Early Christianity*. Edited by Greg H. R. Horsley and Stephen Llewelyn. 10 vols. North Ryde, NSW: The Ancient History Documentary Research Centre, Macquarie University, 1981–. Repr., Grand Rapids: Eerdmans, 1997– |
| NHC | Nag Hammadi Codices |
| NHS | Nag Hammadi Studies |
| NICNT | New International Commentary on the New Testament |
| *NIDNTT* | *New International Dictionary of New Testament Theology*. Edited by Colin Brown. 4 vols. Grand Rapids: Zondervan, 1975–1978 |
| *NIDNTTE* | *New International Dictionary of New Testament Theology and Exegesis*. Edited by M. Silva. 5 vols. Grand Rapids: Zondervan, 2014 |
| NIGTC | New International Greek Testament Commentary |
| NIV | New International Version |
| NIVAC | NIV Application Commentary |
| *NovT* | *Novum Testamentum* |
| NovTSup | Supplements to Novum Testamentum |
| NRSV | New Revised Standard Version (1989) |
| NRSVue | New Revised Standard Version, Updated Edition (2021) |
| NSBT | New Studies in Biblical Theology |
| NTAbh | Neutestamentliche Abhandlungen |
| NTL | New Testament Library |
| NTOA | Novum Testamentum et Orbis Antiquus |
| *NTS* | *New Testament Studies* |
| NTTSD | New Testament Tools, Studies, and Documents |

| | |
|---|---|
| *OCD*[3] | *Oxford Classical Dictionary.* Edited by Simon Hornblower and Antony Spawforth. 3rd ed. Oxford: Oxford University Press, 1996 |
| *OGIS* | *Orientis Graeci Inscriptiones Selectae.* Edited by W. Dittenberger. Supplementum Sylloges Inscriptionum Graecarum. Volumen Alterum. Hildesheim/Zürich/New York: Georg Olms, 1986 (Reprint of Leipzig: Herzel, 1903–1905) |
| ÖTK | Ökumenischer Taschenbuch-Kommentar |
| *PGM* | *Papyri Graecae Magicae: Die griechischen Zauberpapyri.* Edited by Karl Preisendanz. 2nd ed. Stuttgart: Teubner, 1973–1974 |
| *P.Oxy.* | *The Oxyrhynchus Papyri.* Edited by B. P. Grenfell et al. London: Egypt Exploration Fund, 1898– |
| *PRSt* | *Perspectives in Religious Studies* |
| PW | *Paulys Real-Encyclopädie der classischen Altertumswissenschaft.* New edition by Georg Wissowa and Wilhelm Kroll. 50 vols. in 84 parts. Stuttgart: Metzler and Druckenmüller, 1894–1980 |
| PWSup | Supplement to PW |
| QD | Quaestiones Disputatae |
| *RAC* | *Reallexikon für Antike und Christentum.* Edited by T. Klauser et al. Stuttgart: Hiersemann, 1950– |
| *RAr* | *Revue archéologique* |
| *RB* | *Revue biblique* |
| *ResQ* | *Restoration Quarterly* |
| *RevExp* | *Review and Expositor* |
| *RevQ* | *Revue de Qumran* |
| *RGG*[3] | *Religion in Geschichte und Gegenwart.* 3rd ed. Edited by Kurt Galling. 6 vols. Tubingen: Mohr Siebeck, 1957–1962 |
| RGRW | Religions in the Graeco-Roman World |
| RNT | Regensburger Neues Testament |
| *RSPT* | *Revue des sciences philosophiques et théologiques* |
| *SBJT* | *Southern Baptist Journal of Theology* |
| SBLDS | Society of Biblical Literature Dissertation Series |
| SBLMS | Society of Biblical Literature Monograph Series |
| SBLSBS | Society of Biblical Literature Sources for Biblical Study |
| SBM | Stuttgarter biblische Monographien |
| SBR | Studies of the Bible and Its Reception |
| SBS | Stuttgarter Bibelstudien |
| SBT | Studies in Biblical Theology |
| *SEÅ* | *Svensk exegetisk årsbok* |
| *SEG* | *Supplementum Epigraphicum Graecum* |
| *SIG* | *Sylloge Inscriptionum Graecarum.* Edited by Wilhelm Dittenberger. 4 vols. 3rd ed. Leipzig: Hirzel, 1915–1924 |
| SJLA | Studies in Judaism in Late Antiquity |

| | |
|---|---|
| *SJT* | *Scottish Journal of Theology* |
| SKKNT | Stuttgarter kleiner Kommentar, Neues Testament |
| SNT | Studien zum Neuen Testament |
| SNTSMS | Society for New Testament Studies Monograph Series |
| *SNTSU* | *Studien zum Neuen Testament und seiner Umwelt* |
| SP | Sacra Pagina |
| *SR* | *Studies in Religion* |
| STDJ | Studies on the Texts of the Desert of Judah |
| SUNT | Studien zur Umwelt des Neuen Testaments |
| *TAM* | *Tituli Asiae Minoris*. 5 vols. Edited by E. Kalinka et al. Vindobonae: Hoelde-Pichler-Tempsky, 1920–1989 |
| *TBei* | *Theologische Beiträge* |
| *TDNT* | *Theological Dictionary of the New Testament*. Edited by G. Kittel and G. Friedrich. Translated by G. W. Bromiley. 10 vols. Grand Rapids: Eerdmans, 1964–1976 |
| TENTS | Texts and Editions for New Testament Study |
| THGNT | *The Greek New Testament, Produced at Tyndale House, Cambridge*. Edited by Dirk Jongkind and Peter Williams. Wheaton, IL: Crossway, 2017 |
| THKNT | Theologischer Handkommentar zum Neuen Testament |
| *TJ* | *Trinity Journal* |
| TKNT | Theologischer Kommentar zum Neuen Testament |
| *TLZ* | *Theologische Literaturzeitung* |
| TNTC | Tyndale New Testament Commentaries |
| *TQ* | *Theologische Quartalschrift* |
| TR | Textus Receptus |
| TSAJ | Texts and Studies in Ancient Judaism |
| *TTKi* | *Tidsskrift for Teologi og Kirke* |
| TU | Texte und Untersuchungen |
| TUGAL | Texte und Untersuchungen zur Geschichte der altchristlichen Literatur |
| *TynBul* | *Tyndale Bulletin* |
| *TZ* | *Theologische Zeitschrift* |
| UNT | Untersuchungen zum Neuen Testament |
| *VC* | *Vigiliae Christianae* |
| VTSup | Supplements to Vetus Testamentum |
| *WD* | *Wort und Dienst* |
| WGRW | Writings from the Greco-Roman World |
| WGRWSup | Writings from the Greco-Roman World Supplement Series |
| WLAW | Wisdom Literature from the Ancient World |
| WMANT | Wissenschaftliche Monographien zum Alten und Neuen Testament |
| *WTJ* | *Westminster Theological Journal* |

| | |
|---|---|
| ZECNT | Zondervan Exegetical Commentary on the New Testament |
| *ZIBBC* | *Zondervan Illustrated Bible Backgrounds Commentary*. Edited by C. E. Arnold. Grand Rapids: Zondervan, 2002 |
| *ZNW* | *Zeitschrift für die neutestamentliche Wissenschaft und die Kunde der älteren Kirche* |
| *ZPE* | *Zeitschrift für Papyrologie und Epigraphik* |
| *ZRGG* | *Zeitschrift für Religions- und Geistesgeschichte* |
| *ZTK* | *Zeitschrift für Theologie und Kirche* |

# Notes on Texts and Versions

All English translations of the NT are the author's own translation unless otherwise noted by the following convention (e.g., Rom 1:3 NRSV).

All English translations of the OT Apocrypha are from the NRSV. All English translations of the OT Pseudepigrapha are from James H. Charlesworth, ed., *Old Testament Pseudepigrapha*, 2 vols. (New York: Doubleday, 1983).

All English translations of the Dead Sea Scrolls are from Florentino García Martínez, *The Dead Sea Scrolls Translated: The Qumran Texts in English*, 2nd ed. (Grand Rapids: Eerdmans, 1996). The line numbers cited for 1QH will follow García Martínez with the alternative line numbers of Martin Abegg provided in brackets (e.g., [1QH III.]).

All English translations of the Babylonian Talmud are from Jacob Neusner, *The Babylonian Talmud: Translation and Commentary*, 22 vols. (Peabody, MA: Hendrickson, 2006).

All English translations of Greek and Roman literature are from the volumes of the Loeb Classical Library (LCL) unless otherwise indicated.

All English translations of early Christian literature are from the volumes of the Ante-Nicene Fathers (ANF) and Nicene and Post-Nicene Fathers (NPNF) unless otherwise indicated.

Greek texts of papyrus documents are readily available at Papyri.info, https://papyri.info, which aggregates texts and data from the Advanced Papyrological Information System (APIS), the Duke Databank of Documentary Papyri (DDbDP), and other sources.

Greek texts of many inscriptions are readily available at https://epigraphy.packhum.org, a site created by the Packard Humanities Institute.

# General Bibliography


## *Ancient Sources*

### *Editions of the Bible*

*Biblia Hebraica Stuttgartensia.* Edited by K. Elliger and W. Rudolph. Stuttgart: Deutsche Bibelgesellschaft, 1977.

*The Greek New Testament.* United Bible Societies, 5th ed. Edited by B. Aland, K. Aland, J. Karavidopoulos, C. M. Martini, and B. Metzger. Stuttgart: Deutsche Bibelgesellschaft, 2014.

*The Greek New Testament, Produced at Tyndale House, Cambridge.* Edited by Dirk Jongkind and Peter Williams. Wheaton, IL: Crossway, 2017.

*Novum Testamentum Graece.* 28th Revised Edition. Edited by B. Aland, K. Aland, J. Karavidopoulos, C. M. Martini, and B. Metzger. Stuttgart: Deutsche Bibelgesellschaft, 2012.

*Novum Testamenti Graece: Editio Octava Critica Maior.* 2 Vols. Edited by C. Tischendorf. Leipzig: Giesecke and Devrient, 1869, 1872.

*Septuaginta.* Edited by A. Rahlfs. Stuttgart: Deutsche Bibelgesellschaft, 1979.

*Septuaginta.* Edited by A. Rahlfs and R. Hanhart. 2nd ed. Stuttgart: Deutsche Bibelgesellschaft, 2007.

### *Second Temple Jewish Sources*

*The Apocrypha and Pseudepigrapha of the Old Testament.* 2 vols. Edited by R. H. Charles. Oxford: Clarendon, 1913.

*The Babylonian Talmud: Translation and Commentary.* 22 vols. Edited and translated by J. Neusner. Peabody, MA: Hendrikson, 2006.

*The Dead Sea Scrolls: A New Translation.* Edited by M. O. Wise, M. G. Abegg, and E. M. Cook. San Francisco: HarperSanFrancisco, 2005.

*The Dead Sea Scrolls Translated: The Qumran Texts in English.* 2nd ed. Edited by F. G. Martinez. Grand Rapids: Eerdmans, 1996.

*The Mishnah.* Translated with Introduction and Notes by H. Danby. Oxford: Oxford University Press, 1933.

*The Old Testament Pseudepigrapha.* 2 vols. Edited by J. H. Charlesworth. New York: Doubleday, 1983.

*Old Testament Pseudepigrapha: More Noncanonical Scriptures.* Vol. 1. Edited by R. Bauckham, J. R. Davila, and A. Panayotov. Grand Rapids: Eerdmans, 2013.

*Qumran Cave 11: Part 2: 11Q2–18 and 11Q20–31.* Edited by F. G. Martinez, E. J. C. Tigcheaar, A. S. van der Woude, and E. D. Herbert. DJD 23. Oxford: Clarendon, 1998.

*Sepher Ha-Razim: The Book of the Mysteries.* Translated and edited by M. A. Morgan. SBL Texts and Translations 25, Pseudepigrapha Series 11. Chico: Scholars Press, 1983.

*The Shi'ur Qomah: Texts and Recensions.* Translated and Edited by M. S. Cohen. TSAJ 9. Tübingen: Mohr Siebeck, 1985.

*Songs of the Sabbath Sacrifice: A Critical Edition.* Edited with Introduction and Notes by C. Newsom. Harvard Semitic Studies 27. Atlanta: Scholars Press, 1985.

*Synopse zur Hekhlot-Literatur.* Edited by P. Schäfer. TSAJ 2. Tübingen: Mohr Siebeck, 1981.

*Übersetzung der Hekhalot Literatur.* Edited by P. Schäfer et al. 4 vols. TSAJ 17, 22, 29, 46. Tübingen: Mohr Siebeck, 1987–1995.

*Le Testament Grec d'Abraham, Introduction, édition critique des deus recensions grecques, traduction.* Edited by F. Schmidt. TSAJ 11. Tübingen: Mohr Siebeck, 1986.

*The Testament of Solomon*. Translated and Edited by C. C. McCown. Leipzig: J. C. Heinrichs, 1922.

*The Testaments of the Twelve Patriarchs: A Commentary*. Translated and Edited by H. W. Hollander and M. de Jonge. Studia in Veteris Testamenti Pseudepigrapha 8. Leiden: Brill, 1985.

*Traditions of the Rabbis from the Era of the New Testament, Volume I: Prayer and Agriculture*. Translated and Edited by D. Instone-Brewer. Grand Rapids: Eerdmans, 2004.

*The Works of Josephus*. Updated edition. Translated by W. Whiston. Peabody, MA: Hendrickson, 1987. Reprint of 1736 edition.

*The Works of Philo Complete and Unabridged: New Updated Version*. Translated by C. D. Yonge. Peabody, Mass.: Hendrickson, 1993.

## Ancient Greek and Roman Literature

*Note: all citations of Greek and Roman literature are from the volumes of the Loeb Classical Library unless otherwise indicated.*

*Die Fragmente der Vorsokratiker*. Edited by H. Diels. Berlin: Weidmannsche, 1922.

*Galen: On the Doctrines of Hippocrates and Plato*. Translated by Phillip de Lacy. Corpus medicorum Graecorum 4.1.2. Berlin: Akademie, 1978.

*The Greek Alexander Romance*. Translated with an Introduction and Notes by R. Stoneman. New York: Penguin, 1991.

*Hermetica: The Greek* Corpus Hermeticum *and the Latin* Asclepius *in a New English Translation with Notes and Introduction*. Translated and Edited by B. P. Copenhaver. Cambridge: Cambridge University Press, 1992.

*The Homeric Hymns*. Translated with Introduction and Notes by D. J. Rayor. Berkeley; University of California Press, 2014.

*Iamblichus: On the Mysteries*. Translated with Introduction and Notes by E. C. Clarke, J. M. Dillon, and J. P. Hershbell. WGRW 4. Atlanta: SBL Press, 2003.

*The Nag Hammadi Library*. 3rd ed. Edited by J. M. Robinson. San Francisco: HarperSanFrancisco, 1988.

## Christian Texts

*Note: all citations of early Christian texts are from the volumes of the Ante-Nicene Fathers (ANF) and Nicene and Post-Nicene Fathers (NPNF) unless otherwise indicated.*

*The Apostolic Fathers: Greek Texts and English Translations*. 3rd ed. Translated and edited by M. W. Holmes. Grand Rapids: Baker, 2007.

*Eusebius: The History of the Christian Church*. Translated with an introduction by G. A. Williamson. New York: Penguin, 1965. Reprint, 1988.

*New Testament Apocrypha, Volume Two: Writings Relating to the Apostles; Apocalypses and Related Subjects*. Edited by E. Hennecke and W. Schneemelcher. Translated by R. McL. Wilson. Philadelphia: Westminster, 1965.

*Tatian: Oratio ad Graecos*. Pages 268–305 in *Die ältesten Apologeten*. Edited by E. J. Goodspeed. Göttingen: Vandenhoeck & Ruprecht, 1915.

## Papyri

Betz, H. D., ed. *The Greek Magical Papyri in Translation, Volume 1: Texts*. 2nd ed. Chicago: University of Chicago Press, 1996.

Daniel, R., and F. Maltomini. *Supplementum Magicum*. 2 vols. Abhandlungen der Rheinisch-Westfälischen Akademie der Wissenschaften. Sonderreihe, Papyrological Coloniensia 16.1, 16.2. Opladen: Westdeutscher, 1990, 1992.

Janko, R. "The Derveni Papyrus: An Interim Text." *ZPE* 141 (2002): 1–62.

Meyer, M. W., amd R. Smith. *Ancient Christian Magic: Coptic Texts of Ritual Power.* San Francisco: Harper, 1994.

## *Inscriptions*

*Note: see also the editions cited in the abbreviations listed at the beginning of this volume.*

Audollent, A. *Defixionum Tabellae.* Paris: Alberti Fontemoing, 1894.

Gager, J. G. *Curse Tablets and Binding Spells from the Ancient World.* Oxford: Oxford University Press, 1992.

Gregoire, H. *Recueil des inscriptions grecques-chrétiennes d'Asie Mineure.* Amsterdam: Adolf M. Hakkert, 1922.

Kotansky, R. *Greek Magical Amulets: The Inscribed Gold, Silver, Copper and Bronze* Lamellae: *Part I: Published Texts of Known Provenance.* Papyrologica Coloniensia 22/1. Opladen: Westdeutscher, 1994.

McCabe, D. F. *Aphrodisias Inscriptions: Texts and Lists.* The Princeton Project on the Inscriptions of Anatolia. Princeton: Princeton University Press, 1991.

Petzl, G. *Die Beichtinschriften Westkleinasiens.* Epigraphica Anatolica 22. Bonn: Habelt, 1994.

Zwierlein-Diehl, E., ed. *Magische Amulette und andere Gemmen des Instituts für Altertumskunde der Universität zu Köln.* Abhandlungen der Rheinisch-Westfälischen Akademie der Wissenschaften. Sonderreihe, Papyrological Coloniensia 20. Opladen: Westdeutscher, 1992.

## *Coins*

Aulock, H. von. *Münzen und Städte Phrygiens.* Istanbuler Mitteilungen Beiheft 27. Tübingen: Ernst Wasmuth, 1987.

Burnett, A., M. Amandry, P. P. Ripollès. *Roman Provincial Coinage, Volume 1: From the Death of Caesar to the Death of Vitellius (44 BC–AD 69). Part I: Introduction and Catalog.* Paris: Bibliothèque Nationale de France, 1992.

Head, B. V. *Catalogue of the Greek Coins of Phrygia in the British Museum.* London: British Museum, 1906.

Imhoof-Blumer, F. *Kleinasiatische Münzen.* Sonderschriften des Österreichischen Archäologischen Institutes in Wien. 3 Vols. Wien: Alfred Hölder, 1902.

# ***Older Commentaries on Colossians (Arranged by Date)***

## *Ambrosiaster (4th century)*

*Ambrosiaster: Commentaries on Galatians–Philemon.* Translated and Edited by G. L. Bray. Ancient Christian Texts. Downers Grove, IL: InterVarsity Press, 2009.

## *Chrysostom (4th century)*

*John Chrysostom: Homilies on Colossians.* Translated with an introduction and annotations by P. Allen. WGRW 46. Atlanta: SBL Press, 2021.

## *Theodore of Mopsuestia (4th century)*

*Theodore of Mopsuestia: The Commentaries on the Minor Epistles of Paul.* Translated with an Introduction by R. A. Greer. WGRW 26. Atlanta: Society of Biblical Literature, 2010.

## *Theodoret of Cyrus (5th century)*

*Theodoret of Cyrus: Commentary on the Letters of St. Paul.* Vol. 2. Translated with an Introduction by R. C. Hill. Brookline, MA: Holy Cross Orthodox Press, 2001.

### *Thomas Aquinas (c. 1250–1274)*

*St. Thomas Aquinas: Commentary by St. Thomas Aquinas on the Epistle to the Colossians.* Edited by D. A. Keating. Translated by F. Larcher. Naples, FL: Sapientia Press, 2006.

### *Philipp Melanchthon (1527)*

Melanchthon, P. *Paul's Letter to the Colossians.* Translated by D. C. Parker. Sheffield: Sheffield Academic Press, 1989.

### *John Calvin (c. 1550)*

Calvin, J. *The Epistles of Paul the Apostle to the Galatians, Ephesians, Philippians and Colossians.* Calvin's New Testament Commentaries 11. Edited by D. W. Torrance and T. F. Torrance. Translated by T. H. L. Parker. Grand Rapids: Eerdmans, 1965.

### *Johann Albrecht Bengel (1742)*

Bengel, J. A. *Gnomon of the New Testament.* 3rd ed. Vol 4. Edited by M. E. Bengel and J. C. F. Steudel. Translated by J. Bryce. Philadelphia: Smith, English, and Co., 1860.

### *1800s (see below for full bibliography)*

Meyer (1874); Lightfoot (1875); Eadie (1884); Abbott (1897); Peake (1897)

### *1900–1945 (see below for full bibliography)*

Haupt (1902); Williams (1907); Ewald (1910); Dibelius (1st ed.; 1912); Westcott (1914); Strack and Billerbeck (1926); Schlatter (1928); Scott (1930); Lohmeyer (1930); Radford (1931)

## Commentaries on Colossians

Commentaries on Colossians are cited in this commentary by their author's name, followed by a page number(s); for example, Aletti, 112–13; Lightfoot, 84; Wolter, 190.

Abbott, T. K. *The Epistles to the Ephesians and to the Colossians.* ICC. Edinburgh: T&T Clark, 1897.

Aletti, J.-N. *Saint Paul Épitre aux Colossiens.* Études Bibliques 20. Paris: Gabalda, 1993.

Barth, M, and H. Blanke. *Colossians: A New Translation with Introduction and Commentary.* AB 34B. Translated by A. B. Beck. New York: Doubleday, 1994.

Beale, G. K. "Colossians." Pages 841–870 in *Commentary on the New Testament Use of the Old Testament.* Edited by G. K. Beale and D. A. Carson. Grand Rapids: Baker, 2007.

———. *Colossians and Philemon.* BECNT. Grand Rapids: Baker, 2019.

Beare, F. W. "The Epistle to the Colossians." Pages 133–241 in vol. 11 of *The Interpreter's Bible.* Edited by G. A. Buttrick. 12 vols. IB 11. New York: Abingdon, 1955.

Bird, M. F. *Colossians and Philemon.* NCCS 12. Eugene, OR: Cascade, 2009.

Bormann, L. *Der Brief des Paulus an die Kolosser.* THKNT 10/I. Leipzig: Evangelische Verlagsanstalt, 2012.

Bruce, F. F. *The Epistles to the Colossians, to Philemon, and to the Ephesians.* NICNT. Grand Rapids: Eerdmans, 1984.

Caird, G. B. *Paul's Letters from Prison.* New Clarendon Bible. Oxford: Oxford University Press, 1976.

Campbell, C. R. *Colossians and Philemon: A Handbook on the Greek Text.* Baylor Handbook on the Greek New Testament. Waco, TX: Baylor University Press, 2013.

Conzelmann, H. "Der Brief an die Kolosser." Pages 176–202 in *Die Briefe an die Galater, Epheser, Philipper, Kolosser, Thessalonicher und Philemon.* Edited by G. Friedrich and P. Stuhlmacher. 16th ed. NTD 8. Göttingen: Vandenhoeck & Ruprecht, 1985.

Dibelius, M., and H. Greeven. *An die Kolosser, Epheser, an Philemon*. 3rd ed. HNT 12. Tübingen: Mohr Siebeck, 1953.
Dunn, J. D. G. *The Epistles to the Colossians and to Philemon*. NIGTC. Grand Rapids: Eerdmans, 1996.
Eadie, J. *A Commentary on the Greek Text of the Epistle of Paul to the Colossians*. Edinburgh: T&T Clark, 1884.
Ernst, J. *Die Briefe an die Philipper, an Philemon, an die Kolosser, an die Epheser*. RNT. Regensburg: Pustet, 1974.
Foster, P. *Colossians*. BNTC. London: Boomsbury T&T Clark, 2016.
Garland, D. E. *Colossians/Philemon*. NIVAC. Grand Rapids: Zondervan, 1998.
Gnilka, J. *Der Kolosserbrief*. HThKNT 10/1. Freiburg: Herder, 1980.
Gorday, P., ed. *Colossians, 1–2 Thessalonians, 1–2 Timothy, Titus, Philemon*. ACCS: New Testament 9. Downers Grove, IL: InterVarsity Press, 2000.
Gupta, Nijay K. *Colossians*. Smyth & Helwys Bible Commentary. Macon, GA: Smyth & Helwys, 2013.
Harris, M. J. *Colossians and Philemon*. Rev. ed. Exegetical Guide to the Greek New Testament. Nashville: B&H Academic, 2010. First ed., Grand Rapids: Eerdmans, 1991.
Hay, D. M. *Colossians*. ANTC. Nashville: Abingdon, 2000.
Hoppe, R. *Epheserbrief/Kolosserbrief*. 2nd ed. SKKNT 12. Stuttgart: Katholisches Bibelwerk, 2003.
Houlden, J. L. *Paul's Letters from Prison: Philippians, Colossians, Philemon, and Ephesians*. Baltimore: Penguin, 1970.
Hübner, H. *An Philemon, An die Kolosser, An die Epheser*. HNT 12. Tübingen: Mohr Siebeck, 1997.
Lightfoot, J. B. *St. Paul's Epistles to the Colossians and to Philemon*. London: Macmillan, 1875.
Lincoln, A. T. "The Letter to the Colossians." Pages 551–669 in *The New Interpreter's Bible*. Edited by Leander E. Keck. Nashville: Abingdon, 2000.
Lindemann, A. *Der Kolosserbrief*. Zürich Bibel 10. Zürich: Zwingli, 1983.
Lohmeyer, E. *Die Briefe an die Philipper, an die Kolosser und an Philemon*. KEK 9. 13th ed. Göttingen: Vandenhoeck & Ruprecht, 1964 (original publication 1930).
Lohse, E. *Colossians and Philemon*. Translated by W. R. Poehlmann and R. J. Karris. Hermeneia. Philadelphia: Fortress, 1971.
MacDonald, M. Y. *Colossians and Ephesians*. SP 17. Collegeville, MN: Liturgical Press, 2000.
Maisch, I. *Der Brief an die Gemeinde von Kolossä*. TKNT 12. Stuttgart: Kohlhammer, 2003.
Martin, R. P. *Colossians and Philemon*. NCB. Grand Rapids: Eerdmans, 1973.
———. *Colossians: The Church's Lord and the Christian's Liberty*. Exeter: Paternoster, 1972.
———. *Ephesians, Colossians, and Philemon*. IBC. Louisville: Westminster John Knox, 1991.
Mayerhoff, E. T. *Der Brief an die Colosser mit vornehmlicher Berüchsichtigung der drei Pastoralbriefe*. Berlin: Hermann Schultze, 1838.
McKnight, S. *The Letter to the Colossians*. NICNT. Grand Rapids: Eerdmans, 2018.
Melick, R. R. *Philippians, Colossians, Philemon*. NAC 32. Nashville: Broadman, 1991.
Moo, D. J. *The Letters to the Colossians and to Philemon*. Pillar New Testament Commentary. Grand Rapids: Eerdmans, 2008.
Moule, C. F. D. *The Epistles of Paul the Apostle to the Colossians and to Philemon*. CGTC. Cambridge: Cambridge University Press, 1962.
Moule, H. C. G. *The Epistles to the Colossians and to Philemon*. The Cambridge Bible for Schools and Colleges. Cambridge: University Press, 1902.
Murphy-O'Connor, J. "Colossians." Pages 1191–99 in *The Oxford Bible Commentary*. Edited by J. Barton and J. Muddiman. Oxford: Oxford University Press, 2001.
Pao, D. *Colossians and Philemon*. ZECNT. Grand Rapids: Zondervan, 2012.
Patzia, A. G. *Ephesians, Colossians, Philemon*. NIBCNT 10. Peabody, MA: Hendrickson, 1990.

Peake, A. S. "The Epistle to the Colossians." Pages 475–547 in *The Expositor's Greek New Testament*. Edited by W. Roberston Nicoll. London: Hodder & Stoughton, 1897. Repr., Grand Rapids: Eerdmans, 1990.

Pokorný, P. *Colossians: A Commentary*. Translated by Siegfried Schatzmann. Peabody, MA: Hendrickson, 1991.

Radford, Lewis B. *The Epistle to Colossians and the Epistle to Philemon*. Westminster Commentaries. London: Methuen, 1931.

Schlatter, A. *Die Briefe an die Galater, Epheser, Kolosser und Philemon*. Vol. 7 of *Erläuterungen zum Neuen Testament*. Stuttgart: Calwer, 1963.

Schweizer, E. *The Letter to the Colossians*. Translated by A. Chester. Minneapolis: Augsburg, 1982.

Scott, E. F. *The Epistles of Paul to the Colossians, to Philemon, and to the Ephesians*. MNTC. London: Hodder & Stoughton, 1930.

Seitz, C. R. *Colossians*. Brazos Theological Commentary on the Bible. Grand Rapids: Baker, 2014.

Strack, H. L., and P. Billerbeck. *Kommentar zum Neuen Testament aus Talmud und Midrasch*. Vol. 3. München: Beck, 1926.

Still, T. D. "Colossians." Pages 263–360 in *The Expositor's Bible Commentary*. Vol. 12. Revised Edition. Grand Rapids: Zondervan, 2006.

Sumney, J. L. *Colossians: A Commentary*. NTL. Louisville: Westminster John Knox, 2008.

Talbert, C. H. *Ephesians and Colossians*. Paideia. Grand Rapids: Baker, 2007.

Thiselton, A.C. *Colossians: A Short Exegetical and Pastoral Commentary*. Eugene, OR: Cascade, 2020.

Thompson, M. M. *Colossians & Philemon*. Two Horizons New Testament Commentary. Grand Rapids: Eerdmans, 2005.

Thurston, B. *Reading Colossians, Ephesians, and 2 Thessalonians: A Literary and Theological Commentary*. Macon, GA: Smyth & Helwys, 2013.

Wall, R. W. *Colossians & Philemon*. IVP New Testament Commentary 12. Downers Grove, IL: InterVarsity Press, 1993.

Westcott, B. F. *Colossian: A Letter to Asia*. London: MacMillan, 1914.

Williams, A. L. *The Epistles of Paul the Apostle to the Colossians and to Philemon*. Cambridge Greek Testament for Schools and Colleges. Cambridge: Cambridge University Press, 1907.

Wilson, R. McL. *A Critical and Exegetical Commentary on Colossians and Philemon*. ICC. London: T&T Clark, 2005.

Witherington III, B. *The Letters to Philemon, the Colossians, and the Ephesians: A Socio-Rhetorical Commentary on the Captivity Epistles*. Grand Rapids: Eerdmans, 2007.

Wolter, M. *Der Brief an die Kolosser. Der Brief an Philemon*. ÖTK 12. Gütersloh: Gütersloher Verlagshaus, 1993.

Wright, N. T. *Colossians and Philemon*. TNTC. Downers Grove, IL: InterVarsity Press, 1986.

Yates, R. *The Epistle to the Colossians*. Epworth Commentaries. London: Epworth, 1993.

## *Books and Articles*

Aasgaard, R. *"My Beloved Brothers and Sisters": Christian Siblingship in Paul*. JSNTSup 265. London: T&T Clark, 2004.

Achtemeier, P. J. "*Omne Verbum Sonat*: The New Testament and the Oral Environment of Late Western Antiquity." *JBL* 109 (1990): 3–27.

Agersnap, S. *Baptism and the New Life: A Study of Romans 6.1–4*. Aarhus: Aarhus University Press, 1999.

Akurgal, E. *Ancient Civilizations and Ruins of Turkey*. Istanbul: Mobil Oil Türk, 1969.

Aland, K. *Kurzgefasste Liste der griechischen Handschriften des Neuen Testaments.* ANTF 1. Berlin: de Gruyter, 1994.

———. "The Problem of Anonymity and Pseudonymity in Christian Literature of the First Two Centuries." *JTS* 12 (1961): 39–49.

Aland, K., and Aland, B. *The Text of the New Testament.* Grand Rapids: Eerdmans, 1989.

Aletti, J.-N. *Colossiens 1, 15–20: Genre et exégese du texte. Fonction de la thématique sapientielle.* AnBib 91. Rome: Biblical Institute, 1981.

Alexander, P. S. "Incantations and Books of Magic." Pages 342–79 in *The History of the Jewish People in the Age of Jesus Christ.* Revised and edited by G. Vermes, F. Millar, and M. Goodman. Vol. 3, Part 1. Edinburgh: T&T Clark, 1986.

———. "Jewish Elements in Gnosticism and Magic (c. CE 70–c. CE 270)." Pages 1210–19 in *The Cambridge History of Judaism, Volume Three: The Early Roman Period.* Edited by W. Horbury, W. D. Davies, and J. Sturdy. Cambridge: Cambridge University Press, 1999.

Ameling, W. "Die jüdischen Gemeinden im antiken Kleinasien." Pages 29–55 in *Jüdische Gemeinden und Organisationsformen von der Antike bis zur Gegenwart.* Edited by R. Jütte and A. P. Kustermann. Aschkenas, Zeitschrift für Geshichte und Kultur der Juden Beiheft 3. Vienna: Böhlau, 1996.

Anderson, C. P. "Hebrews among the Letters of Paul." *SR* 5 (1975): 258–66.

———. "Who Wrote 'the Epistle from Laodicea'?" *JBL* 85 (1966): 436–40.

Arbesmann, P. R. *Das Fasten bei den Griechen und Römern.* Religionsgeschichtliche Versuche und Vorarbeiten 21. Giessen: Töpelmann, 1929. Repr., 1966.

Argall, R. A. "The Source of Religious Error in Colossae." *CTJ* 22 (1987): 6–20.

Armstrong, A. J. "Roman Phrygia: Cities and Their Coinage." PhD diss., University College, London, 1998.

Arnold, C. E. "Colossians." Pages 370–403 in vol. 3 of *Zondervan Illustrated Bible Backgrounds Commentary.* Edited by C. E. Arnold. Grand Rapids: Zondervan, 2002.

———. *The Colossian Syncretism: The Interface between Christianity and Folk Belief at Colossae.* WUNT 2/77. Tübingen: Mohr Siebeck, 1995.

———. "Do We Really Need to Reconstruct the Background of Colossians to Understand the Letter?" Pages 171–83 in *God's Glory Revealed in Christ: Essays on Biblical Theology in Honor of Thomas R. Schreiner.* Edited by D. Burk, J. M. Hamilton, and B. Vickers. Nashville: B&H Academic, 2019.

———. *Ephesians: Power and Magic. The Concept of Power in Ephesians in Light of Its Historical Setting.* SNTSMS 63. Cambridge: University Press, 1989.

———. "Initiation, Vision, and Spiritual Power: The Hellenistic Dimensions of the Problem at Colossae." Pages 173–86 in *The First Urban Churches 5: Colossae, Hierapolis, and Laodicea.* Edited by J. R. Harrison and L. L. Welborn. WGRWSup 16. Atlanta: SBL Press, 2019.

———. "Jesus Christ: 'Head' of the Church." Pages 346–66 in *Jesus of Nazareth: Lord and Christ. Essays on the Historical Jesus and New Testament Christology.* FS I. H. Marshall. Edited by M. M. B. Turner and J. B. Green. Grand Rapids: Eerdmans, 1994.

———. "Living in Connection to the Resurrected Christ: Discipleship in Colossians and Ephesians." Pages 141–57 in *Following Jesus Christ: The New Testament Message of Discipleship for Today. A Volume in Honor of Michael J. Wilkins.* Edited by J. K. Goodrich and M. L. Strauss. Grand Rapids: Kregel, 2019.

———. "Magical Papyri." Pages 665–70 in *Dictionary of New Testament Background.* Edited by C. A. Evans and S. E. Porter. Downers Grove, IL: InterVarsity Press, 2000.

———. "Returning to the Domain of the Powers: *Stoicheia* as Evil Spirits in Gal 4:3, 9." *NovT* 38 (1996): 55–76.

———. "Sceva, Solomon, and Shamanism: The Jewish Roots of the Problem at Colossae." *JETS* 33 (2012): 7–26.

Arundell, V. J. *A Visit to the Seven Churces of Asia.* London: John Rodwell, 1828.

Arzt, P. "The 'Epistolary Introductory Thanksgiving' in the Papyri and in Paul." *NovT* 36 (1994): 29–46.

Arzt-Grabner, P. "Everyday Life in a Roman Town Like Colossae: The Papyrological Evidence." Pages 187–238 in *The First Urban Churches 5: Colossae, Hierapolis, and Laodicea.* Edited by J. R. Harrison and L. L. Welborn. WGRWSup 16. Atlanta: SBL Press, 2019.

———. "How to Deal with Onesimus? Paul's Solution within the Frame of Ancient Legal and Documentary Sources." Pages 113–42 in *Philemon in Perspective: Interpreting a Pauline Letter.* Edited by D. F. Tolmie. Berlin: de Gruyter, 2010.

Attridge, H. "On Becoming an Angel: Rival Baptismal Theologies at Colossae." Pages 481–98 in *Religious Propaganda and Missionary Competition in the New Testament World.* NovTSup 74. Edited by L. Mormann, K. Del Tredici, and A. Standhartinger. Leiden: Brill, 1994.

Aune, D. E. "The Apocalypse of John and Graeco-Roman Revelatory Magic." *NTS* 33 (1987): 481–501.

———. "Magic in Early Christianity." *ANRW* II.23.2 (1980): 1507–57.

———. *The New Testament in Its Literary Environment.* LEC 8. Philadelphia: Westminster, 1987.

———. *Prophecy in Early Christianity and the Ancient Mediterranean World.* Grand Rapids: Eerdmans, 1983.

———. "Reconceptualizing the Phenomenon of Ancient Pseudepigraphy: An Epilogue." Pages 789–824 in *Pseudepigraphie und Verfasserfiktion in frühchristlichen Briefen—Pseudepigaphy and Author Fiction in Early Christian Letters.* Edited by J. Frey, J. Herzer, M. Janssen, and C. K. Rothschild. WUNT 246. Tübingen: Mohr Siebeck, 2009.

Aune, N. A. "Tro på magi og onde makter—en nøkkel til forståelsen av heresiproblemet i Kolossæ." *TTKi* 2 (1994): 97–105.

Aydaş, M. "New Inscriptions from Asia Minor." *Epigraphica Anatolica* 37 (2004): 121–25.

Baird, R. D. *Category Formation and the History of Religions.* Netherlands: Mouton, 1971.

Balabanski, V. "Where Is Philemon? The Case for a Logical Fallacy in the Correlation of the Data in Philemon and Colossians 1.1–2; 4:7–18." *JSNT* 38 (2015): 131–50.

Balch, D. L. "Household Codes." Pages 25–50 in *Greco-Roman Literature and the New Testament: Selected Forms and Genres.* Sources for Biblical Study 21. Edited by D. E. Aune. Atlanta: Scholar's Press, 1988.

———. *Let Wives Be Submissive: The Domestic Code in 1 Peter.* SBLMS 26. Chico, CA: Scholars Press, 1981.

Balchin, J. F. "Colossians 1:15–20: An Early Christian Hymn? The Arguments from Style." *Vox Evangelica* 15 (1985): 65–94.

Bammel, E. "Versuch zu Kol 1, 15–20." *ZNW* 52 (1961): 88–95.

Bandstra, A. J. "Did the Colossian Errorists Need a Mediator?" Pages 329–43 in *New Dimensions in New Testament Study.* Edited by R. N. Longenecker and M. C. Tenney. Grand Rapids: Zondervan, 1974.

———. *The Law and the Elements of the World: An Exegetical Study in Aspects of Paul's Teaching.* Kampen: Kok, 1964.

———. "Plērōma as Pneuma in Colossians." Pages 96–102 in *Ad Interim: Opstellen over Eschatologie, Apocalyptiek en Ethiek.* FS R. Schippers. Edited by T. Baarda, J. Firet, and G. T. Rothuizen. Kampen: Kok, 1975.

Barbour, R. S. "Salvation and Cosmology: The Setting of the Epistle to the Colossians." *SJT* 20 (1967): 257–71.

Barclay, J. M. G. *Colossians and Philemon.* T&T Clark Study Guides. London: T&T Clark, 1997.

———. *Jews in the Mediterranean Diaspora: From Alexander to Trajan (323 BCE–117 CE).* Berkeley: University of California Press, 1996.

———. "Ordinary but Different: Colossians and Hidden Moral Identity." Pages 237–50 in *Pauline Churches and Diaspora Jews.* WUNT 275. Tübingen: Mohr Siebeck, 2011.

———. *Paul and the Gift*. Grand Rapids: Eerdmans, 2015.

———. "Paul, Philemon, and the Dilemma of Christian Slave Ownership." *NTS* 37 (1991): 161–86.

———. "Paul, Roman Religion and the Emperor: Mapping the Point of Conflict." Pages 345–62 in *Pauline Churches and Diaspora Jews*. Edited by J. M. G. Barclay. WUNT 275. Tübingen: Mohr Siebeck, 2011.

———. "Why the Roman Empire Was Insignificant to Paul." Pages 363–87 in *Pauline Churches and Diaspora Jews*. Edited by J. M. G. Barclay. WUNT 275. Tübingen: Mohr Siebeck, 2011.

Barnett, P. *Paul: Missionary of Jesus*. After Jesus 2. Grand Rapids: Eerdmans, 2008.

Barram, M. "Colossians 3:1–17." *Interpretation* 59 (2005): 188–90.

Barton, S. C., and Horsley, G. H. R. "A Hellenistic Cult Group and the New Testament Churches." *Jahrbuch für Antike und Christentum* 24 (1981): 7–41.

Bauckham, R. "Colossians 1:24 Again: The Apocalyptic Motif." *EvQ* 47 (1975): 168–70.

———. "Pseudo-Apostolic Letters." *JBL* 107 (1988): 469–94.

———. "Where Is Wisdom to Be Found? Colossians 1.15–20 (2)." Pages 129–38 in *Reading Texts, Seeking Wisdom: Scripture and Theology*. Edited by D. F. Ford and G. Stanton. Grand Rapids: Eerdmans, 2004.

Baugh, S. "The Poetic Form of Col 1:15–20." *WTJ* 47 (1985): 227–44.

Baum, A. "Authorship and Pseudepigraphy in Early Christian Literature: A Translation of the Most Important Source Texts and an Annotated Bibliography." Pages 11–64 in *Paul and Pseudepigraphy*. Edited by S. E. Porter and G. P. Fewster. Leiden: Brill, 2013.

———. "Content and Form: Authorship Attribution and Pseudonymity in Ancient Speeches, Letters, Lectures, and Translations—A Rejoinder to Bart Ehrman." *JBL* 136 (2017): 381–403.

———. *Pseudepigraphie und literarische Falschung im Frühen Christentum: Mit ausgewahlten Quellentexten samt deutscher Übersetzung*. WUNT 2/138. Tübingen: Mohr Siebeck, 2001.

Baur, F. C. *Paul the Apostle of Jesus Christ*. Peabody, MA: Hendrickson, 2003. Originally published as *Paulus, der Apostel Jesu Christi*, 1845.

Beale, G. K., and B. L. Gladd. *Hidden but Now Revealed: A Biblical Theology of Mystery*. Downers Grove, IL: InterVarsity Press, 2014.

Beard, M. *The Roman Triumph*. Cambridge: Belknap, 2007.

Beard, M., J. North, and S. Price. *Religions of Rome*. 2 vols. Cambridge: Cambridge University Press, 1998.

Beasley-Murray, G. R. *Baptism in the New Testament*. London: Macmillan, 1962.

———. "The Second Chapter of Colossians." *RevExp* 70 (1973): 469–79.

Beasley-Murray, P. "Colossians 1:15–20: An Early Christian Hymn Celebrating the Lordship of Christ." Pages 169–83 in *Pauline Studies: Essays Presented to Professor F. F. Bruce on His 70th Birthday*. Edited by D. A. Hagner and M. J. Harris. Grand Rapids: Eerdmans, 1980.

Becker, J. *Auferstehung der Toten im Urchristentum*. SBS 82. Stuttgart: KBW, 1976.

Beetham, C. A. *Echoes of Scripture in the Letter of Paul to the Colossians*. BibInt 96. Leiden: Brill, 2008.

Beker, J. C. *Paul the Apostle*. Edinburgh: T&T Clark, 1980.

Benoit, P. "L'hymne christologique de Col i, 15–20. Jugement critique sur l'état des recherches." Pages 226–63 in *Christianity, Judaism and Other Greco-Roman Cults, Part I*. FS M. Smith. Edited by J. Neusner. SJLA 12. Leiden: Brill, 1975.

———. "Pauline Angelology and Demonology: Reflexions on the Designations of the Heavenly Powers and on the Origin of Angelic Evil according to Paul." *Religious Studies Bulletin* 3 (1983): 1–18.

———. "The 'Plèroma' in the Epistles to the Colossians and the Ephesians." *SEÅ* 49 (1984): 136–58.

Best, E. *A Critical and Exegetical Commentary on Ephesians*. ICC. Edinburgh: T&T Clark, 1998.

———. "Who Used Whom? The Relationship of Ephesians and Colossians." *NTS* 43 (1997): 72–96.

Betz, H. D. "The Delphic Maxim 'Know Yourself' in the Greek Magical Papyri." *HistRel* 21 (1981): 156–71.

———. "The Formation of Authoritative Tradition in the Greek Magical Papyri." Pages 161–70 in *Jewish and Christian Self-Definition III*. Edited by B. F. Meyer and E. P. Sanders. London: SCM, 1982.

———. "Fragments from a Catabasis Ritual in a Greek Magical Papyrus." *HistRel* 19 (1980): 287–95.

———. "Magic and Mystery in the Greek Magical Papyri." Pages 209–29 in *Hellenismus und Urchristentum*. Gesammelte Aufsätze I. Tübingen: Mohr Siebeck, 1990.

———. "Magic and Mystery in the Greek Magical Papyri." Pages 244–59 in *Magika Hiera: Ancient Greek Magic and Religion*. Edited by C. A. Faraone and D. Obbink. Oxford: Oxford University Press, 1991.

———. *The "Mithras Liturgy": Text, Translation, and Commentary*. Studies and Texts in Antiquity and Christianity 18. Tübingen: Mohr Siebeck, 2005.

———. "Paul's 'Second Presence' in Colossians." Pages 507–18 in *Texts and Contexts: Biblical Texts in Their Textual and Situational Contexts: Essays in Honor of Lars Hartman*. Edited by F. Fornberg and D. Hellholm. Oslo: Scandinavian University Press, 1995.

Bevere, A. R. *Sharing in the Inheritance: Identity and the Moral Life in Colossians*. JSNTSup 226. Sheffield: Sheffield Academic Press, 2003.

Bing, C. C. "The Warning in Colossians 1:21–23." *BSac* 164 (2007): 74–88.

Bird, M. F. "Reassessing a Rhetorical Approach to Paul's Letters." *ExpTim* 119 (2008): 374–79.

Bird, M. F., and P. Sprinkle, eds. *The Faith of Jesus Christ: Exegetical, Biblical, and Theological Studies*. Peabody, MA: Hendrickson, 2009.

Blackwell, Ben C. "You Are Filled in Him: Theosis and Colossians 2–3." *JTI* 8 (2014): 103–23.

Blanchette, O. A. "Does the Cheirographon of Col. 2,14 Represent Christ Himself?" *CBQ* 23 (1961): 306–12.

Blass, F., A. Debrunner, and R. W. Funk. *A Greek Grammar of the New Testament and Other Early Christian Literature*. Chicago: University of Chicago Press, 1961.

Blau, L. *Das altjüdische Zauberwesen*. Berlin: Verlag von Luis Lamm, 1914.

Blinzler, J. "Lexikalisches zu dem Terminus τὰ στοιχεῖα τοῦ κόσμου." Pages 429–43 in *Studiorum Paulinorum Congressus Internationalis Catholicus*. Vol. 2 AnBib 18. Rome: Pontifical Biblical Institute, 1963.

Blue, B. "Acts and the House Church." Pages 119–222 in *The Book of Acts in Its Graeco-Roman Setting*. Edited by D. W. J. Gill and C. Gempf. Vol. 2 of *The Book of Acts in Its First Century Setting*. Edited by B. W. Winter. Grand Rapids: Eerdmans, 1994.

Böcher, O. *Christus Exorcista: Dämonismus und Taufe im Neuen Testament*. BWANT 16. Stuttgart: Kohlhammmer, 1972.

———. *Dämonenfurcht und Dämonenabwehr: Ein Beitrag zur Vorgeschichte der christlichen Taufe*. BWANT 10. Stuttgart: Kohlhammer, 1970.

———. *Das Neue Testament und die dämonischen Mächte*. SBS 58. Stuttgart: Katholisches Bibelwerk, 1972.

Bock, D. L. "'The New Man' as Community in Colossians and Ephesians." Pages 157–67 in *Integrity of Heart, Skillfulness of Hands: Biblical and Leadership Studies in Honor of Donald K. Campbell*. Edited by C. H. Dyer and R. B. Zuck. Grand Rapids: Baker, 1994.

Bockmuehl, M. N. A. "A Note on the Text of Colossians 4:3." *JTS* 39 (1988): 489–94.

———. *Revelation and Mystery in Ancient Judaism and Pauline Christianity*. WUNT 2/36. Tübingen: Mohr Siebeck, 1990.

Bogh, B. "The Phrygian Background of Kybele." *Numen* 54 (2007): 304–39.

Bohak, G. *Ancient Jewish Magic: A History*. Cambridge: Cambridge University Press, 2008.

Bonner, C. *Studies in Magical Amulets Chiefly Graeco-Egyptian*. Ann Arbor: University of Michigan Press, 1950.

Bormann, L. "Barbaren und Skythen im Lykostal? Epigraphischer Kommentar zu Kol 3:11." Pages 161–98 in *Epigraphical Evidence Illustrating Paul's Letter to the Colossians*. Edited by J. Verheyden, M. Öhler, and T. Corsten. WUNT 2/411. Tübingen: Mohr Siebeck, 2018.

———. "Schriftgebrauch im Kolosser- und im Epheserbrief: Zure Praxis frühchristlicher Text- und Interpretationsgemeinschaften." Pages 217–34 in *Paulinische Schriftrezeption: Grundlagen—Ausprägungen—Wirkungen—Wertungen*. Edited by F. Wilk and M. Öhler. FRLANT 268. Göttingen: Vandenhoeck & Ruprecht, 2017.

———. "Weltbild und gruppenspezifische Raumkonfiguration des Kolosserbriefs." Pages 83–102 in *Kolosser-Studien*. Edited by P. Müller. Biblisch-Theologische Studien 103. Neukirchen-Vluyn: Neukirchener, 2009.

Bornkamm, G. "The Heresy of Colossians." Pages 123–45 in *Conflict at Colossae*. Edited by F. O. Francis and W. A. Meeks. SBLSBS 4. Missoula, MT: Scholars Press, 1973.

———. "Die Hoffnung im Kolosserbrief: Zugleich ein Beitrag zur Frage der Echtheit des Briefes." Pages 56–64 in *Studien zum Neuen Testament und zur Patristik*. FS E. Klostermann. TU 77. Berlin: Akademie, 1961.

Bosch, J. S. "Der Hymnus Kol 1,15–20 in seinem früheren und seinem späteren Kontext." Pages 23–32 in *Kolosser-Studien*. Edited by P. Müller. Biblisch-Theologische Studien 103. Neukirchen-Vluyn: Neukirchener, 2009.

Botha, J. "A Stylistic Analysis of the Christ Hymn (Col 1:15–20)." Pages 238–51 in *A South African Perspective on the New Testament: Essays by South African New Testament Scholars Presented to Bruce Manning Metzger during His Visit in South Africa in 1985*. Edited by J. H. Petzer and P. J. Hartin. Leiden: Brill, 1997.

Böttrich, C. *Weltweisheit, Menschheitsethik, Urkult: Studien zum slavonischen Henochbuch*. WUNT 2/50. Tübingen: Mohr Siebeck, 1992.

Bousset, W. *Kyrios Christos*. Translated by J. E. Steely. Nashville: Abingdon, 1970.

Bousset, W., and H. Gressman. *Die Religion des Judentums im Späthellenistischen Zeitalter*. 3rd ed. HzNT 21. Tübingen: Mohr Siebeck, 1966.

Boustan, R., and J. E. Sanzo. "Christian Magicians, Jewish Magical Idioms, and Shared Magical Culture of Late Antiquity." *HTR* 110 (2017): 217–40.

Boustan, R., J. Dieleman, and J. E. Sanzo. "Introduction: Authoritative Traditions and Ritual Power in the Ancient World." *Archiv für Religionsgeschichte* 16 (2015): 3–10.

Bradley, K. *Slavery and Society at Rome*. Key Themes in Ancient History. Cambridge: Cambridge University Press, 1994.

Branick, V. P. "Apocalyptic Paul?" *CBQ* 47 (1985): 664–75.

Braun, H. *Qumran und das Neue Testament*. 2 Vols. Tübingen: Mohr Siebeck, 1966.

Brashear, W. M. "The Greek Magical Papyri: An Introduction and Survey; Annotated Bibliography (1928–1994)." *ANRW* II.18.5 (1995): 3380–483.

———. "Out of the Closet: Recent Corpora of Magical Texts." *Classical Philology* 91 (1996): 372–83.

Brenk, F. E. "The Exorcism at Philippi in Acts 16.11–40: Divine Possession or Diabolic Inspiration." *Filologia Neotestamentaria* 13 (2000): 3–21.

Breytenbach, C. "Paul's Proclamation and God's 'Thriambos.'" *Neot* 24 (1990): 257–71.

Brown, R. E. *The Semitic Background of the Term "Mystery" in the New Testament*. Facet Books, Biblical Series 21. Philadelphia: Fortress, 1968.

Bruce, F. F. *The Book of Acts*. Rev. ed. NICNT. Grand Rapids: Eerdmans, 1988.

———. "Christ as Conqueror and Reconciler." *BSac* 141 (1984): 291–302.

———. "The 'Christ-Hymn' of Colossians 1:15–20." *BSac* 141 (1984): 99–111.

———. "The Colossian Heresy." *BSac* 141 (1984): 195–208.

———. "Jews and Christians in the Lycus Valley." *BSac* 141 (1984): 3–15.

Brucker, R. *"Christushymnen" oder "epedeiktische Passagen"? Studien zum Stilwechsel im Neuen Testament und seiner Umwelt.* FRLANT 176. Göttingen: Vandenhoeck & Ruprecht, 1997.

Buckler, W. H., W. M. Calder, and C. W. M. Cox. "Asia Minor, 1924. III.—Monuments from Central Phrygia." *JRS* 16 (1926): 53–94.

Bujard, W. *Stilanalytische Untersuchungen zum Kolosserbrief.* SUNT 11. Göttingen: Vandenhoeck & Ruprecht, 1973.

Buls, H. H. "Luther's Translation of Colossians 2:12." *CTQ* 45 (1981): 13–16.

Bultmann, R. *Theology of the New Testament.* 2 Vols. Translated by K. Grobel. New York: Charles Scribner's Sons, 1951, 1955.

Bundrick, D. R. "*TA STOICHEIA TOU KOSMOU* (GAL 4:3)." *JETS* 34 (1991): 353–64.

Buresch, K. *Klaros: Untersuchungen zum Orakelwesen des Späteren Altertums.* Leipzig: Teubner, 1889.

Bürger, C. *Schöpfung und Versöhnung: Studien zum liturgischen Gut im Kolosser- und Epheserbrief.* WMANT 46. Neukirchen: Neukirchener, 1975.

Burns, J. P. "Baptism as Dying and Rising with Christ in the Teaching of Augustine." *JECS* 20 (2012): 407–38.

Burkert, W. *Ancient Mystery Cults.* Cambridge: Harvard University Press, 1987.

———. "ΓΟΗΣ. Zum griechischen 'Schamanismus.'" *Rheinisches Museum für Philologie* NS 105 (1962): 36–55.

Burney, C. F. "Christ as the ARXH of Creation." *JTS* 27 (1926): 160–77.

Busch, P. *Das Testament Salomos: Die älteste christliche Dämonologie, kommentiert und in deutscher Erstübersetzung.* TUGAL 153. Berlin: de Gruyter, 2006.

Cadwallader, A. H. *Fragments of Colossae: Sifting through the Traces.* Adelaide: ATF, 2015.

———. "The Historical Sweep of the Life of Kolossai." Pages 25–68 in *Epigraphical Evidence Illustrating Paul's Letter to the Colossians.* Edited by J. Verheyden, M. Öhler, and T. Corsten. WUNT 2/411. Tübingen: Mohr Siebeck, 2018.

———. "Honouring the Repairer of the Baths: A New Inscription from Kolossai." *Antichthon* 46 (2012): 150–83.

———. "On the Question of Historical Method in Historical Research: Colossae and Chonai in Larger Frame." Pages 105–51 in *The First Urban Churches 5: Colossae, Hierapolis, and Laodicea.* Edited by J. R. Harrison and L. L. Welborn. WGRWSup 16. Atlanta: SBL Press, 2019.

———. "Refuting an Axiom of Scholarship on Colossae: Fresh Insights from New and Old Inscriptions." Pages 151–79 in *Colossae in Space and Time: Linking to an Ancient City.* Edited by A. H. Cadwallader and M. Trainor. NTOA/SUNT 94. Göttingen: Vandenhoeck & Ruprecht, 2011.

———. "Revisiting Calder on Colossae." *AnSt* 56 (2006): 103–11.

Cadwallader, A. H., and J. R. Harrison. "Perspectives on the Lycus Valley: An Inscriptional, Archaeological, Numismatic, and Iconographic Approach." Pages 3–70 in *The First Urban Churches 5: Colossae, Hierapolis, and Laodicea.* Edited by J. R. Harrison and L. L. Welborn. WGRWSup 16. Atlanta: SBL Press, 2019.

Cadwallader, A. H., and Michael Trainor. "Colossae in Space and Time: Overcoming Dismemberment and Anachronicity." Pages 9–47 in *Colossae in Space and Time: Linking to an Ancient City.* Edited by A. H. Cadwallader and M. Trainor. NTOA/SUNT 94. Göttingen: Vandenhoeck & Ruprecht, 2011.

Cahill, M. "The Neglected Parallelism in Colossians 1,24–25." *ETL* 68 (1992): 142–47.

Caird, G. B. *Principalities and Powers.* Oxford: Clarendon, 1956.

Callan, T. *Dying and Rising with Christ: The Theology of Paul the Apostle.* New York: Paulist, 2006.

Callow, J. *A Semantic and Structural Analysis of Colossians.* 2nd ed. Dallas: SIL International, 2002.

Campbell, C. R. *Paul and the Hope of Glory: An Exegetical and Theological Study*. Grand Rapids: Zondervan, 2020.

———. *Paul and Union with Christ: An Exegetical and Theological Study*. Grand Rapids: Zondervan, 2012.

Campbell, D. A. *Framing Paul: An Epistolary Biography*. Grand Rapids: Eerdmans, 2014.

———. "Scythian Perspective." *NovT* 39 (1997): 81–84.

———. "Unravelling Colossians 3.11b." *NTS* 42 (1996): 120–32.

Canavan, R. *Clothing the Body of Christ at Colossae: A Visual Reconstruction of Identity*. WUNT 2/334. Tübingen: Mohr Siebeck, 2012.

———. "Unraveling the Threads of Identity: Cloth and Clothing in the Lycus Valley." Pages 81–104 in *The First Urban Churches 5: Colossae, Hierapolis, and Laodicea*. Edited by J. R. Harrison and L. L. Welborn. WGRWSup 16. Atlanta: SBL Press, 2019.

Caneday, A. B. "'If You Continue in the Faith' (Colossians 1:21–23): An Exegetical-Theological Exercise in Syntax, Discourse, and Performative Speech." *SBJT* 17 (2013): 20–33.

Cannon, G. E. *The Use of Traditional Material in Colossians*. Macon, GA: Mercer University Press, 1983.

Capes, D. B. *The Divine Christ: Paul, the Lord Jesus, and the Scriptures of Israel*. Acadia Studies in Bible and Theology. Grand Rapids: Baker, 2018.

———. *Old Testament Yahweh Texts in Paul's Christology*. WUNT 2/47. Tübingen: Mohr Siebeck, 1992.

Caragounis, C. C. *The Ephesian Mysterion: Meaning and Content*. ConBNT 8. Lund: Gleerup, 1977.

Carr, W. *Angels and Principalities: The Background, Meaning and Development of the Pauline Phrase hai archai kai hai exousiai*. SNTSMS 42. Cambridge: Cambridge University Press, 1983.

———. "Two Notes on Colossians." *JTS* 24 (1973): 492–500.

Carratelli, G. P. "ΧΡΗΣΜΟΙ di Apollo Kareios e Apollo Klarios a Hierapolis in Frigia." *Annuario della Scuola Archeologica di Atene e delle Missioni Italiane in Oriente* 61–62 (1963–64): 351–70.

Cassidy, W. "Introduction (Retrofitting Syncretism)." *Historical Reflections/Réflexions Historiques* 27 (2001): 365–73.

Cavin, R. L. *New Existence and Righteous Living: Colossians and 1 Peter in Conversation with 1QInstruction and the Hodayot*. BZNW 197. Berlin: de Gruyter, 2013.

Cerfaux, L. "Influence des Mystères sur le Judaïsme Alexandrin avant Philo." Pages 65–112 in *Recueil Lucien Cerfaux: Études d'Exégèse et d'Histoire Religieuse de Monseigneur Cerfaux*. 2 Vols. BETL 6–7. Gembloux: Duculot, 1954.

Chamonard, J., and A. Legrand. "Inscriptions de Notion." *BCH* 18 (1894): 216–21.

Chaniotis, A. "Epigraphic Bulletin for Greek Religion 2007." *Kernos* 23 (2010): 271–327.

———. "The Perception of Imperial Power in Aphrodisias: The Epigraphic Evidence." Pages 250–60 in *The Representation and Perception of Roman Imperial Power: Proceedings of the Third Workshop of the International Network Impact of Empire (Roman Empire, 200 B.C.–A.D. 476), Rome, March 20–23, 2002*. Edited by L. de Blois et al. Leiden: Brill, 2003.

Charlesworth, J. H. "A Critical Comparison of the Dualism in 1QS III, 13–IV, 26 and the 'Dualism' Contained in the Fourth Gospel." *NTS* 15 (1969): 389–418.

———. "Jewish Astrology in the Talmud, Pseudepigrapha, the Dead Sea Scrolls, and Early Palestinian Synagogues." *HTR* 70 (1977): 183–200.

———. *The Old Testament Pseudepigrapha and the New Testament: Prolegomena for the Study of Christian Origins*. SNTSMS 54. Cambridge: Cambridge University Press, 1985.

———. *The Pseudepigrapha and Modern Research*. Society of Biblical Literature Septuagint and Cognate Studies 7. Missoula, MT: Scholars Press, 1976.

Chiai, G. F. "Allmächtiger Götter und fromme Menschen im ländlichen Kleinasien der Kaiserzeit." *Millennium* 6 (2009): 61–102.

———. "Die Götter und ihr Territorium: Münzen als Quellen zur *Interpretation* im kaiserzeitlichen Phrygien." *Mediterraneo Antico* 15 (2012): 51–70.

———. "Norm, Kommunikation und Identitat: die jüdische Lebenswelt in den Inschriften des kaiserzeitlichen Phrygien." Pages 117–46 in *Athen, Rom, Jerusalem: Normentransfers in der antiken Welt.* Edited by G. F. Chiai et al. Eichstätter Studien 66. Regensburg: Pustet, 2012.

———. *Phrygien und seine Götter: Historie und Religionsgeschichte einer anatolischen Region von der Zeit der Hethiter bis zur Ausbreitung des Christentums.* Pharos Studien zur griechisch-römischen Antike 46. Rahden/Westphalia: VML, 2020.

———. "Zeus Bronton und der Totenkult im kaiserzeitlichen Phrygien." Pages 135–56 in *Bestattungsrituale und Totenkult in der römischen Kaiserzeit.* Edited by J. Rüpke and J. Scheid. Potsdamer Altertumswissenschaftliche Beitrage 27. Stuttgart: Steiner, 2010.

Cianca, J. *Sacred Ritual, Profane Space: The Roman House as Early Christian Meeting Place.* Studies in Christianity and Judaism 1. Montreal: McGill-Queen's University Press, 2018.

Clark, B. *Completing Christ's Afflictions: Christ, Paul, and the Reconciliation of All Things.* WUNT 2/383. Tübingen: Mohr Siebeck, 2015.

Clark, S. B. *Man and Woman in Christ.* Ann Arbor: Servant Books, 1980.

Classen, C. J. "Can the Theory of Rhetoric Help Us to Understand the New Testament, and in Particular the Letters of Paul?" Pages 13–39 in *Paul and Ancient Rhetoric: Theory and Practice in the Hellenistic Context.* Edited by S. E. Porter and B. R. Dyer. Cambridge: Cambridge University Press, 2016.

Cline, R. H. *Ancient Angels: Conceptualizing Angeloi in the Roman Empire.* RGRW 172. Leiden: Brill, 2011.

———. "Archangels, Magical Amulets, and the Defense of Late Antique Miletus." *Journal of Late Antiquity* 4 (2011): 55–78.

Cohen, S. J. D. *The Beginnings of Jewishness: Boundaries, Varieties, Uncertainties.* Berkeley: University of California Press, 1999.

Cole, H. R. "The Christian and Time-Keeping in Colossians 2:16 and Galatians 4:10." *AUSS* 39 (2001): 273–82.

Collins, B. J. "Necromancy, Fertility and the Dark Earth: The Use of Ritual Pits in Hittite Culture." Pages 224–41 in *Magic and Ritual in the Ancient World.* Edited by P. Mirecki and M. Meyer. RGRW 141. Leiden: Brill, 2001.

Collins, C. J. "Colossians 1,17 'Hold Together': A Co-Opted Term." *Biblica* 95 (2014): 64–87.

Colpe, C. *Die religionsgeschichtliche Schule: Darstellung der Kritik ihres Bildes vom gnostischen Erlösermythus.* FRLANT 78. Göttingen: Vandenhoeck & Ruprecht, 1961.

Comfort, P. W., and D. P. Barrett. *The Text of the Earliest New Testament Greek Manuscripts.* Wheaton, IL: Tyndale House, 2001.

Conzelmann, H. "Paulus und die Weisheit." *NTS* 12 (1966): 231–44.

Copenhaver, A. "Echoes of a Hymn in a Letter of Paul: The Rhetorical Function of the Chist-Hymn in the Letter to the Colossians." *JSPL* 4 (2014): 235–55.

———. *Reconstructing the Historical Background of Paul's Rhetoric in the Letter to the Colossians.* LNTS 585. London: Bloomsbury T&T Clark, 2018.

Cormack, J. M. R. "Inscriptions from Aphrodisias," *Annual of the British School at Athens* 59 (1964): 16–29.

———. "A *Tabella Defixionis* in the Museum of the University of Reading, England." *HTR* 44 (1951): 25–34.

Corsten, T., ed. *A Lexicon of Greek Personal Names. Volume V.A. Coastal Asia Minor: Pontos to Ionia.* Oxford: Clarendon, 2010.

Corsten, T. "Mann oder Frau: Nympha oder Nymphas in Laodikeia?" Pages 215–20 in *Epigraphical Evidence Illustrating Paul's Letter to the Colossians.* Edited by J. Verheyden, M. Öhler, and T. Corsten. WUNT 2/411. Tübingen: Mohr Siebeck, 2018.

Cosgrove, C. H. "The Syntax of Early Christian Hymns and Prayers: Revisiting Relative and Participial Styles for Making Assertions about a Deity." *EC* 9 (2018): 158–80.

Cranfield, C. E. B. *A Critical and Exegetical Commentary on the Epistle to the Romans*. 2 Vols. ICC. Edinburgh: T&T Clark, 1975.

———. "Romans 6:1–14 Revisited." *ExpTim* 106 (1994): 40–43.

Croon, J. H. "Hot Springs and Healing Gods." *Mnemosyne* 20 (1967): 225–46.

Crouch, J. E. *The Origin and Intention of the Colossian Haustafeln*. FRLANT 109. Göttingen: Vandenhoeck & Ruprecht, 1972.

Culianu, I. P. "The Angels of the Nations and the Origins of Gnostic Dualism." Pages 78–91 in *Studies in Gnosticism and Hellenistic Religions*. FS G. Quispel. Edited by R. van den Broek and M. J. Vermaseren. EPRO 91. Leiden: Brill, 1981.

Cumont, F. *Astrology and Religion among the Greeks and Romans*. New York: Putnam's, 1912.

———. "Les Mystères de Sabazius et le Judaïsme." *CRAI* (1906): 63–79.

———. *The Oriental Religions in Roman Paganism*. New York: Dover, 1956.

D'Andria, F. *Hierapolis of Phrygia (Pamukkale): An Archaeological Guide*. Translated by P. Arthur. Istanbul: Ege Yayinlari, 2003.

———. "The Sanctuary of St. Philip in Hierapolis and the Tombs of Saints in Anatolian Cities." Pages 34–57 in *Life and Death in Asia Minor in Hellenistic, Roman and Byzantine Times*. Edited by J. R. Brandt, E. Hagelberg, G. Bjørnstad, and S. Ahrens. Studies in Funerary Archaeology 10. Oxford: Oxbow, 2017.

D'Andria, F., and I. Romeo, eds. *Roman Sculpture in Asia Minor: Proceedings of the International Conference to Celebrate the 50th Anniversary of the Italian Excavations at Hierapolis in Phrygia, Held on May 24–26, 2007, in Cavallino (Lecce)*. JRASup 80. Portsmouth, RI: Journal of Roman Archaeology, 2011.

Daniel, R. "The Testament of Solomon XVIII 27–28, 33–40." Pages 294–303 in *Papyrus Erzherzog Rainer (P. Rainer Cent.): Festschrift zum 100-jährigen Bestehen der Papyrussammlung der Österreichischen National-Bibliothek*. Vienna: Brüder Hollinek, 1983.

Daniell, D. *The Bible in English: Its History and Influence*. New Haven: Yale University Press, 2003.

Davidson, M. J. *Angels at Qumran: A Comparative Study of 1 Enoch 1–36, 72–108 and Sectarian Writings from Qumran*. JSPSup 11. Sheffield: JSOT Press, 1992.

Davies, W. D. *Paul and Rabbinic Judaism: Some Rabbinic Elements in Pauline Theology*. 3rd ed. London: SPCK, 1970.

Davila, J. R. *Descenders to the Chariot: The People behind the Hekhalot Literature*. JSJSup 70. Leiden: Brill, 2001.

———. *Hekhalot Literature in Translation: Major Texts of Merkavah Mysticism*. JJTPSup 20. Leiden: Brill, 2013.

———. "Shamanic Initiatory Death and Resurrection in the *Hekhalot* Literature." Pages 283–301 in *Magic and Ritual in the Ancient World*. Edited by P. Mirecki and M. Meyer. RGRW 141. Leiden: Brill, 2002.

De Boer, M. C. "The Meaning of the Phrase τὰ στοιχεῖα τοῦ κόσμου in Galatians." *NTS* 53 (2007): 204–24.

Deichgräber, R. *Gotteshymnus und Christushymnus in der frühen Christenheit: Untersuchungen zur Form, Sprache und Stil der frühchristlichen Hymnen*. SUNT 5. Göttingen: Vandenhoeck & Ruprecht, 1967.

Deissmann, A. *Bible Studies*. Edinburgh: T&T Clark, 1901.

———. "Ephesia Grammata." Pages 121–24 in *Abhandlung zur semitischen Religionskunde und Sprachwissenschaft*. Edited by W. Frankenberg and F. Kuchler. BZAW 33. Gießen: Töpelmann, 1918.

———. *Light from the Ancient East*. Translated by R. M. Strachan. New York: Doran, 1927.

DeMaris, R. E. *The Colossian Controversy: Wisdom in Dispute at Colossae*. JSNTSup 96. Sheffield: JSOT Press, 1994.

Deschamps, G., and G. Cousin. "Inscriptions du Temple de Zeus Panamaros." *BCH* 12 (1888): 249–73.

deSilva, D. A. *Galatians*. NICNT. Grand Rapids: Eerdmans, 2018.

Dettwiler, A. "Le lettre aux Colossiens: une théologie de la mémoire." *NTS* 59 (2013): 109–28.

Detwiler, D. F. "Church Music and Colossians 3:16." *BSac* 158 (2001): 347–69.

Dibelius, M. *Die Geisterwelt im Glauben des Paulus*. Göttingen: Vandenhoeck & Ruprecht, 1909.

———. "The Isis Initiation in Apuleius and Related Initiatory Rites." Pages 61–121 in *Conflict at Colossae*. Edited by F. O. Francis and W. A. Meeks. SBLSBS 4. Missoula, MT: Scholars Press, 1973. (Originally published in 1917.)

Diels, H. *Elementum: Eine Vorarbeit zum Griechischen und Lateinischen Thesaurus*. Leipzig: Teubner, 1899.

Dieterich, A. *Abraxas: Studien zur Religionsgeschichte des spätern Altertums*. Leipzig: Teubner, 1891.

———. *Eine Mithrasliturgie*. 3rd ed. Darmstadt: Wissenschaftliche Buchgesellschaft, 1966.

Dillon, J. M. "*Pleroma* and Noetic Cosmos: A Comparative Study." Pages 99–110 in *Neoplatonism and Gnosticism*. Edited by R. T. Wallis. Studies in Neoplatonism: Ancient and Modern 6. Albany: State University of New York, 1992.

Doherty, B. "The First Rural Christians: Toward an Explanation of the Christianisation of the Roman Phrygian Countryside." *Phronema* 32 (2017): 71–98.

Dorigny, A. S. "Phylactére alexandrin." *Revue des Études Grecques* 4 (1891): 287–96.

Dörner, F. K. "Eine neue Fluchtafel." *JÖAI* 32 (1940): 64–72.

Drew-Bear, T., and C. Naour. "Divinitès de Phrygie." *ANRW* II.18.3 (1990): 1907–2044.

du Preez, R. *Judging the Sabbath: Discovering What Can't Be Found in Colossians 2:16*. Berrien Springs, MI: Andrews University Press, 2008.

Dübbers, M. *Christologie und Existenz im Kolosserbrief: Exegetische und semantische Untersuchungen zur Intention des Kolosserbriefes*. WUNT 2/191. Tübingen: Mohr Siebeck, 2005.

DuBois, T. A. *An Introduction to Shamanism*. Cambridge: Cambridge University Press, 2009.

Duff, J. "A Reconsideration of Pseudepigraphy in Early Christianity." PhD thesis, University of Oxford, 1998.

Duling, D. "The Eleazar Miracle and Solomon's Magical Wisdom in Flavius Josephus's *Antiquitates Judaicae* 8.42–49." *HTR* 78 (1985): 1–25.

———. "Solomon, Exorcism, and the Son of David." *HTR* 68 (1975): 235–52.

———. "The Testament of Solomon: Retrospect and Prospect." *JSP* 2 (1988) 87–112.

Duman, B. "Tabernae in Tripolis." Pages 109–42 in *Landscape and History in the Lykos Valley: Laodikeia and Hierapolis in Phrygia*. Edited by C. Şimşek and F. D'Andria. Newcastle upon Tyne: Cambridge Scholars, 2017.

Duman, B., and E. Konakçi. "Kolossai: Höyük, Kalinti ve Buluntulan (Colossae: the Mound, Remains and Findings)." *Arkeoloji Dergisi* 8 (2006): 83–109.

———. "The Silent Witness of the Mound of Colossae: Pottery Remains." Pages 247–81 in *Colossae in Space and Time: Linking to an Ancient City*. Edited by A. H. Cadwallader and M. Trainor. NTOA/SUNT 94. Göttingen: Vandenhoeck & Ruprecht, 2011.

Dunand, F. *Le Culte d'Isis dans le Bassin Oriental de la Méditerranée*. Vol. 3. EPRO 26. Leiden: Brill, 1973.

Dunbabin, K. M. D. "*Baiarum Grata Voluptas*: Pleasures and Dangers of the Baths." *Papers of the British School at Rome* 57 (1989): 6–46.

Duncan, G. S. *St. Paul's Ephesian Ministry*. London: Hodder & Stoughton, 1929.

Dunn, J. D. G. "The Colossian Philosophy: A Confident Jewish Apologia." *Biblica* 76 (1995): 153–81.

———. *The Theology of Paul the Apostle*. Grand Rapids: Eerdmans, 1998.

Dunne, J. A. "The Regal Status of Christ in the Colossian 'Christ-Hymn': A Re-Evaluation of the Influence of Wisdom Traditions." *TJ* (2011): 3–18.

Easton, B. S. "New Testament Ethical Lists." *JBL* 51 (1932): 1–12.
Eckhardt, B. "Romanization and Isomorphic Change in Phrygia: The Case of Private Associations." *JRS* 106 (2016): 147–71.
Eckstein, H.-J. "Auferstehung und gegenwärtiges Leben nach Röm 6,1–11: Präsentische Eschatologie bei Paulus?" *TBei* 28 (1997): 8–23.
Edsall, B., and J. R. Strawbridge. "The Songs We Used to Sing? Hymn 'Traditions' and Reception in Pauline Letters." *JSNT* 37 (2015): 290–311.
Egan, R. B. "Lexical Evidence on Two Pauline Passages." *NovT* 19 (1977): 34–62.
Ehrman, B. *Forgery and Counterforgery: The Use of Literary Deceit in Early Christian Polemics*. Oxford: Oxford University Press, 2012.
Eidinow, E. *Oracles, Curses, and Risk among the Ancient Greeks*. Oxford: Oxford University Press, 2007.
Eitrem, S. E. "'EMBATEYΩ: Note sur Col. 2, 18." *ST* 2 (1948): 90–94.
———. *Orakel und Mysterien am Ausgang der Antike*. Albae Vigiliae 5. Zürich: Rhein-Verlag, 1947.
———. *Papyri Osloenses. Fasc. 1. Magical Papyri*. Oslo: Academy of Science and Letters of Oslo, 1925.
———. *Some Notes on the Demonology of the New Testament*. Symbolae Osloenses Fasc. Supplement 12. Oslo: A. W. Brogger, 1950.
Elliott, J. H. *Beware the Evil Eye: The Evil Eye in the Bible and the Ancient World. Volume 2: Greece and Rome*. Eugene, OR: Cascade, 2016.
Elliott, S. *Cutting Too Close for Comfort: Paul's Letter to the Galatians in Its Anatolian Context*. JSNTSup 248. Edinburgh: T&T Clark, 2003.
Ellis, E. E. "Colossians 1:12–20: Christus Creator, Christus Salvator." Pages 415–28 in *Interpreting the New Testament Text: Introduction to the Art and Science of Exegesis*. Edited by D. L. Bock and B. M. Fanning. Wheaton, IL: Crossway, 2006.
———. *The Making of the New Testament Documents*. BibInt 39. Leiden: Brill, 1999.
Engberg-Pedersen, T. "Paul, Virtues and Vices." Pages 608–33 in *Paul in the Greco-Roman World*. Edited by J. P. Sampley. Harrisburg, PA: Trinity Press International, 2003.
Erdemir, H. "Woollen Textiles: An International Trade Good in the Lycus Valley in Antiquity." Pages 104–29 in *Colossae in Space and Time: Linking to an Ancient City*. Edited by A. H. Cadwallader and M. Trainor. NTOA/SUNT 94. Göttingen: Vandenhoeck & Ruprecht, 2011.
Evans, C. A. "The Colossian Mystics." *Bib* 63 (1982): 188–205.
Everling, O. *Die paulinische Angelologie und Dämonologie*. Göttingen: Vandenhoeck & Ruprecht, 1888.
Fairweather, J. "The Epistle to the Galatians and Classical Rhetoric: Part 3." *TynBul* 45 (1994): 211–43.
———. "The Epistle to the Galatians and Classical Rhetoric: Parts 1 & 2." *TynBul* 45 (1994): 1–38.
Fantin, J. *The Imperative Mood in Greek: A Cognitive and Communicative Approach*. Studies in Biblical Greek 12. New York: Peter Lang, 2010.
Farnell, L. R. *Cults of the Greek States*. 4 vols. Oxford: Clarendon, 1896.
Fee, G. D. *God's Empowering Presence: The Holy Spirit in the Letters of Paul*. Peabody, Mass.: Hendrickson, 1994.
———. *Pauline Christology: An Exegetical-Theological Study*. Peabody, MA: Hendrickson, 2007.
Ferguson, E. *Baptism in the Early Church: History, Theology, and Liturgy in the First Five Centuries*. Grand Rapids: Eerdmans, 2009.
———. "Spiritual Circumcision in Early Christianity." *SJT* 41 (1988): 485–97.
Fewster, G. P. "Hermeneutical Issues in Canonical Pseudepigrapha: The Head/Body Motif in the Pauline Corpus as a Test Case." Pages 89–112 in *Paul and Pseudepigraphy*. Edited by S. E. Porter and G. P. Fewster. Leiden: Brill, 2013.

Fischer, K. M. *Tendenz und Absicht des Epheserbriefes*. FRLANT 111. Göttingen: Vandenhoeck & Ruprecht, 1973.

Fitzmyer, J. A. "Another Look at κεφαλή in 1 Corinthians 11.3." *NTS* 35 (1989): 503–11.

———. *The Gospel According to Luke*. 2 vols. AB 28, 28A. New York: Doubleday, 1981, 1985.

———. *Romans: A New Translation with Introduction and Commentary*. AB 33. New York: Doubleday, 1993.

Flemming, D. *Contextualization in the New Testament: Patterns for Theology and Mission*. Downers Grove, IL: InterVarsity Press, 2005.

Foerster, W. "Die Irrlehrer des Kolosserbriefes." Pages 71–80 in *Studia Biblica et Semitica*. FS T. C. Vriezen. Edited by W. C. van Unnik and A. S. van der Woude. Wageningen, Netherlands: Veenman & Zonen, 1966.

Fontenrose, J. *Didyma: Apollo's Oracle, Cult, and Companions*. Berkeley: University of California Press. 1988.

Forbes, C. "Ancient Rhetoric and Ancient Letters: Models for Reading Paul, and Their Limits." Pages 143–60 in *Paul and Rhetoric*. Edited by J. P. Sampley and P. Lampe. New York: T&T Clark, 2010.

Foschia, L. "Le nom du culte, θρησκεία, et ses dérivés à l'époque impériale." Pages 15–35 in *L'Hellénisme d'Époque Romaine: Nouveaux Documents, Nouvelles Approches (Ier s.a.C.–IIIe s.p.C.). Actes du Colloque international à la mémoire de Louis Robert, Paris, 7–8 juillet 2000*. Edited by S. Follet. Paris: de Boccard, 2004.

Fossum, J. "Colossians 1.15–18 in the Light of Jewish Mysticism and Gnosticism." *NTS* 35 (1989): 183–201.

———. "The Image of the Invisible God: Colossians 1.15–18 in the Light of Jewish Mysticism and Gnosticism." Pages 13–39 in *The Image of the Invisible God: Essays on the Influence of Jewish Mysticism on Early Christology*. NTOA 30. Göttingen: Vandenhoeck & Ruprecht, 1995.

Fowl, S. E. *The Story of Christ in the Ethics of Paul*. JSNTSup 36. Sheffield: JSOT Press, 1990.

Francis, F. O. "The Background of EMBATEUEIN (Col 2:18) in Legal Papyri and Oracle Inscriptions." Pages 197–207 in *Conflict at Colossae*. Edited by F. O. Francis and W. A. Meeks. SBLSBS 4. Missoula, MT: Scholars Press, 1973.

———. "Humility and Angelic Worship in Col 2:18." Pages 163–95 in *Conflict at Colossae*. Edited by F. O. Francis and W. A. Meeks. SBLSBS 4. Missoula, MT: Scholars Press, 1973.

———. "A Reexamination of the Colossian Controversy." PhD diss., Yale University, 1964.

Francis, F. O., and W. A. Meeks, eds. *Conflict at Colossae*. SBLSBS 4. Missoula, MT: Scholars Press, 1975.

Frank, N. *Der Kolosserbrief im Kontext des paulinischen Erbes*. WUNT 2/271. Tübingen: Mohr Siebeck, 2009.

———. "Der Kolosserbrief und the 'Philosophia': Pseudepigraphie als Spiegel frühchristlicher Auseinandersetzung um die Auslegung des paulinischen Erbes." Pages 411–32 in *Pseudepigraphie und Verfasserfiktion in frühchristlichen Briefen = Pseudepigaphy and Author Fiction in Early Christian Letters*. Edited by J. Frey, J. Herzer, M. Janssen, and C. K. Rothschild. WUNT 246. Tübingen: Mohr Siebeck, 2009.

Frankfurter, D. *Christianizing Egypt: Syncretism and Local Worlds in Late Antiquity*. Princeton: Princeton University Press, 2018.

———. *Religion in Roman Egypt: Assimilation and Reistance*. Princeton: Princeton University Press, 1998.

Fraser, K. A. "Roman Antiquity: The Imperial Period." Pages 115–47 in *The Cambridge History of Magic and Witchcraft in the West: From Antiquity to Present*. Edited by D. J. Collins. Cambridge: Cambridge University Press, 2015.

Frey, J. "Die paulinische Antithese von 'Fleisch' und 'Geist' und die palästinisch-jüdische Weisheitstradition." *ZNW* 90 (1999): 45–77.

Frey, J.-B. "L'Angélologie Juive au temps de Jésus-Christ." *RSPT* 5 (1911): 75–110.
Furnish, V. P. *Theology and Ethics in Paul*. Nashville: Abingdon, 1968.
Gabathuler, H. J. *Jesus Christus: Haupt der Kirche—Haupt der Welt. Der Christushymnus Colosser 1, 15–20 in der theologischen Forschung der letzten 130 Jahre*. ATANT 45. Zürich: Zwingli, 1965.
Gager, J. G. *Moses in Greco-Roman Paganism*. SBLMS 16. Nashville: Abingdon, 1972.
Gardner, P. D. "Circumcised in Baptism—Raised through Faith." *WTJ* 45 (1983): 172–77.
Gehring, R. W. *House Church and Mission: The Importance of Household Structures in Early Christianity*. Peabody, MA: Hendrickson, 2004.
Geréb, Z. "Paulus als Diener der Kirche: Die Vorstellung des Apostels in Kolosser 1,21–3,5." Pages 33–54 in *Kolosser-Studien*. Edited by P. Müller. Biblisch-Theologische Studien 103. Neukirchen-Vluyn: Neukirchener, 2009.
Gerlitz, P. "Fasten als Reinigungsritus." *ZRGG* 20 (1968): 212–22.
Gese, H. "Die Weisheit, der Menschensohn, und die Ursprünge der Christologie als konsequente Entfaltung der biblischen Theologie." Pages 218–48 in *Alttestamentliche Studien*. Tübingen: Mohr Siebeck, 1991.
Gibbs, J. G. *Creation and Redemption: A Study in Pauline Theology*. NovTSup 26. Leiden: Brill, 1971.
Gielen, M. *Tradition und Theologie neutestamentlicher Haustafelethik: Ein Beitrag zur Frage einer christlichen Auseinandersetzung mit gesellschaftlichen Normen*. BBB 75. Frankfurt am Main: Hain, 1990.
———. "Zur Interpretation der paulinischen Formel ἡ κατ' οἶκον ἐκκλησία." *ZNW* 77 (1986): 109–25.
Giem, P. "*Sabbatōn* in Col 2:16." *AUSS* 19 (1981): 195–210.
Giversen, S. "Solomon und die Dämonen." Pages 16–21 in *Essays on the Nag Hammadi Texts in Honor of Alexander Böhlig*. Edited by M. Krause. NHS 3. Leiden: Brill, 1972.
Gladd, B. L. *Revealing the Mysterion: The Use of Mystery in Daniel and Second Temple Judaism with Its Bearing on First Corinthians*. BZNW 160. Berlin: de Gruyter, 2008.
Glancy, J. A. *Slavery in Early Christianity*. Oxford: Oxford University Press, 2002.
Gloer, W. H. "Homologies and Hymns in the New Testament: Form, Content and Criteria for Identification." *PRSt* 11 (1984): 115–32.
Goetze, A. *Kulturgeschichte des Alten Orients: Kleinasien*. 2nd Ed. Handbuch der Altertumswissenschaft 3.1.3.3.1. München: C. H. Beck'sche, 1957.
Goff, M. J. *4QInstruction*. WLAW 2. Atlanta: Society of Biblical Literature, 2013.
Goodenough, E. R. *Jewish Symbols in the Greco-Roman Period, Volume I: The Archaeological Evidence from Palestine*. New York: Pantheon, 1953.
———. *Jewish Symbols in the Greco-Roman Period, Volume II: The Archaeological Evidence from the Diaspora*. New York: Pantheon, 1953.
———. *Jewish Symbols in the Greco-Roman Period, Volume 10.2: Symbolism in the Dura Synagogue*. Bollingen Series 37. New York: Bollingen Foundation, 1964.
Goodrich, J. R. *Paul as an Administrator of God in 1 Corinthians*. SNTSMS 152. Cambridge: Cambridge University Press, 2012.
Goppelt, L. *Theology of the New Testament*. 2 Vols. Translated by J. E. Alsup. Grand Rapids: Eerdmans, 1982.
Gordley, M. E. *The Colossian Hymn in Context: An Exegesis in Light of Jewish and Greco-Roman Hymnic and Epistolary Conventions*. WUNT 2/228. Tübingen: Mohr Siebeck, 2007.
———. *New Testament Christological Hymns: Exploring Texts, Contexts, and Significance*. Downers Grove, IL: InterVarsity Press, 2018.
———. *Teaching through Song in Antiquity: Didactic Hymnody among Greeks, Romans, Jews, and Christians*. WUNT 2/302. Tübingen: Mohr Siebeck, 2011.
Gordon, R. "Another View of the Pergamon Divination Kit." *JRA* 15 (2002): 188–98.
Goulder, M. "Colossians and Barbelo." *NTS* 41 (1995): 601–19.
Gräbe, P. J. *The Power of God in Paul's Letters*. 2nd ed. WUNT 2/123. Tübingen: Mohr Siebeck, 2008.

———. "Salvation in Colossians and Ephesians." Pages 287–304 in *Salvation in the New Testament: Perspectives on Soteriology*. Edited by J. G. van der Watt. NovTSup 121. Leiden: Brill, 2005.

Graf, F. *Apollo*. Gods and Heroes of the Ancient World. New York: Routledge, 2009.

———. "The Magician's Initiation." *Helios* 21 (1994): 161–77.

———. "An Oracle against Pestilence from a Western Anatolian Town." *ZPE* 92 (1992): 267–79.

Graillot, H. *Le Culte de Cybele: Mere des Dieux, a Rome et dans l'Empire romain*. Bibliotheque des Ecoles Francaises d'Athenes et de Rome 107. Paris: Fontemoing, 1912.

Grässer, E. "Kol. 3:1–4 als Beispiel einer Interpretation secundum homines recipientes." *ZTK* 64 (1967): 139–68.

Griffiths, J. G. *The Isis-Book (Metamorphoses, Book XI)*. EPRO 39. Leiden: Brill, 1975.

Grindheim, S. "A Deutero-Pauline Mystery? Ecclesiology in Colossians and Ephesians." Pages 173–96 in *Paul and Pseudepigraphy*. Edited by S. E. Porter and G. P. Fewster. Leiden: Brill, 2013.

Grundmann, W. *Der Begriff der Kraft in der neutestamentlichen Gedankenwelt*. BWANT 8. Stuttgart: Kohlhammer, 1932.

Guichard, C. "Travels and Traversals in the Hellenistic Oracular Temples at Klaros and Didyma." PhD diss., Columbia University, 2005.

Gundel, H. G. "Imagines Zodiaci: Zu neueren Funden und Forschungen." Pages 438–54 in *Hommages à Maarten J. Vermaseren*. Edited by M. B. De Boer and T. A. Edridge. EPRO 68. Leiden: Brill, 1978.

———. *Weltbild und Astrologie in den griechischen Zauberpapyri*. Münchener Beiträge zur Papyrusforschung und Antiken Rechtsgeschichte 53. München: Beck, 1968.

Gundel, W. *Dekane und Dekansternbilder: Ein Beitrag zur Geschichte der Sternbilder der Kulturvölker*. 2nd ed. Darmstadt: Wissenschaftliche Buchgesellschaft, 1969.

Gunther, J. J. *St. Paul's Opponents and Their Background: A Study of Apocalyptic and Jewish Sectarian Teachings*. NovTSup 35. Leiden: Brill, 1973.

Gupta, N. "What Is in a Name? The Hermeneutics of Authorship Analysis concerning Colossians." *CurBR* 11 (2013): 196–217.

Guthrie, D. *New Testament Introduction*. Rev. ed. Downers Grove, IL: InterVarsity Press, 1990.

Hafemann, S. *Suffering and Ministry in the Spirit: An Exegetical Study of II Cor 2:14–3:3 within the Context of the Corinthian Correspondence*. WUNT 2/19. Tübingen: Mohr Siebeck, 1986.

Hagen Pifer, J. *Faith as Participation: An Exegetical Study of Some Key Pauline Texts*. WUNT 2/486. Tübingen: Mohr Siebeck, 2019.

Hall, A. S. "The Klarian Oracle at Oenoanda." *ZPE* 32 (1978): 263–67.

Hansen, B. *"All of You Are One": The Social Vision of Galatians 3.28, 1 Corinthians 12.13 and Colossians 3.11*. LNTS 409. London: T&T Clark, 2010.

Harland, P. A. "Acculturation and Identity in the Diaspora: A Jewish Family and 'Pagan' Guilds at Hierapolis." *JJS* 57 (2006): 222–44.

Harper, K. "*Porneia*: The Making of a Christian Sexual Norm." *JBL* 131 (2011): 363–83.

Harrison, J. R. *Paul's Language of Grace in Its Graeco-Roman Context*. WUNT 2/172. Tübingen: Mohr Siebeck, 2003.

———. "Paul's Legacy in Romans and the Confession Inscriptions of Asia Minor: The Difficulty of Moving beyond Divine Justice to Mercy in Antiquity." Pages 337–87 in *Romans and the Legacy of St. Paul: Historical, Theological, and Social Perspectives*. Edited by P. G. Bolt and J. R. Harrison. Occasional Series 1. Macquarie Park, NSW: SCD, 2019.

Harrisville, R. A. "The Concept of Newness in the New Testament." *JBL* 74 (1955): 69–79.

Hartmann, L. *"Auf den Namen des Herrn Jesus": Die Taufe in den neutestamentlichen Schriften*. SBS 148. Stuttgart: Katholisches Bibelwerk, 1992.

———. "Code and Context: A Few Reflections on the Parenesis of Col 3:6–4:1." Pages 237–47 in *Tradition and Interpretation in the New Testament: Essays in Honor of E. Earle Ellis*. Edited by G. F. Hawthorne. Grand Rapids: Eerdmans, 1987.

———. "Universal Reconciliation (Col 1,20)." *SNTSU* 10 (1985): 109–21.

Hatch, W. H. P. "Τὰ Στοιχεῖα in Paul and Bardaisan." *JTS* 28 (1927): 181–82.

Hatina, T. R. "The Perfect Tense-Form in Colossians: Verbal Aspect, Temporality and the Challenge of Translation." Pages 224–52 in *Translating the Bible: Problems and Prospects*. JSNTSup 173. Sheffield: Sheffield Academic Press, 1999.

Haufe, G. "Hellenistische Volksfrömmigkeit." Pages 68–100 in *Umwelt des Urchristentums I: Darstellung des neutestamentlichen Zeitalters*. Edited by J. Leipoldt and W. Grundmann. Berlin: Evangelische Verlagsanstalt, 1971.

Haussoullier, B. "L'Oracle d'Apollon a Claros." *Revue de Philologie* 22 (1898): 257–73.

Hauvette-Besnault, A., and M. Dubois. "Inscriptions de Carie." *BCH* 5 (1881): 179–94.

Hay, D. M. "All the Fullness of God: Concepts of Deity in Colossians and Ephesians." Pages 163–80 in *The Forgotten God: Perspectives in Biblical Theology*. Edited by A. A. Das and F. J. Matera. Louisville: Westminster John Knox, 2002.

———. *Glory at the Right Hand: Psalm 110 in Early Christianity*. SBLMS 18. Nashville: Abingdon, 1973.

Hayes, H. D. "Colossians 2:6–19." *Int* 49 (1995): 285–88.

Hayman, P. "Was God a Magician? Sefer Yesira and Jewish Magic." *JJS* 40 (1989): 225–37.

Hefele, C. J. *A History of the Councils of the Church, Volume II: A.D. 326–A.D. 429*. Edinburgh: T&T Clark, 1896.

Hegermann, H. *Die Vorstellung vom Schöpfungsmittler im hellenistischen Judentum und Urchristentum*. TU 82. Berlin: Akademie, 1961.

Heil, J. P. *Colossians: Encouragement to Walk in All Wisdom as Holy Ones in Christ*. SBL Early Christianity and Its Literature 4. Atlanta: Society of Biblical Literature, 2010.

Heilig, C. *The Apostle and the Empire: Paul's Implicit and Explicit Criticism of Rome*. Grand Rapids: Eerdmans, 2022.

Heininger, B. "Soziale und politische Metaphorik im Kolosserbrief." Pages 55–82 in *Kolosser-Studien*. Edited by P. Müller. Biblisch-Theologische Studien 103. Neukirchen-Vluyn: Neukirchener, 2009.

Hellerman, J. *When the Church Was a Family*. Nashville: B&H Academic, 2009.

Hellholm, D. "Die Gattung Haustafel im Kolosser- und Epheserbrief: Ihre Position innerhalb der Paränese-Abschnitte und ihr Hintergrund in der spätantiken Gesellschaft." Pages 103–28 in *Kolosser-Studien*. Edited by P. Müller. Biblisch-Theologische Studien 103. Neukirchen-Vluyn: Neukirchener, 2009.

Helyer, L. "Arius Revisited: The Firstborn over All Creation (Col 1:15)." *JETS* 31 (1988): 59–67.

———. "Colossians 1:15–20: Pre-Pauline or Pauline?" *JETS* 26 (1983): 167–79.

———. "Cosmic Christology and Col 1:15–20." *JETS* 37 (1994): 235–46.

———. "Recent Research on Col 1:15–20 (1980–1990)." *GTJ* 12 (1992): 51–67.

Hemberg, B. "Die Idaiischen Daktylen." *Eranos: Acta philologica suecana a Vilelmo Lundström condita* 50 (1952): 41–59.

Hemer, C. *The Book of Acts in the Setting of Hellenistic History*. Edited by C. Gempf. WUNT 49. Tübingen: Mohr Siebeck, 1989. Repr., Winona Lake, IN: Eisenbrauns, 1990.

———. *The Letters to the Seven Churches of Asia in Their Local Setting*. JSNTSup 11. Sheffield: JSOT Press, 1986.

Hengel, M. "Der alte und der neue 'Schürer.'" *JSS* 35 (1990): 19–72.

———. "Christology and New Testament Chronology: A Problem in the History of Earliest Christianity." Pages 30–47, 156–65 in *Between Jesus and Paul: Studies in the Earliest History of Christianity*. Philadelphia: Fortress, 1983.

———. "Das Chrustuslied im frühesten Gottesdienst." Pages 357–404 in *Weisheit Gottes—Weisheit der Welt.* Edited by W. Baier. St. Ottilien: EOS, 1987.

———. "Hymns and Christology." Pages 78–96 in *Between Jesus and Paul: Studies in the Earliest History of Christianity.* Philadelphia: Fortress, 1983.

———. "Hymnus und Christologie." Pages 3–23 in *Wort in der Zeit: Neutestamentliche Studien.* FS K. H. Rengstorf. Edited by W. Haubeck and M. Bachmann. Leiden: Brill, 1980.

———. *Judaism and Hellenism: Studies in Their Encounter in Palestine during the Early Hellenistic Period.* 2 Vols. Translated by J. Bowden. London: SCM, 1974.

———. *The Pre-Christian Paul.* Philadelphia: Trinity Press International, 1991.

———. *The Son of God.* Philadelphia: Fortress, 1976.

———. "Die Synagogeninschrift von Stobi." *ZNW* 57 (1966): 145–83.

———. "Die Ursprünge der Gnosis and das Urchristentum." Pages 190–223 in *Evangelium—Schriftauslegung—Kirche.* FS P. Stuhlmacher. Edited by J. Ådna, S. J. Hafemann, and O. Hofius. Göttingen: Vandenhoeck & Ruprecht, 1997.

Hengel, M., and A. M. Schwemer. *Paul between Damascus and Antioch: The Unknown Years.* Louisville: Westminster John Knox, 1997.

Henle, F. A. "Der Men- und Mithrakult in Phrgyien: Skizzen zur Vorgeschichte der kolossischen Irrlehre." *TQ* 70 (1888): 590–614.

Hering, J. P. *The Colossian and Ephesian Haustafeln in Theological Context: An Analysis of Their Origins, Relationship, and Message.* AUS 7/260. New York: Lang, 2007.

Herrmann, P., and K. Z. Polatkan. *Das Testament des Epikrates und andere neue Inscriften aus dem Museum von Manisa.* Sitzungsberichte Österreichische Akademie der Wissenschaften, Philosophisch-Historische Klasse 265.1. Vienna: Hermann Böhlhaus, 1969.

Hill, G. F. "Apollo and St. Michael: Some Analogies." *JHS* 36 (1916): 134–62.

Hoehner, H. W. *Ephesians: An Exegetical Commentary.* Grand Rapids: Baker, 2002.

Hofius, O. "'Erstgeborener vor aller Schöpfung'—'Erstgeborener aus den Toten': Erwägungen zu Struktur und Aussage des Christushymnus Kol 1,15–20." Pages 185–203 in *Auferstehung-Resurrection: The Fourth Durham Tübingen Research Symposium.* Edited by F. Avemarie and H. Lichtenberger. WUNT 136. Tübingen: Mohr Siebeck, 2001.

———. "Gemeinschaft mit den Engeln im Gottesdienst der Kirche: Eine traditionsgeschichtliche Skizze." *ZTK* 89 (1992): 172–96.

Hofmann, J. "Christliche Frauen im Dienst kleinasiatischer Gemeinden des ersten und zweiten Jahrhunderts: Eine prosopographische Studie." *VC* 54 (2000): 283–308.

Holbrook, F. B. "Did the Apostle Paul Abolish the Sabbath? Colossians 2:14–17 Revisited." *Journal of the Adventist Theological Society* 13 (2002): 64–72.

Hollenbach, B. "Col. II.23: Which Things Lead to the Fulfilment of the Flesh." *NTS* 25 (1978–79): 254–61.

Holmes, M. W. "Reasoned Eclecticism in New Testament Textual Criticism." Pages 771–802 in *The Text of the New Testament in Contemporary Research: Essays on the* Status Quaestionis. 2nd ed. NTTSD 42. Leiden: Brill, 2013.

Hölscher, A. "Christus als Bild Gottes: Zum Hymnus des Kolosserbriefes." Pages 114–33 in *Religiöse Sprache und ihre Bilder: Von der Bible bis zur modernen Lyrik.* Edited by A. Hölscher and R. Kampling. Berlin: Morus, 1998.

Holtzmann, H. J. *Kritik der Epheser- und Kolosserbriefe auf Grund einer Analyse Ihres Verwandtschaftsverhältnisses.* Leipzig: Wilhelm Engelmann, 1872.

Homolle, T. "Nouvelles et correspondance: Ionie." *BCH* 17 (1893): 638.

Hooker, M. D. "Were There False Teachers in Colossae?" Pages 315–31 in *Christ and Spirit in the New Testament.* FS C. F. D. Moule. Edited by B. Lindars and S. Smalley. Cambridge: Cambridge University Press, 1973.

———. "Where Is Wisdom to Be Found? Colossians 1.15–20 (1)." Pages 116–28 in *Reading*

*Texts, Seeking Wisdom: Scripture and Theology*. Edited by D. F. Ford and G. Stanton. Grand Rapids: Eerdmans, 2003.

Hopfner, T. *Griechisch-Agyptischer Offenbarungszauber*. 2 vols. Studien zur Palaeographie und Papyruskunde. Amsterdam: Adolf M. Hakkert, 1974, 1983. Repr., Leipzig: Haessel, 1921, 1924.

———. "Hekate-Selene-Artemis und Verwandte in den griechischen Zauberpapyri und auf den Fluchtafeln." Pages 125–45 in *Pisciculi: F. J. Dölger zum 60. Geburtstage*. Münster: Aschendorff, 1939.

Hopkins, K. *Conquerors and Slaves*. Sociological Studies in Roman History 1. Cambridge: Cambridge University Press, 1978.

Hoppe, R. *Der Triumph des Kreuzes: Studien zum Verhältnis des Kolosserbriefes zur paulinischen Kreuzestheologie*. SBB 28. Stuttgart: Katholisches Bibelwerk, 1994.

Horsley, G. H. R. "The Inscriptions of Ephesos and the New Testament." *NovT* 34 (1992): 105–68.

Horsley, G. H. R., and S. Llewelyn, eds. *New Documents Illustrating Early Christianity*. 10 vols. North Ryde, NSW, Australia: Macquarie University, 1981–. Repr., Grand Rapids: Eerdmans, 1997–.

Horsley, G. H. R., and J. M. Luxford. "Pagan Angels in Roman Asia Minor: Revisiting the Epigraphic Evidence." *AnSt* 66 (2016): 141–83.

Horst, P. W. van der. "The Great Magical Papyrus of Paris (PGM IV) and the Bible." Pages 173–83 in *A Kind of Magic: Understanding Magic in the New Testament and Its Religious Environment*. LNTS 306. Edited by B. J. L. Peerbolte and M. Labahn. London: T&T Clark, 2007.

———. "The Jews of Ancient Phrygia." *European Journal of Jewish Studies* 2 (2009): 283–92.

Huffman, D. S. *Verbal Aspect Theory and the Prohibitions in the Greek New Testament*. Studies in Biblical Greek 16. New York: Lang, 2014.

Humann, C., C. Cichorius, W. Judeich, and F. Winter. *Altertümer von Hierapolis*. Berlin: Georg Reimer, 1898.

Hunt, J. P. T. "Colossians 2:11–12, the Circumcision/Baptism Analogy, and Infant Baptism." *TynBul* 41 (1990): 227–44.

Hurtado, L. W. *Lord Jesus Christ: Devotion to Jesus in Earliest Christianity*. Grand Rapids: Eerdmans, 2003.

———. *One God, One Lord: Early Christian Devotion and Ancient Jewish Monotheism*. Philadelphia: Fortress, 1988.

Huttner, U. "Colossians, Hierapolitan Coins—and the Young Bearers of Hope." Pages 73–79 in *The First Urban Churches 5: Colossae, Hierapolis, and Laodicea*. Edited by J. R. Harrison and L. L. Welborn. WGRWSup 16. Atlanta: SBL Press, 2019.

———. *Early Christianity in the Lycus Valley*. Translated by D. Green. AJEC 85/ECAM 1. Leiden: Brill, 2013.

———. "Vorkonstantinishes Christentum in Lykos- und Mäandertal: Das Zeugnis der Inschriften." Pages 1–24 in *Epigraphical Evidence Illustrating Paul's Letter to the Colossians*. Edited by J. Verheyden, M. Öhler, and T. Corsten. WUNT 2/411. Tubingen: Mohr Siebeck, 2018.

Immendörfer, M. *Ephesians and Artemis: The Cult of the Great Goddess of Ephesus as the Epistle's Context*. WUNT 2/436. Tübingen: Mohr Siebeck, 2017.

Janowitz, N. *Magic in the Roman World: Pagans, Jews and Christians*. London: Routledge, 2001.

Janssen, M. "Die Themistoklesbriefe zwischen Fälschung und Fiktion—Zur Relevanz griechischer Brieffiktionen für die neutestamentliche Pseudepigraphiefrage." *ZNW* 111 (2020): 161–93.

Jeremias, J. *Jerusalem in the Time of Jesus: An Investigation into Economic and Social Conditions during the New Testament Period*. Philadelphia: Fortress, 1969.

Jervell, J. *Imago Dei: Gen 1, 26f im Spätjudentum, in der Gnosis und in den paulinischen Briefen.* FRLANT 76. Göttingen: Vandenhoeck & Ruprecht, 1960.

Jobes, K. H. "Sophia Christology: The Way of Wisdom?" Pages 79–103 in *The Way of Wisdom: Essays in Honor of Bruce K. Waltke.* Edited by J. I. Packer and S. K. Soderlund. Grand Rapids: Zondervan, 2000.

Johnson, L. T. *The Acts of the Apostles.* SP 5. Collegeville, MN,: Liturgical Press, 1992.

Johnson, S. E. "Asia Minor and Early Christianity." Pages 77–145 in *Christianity, Judaism and Other Greco-Roman Cults II.* FS M. Smith. Edited by J. Neusner. SJLA 12. Leiden: Brill, 1975.

———. "Laodicea and Its Neighbors." *BA* 13 (1950): 1–18.

———. "The Present State of Sabazios Research." *ANRW* II.17.3 (1984): 1583–1613.

———. "Unsolved Questions about Early Christianity in Anatolia." Pages 181–93 in *Studies in New Testament and Early Christian Literature.* FS A. P. Wikgren. Edited by D. E. Aune. NovTSup 33. Leiden: Brill, 1972.

Johnston, S. I. *Ancient Greek Divination.* Blackwell Ancient Religions. Oxford: Wiley-Blackwell, 2008.

———. *Hekate Soteira: A Study of Hekate's Roles in the Chaldean Oracles and Related Literature.* American Philological Association. American Classical Studies 21. Atlanta: Scholars Press, 1990.

Jones, C. P. "A Hellenistic Cult-Association." *Chiron* 38 (2008): 195–204.

Jonge, C. C de. *Between Grammar and Rhetoric: Dionysius of Halicarnassus on Language, Linguistics and Literature.* Mnemosyne Supplements 301. Leiden: Brill, 2008.

Jordan, D. R. "Curse Tablets of the Roman Period from the Athenian Agora." *Hesperia* 91 (2022): 133–210.

———. "A Love Charm with Verses." *ZPE* 72 (1988): 245–59.

———. "New Greek Curse Tablets (1985–2000)." *GRBS* 41 (2000): 5–46.

———. "A Survey of Greek Defixiones Not Included in the Special Corpora." *GRBS* 26 (1985): 151–97.

Jordan, D., and R. Kotansky. "Two Phylacteries from Xanthos." *RAr* 1 (1996): 167–74.

Joshel, S. R. *Slavery in the Roman World.* Cambridge Introduction to Roman Civilization. Cambridge: Cambridge University Press, 2010.

Käsemann, E. "Kolosserbrief." *RGG*³ 3:1727–28.

———. "A Primitive Christian Baptismal Liturgy." Pages 149–68 in *Essays on New Testament Themes.* Translated by W. J. Montague. SBT 41. London: SCM, 1964.

Kearsley, R. A. "Epigraphic Evidence for the Social Impact of Roman Government in Laodicea and Hierapolis." Pages 130–50 in *Colossae in Space and Time: Linking to an Ancient City.* Edited by A. H. Cadwallader and M. Trainor. NTOA/SUNT 94. Göttingen: Vandenhoeck & Ruprecht, 2011.

Keener, C. "Heavenly Mindedness and Earthly Good: Contemplating Matters Above in Colossians." *JGRChJ* 6 (2009): 175–90.

Kehl, N. *Der Christushymnus im Kolosserbrief: Eine motivgeschichtliche Untersuchung zu Kol 1, 12–20.* SBM 1. Stuttgart: Katholisches Bibelwerk, 1967.

Keil, J. "Ein rätselhaftes Amulett." *JÖAI* 32 (1940): 79–84.

Keil, J., and A. Premerstein. *Bericht über eine zweite Reise in Lydien.* Vienna: Hölder, 1911.

Kennedy, G. A. *Art of Persuasion in Greece.* Princeton: Princeton University Press, 1963.

———. *A New History of Classical Rhetoric.* Princeton: Princeton University Press, 2011.

———. *New Testament Interpretation through Rhetorical Criticism.* Studies in Religion. Chapel Hill: University of North Carolina Press, 1984.

Kern, P. *Rhetoric and Galatians: Assessing an Approach to Paul's Epistles.* SNTSMS 101. Cambridge: Cambridge University Press, 1998.

Kerschbaum, S. "Die Apollines von Hierapolis in Phrygien." *Jahrbuch für Numismatik und Geldgeschichte* 64 (2014): 15–42.

Kiley, M. *Colossians as Pseudepigraphy*. The Biblical Seminar. Sheffield: JSOT Press, 1986.

Kim, J. H. *The Significance of Clothing Imagery in the Pauline Corpus*. JSNTSup 268. London: T.&T. Clark, 2004.

Kim, S. *The Origin of Paul's Gospel*. WUNT 2/4. Tübingen: Mohr Siebeck, 1981.

Kim, Y. K. "Palaeographical Dating of $P^{46}$ to the Later First Century." *Biblica* 69 (1988): 248–57.

King, M. *An Exegetical Summary of Colossians*. Dallas: Summer Institute of Linguistics, 1998.

Kirkland, A. "The Beginnings of Christianity in the Lycus Valley: An Exercise in Historical Reconstruction." *Neot* 29 (1995): 109–24.

Kittel, G. "Das kleinasiatische Judentum in der hellenistisch-römischen Zeit." *TLZ* 1.2 (1944): 9–20.

Klauck, H.-J. *Ancient Letters and the New Testament: A Guide to Context and Exegesis*. Waco, TX: Baylor University Press, 2006.

———. *Magic and Paganism in Early Christianity*. Edinburgh: T &T Clark, 2000.

Klutz, T. E. *Rewriting the Testament of Solomon: Tradition, Conflict and Identity in a Late Antique Pseudepigraphon*. LSTS 53. London: T&T Clark, 2005.

Knox, J. *Philemon among the Letters of Paul*. Chicago: University of Chicago Press, 1935.

Knox, W. L. "Jewish Liturgical Exorcism." *HTR* 31 (1938): 191–203.

———. *St. Paul and the Church of the Gentiles*. Cambridge: Cambridge University Press, 1961.

Koester, H. *History and Literature of Early Christianity*. 2nd ed. Berlin: de Gruyter, 2000.

———. *Introduction to the New Testament*. 2 vols. Philadelphia: Fortress, 1982.

Kok, J. "Christology in the Making: The Problem of Worshiping and Honouring Angels in Colossians." Pages 145–69 in *The New Testament in the Graeco-Roman World: Articles in Honor of Abe Malherbe*. Theology in Africa 4. Edited by N. Nel, J. G. van der Watt, and F. J. van Rendsburg. Münster: LIT, 2014.

Kotansky, R. "Incantations and Prayers for Salvation on Inscribed Greek Amulets." Pages 107–37 in *Magika Hiera: Ancient Greek Magic and Religion*. Edited by C. A. Faraone and D. Obbink. Oxford: Oxford University Press, 1991.

———. "A Silver Votive Plaque with a Judicial Prayer against Slander." *GRBS* 60 (2020): 139–57.

———. "Texts and Studies in the Graeco-Egyptian Magic Lamellae: An Introduction, Corpus, and Commentary on the Phylacteries and Amulets Principally Engraved onto Gold and Silver Tablets." PhD diss., University of Chicago, 1988.

Kraabel, A. T. "The Diaspora Synagogue: Archaeological and Epigraphic Evidence Since Sukenik." *ANRW* II.19.1 (1979): 477–510.

———. "Judaism in Asia Minor under the Roman Empire with a Preliminary Study of the Jewish Community at Sardis, Lydia." PhD diss., Harvard University, 1968.

———. "Paganism and Judaism: The Sardis Evidence." Pages 13–33 in *Paganisme, Judaïsme, Christianisme: Influences et affrontements dans le Monde Antique*. Mélanges offerts à Marcel Simon. Edited by A. Benoit, M. Philonenko, and C. Vogel. Paris: de Boccard, 1978.

———. "The Roman Diaspora: Six Questionable Assumptions." *JJS* 33 (1982): 445–64.

———. "ΥΨΙΣΤΟΣ and the Synagogue at Sardis." *GRBS* 10 (1969): 81–93.

Kraft, R. "The Multiform Jewish Heritage of Early Christianity." Pages 174–205 in *Christianity, Judaism and Other Greco-Roman Cults III*. FS M. Smith. Edited by J. Neusner. SJLA 12. Leiden: Brill, 1975.

Kraus, T. *Hekate: Studien zu Wesen und Bild der Göttin in Kleinasien und Griechenland*. Heidelberger Kunstgeschichtliche Abhandlungen 5. Heidelberg: Winter, 1960.

Kreitzer, L. J. "The Plutonium of Hierapolis and the Descent of Christ into the 'Lowermost Parts of the Earth' (Ephesians 4,9)." *Biblica* 79 (1998): 381–93.

Kremer, J. *Was an den Leiden Christi noch mangelt: Eine interpretationsgeschichtliche und exegetische Untersuchung zu Kol. 1,24b*. Bonner Theologischer Studien. Bonn: Haustein, 1956.

Kristensen, T. M. "Earthquakes and Late Antique Urbanism: Some Observations on the Case of the Lykos Valley." Pages 71–78 in *The Lykos Valley and Neighbourhood in Late Antiquity*. Edited by C. Şimşek and T. Kacar. Istanbul: Ege Yayinlari, 2018.

Kümmel, W. G. *Introduction to the New Testament*. Translated by H. C. Kee. London: SCM, 1982.

Kumsar, H., Ö. Aydan, C. Şimşek, and F. D'Andria. "Historical Earthquakes That Damaged Hierapolis and Laodikeia Antique Cities and Their Implications for Earthquake Potential of Denizli Basin in Western Turkey." *Bulletin of Engineering Geology and Environment* 75 (2016): 519–36.

Ladd, G. E. "Paul's Friends in Colossians 4:7–16." *RevExp* 70 (1973): 507–14.

Lähnemann, J. *Der Kolosserbrief: Komposition, Situation und Argumentation*. SNT 3. Gütersloh: Mohn, 1971.

Laks, A., and G. W. Most, eds. *Studies on the Derveni Papyrus*. Oxford: Clarendon, 1997.

Lamp, J. S. "Wisdom in Col 1:15–20: Contribution and Significance." *JETS* 41 (1998): 45–53.

Lampe, G. W. H., ed. *A Patristic Greek Lexicon*. Oxford: Clarendon Press, 1961.

Lampe, P. "Keine 'Sklavenflucht' des Onesimus." *ZNW* 76 (1985): 135–37.

———. "Rhetorical Analysis of Pauline Texts—*Quo Vadit?* Methodological Reflections." Pages 3–21 in *Paul and Rhetoric*. Edited by J. P. Sampley and P. Lampe. London: T&T Clark, 2010.

Lane, E. *Corpus Monumentorum Religionis Dei Menis*. EPRO 19, Part 3. Leiden: Brill, 1976.

———. "Men: A Neglected Cult of Roman Asia Minor." *ANRW* II.18.3 (1990): 2161–74.

———. "Sabazius and the Jews in Valerius Maximus: A Re-Examination." *JRS* 69 (1979): 35–38.

Lane Fox, R. *Pagans and Christians*. New York: Knopf, 1986.

Lang, T. J. "Disbursing the Account of God: Fiscal Terminology and the Economy of God in Colossians 1,24–25." *ZNW* 107 (2016): 116–36.

———. *Mystery and the Making of Christian Historical Consciousness: From Paul to the Second Century*. BZNW 219. Berlin: de Gruyter, 2015.

Lange, A., H. Lichtenberger, and K. F. D. Römheld, eds. *Die Dämonen: Die Dämonologie der israelitisch-jüdischen und frühchristlichen Literatur im Kontext ihrer Umwelt = Demons: The Demonology of Israelite-Jewish and Early Christian Literature in Context of Their Environment*. Tübingen: Mohr Siebeck, 2003.

Laumonier, A. "Inscriptions de Carie." *BCH* 53 (1954): 291–380.

Le Bas, P. and Waddington, W. *Voyage archéologique en Grèce et en Asie Mineure*. Vol. III.v (Inscriptions - Asie Mineure). Bibliotheque des Monuments Figures Grecs et Romains 1. Paris: Firmin-Didot et Cie, 1870.

Lease, G. "Jewish Mystery Cults Since Goodenough." *ANRW* II.20.2 (1987): 858–80.

Lee, J. Y. "Interpreting the Demonic Powers in Pauline Thought." *NovT* 12 (1970): 54–69.

Lee, M. V. *Paul, the Stoics, and the Body of Christ*. SNTSMS 137. Cambridge: Cambridge University Press, 2006.

Lee-Barnewall, M. "Turning Κεφαλή on Its Head: The Rhetoric of Reversal in Ephesians 5:21–33." Pages 599–614 in *Christian Origins and Greco-Roman Culture: Social and Literary Contexts for the New Testament*. Edited by S. E. Porter and A. W. Pitts. TENTS 9/1. Leiden: Brill, 2013.

Leivestad, R. *Christ the Conqueror: Ideas of Conflict and Victory in the New Testament*. London: SPCK, 1954.

Leppä, O. *The Making of Colossians: A Study on the Formation and Purpose of a Deutero-Pauline Letter*. Publications of the Finnish Exegetical Society 86. Helsinki: Finnish Exegetical Society in Helisinki, 2003.

Lesses, R. *Ritual Practices to Gain Power: Angels, Incantations, and Revelation in Early Jewish Mysticism*. HTS 44. Harrisburg, PA: Trinity Press International, 1998.

———. "Speaking with Angels: Jewish and Greco-Egyptian Revelatory Adjurations." *HTR* 89 (1996): 41–60.

Levine, L. I. *The Ancient Synagogue: The First Thousand Years*. 2nd ed. New Haven: Yale University Press, 2005.

Levinskaya, I. A. "Syncretism—The Term and Phenomenon." *TynBul* 44 (1993): 117–28.

Levison, J. R. "*2 Apoc. Bar.* 48:42–52:7 and the Apocalyptic Dimension of Colossians 3:1–6." *JBL* 108 (1989): 93–108.

Lightfoot, J. B. "The Colossian Heresy." Pages 13–59 in *Conflict at Colossae*. Edited by F. O. Francis and W. A. Meeks. SBLSBS 4. Missoula, MT: Scholars Press, 1973.

Lightstone, J. *Commerce of the Sacred: Mediation of the Divine among Jews in the Graeco-Roman Diaspora*. 2nd ed. BJS 59. New York: Columbia University Press, 2006.

Lincicum, D. "Mirror-Reading a Pseudepigraphal Letter." *NovT* 59 (2017): 171–193.

Lincoln, A. T. *Ephesians*. WBC 42. Dallas: Word, 1990.

———. "The Household Code and Wisdom Mode of Colossians." *JSNT* 21 (1999): 93–112.

———. *Paradise Now and Not Yet: Studies in the Role of the Heavenly Dimension in Paul's Thought with Special Reference to His Eschatology*. SNTSMS 43. Cambridge: Cambridge University Press, 1981.

Lincoln, A. T., and A. J. M. Wedderburn. *The Theology of the Later Pauline Epistles*. New Testament Theology. Cambridge: Cambridge University Press, 1993.

Lindemann, A. *Die Aufhebung der Zeit: Geschichtsverständnis und Eschatologie im Epheserbriefes*. SNT 12. Gütersloh: Mohn, 1975.

———. "Die Gemeinde von 'Kolossä': Erwägungen zum 'Sitz im Leben' eines pseudopaulinischen Briefes." *Wort und Dienst* 16 (1981): 111–34.

Lips, H. von. "Die Haustafel als 'Topos' im Rahmen der urchristlichen Paränese: Beobachtungen anhand des 1.Petrusbriefes und des Titusbriefes." *NTS* 40 (1994): 261–80.

Lohse, E. "Christusherrschaft und Kirche im Kolosserbrief." *NTS* 11 (1964–65): 203–16.

———. "Ein hymnisches Bekenntnis in Kolosser 2, 13c–15." Pages 427–35 in *Mélanges bibliques en hommage au R. P. Béda Rigaux*. Edited by A. Descamps and A. Halleux. Gembloux: Duculot, 1970.

———. "Die Mitarbeiter des Apostels Paulus im Kolosserbrief." Pages 189–94 in *Verborum Veritas*. FS G. Stählin. Wuppertal: Broackhaus, 1970.

———. "Pauline Theology in the Letter to the Colossians." *NTS* 15 (1968–69): 211–20.

Löhr, H. "The Early Christian Household Codes in the Light of Epigraphic Evidence." Pages 199–214 in *Epigraphical Evidence Illustrating Paul's Letter to the Colossians*. Edited by J. Verheyden, M. Öhler, and T. Corsten. WUNT 2/411. Tübingen: Mohr Siebeck, 2018.

———. "What Can We Know about the Beginnings of Christian Hymnody?" Pages 157–74 in *Literature or Liturgy? Early Christian Hymns and Prayers in their Literary and Liturgical Context in Antiquity*. Edited by C. Leonhard and H. Löhr. WUNT 2/363. Tübingen: Mohr Siebeck, 2014.

Loke, T. E. A. *The Origin of Divine Christology*. SNTSMS 169. Cambridge: Cambridge University Press, 2017.

Lona, H. E. *Die Eschatologie im Kolosser- und Epheserbrief*. FB 48. Würzburg: Echter, 1984.

Longenecker, B., and S. C. Ryan. "Presenting the Pauline Voice: An Appreciation of the *Letter to the Laodiceans*." *NTS* 62 (2016): 136–48.

Longenecker, R. *Galatians*. WBC 41. Dallas: Word, 1990.

Lövestam, E. *Spiritual Wakefulness in the New Testament*. LUÅ 55/3. Lund: Gleerup, 1963.

Luck, G. *Arcana Mundi: Magic and the Occult in the Greek and Roman Worlds*. Baltimore: Johns Hopkins University Press, 1985.

Lueken, W. *Michael: Eine Darstellung und Vergleichung der jüdischen und der morgenländisch-christlichen Tradition vom Erzengel Michael*. Göttingen: Vandenhoeck & Ruprecht, 1898.

Lührmann, D. "Neutestamentliche Haustafeln und antike Ökonomie." *NTS* 27 (1980): 83–97.

Luttenberger, J. "Der gekreuzigte Schuldschein: Ein Aspekt der Deutung des Todes Jesu im Kolosserbrief." *NTS* 15 (2005): 80–95.

Lyonnet, S. "L'épitre aux Colossiens (Col 2,18) et let mystères d'Apollon Clarien." *Biblica* 43 (1962): 417–35.

———. "Paul's Adversaries in Colossae." Pages 147–61 in *Conflict at Colossae*. Edited by F. O. Francis and W. A. Meeks. SBLSBS 4. Missoula, MT: Scholars Press, 1973.

Macaskill, G. *Union with Christ in the New Testament*. Oxford: Oxford University Press, 2013.

———. "Union(s) with Christ: Colossians 1:15–20." *ExAud* 33 (2017): 92–107.

MacDonald, D. "The Homonoia of Colossae and Aphrodisias." *Jahrbuch für Numismatik und Geldgeschichte* 33 (1983): 25–27.

MacDonald, M. Y. "Beyond Identification of the Topos of Household Management: Reading the Household Codes in Light of Recent Methodologies and Theoretical Perspectives in the Study of the New Testament." *NTS* 57 (2010): 65–90.

———. "Can Nympha Rule This House? The Rhetoric of Domesticity in Colossians." Pages 99–120 in *Rhetoric and Reality in Early Christianities*. Edited by W. Braun. Waterloo, Ontario: Wilfred Laurier University Press, 2005.

———. "Slavery, Sexuality and House Churches: A Reassessment of Colossians 3.18–4.1 in Light of New Research on the Roman Family." *NTS* 43 (2007): 94–113.

MacGregor, G. H. C. "Principalities and Powers: The Cosmic Background of Paul's Thought." *NTS* 1 (1954–55): 17–28.

Mach, M. *Entwicklungsstadien des jüdischen Engelglaubens in vorrabbinischer Zeit*. TSAJ 34. Tübingen: Mohr Siebeck, 1992.

Machen, J. G. *The Origin of Paul's Religion*. New York: Macmillan, 1921.

MacMullen, R. *Paganism in the Roman Empire*. New Haven: Yale University Press, 1974.

Macridy, T. "Altertümer von Notion." *JÖAI* 8 (1905): 155–73.

———. "Antiquités de Notion II." *JÖAI* 15 (1912): 36–67.

Macridy, T., and C. Picard. "Fouilles du Hiéron d'Apollon Clarios a Colophon." *BCH* 39 (1915): 33–52.

MaGee, G. S. *Portrait of an Apostle: A Case for Paul's Authorship of Colossians and Ephesians*. Eugene, OR: Wipf & Stock, 2013.

Magie, D. *Roman Rule in Asia Minor*. 2 vols. Princeton: Princeton University Press, 1950.

Maier, H. O. "Barbarians, Scythians and Imperial Iconography in the Epistle to the Colossians." Pages 385–406 in *Picturing the New Testament*. Edited by A. Weissenrieder, F. Wendt, and P. von Gemünde. Tübingen: Mohr Siebeck, 2005.

———. *Picturing Paul in Empire: Imperial Image, Text and Persuasion in Colossians, Ephesians and the Pastoral Epistles*. London: Bloomsbury, 2013.

———. "Reading Colossians in the Ruins: Roman Imperial Iconography, Moral Transformation, and the Construction of Christian Identity in the Lycus Valley." Pages 212–31 in *Colossae in Space and Time: Linking to an Ancient City*. Edited by A. H. Cadwallader and M. Trainor. NTOA/SUNT 94. Göttingen: Vandenhoeck & Ruprecht, 2011.

———. "A Sly Civility: Colossians and Empire." *JSNT* 27 (2005): 323–49.

Malan, F. S. "Church Singing according to the Pauline Epistles." *Neot* 32 (1998): 509–24.

Malherbe, A. *Moral Exhortation: A Greco-Roman Sourcebook*. Library of Early Christianity 4. Philadelphia: Westminster, 1986.

Manoledakis, M. "Hekate with Apollo and Artemis on a Gem from the Southern Black Sea Region." *Istanbuler Mitteilungen* 62 (2012): 289–302.

Mare, W. H. "Archaeological Prospects at Colossae." *Near East Archaeological Society Bulletin* 7 (1976): 39–59.

Margalioth, M. *Sepher Ha-Razim*. Jerusalem: Yediot Achronot, 1966.

Marshall, I. H. *New Testament Theology: Many Witnesses, One Gospel*. Downers Grove, IL: InterVarsity Press, 2004.

Marshall, P. "A Metaphor of Shame: ΘΡΙΑΜΒΕΥΕΙΝ in 2 Cor 2:14." *NovT* 25 (1983): 302–17.

Martin, D. B. *Slavery as Salvation: The Metaphor of Slavery in Pauline Christianity*. New Haven: Yale University Press, 1990.

Martin, L. H. *Hellenistic Religions*. Oxford: Oxford University Press, 1987.

Martin, R. "Le Didymeion." Pages 297–303 in *La civilisation grecque de l'antiquite a nos Jours*. Vol. 1. Edited by C. Delvoye and G. Roux. Brussels: La Renaissance du Livre, 1967.

Martin, R. P. *2 Corinthians*. 2nd ed. WBC 40. Grand Rapids: Zondervan, 2014.

———. *Reconciliation: A Study of Paul's Theology*. Atlanta: John Knox, 1981.

Martin, T. W. "But Let Everyone Discern the Body of Christ (Colossians 2:17)." *JBL* 114 (1995): 249–55.

———. *By Philosophy and Empty Deceit: Colossians as Response to a Cynic Critique*. JSNTSup 118. Sheffield: Sheffield Academic Press, 1996.

———. "Pagan and Judeo-Christian Time-Keeping Schemes in Gal 4.10 and Col 2.16." *NTS* 42 (1996): 105–19.

———. "The Scythian Perspective in Col 3:11." *NovT* 37 (1995): 249–61.

———. "Scythian Perspective or Elusive Chiasm." *NovT* 41 (1999): 256–64.

Mastrocinque, A. "The Divinatory Kit from Pergamon and Greek Magic in Late Antiquity." *JRA* 15 (2002): 173–87.

Maurer, C. "Die Begründung der Herrschaft Christi über die Mächte nach Kol. 1, 15–20." *WD* 4 (1955): 79–93.

Mayerhoff, E. T. *Der Brief an die Colosser, mit vornehmlicher Berücksichtigung der drei Pastoralbriefe*. Edited by J. L. Mayerhoff. Berlin: Hermann Schultze, 1838.

McCabe, D. F., and M. A. Plunkett. *Miletos Inscriptions: Texts and List*. Princeton Epigraphic Project. Princeton: Institute for Advanced Study, 1984.

McClure, J., and R. Collins. *Bede: The Ecclesiastical History of the English People*. Oxford World's Classics. Oxford: Oxford University Press, 1969. Repr., 1999.

McCown, C. C. "The Ephesia Grammata in Popular Belief." *Transactions of the Ameican Philological Association* 54 (1923): 128–40.

McDowell, S. *The Fate of the Apostles: Examining the Martyrdom Accounts of the Closest Followers of Jesus*. London: Routledge, 2015.

McKechnie, P. *Christianizing Asia Minor: Conversion, Communities, and Social Change in the Pre-Constantinian Era*. Cambridge: Cambridge University Press, 2019.

McRay, J. *Paul: His Life and Teaching*. Grand Rapids: Baker, 2003.

Meade, D. G. *Pseudonymity and Canon: An Investigation into the Relationship of Authorship and Authority in Jewish and Earliest Christian Tradition*. WUNT 39. Tübingen: Mohr Siebeck, 1986.

Medley, M. S. "Subversive Song: Imagining Colossians 1:15–20 as a Social Protest Hymn in the Context of Roman Empire." *RevExp* 116 (2019): 421–35.

Meeks, W. A. *The First Urban Christians*. New Haven: Yale Univerisity Press, 1983.

———. "In One Body: The Unity of Humankind in Colossians and Ephesians." Pages 209–21 in *God's Christ and His People: Studies in Honor of Nils Alstrup Dahl*. Edited by J. Jervell and W. A. Meeks. Oslo: Universitetsforlaget, 1978.

———. "'To Walk Worthily of the Lord': Moral Formation in the Pauline School Exemplified by the Letter to Colossians." Pages 37–58 in *Hermes and Athena: Biblical Exegesis and Philosophical Theology*. Edited by E. Stump and T. P. Flint. University of Notre Dame Studies in the Philosophy of Religion 7. Notre Dame: University of Notre Dame Press, 1993.

Mellor, R. *Tacitus' Annals*. Oxford Approaches to Classical Literature. Oxford: Oxford University Press, 2010.

———. *ΘΕΑ ΡΩΜΗ: The Worship of the Goddess Roma in the Greek World.* Hypomnemata 42. Göttingen: Vandenhoeck & Ruprecht, 1975.

Merisch, N. "Chonai." Pages 222–25 in *Phrygien und Pisidien.* Edited by K. Belke and N. Merisch. Tabuli Imperii Byzantini 7, Österreichische Akademie der Wissenschaften, Philosophisch-Historische Klasse Denkschriften 211. Vienna: Verlag der Österreischischen Akademie der Wissenschaften, 1990.

———. "Kolossai." Pages 309–11 in *Phrygien und Pisidien.* Edited by K. Belke and N. Merisch. Tabuli Imperii Byzantini 7, Österreichische Akademie der Wissenschaften, Philosophisch-Historische Klasse Denkschriften 211. Vienna: Verlag der Österreicheischen Akademie der Wissenschaften, 1990.

Merk, O. "Erwägungen zu Kol 2,6f." Pages 407–16 in *Vom Urchristentum zu Jesus.* FS J. Gnilka. Edited by H. Frankemölle and K. Kertelge. Freiburg: Herder, 1989.

Merkelbach, R. "Ein Orakel des Apollon für Artemis von Koloe." *ZPE* 88 (1991): 70–72.

———. *Philologica: Ausgewählte Kleine Schriften.* Edited by W. Blümel et al. Leipzig: Teubner, 1997.

Merkelbach, R., and J. Stauber. "Die Orakel des Apollon von Klaros." *EA* 27 (1996): 1–54.

Merkelbach, R., and M. Totti. *Abrasax: Ausgewählte Papyri Religiösen und Magischen Inhalts.* 3 Vols. Abhandlungen der Rheinisch-Westfälischen Akademie der Wissenschaften. Sonderreihe, Papyrological Coloniensia 17.1, 17.2, 17.3. Opladen: Westdeutscher, 1990, 1991, 1992.

Merklein, H. "Paulinische Theologie in der Rezeption des Kolosser- und Epheserbriefes." Pages 25–69 in *Paulus in den neutestamentlichen Spätschriften: Zur Paulusrezeption im Neuen Testament.* Edited by K. Kertelge. QD 89. Freiburg: Herder, 1981.

Metzger, B. M. *A Textual Commentary on the Greek New Testament.* 2nd ed. Stuttgart: Deutsche Bibelgesellschaft, 1994.

Metzger, B. M., and B. D. Ehrman. *The Text of the New Testament: Its Transmission, Corruption, and Restoration.* 4th ed. Oxford: Oxford University Press, 2005.

Meyer, M. W. *The Ancient Mysteries: A Sourcebook.* San Francisco: Harper & Row, 1987.

———. *The "Mithras Liturgy."* SBL Texts and Translations 10, Graeco-Roman Religion Series 2. Missoula, MT: Scholars Press, 1976.

Michaelis, W. *Versöhnung des Alls: Die frohe Botschaft von der Gnade Gottes.* Bern: Siloah, 1950.

Miller, C. "The Imperial Cult in the Pauline Cities of Asia Minor and Greece." *CBQ* 72 (2010): 314–32.

Miller, K. M. "Apollo Lairbenos." *Numen* 32 (1985): 46–70.

Mitchell, S. *Anatolia: Land, Men, and Gods in Asia Minor.* 2 vols. Oxford: Oxford University Press, 1995.

———. *Regional Epigraphic Catalogues of Asia Minor II: The Ankara District. The Inscriptions of North Galatia.* British Institute of Archaeology at Ankara Monograph 4. British Archaeological Reports International Series 135. Oxford: British Archaeological Reports Oxford Ltd, 1982.

Moir, I. A. "Some Thoughts on Col 2,17–18. *TZ* 35 (1979): 363–65.

Moo, D. J. *Galatians.* BECNT. Grand Rapids: Eerdmans, 2013.

———. *A Theology of Paul and His Letters.* Grand Rapids: Zondervan, 2021.

Morris, L. *The Apostolic Preaching of the Cross.* Grand Rapids: Eerdmans, 1965.

Morris, S. P. "The Prehistoric Background of Artemis Ephesia: A Solution to the Enigma of Her 'Breasts'?" Pages 135–51 in *Der Kosmos der Artemis.* Edited by U. Muss. Österreichisches Archäologisches Institut, Sonderschriften 37. Vienna: Österreichisches Archäologisches Institut, 2001.

Moulton, J. H. "It Is His Angel." *JTS* 3 (1902): 514–27.

Müller, P. *Anfänge der Paulusschule: Dargestellt am zweiten Thessalonicherbrief und am Kolosserbrief.* Zürich: Theologischer, 1988.

———. "Verehrung der Engel: Kol 2:18 im Licht inschriftlicher Zeugnisse." Pages 123–46 in *Epigraphical Evidence Illustrating Paul's Letter to the Colossians*. Edited by J. Verheyden, M. Öhler, and T. Corsten. WUNT 2/411. Tubingen: Mohr Siebeck, 2018.

———. "Zum Problem der Paulusschule: Methodische und sachliche Überlegungen." Pages 171–97 in *Kolosser-Studien*. Edited by P. Müller. Biblisch-Theologische Studien 103. Neukirchen-Vluyn: Neukirchener, 2009.

Mullins, T. Y. "The Thanksgivings of Philemon and Colossians." *NTS* 30 (1984): 288–93.

Münderlein, G. "Die Erwählung durch das *Plērōma*—Kol 1:19." *NTS* 8 (1962): 264–76.

Munro, W. "Colossians III.18–IV.1 and Eph V.21–VI.9: Evidence of a Late Literary Stratum?" *NTS* 18 (1972): 434–47.

Murphy, R. E. "GBR and GBWRH in the Qumran Writings." Pages 137–43 in *Lex Tua Veritas*. FS H. Junker. Trier: Paulinus, 1961.

Murphy-O'Connor, J. "The Greeters in Col 4:10–14 and Phlm 23–24." *RB* 114 (2007): 416–26.

———. *Paul: A Critical Life*. Oxford: Oxford University Press, 1997.

———. *Paul the Letter-Writer: His World, His Options, His Skills*. Good News Studies 41. Collegeville, MN: Liturgical Press, 1995.

———. "Tradition and Redaction in Col 1:15–20." *RB* 102 (1995): 231–41.

Naveh, J. "Fragments of an Aramaic Magic Book from Qumran." *IEJ* 48 (1998): 252–61.

Naveh, J., and S. Shaked. *Amulets and Magic Bowls: Aramaic Incantations of Late Antiquity*. Leiden: Brill, 1985.

Neugebauer, F. "Das Paulinische 'In Christo.'" *NTS* 4 (1957–58): 124–38.

Neumann, K. J. *The Authenticity of the Pauline Epistles in the Light of Stylostatistical Analysis*. SBLDS 120. Atlanta: Scholars Press, 1990.

Neusner, J. *The Wonder-Working Lawyers of Talmudic Babylonia: The Theory and Practice of Judaism in Its Formative Age*. Studies in Judaism. Lanham, MD: University Press of America, 1987.

Nickelsburg, G. W. E. *Jewish Literature between the Bible and the Mishnah*. 2nd ed. Minneapolis: Fortress, 2005.

Nilsson, M. P. *Geschichte der griechischen Religion*. 2nd ed. 2 vols. Handbuch der Altertumswissenschaft 5.2. München: Beck'sche: 1961.

———. *Greek Popular Religion*. New York: Columbia University Press, 1940. Repr., *Greek Folk Religion*. Harper Torch Books. New York: Harper, 1961.

———. "Letter to Professor Arthur D. Nock on Some Fundamental Concepts in the Science of Religion. May 15, 1947." *HTR* 42 (1949): 71–107. Repr., pages 345–82 in vol. 3 of *Opuscula Selecta*. Lund: Gleerup, 1960.

———. "Die Religion in den griechischen Zauberpapyri." Pages 59–93 in *Kungl. Humanistiska Vetenskapssamfundet i Lund: Årsberattelse 1947–48*. Lund: Gleerup, 1948. Repr., pages 129–66 in vol. 3 of *Opuscula Selecta*. Lund: Gleerup, 1960.

Nitzan, B. "Hymns from Qumran—4Q510–4Q511." Pages 53–63 in *The Dead Sea Scrolls: Forty Years of Research*. Edited by D. Dimant and U. Rappaport. STDJ 10. Leiden: Brill, 1992.

Noack, B. *Satanâs und Soterîa: Untersuchungen zur neutestamentlichen Dämonologie*. København: G. E. C. Gads, 1948.

Nock, A. D. "Astrology and Cultural History." Pages 359–68 in vol. 1 of *Arthur Darby Nock: Essays on Religion and the Ancient World*. Edited by Z. Stewart. Oxford: Clarendon, 1972.

———. *Conversion: The Old and the New in Religion from Alexander the Great to Augustine of Hippo*. Oxford: Oxford University Press, 1933.

———. *Early Gentile Christianity and Its Hellenistic Background*. New York: Harper and Row, 1964.

———. "Eunuchs in Ancient Religion." *Archiv für Religionswissenschaft* 23 (1925–26): 25–33. Repr., pages 7–15 of vol. 1 of *Arthur Darby Nock: Essays on Religion and the Ancient World*. Edited by Z. Stewart. Oxford: Clarendon, 1972.

———. "Greek Magical Papyri." *Journal of Egyptian Archaeology* 15 (1929): 219–35. Repr., pages 176–94 in vol. 1 of *Arthur Darby Nock: Essays on Religion and the Ancient World.* Edited by Z. Stewart. Oxford: Clarendon, 1972.

———. "Religious Symbols and Symbolism I." *Gnomon* 27 (1955): 558–72. Repr., pages 877–94 in vol. 2 of *Arthur Darby Nock: Essays on Religion and the Ancient World.* Edited by Z. Stewart. Oxford: Clarendon, 1972.

———. "Religious Symbols and Symbolism II." Pages 895–907 in vol. 2 of *Arthur Darby Nock: Essays on Religion and the Ancient World.* Edited by Z. Stewart. Oxford: Clarendon, 1972.

———. "Religious Symbols and Symbolism III." *Gnomon* 32 (1960): 728–36. Repr., pages 908–18 in vol. 2 of *Arthur Darby Nock: Essays on Religion and the Ancient World.* Edited by Z. Stewart. Oxford: Clarendon, 1972.

———. "Studies in the Graeco-Roman Beliefs of the Empire." *JHS* 48 (1928): 84–101. Repr., pages 32–48 in vol. 1 of *Arthur Darby Nock: Essays on Religion and the Ancient World.* Edited by Z. Stewart. Oxford: Clarendon, 1972.

———. "Vocabulary of the New Testament." *JBL* 52 (1933): 131–39.

Nock, A. D., C. Roberts, and T. C. Skeat. "The Guild of Zeus Hypsistos." *HTR* 29 (1936): 61–69. Repr., pages 908–18 in vol. 2 of *Arthur Darby Nock: Essays on Religion and the Ancient World.* Edited by Z. Stewart. Oxford: Clarendon, 1972.

Nongbri, B. "The Construction and Contents of the Beatty-Michigan Pauline Epistle Codex ($\mathfrak{P}^{46}$)." *NovT* 64 (2022): 388–407.

———. *God's Library: The Archaeology of the Earliest Christian Maunscripts.* New Haven: Yale University Press, 2018.

Norden, E. *Agnostos Theos: Untersuchungen zur Formengeschichte religiöser Rede.* 4th ed. Stuttgart: Teubner, 1956.

Nordling, J. G. "Onesimus Fugitivus: A Defense of the Runaway Slave Hypothesis in Philemon." *JSNT* 41 (1991): 97–119.

———. "Philemon in the Context of Paul's Travels." *CTQ* 74 (2010): 289–305.

———. "Some Matters Favouring the Runaway Slave Hypothesis in Philemon." *Neot* 44 (2010): 85–121.

O'Brien, P. T. *Introductory Thanksgivings in the Letters of Paul.* NovTSup 49. Leiden: Brill, 1977.

———. "Thanksgiving and the Gospel in Paul." *NTS* 21 (1974–75): 144–55.

Ogereau, J. M. "Χειρόγραφον in Colossians 2:14: The Contribution of Epigraphy to the Philology of the New Testament." Pages 93–122 in *Epigraphical Evidence Illustrating Paul's Letter to the Colossians.* Edited by J. Verheyden, M. Öhler, and T. Corsten. WUNT 2/411. Tübingen: Mohr Siebeck, 2018.

Olbricht, T. H. "The *Stoicheia* and the Rhetoric of Colossians: Then and Now." Pages 308–28 in *Rhetoric, Scripture and Theology: Essays from the 1994 Pretoria Conference.* Edited by S. E. Porter. Sheffield: Sheffield Academic Press, 1996.

O'Neill, J. C. "The Source of Christology in Colossians." *NTS* 26 (1979): 87–100.

Osiek, C., and D. L. Balch. *Families in the New Testament World: Households and House Churches.* Family, Religion, and Culture. Louisville: Westminster John Knox, 1997.

Overfield, P. D. "Pleroma: A Study in Content and Context." *NTS* 25 (1978–79): 384–96.

Özkaya, V. "The Shaft Monuments and the 'Taurobolium' among the Phrygians." *AnSt* 47 (1997): 89–103.

Pao, D. W. *Thanksgiving: An Investigation of a Pauline Theme.* NSBT 13. Downers Grove, IL: InterVarsity Press, 2002.

Papanikolaou, D. "The Aretalogy of Isis from Maroneia and the Question of Hellenistic 'Asianism.'" *ZPE* 168 (2009): 59–70.

Parke, H. W. *The Oracles of Apollo in Asia Minor.* London: Croom Helm, 1985.

Parker, D. C. *An Introduction to the New Testament Manuscripts and Their Texts.* Cambridge: Cambridge University Press, 2008.

Parker, R. *Greek Gods Abroad: Names, Natures, and Transformations*. Oakland, CA: University of California Press, 2017.

Pascuzzi, M. A. "Reconsidering the Authorship of Colossians." *BBR* 23 (2013): 223–46.

Peerbolte, B. J. L. "The *Eighth Book of Moses* (PLeid. J 395): Hellenistic Jewish Influence in a Pagan Magical Papyrus." Pages 184–94 in *A Kind of Magic: Understanding Magic in the New Testament and Its Religious Environment*. LNTS 306. Edited by B. J. L. Peerbolte and M. Labahn. London: T&T Clark, 2007.

Peers, G. *Subtle Bodies: Representing Angels in Byzantium*. Berkeley: University of California Press, 2001.

Pelser, G. M. M. "Could the 'Formulas' *Dying* and *Rising with Christ* Be Expressions of Pauline Mysticism?" *Neot* 32 (1998): 115–34.

Peppard, M. "'Poetry,' 'Hymn,' and 'Traditional Material' in New Testament Epistles or How to Do Things with Indentations." *JSNT* 30 (2008): 319–42.

Percy, Ernst. *Die Probleme der Kolosser- und Epheserbriefe*. Skrifter Utgivna av Kungl. Humanistiska Vetenskapssamfundet i Lund 39. Lund: Gleerup, 1946. Repr., 1964.

Pernot, L. *Rhetoric in Antiquity*. Washington, DC: Catholic University Press of America, 2005.

Perdrizet, P. "Amulette grecque trouvée en Syrie." *Revue des Études Grecque* 41 (1928): 73–82.

Perkins, P. *Gnosticism and the New Testament*. Minneapolis: Fortress, 1993.

Perriman, A. "The Pattern of Christ's Sufferings: Colossians 1:24 and Philippians 3:10–11." *TynBul* 42 (1991): 62–79.

Peterson, J. "'The Circumcision of the Christ': The Significance of Baptism in Colossians and the Churches of the Restoration." *ResQ* 43 (2001): 65–77.

Petrovic, A. "Do Seize, Do Eat, Do Touch—But Mind Your Thoughts: Colossians and Greek Purity Regulations." Pages 147–60 in *Epigraphical Evidence Illustrating Paul's Letter to the Colossians*. Edited by J. Verheyden, M. Öhler, and T. Corsten. WUNT 2/411. Tubingen: Mohr Siebeck, 2018.

Petzl, G. "Vier Inschriften aus Lydien." Pages 745–61 in *Studien zur Religion und Kultur Kleinasiens II*. FS F. K. Dörner. Edited by S. Sahin, E. Schwertheim, and J. Wagner. EPRO 66. Leiden: Brill, 1978.

Pfanz, H., G. Yüce, A. H. Gulbay, and A. Gokgoz. "Deadly CO2 Gases in the Plutonium of Hierapolis (Denizli, Turkey)." *Archaeological and Anthropological Sciences* 11 (2019): 1359–71.

Pfister, F. "Die στοιχεῖα τοῦ κόσμου in den Briefen des Apostels Paulus." *Philologus* 69 (1910): 411–27.

Picard, C. *Éphèse et Claros: Recherches sur les Sanctuaires et les Cultes de L'Ionie du Nord*. Biobliothèque des Écoles Françaises d'Athenes et de Rome 123. Paris: Anciennes Maisons Thorin et Fontemoing, 1922.

———. "Un Oracle d'Apollon Clarios a Pergame." *BCH* 46 (1922): 190–97.

Piccardi, L. "The AD 60 Denizli Basin Earthquake and the Apparition of Archangel Michael at Colossae (Aegean Turkey)." Pages 95–105 in *Myth and Geology*. Edited by L. Piccardi and W. B. Masse. Geological Society, Special Publication 273. London: Geological Society of London, 2007.

Piper, J. *Filling Up the Afflictions of Christ*. Wheaton, IL: Crossway, 2009.

Pitts, A. W. "Paul in Tarsus: Historical Factors in Assessing Paul's Early Education." Pages 43–67 in *Paul and Ancient Rhetoric: Theory and Practice in the Hellenistic Context*. Edited by S. E. Porter and B. R. Dyer. Cambridge: Cambridge University Press, 2016.

———. "Style and Pseudonymity in Pauline Scholarship: A Register Based Configuration." Pages 113–52 in *Paul and Pseudepigraphy*. Edited by S. E. Porter and G. P. Fewster. Leiden: Brill, 2013.

Pizzuto, V. A. *A Cosmic Leap of Faith: An Authorial, Structural, and Theological Invesigation of the Cosmic Christology in Col 1:15–20*. CBET 41. Leuven: Peeters, 2006.

Porter, S. E. "Ancient Literate Culture and Popular Rhetorical Knowledge: Implications for Studying Pauline Rhetoric." Pages 96–115 in *Paul and Ancient Rhetoric: Theory and Practice in the Hellenistic Context*. Edited by S. E. Porter and B. R. Dyer. Cambridge: Cambridge University Press, 2016.

———. *The Apostle Paul: His Life, Thought, and Letters*. Grand Rapids: Eerdmans, 2016.

———. "Ben Witherington on Rhetoric One Last Time (I Hope)." *BBR* 26 (2016): 551–52.

———. *Idioms of the Greek New Testament*. Biblical Languages: Greek 2. Sheffield: JSOT Press, 1992.

———. *Καταλλάσσω in Ancient Greek Literature, with Reference to the Pauline Writings*. Estudios de Filología Neotestamentaria 5. Cordoba: Ediciones El Almendro, 1994.

———. "Paul, Virtues, Vices, and Household Codes." Pages 369–90 in *Paul in the Greco-Roman World: A Handbook*. Edited by J. P. Sampley. London: Bloomsbury T& Clark, 2016.

———. "Pauline Authorship and the Pastoral Epistles: Implications for Canon." *BBR* 5 (1995): 105–23.

———. "P.Oxy. 744.4 and Colossians 3:9." *Biblica* 73 (1992): 565–67.

———. *Verbal Aspect in the Greek of the New Testament with Reference to Tense and Mood*. Studies in Biblical Greek 1. New York: Peter Lang, 1989.

———. "'When It Was Clear That We Could Not Persuade Him, We Gave Up and Said, "The Lord's Will Be Done"' (Acts 21:14: Good Reasons to Stop Making Unproven Claims for Rhetorical Criticism." *BBR* 26 (2016): 533–45.

Porter, S. E., and A. W. Pitts. *Fundamentals of New Testament Textual Criticism*. Grand Rapids: Baker, 2015.

Porter, S. E., and J. T. Reed. "Philippians as a Macro-Chiasm and Its Exegetical Significance." *NTS* 44 (1998): 213–31.

Preisendanz, K. "Die griechischen und lateinischen Zaubertafeln." *APF* 11 (1935): 153–64.

———. "Die griechischen Zauberpapyri." *APF* 8 (1927): 104–67.

———. "Salomon." Pages 660–704 in *Real-Encyclopädie der classischen Altertumswissenschaft*. PWSup 8. Stuttgart: Metzler, 1956.

———. "Ein Wiener Papyrusfragment zum Testamentum Salomonis," *EOS* 48 (1956): 161–67.

Preisigke, F. *Wörterbuch der griechischen Papyruskunden mit Einfluss der griechischen Inschriften Ausschriften Ostraca Mumien Schilder usw. aus Ägypten*. 4 vols. Göttingen: Hubert, 1925–31.

Price, S. R. F. *Rituals and Power: The Roman Imperial Cult in Asia Minor*. Cambridge: Cambridge University Press, 1986.

Puech, É. "11QPsAp[a]: un rituel d'exorcismes: Essai de reconstruction." *RevQ* 55 (1990): 377–408.

———. "Les deux derniers psaumes davidiques du rituel d'exorcisme, 11QPsAp[a] IV 4–V 14." Pages 64–89 in *The Dead Sea Scrolls: Forty Years of Research*. STDJ 10. Edited by D. Dimant and U. Rappaport. Leiden: Brill, 1992.

Ramsay, W. M. "Ancient Mysteries and their Relation to St. Paul." *Athenaeum* (Jan. 25, 1913): 106–7.

———. "Artemis-Leto and Apollo-Lairbenos." *JHS* 10 (1889): 216–30.

———. *The Church in the Roman Empire before A.D. 170*. New York: Putnam's, 1893.

———. *The Cities and Bishoprics of Phrygia*. 2 vols. Oxford: Oxford University Press, 1895, 1897.

———. "The Mysteries in their Relation to St. Paul." *Contemporary Review* 104 (1913): 198–209.

———. "Phrygians." Pages 900–11 in *Encyclopaedia of Religion and Ethics*. Vol. 9. Edited by J. Hastings. New York: Charles Scribner's Sons, 1925.

———. "Sketches in the Religious Antiquities of Asia Minor." *The Annual of the British School at Athens* 18 (1911–12): 37–79.

———. *The Teaching of Paul in Terms of the Present Day*. London: Hodder & Stoughton, 1914.

Rapske, B. M. *Paul in Roman Custody*. Vol. 3 of *The Book of Acts in Its First Century Setting*. Edited by Bruce W. Winter. Grand Rapids: Eerdmans, 1994.

———. "The Prisoner Paul in the Eyes of Onesimus." *NTS* 37 (1991): 187–203.

Redfield, R. *The Primitive World and Its Transformations*. Ithaca: Cornell University Press, 1953.

———. "A Selection from *The Folk Culture of Yucatan*." Pages 337–88 in *Anthropology of Folk Religion*. Edited by C. Leslie. New York: Vintage, 1960. Reprinted from *The Folk Culture of Yucatan*. Chicago: University of Chicago Press, 1941.

Reed, J. T. "Are Paul's Thanksgivings 'Epistolary'?" *JSNT* 61 (1996): 87–99.

Reicke, B. "Caesarea, Rome, and the Captivity Epistles." Pages 277–86 in *Apostolic History and the Gospel: Biblical and Historical Essays Presented to F. F. Bruce*. Exeter: Paternoster, 1970.

———. "Zum sprachlichen Verständnis v. Kol. 2:23." *ST* 6 (1953): 39–53.

Reitzenstein, R. *Hellenistic Mystery Religions: Their Basic Ideas and Significance*. Pittsburgh Theological Monograph Series 15. Pittsburgh: Pickwick, 1978.

Reumann, J. "'Stewards of God'—Pre-Christian Religious Application of *Oikonomos* in Greek." *JBL* 77 (1958): 339–49.

Reynolds, J., and R. Tannenbaum. *Jews and God-Fearers at Aphrodisias: Greek Inscriptions with Commentary*. Cambridge Philosophical Society Supplements 12. Cambridge: Cambridge Philosophical Society, 1987.

Richards, E. R. *Paul and First-Century Letter Writing: Secretaries, Composition and Collection*. Downers Grove, IL: InterVarsity Press, 2004.

———. *The Secretary in the Letters of Paul*. WUNT 2/42. Tübingen: Mohr Siebeck, 1991.

Ricl, M. "Cults of Phrygia Epiktetos in the Roman Imperial Period." *EA* 50 (2017): 133–48.

Riesner, R. *Paul's Early Period: Chronology, Mission Strategy, Theology*. Grand Rapids: Eerdmans, 1998.

Ritti, T. *An Epigraphic Guide to Hierapolis (Pamukkale)*. Translated by P. Arthur. Istanbul: Ege Yayinlari, 2006.

Robert, L. "XXVII. Reliefs votifs: 1. Relief à Hiérapolis." *BCH* 107 (1983): 511–15. Repr., pages 355–59 in *Documents d'Asie Mineure*. Bibliotheque des Écoles Françaises d'Athènes et de Rome 239. Paris: de Boccard, 1987.

———. "Épitaphes d'Eumeneia de Phrygie." Pages 414–39 in *Hellenica: Recueil d'épigraphie de numismatique et d'antiquites grecques*. Vols. 11–12. Paris: Adrien-Maisonneuve, 1960.

———. "Les fouilles de Claros: Conférence donnée à l'université d'Ankara à la fin de quatre campagnes de fouilles." Pages 3–29 in *Opera Minora Selecta*. Vol. 6. Amsterdam: Hakkert, 1989.

———. "Les inscriptions." Pages 247–389 in *Laodicée du Lycos: Le Nymphée*. Edited by J. des Gagiers, et al. Quebec: L'Université Laval, 1969.

———. "L'oracle de Claros." Pages 305–12 in *La civilisation grecque de l'antiquité a nos jours*. Vol. 1. Edited by C. Delvoye and G. Roux. Brussells: La Renaissance du Livre, 1967.

———. "Un oracle gravé à Oenoanda." *CRAI* (1971): 597–619.

———. "Rapport sommaire sur un second voyage en Carie." *RAr* 6 (1935): 152–63.

———. "Reliefs votifs et cultes d'Anatolie. I. Dédicace à Héraclès et aux Nymphes. II. Inscriptions de Lydie. *Anatolia* 3 (1958): 103–36. Repr., pages 402–35 in *Opera Minora Selecta*. Vol. 1. Amsterdam: Hakkert, 1969.

———. *Villes d'Asie Mineure: Etudes de géographie ancienne*. 2nd ed. Paris: de Boccard, 1962.

Robert, L., and J. Robert. *La Carie: Histoire et géographie historique avec le recueil des inscriptions antiequest. Le plateaue de Tabai et ses environs, Volume 2*. Paris: Libraire d'Amérique at d'Orient Adrien-Maissoneuve, 1954.

———. *Claros I: Décrets hellénistiques*. Paris: Éditions Recherche sur les Civilisations, 1989.

Roberts, J. H. "Jewish Mystical Experience in the Early Christian Era as Background to Understanding Colossians." *Neot* 32 (1998): 161–89.

Robertson, A. T. *A Grammar of the Greek New Testament in the Light of Historical Research*. Nashville: Broadman, 1934.

Robinson, B. W. "An Ephesian Imprisonment of Paul." *JBL* 29 (1910): 181–89.

Robinson, D. M. "A Magical Inscription from Pisidian Antioch." *Hesperia* 22 (1953): 172–74.

Robinson, J. A. *St. Paul's Epistle to the Ephesians*. 2nd ed. London: Macmillan, 1907.

Robinson, J. A. T. *The Body*. SBT 5. London: SCM, 1952.

Robinson, J. M. "A Formal Analysis of Colossians 1:15–20." *JBL* 76 (1957): 270–87.

Robinson, L. "Hidden Transcripts? The Supposedly Self-Censoring Paul and Rome as Surveillance State in Modern Pauline Scholarship." *NTS* 67 (2021): 55–72.

Robinson, T. L. "Oracles and Their Society: Social Realities as Reflected in the Oracles of Claros and Didyma." *Semeia* 56 (1992): 59–77.

Rodd, C. S. "Salvation Proclaimed: XI. Colossians 2:8–15." *ExpTim* 94 (1982): 36–41.

Röhser, G. "Der Schluss der Schlüssel: Zu den Epistolaria des Kolosserbriefes." Pages 129–50 in *Kolosser-Studien*. Edited by P. Müller. Biblisch-Theologische Studien 103. Neukirchen-Vluyn: Neukirchener, 2009.

Rojas, J. M. G. "Is the Word of God Incomplete? An Exegetical and Rhetorical Study of Col 1,25." *Biblica* 94 (2013): 63–79.

Rolle, R. *The World of the Scythians*. Translated by F. G. Walls. Berkeley: University of California Press, 1989.

Roller, L. E. *In Search of God the Mother: The Cult of Anatolian Cybele*. Berkeley: University of California Press, 1999.

Rollins, W. G. "Christological *Tendenz* in Colossians 1:15–20: A *Theologia Crucis*." Pages 123–38 in *Christological Perspectives*. FS H. K. McArthur. Edited by R. F. Berkey and S. A. Edwards. New York: Pilgrim, 1982.

Roose, H. "Die Hierarchisierung der Leib-Metapher im Kolosser- und Epheserbrief als 'Paulinisierung': Ein Beitrag zur Rezeption paulinischer Tradition in pseudo-paulinischen Briefen." *NovT* 47 (2005): 117–41.

Rosner, B. *Greed as Idolatry: The Origin and Meaning of a Pauline Metaphor*. Grand Rapids: Eerdmans, 2007.

Rostad, A. *Human Transgression—Divine Retribution: A Study of Religious Transgressions and Punishments in Greek Cultic Regulation and Lydian-Phrygian Propitiatory Inscriptions ("Confession Inscriptions")*. Oxford: Archaeopress, 2020.

Rowland, C. "Apocalyptic Visions and the Exaltation of Christ in the Letter to the Colossians." *JSNT* 19 (1983): 73–83. Repr., pages 220–31 in *The Pauline Writings: A Sheffield Reader*. Edited by S. E. Porter and C. A. Evans. Sheffield: Sheffield Academic Press, 1995.

———. *The Open Heaven: A Study of Apocalyptic in Judaism and Early Christianity*. London: SPCK, 1982.

Royalty, R. M. "Dwelling on Visions: On the Nature of the So-Called 'Colossians Heresy.'" *Biblica* 83 (2002): 329–57.

Rudolph, K. *Gnosis: The Nature and History of Gnosticism*. San Francisco: Harper & Row, 1987.

———. "Syncretism: From Theological Invective to a Concept in the Study of Religion." Pages 68–87 in *Syncretism in Religion: A Reader*. Edited by A. M. Leopold and J. S. Jensen. London: Routledge, 2014.

Rusam, D. "Neue Belege zu den στοιχεῖα τοῦ κόσμου (Gal 4,3.9; Kol 2,8.20)." *ZNW* 83 (1992): 119–25.

Rutherford, I. "Trouble in Snake-Town: Interpreting an Oracle from Hierapolis-Pamukkale." Pages 449–57 in *Severan Culture*. Edited by S. Swain et al. Cambridge: Cambridge University Press, 2007.

Sänger, D. *Antikes Judentum und die Mysterien*. WUNT 2/5. Tübingen: Mohr Siebeck, 1980.

Sappington, T. J. *Revelation and Redemption at Colossae.* JSNTSup 53. Sheffield: JSOT Press, 1991.

Sarri, A. *Material Aspects of Letter Writing in the Graeco-Roman World: 500 BC–AD 300.* Materiale Textkulturen 12. Berlin: de Gruyter, 2018.

Schäfer, P. "The Aim and Purpose of Early Jewish Mysticism." Pages 277–95 in *Hekhalot-Studien.* TSAJ 19. Tübingen: Mohr, 1988.

———. "Communion with the Angels: Qumran and the Origins of Jewish Mysticism." Pages 37–66 in *Wege mystischer Gotteserfahrung: Judentum, Christentum und Islam (Mystical Approaches to God: Judaism, Christianity and Islam).* Edited by P. Schäfer. Schriften des historischen Kollegs 65. Berlin: de Gruyter, 2006.

———. "Jewish Magic and Literature in Late Antiquity and Early Middle Ages." *JJS* 41 (1990): 75–91.

———. *The Origins of Jewish Mysticism.* Princeton: Princeton University Press, 2009.

———. *Rivalität zwischen Engeln und Menschen.* Studia Judaica 8. Berlin: de Gruyter, 1975.

———. "Tradition and Redaction in Hekhalot Literature." Pages 8–16 in *Hekhalot-Studien.* TSAJ 19. Tübingen: Mohr Siebeck, 1988.

Schaff, P. *History of the Christian Church, Volume 1: Apostolic Christianity, A.D. 1–100.* Grand Rapids: Eerdmans, 1910. Repr., 1994.

Schenke, H.-M. *Der Gott "Mensch" in der Gnosis: Ein religionsgeschichtlicher Beitrag zur Diskussion über die paulinische Anschauung von der Kirche als Leib Christi.* Göttingen: Vandenhoeck & Ruprecht, 1962.

———. "Der Widerstreit gnostischer und kirchlicher Christologie im Spiegel des Kolosserbriefes." *ZTK* 61 (1964): 391–403.

Schenk, W. "Christus, das Geheimnis der Welt, als dogmatisches und ethisches Grundprinzip des Kolosserbriefes." *EvT* 43 (1983): 138–55.

———. "Der Kolosserbrief in der neueren Forschung (1945–1985)." *ANRW* II.25.4 (1987): 3327–64.

Scheu, L. E. *Die "Weltelemente" beim Apostel Paulus (Gal. 4, 3.9 und Kol. 2,8.20).* Universitas Catholica Americae 37. Washington, DC: Catholic University of America Press, 1933.

Schille, G. *Frühchristliche Hymnen.* Berlin: Evangelische Verlagsanstalt, 1965.

Schlarb, R. *Wir sind mit Christus begraben: Die Auslegung von Römer 6, 1–11 im frühchristentum bis Origenes.* BGBE 31. Tübingen: Mohr Siebeck, 1990.

Schleiermacher, F. "Ueber Koloss. 1, 15–20." *Theologische Studien und Kritiken* 5 (1832): 497–537.

Schlier, H. *Principalities and Powers in the New Testament.* QD 3. Freiburg: Herder, 1961.

Schmidt, F. "The Two Recensions of the Testament of Abraham: In Which Way Did the Transformation Take Place?" Pages 65–84 in *Studies on the Testament of Abraham.* Edited by G. W. E. Nickelsburg. Septuagint and Cognate Studies 6. Missoula, MT: Scholars Press, 1976.

Schmidt, K. L. "Die Natur- und Geistkräfte bei Paulus." *Eranos Jahrbuch* 14 (1946): 87–143.

Schnabel, E. J. *Early Christian Mission.* 2 vols. Downers Grove, IL: InterVarsity Press, 2004.

———. *Law and Wisdom from Ben Sira to Paul.* WUNT 2/16. Tübingen: Mohr Siebeck, 1985.

Schnackenburg, R. *The Epistle to the Ephesians: A Commentary.* Translated by H. Heron. Edinburgh: T&T Clark, 1991.

Schnelle, U. *Apostle Paul: His Life and Theology.* Grand Rapids: Baker, 2003.

———. *Gerechtigkeit und Christusgegenwart: Vorpaulinische und paulinische Tauftheologie.* GTA 24. Göttingen: Vandenhoeck & Ruprecht, 1983.

———. *Theology of the New Testament.* Translated by M. E. Boring. Grand Rapids: Baker, 2009.

Schniewind, J. *Euangelion: Ursprung und erste Gestalt des Begriffs Euangelium.* Vol. 2. Darmstadt: Wissenschaftliche Buchgesellschaft, 1931.

Scholem, G. *Jewish Gnosticism, Merkabah Mysticism, and Talmudic Tradition*. New York: Jewish Theological Seminary of America, 1960.

———. *Major Trends in Jewish Mysticism*. London: Thames and Hudson, 1955.

Schottroff, L. "Ist Allein in Christus Heil? Das Bekenntnis zu Christus und die Erlösung (Kol 1,15–20)." Pages 79–89 in *Antijudaismus im Neuen Testament? Grundlagen für die Arbeit mit biblischen Texten*. Edited by D. Henze. Gütersloh: Kaiser, 1997.

Schrage, W. *Ethik des neuen Testaments*. GNT 4. Göttingen: Vandenhoeck & Ruprecht, 1982.

Schreiner, Thomas R. *New Testament Theology: Magnifying God in Christ*. Grand Rapids: Baker, 2008.

———. *Paul: Apostle of God's Glory in Christ*. Downers Grove, IL: InterVarsity Press, 2001.

Schubert, P. *Form and Function of the Pauline Thanksgivings*. BZNW 20. Berlin: Töpelmann, 1939.

Schürer, E. *The History of the Jewish People in the Age of Jesus Christ*. Revised and edited by G. Vermes, F. Millar, and M. Goodman. Vol. 3, Part 1. Edinburgh: T&T Clark, 1986.

Schüssler Fiorenza, E. *In Memory of Her: A Feminist Theological Reconstruction of Christian Origins*. New York: Crossroad, 1983.

Schwarz, S. L. "Reconsidering the *Testament of Solomon*." *JSP* 16 (2007): 203–37.

Schweizer, E. "Altes und neues zu den 'Elementen der Welt' in Kol 2,20; Gal 4,3–9." Pages 111–18 in *Wissenschaft und Kirche*. Edited by K. Aland. Bielefeld: Luther-Verlag, 1989.

———. "Christus und Geist im Kolosserbrief." Pages 297–313 in *Christ and Spirit in the New Testament*. FS C. F. D. Moule. Edited by B. Lindars and S. S. Smalley. Cambridge: Cambridge University Press, 1973.

———. "Colossians 1:15–20." *RevExp* 87 (1990): 97–104.

———. "Die 'Elemente der Welt' Gal 4, 3.9; Kol 2, 8.20." Pages 245–59 in *Verborum Veritas*. FS G. Stählin. Edited by O. Böcher and K. Haacker. Wuppertal: Brockhaus, 1970.

———. "Die Kirche als Leib Christi in den paulinischen Antilegomena." Pages 293–316 in *Neotestamentica: Deutsche und Englische Aufsätze, 1951–1963*. Zürich: Zwingli, 1963.

———. "Slaves of the Elements and Worshipers of Angels: Gal 4:3, 9 and Col 2:8, 18, 20." *JBL* 107 (1988): 455–68.

———. "Versöhnung des Alls." Pages 487–501 in *Jesus Christus in Historie und Theologie*. FS H. Conzelmann. Edited by G. Strecker. Tübingen: Mohr Siebeck, 1975.

Schwindt, R. *Das Weltbild des Epheserbriefes: Eine religionsgeschichtlich-exegetisch Studie*. WUNT 148. Tübingen: Mohr Siebeck, 2002.

Scott, J. M. *Adoption as Sons of God: An Exegetical Investigation into the Background of ΥΙΟΘΕΣΙΑ in the Pauline Corpus*. WUNT 2/48. Tübingen: Mohr Siebeck, 1992.

Segal, A. F. "Heavenly Ascent in Hellenistic Judaism, Early Christianity and Their Environment." *ANRW* II.23.2 (1980): 1333–94.

———. "Hellenistic Magic: Some Questions of Definition." Pages 349–75 in *Studies in Gnosticism and Hellenistic Religions*. FS. G Quispel. Edited by R. van den Broek and M. J. Vermaseren. EPRO 91. Leiden: Brill, 1981. Repr., "Hellenistic Magic: Some Questions of Definition." Pages 79–108 in *The Other Judaisms of Late Antiquity*. BJS 127. Atlanta: Scholars Press, 1987.

———. *Two Powers in Heaven: Early Rabbinic Reports about Christianity and Gnosticism*. SJLA 25. Leiden: Brill, 1977.

Sellar, A. M. *Bede's Ecclesiastical History of England: A Revised Translation with Introduction, Life, and Notes*. London: George Bell, 1907.

Sellin, G. "'Die Auferstehung ist schon geschehen': Zur Spiritualisierung Apokolyptisch Terminologie im Neuen Testament." *NovT* 25 (1983): 220–37.

———. "Vom Kolosser- zum Epheserbrief: Eine Entwicklung im Deuteropaulinismus." Pages 151–70 in *Kolosser-Studien*. Edited by P. Müller. Biblisch-Theologische Studien 103. Neukirchen-Vluyn: Neukirchener, 2009.

Sheppard, A. R. R. "Jews, Christians and Heretics in Acmonia and Eumeneia." *AnSt* 29 (1979): 169–80.

———. "Pagan Cults of Angels in Roman Asia Minor." *Talanta* 12–13 (1980–81): 77–101.

Shkul, M. "New Identity and Cultural Baggage: Identity and Otherness in Colossians." Pages 367–87 in *T&T Clark Handbook to Social Identity in the New Testament*. Edited by J. B. Tucker and C. A. Baker. New York: Bloomsbury T&T Clark, 2014.

Shogren, G. "Presently Entering the Kingdom of Christ: The Background and Purpose of Col 1:12–14." *JETS* 31 (1988): 173–80.

Siber, P. *Mit Christus Leben: Eine Studie zur paulinischen Auferstehungshoffnung*. ATANT 61. Zürich: TVZ, 1971.

Simon, M. *Le Christianisme antique et son contexte religieux*. WUNT 23. Tübingen: Mohr Siebeck, 1981.

———. "Remarques sur l'angélolâtrie juive au début de l'ére Chrétienne." *CRAI* (1971): 120–34.

———. *Verus Israel: A Study of the Relations between Christians and Jews in the Roman Empire (135–425)*. Translated by H. McKeating. Oxford: Oxford University Press, 1986.

Şimşek, C. "Kolossai." *Arkeoloji ve Sanat* 24/107 (2002): 1–16.

———. "A Menorah with a Cross Carved on a Column of Nymphaeum A at Laodicea ad Lycum." *JRA* 19 (2006): 343–46.

———. "Regional Cults in the Lycos Valley and Its Neighbourhood." Page 673–90 in *Studies in Honour of Altan Çilingiroğlu: A Life Dedicated to Urartu on the Shores of the Upper Sea*. Edited by H. Sağlamtimur et al. Istanbul: Arkeoloji ve Sanat Yayinlari, 2011.

Smith, I. K. *Heavenly Perspective: A Study of the Apostle Paul's Response to a Jewish Mystical Movement at Colossae*. LNTS 346. London: T&T Clark, 2006.

Smith, J. A. "First-Century Christian Singing and Its Relationship to Contemporary Jewish Religious Song." *Music & Letters* 75 (1994): 1–15.

Smith, M. "The Eighth Book of Moses and How it Grew (*PLEID.* J 395)." Pages 683–93 in *Atti del XVII Congresso Internazionale di Papirologia*. Vol. 2. Napoli: Centro Internazionale per lo Studio Dei Papiri Ercolanesi, 1984.

———. "Goodenough's *Jewish Symbols* in Retrospect." *JBL* 86 (1967): 53–68.

———. "A Note on Some Jewish Assimilationists: The Angels (P. Berlin 5025b, P. Louvre 2391)." *JANESCU* 16–17 (1984–85): 207–12.

Smith, R. R. R. "The Imperial Reliefs from the Sebasteion at Aphrodisias." *JRS* 77 (1987): 88–138.

———. "*Simulacra Gentium*: The *Ethne* from the Sebasteion at Aphrodisias." *JRS* 78 (1988): 50–77.

Sokolowski, F. *Lois sacrées de l'Asie Mineure*. Paris: de Boccard, 1955.

———. "Sur le culte d'angelos dans le paganisme grec et romain." *HTR* 53 (1960): 225–29.

Sokupa, M. M. "The Calendrical Elements in Colossians 2:16 in Light of the Ongoing Debate on the Opponents." *Neot* 45 (2012): 172–89.

Son, S.-W. "Tò σῶμα τοῦ Χριστοῦ in Colossians 2:17." Pages 222–38 in *History and Exegesis*. FS E. E. Ellis. Edited by S.-W. Son. London: T&T Clark, 2006.

Standhartinger, A. "A City with a Message: Colossae and Colossians." Pages 239–56 in *The First Urban Churches 5: Colossae, Hierapolis, and Laodicea*. Edited by J. R. Harrison and L. L. Welborn. WGRWSup 16. Atlanta: SBL Press, 2019.

———. "Colossians and the Pauline School." *NTS* 50 (2004): 572–93.

———. "Der Kolosserhymnus im Lichte epigraphischer Zeugnisse." Pages 69–92 in *Epigraphical Evidence Illustrating Paul's Letter to the Colossians*. Edited by J. Verheyden, M. Öhler, and T. Corsten. WUNT 2/411. Tübingen: Mohr Siebeck, 2018.

———. "The Origin and Intention of the Household Code in the Letter to the Colossians." *JSNT* 79 (2000): 117–30.

———. *Studien zur Entstehungsgeschichte und Intention des Kolosserbriefs.* NovTSup 94. Leiden: Brill, 1999.

———. "'. . . wegen der Hoffnung, die für euch im Himmel bereitliegt' (Kol 1,5)." Pages 1–22 in *Kolosser-Studien.* Edited by P. Müller. Biblisch-Theologische Studien 103. Neukirchen-Vluyn: Neukirchener, 2009.

Stern, M. "The Jewish Diaspora." Pages 117–83 in *The Jewish People in the First Century.* Edited by S. Safrai and M. Stern. CRINT I/1. Philadelphia: Fortress, 1974.

Stettler, C. *Der Kolosserhymnus: Untersuchungen zu Form, traditionsgeschichtlichem Hintergrund und Aussage von Kol 1,15–20.* WUNT 2/131. Tübingen: Mohr Siebeck, 2000.

———. "The Opponents at Colossae." Pages 169–200 in *Paul and His Opponents.* Pauline Studies 2. Edited by S. E. Porter. Leiden: Brill, 2005.

Stettler, H. *Heiligung bei Paulus: Ein Beitrag aus biblisch-theologischer Sicht.* WUNT 2/368. Tübingen: Mohr Siebeck, 2014.

———. "An Interpretation of Colossians 1:24 in the Framework of Paul's Mission Theology." Pages 185–208 in *The Mission of the Early Church to Jews and Gentiles.* Edited by J. Ådna and H. Kvalbein. WUNT 127. Tübingen: Mohr Siebeck, 2000.

Still, T. "Eschatology in Colossians: How Realized Is It?" *NTS* 50 (2004): 125–38.

Stirewalt, M. L. *Paul: The Letter Writer.* Grand Rapids: Eerdmans, 2003.

Stone, M. "Pseudepigraphy Reconsidered." *Review of Rabbinic Judaism* 9 (2006): 1–15.

Stowers, S. K. *Letter Writing in Greco-Roman Antiquity.* LEC 5. Philadelphia: Westminster, 1986.

Strawbridge, J. R. *The Pauline Effect: The Use of the Pauline Epistles by Early Christian Writers.* SBR 5. Berlin: de Gruyter, 2015.

Strecker, G. *Theology of the New Testament.* Translated by M. E. Boring. Berlin: de Gruyter, 2000.

Strelan, R. "The Languages of the Lycus Valley." Pages 77–103 in *Colossae in Space and Time: Linking to an Ancient City.* NTOA 94. Edited by A. H. Cadwallader and M. Trainor. Göttingen: Vandenhoeck & Ruprecht, 2011.

Strubbe, J. H. M. APAI EPITYMBAIOI: *Imprecations against Desecrators of the Grave in the Greek Epitaphs of Asia Minor: A Catalogue.* IGSK 52. Bonn: Habelt, 1997.

———. "Cursed Be He That Moves My Bones." Pages 33–59 in *Magika Hiera: Ancient Greek Magic and Religion.* Edited by C. A. Faraone and D. Obbink. New York: Oxford University Press, 1991.

Strugnell, J. "The Angelic Liturgy at Qumran, 4QSerek Sirot 'Olat Hassabat." Pages 318–45 in *Congress Volume: Oxford, 1959.* VTSup 7. Leiden: Brill, 1960.

Stuckenbruck, L. T. *Angel Veneration and Christology.* WUNT 2/70. Tübingen: Mohr Siebeck, 1995.

———. "Prayers of Deliverance from the Demonic in the Dead Sea Scrolls and Related Early Jewish Literature." Pages 146–65 in *The Changing Face of Judaism, Christianity, and Other Greco-Roman Religions in Antiquity.* Edited by I. H. Henderson, G. S. Oegema, and S. P. Rickers. Studien zu den jüdischen Schriften aus hellensitisch-römischer Zeit 2. Gütersloh: Gütersloher, 2006.

Stuhlmacher, P. *Biblical Theology of the New Testament.* Translated and Edited by D. P. Bailey. Grand Rapids: Eerdmans, 2018.

———. "Christliche Verantwortung bei Paulus und seinen Schülern." *EvT* 28 (1968): 165–86.

Stuhlmann, R. *Das eschatologische Maß im Neuen Testament.* FRLANT 132. Göttingen: Vandenhoeck & Ruprecht, 1983.

Sumney, J. "'I Fill Up What Is Lacking in the Afflictions of Christ': Paul's Vicarious Suffering in Colossians." *CBQ* 68 (2006): 664–80.

———. "'Those Who Pass Judgment': The Identity of the Opponents in Colossians." *Biblica* 74 (1993): 366–88.

Swart, G. "Eschatological Vision or Exhortation to Visible Christian Conduct? Notes on the Interpretation of Colossians 3:4." *Neot* 33 (1999): 169–77.

Swartz, M. D. "The Dead Sea Scrolls and Later Jewish Magic and Mysticism." *DSD* 8 (2001): 182–93.

———. "'Like the Ministering Angels': Ritual and Purity in Early Jewish Mysticism and Magic." *AJSR* 19 (1994): 135–67.

Sweeney, J. P. "Guidelines on Christian Witness in Colossians 4:5–6." *BSac* 159 (2002): 449–61.

Taatz, I. *Frühjudische Briefe: Die paulinische Briefe im Rahmen der offiziellen religiösen Briefe des Frühjudentum*. NTOA 16. Göttingen: Vandenhoeck & Ruprecht, 1991.

Tachau, P. *"Einst" und "Jetzt" im Neuen Testament: Beobachtungen zu einem urchristlichen Predigtschema in der neutestamenlichen Briefliteratur und zu seiner Vorgeschichte*. FRLANT 105. Göttingen: Vandenhoeck & Ruprecht, 1972.

Tannehill, R. C. *Dying and Rising with Christ: A Study in Pauline Theology*. BZNW 32. Berlin: Töpelmann, 1967.

Tanriver, C. "Three New Inscriptions from Tripolis." *EA* 42 (2009): 81–96.

Theophilos, M. P. "Employing Numismatic Evidence in Discussions of Early Christianity in the Lycus Valley: A Case Study from Laodicea." Pages 257–92 in *The First Urban Churches 5: Colossae, Hierapolis, and Laodicea*. Edited by J. R. Harrison and L. L. Welborn. WGRWSup 16. Atlanta: SBL Press, 2019.

Thielman, F. *Romans*. ZECNT. Grand Rapids: Zondervan Academic, 2018.

———. *Theology of the New Testament: A Canonical and Synthetic Approach*. Grand Rapids: Zondervan, 2005.

Thomas, G. "Magna Mater and Attis." *ANRW* II.17.3 (1984): 93–110.

Thompson, J. W. *Moral Formation according to Paul: The Context and Coherence of Pauline Ethics*. Grand Rapids: Baker, 2011.

Thomson, I. H. *Chiasmus in the Pauline Letters*. JSNTSup 111. Sheffield: Sheffield Academic Press, 1995.

Thonemann, P. *The Maeander Valley: A Historical Geography from Antiquity to Byzantium*. Greek Culture in the Roman World. Cambridge: Cambridge University Press, 2011.

Thornton, T. C. G. "Jewish New Moon Festivals, Galatians 4:3–11 and Colossians 2:16." *JTS* 40 (1989): 97–100.

Thurén, L. "Epistolography and Rhetoric: Case Not Closed." Pages 141–59 in *Paul and Ancient Rhetoric: Theory and Practice in the Hellenistic Context*. Edited by S. E. Porter and B. R. Dyer. Cambridge: Cambridge University Press, 2016.

Thurston, B. B. "Paul's Associates in Colossians 4:7–17." *ResQ* 41 (1999): 45–53.

Tidball, D. *In Christ, in Colossae: Sociological Perspectives on Colossians*. Milton Keynes: Paternoster, 2011.

Tinsley, A. *A Postcolonial African-American Re-Reading of Colossians: Identity, Reception, and Interpretation under the Gaze of the Empire*. New York: Palgrave Macmillan, 2013.

Tite, P. L. "Dusting Off a Pseudo-Historical Letter: Re-Thinking the Epistolary Aspects of the Apocryphal Epistle to the Laodiceans." Pages 289–318 in *Paul and Pseudepigraphy*. Edited by S. E. Porter and G. P. Fewster. Leiden: Brill, 2013.

Torijano, P. A. *Solomon the Esoteric King: From King to Magus, Development of a Tradition*. JSJSup 73. Leiden: Brill, 2002.

Trainor, M. F. "Colossae: The State of Forthcoming Excavations." *JSPL* 1 (2011): 133–36.

———. *Epaphras: Paul's Educator at Colossae*. Paul's Social Network: Brothers & Sisters in Faith. Collegeville, MN: Liturgical Press, 2008.

———. "Excavating Epaphras of Colossae." Pages 232–46 in *Colossae in Space and Time: Linking to an Ancient City*. Edited by A. H. Cadwallader and M. Trainor. NTOA/SUNT 94. Göttingen: Vandenhoeck & Ruprecht, 2011.

Trebilco, P. "Christian Communities in Western Asia Minor into the Early Second Century: Ignatius and Others as Witnesses against Bauer." *JETS* 49 (2006): 17–44.

———. "Christians in the Lycus Valley: The View from Ephesus and from Western Asia Minor." Pages 180–211 in *Colossae in Space and Time: Linking to an Ancient City*. Edited by A. H. Cadwallader and M. Trainor. NTOA/SUNT 94. Göttingen: Vandenhoeck & Ruprecht, 2011.

———. *Jewish Communities in Asia Minor*. SNTSMS 69. Cambridge: University Press, 1991.

Trench, R. C. *Synonyms of the New Testament*. London: Macmillan, 1876.

Tripp, D. "(Colossians 1:19, 2:9): Christology, or Soteriology Also?" *ExpTim* 116 (2004): 78–79.

Trudinger, L. P. "A Further Brief Note on Colossians 1:24." *EvQ* 45 (1973): 36–38.

Valiavitcharska, V. *Rhetoric and Rhythm in Byzantium: The Sound of Persuasion*. Cambridge: Cambridge University Press, 2015.

Van Kooten, G. H. *Cosmic Christology in Paul and the Pauline School: Colossians and Ephesians in the Context of Graeco-Roman Cosmology*. WUNT 2/171. Tübingen: Mohr Siebeck, 2003.

Van Lennep, H. J. *Travels in Little-Known Parts of Asia Minor*. 2 vols. London: John Murray, 1870.

Van Nes, J. "*Hapax Legomena* in Disputed Pauline Letters: A Reassessment." *ZNW* 109 (2018): 118–37.

———. "Missing 'Particles' in Disputed Pauline Letters? A Question of Method." *JSNT* 40 (2018): 383–98.

Varhelyi, Z. "Magic, Religion, and Syncretism at the Oracle at Claros." Pages 13–31 in *Between Magic and Religion: Interdisciplinary Studies in Ancient Mediterranean Religion and Society*. Edited by S. R. Asirvatham et al. New York: Rowman & Littlefield, 2001.

Vasser, M. "Grant Slaves Equality: Re-Examining the Translation of Colossians 4:1." *TynBul* 68 (2017): 59–71.

Vergeer, W. C. "Σκιά and Σῶμα: The Strategy of Contextualisation in Colossians 2:17. A Contribution to the Quest for a Legitimate Contextual Theology Today." *Neot* 28 (1994): 379–93.

Vermaseren, M. J. *Corpus Cultus Cybelae Attidisque (CCCA): I. Asia Minor*. EPRO 50. Leiden: Brill, 1987.

———. *Cybele and Attis: The Myth and the Cult*. London: Thames and Hudson, 1977.

———. *The Legend of Attis in Greek and Roman Art*. EPRO 9. Leiden: Brill, 1966.

———. "La sotériologie dans les papyri graecae magicae." Pages 17–30 in *La soteriologia dei culti orientali nell' impero romano*. Edited by U. Bianchi and M. J. Vermaseren. EPRO 92. Leiden: Brill, 1982.

Verner, D. C. *The Household of God: The Social World of the Pastoral Epistles*. SBLDS 71. Chico, CA: Scholars Press, 1983.

Vielhauer, P. "Gesetzesdienst und Stoicheiadienst im Galaterbrief." Pages 543–55 in *Rechtfertigung*. FS E. Käsemann. Edited by J. Friedrich, W. Pöhlmann, and P. Stuhlmacher. Tübingen: Mohr Siebeck; Göttingen: Vandenhoeck & Ruprecht, 1976.

Vögtle, A. *Die Tugend- und Lasterkataloge im Neuen Testaments: Exegetisch religions- und formgeschichtlich Untersucht*. NTAbh 16. Münster: Aschendorff, 1936.

Vollenweider, S. "Hymnus, Enkomion oder Psalm? Schattengefechte in der neutestamentlichen Wissenschaft." *NTS* 56 (2010): 208–31.

Waelkens, M. *Die kleinasiatischen Türsteine: Typologische und epigraphische Untersuchungen der klaeinasiatischen Grabreliefs mit Scheintür*. Mainz: von Zabern, 1986.

Walker-Ramisch, S. "Graeco-Roman Voluntary Associations and the Damascus Document: A Sociological Analysis." Pages 128–45 in *Voluntary Associations in the Graeco-Roman World*. Edited by J. S. Kloppenborg and S. G. Wilson. London: Routledge, 1996.

Wallace, D. B. *Greek Grammar Beyond the Basics: An Exegetical Syntax of the New Testament*. Grand Rapids: Zondervan, 1996.

Walsh, B. J. "Late/Post Modernity and Idolatry: A Contextual Reading of Colossians 2:8–3:4." *ExAud* 15 (1999): 1–17.

Walsh, B. J., and S. C. Keesmaat. *Colossians Remixed: Subverting the Empire*. Downers Grove, IL: InterVarsity Press, 2004.

Walter, N. "Geschichte und Mythos in der urchristlichen Präexistenzchristologie." Pages 224–34 in *Mythos und Rationalität*. Edited by H H. Schmid. Gütersloh: Gütersloher Verlagshaus, 1988.

Walter, N. "Die 'Handschrift in Satzungen' Kol 2:14." *ZNW* 70 (1979): 115–18.

Watson, L. C. *Magic in Ancient Greece and Rome*. London: Bloomsbury Academic, 2019.

Webb, W. J. *Slaves, Women, and Homosexuals: Exploring the Hermeneutics of Cultural Analysis*. Downers Grove, IL: InterVarsity Press, 2001.

Wedderburn, A. J. M. *Baptism and Resurrection: Studies in Pauline Theology against Its Graeco-Roman Background*. WUNT 44. Tübingen: Mohr Siebeck, 1987.

———. "The Theology of Colossians." Pages 1–71 in *The Theology of the Later Pauline Letters*. Cambridge: Cambridge University Press, 1993.

Weidinger, K. *Die Haustafeln: Ein Stück urchristlicher Paränese*. UNT 14. Leipzig: Hinrichs, 1928.

Weima, J. A. D. *1–2 Thessalonians*. BECNT. Grand Rapids: Baker Academic, 2014.

———. *Neglected Endings: The Significance of the Pauline Letter Closings*. JSNTSup 101. Sheffield: JSOT Press, 1994.

———. *Paul the Ancient Letter Writer: An Introduction to Epistolary Analysis*. Grand Rapids: Baker, 2016.

———. "What Does Aristotle Have to Do with Paul? An Evaluation of Rhetorical Criticism." *CTJ* 32 (1997): 458–68.

Weiss, H. "The Law in the Epistle to the Colossians." *CBQ* 34 (1972): 294–314.

Weiss, H.-F. "Gnostische Motive und antignostische Polemik im Kolosser- und Epheserbrief." Pages 311–24 in *Gnosis und Neues Testament*. Edited by K. W. Tröger. Gütersloh: Mohn, 1973.

Weiss, J. *Christ: The Beginnings of Dogma*. Boston: American Unitarian Association, 1911.

Wengst, K. *Christologische Formeln und Lieder des Urchristentums*. SNT 7. Gütersloh: Gütersloher, 1972.

Wessely, K. "Ephesia Grammata aus Papyrusrollen, Inschriften, Gemmen, etc." Pages 3–38 in *Zwölfter jahresbericht über das k. k. Franz-Josef-Gymnasium in Wien*. Vienna: Franz-Joseph-Gymnasium, 1886.

West, M. L. *Greek Meter*. Oxford: Clarendon, 1982.

Westcott, B. F. *A General Survey of the History of the Canon of the New Testament*. 7th ed. Cambridge: Cambridge University Press, 1896.

Westcott, B. F., and F. J. Hort. *The New Testament in the Original Greek: Introduction and Appendix*. New York: Harper & Brothers, 1882.

White, B. L. *Remembering Paul: Ancient and Modern Contests over the Image of the Apostle*. Oxford: Oxford University Press, 2014.

White, J. "The Imprisonment that Could Have Happened (and the Letters Paul Could Have Written There): A Response to Ben Witherington." *JETS* 61 (2018): 549–58.

———. "Paul Completes the Servant's Sufferings (Colossians 1:24)." *JSPL* 6 (2016): 181–98.

Wibbing, S. *Die Tugend- und Lasterkataloge im Neuen Testament und ihre Traditionsgeschichte unter bessonderer Berücksichtigung der Qumran-Texte*. BZNW 25. Berlin: Töpelmann, 1959.

Wiegand, T., ed. *Didyma. Zweiter Teil: Die Inschriften*. Berlin: Gebr. Mann, 1958.

Wilder, T. *Pseudonymity, the New Testament, and Deception: An Inquiry into Intention and Reception*. Lanham, MD: University Press of America, 2004.

Williams, A. L. "The Cult of the Angels at Colossae." *JTS* 10 (1909): 413–38.

Williams, G. *The Spirit World in the Letters of Paul the Apostle*. FRLANT 231. Göttingen: Vandenhoeck & Ruprecht, 2009.

Williamson, L. "Led in Triumph: Paul's Use of Thriambeuo." *Int* 22 (1968): 317–32.

Wilson, M. *Biblical Turkey: A Guide to the Jewish and Christian Sites of Asia Minor.* Istanbul: Ege Yayinlari, 2012.

Wilson, R. McL. "Gnosis and the Mysteries." Pages 451–57 in *Studies in Gnosticism and Hellenistic Religions.* FS G. Quispel. Edited by R. van den Broek and M. J. Vermaseren. EPRO 91. Leiden: Brill, 1981.

———. *Gnosis and the New Testament.* Philadelphia: Fortress, 1968.

———. *The Gnostic Problem.* London: Mowbray, 1958.

———. "Nag Hammadi and the New Testament." *NTS* 28 (1982): 289–302.

Wilson, W. T. *The Hope of Glory: Education and Exhortation in the Epistle to the Colossians.* NovTSup 88. Leiden: Brill, 1997.

Windisch, H. *Paulus und Christus: Ein biblisch-religionsgeschichtlicher Vergleich.* UNT 24. Leipzig: Hinrichs, 1934.

Wink, W. *Engaging the Powers: Discernment and Resistance in a World of Domination.* Minneapolis: Fortress, 1992.

———. *Naming the Powers: The Language of Power in the New Testament.* Philadelphia: Fortress, 1984.

Winter, B. W. "The Entries and Ethics of Orators and Paul (1 Thessalonians 2:1–12)." *TynBul* 44 (1993): 55–74.

Wise, M. O. *Language and Literacy in Roman Judaea: A Study of the Bar Kokhba Documents.* AYBRL. New Haven: Yale University Press, 2015.

Witherington B. "'Almost Thou Persuadest Me . . .': The Importance of Greco-Roman Rhetoric for the Understanding of the Text and Context of the NT." *JETS* 58 (2015): 63–88.

———. "The Case of the Imprisonment that Did Not Happen: Paul at Ephesus." *JETS* 60 (2017): 525–32.

Witherington, B., and G. F. Wessels. "Do Everything in the Name of the Lord: Ethics and Ethos in Colossians." Pages 303–33 in *Identity, Ethics, and Ethos in the New Testament.* Edited by J. G. van der Watt. BZNW 141. Berlin: de Gruyter, 2006.

Witt, R. E. *Isis in the Greco-Roman World.* Ithaca, NY: Cornell University Press, 1971.

Witulski, T. "Gegenwart und Zukunft in den eschatologischen Konzeptionen des Kolosser- und des Epheserbriefes." *ZNW* 96 (2005): 211–42.

Wold, B. G. "Family Ethics in *4QInstruction* and the New Testament." *NovT* 50 (2008): 286–300.

———. *Women, Men and Angels: The Qumran Wisdom Document Musar leMevin and Its Allusions to Genesis Creation Traditions.* WUNT 2/201. Tübingen: Mohr Siebeck, 2005.

Wood, K. H. "The 'Sabbath Days' of Colossians 2:16, 17." Pages 338–42 in *The Sabbath in Scripture and History.* Edited by K. A. Strand and D. A. Augsburger. Washington, DC: Review and Herald, 1982.

Wortmann, D. "Neue magische Texte." *Bonner Jahrbücher* 168 (1968): 56–111.

Wright, N. T. "Monotheism, Christology and Ethics: 1 Corinthians 8." Pages 120–36 in *The Climax of the Covenant: Christ and the Law in Pauline Theology.* Minneapolis: Fortress, 1992.

———. *Paul and the Faithfulness of God.* 2 vols. Christian Origins and the Question of God 4. Minneapolis: Fortress, 2013.

———. "Poetry and Theology in Colossians 1.15–20." *NTS* 36 (1990): 444–68. Repr., with minor revisions, in pages 99–119 of *The Climax of the Covenant: Christ and the Law in Pauline Theology.* Minneapolis: Fortress, 1992.

———. *Resurrection of the Son of God.* Christian Origins and the Question of God 3. Minneapolis: Fortress, 2003.

Wünsch, R. *Antike Fluchtafeln.* 2nd ed. Kleine Texte für Vorlesungen und Übungen 20. Bonn: Marcus and Weber, 1912.

———. *Antikes Zaubergerät aus Pergamon.* Jahrbuch des kaiserlich deutschen archäologischen Instituts. Ergänzungsheft VI. Berlin: Reimer, 1905.

Yamauchi, E. M. "Jewish Gnosticism? The Prologue of John, Mandaean Parallels, and the Trimorphic Protennoia." Pages 467–97 in *Studies in Gnosticism and Hellenistic Religions.* FS G. Quispel. Edited by R. van den Broek and M. J. Vermaseren. EPRO 91. Leiden: Brill, 1981.

———. "Magic in the Biblical World." *TynBul* 34 (1983): 169–200.

———. *Persia and the Bible.* Grand Rapids: Baker, 1990.

———. *Pre-Christian Gnosticism.* 2nd ed. Grand Rapids: Baker, 1983.

———. "Pre-Christian Gnosticism, the New Testament and Nag Hammadi in Recent Debate." *Themelios* 10 (1984): 22–27.

———. "The Scythians—Who Were They? And Why Did Paul Include Them in Colossians 3:11?" *Priscilla Papers* 21 (2007): 13–18.

———. "Sectarian Parallels: Qumran and Colosse." *BSac* 121 (1964): 141–52.

Yates, R. "Christ and the Powers of Evil in Colossians." Pages 461–68 in *Studia Biblica 1978: III. Papers on Paul and Other New Testament Authors.* Edited by E. A. Livingstone. JSNTSup 3. Sheffield: JSOT Press, 1980.

———. "Colossians 2,14: Metaphor of Forgiveness." *Biblica* 90 (1990): 248–59.

———. "Colossians 2.15: Christ Triumphant." *NTS* 37 (1991): 573–91.

———. "Colossians and Gnosis." *JSNT* 27 (1986): 49–68.

———. "A Note on Colossians 1:24." *EvQ* 42 (1970): 88–92.

———. "A Reappraisal of Colossians." *ITQ* 58 (1992): 95–117.

———. "'The Worship of Angels' (Col. 2:18)." *ExpTim* 97 (1985): 12–15.

Yener, B., and P. Ulusoy, Ş. Yener, D. Etik, T. Abali, and M. Ergenç. "Kolossai Antik Kenti ve Territoryumu 2021 Yılı Arkeolojik Yüzey Araştırmaları (1. Sezon)." Pages 215–28 in 38. *Araştırma Sonuçları Toplantısı.* Vol. 1. Edited by C. Keskin. Ankara: T. C. Kültür ve Turizm Bakanliği, 2023.

Yener, B., and P. Ulusoy, Ş. Yener, T. Abali, and M. Ergenç. "Kolossai Antik Kenti ve Territoryumu 2022 Yılı Arkeolojik Yüzey Araştırmaları (2. Sezon)." Pages 299–312 in 39. *Araştırma Sonuçları Toplantısı.* Vol. 1. Edited by E. Evcin. Ankara: T. C. Kültür ve Turizm Bakanliği, 2024.

Yinger, K. "Translating καταβραβευέτω ['Disqualify' NRSV] in Colossians 2.18." *BT* 54 (2003): 138–45.

Yule, G. U. *The Statistical Study of Literary Vocabulary.* Cambridge: Cambridge University Press, 1944.

Zeilinger, F. *Der Erstgeborene der Schöpfung: Untersuchungen zur Formalstruktur und Theologie des Kolosserbriefes.* Wien: Herder, 1974.

Zeller, D. "Die Mysterienkulte und die paulinische Soteriologie (Röm 6,1–11): Eine Fallstudie zum Synkretismus im Neuen Testament." Pages 42–61 in *Suchbewegungen: Synkretismus—kulturelle Identität und kirchliches Bekenntnis.* Edited by H. P. Siller. Darmstadt: Wissenschafliche Buchgesellschaft, 1991.

Zmiejewski, J. *Der Stil der paulinische "Narrenrede."* BBB 52. Bonn: Hanstein, 1978.

# Introduction

Colossians is a remarkable letter. In the span of less than 1600 words, the apostle Paul was able to give expression to one of the most magnificent paeans of praise to Christ in all of Scripture, deliver warnings about a unique and dangerous teaching threatening the health of the church at Colossae, expound on the meaning and implications of union with Christ, voice thanksgiving to God for the Colossian church, report on how he is praying for them, provide incisive instructions on the behavior fitting for new life in Christ, give guidance on what it means to live as Christians in the household, and convey an array of personal greetings and travel plans. And he did this under the constraint and discomfort of the chains of Roman custody.

Many interpreters have justifiably asserted that Christ is the theme of the letter. This is summed up well midway through the letter when Paul exclaims, "but Christ is all and in all" (3:11). He is truly everything—not just for believers but for the entire universe. He created all things and will bring history to a conclusion. He will overcome the problem of evil and will usher in universal and everlasting peace. But tragically this could only be accomplished through the "blood" of his cross (1:20). The horrible death of Jesus not only made it possible for God to forgive sins, but it also resulted in a decisive defeat of the supernatural forces of evil holding humanity in bondage. The apostle thus paints a portrait of redemption that stretches from the individual to the universe.

Until Christ appears in glory, the church is the base of his operation and the means by which God will accomplish his purposes on earth. From the small house churches in the cities of Colossae, Laodicea, and Hierapolis to the vast network of churches comprising the universal body of Christ, Christ is actively and dynamically involved with his people as head of the body. Paul is likewise a steward and servant of this body, and especially of the local churches whose beginnings can be traced to Paul's apostolic ministry. Thus, although he has likely never met the Colossian believers personally, he feels a strong caring and pastoral responsibility for them. When word comes to him that their well-being is being undermined by what he deems to be a threatening and dangerous teaching, he attempts to do what he can to counteract this teaching and set of practices. He does so by writing this letter and dispatching two of his trusted associates to carry it to the Colossians and to minister to them.

The specific shape and contours of this opposing teaching have been somewhat of an enigma to scholars over the years. There are a variety of indicators within the polemical section of the letter that provide specific insight, but how all of these come together into a coherent set of beliefs and practices has been a major point of discussion. I have tried to utilize all of the available and relevant sources for piecing this puzzle together, but I recognize that despite acquiring new puzzle pieces and identifying some pieces that perhaps belong to a different puzzle, the resultant picture remains opaque and tentative. I can only hope that as Colossae is excavated, more information will come to light that will inform our understanding of the nature of this problem.

I also recognize that since 1838 not everyone has seen Colossians as an authentically Pauline letter. I have spent countless hours looking at the evidence and the arguments, but I continue to find the weight of the evidence more strongly on the side of authenticity. I have sought to explain why I believe that this is the case in the section on authenticity.

The purpose of the Word Biblical Commentary series since its inception has been "to serve the needs of professional scholars and teachers, seminary students, working ministers—anyone who seeks to build a theological understanding of Scripture upon a solid foundation of scholarship." Seeking to serve the needs of both scholars and ministers in one volume is a tall order, but I have sought to keep both in mind as I have worked on this commentary. One of the distinctive traits of this series is to bring forth "major discoveries in the historical, textual, and archaeological fields." Much has come to light in recent years in the fields of history and archaeology that has relevance for interpreting the letter to the Colossians. Consequently, readers will find numerous references to inscriptional data and archaeological discoveries in the pages of this volume. There has also been an avalanche of literature on Colossians in the form of monographs and journal articles in the past thirty years. I have drawn from this rich reservoir as much as possible, but I have necessarily had to be selective simply to keep this volume to a manageable size (although some may still protest that I have written too much for such a brief NT letter).

In the sectional bibliographies, I have given a shortened title for each work. The full bibliographic data is provided in the comprehensive bibliography at the front of this volume. I should also note that in the sectional bibliographies, I have not included dictionary articles, Greek grammars, biblical theologies, and editions of texts. I do include all other works that I have cited in the section.

## *1. The City of Colossae*

### *Bibliography*

**Armstrong, A. J.** "Roman Phrygia," 349–57. **Arundell, V. J.** *Seven Churches*, 97–101. **Aulock, H. von.** *Münzen und Städte Phrygiens.* **Cadwallader, A.** "Comparative Method," 105–51. ———. *Fragments.* ———. "Revisiting Calder on Colossae," 103–11. ———. "St. Michael," 323–30. **Cadwallader, A., and J. R. Harrison.** "Perspectives on the Lycus Valley," 3–70. **Canavan, R.** "Threads of Identity," 81–104. **Duman, B., and E. Konakçi.** "Kolossai," 83–109. ———. "Silent Witness," 247–81. **Head, B. V.** *Greek Coins of Phrygia.* **Huttner, U.** "Colossians, Hierapolitan Coins," 73–79. ———. *Early Christianity in the Lycus Valley.* **Imhoof-Blumer, F.** *Kleinasiatische Münzen.* **Levine, L.** *Ancient Synagogue.* **Mare, W. H.** "Archaeological Prospects," 39–59. **Piccardi, L.** "Denizli Basin Earthquake," 95–105. **Ramsay, W. M.** *Cities and Bishoprics of Phrygia.* 2 vols. **Şimşek, C.** "Kolossai," 1–16. ———. "Regional Cults in the Lycus Valley," 673–90. **Standhartinger, A.** "City with a Message,"

239–56. **Theophilos, M. P.** "Numismatic Evidence," 257–92. **Thonemann, P.** *Maeander Valley*. **Trainor, M.** "State of Forthcoming Excavations," 133–35. **Yener et al.** "Kolossai Antik Kenti (2021)," 215–28. ———. "Kolossai Antik Kenti (2022)," 299–312.

## *Location and Setting*

The ancient city of Colossae was located along an important trade route about 120 miles due east of Ephesus (coordinates: N 37°47'20.8", E 29°15'37.8"). It was only eight miles southeast of Laodicea and ten miles south-southeast from Hierapolis. Colossae was situated in the southwestern portion of the territory of Phrygia, which became part of the Roman province of Asia in the second century BC. The highest peak of Asia Minor's Aegean region, Mount Cadmus (8200 feet in elevation), overlooked Colossae a short distance to the south. The city had an ample supply of water from the Lycus River that flowed from the higher elevations from the east, through Colossae, past Laodicea to the north, and joined the Maeander River just south of Tripolis. This length of the Lycus River was part of a fertile agricultural area called the Lycus Valley, which was also part of the upper Maeander Valley.

Some early interpreters were unaware of the location of the site and confused Colossians with the Colossus of Rhodes, resulting in some late NT manuscripts even calling the epistle "the letter to the Rhodians."[1] But the proximity to Laodicea and Hierapolis, both mentioned in Colossians (see 2:1; 4:13, 15, 16), clearly suggests a location in close proximity to those two cities. The general area of the site was identified by the English explorer and antiquarian, Francis Arundell, who traveled through this region in 1826.[2] The site was firmly identified a few years later, in 1835, by William Hamilton.[3] The most thorough subsequent investigation of Colossae and the Lycus Valley was undertaken by William M. Ramsay of the University of Aberdeen in volume 1 of a massive study titled *The Cities and Bishoprics of Phrygia*.[4] One of Ramsay's students, William Calder, took up Ramsay's interest and published a number of inscriptions related to Colossae.[5] Since then, there have been a handful of investigations of the site, but it remains unexcavated. Most of the publications since Ramsay and Calder have focused on the discovery of Colossian coins, inscriptions from the site and nearby area, pottery shards discovered in situ, and observations about the site itself.

When I first visited the site in 1985, it was unmarked and difficult to access—only via a rough dirt road from the nearby village of Honaz. Today it is easily

1 Cadwallader, *Fragments*, 7.

2 Arundell, *Seven Churches*, 90–101.

3 Duman and Konakçi, "Silent Witness," 249n6.

4 Ramsay, *Cities and Bishoprics of Phrygia*, 1:1–121, 208–34. The sixth chapter covered Colossae, whereas chs. 1–3 covered the Lycus Valley, Laodicea, and Hierapolis.

5 These have been published in vol. 6 of the multivolume series, *Monumenta Asiae Minoris Antiqua*, edited by W. H. Buckler and Calder. For an overview of Calder's work on Colossae, see Cadwallader, "Revisiting Calder on Colossae," 103–11.

accessible by a paved road that runs from Honaz to the main highway (D320) that connects to the highway leading to the large city of Denizli (near ancient Attouda), with a population of over seven hundred thousand people, and the road to Pamukkale (ancient Hierapolis).

### *Archaeological Prospects*

The site of Colossae presents an extraordinary opportunity for excavation and discovery. The area is completely unoccupied, and the space around the central part of the city is used for agriculture. Fortunately, at the time of this writing, arrangements are underway for the excavation of Colossae under the direction of Dr. Bariş Yener of the department of archaeology at Pamukkale University.[6]

In previous years, various groups had sought permission and attempted to pull together teams to begin work, but the plans never came to fruition. In the mid-1970s, Harold Mare, representing the Near East Archaeological Society, endeavored to put together a team to undertake a project called "The Joint Expedition to Colossae."[7] During the 1980s and 1990s, no group that I am familiar with was petitioning the Turkish government for permission to excavate the site.[8] In more recent years, Michael Trainor, under the auspices of Flinders University in Australia, renewed the efforts to excavate Colossae.[9] This effort, too, reached a dead end. But now, thanks to the leadership of Celal Şimşek, director of the archaeology department at Pamukkale University (Denizli, Turkey), a number of important sites in the Lycus Valley are being excavated. Beginning in 2003, Şimşek has directed extensive excavations at Laodicea. His emphasis on investment into the careful restoration and preservation of the site has been exemplary and sets a high standard. The pace of the excavation and restoration work has been rapid, along with many significant discoveries. One of Şimşek's students, Bahadir Duman, has been put in charge of the excavations at Tripolis at the northwest end of the Lycus Valley on the Maeander River. Now, and with gratitude from biblical scholars and many classicists, work will begin at Colossae under the direction of yet another of Şimşek's students, Bariş Yener.

Two preliminary surveys were undertaken of portions of the site. In 1997, Şimşek led a team to analyze the tumuli in the necropolis just north of the main part of the city. Then, in 2005, Duman and Erim Konakçi carried out a survey of pottery shards found at the site.[10] Thirty-one inscriptions have been

---

6 See his reports of two area surveys of the site in Yener et al., "Kolossai Antik Kenti (2022)," 299–312, and idem, "Kolossai Antik Kenti (2021)," 215–28.

7 See Mare, "Archaeological Prospects," 39–59.

8 In 1994, Prof. Daria de Barnardi Ferrero, director of the Italian mission currently excavating Hierapolis, informed me (by letter) that she was unaware of any group with plans to excavate the site.

9 See Trainor, "State of Forthcoming Excavations," 133–36.

10 Duman and Konakçi, "Kolossai," 83–109.

discovered that are associated with the city of Colossae. They range in date from the first century BC to the fifth century AD. Most of these are funerary inscriptions.[11] There have also been roughly 190 coins discovered that were minted at Colossae either in the Hellenistic or Roman eras.[12]

For NT scholars, the excavation of Colossae is of monumental significance. There is much to be discovered that could illuminate the text of the letter to the Colossians and, beyond this, to a better understanding of the Roman world and life in the Lycus Valley. With regard to Colossians, the potential for discovery is tantalizing. New light could be shed on the unique contours of the Colossian "philosophy" that Paul describes only in brief catchwords. Because this teaching appears to be a blend of local religious beliefs and practices with local Judaism, there is the potential for helpful insights through the discovery of temples, inscriptions, and Jewish realia. But everything that is discovered at the site will contribute to a better understanding of the social, religious, political, and cultural context of the letter.

### *Site Features*

The most prominent feature on the site of Colossae is a large biconical mound. The lower portion of the mound measures about 130 feet high and the upper portion 210 feet high. The entire mound covers approximately twenty-five acres. Buried within this mound, on top of it, and around the perimeter are the remains of the center of the ancient city of Colossae. There is currently a great deal of building material protruding from the mound, but much of the stone remains of the city have been carried away and used in other building projects over the centuries. Some of these remains were used in the construction of a Byzantine-era fortress about three miles south near the modern village of Honaz. The mound itself was not a natural hill but was likely created for defensive purpose before the Hellenistic era.[13]

The only identifiable structure thus far discovered is a theater built into the eastern side of the mound. It was likely built during the Hellenistic era (perhaps under Seleucid influence) and measures close to 250 feet wide. Cadwallader estimates that the seating capacity would have been in the range of five to seven thousand people.[14] As with other local theaters, it was probably modified during the Roman period.

---

11 Cadwallader and Harrison, "Perspectives on the Lycus Valley," 3, 7, 9–11. The authors provide a full list of these inscriptions and where they were originally published (pp. 9–11).

12 Cadwallader, *Fragments*, 24, Many of these are published in H. von Aulock, *Münzen und Städte Phrygiens*, 24–27, 83–93 (nos. 443–595). An additional forty coins have been published since then (all dating to the second century or later). See also B. V. Head, *Greek Coins of Phrygia*, 154–57; F. Imhoof-Blumer, *Kleinasiatische Münzen*, 260–61. Many of these coins are now catalogued and discussed in the PhD thesis of A. J. Armstrong, "Roman Phrygia," 349–57 (where the Colossian coins are catalogued).

13 Cadwallader, *Fragments*, 97.

14 Cadwallader, *Fragments*, 80–81.

In the area just north of the city center was an extensive necropolis. Some of these graves were cut into the travertine rock and covered with a stone lid. There were also a number of Hellenistic-era tumulus tombs also situated in the travertine rock.[15] Also to the north of the city are the remains of small stone waterways resembling those at Hierapolis. The channels would have distributed water to shops and various other needs.

The Lycus River flowed from the east to the west in its channel just north of the city. No evidence of Jewish presence in the city has yet been discovered, but if a synaogogue were to be found, one might reasonably expect that it would be somewhere along the banks of the Lycus (for access to fresh water for purification purposes).[16]

No other structures have yet been uncovered in the city or its outlying area. We can only speculate as to what might be found in the upcoming excavations. One would expect to find the remains of what is typical in other Phrygian cities: one or more temples (perhaps for Apollo, Zeus, and other deities), a bath house, an odeum, shops, a main street (*plateia*), an agora, a fountain (*nymphaeum*), a city gate, and more. Excavation of the site should also lead to the discovery of more inscriptions, coins, and statuary—all of which would provide significant insight into the social, cultural, economic, political, and religious characteristics of this city.

There is insufficient information to estimate the size and population of the city. The boundaries of the actual city went far beyond the mound. The size of the theater and the area of the necropolis would suggest that Colossae was much smaller than Hierapolis, Laodicea, and Tripolis.

## *History of Colossae*

Colossae may very well have been the oldest and most important city of the Lycus Valley in the early Hellenistic period and in the centuries earlier. The pottery finds from the site provide evidence of settlement in the city as early as the late Chalcolithic age (3800–3400 BC). There are additional ceramic finds that can be dated to Early Bronze (3300–2000 BC), Middle Bronze (2000–1600 BC), and Late Bronze ages (1600–1200 BC). Although it has long been assumed that Laodicea and Hierapolis were founded by Seleucid kings in the second century BC,[17] there is now pottery evidence indicating that the initial settlement at Laodicea may also be as early as as the late Chalcolithic period.[18] Duman has suggested that Colossae was probably the city referred to as Huwalušija in Hittite texts.[19]

15 Şimşek, "Kolossai," 10. Also see ch. 8 ("The Necropolis") in Cadwallader, *Fragments*, 155–80.

16 See Levine, *Ancient Synagogue*, 114.

17 Huttner, *Early Christianity in the Lycus Valley*, 33.

18 Duman and Konakçi, "Silent Witness," 255–59.

19 Duman and Konakçi, "Silent Witness," 250.

There are few references to Colossae in Greek literature predating the introduction of Christianity into the region. The first is found in Herodotus (*Hist.* 7.30), who describes Xerxes leading the Persian army through Phrygia as they marched westward to invade Greece in 480 BC, where they would gain a notable victory at the famous battle of Thermopylae but would eventually suffer a devastating defeat at the battle of Salamis. In his account, Herodotus says that the army came to Colossae after passing by the Phrygian town of Anaua (30 miles east of Colossae). He describes Colossae as "a great city in Phrygia [πόλιν μεγάλην Φρυγίης]." Similar to the account of Cyrus by Xenophon, Herodotus does not mention any other city in the Lycus Valley. The next place the army passed was a town called Carurua (or Cydrara), which was situated at the westernmost edge of the Lycus Valley (seven miles west of where the Lycus flows into the Maeander) and about twenty miles west of the site that came to be the city of Laodicea. The account only makes one other observation about Colossae and that had to do with the Lycus River and not the city itself. Herodotus observes that "the river Lycus plunges into a cleft in the earth out of sight, till it appears again about five furlongs [over a half mile] away and issues like the other river into the Maeander" (Herodotus, *Hist.* 7.30 LCL). Today the Lycus is visible for the entire length since the rock roof over the chasm has collapsed, presumably due to seismic activity in the area over the centuries.

The next reference comes from Xenophon (*Anab.* 1.2.6), who describes the journey that Cyrus the Younger took across Anatolia after conquering the Greek-inhabited territory of Ionia in 401 BC. After leaving Sardis, Cyrus marched eastward with his Persian army through the territory of Lydia, crossed the Maeander River, and entered into Phrygia. He came to the city of Colossae, where he stayed seven days with his army. The account characterizes Colossae as "an inhabited city, prosperous and large [πόλιν οἰκουμένην καὶ εὐδαίμονα καὶ μεγάλην]." From there he marched his troops about fifty-five miles east-northeast to Celaenae (Apamea), which he describes in the same terms as Colossae. It should be observed that no other city of the Lycus Valley is mentioned in this account, leaving the impression that Colossae was the city best suited to meet the needs of the king and his army in that valley.

One further reference to Colossae during the Persian era is found in the histories of Diodorus Siculus (*Hist.* 14.80.6–8). During the reign of the Persian king Artaxerxes II (404–358 BC), Tissaphernes was made satrap of the territory of Lydia, which bordered Phrygia. He was assassinated at Colossae by another Persian official named Tithraustes, with the aid of another Persian satrap, Ariaeus, who apparently lived in Colossae. The text of the account says that Tissaphernes was arrested while he was bathing (λουόμενον). It is not known if this was a public bath house or a private bath in Ariaeus's home.

Nothing is said about Colossae in Greek literature during the Hellenistic and Seleucid periods, yet it was under the Seleucids that Laodicea was established and that Hierapolis became a significant city. We know that Colossae continued to be occupied during the Hellenistic era because of the discovery of Hellenistic pottery on the site.[20] What happened to Colossae during this dark period remains a mystery that may partially be solved by discoveries in the future excavation.

In the Roman era, Strabo (*Geogr.* 12.8.13) includes Colossae in his list of the cities of Phrygia. He describes Laodicea and Apamea as the largest (μέγισται) of the Phrygian cities, whereas he characterizes Colossae, along with Themisomium, Sanaüs, Metropolis, Apollonias, and Aphrodisias, as "small towns" (πολίσματα). Unfortunately, the text is broken away in this paragraph, and a portion (approximately fifteen letters) is missing, which has led some to wonder if the categorization of Colossae as one of the "small towns" is appropriate.[21] There may be merit to this question since Aphrodisias does not seem to fit the description of a small town, although it would be appropriate for the others listed. What is perhaps most important to observe is that Laodicea has now eclipsed Colossae in terms of size and significance in the Lycus Valley. Duman is probably correct in concluding that by the first century BC, Colossae "was considerably diminished from its old magnificence and size."[22] A handful of ancient sources describe a devastating earthquake that struck in the Lycus Valley in the early 60s AD. I will discuss this in more detail below.

Pliny the Elder (AD 23–79) lists Colossae along with Celaenae as one of the most famous towns (*oppida celeberrima*) of Phrygia (Pliny the Elder, *Nat.* 5.41) in a work that he wrote in the 70s AD. Not included in this list are Laodicea and Hierapolis. But he may have characterized Colossae as famous because of its historic significance, which may explain the absence of the other two cities.[23] As Ramsay notes, "there is no doubt that in early time Colossai was the great city of the Lycos valley."[24] Pliny also mentions a flower that is "Colossae purple" (*flos colossinus*) in color (Pliny the Elder, *Nat.* 21.27) and the petrifying effect that the Lycus River has on bricks when they are submerged in its water (Pliny the Elder, *Nat.* 31.20).

Colossae was likely one of the places that the emperor Hadrian visited in his pan-Hellenic tour in AD 129.[25] This is suggested by an honorific inscription for Hadrian set up in Colossae at that time (*IGRR* 4.869) and by the coins honoring Hadrian minted following the visit.[26] From this point forward, Colossae and the letter to the Colossians are mentioned extensively in Christian literature, but few secular sources mention the city.

---

20 Duman and Konakçi, "Silent Witness," 262–69.

21 E.g., Mare, "Archaeological Prospects," 42.

22 Duman and Konakçi, "Silent Witness," 250–51.

23 Duman and Konakçi, "Silent Witness," 251, however, suggest that "Colossae appears to have revived early in the second century CE and become again one of the significant cities of the region." They attribute this growth to the reconstruction efforts after the earthquake.

24 Ramsay, *Cities and Bishoprics of Phrygia*, 1:35.

25 Cadwallader and Harrison, "Perspectives on the Lycus Valley," 12.

26 See Cadwallader and Harrison, "Perspectives on the Lycus Valley," 12–13.

In the late Roman era (4th c. AD), a church was built in the vicinity of Colossae dedicated to Michael the archangel. Nothing remains of this church today, yet Ramsay says that its ruins were plainly visible in 1881.[27] He located it northeast of the city on the north bank of the Lycus River before it enters the gorge. The founding legend of the church claims that Michael saved the city of Colossae from flood waters raging toward it when a nearby dam was ruptured with malicious intent.[28] Michael intervened by creating a deep ravine into which the waters could be diverted to the lower part of the valley, and thus he preserved the city from inundation and loss of life. This story about an angel saving the city is significant as a continuation of a strong tradition in this area regarding angels as the source of deliverance. As will be seen in my discussion of "worship of angels" in Col 2:18, I contend that the phrase should be interpreted as the ritual invocation of angels for help, protection, and deliverance.

Colossae continued to be an active city through the Byzantine period. Duman and Konakçi have discovered early Byzantine pottery on the site.[29] Colossae is also mentioned in connection with the Second Council of Nicaea (AD 787).[30] The site was likely abandoned during the Arab invasions of the seventh and eighth centuries, although some settlement remained.[31] By AD 800, the site was deserted, with much of the population relocating to the village of Honaz, which was about two-and-a-half miles to the south on the slope of Mt. Cadmus.

## *2. The Lycus Valley*

### *Bibliography*

**Ameling, W.** "Die jüdischen Gemeinden," 29–55. **Armstrong, A. J.** "Roman Phrygia," 1–394. **Arzt-Grabner, P.** "Everyday Life in a Roman Town," 187–238. **Aulock, H. von.** *Münzen und Städte Phrygiens.* **Barclay, J. M. G.** "Paul, Roman Religion and the Emperor," 345–62. ———. "Why the Roman Empire Was Insignificant to Paul," 363–87. **Beard, M., J. North, and S. Price.** *Religions of Rome.* **Bogh, B.** "Phrygian Background of Kybele," 304–39. **Bormann, L.** "Barbaren und Sykthen," 161–98. **Cadwallader, A.** "Comparative Method," 105–51. ———. *Fragments.* ———. "Honouring the Repairer of the Baths," 150–83. ———. "Refuting an Axiom of Scholarship," 151–79. **Cadwallader, A., and J. R. Harrison.** "Perspectives on the Lycus Valley," 3–70. **Canavan, R.** "Threads of Identity," 81–104. **Chaniotis, A.** "Epigraphic Bulletin," 271–327. ———. "Imperial Power in Aphrodisias," 250–60. **Chiai, G. F.** "Allmächtiger Götter," 61–106. ———. "Die Götter und Ihr Territorium," 51–70. ———. "Jüdische Lebenswelt," 117–46. ———. *Phrygien und seine*

27 Ramsay, *Cities and Bishoprics of Phrygia*, 1:214–15.

28 See the discussion of this legend in Cadwallader, *Fragments*, ch. 8 ("The Mighty Angel"), 181–202; Cadwallader, "St. Michael," 323–30 (an English translation of the legend); Huttner, *Early Christianity in the Lycus Valley*, 372–76; Ramsay, *Church in the Roman Empire*, 465–80 (= ch. 19, "The Miracle at Khonai"); Ramsay, *Cities and Bishoprics of Phrygia*, 1:214–15.

29 Duman and Konakçi, "Silent Witness," 252.

30 Duman and Konakçi, "Silent Witness," 251.

31 Duman and Konakçi, "Silent Witness," 251–52.

*Götter.* ———. "Zeus Bronton," 135–56. **Cumont, F.** *Oriental Religions.* **D'Andria, F.** *Hierapolis of Phrygia.* ———. "Sanctuary of St. Philip," 34–57. **Deissmann, A.** *Light from the Ancient East.* **Doherty, B.** "Roman Phrygian Countryside," 71–98. **Duman, B.** "Tabernae in Tripolis," 109–42. **Duman, B., and E. Konakçi.** "Kolossai," 83–109. ———. "Silent Witness," 247–81. **Eckhardt, B.** "Romanization and Isomorphic Change in Phrygia," 147–71. **Erdemir, H.** "Woollen Textiles," 104–29. **Harland, P. A.** "Acculturation and Identity," 222–44. ———. *Associations, Synagogues, and Congregations.* **Heilig, C.** *The Apostle and the Empire.* **Hemer, C.** *Book of Acts.* **Hengel, M., and A. M. Schwemer.** *Paul: Between Damascus and Antioch.* **Horst, P. W. van der.** "Jews of Ancient Phrygia," 283–92. **Huttner, U.** "Colossians, Hierapolitan Coins," 73–79. ———. *Early Christianity in the Lycus Valley.* **Immendörfer, M.** *Ephesians and Artemis.* **Kearsley, R. A.** "Epigraphic Evidence," 130–50. **Kerschbaum, S.** "Die Apollines von Hierapolis," 15–42. **Kittel, G.** "Kleinasiatische Judentum," 9–20. **Kraabel, A. T.** "Judaism in Western Asia Minor." ———. "Roman Diaspora," 445–64. **Kristensen, T. M.** "Earthquakes and Late Antique Urbanism," 71–78. **Kumsar, H.** "Historical Earthquakes," 519–36. **Lane, E.** *Corpus Monumentorum Religionis Dei Menis.* ———. "Men," 2161–74. **Lease, G.** "Jewish Mystery Cults," 858–80. **Lindemann, A.** "Die Gemeinde von 'Kolossä,'" 111–34. **MacDonald, D.** "Homonoia of Colossae and Aphrodisias," 25–27. **Magie, D.** *Roman Rule.* 2 vols. **Maier, H. O.** "Colossians and Empire," 323–49. ———. *Picturing Paul in Empire.* ———. "Reading Colossians in the Ruins," 212–31. **McDowell, S.** *Fate of the Apostles.* **Mellor, R.** *Tacitus's Annals.* ———. *ΘΕΑ ΡΩΜΗ.* **Miller, K. M.** "Apollo Lairbenos," 46–70. **Mitchell, S.** *Anatolia.* 2 vols. **Morris, S. P.** "Artemis Ephesia," 135–51. **Nilsson, M. P.** *Geschichte der griechischen Religion.* 2 vols. **Özkaya, V.** "Shaft Monuments," 89–103. **Piccardi, L.** "The AD 60 Denizli Basin Earthquake," 95–105. **Price, S. R. F.** *Rituals and Power.* **Ramsay, W. M.** "Artemis-Leto and Apollo-Lairbenos," 216–30. ———. *Cities and Bishoprics of Phrygia.* 2 vols. ———. "Sketches in the Religious Antiquities," 37–79. **Ritti, T.** *Epigraphic Guide to Hierapolis.* **Robert, L.** "Les Inscriptions," 247–389. **Robinson, L.** "Hidden Transcripts?," 55–72. **Roller, L.** *In Search of God the Mother.* **Schwindt, R.** *Das Weltbild.* **Şimşek, C.** "A Menorah with a Cross," 343–46. ———. "Regional Cults in the Lycus Valley," 673–90. **Smith, I. K.** *Heavenly Perspective.* **Smith, R. R. R.** "*Ethne* from the Sebasteion at Aphrodisias," 50–77. ———. "Imperial Reliefs from the Sebasteion at Aphrodisias," 88–138. **Standhartinger, A.** "City with a Message," 239–56. **Strelan, R.** "Languages of the Lycus Valley," 77–103. **Theophilos, M. P.** "Numismatic Evidence," 257–92. **Thomas, G.** "Magna Mater and Attis," 93–110. **Thonemann, P.** *Maeander Valley.* ———. *Roman Phrygia.* **Trebilco, P.** *Jewish Communities in Asia Minor.* **Van Kooten, G. H.** *Cosmic Christology.* **Walsh, B. J.**, and **S. C. Keesmaat.** *Colossians Remixed.* **Wilson, M.** *Biblical Turkey.*

Colossae lay in the eastern portion of the Lycus Valley only a day's walk from Laodicea and Hierapolis. These three cities were in a close relationship with each other, not only because of proximity but because of shared culture, religions, and economy. It is likely that Epaphras was instrumental in the founding of the churches not only in Colossae but also in Laodicea and Hierapolis. It is clear that Epaphras felt a responsibility for believers in all three of these cities and labored intensely for them in prayer while he was with Paul (4:12–13). Paul explicitly states in his letter to the Colossians that he is struggling for the believers in Laodicea and Hierapolis as well (2:1). He even directly greets Christians at Laodicea and a particular house church there in his final greetings (4:15). He also wrote a separate letter to the believers in Laodicea (4:16) that has, unfortunately, been lost.

It is important for us to explore the major features of the Lycus Valley as we consider Colossians. There were many shared characteristics among the people living in its cities and villages of this region. Cadwallader and Harrison have rightly noted, "Until Colossae itself is finally excavated, perhaps the archaeological, epigraphic, numismatic, and iconographic evidence of Hierapolis and Laodicea can continue to provide some indirect light from the Lycus Valley on the epistle to the Colossians."[32] Nevertheless, Colossae remains a distinctive city that, in certain respects, is different than Laodicea and Hierapolis.[33] In the discussion that follows, where there is evidence, I will highlight some of those distinctive features.

## *The Lycus Valley in the Context of Phrygia*

The Lycus Valley was a small, fertile valley about thirty-five miles in length (east to west) and as much as ten miles across at its widest point. It was bounded on the south by Mount Cadmus and Mount Salbakos (west of Mount Cadmus) and a small range of mountains on the north. Colossae was situated on the southeast edge of the valley on a higher plain just below the slopes of Mount Cadmus. Hierapolis was located on the northeast portion of the valley on a plateau just below the Mossyna range. Laodicea was on the lower plain in the center of the valley eight miles northwest of Colossae and five miles south of Hierapolis. In the extreme edge of the northwest portion of the valley lies Tripolis, which was on the upper Maeander River just north of where the Lycus River flows into the Maeander. In the southwest portion of the valley were Attouda and Karoura (just west of modern Denizli).

The Lycus Valley was at the southwest portion of the ancient ethnic territory of Phrygia. Of course, by the time Paul wrote Colossians, the older territorial distinctions made no difference politically since the entirety of Anatolia was under Roman rule. But these distinctions were important culturally. Phrygia was bordered on the southwest by Caria (which included the city of Aphrodisias), Lydia to the northwest (which encompassed Sardis, Philadelphia, and Thyatira), Bithynia to the north, Galatia to the east, and Lycaonia to the southeast. The Lycus Valley was in close proximity to the borders of Lydia and Caria.

The indigenous peoples of the Lycus Valley maintained a consciousness of

32 Cadwallader and Harrison, "Perspectives on the Lycus Valley," 59. Similarly, Kearsley, "Epigraphic Evidence," 130, observes, "Laodicea and Hierapolis are likely to have had much in common with Colossae and are likely to provide a useful cultural framework."

33 Cadwallader, "Comparative Method," 113, suggests that, "Colossae's *polis*-pride may have led it to assert itself through a display of distinctive iconography." But this is simply not knowable until the site is excavated. He speculates that the civic officials of Colossae may have suffered a bruised pride when Colossae was overlooked ("spurned") in favor of Laodicea by Antiochus II in the mid-third century BC, when he renamed Diospolis after his wife, Laodikeia, and showed favor to that city (Cadwallader, "Comparative Method," 129). But this, too, is not substantiated with any evidence and remains highly speculative.

Phrygian identity.[34] In terms of language, the majority of people in this area were bilingual—maintaining some facility in the Phrygian language while speaking Greek.[35] Despite Ramsay's contention that "the native languages died out completely in the reign of Augustus, if not earlier,"[36] the Phrygian language persisted in the Lycus Valley. This likely extended to Phrygian pronunciations of Greek. The continuous use of Phrygian was probably more extensive in rural villages and estates than in the cities. A Colossian inscription published in 2007 honors a certain official named Markos who served as "chief interpreter [ἀρχερμενεύς] and translator [ἐξηγητής] for the Colossians."[37] This person likely served in the agora, fulfilling the practical need for translation and mediation in business and legal matters in light of the multiple languages spoken.[38] While Greek would have functioned as the commercial language, situations requiring accurate understanding of technical matters would have been faciliatated by an interpreter.

While many indigenous Phrygian people lived in the Lycus Valley, it was also occupied by Carians and Lydians (and perhaps others from adjacent territories) along with Persians, Greeks, Romans, and Jews.[39] A first-century AD inscription from Colossae discovered in 2005 honors a man named Korumbos who repaired the baths at Colossae at his own expense. The text goes on to list the names of sixty-six additional donors.[40] Greek names predominate in the text, but there are names reflecting Phrygian, Thracian, Scythian, and possibly Lydian and Carian backgrounds. As Cadwallader notes, "The presence of names of other backgrounds [than Greek] ought not be dissociated from the languages of those backgrounds."[41] One might also add that if different linguistic backgrounds are present, other facets of their cultural background would have accompanied this. There was thus extensive ethnic diversity in the Lycus Valley.

The economy of the Lycus Valley was supported by agriculture, the raising of livestock, textile production, mining, and trade. One of the main agricultural

---

34 Huttner, *Early Christianity in the Lycus Valley*, 27.

35 Mitchell, *Anatolia*, 1:174–75; Strelan, "Languages of the Lycus Valley," 89–97; Huttner, *Early Christianity in the Lycus Valley*, 28.

36 Ramsay, *Cities and Bishoprics of Phrygia*, 1:12. Deissmann, *Light from the Ancient East*, 66–67, reached a similar conclusion. He notes that not only did people no longer speak the popular colloquial languages but that "in this Hellenised world . . . men no longer spoke local dialects of Greek."

37 Cadwallader, "Inscriptions from Colossae," 112–18.

38 Chaniotis, "Epigraphic Bulletin," 285–86, asserts that the translation needs of Colossae could not have been so substantial as to require a board of translators headed by a chief translator. He contends, rather, that "it is more probable that we are dealing with religious functions, possibly of an interpreter of oracles." Bormann, "Barbaren und Skythen," 193–96, contends that it simply refers to Markos providing legal and administrative assistance and not with the interpretation of languages. The weight of evidence, however, supports Cadwallader's suggestion.

39 See Strelan, "Languages of the Lycus Valley."

40 Cadwallader, "Honouring the Repairer of the Baths," 150–83.

41 Cadwallader, "Honouring the Repairer of the Baths," 170. On this topic, see Mitchell, *Anatolia*, 1:175.

products was grapes. The soil and climate were conducive to viticulture.[42] The rich and fertile land likely also enabled the populace to raise numerous subsistence-level crops and other produce that would have been brought to the city agoras and sold or traded. The main livestock raised in the region would have been sheep, along with some hogs and cattle.[43] Wool production was a key contributor to the economic vitality of the valley. In fact, this area "formed the most important centre of textile production in Asia Minor, if not the whole eastern Mediterranean."[44] The extensive wool production led to many associated trades that included wool washers, wool beaters, dyers, weavers, tailors, dress makers, and leather workers.[45] According to Strabo, the hot mineral waters of Hierapolis are "remarkably adapted also to the dyeing of wool, so that wool dyed with the roots [the Madder root] rivals that dyed with the coccus or with the marine purple (*Geogr.* 13.4.14). All three cities, however, were known for the quality of their wool and its brilliant colors, especially purple. Colossae was particularly known for the glossy, dark violet wool produced there.[46]

Mining was another important industry in the Lycus Valley. North of the city of Colossae beyond the Lycus River was a travertine quarry that had been mined in antiquity.[47] At the foot of Mount Cadmus was an additional travertine quarry and a marble quarry.[48] But there were also limestone quarries and at least two high-quality marble quarries in the valley.[49]

The products of the valley and its location on the main road from the east to the west enhanced the ability of merchants to extend their trade. A first-century funerary inscription of a merchant from Hierapolis named Titus Flavius Zeuxis recounts the extraordinary amount of travel he undertook in marketing the products of the Lycus Valley.[50] Another tomb inscription from Hierapolis honors M. Aurelius Alexander as "a decurion and purple-seller."[51] A second-century inscription from Colossae honors an esteemed citizen named Zosimos, who served the city through a number of offices he held related to trade.[52]

## *The Earthquake of AD 60*

A severe earthquake struck this region sometime between AD 60 and 64 during the reign of Nero. Tacitus, who dates the earthquake to AD 60, reports,

42 See Thonemann, *Maeander Valley*, 193.
43 Erdemir, "Woolen Textiles," 123.
44 Thonemann, *Maeander Valley*, 186.
45 Erdemir, "Woolen Textiles," 123.
46 Cadwallader, *Fragments*, 113.
47 Huttner, *Early Christianity in the Lycus Valley*, 22.
48 Cadwallader and Harrison, "Perspectives on the Lycus Valley," 30.
49 Huttner, *Early Christianity in the Lycus Valley*, 22–23.
50 Huttner, *Early Christianity in the Lycus Valley*, 20. See Thonemann, *Maeander Valley*, 189, for a picture of his elaborate mausoleum and the inscription.
51 Thonemann, *Maeander Valley*, 189.
52 Cadwallader, *Fragments*, 129–30.

"Laodicea, one of the famous Asiatic cities, was laid in ruins by an earthquake, but recovered by its own resources, without assistance from ourselves" (Tacitus, *Ann.* 14.27). According to the Roman-Christian historian Orosius, the temblor destroyed Laodicea, Hierapolis, and Colossae (Orosius, *Historiarum adversus paganos* 7.7.12). In Jerome's translation of Eusebius's *Chronicle*, the earthquake is dated immediately after Nero's burning of Rome in AD 64. The *Chronicle* states, "In Asia, three cities were ruined in an earthquake: Laodicea, Hierapolis and Colossae."[53] No other ancient sources comment on the earthquake.

It is difficult to fix the precise date of this quake, but it is clear that it occurred in close proximity to the Colossian church receiving the letter from Paul (assuming the authenticity of the letter). The date hinges on the interpretation of the key texts and evidence from the site; the science of palaeogeology cannot determine the date exactly. Eusebius wrote nearly three centuries after the event, and his accuracy has been called into question by some scholars.[54] Furthermore, it is possible that Eusebius intentionally placed the earthquake after the burning of Rome. Hemer notes, "It seems likely that the dating of the earthquake in Christian writers is coloured by a tradition making it one of a series of judgments on the pagan world for the Neronian persecution of 64."[55] The date set by Tacitus appears to be the more reliable.[56] The series of events he narrates takes place "in the consulate of Nero—his fourth term—A.V.C. 813 [= AD 60] and of Cornelius Cossus" (Tacitus, *Ann.* 14.20 LCL). It falls close to the end of the episodes he relates that took place during that year and then begins his account of the episodes of A.V.C. 814 (= AD 61) (see Tacitus, *Ann.* 14.29). This could suggest that the earthquake took place toward the end of AD 60.

The geology of the Lycus Valley has made it prone to serious earthquakes. Strabo commented that "the country is full of holes and subject to earthquakes; for if any other country is subject to earthquakes, Laodicea is, and so is Carura in the neighbouring country" (*Geogr.* 12.16). There is historical record of additional serious earthquakes occuring in AD 494, the early seventh century, the second half of the seventh century, 1358, 1651, and more.[57] A magnitude 5.7 earthquake shook Honaz in 1965, causing nine miles of surface rupture. Yet another hit Honaz in 2000, registering as a magnitude 5.2.[58] The city of Laodicea was

53 Jerome, "Chronicle," p. 265, Tertullian.org, www.tertullian.org/fathers/jerome_chronicle_03_part2.htm. See the note by Magie, *Roman Rule*, 2.1421.

54 See Cadwallader, "Refuting an Axiom of Scholarship," 165.

55 Hemer, *Book of Acts*, 274n60.

56 Not only does Tacitus reflect a concern to place events in their proper chronological sequence consistent with his purpose in writing the *Annals*, but he lived in the latter part of the first century and was in much closer proximity to the events. For a positive appraisal of Tacitus's accuracy as a historian, see Mellor, *Tacitus's Annals*, 22–41.

57 Kumsar et al., "Historical Earthquakes," 524.

58 Kumsar et al., "Historical Earthquakes," 524.

abandoned after the extensive damage caused by the earthquake in the early seventh century AD with an estimated magnitude of 6.5.[59]

The devastation caused by this earthquake is consistent with recent geological studies of faults in the area of the Lycus Valley (the Denizli basin). The Pammukale Fault is the main active fault in the region and is capable of producing an earthquake as large as magnitude 6.5 or more. The largest possible earthquake in the Denizli basin could range as high as magnitude 7.1.[60] As a point of comparison, a 7.0 magnitude earthquake struck in the Aegean Sea on October 30, 2020. The epicenter was just north of the island of Samos and about forty miles south of Izmir. According to the International Blue Crescent (IBC) report, 115 people lost their lives, 1034 people were injured, 17 buildings were demolished, and at least another thousand buildings would need to be destroyed.[61] The destruction that would have been caused by a similar-sized earthquake in the first century would be magnified many times over. There were none of the earthquake safety measures in construction that are in place today. Public structures made with marble, limestone, or travertine and not reinforced with steel would easily have toppled. The kind of flexible steel that is used today for reinforcement was not available to them at that time. Iron reinforcement would easily have fractured. Colossae likely experienced massive damage. The critical question is whether Colossae was rebuilt after that earthquake.

Laodicea recovered on its own, but Hierapolis required help from the Roman government.[62] Based on the accounts by Orosius and Jerome, it has long been assumed that Colossae was utterly destroyed and never rebuilt and that it was probably at this time that the population relocated to Honaz and elsewhere.[63] Lindemann argued that since Colossae was depopulated and no Christian tradition developed there, the risk that a letter fictitiously directed to that city could be detected as fictitious was very small by the 70s or 80s, which is something the author of Colossians took advantage of for writing this letter.[64] Van Kooten mounted a similar argument, stating that "this earthquake presented an ideal opportunity to disguise the letter's pseudepigraphic origins."[65]

Cadwallader has marshalled new evidence and gathered old evidence to refute the long-held "axiom of scholarship"—namely, that Colossae met its

59 Kumsar et al., "Historical Earthquakes," 528.

60 Kumsar et al., "Historical Earthquakes," 519; Kristensen, "Earthquakes and Late Antique Urbanism," 71–78; Piccardi, "The AD 60 Denizli Basin Earthquke," 97, concludes that, based on fault length, this fault was "capable of earthquakes of at least magnitude 6."

61 See International Blue Crescent, "Izmir Earthquake Assessment Report of IBV," November 11, 2020, https://reliefweb.int/sites/reliefweb.int/files/resources/IBC%20Izmir%20Assessment%20Report%20November%202020.pdf.

62 Cadwallader and Harrison, "Perspectives on the Lycus Valley," 22.

63 E.g., Lindemann, "Die Gemeinde von 'Kolossä,'" 128; Lohse, 9.

64 Lindemann, "Die Gemeinde von 'Kolossä,'" 128–29.

65 Van Kooten, *Cosmic Christology*, 137.

demise by the earthquake of AD 60 and was never rebuilt.[66] He concludes that quite the opposite was the case and that Colossae maintained "considerable prestige of presence and influence well beyond the first century."[67] Part of the new evidence comes from two inscriptions dating to the late first- or early second-century. One inscription refers to "a chief interpreter and translator" who performed an important commercial function in the agora. Another refers to a man named Korumbos who engineered the repair of the baths at Colossae at his own expense.[68] Although why the baths needed repair is not stated, the ostensible cause could have been the destruction the city faced as a result of the earthquake. He also points to many coins naming Colossae that range in date throughout the entire Roman period.[69] Duman and Konakçi reached a similar conclusion and noted that "it may be said that the city had lost its previous importance in the first century BC but appears to have revived early in the second century AD and become again one of the significant cities of the region."[70]

Colossae may not have been as rich a city as Laodicea and possibly did not benefit from imperial munificence for its rebuilding, but it is likely that Colossae was rebuilt. While its neighbors continued to grow in population, size, and in public buildings, Colossae nevertheless persisted and remained a significant city in the Lycus Valley.

### *Cities of the Lycus Valley*

The close proximity of Colossae to Laodicea and Hierapolis means that the cities shared many common characteristics. The work of Epaphras in evangelizing and planting churches apparently extended to these cities as well, since Paul mentions Epaphras's ongoing labor in prayer for them (4:13). It will be informative to look at each of these cities, and other cities in the Lycus Valley, for filling out the picture of the principal features of this area and its people.

#### Laodicea

The Hellenistic city of Laodicea was "founded" about 253 BC under the Seleucid king, Antiochus II Theos (261–246 BC), who named the city after his wife, Laodice. His grandfather, Seleucus I Nicator, had been one of the generals (*Diadochoi*) of Alexander the Great. The Seleucid Empire had expanded to include the entirety of Anatolia. The roots of the city reach much earlier, however. Pliny says it was first named Diospolis ("city of Zeus") (Pliny the Elder, *Nat.* 5.105). But more recent excavations have revealed finds that show occupation on the site reaching back to the late Chalcolithic period.[71] The city

66 Cadwallader, "Refuting an Axiom of Scholarship," 151–79.
67 Cadwallader, "Refuting an Axiom of Scholarship," 174.
68 Cadwallader, "Refuting an Axiom of Scholarship," 170–74.
69 Cadwallader, "Refuting an Axiom of Scholarship," 162–65.
70 Duman and Konakçi, "Silent Witness," 251.
71 Şimşek, "Regional Cults in the Lycus Valley," 673.

was located in a portion of Phrygia close to the border of the ethnic territory of Caria. It was at the cross point of roads emanating to the north, south, east, and west[72] and thus functioned as an important hub for trade. Laodicea became the center for Roman government in the region, which is understandable given its strategic position on the main roads.[73] Along with Hierapolis, the two cities became popular destinations for Romans to establish homes and businesses.[74]

After the Pergamene king Attalus III bequeathed his kingdom to Rome, Laodicea and all of the cities of the Lycus Valley came under Roman rule. Laodicea grew in political and civic status throughout the Roman era. The city built many of the typical structures of a Roman city. Among its public buildings included two theaters (one to the west that had a capacity of eight thousand people and one to the north with a capacity of twelve thousand), a stadium (with a capacity of up to twenty-five thousand people), two nymphaeums, a central agora, a *plateia* (central street) extending over a half mile, two bath complexes, a bouleuterion, and monumental gates. Not all of these structures date to the first century AD, but they were all made during the Roman period. The notoriety and prominence Laodicea was achieving was formally recognized by the emperor Claudius when he gave his name to games held in his honor in Laodicea.[75]

Our knowledge of many features of Laodicea is being expanded greatly by the extensive excavations being carried out since 2003 under the direction of Celal Şimşek and Pamukkale University.[76] Excavation was first begun in 1961, but the pace has increased dramatically under Simsek's leadership.

## Hierapolis

Located at the northeast end of the Lycus Valley, one of the distinguishing marks of Hierapolis was the white travertine cascades along the edge of the plateau descending from the city into the valley. These were created over the centuries by the mineral-rich water from multiple hot springs flowing down the hillside and creating numerous terraces. The snow-white deposits resulted in its current Turkish name, Pamukkale ("cotton castle").[77] But these hot springs were also an indication that this area was geologically active, leading to its proneness to earthquakes. The city was also famous because of a cave descending deep into the ground that was widely thought to be an opening into the underworld, a Plutonium (see below for more discussion). The cave was not only used for mantic inspiration by local priests but may also have led to the extensive necropolis because of the proximity of this portal to the underworld.

72 Şimşek, "Regional Cults in the Lycus Valley," 673.

73 Kearsley, "Epigraphic Evidence," 131.

74 Kearsley, "Epigraphic Evidence," 131.

75 Mitchell, *Anatolia*, 1:219.

76 Cadwallader and Harrison, "Perspectives on the Lycus Valley."

77 In 1988, Hierapolis was designated as a UNESCO World Heritage Site (https://whc.unesco.org/en/list/485/).

Like Laodicea, the city was founded during the Seleucid period (third century BC), but it shows evidence of earlier settlement on the site. The city was laid out according to a Hellenistic (Hippodamean) urban grid plan.[78] There was a forty-six-foot wide *plateia* ("Frontinus Street") that ran nearly a mile between the north gate of the city and the southern gate.[79] There are ruins of theater in the north part of the city that dates to Hellenistic times.[80] Most of the remaining structures, however, date from the Roman period, with many dating to the second century AD and later. In the middle of the city was a Roman theater, with the initial structure dating to the first century, although it was rebuilt and expanded in subsequent years. With a seating capacity of up to ten thousand spectators, it looked out over the Lycus Valley in the direction of Colossae. There was an immense agora in the northern part of the city measuring over three hundred yards in length. Many of the typical Roman public buildings were present in the city, including a nymphaeum, a bath house, and a gymnasium. There were also temples in the city, but the most prominent was the temple of Apollo located just below the theater adjacent to the Plutonium. The present structure dates to the third century AD, but recent excavations have uncovered the remains of pottery cups used for libation rituals and lamps that date as early as the first century BC and give evidence of cult ceremonies that took place in the earlier temple.[81] Apollo was the principal deity of the city along with Artemis. This is confirmed by the busts of the two deities discovered in the temple nymphaeum and the multiple scenes of the lives of the two deities depicted in the architectural backdrop of the theater. The city likely derived its name (Hierapolis means "sacred city") early in its history from its dedication to one of these deities or perhaps to the Great Mother (Cybele).

The enormous necropolis that extends over the span of one and a quarter miles to the north of the city had over a thousand tombs that have survived. The oldest are a series of tumulus tombs that date to the Hellenistic period, with the remaining dating to the Roman era. Some of the saracophagi have Greek inscriptions. Well-known are the warning inscriptions on a number of the tombs, such as one that issues this stern threat: "after death the infernal gods should be the angry tormentors of whoever orders construction or tampering and whoever carries out the orders!"[82]

It is difficult to know the size of the city during its peak in the Roman era. Some have estimated the population to be as many as a hundred thousand. Inscriptional evidence from family tombs in the necropolis also points to a sizeable Jewish population in the city of Hierapolis through the Roman period.[83]

---

78 D'Andria, *Hierapolis of Phrygia*, 34.
79 D'Andria, *Hierapolis of Phrygia*, 74–79.
80 D'Andria, *Hierapolis of Phrygia*, 111–12.
81 D'Andria, *Hierapolis of Phrygia*, 141.
82 As cited in D'Andria, *Hierapolis of Phrygia*, 58.
83 Harland, "Acculturation and Identity," 227.

Hierapolis is well-known as being the home of the Greek church father, Papias (AD 60–135), who served as a bishop among the churches in Hierapolis and is frequently cited as an important source on the oral tradition standing behind the Synoptic Gospels. There is also a widespread tradition that the apostle Philip (or possibly the evangelist/deacon Philip from Caesarea) spent his final years in this city.[84] An octagonal *martyrion* was erected in the late fourth or early fifth century in his honor.

The Italian Archaeological Mission under the leadership of P. Verzone began excavating the city in 1957, with D. de Bernardo Ferrero directing the excavations beginning in 1978. The site is currently being excavated under the direction of F. D'Andria.

## Tripolis

Although overshadowed by the larger cities of Laodicea and Hierapolis, Tripolis was a significant Roman city on the northwest edge of the Lycus Valley on the Maeander River about five miles north of where the Lycus River joins the Maeander. Tripolis was located about fifteen miles northwest of Hierapolis and about twenty-five miles northwest of Colossae. It lay on the border of Phrygia, Lydia, and Caria, which may have been the source of its name in the first century BC as the "triple city." It first bore the name Apollonia and then, for a short time, was called, Antoniopolis. Tripolis was on a major trade road leading westward from Apameia through Colossae, Laodicea, and Hierapolis and from Tripolis on to Philadelphia and Sardis. The site has been the focal point of excavations only recently, beginning in 2012 under the direction of B. Duman under the auspices of the directorate for museums in Denizli and the department of archaeology at Pamukkale University.

This city thrived under Roman rule and had many structures typical of other Roman cities. The main street through the city ran north and south, was a quarter mile long, and was lined by columns. The city had an agora, a theater (with a capacity of eight thousand people), a stadium, two bath houses, a nymphaeum, a bouleuterion, a structure consisting of fifteen arches that may have been used for workshops and storage, and more than one necropolis. Some of the most recent excavations have uncovered a series of three *tabernae* (shops).[85]

---

84 For an in-depth discussion of the sources related to this problem, see McDowell, *Fate of the Apostles*, 193–210. He contends that there was consistent testimony from the early second century affirming that the apostle went to Hierapolis, but that this was later confused by Eusebius, who conflated the work of the apostle with a tradition about Philip the Evangelist. Reaching a similar conclusion, Wilson (*Biblical Turkey*, 243–45) argued that the testimony of Proclus and Polycrates should be trusted over that of Eusebius on this issue since they were both second-century church leaders from Roman Asia. See also D'Andria, "Sanctuary of St. Philip," 50, who concludes that "together with textual sources, the extaordinary complexity of the buildings and ritual practices now identified on the eastern hill of Hierapolis allows us to attribute the sanctuary and the tomb at the centre of the church to Philip the Apostle."

85 Duman, "Tabernae in Tripolis," 109–42.

The city is not mentioned in the NT, but we can probably safely assume that Christianity spread there in the mid- to late- first century.

## Trapezopolis, Attouda, and Karoura

There were three other smaller cities that were part of the Lycus Valley. Trapezopolis lay about sixteen miles west of Colossae and about ten miles west of Laodicea in the south-central portion of the Lycus Valley and just inside the territory of Caria. It was situated on the southwestern slope of the Cadmus range and was the closest city to the sanctuary of Mēn Karou, which was just three miles to the north. A few inscriptions have been discovered there, with one of them extolling the victory in an *agōn* of one of its wrestlers, Hermes, in the local games held in honor of the Pythian Apollo.[86] The city of Attouda lay six miles to the west of Trapezopolis. This city, too, had a close connection with the temple and healing center of Mēn Karou. A handful of silver coins are known to have come from there.[87] Karoura was located at the extreme western end of the Lycus Valley on the upper Maeander River. It was eighteen miles due west of Laodicea and about five miles north of Attouda. According to Strabo, this village (κώμη) had hot springs that flowed into the Maeander River (*Geogr.* 12.17). There were also many additional villages that dotted the landscape of the Lycus Valley.

## *Religions of the Lycus Valley*

Since Colossae has not yet been excavated, we have limited sources on the gods worshiped in that city. No statue of a deity has yet been discovered there. At the present time, we are reliant on the few inscriptions that have come from Colossae and the hundred plus coins that were minted at Colossae. When we examine these sources, there is evidence for an extensive array of deities worshiped in this city. These include: Zeus, Apollo, Mēn, the Ephesian Artemis, the Greek Artemis, Cybele (the Great Mother), Asclepius, Demeter, Dionysus, Helios, Selene, Athena, Sarapis, Isis, Hygeia, Tyche, the "River God" (*Lykos*), and more.[88] Although it may be an overstatement to say that "most gods at Colossae probably had a 'mystery cult' practice connected with their observance,"[89] many no doubt did. There was likely some variation in the deities worshiped at Colossae from the other cities of the Lycus Valley, yet many would have been the same, and there would have been commonalities in the manner of their worship in each locale—especially in Laodicea, Hierapolis, and Colossae. The proximity of these cities to each other would also have given the people living at Colossae exposure to the deities and their worship in these other cities.

86 *MAMA* 6.61 (= *SEG* 26.1233). The inscription is discussed in Huttner, *Early Christianity in the Lycus Valley*, 45.

87 Ramsay, *Cities and Bishoprics of Phrygia*, 1:166.

88 Cadwallader, *Fragments*, 68. See also von Aulock, *Münzen und Städte Phrygiens*, 27, and my "Colossae," *ABD* 1:1089. Unfortunately, most of the coins date from the time of Hadrian onward.

89 Cadwallader, *Fragments*, 54.

I will offer a brief survey of what we know of the worship of the prominent deities in this area and, when there is specific evidence about their presence at Colossae, will include that.

## Zeus

Zeus is attested on a coin from Colossae dating to the early first or second century BC,[90] as well as on coins from the time of Hadrian and later.[91] Cadwallader goes so far as to suggest that Zeus was possibly the patron deity of Colossae and that his temple remains may eventually be found on the top of the Colossian mound.[92] This, of course, is highly speculative, and there are other contenders for the most prominent rôle at Colossae, including Apollo. The future excavation of the site will reveal much about the religious climate there.

There is no doubt that Zeus was the most important deity of Laodicea, especially as evidenced by the numerous local coins with the name, Zeus Laodikenus.[93] Before Antiochus II's renaming of the city in the mid-third century, it was called Diospolis—the city of Zeus. The image of the god appears on many coins from the Roman imperial period at Laodicea.[94] He was worshiped under various other epithets, including Zeus Aetophoros and Zeus Bronton (Zeus the Thunderer) as well as Zeus Ktesios Patrios, "the defender father of the shepherds."[95]

## Apollo

Apollo was the principal deity of the city of Hierapolis where he appeared in two forms—Apollo Archegetes and Apollo Lairbenos. He was also worshiped at Laodicea, where he appears on coins as early as the time of Claudius.[96] We have limited evidence of the worship of Apollo at Colossae, but given his prominence throughout the Lycus Valley, we should expect that he had a similar prominence in Colossae. A Colossian inscription found in Honaz mentions *Nea Olympia Apollonia* games held every four years in honor of the god.[97] There is also a second-century BC coin from Colossae that bears the image of Apollo with a lyre.[98]

---

90 Von Aulock, *Münzen und Städte Phrygiens*, 26, 83. See also Huttner, *Early Christianity in the Lycus Valley*, 44.

91 von Aulock, *Münzen und Städte Phrygiens*, 84–85, 88–89, 92–93 (nos. 458–60; 470–82; 534–36; 547; 588, 590).

92 Cadwallader, *Fragments*, 66–67, 76.

93 G. F. Chiai, "Phrygia," *RAC* 27:701.

94 Huttner, *Early Christianity in the Lycus Valley*, 43.

95 Şimşek, "Regional Cults in the Lycus Valley," 680. See also Canavan, "Unraveling the Threads of Identity," 86.

96 Armstrong, "Roman Phrygia," 282.

97 *MAMA* 6.40 (p. 15). See the discussion in Huttner, *Early Christianity in the Lycus Valley*, 45.

98 See the image published in Cadwallader, "Comparative Method," 111. Cadwallader suggests, however, that the image could be that of Helios.

The sanctuary of Apollo was the religious center of the city of Hierapolis.[99] He was given the epithet, ἀρχηγέτις, "first leader" or "founder" of the city. As such, he was the leading god of Hierapolis.[100] His cult formed the religious and political backbone of Hierapolis.[101] His temple was located in the very center of the city adjacent to the Plutonium grotto. Numerous shards of pottery dating from as early as the first century BC attest to libation rites held in the temple. The numerous lamps discovered are "presumably linked to cult ceremonies that took place in the sanctuary."[102] The temple was located in close proximity to the theater, which was dedicated to Apollo.[103] A series of reliefs behind the stage of the theater depict various scenes from the lives of Apollo and his sister, Artemis. One panel (no. 11) depicts Apollo as the god of purification, as he sprinkles water with his laurel branch. As such, he is invoked to protect the city from pestilence.[104] Another panel portrays dancing maidens who are linked to the purification rites "and evokes the cathartic function of Apollo during epidemics that struck the city."[105]

Apollo is the official reprentative of the city in its bronze coins, homonoia coins, and the Cistophoren.[106] But this Apollo was also known as the Pythios and Delphos, suggesting a close connection to the Apollo at Delphi.[107] This connection is further evidenced by the Pythian games that were held in Hierapolis.[108]

Both the proximity of Apollo's temple to the Plutonium and the relief scenes at the theater point to the oracular and prophetic function of Apollo as well as his role as a healing god.[109] Apollo was represented as a god who was concerned about his people—both in the city and the rural territories.[110] So far there has not been sufficient evidence to infer that there were mystery initiation rituals done in the sanctuary of Apollo at Hierapolis, but this remains a distinct possibility.

Approximately six miles to the northeast of Hierapolis was another Apollo sanctuary—the temple of Apollo Kareios. He was worshiped in Hierapolis as an indigenous oracle god.[111] He was also worshiped alongside Apollo Archegetes in the main temple at Hierapolis. The name Kareios may be derived from Kareios, the son of Zeus and Torrhebia. This Kareios had a son named Attis, which may

99 Şimşek, "Regional Cults in the Lycus Valley," 675.
100 Kerschbaum, "Die Apollines von Hierapolis," 15.
101 Kerschbaum, "Die Apollines von Hierapolis," 33.
102 D'Andria, *Hierapolis of Phrygia*, 16.
103 Huttner, *Early Christianity in the Lycus Valley*, 46.
104 D'Andria, *Hierapolis of Phrygia*, 168–70.
105 D'Andria, *Hierapolis of Phrygia*, 168–70.
106 Kerschbaum, "Die Apollines von Hierapolis," 16.
107 Şimşek, "Regional Cults in the Lycus Valley," 675; Kerschbaum, "Die Apollines von Hierapolis," 17.
108 D'Andria, *Hierapolis of Phrygia*, 109.
109 Cadwallader and Harrison, "Perspectives on the Lycus Valley," 49.
110 Kerschbaum, "Die Apollines von Hierapolis," 33.
111 Kerschbaum, "Die Apollines von Hierapolis," 19.

be the Phrygian Attis, the consort of Cybele.[112] An alphabet oracle was built into the cella of the temple of Apollo.[113] A statue of Apollo Kareios (without the head) with the inscription *Kareios Apollon* on the base, was discovered in the theater at Hierapolis and is now on display in the Hierapolis Museum.[114]

There is yet another sanctuary of Apollo about eighteen miles north of Hierapolis, serving the cult of Apollo Lairbenos.[115] The site was roughly a mile from the ancient town of Motella. This cult was in close relationship to its counterpart in Hierapolis and was possibly even governed by it.[116] The site is situated on a bluff overlooking the upper Maeander River and remains unexcavated.[117] The temple measured 42 x 97 feet and is slightly bigger than the temple of Apollo in Hierapolis. There is another small building that stood west of the temple. Several statues and many inscriptions were discovered at the site. One of these inscriptions honors Apollo as the god who wards off evil (ἀλεξίκακος).[118] Many of the images of Apollo Lairbenos depict him wielding a double-headed axe rather than a cithara. In a few of these inscriptions, Apollo Lairbenos is identified with the god, Helios. A number of the inscriptions from this site are part of a larger genre of inscriptions referred to as *confessional inscriptions* (or *propitiation inscriptions*), where the suppliant confesses a sin to the deity to avert his wrath and alleviate the effect of a divine punishment. It is not known whether there were any permanent residents living at the site when it was active. The sanctuary did attract many visitors from surrounding cities and villages coming to consult the god, to appease him for a ritual or ethical violation or to perform a vow. Ramsay contends that mystery rites were performed in this cult.[119]

One of the most magnificent temples on the main *plateia* of Laodicea (referred to as "Temple A") was established as early as the first century AD and may have served as a sanctuary of Apollo. Among the many inscriptions mentioning Apollo at Laodicea, twenty-five of them provide record of delegations traveling to the oracle sanctuary of Apollo at Claros.[120] Huttner notes that "during the high empire, Laodicea sent cultic embassies to the oracle every year."[121] This is highly significant for my contention that the term ἐμβατεύω (*embateuō*) in Col 2:18 would have been familiar to people living in the Lycus Valley as a technical

112 Kerschbaum, "Die Apollines von Hierapolis," 20.

113 *SEG* 39.1377. See Şimşek, "Regional Cults in the Lycus Valley," 675; D'Andria, *Hierapolis of Phrygia*, 228, provides the Greek text and an English translation of the inscription.

114 D'Andria, *Hierapolis of Phrygia*, 227.

115 See Miller, "Apollo Lairbenos," 46–70; Huttner, *Early Christianity in the Lycus Valley*, 48–52.

116 Şimşek, "Regional Cults in the Lycus Valley," 677. Kerschbaum, "Die Apollines von Hierapolis," 23, sees the temple as under the influence of Hierapolis, but as independent to some degree.

117 See Mitchell, *Anatolia*, 1:187.

118 *MAMA* 4.275 A. See Miller, "Apollo Lairbenos," 51.

119 Ramsay, "Artemis-Leto and Apollo-Lairbenos," 226.

120 Robert, "Les Inscriptions," 299–303. See the discussion in Cadwallader and Harrison, "Perspectives on the Lycus Valley," 43.

121 Huttner, *Early Christianity in the Lycus Valley*, 45. Robert, *Les Inscriptions*, 303.

term for the higher stage of ritual initiation that certain delegations performed when they consulted the Clarian Apollo. Many of these inscriptions speak of a prophet of Apollo, living in Laodicea, who served annually.[122] Ironically, this prophet was the intermediary for the Clarian Apollo and not the local Apollo.[123] The prophet would travel regularly to Claros and then return with the rites to be performed by the city to ward off epidemics and other problems. There were also delegations that traveled to Claros to consult the oracle from nearby Herakleia Salbakes (eighteen miles southwest of Colossae) and Tabai (twenty-four miles south-southwest of Colossae).[124]

## Mēn

About thirteen miles west of Laodicea (and eighteen miles west of Colossae) was the temple of Mēn Karou. According to Strabo, this sanctuary was held in "remarkable veneration" (τιμώμενον ἀξιολόγως) and was an important healing center.[125] There was even a school of medicine associated with it (Strabo, *Geogr.* 12.20). Roman coins from Colossae confirm that Mēn was worshiped in that city. The coins depict Mēn in a Phrygian cap with a crescent moon.[126] He is also depicted on many coins from Laodicea.[127]

Mēn is a uniquely Asia Minor deity and is seldom mentioned in ancient literature.[128] He is known primarily from epigraphical and numismatic evidence. He is typically portrayed in Phrygian apparel with the crescent moon in the background.[129] In addition to his temple in the Lycus Valley, he had a temple in Pontus and in Pisidian Antioch, which was excavated by W. M. Ramsay in 1912. Many inscriptions mentioning Mēn have been discovered in northeast Lydia, where he was an important and feared territorial deity. He was worshiped with the epithets κύριος, βασιλεύς, and τύραννος ("absolute ruler") and was said to wield great power. This can be seen in an altar inscription from Saittai (Lydia) where he is extolled as "the one god in heaven, the great heavenly Mēn, the great power of the invisible god."[130] He was severe in his punishment of those who violated his ethical standards or required ritual perfomances.[131] Lane comments, "From these inscriptions, I think that it is clear what an important role Men

122 Robert, "Les Inscriptions," 304.

123 Robert, "Les Inscriptions," 305.

124 Robert, "Les Inscriptions," 303.

125 Ramsay, *Cities and Bishoprics of Phrygia*, 1:52, identified Mēn with Asclepius, but Mēn may have been a healing god in his own right; see Huttner, *Early Christianity in the Lycus Valley*, 52.

126 von Aulock, *Münzen und Städte Phrygiens*, 84, 93 (no. 453 and 591).

127 Cadwallader and Harrison, "Perspectives on the Lycus Valley," 39.

128 It is possible that Mēn may reflect a Persian derivation from the lunar deity, Mao. His consort, Artemis Anaetis, also likely had Persian roots from the water spirit, Anahita. See Lane, "Men," 2170.

129 Lane, "Men," 2161.

130 *TAM* V,1.75. See the discussion in Nilsson, *Geschichte der griechischen Religion*, 2:657.

131 Lane, "Men," 2164.

and the divinities associated with him played in the life of the common people of this area."[132]

Mystery rites for Mēn are attested in an inscription from the Cayster Valley (Lydia).[133] Ramsay made the claim that the structure and layout of the temple of Mēn in Antioch of Pisidia suggests that there was a two-stage mystery initiation ritual that was practiced there.[134] He compared it explicitly to the two-stage ritual initiation at Claros, where the climax of the mystery rite was called *embateuein* (see Col 2:18).[135] This opens the door to the possibility that the sanctuary of Mēn Karou also offered a ritual initiation ceremony, perhaps as part of the procedure for those who came to the god seeking healing.

Because of his power, Mēn could be called upon for protection. People could invoke him to ward off evil from their farms and property.[136] Although Mēn was a lunar god as evidenced by the crescent moon that was normally depicted behind his head and shoulders, he was also given the title Μὴν καταχθόνιος, "the underworld Mēn," and was called upon to protect graves.[137] The worship of Mēn highlights many of the common spiritual and religious concerns of people living in the Lycus Valley, including healing, protection, and fear of underworld spirits and other spirit powers.

## The Great Mother (Cybele)

The Great Mother was the most important deity in Phrygia.[138] Thus far, however, there is no epigraphic, numismatic, or statuary evidence of the worship of the Great Mother at Colossae. But given her pervasive presence throughout central Anatolia, Phrygia, and the Lycus Valley, it is only a matter of time until material evidence is discovered. Cadwallader rightly notes, "It is hard to imagine a site replete with water, vegetation and mountain having no influence from her power."[139] There is evidence of her cult in Laodicea, Hierapolis, Tripolis, Attouda, and Trapezopolis.[140] She was worshiped in the area long before the Phrygians settled there.[141] Small idols of the mother goddess have been discovered in Hierapolis that date to the Copper Age or Chalcolithic era (3800–3400 BC).[142] Şimşek suggests that the Hierapolis Plutonium was originally the holy place of

132 Lane, *Corpus Monumentorum Religionis Dei Menis*, 1.31.

133 Lane, *Corpus Monumentorum Religionis Dei Menis*, 1.75. See also Nilsson, *Geschichte der griechischen Religion*, 2:657, and A. Lesky, "Men," PW 15/1.696.

134 Ramsay, "Sketches in the Religious Antiquities," 37–44.

135 Ramsay, "Sketches in the Religious Antiquities," 44–54.

136 Cumont, *Oriental Religions*, 61.

137 Lane, "Men," 2165.

138 Roller, *In Search of God the Mother*, 64.

139 Cadwallader, *Fragments*, 51.

140 Huttner, *Early Christianity in the Lycus Valley*, 53.

141 Şimşek, "Regional Cults in the Lycus Valley," 674.

142 D'Andria, *Hierapolis of Phrygia*, 215.

Cybele.[143] Strabo reports the presence of the castrated Galli, the cultic servants of Cybele, serving in the Plutonium (*Geogr.* 13.4.14).[144] There was also a statue of the god, Attis, the emasculated partner of Cybele, found in Hierapolis and now on display in the museum. Cybele also appears on a number of Laodicean coins.[145] Huttner suggests that the very name of the city, "Colossae," is a toponym that points to a sanctuary of the Anatolian mother goddess in that place.[146] He reasons that the name of the city is derived from the Greek term, κολοσσός, "statue," and that this may refer to the most important deity of the area. The feminine plural form, κολοσσαί, may refer to statues of more than one female goddess. While this is possible, it remains highly speculative.[147]

The Great Mother went by a variety of names in the Roman era, including Μήτηρ ("Mother"), Μήτηρ Μεγάλη ("Great Mother"), Μήτηρ θεῶν ("Mother of the Gods"), Μήτηρ Ὀρεία ("Mountain Mother"), Κυβέλη ("Kybele"), and in Latin, *Magna Mater.* She could also be addressed with local place-name epithets. The Greeks identified her with the goddess Rhea, the daughter of Uranus and Gaia.[148]

Despite her name and titles, she does not fit the conventional roles of motherhood. It would be inaccurate to project onto her notions of conception, pregnancy, fertility, and nurture. She is never shown, for instance, holding or nurturing a child.[149] There is also nothing about her cultic image that suggests that she is a fertility deity.[150] It is also germane to observe that her divine consort, Attis, was emasculated.

One of the most common motifs on various depictions of her is the presence of lions, birds of prey, and fantastic creatures, like a sphinx.[151] This conveys the assurance that this deity had power and control of wildlife and nature.[152] She was worshiped as the guardian of the Phrygian people and "as the protector of individuals and their families."[153] The turreted crown on her head suggests that she was worshiped as the supporter and protector of the city.[154] But she was also the guardian of the countryside—extending her protection to farmers, shepherds, and keepers of livestock. The lions, which are commonly depicted by her side in the Roman era, may have been apotropaic symbols—that is, warding off evil spirits.[155]

143 Şimşek, "Regional Cults in the Lycus Valley," 674.

144 Huttner, *Early Christianity in the Lycus Valley*, 56.

145 Huttner, *Early Christianity in the Lycus Valley*, 54.

146 Huttner, *Early Christianity in the Lycus Valley*, 53–54.

147 Lightfoot, 16–18n4, expresses uncertainty about the derivation of the city name from the Greek term, κολοσσός, since it could alternatively be derived from one of the languages of the eastern nations that swept through the area.

148 See Bogh, "Phrygian Background of Kybele," 317.

149 Roller, *In Search of God the Mother*, 114.

150 Roller, *In Search of God the Mother*, 6, 114.

151 Bogh, "Phrygian Background of Kybele," 316.

152 Roller, *In Search of God the Mother*, 109, 114.

153 Roller, *In Search of God the Mother*, 6, 342. See also Bogh, "Phrygian Background of Kybele," 317.

154 Roller, *In Search of God the Mother*, 330.

155 See Bogh, "Phrygian Background of Kybele," 324.

One of the appealing features of her cult to many were the ecstatic rites performed as part of her worship. The wild music (with flutes, drums, and castanets), chanting, frenzied movement, and dance would have given her devotees an escape from the doldrums of daily life.[156] A person could become "seized by Meter" (μητρόληπτος) and enter an altered state of consciousness.[157] The first-century BC Roman poet Catullus describes some of the experience—no doubt with some degree of hyperbole (Catullus, *Poems* 63.1–93). He speaks of the emasculated *Galli* leading the worshipers through the Phrygian forests "where the noise of cymbals sounds, where timbrels re-echo, where the Phrygian flute-player blows a deep note on his curved reed, where the Maenads ivy-crowned toss their heads violently, where with shrill yells they shake the holy emblems . . . [and] to hasten with rapid dances" (63.18–26). Then, once they have reached the house of Cybele faint and weary, "the delirious madness of their mind departs in soft slumber" (63.36–37). The poem ends with the exclamation, "O my queen; others drive thou in frenzy; others drive thou to madness" (63.91–93).

The consort of the Great Mother was the god Attis. The myth of Attis, which may have been a Hellenistic development,[158] depicts the Great Mother entertaining suspicions about the fidelity of his love for her and driving him into a mad frenzy. This led him to violently castrate himself with a sharp flint rock (Catullus, *Poems* 63.1–9).[159] Following the example of Attis, the priests of Cybele, called *Galloi*, emasculated themselves in frenzied worship of Cybele.[160] They also "emphasized their artificial femininity through feminine dress and manners, so their high-pitched voices, long wild hair, and garish costume made them immediately recognizable."[161] Despite their castration, they engaged in erotic activities with both men and women.[162]

Part of the worship of Cybele included mystery initiation rituals.[163] These rites occurred in the night and were illuminated by the use of torches. One of the associated rituals was called the *taurobolium* (the slaughter of a bull) or the *criobolium* (the slaughter of a ram). In this rite, the initiate would descend into an underground pit. The pit would then be partially covered with wooden planks, and numerous holes would be cut into the timber. Walking out on to the wooden covering, the priests of Cybele would slaughter the bull (or the ram) and allow its blood to pour through the openings of the wood, drenching the initiate in the pit below. The Latin Christian writer Prudentius vividly describes the rite: "Through the thousand crevices in the wood, the bloody dew runs down into

156 See Beard, North, and Price, *Religions of Rome*, 1:97.
157 Roller, *In Search of God the Mother*, 156.
158 Bogh, "Phrygian Background of Kybele," 320.
159 See the discussion in Beard, North, and Price, *Religions of Rome*, 1:164–65.
160 See Thomas, "Magna Mater and Attis," 1526.
161 Roller, *In Search of God the Mother*, 301.
162 Roller, *In Search of God the Mother*, 301.
163 See the discussion in Roller, *In Search of God the Mother*, 349–51.

the pit. The neophyte [initiate] receives the falling drops on his head, clothes and body. He leans backward to have his cheeks, his ears, his lips and his nostrils wetted; he pours the liquid over his eyes, and does not even spare his palate, for he moistens his tongue with blood and drinks it eagerly."[164] Written records of this practice are quite rare, but there is an inscription from Lugdunum (Lyons) attesting the rite in this city in AD 160.[165] Some have questioned whether the *taurobolium* was ever practiced in Anatolia,[166] but a series of five underground shaft monuments discovered in Phrygia and associated with the worship of the Great Mother may provide material evidence of the practice. A study of these shafts by V. Özkaya has demonstrated the plausibility that these shafts "could have been used for a full-scale *taurobolium* rite."[167]

## The Ephesian Artemis and the Greek Artemis (Artemis the Huntress)

One third of the coins from Colossae feature a form of Artemis—either the Ephesian Artemis or the huntress Artemis.[168] There is also material evidence of her worship at Laodicea and Hierapolis.[169] There was likely a sanctuary of Artemis in Laodicea as early as the second century BC.[170] At Hierapolis, there was an entire cycle of reliefs on the back stage of the theater depicting various scenes in the life of Artemis.[171] These reliefs showed a preference for the Ephesian Artemis and local traditions about Artemis to the classical myths.[172] The frieze begins with the classical Artemis, and then "a radical change of theme" to the Ephesian deity takes place.[173] One panel depicts the sacrifice of a bull and thereby helps to "demolish one of the most widely held beliefs that the cult of Ephesus did not include blood sacrifice."[174] The prominence of the Ephesian Artemis in the Lycus Valley and at Colossae is of special interest. One wonders if it may have

164 As cited in Cumont, *Oriental Religions*, 66. See also the full text and discussion in Beard, North, and Price, *Religions of Rome*, 2:160–62.

165 *CIL* 13.1751. See the text and discussion in Beard, North, and Price, *Religions of Rome*, 2:162.

166 Roller, *In Search of God the Mother*, 338, asserts that "there is no evidence to indicate that this type of taurobolium was ever practiced in Anatolia."

167 Özkaya, "Shaft Monuments," 103. Roller, *In Search of God the Mother*, 339, is familiar with the shaft monuments, but asserts that they were likely used for depositing votive offerings. Özkaya, however, points to Hittite texts from Anatolia that talk about ritual pits dug in the ground where victims were sacrificed (p. 100). These pits were associated with the underworld, and the gods of the underworld were then invited by calling out to them. It seems to me far more likely that the *taurobolium* ritual emerged in Phrygia than in Rome.

168 Cadwallader, *Fragments*, 56, 58.

169 See Şimşek, "Regional Cults in the Lycus Valley," 675, and Huttner, *Early Christianity in the Lycus Valley*, 54.

170 Huttner, *Early Christianity in the Lycus Valley*, 55. An inscription from Priene refers to a deposit that was to be made in the treasury of the Laodicean Artemis.

171 For a diagram and pictures of these reliefs, see D'Andria, *Hierapolis of Phrygia*, 171–81.

172 Cadwallader and Harrison, "Perspectives on the Lycus Valley," 48.

173 D'Andria, *Hierapolis of Phrygia*, 176.

174 D'Andria, *Hierapolis of Phrygia*, 178.

had to do with the protective and apotropaic power of the deity over various kinds of spiritual powers—astral, chthonic, and underworld. Her zodiacal necklace represented her power over astrological fate and various spiritual powers in the heavenly spheres; she was ruler of the cosmos and queen of heaven.[175] The reliefs of various kinds of frightful animals on her ἐπενδύτης (wrapped skirt) represent her power over the spirits of wildlife and nature as indicated by their posture of surrender to the goddess.[176] And the bulbous objects on her chest are not breasts but likely represent goatskin pouches filled with magical material and used as fetishes.[177] They would have been known as *kurša* in ancient Anatolia and are known from Hittite practices. They would have functioned as symbols for the fecundity, spiritual power, and protection that the Ephesian Artemis provides to her devotees. Mystery rites were also an important part of this cult.[178]

## Other Deities Worshiped in the Lycus Valley

In addition to the Great Mother and Artemis, there were an array of other female deities worshiped in the Lycus Valley. Leto, the mother of Apollo and Artemis, was worshiped in the area. A Colossian coin with the image of Marcus Aurelius depicts Leto on the reverse side with both of her children.[179] Pieces of sculpture and coins of Leto were discovered at Hierapolis.[180] In Anatolia, Leto was worshiped as the powerful goddess who makes possible the impossible.[181] Tyche, the Greek goddess of fortune, appears on a number of Colossian coins, the earliest dating to the second century BC.[182] She is also honored on the base of the Korumbus inscription recently discovered at Colossae.[183] Demeter also is depicted on a handful of Colossian coins.[184] In each of these she is wielding a scepter. She is also depicted in the theater reliefs at Hierapolis in a scene portraying the abduction of Persephone by Hades. This is not surprising given the prominence of the god, Hades, at Hierapolis. Because of the extensive agriculture in the Lycus Valley, one would expect her to be worshiped at a place like Colossae. There is still no evidence of the worship of Aphrodite at Colossae despite the close proximity of the city to Aphrodisias. She is, however, depicted on Laodicean coins.[185] A number of coins attest the worship of Isis at Colossae.[186]

175 Immendörfer, *Ephesians and Artemis*, 152.
176 Schwindt, *Weltbild*, 123, argues that the animals have apotropaic significance.
177 This is the thesis of Morris, "Artemis Ephesia," 135–51.
178 See Immendörfer, *Ephesians and Artemis*, 171–74.
179 Von Aulock, *Münzen und Städte Phrygiens*, 91 (no. 564); Armstrong, "Roman Phrygia," 351.
180 Şimşek, "Regional Cults in the Lycus Valley," 675.
181 Mitchell, *Anatolia*, 1:192.
182 Von Aulock, *Münzen und Städte Phrygiens*, 85, 88, 92, 93 (nos. 470, 537–39, 540, 585, 589, 592–93).
183 Cadwallader, "Honoring the Repairer of the Baths," 150–83, esp. 154–55.
184 Von Aulock, *Münzen und Städte Phrygiens*, 83–84 (nos. 447, 455–57).
185 See Huttner, *Early Christianity in the Lycus Valley*, 87, and Cadwallader and Harrison, "Perspectives on the Lycus Valley," 39.
186 Von Aulock, *Münzen und Städte Phrygiens*, 87–89 (nos. 518–33, 543–44).

She is regularly depicted on these issues with Sarapis. A sculpture of Isis was found in the nymphaeum at Laodicea.[187] Athena, also, is depicted on a few Colossian coins.[188] A statuary head of Athena was unearthed in Laodicea in the 2015 excavations. Her worship in this area is consistent with her association with the weaving and clothing industry.[189] And, finally, an additional female deity worshiped in the Lycus Valley was the moon goddess, Selene. She is depicted in a pediment relief from the nymphaeum in Hierapolis.[190] She is often identified with Artemis in magical texts.

The famed god of wine and revelry, Dionysus, had a place at Colossae. One Colossian coin depicts the head of Dionysus with his typical ivy wreath.[191] Cadwallader and Harrison report the discovery (on the numismatic market) of two Colossian coins with what they interpret to be a votive altar to Bacchus.[192] Despite the paucity of evidence for Dionysus at Colossae, Cadwallader and Harrison speak of the likelihood of "a significant Dionysian cult in the city."[193] While this is a speculative assumption and lacks evidence, Cadwallader is correct in obseriving that "Dionysus (also known as Bacchus) flourished where there were mountains, caves, springs, lavish vegetation—all offered by Colossae and its surrounds."[194] Dionysus worship is attested for Laodicea and Hierapolis. His image is on a theater relief at Hierapolis.[195] There is also inscriptional evidence from Hierapolis that may suggest the presence of a mystery initiation ritual in the cult of Dionysus in that city. The text speaks of the dedication of a *hierophant* (ἱεροφάντης, an initiate).[196]

There were a variety of other gods worshiped at Colossae and represented on coins. One of these is the river-god Lykos. He is attested on a number of Colossian coins.[197] Also, the image of a wolf (the Greek term is λύκος *lykos*) on some Colossian coins may be a representation of the river-god. Others include Asclepius, Hygieia, Helios, Nike, and Sarapis.

There are a few other gods who may have been worshiped at Colossae, but we are lacking evidence of their presence in the city at this point. These would include Hermes, Hades, Hekate, Theos Hypsistos, Hosios and Dikaios, and Sabazios. These deities are amply attested, however, in western Asia Minor during the Roman era.

187 Cadwallader and Harrison, "Perspectives on the Lycus Valley," 33.
188 Von Aulock, *Münzen und Städte Phrygiens*, 85, 89, 91 (nos. 465–68, 548, 563).
189 Canavan, "Threads of Identity," 85.
190 Şimşek, "Regional Cults in the Lycus Valley," 680.
191 Armstrong, "Roman Phrygia," 355 (no. 11).
192 Cadwallader and Harrison, "Perspectives on the Lycus Valley," 17–18.
193 Cadwallader and Harrison, "Perspectives on the Lycus Valley," 17–18.
194 Cadwallader, *Fragments*, 53.
195 Cadwallader and Harrison, "Perspectives on the Lycus Valley," 49.
196 For the text and discussion, see Huttner, *Early Christianity in the Lycus Valley*, 131.
197 Von Aulock, *Münzen und Städte Phrygiens*, 83–84, 92 (no. 448–52, 581–84).

### *Judaism in the Lycus Valley*

There is presently no direct evidence of a Jewish community in Colossae. No synagogue has been discovered, no Jewish inscriptions, no symbols of Jewish presence, and no literary references to Jews living in the city. Nevertheless, there has long been an assumption that there was a strong Jewish presence in Colossae because of the abundant evidence of Jews living in the Lycus Valley. Dunn infers that "a significant feature of the Lycus Valley cities, including presumably Colossae, was the presence of a substantial Jewish minority."[198] This assumption is foundational for Dunn in that he concludes that the opposing teaching at Colossae was external and could be located as coming from "one of the Colossian synagogues."[199] In fact, those who identify the problem at Colossae as having its roots in Jewish mysticism make a similar assumption.[200] But this assumption has been challenged in recent scholarship. Cadwallader, for instance, has argued that "the evidence for a *significant* Jewish population at Colossae is lacking."[201] In addition to observing that none of the 250 Jewish inscriptions in Asia Minor come from Colossae,[202] he infers that Colossae was probably not one of the Lydian or Phrygian cities considered by the Seleucid king, Antiochus III, for population by Jewish people (see below).[203] He also finds a subtle suggestion of a minimal Jewish population in the city by the reversal of the word order of "Jews and Greeks" in Col 3:11 to "Greeks and Jews."[204] This reticence to assume a Jewish population in Colossae has found its way into some commentaries.[205]

It must be remembered, however, that there are very few references to Colossae in the literature leading up to the first century AD, very few inscriptions of any kind from the city, and, at the time of this writing, no excavation of the site. So any definitive judgment about the extent of Jewish settlement in the city must be suspended until more information is forthcoming through archaeological discovery. Nevertheless, I believe that it is reasonable to infer at least some Jewish presence in the city and possibly a synagogue somewhere along the Lycus River near the city. This can reasonably be deduced from the abundant evidence of Jewish presence throughout the Lycus Valley and Phrygia.

The earliest evidence of Jewish settlers in Phrygia comes from Persian times when Jews came as slaves, soldiers, and travelers into the territory.[206] The most significant wave of Jewish migration, however, came between 212–205 BC

198 Dunn, 21.
199 Dunn, 34.
200 E.g., Smith, *Heavenly Perspective*, 3–5.
201 Cadwallader, "Comparative Method," 117.
202 Cadwallader, "Comparative Method," 131.
203 Cadwallader, "Comparative Method," 140.
204 Cadwallader, "Comparative Method," 140.
205 E.g., Foster, 15, comments: "Therefore, in the face of no extant evidence from Colossae, all that can be said is that there is no conclusive evidence for the existence of Jews in the city. Furthermore, the letter does not betray any significant interest in Jewish matters."
206 Ameling, "Die jüdische Gemeinden," 32.

when the Seleucid king, Antiochus III the Great, who reigned over Syria and Anatolia (222–187 BC), resettled two thousand Jewish households (as many as ten thousand people) in Lydia and Phrygia (Josephus, *Ant.* 12.147–52).[207] He sent these Jews to settle in the area as a way of helping to quell the sedition and uprisings that were beginning to occur against him. It is important to note that these Jewish settlers did not come from Judea or Galilee but from Mesopotamia. Antiochus had high regard for their piety and loyalty and believed that they would become "loyal guardians of our interests" in Phrygia (Josephus, *Ant.* 12.150). As part of his goodwill toward them, Antiochus ensured that they would be given land, exemption from taxes for ten years, and the freedom to follow their laws. This privileged status would be lost after the first generation when these territories passed into the hands of other regimes. But these resettled Jewish households became the nucleus of what later became a numerous Jewish presence in Lydia and Phrygia.[208] Cadwallader's assumption that the Seleucid-founded cities would have received most of the Jewish settlers from Mesopotamia may be correct,[209] but it is just as likely that other cities were the hotbed of sedition and may have been the primary focal points of the resettlement for strategic purposes. If the latter is true, Colossae may have been a likely candidate for receiving some of the Jewish settlers.

Cicero provides literary evidence in the mid-first century BC of a sizeable number of Jews living in the Lycus Valley and, especially, at Laodicea. The testimony comes in the context of his defense of the governor of the Roman province of Asia, L. Valerius Flaccus, who was accused of confiscating gold from the Jews in Asia that was being sent to the temple in Jerusalem. In the process of making his defense, Cicero reveals that the Jews in Laodicea had collected over twenty pounds of gold for the temple (Cicero, *Flac.* 68–69). It is difficult to calculate from this amount of gold just how many Jews this represents, given the typical annual contribution of two drachmas, because we do not know the geographical extent of this collection (does it include all of the cities of the Lycus Valley?), nor the number of years of savings it represents.[210] But it does point to Laodicea as a Jewish center and a considerable Jewish population in the Lycus Valley. It is also significant that Cicero mentions that nearly one hundred pounds of gold was confiscated from the Jewish community at Apamea (fifty-five miles west of Colossae).

Luke mentions that there were Jews from Phrygia who were present in Jerusalem on the day of Pentecost (Acts 2:10). One can only wonder if any of these Phrygian Jews were from the Lycus Valley and returned to their home cities and villages with newfound conviction that Jesus of Nazareth was the long-anticipated

207 See the discussion in Ameling, "Die jüdische Gemeinden," 32; van der Horst, "Jews of Ancient Phrygia," 284; Trebilco, *Jewish Communities in Asia Minor*, 6.

208 Ameling, "Die jüdische Gemeinden," 34.

209 Cadwallader, "Comparative Method," 136.

210 See the discussion in Huttner, *Early Christianity in the Lycus Valley*, 70–71, and van der Horst, "Jews of Ancient Phrygia," 284.

Messiah and that the promised Spirit had arrived in power. Could Jewish delegates from the Lycus Valley (perhaps Colossae) have been among their number, and were they the first to bring the gospel back to this region (with the gentile Epaphras shortly later becoming the most prominent convert and teacher)?

Of the many Jewish inscriptions discovered in Asia Minor, forty-eight are from Phrygia and almost half of these (twenty-three) are from Hierapolis.[211] Most of these are epitaphs from Jewish burials in the necropolis at Hierapolis. From these inscriptions we learn that Jews were involved in the purple dyeing industry of the city, that they observed the important festivals of Judaism, and that they may even have had their own living quarter within the city.[212] Although no synagogue has been discovered in the excavations at Hierapolis, one inscription makes reference to "the most holy synagogue" (τῇ ἁγιωτάτῃ συναγωγῇ).[213] Harland observes that several inscriptions refer to groups or associations of Jews that may be suggestive of a local synagogue (or even several synagogues over time).[214] But we also learn of a Jew who participated in an ἀγών, which was typically frowned upon by the more orthodox.[215]

Only two Jewish inscriptions have thus far been discovered at Laodicea. One is a third- or fourth-century Greek burial inscription that includes some Hebrew letters.[216] The other is a sarcophagus inscription for L. Nonius Glykon that warns against anyone else being interred in the tomb or they would suffer the curses written in Deuteronomy.[217] The allusion here is likely to the curses for covenant disobedience in Deut 28:22–36.[218] More recently, Şimşek discovered a menorah carved into a column of the nymphaeum at Laodicea.[219] Inscribed to the left of the menorah was a palm branch (lulab) and to the right was a horn (shofar). He notes that "the schematic style of our menorah, palm and horn is similar to those drawn on some tombs of the 1st c. AD in the necropolis at nearby Hierapolis."[220] In the middle of the menorah and added much later is a globe with a large cross above it. Şimşek suggests that this association of the cross with the menorah implies that part of the Jewish community at Laodicea had accepted Christianity.[221]

One of the more interesting and significant Jewish inscriptions from Phrygia comes from the city of Acmonia (about seventy miles north-northeast of Colossae). The inscription represents the earliest evidence of a synagogue in

211 See *IJO* 2.187–209 (pp. 398–440). These inscriptions are discussed in Harland, "Acculturation and Identity," 222–44. See also van der Horst, "Jews of Ancient Phrygia," 285.
212 Van der Horst, "Jews of Ancient Phrygia," 286.
213 *IJO* 2.191. See also Harland, "Acculturation and Identity," 226.
214 Harland, "Acculturation and Identity," 224.
215 See Huttner, *Early Christianity in the Lycus Valley*, 76.
216 *IJO* 2.212 (pp. 444–46).
217 *IJO* 2.213 (pp. 446–47).
218 Van der Horst, "Jews of Ancient Phrygia," 288.
219 Şimşek, "Menorah with a Cross," 343–46.
220 Şimşek, "Menorah with a Cross," 345.
221 Şimşek, "Menorah with a Cross," 346.

Phrygia. The text refers to a woman named Julia Severa, who contributed funds for the building of the synagogue.[222] She is well-known in this region through other references to her on coins and inscriptions.[223] Based on this evidence, it appears that she was involved in civic affairs in the 50s and 60s, which means that the synagogue was likely constructed in the mid-first century. It is particularly significant to note that Julia Severa was probably not Jewish;[224] she was a high priestess in the imperial cult and served as an ἀγωνοθέτις, an official who presided over the games.[225] She thus served as an important benefactor for the Jewish community[226] and may have been a "Gentile sympathizer."[227] Hengel notes that the diaspora synagogue—"with its prayer, hymn-singing, interpretation of scripture, and presentation of doctrine and ethical admonition in a sermon"—had a strong power of attraction to many gentiles, especially on members of the urban middle and upper classes, and particularly women from those classes.[228] The ethical monotheism of Judaism was quite appealing to many of the urban elites. What we do not know in the case of the synagogue at Acmonia is the degree to which the influence went both ways. In other words, to what extent did Julia Severa and other influential gentile sympathizers and patrons lead these Jews to deeper levels of cultural and religious assimilation? To be sure, the influence was not only in one direction.

There was no doubt that Jewish communities in Phrygia engaged in a high degree of cultural integration with the surrounding gentile society. The inscriptional evidence suggests that Jews maintained good relationships with their gentile neighbors, that they participated in important cultural events (sports and music), that they adopted some of the local customs (such as funerary customs), and that they were involved in local businesses and industry.[229] This is consistent with how the Sardis Jewish community related to their gentile neighbors.[230]

The degree of syncretism among the Jewish communities of Asia Minor has sometimes been overstated in the past, especially when it is based on interpreting the cults of Theos Hypsistos and Sabazios as syncretistic Jewish groups.[231] This has rightly been corrected by more recent scholarship, which has pointed out

222 *IJO* 2.168 (pp. 348–55).

223 See Trebilco, *Jewish Communities in Asia Minor*, 50.

224 Contra Ramsay, *Cities and Bishoprics of Phrygia*, 1.2.650.

225 Trebilco, *Jewish Communities in Asia Minor*, 59–60; Harland, *Associations, Synagogues, and Congregations*, 227–28.

226 Harland, *Associations, Synagogues, and Congregations*, 228.

227 Trebilco, *Jewish Communities in Asia Minor*, 59–60.

228 Hengel and Schwemer, *Paul: Between Damascus and Antioch*, 61–62. See his entire excursus, "The Problem of the 'Sympathizers' and Jewish Propaganda" (pp. 61–76). He cites Julia Severa as an example of that group (pp. 68–69).

229 Van der Horst, "Jews of Ancient Phrygia," 292.

230 See Mitchell, *Anatolia*, 2:32–33, on the integration of the Sardis Jewish community into the civic life.

231 E.g., Kittel, "Kleinasiatische Judentum," 9–20, and Cumont, *Oriental Religions*, 63–65. Lease, "Jewish Mystery Cults," 874, rightly concludes that "we must also acknowledge that the existence

the pagan background and worship of both of these deities.[232] However, in the realm of Jewish magic, there was a strong syncretistic impulse that led to the assimilation of pagan rituals, invocation of pagan deities and divine assistants, astrological beliefs, and a variety of other practices (see below).[233] It is important to note that despite the popularity of the Jewish mystical view of the Colossian "philosophy," there is no evidence of Jewish mysticism in Phrygia.

## *Roman Empire and Imperial Authority*

At the time that Paul wrote his letter to the Colossians, the Lycus Valley had been under Roman rule for nearly two hundred years, Nero was princeps of the empire, and Colossae and the Lycus Valley were part of the Roman province of Asia. In a matter of months after the letter arrived, there would be major upheaval. Colossae would be devastated by a major earthquake that would destroy many of its principal buildings. A similar fate would be experienced by Laodicea and Hierapolis. In Rome, ten of its fourteen districts would burn in an enormous conflagration that many attributed to Nero's increasingly deranged thinking and actions. For many living in the Lycus Valley, the touted *Pax Romana* would surely have felt less certain.

Roman rule had, however, provided a great deal of security and stability for people in Phrygia and Asia Minor following a number of regime changes. Prior to the Pergamene king, Attalus III (reigned 138–133 BC), bestowing his kingdom on the Roman Empire upon his death in 133 BC, the area had passed from Lydian rule, to Persian rule (546 BC), and then was retaken by Alexander the Great. Following Alexander's death in 323 BC, the region came under the control of the Seleucids and the Attalids (of Pergamum). It was the Seleucid king, Antiochus II (reigned 261–246 BC), who founded the city of Laodicea and named it after his wife. In 129 BC, the Roman provice of Asia was established, and Phrygia was incorporated into this province at some point between 122 and 116 BC.[234] For a brief period of time (56–50 BC), the Lycus Valley became part of the Roman province of Cilicia while it was governed by Cicero, but then was reincorporated into the province of Asia.[235]

Roman rule did not lead to the kind of widespread change that had taken place under the reign of the Greeks. The Hellenization process had been

of a peculiarly Jewish mystery cult, conceptualized and patterned after the Hellenistic mystery cults, is without evidence and unsupportable."

232 See esp. Kraabel, "Roman Diaspora," 450–51.

233 Surprisingly, Kraabel does not treat the matter of Jewish magic in his later essays, where he mounts a case against the notion of a "syncretistic Judaism" in Asia Minor despite his extensive treatment of magic in his unpublished Harvard dissertation. He goes so far as to speak of a pagan "Lydian-Phrygian piety, in which Anatolian Judaism has already participated," which he sees as an explanation for the role of the στοιχεῖα (*stoicheia*) and the "worship of angels" in Colossians (Kraabel, "Judaism in Western Asia Minor," 145).

234 Thonemann, *Roman Phrygia*, 29.

235 Huttner, *Early Christianity in the Lycus Valley*, 38.

thorough and long-lasting. The regional languages (such as Phrygian) were supplanted by the use of Greek. There was significant reorganization of civic structures, which were brought into alignment with Greek municipal organization that included a βουλή, a δῆμος, and the full range of Greek civic magistrates. Much of Greek culture came to Phrygia during this era, with benefits that included sporting events, festivals, theater, and more. Greek deities were introduced, and many of the local deities were identified with what the newcomers considered to be their Greek counterparts through a process often referred to as *interpretatio graeca*. Hellenization in the Lycus Valley was probably accelerated through the establishment of the new Seleucid city called Laodicea in the early 250s BC and the development of the city of Hierapolis under a Hippodamian grid plan.[236] By the time of the Roman imperial period, the Lycus Valley was "culturally indistinguishable from the Hellenized regions of lowland Asia Minor."[237]

Roman rule in Phrygia was only superficially established and, in the words of Thonemann, was only "paper thin."[238] It did not originate through violent military subjugation but by the last testament of an Attalid ruler and the peaceful transition of power. No Roman legion came to be stationed in Asia, whereas Syria had four different legions garrisoned there. Most of the municipal structures remained untouched. The Latin language was not imposed on the people, and very little of Italian culture was brought to this region. The most intrusive aspect of Roman rule was the poll tax and the regular census, both of which served as important reminders of Roman hegemony.[239] For many civic leaders, the goal was to curry favor with Rome, which many thought would lead to greater honor or funds for civic projects coming their way, such as Hierapolis received to rebuild after the great earthquake in the early 60s. The relative peace under the empire, the extensive road system, and the enhancement of trade resulted in a wider economic prosperity to the region.

The large imperial temple and sanctuary complex at nearby Aphrodisias (about forty miles west-southwest of Colossae) gives a different impression of Roman rule in this area of Asia Minor. Discovered in 1979 by K. T. Erim, this temple was constructed between AD 20 and 60 in honor of the goddess Aphrodite and the Julio-Claudian emperors (the *Theoi Sebastoi Olympioi*). The impressive temple complex was a long rectangular structure (about 300′ x 46′) consisting of a processional roadway flanked by a three-story porticoed structure on both sides. The second and third stories contained marble reliefs framed by

236 Thonemann, *Roman Phrygia*, 22.

237 Thonemann, *Roman Phrygia*, 22.

238 Thonemann, *Roman Phrygia*, 3. See also Doherty, "Roman Phrygian Countryside," 81. Eckhardt, "Romanization and Isomorphic Change in Phrygia," 147, notes that "Romanization in the province of Asia did not manifest itself in linguistic or cultural changes, but is very visible in a trend towards corporate organization."

239 Arzt-Grabner, "Everyday Life in a Roman Town," 206.

the columns. Eighty reliefs have been recovered in the excavation, but there would have been an estimated two hundred reliefs in the entire complex. Many of the statuary reliefs depict the conquest of Roman imperial power over numerous *ethnē* (people groups) from the edges of the empire. The inscriptions identify thirteen different *ethnē* and peoples from three different islands. They include the Rhaetians (between the Danube and the Rhine), the Trumpilini (in the Alps north of Italy), the Callaeci (northwest of Spain), the Iapodes (Illyricum), the Andizeti and Piourstae (Pannoia), the Dardani and the Bessi (south of the Danube), the Dacians, the Bosporans (north of the Black Sea), as well as the Egyptians, Judeans, and Arabs. Three islands are included—Crete, Cyprus, and Sicily. Smith notes that "in the Sebasteion the selection of outlandish peoples was meant to stand as a visual account of the extent of the Augustan Empire, and by the sheer numbers and impressive unfamiliarity of the names, to suggest that it is coterminous with the ends of the earth."[240] To all from this region viewing the reliefs, they represented a new world order ruled by the succession of Roman emperors, who brought peace and stability through their subjugation and rule.[241] This was a political order thought to be aligned with the divine order. Indeed, the divine Augustus was believed to have descended from Aphrodite through Iulus, son of Aeneas.[242] The structure brought great honor to Roman imperial rule and the reign of the emperors from Tiberius to Nero.

Harry Maier has drawn attention to the Sebasteion in a series of publications and contends that it provides insight into the extensive imperial language and imagery in the letter to the Colossians.[243] He has pointed to the image of the Roman triumphal procession in Col 2:15, the reference to Christ making peace (1:20), the cosmic supremacy of Christ in relation to all powers, and the order represented by the household code as pointing to the Colossian author's representation of the new order Christ has inaugurated vis-à-vis the Roman Empire. Maier is to be commended for compiling and correlating a great deal of data illustrating Roman rule to the language and imagery of Colossians in a way that enhances our understanding of the letter. One wonders, however, if his thesis is overstated to the exclusion of other important sources for understanding the terminology and metaphors of the letter, especially the Jewish background of

240 Smith, "Ethne from the Sebasteion at Aphrodisias," 77.

241 Maier, "Reading Colossians in the Ruins," 212–31, sees these images as snapshots of a world in transformation and renewal: "Observers were to see themselves belonging to a social order of transformation and renewal. Classical forms were used to depict the self-control and moderation of Roman rule realizing a worldwide imperium while Hellenistic forms helped to communicate the dynamic unfolding of that rule through the labour and effort of Roman rulers" (p. 221).

242 Smith, "Imperial Reliefs," 90.

243 See Maier, *Picturing Paul in Empire*, 63–102; idem, "Colossians and Empire," 323–49, idem, "Reading Colossians in the Ruins," 212–31. He makes the sweeping assertions that "Colossians is a letter charged with imperial picture language" (*Picturing Paul in Empire*, 63) and "everywhere Colossians makes use of imperial themes and commonplaces" ("Reading Colossians in the Ruins," 215).

much of the terminology and conceptuality as well as the relevance of the local religious traditions. Aside from the term for Roman triumph that appears in 2:15 (θριαμβεύω), there are no other terms and images that are explicitly Roman. Nevertheless, the Colossian hymn represents Christ as supreme over all things "in heaven and on earth, visible and invisible" (1:16; see also 1:20), which, no doubt, was intended to extend to the Roman imperium. Although the people of Phrygia and Caria (where Aphrodisias was located) heard the tales of military victory by Pompey, Julius Caesar, and the succeeding emperors, they were not a people who were subjugated by force. Their concerns had to do more with navigating the political and economic realities of Roman rule for the benefit of their communities. This would have involved currying favor with Rome for their economic well-being and for gaining honor in Roman society. Aphrodisias had handled this well and had managed to gain an elevated status with Rome (an ἐλεύθερος, or "free" city) that privileged it above all other cities in Caria, Phrygia, and Lydia.[244] Aphrodisias was proud of their special relationship with Rome and undertook public works to honor their imperial patron. Their status of being a "free city" brought to them a degree of autonomy and even freedom from taxation—an enormous benefit.[245] Caesar Augustus described his conferral of this status on Aphrodisias in a letter: "I have freed Zoilos' city. . . . This one city I have taken for my own out of all Asia. I wish these people to be protected as my own townsmen."[246] Part of their response to this was the establishment of the emperor cult in the city and a grand temple to honor all of the emperors.

Although not possessing the same status and privileges as Aphrodisias, the cities of Laodicea and Hierapolis also honored the emperors in many ways and established the ruler cult. During the reign of Caesar Augustus, they began to mint coins with his image in place of the image of one of the gods. This practice continued with the other emperors. There is also inscriptional evidence of their worship in Hierapolis. A cylindrical altar was found in the theater with an inscription dedicating it to "Gaius Caesar, son of Augustus, ruler of youth, and to the goddess Roma [Γαΐῳ Καίσαρι Σεβαστοῦ υἱῷ, ἡγεμόνι τῆς νεότητος, καὶ Θεᾶι Ῥώμῃ]."[247] There are two twin marble altars found in 2001 that each have the inscription: "to Apollo Archegetes and to the lord emperor [τῶι κυρίωι Αὐτοκράτορι]."[248] Hierapolis also held games in honor of the emperor Augustus.[249] In Laodicea, an inscription commemorates a dedication made to Zeus Soter and the divine emperors (Θεοὶ Σεβαστοί).[250] Numismatic evidence from both cities document that each city constructed a temple in honor of the emperors—in

244 See Chaniotis, "Imperial Power in Aphrodisias," 250–60.
245 Chaniotis, "Imperial Power in Aphrodisias," 252.
246 As cited in Chaniotis, "Imperial Power in Aphrodisias," 253.
247 Ritti, *Epigraphic Guide to Hierapolis*, 150–52 (no. 34).
248 Ritti, *Epigraphic Guide to Hierapolis*, 88–89 (no. 14).
249 Huttner, *Early Christianity in the Lycus Valley*, 62.
250 Huttner, *Early Christianity in the Lycus Valley*, 62.

Hierapolis during the reign of Claudius and in Laodicea under Domitian.[251] The sparse evidence available for the ruler cult in the Lycus Valley, however, is in no way comparable to the abundance of evidence related to the worship of the local gods and goddesses.

There was a substantial difference between the worship of the traditional gods and the worship of the emperors despite the many points of overlap. It is important to observe that there were no accounts of healing that took place in the emperor temples or of the thwarting of a plague. No one ever sought out *Thea Roma* (the goddess Roma) or any of the divine emperors for oracular advice. There are no reports of divine emissaries (*angeloi*) of the emperors appearing to people in the night and no accounts of being "struck" by a deified emperor as we find in the testimonies coming from those honoring the local territorial gods. In fact, the local gods could assert their hegemony over Roman imperial might. When a woman brought Roman soldiers into the sanctuary of Apollo Lairbenos to settle a private dispute, she was forced by Apollo to admit and atone for her fault.[252] As Price notes, there was an important distinction between the emperors and the traditional gods. The emperor was regarded as midway between human and divine and needed the divine protection that came from sacrifices made to the traditional deities.[253] When an emperor shared a sanctuary with a traditional god, he was subordinated to that deity.[254] The high priest of the emperor cult at Aphrodisias sacrificed to the ancestral gods.[255] Mellor is not far off the mark when he concludes that "it was a cult based on political, rather than religious, experience."[256] It served to enhance the status of cities and its more influential citizens. But it also served as a constant reminder of the pervasive nature of Roman rule in the Lycus Valley, Phrygia, and all of the province of Asia.

As we will see throughout the letter to the Colossians, Paul presents a vision of Christ's supremacy and lordship that has significant implications for Roman rule. But Colossians is not principally a critique of Roman power and domination.[257] That would be to sell it short. Paul's understanding of Christ's reign and power extends far beyond that to the realm of "the invisible" (τὰ ἀόρατα; see 1:16). It is truly a cosmic, universal, and supernatural framework of

251 Price, *Rituals and Power*, 264–65, and Huttner, *Early Christianity in the Lycus Valley*, 62.

252 Mitchell, *Anatolia*, 1:197.

253 Price, *Rituals and Power*, 233.

254 Price, *Rituals and Power*, 232.

255 Price, *Rituals and Power*, 211 (see ch. 8: "Sacrifices for the Emperor").

256 Mellor, *ΘΕΑ ΡΩΜΗ*, 16.

257 Contra Walsh and Keesmaat, *Colossians Remixed*, 62, who contend that "in Colossians Paul is telling a story that is an alternative to the mythology of empire." I remain rather skeptical of the recent trend to find "hidden" or "coded" anti-imperial transcripts embedded in the letters of Paul and Colossians in particular. See the recent critique of these approaches in Robinson, "Hidden Transcripts?," 55–72, and Barclay, "Paul, Roman Religion, and the Emperor," 344–62, and idem, "Why the Roman Empire Was Insignificant to Paul," 363–87. Heilig, *Apostle and the Empire*, has attempted to nuance the issue and provide new argumentation for finding criticism of Roman power in Paul's letters. The issue is beyond the scope of what can be adequately handled here.

understanding. Paul goes behind the denizens of Roman imperial power to the spiritual forces that influence and drive the emperors and declares that the status, power, and might of Christ is infinitely superior. Colossians is not a manifesto for political subversion but a plan for something far more grand. Paul is not as concerned about the princeps, the consuls, the provincial governors, or even his own chains that represent his Roman custody as much as he is about the spiritual powers that hold them, and all who have not come to faith in Jesus Christ, as captives. These ultimate enemies are the power of sin and the principalities and powers. In his view, the only hope is found in the gospel of the Lord Jesus Christ that brings forgiveness of sin and deliverance from the authority of darkness.

## *3. Magic, Phrygian Local Belief, Jewish Shamanism, and Syncretism*

### *Bibliography*

**Alexander, P. S.** "Incantations and Books of Magic," 342–79. **Arnold, C. E.** *Colossian Syncretism.* ———. *Ephesians: Power and Magic.* ———. "Sceva, Solomon, and Shamanism," 7–26. **Audollent, A.** *Defixionum Tabellae.* **Aune, D. E.** "Magic in Early Christianity," 1507–57. **Aydaş, M.** "New Inscriptions from Asia Minor," 121–25. **Baird, R. D.** *Category Formation.* **Barclay, J. M. G.** *Jews in the Mediterranean Diaspora.* **Betz, H. D.** "Catabasis Ritual," 287–95. ———. *Greek Magical Papyri in Translation.* ———. "Magic and Mystery in the Greek Magical Papyri," 209–29. ———. *"Mithras Liturgy."* **Bohak, G.** *Ancient Jewish Magic.* **Bonner, C.** *Studies in Magical Amulets.* **Boustan, R., and J. E. Sanzo.** "Christian Magicians," 217–40. **Boustan, R., J. Dielemann, and J. E. Sanzo.** "Authoritative Traditions and Ritual Power," 3–10. **Brashear, W. M.** "Greek Magical Papyri," 3380–483. ———. "Recent Corpora of Magical Texts," 372–83. **Brenk, F. E.** "Exorcism," 3–21. **Buckler, W. H., W. M. Calder, and C. W. M. Cox.** "Monuments from Central Phrygia," 53–94. **Burkert, W.** *Ancient Mystery Cults.* ———. "ΓΟΗΣ," 36–55. **Busch, P.** *Das Testament Salomos.* **Cadwallader, A., and J. R. Harrison.** "Perspectives on the Lycus Valley," 3–70. **Carratelli, G. P.** "ΧΡΗΣΜΟΙ di Apollo Kareios," 358–65. **Cassidy, W.** "Introduction (Retrofitting Syncretism)," 365–73. **Chiai, G. F.** "Norm, Kommunikation und Identität," 117–46. **Cline, R.** *Ancient Angels.* ———. "Archangels," 55–78. **Collins, B. J.** "Necromancy," 224–41. **Cormack, J. M. R.** "*Tabella Defixionis*," 25–34. **Croon, J. H.** "Hot Springs and Healing Gods," 225–46. **D'Andria, F.** *Hierapolis of Phrygia.* **Daniel, R.** "Testament of Solomon," 294–303. **Daniel, R., and F. Maltomini.** *Supplementum Magicum.* **Davila, J. R.** *Descenders to the Chariot.* **Dorigny, A. S.** "Phylactère alexandrin," 287–96. **DuBois, T. A.** *Shamanism.* **Duling, D.** "Testament of Solomon," 87–112. **Eidinow, E.** *Oracles, Curses, and Risk.* **Eitrem, S.** *Magical Papyri.* **Elliott, J. H.** *Evil Eye.* 2 vols. **Farnell, L. R.** *Cults of the Greek States.* 4 vols. **Frankfurter, D.** *Christianizing Egypt.* **Fraser, K. A.** "Roman Antiquity," 115–47. **Gager, J. G.** *Curse Tablets.* **Goetze, A.** *Kulturgeschichte Kleinasiens.* **Goodenough, E. R.** *Symbols.* **Graf, F.** *Magic in the Ancient World.* ———. "Magician's Initiation," 161–77. ———. "Oracle against Pestilence," 267–79. **Gundel, W.** *Dekane und Dekansternbilder.* **Head, B. V.** *Greek Coins of Phrygia.* **Homolle, T.** "Nouvelles et correspondance: Ionie," 638. **Hopfner, T.** "Hekate-Selene-Artemis," 125–45. **Horst, P. W. van der.** "Jews of Ancient Phrygia," 283–92. **Janowitz, N.** *Magic in the Roman World.* **Jeremias, J.** *Jerusalem in the Time of Jesus.* **Johnston, S. I.** *Hekate Soteira.* ———. *Divination.* **Jordan, D. R.** "Curse Tablets of the Roman Period," 133–210. ———. "New Greek Curse Tablets," 5–46. ———. "Survey of Greek Defixiones," 151–97. **Jordan, D. R.,**

**and R. D. Kotansky.** "Two Phylacteries from Xanthos," 167–74. **Keil, J.** "Ein rätselhaftes Amulett," 79–84. **Klauck, H.-J.** *Magic and Paganism.* **Klutz, T. E.** *Rewriting the Testament of Solomon.* **Kotansky, R. D.** "Silver Votive Plaque," 139–57. **Kraabel, A. T.** "Judaism in Western Asia Minor." **Kraus, T.** *Hekate.* **Lane Fox, R.** *Pagans and Christians.* **Lange, A., H. Lichtenberger, and K. F. D. Römheld.** *Die Dämonen.* **Laumonier, A.** "Inscriptions de Carie," 291–380. **Lesses, R. M.** *Ritual Practices to Gain Power.* **Levinskaya, I. A.** "Syncretism." **Lightstone, J.** *Commerce of the Sacred.* **Luck, G.** *Arcana Mundi.* **Magie, D.** *Roman Rule.* 2 vols. **Manoledakis, M.** "Hekate with Apollo and Artemis," 289–302. **McCown, C. C.** "Ephesia Grammata in Popular Belief," 128–40. ———. *Testament of Solomon.* **Merkelbach, R.** "Ein Orakel des Apollo," 70–72. **Merkelbach, R., and J. Stauber.** "Orakel des Apollon," 1–54. **Meyer, M. W., and R. Smith.** *Ancient Christian Magic.* **Mitchell, S.** *Anatolia.* 2 vols. **Morgan, M.** *Sepher Ha-Razim.* **Naveh, J.** "Fragments of an Aramaic Magic Book," 252–61. **Naveh, J., and S. Shaked.** *Amulets and Magic Bowls.* **Nilsson, M. P.** *Geschichte der griechischen Religion.* 2 vols. ———. *Greek Popular Religion.* **Nock, A. D.** "Greek Magical Papyri," 176–94. **Parke, H. W.** *Oracles of Apollo.* **Pfanz, H., et al.** "Deadly CO2 Gases in the Plutonium of Hierapolis, 359–71. **Piccardi, L.** "Denizli Basin Earthquake," 95–105. **Preisendanz, K.** "Ein Wiener Papyrusfragment," 161–67. ———. "Salomon," 660–704. **Ramsay, W. M.** *Cities and Bishoprics of Phrygia.* 2 vols. **Ritti, T.** *Epigraphic Guide to Hierapolis.* **Robert, L.** "Épitaphes d'Eumeneia de Phrygie," 414–39. **Rudolph, K.** "Syncretism," 68–87. **Schäfer, P.** *Origins of Jewish Mysticism.* **Schniewind, J.** *Euangelion.* **Schwarz, S. L.** "Reconsidering the *Testament of Solomon*," 203–37. **Segal, A. F.** "Hellenistic Magic," 79–108. **Sheppard, A. R. R.** "Jews, Christians and Heretics," 169–80. **Simon, M.** *Verus Israel.* **Smith, M.** "Jewish Assimilationists," 207–12. **Strubbe, J. H. M.** "Cursed Be He that Moves My Bones," 33–59. ———. *Imprecations against Desecrators.* **Swartz, M. D.** "Jewish Magic and Mysticism," 182–93. **Torijano, P. A.** *Solomon the Esoteric King.* **Van Lennep, H. J.** *Travels.* **Watson, L. C.** *Magic.* **Wessely, K.** *Ephesia Grammata.* **Williams, G.** *Spirit World.* **Wünsch, R.** *Antikes Zaubergerät.*

> I adjure you by God who created the earth and the heavens.
> I adjure you by the angels, Cherubim, the harmony above.
> [I adjure you] by Michael, Raphael, Abrasax . . .
> That I might be averted from injury!

This magical text was inscribed on a silver scroll, rolled up, inserted in a silver tube, and placed in a tomb in the necropolis of Hierapolis during the Roman era. It was published in 2004 by M. Aydaş shortly after it was discovered.[258] This invocation well illustrates many of the contentions that I will make in this section and throughout the commentary: that magic was practiced in the Lycus Valley, that an important part of magic consisted of invoking angels, spirits, gods, and divine helpers, and that magic was inherently syncretistic. This text, in particular, illustrates calling on angels for help and deliverance and thereby provides us with insight into "the worship of angels" in Col 2:18. If this invocation text belonged to a Jew, which is quite possible because of the predominance of Jewish names and themes, it is surprising to see that the pagan

258 Aydaş, "New Inscriptions from Asia Minor," 124. The translation is by Aydaş, but I have introduced a few minor modifications.

god, Abrasax, is invoked alongside Michael and the creator God. The existence of this text also presupposes that there was someone in this community with the requisite wisdom and knowledge of matters pertaining to the spirit world to create the text. Such an individual, whom we might call a "magician" or a "shaman," may have served the community by creating such texts and may have been called in to help when an individual, or part of the community, was afflicted by illness, disease, a curse, or the evil eye.

There is little doubt that many in the Lycus Valley (including Colossae) would have engaged in magical practices and consulted practitioners with arcane knowledge and wisdom for help. Although no magical texts or materials have been found in Colossae, it is only a matter of time until future excavation makes these discoveries. Magical practices are attested in the Lycus Valley and throughout Roman Asia, including its provincial capital, Ephesus. It is also likely that some of the Jews of this area practiced magic—especially because of the widely attested evidence of the invocation of Jewish angels and the presence of the Solomonic magical tradition in Asia Minor.

## *Magic*

In the ancient world, magic represented a ritual means of gaining spiritual power and managing life's issues with ritual practices, incantations, invocations, and formulas that solicited help from supernatural beings. There were a multiplicity of uses for magic that included protection, healing, and revelatory insight. But there was also a darker side to magic that involved malevolent intent and bringing harm to individuals. Graf notes that magic was "omnipresent in classical antiquity,"[259] and this continued throughout the Hellenistic, Roman, and Byzantine eras. The increasing evidence of the practice of magic that is becoming available through archaeological discovery is crucial for understanding the lives of common people throughout the Roman world. As Brashear comments, "These relics of a bygone age are direct and eloquent testimony to the thoughts and beliefs of the man and woman in the street, briefly lifting the veil that otherwise obscures so much of their lives."[260] This is true not only of pagans but also of Jewish people, as Alexander stresses:

> Incantations and books of magic . . . open up areas of popular religion which are often inadequately represented in the official literary texts, and which are in consequence frequently ignored by historians. As an indicator of the spiritual atmosphere in which large sections of the populace lived—rich and poor, educated and ignorant—their importance can hardly be overestimated. Magic flourished among the Jews despite strong and persistent condemnation by the religious authority.[261]

259 Graf, *Magic in the Ancient World*, 1.
260 Brashear, "Recent Corpora of Magical Texts," 383.
261 Alexander, "Incantations and Books of Magic," 342.

This was particularly true in Asia Minor of pagans, Jews, and also of Christians. Thus, the phenomenon of magic is something that we cannot ignore in the interpretation of the NT, and especially, Colossians.

## Defining Magic

The definition of *magic* has been widely debated in recent years. The topic is fraught with complexity, especially in attempts to differentiate "magic" from "religion." Scholars of a previous generation portrayed magic as a perversion of the purity of religion. In his 1925 introduction to the publication of some magical papyri, S. Eitrem characterized these texts as "interesting relics of degenerate religions and of the human mind gone astray."[262] In his magisterial work on Greek religion, M. Nilsson's chapter on magic is titled, "Der niedere Glaube" (i.e., "low," "base," or "ignoble" belief).[263] But identifying a sharp line of demarcation has proven to be elusive. There are many concepts and practices in the magical papyri that would fit the traditional understanding of religion—such as prayers, hymns, initiation rituals, and seeking oracular information. Conversely, there are practices in the traditional religious cults that have the appearance of what has often been termed magic.

More recent attempts to define magic have considered it from the vantage point of the anthropological concepts of "insider" (emic) and "outsider" (etic) perspectives. This gives proper consideration to the social contexts of those who use the term "magic," and the related terminology.[264]

From the insider view, one can observe that a practitioner of magic could self-identify as a "magician" (μάγος),[265] "wise man" (σοφιστής),[266] "priest" (ἱερεύς),[267] or even "prophet" (προφήτης).[268] These adepts understood what they did as a specialized art that they could practice privately or even within the context of the sanctioned cult. They claimed to possess special insight into the realm of supernatural powers and could use their wisdom and knowledge to accomplish a variety of purposes for individuals or for the benefit of the community. They alone knew the right spirits or gods, names, symbols, invocations, and rituals to accomplish specific tasks. This is why desperate people dealing with the effects

262 Eitrem, *Papyri Osloenses. Fasc. 1. Magical Papyri*, preface (as cited in Aune, "Magic in Early Christianity," 1511n7). See also the discussion in Graf, *Magic in the Ancient World*, 13–14.

263 Nilsson, *Geschichte der griechischen Religion*, 2:520. Elsewhere, Nilsson referred to magic as "the decay of old religion" (see his *Greek Popular Religion*, 115).

264 Segal, "Hellenistic Magic," 81, astutely observed that "no definition of magic can be universally applicable because 'magic' cannot and should not be construed as a properly scientific term. Its meaning changes as the context in which it is used changes."

265 See *PGM* IV.243, 2081, 2289, and LXIII.4–5.

266 See *PGM* IV.157.

267 The term *magos* came from the Persians and designated a priest; see Graf, *Magic in the Ancient World*, 20. Much of the material in the Greek magical papyri reflects the spells of Hellenized Egyptian priests.

268 See *PGM* III.254; VII.323.

of a curse, for instance, would seek out such individuals and pay them money for their expert help. Or, alternatively, magic could be used to place a curse upon an enemy. This can be seen, for instance, in a spell reportedly originating from the Egyptian prophet/magician Pachrates (perhaps the same person described by Lucian [*Philops.* 34]), which twice uses the term "magic" (μαγεία) to describe the practice:

> Pachrates, the prophet of Heliopolis, revealed it [the spell] to the emperor Hadrian, revealing the power of his own divine magic [μαγείας]. For it attracted in one hour; it made someone sick in 2 hours; it destroyed in 7 hours, sent the emperor himself dreams as he thoroughly tested the whole truth of the magic [μαγείας] within his power. And marveling at the prophet, he ordered double fees to be given to him. (*PGM* IV.2445–55)

Magic was regularly judged by its effectiveness (e.g., "for the invocation to Selene is very effective [ποιεῖ μεγάλως]," *PGM* VII.879, or "[this charm to restrain] works on everything," *PGM* XXXVI.1), which contributes to an understanding of the utilitarian character of magic. L. Watson thus rightly notes that magic was "highly pragmatic" and "goal focused"; it was believed to work.[269] A. D. Nock differentiated magic from later Gnosticism by asserting that the readers of the gnostic work Pistis Sophia "were passionately eager to know how the wheels went round, the authors and readers of the magic papyri desired simply to be able to make them turn."[270]

F. Graf thus understands magic as "an autonomous domain within religious practice" that emerged as early as the classical era of Greek history.[271] He is right not to distinguish magic sharply from the traditional religions because the practitioners of magic would not have done so. Magicians and sorcerers in the Roman world were adherents to the traditional Greek and Roman religions and would not have seen their practices as falling outside the boundaries of the cult. They simply had acquired specialized knowledge on how to access the power of the deity and its associated spirits for accomplishing certain purposes. They were also recognized by their respective communities as experts who could render assistance to members of the community to address various kinds of problems. In his earlier essay on the definition of magic, Aune rightly characterized it as "a substructure of religious systems."[272] This persective on magic may help to understand how the leader(s) behind the problem at Colossae

269 Watson, *Magic*, vii, 3.

270 Nock, "Greek Magical Papyri," 193.

271 Graf, *Magic in the Ancient World*, 30. See also Janowitz, *Magic in the Roman World*, 1–8.

272 Aune, "Magic in Early Christianity," 1557. Similarly Fraser, "Roman Antiquity," 122, comments that in Hellenistic and Roman Egypt, "the self-definition of the priest-as-magus should be viewed not as an external stereotype, but as an image elaborated within Egyptian priestly circles over the course of centuries, beginning in Ptolemaic times with figures like Manetho."

saw no problem in combining their arcane insights into the spiritual realm with their recently acquired acceptance of Jesus Christ and their commitment to the local church.

Nevertheless, magic could also involve a set of malevolent practices that were not authorized by the cult and certainly not by civic authorities. Curses and *defixiones* were intended to harm people and clearly ran afoul of ordered society. This often let to proscriptions against magic by civic officials. In these cases, a sharp distinction was made between magic (which was illegal) and the practices of the local religions (which were legal). It is unknown whether the practitioners of magic at Colossae would have limited themselves only to protective magic and avoided other forms that sought to bring harm.

The terms used for "magic" could thus be used in a pejorative and accusatory sense by outsiders. Roman elites like Pliny sought to maintain the purity of Roman religion and characterized magic as "monstrous rites" worthy of eradication and something to be feared and avoided.[273] This stems primarily from the forms of "black" magic and curses that were a constituent part of the traditions and practices. But "witchcraft accusations" could be a handy way of denigrating and defaming one's enemies in the ancient world.

Because of the theoretical confusion regarding the term magic, some have begun speaking of the phenomena as performances of "ritual power." Meyer and Smith thus subtitle their collection of Christian magical papyri as "texts of ritual power."[274] They find this expression to be a less value-laden description than "magic" or "religion." They contend that the descriptive label "ritual power" best represents the nature of these texts. As texts of ritual power, "they direct the user to engage in activities that are marked off from normal activity by framing behavior through rules, repetitions, and other formalities."[275] Similarly, in her important monograph on the Hekhalot literature, R. Lesses concludes that a more useful way of analyzing these practices is "as ritual performances to gain power."[276] Other scholars have followed suit.[277] I have noted elsewhere that the expression "texts of ritual power" is accurate in describing magical documents and the practices they prescribe, but it is not sufficient to describe the common characteristics of what have traditionally been called magical texts. In other words, it is possible to be much more specific regarding what constitutes "ritual" in the expression, "ritual power." The following characteristics should also be included:

---

273 Pliny the Elder, *Nat.* 30.13; see the discussion in Fraser, "Roman Antiquity," 115, 125–26.

274 Meyer and Smith, *Ancient Christian Magic*.

275 Meyer and Smith, *Ancient Christian Magic*, 4.

276 Lesses, *Ritual Practices to Gain Power*, 11.

277 E.g., Boustan, Dieleman, and Sanzo, "Authoritative Traditions and Ritual Power," 3–10; Davila, *Descenders to the Chariot*, 40, notes, "I will avoid the term 'magic' in favor of 'ritual power'"; Schwarz, "Reconsidering the *Testament of Solomon*," 213; et al.

1. There is an identifiable form to the charms and spells. Most of the so-called magical texts can be observed to have two or three of the following elements: (a) a rite to perform, (b) an invocation (including a list of the appropriate names to call upon), and (c) a statement of command (versus request), usually given in the aorist imperative (in Greek texts).
2. As we have already seen above, magic was perceived to guarantee results; it was understood to be effective (ἐνέργεια). If one followed all the details of the instructions for the prescribed rite and invocation, it was thought that one would experience success.
3. Magical documents have an array of terminology given specialized significance. Perhaps the most common is the term for conjuration that appears in the vast majority of the documents: ὁρκίζω or ἐξορκίζω. For example, in one Jewish exorcistic recipe (*PGM* IV.3007–86), the phrase, "I conjure you" (ὁρκίζω σε) appears fourteen times.
4. The documents invariably include a series of names or characters (often unknown to the modern interpreter). Scholars sometimes refer to these as "Ephesia Grammata."[278] The document may also include a figure or drawing, thought to be laden with power.[279]

These were constituent elements of the magician's technique that set them apart from other religious functionaries in a cult. From an emic perspective, these were essential ingredients of the art. But from an etic perspective, evidence of these practices could attract the charge of "magic" or "sorcery." In summary, although there is much more that can be said on this topic, I will use the term "magic" throughout this commentary as "the art of the *magos*," which is the sense used by many of the ancients.[280]

## Shamanism

I will also make use of the anthropological concept of *shamanism*, an etic term, to characterize the practitioners of magic. A shaman figure serves his community through his knowledge of spiritual power.[281] Persons afflicted or harassed by evil spirits go to the shaman for help and deliverance because he has wisdom about such things and knows the rituals of power that will be effective.[282] Visionary experience is often foundational to becoming a shaman since it is

278 See Wessely, *Ephesia Grammata*, 1–38.

279 Taken from my *Colossian Syncretism*, 14–15.

280 Thus also Graf, *Magic in the Ancient World*, 18, 20.

281 Taken from my article, "Sceva, Solomon, and Shamanism," 19–20.

282 DuBois, *Shamanism*, 82, notes, "Human beings find themselves in a mysterious web of seen and unseen forces. Frail and limited figures in themselves, they are set in largely unconscious relation to a vast array of powerful sentient beings who hold the keys to success or failure in their lives. Amid this complex and threatening world, the shaman emerges as a crucial mediating figure."

through a personal vision that the shaman gains his power.[283] In addition, ascetic practices such as fasting, dietary restrictions, abstinence from sex, and other taboos are essential for a shaman to have a visionary experience.[284]

A generation ago, W. Burkert wrote an important article establishing the importance of the concept of shamanism to describe the significant role played by practitioners of magic in the Greek world. He contended that the term was coextensive with the Greek term γόης, "sorcerer,"[285] and that this figure was not only closely connected with the cultic form of the Greek mysteries but was central to the practice of Greek religion.[286] He notes that from the earliest stage of Greek religion there have been individuals who, because of their special knowledge and abilities, served as medicine men, magical priests, and shamans.[287]

Other scholars have now been using the term *shaman* to describe the function and role of the figures practicing magic within communities—even within Judaism. In his important monograph *The Commerce of the Sacred*, J. N. Lightstone argued that the Jewish text, Sepher ha-Razim, is an important piece of evidence demonstrating the presence of certain Jewish holy men functioning as shamans in the diaspora.[288] The visionary ascent to heaven, according to him, "grounds the authority of the theurgist and provides the measure of the extent of that authority."[289] This shaman figure therefore wields spiritual insight, power, and authority that he can use to help others within the community deal with the influence of these hostile forces.

Similarly, J. Davila has argued convincingly that the adepts described in the Hekhalot literature correspond to the anthropological model of shamanism.[290] He argues that "a central element of the Hekhalot texts themselves is the quest for ritual power."[291] Davila rightly explains that the control of spirits is a central feature of shamanism in all cultures. It also plays a significant role in the Hekhalot writings. In these documents, the spirits controlled by the shaman are angels.[292] Through rituals of power, the Jewish shaman adjures the angels and controls them for various practical purposes in the community—for example, to grant revelations, to serve as guides in otherworldly journeys, to grant wishes, to provide protection from demonic spirits, and to bring healing.[293] As Davila notes, one of the Hekhalot documents, the Ma'aseh Merkavah, "provides seals,

283 See Davila, *Descenders to the Chariot*, 47.
284 Davila, *Descenders to the Chariot*, 306.
285 See Burkert, "ΓΟΗΣ," 36–55.
286 Burkert, "ΓΟΗΣ," 40–41.
287 Burkert, "ΓΟΗΣ," 43.
288 Lightstone, *Commerce of the Sacred*, 16–22.
289 Lightstone, *Commerce of the Sacred*, 31.
290 Davila, *Descenders to the Chariot*, 49, 306.
291 Davila, *Descenders to the Chariot*, 42.
292 Davila, *Descenders to the Chariot*, 211.
293 Davila, *Descenders to the Chariot*, 212.

invocations, and rituals for protection from hostile angels and harmful demons" (§§560–66) as well as incantations "designed to protect against 'angels and harmful demons.'"[294]

The concept of shamanism appropriately emphasizes the role that the ritual expert plays for the well-being of the community. It also provides an important corrective to the notion of Nock and others that with magic we are now "in the sphere of individualist religion."[295] There certainly can be an individualist element to magic, but the practitioner also serves the needs of the community.

I have argued elsewhere that the Jewish exorcist and priest identified by Luke as Sceva in Acts 19 functions as a shaman for Ephesus and the surrounding communities.[296] One of my contentions in this commentary will be that the opposing teacher at Colossae is a Sceva-like figure functioning as a shaman for Colossae and elsewhere in the Lycus Valley.

## Sources for Understanding Magic

Our knowledge of magic in the Roman era has been enhanced significantly in recent years through the discovery of many documents and artifacts related to its practice. These include papyri, inscribed magical gems and thin sheets of metal (amulets or phylacteries), and lead tablets. Some of these discoveries have come from Phrygia and western Asia Minor, which I will note below.

*Magical Papyri.* One of the most significant finds in the last century and a half has been the discovery of roughly 250 magical papyri in Egypt.[297] These texts include rituals, spells, charms, formulae, invocations, magical words and symbols, curses, recipes for amulets, and all of the rest of the phenomena that is typical of Roman-era magical practices. These texts have been published in a two-volume set called the *Papyri Graecae Magicae* (*PGM*), edited by K. Preisendanz.[298] These Greek texts and a handful of Egyptian demotic texts have been translated into English and made available in a volume edited by H. D. Betz titled, *The Greek Magical Papyri in Translation* (2nd ed.). All of these papyri come from Egypt; none have been found in Asia Minor or elsewhere. But this has strictly to do with Egypt's climate, which has been conducive to the preservation of papyri—not only magical texts but papyrus fragments and copies of the NT as well. Graf rightly observes that "it must be assumed that such magic texts also had existed on papyrus outside of Egypt."[299] Luke's account of the burning of the magical texts in Ephesus (Acts 19:19) provides independent attestation of the use of magical papyri in western Asia Minor. The *PGM* texts

294 Davila, *Descenders to the Chariot*, 210.
295 Nock, "Greek Magical Papyri," 231.
296 "Sceva, Solomon, and Shamanism," 6–26.
297 See my "Magical Papyri," *DNTB* 665–70.
298 See also Daniel and Maltomini, *Supplementum Magicum*.
299 Graf, *Magic in the Ancient World*, 3.

represent a strong affinity of type with the kind of magical texts that would have been in use in Ionia, Caria, Lydia, and Phrygia.

*Amulets.* Amulets provide another important source of evidence for understanding magic in antiquity. They were charms either worn or carried by a person for protection from attacks by evil spirits or as a means of enhancing one's power or influence.[300] They often contain texts of invocations along with magical symbols, words, names, and figures that were inscribed on gems or stones or on thin pieces of metal (including gold or silver). Hundreds of amulets have been discovered throughout the Mediterranean world and many from western Asia Minor. A surprising number of Jewish amulets have also been found. Numerous amulets are unprovenanced because they have found their way onto the black market. There are two important corpora of magical amulets: one compiled by R. Kotansky titled, *Greek Magical Amulets*, and another by E. Zwierlein-Diehl titled, *Magische Amulette und andere Gemmen*.[301] Kotansky's collection includes four from Asia Minor (nos. 34, 35, 36, and 37). No. 36 is a silver lamella that comes from Amisos (Pontus) and dates to the first century BC or first century AD. No. 37 is a gold lamella dating as early as the second century AD from Ephesus. In a more recent article, Kotansky published a second-century AD silver lamella that may have originated in Phrygia.[302] In 1890, the Athens Institute discovered at Pergamum a magical apparatus that included three burnished black stone amulets, which was subsequently published by R. Wünsch.[303] Fourteen lines of the inscription on the amulets consist of magical names and characters, but the fifth line is remarkable because it includes the names of four Jewish angels: Michael, Gabriel, Ragouel (two of the three spell it "Ragousel"), and Raphael. They are invoked next to the pagan deities, Sthenno and Mercury. The underworld goddess, Hekate, figures prominently in the rest of the apparatus. A number of other amulets, especially of a Jewish character, have been discovered in Asia Minor (see below).

*Defixiones. Defixiones* or curse tablets represented a form of malevolent magic that was present throughout the Mediterranean world, including Phrygia and western Asia Minor. Over sixteen hundred of these have been discovered, and that number continues to increase.[304] Unlike papyri, which deteriorated with age and weather, lead curse tablets survived in about any climate. D. R. Jordan describes them as texts that were "intended to influence, by supernatural means, the actions or welfare of persons or animals against their will."[305] Many of these

300 See my article, "Amulets," *ESTJ* 2:24–25.

301 See also C. Bonner, *Studies in Magical Amulets* (1950). For Jewish magical amulets, see J. Naveh and S. Shaked, *Amulets and Magic Bowls* (1985) and E. R. Goodenough, *Jewish Symbols in the Graeco-Roman Period, Volume 2: The Archaeological Evidence from the Diaspora* (1952).

302 Kotansky, "Silver Votive Plaque," 139–57.

303 Wünsch, *Antikes Zaubergerät.*

304 Gager, *Curse Tablets*, 3.

305 Jordan, "Survey of Greek Defixiones," 151.

were written on thin sheets of lead, rolled up, and deposited in a tomb or a well. There are two main corpora of texts: one published by R. Wünsch titled, *Antike Fluchtafeln* (originally published in 1897 with a second edition appearing in 1912), and another compiled by A. Audollent titled, *Defixionum Tabellae* (1894). Since these two volumes were published, numerous additional texts have been discovered, but no recent corpus of texts has been published. Jordan announced in 1985 that he was preparing a corpus of Greek *defixiones*,[306] but he was unable to complete this task, and no one else has taken it up. He has, however, published two important checklists of Greek *defixiones* that are not included in the published copora.[307] J. Gager has published an English translation of select *defixiones* in his *Curse Tablets and Binding Spells from the Ancient World* (1992). Of special interest is a tablet found in the upper Maeander Valley (not far from Colossae) dating to the second century.[308] On one side, the text reads (following a series of magical signs): "I adjure you, demons, according to the written name, to make my opponents and whoever else pleads for them to be judged guilty." Six victims are then named. The other side of the tablet begins with the same curse, but then invokes Gē, Hekate, Hermes, and underworld gods. Gager includes a lead tablet in his volume coming from Claudiopolis (Bithynia), in which a man seeks to bind a large number of men and women to stop them from informing against him. The spell invokes a number of divine beings (indicated by magical names) along with "lord gods" (κύριοι θεοί), angels (ἄγγελοι), Abrasax, Ereschigal, and Iao in an extraordinary syncretistic mix.[309] In his collection of texts, Audollent publishes thirteen from Cnidus in Caria (the region just southwest of Colossae) that range in date from 300 BC to 100 BC, and one from Phrygia.[310] The Cnidus texts overlap with what some scholars are calling judicial prayers. One example from this group reads: "Artemis 'dedicates' to Demeter and Kore and all the gods with Demeter, the person who would not return to me the articles of clothing, the cloak and the stole, that I left behind . . . let him burn, and let him publicly confess his guilt. . . . For I have been wronged, Mistress Demeter."[311] On a number of tombs and grave markers in Phrygia are inscriptions bringing curses against anyone who would inter someone in the private tomb.[312]

*Inscriptions.* In addition to the inscriptions found on amulets and *defixiones*, other inscriptions illustrating the practice of magic in western Asia Minor have been discovered. Kotansky published a silver plaque that records a woman's invocation of a local deity, in which she seeks vengeance against certain people slandering her by accusing her of using a magical spell (φάρμακος) against

306 Jordan, "Survey of Greek Defixiones," 154.

307 See Jordan, "Survey of Greek Defixiones," 151–97, and idem, "New Greek Curse Tablets," 5–46.

308 Jordan, "Survey of Greek Defixiones," 194 (no. 168).

309 Gager, *Curse Tablets*, 137–38 (no. 47). The Greek text is in Cormack, "*Tabella Defixionis*," 26.

310 Audollent, *Defixionum Tabellae*, 5–20 (nos. 1–14).

311 Audollent, *Defixionum Tabellae*, 8 (no. 2); translation by Kotansky, "Silver Votive Plaque," 140–41.

312 Chiai, "Phrygia," *RAC* 27:706.

her husband.[313] The famed *Ephesia Grammata*, said by Pausanias (the Atticistic lexicographer) to have been inscribed on the cultic image of the Ephesian Artemis, may have had a Phrygian origin.[314] These six names, representing powerful and active spirits, are attested in many documents beginning in the fourth century BC. Graf published an inscription found on a stone slab in Ephesus that speaks of a pestilence caused by the evil art of a sorcerer (this will be more fully discussed below).[315] A bronze tablet from Asia Minor dating to the early Roman era records an invocation to "the mother of the gods" (probably Cybele), appealing to her for the return of stolen property and seeking the punishment of the thief.[316] And, finally, to the east of Colossae in the territory of Pisidia is a relief carved on a rock face, depicting an evil eye pierced by a spear and a dagger with animals attacking it (including a scorpion, a snake, and a crab).[317] These represent simply a sampling of the kinds of inscriptions discovered in western Asia Minor.

## The Issue of Date

The phenomenon of magic was not only widespread throughout the Mediterranean world and ancient Near East but was continuously practiced in every society from the time of earliest written records and throughout the Hellenistic and Roman periods. Whereas a religion such as Gnosticism had a definite point of origin (most likely at the end of the first or early second century), the practice of magic reaches back as early as the Hittite era in Anatolia.[318]

Over sixteen hundred Greek curse tablets (*defixiones*) have now been discovered, with the earliest dating to the sixth century BC and with many dating to the Hellenistic and Roman era.[319] They continue to be discovered in ancient wells and tombs. Most recently, a collection of thirty *defixiones* dating to the Roman era were found in a cistern and various wells in the Kerameikos area of ancient Athens and have now been published by D. R. Jordan.[320] All of these Greek *defixiones* possess an affinity of type with the Greek magical papyri, which contain recipes on how to construct them and what to inscribe on them (e.g., "take a lead tablet and write . . ."; *PGM* IV.329).

Similarly, the Greek amulets range in dates throughout the Hellenistic and Roman eras. The magical papyri contain instructions on how to create amulets and lamellas (e.g., "on a jasperlike agate engrave . . ."; *PGM* V.447).

Most of the Greek magical papyri in the Preisendanz collection are later than

313 Kotansky, "Silver Votive Plaque," 139–57.

314 McCown, "Ephesia Grammata in Popular Belief," 140.

315 Graf, "Oracle against Pestilence," 267–79.

316 Gager, *Curse Tablets*, 190–91 (no. 90).

317 Elliott, *Evil Eye*, 2:242.

318 See Goetze, *Kulturgeschichte Kleinasiens*, 151–61. He notes, "As with all ancient oriental people, so also with the Hittites, the magical occupies a large space alongside the religious."

319 Eidinow, *Oracles, Curses, and Risk*, 141.

320 See Jordan, "Curse Tablets of the Roman Period," 133–210.

the NT and date to the second, third, and fourth centuries. This has caused some scholars to question the use of them for illuminating the NT world and for interpreting Colossians.[321] Yet, one needs to take into account five important considerations: (1) the practice of magic did exist in the first century AD and much earlier. This is clear from the abundant literary testimony, as well as the evidence from amulets and *defixiones*. (2) The NT itself attests to the practice of magic. This is especially seen in the book of Acts—most notably the burning of the magical texts in Ephesus in the mid-first century AD (Acts 19:19), but also the situation involving Bar-Jesus/Elymas on Cyprus, who was a Jewish magician (μάγος) attached to the proconsul, Sergius Paulus (Acts 13:6–12), as well as Simon "who practiced magic" (μαγεύων) in Samaria (Acts 8:9–25). (3) There are magical papyri that date to the first century AD and earlier. The oldest Greek magical text on payrus (and one of the oldest Greek papyri every discovered) is *PGM* XL, which dates as early as the time of Alexander the Great (4th c. BC).[322] The next three oldest texts date to the first century BC (*PGM* XX, CXVII, and CXXII).[323] Some texts date to the first century AD (*PGM* XVI and CXI).[324] (4) Many of the formulas, spells, and traditions in the magical papyri were prized by those who wrote these texts as old and venerable. Brashear has noted that the papyrus texts as we have them today "cannot be the original works of the scribes who penned them, but are rather compilations from a multitude of various sources."[325] Similarly, Luck comments, "Although their [the magical papyri] date is relatively late (third or fourth century AD), they reflect much older ideas, and the doctrines and techniques they embody were probably developed in the late Hellenistic period. Many are considered to be copies of copies."[326] In fact, the preservation, transmission, and use of spells thought to be ancient was fundamental to the practice of magic. Thus, some of the spells in the third- and fourth-century papyri may have actually been created in the first century and earlier. For instance, based on a tradition-historical study of *PGM* I.300–305 and *PGM* III.211–24 (the final form of which both date to the fourth century), M. Smith has argued that these spells originated in the first century AD or even the first century BC.[327] Regarding the largest of the magical texts, the Great Paris Magical Papyrus (*PGM* IV), Brashear has asserted that although the papyrus was written early in the fourth century AD, it "has more the character of a text composed two hundred years earlier."[328] He also suggests that some of the hymns embedded in

321 See, e.g., Witherington, 109–10.

322 See Brashear, "Greek Magical Papyri," 3413. It is incorrectly labeled as fourth century AD in the list of dates of the papyri in the introduction to Betz, *Greek Magical Papyri in Translation*, xxiv.

323 Brashear, "Greek Magical Papyri," 3413.

324 Brashear, "Greek Magical Papyri," 3414.

325 Brashear, "Greek Magical Papyri," 3415–16.

326 Luck, *Arcana Mundi*, 16. With respect to Jewish magic, compare the same contention of Alexander, "Incantations and Books of Magic," 344. See also Meyer and Smith, *Ancient Christian Magic*, 7.

327 Smith, "Jewish Assimilationists," 207–12, esp. 212.

328 Brashear, "Greek Magical Papyri," 3419.

the papyri may date to the first century BC.[329] (5) There is a significant similarity of form, content, and language between the third- and fourth-century Greek magical papyri and their first-century counterparts. This evidence suggests that we should use the Greek magical papyri in NT studies, but we need to do so with caution. Specific lexical items only attested in third- and fourth-century texts, for instance, should only be used tentatively and provisionally.

## *Magic and Ritual Power in Phrygian, Carian, and Lydian Local Belief*

> I adjure you, demons, by the name written [on this tablet],
> that you would carry out judgment on Marius Macrinus . . .
> I adjure you by her—Ge, Chthon, Hekate, chthonic Hermes,
> underworld Lethe—
> I adjure you by them and the rest of the gods
> that you would carry out judgment on Macrinus . . .
> I adjure you, demons, by the underworld gods . . .

This magical text was discovered in the upper Maeander region, which places it near the western end of the Lycus Valley, just a few miles west of Colossae. This lead tablet, dated to the second century, was published in 1940 by F. K. Dörner,[330] but it has largely been unnoticed in scholarship, and not at all noticed by NT scholars despite its proximity to Colossae and Laodicea. The person who wrote this curse wants vengeance against Marius Macrinus for making a claim against his vineyard. The Greek text is accompanied by a series of magical symbols (*characteres*). The suppliant invokes a number of underworld deities who are summoned to cause harm to Marius Macrinus. Among the deities invoked is Hekate—an underworld deity frequently associated with curses.

### Hekate: The Goddess of Witchcraft and Magic

Hekate was an Anatolian deity whose cult center was in Lagina (Caria), about seventy miles southwest of Colossae (near Stratonikeia).[331] She was widely worshiped and invoked throughout Phrygia and certainly would have been known and revered in Colossae. Although never mentioned in Homer or the Homeric fragments, Hekate is frequently called upon in curse tablets and magical texts. For Christians living in the Lycus Valley, she would have been a source of fear since she was the supernatural functionary of curses from whom they would need protection.

As the principal goddess of magic, witchcraft, and sorcery, she was regularly invoked in magic. She fulfilled this role because she was believed to wield power

329 Brashear, "Greek Magical Papyri," 3421.

330 Dörner, "Eine neue Fluchtafel," 64–71.

331 Kraus, *Hekate*, 31, 51.

over demons, spirits, and the souls of the dead, which she could order to do her bidding. Alois Kehl remarks that "in the common belief of Greco-Roman civilization, Hekate appeared above all as the ruler of darkness, of terror, of the dead, of demons, and of magic."[332] As the goddess who possessed the "keys of Hades," she controlled the passageway to the underworld,[333] and because of this she had the ability to control the apparitions or souls who ascended to do the magician's bidding.[334] She could inflict sickness, bring night terrors, cause calamities, capture a lover, or bring insanity. But she could also be called upon to avert evil. In folk belief, the intersection of roads was commonly thought to be a dangerous place and potentially haunted by evil spirits. As "goddess of the crossroads," a well-known epithet of Hekate,[335] her statue was set up at various intersections of roads in Asia Minor.

The statuary and depictions of Hekate often represent her as a three-sided figure (*triformis*). Whether this signifies her connection to Artemis, Selene, and Persephone, the sway she held over the moon, the earth, and the underworld, her association with the moon in its three phases, or because she is the goddess of the crossroads is unknown. One of the epithets by which she was known was ἄγγελος, "angel/messenger,"[336] which may emphasize her mediatorial role with the underworld and the supernatural world. She was also worshiped as θεῖος ἀγγελικός, "divine messenger," in Stratonikeia, where she was seen as an underworld deity and associated with Zeus.[337]

The important role she played in the folk belief of Asia Minor (and Phrygia, in particular) is often neglected in scholarship. She completely escapes the notice of Huttner in his otherwise important volume on the Lycus Valley.[338] And she receives only a passing mention by Mitchell in his two-volume work on Anatolia.[339] Nevertheless, she features prominently in the material evidence of Phrygia. Kraus lists seventeen different cities and areas of Caria for which evidence of Hekate worship exists (including Aphrodisias, Straonikeia, and Lagina). He provides the evidence for nineteen different cities of Phrygia.[340] This includes the Lycus Valley cities of Hierapolis and Laodicea, in which coins depicting the three-formed Hekate have been discovered. One of these coins depicts Hekate with a moon crescent at her shoulders and carrying two torches with

332 A. Kehl, "Hekate," *RAC* 14:315 (translation mine).

333 Kraus, *Hekate*, 50–51; Kehl, "Hekate," 320; J. Heckenbach, "Hekate," PW 7.2773.

334 See Johnston, *Hekate Soteira*, 146.

335 E.g., *PGM* IV.1432: "O mistress Hekate . . . O Lady of the Crossroads."

336 See Farnell, *Cults of the Greek States*, 2:517–18, 601.

337 Laumonier, "Inscriptions de Carie," 337–39.

338 Huttner, *Early Christianity in the Lycus Valley*.

339 Mitchell, *Anatolia*.

340 See Kraus, *Hekate*, 166–68 (= appendix 1, "Hekate-Zeugnisse aus Karien und Phrygien"). See also Buckler, Calder, and Cox, "Monuments from Central Phrygia," 88–89, who cite evidence from the Phrygian cities of Acmonia, Amorium, Apamea, Appia, Cotiaeum, Tiberiopolis, Ancyra, Peltae, Laodicea, Cibyra, and Lysias.

an inscription of the city name, Hierapolis.[341] A coin from Laodicea bears the image of the triform Hekate with each holding torches, a dagger, a whip, and a serpent.[342] An altar dedicated to Hekate was found at Sebaste (about forty-five miles north of Colossae) with the inscription, "belonging to Hekate: the village of the oracle."[343]

The syncretistic character of religion in the Roman era is illustrated by a second-century AD invocation of Isis in an Egyptian papyrus that claims that in Caria, Isis was worshiped as Hekate (*P.Oxy.* 1380.113). The text describes other ways that Isis was identified with other gods.

Her local connections to magic, witchcraft, and divination are not only seen in the curse tablet from the upper Maeander (cited above), but also in the way she figures prominently in a magical apparatus discovered in Pergamum. She is depicted holding the keys to the underworld on the three corners of a bronze divination table discovered there.[344] This is consistent with the pervasive role she plays in the Greek magical papyri where she is commonly invoked in various spells.[345]

## The Association of Artemis with Hekate

In the magical texts, Hekate had a strong connection to Artemis as well as the moon goddess, Selene.[346] There were, in fact, a number of hymns in the magical papyri dedicated to Hekate-Selene-Artemis.[347] All of these deities wielded power over threatening spirits. They could be called upon for protection or invoked to effect a curse.

We know that Artemis was worshiped at Colossae (see above). Because of this, it is likely that Hekate worship was present at Colossae. Farnell has asserted that "any centre of the cult of Artemis was likely to attract the worship of the kindred goddess," as was the case with the presence of a Hekate statue in the precincts of the sanctuary of Artemis at Ephesus.[348]

---

341 Head, *Greek Coins of Phrygia*, 236.

342 Head, *Greek Coins of Phrygia*, 323.

343 Buckler, Calder, and Cox, "Monuments from Central Phrygia," 88–89.

344 Wünsch, *Antikes Zaubergerät*, 11–13. See also Heckenbach, "Hekate," 2773.

345 See, e.g., *PGM* III.47; IV.1432, 1443, 1462, 2119, 2610, 2632, 2692, 2714, 2727, 2730, 2745, 2751, 2815, 2880, and 2957. For an indication of how often she is invoked in *defixiones*, see Audollent, *Defixionum Tabellae*, 461–70 (= index IV: "Nomina et Cognomina Deorum Daemonumque Invocatorum").

346 See esp. Hopfner, "Hekate-Selene-Artemis," 125–45. See also Heckenbach, "Hekate," 2770–71; Kraus, *Hekate*, 34–36; and my *Ephesians: Power and Magic* (ch. 2, the section titled "Artemis and Magic").

347 See Preisendanz, *PGM* (Stuttgart edition) 250–60, for hymns 18 (= *PGM* IV.2786–870), 19 (= *PGM* IV.2574–610 and 2643–74), 20 (= *PGM* IV.2522–67), and 21 (= *PGM* IV.2714–83). For further discussion, see Hopfner, "Hekate-Selene-Artemis," 125–45, who devotes special attention to the variety of epithets ascribed to these deities.

348 Farnell, *Cults of the Greek States*, 2:506, cited approvingly in Manoledakis, "Hekate with Apollo and Artemis," 295.

The people of Asia Minor would have been familiar with invoking Artemis and Hekate as ἄγγελοι, "angels/messengers," in the context of seeking ritual power. This term was a well-known epithet in Asia Minor and beyond for both of these deities.[349]

## Artemis and Apollo Conquering a *Defixio* of a Magician

An important inscription that helps fill out the picture of the practice of magic in western Asia Minor was found in a pavement block in the city of Ephesus and published in 1991.[350] The text refers to a devastating plague that struck the area around Sardis and quite possibly a much broader area. Graf and others have suggested that it refers to a great plague that was carried from Mesopotamia to Asia Minor by the armies of Lucius Verus in AD 165 (during the reign of Marcus Aurelius).[351] This plague is mentioned by ancient historians and a number of oracle texts from various locations. A delegation was sent form the city of Sardis to consult the oracle of Apollo at Claros. The inscription provides the response from the god. Most notably, Apollo attributes the source of the plague to the work of a magician and points to the Ephesian Artemis as the means of their deliverance:

> For help, you have to look to Artemis with the golden quiver. . . . Her form bring in from Ephesus, brilliant with gold. Put her up in a temple, full of joy: she will provide deliverance from your afflication and will dissolve the poison (or: magic, φαρμάκα) of pestilence, which destroys men, and will melt down with her flame-bearing torches in nightly fire the kneaded works of wax, the signs of the evil art of a sorcerer (μάγος).[352]

Graf suggests that the text is referring to a magician who constructed a *defixio* and performed the associated rituals of power.[353]

Although Artemis could be invoked to effect a curse, she could also be called upon to come to the aid of those who worship her. Because of the covenant bond she had with the city of Ephesus, she had a special interest in the well-being of that population. It is unsurprising that the Clarian Apollo would point the petitioners to the Ephesian Artemis for help. Not only was she the sister of Apollo, with both of them descended from Leto, but Artemis was revered in magic as having power over the underworld, terrestrial spirits, and astral spirits. She held sway over the powers ritually invoked by the sorcerer. The torches she

349 For the texts, see Schniewind, *Euangelion*, 2:223–35.
350 Merkelbach, "Ein Orakel des Apollo," 70–72.
351 Graf, "Oracle against Pestilence," 271. See also Magie, *Roman Rule*, 1:663.
352 Translation from Graf, "Oracle against Pestilence," 268–69.
353 Graf, "Oracle against Pestilence," 269, 276. So also J. R. Harrison, "Artemis Triumphs over a Sorcerer's Evil Art," *NewDocs* 10:40 (§8).

carries associates her with Hekate, and "Hecate easily leads to magic."[354] Here she functions as Artemis Soteira, which also overlaps with the role in deliverance Hekate could play as Hekate Soteira.[355]

This pestilence oracle likely describes the same plague referenced in a series of oracles given to other cities of western Asia Minor. What is of special interest to us here is an oracle of the Clarian Apollo to the people of Hierapolis. In what Ritti has described as "one of the most interesting religious texts of the town,"[356] the text of the inscription reflects a situation in which the people of Hierapolis turned first to Apollo Karieos for answers on how to be delivered from the pestilence they were facing, but ultimately decided to consult the Apollo of Claros. The delegation returned with an answer from the god, and it was inscribed on stone and set up in the city.[357] Here are some of the words from that oracle:

> You are not the only ones to have been hit by the destructive miseries of the mortal pestilence, hard to heal. Many are, instead, the towns and the people afflicted by the vindictive malevolence of the gods. I order you to avoid the anger of the deities that brings pain, through thorough libations and feasts and hecatombs. In the first place you must offer to Earth [Γαίῃ], mother of all, a cow . . . Then offer to the Ether [Αἰθέρι] and to the gods of the heavens [ἐπουρανίοις τε θεοῖς] a whole lamb . . . Then, as is your custom, perform rites addressed to Deo [Δηοῖ, Demeter] and to the subterranean gods [ἐνερτερίοις τε θεοῖσιν] with immaculate victims, and offer libations to the infernal heroes beneath the earth [ἥρωσίν τε χοὰς χθονίοις], according to the rites . . . And in front of all the gates of your town consecrate precincts that contain a sacred image of Phoebus Clarius [Apollo of Claros], armed with his bow that kills the malady, in order to drive away with the arrows the insatiable malady. And furthermore, when the evil forces of the dead will return placated . . .[358]

Unlike the previous oracle, this inscription does not comment on whether the indirect cause of the malady could be attributed to a sorcerer who summoned these deities and spirits. These powers not only need to be appeased, but the god, Apollo of Claros, needs to avert the evil with his arrows. It is rather surpising that given the prominence of three local forms of Apollo at or near Hierapolis—that is, Apollo Archegetes, Apollo Lairbenos, and Apollo Kareios, that the city would send an embassy to consult the Apollo at Claros. This may have

354 Graf, "Oracle against Pestilence," 275.

355 Graf, "Oracle against Pestilence," 275–77.

356 Ritti, *Epigraphic Guide to Hierapolis*, 97.

357 The text of the inscription was initially published by Carratelli, "ΧΡΗΣΜΟΙ di Apollo Kareios," 358–65. See also R. Merkelbach and J. Stauber, "Orakel des Apollon," 1–54, and J. R. Harrison, "Artemis Triumphs over a Sorcerer's Evil Art," in *NewDocs* 10:37–47 (§8). The translation here depends on Ritti, *Epigraphic Guide to Hierapolis*, 96.

358 Ritti, *Epigraphic Guide to Hierapolis*, 96.

something to do with the Clarian Apollo's antiquity, prominence, and special reputation for averting plagues.[359] Once the plague is averted, the people of Hierapolis are instructed to send a delegation to Colophon (Claros) and provide a thank offering to Apollo.

It is instructive to note that many delegations from cities who traveled to Claros to consult the oracle were required to perform ritual initiation as essential preparation for receiving the oracle. As I will show later (in the commentary on 2:18), the second stage of this ritual initiation was called "entering" (ἐμβατεύω) at Claros—the very word that Paul uses to describe a certain feature of the competing teaching at Colossae. It may be likely that they did go through this two-stage initiation at Claros since, as W. Burkert notes, the central idea of mystery initiation had to do with appeasing the active powers of destruction that are a threat to daily life in the present.[360]

This inscription underlines the local belief in the reality of evil powers (or gods) who can bring destruction and harm. This was a concern for people living in the Lycus Valley (and beyond) that would not have disappeared once they became followers of Christ and joined the local Christian communities. The issues for them could be formulated in two questions: "What difference does Christ make?" and, "Do I continue to use these traditional means of dealing with plagues, curses, and various forms of evil?"

## The Plutonium of Hierapolis and Underworld Beliefs

In the excavations of Hierapolis taking place in 1962–1965, archaeologists uncovered an opening in the ground emitting noxious fumes that was located immediately adjacent to the temple of Pluto.[361] This was identified as the famed Plutonium—an entrance to the underworld. More recent excavations carried out by D'Andria in 2011–2014, however, uncovered a subterranean grotto beneath the rows of stone seats within the sanctuary of Pluto. This grotto was an integral part of the sanctuary of Pluto (Hades) and Kore (Persephone). The new location for the Plutonium was confirmed by an inscription, "to Pluto and Kore," inscribed under the seats in a stone row.[362] The ancient geographer, Strabo, provided a detailed account of his observations of the Plutonium. He characterizes it as "an opening of only moderate size, large enough to admit a man, but it reaches a considerable depth" and "is full of a vapour so misty and dense that one can scarcely see the ground" (*Geogr.* 13.14 LCL). He goes on to describe how bulls that are led into it fall dead because of the vapor, but notes how the eunuch priests of Cybele, the *Galli*, were immune to the effects of the vapor. The gas emission coming from this site has been identified as primarily

359 Parke, *Oracles of Apollo*, 155.

360 Burkert, *Ancient Mystery Cults*, 24.

361 See D'Andria, *Hierapolis of Phrygia*, 142–44.

362 Pfanz et al., "Deadly CO2 Gases in the Plutonium of Hierapolis," 1361–62.

carbon dioxide ($CO_2$), but also traces of hydrogen sulfide ($H_2S$), methane ($CH_4$), and other gasses are present and still in strong enough concentrations to kill insects, birds, and mammals, and a human being within a minute.[363] The origin of these gasses is related to Hierapolis being located over an active fault, the Babadag fracture zone.[364] This is associated with the intense thermal activity of the area, resulting in the hot springs that have produced the travertine deposits.

As an opening to the underworld, the Plutonium would have been understood as a place of access to the underworld gods and souls of the departed. The existence of the Plutonium in Hierapolis may explain, in part, why there was such an extensive necropolis that extended to the north nearly two miles, with over two thousand tombs identified thus far. But these chthonic deities and the spirits they command could emerge from the underworld to cause terror and be summoned for curses (see below on the Phrygian practice of cursing tomb desecrators).

For centuries before the Roman era, such openings were seen as avenues for commerce with underworld spirits and gods. As far back as the Hittite era, pits served "as a channel for the chthonic deities."[365] Similarly, hot springs were also a gateway for supernatural powers. One scholar notes that "in the religious experience of the ancient rural population hot spings were products of awesome supernatural chthonic powers."[366] Rituals of power could be employed to invoke these deities and spirits. As we have seen with the *defixiones*, these underworld gods were frequently called upon to effect curses.

Although the Plutonium at Hierapolis was often associated with Cybele, it came to have a stronger connection with the chthonic god of the underworld, Hades (Pluto). A statue of Hades was discovered in the city and is now on display in the Hierapolis Museum.[367] A number of coins from Hierapolis depict the abduction of Persephone by Hades.[368] The drama was also depicted in series of reliefs in the theater of Hierapolis.[369]

## The Phrygian Custom of Putting a Curse on Tomb Desecrators

Another form of cursing that was practiced in Phrygia (and throughout Asia Minor) was the creation of imprecations against anyone despoiling a tomb.[370] These funerary imprecations were inscribed on the tomb and warned any potential violator that evil would come upon them if they were to defy the warning.

363 Pfanz et al., "Deadly CO2 Gases in the Plutonium of Hierapolis," 1359.

364 Piccardi, "Denizli Basin Earthquake," 97–98.

365 Collins, "Necromancy," 226.

366 Croon, "Hot Springs and Healing Gods," 246.

367 D'Andria, *Hierapolis of Phrygia*, 226 (fig. 207).

368 See Head, *Greek Coins of Phrygia*, 233, 242, 254.

369 D'Andria, *Hierapolis of Phrygia*, 180, 222 (fig. 202), 226–27.

370 See the discussion in Strubbe, "Cursed Be He that Moves My Bones," 33–59 (his essay is based on his 1983 PhD dissertation).

Such grave curses were seldom used outside of Asia Minor,[371] which is likely due to the fact that this was an indigenous Anatolian practice. Over three hundred and fifty of these texts have now been discovered in Asia Minor.[372] The earliest instances of these inscriptions begin at the fourth century BC, but a large number date to the Roman imperial period. The gods most commonly called upon in these tomb inscriptions were the underworld gods (χθόνιοι, καταχθόνιοι, or ὑποχθόνιοι θεοί) sometimes along with the heavenly gods (οὐράνιοι θεοί). But the moon gods, Mēn and Selene, were also commonly invoked as well as Hekate.[373]

One example of this form of imprecation comes from the tomb of P Ail. Apollinarios Makedon in Hierapolis. This second-century inscription reads:

> The man who does anything against the prescriptions will be liable to fines, and may he not know the pleasure of children and of life, may the earth be not accessible and the sea not navigable, but may he die with all sufferings, childless and destitute and deformed, and may he find after his death the gods of the underworld [τοὺς ὑποχθονίους θεούς] punishing and enraged, both the man who has ordered it to be built or made, and the workman.[374]

D'Andria notes that this menacing warning "has led to this tomb being nicknamed the 'Tomb of the Curse.'"[375] Another inscription from northern Phrygia threatens the potential violator that if anyone commits an offense "against the stele or the heroon, he would have to reckon with Heavenly Hekate in her wrath."[376]

Inscriptional evidence from Judaism in Phrygia demonstrates that some of the Jews took over this Anatolian practice and implemented it in their own burial rites. A Jewish grave epitaph discovered in Laodicea threatens that anyone who places another body into the tomb other than the deceased for whom it had been constructed will be liable to "the curses that are written in Deuteronomy."[377] Van der Horst thinks that the reference is to the curses of Deut 28 (although the contexts are quite different). Chiai suggests that the mention of Deuteronomy should perhaps be interpreted against the background that Jews in the Roman era were often involved in magic and sorcery.[378] Here we have an example of

371 Strubbe, "Cursed Be He that Moves My Bones," 38.

372 Strubbe, "Cursed Be He that Moves My Bones," 36.

373 Strubbe, "Cursed Be He that Moves My Bones," 46.

374 *CIG* 3915. Cited from Cadwallader and Harrison, "Perspectives on the Lycus Valley," 52. Greek text published in Strubbe, *Imprecations against Desecrators*, §285.9–12, and in Ritti, *Epigraphic Guide*, 56–59 (who also includes pictures of the tomb).

375 D'Andria, *Hierapolis of Phrygia*, 58.

376 Cited in Mitchell, *Anatolia*, 1:188.

377 *IJO* 2.213. See the discussion in van der Horst, "Jews of Ancient Phrygia," 287. Two similar texts were discovered in Acmonia (*IJO* 2.173, 174).

378 Chiai, "Norm, Kommunikation und Identität," 129.

local Jews adopting some of the local practices and justifying it under the veneer of a scriptural warrant.

A grave inscription in Eumenia (fifty-one miles NNE of Colossae) warns the potential tomb violator with the following consequence:

> (Property) of one who still lives. I, Lycidas, cite God as my witness, that I build the heroon by my own labours, as my brother Amianus was reluctant, and I authorize only my sisters Phronime and Mixima to be placed (in it). If anyone inters another [here], he will have to reckon with God and the angel of Roubes [τὸν ἄνγελον τὸν Ῥουβῆδος].[379]

Roubes (or Reuben) is a distinctively Jewish name, which has led some interpreters to regard this inscription as Jewish. It is not completely certain whether the inscription is Jewish or Christian, but even if it is Christian,[380] it demonstrates that the Jewish idea of calling upon angels for protection also penetrated early Christianity.

### *Mystery Initiation, Visionary Experience, and Spiritual Knowledge*

The evidence suggests that the Colossian "philosophy" had some connection to mystery initiation ritual, visionary experience, and esoteric knowledge that was imparted through the rite (see below in the section titled "The Rival Teaching"). Initiation rituals into the mysteries of the deities were common to the local religions of western Asia Minor. Many of the deities worshiped in Asia Minor were known to have mystery initiation rituals, such as Cybele (*Magna Mater*, or the Great Mother), the Ephesian Artemis, Apollo, Dionysus, Aphrodite, Sabazios, and other territorial deities. The language of the mysteries is found in some of the inscriptions of Asia Minor with such terms as μυστήρια, ἐπιτελέω, μύησις, μυέω, τελετή, and more, appearing in them with reference to these rituals. It is of great significance that a technical term for the highest stage of ritual initiation in the cult of Apollo at Claros, ἐμβατεύω, actually appears in Col 2:18 as part of Paul's description of the teaching of the faction he opposes. Although this term has not yet been attested in the inscriptions of the Lycus Valley, we know that Hierapolis and Laodicea both had embassies that traveled to Claros to consult Apollo. A Clarian epigraphic oracle was also found at Hierapolis. We have already observed that the god Apollo was very significant at Hierapolis and was worshiped at Colossae.

All interpreters are agreed that visionary experience of some sort was a key component of the experience of the rival teachers at Colossae. But this visionary

379 Robert, "Épitaphes d'Eumeneia de Phrygie," 429–30. The translation here is from Sheppard, "Jews, Christians and Heretics," 175–76.

380 This is the opinion of Robert, "Épitaphes d'Eumeneia de Phrygie," 432, Sheppard, "Jews, Christians, and Heretics," 176, and Lane Fox, *Pagans and Christians*, 294–95, who regards "Roubes" as a Christian (although possibly a converted Jew).

experience is closely connected to mystery initiation ritual, as suggested by the linkage of the term ἐμβατεύω to ὁράω in Col 2:18 (ἃ ἑόρακεν ἐμβατεύων). Visionary experience was a significant part of all mystery initiation rituals. The celebrated mysteries of Demeter and Kore at Eleusis culminated in a vision called the ἐποπτεία—a cognate term of ὁράω (ὀπτεύω = ὁράω).[381]

Although one needs be mindful of the unique features of the mystery initiation rituals in the cults of individual deities, as well as of the variety of motivations adherents may have had in undergoing an initiation rite, there were commonalities. What I would stress here is that the revelation of the deity in the culminating vision would lead to the possession of secret knowledge.[382] The acquisition of such spiritual knowledge and arcane wisdom was foundational to the practice of magic. A prospective magician, or shaman, would seek initiation so that he could effectively perform his practices.[383] Graf has written specifically on this matter in a book chapter titled, "How to Become a Magician: The Rites of Initiation."[384] He notes that there is a "close relationship between magic and mysteries."[385] "The magician," he says, "without any doubt, considered himself the adept of a mystery cult, who underwent a ritual, an experience very close to that of the well-known mystery cults." Initiation would change the status of an individual and bring the adept under the care of the deity.[386] Fraser observes that "it was not by setting himself against the gods of heaven, but by aligning himself with them, that the magician is able to harness the powers of the underworld."[387] He concludes that the magician "understands himself first and foremost as an initiate, specially consecrated and empowered through his intimate connection to the Supreme Deity."[388]

The magical papyri are full of references to the performance of initiatory rites and describe the benefits accruing to the initiate. Betz has described this phenomena in an important essay titled, "Magic and Mystery in the Greek Magical Papyri."[389] I will provide three examples from the magical papyri:

- One passage describes how to acquire a supernatural assistant through initiation: "He will serve you suitably for [whatever] you have in mind, O blessed initiate [ὦ μακάριε μύστα] of the sacred magic [μαγείας], and will accomplish it for you, this most powerful assistant [πάρεδρος], who is also the only lord of the air. . . . Share this great mystery [μυστήριον] with

---

381 See LSJ, s.v. ὀπτεύω.

382 Fraser, "Roman Antiquity," 115.

383 Graf, "Magician's Initiation," 97.

384 Graf, *Magic in the Ancient World*, 89–117. See also his essay, "The Magician's Initiation," 161–77.

385 Graf, *Magic in the Ancient World*, 97.

386 Graf, "Magician's Initiation," 170.

387 Fraser, "Roman Antiquity," 136.

388 Fraser, "Roman Antiquity," 136.

389 Betz, "Magic and Mystery in the Greek Magical Papyri," 209–29.

no one else, but conceal it, by Helios, since you have been deemed worthy by the lord god" (*PGM* I.127–31).

- Another text demonstrates how a magician draws on his initiation for a protective charm: "Charm of Hekate Ereschigal against fear of punishment: "I have been initiated [τετέλεσμαι], and I went down [κατέβην] into the [underground] chamber of the Dactyls, and I saw [εἶδον] the other things down below . . . say it . . . it will save you [σώσει σέ]" (*PGM* LXX.4–25). Betz has written an essay contending that this text contains actual elements of the initiation liturgy of the Idaean Dactyls, dwarfish sprites associated with the Great Mother worshiped in Phrygia, Cybele.[390]
- This final text comes from the so-called Mithras Liturgy and refers to the handing down of mysteries from Mithras through the mediation of an archangel as part of an initiation ritual: "Be gracious to me, O Providence and Psyche, as I write these mysteries [μυτήρια] handed down [παραδοτά] [not] for gain but for instruction; and for an only child I request immortality, O initiates [μύσται] of this our power . . . which the great god Helios Mithras ordered to be revealed to me by his archangel [ἀρχαγγέλου], so that I may ascend into heaven as an inquirer and behold the universe" (*PGM* IV.475–86).[391]

Intiation provides the suppliant with knowledge of supernatural things and elevates the status of the individual from a mere mortal. Through the ritual, the initiate has a vision of divine realities, with the secrets of the supernatural realm unlocked before his eyes. Graf states that "the idea that knowledge is divinely bestowed during an initiatory process was widespread in Imperial times and certainly was not confined to magic alone."[392] During initiation, the magician could obtain the secret names of the gods and unintelligible magical names (*voces magicae*), which were essential to the operation of magic. The initiation would also bestow the adept with authority to command lesser *daimones* and spirits. As Fraser notes, "the knowledge of the divine names demonstrated the magician's attainment of this initiated status and empowered him to command infernal spirits."[393] But initiation could also bestow upon the magician a πάρεδρος (*paredros*)—a supernatural spirit assistant who could help in the performance of magical rituals, divination, and obtaining dreams.[394]

390 Betz, "Catabasis Ritual," 287–95.

391 Betz, "Magic and Mystery in the Greek Magical Papyri," 228, argued that this text contained actual liturgy from the mystery initiation rites of the god, Mithras. However, he contended that the text was adapted for the purposes of the magician and would have meant "dragging the great tradition down into the muddy waters of 'magic.'" See also his entire volume devoted to the discussion and commentary on this text: *The "Mithras Liturgy": Text, Translation and Commentary*.

392 Graf, "Magician's Initiation," 162.

393 Fraser, "Roman Antiquity," 137 (see also p. 115).

394 Graf, "Magician's Initiation," 168.

To be sure, not everyone who was initiated into the mysteries of a deity became a magician.[395] But a magician needed to be initiated in order to be an effective shaman. Magicians also had some of their own rituals of initiation outside of the official cults. But Betz is correct in noting that for the magician, "magic and religion are a single entity,"[396] even though it may not have been perceived the same way by the official cult.

A ritual specialist initiated into the mysteries, a shaman figure, could serve the community well by providing healing remedies, protection from curses, deliverance from harmful spirits, and mediating supernatural insights. This person would be highly sought after because of their specialized spiritual knowledge. Because of this, the magician possessed an unofficial authority within the community to deal with issues and problems. Such an individual may very well have been the person Paul perceived to be disrupting the Colossian community.

### *Jewish Magic and Practitioners of Ritual Power*

Jewish involvement in magical practices is well-attested for the Roman era in Palestine and throughout the Mediterranean world.[397] Jews living in Asia Minor, Phrygia, and the Lycus Valley also embraced many of these practices. A. T. Kraabel was the first to compile much of the evidence for Asia Minor, including Phrygia, in his (unfortunately) unpublished 1969 Harvard PhD dissertation.[398] The Phrygian evidence was sufficient for M. Simon to conclude that the syncretism underlying magic was common in the Judaism of Phrygia.[399] He saw this syncretism as essential for understanding the problem at Colossae. Regrettably, few scholars on Colossians followed his lead on this explanation of the Colossian "philosophy."

Much of the local evidence for Jewish magic in western Asia Minor can be seen in the amulets, tomb inscriptions, and curse tablets that have been discovered. Of course, the climate was not conducive to the preservation of papyri, so we should not expect to find any magical papyri (or papyri of any kind). We are also hindered in our search because magical traditions were generally transmitted orally, so we are limited in what we can expect to find. Yet there is

---

395 Johnston, *Divination*, 156, observes that "mainstream mystery initiations sought contact with the gods to ensure prosperity and a happy afterlife; magical mystery initiations, as we see them in the papyri spells, sought contact in order to learn."

396 Betz, "Magic and Mystery in the Greek Magical Papyri," 217. He claims that the evidence from the Greek mystery cults "definitely suggest that magic was a constiuent element in the rituals of the mysteries" and that "one can assume that magic was a constitutive element of the mystery-cults from their inception" (220).

397 There is an extensive bibliography on this topic, but see especially Bohak, *Ancient Jewish Magic*; Lange, Lichtenberger, and Römheld, *Die Dämonen*; Lightstone, *Commerce of the Sacred*; Lesses, *Ritual Practices to Gain Power*; Goodenough, *Symbols*, vol. 2; Simon, *Verus Israel*, ch. 12 ("Superstition and Magic"), Alexander, "Incantations and Books of Magic," 342–79.

398 Kraabel, "Judaism in Asia Minor under the Roman Empire."

399 Simon, *Verus Israel*, 341, 367–68.

the possibility of some literary remains associated with Asia Minor that we will examine at the end of this section.

## Amulets

A characteristic feature of Jewish amulets is the tendency to invoke angels to fight against the demonic powers. The invocation of angels in Jewish rituals of power to expel demons and ward off attack (see Col 2:18) is a staple part of this folk tradition within Judaism. Bohak notes, "The appeal to angels, which is echoed in *Tobith* and is apparent in the exorcistic texts, seems to have grown hand in hand with the Jewish demonology and angelology of the last few centuries BCE, but it will remain a permanent fixture of Jewish magic for many centuries to come."[400] The Jewish magical amulets dating from the Roman period and late antiquity continue this tradition. These were generally worn around the neck or somewhere on the body and were ritually empowered to fend off evil spirits.

A simple example of this is an unprovenanced amulet that is housed in the Kelsey Museum at the University of Michigan.[401] The amulet depicts an anguipede (a man's body with a rooster's head and snakes as legs). Both of these figures are common in apotropaic magic. The inscription on the upper right side of the amulet reads: "Michael, Raphael, Gabriel, Ouriel." Another unprovenanced Jewish amulet invokes angels, but also features Solomon. This limonite stone amulet on one side depicts Solomon as a mystagogue, haloed, and holding a scroll.[402] A snake is portrayed beside him, perhaps a symbol of the demonic over which Solomon has power. The inscription reads, βοήθι, "help." On the reverse side is the inscription, "Ouriel, Sabao, help!," a clear invocation of two angels widely known in Judaism. The Semitic characters at the top probably represent magical words of some kind.

Admittedly, the discovery of Jewish amulets in the Lycus Valley is quite sparse for now. But because of the strong Jewish presence in the area, I would expect that more will come to light in the future. Nevertheless, Jewish amulets have been found west, south, north, and east of the Lycus Valley. Many have also been found in Palestine and elsewhere. What follows is a summary of the known Jewish amulets from western Asia Minor. Note the magical words at points.

*Thiounta (just north of Hierapolis, Phrygia).* The inscription on this amulet reads, "Lord, help! aaaa Michael e Gabriel, Istrael, Raphael." Ramsay, who first published this document, noted that the inscription "is interesting in view of the early prevalence of the worship of angels in the Lycos Valley (Thiounta was subject to Hierapolis)."[403]

---

400 Bohak, *Ancient Jewish Magic*, 141.

401 Bonner, *Studies in Magical Amulets*, 281 (§172).

402 See the discussion of this amulet in Goodenough, *Symbols*, 2:232. See also Bonner, *Studies in Magical Amulets*, 310 (§339).

403 Ramsay, *Cities and Bishoprics of Phrygia*, 1:541 (no. 404).

*Philadelphia (Lydia).* Two fragments from a marble plaque found in Philadelphia represent an incantation to prevent hail.[404] The text invokes Sabaoth, "the throne of the Lord," and the angels Raphael, Ragouel, and Istrael alongside a series of magical vowels. It is possible that it is a pagan invocation heavily influenced by Judaism, but it is more likely a Jewish invocation.

*Cyzicus (Mysia).* An amulet discovered in a Roman cemetery in the city of Cyzicus (Mysia) bears the inscription,[405] "Michael, Gabriel, Ouriel, Raphael, protect the one who wears this. Holy, holy, holy. ΠΙΠΙ[406] RPSS." On the reverse side it reads, "Angel Araaph, Flee, O hated one: Solomon pursues you." In the center of the amulet is the figure of a horseman (probably best interpreted as Solomon) led by an angel and depicted spearing a demonic figure and a snake.[407] The motifs of the amulet are predominantly Jewish—the angel names, the mention of Solomon, the trisagion, and the Greek imitation of the divine name. But there are also depictions of pagan deities and a drawing of the evil eye, demonstrating its syncretistic character. The demonic name "Araaph" is otherwise unattested except in one other amulet from Carthage.[408] A similar name, "Arapha" (Arapha) appears in *PGM* XIII.778 as part of a series of magical names—including some Jewish names—in an invocation of the god, Agathos Daimon. Dorigny surmised that it was cognate to the Arabic word for a nosebleed.[409]

*Smyrna.* A similar amulet was found in Smyrna that has many of the same features: the mention of Solomon, an evil angel named Araaph, and the trisagion, "holy, holy, holy."[410] The inscription on the obverse side reads, "Seal of the living God. Protect the one who wears this. Holy, holy, holy Lord. Sabaoth, the heaven and earth is full of [your] glory." On the reverse side around the edges, the inscription is: "Flee, hated one, O angel Araaph. Solomon pursues you from the one wearing this." The mention of the "seal" evokes the Solomonic magical tradition, especially as represented by the Testament of Solomon (see below). Although the exemplar of the amulet Jewish themes, this particular amulet was likely appropriated for Christian use since on the front side an image of Christ appears between the sun god and the moon god, while on the reverse side the

404 *TAM* V.3.1659. See H. Gregoire, *Recueil des inscriptions grecques-chrétiennes d'Asie Mineure*, 1.124 (no. 341).

405 Dorigny, "Phylactère alexandrin," 287–96; Goodenough, *Symbols*, 2:229–30 (fig. 1052); Preisendanz, "Salomon," 682; Cline, "Archangels," 69–72. Dorigny dates it to the middle of the second to early third century.

406 These four Greek letters represent a crude way of writing the Tetragrammaton in Greek script. Torijano, *Solomon the Esoteric King*, 136, takes it as constituting "further evidence of the age of the charm and of its probable Jewish origin."

407 Goodenough, *Symbols*, 2:229, contends that Araaph is a good angel in league with Solomon. But it is better to follow Dorigny, "Phylactère alexandrin," 290, and take Araaph as an evil spirit that Solomon fights. So also Cline, "Archangels," 71.

408 Preisendanz, "Salomon," 683.

409 Dorigny, "Phylactère alexandrin," 294.

410 Homolle, "Nouvelles et corresponance: Ionie," 638.

cavalier Solomon carries the cross.[411] The amulet provides an important example of the use of the Solomonic magical tradition in Christian circles in Asia Minor. Like many of the other amulets, it also illustrates how syncretism occurred in the context of magic. Yet another amulet discovered in Smyra simply bears the inscription, "seal of Solomon, help!"[412] In the mid-1800s, van Lennep reported seeing "many signet stones having the same characters, and all coming from the regions south of Smyrna."[413] One of these had a representation of the Jewish menorah. Another made reference to the name "Abrasax," a popular deity in magic appearing frequently in Jewish magic,[414] along with other magical names.[415]

*Ephesus.* An amulet found in Ephesus contains an invocation to the "ever living Adonai" on one side and, on the other, contains eleven letters in a Hebrew cryptographic scheme known as athbash.[416] A gold lamella from Ephesus lists the cosmic powers of twenty-six angels known in Judaism.[417]

*Xanthos (Lycia).* The text of a silver phylactery discovered near a tomb in the city of Xanthos (about 110 miles due south of Colossae) reads: "holy *oistuchia* [read *stoicheia*], holy *characteres* powerful and strong, drive away every wicked demon, occurence or happening or encounter or evil eye, drive and chase them away from Ioannes, whom Thoktiste bore, now, now, quickly, quickly!"[418] The first thirteen lines contain numerous magical *characteres*, names, and letters; the final eight lines of the text do the same. Among the names mentioned are a handful of Jewish names including Adonai, Sabaoth, and Iao. This does not automatically render the text Jewish, but it remains a possibility. The only known pagan deity named is the Egyptian god, Ptah. Significantly for the interpretation of Col 2:8, 20 is that this text represents the only known instance of στοιχεῖα being invoked in a magical text in Asia Minor.

The city of Xanthos yielded another phylactery lamella. This amulet belonged to an otherwise unknown Christian named Epiphanius and reveals not only a dependence on the Solomon tradition but the prevalent impulse to syncretize by invoking a pagan deity alongside Christ (the Lord) and Jewish angels. It reads:

> Lord, help the bearer [of this tablet] Epiphanius, whom Anastasia bore. I adjure you Solomon, the great Angel Michael, Gabriel, Ouriel, Raphael. I adjure you

411 See the image in Homolle, "Nouvelles et corresponance: Ionie," 638, and a discussion in Goodenough, *Symbols*, 2:231.

412 Preisendanz, "Salomon," 676.

413 Van Lennep, *Travels*, 20.

414 See Bohak, *Ancient Jewish Magic*, 248.

415 See Goodenough, *Symbols*, 2.221

416 Keil, "Ein rätselhaftes Amulett," 79–84.

417 Fitzwilliam Museum (Cambridge): GR 63.1905. See the mention in Brenk, "Exorcism," 11n18. The lamella remains unpublished. I possess photographs of it.

418 Jordan and Kotansky, "Two Phylacteries from Xanthos," 167–74.

> Abrasax. I adjure you in Hebrew: thaobarao Sabaoth, Epiphanius . . . Iaw . . . Iao . . . noeitho . . .[419]

This amulet reveals why canon 35 of the synod held in Laodicea sometime near AD 350 found it necessary to prohibit the invocation of angels and referred to the practice as a secret idolatry.[420]

In addition to the Jewish amulets that I have cited are numerous published amulets invoking angels that cannot be identified as specifically Jewish, pagan, or Christian because of their syncretistic character.[421] It is precisely here in the practices of ritual power in the ancient world where syncretism reaches its high points.

All of these amulets are notoriously difficult to date. They could date from anywhere in the Roman period or even into late antiquity. They are, however, consistent with what we know of the Jewish, Solomonic magical tradition. They represent a calling on the names of angels for deliverance from demonic powers. This is a form of Judaism that is not well-known and has been neglected in previous decades of academic study. Neverthless, it is an important window for understanding how many Jews in Israel and throughout the Roman world dealt with the reality of demonic influence and intrusion in their lives.

## The Solomonic Magical Tradition

This magical tradition about how to perform exorcisms and deal with the influence of demonic powers was long-standing within Judaism and purportedly was passed down from Solomon himself. Because of its widespread popularity, P. Torijano has noted that "one could say that the connection of ritual power and Solomon in some circles almost obscured the 'normative' representation of the biblical king."[422] As we have seen, this Solomonic tradition is reflected in many of the Jewish magical amulets. The tradition is initially mentioned in

---

419 Jordan and Kotansky, "Two Phylacteries from Xanthos," 167–74. See the discussion in Cline, *Ancient Angels*, 146–51.

420 For the text and translation, see Hefele, *History of the Councils*, 2:317–18. Hefele contended that "it hardly needs to be observed that this canon does not exclude a regulated worship of angels, such as is usual in the Church, although on the Protestant side it has often been so interpreted." Cline, *Ancient Angels*, 146–65, concurs (although he seems unaware of Hefele's statement) and attempts to make the case that part of the purpose of these decrees of the synod was to create an acceptable space for angel invocations within the church. Part of the positive evidence he cites for this kind of acceptable angel invocations does not work, however. The examples he gives from John Chrysostom represent prayers to God for the ministry of angels and not a direct invocation of the angels themselves; see Cline, *Ancient Angels*, 156–57.

421 One important publication of amulets depicts sixteen that include the name of angels. See Bonner, *Studies in Magical Amulets*, 280 (§168), 281 (§§171–72), 283 (§179), 288 (§208), 291 (§227), 300 (§280), 302 (§298), 304 (§§309, 310, 311), 305 (§313), 310 (§§338, 339, 342), 314 (§361). Numerous additional amulets invoking angels have been published in a wide array of journals. A complete corpus of amulets has yet to be published.

422 Torijano, "Solomon and Magic," 122.

the first-century BC Wisdom of Solomon. There the author claims that God gave Solomon "unerring knowledge of what exists" (Wis 7:17). This knowledge extended to the spiritual domain and included wisdom about "the powers of spirits" (πνευμάτων βίας; v. 20), the constellations of the stars (ἄστρων θέσεις; v. 19), and the powerful workings of the *stoicheia* (ἐνέργειαν στοιχείων; v. 17), which here should be understood as astral spirits or evil spirits.

The theme of Solomon's esoteric knowledge and abilities is also developed by Josephus in the eighth book of the *Antiquities*. Josephus describes how Solomon's extensive wisdom included insight on how to get rid of evil spirits. He says, "God also enabled him to learn that skill which expels demons. . . . He left behind him the manner of using exorcisms, by which they drive away demons, so that they never return" (Josephus, *Ant.* 8.45). In Josephus's view, this powerful, secret wisdom was then passed down for generations. He then describes a dramatic situation in which a Jewish man named Eleazar cast an evil spirit out of a man in front of a distinguished Roman audience that included the emperor Vespasian and his sons, Titus and Domitian (who also would, in turn, serve as Roman emperors). Also present for the event were a number of Roman officers and soldiers (*Ant.* 8.46–49). As Bohak notes, Josephus presents Eleazar as "an experienced, and we might even say professional, exorcist, who had the special implements and texts needed for this kind of ritual."[423] This Eleazar has much in common with the Sceva of Acts 19.

## The Testament of Solomon

The Solomonic magical tradition is well-illustrated in a Jewish magical handbook called the Testament of Solomon.[424] This document is a compilation of adjurations and magical wisdom that, in its final form, postdates the NT, but likely contains many traditions that were current during the time of Jesus and Paul. Like dealing with the rabbinic literature, one needs to be cautious in using this document, for it is often extremely difficult to discern which traditions are early and which are late.

There is one portion of this text, however, that may date as early as the first century BC. That is the eighteenth chapter. In his monograph titled *Rewriting the Testament of Solomon*, Klutz argued that the Testament reached its full form some time between the last quarter of the second century and the middle of the third.[425] Nevertheless, he contends (along with W. Gundel and others) that the

423 Bohak, *Ancient Jewish Magic*, 103.

424 Still the only critical edition of the Greek text (although badly in need of updating) is that of McCown, *Testament of Solomon*. The most recent translation and (only) commentary on the text is by P. Busch, *Das Testament Salomos*.

425 Klutz, *Rewriting the Testament of Solomon*, 35. Schwarz, "Reconsidering the *Testament of Solomon*," 203–37, argues that the final form of the testament came together later than Klutz posits. Nevertheless, she recognizes that "the individual spells were ancient elements, gathered over time into a spellbook collection" (208).

eighteenth chapter should perhaps be dated as early as the first or second century BC.[426] Part of the basis for this was the discovery of a fifth-century papyrus fragment of this chapter as well as the astrological decan tradition. Because this is one portion of the text that can be dated as existing before the NT era with reasonable certainty, I will only use this portion of the text for my purposes here.

A modern psychological reading of the text of Testament of Solomon 18 might regard it as an ancient version of the DSM-5 (the diagnostic manual for various diseases). The difference is that every ailment it lists traces the etiology of the problem to a demonic spirit and then prescribes how the spirit can be expelled. In this text, Solomon interrogates thirty-six demons, requiring them to divulge the nature of their assignments and how they can be defeated. These particular demons are astral spirits and correspond to every 10 degrees of the heavenly sphere. They describe themselves to Solomon as στοιχεῖα—the same term used in Wis 7:17 and that Paul uses in Col 2:8, 20 that is often translated as "elementary spirits" (T. Sol. 18.2). They also call themselves κοσμοκράτορες, "world rulers," another designation for spiritual powers that Paul uses in Eph 6:12 (T. Sol. 18.2). I am convinced that it is precisely from this kind of Jewish folk belief that Paul derives these terms.[427] It is highly doubtful that Paul coined these words for spirits himself. He more likely chose terms that would have been widely known among Jews to refer to demonic powers.

One by one these evil spirits, or στοιχεῖα, appear before Solomon and are forced to surrender the information that he seeks. When Solomon summons the first spirit, he says to him, "Who are you?" (T. Sol. 18.4). The spirit replies, "I am the first decan of the zodiac and I am called Ruax. I cause heads of men to suffer pain and I cause their temples to throb. Should I hear only, 'Michael, imprison Ruax,' I retreat immediately."

And so it goes on, one after the other, with each spirit revealing its name, a particular evil it accomplishes, and how it can be thwarted. Many of the spirits

---

426 Klutz, *Rewriting the Testament of Solomon*, 35. See also Gundel, *Dekane und Dekansternbilder*, 45, 92. Part of the evidence for this is the discovery of a fifth- or sixth-century papyrus containing a portion of T. Sol. 18; see Preisendanz, "Ein Wiener Papyrusfragment," 161–67 and Daniel, "The Testament of Solomon," 294–303. Schwarz, "Reconsidering the *Testament of Solomon*," 219, notes, "Such decan lists [as contained in T. Sol. 18] are known from earlier Egyptian sources, and, based simply on its form and content, this version could easily once have been an independent document. It is quite plausible that this chapter was one of the oldest portions of the story, and that it circulated independently of the rest until it was agglomerated with other Solomonic incantation materials at some later point."

427 Williams, *Spirit World*, 164–65, suggests that the later editor/compiler of Testament of Solomon may have been familiar with these terms from the NT and imported them into the document. That is possible, but this position presumes that Paul would have coined these terms, which is highly doubtful. As Duling, "Testament of Solomon," 201, rightly notes, "It is perhaps in this area of demonology (and angelology) that the Testament offers information which could be exploited for New Testament interpretation. . . . As commentators on the Pauline latters [sic] have observed, the selections on the *stoicheia* in *T. Sol.* 8 and 18 may provide background for attempting to understand the Galatian and Colossian heresies."

cause physical ills (such as damage to the eyes or ears, tumors, problems with the internal organs, fevers, convulsions, hysteria, and paralysis). Others incite relational problems in the home and the community (such as conflicts between husbands and wives, jealousies, strife, dissension, and perversions).

In sum, the eighteenth chapter of the Testament of Solomon is essentially a Jewish shaman's diagnostic manual. By looking at the presenting symptom, the holy man can identify the name of the demon causing the problem and then perform the appropriate spiritual intervention to alleviate the demonic attack and thus bring healing to the person.

What is of special interest to us here is that the demon is driven out by invoking an angel to perform the deliverance. But it cannot be just any angel. The Jewish healer needs to know the precise angel who has power to defeat the particular afflicting spirit. It does no good, for instance, to call on Gabriel if the person has a tumor. The angel who is effective for this is one named Sabael (T. Sol. 18.10).

I would suggest that it was precisely this kind of Jewish folk tradition that was behind the methodology Sceva and his sons employed in their itinerant ministry of exorcism within the Jewish communities of Asia Minor and, as I hope to further demonstrate, this tradition was at the heart of the problem at Colossae.

This magical tradition purportedly stemming from Solomon became well-known—even among the gentiles—in the Mediterranean world as very effective in dealing with harmful spirits. In a recent monograph published by Cambridge University Press titled *Ancient Jewish Magic*, G. Bohak argued that these magical traditions were generally passed on orally throughout the Second Temple period and only came to be written down in the third century and beyond.[428]

There is also first-century testimony about this Solomonic magical tradition at Qumran. The text is 11Q11, also known as 11QApocryphal Psalms[a] (or 11QPsAp[a]),[429] which dates to the middle of the first century AD. It is a five-column text, inscribed on vellum, and written in Hebrew. The overall function of this fragmentary text is apotropaic—that is, to drive away evil spirits, indicated in part by the words "exorcising" and "the demon" in the first column. In the beginning of column one, Solomon is mentioned, followed by the statement, "he will invoke" before it breaks away. The text goes on to speak of spirits and demons. In column two, the text begins with the same question of interrogation of the demons—"Who are you?"—that we find in the Testament of Solomon, especially chapter 18, where this question is posed to each of the

428 Bohak, *Ancient Jewish Magic*, 138. He notes, "It thus seems quite clear that most of Second Temple Jewish magic was transmitted orally, and even when it was trasmitted in writing, as in the case of some exorcistic hymns, its 'performance' normally included an oral recitation but no writing." Torijano, *Solomon the Esoteric King*, 86, notes, "It is most probable that the traditions that contained information about Solomon and the demons were quite common as early as the second century BCE."

429 See *Qumran Cave 11: Part 2*, 376–78.

thirty-six demons of the zodiac that Solomon questions.[430] Column three speaks of a powerful angel who fights against an evil spirit and then once again uses the same interrogation formula ("who are you?") that reminds us of the Testament of Solomon. Column four refers to "those possessed" and then mentions that the angel Raphael will heal them. The text ends with a recitation of Psalm 91—a biblical text often cited in connection with exorcism and protection from demons. Pablo Torijano rightly points to a fourfold structure that this text has in common with the Testament of Solomon: (1) an identifying formula ("who are you?"); (2) a description of the demon; (3) the threat of binding at the hands of YHWH; and (4), the rhetorical invocation of an angel.[431] These commonalities suggest that the date of this Solomonic exorcism tradition is certainly earlier than the mid-first century AD when this text was copied. It also corroborates our observation that the Jewish exorcism formula encapsulated in Testament of Solomon 18 predates the NT.

One final but significant point is that there is a possibility that the Testament of Solomon may have originated in Asia Minor. This was the conclusion of the editor of the first critical edition of the document,[432] although this remains highly speculative. It is based, in part, on some distinctive knowledge of western Asia Minor revealed in the document.

## Other Sources for Understanding Jewish Magic

Another fascinating document illustrating Jewish magic is 4Q560, also called 4QExorcism, an Aramaic fragment dated to 50 BC. Naveh claims that it has all the signs of being a "magical manual" and that it "bears clear evidence for the existence of such books at least as early as the Hasmonaean period."[433] Swartz agrees with Naveh's assessment and concludes that it confirms the existence of magical manuals in antiquity.[434] The text speaks of certain kinds of evil spirits that produce a variety of illnesses and maladies. The names of these spirits correspond to certain demons invoked in the Babylonian incantation bowls many years later.

Finally, I might also mention 4Q510 and 511, also known as 4QSongs of the Sage. Although not a recipe book of invocations as we have in the Testament of Solomon, 11Q11, or 4Q560, they do represent hymns that were probably recited to ward off the influence of demons. In the spirit of Psalm 91, this song emphasizes trust in God as the principal means of protection. The text begins,

430 Torijano, *Solomon*, 51–52, contends that this interrogation technique and the name of Solomon were linked in a popular exorcistic tradition that was probably widespread in Judaism from the first century BC.

431 Torijano, *Solomon*, 52.

432 McCown, *Testament*, 110. So also M. R. James, review of *Testament of Solomon*, by C. C. McCown, *JTS* 24 (1922): 468.

433 Naveh, "Fragments of an Aramaic Magic Book," 261.

434 Swartz, "Jewish Magic and Mysticism," 191.

"And I, the Sage, declare the grandeur of his radiance in order to frighten and terr[ify] all the spirits of the ravaging angels and the bastard spirits, demons, Liliths, owls, and [jackals . . . ] and those who strike unexpectedly . . ." (1.4–6). The identity of the sage is never explicitly revealed, but Solomon is the likely candidate. And although angels are not invoked by name as in the Testament of Solomon, angels figure prominently in this text.

This tradition involving knowledge of angelic names, the adjuration of angels, and various magical techniques can be traced in a trajectory that can be seen in a variety of Jewish documents that extend to the Middle Ages and beyond. It can be seen especially in the Sepher ha-Razim and in the Hekhalot literature.

The Sepher ha-Razim—that is, the "Book of Mysteries," is a manual of Jewish magic consisting of roughly eight hundred lines that may date to the late third or early fourth century AD.[435] M. Morgan, the translator of the text for the SBL Texts and Translations series, notes that "it is crucial to recognize that what fascinates us most about this text, the magic, is part of a folk tradition which dates from an earlier time."[436] The volume begins by attributing the source of its esoteric content to Solomon: "the Books of the Mysteries were disclosed to him [Solomon] and he became very learned in books of understanding, and (so) ruled over everything he desired, over all the spirits and demons that wander in the world, and from the wisdom of this book he imprisoned and released, and sent out and brought in, and built and prospered" (lines 26–28). Among the various spells in the document are some for warding off demons, and central to dealing with these demons is calling on angels. The names of nearly seven hundred angels are mentioned in this book. For instance, in one portion of the document, sixteen different angels are named and described. The reader is told that "in a place where their name is invoked an evil spirit cannot appear" (2.123 [p. 54]). The reader is then told how to make a gold lamella with the names of these angels inscribed upon it "if you wish to drive off an evil spirit so it will not come to a woman when she is in childbirth and so it will not kill her child" (2.124–25 [p. 54]).

In his important monograph, *Commerce of the Sacred*, J. N. Lightstone argued that the Sepher ha-Razim is an important piece of evidence demonstrating the presence of certain Jewish holy men functioning as shamans in the diaspora.[437] The visionary ascent to heaven, according to him, "grounds the authority of the theurgist and provides the measure of the extent of that authority."[438] This shaman figure therefore wields spiritual insight, power, and authority that he

435 M. Morgan has provided an English translation of the text in his 1983 edition of the Sepher ha-Razim. Regarding the date of the document, he notes, "the consensus of those scholars who have worked with the text is to support Margalioth's dating of SHR to the early fourth or late third century CE" (p. 8).

436 Morgan, *Sepher Ha-Razim*, 9.

437 Lightstone, *Commerce of the Sacred*, 16–22.

438 Lightstone, *Commerce of the Sacred*, 31.

can use to help others within the community deal with the influence of these hostile forces. His comments also show that there can be a strong connection between Jewish mysticism and Jewish magic.

A final group of texts that reflect this tradition are the Hekhalot writings.[439] These are a collection of Jewish esoteric and revelatory texts produced in late antiquity or the early Middle Ages. They detail the ascent-to-heaven experiences of a number of Jewish rabbis, wherein they describe what they have seen, heard, and learned in the heavenly palaces (the *hekhalot*) in their visionary experience. At the beginning of the twentieth century, S. Schechter of Cambridge University discovered about two dozen Hekhalot fragments among the thousands of other Jewish writings in the Cairo Geniza. Bohak has noted that "it is quite possible that the lore contained within them was passed orally for many generations before being first committed to writing."[440]

These texts have often been described as reflecting Jewish mysticism. In a recent monograph titled *Ancient Jewish Mysticism*, P. Schäfer raises serious questions about this categorization since they do not reflect a mystical union (*unio mystica*) with the deity that is central to the common understanding of mysticism.[441] Rather, he speaks of them as representing a "liturgical communion" of the suppliant with the angels in heaven.

Although the Hekhalot writings are often mined for their contribution to an understanding of *merkabah* mysticism, what has been missed is their contribution to understanding Jewish magic. The texts are filled with esoteric knowledge about the names of the angels, magical formulas and charms, and techniques for adjuring the angels. These adjurations were the subject of a study by R. Lesses in a Harvard Theological Studies monograph. She noted that "one best understands the adjurations of the Hekhalot literature within the overarching category of ritual practices involving the use of divine or angelic names in order to gain power of various kinds."[442] She argued that these texts functioned as "instructions for performances" rather than merely literary accounts.[443] As such, they enable the holy man to serve the Jewish community to fulfill a variety of human needs.

## Sceva and Jewish Shamanism

This kind of Jewish shamanism can be seen within the NT itself—and in Asia Minor. A Jewish man named Sceva served in Ephesus about the time that the church at Colossae was being planted by Epaphras. We meet Sceva in Acts

439 These Hebrew and Aramaic texts have been compiled and edited by P. Schäfer (with the assistance of M. Schlüter and H. G. von Mutius) in a large folio volume titled *Synopse zur Hekhalot-Literatur*, TSAJ 2 (Tübingen: Mohr Siebeck, 1981). A German translation is available in the four-volume set edited by P. Schäfer, *Übersetzung der Hekhalot Literatur* (Tübingen: Mohr Siebeck, 1987–1995).

440 Bohak, *Ancient Jewish Magic*, 330.

441 Schäfer, *Origins of Jewish Mysticism*, 354–55.

442 Lesses, *Ritual Practices to Gain Power*, 367.

443 Lesses, *Ritual Practices to Gain Power*, 378.

19 where his seven sons are singled out by Luke as part of a larger group of Jews who functioned as itinerant exorcists (Acts 19:13–14).[444] This story is told to us by Luke as a way of describing how God sovereignly worked to convict a number of Ephesian Christians to give up their magical practices. Apparently the tendency to syncretize their faith with some of their traditional beliefs and practices overwhelmed quite a number of believers despite Paul's teaching and the inner working of the Holy Spirit.

We do not know where Sceva was from or where he lived at the time he was in Ephesus. He could have been a resident in Ephesus, or he may have come from another Jewish community in Asia Minor. Luke is clear, however, that the seven sons of Sceva went from place to place (περιερχόμενοι) offering their services as those who had special knowledge and access to spiritual power for bringing healing and release from demonic spirits. A modern anthropologist would refer to such figures as shamans for the Jewish community—that is, they functioned as medicine men, village healers, sages with esoteric knowledge, or holy men.

Luke refers to Sceva as a "chief priest" (ἀρχιερεύς). Some commentators have thought that this was downright false advertising designed to enhance his reputation and thus gain more business.[445] Klauck even refers to it as a "stage name" to make people think he was authorized to utter the divine name and had access to sacred skills.[446] But Luke shows no sign of questioning this designation; he narrates it as though it were true. Perhaps the best explanation is that Sceva was from the high-priestly clan, a distant descendent of Zadok. As J. Jeremias notes, even though members of the Zadokite clan did not hold the priestly office during the time of Jesus and Paul, they "stood in the popular view high above the influential but illegitimate high-priestly families."[447] Functionally, Jews in this diaspora community may have looked to him and his sons as those who could serve as spiritual intermediaries for them.

It is likely that Sceva himself was also involved in this work. Presumably his seven sons were adults since this is the kind of ministry that would not be undertaken by children. Whether they independently operated as itinerant exorcists in various places is not known, but it is quite possible. In this situation, it appears that they joined together as a team of eight people to help a severely demonized man. As we already know, the situation turned ugly, with the demonized man exhibiting superhuman strength and physically overpowering all eight of the men there to deliver him from these forces.

Luke says that the reason they were unsuccessful in the exorcism is that the team used the name of Jesus (whom Paul proclaims) in their ritual adjuration.

444 Johnson, *Acts*, 340, rightly notes that "by his language, Luke suggests that there were a number of such exorcists besides these, who 'wandered' (*perierchomenoi*) through the cities of Asia."

445 See Bruce, *Acts*, 411.

446 Klauck, *Magic and Paganism*, 100.

447 Jeremias, *Jerusalem in the Time of Jesus*, 193.

The demonized man successfully challenged their authority to use this name, and they were unable to restrain him.

One of the questions that is not often asked about this Jewish exorcist and his team is: "How did they do it?" How did a first-century Jew living in the Greek world (over seven hundred miles from the land of Israel) perform exorcisms? What names of authority did they typically use in their ritual invocations for exorcism?

Based on the evidence we have from folk Jewish practices during the Roman period, this is an easy question to answer. They called on the names of angels. The names they called upon were Michael, Gabriel, Ouriel, Raphael, and dozens of others. The invocation of angels was the common way within Judaism to conduct exorcisms in the Second Temple period and beyond.

## *Syncretism*

Throughout this volume and in my 1995 monograph (*Colossian Synyncretism*), I use the term *syncretism* to describe not only the nature of the competing teaching at Colossae but also the phenomena of magic. At the outset of that volume, I set forth how I am using the term:

> The use of the term "syncretism" here and in the title of the book is not intended to prejudge the teaching of the opponents as bad, heretical, or unorthodox (thus, the previous references to "the Colossian heresy," or "die kolossische Irrlehre"). The designation is descriptive insofar as the competing teaching represents a blending of a variety of religious traditions. Of course, as we will see in the course of this investigation, the author of the letter has significant problems with the particular set of beliefs that combine to form the Colossian "philosophy."[448]

In the intervening years, there has been extensive discussion about the propriety of using the term *syncretism*. Some have seen it as an inappropriate term in the study of the history of religions because it is laden with overtones by privileging one tradition as pure and the inclusion of other religious elements as adulterating or corrupting it.[449] They contend that it is thus a pejorative term that should be avoided. R. Baird, for instance, concluded, "Since syncretism in its historical sense is universally applicable and since in its theological sense it is a barrier to authentic religio-historical understanding, its use in religio-historical inquiry should be abandoned."[450] I will provide three points of response clarifying why I will continue to use the term.

First, there are many history-of-religions scholars who continue to use the

448 *Colossian Syncretism*, 1n1.

449 See Cassidy, "Introduction (Retrofitting Syncretism)," 365, who describes an SBL panel inquiry into the term since "syncretism is the product of an older scholarship laden with theological presuppositions rejected by contemporary historians of religions."

450 Baird, *Category Formation*, 152.

term and find it to be a helpful analytical tool. D. Frankfurter, for example, contends that the term can convey a more neutral sense to describe the constant blending of traditions that occurs in religions. He notes that "all these alleged 'systems' are themselves endlessly mutating and shifting bricolages taking place in many different regional and local contexts."[451] R. Boustan and J. Sanzo concur and claim that "this model of syncretism is especially useful for describing the creative agency of ritual experts at specific moments of cultural transition."[452] They contend that the field should move beyond assigning labels to religious phenomena based on their historical origins to "consider the fluctuating nature of religious idioms and communal boundaries."[453] When Paul writes to the Colossians, Christianity in the Lycus Valley is at just such a moment of cultural transition, with a ritual expert offering a different and hybrid form of Christianity. *Syncretism* is a useful and appropriate way of describing the various strands of belief, ritual, and practices that this person is advocating. Part of my goal is to identify the nature and context of these new elements being combined into the new system. I have no reason to doubt that the purveyor of this teaching saw that there was at least some modicum of coherence and meaning in the new system, even if coherence were not his primary concern.

Second, when it comes to the phenomena of magic, *syncretism* seems to be a particularly appropriate way to characterize these beliefs, rituals, and practices. Baird conceded that "the only meaningful use of the term syncretism is to describe a situation in which conflicting ideas or practices are brought together into a new complex which is devoid of coherence."[454] But this is precisely what happens in magic and shamanism. Concern for theological coherence or fidelity to a system of thought gives way to an overriding concern for spiritual power and what will work. For the shaman, the issue is not, "What will please God?" or "What is the will of the deity?" but "What do I need to do to effect this cure (or curse)?" J. M. G. Barclay senses this when he creates a taxonomy of three different levels of assimilation that can be detected in diaspora Judaism, but when it comes to Jewish magic, he places it under the category "unknown assimilation" and then proceeds to describe it as syncretism.[455]

Third, and finally, from the emic vantage point of the author of Colossians, fidelity to the tradition is vitally important. Thus, theology does have a place, and syncretism would be understood as a declension from the purity of the tradition they received. But Paul never uses the term *syncretism* in his polemic. He simply describes the elements of the rival beliefs and practices that he finds unacceptable and urges the Lycus Valley Christians to "continue in the faith,

451 Frankfurter, *Christianizing Egypt*, 16.

452 Boustan and Sanzo, "Christian Magicians," 223.

453 Boustan and Sanzo, "Christian Magicians," 219.

454 Baird, *Category Formation*, 151.

455 Barclay, *Jews in the Mediterranean Diaspora*, 119–24.

stable and steadfast, not shifting from the hope of the gospel" (1:23) and to be "established in the faith" (2:7). For Paul, his use of the articular term "the faith" assumes a common confession and set of practices that are being passed on. I have no doubt that, had he thought of it, Paul could have used syncretism in this pejorative sense to refer to the advocates of the philosophy. Yet, I need to make it clear that this is not the sense in which I am using *syncretism* to describe either the phenomena of magic or the rival teaching at Colossae.

## *4. The Issue of Authenticity*

### *Bibliography*

**Achtemeier, P. J.** "*Omne Verbum Sonat*," 3–27. **Aland, K.** "Anonymity and Pseudonymity," 39–49. **Arnold, C. E.** *Colossian Syncretism.* ———. "Jesus Christ: 'Head' of the Church," 346–66. **Aune, D. E.** "Ancient Pseudepigraphy," 789–824. **Barclay, J. M. G.** *Colossians and Philemon*, 18–36. **Bauckham, R.** "Pseudo-Apostolic Letters," 469–94. **Baum, A.** "Authorship and Pseudepigraphy," 11–64. ———. "Authorship Attribution and Pseudonymity," 381–403. *Pseudepigraphie und literarische Falschung.* **Baur, F. C.** *Paul the Apostle.* **Becker, J.** *Auferstehung der Toten.* **Beker, J. C.** *Paul.* **Best, E.** "Who Used Whom?," 72–96. **Betz, H. D.** "Paul's 'Second Presence' in Colossians," 507–18. **Bevere, A.** *Sharing in the Inheritance.* **Bornkamm, G.** "Hoffnung," 56–64. **Bujard, W.** *Stilanalytische Untersuchungen.* **Campbell, D. A.** *Framing Paul*, 260–338. **Canavan, R.** *Clothing the Body of Christ.* **Cannon, G. E.** *Traditional Materials.* **Conzelmann, H.** "Paulus und die Weisheit," 231–44. **Duff, J.** "A Reconsideration of Pseudepigraphy." **Dunn, J. D. G.** *Theology of Paul.* **Ehrman, B. D.** *Forgery and Counterforgery.* **Frank, N.** *Kolosserbrief im Kontext.* ———. "Kolosserbrief und die 'Philosophia,'" 411–32. **Gupta, N.** "What Is in a Name?," 196–217. **Huttner, U.** *Early Christianity in the Lycus Valley.* **Janssen, M.** "Themistoklesbriefe zwischen Fälsche und Fiktion," 161–93. **Käsemann, E.** "Kolosserbrief," 3:1727–28. **Kiley, M.** *Colossians and Pseudepigraphy.* **Klauck, H.-J.** *Ancient Letters.* **Koester, H.** *Introduction.* 2 vols. **Kümmel, W.** *Introduction.* **Leppä, O.** *Making of Colossians.* **Lincicum, D.** "Mirror-Reading a Pseudepigraphical Letter," 171–93. **Lincoln, A. T.** *Paradise Now and Not Yet.* **Lindemann, A.** "Die Gemeinde von 'Kolossä,'" 111–34. **Longenecker, B., and S. C. Ryan.** "Presenting the Pauline Voice," 136–48. **MaGee, G. S.** *Portrait of an Apostle.* **Mayerhoff, E. T.** *Colosser.* **Meade, D.** *Pseudonymity and Canon.* **Merklein, H.** "Rezeption," 25–69. **Müller, P.** *Anfänge der Paulusschule.* **Murphy-O'Connor, J.** *Paul*, 231–51. ———. *Paul the Letter-Writer.* **Neumann, K. J.** *Authenticity of the Pauline Epistles.* **Pascuzzi, M. A.** "Reconsidering the Authorship of Colossians," 223–46. **Percy, E.** *Probleme.* **Pitts, A. W.** "Style and Pseudonymity in Pauline Scholarship," 113–52. **Porter, S. E.** *Apostle Paul*, 354–75. ———. "Pauline Authorship and the Pastoral Epistles," 105–23. **Richards, E. R.** *Paul and First-Century Letter Writing.* ———. *Secretary in the Letters of Paul.* **Sarri, M.** *Material Aspects of Letter Writing.* **Schenk, W.** "Kolosserbrief in der neuren Forschung," 3227–64. **Schnelle, U.** *Apostle Paul.* **Schweizer, E.** "Christus und Geist," 297–313. **Standhartinger, A.** "City with a Message," 239–56. ———. "Colossians and the Pauline School," 572–93. ———. *Studien zur Enstehungsgeschichte.* **Stettler, C.** *Kolosserhymnus.* ———. "Opponents at Colossae," 169–200. **Stettler, H.** *Heiligung.* **Still, T.** "Eschatology in Colossians," 125–38. **Stone, M.** "Pseudepigraphy Reconsidered," 1–15. **Strawbridge, J. R.** *The Pauline Effect.* **Stuhlmacher, P.** "Christliche Verantwortung," 165–86. **Tannehill, R. C.** *Dying and Rising.* **Tite, P.** "Dusting Off a Pseudepigraphical Letter," 289–318. **Van Nes, J.** "*Hapax Legomena* in Disputed Pauline Letters," 118–37. ———. "Missing 'Particles,'" 383–98. **Wedderburn, A. J. M.** *Baptism and Resurrection.* ———. *Theology of the Later Pauline Letters*, 3–77. **Westcott, B. F.** *Canon.* **Wilder, T. L.** *Pseudonymity.* **Wright, N. T.** "Monotheism, Christology and Ethics," 120–36. **Yule, G. U.** *Statistical Study.*

A careful reading of the letter to the Colossians would not lead one to conclude that the letter was written by anyone other than the apostle Paul. Paul is explicitly named as the author of the letter at the outset: "Paul, an apostle of Christ Jesus by the will of God, and Timothy our brother." In fact, the beginning of his second letter to the Corinthians (2 Cor 1:1) is worded in precisely the same way. All of Paul's accepted letters begin by naming him as the author.

Timothy is named as the coauthor not only of Colossians and 2 Corinthians but also of Philippians, Philemon, and 1 and 2 Thessalonians. But early in the body of Colossians, the focus narrows to the first person, Paul himself, when, in speaking of the gospel, he says, "of which I, Paul, became a servant" (1:23). This is followed by a series of twelve first-person singular verbs where the apostle Paul is the clear subject (1:24, 25, 29; 2:1, 4, 5; 4:3, 4, 8, 13) and Timothy's coauthorship is no longer explicitly in view.

Pauline authorship of Colossians was never in doubt throughout the pre-Nicene and post-Nicene church, throughout the Byzantine era, through the medieval period, or by any of the Reformation scholars. From Chrysostom to Calvin, Ignatius to Aquinas, Eusebius to Erasmus, Origen to Luther, all the teachers and scholars throughout the history of the church presumed Paul to be the author and regarded the content of this book to accurately reflect the apostle's thoughts.[456] No one raised a concern until 1838—the year E. T. Mayerhoff published a detailed study of the letter to the Colossians and concluded that Paul may not have been the author.[457] He built his argument on a variety of factors, including the high number of hapax legomena, stylistic differences with the other Pauline letters, the absence of key Pauline concepts, a polemic against a teaching that reflects a later period of time, and what he concluded to be a literary dependence on the letter to the Ephesians.

A few years later in his highly influential study on Paul, F. C. Baur raised considerable questions about the authenticity of Colossians (and Ephesians).[458] Focusing less on stylistic matters, Baur looked at the theological content of the letters, which he saw as reflecting a postapostolic context. In the first instance, he was struck by the fact that "the eye of the writer is directed chiefly to the transcendantal regions of the spirit-world."[459] Rather than seeing this as part of mid-first-century folk belief, he contended that it belonged "to the period of Gnosticism."[460] He went a different direction than Mayerhoff on the matter of the relationship between Ephesians and Colossians, arguing that the author of Ephesians exhibited literary dependence upon Colossians.

This was the beginning of a large stream of scholars over the next century

---

456 Strawbridge, *Pauline Effect*, 135, notes that "early Christian writers from Justin Martyr to Methodius, Irenaeus to Eusebius assume Pauline authorship of the Colossian epistle."

457 Mayerhoff, *Colosser*, 1–162.

458 Baur, *Paul the Apostle*, 2.1–44. The German original was published in 1845.

459 Baur, *Paul the Apostle*, 2.6.

460 Baur, *Paul the Apostle*, 8.

and a half, especially on the continent, who entertained serious doubts about the Pauline authorship of Colossians. There have been notable exceptions, such as E. Percy, a Swedish scholar who wrote a 517-page monograph in 1946 defending the Pauline authorship of Colossians and Ephesians.[461] Percy's treatment of the matter included a detailed fifty-page analysis of the language and style of Colossians, a seventy-page evaluation of the theology, a forty-page assessment of the opponents, and a seventy-page section on the relationship of Colossians to Ephesians. This comprehensive assessment of the authorship of Colossians has never been matched in the literature. But it has often been ignored.

In 1973, W. Bujard published a detailed analytical study of the grammar and style of Colossians titled *Stilanalytisiche Untersuchung zum Kolosserbrief.* Bujard compared specific elements of the style of Colossians—from conjunctions to infinitives and participial constructions to aspects of the rhetorical structure of the letter—with the accepted Pauline epistles. He engaged with Percy's observations and arguments regarding the style but endeavored to bring more specificity and detail to the question of style. He concluded that the author of the letter could not have been the apostle Paul based on the divergent stylistic qualities. Bujard's monograph has been highly influential, with some scholars viewing it as a definitive case against Pauline authorship. Surprisingly, no one has ever written a thoroughgoing response to Bujard's case. Although a commentary is not the place for a comprehensive response, I will raise a few preliminary questions and concerns about Bujard's study and bring in some new data (see *Excursus* below).

There remains no consensus on the authorship of Colossians. My sense is that on the continent, the majority of scholars would see the letter as pseudepigraphical. In the UK and USA, however, there seems to be a more even divide. I made a similar observation in my 1995 monograph, indicating that there is "a fairly strong stream of scholarship" accepting Colossians as authentic.[462] This was challenged by O. Leppä, who claimed that this "does not describe the situation properly."[463] But in 1959, E. Käsemann could say that "the authenticity is today nearly generally recognized."[464] He probably had in mind influential commentators such as E. Lohmeyer, M. Dibelius, C. F. D. Moule, E. F. Scott, C. Masson, and others. P. Foster conducted a survey of 109 scholars and students attending a British New Testament Studies Conference in 2011. He found that 51.4 percent were in favor of Pauline authorship, while only 15.6 percent were decidedly against that position; the remaining 33 percent were undecided.[465] C. Stettler has observed that "in recent years there has been a growing tendency to regard

461 Percy, *Probleme.*

462 *Colossian Syncretism*, 7.

463 Leppä, *Making of Colossians*, 10.

464 E. Käsemann, "Kolosserbrief," *RGG*³ 3:1727.

465 Foster, 67.

it as possible or even probable that Colossians was written by Paul himself, or at least in Paul's lifetime and on behalf of Paul by a secretary (cf. 1:1 and 4:18) whose theology was very close to Paul's."[466] In the last thirty-five years, many commentaries, academic monographs, journal articles, book chapters, and biblical theologies have been written that affirm Pauline authorship—certainly enough to affirm "a fairly strong stream of scholarship." I will provide a representative list from the last thirty years in the note below.[467]

Although some would say that the stakes are not high for Christians on the issue of authorship because whether the letter is from the hand of Paul or not, it is still in the canon of Scripture and has been used profitably by the church for centuries. While this is true and Colossians remains canonical, one's convictions about authorship do indeed have an impact on how the theology of the letter is understood. For many who regard Colossians as a pseudepigraphical letter, much of the content is deemed inconsistent with Paul's thought as reflected in his accepted letters. Some judge the Christology to be too high, the eschatology too realized, the ecclesiology too developed, and the representation of Paul himself to be too grandiose. Thus, U. Schnelle concludes that "the deutero-Paulines deviate from Paul's own theology in essential points."[468] Relatedly, it is also important to observe that one's conclusion on this matter alters an understanding of Paul himself and the array of his convictions. An overall portrait of Pauline eschatology will look different between scholars who hold to Paul's authorship of Colossians and those who do not. This is readily observable in many works describing the theology of Paul. For some, Colossians is not even included in the description of the theology unless its deviations are noted in a footnote, or an appendix discusses post-Pauline developments.

I have previously gone into print advocating the Pauline authorship of Colossians.[469] As I have reflected on this matter further, read many more treatments of the relevant arguments on both sides, and examined the pivotal issues much more deeply, I continue to be convinced that the weight of the evidence

---

466 Stettler, "Opponents at Colossae," 169.

467 *Commentaries:* Thiselton (2020); Beale (2019); McKnight (2018); Thurston (2013); Gupta (2013); Campbell, C. R. (2013); Pao (2012); Harris (2010); Bird (2009); Moo (2008); Witherington (2007); Still (2006); Thompson (2005); Garland (1998); Wright (1986); Barth and Blanke (1994). *Monographs:* Copenhaver (2018); Gordley (2018, 2007); Magee (2013); Cavin (2013); Pate (2013); Heil (2010); Beetham (2008); Smith (2006); Kim, J. H. (2004); Wilder (2004); Schnabel (2004, 1985); Richards (2004, 1991); Sappington (1991); Bockmuehl (1990). *Introductions and Biblical Theologies:* Moo (2021); Campbell, C. R. (2020, 2012); Porter (2016); Campbell, D. A. (2014); Wright (2013); Tidball (2011); Barnett (2008); Schreiner (2008, 2001); Fee (2007, 1994); Thielman (2005); Marshall (2004); McRay (2003). *Journal Articles and Book Chapters:* Allen (2018); Macaskill (2017); Blackwell (2014); Pascuzzi (2013); Gupta (2013); Dunne (2011); Ellis (2006); Stettler, C. (2005); Still (2004); Stettler, H. (2000); Bock (1994); Helyer (1994).

468 Schnelle, *Apostle Paul*, 151.

469 See my *Colossian Syncretism*, 6–7; "Colossians," *ZIBBC*, 370–403; "Colossians," in the *ESV Study Bible*, 2289–2300.

tips more strongly on the side of the Pauline authorship of Colossians. I will set forth some of that evidence in the pages that follow.

### *The Spectrum of Views on the Authorship of Colossians*

A continuum of perspectives exists concerning the authorship of the letter. The matter cannot simply be explained as a choice between Pauline authorship or pseudepigraphy. I will provide a few representative examples of the proponents of each of the five positions mentioned below.

Before doing so, however, it is important to define what I mean by "author" in an ancient letter-writing context. The study of the authorship of an ancient letter needs to take into account the use of an amanuensis, or secretary, in the composition of the document. The fact that Paul used a secretary in writing his letters is confirmed when Paul's scribe, Tertius, includes his own greeting to the Roman church: "I Tertius, who wrote this letter [ὁ γράψας τὴν ἐπιστολήν], greet you in the Lord" (Rom 16:22). There is no similar greeting by a secretary at the end of Colossians, but in his closing remarks Paul says, "This greeting is with my own hand—from Paul" (4:18). This would imply that the letter itself was written by the hand of another, presumably the secretary. If we are to take 1:1 seriously, this could mean that Timothy served as the secretary for Paul. Yet the evidence could also suggest that a professional scribe was hired to serve both of the coauthors.

E. R. Richards has investigated the function and role of an amanuensis (a literary secretary) in his 1991 monograph, *The Secretary in the Letters of Paul*.[470] He suggests that the secretary was likely a specially contracted individual who was trained with the requisite skills rather than a team member.[471] He also argues that the secretary was afforded some degree of latitude in the composition of the letter that would have resulted in minor influences on stylistic matters such as vocabulary and grammar.[472] This is a factor that is seldom taken into account in discussions about Colossians as pseudepigraphy.

#### The Letter Was Composed by the Apostle Paul

This has been the historic position of the church until 1838 and continues to be held by a wide array of scholars. Most who take this position recognize the uniqueness of the style of the letter and the distinctive theological emphases. Yet they would contend that the style is not inconsistent with the main Pauline letters and that the theology reflects some new accents but was motivated by the situation Paul was addressing and is a natural extension of his thought (see more on this below).

470 The results of his research have now been updated and made available to a broader audience in a volume titled, *Paul and First-Century Letter Writing* (2004). See also Klauck, *Ancient Letters*, 58–60.

471 Richards, *Letter Writing*, 230.

472 Richards, *Letter Writing*, 230.

## The Letter Was Composed by One of Paul's Disciples and Received His Approval

Some writers see the letter as sufficiently consistent with Paul's undisputed letters in language, style, and theology but are open to the possibility that the letter could have been primarily composed by one of Paul's associates as a way of explaining some of the stylistic variations. H. Stettler writes, "Since neither the language and style nor the teaching of the letter can definitely be identified as un-Pauline and the letter can also be accommodated within the framework of what we know about Paul's life, a Pauline authorship cannot be ruled out from the outset. In any event, if the letter is not written by Paul himself, it was either written on his behalf by a secretary or by one of his closest disciples and associates."[473] But the idea of Paul using an associate as a secretary or hiring a secretary to compose the letter on his behalf is tantamount to affirming Pauline authorship.

The stylistic differences between Colossians and the accepted letters lead some to conclude that the letter must have been written by one of his missionary colleagues. The candidate usually put forward for this is Timothy. E. Schweizer suggested this solution in his influential commentary on the letter.[474] Although he reasoned that there was no insurmountable problem in reconciling the theological constructs of Colossians with the undisputed letters, he regarded the differences in style as pointing to an author other than Paul. Schweizer found Bujard's 1973 monograph as completely convincing on this score. Thus, he argued that the author of Colossians was one "who, although following Paul completely in vocabulary and theological concepts, differs from him altogether in his mode of argument."[475] As one who was "steeped to a large extent in Paul's style and train of thought," Timothy surfaces as the most likely candidate.[476]

This view was reaffirmed by J. D. G. Dunn in his commentary on Colossians. He postulated that Paul outlined "his main concerns to a secretary (Timothy) who was familiar with the broad pattern of Paul's letter writing" and accorded Timothy a fair degree of license in composing the letter.[477] He suggested that the conditions of Paul's imprisonment may have kept Paul from doing anything other than adding a brief personal conclusion. He says that "if Timothy did indeed write for Paul at Paul's behest, but also with Paul's approval of what was in the event written (prior to adding 4:18), then we have to call the letter 'Pauline' in the full sense of the word, and the distinction between 'Pauline' and 'post-Pauline' as applied to Colossians becomes relatively unimportant."[478] While agreeing with Schweizer that "the style is consistently and markedly

473 Stettler, *Heiligung*, 543.
474 Schweizer, 15–24.
475 Schweizer, 18–19.
476 Schweizer, 23–24.
477 Dunn, 38.
478 Dunn, 38.

different" from the accepted Pauline letters, Dunn goes beyond Schweizer by contending that the theological content "is significantly different from what we are accustomed to in all the undisputed Paulines."[479] He points in particular to the Christology, ecclesiology, and eschatology of the letter. But this raises an interesting conundrum for Dunn since he believes that Paul was still alive and likely even approved the content of the letter. As Leppä notes, it seems "unlikely that during Paul's lifetime some of his disciples would have written a letter which puts forth a theology which diverges so much from Paul."[480] Although Dunn does not reflect further on this, the theory would suggest that the way Timothy describes the theology of the letter and develops the Christology, ecclesiology, and eschatology is completely consistent with Paul's own thought. Otherwise, how could he endorse it?

One also needs to consider the large number of autobiographical elements and personal greetings in the letter (more than in most of his other letters). It seems rather surprising that someone writing in his name would include more personal detail than Paul normally includes himself. When this is combined with the theological differences, this theory of authorship becomes more difficult to accept.

Others have followed suit and asserted Timothy as the author but have not seen the theology as discontinuous with Paul. A. Bevere, for instance, sees the style as decisive, but says that the theology "is not so great that authenticity can be excluded."[481]

## The Letter Was Composed Shortly after Paul's Death by One of His Disciples

Those who have understood both the theology and style of the letter as substantially different than how Paul would have expressed himself have tended to argue that the letter was written sometime after his death. The author is often seen as one who was acquainted with and appreciated the Pauline legacy—either in its oral or written form.[482]

M. MacDonald takes this approach in her commentary. She is in favor of regarding the letter as "deutero-Pauline" because of the style, some of the content (such as the household code), and the transformed nature of the theology, but she does not want to distance it too far from Paul. She sees it composed at the very end of Paul's career or shortly after his death.[483] With Schweizer and Dunn, she thinks Timothy could have been the author.

479 Dunn, 36.

480 Leppä, *Making of Colossians*, 11.

481 Bevere, *Sharing in the Inheritance*, 54–55.

482 In addition to those mentioned below as advocates of this view, see also Huttner, *Early Christianity in the Lycus Valley*, 148; Canavan, *Clothing the Body of Christ*, 24–29 (she favors Epaphras as the possible author).

483 MacDonald, 6–10.

P. Foster makes a similar argument but is open to a later dating. He sees the writer of Colossians as co-opting Paul's apostolic authority to respond to a perceived misleading teaching in Colossae.[484] He observes that "the changes in theology, when taken in combination, raise sufficient doubts to make the attribution of authorship to Paul difficult, although admittedly not impossible."[485] He sees the date of the later as possibly ranging anywhere from AD 65–80.

Because of the cumulative impact of observing the differences in style and especially theology, J. Sumney reaches the conclusion that "the letter was composed soon after Paul's death, perhaps even in the wake of this loss to the church" by an associate (which he does not name) in AD 62–64.[486] He also notes that the early date helps to explain why Colossians draws heavily on Philemon.

One of the difficulties of this view is that it does not adequately factor in the impact of the devastating earthquake in the early 60s. A. Lindemann goes so far as to say that if the city of Colossae lay in ruins from the year AD 61 or 62, "then the inevitable consequence is that the post-Pauline drafting of a letter directed to Colossae can be ruled out."[487] Contrary to Lindemann and others who see the earthquake as utterly devastating the city and perhaps forcing a relocation of the population, the material evidence suggests that the city was rebuilt and existed as a viable city in the years ahead. Nevertheless, the absence of any reference or allusion to the earthquake would be surprising in a letter written to Colossae (or Laodicea) in the mid-60s. The severity of the earthquake would have altered much about the situation in Colossae. Sumney, however, senses this difficulty and suggests that if Paul is not the author of the letter, then the churches of Colossae are probably not its actual recipients. Consequently, he sees the letter addressed to a broader group of Christians in Asia Minor.[488] But the theory of a much broader readership would seem to falter on the specificity of the factional teaching that is so strenuously opposed in the contents of Colossians.

## The Letter Was Composed a Decade or Two after Paul's Death by One or More Members of a "Pauline School"

An increasingly popular way of accounting for the origin of Colossians, especially by European scholarship, is by conjecturing that the letter is the product of a "Pauline school." H. Conzelmann was the first to posit the idea of Paul gathering a circle of his followers into a school of wisdom (perhaps in Ephesus).[489] This so-called school would have continued its work after Paul's death. He contended that Colossians, Ephesians, 2 Thessalonians, and the Pastoral Epistles

484 Foster, 79.

485 Foster, 80.

486 Sumney, 9.

487 Lindemann, "Die Gemeinde von 'Kolossä,'" 115.

488 Sumney, 9–10.

489 Conzelmann, "Paulus und die Weisheit," 231–44.

were all a product of the work of this school after Paul's death.[490] The unique theological developments in Colossians (and the other deutero-Paulines) are all attributed to this school.

This theory was taken up and elaborated by a steady stream of other scholars, including E. Lohse, A. Standhartinger, O. Leppä, P. Stuhlmacher, and others.[491] In his highly influential Hermeneia commentary on Colossians, Lohse contended that the letter was written around AD 80 by a member of the Pauline school at Ephesus. The letter was not written to believers in Colossae but to a larger circle of readers in Asia Minor, with the purpose of instructing them on "how they should conduct themselves in true obedience to their Lord, in the face of the menace of syncretism."[492] Although Lohse pointed out what he regarded to be many substantive differences between Colossians and the main Pauline letters in language and style,[493] it was the significant theological differences that he urged must not be overlooked. He went so far as to say:

> The appearance of non-Pauline concepts and expressions cannot be explained simply by saying that they were coined by the specific circumstances of this controversy [i.e., "the philosophy"]. Rather Pauline theology has undergone a profound change in Col, which is evident in every section of the letter and has produced new formulations in Christology, ecclesiology, the concept of the apostle, eschatology, and the understanding of baptism. Therefore, Paul cannot be considered to be the direct or indirect author of Colossians.[494]

For Lohse, the author of Colossians was intimately familiar with the letters of Paul, as he read them over and over in the Pauline school. He responded to the challenges that the church of his day faced from "the philosophy" by "applying Pauline theology to this new problem."[495] He found Colossae to be the ideal location for the fictive address because Colossae may never have been rebuilt after the severe earthquake of the early 60s and because the letter of Philemon gave him a list of greetings that would make the letter more vivid and would ensure "that his letter will gain a hearing as a message from Paul."[496] In other words, "it would be very advantageous for an author who wrote at a later date to bolster the authority of his writing by statements about individual persons and by more detailed information."[497] Lohse never discusses the possible ethical

490 Conzelmann, "Paulus und die Weisheit," 234.

491 See Leppä, *Making of Colossians*, 9–15; Müller, *Anfänge der Paulusschule*, 13–19, 270–325; Schnelle, *Apostle Paul*, 150–51.

492 Lohse, 181.

493 Lohse, 84–91.

494 Lohse, 180–81.

495 Lohse, 182.

496 Lohse, 177.

497 Lohse, 176–77 (n59).

problem the author would face in this explicit effort to deceive his potential hearers into thinking this was an actual letter from Paul. Nor does he make any attempt to defend pseudepigraphy as an acceptable literary form. What is clear is that Lohse would categorically reject the first three options discussed above by contending that these views all minimize the theological differences between the theology of Colossians and the accepted Pauline letters.

In her study *The Making of Colossians*, O. Leppä follows previous scholarship in asserting the presence of a Pauline school (perhaps in Ephesus). She sees the author of Colossians as writing in the name of Paul, not with malicious intent but with a motivation of respect and admiration. This person "wants to write in a new situation in a way he thinks Paul would have done if he were still alive."[498] She suggests that believers at Colossae were pseudo-addressees because it would have been "more reasonable to set a fictive writing in a possibly non-existent town [assuming Colossae was destroyed in the earthquake] rather than in a living and well-known city."[499] She sees the intended readers as Christian congregations throughout Asia Minor.[500] The teaching the author opposes was an apocalyptic visionary group that observed Jewish regulations, whereas the author asserts Paul's heritage of Christian liberty.[501] She speculates that the author may have been Tychicus and that he wrote in the 80s from Ephesus, the seat of the Pauline school.[502] Leppä's unique contribution to the debate is the contention that the author of Colossians was familiar with all of Paul's undisputed letters and used them in the composition of Colossians while using Philemon as the frame.

A. Standhartinger continues the assumption of a Pauline school without speculating on a location for it. For her, the school functioned as a circle of Paul's disciples who were intimately familiar with his oral teaching and spent many hours discussing it. She suggests that Colossians was written by a group of authors from this school in the early post-Pauline years to address "uncertainty and tendencies toward disintegration" faced by Christians in the Pauline churches throughout the Roman world.[503] In particular, she supposes that "Paul's death led to uncertainty within the churches," especially by the fact that "the parousia of Christ, expected by Paul within his lifetime, remained unrealized."[504] This resulted in the community feeling threatened and ready "to give up and collapse."[505] With H. D. Betz,[506] she characterizes Colossians as a "heavenly

498 Leppä, *Making of Colossians*, 12.
499 Leppä, *Making of Colossians*, 14.
500 Leppä, *Making of Colossians*, 262.
501 Leppä, *Making of Colossians*, 262–63.
502 Leppä, *Making of Colossians*, 263.
503 Standhartinger, "Colossians and the Pauline School," 586, 592.
504 Standhartinger, "Colossians and the Pauline School," 585.
505 Standhartinger, "Colossians and the Pauline School," 585.
506 Betz, "Paul's 'Second Presence' in Colossians," 513.

letter" purportedly sent from Paul intended to convey his spiritual presence to replace his bodily presence with the churches.[507] The author chose "Colossians" as the fictive addressees because, as a small town in the interior of Asia Minor, it symbolizes the spread of the gospel to the furthest corners of the Roman Empire.[508] The theology expressed in the letter represents a transformation of Paul's thought for the conditions of this new era.

P. Stuhlmacher also sees Colossians as the product of the Pauline school, but would push the date earlier than most and would contend for more theological continuity with the accepted letters.[509] For Stuhlmacher, the school arose among Paul's pupils because of the need "to develop lasting church structures and firm criteria for the Christian life, but also to protect themselves against the undermining of their faith by false teachers in their own midst" in the latter years of Paul and the era following his death.[510] He contends that Paul founded the school himself before he died. He sees the composition of Colossians as taking place in the very early years of this school. He argues that Colossians "was probably written by Timothy at Paul's request while in prison and only 'countersigned' by Paul himself (cf. Col 4:8)."[511] Thus, his view has much in common with that of Schweizer and Dunn, who also see Timothy as the author.

Although there are a wide array of scholars affirming the Pauline-school hypothesis, there is significant divergence among them in when they see the letter written, by whom, the purpose of the letter, and the portrayal of the theological concepts. For all of them, the language and style of Colossians prevents them from affirming Pauline authorship. They also regard the theology and historical content as reflecting a later date and, for many, addressing the concerns of a later generation.

### The Letter Was Composed by a Lone Author One to Three Decades after Paul's Death

There are a number of scholars who do not appeal to a Pauline-school tradition and see the writer as a lone author writing sometime in the post-Pauline era. For some, the author of Colossians was attempting to faithfully interpret the Pauline legacy for a new generation and the challenges it faced. For others, the author was more creative. All of these interpreters see the style and theology of the letter as inconsistent with the recognized Pauline letters.

After arguing that the style, vocabulary, and theological emphases in Colossians are not Pauline, A. T. Lincoln concludes that the cumulative weight

507 Standhartinger, "Colossians and the Pauline School," 582–83.

508 Standhartinger, "Colossians and the Pauline School," 586. See also idem, *Studien zur Entstehungsgeschichte*, 15–16.

509 See Stuhlmacher, *Biblical Theology*, 431–33. See also his earlier essay, "Christliche Verantwortung," 165–86.

510 Stuhlmacher, *Biblical Theology*, 432.

511 Stuhlmacher, *Biblical Theology*, 432.

of the evidence demonstrates that Colossians was likely written by a follower after the apostle's death.[512] He contends that the author attempted "to be both faithful and creative in its interpretation of the Pauline tradition in a later situation."[513] For Lincoln, it is important to conceive of pseudonymity in this case as an accepted literary device for passing on authoritative tradition. He finds the author of Colossians as reflecting a broad Jewish tradition of pseudonymity as a way of asserting authoritative tradition. But for the letter genre, in particular, he sees the Greco-Roman literary precedents as decisive. He finds the authors of such letters as attempting "to convey the presence of the sender to the readers and in doing so would invent personal references and extraneous mundane details for the sake of versimilitude."[514] Lincoln understands that the purpose "was to provide the occasion for passing on philosophical teaching and portraying a particular philosopher as a model."[515]

A. Lindemann attempts to make the case (against Schweizer and others) that the letter could not have been written by a disciple of Paul's in the immediate years following his death. As I have already noted (above), he thinks such a view is ruled out by the severe earthquake rocking that region, which would have left the city in shambles.[516] He also finds it unlikely that Paul would have accepted the epistle's theological thought and endorsed it as his own, especially if Timothy was, in fact, the author of the letter as some have asserted.[517] Rather, the author of the letter created a fictional situation at Colossae as a means of addressing an actual situation in Laodicea in the 70s or 80s.[518] The readers in Laodicea, when they encountered the letter, would have recognized in the contents of Colossians their own situation and that Paul's arguments from twenty years ago applied to them at the time they were reading it.

B. Ehrman likewise argues strenuously against seeing an associate of Paul as the author of the letter.[519] He, too, contends that the differences in theology, particularly the eschatology, stand at odds with Paul's thought. Arguing in a different way than Lindemann, Ehrman thinks that an associate of the apostle Paul, such as Timothy, would not have been willing to endorse the teaching expressed in the letter, especially the eschatology.[520] He contends that the same issues would rule out the possibility that a member of the so-called Pauline school authored the letter. For Ehrman, the entire theory of a Pauline school should "probably be put to rest."[521] He concludes that "there in fact is no evidence that students

---

512 Lincoln, "Colossians," 577–83.
513 Lincoln, "Colossians," 582.
514 Lincoln, "Colossians," 582.
515 Lincoln, "Colossians," 582.
516 Lindemann, "Gemeinde von 'Kolossä,'" 115.
517 Lindemann, 11.
518 Lindemann, "Gemeinde von 'Kolossä,'" 115.
519 Ehrman, *Forgery and Counterforgery*, 171–82.
520 Ehrman, *Forgery and Counterforgery*, 171.
521 Ehrman, *Forgery and Counterforgery*, 172.

produced pseudonymous writings in the names of their teachers with impunity in the philosophical schools of the first century (or before or after)."[522] Rather, he argues, and probably rightly so, that education took place in the context of the local churches—not in a scholastic context. Colossians was therefore written by an individual in the post-Pauline era who composed the letter in Paul's name, "wanting his readers to think he is Paul."[523] Ehrman is sharply critical of NT scholars who will go to extraordinary lengths "to absolve the author of any intent to deceive."[524] He agrees with Standhartinger that there is a universal tendency to the contents of the letter and that the choice of Colossae as the destination may have symbolic value, suggesting that the gospel has reached into the remote corners of the empire.[525] This conclusion, however, seems at odds with his contention that the opponents are real and that the author is using Paul's authority to attack them. The contours of the so-called philosophy are too narrow and idiosyncratic to universalize them to the whole of Asia Minor (and beyond).

Many others argue for some form of this view under the assumption that Colossians is clearly not Pauline in language, style, and theology and that it reflects the conditions of second- or third-generation Christianity after the apostle Paul's death. Generally, all would see some continuity with Paul and contend for seeing Colossians as some form of interpretation of Pauline tradition for a later generation experiencing its own unique challenges.[526]

### *Language, Style, Theology, and Historical Plausibility*

Arguments (and assumptions) regarding the pseudonymity of Colossians generally revolve around these four categories. As we will see (below), there are a wide variety of opinions about which of these areas carry the most weight.[527] Some see the language and style as decisively against Pauline authorship. Other see those matters as no problem but contend that some of the theological constructs are discontinuous with Paul. Still others see problems with all the above. I will examine, in turn, each of these areas and offer some analysis.

#### Language

The matter of hapax legomena in Colossians has been cited by many scholars as a problem for Pauline authorship. Lohse provides a list of thirty-four different

522 Ehrman, *Forgery and Counterforgery*, 173 (see also pp. 105–19 where he presents the evidence to support his position).

523 Ehrman, *Forgery and Counterforgery*, 178.

524 Ehrman, *Forgery and Counterforgery*, 178.

525 Ehrman, *Forgery and Counterforgery*, 182.

526 See, e.g., Frank, *Kolosserbrief im Kontext*, 1–5, 26–31, and idem, "Kolosserbrief und die 'Philosophia,'" 411–32.

527 Porter, "Pauline Authorship and the Pastoral Epistles," 110, aptly observes that "the methods used to determine authorship are almost as varied as those scholars doing the calculations, with very little control on what criteria are being used and what would count as an adequate test of the method."

terms that appear in Colossians and nowhere else in the NT and presents this as one of a number of reasons to judge Colossians inauthentic.[528] What Lohse does not take into account is the fact that three of the terms come from cited traditional material, the Colossian hymn (ὁρατός, πρωτεύω, εἰρηνοποιέω), five represent likely catchwords from the Colossian "philosophy" (φιλοσοφία, νεομηνία, ἐμβατεύω, ἐθελοθηρσκία, ἀφειδία), and six are part of the author's polemic against this unique oppositional teaching (πιθανολογία, σαλαγωγέω, καταβραβεύω, δογματίζω, ἀπόχρησις, πλησμονή). If these fourteen terms are set aside, then the number of hapax legomena is reduced to twenty—completely within the range (or even less) than the number of hapax legomena in Paul's accepted letters. Nevertheless, thirty-four is not an unreasonable number of unique terms, especially when we take into account that Philippians—an undisputed letter—actually contains more (thirty-six) than Colossians. A detailed study of this matter by J. van Nes has confirmed that hapax legomena "are not overused" in Colossians compared to their use in the accepted Pauline letters.[529] Consequently, some advocates of seeing Colossians as pseudepigraphy discount this criterion in its application to Colossians.[530]

Lohse also points out that there are twenty-eight words in Colossians that are found elsewhere in the NT, but not in other Pauline letters. Once again, this number should be reduced by the same criteria—that is, there are two words that appear in the Colossian hymn (θρόνος, συνίστημι[531]), four words that are catchwords of "the philosophy" (ἑορτή, θρησκεία, γεύομαι, θιγγάνω), and four words that are part of the polemic (παραλογίζομαι, σκία, κρατέω, ἔνταλμα). This reduces the total to an insignificant number (a total of eighteen). And once again, as Kiley observes, Philippians actually has more (forty-three) such words.[532]

Some have also pointed out that there are a number of terms that appear in the undisputed letters that are not present in Colossians. But this is an unconvincing way to argue when one considers that (1) Colossians is substantially smaller than the main Pauline letters (e.g., Romans is 7105 words compared to 1575 in Colossians), (2) the different subject matter and themes represented in the letters (e.g., the Judaizing problem is absent in Colossians), and (3) the apostle Paul shows a substantial versatility in his use of vocabulary. This argument would bear more weight if Colossians were a summary of the Pauline gospel, but it is very much an ad hoc composition designed primarily to warn against the incursion of a teaching the Paul finds out of sync with his teaching.

---

528 See Lohse, 85–86.

529 Van Nes, "*Hapax Legomena* in Disputed Pauline Letters," 118–37, esp. 137.

530 E.g., Kiley, *Colossians as Pseudepigraphy*, 44.

531 Lohse, 85, includes this term in his list, but it actually appears thirteen other times in Paul's accepted letters. This is the only time, however, that it appears in the perfect tense with the meaning "hold together," but Paul is certainly quite familiar with the lexical item.

532 Kiley, *Colossians as Pseudepigraphy*, 44.

## Style

In recent years, far more weight has been given to observations regarding the grammar, syntax, and specific rhetorical features of the letter. Some believe that the author's use of such compositional features as his use of conjunctions, prepositions, infinitival and participial constructions, repetition, parallelism, redundancy of thought, fullness of expression, sentence length, and more betray the fingerprints of a pseudepigrapher. One 259-page monograph has been especially influential in galvanizing the opinions of many who are strongly on the side of pseudepigraphy. As mentioned already, in 1973 W. Bujard published the results of his extensive Heidelberg dissertation research on the style of Colossians (under the direction of K. G. Kuhn) in a detailed work titled, *Stilanalytische Untersuchungen zum Kolosserbrief.* Many have viewed this book as settling the case for the pseudonymity of Colossians once for all. Kiley concludes that "Bujard has established beyone a reasonable doubt that Paul's authorship of Col is highly unlikely."[533] Similarly, Standhartinger notes that "Walter Bujard convinced most scholars, including myself, that Colossians was written not by Paul himself but rather by one or more of Paul's friends and companions, most likely after Paul's death, which occurred sometime after 65 CE."[534] W. Schenk says that Bujard's study not only confirms the obervations and arguments of Mayerhoff but has raised them to a new level because of the explanatory power of his methodology.[535] In the years since Bujard published his work, there has been no thoroughgoing response to his case. What is needed is a monograph-length evaluation of his methodology in light of modern linguistic studies and grammar. Both his methodology and his statistical analyses are not unassailable. For the purposes of a commentary, I can in no way provide a detailed response, but I do want to raise some questions about his study and make some of my own obervations about the style of Colossians.

533 Kiley, *Colossians as Pseudepigaphy*, 59.

534 Standhartinger, "City with a Message," 239.

535 W. Schenk, review of Bujard, *Stilanalytische Untersuchungen*, *TLZ* 99 (1974): 918–19.

# Excursus: A Brief Analysis of W. Bujard's *Stilanalytische Untersuchungen zum Kolosserbrief*

Bujard's study consists of three major sections: an analysis of how the author constructs his sentences (including the frequency and use of conjunctions, infinitives, participles, and relative clauses), an assessment of the author's thought development (with observations on the use of repetition, antithetical elements, and parallel expressions), and what he calls "rhetorical engagement"—not formal rhetoric as such, but persuasive devices, such as the fullness of the author's style (e.g., the frequency of synonyms and genitive expressions) as well as considerations about the sound of the expressions, especially considering the oral reading of the text. The details of this study are considerable, indeed overwhelming, and certainly give it the appearance of a scientific case that will not easily be supplanted.

At the outset of this review, I will mention four methodological problems that flow through Bujard's entire study. First, at no place in his monograph does he establish criteria for determining when a difference is statistically significant for the determination of authorship. In other words, what amount of deviation is needed to judge that the author's use of a particular conjunction is outside the parameters of what would be deemed genuine Pauline usage? Bujard merely presents the statistics and then often draws the judgment that the differences between Colossians and the accepted Paulines are too great for Colossians to be authentic. But no scientific basis rooted in the science of statistical analysis is ever provided.[536] His judgments appear quite subjective, and the evidence he presents seems certainly capable of different interpretations than he makes. Since Bujard published his monograph, K. J. Neumann undertook a computer-assisted, discriminant statistical analysis of linguistic phenomena in Paul's letters and concluded that there was a high degree of statistical affinities between Colossians and the accepted letters of Paul.[537] Nevertheless, these kinds of analyses are laden with variables that can skew the data and make a scientific judgment very difficult. Thus, I think the most that is possible is to observe variations and seek to understand and explain them.

---

536 So also, Barclay, *Colossians and Philemon*, 30, who notes, "What Bujard's case lacked was a thorough grounding in statistics, by which alone one may judge how significant is a result that shows deviation from a Pauline 'norm.'" This problem is not isolated to Bujard. Pitts, "Style and Pseudonymity in Pauline Scholarship," 116, points out that "one of the primary shortcomings of assessments of Pauline authorship in biblical studies up to this point remains the lack of a developed, sound linguistic methodology by which to interpret the data."

537 Neumann, *Authenticity*, 194–99.

Second, there are also other features of the style that he overlooks. What about the relative uses of verb tense? The relative use of cases? The frequency of imperative verbs? The use of adjectives? Adverbs? In other words, why did he select the elements of style that he chose to assess and to leave others out? I will include some of the missing data in my brief analysis below.

Third, there is no comparative data from outside of the NT. In other words, how does the data from Colossians not only compare with the other Pauline letters but from documents in the NT world?

Fourth, in an important monograph titled *The Statistical Study of Literary Vocabulary*, U. Yule concluded that a minimum sample of ten thousand words is necessary for attaining trustworthy results in literary statistics.[538] The text of Colossians, amounting to 1575 words, falls 8425 words short of this statistical benchmark. Bujard does not explain the basis for his confidence in the conclusions he draws from his statistical results.

What I intend to do in this brief review is to examine some of the stylistic features of Colossians—some that Bujard investigated and some he did not—through a slightly different lens. Paul's first letter to the Thessalonians and his letter to the Philippians are both undisputed letters in terms of their Pauline authorship, and they are roughly the same size as Colossians. First Thessalonians is 1475 words, and Philippians is 1625, whereas Colossians falls between them at 1575. Because of their relative sizes, any statistical analysis is more visibly comparable using these three letters. First Thessalonians is one of the first letters that Paul wrote (perhaps as early as AD 50), whereas Philippians would be one of the final letters he wrote (10–12 years later in AD 60–62). Thus, they provide a beginning point and end point in terms of any possible theological development in Paul's thought. Both 1 Thessalonians and Philippians were written to churches in the same Roman province (Macedonia), which could suggest some similarity in expression if there is any contextualization of expression taking place; whereas Colossians was written to Asia Minor, suggesting that there should be even greater dissimilarity with the two. The pseudepigraphical hypothesis, especially the way it has been articulated by Bujard, would lead one to assume that the stylistic differences between these two letters and Colossians should be evident.

I will also include in the statistical data information from two other documents from that era: Ignatius's letter *To the Ephesians*, and the Testament of Naphtali (from the Testaments of the Twelve Patriarchs).[539] Both are of comparable size to the other three letters, with *To the Ephesians* as the largest (1772 words) and

---

538 Yule, *Statistical Study*, 281. He concludes, "We judged that it was best, if fairly trustworthy results were wanted, not to take a sample of much less than some 2000 occurrences of a noun. This would imply a sample of something like 10,000 words, more or less."

539 I compiled the statistical data by using the morphologically tagged databases of the documents in the BibleWorks software program. The Greek text of the Apostolic Fathers in BibleWorks is an eclectic text drawing on both the Lightfoot and Lake editions. The Greek text of T. Naph. is from the electronic edition of the OT Pseudepigrapha prepared by Craig Evans. It draws on all available Greek texts of the T. 12 Patr.

Testament of Naphtali almost exactly the same size (1467) as Paul's letter to the Philippians (1475). With all five documents of a similar size, a quick visual comparison in the charts will be much easier. I have chosen Ignatius's letter because it is not too distant in date from Colossians, contains some of the same themes, and addresses churches in Asia Minor. Testament of Naphtali was selected because it is written by a Jewish author around the time of the first century and contains moral exhortation for the people of God, thus sharing some of the same characteristics as Colossians. It is also a Jewish pseudepigraphon (not written by Naphtali) and was used and perhaps slightly edited by Christians. Both of these letters also supply a point of reference for grammar and style usage outside the Pauline corpus.

## *Terms and Grammatical Forms*

In the charts that follow, I do not follow the overall structure of Bujard's monograph. Part of the reason for that is that he misses some data points that I would regard as important for gaining a clearer picture of the fingerprint of the author of these letters. *Italics* are placed on the numbered occurrences of the noncanonical texts to aid the reading of the tables.

### *Conjunctions (Coordinating, Adversative, and Causal)*

| | καί | τέ | δέ | ἀλλά | γάρ | ὅτι |
|---|---|---|---|---|---|---|
| 1 Thess | 102 | 0 | 15 | 13 | 23 | 13 |
| Phil | 107 | 1 | 27 | 15 | 13 | 21 |
| Col | 101 | 0 | 5 | 3 | 6 | 6 |
| Ign. *Eph.* | *82* | *3* | *20* | *7* | *20* | *5* |
| T. Naph. | *146* | *0* | *12* | *1* | *13* | *16* |

In the first part of his study, Bujard focuses on various conjunctions and their distribution of usage throughout the Pauline letters. Conspicuous in its absence from Bujard's tables is any tabulation of the most common conjunction of all, καί (or, for that matter, τέ). There is obviously a very similar amount of occurrences of καί among the three letters and a very sparing use of τέ. This should be regarded as a highly significant element of style and a major oversight by Bujard.[540]

There are some noticeable differences of usage when it comes to the adversative and causal conjunctions, a difference that Bujard stresses in his monograph.[541]

540 He does discuss a study of καί frequency conducted by H. K. McArthur at the end of the monograph (232–33). But the absence of his treatment of this in his section on conjunctions remains suspicious, especially since the evidence runs counter to his thesis. I agree, however, with Bujard that a full study of the usage of καί should take into account its varied usage.

541 Bujard, *Stilanalytische Untersuchungen*, 26–27.

It is difficult to know how to account for these variations. One possible explanation is the several styles exhibited within Colossians—the presence of a hymn, a household code, a series of admonitions, and a long list of greetings—may explain some of this variation. Nevertheless, there is a distinctly different pattern of usage between Colossians and the other letters with the adversative and causal conjunctions.

The frequency of καί is quite different in Ign. *Eph.* and T. Naph., with a much lower frequency in Ign. *Eph.* and a much higher frequency in T. Naph. than the three NT letters. T. Naph. also uses the adversative conjunction ἀλλά only once, and Ign. *Eph.* uses the conjunction ὅτι less than the other documents.

*Conjunctions (Comparative)*

| | **κάθως** | **ὡς** | **καθάπερ** |
|---|---|---|---|
| 1 Thess | 13 | 9 | 4 |
| Phil | 3 | 7 | 0 |
| Col | 5 | 7 | 0 |
| Ign. *Eph.* | *0* | *14* | *0* |
| T. Naph. | *1* | *17* | *1* |

When it comes to comparative conjunctions, 1 Thessalonians is slightly out of step with Philippians and Colossians by making far more use of these terms and the constructions they introduce. Both Ign. *Eph.* and T. Naph. show a stronger stylistic preference for ὡς.

*Conjunctions (Inferential and Purpose)*

| | **οὖν** | **διό** | **ἄρα** | **ἵνα** | **ὥστε** |
|---|---|---|---|---|---|
| 1 Thess | 2 | 2 | 1 | 7 | 3 |
| Phil | 5 | 1 | 0 | 12 | 3 |
| Col | 5 | 0 | 0 | 13 | 0 |
| Ign. *Eph.* | 15 | 0 | 1 | 16 | 0 |
| T. Naph. | 6 | 0 | 0 | 3 | 1 |

There is a similar pattern of usage of these conjunctions in Philippians and Colossians, but 1 Thessalonians differs significantly. There are far fewer occurrences of οὖν and ἵνα in that letter. In the two noncanonical letters, Ign. *Eph.* has a strong preference for the use of οὖν, and T.Naph. seldom uses ἵνα.

### *Negatives*

| | οὐ, οὐκ, οὐχ | μή | οὐδέ | οὔτε | μηδέ | μήτε |
|---|---|---|---|---|---|---|
| 1 Thess | 18 | 15 | 3 | 5 | 0 | 0 |
| Phil | 13 | 6 | 1 | 0 | 1 | 0 |
| Col | 8 | 10 | 0 | 0 | 2 | 0 |
| Ign. *Eph.* | 8 | 14 | 6 | 0 | 0 | 0 |
| T. Naph. | 9 | 6 | 1 | 0 | 1 | 0 |

Once again, it is 1 Thessalonians that exhibits a different pattern of usage with negative particles and conjunctions by using nearly twice as many (41) as Philippians (21) and Colossians (20). Ign. *Eph.* also makes ample usage of the negative particle μή.

### *Particles (Conditional)*

| | εἴ | ἐάν | ἄν |
|---|---|---|---|
| 1 Thess | 1 | 2 | 2 |
| Phil | 13 | 0 | 1 |
| Col | 4 | 4 | 0 |
| Ign. *Eph.* | *5* | *7* | *0* |
| T. Naph. | *1* | *2* | *2* |

With respect to the use of conditional particles, Colossians (8) falls between 1 Thessalonians (5) and Philippians (14) in the number used. Ign. *Eph.* tends to use more conditional clauses introduced by ἐάν than any of the other letters.

### *Particles (Temporal)*

| | ποτέ | νῦν | ὅτε | ὅταν | ἄχρι |
|---|---|---|---|---|---|
| 1 Thess | 1 | 1 | 1 | 1 | 0 |
| Phil | 1 | 5 | 1 | 0 | 2 |
| Col | 2 | 2 | 1 | 2 | 0 |
| Ign. *Eph.* | *0* | *2* | *0* | *3* | *0* |
| T. Naph. | *1* | *0* | *0* | *1* | *1* |

There is nothing remarkable about the pattern of usage of the temporal particles between the three NT letters (or with Ign. *Eph.* and T. Naph.).

In summarizing these previous five categories, a significant study by J. van Nes should be noted. He researched what he called "indeclinables" (numerals, adverbs, prepositions, connectives, particles, and interjections) in Paul's letters.[542] He observes that the results will vary depending on whether one takes a seven-letter approach or a thirteen-letter approach in the statistical investigation. Regardless, he concludes that "none of the statistical data presented above should be taken as conclusive evidence for the pseudonymity of Pauline letters, whether disputed or not."[543]

### *Pronouns (Personal)*

| | ἡμεῖς[1] | ὑμεῖς | ἐγώ[2] | σύ | αὐτός[3] |
|---|---|---|---|---|---|
| 1 Thess | 49 | 84 | 1 | 0 | 24 |
| Phil | 6 | 51 | 52 | 1 | 31 |
| Col | 13 | 57 | 11 | 0 | 45 |
| Ign. *Eph.* | *14* | *61* | *16* | *1* | *40* |
| T. Naph. | *13* | *25* | *26* | *5* | *66* |

[1] For the first four pronouns, the chart tabulates the usage of the pronoun in all cases.
[2] This includes the following forms: ἐγώ, ἐμοῦ, ἐμοί, ἐμέ, μου, μοι, με.
[3] The numbers reflect all cases, singular and plural, for this pronoun.

There are some enormous variations in the use of personal pronouns among the three NT letters. First Thessalonians uses proportionally a far greater amount of the first-person plural and second-person plural pronouns than the other two letters. Philippians uses proportionally a far greater number of first-person singular personal pronouns than the other two letters. Since many advocates of the pseudepigraphical hypothesis think that the author of Colossians was presenting an exalted view of the apostle, one might have expected Colossians to use far more first-person singular personal pronouns. There is little that is noteworthy with the two other documents. T. Naph. uses the second-person plural pronoun far less than all the other letters and the third-person pronoun substantially more.

542 Van Nes, "Missing 'Particles,'" 383–98.
543 Van Nes, "Missing 'Particles,'" 392.

*Words Relating to God, Christ, and the Holy Spirit*

| | θεός | κύριος | Χριστός | Ἰησοῦς | πνεῦμα | πατήρ |
|---|---|---|---|---|---|---|
| 1 Thess | 36 | 25 | 10 | 16 | 5 | 5 |
| Phil | 23 | 15 | 37 | 22 | 5 | 4 |
| Col | 21 | 16 | 25 | 7 | 2 | 5 |
| Ign. *Eph.* | *43* | *9* | *33* | *33* | *3* | *10* |
| T. Naph. | *10* | *20* | *0* | *0* | *3* | *13* |

As we might expect, all three NT letters make ample use of these terms. There is nothing unusual about the frequency of these terms in Colossians compared to the other two letters. Christology is a major theme in Colossians, and the term Χριστός appears twenty-five times in the span of four chapters. But the title appears even more frequently in Philippians, which also contains a hymn of praise to Christ. First Thessalonians does not make use of a hymn, and the number of references to Christ is considerably less than the other two letters.

Ign. *Eph.*, because it is a Christian document, makes use of all these terms, but especially the name "Jesus," which it uses more than all the other documents. It it consistently paired with "Christ" ("Christ Jesus") in the letter. Not surprisingly, since it is a pre-Christian Jewish document, T. Naph. never mentions "Christ" or "Jesus." It shows a preference for "Lord" over "God," but both are frequent in the document.

*Common Pauline Words*

| | πίστις, πιστεύω | ἐλπίς, ἐλπίζω | ἀγαπή, ἀγαπάω | εἰρήνη | χάρις | χάρα, χαίρω |
|---|---|---|---|---|---|---|
| 1 Thess | 13 | 4 | 7 | 3 | 2 | 7 |
| Phil | 6 | 3 | 4 | 3 | 3 | 14 |
| Col | 5 | 3 | 7 | 2 | 5 | 3 |
| Ign. *Eph.* | *14* | *5* | *17* | *1* | *2* | *3* |
| T. Naph. | *2* | *0* | *3* | *1* | *0* | *0* |

There is a rather similar pattern of usage among the letters with this array of common Pauline terminology, with two exceptions. Philippians has substantially more references to "joy" than the other two NT letters, which is consistent with the common understanding that joy is a major theme in the letter. First Thessalonians doubles the number of references to "faith/believe" contained in each of the other letters. This is understandable given the different circumstances of the letter. Paul had planted the Thessalonian church less than a year earlier and was forced to leave them because of hostilities that had arisen. A major concern for him was how their faith was faring since he had departed. He wrote to them, "I sent to learn about your faith, for fear that somehow the tempter had tempted you and our labor would be in vain" (1 Thess 3:5 ESV).

Although these are not distinctively Christian terms, they are all used with far less freqency in T. Naph. "Love" surfaces as a major theme in Ignatius's letter, and "faith" is not far behind. Ignatius urges his readers to have "perfect faith and love toward Jesus Christ" since "everything else that contributes to excellence follows from them" (Ign. *Eph.* 14.1).

### *Common Pauline Words*

| | εὐαγγέλιον | προσευχή, προσεύχομαι | περιπατέω | ἅγιος | ἀδελφός | ἀληθεία |
|---|---|---|---|---|---|---|
| 1 Thess | 6 | 3 | 4 | 5 | 19 | 0 |
| Phil | 9 | 2 | 2 | 3 | 9 | 1 |
| Col | 2 | 5 | 4 | 6 | 5 | 2 |
| Ign. *Eph.* | *0* | *7* | *0* | *2* | *2* | *2* |
| T. Naph. | *0* | *1* | *0* | *2* | *3* | *0* |

Again, there is nothing remarkable about the pattern of usage with these common Pauline words. The one variation is that 1 Thessalonians uses the fictive kinship term, ἀδελφός, far more than the other two letters. This could serve part of Paul's pastoral purpose of encouraging these new believers in their faith by stressing their close filial connection with him and one another in the assembly. Paul tells them that "you know that we dealt with each of you as a father deals with his own children" (1 Thess 2:11 NIV). There are fewer occurrences of these words in Ign. *Eph.* and T. Naph., with the exception of the terms for "prayer," which are frequent in Ignatius's brief letter.

### *Key Pauline Theological Words in the Accepted Letters*

| | δικαιοσύνη | νόμος | δικαιόω | ἀπολύτρωσις | ἱλαστήριον | ἁμαρτία |
|---|---|---|---|---|---|---|
| 1 Thess | 0 | 0 | 0 | 0 | 0 | 3 |
| Phil | 4 | 3 | 0 | 0 | 0 | 0 |
| Col | 0 | 0 | 0 | 1 | 0 | 1 |
| Ign. *Eph.* | *0* | *0* | *0* | *0* | *0* | *0* |
| T. Naph. | *1* | *4* | *0* | *0* | *0* | *1* |

None of these theological terms appear with a great deal of frequency in the three NT letters. It is very conspicuous that Paul uses none of these terms (except "sin") in his letter to the Thessalonians. Nevertheless, some advocates of the pseudonymity of Colossians contend that the absence of these terms is a sign that the letter was written by someone other than Paul. If that contention is valid, then it impugns the Pauline authorship of 1 Thessalonians and Philippians as well. Philippians does make use of the terms for "righteousness" and "law," but we know that the Judaizing controversy had emerged in that context to some extent, whereas it was not present in the other two communties when the letters were written. These terms are largely absent from Ign. *Eph.* and T. Naph. except for the term "law," which appears four times in T. Naph.

### *Basic Vocabulary*

| | ἔρχομαι | γίνομαι | εἰμί | ἔχω | δίδωμι | τίθημι |
|---|---|---|---|---|---|---|
| 1 Thess | 4 | 12 | 12 | 8 | 2 | 1 |
| Phil | 3 | 6 | 17 | 10 | 0 | 0 |
| Col | 2 | 5 | 26 | 7 | 1 | 0 |
| Ign. *Eph.* | *1* | *11* | *53* | *5* | *0* | *0* |
| T. Naph. | *3* | *5* | *19* | *1* | *2* | *0* |

These basic terms can be one helpful indicator of an author's stylistic preferences. There are two variances here that should be noted among the canonical letters. There are twice as many occurences of γίνομαι in 1 Thessalonians than there are Philippians and Colossians. It is also notable that Colossians uses εἰμί substantially more than it is used in 1 Thessalonians and Philippians. What is surprising is the extraordinary amount of times Ignatius's letter uses εἰμί compared to the four other documents.

### *Distribution of Mood in Finite Verbs*

| | **Indicatives** | **Subjunctives** | **Imperatives** | **Optatives** |
|---|---|---|---|---|
| 1 Thess | 96 | 19 | 21 | 5 |
| Phil | 117 | 19 | 26 | 0 |
| Col | 96 | 23 | 30 | 0 |
| Ign. *Eph.* | *129* | *45* | *13* | *5* |
| T. Naph. | *155* | *11* | *6* | *1* |

There is nothing remarkable about the number of indicatives, subjunctives, and imperatives in the three NT letters when compared with one another. Philippians has slightly more indicative verbs. Perhaps it is most remarkable that there is such similarity.

It is also noteworthy that T. Naph. uses the indicative mood far more than the other documents and the subjunctive mood substantially less. Ignatius's letter uses the indicative mood more than the NT letters.

*Distribution of Tenses in Finite Verbs*

| | **Pres** | **Impf** | **Fut** | **Aor** | **Perf** | **Plpf** |
|---|---|---|---|---|---|---|
| 1 Thess | 72 | 3 | 6 | 47 | 13 | 0 |
| Phil | 82 | 5 | 16 | 48 | 11 | 0 |
| Col | 77 | 3 | 6 | 56 | 7 | 0 |
| Ign. *Eph.* | *108* | *11* | *5* | *57* | *10* | *0* |
| T. Naph. | *42* | *17* | *33* | *73* | *7* | *1* |

*Distribution of Tenses across Moods of Finite Verbs*

| | | **1 Thess** | **Phil** | **Col** | **Ign. *Eph.*** | **T. Naph.** |
|---|---|---|---|---|---|---|
| Indic | Pres | 40 | 51 | 48 | 74 | 40 |
| | Impf | 3 | 5 | 3 | 11 | 17 |
| | Fut | 6 | 16 | 6 | 5 | 33 |
| | Aor | 34 | 34 | 32 | 29 | 57 |
| | Perf | 13 | 11 | 7 | 10 | 7 |
| | Plpf | 0 | 0 | 0 | 0 | 1 |
| Subj | Pres | 12 | 8 | 6 | 23 | 0 |
| | Aor | 7 | 11 | 17 | 22 | 11 |
| Impv | Pres | 20 | 23 | 23 | 11 | 2 |
| | Aor | 1 | 3 | 7 | 1 | 4 |
| Opt | Aor | 5 | 0 | 0 | 5 | 1 |

Similarly, with the use of tenses in finite verbs, there is a suprisingly even distribution of the various tenses among the three NT letters. It is a different story when one turns to the letter from Ignatius. There is a substantially greater use of the present tense both in the indicative mood and in the subjunctive mood. T. Naph. also uses the aorist indicative and the future tense far more than the other documents.

### *Participles and Infinitives*

| | Participles | Infinitives |
|---|---|---|
| 1 Thess | 58 | 45 |
| Phil | 56 | 39 |
| Col | 77 | 11 |
| Ign. *Eph.* | *80* | *53* |
| T. Naph. | *42* | *19* |

Colossians tends to use substantially more participles and significantly fewer infinitives than the other two NT letters, while Ignatius's letter uses far more participles and significantly more infinitives than all the other documents.

### *Distribution of Tenses in Participles and Infinitives*

| | Participles | | | Infinitives | | |
|---|---|---|---|---|---|---|
| | *Pres* | *Aor* | *Perf* | *Pres* | *Aor* | *Perf* |
| 1 Thess | 42 | 13 | 3 | 24 | 19 | 2 |
| Phil | 36 | 13 | 7 | 29 | 8 | 2 |
| Col | 50 | 17 | 10 | 1 | 8 | 2 |
| Ign. *Eph.* | *49* | *14* | *17* | *34* | *18* | *1* |
| T.Naph. | *21* | *19* | *2* | *6* | *13* | *0* |

There is a fairly consistent pattern in the use of tense among participles with the three NT letters. It is noteworthy that there is only one present infinitive in Colossians, whereas there are twenty-four and twenty-nine respectively in 1 Thessalonians and Philippians.

### *Distribution of Cases among Nouns*

| | Nominative | Genitive | Dative | Accusative |
|---|---|---|---|---|
| 1 Thess | 57 | 97 | 78 | 71 |
| Phil | 56 | 113 | 93 | 94 |
| Col | 73 | 117 | 110 | 89 |
| Ign. *Eph.* | *104* | *115* | *120* | *94* |
| T. Naph. | *120* | *101* | *62* | *109* |

The distribution of the cases among nouns is unremarkable between the three NT letters. Colossians is sometimes singled out for an abundant use of genitive cases, but the proportion of its use of the genitive case is proportional to the other two letters. Ignatius's letter and T. Naph. show a much greater use of the nominative case.

## *Prepositions*

| | **All** | ἀπό | διά | εἰς | ἐκ | ἐν | ἐπί | κατά |
|---|---|---|---|---|---|---|---|---|
| 1 Thess | 153 | 9 | 10 | 29 | 3 | 55 | 5 | 0 |
| Phil | 170 | 4 | 14 | 27 | 10 | 66 | 7 | 11 |
| Col | 192 | 9 | 14 | 21 | 11 | 88 | 6 | 14 |
| Ign. *Eph.* | *166* | *3* | *17* | *32* | *8* | *65* | *3* | *18* |
| T. Naph. | *128* | *5* | *6* | *23* | *4* | *42* | *16* | *10* |

| | παρά | περί | πρό | πρός | σύν | ὑπέρ | ὑπό |
|---|---|---|---|---|---|---|---|
| 1 Thess | 2 | 8 | 0 | 13 | 3 | 2 | 3 |
| Phil | 1 | 4 | 0 | 4 | 4 | 7 | 2 |
| Col | 1 | 4 | 1 | 6 | 7 | 7 | 2 |
| Ign. *Eph.* | *1* | *3* | *2* | *6* | *0* | *6* | *5* |
| T. Naph. | *1* | *1* | *0* | *7* | *2* | *0* | *2* |

The author of Colossians uses more prepositions than the other two NT letters, perhaps substantially more than 1 Thessalonians. Where this is most evident is in the use of the preposition ἐν. There are thirty-three more occurrences of this preposition in Colossians than 1 Thessalonians, and twenty-two more than Philippians. This is the only place where there is significant variation by Colossians from the other two letters. First Thessalonians is different from the other two by never making use of the preposition κατά, whereas Philippians and Colossians use it eleven and fourteen times respectively. First Thessalonians also shows a preference for the preposition πρός.

Part of the reason for the abundance of occurrences of ἐν in Colossians likely has to do with the author's overt theological emphasis on union with Christ. This comes to expression prominently in the early part of the second chapter: "all the treasures of wisdom and knowledge are *in him*" (2:3); "walk *in him*" (2:6); "rooted and grounded *in him*" (2:7); "you have been filled *in him*" (2:10); "you were circumcised *in him*" (2:11); and "you were raised *in him*" (2:12). This accords with the increased use of σύν in Colossians, another preposition that the author uses to express union *with Christ*.

Both Ign. *Eph.* and T. Naph. have a comparable distribution of prepositions to the NT letters, with some minor variations. T. Naph. makes greater use of ἐπί than all the other documents and never employs ὑπέρ.

## *Relative Pronouns*

| | **Relative Pronouns** |
|---|---|
| 1 Thess | 5 |
| Phil | 26 |
| Col | 42 |
| Ign. *Eph.* | *39* |
| T. Naph. | *9* |

When it comes to the frequency of relative pronouns, 1 Thessalonians is more the outlier than Colossians when the three NT letters are compared. Although Philippians has twenty-one more relative pronouns than 1 Thessalonians, Colossians still has sixteen more than Philippians. Thus, the use of relative pronouns is a unique stylistic feature of Colossians. It is very close in the frequency of usage to Ign. *Eph.*, but T. Naph. is much closer to 1 Thessalonians.

## *Conclusion*

Based on this array of data, much of which was not used by Bujard, we can draw the following preliminary conclusions.

(1) The vast majority of this data shows that the vocabulary and grammatical forms used by the author of Colossians display a great deal of consistency with Paul's first letter to the Thessalonians and his letter to the Philippians. Something as mundane as the frequency of the use of the conjunction καί is almost identical among the three letters. Most of the differences in frequency of particular vocabulary and specific forms are unremarkable.

(2) There are a handful of places where 1 Thessalonians showed substantial variation from the other two NT letters. This is evident in that letter's use of the first- and second-person personal pronouns, a significantly greater number of uses of πίστις/πιστεύω and ἀδελφός than the other letters, a more extensive use of γίνομαι, and the absence of the preposition κατά.

(3) There are also a variety of places where Philippians varies significantly in its use of vocabulary and certain grammatical forms from the other two letters. This letter uses an enormously greater number of first-person singular personal pronouns than the other NT letters. Philippians also makes greater use of the terms Χριστός and χάρα/χαίρω than 1 Thessalonians and Colossians. As for grammatical forms, Philippians has a great deal more indicative verbs than its counterparts. Philippians also is the only one of the three letters to use the terms νόμος and δικαιοσύνη.

(4) Colossians does, in fact, have a handful of unique features. This letter makes significantly less use of the conjunctions δέ and ἀλλά, as well as the causal conjunctions γάρ and ὅτι. The author of Colossians also employs the copulative εἰμί quite a bit more than the other letters and makes far greater use of relative pronouns. It also employs noticeably more participles and fewer infinitives than its counterparts. And, finally, Colossians uses the preposition ἐν proportionally more than the other letters, while displaying a consistency with the use of the other prepositions.

(5) While this analysis clearly reveals that Colossians displays some unique tendencies with the use of vocabulary and grammatical forms, the same can be said for 1 Thessalonians and Philippians. Do the differences revealed for Colossians cause one to question its authenticity as a letter from Paul? It would be hard to make that case from this data.

(6) The other two non-NT documents, Ignatius's letter *To the Ephesians* and the Testament of Naphtali, actually reveal a great deal of similarity of usage with the three NT letters. Nevertheless, there are many significant differences, which might be expected with altogether different authors and with different purposes. Elements of style such as the frequency of use of the conjunctions—καί, ἀλλά, ὡς, οὖν, and ἵνα—are markedly different than the three NT letters. Similarly, there is a noteworthy difference with the use of εἰμί, the indicative and subjunctive moods, the present and future tenses, participle and infinitives, and the use (or nonuse) of certain prepositions. Understandably, T. Naph. makes no use of christological names and little use of common Pauline theological terms. This comparison makes it clear that Colossians lines up far more closely with 1 Thessalonians and Philippians than with these other documents.

## Thought Development in Colossians

In the second part of his monograph, Bujard examines the way that the author of Colossians constructs and develops his line of thought in sections of the letter, especially 1:3–8 and 2:6–15.[544] He observes that the author tends to use participles and relative clauses while avoiding the use of conjunctions to express the logical relations. He characterizes this as a loosely associative manner of developing the thought, as opposed to a more precise and logical development, and concludes that this stylistic trait represents "an essential difference" between Colossians and the accepted Pauline letters.[545] He also examines some other stylistic tendencies of the letter, including the repetition of words and word groups, the use of antitheses, and the frequency of the use of the preposition ἐν. Although this section of Bujard's monograph deserves a full and detailed response, I can only here make a few preliminary remarks about this portion of his study.

544 Bujard, *Stilanalytisches Untersuchungen*, 76–129.

545 Bujard, *Stilanalytisches Untersuchungen*, 129. Barth and Blanke, 120, refer to Bujard's indictment against the logical order of individual sentences and drawn out thoughts as a set of "wild accusations."

First, one must take into account that the sample that Bujard focuses on here is quite small—that is, 1:3–8 and 2:6–15. It is one thing to *describe* the characteristics of the style in each of these passages, but it is quite another to *render a judgment* about the style as non-Pauline. This is particularly true when the judgment is made on the basis of the frequency of a particular stylistic characteristic in each section on aspects of style that Paul clearly knows and employs.

Second, regarding the repetition of words and word groups, Bujard argues in a different direction by observing that this phenomena appears with *less* frequency in Colossians than in the accepted Pauline letters. Although he acknowledges the presence of repetition in Colossians (e.g., 1:11: ἐν πάσῃ δυνάμει δυναμούμενοι) and tabulates the occurrences, his argument is once again based on the quantification of occurrences to judge authenticity. But his case actually goes a step further when he contends that Paul uses repetition to further his argument, whereas in Colossians this function is absent and the repetition merely has a simple rhetorical purpose (as in 1:11, 29; 2:19).[546] But even this rhetorical use of repetition is something Bujard admits is present in Paul, which, once again, renders this a judgment about frequency. In a similar way, Bujard finds a higher degree of antithetical formulations in Colossians than occurs in the undisputed letters.

Third, I would acknowledge (with Bujard) that there is a much greater use of the preposition ἐν in the letter to the Colossians (see the table above).[547] What Bujard fails to do is to ask the question, "Why?" Might there be a theological reason for the more extensive use of this preposition? The apostle Paul uses the preposition ἐν forty-six times in Rom 5–8. Part of his purpose in that context is to emphasize the union of believers with Christ (e.g., "consider yourselves dead to sin and alive to God *in Christ Jesus*," Rom 6:11; "the gift of God is eternal life *in Christ Jesus* our Lord," Rom 6:23; "there is therefore now no condemnation for those who are *in Christ Jesus*," Rom 8:1). In a similar way, there is a strong rhetorical emphasis on union with Christ expressed by the author of Colossians, especially in the second chapter (e.g., "all the treasures of wisdom and knowledge are *in him*" [2:3]; "walk *in him*" [2:6]; "rooted and grounded *in him*" [2:7]; "you have been filled *in him*" [2:10]; "you were circumcised *in him*" [2:11]; and "you were raised *in him*" [2:12]). It is not inconceivable that the apostle would put a greater emphasis on union with Christ in some letters over others.

## The "Plerophoric" Character of the Style of Colossians

The final section of Bujard's monograph focuses on what he calls the author's "rhetorical engagement" in the letter. This does not refer to the schools of rhetoric of the Hellenistic and Roman eras but on a variety of stylistic elements in the letter. Much of his discussion has to do with the "plerophoric" style of the letter—that is, a "fullness" of style, such as the use of synonyms, appositions,

546 Bujard, *Stilanalytisches Untersuchungen*, 96.

547 Bujard, *Stilanalytisches Untersuchungen*, 121–28.

the frequency of the use of genitives, etymological cognates, and the frequent use of πᾶς.[548] In this section, I intend to raise a few questions and points of concern about Bujard's method and his interpretation of the results.

Following Mayerhoff, Bujard observes the great frequency of the use of synonyms in Colossians and constructs a list of twenty-eight different synonymous expressions that occur in the four chapters of the letter.[549] However, there are many alleged synonymous expressions in this list that I would not regard as synonymous. For many of these, there is some degree of semantic overlap, but it is insufficient for any of them to be construed as synonymous. In the phrase "holy and faithful" (ἁγίοις καὶ πιστοῖς, 1:2), "holy" has a much broader frame of reference than "faithful," although faithfulness would certainly be included in its meaning. The same should be said of "holy and beloved" (ἅγιοι καὶ ἠγαπημένοι, 3:12) and "faithful and beloved" (τῷ πιστῷ καὶ ἀγαπητῷ, 4:9), which Bujard also regards as synonymous expressions. "Beloved" could be regarded as semantically distinct from both "holy" and "faithful." "Philosophy and empty deceit" (τῆς φιλοσοφίας καὶ κενῆς ἀπάτης, 2:8) are not synonymous expressions, but rather "the philosophy" is a self-characterization of the oppositional faction at Colossae, and "empty deceit" represents an adjectival description of it from the author's perspective. Bujard also regards "humility and the worship of angels" (ταπεινοφροσύνη καὶ θρησκείᾳ τῶν ἀγγέλων, 2:18) as synonyms, but they refer to two entirely distinct practices. The first refers most likely to ascetic practices (such as fasting and taboos), while the latter refers to a ritual invocation of angelic beings. This should be adequate to demonstrate that there are significant problems wth Bujard's classification of what constitutes synonymous expressions. E. Percy argued that Philippians actually has more synonymous expressions than Colossians, thus suggesting that Colossians is not outside the scope of Pauline usage.[550] Bujard, of course, took exception to Percy's observation, but when Bujard's inflated list of synonymous expressions is reduced, Percy is justified in his conclusion.

Bujard also looks at appositional expressions in Colossians and concludes that their frequency and manner of usage in no way corresponds with Paul's writings.[551] He points to modifiers such as the genitive τῆς ἐκκλησίας in the clause "he is the head of the body, the church" (αὐτός ἐστιν ἡ κεφαλὴ τοῦ σώματος τῆς ἐκκλησίας, 1:18). This, of course, is a problematic passage to cite because it occurs in the Colossian hymn and may not represent Paul's style here, unless it is an editorial insertion to reinterpret the meaning of "the body." Nevertheless, it is likely that Bujard overstates the discontinuity between Paul's usage and Colossians since, as Kiley notes, this kind of specification "is present in Paul."[552]

---

548 Bujard, *Stilanalytisches Untersuchungen*, 130–219.

549 Bujard, *Stilanalytisches Untersuchungen*, 148.

550 Percy, *Probleme*, 21–22.

551 Bujard, *Stilanalytisches Untersuchungen*, 153.

552 Kiley, *Colossians as Pseudepigraphy*, 56.

He also finds this fullness of expression in a handful of circumstantial definitions with prepositional phrases beginning in ἐν. He cites fifteen examples of this "stylistic peculiarity,"[553] such as "a portion of the share of the saints *in the light*" (ἐν τῷ φωτί, 1:12). Kiley reduces the number to eleven after eliminating formulaic constructions or predicate completions.[554] Applying his criteria of what constitutes this kind of circumstantial definition, Bujard compiles a list of sixteen instances in the recognized letters of Paul and then infers that the relative frequency of this stylistic trait puts Colossians beyond the pale of accepted Pauline usage. Without arguing over his criteria or the application of them to certain passages, we are once again in a situation where he makes relative quantifications that serve as his basis for judging authenticity. It is one thing to say that this is a stylistic characteristic that the apostle Paul never used and Colossians uses repeatedly. But that is not the case. Paul was indeed aware of this element of style and used it. The authenticity question, for Bujard, once again revolves around frequency and the matter of how many is too many for the letter to come from the same author as the accepted Paulines. Bujard appears to have unwarranted confidence in his judgments on such issues as this.

Mayerhoff was the first to point to the stringing together of genitive cases in Colossians as a stylistic trait.[555] Bujard has noticed this, too, but (with Percy) has sharpened the focus to the pairing of genitives where both are substantives and the first stands as a designation for the second, as in "the word of truth, the gospel" (τῷ λόγῳ τῆς ἀληθείας τοῦ εὐαγγελίου, 1:5).[556] He compiles a list of five occurrences in Colossians whereas, he contends, there are only eight instances of this phenomenon in the accepted Pauline letters (with five of these in Romans). But the list does not fit the criteria that he has established in every instance. In 1:13, the second genitive functions adjectivally to describe the first genitive—that is, "the kingdom of his beloved son" (τὴν βασιλείαν τοῦ υἱοῦ τῆς ἀγάπης αὐτοῦ). In 1:27, the first genitive actually modifies the preceding nominative noun adjectivally and does not stand appositionally to the second genitive: "the glorious wealth of this mystery" (τὸ πλοῦτος τῆς δόξης τοῦ μυστηρίου τούτου). This reduces the number of his examples in Colossians to three—an unremarkable difference. Furthermore, his observation about Pauline usage of genitives is simply wrong; he overlooks other instances in the accepted letters. Notice, for instance, the use of the genitives in 1 Thess 1:3: "remembering before our God and Father your work of faith and labor of love and steadfastness of hope in our Lord Jesus Christ" (μνημονεύοντες ὑμῶν τοῦ ἔργου τῆς πίστεως καὶ τοῦ κόπου τῆς ἀγάπης καὶ τῆς ὑπομονῆς τῆς ἐλπίδος τοῦ κυρίου ἡμῶν Ἰησοῦ Χριστοῦ ἔμπροσθεν τοῦ θεοῦ καὶ πατρὸς ἡμῶν). The first genitive in each of the three

553 Bujard, *Stilanalytisches Untersuchungen*, 153.
554 Kiley, *Colossians as Pseudepigraphy*, 56.
555 Mayerhoff, *Colosser*, 37.
556 Bujard, *Stilanalytisches Untersuchungen*, 156.

pairs is a designation for the second; in other words, the work is faith, the labor is love, and endurance is hope.[557]

The adjective πᾶς occurs a total of thirty-nine times in Colossians, whereas it appears only eighteen times in 1 Thessalonians and fifteen times in Galatians (although it occurs 111 times in 1 Corinthians and 71 times in Romans). Bujard makes a distinction within its usage where there are certain instances that he characterizes as having a "plerophoric character" that semantically serves to strengthen an expression, such as in Col 1:11: "with *all* power being strengthened" (ἐν πάσῃ δυνάμει δυναμούμενοι).[558] He counts thirteen instances of this in Colossians (1:6, 9, 10 [2x], 11 [3x], 23, 28; 2:3; 3:9, 16; 4:12), whereas he finds only three in 1 Thessalonians and none in Galatians (but two in 1 Corinthians and five in Romans). Although this stylistic trait does appear in Paul, it is more pronounced in Colossians, as Bujard has demonstrated. Nevertheless, he counts eight occurences of the plerophoric πᾶς in Philippians. So if Paul could use it that many times in another small letter, why is it unreasonable to think of him using it a few more times in another letter without inferring that there must be another author at work?

Finally, Bujard observes that the author of Colossians makes use of different "fullness" language than Paul in his accepted letters. He notes that Paul tends to use forms of περισσός, πλεῖον, and ὑπερέχω, whereas the author of Colossians employs forms of πληρόω.[559] This observation is accurate, although it must be said that Paul also uses forms of πληρόω and Colossians likewise uses forms of περισσός and πλεῖον, albeit with less frequency. What Bujard does not take into account is the potential influence of the Christ-hymn where the term πλήρωμα plays a significant role in this poetic declaration of Christology ("for in him all the fullness of God was pleased to dwell," 1:19). This likely influenced the author to use this term and its verbal cognate elsewhere in the letter (1:9, 25; 2:9, 10).

## Conclusions

Bujard's monograph remains the most thoroughgoing study of the grammar and style of Colossians that has ever been undertaken. His work surpasses both Mayerhoff and Percy by sharpening the focus to include an array of very nuanced aspects of style.

One of his primary objectives was to overcome the problem of the widespread use of isolating (non-contextual) and quantifying methods of previous forms of literary-critical language and style comparisons.[560] His stated approach was to set stylistic observations next to each other, order their functions, and interpret

557 My interpretational preference in this passage, however, is to take the second genitive of each of the three pairs as a subjective genitive, but this would still fit the criteria that Bujard established.

558 Bujard, *Stilanalytisches Untersuchungen*, 159–60.

559 Bujard, *Stilanalytisches Untersuchungen*, 160–64.

560 Bujard, *Stilanalytisches Untersuchungen*, 7.

the whole as a way of overcoming the limitations of a quantifying approach. Unfortunately, Bujard never seems to surmount the quantifying approach himself as he executes his study. His volume is replete with references to the amount of occurrences (*die Häufigkeit*) of a term or grammatical item in Paul compared to its use in Colossians. A disparity in frequency almost always becomes his criterion for judging Colossians to be out of sync with Paul and therefore an indication of its pseudonymity. Yet nowhere does he provide us with any kind of criteria for making these judgments. They are generally his own subjective impressions based on the statistics that he has compiled.

Although part of Bujard's method is to stay rigorously focused on matters of grammar and style, this is also the Achilles' heel of his work. He does not take into account a variety of factors going into the composition of Colossians that would undoubtedly have exerted a significant influence on how it was written. In particular, he includes no discussion of the opposing teaching that is being addressed by the letter, nor the way that the author is polemicizing against it. Nor does he take into account the use of traditional material—especially the Christ-hymn—and how this may have influenced the compositional tendencies of the author. He also does not take into account some of the unique stylistic features of the various other subunits of thought within the letter, such as thanksgiving, prayer reports, the household code, and the long list of greetings and how these would have had an impact on vocabulary, grammatical forms, and the rhetorical style of the author of the letter.

Finally, Bujard never considers the possible influence of the ostensible cowriter of the letter (Timothy) and the likely use of a secretary. One can safely attribute some degree of grammatical, stylistic, and rhetorical influence to these individuals in the letter-writing process, which could very well account for some or most of the differences that Bujard has tabulated. At the minimum, the possibility that Paul used a secretary in the composition of Colossians should temper one's conclusion about the pseudonymity of the letter.

In the end, Bujard exercises an unwarranted sense of confidence in the conclusions he has drawn from the results of his study. He ends his monograph with the cavalier statement, "This holistic view of the style and its evaluation for the solution of the authenticity problem have fully proven themselves. With their help it was possible to prove that the difference between the style of Colossians and that of the Pauline letters in terms of uniformity, type, and size is so serious, that Paul's authorship of Colossians must be ruled out for that reason alone."[561] Unfortunately, this conclusion has proven highly influential in a broad swath of higher critical scholarship. But it needs to be seriously questioned. What I have attempted here is to offer some preliminary observations, data, and questions to begin that process. One needs to begin with Bujard's underlying assumption that style alone can determine authorship or pseudonymity.

561 Bujard, *Stilanalytisches Untersuchungen*, 220.

### *Theological Content*

For some interpreters, the distinctive theological traits of Colossians are the most decisive argument against Pauline authorship. Yet for others, the theology of Colossians is thoroughly consistent with Paul's accepted letters, and the alleged differences should not be treated as new developments by another author but as accents or emphases within the larger framework of Pauline theology. The latter option reflects my own approach to this issue. In my previous work on the letter, I discussed this in an extended section titled "The Contextualized Theology of Colossians," where I suggested that the unique situation at Colossae called forth certain theological emphases by Paul out of his pastoral care for these churches.[562] I still find this the most compelling explanation for some of the unique theological emphases in Colossians. The putative differences between the theology of this letter and the accepted letters revolve around certain aspects of the Christology, eschatology, and the ecclesiology reflected in Colossians. Scholars have also expressed concern about the absence of some prominent Pauline themes.

#### Christology

It has long been recognized that there is a "cosmic Christology" in Colossians. There is a strong emphasis on Christ's supremacy to everything (τὰ πάντα) in heaven and on earth. This theme is especially pronounced in the Christ-hymn where Jesus is extolled as the creator and sustainer of the universe and the one who will bring final peace and restoration to everything. He is therefore preeminent above all. But he is especially proclaimed as supreme over all the visible powers (which would include the Roman Imperium) and the invisible powers, which the hymn delineates as "thrones, dominions, principalities, and authorities" (1:16). This theme is then developed through the letter, reaching a high point in 2:15 where Jesus's victory over the principalities and authorities is declared in the most dramatic terms. His lordship over these powers is made ecclesiologically relevant in 2:10 where the writer asserts that "in him all the fullness of the deity dwells bodily, and you have been filled in him, who is the head of every principality and authority."

The idea that Christ is supreme over all of creation is already present in Paul. The Philippian Christ-hymn extols Christ in his exalted status and proclaims that "at the name of Jesus every knee should bow, in heaven and on earth and under the earth, and every tongue confess that Jesus Christ is Lord" (Phil 2:10–11 ESV). Paul also announced the supremacy and lordship of Christ to the Corinthians when he placed Jesus alongside God the Father and announced that he is the creator and sustainer of all things (1 Cor 8:6).[563] He sums it up

562 *Colossian Syncretism*, 245–309.

563 Wright, "Monotheism, Christology and Ethics," 136, has referred to this as "the emergence of a strikingly new phenomenon: christological monotheism."

concisely in Romans in his ascription of praise to Christ as the one "who is over all, God blessed forever" (NRSV; ὁ ὢν ἐπὶ πάντων θεὸς εὐλογητὸς εἰς τοὺς αἰῶνας; Rom 9:5).

There should be very little dispute that the theme of hostile supernatural powers opposing God and the church is a major concern of the letter (regardless of how one interprets the nature of "the philosophy"). This alone is sufficient to call forth an emphasis by the author on the supremacy and lordship of Christ. Yet if I am correct in describing the allurement of the opposing teaching as rooted in a deep concern on the part of the readers about the influence of spiritual forces on daily life that is prompting them to give heed to a local Christian shaman figure, the cosmic Christology is even more understandable. The solution that Paul points them to is christological—that is, to hold on tight to Christ who is the head of the body (2:19). He is supreme over all of these forces.

The theme of Christ's supremacy over the powers is present in the Pauline letters. They presently do not possess the power and ability to separate God's people from the love of Christ (Rom 8:38–39), and in the eschatological future they will be completely destroyed (1 Cor 15:24). All that the author of Colossians says about the lordship of Christ over the powers in Colossians is consistent with what is said in the accepted Paulines.[564]

## Eschatology

Some have asserted that there is a complete loss of future eschatology in Colossians and that this Pauline emphasis has been replaced by a completely realized eschatology. Others go so far as to say that the Jewish apocalyptic, two-age understanding has been jettisoned in favor of a Hellenistic spatial perspective. For G. Bornkamm, this particularly came to expression with the concept of hope in Colossians. It is no longer in the age to come, but hope is now placed in what is "above" and not on what is "below."[565] The expectation of an imminent parousia has receded, and far more often the emphasis is on salvation in the present.[566] A. J. M. Wedderburn has wisely cautioned, however, that Colossians shares the worldview of Jewish apocalyptic where those writings "combined both spatial and temporal categories in their imagery."[567]

A significant part of the concern of those who see a disjuncture with Paul's eschatology is the author's declaration that believers not only have participated with Christ in his death, but *also in his resurrection* (2:12–13). Many interpreters see Paul as maintaining an "eschatological reserve"—that is, he consistently

564 Sumney, 5, who takes the letter as pseudepigraphical, concludes that "thus, Colossians' cosmic Christology does not exclude the possibility that Paul wrote this letter."

565 Bornkamm, "Hoffnung," 56–64. See also Merklein, "Rezeption," 46–47; Müller, *Anfänge der Paulusschule*, 80–82; et al.

566 Müller, *Anfänge der Paulusschule*, 67. Lohse, 180, asserts that "the expectation that the Lord would soon appear has disappeared."

567 Wedderburn, *Theology of the Later Pauline Letters*, 52–53.

speaks of resurrection as a future event and always stops short of characterizing it as a present experience. Thus, when Paul speaks of the baptismal experience as representing a union with Christ in his death in Rom 6, he does not continue this line of thought by explicitly saying that we are likewise united with him in his resurrection. Rather, he says, "we *will be* [ἐσόμεθα] united with him in a resurrection like his" (Rom 6:5). Some think that Paul is here, in part, polemicizing against a Hellenistic church tradition that espouses an overrealized eschatology (similar to what we find in the theology of the opponents at Corinth, but perhaps not as realized as the enthusiasts in view in 2 Tim 2:18 [τὴν ἀνάστασιν ἤδη γεγονέναι]).[568] The roots of this notion ostensibly stem from a Hellenistic church that derives its view of dying and rising from mystery-cult theology.

Wedderburn has argued convincingly against the view that Paul is setting out to correct an alleged Hellenistic-Christian view of overrealized eschatology in Rom 6.[569] He points out that initiates into the mysteries did not see their relationship to the deity as "dying" and "rising." Rather, they put their hope in the power of the deity with whom they were now related through initiation.[570] Consequently, he concludes that it is possible that the future tenses of Rom 6:5, 8 "are as much logical as temporal, or, putting it another (perhaps better) way, they refer to a state of affairs that already obtains in some measure, however much it still looks to the future for its full consummation (as in 5:19?)."[571] When he turns to Col 2:12, Wedderburn then argues that the declaration of co-resurrection with Christ does not go back to a tradition already in existence and opposed by Paul in Rom 6, nor does it reflect a mystery religion or gnostic influence on the writer of Colossians; rather, the author has here given expression to the meaning of baptism in terms borrowed from Rom 6.[572] For Wedderburn, this is a logical and natural development of the themes in Rom 6 that came into expression because of the nature of the situation facing the church at Colossae. But the seeds of realized eschatology are also present in Paul's statement that by virtue of their identification with Christ and the fact that Christ was raised from the dead, believers can now "walk in newness of life" (ἐν καινότητι ζωῆς περιπατήσωμεν, Rom 6:4). This newness of life is a logical entailment of identifying with Christ in his resurrection. Lincoln summarizes well the scope of Paul's thought on this issue when he states that "there are two poles to Paul's thinking about resurrection life. That life has been entered on by the believer in union with Christ yet its consummation still lies in the future."[573] This encapsulates the thought of the apostle in Romans, but also in Colossians.

568 See, e.g., L. Hartmann, "Baptism," *ABD* 1:589; Koester, *Introduction*, 2:266; Schweizer, 144–45; Tannehill, *Dying and Rising*, 10–11; Becker, *Auferstehung der Toten*, 55; Lohse, 103; Beker, *Paul*, 163.

569 Wedderburn, *Baptism and Resurrection*.

570 Wedderburn, *Baptism and Resurrection*, 356–57.

571 Wedderburn, *Baptism and Resurrection*, 44.

572 Wedderburn, *Baptism and Resurrection*, 73–74.

573 Lincoln, *Paradise Now and Not Yet*, 122. See also his "Colossians," 624, and idem, *Ephesians*, 105–6.

But Colossians also has not lost sight of future fulfillment. As much as Paul uses spatial categories and emphasizes a realized eschatology, the future hope is preserved. The expectation of a future return of Christ shines brightly in Col 3:4 (see also 1:22, 28), and, at the same time, the anticipation of future judgment is brought out in Col 3:6 and 24. The hope of future peace is declared brilliantly in the last line of the hymn where universal reconciliation through Christ is promised (1:20). In an important study of the eschatology in Colossians, T. Still has argued that future eschatology in the letter is more pervasive than is frequently supposed and that there is "less variance between the eschatological perspectives of Colossians and Paul than is typically recognized."[574] He also notes that spatial terminology and thought is present in the accepted Pauline letters.[575] In Philippians, the apostle Paul can say, "I press on toward the prize of the upward call of God [τῆς ἄνω κλήσεως τοῦ θεοῦ] in Christ Jesus" (3:14). The adverb ἄνω is the same term appearing in Colossians when believers are urged to "seek the things above" (3:1) and "think on the things above" (3:2). Paul also tells the Philippian believers that their "citizenship is in heaven" (Phil 3:20).

It is consequently more accurate to describe the distinctive accents in Colossians as a matter of emphasis and not of discontinuity with Paul.[576] The emphasis on the present is in line with the purpose of Colossians in helping believers see the full implications of their incorporation into Christ so they will have the security and strength to refuse the demands placed upon them by the teachers of this faction, as well as to live the lifestyle that God has called them to live. But the emphasis on co-resurrection goes even deeper than this. The concern of the Colossians, and for Paul, was the influence of the powers on daily life in the here and now. The concept of co-resurrection affirms their participation with Christ in his exaltation and defeat of the powers (cf. Col 2:15) and what this means for them (2:9–10, 20).

## Ecclesiology

The ecclesiology of the letter is very closely tied to its Christology.[577] Christ is filled with "all the fullness of God," and believers "have been filled in him" (2:9–10). Christ is the "head" of the corporate community of believers—his "body" (1:18).

The notion of Christ as "head" of the body is often singled out as a significant theological development that goes beyond what Paul said (or perhaps would have said). It is mentioned first in the middle stanza or refrain of the Christ-hymn (1:18a). But there is significant debate among scholars on whether τῆς ἐκκλησίας

574 Still, "Eschatology in Colossians," 125–38.

575 Still, "Eschatology in Colossians," 132.

576 So also Lincoln, "Colossians," 624, who concludes, "Since this is a shift in emphasis rather than a major change of thought, it should not be made a decisive factor in the issue of authorship."

577 See also Lohse, 179.

was part of the original hymn or reflects an editorial addition. Either way, because it is in the final form of the letter, it reflects precisely what the author wanted to communicate. The term "head" appears in connection with "body" one additional time in Colossians, where the physiological metaphor is elaborated with reference to joints and ligaments as well as being supplied (nourished), "held together," and "growth" (2:19). The context is Paul's appeal to the Colossians to hold tight to Christ who, as head, provides them with direction, nourishment, and unity. The implication is that the church can only overcome the influence of "the philosophy" by submitting to the resurrected Christ's leadership and receiving from him empowerment and support.[578]

Although Paul never refers to Christ as "head" in his undisputed letters, the conceptuality that the metaphor expresses is present in Paul's writings, especially through the terms "grace," "power," and "Spirit" (expressing his provision for the church), as well as "Lord" (expressing his leadership of the church). For Paul to express these ideas through the addition of the word "head" to the body metaphor is a natural extension of the metaphor that would not run counter to his previous thought. The other occurrence of "head" in Colossians is the author's assertion of Christ's lordship over the principalities and authorities (2:10) and not to his role in relation to the church.

Colossians represents the first time in the Pauline corpus that the term ἐκκλησία, "church," (or "body," for that matter) is universalized to speak of the entire aggregate of local assemblies as one corporate entity (1:18, 24). This, too, is sometimes seen as a development that reflects later (and not Pauline) usage. But the question is whether this is inconsistent with Paul's thought or is a direction in the use of the terms that Paul himself would not have developed. As Dunn has explained, Paul's use of the term ἐκκλησία depends on the LXX usage and Israel's self-identity as the "assembly of God" (קְהַל אֱלֹהִים, *qahal elohim*, ἐκκλησία θεοῦ) or "the assembly of Israel."[579] Like ancient Israel, the newly constituted people of God met in local assemblies, but the entire collection of these "churches" would represent "the church of God." Paul appears to be using the expression this way in Gal 1:13 where he reflects on "how I persecuted *the church of God* violently and tried to destroy it." This would refer to more than one local assembly.[580] The reference here is primarily to multiple gatherings of Jewish believers within Jerusalem, but likely also throughout Judea and perhaps somewhat beyond. It does not strain credulity to conceive of Paul endorsing what he has found in traditional material (the Christ-hymn) and building upon it, since it fits his larger conceptual framework for the identity of the church. This would fit with his concern to locate the group of house churches at Colossae in the larger network of churches in the Lycus Valley and in the world where the gospel has spread (1:5–6).

578 See my full discussion in "Jesus Christ: 'Head' of the Church," 346–66.

579 Dunn, *Theology of Paul*, 537–38.

580 So also Moo, *Galatians*, 100, and Longenecker, *Galatians*, 23.

It is important to observe that Colossians reflects no steps toward the institutionalization of the Pauline communities. There are no mention of church offices of any kind in the letter. It would be wrong to take Paul's admonition to Archippus to "fulfill the ministry [διακονίαν]" he has received as an allusion to a church office (4:17).[581] The lack of reference to bishops, overseers, and deacons is a problem for those who push the date closer to the time of Ignatius. This is particularly true in the way that the author of Colossians has handled the problem of "the philosophy." One might expect an appeal to obey or be subject to the bishop (cf., e.g., Ign. *Eph.* 2.2; 5.3; *Magn.* 6.2; 13.2; *Trall.* 2.1–2; 13.2).

## Absent Themes

Another ostensible indicator that Colossians was penned by a pseudonymous author is the absence of a number of themes that are believed to be central to Paul's thought. What these are may vary from scholar to scholar, but there are a handful that need to be addressed.

W. Kümmel expressed skepticism about this argument from silence, saying that "the absence of well-known Pauline concepts proves nothing, because analogous observations can also be made about other Pauline epistles."[582] It also needs to be acknowledged that Colossians is a relatively brief letter (1575 words) compared to some of Paul's main letters (e.g., Romans [7111 words] or 1 Corinthians [6830 words]). One cannot reasonably expect Paul to include the major themes of his theology in the smaller letters. Certainly scholars do not expect this of Philemon.

It is also important to keep in mind that all of Paul's letters are ad hoc pieces of correspondence in which he addresses specific issues and matters of concern within each of the respective congregations. They do not represent summaries of his theology distributed to broad audiences.

It is quite conspicuous that the author of Colossians never mentions "law" (νόμος), "righteousness" (δικαιοσύνη), and "justification" (δικαιόω). By contrast, in Galatians, νόμος occurs thirty-two times, δικαιοσύνη four times, and δικαιόω eight times. Yet the situation addressed by each of these letters is substantially different. In Galatians, Paul polemicizes against law-observant Jewish Christians who want to impose aspects of law observance on gentile Christians. Whereas in Colossians, there are aspects of the law mentioned (e.g., Sabbath, festivals, and new-moon celebrations), but not with the same motivation. The opponents at Colossae were not advocating law observance as a way of pleasing the one true God, but were rather advocating certain rituals, taboos, and ascetic practices that would assist them in their struggle with spiritual forces. Thus the array of terminology in the polemical portion and in the contextualized theology of the letter is quite different from Galatians. One should also note that many of these

581 So also Huttner, *Early Christianity in the Lycus Valley*, 86.

582 Kümmel, *Introduction*, 241, cited approvingly by Thiselton, 10.

words are also missing from 2 Corinthians, which is addressing yet different matters. "Law" and "justification" never appear. And, similarly, none of these terms appear in Philemon, yet it is an accepted Pauline letter.

The term "Spirit" (πνεῦμα) only appears twice in Colossians (1:8; 2:5). In the second reference, the author tells the Colossians, "I am absent in body, yet I am with you in spirit," which could be a reference to the human spirit.[583] Although I think this is a way of referring to the common bond that the author shares with the community through the Spirit-indwelt body of Christ, the Holy Spirit receives very little attention compared to the accepted Pauline letters. Sumney says that this "represents a significant departure" and "a considerable modification to the emphasis Paul gives the role of the Spirit in believers' lives."[584] But this ignores the fact that despite the numerous references to πνεῦμα in Romans (34), 1 Corinthians (40), 2 Corinthians (17), and Galatians (18), Philippians only mentions πνεῦμα five times, and two of these occurrences should be interpreted anthropologically (Phil 1:27; 4:23). This has caused Schweizer to be more circumspect in his special study on the Spirit in Colossians by asserting that the paucity of references does not necessarily lead to the conclusion that Paul was not the author.[585] He appeals to the situation at Colossae involving "the philosophy," which called for a more christological focus. While this may be true, I would contend that the idea of the work of the Holy Spirit is represented in the use of the πληρῶμα language. This was not a catchword of the opponents, but both the noun and the verb were used to speak of the Spirit in ways that echoed the "filling" of the temple with the glory of God in the prophets. The term πληρῶμα has thus become a circumlocution for the Spirit (see my comments on 1:19 and 2:9–10). The Spirit is portrayed as filling (or dwelling in) Christ, and the Colossian believers have likewise been "filled" (with the Spirit).

### *Historical Matters and Plausibility*

It is important for us to look closely at the content of the letter to determine if it fits in a time frame late in Paul's life or whether there are subtle indicators that it must indeed be attributed to some time after the apostle had died. Some interpreters believe that they have detected a few clues that suggest pseudonymity and a later date. Nevertheless, much of the letter corresponds well with the historical circumstances in the late 50s or early 60s and plausibly represents the kind of letter that the apostle would have written in this ostensible situation.

#### Events in the Lycus Valley, Rome, and Jerusalem

There were enormous—indeed, cataclysmic—events that took place in each of these areas in the decade of AD 60–70. At the end of AD 60, a massive

583 Schweizer, "Christus und Geist," 308, says it is likely purely anthropological.

584 Sumney, 3.

585 Schweizer, "Christus und Geist," 310.

earthquake struck the Lycus Valley, leaving many structures destroyed and profound economic loss to the area (see the full discussion above). If the letter were written during Paul's Roman imprisonment, it would need to have been written very early in this time period. It is difficult to imagine that the letter would have been written subsequent to the earthquake with no expressions of condolence, no encouragement to many who were displaced and profoundly affected, no collection for the church, or even any hint that there was a devastating earthquake. This fact calls into question any view of pseudonymity that sees the letter written sometime in the period of AD 61–70.

Just three to four years after the earthquake, Rome itself burned in a fiery conflagration in AD 64. According to Tacitus, this led to an intense time of persecution for Christians living in the capitol city. There is nothing in Colossians to suggest that this event was on the author's mind or in the author's recent experience or awareness.

And, finally, in the last four years of the decade, Titus's armies invaded the land of Israel and engaged in a bloody and extensive war with the Jewish people. Beginning in Galilee and moving south, the Roman military left a wide swath of destruction and death, culminating in the siege of Jerusalem. In AD 70, Jerusalem was leveled, and the temple was destroyed. The apocalyptic hope of the people of Israel that God would intervene to crush the arrogance of the gentile sinners like a potter's jar had been completely taken away from them. It is difficult to imagine a Jewish, even Jewish-Christian, writer not being profoundly affected by this event and for this not to be evident in some fashion in his writing.

The combination of these three episodes of historic upheaval would suggest that Colossians was written sometime before AD 61. Of course, this would not apply if there was an attempt to deceive on the part of the author, and he were to have written much later but in a way to give the appearance of a letter written before these events (as some advocates of pseudonymity have suggested).

## Paul's Autobiographical Material

There is a surprisingly large amount of material in Colossians that is autobiographical or provides personal details of various sorts. This becomes very difficult to explain on the basis of the theory of pseudonymity. Explanations usually revolve around the contentions that (1) the inclusion of this material gives verisimilitude to the claim of Pauline authorship, and/or (2) the material serves a literary purpose for enhancing one of the thematic purposes of the actual author (e.g., an encouragement to pray because Paul did so). Some of these explanations, at times, appear deeply strained. What follows is a brief summary of the autobiographical material:

- Paul and Timothy report how they regularly give thanks in prayer to God for the Colossian believers (1:3–5).

- Paul and Timothy recount that Epaphras has let them know about the way the Colossian believers are showing love in the community (1:8).
- Paul and Timothy explain how they engage in unceasing prayer for the Colossians. They summarize the essence of what specific things they are praying for the Colossian believers (1:9–14).
- Paul speaks of the fact that he has become a servant (διάκονος) of the gospel (1:23).
- Paul mentions his suffering on behalf of the gospel and its implications for the Colossians. He gives an additional description of his service for the church and his stewardship of the word of God that was entrusted to him (1:24–25).
- Paul and Timothy describe the ministry of proclamation, admonishment, and teaching that they have, with the goal of helping believers grow in Christ. Paul explains that he is able to labor so intensively because he does so through the empowerment that Christ provides him (1:27c–29).
- Paul once again expresses what a great struggle he is having on behalf of the believers in Colossae and Laodicea (2:1–3).
- Paul begins to express his concerns to them about being misled by the dangerous teaching. He assures them that although he is absent from them in the flesh, he is with them in spirit. He tells them that he is rejoicing at the firmness of their faith in Christ (2:4–5).
- Paul asks the Colossians to pray for him and Timothy, especially for an opportunity to proclaim the mystery of Christ (4:3–4).
- Paul assures the Colossians that Timothy will share with them news about how he is doing (4:7).
- Paul tells the Colossians that he has dispatched Tychicus and Onesimus to travel to Colossae to be with them. He also tells them that these two will let them know all that is happening with him and his companions in Rome (4:8–9).
- Paul informs the Colossians that they have received instructions regarding Mark when he travels to Colossae to be with them (4:10).
- Paul shares with them that Aristarchus, Mark, and Jesus Justus have faithfully served the kingdom of God and that they have proven to be a great comfort to Paul during this time (4:10–11).
- Paul tells them that Epaphras has labored in prayer for them and has experienced much pain in his service for them and the believers in Laodicea and Hierapolis (4:12–13).
- Paul closes the letter with a greeting in his own hand and urges them to remember him, as he is in chains (4:18).

The extent of first-person information that is detailed in Colossians is highly unusual for a pseudepigraphical letter. In his commentary, Lohse ignores the weight of this and comments on the individual passages as though they were authentic personal remarks. He simply observes that "it would be very advantageous for an author who wrote at a later date to bolster the authority of his writing by statements about individual persons and by more detailed information."[586] Leppä concludes similarly that the author of Colossians utilizes "the style of Paul in order to give an apostolic authorization to the letter."[587] Likewise, Lincoln repeatedly comments that these personal features are an attempt to provide verisimilitude to Colossians as an authentic Pauline letter.[588] But the aggregate of all these personal comments seem to quite surpass what would be necessary to achieve the purpose of causing the actual readers to believe that it was an authentic letter. Even if we were to assume that pseudonymity was a well-known and accepted literary device for passing on tradition, the amount of personal details seems entirely unnecessary.[589] It also seems suprising that in a letter where the author has admonished the readers, "Do not lie [μὴ ψεύδεσθε] to one another" (3:9), he would fabricate such an extensive array of details as are represented here.

## The Long List of Personal Greetings

At the end of the letter, Paul extends greetings to the Colossian church from six different individuals (4:10–14), greets believers in Laodicea and the house church of Nymphas (4:15),[590] and admonishes Archippus to fulfill his ministry (4:17). Five of the six names of those greeting the Colossians are also found in a similar greeting in Philemon (Phlm 23–24). The greetings in Colossians, however, are more expansive, with remarks about some of these individuals and instructions to the Colossians about one of them for when he comes to visit. As noted above, many interpreters who see Colossians as pseudepigraphy contend that these names are added to provide a guise of authenticity to the letter.

As I will note later in the commentary, the nature of the personal comments about each individual strains the pseudepigraphical hypothesis to a breaking point. There is insufficient reason to extend the fiction with the kinds of details that are expressed, such as indicating that Mark would be coming to visit the Colossians and that they should prepare for his arrival (4:10), adding a name like Nymphas when it appears nowhere else in Paul's letters (4:15), urging Archippus to fulfill his ministry (4:17), and more. Schweizer sums up this difficulty well: "I confess that as far as I am concerned a clever forgery of this kind remains inconceivable, especially in a letter that is so very close to Paul, and would

---

586 Lohse, 176–77n59.

587 Leppä, *Making of Colossians*, 208.

588 Lincoln, "Colossians," 664–69.

589 Moo, 29, correctly sees this problem and writes, "Any ultimately convincing alternative to Pauline authorship will have to deal adequately with this rather extensive series of details."

590 "Nymphas" is a masculine form, and "Nympha" is feminine. See my comments on 4:15 and the text-critical issue regarding the gender of this person. I reach the conclusion that that text should read "Nymphas."

therefore presumably be the first to be seized as inauthentic. Furthermore, there does not seem to be a parallel case of such a forgery in antiquity."[591] It should also be mentioned that known Christian pseudepigraphical letters, such as 3 Corinthians and the Epistle to the Laodiceans, completely lack personal greetings. The Epistle to the Laodiceans does give a closing greeting, but only in the most general terms ("the saints salute you").

## Paul's Reflections on His Sufferings (1:24) and His Role as a Servant of the Gospel (1:23, 25)

As Paul reflects on his suffering on behalf of the Colossians, he makes the startling statement, "I fill up in my flesh what is lacking in the afflictions of Christ for his body, which is the church" (1:24). This one announcement has resulted in the publication of numerous articles and even monographs, written with the intent of probing what Paul means. On the surface, it appears that Paul is saying that his suffering may have atoning significance that remedies something that was deficient in Christ's suffering on the cross. In fact, Kiley says that "the absence in Col of a qualifier protesting against just such an inference as Windisch's [who takes Paul's suffering here as having expiatory significance] is to me a sure sign that 1.24 is not the voice of Paul."[592] But Kiley is assuming that Paul's initial readers would not have understood what he is saying, which very well may not have been the case.

There are at least nine different views (with variations on some of these views) on how to explain this enigmatic text (see the *Excursus*, "Filling Up What Is Lacking in the Afflictions of Christ"). For Sumney, this passage tips the balance for seeing Colossians written after Paul's death by an associate.[593] This is because his sufferings are presented in a way to inspire imitation by the readers.[594] For many who hold to the theory of pseudonymity, this passage presents an exalted view of the apostle that is somewhat out of sync with how Paul would represent himself and fits better with the period after his death.

My own conclusion on this text is that it has to do with Paul completing the mission of the servant of the Lord to take the gospel to the nations and to endure the afflictions that would accompany this service (see my extensive discussion in the commentary). As such, it fits well within Paul's own conception of his ministry of the gospel within his own lifetime.

The letter does emphasize Paul's unique and exemplary role as a servant (διάκονος) of the gospel—a stewardship divinely bestowed upon him (1:23, 25). He labors tirelessly and strenuously in his ministry of the word of God, sustained by the infusion of divine power into his life (1:29). His labor extends not only to

591 Schweizer, 21.

592 Kiley, *Colossians as Pseudepigraphy*, 60.

593 Sumney, 8.

594 See Sumney, 110–11.

the believers in the Lycus Valley (2:1), but throughout the Mediterranean world (1:6, 23). For the Colossians, these statements would justify his interest in their community and concern for its well-being. But they would also reaffirm his authority to speak into their situation and cause them to heed the warnings he is delivering to them.[595] But Paul's appeals to them are not based simply on his divine commission but on the shared traditions and the common faith.

Regardless of the view that one takes on this particular issue, it is easier to see the apostle Paul exercising the creativity to make this kind of statement than to posit a pseudepigrapher. If the latter were trying to make Pauline tradition relevant to a new situation, it is difficult to see what he is drawing on in Paul's writings. If the author was attempting to escape detection, by adding something so distinctive (and, to some, quite troubling), he has not done well at concealing his efforts.

## The Household Code

This is the first time in the Pauline corpus (and for that matter, in early Christianity) where a household code has been included as part of a letter. The code contains a specific set of instructions to various pairs of members within a household—wives and husbands, children and fathers, and slaves and masters (3:18–4:1). Some interpreters have taken this as evidence that Colossians is reflective of the post-Pauline years. MacDonald, for instance, reasons that the code provides an indication "that the author of Colossians stands at some distance from the Paul of 1 Corinthians 7 who preferred celibacy—the ultimate sign that the world was passing away!"[596] Lincoln sees the death of the apostle and the delay of the parousia as secondary to the primary motivating factor for the creation of the household code, which was that it "reflects a stage in which Christians were conscious of subverting the social order and of the need to adjust to living as Christians in the Greco-Roman world without unnecessarily disrupting the status quo."[597]

But the household code may be nothing more than Paul's efforts to provide the readers with instruction about how to live in a way that pleases God in a manner that is consistent with the Jewish wisdom tradition rooted in God's revelation of himself and his ways in the Torah. The heart of the passage is expressed in 3:24: "serve the Lord Christ." The sevenfold reference to Christ as Lord in the passage (3:18, 20, 22, 23, 24 [2x]; 4:1) strongly suggests that the code is a set of instructions designed to portray what it means to live under the lordship of Christ in every relationship within the household (see the more extended discussion of the code in the *Excursus*, "The Household Code"). It is therefore unnecessary to find recourse to explanations of the code that locate it in the post-Pauline era.

595 Barth and Blanke, 71, notes that the intention of these statements "include a confirmation and reinforcement of his teachings."

596 MacDonald, 8.

597 Lincoln, "Colossians," 654.

## Financial Transaction for the Sake of the Mission

In his 1986 monograph, M. Kiley observed that all seven undisputed epistles of Paul show him engaged in some kind of financial transactions on behalf of the mission.[598] Conversely, in the six disputed epistles, there is a consistent absence of financial transaction on behalf of the mission. Therefore, he advances the thesis that "the lack of such mission finances in Col (as well as in Eph, 2 Thess, and the Pastorals) suggests that they are spurious."[599] First of all, it needs to be observed that whereas Paul undertook a collection for the impoverished believers in Jerusalem (Rom 15:26; 1 Cor 16:1–4; 2 Cor 8–9), that collection was completed prior to the composition of five of the six letters he mentions in which financial transaction is absent. His larger construct of "financial transaction for the sake of the mission" is artificial, and he strains the textual evidence in places to make it fit the thesis. For instance, can the report of the Jerusalem leaders' request that the gentile churches should remember the poor in Gal 2:10 accurately be called a financial transaction on behalf of a mission? And can Paul's offer to reimburse Philemon for any damages incurred by Onesimus fit the criterion of a financial transaction on behalf of his mission?[600] And, finally, can Paul's reminder to the Thessalonians that he and his companions worked night and day not to burden them (1 Thess 2:9) likewise be considered a financial transaction for the mission? In sum, I do not find this aspect of his case to be a convincing argument.[601]

## The Relationship of Colossians to Ephesians

There is a very close relationship in matters of vocabulary, style, and theological content when Colossians is compared to Ephesians. In his comparison of the letters, Mayerhoff concluded that the author of Colossians displayed literary dependence upon the letter to the Ephesians.[602] The consensus of recent scholarship, however, among those who see Colossians as a pseudepigraphical letter, is that there was literary dependence, but it went the other direction—the author of Ephesians depended on Colossians. In a detailed study of this problem, E. Best reached the conclusion that there are insuperable difficulties in seeing the author of either of the letters depending on the other.[603] Of course, another alternative is to see the letters written at roughly the same time by the same author but for different overall purposes, yet also with some overlapping purposes. I will not discuss the matter in detail here. Barth and Blanke have provided an excellent

598 Kiley, *Colossians as Pseudepigraphy*, 46–51.
599 Kiley, *Colossians as Pseudepigraphy*, 72–73.
600 For a more detailed engagement with Kiley's thesis, see my review in *EvQ* 60 (1988): 69–71.
601 Similarly, Barclay, *Colossians*, 24, writes, "Kiley's argument (pp. 46–51) that the lack of reference to financial transactions is suspicious can hardly be taken seriously."
602 Mayerhoff, *Colosser*, 72–106.
603 Best, "Who Used Whom?," 72–96.

fifty-page treatment of this issue in their commentary.[604] I will discuss some of the specific problems and issues at the relevant portions of this commentary.

### *Eleven Factors Not Sufficiently Taken into Account By Those Advocating Pseudepigraphy*

Although every commentary and many monographs on Colossians include a discussion of the authorship question, some do not take into account one or more of a variety of factors that should have a bearing on one's decision about authenticity. I will provide a brief discussion of some of these factors. Each of these topics warrants a far more extensive discussion than I have provided, but this diverse array of considerations should cause one to pause before assuming that the so-called scholarly consensus on the pseudepigraphical nature of Colossians is correct.

#### The Unique Situation at Colossae

The opponents reflected in the letter to the Colossians are unlike the opposition in any of the other letters attributed to Paul. Yet as I have noted earlier, many of the hapax legomena of Colossians are terms associated with the factional teaching at Colossae (see above). Not only would the distinctive contours of this teaching influence the author's language and word choices in referring to the issue, but it would also have had an impact on the nature of his rhetoric and polemic against it. This will be discussed in more detail in the "Form, Structure, and Setting" portions of each section of the commentary.

#### The Incorporation of Traditional Material

In an important monograph on this topic, G. E. Cannon has discussed the author's extensive use of traditional material and has argued that much of the vocabulary and thought of Colossians was shaped by its use.[605] Although showing no awareness of Cannon's study, Barth and Blanke have independently argued for the importance of weighing the impact of the varied traditional materials used throughout Colossians.[606] Each of these authors contend that one needs to consider such appropriated material as the Christ-hymn (1:15–20), the baptismal liturgical language (2:9–15), the paraenetic language, including language from virtue and vice catalogs (3:5–17), and the *Haustafel* tradition (3:18–4:1). Although one may disagree over the extent of the use of traditional material

604 Barth and Blanke, 72–114.

605 Cannon, *Traditional Materials*. Cannon is perhaps overly optimistic to conclude that "it seems justifiable to believe that the author of Colossians was Paul the Apostle" (p. 229). The authorship question needs to be decided on the full array of issues that are relevant to this determination. Nevertheless, his conclusion does not diminish the fact that he can justly conclude that the use of traditional materials is wholly consistent with Pauline authorship.

606 Barth and Blanke, 64–72.

in Colossians, the purpose for its use, or even how it is used, the presence of this material still needs to be regarded as having a bearing on the language and style of the letter. Specific passages will be discussed in the "Form, Structure, and Setting" sections.

## The Range of Styles Represented in the Letter

Colossians is not simply a prose letter with an introductory address and a closing. It is much more complex and artistic in its composition. Not only does the author polemicize against the so-called philosophy and utilize traditional material in what he writes, but he employs a variety of other styles and language appropriate to his purposes in each section of the letter. This includes beginning the letter with a thanksgiving (1:3–5) followed by a prayer report (1:9–14). The heavily doctrinal portion of the letter (2:6–15) is followed by the intensely polemical segment with its own stylistic traits (2:16–23). The third chapter is largely paraenetic, with a portion of it conforming to the pattern of the *Haustafel* tradition (3:5–4:1). The last portion of the letter includes an expansive list of greetings (4:7–21). Although this summary does not encompass every portion of the letter, it does show the rich variety of styles that the author of Colossians employed in composing the letter. This array of styles renders the process of making a determination of authorship far more complex. Some scholars, such as Bujard, tend to overlook the manifold styles represented within Colossians. But this skews the overall assessment of the language and style of the letter.

A. W. Pitts has expressed concern over simplistic statistical analyses of language usage in the Pauline corpus as a basis for making decisions about authorship and has argued for a sociolinguistic approach that is based on register—that is, "contexts for language varieties ranging from literary genres to social situations."[607] Such an approach has far more promise than a computational method as exemplified by Bujard and others. Pitts notes that "a register design model of style-shift predicates a substantial degree of language change in response to social change so that significant co-textual variation can often be anticipated as the result of register rather than author variation."[608]

## Overconfidence in What Constitutes Paul's Style

Nearly fifty years ago, H. Chadwick quipped that "the case against the authenticity of Colossians depends . . . above all on a capacity gravely to underestimate Paul's versatility and intelligence."[609] This comment bears repeating because of Paul's ability to use an array of vocabulary, styles, and literary forms within his letters. And this is often underappreciated.

Conversely, those advocating the pseudonymity of Colossians also tend to

---

607 Pitts, "Style and Pseudonymity in Pauline Scholarship," 117.

608 Pitts, "Style and Pseudonymity in Pauline Scholarship," 151.

609 As cited in Barclay, *Colossians*, 28.

overestimate their ability to discern quite precisely what constitutes Paul's style and to detect what falls outside the bounds of what they have determined to be the parameters of Paul's literary abilities. M. Barth has rightly protested against methods that oversimplify difficult issues and too rashly draw conclusions on the basis of statistics. He warns against reaching conclusions about the authorship of a letter by assuming one sole form of diction.[610]

In a related sense, it is inappropriate to assume that the language and style of one or two of an author's letters—such as Galatians and Romans—should characterize the stylistic elements of another letter by the same author (such as Colossians). S. McKnight has made this point a major premise of his argument for the Pauline authorship of Colossians. He regards the assumption that the accepted letters of Paul represent the pure and authentic voice of the apostle, from which the other letters cannot vary, as a major historical error repeated over and again by most everyone who denies the Pauline authorship of Colossians.[611] He argues that the argument from style "slides down the mountainside" when "there is simply not enough evidence to know what many think they know" about the language and style of the apostle Paul.[612] In addition to Paul's versatility in his composition and in the themes he chooses to address are the complicating factors of the use of a secretary and the employment of traditional materials.

### That Paul Might Reflect Some of the Language, Wording, and Thoughts He Has Expressed in Other Letters

There has been much discussion in the literature about potential literary dependence by the author of Colossians on Philemon, Philippians, and other letters of Paul and whether this may reflect the secondary nature of Colossians. Kiley, for instance, attempts to make the case for the direct literary dependence of Colossians on Philemon and Philippians.[613] In his review of Kiley's monograph, C. F. D. Moule summarizes his own evaluation of Kiley's evidence and argumentation, saying that "all in all, one is tempted to ask whether it would not be simpler to postulate that Paul himself was writing with some of the language of Philippians and Philemon in his mind."[614] In general, I think this is an appropriate question to ask of all the passages where there is alleged literary dependence, to avoid the kind of judgment that Moule leveled against Kiley: "the alleged resemblances are sometimes far-fetched."[615] I will address many of these instances throughout the commentary.

---

610 Barth and Blanke, 57.

611 McKnight, 7.

612 McKnight, 9.

613 Kiley, *Colossians as Pseudepigraphy*, 76–91.

614 C. Moule, review of *Colossians as Pseudepigraphy*, by M. Kiley, *JTS* 38 (1987): 509.

615 C. Moule, review of *Colossians as Pseudepigraphy*, 509.

## That Pseudepigraphy Was Not Common in *Letters* in Jewish and Christian Circles

It is beyond dispute that pseudepigraphy was common within the literature of Second Temple Judaism. This is especially true of the apocalyptic literature. But these documents set themselves apart from the kind of alleged pseudepigraphy in the NT letters in that none are attributed to figures contemporary in the NT world. The apocalyptic documents "were attributed to figures who are already known from earlier biblical sources,"[616] such as Enoch, Abraham, Moses, and the patriarchs. There is also some question about how these documents would have been understood by first-century Jews. Stone observes that "rabbinic literature regarded these ideas about Enoch with great suspicion, seeking to minimize Enoch's role."[617]

But Jewish pseudepigraphical letters written during the Hellenistic and Roman eras are quite rare. Bauckham has identified four such letters that he has classified as didactic letters: the Epistle of Jeremiah and three letters embedded in apocalyptic documents—the Epistle of Enoch (1 En. 92–105), Baruch, and 2 Bar. 78–87.[618] But these are all associated with ancient biblical figures—Enoch, Jeremiah, and Jeremiah's scribe, Baruch. The authors of these pseudepigraphical letters use these famous figures to address real readers centuries later and their contemporary situations.[619] We have no examples within Judaism of a pseudepigraphical author writing in the name of someone who lived a few years or even a few decades earlier. Each of these (apart from the Epistle of Jeremiah) are also not actually letters of the type we find in the NT but are testamentary documents or farewell sermons.

Some have also pointed to the Letter of Aristeas as an example of a Jewish pseudepigraphical letter. But this is not an actual letter and, as Bauckham notes, should be classified as "a dedicated treatise."[620]

There are a handful of Christian pseudepigraphical letters attributed to the apostle Paul: 3 Corinthians, the Epistle to the Laodiceans, and the Epistle to the Alexandrians. The latter is not extant and is only known because it is mentioned by name in the Muratorian Fragment. The fragment notes, "There is in circulation an Epistle to the Laodiceans [and] another to the Alexandrians forged under the name of Paul bearing on the heresy of Marcion."[621] The document goes on to say that there were "several others which cannot be received into the Catholic Church. For gall ought not to be mixed with honey."[622] More will be said below about the first two.

---

616 Stone, "Pseudepigraphy Reconsidered," 3.
617 Stone, "Pseudepigraphy Reconsidered," 6.
618 Bauckham, "Pseudo-Apostolic Letters," 469–94.
619 See Bauckham, "Pseudo-Apostolic Letters," 481.
620 Bauckham, "Pseudo-Apostolic Letters," 478.
621 See Westcott, *Canon*, 221.
622 Westcott, *Canon*, 221.

All of these Jewish and Christian pseudepigraphical letters are quite distinct in character from Colossians. Bauckham concludes that "none of these letters achieves anything like the particularity of the major Pauline letters, or even of such allegedly pseudepigraphal letters as Colossians and Jude."[623] And the fact remains that "*pseudepigraphal* letters from that period are rare."[624]

## The Claim that Disciples Would Write in the Name of their Master

It has become commonplace for advocates of the hypothesis that Colossians is pseudepigraphy to claim that it was a widespread and well-known practice for disciples to write in the name of their master. Such a practice, it is argued, was honoring to a great teacher and a way of preserving their legacy and teaching for a new generation. It was thus an acceptable literary technique widely accepted in the world of the NT.

Nevertheless, Kiley admits that "evidence of a praiseworthy motive for the creation of pseudepigraphical writing is almost non-existent,"[625] yet he upheld such a conjecture by arguing that Epaphras wrote in the name of Paul in the context of a Pauline school.[626] A. Baum has observed that there is a growing number of scholars "who have raised substantive doubts regarding the once-popular thesis of innocent ancient pseudepigraphy."[627] A highly significant work in this regard is a 1998 Oxford PhD thesis written by J. Duff. He notes, "The studies within this thesis cast doubt on the suggestion that pseudepigraphy was seen as some form of acceptable literary technique by the early Christians. . . . Thus the claim that pseudepigraphy was an accepted literary technique among the early Christians is left without any support."[628] Baum's own monograph, *Pseudepigraphie und literarische Fälschung* (2001), has been joined by the work of B. Ehrman, *Forgery and Counterforgery* (2012), in making the case that pseudepigraphical works were written to deceive and were regarded as deceptive by their readers. Baum contends that "pupils had to publish their own philosophical, medical, or theological ideas under their own names. Otherwise they were regarded as literary forgers."[629]

Proponents of the pseudonymous nature of Colossians often appeal to the many pseudepigraphical documents attributed to Pythagoras but written by his students as an example of the acceptability of this form of pseudepigraphy. They

623 Bauckham, "Pseudo-Apostolic Letters," 488.

624 Bauckham, "Pseudo-Apostolic Letters," 487 (emphasis original).

625 Kiley, *Colossians as Pseudepigraphy*, 21.

626 Kiley, *Colossians as Pseudepigraphy*, 96–103.

627 Baum, "Authorship Attribution and Pseudonymity," 381.

628 Duff, "Reconsideration of Pseudepigraphy," 269.

629 Baum, "Authorship Attribution and Pseudonymity," 381. For a discussion of the evidence, see his *Pseudepigraphie und literarische Fälschung*, 51–63. He does note that pupils were allowed to publish "*their teachers' thoughts*" under the names of their teachers (Baum, "Authorship Attribution and Pseudonymity," 392 [emphases original]). But Ehrman, *Forgery and Counterforgery*, 107, disagrees unless it is the exact wording from the teacher.

point to a statement made by Iamblichus in his work *On the Pythagorean Way of Life* as illustrating this method of pupils honoring their master and perpetuating his teaching: "it was a fine custom of theirs also to ascribe and assign everything to Pythagoras, and only very seldom to claim personal fame for their discoveries, for there are very few of them indeed to whom works are ascribed personally" (Iamblichus, *On the Pythagorean Way of Life*, 198). But the editors of this text, J. Dillon and J. Hershbell, dispute the accuracy of this statement. They note that "this statement might have validity in Aristoxenus' time [4th c. BC], but hardly makes much sense subsequent to the publication of the pseudo-Pythagorean writings [roughly 43 authors]."[630] Furthermore, no mention is made of this practice in other extant ancient biographies of Iamblichus. As Duff notes, "It is far more likely to be Iamblicus' own explanation of the pseudonymity of the texts which he has before him, in exactly the same way as modern scholars might construct explanations."[631]

Kiley further supports the notion of a praiseworthy motive for pseudepigraphy by the remarks of the fifth-century church leader, Salvian. The presbyter had written a brief document under the name of the apostle Paul's companion, Timothy, admonishing the church of his day to reject luxury and wealth.[632] When confronted by his bishop, Solonius, about the literary forgery, Salvian defended himself by saying that he composed this out of humility. But the more likely explanation is that it represented the excuse "of a man caught out and attempting to retain his office."[633] It also needs to be observed that the reaction of the bishop illustrates the attitude of church leadership regarding pseudepigraphy.

Finally, Kiley also marshalls additional evidence for his thesis by citing the sixth-century AD Neoplatonist author Olympiodorus, who mentions "the goodwill of disciples" as a motive for the pseudepigraphical works present in the Pythagorean corpus.[634] But not only is this comment made five hundred years after the writing of the documents under question, it also likely represents a positive spin justifying the many pseudonymous works written under the name of Pythagoras, without any firsthand knowledge of the origin of these documents.

In summary, this is very thin evidence for constructing a thesis that NT pseudepigraphical writings, and Colossians in particular, were written with the praiseworthy motive of honoring a master teacher. Both Iamblichus and Olympiodorus made their comments centuries after the composition of the pseudepigraphical Pythagorean collection. Far more compelling would be a

630 Clarke, Dillon, and Hershbell, *Iamblichus*, 203n12.

631 Duff, "Reconsideration of Pseudepigraphy," 131.

632 Kiley, *Colossians as Pseudepigraphy*, 21–22.

633 Duff, "Reconsideration of Pseudepigraphy," 40.

634 Kiley, *Colossians as Pseudepigraphy*, 22–23.

document written by a contemporary with firsthand knowledge of the motives for the origin of these works. But such evidence does not exist.

## Comparison with Unequivocal Examples of Pseudepigraphical Pauline Letters

We have two extant examples of pseudepigraphical letters written under the name of the apostle Paul—the Letter to the Laodiceans and 3 Corinthians. A surface comparison of Colossians to these two letters reveals striking differences, which raises further doubts about the alleged pseudepigraphical nature of Colossians.

The Letter to the Laodiceans was written in the second half of the second century, presumably to fill the gap presented by the letter to the Colossians, when the latter's author encouraged his original audience to also read the letter he wrote to the Laodiceans (Col 4:16). The actual letter to the Laodiceans was probably lost, and the hypothesis that Ephesians is actually the lost letter to the Colossians is unconvincing. Although the text is only extant in Latin, the original composition was probably in Greek. Contrary to W. Schneemelcher, who characterized it as a "clumsy forgery,"[635] and Bauckham's quip that it is "a remarkably imcompetent attempt to fill the gap."[636] B. W. Longenecker and S. C. Ryan have convincingly argued that it is thoughtfully and carefully composed and represents "an engaging attempt to speak Paul's voice in a compositionally coherent presentation."[637] Regardless of the compositional abilities of the author of this document, it does show extensive dependence on the wording and content of Philippians as well as wording from some of Paul's other letters. There is only a residue that is unique to this writer.

Third Corinthians is found embedded in the late second-century apocryphal Acts of Paul.[638] Although it purports to be an actual letter by the apostle Paul to the Corinthian church in response to a letter they sent to him while he was in Philippi, Bauckham rightly concludes that "all the indications are that it was composed for its context in the Acts of Paul and only later circulated separately as an extract."[639] The author of this document polemicizes against the gnostic controversies of his own time and retrojects that back into the first century. Putting Paul's name on the letter grants it the authority to carry a strong persuasive appeal to churches and Christians throughout the Roman Empire.

Although I do not intend to provide a full comparison of these documents with Colossians here, I am simply observing that there is a lacuna in the

635 Hennecke and Schneemelcher, *New Testament Apocrypha*, 2:141.

636 Bauckham, "Pseudo-Apostolic Letters," 485.

637 Longenecker and Ryan, "Presenting the Pauline Voice," 148. P. Tite, "Dusting Off a Pseudepigraphical Letter," 313–15, reaches the same conclusion through the application of epistolary analysis.

638 See Hennecke and Schneemelcher, *New Testament Apocrypha*, 2:374–78.

639 Bauckham, "Pseudo-Apostolic Letters," 486.

scholarship of the pseudepigraphy of Colossians, where Colossians is never compared with actual pseudepigraphical documents attributed to the apostle. This has been remedied, in part, by the study of G. S. MaGee,[640] but more work remains to be done. MaGee concludes that these two letters "represent methodical and deliberate attemps to recreate the voice of Paul in a later generation."[641]

## The Concern of Ancient Writers over Literary Forgeries in the Roman World

Authentication was very important to recipients of letters in the Greek and Roman world.[642] The handwriting and overall layout was one of the means of authenticating the source.[643] If a letter was written by a secretary, the author of the letter would include a closing greeting in his or her own hand.[644] This appears to be the case in Colossians where it says, "this greeting is with my own hand—from Paul" (4:18a).

Concern about forgery extended beyond letters to other kinds of literary documents. One example concerns the second-century AD doctor and philosopher Galen, who expressed his frustration over pseudepigraphical documents that were written under his name and sold in Rome:

> I was recently in the Sandalarium, the area of Rome with the largest concentration of booksellers, where I witnessed a dispute as to whether a certain book for sale was by me or someone else. The book bore the title: *Galen the doctor.* Someone had bought the book under the impression that it was one of mine; someone else—a man of letters—struck by the odd form of the title, desired to know the book's subject. On reading the first two lines he immediately tore up the inscription, saying simply: "This is not Galen's language [λέξις]—the title is false [ψευδῶς ἐπιγέγραπται τουτὶ τὸ βιβλίον]." (Galen, *On My Own Books* 19.8–9)[645]

Baum comments, "This erudite reader appears to have made his judgment on the assumption that usually an author himself put pen to paper and wrote his book in his own style."[646] Galen goes on to complain that some of the works with his name attached to them vary in their styles and theoretical content from his own writings. He says they are "neither complete nor perfectly accurate in their teaching" (Galen, *On My Own Books* 19.11). He says that "my books have been subject to all sorts of mutilations" (19.11). In some instances, people had published Galen's books in their own names "with all sorts of cuts, additions,

640 MaGee, *Portrait of an Apostle*, esp. 63–79.

641 MaGee, *Portrait of an Apostle*, esp. 78–79.

642 See Sarri, *Material Aspects of Letter Writing*, ch. 4 ("Authentication"), 125–92.

643 Sarri, *Material Aspects of Letter Writing*, 127.

644 Sarri, *Material Aspects of Letter Writing*, 128, 140–76, 191–92.

645 Translation by Singer, *Galen: Selected Works*, 3.

646 Baum, "Authorship Attribution and Pseudonymity," 386.

and alterations," and subsequently Galen's name was reattached to them. The motivation of some pseudepigraphers may have been financial since the major libraries of the ancient world, such as at Pergamum and Alexandria, paid well to stock their shelves with important authors.[647]

Galen's irritation at what has happened to his books is understandable in that not only was his own intellectual property being sold on the market and his professional reputation being sullied, but incomplete and even false (or harmful) medical knowledge was being disseminated. As Duff notes, "this story reveals that false attribution was relatively common, but was seen as unacceptable by both readers and authors."[648] Consequently, Galen followed the advice of his friend Bassus and created a catalogue of his extant books—effectively establishing his own "canon." This would help people to avoid works that are falsely attributed to him.

Duff has pointed out that Galen's concern over false attributions extended to the Hippocratic corpus, where he discerned that "there were interpolations and texts falsely attributed to Hippocrates many times in his works."[649] Duff summarizes the evidence well in saying, "Galen demonstrates that his readers would have understood the difference between the genuine work of Hippocrates and work falsely attributed to him, and would have seen this as an important distinction."[650]

Alteration of texts was also a matter of great concern in the Roman world. The librarian at Pergamus, the Stoic Athenodorus, lost his job when it was discovered that he had altered some of the texts of Zeno.[651] Herodotus revealed that Onomacritus was sent into exile when an investigation revealed that he had made interpolations into the oracles of Musaeus (Herodotus, *Hist.* 7.6).[652] Many additional instances could be mentioned.

In summary, the notion of literary property was important in the ancient world. This is not a modern construct.

## Early Church Concern about Forgeries

The same kind of concern about forgeries was shared by the early church. There are a handful of texts that directly address this matter.

One of the more remarkable testimonies in this regard comes from Tertullian. He refers to a presbyter from the Roman province of Asia who, after confessing to writing the apocryphal Acts of Paul, was convicted by church leaders and removed from his office despite his claim that "he had done if from a love of Paul" (Tertullian, *Bapt.* 17). This document included the so-called letter from Paul known as 3 Corinthians and the Acts of Paul and Thecla.

647 See Wilder, *Pseudonymity*, 27n21, 44; Ehrman, *Forgery and Counterforgery*, 97.

648 Duff, "Reconsideration of Pseudepigraphy," 126.

649 Duff, "Reconsideration of Pseudepigraphy," 127.

650 Duff, "Reconsideration of Pseudepigraphy," 130.

651 See the discussion in Ehrman, *Forgery and Counterforgery*, 84, and Wilder, *Pseudonymity*, 47.

652 Wilder, *Pseudonymity*, 47.

Tertullian characterized the Acts of Paul as "writings which wrongly [*perperam scripta*] go under Paul's name."[653] The text provides unequivocal evidence that the early church was not indifferent to pseudepigraphical writings regardless of the motives of the author. As we saw earlier, 3 Corinthians was denounced in the Muratorian Canon.

In the late second century AD, the bishop of Antioch, Syria (Serapion) strongly denounced pseudepigraphical writings: "we, my brothers, receive Peter and all the apostles as we receive Christ, but the writings falsely attributed to them we are experienced enough to reject, knowing that nothing of the sort has been handed down to us" (cited in Eusebius, *Hist. eccl.* 6.12.3).[654] The context of these remarks has to do with the so-called Gospel of Peter. According to Eusebius, some members of a nearby Christian community had gone astray due to its influence. It seems clear in Serapion's remarks that he and other Christian leaders were familiar with additional pseudepigraphical works attributed to the apostles, but that they rejected all of them. Verifying the authenticity was crucial for them. Serapion's remarks would call into question the widespread acceptance that pseudepigraphy was a commonly accepted literary device that honors a teacher.

Cyril of Jerusalem articulates a similar concern about pseudepigrapha. In commenting on the books that should be read openly in the churches as Scripture, he notes, "Then of the new Testament there are the four Gospels only, for the rest have false titles (ψευδεπίγραφα) and are mischievous" (Cyril of Jerusalem, *Catechetical Lectures* 4.36). He goes on to limit the Pauline corpus to fourteen books (he includes Hebrews).

Although additional texts could be added to this summary, this is adequate to show that the early church was concerned about forgeries and authorship. Nowhere in the documents of the pre-Nicene and post-Nicene church do we find any hesitation in the acceptance of Colossians.

Thus, contrary to the conclusion of Hay (and many others) that, "so far as we can tell, the ethos of the environment of early Christianity did not discourage pseudonymous authorship,"[655] the evidence appears to point in precisely the opposite direction. There was a strong concern to root out any documents falsely attributed to an apostle.

## Early Christian Use of Colossians as a Pauline Letter

Concurrent with the universal acceptance of Colossians as a Pauline letter in the early church was the use of the contents of the letter in establishing doctrine and norms of Christian practice. Barth and Blanke have provided a summary of this usage in their commentary.[656] Strawbridge has noted that

653 Tertullian, *On the Power of Conferring Baptism* 17.

654 Translation by G. A. Williamson, *Eusebius*, 252.

655 Hay, 20.

656 Barth and Blanke, 117–18.

the letter as a whole is not cited as frequently as the other Pauline epistles, but Col 1:15–20 "is amongst the most highly cited Pauline passages in ante-Nicene Christianity," with portions of it "used more than 670 times in 50 different pre-Nicene authors."[657] She goes on to say that "early Christian writers from Justin Martyr to Methodius, Irenaeus to Eusebius assume Pauline authorship of the Colossian epistle."[658] Even Marcion, the Valentinians, and other gnostic groups made extensive use of Colossians.

### *Conclusion*

Although it is impossible to provide a comprehensive discussion of the authorship of Colossians within the space constraints of a commentary, I have sought to make a sufficient number of observations and raise enough questions to call the pseudepigraphical hypothesis into question. The conclusion that Colossians is a pseudepigraphical text should no longer be seen as an assured result of scientific scholarship on the letter. In fact, I believe that the aggregation of evidence tips strongly in favor of viewing it as an authentic Pauline letter. As Barth and Blanke have aptly noted, seeing Colossians as inauthentic "leads to a depreciation and devaluation of some elements, at times even of the essential substance and character of the letter."[659] Renewed consideration needs to be given to viewing Colossians as an authentic Pauline letter and its contents included in the representation of Pauline theology.

## *5. The Rival Teaching at Colossae*

### *Bibliography*

**Argall, R. A.** "Religious Error," 6–20. **Arnold, C. E.** *Colossian Syncretism*. ———. "Initiation, Vision, and Spiritual Power," 173–86. ———. "Sceva, Solomon, and Shamanism," 7–26. **Attridge, H.** "On Becoming an Angel," 481–98. **Aune, N. A.** "Heresiproblemet i Kolossæ," 97–105. **Bandstra, A. J.** "Colossian Errorists," 329–43. **Beetham, C. A.** *Echoes of Scripture*, 193–218. **Bevere, A.** *Sharing in the Inheritance*. **Bornkamm, G.** "Heresy of Colossians," 123–45. **Bruce, F. F.** "Colossian Heresy," 195–208. **Carr, W.** *Angels and Principalities*. ———. "Two Notes on Colossians," 492–500. **Culianu, I.** "Origins of Gnostic Dualism," 78–91. **Davila, J. R.** *Descenders to the Chariot*. **Demaris, R.** *Colossian Controversy*. **Dibelius, M.** "Isis Initiation," 61–121. **DuBois, T. A.** *Shamanism*. **Dunn, J. D. G.** "Colossian Philosophy," 153–81. **Eitrem, S. E.** "ΈΜΒΑΤΕΥΩ," 90–94. ———. *Orakel und Mysterien*. **Evans, C. A.** "Colossian Mystics," 188–205. **Fee, G.** *Christology*. **Foerster, W.** "Irrlehrer," 71–80. **Francis, F. O.** "EMBATEUEIN," 197–207. ———. "Humility and Angelic Worship," 163–95. ———. "Reexamination of the Colossian Controversy." **Goulder, M.** "Colossians and Barbelo," 601–19. **Gunther, J. J.** *Paul's Opponents*. **Hegermann, H.** *Schöpfungsmittler*. **Hengel, M.** "Ursprünge der Gnosis," 190–223. **Hooker, M. D.** "False Teachers," 315–31. **Horst, P. W. van der.** "Great Magical Papyrus of Paris," 173–83. **Lähnemann, J.** *Kolosserbrief*, 134–52. **Lease, G.** "Jewish Mystery Cults Since Goodenough," 858–80. **Lightfoot,**

657 Strawbridge, *Pauline Effect*, 135.

658 Strawbridge, *Pauline Effect*, 135.

659 Barth and Blanke, 114.

**J. B.** "Colossian Heresy," 13–59. **Lincoln, A. T.** *Paradise Now and Not Yet.* **Lyonnet, S.** "Adversaries," 147–61. ———. "Mystères d'Apollon Clarien," 417–35. **Machen, J. G.** *Origin of Paul's Religion.* **Macridy, T.** "Antiquités," 36–67. **Martin, T. W.** *By Philosophy and Empty Deceit.* **Peerbolte, B. J. L.** "The *Eighth Book of Moses*," 184–94. **Perkins, P.** *Gnosticism and the New Testament.* **Ramsay, W. M.** "Mysteries," 198–209. ———. "Sketches," 37–79. ———. *Teaching of Paul.* **Roberts, J. H.** "Jewish Mystical Experience," 161–89. **Rowland, C.** "Apocalyptic Visions," 220–31. **Rudolph, K.** *Gnosis.* **Sappington, T. J.** *Revelation and Redemption.* **Schenke, H.-M.** "Widerstreit," 391–403. **Schweizer, E.** "Slaves of the Elements," 455–68. **Segal, A.** *Two Powers in Heaven.* **Smith, I. H.** *Heavenly Perspective.* **Stettler, C.** "Opponents," 169–200. **Sumney, J.** "Opponents," 366–88. **Tidball, D.** *In Christ, in Colossae.* **Wedderburn, A. J. M.** *Baptism and Resurrection.* **Williams, A. L.** "Cult of the Angels," 413–38. **Yamauchi, E.** "Jewish Gnosticism," 467–97. **Yates, R.** "Colossians and Gnosis," 49–68. ———. "Worship of Angels," 12–15.

Colossians was not just a general letter of encouragement and instruction for the Colossian believers. There was trouble at Colossae, and the author felt it his duty to direct a series of stern warnings to them: "let no one judge you" (2:16); "let no one condemn you" (2:18); and the pointed question, "Why do you comply with their dictates?" (2:20). These three warnings form the backbone of a polemical section in the letter that also includes descriptive comments of a rival teaching and concise but sharp critique (2:16–23). The warnings began even earlier in the letter when the apostle asserts, "I am saying this so that no one may deceive you with plausible arguments" (2:4 NRSV). And then a few lines later he makes some of his strongest comments of all: "see to it that no one takes you captive through philosophy and empty deceit, according to human tradition, according to the elemental spirits of the universe, and not according to Christ" (2:8 NRSV). The seriousness of the warnings and the detailed and specific nature of the polemic make it impossible to agree with M. Hooker, who has asserted that "the letter is written out of general pastoral concern"[660] and with an "extraordinary calm."[661]

The first warning (2:8) and the polemical section of the letter (2:16–23) contain a number of explicit indicators of the nature of the rival teaching at Colossae. These elements have been the focus of extensive scholarly investigation over the years, but they are very difficult to interpret. Part of the reason for this is that they are stated in a shorthand form that was sufficient for the readers to know what Paul was referring to, but difficult for modern interpreters to grasp without the larger context. It is similar to an American making a reference to "runs, hits, and errors." This expression would be lost on anyone who does not understand baseball. For the Colossian situation to make sense, the larger picture needs to be inferred, but we only have bits and pieces from which to make this inference. The crucial question to ask is how do all of the various and disparate elements cohere? How do we paint a portrait of the situation that takes

660 Hooker, "False Teachers," 320.
661 Hooker, "False Teachers," 316.

into account both the explicit and implicit elements, accounts for the nature of the polemic, and explains why the author chose to emphasize certain theological themes? Of course, this is a process fraught with danger, because it is so easy to misinterpret one or more of the elements and thus reconstruct a skewed picture of the problem at Colossae. But it is the task of the interpreter to do interpretive work. It is not helpful or appropriate for the historian or exegete to give up prematurely and complain that the interpretive dilemma is simply insoluble.[662] There is a solution to the conundrum despite how hard it may be to achieve it. The very process of examining the relevant historical and textual data will yield insights that contribute to gaining greater clarity about the situation and how to interpret the text. Nevertheless, the complexity of this problem should temper the confidence of the interpreter and solicit a degree of humility.

One of the challenges of interpreting the various elements of the opposing teaching is in identifying the background of each item and, more importantly, their relevant context at the time of the writing of the letter. Some elements, such as Sabbath observance, have a clearly Jewish background and may be assumed to reflect the practices of a law-observant and faithful Jew in the diaspora setting. But this may not be a correct assumption. A Sabbath might be observed—even by a gentile—but for a different purpose than in common Judaism. Such a situation can be seen in the testimony of Hippolytus about the sect of Elchasai. In that context, Sabbath observance is motivated primarily by astrological reasons (Hippolytus, *Haer.* 9.11.4). For nearly every specific indicator of the rival teaching at Colossae, the conclusions of the interpreters range somewhere on the spectrum of Torah-observant Judaism to a purely pagan background. And this has been true of the overall portrait of the Colossian problem. Some have argued that it is purely Jewish; others have argued that it is purely pagan. Most, however, see some kind of syncretistic mix.

Before we examine the various theories about the nature of the rival teaching at Colossae, it would be helpful to survey the explicit indicators of the problem from the warning at 2:8 and the polemical section of the letter (2:16–23).[663] It is exceedingly difficult to separate cited slogans and self-descriptions of the rival group from the author's own characterization of the teaching and practices. While it is possible—and even likely—that additional allusions are made to the factional group outside of the direct polemic, these are the most crucial data points for inferring any reconstruction of the rival teaching.

662 Barclay, *Colossians and Philemon*, 54, concludes his discussion with the comment that the situation at Colossae is "an unsolved, and unsoluble mystery." Similarly, Bormann, 51, recognizes that there are concrete opponents, but the precise details are unknown.

663 For a helpful discussion of a methodology for discerning the teaching of the opponents (with which I am in essential agreement), see Sumney, "Identity of the Opponents," 366–67. He notes, "This method focuses on the primary text itself, strictly limiting what parallels outside the letter can contribute." This is the proper place to begin, but at some point, one must correlate this data with what is known in the religious environment.

*"Worship of angels"* (2:18). This is widely recognized to be a crux expression for interpreting one of the practices of the rival teachers. But interpreters are divided on whether the genitive is objective or subjective; in other words, are the angels receiving worship or are they performing it? The word for worship is also not the common Pauline word for worship. So there is a question about what is entailed by this particular word choice.

*Visionary experience and "entering"* (2:18). The term ἐμβατεύω is also a crux for discerning the nature of the teaching. Is it a technical term giving expression to the second and highest stage of a pagan mystery initiation ritual—derived from "entering" the oracle grotto of the Apollo temple at Claros? Or is it simply a common expresson for "entering" something, "investigating" something, or "going into detail" about a matter? Some have seen this as proof of the syncretistic nature of the problem at Colossae, since it suggests that ritual initiation had something to do with the rival teaching. All are agreed, however, that ἃ ἑόρακεν, "what he has seen," indicates that there was some kind of visionary experience that was integral to the practices of the opponents. But was this a Jewish ascent to heaven visionary experience, the visions of someone initiated into a pagan ritual, or some other kind of visionary experience?

*"The philosophy"* (2:8). The author explicitly refers to the factional teaching as "the philosophy," which he immediately judges to be empty and deceitful. The question here is whether we are to think of this group as advocates of one of the contemporary school philosophies, such as Platonism, Pythagoreanism, Epicureanism, Cynicism, or even philosophy in general. Each of these has had an advocate in the history of interpretation. Or do we regard it as a characterization of a segment of Judaism—much as Josephus used "philosophy" to describe the Pharisees, Sadducees, and the Essenes? Or could it be a reference to an arcane "philosophy" consisting of rituals of power?

*"A festival or new moon or Sabbath"* (2:16). Calendar observances apparently played an important role in the practice of the opponents. Sabbath observance would appear to be proof positive that the rival teaching had its roots in Judaism. But one needs to be cautious in making this assumption (as noted above). Similarly, although new-moon festivals are found in Judaism, they are also significant for local moon gods, such as Mēn and Selene. The root issue is to discern how these observances were appropriated by a group of Jewish and gentile Christians in the Lycus Valley.

*"Food and drink"* (2:16). Rules regarding food and drink were also a constituent part of the opponents' teaching and practice. But what was the intent of these regulations? Were they reflective of Torah observance in obedience to God? Or, were they preparatory practices in the anticipation of a heavenly journey or a visionary experience?

*"Do not handle! Do not taste! Do not touch!"* (2:21). Many English translations place these three commands in quotation marks since they appear to be slogans from the rival group. Once again, what was the intent of these various taboos? And did they go beyond food and drink prohibitions to the avoidance of sexual contact and other matters?

*Asceticism* (2:18, 23). The term "humility" is twice used to characterize the opponents' practices, which, almost all interpreters agree, refers to ascetic practices that would include fasting. What purpose did fasting have in this group?

*Severe treatment of the body* (2:23). Is this a reference to the extreme asceticism of the group? Or is it a possible allusion to the practice of circumcision, which some have seen as important to the rival teachers? Or could it even be an allusion to some kind of bodily mutilations that were mediated to the group through local religious practice?

*"A reputation for wisdom"* (2:23). Was this a reputation within the gentile community or the Jewish community? Is the wisdom referred to here a philosophical wisdom or a wisdom associated with the Jewish wisdom tradition? Or was it even an esoteric and arcane wisdom connected to secret arts?

*Demonic spirits of the world* (2:8, 20). Although this expression (τὰ στοιχεῖα τοῦ κόσμου) is not unique to Colossians (it also appears in Gal 4:3, 9), it appears twice in the polemical material in this letter. Some interpreters have taken it as an indication that the opponents were advocates of a cult to the *stoicheia*. Others have seen it as reflective of a gnostic cosmology. Still others have seen the expression as part of Paul's reservoir of terminology for demonic powers and that it is functioning as part of his polemic and not as a descriptor of the practices of the group. What role did demonic powers have in the Colossian philosophy? Or should the expression be interpreted as fundamental principles or as a reference to the four or five foundational elements (earth, air, fire, water, and perhaps ether)?

*"Freely chosen worship"* (2:23). Does this expression reveal an alignment with Greco-Roman voluntary societies or elective participation in mystery rites?

*"Honor"* (2:23). The philosophy claimed to be honorable (which the author denies), but did this claim extend to an affirmation of its honor in a general Greco-Roman sense in the context of an honor-shame culture? Or did it have a more specific function of indicating the honor that accrues to an individual who has a visionary experience or is honored with the appearance of a divine being?

In addition to these explicit indicators are some terms and practices outside the polemical section that could yield allusions to the rival teaching. An even greater caution is needed for this level of inquiry, since what might be taken as a catchword of the opponents or as a feature of their teaching may simply be part of the author's own theology. Among the elements proposed for contributing to a portait of "the philosophy" are the following:

*Pleroma* (1:19; 2:9). This characterization of Christ as possessing the "fullness" of God is sometimes seen as a direct counter to the teaching of the opponents. This is particularly true of those who see some form of gnostic background to the problem since the term πλήρωμα features prominently in some gnostic systems. But could it simply be an expression of the writer's own theology?

*Circumcision* (2:11). The mention of a spiritual circumcision in 2:11 is thought by some to counter the group's advocacy of literal physical circumcision. But, once again, could this notion be a positive expression of theology apart from a direct allusion to a practice of "the philosophy"?

Finally, one needs to ask whether the theological emphases of the letter contribute some insight into the nature of the problem at Colossae. Although this is more slippery ground for inferring the contours of the rival teaching, it is entirely reasonable to think that the author would have this concern in mind when he selects theological themes to address and shapes them into a relevant discourse for his readers. Yet an even greater degree of tentativeness is important for this kind of "mirror reading" of a letter.

*Thrones, dominions, principalities, authorities, "the invisible," "things in heaven," demonic spirits of the world, and "the powerful realm of darkness"* (1:13, 16, 20; 2:8, 10, 15, 20). There is an extraordinary emphasis on demonic powers in Colossians. What role do these demonic powers play in the Colossian "philosophy"? Have the rival teachers set up a cult through which these spirits can be appeased, as some have asserted? Are they powers that control the heavenly spheres and endeavor to block access to the highest heaven? Or does the teaching of the passage address the common fear of demonic spirits that most people entertained?

*Exaltation Christology.* There is a pronounced emphasis on Jesus as Lord of all in this letter. Christ is celebrated as preeminent over everything in heaven and on earth. He is eloquently portrayed as the one who has won a decisive and humiliating victory over the principalities and powers. Is this theological emphasis called forth by the needs of the readers, who are tempted to yield to the demands of "the philosophy"? And, if so, how?

*Realized eschatology.* More than the main letters of Paul, Colossians stresses the participation of believers with Christ in his resurrection and in his exalted status. Believers have been rescued from the dominion of darkness and participate with Christ in his authority over these evil beings. Once again, we must ask if there is something unique to the situation that elicits this theological emphasis by the author.

At this point we must ask how all of these elements cohere to contribute to an overall portait of the situation at Colossae. This has been a major problem in the history of NT scholarship, which has prompted numerous articles and monographs in the attempt to solve the riddle. Nevertheless, still no solution has emerged that has commanded the assent of most scholars, resulting in a consensus position. At various intervals in the history of interpretation, it has appeared that scholarship was closing in on a particular view, only for this agreement to be disrupted by new historical data or a new way of looking at the evidence.

Many commentaries cite J. J. Gunther's tabulation of forty-four different views of the Colossian philosophy, to stress the dizzying array of possibilities and the almost hopeless difficulty of achieving a solution.[664] My count is actually more than this. But this way of characterizing the problem is somewhat misleading. The various perspectives on the nature of the problem can be reduced to variations on about a half dozen views. These would include those who take the problem as purely Hellenistic (e.g., a Hellenistic philosophy or a pagan mystery cult), purely Jewish (either observant Judaism or a mystical Judaism) or a syncretistic blend (gnosis/Gnosticism, Essene Judaism influenced by Gnosticism, or Jewish folk belief). Among these views there are various permutations and blends. I will survey each of the major approaches in turn and provide some general critique. A full assessment of each view is beyond the scope of what is possible in the commentary. Many of the arguments for these views, however, will be handled in the exegesis of the relevant passages.

### *Hellenistic Philosophy*

A stream of scholars has taken the explicit reference to "the philosophy" (2:8) quite seriously. This began as early as Tertullian, who identified the Colossian problem as philosophy in general.[665] Most others, however, have attempted to correlate the information given about the rival teaching with a known school philosophy. Clement associated it with Epicureanism.[666] Grotius suggested Pythagoreanism.[667] This notion was picked up by E. Schweizer in more recent years, who compared the elements of the Colossian "philosophy" with what we know of Neopythagorean thought and practice.[668] Nevertheless, he held open the possibility that the Colossian teaching "may also have included some kind of mystery rite" that would "ensure the soul's ascent to the upper world."[669] Others have tended to see some Judaism in the mix. E. Percy thought that the evidence of Colossians was best described as a Jewish sort of Christian faith with strong

664 Gunther, *Paul's Opponents*, 3–4.

665 Tertullian as cited in Eadie, xxxiv.

666 Clement as cited in Meyer, 195.

667 Grotius as cited in Eadie, xxxiv.

668 See Schweizer, 132. He cites, in particular, a text in Diels, *Fragmente der Vorsokratiker*, 1.448.33–451.19.

669 Schweizer, 133.

influence of late Greek speculation (Neopythagoreanism and Neoplatonism) along with ascetic piety.[670] M. Wolter has likewise leaned in this direction by explaining the rival teaching as an esoteric revelatory wisdom of Hellenistic-Jewish provenance, with food-asceticism regulations that are found above all in Neopythagoreanism.[671]

R. DeMaris has argued that the Colossian "philosophy" is best interpreted as an expression of Middle Platonism (albeit within a syncretistic mix of ideas).[672] He draws on Plutarch and other writers in the Middle Platonic tradition as representing the most important sources for interpreting the core features of the rival teaching. In the final analysis, he contends that the teaching is syncretistic, with "a distinctive blend of popular Middle Platonic, Jewish, and Christian elements that cohere around the pursuit of wisdom."[673] DeMaris provides us with a thoroughgoing critique of Schweizer's view. He rightly criticizes Schweizer for not recognizing the distinctively Jewish elements of the Colossian "philosophy" and for too readily accepting claims of ancient sources to represent Pythagoreanism when they are more accurately described as Platonic or eclectic.[674]

T. Martin contends that the Colossian "philosophy" should be read against the background of Cynic philosophy.[675] He eschews any notion of syncretism and argues that the Colossian teaching is "a consistent, coherent expression of Cynic philosophy." The catalyst for the letter is a situation in which a group of itinerant Cynic philosophers visited the church at Colossae and critiqued what they saw based on their own worldview assumptions and convictions.[676] Colossians was then written to counter this critique. Yet it is difficult to see how Martin can avoid seeing Jewish features to the rival teaching. He does so through a dubious interpretation of the calendar observances in 2:16 ("festivals, new moons, and Sabbaths") as observances that the Colossian Christians were already practicing and that the Cynics observe and critique.[677] But this misses the pattern of Paul's polemic in 2:16–23 wherein he includes a characterization of the practices of the opponents immediately after each of the three warnings. Overall, as F. G. Downing has noted, "it is not a little odd that this writer to the Colossian congregation opposes a Cynic infiltrator without using any of the traditional polemical commonplaces."[678]

One of the difficulties of these purely philosophical views is the problem of social location. It must be remembered that Colossae was not a prominent

670 Percy, *Probleme*, 143.
671 Wolter, 162.
672 DeMaris, *Colossian Controversy*, 17, 134–45.
673 DeMaris, *Colossian Controversy*, 17.
674 DeMaris, *Colossian Controversy*, 88, 92.
675 Martin, *By Philosophy and Empty Deceit*, 206.
676 Martin, *By Philosophy and Empty Deceit*, 205.
677 Martin, *By Philosophy and Empty Deceit*, 124–34.
678 F. G. Downing, review of *By Philosophy and Empty Deceit*, by T. Martin, *JBL* 117 (1998): 543–44.

metropolis such as Athens, Alexandria, or even Ephesus; it was a small community in a rural area with farmers, miners, and textile workers, with a population that was less educated than the urban centers. It is unlikely that any of the school philosophies would have gained a strong hearing and proven to be enticing to the common folk of this place. Some of the advocates of this view wrongly downplay the Jewish features of the teaching and practices of the opponents. And, finally, this group of interpreters presents strained interpretations of aspects of the rival teaching that do not fit well into the respective systems. For instance, Martin suggests that the angels of 2:18 were human messengers who communicated the gospel to the Colossians,[679] and ἃ ἑώρακεν ἐμβατεύων, "entering what he has seen," is interpreted as a Cynic infiltrator entering the Colossian worship service to observe and then to critique.[680] Of all these interpreters, DeMaris makes the best case for a recognized philosophy (in his view, Middle Platonism), but in the end he does not provide the most compelling set of explanations for the exegetical details and for how the various and disparate elements cohere. Much of his case rests on interpreting τὰ στοιχεῖα τοῦ κόσμου as actual quotations from the opponents (2:8, 20) that he sees pointing "unequivocally to a philosophical background" and referring to "the fundamental elements of the world," that is, the "guiding principles of the world."[681] Yet his analysis fails to give adequate weight to Paul's own polemical use of the phrase in Gal 4:3, 9 and the evidence that points to a more likely personal interpretation of the phrase as spirits. In sum, the philosophical interpretation of the Colossian problem has fallen short of attracting many adherents among scholars.

### *Local Religious Influence: A Pagan Mystery Cult*

In 1905, with the help of local peasants, archaeologist Theodor Macridy (who later became director of the Istanbul Archaeological Museum) discovered the famous temple of Apollo at Claros. The site was located about fourteen miles northwest of Ephesus and slightly over a mile north of the Roman city of Notion. Numerous inscriptions were subsequently discovered at the site, along with some that had been taken from the site for secondary use in a nearby Byzantine era church.[682] Among the inscriptions were two from the Byzantine church nearby and one from a marble column of the propylon at Claros, all of which made use of the term ἐμβατεύω, "enter"—the very word that had been so difficult to interpret from the description of the practice of the opponents in Col 2:18.

About a decade later (1917), M. Dibelius wrote the seminal and influential study "The Isis Initiation in Apuleius and Related Initiatory Rites," in which he argued that ἐμβατεύω was used in the Claros inscriptions as a technical

679 Martin, *By Philosophy and Empty Deceit*, 159.

680 Martin, *By Philosophy and Empty Deceit*, 108, 113, 149.

681 DeMaris, *Colossian Controversy*, 55.

682 Macridy, "Antiquités," 41–45.

expression signifying the second stage of a mystery initiation rite practiced at the Apollo temple.[683] He concluded that the pattern of ritual initiation at Claros was similar to the ritual at Eleusis in that there was a lower and higher stage of initiation. The lower stage was the initiation proper (called the μύησις), and the higher stage was called "entering" (ἐμβατεύω), which corresponded to the "Epoptia" at Eleusis.[684] Dibelius then argued that the enigmatic term in Col 2:18 could now be explained on the basis of these inscriptions. He contended that members of the church at Colossae had been initiated into a mystery cult and were creating a hybrid structure of belief and practice that combined pagan practice with Christianity.[685] He concluded that a group from Colossae had been initiated into a "cult of the 'elements,'" which had already been influenced to some degree by gnosis. The end result was a new syncretistic group within the Colossian church who strove "by means of a revelatory religion to set man free from cosmic compulsion and to make him master of his fate."[686] He interpreted all the other features of the Colossian "philosophy" on the basis of this and minimized the Jewish features of the teaching.

Independently from Dibelius and without an awareness of his work, W. M. Ramsay reached essentially the same conclusion about the relevance of the Claros inscriptions for interpreting ἐμβατεύω in Col 2:18.[687] Ramsay also concludes that ἐμβατεύω was indeed a technical term from the mysteries familiar to Phrygian readers and that Paul used it because it was a technical term. Like Dibelius, he drew a parallel with the two-stage Eleusinian rites and argued that ἐμβατεύω "implied the whole epoptika" and should be translated, "performed the higher stage of the ritual."[688] He concludes that "a leader in the congregation, prominent in teaching a certain new theosophic and mystic form of Christianity, was introducing ideas which he had brought over from his old belief in the Mysteries."[689] The "worship of angels" he took as a homage paid to angels or powers that are intermediaries between God and humanity.[690] These "elemental powers" (2:8, 20) were believed to enslave human beings and control their fate. The Colossian "philosophy" thus offered a means of escape. As Ramsay notes, the mystery rites, such as at Claros, offered "prayers, rites, incantations, magic arts, [and] purifications . . . to aid the struggling soul."[691]

To Ramsay's credit, he recognized the Jewish contribution to the syncretistic teaching at Colossae, which Dibelius completely dismissed. He claimed that "the

683 Dibelius, "Isis Initiation," 61–121.
684 Dibelius, "Isis Initiation," 87.
685 Dibelius, "Isis Initiation," 90–91.
686 Dibelius, "Isis Initiation," 100.
687 Ramsay, *Teaching of Paul*, 283–305; idem, "Mysteries," 198–209; idem, "Sketches," 44–51.
688 Ramsay, *Teaching of Paul*, 296.
689 Ramsay, *Teaching of Paul*, 300.
690 Ramsay, *Teaching of Paul*, 298.
691 Ramsay, *Teaching of Paul*, 302.

order of ritual" practiced by the opponents was "largely Jewish."[692] But he also made an important correlation to Jewish folk belief when he contended that the opponents combined mystery-cult teaching and practice "with Jewish thought in a popular superstitious form," alluding to a possible connection with Jewish magic (Acts 19:13). Unfortunately, Ramsay's study has gone largely unnoticed, and the view that the Colossian "philosophy" has something to do with local mystery religions has been attacked mainly on the refusal of Dibelius, Lohse, and others to take seriously the Jewish features of the teaching.

In his important Hermeneia commentary, E. Lohse has adopted the substance of Dibelius's conclusions and has contended that the Colossian teaching was syncretistic and "probably took the form of a mystery."[693] Due to their concern to gain security against the cosmic principalities and the powers of fate, the rival teachers advocated paying homage to the angels in a cultic worship.[694] Lohse also saw gnosis as part of the mix and suggested that the rival teachers were attempting "to gain entry to the *pleroma* (2:9) and participate in the divine fullness."[695] The myopic exclusion of admitting any Jewish elements to this teaching has rightly earned this view a great deal of criticism.

Although Dibelius and Lohse are often seen as the primary representatives of the mystery-cult view, numerous others have been convinced by the relevance of the Claros inscriptions for seeing some connection to the mysteries.[696] All of these interpreters contend that there is a syncretistic blend of teachings, but there has been a range of opinions expressed regarding the nature and amount of Jewish features. Hegermann, for instance, builds upon Dibelius, arguing that the nearest parallel to the Colossian teaching is the so-called Mithras liturgy, but he contends that the origin of the Colossian "philosophy" is in heretical, syncretistic Judaism.[697] Argall argued that the rival teaching originated "in the realm of the Hellenistic mystery religions rather than of Jewish apocalyticism,"[698] but contended (contra Lohse and others) that the polemic in Colossians is against idolatry and not against gnosis. Nevertheless, he saw the syncretistic mix "did indeed include some patently Jewish elements (e.g., Sabbath observance)."[699]

The discovery of the Claros inscriptions and their explanatory power for accounting for the presence of ἐμβατεύω in Col 2:18 is compelling. Some form of connection to mystery ritual initiation appears to be well established. Where many of the articulations of this view fall short is in overemphasizing the

692 Ramsay, *Teaching of Paul*, 298.
693 Lohse, 129.
694 Lohse, 128.
695 Lohse, 128.
696 Pokorný, 115–17, 146–47; Argall, "Religious Error," 14–15; Martin, 94–95; Lähnemann, *Kolosserbrief*, 86, 138; Houlden, 198; Beare, 202–4; Scott, 55; Eitrem, "EMBATEYΩ," 90–94; idem, *Orakel und Mysterien*, 73; et al.
697 Hegermann, *Schöpfungsmittler*, 161–65.
698 Argall, "Religious Error," 7.
699 Argall, "Religious Error," 20.

mystery-cult connection to the exclusion of the Jewish elements. Yet it is difficult to find examples in Second Temple Jewish literature of a kind of syncretistic Judaism that compromised so far with the pagan environment that they assimilated mystery-cult rituals. It is a shame that no one has followed up on Ramsay's brief suggestion that the kind of folk Judaism we see reflected in the account of Sceva in Acts 19 may be the kind of Judaism reflected here.

### *Judaism*

There is an opposite stream of scholarship that has argued that everything about the Colossian "philosophy" is thoroughly Jewish and contains no local pagan religious elements or any Hellenistic influence. A. S. Peake, for instance, writing in the late 1800s, argued that the false teaching was Jewish and contained no elements of Gnosticism or even Essene Judaism.[700] Writing before the discovery of the Claros inscriptions, he contended that all of the features of the Colossian problem can be explained by a concern to obey the Mosaic law and by traditions within Judaism. For instance, he notes that what Paul attacks in Col 2:16 "is the view that the Sabbath law should be regarded as still binding."[701] The angels who are worshiped in 2:18 are the angels who mediated the giving of the law.[702] He finds the reference to circumcision in 2:11 as demonstrating that the rival teachers found value in it. For Peake, the opponents were Christians and part of the Colossian church; they simply did not give Christ the place he deserved.[703]

N. T. Wright took a similar position, but has argued that the opposition did not actually belong to the church. He concluded that it is "a warning against Judaism," and the temptation that gentiles at Colossae would face to think of the path to maturity would functionally "lie in their becoming Jews."[704] He observes, "There is, in fact, nothing in the letter which *requires* us to postulate that Paul is opposing actual false teachers who were already infiltrating the church."[705] J. D. G. Dunn has brought further definition to this view by describing the opponents as Jewish outsiders (not Christians) who are part of a local synagogue.[706] They were not evangelistic as much as they were concerned to defend the purity of their synagogue community, especially against "a (quasi-) Jewish sect so recently arrived on the scene."[707] They presented a "Jewish apologia, confident of Israel's privileged status before the one God and consequently dismissive of would-be claimants to share in that status."[708] Thus, as Garland notes,

700 Peake, 484–88.
701 Peake, 486.
702 Peake, 482–83.
703 Peake, 485.
704 Wright, 27.
705 Wright, 27.
706 Dunn, 33–35; idem, "Colossian Philosophy," 153–81.
707 Dunn, "Colossian Philosophy," 158.
708 Dunn, "Colossian Philosophy," 159–60.

the "newly formed Gentile Christians in Colosse are being badgered about their faith by contentious Jews who took affront over their claims."[709]

Barclay is correct in raising the concern that those who take a purely Jewish view can't explain why Colossians is so different from Galatians.[710] This is especially striking when one considers that the term νόμος, "law," appears thirty-two times in Galatians and not once in Colossians. There is also an assumption that because Paul speaks of a spiritual circumcision in 2:11 that this must be in opposition to a group that advocates a literal circumcision.[711] But it must be observed that the mention of circumcision in Colossians is not part of the polemical section of the letter (2:16–23), and Paul elsewhere speaks of a spiritual circumcision (Rom 2:28–29) in dependence on biblical tradition (Deut 10:16; 30:6; Jer 4:4). This view also undervalues the weight of the evidence for interpreting ἐμβατεύω as a technical term of local mystery initiation rites.

Moving away from an explanation rooted in orthodox Judaism, B. F. Westcott argued that the Colossian "philosophy" bore a deep resemblance to Essene Judaism, which he referred to as a group of Jewish mystics.[712] He claimed that no pagan sources were necessary to explain the unique characteristics of the Colossian teaching. The emphasis on angel veneration, the multiplication of rules and regulations, the rigorous asceticism, and the various kinds of appeals to abstinence all point to the influence of the Essenes.[713] Although Westcott's view did not have any impact on subsequent scholarship, the view of his predecessor at Cambridge, J. B. Lightfoot, did. Lightfoot also contended that the root of the Colossian "philosophy" was in Essene Judaism, yet he argued for a complex mixture of elements that included a substantial gnostic stream.[714] More will be said about Lightfoot's views below.

### *Jewish Mysticism*

In recent years, if there is any view that has come close to commanding a consensus, it would be Jewish mysticism. Advocates of this view have also tended to deny any Hellenistic or local religious influence. One of the distinctive features of this view has been to take θρησκεία τῶν ἀγγέλων, "worship of angels," as a subjective genitive and to interpret it as a worship *with* the angels around the heavenly throne, following a visionary ascent-to-heaven experience. Advocates of this view tend to deny any technical significance to ἐμβατεύω and deny that the Colossian "philosophy" has any connection to mystery cults, local religions, or gnosis.

709 Garland, 27. See also Bevere, *Sharing in the Inheritance*, 44–46.

710 Barclay, *Colossians*, 54.

711 E.g., Dunn, "Colossian Philosophy," 160.

712 Westcott, 25.

713 Westcott, 23–24.

714 Lightfoot, "Colossian Heresy," 13.

The catalyst for this view were two highly influential essays published by F. O. Francis[715] that were based on his 1964 Yale University dissertation.[716] His research on the crux text—Col 2:18—challenged the mystery-cult interpretation of ἐμβατεύω and the consensus view that angels were the objects of veneration. Numerous scholars have accepted his conclusions on these two issues and have built on the foundation that he has laid.[717]

Francis pointed to a variety of Jewish texts that point to human participation in the angelic liturgy (e.g., Ascen. Isa. 7.37; 8.17; 9.28, 31, 33; T. Job 48–50; 3 En. 1.12; Apoc. Abr. 17), including texts from Qumran that speak of humans sharing in the lot with the angels (e.g., 1QH 3.20–22; 1QSb 4.25–26).[718] T. J. Sappington expanded this base by providing a thorough overview of the theme of ascetic-mystical piety in Jewish apocalyptic texts.[719] His study served to reinforce Francis's view but narrowed the focus to "Jewish apocalypticism as the religious movement most relevant for the study of Colossians."[720] He concluded that the Colossian error was "a type of Jewish/Gentile Christianity that was strongly oriented toward the ascetic-mystical piety of Jewish apocalypticism."[721] Most of Sappington's conclusions have been upheld by the important study of I. H. Smith.[722] He expands the base, however, by looking at mystical trends at Qumran and in the relevance of *merkabah* mysticism, a movement focused on visionary experience of the throne of God.[723] Although reaching many of the same conclusions, Smith correctly finds an overarching emphasis in Colossians on evil spirits and, contrary to Francis and Sappington, interprets the τὰ στοιχεῖα τοῦ κόσμου (2:8, 20) as evil spiritual forces that the Colossians were trying to overcome.[724] Part of their motivation for heavenly-ascent experience was a dualistic understanding that caused them to long to be released from this world and participate in the heavenly worship.

While identifying the Colossian "philosophy" as a Christianized form of Jewish mysticism appropriately shifts the focus from a purely pagan and Hellenistic background to Judaism, it goes too far in denying any form of syncretism or assimilation of pagan ideas and practices. Although many features

715 Francis, "Humility and Angelic Worship," 163–95; idem, "EMBATEUEIN."

716 Francis, "Reexamination of the Colossian Controversy."

717 E.g., Beetham, *Echoes of Scripture*, 205; Bird, 20–24; Witherington, 109–110; Sappington, *Revelation and Redemption*, 158–64, 225; Sumney, 10–12; idem, "Opponents," 377–78; Carr, *Angels and Principalities*, 69–72; idem, "Two Notes on Colossians," 499–500; Yates, xv; idem, "'Worship of Angels,'" 12–15; idem, "Colossians and Gnosis," 49–68; Rowland, "Apocalyptic Visions," 73–83; Evans, "Colossian Mystics," 188–205; Lincoln, *Paradise Now and Not Yet*, 111–12; Bandstra, "Colossian Errorists," 329–43, esp. 39.

718 Francis, "Humility and Angelic Worship," 178–79.

719 See Sappington, *Revelation and Redemption*, 26–137.

720 Sappington, *Revelation and Redemption*, 225.

721 Sappington, *Revelation and Redemption*, 225.

722 Smith, *Heavenly Perspective*.

723 Bruce, "Colossian Heresy," 201–4, also underlined the importance of *merkabah* mysticism.

724 Smith, *Heavenly Perspective*, 143–44.

of the rival teaching can be explained by Jewish influence of some sort, not every element fits this interpretive grid without straining credulity. This is most notable with the term ἐμβατεύω, which now, because of the discovery of the Claros inscriptions, likely demonstrates that the Colossian "philosophy" had some connection with mystery-cult initiatory rites. The fact that delegations from the Lycus Valley came to Claros to consult the oracle makes this even more probable. The interpretation of θρησκεία τῶν ἀγγέλων as a worship *with* the angels (subjective genitive) is also improbable. The linguistic patterns of usage with θρησκεία followed by a genitive case throughout Greek literature of the time demonstrate that the genitive is invariably objective. If these two cornerstones of the Jewish-mysticism view as articulated by Francis and his followers are not tenable, then the view needs substantial modification. Most importantly, it opens the door to explaining "the philosophy" as some form of Jewish syncretism. Yet one needs to ask what kind of syncretism best explains the phenomena and brings coherence to the whole.

### *Gnosticism, Gnosis, Incipient Gnosticism, and Jewish Gnosticism*

Of course, the most syncretistic religion of all in Greco-Roman antiquity was Gnosticism. Until the post World War II era, there was a widespread consensus that some form of Gnosticism constituted the essence of the Colossian "philosophy." In Gnosticism (or gnosis, as continental historians prefer) there is a convergence of many varied religious and philosophical streams that often include Persian religion, Judaism, Platonism, mystery-cult theology and practice, astrology, magic, and Egyptian religion. Of course, there are numerous forms of gnosis, with certain contributing streams receiving greater emphasis than others, depending on the system. Advocates for some form of gnosis behind the Colossian problem represent a broad range of perspectives, but the crucial distinction is how much and what kind of Judaism they see as part of the mix.

At the heart of a gnostic worldview, especially as we see it in some of its prominent proponents in the second century, is the revelation of a secret, unknown God eternally existing in a kingdom of light, who is distinct from the creator God (the demiurge) of Gen 1–3. Consistent with this theology is a thoroughgoing dualism that denigrates material existence and prompts a longing within people to be freed from the body and united with the invisible God in the highest heaven. The earth is surrounded by heavenly planetary spheres that are populated with dangerous astral spirits, which in some systems could be referred to as the *pleroma*. The transcendent God has mercifully sent a redeemer figure to spread a secret *gnosis* showing the way of salvation from the shackles of material existence and the path through the heavenlies to be reunited with the ultimate God.

Proponents of a gnostic background to Colossians have often contended that this was a worldview that permeated the entire Mediterranean world in the Roman period and influenced most religious traditions. But this assumption is now seriously questioned, both in terms of the date of the rise of Gnosticism and in terms of the nature and extent of its sphere of influence. Most scholars are now less certain of a pre-Christian origin for Gnosticism, and some have argued that it may not have come into existence until after the Jewish War of AD 66–70. Because of the predominance of Jewish vocabulary, mythemes, and historiola in the Nag Hammadi documents, there is a tendency now in scholarship to see Gnosticism emerging in a Jewish context. Although many scholars are uncertain what the catalyst in Judaism would have been, some are suggesting that the dualism may have begun as a theodicy in the aftermath and disillusionment following the horrific losses of the Jewish War. In other words, the only way to explain the crushing defeat of the apocalyptic hope for some groups within Judaism was by postulating that God had a rival in heaven.[725]

The uncertainty about the origins of gnostic systems has tempered the approach of many interpreters, who hesitate in affirming that the Colossian "philosophy" was gnostic and simply assert that it is proto-gnostic or incipient Gnosticism. But this is really to say nothing of substance about the rival teaching, since many different religious streams converged into Gnosticism.

It is easy to see why numerous scholars in the history of the interpretation of the Colossian problem saw Gnosticism as the culprit. The concern about heavenly powers and astral spirits (*stoicheia*), the references to *pleroma*, the veneration of angels, asceticism as a means of fleeing from the world, the author's emphasis on Christ as Lord of heaven and earth, the above and below distinction, and many other features could fit with a gnostic explanation of the problem.

Thus, in the early 1800s Mayerhoff suggested that the false teaching at Colossae was Cerinthian Gnosticism.[726] In a similar vein, conservative scholar J. G. Machen argued that the Colossian errorists "were gnostics, engaged in unhistorical speculations, and as far removed as possible from anything that primitive Palestinian Christianity might conceivably have been."[727] Many others have explained "the philosophy" on the basis of some form of gnosis—usually also acknowledging that there are some Jewish features to the teaching that are part of the mix.[728] One of the most recent articulations of this view has been by P. Pokorný. He observes that "elements of mystery piety and of Jewish conceptions are also combined in Gnosticism, which is not unequivocally attested until the beginning of the second century, however, but which must have had its roots a few decades prior to the first documented evidence."[729]

In his profoundly influential commentary on Colossians, J. B. Lightfoot

---

725 Hengel, "Ursprünge der Gnosis," 190–223, esp. p. 222. See also Culianu, "Origins of Gnostic Dualism," 78–80, and Segal, *Two Powers in Heaven*, 265.

726 Mayerhoff, *Colosser*, 148–62.

727 Machen, *Origin of Paul's Religion*, 129–30.

728 E.g., Lindemann, 42, 83–84; Schenke, "Widerstreit," 391–403; Bultmann, *Theology*, 2:149; Bornkamm, "Heresy of Colossians," 123–45; Lohmeyer, 40–41.

729 Pokorný, 117.

advanced the thesis that the Colossian "heresy" was not only gnostic but shared an essential affinity of type with Essene Judaism, which he characterized as a gnostic Judaism.[730] He made these observations, however, prior to the discovery of Qumran and the Dead Sea Scrolls, so we now know that his identification of Essene Judaism with Gnosticism was in error. He argued that the principalities, powers, authorities, and thrones were different grades of angelic mediators that demanded worship and obeisance. The Colossian aberration thus consisted of a doctrine of intermediate agencies who were involved in creation and now governed the world and constituted the *pleroma*. The temptation for the Colossians was to worship these beings as their link to God.[731] Consistent with Mayerhoff, Lightfoot contended that Cerinthus illustrates the kind of transitional link that was taking place between Judaism and Gnosticism and "between the incipient gnosis of the Colossian heretics and the mature gnosis of the second century."[732] Nevertheless, for Lightfoot, the Colossian "philosophy" was profoundly gnostic, to the extent that he could assert that "the view that the writer of this epistle is combating a Gnostic heresy seems free from all objections."[733] For him, the cosmogony, the angelology, the *pleroma* doctrine, and the strong asceticism all point to a robust gnostic worldview.

Not all agreed with Lightfoot's hypothesis, however. B. F. Westcott quipped that "the famous Essay of Bishop Lightfoot is a marvel of erudition, but it invests the Colossian trouble with a complexity which one would think can hardly belong to it."[734] Westcott himself saw "the philosophy" as Essene Judaism but discounted any connection of either of them with Gnosticism. Many, however, happily affirmed the Lightfoot proposal.[735]

Although the assumption of a Hellenistic, gnostic worldview that permeated the entire Mediterranean world as early as the first century BC has long held sway in NT scholarship, the validity of this assumption is now seriously questioned. The appropriateness of illustrating first-century tendencies and practices on the basis of later well-developed gnostic systems is anachronistic and inaccurate. I have argued in a different context that priority should be given to exploring traditions that were *known* to exist in the first century before appealing to later developments,[736] especially if the catalyst for the development of the anticosmic dualism and the demiurge concept in gnosis may postdate the composition of Colossians.[737] Although the origins of Gnosticism "may well have emerged

730 Lightfoot, "Colossian Heresy," 24–25.
731 Lightfoot, "Colossian Heresy," 29–31.
732 Lightfoot, "Colossian Heresy," 35.
733 Lightfoot, "Colossian Heresy," 37.
734 Westcott, 25.
735 P. Schaff affirmed Lightfoot's view in his influential *History of the Christian Church*, 772–73. See also, e.g., Moule, 31–33; Meyer, 195–97; Guthrie, *Introduction*, 568–71.
736 See my *Ephesians: Power and Magic*, 7–13.
737 See Culianu, "Origins of Gnostic Dualism," 78–80; Segal, *Two Powers in Heaven*, 265; Yamauchi, "Jewish Gnosticism?," 491.

among nonobservant, assimilating Jews,"[738] the fact remains that "identifiable gnostic sects do not appear prior to the emergence of Christianity."[739] K. Rudolph has also noted that once gnosis developed, it was "essentially a city religion" found in the major centers of the Mediterranean world.[740] As a small rural town, Colossae was anything but a major metropolis. One would also wonder about the appeal of gnosis to peasants, farmers, herders, and miners in a rural area.

Most problematic for the gnostic view of "the philosophy" is that the letter gives no indication that the proponents were advocating any of the core beliefs of later gnosis. Missing from the key indicators of "the philosophy" are a revelation of an unknown God differentiated from the creator, a thoroughgoing dualism, and a concern about the dangers of the ascent of the soul on the day of death. There is also no sense that the hostile *stoicheia* and the principalities and powers were represented as an obstacle for the future heavenly ascent on the day of death; they are an immanent threat in the present. Wilson is therefore correct in noting that "the Colossian 'heresy' is beyond question not yet a developed Gnosticism such as we find in the 'classic' systems of the second century."[741] But neither does it help to refer to the teaching at Colossae as "incipient Gnosticism" or even "proto-Gnosticism," since the core elements are missing, and these labels lack precision.

### *Jewish Folk Belief (Shamanism)*

Past generations of scholarship have been correct in identifying the Jewish roots to many elements of the Colossian teaching. Likewise, previous scholarship has also been right to point to the Hellenistic and local religious background to some facets of "the philosophy." The two crucial elements that unlock perspective on the nature of the problem are θρησκεία τῶν ἀγγέλων, "the worship of angels," and ἃ ἑόρακεν ἐμβατεύων, "entering what he has seen" (2:18).

Although the interpretations of both expressions are widely disputed, there are plausible solutions to each that lead to a coherent picture of the seemingly disparate elements of the Colossian problem. The "worship of angels" should not be seen either as a cultic praise and veneration of angels nor as a participation with angels in the worship of God around the heavenly throne, but rather as ritual performances in relationship to angels that included invoking them for help and protection.[742] This approach to angels was very common in folk Judaism and is attested in the Solomonic magical traditions (especially as seen in T. Sol. 18 from the 1st c. BC) and in the Qumran magical handbooks (4Q510, 511, 4Q560; 11Q11). Yet it is also exceedingly common in the hundreds of Jewish amulets from antiquity—including amulets discovered in Asia Minor.

---

738 Perkins, *Gnosticism and the New Testament*, 42.

739 Perkins, *Gnosticism and the New Testament*, 10.

740 Rudolph, *Gnosis*, 291.

741 Wilson, 57.

742 See my "Sceva, Solomon, and Shamanism," 7–26, and *Colossian Syncretism*, 8–102.

This tradition involving knowledge of angelic names and adjuring them for help continued throughout the Roman period and beyond, as seen in the Sepher ha-Razim and the Hekhalot writings. Angels figured prominently in Jewish exorcisms and rituals of power.

The invocation of angels is in some way connected to ritual initiation and visionary experience.[743] It is highly significant that the NT hapax legomenon ἐμβατεύω (Col 2:18) was found in a series of inscriptions in the Apollo temple of Claros, where it was used in a technical sense of the second and highest stage of mystery initiation. Given that delegations from the Lycus Valley traveled to Claros to consult Apollo reinforces the notion that people living in this area were familiar with the term and its usage for ritual initiation. Visionary experience was an integral part of this initiation experience. This explanation contrasts sharply with the fact that the term ἐμβατεύω is nowhere attested in a Jewish context for entry into heaven in a visionary sense (or in any other way). The evidence strongly inclines us to interpret it as a technical expression of the mysteries with attendant visionary experience and then to ask how this practice coheres with the other practices and features of the Colossian opponents.

In recent years, many scholars have refused to acknowledge either of these lines of interpretation—despite the evidence—because there is little to no evidence in Second Temple Jewish literature of Jews worshiping angels or participating in ritual mystery initiation. This level of syncretism within Judaism and, by extension, into a church with a strong Jewish-Christian presence is unthinkable.

Yet there was one form of Judaism where extensive and broad-level syncretism did take place. That was in the context of Jewish folk belief—that is, in Jewish magic. This was the Judaism of the common people where rituals of power, the use of amulets, and the practice of exorcism took place. This is a form of Judaism that has received little attention for its potential contribution to an understanding of the Colossian problem. It is the kind of Judaism that can be seen narrated by Luke in Acts 19 when he describes the situation involving a Jewish priestly figure named Sceva who served, along with his sons, as an itinerant exorcist (Acts 19:13). They served as shaman figures for the Jewish community in Ephesus and perhaps beyond. They functioned as medicine men, healers, and holy men with esoteric knowledge. Presumably they were sought out when a member of the community sought healing, deliverance from an evil spirit, protection from the evil eye, or a means of breaking a curse.

Although we have no direct information about these individuals apart from the text of Acts 19, we have gained a great deal of information in recent years about how someone like them would have operated and the belief structure that would have informed their practices. The Jewish magical texts, the amulet tradition, curse tablets, and the magical papyri (especially those containing

743 See my "Initiation, Vision, and Spiritual Power," 180–84, and *Colossian Syncretism*, 103–57.

Jewish elements) combine to fill out a picture of how a Jewish shaman would have operated. What is clear is that there was a higher degree of syncretism in Jewish magic than in any other Jewish tradition or practice.[744] This is precisely because the overriding concern is in power and in what works rather than what is orthodox. It is also clear that the practice of invoking angels was fundamental to Jewish folk belief.

Visionary experience is also foundational to shamanistic practice. It is through a personal vision that a shaman gains his power.[745] Ritual initiation provided the context in antiquity for someone to have direct contact with the deity through visionary experience and thus acquire spiritual knowledge, wisdom, and power. In animist cultures, a ritual initiation is often foundational and prerequisite for becoming a community healer, wise man, or shaman.[746] Although there is little evidence for Jewish involvement in pagan ritual initiation,[747] there is some—precisely in the realm of magic and folk belief. The initiation experience is central in the so-called Eighth Book of Moses,[748] a handbook for magic/religious ritual that serves as an important "witness to the rich interpenetration of Judaism and paganism in late antiquity."[749] This highly syncretistic text, combining Jewish, Egyptian, and Greek magical practices, contains numerous references to ritual initiation, usually with the terms τελετή or τελέω (see *Moses VIII*.31, 37, 90, 100, 230, 610, 655, 669). The climax of initiation is the appearance of a god: "come to me, Lord, . . . for I have been initiated [τετέλεσμαι]" (*Moses VIII*.89–90). When this visionary experience of the god takes place, the text promises that the deity will impart esoteric information and wisdom. The text also emphasizes a variety of ritual preparations that are essential to be filled prior to the initiation proper.[750] This includes seven days of purification (involving various taboos) and a set of rituals that begin with the new moon. This

744 Horst, "Great Magical Papyrus of Paris," 177, notes that "if syncretism is to be found anywhere, it is in the world of ancient magic."

745 Davila, *Descenders to the Chariot*, 19.

746 On the topic of shamanism, see DuBois, *Shamanism*, 56.81.

747 See Lease, "Jewish Mystery Cults Since Goodenough," 874. Unfortunately, Lease did not include the realm of magic and a text like the Eighth Book of Moses in his analysis.

748 The Eighth Book of Moses corresponds to *PGM* XIII in Preisendanz's collection. It is the Leiden Papyrus J 395, a codex that dates to about AD 350.

749 T. Klutz, "The Eighth Book of Moses," in Bauckham, Davila, and Panayotov, *Old Testament Pseudepigrapha*, 189. It is possible that the Jewish contributions to this text should be kept completely separate from the references to initiation and that we should assume that no Jew crossed the line by engaging in this kind of ritual. But because of the widespread use of Jewish names and themes in the text and the tendency of magical practitioners to use anything that is powerful and is deemed to work, I would find it likely that there were some Jewish shamans who did, in fact, practice ritual initiation to obtain the power and knowledge it would provide.

750 This text was ultimately pagan but is infused with a number of Jewish elements reflecting the kind of Jewish magic and shamanistic practices of the Roman era. J. B. L. Peerbolte, "The *Eighth Book of Moses*," 192, notes that "next to the mention of the temple in Jerusalem, there are more Jewish elements in *Moses VIII* that are difficult to account for if not by postulating some kind of interaction between Jewish and pagan sorcerers."

particular initiation is closely associated with the god Apollo. The book is replete with invocations of spirits and gods. The end result is that the initiate is endowed with wisdom and spiritual power that enables him to serve the community, such as in providing healing for assorted ailments and casting demons away from people. Because of the reference to the Jerusalem temple in line 233 ("as I made you swear, child, in the temple of Jerusalem, when you have been filled with the divine knowledge, put the book in a place where it cannot be found"), J. B. L. Peerbolte has suggested that "the magician's manuals we find in this papyrus are part of a tradition of magic, which was somehow connected to Judaism, perhaps even to the period of the Second Temple."[751]

Of course, we do not even know for sure if the ringleader of the Colossian teaching was Jewish. It remains possible that this person was a gentile Christian who had appropriated many Jewish practices.

## *Conclusion*

Although the rival teaching and practice at Colossae has received a multitude of interpretations, ranging from such diverse explanations as Torah-observant Judaism to Cynic philosophy, no one interpretive scheme has yet become the consensus opinion. For a long period of time, it appeared that some form of Gnosticism may have attained that status. Then, beginning in the 1970s, Jewish apocalyptic and mysticism seemed to be winning the day. Yet each of these major views has significant explanatory deficiencies that has prevented it from gaining widespread acceptance as the key to unlocking the secrets of the nature of the Colossian "philosophy."

Because of the disparate nature of the problem, the limited data for inferring a solution, and the different interpretations that each feature of the Colossian "philosophy" is capable of bearing, whatever solution one opts for needs to be held with a degree of tentativeness and humility. Nevertheless, there is an emerging solution that may provide the coherence and explanatory power that has been missing in previous postulations.[752]

The combined evidence of the letter now suggests that the ringleader behind the beliefs and practices of the opposing teaching at Colossae was a Jewish (now Christian) shaman-like figure who served the community as a wise man and spiritual healer. The closest analogy to this person is Sceva and his sons in Acts 19 who served as itinerant exorcists in Ephesus and its environs. The Colossian leader was someone of stature within the community and highly regarded for his arcane wisdom, spiritual wisdom, and expertise regarding spiritual power.

---

751 Peerbolte, "The *Eighth Book of Moses*," 191. Klutz, "Eighth Book of Moses," 196–98, however, thinks the reference to the temple is rhetorical and that the preceding preposition might best be rendered with "by" rather than "in"—thus, "swearing by the temple."

752 Agreeing with me on the general contours of the problem at Colossae are, e.g., Beale, 12–16; Moo, 57–60; Tidball, *In Christ, in Colossae*, 8–10, 181; Fee, *Christology*, 290.

He was the go-to person in the community for matters related to healing, exorcism, and protection from various forms of evil.

The various identifiable features of the Colossian "philosophy" cohere well with this kind of person's role and operation within the community. Ritual initiation and visionary experience serve as a basis for his wisdom and knowledge in matters related to spirits and healing. This person also possesses knowledge of angels and intermediary spirits and their functions and can thereby invoke the right angels and perform the proper rituals necessary to the problem at hand. Because of his knowledge, this person can prescribe ritual measures for counteracting curses and providing protection and deliverance from harmful spirits.

The apostle Paul takes strong exception to this person and his ritual methods. In his view, the rival teacher is full of pride, and his arrogance is leading him to exploit the church. Although claiming to be spiritual, the leader is not in close connection to Christ. Paul therefore admonishes the Colossians to reject this person's leadership and teaching. They should rather hold on tight to Christ, immerse themselves in the teaching of and about Christ, and grow in the knowledge of who Jesus is and who they are in him.

The title of heresy is too strong for the teaching of the Colossian "philosophy." Some might regard the term as also anachronistic, given the fact that a settled orthodoxy had not yet been established among the churches of the Mediterranean world. Yet Paul can speak in Colossians of "the faith" (Col 1:23; 2:7), which assumes some level of agreed upon core of beliefs that the Colossians shared with other believers and other churches, presumably stemming from the Judean church and the teaching of the apostles.

Nevertheless, one wonders if the primary teacher of "the philosophy" would deny any of the core truths that comprised "the faith." The issue appears to be more in the area of praxis. Paul's principal critique in 2:19 is that he is "not holding tight to the head." In other words, the confession may be "orthodox," but the way he was living and teaching was inconsistent with the implications of the teaching about Christ, creation, and union with the risen Lord.

## *6. The Colossian Church and the Purpose of the Letter*

### *Bibliography*

**Hemer, C.** *Hellenistic History*. **Huttner, U.** *Early Christianity in the Lycus Valley*. **Mare, W. H.** "Archaeological Prospects at Colossae," 39–59. **Reicke, B.** "Historical Setting of Colossians," 429–38. **Schnabel, E. J.** *Early Christian Mission*. **Trebilco, P.** "Christians in the Lycus Valley," 180–211.

### *The Beginnings of the Church at Colossae*

How the church at Colossae got its start is shrouded in obscurity. The book of Acts provides no narrative about the proclamation of the gospel in the Lycus Valley. The only evidence we have is from Colossians itself, where Paul says that they heard the gospel from Epaphras (1:7), who was one of their own (see 4:12). Just how and when Epaphras learned the gospel and became a follower of Jesus Christ is a matter of reasoned speculation. The most likely explanation is that Epaphras encountered Paul and his preaching during the apostle's three-year ministry in Ephesus (AD 53–55). This is the consensus view among scholars.[753] Luke informs us that Paul spoke daily in a lecture hall (σχολή) belonging to a certain Tyrannus for a period of two years and, during this time, "all the Jews and Greeks who lived in the province of Asia heard the word of the Lord" (Acts 19:9–10 NIV). Luke also reports the leader of the guild of silversmiths as saying that "in almost all of Asia, this man Paul has persuaded and misled a considerable number of people" (Acts 19:26). It would not be surprising for business people from the Lycus Valley to travel to Ephesus regularly for trade and commerce, since it was the chief port city and the economic hub of Roman Asia. Whether Epaphras's conversion happened early in Paul's ministry (e.g., AD 53) or later (e.g., AD 55) is unknown. But he became sufficiently grounded in the gospel to take it back to the Lycus Valley, shared it with many people who turned to Christ, and facilitated the establishment of a number of house churches not only in Colossae but also in Laodicea and Hierapolis.

There have been other suggestions about the origin of the churches in the Lycus Valley. Some have suggested that the area may have been evangelized by those who had become Christians in Pisidian Antioch. Luke indicates that following Paul's preaching in that city, "the word of the Lord was spreading throughout the whole region [χώρα]" (Acts 13:49).[754] This would push the date for the beginnings of the churches in the Lycus Valley five to ten years earlier. But Pisidian Antioch was nearly 120 miles distant from Colossae, and it is doubtful that the term for "region" (χώρα) would extend that far—that is, from Pisidia to this portion of Phrygia. This view also diminishes the role of Epaphras, unless, of course, Epaphras had happened to be in Pisidian Antioch while Paul was preaching there. Reicke finds evidence for this view in the fact that the Colossians seem to be aware of Mark, whom Paul asks for them to be prepared to receive as a guest when he comes (Col 4:10). Reicke suggests that they would have been familiar with Mark through his cousin, Barnabas, who was with Paul during his evangelization of Pisidian Antioch. But, as Barth notes, Barnabas was a significant enough figure among Paul's missionary companions that they may have heard about him by other means.[755]

There is no hint in the letter to the Colossians that Paul had ever come to the city previously either to evangelize or to teach and encourage the believers there, although it is possible that he had passed through the Lycus Valley. It is

753 E.g., Lightfoot, 30; Barth and Blanke, 18.

754 E.g., Reicke, "Historical Setting of Colossians," 432; Mare, "Archaeological Prospects at Colossae," 43.

755 Barth and Blanke, 18.

not likely that he went through this region on his second journey as he made his way to Troas, since he was hindered by the Spirit from speaking the word at this time in the Roman province of Asia (Acts 16:6), which probably means that he took a more northerly route toward Bithynia. But he may have traveled through Colossae and Laodicea on his way to Ephesus at the beginning of his third journey. Luke says that he went through "the region of Galatia and Phrygia [τὴν Γαλατικὴν χώραν καὶ Φρυγίαν], strengthening all the disciples" (Acts 18:23). Thus, after revisiting the cities where he had planted churches—Pisidian Antioch, Iconium, Lystra, and Derbe (all part of the Roman province of Galatia)—he traveled with haste westward to rejoin Priscilla and Aquila in resuming his ministry in Ephesus, where he would spend the next three years. Luke says that "Paul passed through the interior [ἀνωτερικὰ μέρη] and arrived at Ephesus" (Acts 19:1). Both Hemer and Schnabel think that this means that Paul followed a more northerly route on a hill road that reached Ephesus by the Cayster Valley north of Mount Messogis.[756] Schnabel suggests, more specifically, that he traveled on a route that led from Pisidian Antioch to Apameia, Eumeneia, Sebaste, Akmonia, Blaundos, and down the Cayster Valley to Ephesus.[757] But the faster and more direct route would have been for Paul to travel from Pisidian Antioch to Apameia and then west through the Lycus Valley to the Maeander Valley and on to Ephesus. This would have taken him through Colossae and Laodicea, but he probably would not have taken the time to proclaim the gospel throughout this region because of the urgency to resume his ministry in the great metropolis of Asia.[758] But it would only be a short time later that Epaphras would hear the gospel during Paul's preaching and teaching in Ephesus and then evangelize the Lycus Valley.

### *The Church at Colossae*

Paul writes his letter to the Colossians roughly five to seven years after the introduction of Christianity to that city. Since the initial evangelistic work of Epaphras in AD 54–55, presumably many additional people had become acquainted with the gospel, were converted, and joined one of the house churches in the region. Thus, many of the believers at Colossae, Laodicea, and Hierapolis were still relatively new Christians when Paul wrote his letter.

The "church" likely consisted of multiple house churches in Colossae and the other cities of the Lycus Valley. Paul explicitly mentions two of these: (1) he urges the readers of Colossians to greet Nymphas and the church in his home (τὴν κατ'

---

756 Hemer, *Hellenistic History*, 120. See also Schnabel, *Early Christian Mission*, 2:1199–1204.

757 Schnabel, *Early Christian Mission*, 2:1200.

758 Reicke, "Historical Setting of Colossians," 433, thinks he took this route, but contends that Paul would have encouraged and strengthened the believers in the Lycus Valley as he passed through, since he sees the area evangelized after Paul's original ministry in Antioch of Pisidia. Paul's reference to "those who have not seen me face to face" (Col 2:1) would seem to preclude this (so also Barth and Blanke, 19).

οἶκον αὐτοῦ ἐκκλησίαν; 4:15),[759] which may have been in Hierapolis (or possibly Laodicea), and (2) he addresses the letter we call Philemon to Philemon (as well as to Apphia and Archippus) and "the church in your home" (καὶ τῇ κατ' οἶκόν σου ἐκκλησίᾳ; Phlm 2), referring to the home of Philemon, which was probably in Colossae. Just how many house churches there were in Colossae and its environs, and the number of believers who were gathering regularly, is impossible to know. With the combined testimony of Colossians and Philemon, we are acquainted with the names of a few of the Colossian and Laodicean Christians. They include Epaphras (who is with Paul at the time of writing), Archippus (4:17; Phlm 1), Philemon (Phlm 1), Apphia (Phlm 2), Nymphas (Col 4:15), and Onesimus (who returned to Colossae with the letters; Phlm 10–21).

As for the ethnic blend in these house churches, and especially the proportion of Jewish believers to gentile believers, it is very difficult to determine. Whereas Paul himself followed the pattern of proclaiming the gospel first to the Jews of a city (Rom 1:16), which the book of Acts confirms with examples of Paul beginning his evangelistic work in the synagogues, Epaphras was a gentile and did not necessarily take the gospel first to the Jewish population of the Lycus Valley. Nevertheless, because of Paul's example, Epaphras would have endeavored to share the gospel with them too. Undoubtedly there were many Jews in this area who eventually embraced Jesus as their Messiah, but it is likely that the majority of believers in these three cities were gentiles. Barth thinks that the church was composed exclusively of gentile believers,[760] but this is speculative and overreaches the evidence. As Trebilco notes, "The reference in Colossians 2:13 to 'the uncircumcision of your flesh' . . . suggests the community was predominantly Gentile, but Wilson notes that 'it would seem unwise to deny the possibility that there was also a Jewish element' in the Christian community."[761]

The inclusion of the statement that in the new community of believers "there is no Greek or Jew, circumcision or uncircumcision, barbarian, Scythian, slave, or free," but that one's primary identity is found in Christ (3:11), may suggest that there is ethnic diversity in the house churches of Colossae and the Lycus Valley. In addition to Jewish believers, the church would have been composed of a wide ethnic variety of gentile believers. Some may have retained a semblance of their older, territorial, ethnic identies as Phrygians, Carians, and Lydians. But there would have been Italians from Rome and elsewhere, those of Persian descent, and perhaps some Macedonians, Achaians, Syrians, Egyptians, and possibly some of Celtic descent.

It is important to remember that the gentile believers in Colossae did not

759 There is a text-critical problem here related to the gender and number of the pronoun. I conclude that it is masculine singular; see my comments on 4:15.

760 Barth and Blanke, 18.

761 Trebilco, "Christians in the Lycus Valley," 187 (citing Wilson, 6n10).

enter the church devoid of religious backgrounds but, like the Thessalonians, would have "turned to God from idols to serve the living and true God" (1 Thess 1:9). This would have included devotion to one or more of the many gods and goddesses worshiped in the Lycus Valley, such as Apollo, Zeus, the Great Mother, Mēn, and others. In addition, these people would have had a vibrant belief in various kinds of chthonic, astral, and terrestrial spirits, which could cause them great harm. They would have feared the regular dangers of coming under a curse or being afflicted by the evil eye. And, in addition, as is widely attested by the inscriptional data, they would have feared violating any of the ritual or moral demands of the territorial gods, who would have "struck" them for any such transgressions.

### *The Purpose of the Letter*

Epaphras had journeyed to Paul in his Roman custody and informed him of all that was happening in the Colossian church and the churches of nearby Laodicea and Hierapolis. A significant part of what he had to share with Paul was the unhealthy influence of the so-called "philosophy." Paul saw these churches as coming under the sphere of his care since they got their start as a result of his mission in Ephesus. *His principal reason for writing Colossians was to directly address the threat of "the philosophy" and to encourage these believers to wholeheartedly renew their allegiance to Christ and to understand and act upon the full implications of what it means to be united with Christ.*

In addition to this overarching purpose are four additional aims he has in writing:

1. to help these relatively new believers become more firmly grounded in their faith by giving them perspective on the identity and work of the Jesus they have come to serve;
2. to encourage and facilitate their ethical development as believers and within the context of the Christian household;
3. to encourage them by his reports and assure them of his prayers (as well as those of Timothy and Epaphras); and
4. to let them know of the impending visit of Mark.

## *7. The Author's Situation and the Date of the Letter*

### *Bibliography*

**Deissmann, A.** *Light from the Ancient East.* ———. *Paul.* **D'Andria, F.** *Hierapolis of Phrygia.* **Duncan, G. S.** *St. Paul's Ephesian Ministry.* **Ellis, E. E.** *Making.* **Ramsay, W. M.** *St. Paul the Traveler.* **Rapske, B. W.** *Paul in Roman Custody.* **Reicke, B.** "Caesarea, Rome, and the Captivity Epistles," 277–86. ———. "Historical Setting of Colossians," 429–38. **Ritti, T.** *Epigraphic Guide to Hierapolis.* **Robinson, B. W.** "Ephesian Imprisonment," 181–89. **White, J.** "Imprisonment," 549–58. **Williams, G.** "'Beast Fight' in Ephesus," 42–56. **Witherington, B.** "Imprisonment," 525–32.

### *Paul's Situation after Ephesus (AD 55–62)*

Paul's three-year ministry in Ephesus (AD 52–55) was a fruitful and productive season for the progress of the gospel. Luke characterizes this as a time when "all the residents of Asia heard the word of the Lord" (Acts 19:10). It was at this time that Epaphras carried the gospel to the Lycus Valley, and the church at Colossae was started. But it was likely also the time when many other churches were established in Roman Asia.

Paul's sojourn in Ephesus ended abruptly with a dramatic uprising instigated by the leaders of a trade guild of silversmiths who made shrines and votive images of the Ephesian Artemis (Acts 19:23–41). This urban uprising nearly ended in Paul's death. By remaining in Ephesus, his presence could have resulted in significant difficulties for the believers there. So, immediately after this volatile situation had subsided, Paul bid the disciples "farewell" and traveled across the Aegean to Macedonia (Acts 20:1). He used this as an opportunity to encourage believers in the churches he had established in Philippi and Thessalonica (Acts 20:2). During this time, he wrote his second letter to the Corinthians (c. AD 56).

Shortly after penning that letter, he journeyed to Corinth, where he spent three winter months and took a collection for the impoverished churches of Judea (Acts 20:2–3a; see also 2 Cor 2:12–13; 7:5; 8:1–5; 9:2). He likely wrote his letter to the Romans early in AD 57 while at Corinth. Luke indicates that Paul returned to Macedonia after this for a brief visit with the churches (Acts 20:3b) and then journeyed to Troas (vv. 5–6). Shortly later, Paul sailed to the coastal city of Miletus, where he met with the elders of the church of Ephesus (vv. 13–38). This was in the spring of AD 57, nearly two years after he had left Ephesus.

He then boarded a vessel and traveled to Jerusalem, where he delivered the relief offering to the Judean believers and visited with the leaders of the Jerusalem church, telling them of all that God had accomplished among the gentiles (Acts 21:15–26). As he fulfilled a Nazirite vow he had taken, he was arrested at the temple and charged with bringing a gentile into the inner courts of the temple beyond the barrier restricting gentiles (vv. 27–35). He was eventually transferred from Jerusalem to Caesarea Maritima, where he was remanded to Roman custody for a period of two years (AD 57–59).

Midway through AD 59, Paul successfully appealed to have his case heard by the emperor himself in the city of Rome. Shortly thereafter he began his voyage to Rome—a journey that turns into a dramatic and harrowing disaster that results in a shipwreck on the island of Malta (Acts 27). After Paul finally arrived in Rome in the spring of AD 60, he spent another two years in Roman detention waiting to be heard by the emperor Nero (AD 60–62).

### *Paul's Roman Custody*

If Paul is indeed the author of Colossians, then his self-references in multiple places (4:3, 10, 18; see also 1:24) and also in Philemon (9, 10, 13, 23) indicate that he was in Roman custody:

- "I am in chains [δέδεμαι]" (4:3);
- he refers to Aristarchus as "my fellow prisoner [συναιχμάλωτος]" (4:10); and
- he concludes his letter with the appeal, "remember my chains [τῶν δεσμῶν]" (4:18).

He never mentions the nature of his custody or its location. It is noticeable that he was accorded a great deal of freedom during this detention. He has regular guests, as evident from the many people he mentions, he has the freedom to pray for the Colossians together with his associates, he is able to compose letters (most likely with the assistance of a secretary who would have had access to him), and he has an expectation that he will be released from his custody (Phlm 22). Paul does not explicitly mention "chains" (ἅλυσις) as the form of his bondage, but if the testimony of Ephesians is authentic for this time, the apostle declares that he is "an ambassador in chains [ἐν ἁλύσει]" (Eph 6:20).

The location of this custody has been a matter of debate, with three major locations that have been proposed. I will discuss the merit of each of these proposals in turn.

### *Was Paul in Roman Custody in Ephesus, Caesarea, or Rome?*

#### Ephesian Custody

Although neither the book of Acts nor Paul ever mention an imprisonment during his three-year ministry in Ephesus (AD 52–55), it is possible to infer this from Paul's statement to the Corinthians that he has been imprisoned multiple times (ἐν φυλακαῖς περισσοτέρως; 2 Cor 11:23; see also 2 Cor 6:5). He says this prior to the time of his Caesarean and Roman imprisonments. One of these times could very well have taken place during his ministry in Ephesus since he spent more time there than anywhere else.

This theory was first advanced by B. W. Robinson in 1910[762] and then adopted by A. Deissman,[763] whose stature gave it a broader accepability. It was then taken up and supported in a three-hundred-page monograph by British scholar G. S. Duncan, titled *St. Paul's Ephesian Ministry.* An array of more recent scholars have supported this view, also contending that this was the time when Colossians (and Philemon) was written.[764]

There are four principal arguments in support of this view. (1) It is first of all built on the assumption that Paul was, in fact, imprisoned while he was in Ephesus, based upon the two references to imprisonments in 2 Corinthians.

762 Robinson, "Ephesian Imprisonment," 181–89.

763 Deissmann, *Light from the Ancient East*, 237–38; idem, *Paul*, 16, 222. For this view, Deissmann cites the influence of M. Albertz and B. W. Robinson.

764 See, e.g., White, "Imprisonment," 549–58; Beale, 8 (he says he leans to this view, but is not confident); McKnight, 34–39; Bird, 55–57; Murphy-O'Connor, "Colossians," 1192; Wright, 34–39; Martin, 30; Schweizer, 24–26.

With this hypothesis, I have no dispute.[765] It seems rather likely that Paul would have experienced one or even more of these incarcerations during this period. But given all that Paul accomplished while he was in Ephesus (including a visit to Corinth), it is likely that any such incarceration would have been brief. The imprisonment reflected in Colossians, Philemon, Philippians, and Ephesians (assuming its authenticity) would necessitate a longer period of time for Paul to write letters and receive the ministry from people (such as Onesimus) that he alludes to in his letters. (2) Duncan and others interpret Paul's statement that he "fought with beasts [ἐθηριομάχησα] at Ephesus" (1 Cor 15:32) as a literal reference to a beast fight in an arena and as direct evidence of Paul taken into Roman custody while in Ephesus.[766] But this is better interpreted as a metaphor for Paul's human adversaries,[767] or even the demonic powers that stood behind his opposition.[768] (3) Perhaps the strongest argument for this view is that the distance between Ephesus and Colossae (slightly over a hundred miles) would make the journeys of Paul's associates more realistic. This is especially relevant to Onesimus, for whom three different journeys are envisioned—his original trip to the city where Paul is in custody, his return to Colossae with Tychicus, and his possible trip back to Paul where he can continue to serve the apostle during his custody.[769] By contrast, the distance between Colossae and Rome is about thirteen hundred miles and would have required many days for the journey (two weeks to two months, depending on the weather).[770] This argument based on the relative distances is by no means an insurmountable obstacle, as I will show below. (4) The second-century Marcionite prologue indicates that Paul wrote Colossians from Ephesus.[771] While this is early testimony, it stands alone, and there is substantially more ancient testimony associating Paul's writing of the Prison Epistles from Rome (see below).

One of the weightiest arguments against this view is that the "we" passages in the book of Acts do not place Luke in Ephesus during Paul's ministry there, whereas Colossians and Philemon indicate that Luke was with Paul when he wrote these letters. Of course, this argument falls if the "we" passages in Acts

---

765 Other interpreters find the supposition of an Ephesian imprisonment much too speculative. Barth and Blanke, 128, for instance, dismiss it because "there is no clear-cut proof of an Ephesian captivity of Paul either in Paul's letters or in the Acts of the Apostles." Reicke, "Historical Setting," 435, quips that "it is pure imagination to speak of any captivity in Ephesus."

766 See Duncan, *Ephesian Ministry*, 66–67.

767 Witherington, "Imprisonment," 526–29. Witherington suggests that Paul was "speaking metaphorically about his heated rhetorical debates in Ephesus."

768 Williams, "'Beast Fight' in Ephesus," 45, has convincingly argued that the metaphor of fighting with wild beasts refers to "the confrontations and physical threats that he experienced in Ephesus as instigated by the evil spirits, or 'beasts,' at work in the demon-possessed sorcerers and idolaters of the city."

769 So Wright, 35, and Schweizer, 26.

770 See White, "Imprisonment," 555–56.

771 White, "Imprisonment," 550.

are not Luke's self-references or if Luke did not write Acts.[772] Witherington also rightly observes that there was no praetorian guard in Ephesus.[773] This is relevant only if Philippians was written from the same imprisonment as Colossians, since Paul declares that his imprisonment "has become known throughout the whole praetorian guard [πραιτώριον]" (Phil 1:13).

## Caesarean Custody

A handful of scholars have suggested that Colossians was written during Paul's Roman detention at Caesarea Maritima.[774] This has a number of advantages over the Ephesian imprisonment view: (1) Caesarea was the location of a historically attested imprisonment of Paul (Acts 23:31–26:32); (2) since it was nearly two years in duration, there is an adequate amount of time for Paul's letter writing and the ministry of his associates; (3) it is relatively closer to Colossae than Rome, which may make some of the journeys of Paul's companions more plausible.

One of the difficulties of this view is that if Onesimus was a fugitive slave seeking anonymity after his escape, Rome was a far more likely destination for him than Caesarea because of its size.[775] It is far easier to go unrecognized in a city of a million people. Although Caesarea is a more attractive option than Ephesus, the arguments for a Roman custody are the most compelling.

## Custody in Rome

Over the years, the vast majority of scholars who have seen Colossians as an authentic Pauline letter have contended that Colossians (and Philemon) were written during Paul's Roman imprisonment.[776] There are many good reasons for this conclusion.

This view retains some of the advantages of the Caesarea hypothesis, such as Rome is historically attested by Luke as the place where Paul faced a detention, and the two-year duration of this confinement meant that there was adequate time for the ministry activities Paul describes. The biggest stumbling block in accepting the Roman imprisonment as the place of writing is the enormous distance between Colossae and Rome. I have already noted that it is some thirteen hundred miles. But an inscription has been discovered at Hierapolis (near Colossae) that demonstrates that there were people who made the journey from the Lycus Valley to Rome many times. Near one of the city gates of Hierapolis

---

772 Schweizer, 26, notes that the presence of Luke in Colossians and Philemon causes no problems unless he wrote Acts!

773 Witherington, "Imprisonment," 528.

774 See Reicke, "Historical Setting," 435–38, and his "Caeasarea, Rome, and the Captivity Epistles," 278, 282–86. See also Ellis, *Making*, 23; Lohmeyer, 24, and Meyer, 198–99.

775 See also Hoehner, *Ephesians*, 93.

776 See, e.g., Pao, 23–24; Moo, 41–46; Barth and Blanke, 134; Witherington, 22–24; Dunn, 39–41; Harris, 4; Garland, 22, 308; Bruce, 32; Scott, 5; Abbott, lix.

is a tomb belonging to a merchant from the city named Titus Flavius Zeuxis. The tomb and its inscription can be dated to the end of the first century (or the first years of the second century). Above the entrance to a large subterranean room of the tomb is a panel bearing the following inscription:

> Titus Flavius Zeuxis, merchant,
> who navigated around Cape Maleus towards Italy during seventy-two sailings,
> built the monument for himself
> and his sons Flavius Theodoros and Flavius Theudas,
> and for whoever shall obtain the concession from them.[777]

Zeuxis made the trip to Italy some seventy-two times during his career as a "workman" (ἐργαστής), which is probably best understood in this context as a merchant. Since Hierapolis was known for its woolen garments, perhaps this is what he traded.[778] Each journey it was necessary for the ship he was on to round Cape Maleus (modern Matapan), the southernmost point of the Peloponnese, here mentioned because of the danger this presented during a storm. Ritti surmises that Zeuxis may have made the trip to Rome twice per year, which would have required at least a thirty-six-year long career as a merchant.[779] He likely boarded a ship for each voyage at the harbor of Ephesus with his goods. Since Ephesus was the principal port for Roman Asia, there would have been ships arriving and departing for Rome weekly or even multiple times per week. For Paul or any of his companions, booking passage from Ephesus to Rome or from Rome to Ephesus would have been easy to do.

There is also a strong historical tradition that Colossians (and the other so-called Prison Epistles) were written by Paul from Rome. This can be seen in the subscripts in the manuscript tradition. Many manuscripts add colophons indicating that the letter was written from Rome:[780]

- Codex Alexandrinus (A): "to the Colossians from Rome";
- Codex Vaticanus (B), corrector "c": "to the Colossians written from Rome";
- Codex P: "to the Colossians written from Rome";
- Codex L: "a letter from the holy Paul written from Rome [to be delivered] through Tychicus and Onesimus";
- Codex K: "to the Colossians written from Rome [to be delivered] through Tychicus and Onesimus";

777 Translation and text in Ritti, *Epigraphic Guide*, 68, no. 9. See also the discussion in D'Andria, *Hierapolis of Phrygia*, 66–68.

778 Ritti, *Epigraphic Guide*, 68.

779 Ritti, *Epigraphic Guide*, 68.

780 For the textual evidence, see Tischendorf, *Novum Testamentum Graece* (1872), 748–49; Metzger, *Textual Commentary*, 560.

- Minuscules 82, 101, 122, 431, 460, 1907, 1924: "to the Colossians written from Rome [to be delivered] through Tychicus and Onesimus";
- Euthalian apparatus: "written to the Colossians from Rome by Paul and Timothy [to be delivered] through Tychicus and Onesimus";
- Some Syriac and Old Latin manuscripts add "from Rome."

The earliest of these testimonies comes from the fourth century, but the tradition behind it comes from much earlier.

The combined evidence thus weighs more strongly in favor of the tradition that Paul wrote Colossians while he was in custody in Rome, awaiting his trial before the princeps. I would suggest that Paul composed four letters at that time—Colossians, Philemon, the (lost) letter to the Laodiceans, and Ephesians.[781] He sent Tychicus, accompanied by Onesimus (Col 4:7–9), to carry these letters to their destinations, likely stopping first in Ephesus and then on to the Lycus Valley. Philippians was written later during the Roman imprisonment, with Timothy being dispatched by Paul to carry that letter to Macedonia (Phil 2:19).

Paul's custody in Rome (see Acts 28:16–31) was not as harsh as some forms of Roman custody. He was permitted to live in a hired lodging at his own expense (v. 30).[782] He "probably occupied an economical third floor apartment in one of the thousands of tenement buildings in the capital."[783] The most difficult part of his custody would have been the constraint and shame of the actual chain that bound him (expressed with the term ἅλυσις; v. 20; see also Eph 6:20).[784] Although Paul could not have engaged in his trade,[785] he was apparently able to receive guests. This made it possible for him to engage in extended prayer with his coworkers for believers in each of the churches he had either planted or over which he felt some level of responsibility for their well-being. It also provided him the opportunity to explain the gospel and the message of the kingdom of God to any who came to visit him (Acts 28:30–31). This likely included both evangelism and catechesis.[786]

## Date of the Letter

A wide array of dates have been suggested for the writing of Colossians. All of these are closely tied to the circumstances surrounding the letter and its provenance. Those who see the letter as pseudonymous have dated the

781 I have argued for the authenticity of Ephesians elsewhere. See my *Ephesians*, 46–50.

782 Rapske, *Paul in Roman Custody*, 326, follows Ramsay, *St. Paul the Traveler*, 311–12, in suggesting that Paul was able to support himself from funds derived from hereditary property. He also thinks that Paul may have received support from fellow Christians either in Rome or elsewhere.

783 Rapske, *Paul in Roman Custody*, 326.

784 For a description of what prisoners in Roman custody faced in wearing chains, see Rapske, *Paul in Roman Custody*, 206–9.

785 Rapske, *Paul in Roman Custody*, 326.

786 Rapske, *Paul in Roman Custody*, 364.

letter anywhere from the mid-60s to as late as the 90s. Those who see the letter as authentic necessarily associate the date with the period of Paul's imprisonment. Thus, those who argue for an Ephesian imprisonment contend that the letter was written within the range of AD 52–55 (although some date the imprisonment later, i.e., AD 55–57[787]). Those contending for a Caesarean imprisonment see the date of the letter between AD 57–60. And those advocating for a Roman imprisonment generally see the letter written sometime between AD 60–62 (although some see it extending to AD 63 and would date the letter then[788]).

I would thus suggest that the letter was written between AD 60–62, but would argue for the earlier part of that range. The letter was sent before the great earthquake, a cataclysm that Tacitus dates to AD 60. If the earthquake occurred in the latter part of that year, then the letter was likely written early to mid-60.

## *8. The Text of Colossians*

### *Bibliography*

**Aland, K.** *Kurzgefasste Liste.* **Aland, K.,** and **Aland, B.** *Text of the New Testament.* **Comfort, P. W., and D. P. Barrett.** *Greek Manuscripts*, 204–6. **Holmes, M. W.** "Reasoned Eclecticism," 771–802. **Kim, Y. K.** "Paleographical Dating of P46," 248–57. **Metzger, B. M.,** and **B. D. Ehrman.** *Text of the New Testament.* **Nongbri, B.** *Early Christian Manuscripts.* **———.** "Pauline Epistles Codex (P46)," 388–407. **Parker, D. C.** *New Testament Manuscripts.* **Porter, S. E.,** and **A. W. Pitts.** *Textual Criticism.*

### *Manuscript Base*

The text of Colossians is very well preserved in an array of ancient papyri, majuscules, minuscules, lectionaries, other language versions, and patristic quotations. The earliest form of Colossians dates to about AD 200[789] (or possibly the late first century if Y. K. Kim is correct in his reassessment of the dating),[790] in a papyrus document in the Chester Beatty collection in Dublin commonly referred to as 𝔓46. Colossians is also transmitted to us in the two earliest codices of the NT—Codex Vaticanus (B, 03) and Codex Sinaiticus (א, 01)—both of which date to the fourth century and are widely regarded as highly accurate witnesses to the text of the NT.

In addition to 𝔓46, a portion of the text of Colossians is preserved in an eighth-century papyrus fragment known as 𝔓61. This text contains 1:3–7, 9–13, and 4:15. These are the only papyrus witnesses to the text of Colossians.

787 E.g., Bird, 55–57.

788 E.g., Lightfoot, 37; Abbott, lix.

789 Parker, *New Testament Manuscripts*, 257; Aland and Aland, *Text of the New Testament*, 99; Metzger and Ehrman, *Text of the New Testament*, 54–55.

790 Kim, "Paleographical Dating of P46," 248–57.

There are twenty-four majuscules that have all or a significant portion of Colossians:

| Siglum | Gregory–Aland no. | Date | Name, Current Location, and Contents[1] |
|---|---|---|---|
| א | 01 | 4th | Codex Sinaiticus. British Library, London. |
| A | 02 | 5th | Codex Alexandrinus. British Library, London. |
| B | 03 | 4th | Codex Vaticanus. Vatican Library, Rome. |
| C | 04 | 5th | Codex Ephraimi Rescriptus. Bibliothèque Nationale, Paris.<br>• Colossians 1:2–4:18 |
| D | 06 | 6th | Codex Claromontanus. Bibliothèque Nationale, Paris. |
| F | 010 | 9th | Codex Augiensis. Trinity College, Cambridge. |
| G | 012 | 9th | Codex Boernianus. Sächsische Landesbibliothek, Dresden.<br>• Colossians 1:1–2:1; 2:8–4:18 |
| H | 015 | 6th | Codex Coislinianus. Bibliothèque Nationale, Paris.<br>• Colossians 1:26–2:8; 2:20–3:4 |
| I | 016 | 5th | Codex Freerianus. Freer Gallery, Washington, DC.<br>• Colossians 1:1–4, 10–12, 20–22, 27–29; 2:7–9, 16–19; 3:5–8, 15–17; 3:25–4:2; 4:11–13. |
| K | 018 | 9th | Codex Mosquensis. State Historical Museum, Moscow. |
| L | 020 | 9th | Codex Angelicus. Biblioteca Angelica, Rome. |
| P | 025 | 9th | Codex Porphyrianus. National Library of Russia, Saint Petersburg.<br>• Colossians 1:1–3:15; 4:9–18 |
| Ψ | 044 | 9th | Codex Athos Lavrensis. Monastery of Megisti Lavra, Athos. |
|  | 048 | 5th | Vatican Library, Rome.<br>• Colossians 1:20–2:8; 2:11–14, 22–23; 3:7–8; 3:12–4:18 |
|  | 049 | 9th | Monastery of Megisti Lavra, Athos. |
|  | 056 | 10th | Bibliothèque Nationale, Paris. |
|  | 075 | 10th | National Library of Greece, Athens. |
|  | 0142 | 10th | Bayerische Staatsbibliothek, Munich. |

| Siglum | Gregory–Aland no. | Date | Name, Current Location, and Contents[1] |
|---|---|---|---|
| | 0150 | 9th | Saint John Monastery, Patmos. |
| | 0151 | 9th | Saint John Monastery, Patmos. |
| | 0198 | 6th | British Library, London<br>• Colossians 3:15–16, 20–21 |
| | 0208 | 6th | Bayerische Staatsbibliothek, Munich.<br>• Colossians 1:29–2:10, 13–14 |
| | 0278 | 9th | St. Catherine's Monastery, Sinai.<br>• Colossians 1:17–3:13; 3:21–4:18 |
| | 0319 =D[abs1] | 9th | Codex Sangermanensis. National Library of Russia, Saint Petersburg. |

[1] Compiled on the basis of Aland, *Kurzgefasste Liste*, 19–44, and the Institut für neutestamentlich Textforschung's website (https://ntvmr.uni-muenster.de/liste/). Contents only noted when the manuscript contains a partial text of Colossians.

There are hundreds of minuscule manuscripts containing the text of Colossians, dating from the ninth century (e.g., 33) to the fifteenth century. The vast majority of these reflect a Byzantine form of the text. There are also hundreds of lectionary manuscripts (out of the nearly 2500 lectionaries) containing portions of the text of Colossians, dating from the sixth century to the fifteenth century. In addition, there are numerous ancient manuscripts representing translations of Colossians into other languages, including Old Latin (*Vetus Latina*), the Latin Vulgate, Syriac, Coptic, Armenian, Georgian, Ethiopic, and Old Church Slavonic. Some of these texts date very early, such as the Latin portion of the bilingual codex D (6th c.), the Vulgate Codex Fuldensis (6th c.), and some Syriac manuscripts (5th–6th c.).

Finally, the text of Colossians is also preserved in the citations of various church fathers dating as early as the third century. Those cited regularly in the NA[28] and the UBS[5] include, by century, Origen (3rd), Tertullian (3rd), Ambrosiaster (4th), Basil (4th), Athanasius (4th), Hilary (4th), Priscillan (4th), Augustine (5th), Chrysostom (4th–5th), Irenaeus (4th–5th), Didymus (4th–5th), Gregory of Nyssa (4th–5th), Jerome (5th), Ambrose (5th), Theodore of Mopsuestia (5th), Cyril of Alexandria (5th), Theodoret (5th), Paulinus-Nola (5th), Pelagius (5th), Severian (5th), Speculum (5th), Varimadum (5th), among others.

### *Summary of Key Variants*

In the notes of this commentary following the translation of each of the passages, I have discussed a total of seventy-three variant readings. These are certainly not all of the possible variants that could be discussed, but these represent those that are the more difficult to decide because the manuscript testimony is divided and have the most significance for interpreting the letter. Most of these are delineated in the apparatus of the NA[28]. The UBS[5] presents twenty-eight of these variants.

Of the seventy-three variants I discuss, the testimony of Sinaiticus (א) and Vaticanus (B) was split in nearly half of the cases (33x). In these instances, I disagreed with the reading of Vaticanus nineteen times and with Sinaiticus fifteen times. In the readings where Sinaiticus and Vaticanus were aligned, I found myself disagreeing with their combined testimony only once. Among the readings attested by 𝔓[46] within these seventy-three variants, I disagreed with its testimony thirteen times. In general, my judgments on the variants supported the readings adopted by the NA[28] and UBS[5] and only disagreed six times.

There were a variety of different kinds of variation represented in these seventy-three different readings. These included:

- Different spellings of a word (e.g., 1:2: "Colossae" or Colassae");
- Different grammatical form of a word (e.g., 2:2: a nominative case versus a genitive case);
- Singular pronoun versus a plural pronoun (e.g., 2:17: singular or plural relative pronoun);
- First-person pronoun versus a second-person pronoun (e.g., 1:7: "our" or "your");
- Grammatical smoothing (e.g., 1:27: the alteration of a neuter relative pronoun to a masculine);
- Words or phrases added to clarify (e.g., 2:7: the addition of a preposition to clarify the case relations);
- Incidental omission of one or more words (e.g., 4:2: the omission of "with thanksgiving" after "watching in it");
- Additions for indeterminate reasons (e.g., 2:18: "worship of the *coming* angels");
- Additions of historical data (e.g., 2:1: "and those in Hierapolis");
- Omission to soften the impact of a statement (e.g., 3:22: "slaves obey *in everything*").

Many of the variations can be traced to assimilation or harmonization with another passage in Colossians, Ephesians, or of the Pauline letters (e.g., 1:2: the addition of "and the Lord Jesus Christ" in the introductory greeting as a scribal assimilation to the greetings of Eph 1:2; Rom 1:7; 1 Cor 1:3; 2 Cor 1:2; Phil 1:2; 1 Thess 1:1; Phlm 3; 2 Thess 1:1). But there are some alterations that appear to be for theological reasons (e.g., 1:14: the addition of "through his blood"; 2:18: "what he has *not* seen [in visions]; 2:2 and 4:3: various alterations to "the mystery of God, which is Christ"). Other variants can best be explained as errors of hearing or eyesight (e.g., 1:9: the omission of "and asking" after "praying" due to the identical ending of the previous participle).

Although most every variant affects the meaning of the text to some degree, there are certain variants that have greater significance than others. None of the variants I have assessed in Colossians would alter the representation of the theology of Colossians. I would summarize the five most significant variants impacting the meaning of the text as follows (I would encourage readers to consult my notes on these for a full discussion):

1. 1:12: Did God "call" (καλέσαντι) or "qualify/authorize" (ἱκανώσαντι) believers to share in the inheritance?
2. 2:2 (and 4:3): Should the text read, "the mystery of God, which is Christ," "the mystery of God, both of the Father and of Christ," "the mystery of God, the Father of Christ," "the mystery of Christ," "the mystery of God in Christ," or "the mystery of God the Father, which is Christ"?
3. 3:13: Should the text read, "forgive one another if any of you has *blame* [μομφή] against someone" or "a *reason for complaint*" (μέμψις), or "wrath" (ὀργή)?
4. 4:13: Does Paul say that Epaphras has engaged in much "toil of war" (πόνον) for the Colossians, or "labor" (κόπον), or "longing" (πόθον), or "zeal" (ζῆλον), or "struggle" (ἀγῶνα)?
5. 4:15: Should the text read, "Nympha and the church in *her* house," or "Nymphas and the church in *his* house," or "Nympha/Nymphas and the church in *their* house"?

## *Method of Analysis*

For identifying variants and their textual evidence, I have consulted the NA[28], the UBS[5], and Tischendorf (1869). Pauline scholarship still awaits the completion of the Pauline-letters volume of *Novum Testamentum Graecum: Editio Critica Maior.* I follow an eclectic method (often referred to as "reasoned eclecticism") and do not give preference to any one manuscript or grouping of manuscripts. Nor do I make the assumption that earliest is best in weighing manuscript evidence. I have taken into consideration the geographical spread and the genealogical relationships of manuscripts (as represented by the classical text groupings of "families" of manuscripts commonly referred to as the Alexandrian, Western, and Byzantine).[791] I have attempted to give balanced weight to both the external and internal evidence of readings. As a matter of priority, I have tried to determine in each case the reading that best explains the origins of the others. This often turned out to be the more difficult reading.

791 See the discussion of "text types" in Holmes, "Reasoned Eclecticism," 793–94.

## 9. *Rhetoric and Composition*

### *Bibliography*

**Bird, M. F.** "Rhetorical Approach," 374–79. **Classen, C. J.** "Theory of Rhetoric," 13–39. **Copenhaver, A.** *Paul's Rhetoric in the Letter to the Colossians.* **Fairweather, J.** "Galatians and Classical Rhetoric," 1–38. ———. "Galatians and Classical Rhetoric: Part 3," 211–43. **Forbes, C.** "Ancient Rhetoric and Ancient Letters," 143–60. **Heil, J. P.** *Colossians.* **Hengel, M.** *Pre-Christian Paul.* **Hooker, M. D.** "False Teachers," 315–31. **Jonge, C. C. de.** *Between Grammar and Rhetoric.* **Kennedy, G. A.** *Art of Persuasion in Greece.* ———. *New History of Classical Rhetoric.* ———. *New Testament Interpretation.* **Kern, P.** *Rhetoric and Galatians.* **Lampe, P.** "Rhetorical Analysis of Pauline Texts," 3–21. **Pernot, L.** *Rhetoric in Antiquity.* **Pitts, A. W.** "Paul's Early Education," 43–67. **Porter, S. E.** "Ben Witherington on Rhetoric," 551–52. ———. "Popular Rhetorical Knowledge," 96–115. ———. "Unproven Claims," 533–45. **Porter, S. E.,** and **B. R. Dyer.** "Paul and Ancient Rhetoric," 1–10. **Porter, S. E.,** and **J. T. Reed.** "Philippians as a Macro-Chiasm," 213–31. **Thomson, I. H.** *Chiasmus.* **Thurén, L.** "Epistolography and Rhetoric," 141–59. **Valiavitcharska, V.** *Rhetoric and Rhythm.* **Weima, J. A. D.** "Evaluation of Rhetorical Criticism." **Winter, B. W.** "Entries and Ethics of Orators," 55–74. **Witherington, B.** "Greco-Roman Rhetoric," 63–88.

In all of his letters and especially in Colossians, Paul endeavors to persuade his readers about a particular set of beliefs and a specific course of action. In this letter, he wants the Colossians to resist the persuasive appeal of dangerous teaching, to believe and internalize a set of convictions about Jesus Christ, and to conduct their lives in a way that is pleasing to God. In the most general sense, rhetoric is the art of persuasion, and Paul unequivocally seeks to persuade these believers. At issue is whether he employs classical rhetorical techniques that he has learned in his earlier education (or possibly has acquired over the years through observation and hearing various orators).

There are three major types of rhetoric that were widely known and used in the ancient world. According to one well-known handbook, they can be described as follows:

> There are three kinds of causes which the speaker must treat: Epideictic, Deliberative, and Judicial. The epideictic kind is devoted to the praise or censure of some particular person. The deliberative consists in the discussion of policy and embraces persuasion and dissuasion. The judicial is based on legal controversy, and comprises criminal prosecution or civil suit, and defence.[792]

In addition to this are many rhetorical techniques that can be used within each of these overarching categories.

Some scholars are convinced that Paul was familiar with the methods of classical rhetoric and employed them in his letters to achieve his purposes. They seek to identify the overall rhetorical approach of the letter to the Colossians

792 *Rhetorica ad Herennium* 1.2 (LCL).

and then to label the various rhetorical techniques that the writer uses section-by-section of the letter.

B. Witherington has been a major advocate of the importance of interpreting Paul's letters through the lens of rhetorical criticism. He contends that Colossians can best be described as an example of deliberative rhetoric and represents the structure of the letter based upon the following rhetorical descriptors:

*Witherington: Deliberative Rhetoric*[1]

| |
|---|
| Prescript and Greetings (1:1–2) |
| Exordium (1:3–14) |
| Narratio (1:15–20) |
| Propositio (1:21–23) |
| Probatio (1:24–2:5) |
| Exhortatio (2:6–4:1) |
| Peroratio (4:2–6) |
| Closing Greetings and Instructions (4:7–18) |

[1] Witherington, 20, 104.

J.-N. Aletti and A. T. Lincoln would agree with Witherington that the writer of Colossians uses deliberative rhetoric, but they differ on how they would identify the functions of the various sections of the letter:

*Aletti: Deliberative Rhetoric*[1]

| |
|---|
| Salut Initial (1:1–2) |
| Exordium (1:3–23) |
| Partitio (1:21–23) |
| Probatio (1:24–4:1) |
| Perorate (4:2–6) |
| Reprise du cadre épistolaire (4:7–18) |

[1] Aletti, 39.

*Lincoln: Deliberative Rhetoric*[1]

| |
|---|
| Letter Opening (1:1–2) |
| Exordium (1:3–23) |
| Probatio (1:24–4:1) |
| Peroratio (4:2–6) |
| Body Closing (4:7–9) |
| Letter Closing (4:10–18) |

[1] Lincoln, "Colossians," 556–60, follows Aletti, with some modifications.

M. Wolter also identifies Colossians as an example of deliberative rhetoric but limits his rhetorical analysis to what he identifies as the body of the letter (2:6–4:6). His analysis of the various sections of the letter differs substantially from the previous authors. One significant difference is his assessment that 3:1–4 functions as the *peroratio* (a recapitulation of the major themes) of the letter, and not 4:2–6. He also does not see Paul as making use of an *exordium* in the letter.

*Wolter: Deliberative Rhetoric*[1]

Präskript (1:1–2)
Proömium (1:3–23)
Selbstvorstellung des Autors (1:24–2:5)
Briefcorpus (2:6–4:6)
  Partitio (2:6–8)
  Argumentatio (2:9–23)
    Probatio (2:9–15)
    Refutatio (2:16–23)
  Peroratio (3:1–4)
  Exhortatio (3:5–4:6)
Briefschluss (4:7–18)

[1] Wolter, 115–16.

These interpreters rely on the categories of analysis and use the technical terminology reflected in the rhetorical handbooks and in authors who wrote about rhetoric in the Hellenistic and Roman eras. These include, especially, Quintillian, Cicero, the *Rhetorica ad Herennium*, Demetrius, and Longinus.

The vast majority of commentators on Colossians, however, do not make use of classical rhetoric for analyzing the persuasive strategy of Paul in this letter. For instance, the commentaries authored by Maisch, Moo, Foster, Beale, Thiselton, Bormann, Hoppe, MacDonald, Hübner, Thompson, Barth and Blanke, Dunn, Hay, and Wright completely disregard rhetorical-critical theory and its categories of analysis in describing the development of thought in Colossians. This is not altogether a lamentable oversight; there are some good reasons for not using the rhetorical handbooks and theorists for interpreting the letter.

### *The Limitations of Rhetorical Criticism for Interpreting Paul's Letters*

There has been resistance among a broad group of NT scholars who are concerned about the appropriateness of using rhetorical criticism for analyzing the style of Paul's letters. S. E. Porter has raised the strongest objections and observes that those employing this methodology "often provide nothing more than exercises in labeling and providing taxonomies of parts of the letters and attempts to identify their species, even though all these are artificial contexts and situations imposed upon the letters."[793]

One of the principal objections is that the ancients used rhetorical theory to craft speeches and not for informing how to write letters. Letter form is seldom

793 Porter, "Popular Rhetorical Knowledge," 112.

discussed in the rhetorical handbooks, and it is sometimes contrasted with writing letters.[794] At the outset of *Rhetorica ad Herennium*, the author makes it clear that his work is about crafting a speech—"your desire, Gaius Herennius, has spurred me to compose a work on the Theory of Public Speaking [*de ratione dicendi conscriberemus*]" (*Rhetorica ad Herennium* 2)—yet this volume is frequently used to assess the rhetoric of Paul's letters. Similarly, Cicero's *Orator* conveys his thoughts about shaping an effective oration, but also about delivery, memory, gesturing, countenance, and intonation, which have nothing to do with letter writing.

It is also uncertain that Paul would have had the opportunity to acquire a Greek education in rhetoric. Although Paul was born in Tarsus and received the initial stages of his education in this deeply Hellenized city known for its rhetoricians, it is likely that Paul never received formal rhetorical training there. Luke makes it clear that Paul received at least his secondary education in Jerusalem under the tutelage of a renowned Jewish rabbi, Gamaliel (Acts 22:3). This may also suggest that Paul's parents were strict, law-observant Jews who would not have wanted their son to be tainted by the corrupting influence of a Hellenistic early education. As such, Paul's elementary education may have been at the feet of a Jewish γραμματιστής. A. Pitts notes also that there was "a well-established tradition among Tarsians to pursue their advanced education outside this city."[795] This means that Paul's peers would have traveled to places like Rhodes, Athens, or Alexandria to pursue formal education in philosophy, rhetoric, and literature. By contrast, Paul traveled to Jersusalem and studied Torah. Nevertheless, under the instruction of his (Jewish) *grammatistēs* in Tarsus, he probably learned Greek literacy skills that may have included some foundational rhetoric knowledge,[796] but this likely did not include the literature of Homer to Euripides.[797] Certainly the Greek Bible would have been an important text in his early education, which would have been constantly reinforced at home.

M. Hengel contends that the forms of rhetoric that Paul would have learned probably came from his training in Jerusalem in the context of "a Jewish Hellenistic school established for effective teaching and proclamation" in the Hellenistic synagogues.[798] Although this scenario is plausible, it is also rather speculative. While Paul may have continued to learn some elemental forms of rhetoric in Jerusalem, especially for ministry in Hellenistic synagogues, Hengel is probably correct that this education "did not correspond to the Attic-style school rhetoric of the time" and was "essentially different from the literary style of the Greek schools."[799]

794 See Kennedy, *New History of Classical Rhetoric*, 90; Porter, "Popular Rhetorical Knowledge," 112.
795 Pitts, "Paul's Early Education," 65.
796 Even Porter, "Unproven Claims," 537, says that "I am willing to admit that Paul had some rudimentary education in rhetoric" in Tarsus. But this falls far short of a full rhetorical education.
797 Hengel, *Pre-Christian Paul*, 38.
798 Hengel, *Pre-Christian Paul*, 58.
799 Hengel, *Pre-Christian Paul*, 58, 61.

It is also not to be overlooked that in his self-reflections on his background and education, Paul gloried in the Jewishness of his education and never mentions any formal Greek education (e.g., Gal 1:14–16; Phil 3:4–6). This is consistent with the fact that he never cites or makes allusion to Homer or any of the principal Greek philosophers (Plato, Aristotle, or others) in any of his letters.

Nevertheless, whatever level of rhetorical training that Paul achieved, he explicitly resisted using the devices and techniques of formal school rhetoric, so that the focus of his message would remain on Christ and his work. This is likely true even of Galatians despite the efforts of H. D. Betz and other scholars to describe this letter in terms of classical rhetoric. P. H. Kern has convincingly argued that classical handbook rhetoric is not found in Galatians.[800]

B. Winter observes that Paul as a preacher had reflected "on the use of classical rhetoric for the presentation of his message and rejected it."[801] As Paul told the Corinthians, he did not come to them "with eloquence [καθ' ὑπεροχὴν λόγου]" and that his "message" and "preaching were not with wise and persuasive words [ἐν πειθοῖς σοφίας λόγοις], but with a demonstration of the Spirit's power" (1 Cor 2:1, 4 NIV). This, of course, does not mean that he did not try to persuade through his speech and his letters but rather that he did not employ the kind of rhetoric that was used by the Sophists and others trained in the formal use of rhetoric.

## *Did Paul Use "Asiatic Rhetoric" for Composing Some of His Letters?*

In his socio-rhetorical commentary on Colossians, B. Witherington has argued that Paul has employed a specific form of rhetoric in Colossians (and Ephesians) known as Asiatic rhetoric. He observes that "the expansive and redundant nature of the style of Colossians is . . . characteristic of Asiatic rhetoric, which was characterized by long lugubrious sentences, piling up of synonyms for rhetorical effect, and the absence of conjunctions so that the sentences keep flowing in a torrent of eloquence."[802]

But, as I have noted, it is doubtful that Paul used any type of formal rhetoric in the composition of his letters, and it would be particularly surprising to see him use Asiatic rhetoric. It was not a movement or a school; it was regarded as a declension from the proper standard. G. A. Kennedy observes that "'Asian' often means any style perceived as inflated and faulty."[803] L. Pernot has noted that "most ancient authors have a qualified or pejorative opinion of the Asiatic style, reproaching it for its excesses and lapses of taste."[804] V. Valiavitcharska says that "'Asianism' as a term is only known—and perhaps created—by its vocal

800 Kern, *Rhetoric and Galatians*, 256–60. See also Fairweather, "Galatians and Classical Rhetoric: Part 3," 213–43.

801 Winter, "Entries and Ethics of Orators," 74.

802 Witherington, 18.

803 Kennedy, *New History of Classical Rhetoric*, 154.

804 Pernot, *Rhetoric in Antiquity*, 82.

opponent, Atticism, which as a movement seems to have appeared around the first century BC, in response to stylistic extremes associated with the oratory of Asia Minor."[805]

Cicero took a very dim view of the Asian style, seeing it as a departure from the elegance and beauty of the Attic standard. He refers to it as a "fat and greasy" style of diction used in the popular oratory of cities in Caria, Phrygia, and Mysia (Cicero, *Orator* 25). He dismissed one second-century BC practitioner of Asiatic rhetoric, Agatharkhides of Knidos, as "an example of ineptitude" (Cicero, *Orator* 226). Dionysius of Halicarnassus likens Attic rhetoric to a dignified and noble wife who is driven out by a shameless harlot from Asia. He speaks of it as arriving from "some Asiatic death hole" (*Ant. or.* 1.4.7–13).[806] In his history of rhetoric, Kennedy notes how the Attic orators of the first century BC castigated Asian rhetoric (or the "Asianists"). He notes that "Asianism is thus descriptive of a style of oratory in much the way that nineteenth-century Southern oratory might be if used by a twentieth-century northern professor of speech."[807]

It is highly doubtful that Paul would have contextualized his preaching and his writing in a form of rhetoric that would have been deplored by some in his audience. But it is likely that he was never schooled in this form of rhetoric. Furthermore, some of the elements of the style that Witherington terms as Asiatic rhetoric, such as the piling up of synonyms, can be seen as part of the style of certain Jewish texts, such as the sectarian texts of Qumran.

### *Copenhaver's Rhetorical Analysis of Colossians*

The most substantive and full-scale approach to Colossians through the lens of Roman rhetoric is the monograph by A. Copenhaver, *Reconstructing the Historical Background to Paul's Rhetoric in the Letter to the Colossians.* Copenhaver describes the letter as a species of deliberative rhetoric and categorizes the other major elements of the letter as follows:[808]

*Copenhaver: Deliberative Rhetoric*[1]

|  |
|---|
| Letter Opening (1:1–2) |
| Exordium (1:3–2:5) |
| Major Transitio (2:6–7) |
| Paraenesis (2:8–4:6) |
| Peroratio (4:2–6) |
| Letter Closing (4:7–18) |

[1] Copenhaver, *Paul's Rhetoric in the Letter to the Colossians*, 91.

805 Valiavitcharska, *Rhetoric and Rhythm*, 57–58.

806 See the discussion in de Jonge, *Between Grammar and Rhetoric*, 11, and Valiavitcharska, *Rhetoric and Rhythm*, 57–58.

807 Kennedy, *Art of Persuasion in Greece*, 303.

808 Copenhaver, *Paul's Rhetoric in the Letter to the Colossians*, 139. The central section of his book (ch. 3) represents a "rhetorical analysis of Colossians and the rhetorical situation" (81–143).

His overall assessment of the body of the letter varies significantly, however, from his predecessors, who analyze Colossians according to classical-rhetoric categories. The first half of the body of the letter he characterizes as an *exordium*, which he describes as functioning as "the introduction of the speech and can contain a variety of elements and functions, namely seeking the good will of the audience, establishing the ethos of the speaker, and introducing the discourse."[809] Whereas, the second half of the letter, following a major *transitio* (2:6–7), he describes as *paraenesis* (2:8–4:6).

The crucial point of departure from the vast majority of interpreters is his assessment that there were no actual opponents against whom the author is polemicizing. He sees "the oppositional rhetoric" of 2:16–23 as simply contributing to the deliberative appeal—that is, "by demonstrating the emptiness of other religious practices and regulations in contrast to the fullness in Christ."[810] He contends that those who argue for a particular set of opponents narrow and weaken Paul's overall purpose and intent behind the letter "by not addressing the full breadth of the world in contrast to Christ."[811] Thus, for Copenhaver, the opposition is the full array of beliefs, practices, and lifestyle influences of the world that threatens the faith and health of this group of young and immature believers at Colossae. Paul is calling them to resist the regulations and practices that belong to the world and to develop a new lifestyle consistent with their new life in Christ.

In many ways, Copenhaver's study endeavors to further substantiate the thesis of M. Hooker, who likewise argued that there were no specific opponents at Colossae.[812] He also points to N. T. Wright's conclusion that in Colossians Paul is warning Christians against submitting to the Jewish law and not engaging a particular opponent,[813] yet Copenhaver thinks that "the world" that threatens Colossians is more than Judaism and should include the pagan religions of the Lycus Valley. The challenge of accepting Copenhaver's proposal, which I see as an insuperable difficulty, is the specificity of Paul's descriptive remarks about the teaching of the opponents in the letter. Nearly all interpreters have understood these descriptive statements as pointing to a particular threat to the church. It begins with Paul's reference to the teaching as "the philosophy" (2:8) and his multiple references to specific practices, such as worshiping angels (v. 18), visionary experience (v. 18), ascetic practices (vv. 18, 23), drawing on insights from ritual mystery initiation (v. 18), observance of festivals and Sabbaths (v. 16), and following various taboos (v. 21). But it also extends to the manner of his warnings to the Colossians, such as "watch out that someone does not lead you

809 Copenhaver, *Paul's Rhetoric in the Letter to the Colossians*, 92.
810 Copenhaver, *Paul's Rhetoric in the Letter to the Colossians*, 142; see also 126.
811 Copenhaver, *Paul's Rhetoric in the Letter to the Colossians*, 142.
812 Hooker, "False Teachers," 315–31.
813 Wright, 28, discussed in Copenhaver, *Paul's Rhetoric in the Letter to the Colossians*, 35–36.

away as a captive" (v. 8), "let no one judge you" (v. 16), and "let no one condemn you" (v. 18). The case for each of these referring to a specific form of opposition will be made when each of these characteristics is discussed at various intervals throughout the commentary.

## *Is There a Macro-Chiastic Structure to Colossians?*

Another significant monograph on the composition of Colossians is J. P. Heil's *Colossians*.[814] He claims to take a rhetorical approach to Colossians, but in a general sense, as he does not apply the categories of ancient Greco-Roman rhetoric. Rather, he analyzes the letter in terms of a literary-rhetorical method by which he seeks to discern Paul's persuasive strategy through noticing the chiastic structures used throughout the letter. In particular, he contends that there is a macro-chiasm that spans the entire letter and ten micro-chiastic units of thought that likewise encompass the entire letter and together comprise the macro structure (see below). He also finds a number of mini-chiasms embedded within the micro-chiasms of the letter.

*Heil's Macro-Chiastic Structure of Colossians*

| | |
|---|---|
| A | 1:1–2 |
| B | 1:3–14 |
| C | 1:15–23 |
| D | 1:24–2:5 |
| E | 2:6–23 |
| E′ | 3:1–7 |
| D′ | 3:8–16 |
| C′ | 3:17–4:1 |
| B′ | 4:2–6 |
| A′ | 4:7–18 |

In general, the prospect of identifying macro-chiasms (especially going beyond fifteen verses) remains a highly disputed issue in NT studies.[815] I do not find his proposal for the macro-chiastic structure of Colossians compelling. For instance, the two micro-chiasms that form the chiastic center of the book are 2:6–23

814 The full title is *Colossians: Encouragement to Walk in All Wisdom as Holy Ones in Christ*.

815 See, e.g., Porter and Reed, "Philippians as a Macro-Chiasm," 213–31; Thompson, *Chiasmus in the Pauline Letters*, 24–25n6, who says that he continues "to find the concept of macro-chiasmus fraught with difficulties."

and 3:1–7. But 2:6–23 seems to me to represent two distinct units of thought: a theological basis for the polemic (2:9–15) followed by the polemic against the oppositional teaching framed by three warnings (2:16–23). Similarly, 3:1–4 forms the theological basis for the ethical exhoration that follows, while 3:5–7 begins the exhortations. Furthermore, 3:5–11 forms one coherent section of ethical exhortations framed around commands to desist ("put to death" and "take off from yourselves"; 3:5 and 3:8 respectively). In addition, 3:12–17 should be taken closely with 3:5–11 since they are framed with terms for "taking off" and "putting on" clothing as a metaphor for vices and virtues. There are additional concerns I would have about the coherence of some of the sections he proposes.

It is also difficult to see the parallelism between some of the micro-chiasms, such as D and D′. It is not altogether apparent what the "clear parallelism" is between Paul's reflections on his suffering and labor for the Colossians in 1:24–2:5 and the injunction to the Colossians to strip off vices in 3:8–11, coupled with the appeal to appropriate virtues in 3:12–16.

I will discuss some of the proposals for chiastic arrangements in the "Form, Structure, and Setting" section of the commentary for some of the passages where there is the presence of a potential chiastic arrangement that may be more convincing.

### *Conclusion*

Although I find the letter to the Colossians to be highly rhetorical in the broader sense of a persuasive argument (or group of arguments) for the Colossians, I am hesitant to analyze the letter in terms of the formal categories of Greco-Roman school rhetoric as found in the classical rhetorical handbooks. I will assess each coherent unit of thought on its own merit without appealing to Aristotle, Quintilian, the *Rhetorica ad Herennium*, or any of the other classical sources. This will help to ensure that due consideration is given to the individual stylistic tendencies and idiosyncrasies of the author of Colossians.

## *10. An Outline of Colossians*

I. Greeting (1:1–2)
II. Thanksgiving (1:3–8)
    A. Thanksgiving (vv. 3–5a)
    B. Excursus on the Gospel (vv. 5b–8)
III. Prayer (1:9–14)
    A. Content and Purpose of the Prayer: To Walk Worthily (vv. 9–10a)
    B. The Means of Walking Worthily (vv. 10b–14)
IV. Hymnic Praise to Christ (1:15–20)
    A. Christ Is Lord of the Creation of All Things (vv. 15–16)
        • Bridge: The Lord of Creation Is Head of the Church (vv. 17–18a)

- B. Christ Is Lord of the Reconciliation of All Things (vv. 18b–20)

V. Reconciliation of the Colossians to God (1:21–23)
- A. Once: Estrangement from God (v. 21)
- B. Now: Reconciled to God (vv. 22–23)

VI. The Apostle Paul's Labor for the Gospel (1:24–2:5)
- A. Paul's Suffering and Stewardship of the Mystery (1:24–29)
  1. Paul's Role as a Servant of the Gospel with Its Attendant Afflictions (vv. 24–25)
  2. The Revelation of the Mystery (vv. 26–27)
  3. The Proclamation of the Gospel (vv. 28–29)
- B. Paul's Labor for the Colossians (2:1–5)
  1. Paul's Efforts to Encourage Their Hearts (vv. 1–3)
  2. A Warning about Being Deceived by Persuasive Teachings (vv. 4–5)

VII. Living for Christ and Resisting a Dangerous Set of Teachings (2:6–15)
- A. A Call to Walk in Union with Christ (vv. 6–7)
- B. Warning about a Deceptive Teaching (v. 8)
- C. Help for the Danger: Resources in Christ (vv. 9–15)
  1. Filled in Him (vv. 9–10)
  2. Circumcised in Him (v. 11)
  3. Buried and Raised with Him (v. 12)
  4. Made Alive with Him (vv. 13–15)
     - a. He Took Away the Guilt of Sin (vv. 13–14)
     - b. He Defeated the Principalities and Powers (v. 15)

VIII. Warnings against the "Philosophy" (2:16–23)
- A. First Warning: Do Not Be Judged (vv. 16–17)
- B. Second Warning: Do Not Be Condemned (vv. 18–19)
- C. Third Warning: Do Not Comply with Their Dictates (vv. 20–23)

IX. Focusing Thoughts and Affections on Christ (3:1–4)
- A. Seek the Things Above (v. 1)
- B. Set Your Mind on the Things Above (vv. 2–4)

X. Dealing with the Sins of the Past (3:5–11)
- A. Putting to Death Sexual Impurity (vv. 5–7)
  1. Confronting Five Vices Related to Sexual Impurity (v. 5)
  2. Reason: These Vices Result in God's Wrath (vv. 6–7)
- B. Eliminating Socially Destructive Behaviors (vv. 8–11)
  1. Confronting Six Socially Destructive Vices (vv. 8–9a)
  2. Basis: Your "Old Self" Has Been Removed (v. 9b)
  3. Basis: You Possess a New Identity in Christ (vv. 10–11)

XI. Putting on the Virtues of God's Chosen People (3:12–17)
- A. Ten Virtues That Should Characterize God's People (vv. 12–15)
- B. The Means: Through the Word of Christ (v. 16)
- C. Conclusion: Do Everything in the Name of the Lord Jesus (v. 17)

XII. Living in the Christian Household (3:18–4:1)
   A. Instructions for Wives and Husbands (vv. 18–19)
   B. Instructions for Children and Fathers (vv. 20–21)
   C. Instructions for Slaves and Masters (3:22–4:1)
XIII. Communicating the Gospel (4:2–6)
   A. Devote Yourselves to Prayer (vv. 2–3)
   B. Walk in Wisdom (vv. 4–5)
   C. Speak with Grace (v. 6)
XIV. Personal Greetings and Instructions (4:7–17)
   A. Remarks about the Messengers Carrying the Letter (vv. 7–9)
   B. Greetings to the Colossians from Paul's Associates (vv. 10–14)
   C. Request to Greet the Christians in Laodicea (v. 15)
   D. Request to Arrange an Exchange of Letters with Christians in Laodicea (v. 16)
   E. Request to the Community to Encourage Archippus in His Ministry (v. 17)
XV. Letter Closing (4:18)

# Colossians

# Greeting (1:1–2)

## *Bibliography*

**Aulock, H. von.** *Münzen und Städte Phrygiens.* **Aune, D. E.** *Literary Environment.* **Harrison, J. R.** *Paul's Language of Grace.* **Hellerman, J.** *When the Church Was a Family.* **Klauck, H.-J.** *Ancient Letters.* **Murphy-O'Connor, J.** *Paul the Letter-Writer.* **Richards, E. R.** *Letter Writing.* ———. *Secretary.* **Stirewalt, M. L.** *Letter Writer.* **Stowers, S. K.** *Letter Writing.* **Taatz, I.** *Frühjudische Briefe.* **Weima, J. A. D.** *Ancient Letter Writer.* **Wise, M. O.** *Language and Literacy in Roman Judaea.*

## *Translation*

*To the Colossians*[a]

[1]*Paul, an apostle of Christ Jesus through the will of God and Timothy, our brother.* [2]*To the saints and faithful brothers and sisters in Christ*[b] *at Colossae.*[c] *Grace and peace to you from God our Father.*[d]

## *Notes*

a. The superscription of the letter is spelled differently among the manuscripts. See, the discussion below (under [c]) where the variant spellings of Colossae and Colossians are discussed.

b. [1:2] The Western text (D F G Vulgate) and a few Alexandrian witnesses (A 33 104) add Ἰησοῦ in 1:2: "in Christ Jesus." This is most likely a scribal assimilation to the wording of 1:1a, 3a, and 4a, which have "Christ Jesus."

c. [1:2] The textual tradition reflects two different ways of spelling Colossae in Greek, one with an omicron in the second syllable (Κολοσσαῖς) and the other with an alpha (Κολασσαῖς). The same issue pertains to the title of the letter, where it is spelled either Κολοσσαεις (or Κολοσσεις) or Κολασσαεἰς. The witnesses ℵ, B, and D spell it with the omicron, with the Old Latin and Vulgate appearing to follow suit by rendering it *Colossis.* 𝔓[46] and A support the alpha spelling (adding also an additional alpha before the ending: Κολασσαεῖς), along with some other important Alexandrian witnesses (I P Ψ 33 81 104 326). The Majority Text is surprisingly split on the issue. The spelling is only of historical interest and has no impact on the interpretation of the text. In the few places that Colossae is mentioned in secular literature, it is invariably spelled with an omicron (see, e.g., Herodotus, *Hist.* 7.30; Xenophon, *Anab.* 1.2.6; Diodorus Siculus, *Hist.* 14.80.8). Roman-era coins similarly use the omicron, but the city name is often spelled Κολοσσηνων (and sometimes Κολοσηνων or Κολοσσηνοις), reflecting the adjectival termination (-ηνος).[1] The omicron is thus historically correct, but the alpha entered the textual tradition very early (as attested by its appearance in 𝔓[46]), possibly reflecting a dialectical pronunciation[2] or even as an error of hearing or eyesight. See the extensive discussion in Lightfoot, 16–18.

d. [1:2] The Byzantine text along with a few Western (F G and some Old Latin and Vulgate manuscripts) and Alexandrian (ℵ A C I 104) witnesses add "and the Lord Jesus

---

1 See von Auluck, *Münzen*, 24–27, 83–93.

2 See Robertson, *Grammar*, 184–85.

Christ" (καὶ κυρίου Ἰησοῦ Χριστοῦ). Codices Vaticanus (B) and Bezae (D) and other assorted witnesses from all three text types retain the simpler reading that ends with "God our Father." The addition is most easily explained as a scribal insertion to bring the greetings in the Colossian letter into conformity with Paul's other letters containing this phrase (see Rom 1:7; 1 Cor 1:3; 2 Cor 1:2; Phil 1:2; 1 Thess 1:1; Phlm 1:3; see also 2 Thess 1:1; Eph 1:2). Sumney reads too much into the omission when he speculates that the absence of "and the Lord Jesus Christ" does "cast serious doubt on the thesis that the main issue of Colossians centers on Christology."[3]

## *Form/Structure/Setting*

The form of the salutation of the letter to the Colossians substantially corresponds to any other Greek letter written during the Roman era. The letter writer is indicated in the nominative case and the recipient(s) in the dative, which is then followed by a brief greeting (usually χαίρειν, "greetings"). The salutation form is standard regardless of the specific letter type (personal, royal correspondence, etc.). These conventions are illustrated in a few examples from letters of this era:

1. A Letter from Upper Egypt (AD 58) (*P.Mert.* 1.12.1–2)
   Chairas to his dearest Dionysius, many greetings and continual health.
   Χαιρᾶς Διονυσίωι τῷ φιλτάτωι πλεῖστα χαίρειν καὶ διὰ παντὸς ὑγιαίνειν

2. A Letter from Karanis, Egypt (2nd c. AD) (P.Wisc. 71.1–2)
   Ptolemaios to Kassianos his brother, many greetings.
   Πτολεμαῖς Κασσιανῷ τῷ ἀδελφῷ πλεῖστα χαίρειν

3. A Letter from Antiochus III (205 BC) (IMagnesia 18.1–3; *OGIS* 231.1–3)
   King Antiochus to the council and people of Magnesia, greetings.
   Βασιλεὺς Ἀντίοχος Μαγνήτων τῆι βουλῆι καὶ δήμωι χαίρειν

Paul expands each element of the salutation—a practice entirely within the bounds of proper letter form. In his self-designation as the sender, he not only indicates his title but speaks of his divine authorization to fulfill this role. This provides part of the warrant for him to write this letter to this community of believers whom he did not know in a city that he had presumably never visited. Timothy is named as the coauthor of the letter. Timothy was probably not the secretary for writing the letter (which required specialized skills), but likely contributed substantially to the content and possibly even to the style of the letter. Paul also elaborates on the naming of the Colossians as the recipients of the letter by describing them in their own relationship to God and himself. The most remarkable variation from the typical letter form comes in his greetings,

3 Sumney, 29.

where he avoids the traditional greeting χαίρειν, "greetings," for his own distinctive greeting of "grace and peace," which is common to all his letters. He thus transforms the traditional convention into an invocation that God would bestow on them two of the most important blessings of the new covenant.

Paul is writing the letter while he is in Roman custody (4:18), most likely in Rome. Timothy is with him and participates meaningfully in the composition of the letter. Paul had probably contracted a secretary (or amanuensis) to actually write the letter. The precise role of the secretary was probably more substantial than taking word-for-word dictation. Richards envisions a situation in which Paul and Timothy would gather to work on the letter. Paul would express what he wanted to say in the letter, while the secretary would take notes in as detailed and complete a manner as possible. The secretary "then prepared a rough draft, probably on washable papyrus sheets or stacks of wax tablets. Paul and his team heard the letter read and made corrections and additions."[4] Once the process was complete and the content and wording of the letter had met with the approval of Paul and Timothy, the final draft of the letter would be composed and prepared to be sent.

There was no organized postal system in the Roman world. A letter was sent through someone who agreed to be the carrier of the letter. In this case, Tychicus and Onesimus were traveling to Colossae and were the bearers of this letter (4:7–9). Upon arriving at the destination and when the community of believers had gathered, there would likely have been an oral reading, probably by Tychicus himself. Stirewalt notes that "such a reading aloud served several purposes, but above all the living voice of the reader underscored the sense of the writer's personal presence, thereby strengthening the relationship between sender and receiver."[5]

## *Comment*

**1** Παῦλος, "Paul." The first word of the letter is the self-designation of the letter writer. This is precisely the way Romans, 1 Corinthians, 2 Corinthians, Galatians, 1 Thessalonians, Philippians, and Philemon each begin. The self-reference also appears in this letter in 1:23 and 4:18. Nevertheless, many interpreters have questioned whether "Paul" should be undersood as the author of the letter in the same way as in the seven letters just named. Our conclusion is that the balance of evidence does tip in favor of the authenticity of the letter (see the full discussion in the introduction).

Although there is no indication that Paul had ever visited the small city of Colossae, he would certainly have been well-known to the Christians there. Luke makes the claim that during Paul's Ephesian ministry (ca. AD 52–55),

4 Richards, *Letter Writing*, 93.

5 Stirewalt, *Letter Writer*, 4–5.

"all Asia heard the word of the Lord" (Acts 19:10). It was at this time that one of their own, Epaphras, likely heard Paul's preaching of the gospel (perhaps while he was in Ephesus), was converted, and took the message of salvation back to the people of the Lycus Valley (1:7). If one accepts the authenticity of the letter and a Caesarean or Roman imprisonment of Paul as the place of writing, six to ten years have passed since the founding of the church. This is more than adequate time for the church to have grown numerically (perhaps with the founding of several house churches in or near the city of Colossae) and for the development of a rival teaching.

ἀπόστολος Χριστοῦ Ἰησοῦ διὰ θελήματος θεοῦ, "an apostle of Christ Jesus through the will of God." Right at the outset of this letter, Paul articulates his warrant for writing to the Colossian believers. By appropriating the title of "apostle" to himself, he claims the same level of leadership and authority in the church as the Twelve (1 Cor 15:7, 9). There were others in the church who were called "apostles," but they did not bear the same level of authority (e.g., Andronicus and Junias in Rom 16:7). This is comparable to the way Paul begins his first letter to the Corinthians (1 Cor 1:1; but see also Eph 1:1; 1 Tim 1:1; 2 Tim 1:1; Titus 1:1), although there he includes the word "called" (κλητός).

The term ἀπόστολος, "apostle," continues to carry the same force as its verbal Hebrew counterpart (שָׁלַח, *šālaḥ*), designating the sending of a person for a specific task or mission as an authorized representative of another. In the OT, God often sent out an individual envoy on an official mission, as seen especially in the sending out of the prophets (Isa 6:8; Jer 1:7; 25:4; 26:5; 35:15; Ezek 2:3–4). "Sending" also evokes the memory of Jesus sending out (ἀποστέλλω) the Twelve to proclaim the kingdom of God (Matt 10:5, 16; Mark 3:14; Luke 9:2; cf. also the sending of the seventy-two, Luke 10:1, 3). The larger context of Colossians bears witness to the fact that Paul clearly understood himself as engaged in the proclamation of the kingdom (Col 1:13; cf. 1:24–2:5). Making known the kerygma and establishing it as central to the forming of Christian communities was the foundational task of an apostle (1:29).

Χριστοῦ Ἰησοῦ, "Christ Jesus," is the one who has commissioned Paul to this role. The genitive case could be interpreted either as a genitive of source ("an apostle *sent from* Christ Jesus") or a genitive of possession ("an apostle belonging to Christ Jesus"). The title "Christ" (Χριστός) identifies Jesus as the Jewish Messiah and encompasses all of the apostolic teaching regarding his coming in fulfillment of the Jewish hope as expressed throughout the Hebrew Scriptures. Since the identity of Jesus as the Messiah was such a divisive issue in the diaspora synagogue, it is doubtful that Dunn is correct in asserting that "'Christ' was already well on the way to becoming simply another name for Jesus."[6]

διὰ θελήματος θεοῦ, "through the will of God," indicates that Paul had a clear sense of divine vocation for his ministry as an apostle. He will elaborate

6 Dunn, 45.

on the nature of this calling in 1:24–2:5. His mention of it here anticipates that discussion. Paul has elsewhere used this expression to refer to the unfolding of God's plan of redemption by which he frees people from their bondage to sin in the present evil age (Gal 1:4; see also Eph 1:9, 11). Paul is cognizant of the fact that God had chosen him to play a foundational role in the unveiling and actualization of this plan. This phrase became a common way for Paul to characterize the basis of his apostolic call and ministry (1 Cor 1:1; 2 Cor 1:1; see also Eph 1:1; 2 Tim 1:1), and is undoubtedly rooted in the resurrected Jesus's revelation to him on the Damascus Road (Acts 9:1–31; 22:3–11; 26:2–18; Gal 1:11–12).

καὶ Τιμόθεος ὁ ἀδελφός, "and Timothy, our brother." The naming of Timothy as a co-sender of the letter, as Paul does also in 2 Cor 1:1, Phil 1:1, 1 Thess 1:1, 2 Thess 1:1, and Phlm 1, raises a question about the extent of Timothy's involvement in composing the letter. Does this indicate that he was equally responsible with Paul for the content and style of the letter? Is it a way of acknowledging him as Paul's amanuensis (or secretary) in writing the letter? Or does it provide our first indication that Timothy had a major role in writing the letter, as some would maintain?[7] A careful analysis of the rest of the letter with this question in mind suggests that Paul is the principal author of the letter. This is strongly intimated by the fact that the letter writer switches to the first-person singular at 1:23 (ἐγὼ Παῦλος) and retains that form through 2:5, where Paul describes his suffering and labor on behalf of the gospel and the Colossians. The first-person form is once again taken up in 4:7 and used throughout the remainder of the letter (with the possible exception of 4:8, where there is a textual corruption). The letter then ends with Paul's own personal greeting (ὁ ἀσπασμὸς τῇ ἐμῇ χειρὶ Παύλου, "Greetings from Paul with my own hand"), without anything comparable from Timothy (4:18). Thus it is inappropriate to regard Timothy as the principal author of the letter,[8] but since he is named as the coauthor, his role in formulating and composing the letter should be regarded as substantial.[9] Although it is possible that Timothy may have served as Paul's secretary,[10] we have no way of knowing this with certainty, and we have no indication that he was ever trained as a literary secretary. The more likely scenario is that Paul

---

7 E.g., Richards, *Letter Writing*, 35–36; Dunn, 47.

8 Schweizer, 23–24.

9 Weima, *Ancient Letter Writer*, 29–31, objects to the idea that the co-sender had a significant role in the writing of the letter. Rather, he contends that the co-sender was included because he had a special relationship with the addressees of the letter. For Colossians, he says that Timothy is listed as co-sender "perhaps because of his past work, personal connection, and/or positive reputation in these congregations." But this unnecessarily diminishes Timothy's role, and there is no evidence that Timothy was known in the Colossian church. Although Paul was the principal author of the letter, one needs to take seriously the first-person plural verbs referring to Paul and Timothy, along with the dependent plural participles (e.g., "we give thanks . . . praying, hearing," 1:3; "we heard . . . we have not ceased giving thanks, praying and asking," 1:9) as well as the first-person plural pronouns (e.g., Epaphras as "our beloved fellow servant," 1:7).

10 Thus Barth and Blanke, 137.

hired someone with the requisite skills to serve as secretary (perhaps a member of the believing community). Paul and Timothy then met with this person and expressed what they wanted to say in the letter, while the secretary took notes and subsequently produced a final draft.

Timothy had a particularly close relationship with Paul as his assistant and coworker. According to Luke, Timothy joined Paul's ministry team over fifteen years earlier (in the late 40s) during Paul's second visit to the small cities of Derbe and Lystra in the south of the Roman province of Galatia (Acts 16:1–4). In some ways, Timothy was well-suited to the mission because of his background of growing up with a gentile father and a Jewish mother. The gentile influence may have been stronger since he had not been circumcised before joining Paul's missionary team (16:3). Timothy worked alongside Paul in evangelizing the Macedonian cities of Philippi, Thessalonica, and Berea (17:14–15), Corinth (18:5; 2 Cor 1:19), and Ephesus (Acts 19:22). Paul began to show a great deal of trust in Timothy during his Ephesian ministry, where he served as Paul's emissary to handle some very delicate ministry situations there (1 Cor 4:17; 16:10). He served Paul in the same way with matters in the churches at Philippi (Phil 2:19) and Thessalonica (1 Thess 3:2, 6). Paul's affection for Timothy is summed up well in a comment he makes to the Philippian church: "as a son with his father he has served with me in the work of the gospel" (Phil 2:22).

Paul could have begun his letter, then, by referring to him as "Timothy, my son," but rather he refers to him as "our brother" (literally, "the brother"). This is Paul's way of commending Timothy to the Colossians as a fellow believer, thus identifying him with himself and especially the readers (so the translation, "*our* brother"). "Brothers" (ἀδελφοί) was the most common word in early Christianity for referring to fellow Christians. They experienced a new bond of kinship based on confessing Jesus as Messiah and Lord and possessing the new-covenant gift of the Spirit. Strikingly, Paul does not refer to Timothy here as an "apostle" (although he possibly could have because of the nature of Timothy's ministry with Paul). Reserving "apostle" for himself may be consistent with the emphasis he places on his unique role as a steward of the mystery (Col 1:24–2:5, esp. vv. 25–26), which carries with it a responsibility to admonish and teach the Colossians (1:28), especially in light of the looming threat to the church.

**2 τοῖς ἐν Κολοσσαῖς ἁγίοις καὶ πιστοῖς ἀδελφοῖς ἐν Χριστῷ**, "to the saints and faithful brothers and sisters in Christ at Colossae." With the dative case, Paul names the recipients of the letter. (For a more extended discussion of the city of Colossae and the beginning of Christianity there, see the introduction.) The form of the address is somewhat simpler than in his other letters, where he sometimes addresses a letter "to the *church* of the . . ." (1 Thess 1:1; 2 Thess 1:1), "to the church of God that is in . . ." (1 Cor 1:2; 2 Cor 1:1), "to those who are in . . ." (Rom 1:7; Phil 1:1; see also Eph 1:1), or "to the churches of . . ." (Gal 1:2). These variations should caution one about making too much of the differences in the manner of addressing the recipients here.

Although ἁγίοις, "holy," could be taken as an attributive adjective modifying ἀδελφοῖς, "brothers," it is better to take it as a substantival adjective ("to the saints and faithful brethren") as most of the versions render it. This is more typical of Paul's usage of the term in the introductions to his letters (e.g., Rom 1:7; 1 Cor 1:2). Nevertheless, the "saints" and "faithful brothers," which stand under the one article (τοῖς), are the same group of people and not two different groups within the Colossian church.[11] The terms characterize the believers in terms of their status before God and in terms of their response to the gospel.

In speaking of the Colossian believers as "brothers" (ἀδελφοί), Paul again employs the language of family (i.e., fictive kinship terminology) that was constitutive of the relationships among members of the Jesus movement. Jesus himself had probably initiated the use of this language when he observed a group of his disciples sitting around him and exclaimed, "Here are my mother and my brothers! Whoever does God's will is my brother and sister and mother" (Mark 3:34–35 NIV). Paul uses this term 133 times in his letters to describe the relationships within the new surrogate family, along with other familial terms (such as "father," "son," and "child"). This was not a casual use of language for Paul; his usage demonstrates that the term conveyed affective solidarity, family unity, material solidarity, and family loyalty.[12]

He characterizes these believers not only as "saints" (ἅγιοι) but also as "faithful ones" (πιστοί). This collocation only appears elsewhere in the NT in Eph 1:1, and the plural πιστοί, "faithful ones," only in the Pastorals (1 Tim 4:3, 10, 12; 6:2; 2 Tim 2:2). "Saints" (ἅγιοι), which could also be translated "holy/pure ones," is one of Paul's favorite and most common ways of referring to Christians in his letters. He uses the plural of this term some forty-three times to refer to the new-covenant people of God. His usage has continuity with the OT description of the people of God as a "holy nation" (ἔθνος ἅγιον; Exod 19:6). They are a "holy people" (λαὸς ἅγιος) because God has chosen them to be his very own and has bestowed his blessings upon them (Deut 7:6; 14:2; cf. Lev 20:26). The term "saints" is frequent in Daniel (ἅγιοι; LXX Dan 7:18, 21, 22, 25; 8:25; see also Ps 34:9 [33:10 LXX]). For Paul, believers in Christ are holy because they have received God's merciful salvation and a new status before him. They have experienced the redemptive work of Christ and have had their sins atoned for through the blood of Christ on the cross and are thus ἡγιασμένοις ἐν Χριστῷ Ἰησοῦ, "sanctified/set apart in Christ Jesus" (1 Cor 1:2).

As πιστοί, the Colossians believers are "faithful" to Christ (as almost all versions render it). Although the term can also mean "believing" (Tyndale renders it, "brethren that believe in Christ"),[13] this sense is already assumed in their description as "brothers," "saints," and "in Christ." Faithfulness is a

11 See Wallace, *Grammar*, 281–83.

12 Hellerman, *Family*, 78–79.

13 Lohse, 9, takes it as such here.

characteristic of God himself that can be seen in his reliability in fulfilling his covenant promises (1 Cor 1:9; 2 Cor 1:20; 1 Thess 5:24; see Deut 7:9; 32:4). Paul applies this term to the Colossian believers to describe their unswerving obedience to God and their consistency in living out what it means to be followers of Christ. Paul has already described Timothy as "faithful" (1 Cor 4:17), and later in this letter he will call both Epaphras (Col 1:7) and Tychicus (4:7) "faithful." The latter two instances are the only other uses of the term in Colossians and give further support to the idea of taking it as "faithful" and not simply "believing." In none of his previous letters did Paul address the recipients as "faithful." Paul may be taking this unique step here as a way of affirming their fidelity to his gospel up to this point, despite the enticements they faced to embrace a contrary teaching. Lightfoot goes too far in speculating that Paul is making an oblique and indirect reference to the near defection of some in the congregation by addressing the "faithful."[14] He is addressing the whole community of believers and can commend them as "faithful" thus far in their fidelity to Christ.

Their status before God as "pure ones," and their close familial relationship to one another, is based on their union with Christ. The expression ἐν Χριστῷ, "in Christ," indicates the sphere, or realm, in which they now live. They no longer live in solidarity with Adam (1 Cor 15:22), but in a present, dynamic relationship with the resurrected and ascended Christ. It also points to their participation with Christ in the key events of his redeeming work—that is, his death and resurrection (Col 2:12). The present union with the exalted Christ is why Paul can speak of the importance of "holding on tight" to him (2:19) and experiencing his peace (3:15).

This phrase stands at the heart of Paul's theology. Dunn aptly notes, "Paul's perception of his whole life as a Christian, its source, its identity, and its responsibilities, could be summed up in these phrases."[15] "In Christ" is thus expressive of their new identity and points to Jesus Christ as the sole and exclusive focus of their new allegiance. Paul uses the expression and its correlates many times in Colossians (ἐν Χριστῷ, "in Christ" [1x]; ἐν Χριστῷ Ἰησοῦ, "in Christ Jesus" [1x]; ἐν ᾧ, "in whom" [4x]; ἐν αὐτῷ, "in him" [8x]; ἐν κυρίῳ, "in the Lord" [4x]). As will be seen in the course of the commentary, its usage here is thoroughly consistent with Paul's usage elsewhere.

χάρις ὑμῖν καὶ εἰρήνη ἀπὸ θεοῦ πατρὸς ἡμῶν, "Grace and peace to you from God our Father." With this greeting, Paul wishes for them to experience the full set of blessings that they can now experience through their membership in the new covenant. This is precisely the same greeting that he uses in most of his other letters (Rom 1:7; 1 Cor 1:3; 2 Cor 1:2; Gal 1:3; Phil 1:2; Phlm 3), except for the absence of "and our Lord Jesus Christ" (which is present in some manuscripts but is most likely a later scribal assimilation; see *Notes*, note d.).

---

14 Lightfoot, 132.

15 Dunn, *Theology*, 399.

A shorter form is also found in 1 Thess 1:1, where he has simply "grace and peace to you." It is somewhat surprising that it is absent in a letter that is so overtly christological in orientation, yet probably no theological motive should be ascribed to Paul in varying his expression here.

A verb is assumed rather than expressed in the greeting. Probably one should supply the optative εἴη, "may it be" (e.g., Ps 113:2 [112:2 LXX]), the imperative ἔστω, "let it be" (e.g., Ps 72:17 [71:17 LXX]), or even the verb πληθυνθείη, "may it be multiplied [to you]" (e.g., Jude 2). When compared with other letters during the Greco-Roman era, Paul's greeting is unique in that it does not contain the normal form χαίρειν (or χαῖρε), "greetings," that was typical in papyrus letters.[16] Rather, Paul uses χάρις, "grace," a term that is expressive of his understanding of the dawning of the new covenant in Christ and yet possesses a certain assonance with χαίρειν, "greetings."

He not only begins the letter with the wish for God's grace to be bestowed on them, but ends the letter on the same note, "grace be with you" (4:18). For Paul, χάρις, "grace," summed up the good news that he preached. It is at the very center of his whole theology. God had unilaterally chosen to bestow his divine favor, blessing, and mercy upon his people through the gift of his Son. The resulting salvation is a benefaction that people receive freely as a gift. His understanding of grace is deeply rooted in the OT usage of the word *ḥēn* (חֵן; "grace," "favor") and, more particularly, *ḥesed* (חֶסֶד; "lovingkindness," "love," "mercy," "faithfulness"). The latter term often occurs in connection with God's covenant with his people and speaks of his faithfulness in fulfilling his covenant obligations out of a heart that is filled with mercy, compassion, and love. Thus it is often translated by "mercy" (ἔλεος) in the LXX. Accordingly, God reveals himself as "the compassionate [חַנּוּן] and gracious God, slow to anger, abounding in love [חֶסֶד] and faithfulness, maintaining love [חֶסֶד] to thousands, and forgiving wickedness, rebellion and sin" (Exod 34:6–7 NIV; see also Num 14:17–19) when he establishes his covenant with Israel on Mount Sinai. His covenant love and faithfulness are the basis for praising God repeatedly throughout the book of Psalms (e.g., Pss 5:8; 6:5; 13:5; 17:7).

Although the plural of the term (χάριτες) was widely known in the Greco-Roman world as "the *leitmotiv* of the first-century reciprocity system" of benefaction,[17] Paul only uses the singular of the term and focuses primarily on the unilateral benefaction of the Father. Paul expresses this eloquently in Romans, where he characterizes justification and righteousness as a free gift that stems from God's grace (Rom 3:24; 5:15, 17). Foundational, then, to Paul's understanding of grace is that it is truly unmerited favor from God to provide salvation for sinners through the work of Christ on the cross. This is his gospel and what motivates him to expend all of his strength in proclaiming it and teaching it

---

16 See Klauck, *Ancient Letters*, 18.

17 So Harrison, *Paul's Language of Grace*, 345.

(Col 1:24–2:5). Yet for Paul, grace is even more than redemption and forgiveness. Grace results in a union with Christ that provides power for living according to the ethical demands of the gospel (2:9–12). Paul's own example is instructive for his readers when he reflects on God's message to him: "my grace is sufficient for you, for my power is made perfect in weakness" (2 Cor 12:9). Grace is God's sustaining provision for his people (2 Cor 4:7–18, esp. 4:15). Thus, when Paul begins his letter invoking God's grace upon his readers, he not only wants them to increasingly appreciate their new status in life as forgiven by God but to grow in their experience of supernatural empowerment that flows from their union with Christ.

In addition to praying for God's grace to be upon them, Paul also calls upon God to give them peace (εἰρήνη). The wish of peace in the greetings of a letter is not at all typical in Greek and Roman letters of the period, but it does appear in some Jewish letters. In fact, the typical opening form of the Aramaic Bar Kokhba letters included the wish of שָׁלוֹם ("peace").[18] It is doubtful that Paul was following a literary convention in including this form of greeting. Rather, the greeting flows out of his desire that the Colossians (as well as all of his churches) experience the blessings of the new covenant. The blessing of peace fits well with grace since the prophets anticipated the messianic era to be an age of peace. Isaiah declared that the Messiah would be the "Prince of Peace" (Isa 9:6), and Zechariah describes him as a humble king who would come and speak peace to the nations (Zech 9:9–10). In his description of the new covenant, the prophet Ezekiel said that God would "make a covenant of peace [εἰρήνη; שָׁלוֹם]" that would be an everlasting covenant (Ezek 37:26). In John's Gospel, Jesus declares this to be fulfilled in himself when he says, "Peace I leave with you; my peace I give you" (John 14:27 NIV). Luke reports that an angel proclaimed that the new era of peace had begun when he announced the birth of the Messiah (Luke 2:14). Paul understood this peace to refer to the experience of all people who put their faith in Christ and are no longer estranged from the one true and living God. Thus peace with God is the result of justification (Rom 5:1).

Of course, in Roman imperial propaganda, Augustus introduced an age of peace and security (*pax et securitas*) symbolized by the Altar of Peace (*Ara Pacis*) in Rome and proclaimed in the *Res Gestae Divi Augusti*, where it is reported that the senate voted to consecrate an altar to the *Pax Augusta* in the Campus Martius in Rome (*Res Gestae* 12) and that his many military victories brought a state of peace (*Res Gestae* 26; see also Suetonius, *Aug.* 22). Yet this peace was a mere chimera that would not be long-lasting and would ultimately be shattered by Christ's return in judgment (1 Thess 5:3). Christ did not introduce an era of political peace in his first coming but an opportunity for all, not only Jews but now gentiles, to experience peace with the one true God through the Lord Jesus Christ (Eph 2:14–16). This peace would pervade the souls of individuals through

18 Wise, *Language and Literacy in Roman Judaea*, 209–10. See also 2 Bar. 78.2, "mercy and peace."

the presence and nearness of God's Spirit (Gal 5:22). Despite the difficulties and upheavals in life, God's presence would provide a tranquility that would guard their hearts and souls (Phil 4:6–7). Paul will later encourage the Colossians to allow God's peace to sweep over them and control their emotions (Col 3:16). The Colossians need the assurance of God's peace because of the mental and emotional turmoil that the pushy advocates of "the philosophy" have stirred.

Paul ends his greeting by rooting the source of the grace and peace in God the Father (ἀπὸ θεοῦ πατρὸς ἡμῶν). Although in his other greetings he includes "and the Lord Jesus Christ," there is no deemphasis on Christ here since he is mentioned as the source of Paul's apostleship (1:1), the basis for the sanctified status and brotherhood of the Colossians (v. 2), the one worthy of thanksgiving together with the Father (v. 3), and the object of their faith (v. 4).

## *Explanation*

In chains and unable to visit the Colossian believers who are threatened by a teaching that Paul deems dangerous, the apostle and his close associate, Timothy, write a letter to these believers. The letter will take the place of Paul's personal presence.

By writing them as a divinely appointed apostle, Paul intends for his remarks to be heard and understood as having a significant authority and claim on their belief and practice. Paul has been commissioned by the resurrected Christ himself and carries out his apostolic task in accordance with the will of God. Paul addresses the Colossians as fellow believers who have been set apart for the Lord and are the recipients of a new status, as those who are holy and pure because of the work of Christ on their behalf. Up to this point, the Colossians have been faithful to the Lord, but as the rest of the letter will show, Paul writes out of a concern that they remain faithful to Christ.

He calls on God to bestow upon them the full measure of Christ's work of salvation in his prayer for "grace." Part of this grace is the understanding that their incorporation into Christ represents the source of divine power and provision to live out their Christian lives. In addition, Paul invokes God to extend to them deeper experiences of his peace. Both grace and peace constitute distinct blessings of the new covenant.

# Thanksgiving (1:3–8)

## *Bibliography*

**Arzt, P.** "Epistolary Introductory Thanksgiving," 29–46. **Bird, M. F.,** and **P. Sprinkle,** eds. *The Faith of Jesus Christ.* **Beetham, C. A.** *Echoes of Scripture,* 41–59. **Bornkamm, G.** "Hoffnung," 56–64. **Cadwallader, A.,** and **J. R. Harrison.** "Perspectives on the Lycus Valley," 3–70. **Doty, W. G.** *Letters in Primitive Christianity.* **Fee, G. D.** *Empowering Presence.* **Frank, N.** *Kolosserbrief im Kontext,* 44–50. **Grässer, E.** "Kol. 3:1–4," 139–68. **Hagen Pifer, J.** *Faith as Participation.* **Humann, C.,** et al. *Alt. v. Hierapolis.* **Huttner, U.** *Early Christianity in the Lycus Valley.* **Lindemann, A.** *Aufhebung der Zeit.* **Martin, D. B.** *Slavery As Salvation.* **Mullins, T. Y.** "Thanksgivings," 288–93. **O'Brien, P. T.** *Introductory Thanksgivings.* **Pao, D. W.** *Thanksgiving.* **Reed, J. T.** "Are Paul's Thanksgivings 'Epistolary'?," 87–99. **Schubert, P.** *Pauline Thanksgivings.* **Schweizer, E.** "Christus und Geist," 297–313. **Smith, R. R. R.** "*Ethne* from the Sebasteion at Aphrodisias," 50–77. **Standhartinger, A.** *Entstehungsgeschichte.* **Still, T.** "Eschatology in Colossians," 125–38. **Trainor, M.** *Epaphras.* **Wise, M. O.** *Language and Literacy in Roman Judaea.*

## *Translation*

*[3]We give thanks to God, [the][a] Father of our Lord Jesus Christ[b] always for[c] you as we pray, [4]because
we heard about your faith in Christ Jesus and the love that you have[d] for all the saints [5]because of the
hope stored up for you in the heavens. [This is the hope] that you heard about earlier in the word of
truth, the gospel, [6]which came to you (and is present[e] in you)[f]—just as it also is in the entire world,
bearing fruit and growing, just as it is in you—from the day you heard and came to know the grace of
God in truth. [7]For[g] you learned it from Epaphras, our beloved fellow slave. He is a faithful servant of
Christ for you,[h] [8]who also informed us of your love in the Spirit.*

## *Notes*

a. [1:3] Following εὐχαριστοῦμεν, "we give thanks," in 1:3, a number of important witnesses insert a καί, "and," between θεῷ, "God," and πατρί, "Father": "to the God *and* Father." Some manuscripts of the Western text (D F G) insert the masculine article τῷ, "to God *the* Father," but the testimony here is too slight for it to be considered original. The external evidence is fairly evenly split between the insertion and omission of καί, "and" (including a split between the two uncials א and B). In support of the inclusion of καί, "and," is the Byzantine text and the Vulgate (and some Old Latin manuscripts [it$^{ar, f}$]), as well as some important Alexandrian witnesses (א I Ψ 33 81 104). The omission of the conjunction also has in its favor some significant Alexandrian (B C 1739 cop$^{sa, bo}$ and possibly the support of 𝔓$^{61}$) and Western witnesses (some Vulgate manuscripts, it$^{mss}$ and Augustine, as well as the testimony of D, F, and G since they attest a form of the text without the conjunction). The shorter and more difficult reading would be the form of the text without the conjunction. The presence of καί, "and" (or the article) in some manuscripts can best be explained as scribal smoothing of the text and conforming it to many other places in Paul's letters where a καί, "and," connects "God" and "Father" (e.g., 1 Cor 15:24; Rom 15:6; 2 Cor 1:3; 11:31; Gal 1:4).

b. [1:3] Codex Vaticanus and a few other witnesses (1739 1881 vg$^{ms}$) omit "Christ." Although there is not a strong reason to explain why a scribe might omit "Christ," thus providing a strong internal argument for the omission, the reading should still be rejected because of the slim manuscript support (contra Barth and Blanke, 151, who argue for the omission).

c. [1:3] Sinaiticus and Vaticanus are split on whether the preposition at the end of 1:3 should be περί, "for" (א along with A C I Ψ 1739 and the Byzantine text; adopted by NA$^{28}$) or ὑπέρ, "for" (B along with D F G 33). In contexts of prayer and thanksgiving for his people, Paul uses both in his other letters: περί, "for," in 1 Cor 1:4; 1 Thess 3:9; 2 Thess 1:3, 11; 2:13, and ὑπέρ, "for," in 2 Cor 9:14; Eph 1:16; 3:1. He subsequently uses ὑπέρ, "for," in his prayer report in Col 1:9. A slight preference should be given for περί, "for," since a scribe may have been motivated to bring 1:3 into conformity with 1:9.

d. [1:4] The Majority text varies from the NA$^{28}$ by reading τήν, "that [is]," in 1:4 instead of the more expansive ἣν ἔχετε, "that you have." Codex Vaticanus is alone in reading neither. The weight of the external evidence lies clearly on the side of the relative clause (א C D F G P 075 81 104). Since a scribe may have sought to conform this passage to Eph 1:15 (τὴν ἀγάπην τὴν εἰς πάντας τοὺς ἁγίους, "the love that is for all the saints"), the longer reading with the relative clause is most likely original.

e. [1:6] There is only one verb here, the participle παρόντος. I will contend in the commentary that this term has the dual idea of "coming" and "being present with" in this context.

f. [1:6] The Majority text along with a few uncials (F G Ψ 075) insert a καί, "and," in 1:6 between κόσμῳ, "world," and ἐστίν, "is." This results in a different understanding of the syntax as reflected in the translation of the NKJV: "[5]the hope . . . of which you heard before in the word of the truth of the gospel, [6]which has come to you, as *it has* also in all the world, and is bringing forth fruit, as *it is* also among you. . . ." In this reading, the καί, "and," coordinates "[the gospel] has come to you" with "[the gospel] is bringing forth fruit" instead of seeing the "bringing forth fruit" as an explanation of what the gospel is doing in all the world. The reading with καί leaves a grammatical problem that renders it unlikely, especially when seen with the weight of external evidence that tips heavily in favor of omission. The first clause modifying "gospel" would be a participial clause in the genitive case that functions like an attributive modifier (τοῦ παρόντος εἰς ὑμᾶς, "which came to you"), whereas the second parallel clause is a periphrastic participial construction (ἐστὶν καρποφορούμενον καὶ αὐξανόμενον, "is bearing fruit and growing"). The coordinate construction could only work if the latter clause paralleled the genitive construction of the previous parallel clause, that is, τοῦ καρπορφορουμένου καὶ αὐξομένου, "which bears fruit and is growing."

g. [1:7] Some manuscripts insert a καί, "also," after καθώς, "just as," here translated "for," at the beginning of 1:7 (𝔐 Ψ 075 1739). The insertion can easily be explained as scribal assimilation to the two previous clauses that begin with καθὼς καί, "just as also," in 1:6.

h. [1:7] At the end of 1:7, the NA$^{28}$/UBS$^{5}$ part company with 𝔓$^{46}$ א B (as well as D F G) and agree with the Byzantine text (along with C Ψ 075 33 1739 it syr$^{p}$ cop$^{sa\ bo}$) in support of "your" (ὑμῶν) over "our" (ἡμῶν). The versions are split in their support, with some (NRSV; ESV; NAB; NLT; KJV) favoring "your" (ὑμῶν), and others (NIV; NASB; NET; NJB) opting for "our" (ἡμῶν). Since Paul has just described Epaphras as "*our* beloved fellow slave" in the previous clause, it only seems natural that he would continue his praise of Epaphras's value to himself and his team by also stating that he is "a faithful servant of Christ for *us*." Yet this might also be a powerful scribal motive for changing the text from "your" to "our." Fee has argued, however, that a scribe may have been motivated to change the pronoun from "our" to "your" under the supposition that

Paul was trying to say that the direction of the thanksgiving and Epaphras's teaching of the gospel was "for your sakes."[1] Since both readings could fit plausibly within the context, the argument of attraction better explains the origin of this variant; therefore, the internal evidence slightly favors "your" (ὑμῶν).

## *Form/Structure/Setting*

### *Form (and Literary Context)*

Immediately following the greeting, Paul and Timothy begin the letter with an introductory thanksgiving—a form that Paul employs in most of his letters. There has been extensive discussion in the literature about whether such a form was obligatory because it was common in Greco-Roman letter-writing practice. In an important and influential monograph written nearly two generations ago, Schubert successfully made the case that the many papyrus letters discovered from the Greco-Roman era "convincingly attest a wide-spread conventional use of an epistolary, religious or non-religious, introductory thanksgiving."[2] Schubert's view regarding the form was upheld by P. T. O'Brien in his own monograph on the theme, but with the crucial caveat that the content of Paul's thanksgivings reflected OT and Jewish influence, early Christian worship and apostolic preaching, and expressions of his own thoughts and concerns relevant to his audience.[3] More recently, P. Arzt has challenged Schubert's conclusion after a reexamination of the papyrus evidence and has asserted that "there are no formal 'introductory thanksgivings' in the prooemia of letters contemporaneous with the Pauline and other New Testament letters; hence, any reconstruction of such an 'introductory thanksgiving' lacks evidence."[4] J. T. Reed has disputed Arzt's methodology and conclusions, providing a compelling case in support of this epistolary form.[5] Reed argued that Arzt inappropriately excluded second-century papyrus letters as evidence (and a mass of preserved letters come from the second century) and that an examination of these letters gives a number of relevant examples of this form.[6] Furthermore, Reed is also able to provide citations from a variety of papyrus texts and ostraca that illustrate a person rendering thanks to a god in a letter, such as *P.Mich.* 8.465.14 (AD 104): εὐχαριστῶ δὲ τῷ Σαραπίδι καὶ Ἀγαθῇ Τύχῃ ὅτι . . . , "I give thanks to Sarapis and Agathe Tyche because . . ."[7] He also points out that Arzt unnecessarily limits what he considers valid examples of thanksgivings to those in a context where there is a

1 Fee, *Empowering Presence*, 638n9.
2 Schubert, *Thanksgivings*, 180.
3 O'Brien, *Introductory Thanksgivings*, 259–65.
4 Arzt, "Epistolary Introductory Thanksgiving," 44.
5 Reed, "Are Paul's Thanksgivings 'Epistolary'?," 87–99.
6 Reed, "Are Paul's Thanksgivings 'Epistolary'?," 91.
7 See other examples cited in Reed, "Are Paul's Thanksgivings 'Epistolary'?," 92.

formulaic health wish (*formula valetudinis*, e.g., "I thanked the gods for your well-being . . ."). Reed is able to show many examples of expressions of thanksgiving to the gods in letters disconnected from this formula.[8]

In sum, there was an epistolary convention that can properly be termed an introductory thanksgiving.[9] As Gnilka has noted, Paul does not follow this schema slavishly but adapts the form to suit his own purposes and fills his thanksgivings with rich theological content reflective of his deep convictions and passions.[10] One of the most notably absent features of Paul's many introductory thanksgivings in his letters is any mention of gratitude to God for his own health or welfare. His thanksgivings focus exclusively on the evidences of God's work among the believers he addresses or of the blessings of the wonders of the salvation that he has been called to proclaim.

In his excellent study of the theme of thanksgiving in Paul, Pao has expressed concern that the focus of scholars on the form of the introductory thanksgivings in the letters has caused them to overlook Paul's emphasis on thanksgiving beyond the introductory paragraphs and that extends into the whole of his letters.[11] This is an important observation and accords well with Paul's admonition later in Colossians, when he appeals to them to make thanksgiving a regular and characteristic part of their lives (Col 3:15). Pao finds Paul's introductory thanksgivings and his attitude about thanksgiving to God as profoundly influenced by the apostle's understanding of God's covenant with his people. He notes, "In biblical-theological terms, thanksgiving is a covenantal act."[12] By this he means that thanksgiving is a way of life that should characterize all of the people of God. As the psalmist declares, "He who sacrifices thank offerings honors me, and he prepares the way so that I may show him the salvation of God" (Ps 50:23). In summarizing the scriptural tradition, Pao contends that expressions of thankfulness to God are based on the recognition that he is the one and only God and lord of all. It is also based on God's covenantal relationship with his people that spans the past, present, and future. Thankfulness recognizes God's redemptive work in the past, the powerful activity of God in the present, and the anticipation of his future salvation when the covenantal promises will finally be fulfilled.

Some who contend that Paul follows Greco-Roman formal rhetoric identify this passage as an *exordium*.[13] The function of this device is to incline the readers

---

8 Reed, "Are Paul's Thanksgivings 'Epistolary'?," 93–94.

9 So also Copenhaver, *Paul's Rhetoric in the Letter to the Colossians*, 93. Pao, 42, however, remains reticent to accept this as an an epistolary convention. He notes that "the few letters that do contain a thanksgiving section point to actual circumstances where the authors need to acknowledge certain gifts and favors."

10 Gnilka, 30.

11 Pao, *Thanksgiving*, 18–19.

12 Pao, *Thanksgiving*, 53.

13 So Lincoln, 589–90; Witherington, 118–19. So also Copenhaver, *Paul's Rhetoric in the Letter to the Colossians*, 92, but he sees the *exordium* extending to 2:5.

to receive the later exhortations of the letter in a more positive manner. Lincoln sees Paul combining the epistolary form of thanksgiving with this rhetorical purpose.[14] Witherington, however, says, "If we ask whether this section of Colossians is more influenced by epistolary or rhetorical conventions, the answer must be rhetorical."[15] Although it is doubtful that Paul is following the school rhetoric of his day (see the *Introduction*, sec. 9), describing this passage strictly as an *exordium* only superficially reflects the function and content of the text. While the passage may partly function to make the readers more conducive to receiving Paul's later admonitions and instruction, this is only a secondary intent. The primary purpose of the passage is to give public recognition and praise to God for his powerful redemptive work among the believers of Colossae, for his continued work of inspiring and empowering them to show love for one another, and for the gospel itself, which stands as the foundation of all that God is doing in Colossae and throughout the world. As Pao has noted, thanksgiving to God for his powerful redemptive work is the proper covenantal response to him. Paul is thus offering a sacrifice of praise to God.

There is no compelling evidence for literary dependence on Philemon or any other book in the composition of this passage. Frank, for instance, contends that the author of Colossians used Philemon as his primary literary exemplar in writing this introductory thanksgiving because of the lexical and syntactical points of correspondence.[16] But this could be easily explained on the assumption of a common author writing to some of the same recipients at approximately the same time.

### *Structure*

The verb εὐχαριστοῦμεν, "we give thanks," governs the entire section stretching from 1:3 to 1:8. It is modified by two dependent adverbial clauses, the first of which gives the occasion for the thanksgiving (προσευχόμενοι, "as we pray") and the second (ἀκούσαντες, "because we heard") provides the basis for their thanks. Recognition of the faith and love of the Colossian Christians explains their gratitude, whereas hope, the third member of Paul's common triad, is not an additional reason for his thanks but rather explains how these believers are able to demonstrate love to one another. Hope is part of a causal expression (διά, "because of" + the accusative) that modifies the immediately preceding τὴν ἀγάπην ἣν ἔχετε, "the love that you have." Paul then makes it clear that the Colossian believers embraced this heavenly hope when they received the gospel. The progression of thought can be visually represented as follows:

---

14 Lincoln, 589.

15 Witherington, 118.

16 Frank, *Kolosserbrief im Context*, 44–50; Standhartinger, *Entstehungsgeschichte*, 81–85.

Thanksgiving: εὐχαριστοῦμεν τῷ θεῷ (1:3a)
  Occasion: προσευχόμενοι (1:3b)
  Basis: ἀκούσαντες . . . τὴν ἀγάπην ἣν ἔχετε (1:4)
    Reason for Their Love: διὰ τὴν ἐλπίδα τὴν ἀποκειμένην (1:5a)
      The Source of The Hope: ἣν προηκούσατε ἐν τῷ λόγῳ (1:5b)
Thanksgiving: We give thanks to God (1:3a)
  Occasion: as we pray (1:3b)
  Basis: because we heard of . . . the love that you have (1:4)
    Reason for Their Love: because of the hope stored up (1:5a)
      The Source of The Hope: that you heard about earlier (1:5b)

The second part of the introductory thanksgiving (1:5b–8) is a descriptive expansion on "the gospel." Gnilka correctly refers to it as a short excursus.[17] Paul first calls the gospel "the word of truth" (1:5b), which is followed by a simple genitive of apposition (τοῦ εὐαγγελίου, "the gospel") to clarify that he is, in fact, referring to the gospel. This is followed by a second appositional genitive (τοῦ παρόντος, "which came to you [and is present in you]"), in which he characterizes the gospel as having come to the Colossians and now being present with them (1:6a). In a third and final descriptive clause, Paul uses two adjectival participles (in the neuter case in agreement with τὸ εὐαγγέλιον, "the gospel") to declare that the gospel continues to bear fruit and increase (1:6c). These final two clauses are both, in turn, modified by comparative clauses introduced by the adverb καθώς, "just as." They explain the impact of the gospel first "in the entire world" (1:6b) and then "in you" (1:6d). The relationships can be clarified in a simplified diagram of the flow of thought in which the subordinate ideas are indented:

προηκούσατε (1:5b)
  ἐν τῷ λόγῳ τῆς ἀληθείας (1:5b)
    τοῦ εὐαγγελίου (1:5c)
    τοῦ παρόντος εἰς ὑμᾶς, (1:6a)
        καθὼς καὶ ἐν παντὶ τῷ κόσμῳ ἐστὶν, (1:6b)
    καρποφορούμενον καὶ αὐχανόμενον (1:6c)
        καθὼς καὶ ἐν ὑμῖν, (1:6d)

You heard about it earlier (1:5b)
  in the word of truth (1:5b)
    the gospel (1:5c)
    which came to you (and is present in you), (1:6a)
        just as it is also in the entire world (1:6b)
    bearing fruit and growing (1:6c)
        just as it is also in you. (1:6d)

17 Gnilka, 30.

This explanation results in four parallel expressions all speaking about the gospel. The two καθώς, "just as," clauses each modify the third and fourth statements about the gospel respectively and are parallel with each other—the first speaking about its presence in the world and the second describing its impact among the Colossians.[18] The passage concludes with a reminder of how they came to know the gospel through the ministry of Epaphras (1:7–8). The final καθώς, "just as," clause (1:7a) thus differs in usage from the previous two by here functioning as an expression of manner, "how."

Arguments for a macro-chiastic structure for the passage have not proved convincing. Dibelius and Greeven, for instance, suggested an A B C D D′ C′ B′ A′ structure for 1:3–9, with the center point of the chiasm the two καθώς, "just as," clauses: καθὼς καὶ ἐν παντὶ τῷ κόσμῳ, "just as it also is in the entire world" (= D, 1:6b) and καθὼς καὶ ἐν ὑμῖν, "just as it is in you" (= D′, 1:6d).[19] The difficulty with this proposal is that it does not take into account the intervening, καρποφορούμενον καὶ αὐξανόμενον, "bearing fruit and growing" (1:6c). It also results in some corresponding members of the chiasm of very unequal length, such as C and C′, which are thirteen words (ἣν προηκούσατε . . . εἰς ὑμᾶς, "that you heard about earlier . . . to you"; 1:5b–6a) and twenty-eight words (ἀφ' ἧς ἡμέρας ἠκούσατε . . . διάκονος τοῦ Χριστοῦ, "from the day you heard . . . servant of Christ"; 1:6e–7b) respectively. The most significant problem, however, is the identification of 1:9 (the beginning of the intercessory prayer report) as the corresponding member (A′) to 1:3a (A: εὐχαριστοῦμεν . . . περὶ ὑμᾶς, "we give thanks . . . for you"). Verse 9 begins a new section of the letter and does not provide the end bracket to 1:3–8.

There is an instance of *inclusio* that marks this passage off as a distinct literary unit. The passage begins and ends on a note of love. At the outset of the passage, Paul says that the reports of their love for one another serve as the basis for his thanksgiving (1:3–4). At the conclusion of the passage, he once again refers to the reports of their love that he had received from Epaphras (1:8).

## *Setting*

Under the assumption of Pauline authorship, two remarks can be made about the setting. The passage fits well with this assumption as a report to the Colossians about how Paul and Timothy regularly meet to pray for these believers and include in their times of prayer expressions of thanksgiving to God.

Although this letter is written specifically to address the challenge of the competing teaching, not all of the letter directly addresses this. This portion is not part of Paul's polemic against "the philosophy," but it is surely not absent from his mind as he writes this. Some of his theological emphases are particularly appropriate to the situation, most notably, (1) the presentation of hope as

---

18 This is also the view of Lohse, 19–20; Peake, 497.

19 Dibelius and Greeven, 5.

reserved in heaven, and (2) the excursus on the truth of the gospel, and (3) the reliability of Epaphras as their teacher.

## *Comment*

**3** Εὐχαριστοῦμεν τῷ θεῷ πατρὶ τοῦ κυρίου ἡμῶν Ἰησοῦ Χριστοῦ πάντοτε περὶ ὑμῶν προσευχόμενοι, "we give thanks to God the Father of our Lord Jesus Christ always for you as we pray." Paul and Timothy begin the body of his letter with an expression of thanksgiving and gratitude to God for the Colossian believers, especially for the evidence of true spiritual vitality in their lives. With the exception of Galatians (and the Pastorals), Paul begins all his letters with a thanksgiving. Since he names Timothy as his coauthor in 1:1, it is natural for him to use the first-person plural of the verb here. It is possible that the "we" extends even further to additional members of his ministry team that send their greetings in this letter, such as Aristarchus, Mark, Jesus Justus, Epaphras, and Luke, as well as Tychicus and Onesimus (4:7–14). When these men met with Paul either as individuals or as a group, it is quite conceivable to think of them joining Paul in praying and giving thanks for the Colossian Christians. This would be consistent with their desire to greet the Colossian church, and it fits well with Paul's claim that Epaphras was laboring for them in prayer (4:12).

The present tense of the verb should be seen in its imperfective aspect, which is confirmed by the adverb πάντοτε, "always," at the end of the line.[20] Despite the adverb's closer proximity to προσευχόμενοι, "praying," it should be understood as modifying the main verb, εὐχαριστοῦμεν, "we give thanks."[21] The combination of these two terms in the introductory thanksgiving is typical for Paul (e.g., 1 Cor 1:4; 1 Thess 1:2; 2 Thess 1:3; Phlm 4). The difference is small, however, since "praying" occurs in conjunction with the thanksgiving. The incessant praying and thanksgiving should not be overinterpreted to mean nonstop praying around the clock or underinterpreted to mean an attitude or disposition of thankfulness. Rather, it implies frequent and regular times of prayer that likely went beyond the traditional Jewish pattern of praying three times a day.

Using this term (εὐχαριστοῦμεν, "we give thanks") to render thanksgiving to a deity was not unknown in western Asia Minor. An inscription from Ephesus memorializes the public thanksgiving that four civic leaders wanted to extend to Hestia Boulaia, "the Incorruptible Fire," Demeter, Kore, the Clarian Apollo, and "and all the gods" (εὐχαριστοῦμεν Ἑστίᾳ Βουλαίᾳ . . . καὶ πᾶσιν τοῖς θεοῖς, "we give thanks to Hestia Boulaia . . . and to all the gods") because they completed the entire year prosperously (*IEph* 1072.10–14). In another inscription from nearby Stratonikeia, private individuals give public thanksgiving to "the angelic divinity" for some sort of deliverance (θείῳ Ἀγγελικῷ εὐχαριστοῦμεν ὑπὲρ

---

20 So also Campbell, 3.

21 Contra Sumney, 33.

σωτηρίας, "we give thanks to the angelic divinity for deliverance" [*IStratonikeia* 1119]). In contrast to these and many other expressions of thanksgiving to local gods and goddesses, Paul and his team give thanks to the one true God. Their heart of thanksgiving is not for some personal benefit they have received but for God's presence and work among the Colossian believers. Their personal comfort and gain are secondary (and perhaps even irrelevant) in comparison to seeing God's purposes fulfilled in the community of believers.

By characterizing God as "the Father of our Lord Jesus Christ," Paul affirms the close filial relationship between Jesus of Nazareth, the Messiah of Israel, and the Father. Although this letter has a strong and overt emphasis on the person of Christ, this designation indicates that a strong distinction between the Father and the Son should not be made. The absence of the connective καί, "and," before "Father" (see *Notes*, note a., on the text-critical issue) ends up stressing God's role as Father in relationship to the Lord Jesus Christ. Here he is not both God *and* Father of the Lord Jesus (as Paul usually expresses it), but simply the Father of Jesus. The absence of the article before "Father" certainly conveys no indefiniteness; the article may be left out to stress the quality rather than the particularity of the Father in this instance.[22]

One of the central themes of this letter that is signaled here at the outset is the role of Jesus Christ as "Lord" (κύριος). The term itself appears thirteen times in the letter with reference to Jesus, but his function as Lord of creation and the Lord of redemption is beautifully extolled in the Christ-hymn of 1:15–20.

The present participle προσευχόμενοι, "praying," is grammatically dependent on εὐχαριστοῦμεν, "we give thanks," and should be interpreted as having a temporal force. Thus Paul is saying that he and his companions give thanks to God "as we pray" or "when we pray." In other words, the times of prayer he and his colleagues have for the Colossians are not only marked by requests that they make to God on behalf of these believers, but are constantly characterized by gratitude to God for his work among them.

**4** ἀκούσαντες τὴν πίστιν ὑμῶν ἐν Χριστῷ Ἰησοῦ, "hearing about your faith in Christ Jesus." Paul now gives the reason he can express such gratitude to God for the Colossians. With most versions and commentators, it is best to take this adverbial participle as causal, "because of your faith . . . and love." The aorist tense could imply that Paul and his colleagues had recently heard a report (see the use of the aorist participle of ἀκούω, "hear," in Matt 14:13), but the tense alone would be insufficient reason to necessarily limit it to one report. Paul expresses the very same reasons for giving thanks to God when he writes to Philemon (Phlm 5).

Faith, hope, and love are three marks of authentic Christianity that Paul consistently looks for in evaluating the spiritual health and vitality of his communities. He sees the tangible display of these three as evidence that the Thessalonian believers have been chosen by God (1 Thess 1:3–4). To the Corinthians, he extols

22 See Porter, *Idioms*, 105.

these virtues as having paramount importance (1 Cor 13:13). Thus he calls on believers to appropriate them and practice them (1 Thess 5:8).

When Paul mentions this trio (or just the duo of faith and love), he invariably mentions faith (πίστις) first. Faith is foundational because belief in Christ is the response to the proclamation of the gospel that brings one into union with the resurrected Christ (Rom 3:22–26; 10:14; Gal 3:5; Eph 1:13). Faith is also the daily response to Christ that maintains this relationship and results in Christ's provisions and resources to his people (2 Cor 5:7; Gal 2:20).[23] Paul's mention of faith here should not be taken as a reference to their "faithfulness."[24] Neither should it be taken solely in terms of the content of belief—that is, as "the faith" as in 1:23 and 2:7.[25] In the Pauline correspondence, whenever "faith" occurs in conjunction with "love" and/or "hope," it is always understood in the active sense of "trusting in" or "believing in." Elsewhere in Colossians, Paul has shown a preference for using πίστος to express "faithfulness" or "reliability" (1:2, 7; 4:7, 9). Dunn has observed that this is the only time in the accepted Pauline writings that πίστις ἐν, "faith in," is used with reference to Christ.[26] Normally, he uses the noun followed by the genitive as the object—that is, πίστις Χριστοῦ or its equivalent (Rom 3:22, 26; Gal 2:16, 20; 3:22; Phil 3:9; although these texts are extensively debated, with some thinking that the expression should be understood as "the faith/faithfulness of Christ"[27]). Even when he uses the verb πιστεύω, "believe," Paul tends to use the preposition εἰς, "in," or ἐπί, "in," to mark the object of belief. This has led many interpreters to interpret ἐν Χριστῷ Ἰησοῦ, "in Christ Jesus," here not as the object of belief but as the sphere of believing. Thus Lohse comments that it "does not refer to the content, but rather the realm in which 'faith' lives."[28] Nevertheless, πίστις ἐν, "faith in," is used in the later Pauline letters for faith in Christ as the object of belief (Eph 1:15; 1 Tim 3:13; 2 Tim 3:15). Moo is correct, however, in minimizing a strong distinction in meaning when the simple dative, ἐν, "in," ἐπί, "in," or εἰς, "in," follows the verb πιστεύω, "believe," to indicate the object of belief in Paul. He notes that "these constructions are probably roughly equivalent to πίστις ἐν Χριστῷ Ἰησοῦ here."[29]

καὶ τὴν ἀγάπην ἣν ἔχετε εἰς πάντας τοὺς ἁγίους, "and the love that you have

---

23 On faith in the major Pauline letters, see Hagen Pifer, *Faith as Participation*. She emphasizes that faith is knowledge of Christ's act of redemption and is "self-involving in the Christ-mediated process of salvation" (217). Because faith is a dynamic phenomenon, it "has the potential to grow or wane" (218). This potential is no doubt why Paul was looking for evidence of faith and can give thanks to God for it when he hears about it in the lives of Christians.

24 Contra Barth and Blanke, 152.

25 Contra Gnilka, 32.

26 Dunn, 57.

27 See now the discussion in Bird and Sprinkle, *Faith*. Hagen Pifer, *Faith as Participation*, 222, warns that the subjective-genitive interpretation can obfuscate the human self-involvement in the work of Christ. She notes that "faith reflects the importance of placing oneself in a posture of humility, dependence, and self-involvement in the Christ-event."

28 Lohse, 16; so also Sumney, 34.

29 Moo, 84n13.

for all the saints." Love as expressed through concrete acts in the life of the community is the additional reason Paul has for his regular exclamations of gratitude to God for the Colossians. Paul had undoubtedly heard numerous stories about various members of the church there and how they demonstrated love in a way that went beyond typical neighborly kindness among people living in the Roman world. The ultimate example of love for Paul is what God himself showed in sacrificing his own Son as an atoning sacrifice for sin (Rom 5:8). All who put their faith in Christ, receive forgiveness for sin, and are now indwelt by the Holy Spirit have the love of God dynamically transfused into their hearts by the Spirit (Rom 5:5). This is why Paul looks for concrete acts of sacrificial love as a sign of genuine conversion and true life in the Spirit. Since Jesus presented loving one's enemies as a duty for his disciples (see Matt 5:44; Luke 6:35), it is quite possible that Paul may have heard of specific instances of this kind of love being lived out among the Colossians. It also bears remembering that in John's Gospel, love is the hallmark sign of genuine Christianity: "By this everyone will know that you are my disciples, if you have love for one another" (John 13:35 NRSV).

**5** διὰ τὴν ἐλπίδα τὴν ἀποκειμένην ὑμῖν ἐν τοῖς οὐρανοῖς, "because of the hope stored up for you in heaven." Rather than coordinating faith, love, and hope, Paul makes hope the basis for love. This explanation is disputed, however. Some interpreters have argued that the prepositional phrase, διὰ τὴν ἐλπίδα, "because of the hope," goes all the way back to the main verb of the section, εὐχαριστοῦμεν, "we give thanks," and thus provides an additional reason for the thanksgiving.[30] This is too great a distance (twenty-eight words), however, and fails to explain why Paul would not coordinate it with faith and love under the causal participle, ἀκούσαντες, "because we heard." Furthermore, it is quite without precedent in Paul's writings to follow the verb εὐχαριστέω with διά, "because of," to express the basis for thanksgiving. The most common interpretation has been to see διὰ τὴν ἐλπίδα, "because of the hope," as providing the basis for *both* faith and love in 1:4.[31] Thus Moo says that "their present experience of faith and love rests on the solid foundation of what God has committed to do for them in the future."[32] Although this interpretation is plausible, it does not offer the best sense of the syntax and meaning of the text.

The most convincing explanation is to interpret the prepositional phrase, διὰ τὴν ἐλπίδα, "because of the hope," as connected to the verb (ἔχετε, "you have") of the immediately preceding clause and thereby functioning to provide one of the reasons for the love that members of the Colossian community have demonstrated to each other.[33] This is the most natural explanation of the syntax

30 Eadie, 9; Abbott, 195–96; Bengel, 157.

31 E.g., Dunn, 58; Wolter, 52; Lohse, 17.

32 Moo, 85.

33 Peake, 496; Meyer, 210; Melanchthon, 33–34; Calvin, 301–2; contra Bornkamm, "Hoffnung," 206; Hübner, 45.

since ἔχετε is the nearest antecedent. It is awkward and less likely gramatically to understand the force of the ἔχετε, "you have," clause as extending back to cover both objects of ἀκούσαντες, "because we heard [of your]" love and faith. There is also precedent in Paul and in other literature for a prepositional phrase introduced by διά, "because of," to give the ground or reason for an action expressed by the verb ἔχω, "have" (see, e.g., 1 Cor 11:10: "a woman ought to have [ἔχειν] a symbol of authority on her head, because of the angels [διὰ τοὺς ἀγγέλους]"; see also Jas 4:2; cf. Isa 3:24 LXX; Wis 8:10, 13).

The meaning would then be that the love the Colossians show to one another is somehow motivated or inspired by the hope that is stored for them in heaven. This, of course, does not mean that they are stimulated to love one another because of the thought of rewards that they are amassing in heaven.[34] Calvin commented that "meditation on the heavenly life ravishes our affections to the worship of God and to exercises of love."[35] Melanchthon rightly observes that their awareness of the profound blessings of the heavenly hope "stir[s] them up and set[s] them on fire, so that they long to please God in their turn, and to show all the gratitude they can."[36] Thus a knowledge of hope incites enormous gratitude in believers that, in turn, motivates them to show love to one another as Christ has commanded them and modeled for them.

Paul's use of the term "hope" (ἐλπίς) is different here than his typical pattern of usage in his other letters. Here the emphasis is on the content of what is hoped for rather than the action of hoping. Thus Paul can use the metaphor of it being "stored away" or "reserved" (ἀποκειμένην) in heaven. The precise meaning of "hope" here has been extensively debated. It has long been understood to be the eager anticipation of the promised final deliverance that believers will experience at the end of time when they will escape the wrath of God and enjoy eternity together with God because of the work of Christ on the cross. This view was challenged, however, by G. Bornkamm in a very influential essay he published in 1961 titled, "Die Hoffnung im Kolosserbrief." In the essay, Bornkamm argued that "hope" in Colossians was totally devoid of eschatological expectation. The Jewish linear understanding of time, involving this age and the age to come, had given way to a vertical, spatial perspective of above and below. The author of Colossians thus stressed the presence of salvation to the complete exclusion of a future hope. Bornkamm acknowledged that in late Jewish texts a spatial understanding of heaven functioned alongside of the temporal perspective.[37] Nevertheless, he contended that the author of Colossians shifted entirely away from a temporal eschatological perspective to a spatial perspective. The changed perspective was influenced substantially by Hellenistic

34 Melanchthon, 33–34, argues strenuously to make this clear.

35 Calvin, 302.

36 Melanchthon, 34.

37 Bornkamm, "Hoffnung," 59–60.

and gnostic categories of thought, in which αἰῶνες were seen as personal powers, and "above" and "below" were two spheres of power and influence. He saw this shift also reflected in the writings of Ignatius where, he contended, the apocalyptic tradition no longer plays a role.

Bornkamm's perspective had a profound impact on scholarship, especially in the German-speaking world. His case was taken up and argued by E. Grässer and by A. Lindemann, who expanded the argument to include Ephesians.[38] Lindemann notes, "With this shift, a growing tendency begins, first of all with Colossians and even more clearly in Ephesians, for one to speak no more of the temporal 'ahead'-situated future, but of an 'above'-situated beyond."[39] This view of "hope" in Col 1:5 (as well as in 1:23, 27) depends on a reinterpretation of all the statements in Colossians that have been traditionally understood as pointing to a futurist eschatology. This is highly problematic, as will be brought out in the relevant portions of this commentary as each passage is discussed. The future hope in Colossians has not completely given way to spatial categories.[40] While the author does use the categories of "above" and "below" and emphasizes a realized eschatology, the future hope has been preserved. The expectation of a future return of Christ is, in fact, declared in 3:4 as well as in 1:22–23, 28. In addition to this, the anticipation of future judgment is brought out in 3:6, 24. This teaching would constitute part of the objective content of "the hope" associated with the gospel.

Nevertheless, the way Paul uses the term "hope" for the content of what believers hope for is unique in comparison to his other letters. That content is certainly assumed when he speaks elsewhere of "hope," but his use of the word is more focused on the response of believers to that content. One passage in the accepted Paulines, however, closely approximates his usage here. When he encourages the Thessalonians to put on as a helmet "the hope of salvation [ἐλπίδα σωτηρίας]" (1 Thess 5:8), it is best to interpret the genitive as one of apposition, thus giving the sense, "hope, which is salvation." He then explains that this salvation consists of the avoidance of God's end-time wrath, obtaining complete deliverance, and spending eternity with the Lord who loved them so much that he died for them (1 Thess 5:9–10). For the Thessalonians, "putting on hope" is tantamount to growing in their knowledge of all that "salvation" entails. It was this deficit in their knowledge of salvation that, in large measure, prompted Paul to write this letter. Ultimately, their awareness of the content of their salvation—that is, their "hope," will give them comfort (1 Thess 5:11). Thus one cannot separate the content of hope too far from the act of hoping.

Others have also pointed out that Paul earlier used spatial categories with

38 Grässer, "Kol 3,1–4," 139–68; Lindemann, *Aufhebung der Zeit*, esp. 193–96.

39 Lindemann, *Aufhebung der Zeit*, 18.

40 For a full defense of seeing future eschatology in Colossians, see Still, "Eschatology in Colossians," 125–38.

reference to the concept of hope. Hübner observed that Paul spoke this way when he wrote to the Philippians: "but our citizenship is in heaven, and it is from there that we are expecting a savior, the Lord Jesus Christ" (Phil 3:20).[41] Paul thus speaks of an objective reality that exists "above" in heaven and will be fully realized at some point in the future, but still has present implications for the believers' sense of identity and confidence.

This comes very close to the way that Paul uses "hope" here. It exists in heaven as an objective reality that gives the Colossian believers identity, purpose, security, and motivation for the present. The term "stored up" (ἀποκειμένην), an attributive participial adjective, is probably best interpreted as indicating that this objective content is safe and secure—that is, there is no power on earth or in heaven that can take it away. The term was commonly used for stowing something away in a place where it was safe from thieves and sheltered from the weather. Josephus illustrates this usage well when he tells about Archelaus taking possession of the vestments of the high priest and having them stored away in a stone chamber (ἀποκειμένης ἐν οἴκῳ λίθοις οἰκοδομηθέντι; "stored away in a house built with stone") under the seal of the priests (Josephus, *Ant.* 18.93). The Pastoral Epistles speak of a crown of righteousness that the Lord has stored away to give to all those who have longed for his appearance (2 Tim 4:8). The concept of future salvation stored away in heaven as a treasure is present in Jewish apocalyptic, as Bornkamm had conceded.[42] Referring to this hope, 4 Ezra 7.14 says, "Therefore unless the living pass through the difficult and vain experiences, they can never receive those things that have been reserved for them." This idea is also taken up by 1 Peter, who, like the author of Colossians, combines the spatial and temporal when he speaks of an inheritance "kept in heaven for you" and then subsequently describes it as "the salvation that is ready to be revealed in the last time" (1 Pet 1:4–5).

The heavenly location (ἐν τοῖς οὐρανοῖς) of this treasure places it where Christ presently is, at the right hand of God (see Col 3:1–4 and 4:1). The thought here corresponds to Paul's assurance to the Corinthians that they have an eternal dwelling awaiting them in heaven: "we have a building from God, a house not made with hands, eternal in the heavens" (2 Cor 5:1).

This unique comment about hope in Colossians is well-suited to a readership that would have entertained concerns about astral fate. Because of Christ's supremacy over all the powers in heaven (1:16; 2:10) and because he has defeated all the hostile powers on the cross (2:15), their future is firm and secure. Furthermore, this hope motivates and impels them to love one another within the community of believers. The certainty of their future, along with their gratitude to Christ for his redemptive work, provides them with a strong impetus to love.

41 See Hübner, 45; Sumney, 35.

42 Bornkamm, "Hoffnung," 60.

ἣν προηκούσατε ἐν τῷ λόγῳ τῆς ἀληθείας τοῦ εὐαγγελίου, "that you heard about earlier in the word of truth, the gospel." The hope of which Paul speaks was not something new to the Colossians. They learned about it as part of their instruction in the gospel as delivered to them by Epaphras. The compound verb that Paul uses (προακούω, "hear about earlier") only appears here in the NT or LXX, but the meaning corresponds with its component parts. Rather than intensifying the verb, the preposition (πρό, "before") serves as a temporal indicator and signals to the readers that they heard about the hope earlier than their reading of this letter.[43] Lightfoot overinterprets the preposition when he says that Paul uses it to contrast the Colossians' initial hearing of the gospel with the gospel that they are now hearing from the opponents.[44]

Paul describes the gospel as "the word of truth," or as it is perhaps better understood here, "the discourse about the truth," since it is important for the contemporary reader not to think of an individual word. This precise description of the gospel (ὁ λόγος τῆς ἀληθείας, "the word of truth") only elsewhere appears in Eph 1:13, 2 Tim 2:15, and in 2 Cor 6:7 (without the articles). Elsewhere, Paul can simply refer to it as "the truth" (Gal 5:7) or modify the truth with a genitive of apposition, "the truth, which is the gospel" (ἡ ἀληθεία τοῦ εὐαγγελίου [Gal 2:5]). In Col 1:5, Paul is anticipating his subsequent disclosure that the teaching of his opponents is "empty deceit" (2:8), whereas his own teaching about Christ is truth and worthy of their confidence.

The genitive case of "the gospel" (τοῦ εὐαγγελίου) should be taken as a genitive of apposition: "the word of truth, that is, the gospel." This is the term that Paul shares with all of the leaders in the early Christian movement that sums up the redemptive work of the one living and true God in Jesus Christ. According to Paul, this message represents the power of God to bring salvation to people who trust in it (Rom 1:16–17).

**6** τοῦ παρόντος εἰς ὑμᾶς, "which came to you (and is present in you)." The mention of the gospel prompts Paul to expand on its significance through a brief excursus (1:6–8). The gospel that the Colossians received was not one of the indigenous local religions. It came to them in a chain of transmission that extended from Epaphras through the apostle Paul and back to Jerusalem. Paul does not choose the common word for "coming" (ἔρχομαι) here, but selects a term that also communicates the idea of being "present."[45] The verb (πάρειμι) was used frequently in Josephus, for instance, of someone or a group coming to a city (e.g., "they came to Haran" [παρῆν εἰς τὴν Χαρράν; Josephus, *Ant.* 1.285] or "they came to Caesarea" [παρῆσαν εἰς Καισάρειαν; *Ant.* 18.57]). But the term was also used to express the presence of someone at a location, such as in John's Gospel when Martha called to her sister Mary and exclaimed, "The teacher

43 So BDAG, s.v. προακούω.

44 See Lightfoot, 134.

45 See BDAG, s.v. πάρειμι.

is here" (ὁ διδάσκαλος πάρεστιν [John 11:28]). In his other letters, Paul only uses the verb in this sense (1 Cor 5:3 [2x]; 2 Cor 10:2, 11; 11:9; 13:2, 10; Gal 4:18, 20). It is likely here that Paul had both ideas in mind—that is, the gospel came to the Colossians and was now present with them. This would correspond with the two participles (καρποφορούμενον καὶ αὐξανόμενον, "bearing fruit and growing") later in the verse that refer to the gospel as producing growth within individuals and then to the gospel as spreading to others. Many commentators have appropriately cited Chrysostom's comments on this verse, which bring out both aspects: "he means, it did not come and go away, but that it remained, and was there."[46]

καθὼς καὶ ἐν παντὶ τῷ κόσμῳ ἐστὶν καρποφορούμενον καὶ αὐξανόμενον καθὼς καὶ ἐν ὑμῖν, "just as it is in the entire world, bearing fruit and growing, just as it is in you." Although the Christian movement began a few years earlier in Jerusalem, it had spread extensively throughout the world and was having a powerful and positive impact on people's lives. The syntax of this clause in relationship to those around it presents some difficulties and has led to a variety of interpretations reflected in the manuscript tradition, critical editions of the Greek text, and the versions (see *Notes* [e.]). The ambiguity revolves around an interconnected set of syntactical issues—namely, determining the referent of the first καθώς, "just as," clause, identifying the function of ἔστιν, "is," interpreting the usage of the two participles, and explaining the potential redundancy of the second καθώς, "just as," clause. The most compelling explanation sees the first καθώς, "just as," clause in a dependent relationship to παρόντος, "came . . . and is present" ("it came and is present [in you] just as it is in the entire world"), the ἐστίν, "is," going with the prepositional phrase (ἐν παντὶ τῷ κόσμῳ, "in the entire world"), the two participles in an appositional and thus explanatory relationship to τοῦ εὐαγγελίου, "the gospel" ("the gospel . . . [which is] bearing fruit and increasing"), and the second καθώς clause modifying the two participles ("bearing fruit and increasing as it is in you"; see the graphical layout and additional discussion in the *Form/Structure/Setting*).

The Majority text sought to solve some of the grammatical ambiguity by inserting a καί, "and," in front of the ἐστίν, "is" (see *Notes* [e.]), thus turning the two participles into periphrastic constructions ("is bearing fruit and increasing") and thereby making an additional statement about the gospel. The sense of this emendation is correct, but the grammatical adjustment was unnecessary since the same idea is achieved through understanding them as adjectival participles in apposition to "the gospel."

Many of the versions interpret the two καθώς, "just as," clauses as correlative: "*just as* the gospel is bearing fruit in the entire world, *so also* is it in you" (e.g., NRSV; NAB; NET).[47] From this perspective, the first καθώς, "just as,"

46 Chrysostom, *Homilies on Colossians* 1 (*NPNF*[1] 13:259).

47 On this view, see Wilson, 91–92.

clause does not modify the previous clause but starts a new sentence. The major problem with interpreting the clauses in this fashion is that Paul's normal way of expressing this construction is with the combination καθώς . . . οὕτως, "just as . . . so [also]" (2 Cor 1:5; 8:6; 10:7; 1 Thess 2:4), which is precisely the construction used later in Colossians (3:13). In fact, no example of the correlative use of καθώς . . . καθώς, "just as . . . just as," can be found in the NT.

In summary, there are two assertions here made about the gospel, and both are modified by comparative clauses: (1) the gospel came to you (and is present in you), *just as* it is in the entire world (1:6a–b), and (2) the gospel is bearing fruit and growing, *just as* it is in your lives.

In the first instance, Paul is affirming that the gospel has come all the way to the Anatolian territories of Caria and Phrygia, just as it has come to "all the world" (ἐν παντὶ τῷ κόσμῳ). This is no doubt hyperbole to speak of the amazing spread throughout a vast area in the thirty or so years since the beginning of the movement. Paul engages in the same kind of rhetoric in 1:23 where he claims that the gospel "has been proclaimed to every creature under heaven." By the early 60s, the word of God had spread throughout Judea, Nabatea, Syria, Ethiopia, Cilicia, Cyprus, Galatia, Asia, Macedonia, Achaia, and Italy. This represents only the regions for which we have a firm historical record in the NT itself. Through the ministry of the other apostles and Jewish pilgrims returning from Pentecost to their homes, it is likely that the gospel had reached into lower and upper Egypt, Parthia, Mesopotamia, north Africa, and probably elsewhere. Moo may be correct in reaffirming the views of earlier commentators that "the widespread experience of the gospel is testimony to its truthfulness over against the claims of the false teachers, who are propagating a local heresy."[48]

This reference to the gospel spreading throughout the whole world would undoubtedly have evoked comparisons with Roman imperial propaganda regarding the spread of the imperium under Octavian. The introductory paragraph to the *Res Gestae* lauds "the acts of the deified Augustus by which he placed the whole world under the sovereignty of the Roman people" (*Res Gestae*, introduction). The Sebasteion in nearby Aphrodisias provides inhabitants of the area inscriptional and visual evidence (through the statuary and reliefs) of the conquest and capture of people groups at the frontiers of the known world.[49] For Paul, it is "the kingdom of the beloved son" (Col 1:13) that is now advancing and has priority over the lives of people.

Here and Col 1:10 are the only places in the NT where the two verbs (καρποφορέω, "bear fruit," and αὐξάνω, "grow") are used together. Paul does use both terms elsewhere, but separately. The first term was commonly used for plants and trees that bear fruit. It is used by the Synoptics in the parable of the soils to describe what happens to the seed sowed in the good soil (Matt 13:23;

48 Moo, 89.

49 See Smith, "*Ethne* from the Sabesteion at Aphrodisias," 50–77.

Mark 4:20, 28; Luke 8:15). This usage illustrates well the transition to the metaphorical sense of fruitbearing as a response to the gospel. Paul only uses it in a metaphorical sense to speak of bad deeds produced by sinful passions (Rom 7:5) or the virtues and good deeds a Christian displays to honor God (Rom 7:4). Of course, Paul also speaks of a "fruit" (καρπός) produced by the Spirit in the lives of believers that represent the key Christian virtues (Gal 5:22–23). The middle voice of the participle here should be interpreted as intensive, with the stress placed on the gospel as the catalyst for the fruitbearing.

Paul combines "bearing fruit" with another agricultural metaphor, "increase" (αὐξάνω), that originally referred to the growth in size of a plant or tree. Luke uses it repeatedly to speak of the increase in the number of converts as the message of the gospel spread (Acts 6:7; 12:24; 19:20). Paul uses it in the same way to speak of people coming to faith through the work of ministers who "plant" and "water," but he is careful to attribute the "increase" to God (1 Cor 3:6–7).

These two neuter participles are in apposition to "the gospel" and provide a further description of its impact. It is doubtful that Paul is echoing the creation mandate of "be fruitful and multiply" given in Gen 1:28 and now applied in a transformed sense to the church to fulfill a worldwide mission.[50] The wording of the LXX is "increase, and multiply, and fill the earth, and subdue it" (NETS; αὐξάνεσθε καὶ πληθύνεσθε καὶ πληρώσατε τὴν γῆν καὶ κατακυριεύσατε αὐτῆς). The only term held in common is the term "increase." Fruitbearing in Col 1:6 has to do with developing Christian virtue, an idea that is absent in the Genesis passage.[51] The combined effect of both participles suggests the idea of conversion (αὐξάνω, "grow") and Christian growth (καρποφορέω, "bear fruit")—an interpretation that is widely held among the commentators.[52] The powerful impact of the gospel should serve to encourage the Colossians to hold on tight to it in the form they originally received it and to resist the enticement coming from "the philosophy."

καθὼς καὶ ἐν ὑμῖν, ἀφ᾽ ἧς ἡμέρας ἠκούσατε, "just as it is in you—from the day you heard." With this second καθώς, "just as," clause, Paul reaffirms the evident work and power of the gospel in reaching the Colossians and producing in them a lifestyle consistent with its message and the call of the God they now serve. Paul locates the beginning of the work of the gospel at the time when they first heard it, presumably from the proclamation and teaching of Epaphras who brought it out to the Lycus Valley (1:7). This repeats his earlier statement that "you heard the word of truth" (1:5) and emphasizes the role of hearing the gospel, an idea that is important to Paul (Rom 10:4).

---

50 Contra Moo, 88.

51 In my view, it is too big of a stretch to reason that Paul was working with a typological framework in which he saw the numerical growth of the creation mandate as "a type for the new creation that had been inaugurated with Christ" and then to see "increase" and "multiply" now as reference to Christian growth in virtue as Beetham, *Echoes of Scripture*, 41–59, has argued.

52 E.g., Abbott, 198; Lightfoot, 135.

καὶ ἐπέγνωτε τὴν χάριν τοῦ θεοῦ ἐν ἀληθείᾳ, "and came to know the grace of God in truth." The Colossians not only heard the gospel but responded to it by embracing its message as the truth. "Hearing" and "knowing" is not a hendiadys[53] since it refers to two distinct steps in the process that leads to conversion. No significance should be attributed to the fact that Paul uses the compound form of the verb with the preposition ἐπί, "upon." There is no discernible difference in usage between the two. As Bultmann notes, the simple and compound forms are used interchangeably in the papyri.[54] The context here would suggest that the Colossians not only grasped the intellectual tenets of the gospel, but they put their trust in it as authentic and true revelation from the one God. Paul uses the simple form of the verb in conjunction with God's grace in addressing the Corinthians: "for you know [γινώσκετε] the grace of our Lord Jesus Christ" (2 Cor 8:9). The aorist tense of the two verbs simply report the event; the Colossians "heard" and "believed" with no comment on the duration or progress of the action.

As Lightfoot observes, "the grace of God" (ἡ χάρις τοῦ θεοῦ) is "Paul's synonym for the Gospel."[55] The content of the gospel message is one of grace. As Luke puts it, this is "the gospel of the grace of God" (Acts 20:24). (For a more complete discussion of "grace" in Paul's thought, see *Comment* on 1:2). This is an expression that Paul uses frequently and by it communicates the manifold blessings of the new covenant that are conveyed to people through the proclamation of the gospel. As noted earlier, however, the term also refers to the continuing manifestation of God's presence and power in their lives enabling them to live the Christian life and engage in mission. The gospel message itself that leads to faith in Christ is probably the emphasis here and as such correponds with his usage in Rom 5:15: "for if the many died through the one man's trespass, much more surely have the grace of God [ἡ χάρις τοῦ θεοῦ] and the free gift in the grace of the one man, Jesus Christ, abounded for the many" (NRSV).

"In truth" (ἐν ἀληθείᾳ) should be understood as modifying "the grace of God" and not as an adverbial expression that goes with the verb (e.g., "you truly came to know"). Thus it characterizes the message as one of truth in a way that is similar to 1:5: "the word of truth."[56] The NIV 1984 brings this out in the translation, "in all its truth," as does the NLT, "the truth about God's wonderful grace." This second reference to the gospel as truth is probably designed to reaffirm for the Colossians the importance of holding on tight to the teaching that they had already received and not succumbing to the opposing teaching that Paul will soon criticize in this letter.

**7 καθὼς ἐμάθετε ἀπὸ Ἐπαφρᾶ**, "for you learned it from Epaphras." This clause clarifies that it was not Paul himself who originally taught them the

53 As Barth and Blank, 159, assert.

54 R. Bultmann, "γινώσκω, κτλ.," *TDNT* 1:703.

55 Lightfoot, 136.

56 So also Wilson, 94.

gospel, but one of their own, Epaphras. This third καθώς, "for," clause differs from the other two in that it is not followed by a καί, "also" (see *Notes* [f.]), and it does not convey a comparison. It functions to introduce how the Colossians heard the gospel.[57] A good illustration of this usage of the term can be seen in Acts 15:14: "Simon has described to us how [καθώς] God at first showed his concern. . . ." Since the English term "how" would not offer a good English rendering, some versions simply leave it untranslated (e.g., NIV; NRSV; CSB). Translating it with "just as" (e.g., ESV; NASB) would imply a comparison and would thus be inappropriate.

Rather than saying that Epaphras "preached" (κηρύσσω) or "proclaimed" (καταγγέλλω) the gospel to them, Paul speaks from the vantage point of the Colossians and indicates that they "learned" (μανθάνω) the gospel. In the LXX, this verb commonly translates the Hebrew לָמַד (*lāmad*), "to learn" or "to be instructed in," from which the noun תַּלְמִיד (*talmid*) is derived. Jesus appropriated this language to describe the proper response to him that leads to a path of discipleship.[58] It is possible that Paul only used this term in the generic sense of "learn," but in a context such as this that begins with receiving the gospel and putting one's faith in Christ Jesus (1:4), it is entirely possible that Paul is echoing the use of μανθάνω, "learn," and the far more frequent μαθητής, "disciple" from the Jesus tradition as recorded in the Synoptic Gospels. If so, the term would imply that these Colossians had become devoted followers of the risen Lord Jesus Christ, that they had applied themselves to his teachings (much of which were likely available to them in oral form), and had learned the teaching of the apostles as mediated through Paul (via Epaphras). Jesus told his disciples, "Take my yoke upon you and learn [μάθετε] from me, for I am gentle and humble in heart" (Matt 11:29). Certainly Paul—and the rest of the apostles—understood their responsibility to pass on the teaching of Jesus as they evangelized and planted churches.

The name Epaphras (Ἐπαφρᾶς) is a shortened form of the full name, Epaphroditus (Ἐπαφρόδιτος).[59] "Epaphras" is widely attested in inscriptions from the regions of Caria, Lydia, Phrygia, and Ionia. Below are a few examples:

- One inscription from Lagina (near Statonikeia) lists Epaphras as the nomen of a man named Dionysius Epaphras Thrason who was a priest of Zeus Panamara. His wife also served as a priestess of the god. The last

57 See LSJ, s.v. καθώς 2; Lohse, 21–22; Peake, 498; Lightfoot, 136.

58 M. Silva, "μανθάνω," *NIDNTTE* 3:223–24. He notes, "Learning is no mere intellectual process by which one acquires teaching about Christ. It implies acceptance of Christ himself, rejection of the old existence, and the beginning of a new life of discipleship in him" (224).

59 See BDAG, s.v. Ἐπαφρᾶς, and Trainor, *Epaphras*, 7; although Horsley, *NewDocs* 4:22 (§5), observes that in his review of the occurrences of both names in texts from this era, he knows of no one person called by both names; thus he contends that those named "Epaphras" may have only gone by that name.

line of the inscription mentions a colleague who served as the steward of the mysteries at the shrine (*IStratonikeia* 676.1–10).

- An inscription found in Ephesus and dated to AD 54 mentions a certain Epaphras son of Tryphona who was listed among the fishermen and fish sellers who dedicated a customs house to Nero (*IEph* 20.A.a.47). The name Epaphras appears later in a fragmentary portion of the manuscript, presumably referring to another person of the same name (*IEph* 20.B.b.25).
- A funerary inscription from Ephesus gives Epaphras as a cognomen: Gaius Sornatius Epaphras (*SEG* 34.1149.1–2).
- An honorific inscription in Ephesus dated to AD 14 honors a certain Epaphras as priest of *Theos Augustus* (*IEph* 803.1–5).
- "Epaphras" occurs several times on inscriptions from Cibyra, about forty-five miles south of Colossae.[60]

Perhaps most significant is the fact that the name Epaphras is attested as current in the Lycus Valley. An inscription from the temple of Apollo dated to AD 129/30 records an embassy from Laodicea on the Lycus who came to consult the oracle of Apollo at Claros. Among them was one Marcus Antonius Epaphras, who led the hymn of praise to the god.[61] Cadwallader and Harrison report the discovery of a second- or third-century coin from Colossae that mentions a certain Epaphras, perhaps a benefactor of the city.[62]

The full name Epaphroditus is even more widely attested. At Rome it is the thirteenth most frequently attested Greek personal name.[63] It appears numerous times in inscriptions from Caria and occurs in a burial inscription in nearby Hierapolis: "the tomb of Marcus Neratius Epaphroditus" (τὸ μηεῖον Μάρκου Νε[ρα]τίο[υ Ἐπαφ[ροδίτου]).[64]

Epaphroditus means "lovely," "fascinating," or "charming" of persons.[65] It is a name that is associated with the Greek goddess Aphrodite (ἐπ' + Ἀφροδίτη).[66] It is possible that Epaphras's parents named him after the goddess to honor her or possibly even to dedicate their son to this goddess since the city of Aphrodisias lay just thirty miles west-southwest of Colossae in a valley on the opposite side of Mount Cadmus from Colossae. Epaphras's gentile roots are confirmed by the fact that he is not included in Paul's list of coworkers whom he says are "of the circumcision"—that is, fellow Jewish Christians (Col 4:10–11).[67] Paul makes

60 For references, see Huttner, *Early Christianity in the Lycus Valley*, 87.
61 Macridy, "Altertümer," 167.
62 Cadwallader and Harrison, "Perspectives on the Lycus Valley," 17.
63 *NewDocs* 4:21 (§5).
64 W. Judeich, "IV. Inschriften," in Humann et al., *Alt. v. Hierapolis*, 157 (no. 283).
65 See LSJ s.v. ἐπαφρόδιτος.
66 Huttner, *Early Christianity in the Lycus Valley*, 87.
67 So also Huttner, *Early Christianity in the Lycus Valley*, 88. But contra Trainor, *Epaphras*, 8, who concludes that "he was probably a Hellenized Israelite."

it clear that he is a native of Colossae (ὁ ἐξ ὑμῶν, "who is from you" [4:12]). Presumably Epaphras had traveled to Ephesus during Paul's ministry in that city, heard the gospel from Paul, and put his faith in Christ. He spent enough time listening to Paul's teaching, learning the Jesus tradition, and becoming well-versed in the Christian faith that he could return to his home city and fully proclaim and teach the gospel there and in the nearby cities of Laodicea and Hierapolis (see 4:13). Besides these two references in Colossians, he is also mentioned in Phlm 23, where Paul says that Epaphras extends his greetings to Philemon and the house church he hosts. It is doubtful that he is the same person as the Epaphroditus mentioned by Paul in his letter to the Philippians, who risked his life in the service of the gospel (Phil 2:25; 4:18).

τοῦ ἀγαπητοῦ συνδούλου ἡμῶν, "our beloved fellow slave." Paul elevates Epaphras to a position of honor in the eyes of the Colossians by according him the same title that he himself bears, "a slave of Jesus Christ" (see Rom 1:1; Gal 1:10; Titus 1:1). Elsewhere he only names Timothy (Phil 1:1) and Tychicus (Col 4:7, the only other time Paul uses σύνδουλος, "fellow slave") as fellow slaves. D. B. Martin has demonstrated that the title "slave" was not necessarily a dishonorable term among the lower classes. What mattered most was whom the slave was attached to. Thus by calling himself a "slave of Christ" (see, e.g., Rom 1:1), Paul was presenting himself as attached to an important person and thus as sharing in Christ's authority and honor.[68] Far more important than honorific, this was a title of total dedication, belonging, and dependence. Because the slave was owned, the will of the master was all important and it was the duty of the slave to carry it out.[69] Throughout the OT, many key leaders among the people of God are called a "slave" of Yahweh, such as Abraham (Gen 26:24), Job (Job 1:8; 2:3), Moses (Num 12:7–8; Josh 1:2, 7), and "the prophets" (Jer 7:25). Above all, David was repeatedly called God's slave (see the numerous places where David is called עַבְדִּי, "my servant"—an expression regularly translated δοῦλος μου, "my servant," in the LXX; e.g., 2 Sam 3:18; 7:5, 8; 1 Kgs 11:13, 32, 34, 36, 38; Ps 89:4, 21 [88:4, 21 LXX]).

Paul's affections for Epaphras exude in his description of him as "beloved" (ἀγαπητός). This was an expression that Paul used quite frequently in his writings to characterize his feelings generally toward believers in the Christian communities (Rom 12:19; 1 Cor 10:14; 15:58; 2 Cor 7:1; 12:19; Phil 2:12; 4:1; 1 Thess 2:8) and, on occasion, for specific members he singles out as people for whom he had a particular affection, such as Timothy (1 Cor 4:17; 2 Tim 1:2), Tychicus (Col 4:7; Eph 6:21), Onesimus (Col 4:9), Luke (4:14), Philemon (Phlm 1), Epenetus (Rom 16:5), Ampliatus (Rom 16:8), Stachys (Rom 16:9), and Persis (Rom 16:12). For Paul, this expression of tender feeling was not a trite statement or a rhetorical maneuver to achieve a certain outcome; it represented a genuine

68 Martin, *Slavery*, 132.

69 See also Dunn, *Romans*, 1:7.

emotion that bonded him with these people. He understood this kind of love as a gift of the Holy Spirit (Gal 5:22) who infuses it into his heart and into the hearts of all believers (Rom 5:5). The personal pronoun (ἡμῶν, "our") at the end of the line indicates that this was an affection that Timothy shared also toward Epaphras.

ὅς ἐστιν πιστὸς ὑπὲρ ὑμῶν διάκονος τοῦ Χριστοῦ, "he is a faithful servant of Christ for you." The relative clause introduces another description of Epaphras in Paul's commendation of him to the Colossians. As with "slave" (δοῦλος), "servant" (διάκονος) is also an appellation that Paul uses to characterize his own ministry (1:23, 25). Here Paul does not use διάκονος, "servant," in the technical sense of a particular office or position of leadership in the church (as he does in 1 Tim 3:8, 12 and possibly also in Phil 1:1). Rather, the meaning here retains its basic sense of rendering assistance to someone. Lying behind this is the conception that Paul advances in 2 Cor 3:6 that God has qualified all believers to serve as "ministers" (διάκονοι) of the new covenant. The nature of this service is qualified by Jesus's self-denying example of humble service (Mark 10:45; Matt 20:28; see also Luke 22:27). There is a slight but important distinction between a "slave" and a "servant," as K. Hess notes: "*doulos* stresses almost exclusively the Christian's complete subjection to the Lord; *diakonos* is concerned with his service for the church, his brothers and fellow-men, for the fellowship, whether this is done by serving at table, with the word, or in some other way."[70] The genitive τοῦ Χριστοῦ, "of Christ," should be interpreted as a possessive genitive, a servant belonging to Christ.

Paul commends Epaphras for being "faithful" or "reliable" (πιστός) in his ministry for the Colossians. No doubt Paul had heard reports from Tychicus regarding Epaphras's hard work, careful teaching, and regular prayer not only for the Colossians but also for the other house churches in the Lycus Valley. At the end of the letter, Paul speaks of the strenuous effort that Epaphras gives to praying for the Colossians (4:12). Because of Paul's praise of Epaphras at the outset of the letter, he is probably attempting to increase the readers' respect for him and assure them that what he teaches is in line with the Pauline gospel. This is important for the challenges he will face in helping the Colossian believers resist the enticements of the new teaching that threatens the health and stability of the church.

**8** ὁ καὶ δηλώσας ἡμῖν τὴν ὑμῶν ἀγάπην ἐν πνεύματι, "who also informed us of your love in the Spirit." In a third descriptive statement (although no longer a commendatory remark about Epaphras), Paul explains that it was Epaphras himself who had come and given him and Timothy a report about their status. The verb δηλόω, "inform," can be used for a simple report, but it may have the idea of revealing something that was previously unknown (thus it was used in

70 K. Hess, "Serve, Deacon, Worship," *NIDNTT* 3:548.

the LXX of Daniel for revealing the meaning of a dream; see, e.g., Dan 2:5, 6, 9, 11, 16, 23, 24). This is probably the meaning of the verb here.

As a prime indicator of their spiritual health, Paul looks for indications of genuine displays of love in the Christian community (see also 1 Thess 3:6). Epaphras's report was probably deeply encouraging to Paul and Timothy. Paul interpreted the stories he heard from Epaphras as examples of love inspired by and produced by the Holy Spirit. It is more appropriate to this context to see the preposition ἐν, "in," as having more of an instrumental sense rather than a dative of sphere ("in the realm of the Spirit"). The NLT gives this sense by rendering it, "the love for others that the Holy Spirit has given you." The recipients of that love Paul is referring to would refer primarily to the reciprocal love between believers in Colossae and in the Lycus Valley. The expression may very well acknowledge their love for Paul himself, but Paul is primarily concerned about seeing the evidence of their love for one another in the report from Epaphras.[71] This is how he assesses the health and vitality of his churches.

Schweizer has argued, however, that the reference here is not to the Holy Spirit and that "the point presumably is only that a spiritual love is to be distinguished from one that is purely worldly."[72] No other commentator has followed Schweizer in this view and with good reason. As Fee asserts, "The association of the Spirit with love is a particularly Pauline understanding of the Spirit's activity."[73] The use of the preposition ἐν, "in," with the dative is a Pauline construction (see Rom 14:17: χαρὰ ἐν πνεύματι ἁγίῳ, "joy in the Holy Spirit"). It is also consistent with Paul's emphasis on the Spirit inspiring love in the hearts of believers (Rom 5:5; 15:30; Gal 5:22). Finally, the overt christological emphasis in Colossians that Schweizer rightly recognizes does not necessarily preclude the possibility of references to the work of the Spirit.[74]

## *Explanation*

Paul and Timothy are truly exuberant over the unmistakable evidence of God's presence and powerful work among the Colossian believers. Paul thus begins his letter with a report of how he and Timothy regularly offer praise to God for the Colossians. An introductory thanksgiving is typical for Greek letters, but this introduction is distinctive in four ways: (1) it is a report of regular thanksgiving to God for them, (2) the thanksgiving is for the recipients and not about the welfare of the writers, (3) the thanksgiving itself is an expression of the writers' sense of appropriate response to the blessings of God that are consistent with

71 Contra Fee, *Empowering Presence*, 639.
72 Schweizer, 38; see also "Christus und Geist," 308–9.
73 Fee, *Empowering Presence*, 638–39.
74 See Fee, *Empowering Presence*, 636–57.

their covenant relationship to him, and (4) there is a lengthy excursus pointing to the truthfulness of and foundational importance of the gospel.

Their thanksgiving to God is principally for the clear and unmistakable evidence of spiritual life and vitality among the Colossians. Consistent with his earlier letters, Paul looks for signs of faith, hope, and love as the marks that they truly know God, are united with Christ, and are empowered by his Spirit. From the reports he has received, it is evident that all three of these indicators are present and thus become the motivation for him and Timothy to offer sacrifices of praise to God.

Paul's primary purpose in writing this letter is to warn the readers about the dangers of "the philosophy," but his direct polemic does not begin until 2:4. Nevertheless, the beginning of the letter lays important groundwork for the exhortations and warnings he will soon deliver. There are four ways that he does this in this passage.

First, Paul validates the authenticity of their conversion and the reality of their experience with God. He speaks of how they heard the gospel (1:5, 6), came to know the grace of God (1:7), put their faith in Christ (1:4), became true followers of Christ, learning the Christian traditions (1:7), and showed the key signs of authentic conversion, especially the manifestation of love for one another in the community (1:4, 8). By emphasizing the genuineness of their experience as believers, Paul implicitly invalidates the claims of the leaders of "the philosophy" who were judging them and disqualifying them (see 2:18).

Second, Paul's unique emphasis here on the security of their hope—expressed as "stored up for you in the heavens" (1:5)—appears to be tailored to reassuring them about a potential concern they would have because of the religious context in which they lived. Despite their past (perhaps continuing for some) fear of astral fate and the power of certain gods, goddesses, daimons, and *stoicheia* over that fate, they have no reason to fear. Their future is entirely secure with God in heaven. This is a spatial as well as temporal assurance. What God has planned, he will carry out. God will bring into subjection every power in heaven and on earth (1:20). They will receive their inheritance as God's children (1:12; 3:24).

Third, Paul's excursus on the gospel (1:5b–8) would reaffirm to them the absolute importance of the message that they heard and received from Epaphras. This is underlined in a number of ways: (a) Paul twice declares that it is a message of truth (1:5, 6). This contrasts sharply with the teaching of "the philosophy" that he will characterize as "empty deceit" (2:8). (b) It is the message about their hope (1:5), which, Paul has reminded them, has served as a powerful motivator to love each other in the house-church communities of faith. (c) What they received from Epaphras is the same message that is going out into all the world (1:6b). In saying this, Paul is making the enormous assumption that there is, in fact, a common gospel that is being proclaimed throughout the Mediterranean world and beyond. It encompasses the traditions that would be passed along orally, summarizing the heart of the message (1 Cor 15:1–3), and constitutes what the writer of Ephesians refers to as the "one faith" (Eph 4:5). (d) This gospel is "bearing fruit" in that it is resulting in many people entering a relationship and union with Jesus Christ. It is also working powerfully to create communities of believers and uniting them to one another in bonds of love. (e) Finally, it is a message about the grace of God (1:6). It has strong lines of continuity with God's covenantal faithfulness to his people in the past and now, through Christ, into the present. This message and this message alone is what God is using to bring people into an authentic relationship with him in Colossae and throughout the world. Paul's substantial and significant teaching about the gospel here effectively cuts the ground out from under the advocates of "the philosophy," who endeavor to assert that the Colossian believers have not had adequate spiritual experience and for whom the message of the gospel is inadequate.

Finally, Paul strongly asserts the credibility and trustworthiness of Epaphras (1:7–8). In case anyone doubted him or his reliability in the message that he initially passed on to them, Paul strongly supports Epaphras by terming him a "fellow slave" and a "servant" of Christ who is reliable and faithful. This is additionally important in the event that Epaphras travels back to the Lycus Valley and resumes his ministry there, as appears likely. They should trust Epaphras more than the ringleaders of "the philosophy."

As a concluding theological reflection on the passage, one should observe the way Paul weaves together the work of the Father, Christ, and the Spirit in this section. God is presented as the one who receives the offering of thanksgiving (1:3), which is consistent with the covenantal responses of the people of God in the OT. He is also represented as the Father of the Lord Jesus Christ (1:3) and the source of grace (1:6). Christ is represented as the Son of God (1:3; implicit in his relationship to the Father), the Lord (1:3), the object of believers' faith (1:4), and one who commissions servants to help him carry out his purposes (1:7). And, finally, the Spirit is described as an empowering presence with believers who inspires and empowers them to love one another in the household of faith (1:8).

# Prayer (1:9–14)

## *Bibliography*

**Arzt, P.** "Epistolary Introductory Thanksgiving," 29–46. **Beetham, C. A.** *Echoes of Scripture*, 61–112. **Crump, D.** *Knocking on Heaven's Door.* **Deichgräber, R.** *Gotteshymnus und Christushymnus.* **Fee, G. D.** *Empowering Presence.* **Käsemann, E.** "Baptismal Liturgy," 149–68. **Kiley, M.** *Colossians as Pseudepigraphy.* **Mitchell, S.** *Anatolia.* 2 vols. **Norden, E.** *Agnostos Theos.* **O'Brien, P. T.** *Introductory Thanksgivings*, 62–104. **Ramsay, W. M.** *Cities and Bishoprics of Phrygia.* 2 vols. **Reed, J. T.** "Are Paul's Thanksgivings 'Epistolary'?," 87–99. **Shogren, G.** "Presently Entering the Kingdom," 173–80.

## *Translation*

9 *For this reason we have also not stopped praying and interceding*[a] *for you from the day we heard. [We pray] that you may be filled with the knowledge of his will with a full measure of wisdom and insight that comes from the Spirit,* 10 *so that*[b] *you walk worthily of the Lord, pleasing him in every way by bearing fruit and increasing in every good work through the knowledge*[c] *of God,* 11 *by being strengthened with all power in accordance with the might of his glory so that you may have great endurance and patience, [and]* 12[d] *by giving thanks*[e] *with joy to*[f] *the Father who qualified*[g] *us*[h] *[to receive] a portion of the inheritance of the saints in the [realm of] light.* 13 *He rescued us from the powerful realm of darkness and transferred us into the kingdom of his beloved Son,* 14 *in whom we have redemption,*[i] *the forgiveness of sins.*

## *Notes*

a. [1:9] καὶ αἰτούμενοι, "and interceding," is missing from Codex Vaticanus (B) (as well as from the ninth-century Codex Mosquensis [K] and a manuscript of the Vulgate). The omission probably originated as an error of eyesight or hearing because of the identical ending of the previous participle (-μενοι).

b. [1:10] The Majority text (along with Ψ 075 and correctors to ℵ and D) insert ὑμᾶς, "you," after the infinitive to make more explicit the subject of "walk worthily." This is unnecessary, however, because the subject is implicit from the main verb of the primary clause that is second-person plural. This smoothing of the text could also have resulted from an effort to bring the text into conformity with the many other Pauline passages where the infinitive is followed by this pronoun (e.g., Rom 1:11; 12:2; 2 Cor 10:9; 13:7; Gal 4:17; Eph 1:18; Phil 1:10; 1 Thess 2:12; 3:2).

c. [1:10] The reading adopted here and in the NA[28]/UBS[5] has the simple dative: τῇ ἐπιγνώσει, "in the knowledge." It has the support of the major Alexandrian (𝔓[46] ℵ A B C I P 33 81) and Western (D F G vg[mss]) witnesses. In two other readings, a preposition is inserted. A handful of manuscripts add an ἐν, "in" (Ψ 075 104 1175 1505 and the Old Latin), and the Majority text adds an εἰς, "in/to" while changing the case of the substantive to accusative and adding an article (εἰς τὴν ἐπιγνώσιν). Both readings are attempts to simplify the construction[1] and probably also to bring it into conformity with the use of prepositions within the passage. Note the use of the two prepositional phrases with ἐν, "in," preceding (1:10b) and following (1:11a) τῇ ἐπιγνώσει, "through the

1 So, rightly, Abbott, 204.

knowledge," that modify two other participles in the passage. Similarly, there are two instances of εἰς-phrases in the passage modifying two other participles (see 1:11d, 12c).

d. [1:12] 𝔓[46] inserts a καί, "and," here. This is a scribal addition to ensure that the two participles (δυναμούμενοι . . . εὐχαριστοῦντες, "being strengthened . . . giving thanks") are seen as coordinate. "And" has been included in the English translation in brackets, not in agreement with this reading but because it is required for English style to complete the series of four participial expressions.

e. [1:12] 𝔓[46] and Vaticanus (B) add the adverb ἅμα, "at the same time," after εὐχαριστοῦντες, "giving thanks." Although the combined testimony of these two manuscripts is impressive and early, the reading lacks any additional manuscript support. One is hard-pressed to find a reason for it dropping out of the manuscript tradition, whereas it may have been added as a natural clarification to the fact that Paul has already said that he is "praying and interceding" for them (1:9b) and to harmonize it with προσευχόμενοι ἅμα, "praying at the same time," in 4:3.

f. [1:12] Codex Sinaiticus (א) and a few other manuscripts and versions add θεῷ, "God," just before πατρί, "Father" (F G 365 along with some manuscripts from the Old Latin, Clementine Vulgate, Syriac Peshitta, Armenian, and Coptic versions [some have θεῷ καί: 075 6 104 326 et al.]). Despite this array of evidence from a variety of different geographical locations, the internal evidence and the weight of the external evidence are strongly in favor of the omission. Metzger writes that "the strangeness of designating God simply as ὁ πατήρ, 'the Father,' when Christ has not been named in the immediate context doubtless prompted copyists to add" the clarifying designation.[2]

g. [1:12] Instead of ἱκανώσαντι, "qualified," a number of important Western witnesses (D F G it[b, d, g, mon, o] vg[ms]) have καλέσαντι, "called." This is most likely a transcriptional error based on confusion between the similar-looking expressions when seen in uncial script: ΤΩΙΚΑΝΩΣΑΝΤΙ versus ΤΩΙΚΑΛΕΣΑΝΤΙ.[3] Codex Vaticanus (B) commits the error that is more typically found in the Byzantine—the conflation of both variants: καλέσαντι καὶ ἱκανώσαντι, "called and qualified."

h. [1:12] There is a fairly even divide between witnesses attesting ὑμᾶς, "you," after ἱκανώσαντι, "qualified," and those attesting ἡμᾶς, "us." The second-person plural pronoun, "you," is supported by most of the principal witnesses of the Alexandrian text (א B), other Alexandrian witnesses (104 1739 Coptic [Sahidic]), along with some Western witnesses (vg[mss]). Based on the strength of this testimony, combined with the observation that the offending scribe most likely sought to harmonize this pronoun with the first-person plural pronoun of 1:13, the NA[28]/UBS[5] have adopted ὑμᾶς, "you." This is the reading followed by most English-language versions (NRSV; NIV; ESV; NJB; NAB; et al.). Nevertheless, a stronger case can be made for reading ἡμᾶς, "us." (1) There is good manuscript evidence from every textual family: Alexandrian (A C Ψ 33 Coptic [Boharic]), Western (D F G 1912; Old Latin; Vulgate; Syriac), and Byzantine (K L P 𝔐). (2) It would be just as easy to argue that the scribe changed the original ἡμᾶς, "us," to ὑμᾶς, "you," since "you" has been the presumed subject of each of the participles up to this point and would thus here be the logical object of the participle ἱκανώσαντι, "qualified." This is the reading adopted here and is also present in a few English versions (KJV; RSV; NASB; Douay-Rheims).

i. [1:14] A few manuscripts (424 614 630 1505 1912 and some versional evidence) insert διὰ τοῦ αἵματος αὐτοῦ, "through his blood," after ἀπολύτρωσιν, "redemption." The expanded reading became a part of the Textus Receptus and is represented in Tyndale, Geneva, KJV, Douay-Rheims, and NKJV. This is clearly a scribal assimiliation to Eph 1:7.

---

2 Metzger, *Textual Commentary*, 553.

3 So Abbott, 206; Lightfoot, 251; Metzger, *Textual Commentary*, 553.

## *Form/Structure/Setting*

### *Form (and Literary Context)*

Paul transitions from a report of his constant prayers of thanksgiving for the Colossians to informing them about his regular prayers of intercession for them. The introductory διὰ τοῦτο, "because of this," refers to the basis for his thanksgiving that he provides in 1:4–5: the Colossian believers have put their faith in Jesus Christ, and they are actively demonstrating love for one another in the Christian community. Because of their authentic conversion and the tangible signs of fruit in their lives, he and Timothy now pray for their ongoing growth in knowing God's plan for their lives and that they would live in a manner that would please the Lord.

This section is closely related to the previous in that both are prayer reports, but one is thanksgiving and the other is intercession. Thus, it would be incorrect to say that 1:9–14 is a continuation of the thanksgiving. Sumney accurately refers to 1:3–14 as a prayer with two parts.[4]

Intercessory prayer reports were common in Paul's letter writing, but vary in length and content according to the situation and purpose behind the respective letters. In most of his letters to churches, Paul begins with a thanksgiving report and then moves to an account of his intercession for them. In Romans, he expresses a brief thanksgiving (1:8–9), followed by a very short prayer report, although in this instance he says nothing of his prayers for the readers, only that he was asking God to enable him to visit them (1:10). Philippians, Philemon, 2 Thessalonians, and Ephesians are closer to the pattern exhibited in Colossians (see Phil 1:3–11; Phlm 4–7; 2 Thess 1:3–12; Eph 1:15–23). First Corinthians, 2 Corinthians, and Galatians do not have intercessory prayer reports. Colossians 1:3–14 thus constitutes the longest combined thanksgiving and prayer report among the letters attributed to Paul.

P. Arzt has demonstrated that prayer reports were an epistolary convention that formed a part of many Hellenistic letters.[5] One example can be seen in a second-century BC letter from an unknown writer to a man named Ptolemaios: "if you are well together with Berenike and the children and everything else runs according to your mind, then it is as we are continually praying to the gods [τοῖς θεοῖς εὐχόμενοι]."[6] Another letter, also dated to the second-century BC, is from a mother to her children. After the usual wish for health and well-being, she reports, "I pray [εὔχομαι] to the gods to see you well . . . I was praying [εὐχόμαην] to the gods daily for your sake."[7] Paul's prayer reports—here and elsewhere in his letters—are far more expansive and go well beyond a prayer for good health.

---

4 Sumney, 44.

5 Arzt, "Epistolary Introductory Thanksgiving," 38–44. Reed, "Are Paul's Thanksgivings 'Epistolary'?," 89, concurs with his conclusion.

6 *BGU* 10.1–3, as cited in Arzt, "Epistolary Introductory Thanksgiving," 38–39.

7 P.Monac. 3.57, as cited in *NewDocs* 9:57 (§20).

He is primarily concerned before God about their spiritual well-being, that they are making progress in the faith, and that they are demonstrating love and other virtues to others within the Christian community.

Although there is no precedent for a combined thanksgiving and prayer report in Jewish letters during the Roman era, there is evidence of a letter written to Jews in Egypt in the first century BC that gives an intercessory prayer report:

> May God do good to you, and may he remember his covenant with Abraham and Isaac and Jacob, his faithful servants. May he give you all a heart to worship him and to do his will with a strong heart and a willing spirit. May he open your heart to his law and his commandments, and may he bring peace. May he hear your prayers and be reconciled to you, and may he not forsake you in time of evil. We are now praying for you here. (2 Macc 1:2–6)

This is more of an actual prayer for the readers than a report of how the senders are regularly praying. It varies from Paul's normal style by the use of optative verbs throughout (although Paul can use this form from time to time; see Rom 15:5, 13; 1 Thess 3:11–12; 5:23; 2 Thess 2:17; 3:5, 16). However, it does have in common with the Colossian prayer a request for doing God's will and an emphasis on covenant status.

One of the striking characteristics of Paul's prayer report are the numerous deliberate points of contact with the thanksgiving: (1) both speak of the incessant nature of the prayers (the first using the present-tense verb with πάντοτε, "always" [1:3], and the second with οὐ παυόμεθα, "we do not stop" [1:9]); (2) both use the participle προσευχόμενοι, "praying" (1:3, 9); (3) both prayers are rooted in "hearing" about the spiritual status of the Colossians (1:4, 9); (4) both stress the importance of "knowing"—the first about how they came to know (ἐπέγνωτε) the grace of God (1:6) and the second about growing in a knowledge (τῇ ἐπιγνώσει) of God and his will (1:9–10); (5) both use the participles καρποφοροῦντες καὶ αὐξανόμενοι, "bearing fruit and increasing," although in the first with refererence to the gospel and in the second referring to the Colossian believers (1:6, 10); (6) both use the language of "thanksgiving" (εὐχαριστέω)—the first with reference to Paul and Timothy and the second as the prescribed practice of the Christians at Colossae (1:3, 12); (7) both speak of the inheritance of the readers—the first through the image of a hope stored up for them in heaven (1:5) and the second through a specific reference to "the inheritance of the saints in the light" (1:12); (8) for both, thanksgiving is ultimately rooted in the impact of the gospel, with the first including a major excursus on the gospel (1:5b–8) and the second describing the transformative message of the gospel (1:12–14); (9) both refer to Christians as ἅγιοι, "saints" (1:4, 12); (10) both address thanksgiving to "the Father" (τῷ πατρὶ; 1:3, 12); (11) both stress the role of Christ in the salvation of the Colossians (1:3, 4, 7; 1:13–14); and (12) both mention the work of the Spirit

(1:8, 9). The content of these many points of contact demonstrate that the two passages are closely related, but serve two overlapping but distinct purposes.

The intercessory prayer also fulfills an important epistolary role by announcing many of the important themes of the letter. These include: (1) the role of prayer (cf. 4:2, 3, 12); (2) expressing "thanksgiving" to God (1:12; cf. 1:3; 2:7; 3:17; 4:2); (3) the need to acquire the right kind of knowledge (1:9–10; cf. 2:2–3; 3:10); (4) following the will of God (1:9; cf. 1:1; 4:12); (5) forgiveness of sins (1:14; cf. 2:13–14; 3:13); (6) redemption and deliverance (1:13–14; cf. 2:9–15, 20; 3:1); (7) the realm of darkness and the hostile powers (1:13; cf. 1:16; 2:8, 10, 15, 20); (8) the realm of Christ and the new identity of believers in Christ (1:12–14; cf. 1:15–20, 21–23, 27–28; 2:2–3, 5, 6–7, 9–15, 19, 20; 3:1–4, 8–11); (9) the language of "fullness/filling" (1:9; cf. 1:19; 2:9–10); (10) the divine empowerment of believers (1:11; cf. 1:29; 2:10); (11) wisdom (1:9; cf. 1:28; 2:3, 23; 3:16; 4:5); (12) the "walk" of believers (1:10; cf. 2:6; 3:7; 4:5); (13) "growing" (1:10; cf. 1:6; 2:19); (14) love (1:13; cf. 1:4, 8; 2:2; 3:14); (15) patience (1:11; cf. 3:12); (16) the glory of God (1:11; cf. 1:27; 3:4); and (17) the future inheritance of believers (1:12; cf. 3:24).

In the history of scholarship on this passage, there has been a great deal of discussion about whether the prayer report extends to 1:14 or whether it comes to an end at 1:11 and a new section begins at 1:12. In a very influential essay, E. Käsemann built on E. Norden's suggestion that 1:12 marked the beginning of a liturgical introduction to the Christ-hymn. Both scholars argued that the verse was stylized in a liturgical fashion, evidenced by the participial construction τῷ ἱκανώσαντι, "who qualified you" (which is not used in the same sense as Paul uses it in 2 Cor 3:6), the "heaping-up of relative clauses," and the unqualified expression τῷ πατρὶ, "to the Father," which is thought to fit well into a liturgy.[8] Käsemann then suggested that the participle εὐχαριστοῦντες, "giving thanks," is used here in the sense of an introduction to a confession of faith.[9] Many scholars have accepted their analysis.[10]

There are a number of insurmountable difficulties with this view, however. First, there is no clear signal at 1:12 of a transition to a new section.[11] In fact, the opposite is the case since the participle εὐχαριστοῦντες, "giving thanks," is best explained as the fourth in a series of coordinate participles explaining what it means to walk in a way that is pleasing to the Lord (1:10–14). There is further symmetry in that each of these participial units is preceded by a prepositional phrase. Second, there is no "heaping-up" of relative clauses in the section. There is only one in the entire passage (ὃς ἐρρύσατο, "who rescued us," in 1:13). Third, τῷ πατρὶ, "to the Father," does not stand alone in an unqualified way but is modified by an appositional dative expression, τῷ ἱκανώσαντι ὑμᾶς, "who qualified you."

---

8 Käsemann, "Baptismal Liturgy," 38–39; Norden, *Agnostos Theos*, 250–54.

9 Käsemann, "Baptismal Liturgy," 39.

10 See, e.g., Hübner, 51–52; Hay, 47–48; Lohse, 24, 32–33; Martin (NCB), 53; Schweizer, 40.

11 So Wolter, 58.

In summary, εὐχαριστοῦντες, "giving thanks" (1:12), should be taken as introducing the concluding portion of the prayer report. It thus forms an *inclusio* with the beginning of the section, so that the introductory prayer begins with "we give thanks to the Father" (1:3) and ends with Paul urging the Colossian believers to "give thanks to the Father."

Although 1:12–14 does not form a single literary unit that the author is citing as an introit to the hymn, it does contain many traditional words and phrases. This is perhaps the best explanation for τῷ ἱκανώσαντι, "who qualified you," as well as the unique expression for inheritance (εἰς τὴν μερίδα τοῦ κλήρου) and for incorporation into Christ (μετέστησεν εἰς τὴν βασιλείαν) and possibly even the reference to "forgiveness of sins" (τὴν ἄφεσιν τῶν ἁμαρτιῶν) in 1:14. It may also explain why the writer shifted to a nominative relative clause and to the first-person plural (ὃς ἐρρύσατο ἡμᾶς, "who rescued us") in 1:13. While it is possible that this language could be interpreted as coming from a baptismal context,[12] this hypothesis is certainly unnecessary and is quite speculative.

Dunn has rightly pointed to "the very Jewish character of the language" of 1:9–14 and the resulting emphasis on the Jewish character of the gospel that the Colossian Christians received.[13] I would add that this is particularly true of the language of 1:12–14. Yet Dunn infers far too much when he notes that the reason for this is the counter the author of the letter is making to the threat to the Christian community, presented by "local Jews who were confident of the superiority of their own religious practice and who denigrated the claims of these Gentiles to share in their own Jewish heritage."[14] The language is best explained by the fact that Colossians has a Jewish author who not only writes like a Jew but sees the Christian faith as the fulfillment of Israel's hope.

### *Structure*

The prayer report consists of one long sentence of 106 words. Since 1:15 begins with a relative pronoun, some interpreters have considered 1:15–20 to be a continuation of this sentence.[15] The introductory διά τοῦτο, "because of this," connects this prayer very closely with the preceding thanksgiving, and especially the report that their faith and love are flourishing (1:4–5). The repetition of the word "hearing" (ἠκούσαμεν) in 1:9 clarifies the precise nature of this connection to the thanksgiving.

There is one main verbal expression that governs the entire passage: οὐ παυόμεθα . . . προσευχόμενοι καὶ αἰτούμενοι, "we have not stopped . . . praying and interceding" (1:9), consisting of a finite verb and two complementary participles. The rest of the passage is grammatically dependent upon this expression. The skeleton of the passage could be graphically displayed as follows:

12 So Käsemann, "Baptismal Liturgy," 159–64.

13 Dunn, 68–69.

14 Dunn, 68–69.

15 See Hay, 44.

οὐ παυόμεθα . . . προσευχόμενοι καὶ αἰτούμενοι (*prayer*)
    ἵνα πληρωθῆτε τὴν ἐπίγνωσιν (*content of the prayer*)
        περιπατῆσαι ἀξίως (*purpose of the acquired knowledge*)
            1. καρποφοροῦντες καὶ αὐξανόμενοι (*means of walking worthily*)
            2. δυναμούμενοι
            3. εὐχαριστοῦντες

"We have not stopped . . . praying and interceding (1:9a)
    that you may be filled with the knowledge (1:9b)
        so that you walk worthily (1:10a)
            1. by bearing fruit and increasing (1:10b)
            2. by being strengthened (1:11)
            3. by giving thanks" (1:12–14)

The ἵνα, "so that," clause at v. 9b introduces the content of the prayer, which is a request for God to impart knowledge to them of his will for their lives. Paul then expresses the goal in acquiring this knowledge with a simple infinitive (v. 10a). His aim is that they would conduct their lives in a way that is worthy of the Lord Jesus Christ. The four participles then convey the means by which they can walk in a way that pleases the Lord. The first two (καρποφοροῦντες καὶ αὐξανόμενοι, "bearing fruit and increasing") form a unit and should be seen together. The final participle, εὐχαριστοῦντες, "giving thanks," draws the reader back to the beginning and the way Paul started the letter with εὐχαριστοῦμεν, "we give thanks," and thereby forms an *inclusio*. This literary touch brackets the entire prayer of 1:3–14 and marks it as a coherent unit of thought. 1:12–14 should therefore not be seen as separate from the prayer. This would call into question the analysis of those who characterize 1:11 as the conclusion of the prayer report and see 1:12–14 as a specially crafted introduction to the Christ-hymn. It would also render unlikely the macro-chiastic structure that Pokorný finds in 1:3–14, consisting of A, thanksgiving (1:3–9), B, intercession (1:9–11), and A′, thanksgiving (1:12–14).[16]

Nevertheless, Paul's shift to the relative pronoun ὅς, "who," in 1:13 and the presence of traditional language signal a change in function for 1:13–14. Grammatically the relative pronoun continues the series of benevolent actions that characterize the Father, but they also prepare the reader for the hymn of praise about Christ, who is the agent used to fulfill these redemptive acts of the Father. These two verses thus have a transitional function. They provide reasons for thanking God (1:12), but they also begin to describe the redemptive activity of the Lord Jesus Christ, which prepares the way for the poetic praise of his work in creation and redemption in 1:15–20.[17]

16 Pokorný, 45–46.

17 See also, Lincoln, 595–96; Sumney, 55–60.

## *Setting*

This prayer report is sufficiently general that it could be characteristic of the way that Paul would pray for any of his churches. The goal of walking worthily of the Lord and pleasing him is relevant for all Christians at all times. Yet the content of this prayer does seem particularly timely and relevant to the Colossians in light of the pressure that they are facing from the advocates of "the philosophy."

The emphasis in the prayer on "being filled" with a knowledge of his will was particularly urgent for the readers in light of the temptation they faced to embrace a teaching that Paul regarded as counter to the will of God that amounted to "empty deceit" (2:8). In light of the role of the hostile powers in the background of the letter, the aspects of the prayer that touch on their redemption from the authority of darkness, their present experience in the realm of Christ, and the divine power that is available to strengthen them all appear to be crucial to their present situation.

## *Comment*

**9** Διὰ τοῦτο καὶ ἡμεῖς, ἀφ' ἧς ἡμέρας ἠκούσαμεν, οὐ παυόμεθα ὑπὲρ ὑμῶν προσευχόμενοι καὶ αἰτούμενοι, "for this reason we have also not stopped praying and interceding for you from the day we heard." The transition from the thanksgiving to the intercessory prayer report is marked by a causal expression (διά τοῦτο, "for this reason") that roots his prayer in the entirety of 1:3–8, but especially 1:4–5 and the report of how their faith in Christ and love for one another are flourishing. The ἠκούσαμεν, "we heard," here signals the reader to recall the content of the ἀκούσαντες, "hearing," of 1:4. The καί, "also/and," that follows has been interpreted (1) as attached to ἡμεῖς, "we," and interpreted in an adjunctive sense, thus "we also" (KJV; NET) or "we, for our part";[18] or (2) as going with the main verb and thus providing an additional response of Paul and Timothy to the reports of their faith and love; thus, they not only give thanks to God but they also intercede for the Colossians.[19] Most of the English versions simply leave the καί, "and/also," untranslated. The best solution is the second—that is, taking καί, "and/also," with the main verb. This is consistent with the flow of thought in which Paul and Timothy receive the encouraging report of their faith and love, which causes them not only to well up with gratitude but also to pray for them. The adjunctive view would only work if Paul and Timothy were joining a group of others in praying for the Colossians. The variation of that, "we, for our part," is quite without precedent in interpreting καί, "and/also,"[20] and should thus be avoided.

18 Wilson, 98–99; Lightfoot, 137.

19 Harris, 25–26; Lohse, 24.

20 See BDAG, s.v. καί.

Paul claims that he and Timothy have engaged in ceaseless prayer for the Colossians after receiving the good reports of their spiritual well-being. The precise manner of expression, οὐ with παυόμαι, "I do not stop," followed by a participle, only appears in Paul elsewhere in Eph 1:15, but was used in the LXX (Isa 38:20; Jer 51:10 [44:10 MT]), Judaism (e.g., Josephus, *Ant.* 6.317; Philo, *Alleg. Interp.* 1.18; 3.14; *Cherubim* 67; *Sacrifices* 1.38), and elsewhere in the NT (Acts 5:42; 6:13; 20:31; Heb 10:2). It is the semantic equivalent of προσεύχομαι πάντοτε, "I pray always" (2 Thess 1:11). This expression is not the fingerprint of a pseudepigraphical author as much as a rhetorical variation on εὐχαριστοῦμεν . . . πάντοτε . . . προσευχόμενοι, "we give thanks . . . always . . . praying" (Col 1:3).

"Praying and interceding" (προσευχόμενοι καὶ αἰτούμενοι) should be understood as a hendiadys (as most commentators suggest). The addition of αἰτούμενοι, "interceding," puts the emphasis on making requests of God and thus "interceding" for the readers. This is the only time that Paul uses the verb αἰτέω, "ask," in the context of prayer, but he does use the noun αἰτήματα, "requests" (Phil 4:6). The combination of the two verbs occurs in Mark's Gospel when Jesus says, "Therefore I say to you, all things for which you pray and ask [προσεύχεσθε καὶ αἰτεῖσθε], believe that you have received them, and they shall be granted you" (Mark 11:24; cf. 1 Macc 3:44). There is no exegetical significance to the middle voice of αἰτέω, "ask," since the active and middle voices appear to be used interchangeably.[21]

ἵνα πληρωθῆτε τὴν ἐπίγνωσιν τοῦ θελήματος αὐτοῦ, "that you may be filled with the knowledge of his will." The particle (ἵνα, "that") serves not to introduce a purpose statement but to indicate the content of the regular prayers of Paul and Timothy for the Colossians. The heart of the prayer is that they would acquire a knowledge of God's will that would enable them to live in a way that is pleasing to the Lord. Knowing and doing the will of God was a defining feature of the people of God under the old covenant. The psalmist exclaimed, "I desire to do your will, O my God; your law is within my heart" (Ps 40:8). In another passage, while seeking God's powerful rescue from his enemies, the psalmist prays, "Teach me to do your will, for you are my God" (Ps 143:10). The people of Israel could know the will of God for their lives since the Lord had revealed it to them in his word. The Judaism of the Second Temple period similarly emphasized the importance of learning and living God's will. This comes to emphatic expression at Qumran, where the instructor of the community is charged with living in a way that epitomizes what it means to live according to the will of God: "He should perform (God's) will in all that his hand should tackle and in all that he controls, as he commanded. And all that happens to him he should welcome freely and be gratified by nothing except God's will" (1QS 8.24). Anyone who seeks membership in the community must swear a binding oath to "walk according to his will" and to learn from the priests who

21 See BDAG, s.v. αἰτέω; Harris, 26.

"interpret his will" based on "the Law of Moses with all that it decrees" (1QS 5.8–10). Thus, the members of the community endeavor to "always seek his will" (4Q416 frag. 2 III.12; see also CD 3.15).

In the teaching of Jesus as reflected in the Synoptic Gospels, there is a strong emphasis on knowing the will of God. Only the one "who does the will of my Father in heaven" can claim an authentic relationship with Jesus (Matt 12:50; Mark 3:35; Luke 8:21) and can enter heaven (Matt 7:21). Jesus teaches his disciples to pray that the will of the Father would be done on earth as it is in heaven (Matt 6:10). Jesus reveals, however, that his passion and death on the cross was part of the will of the Father (Matt 26:39, 42; Mark 14:36; Luke 22:42). John's Gospel continues this emphasis by stressing the role of Jesus in obediently fulfilling the Father's will for him to come and complete the work (his atoning death) that the Father had commissioned him to do (John 4:34; 5:30; 6:38). Looking to Jesus as the source of life is thus the Father's will in the new-covenant era: "for my Father's will is that everyone who looks to the Son and believes in him shall have eternal life, and I will raise him up at the last day" (John 6:40 NIV). Likewise, Paul declares that Christ's role as redeemer is central to a proper understanding of the will of God. Thus, he proclaims that it was "according to the will of our God and Father" that Christ "gave himself for our sins to rescue us from the present evil age" (Gal 1:4 NIV). This theme is strongly emphasized in Ephesians (1:5, 9, 11). Nevertheless, in line with his OT and Jewish roots, Paul also stresses obedience to the revealed will of God as essential for God's people. Thus, appropriating holiness and purity is incumbent upon Christians just as it was for the old-covenant people of God for living according to the will of God (1 Thess 4:3; cf. Lev 11:44–45). Doing God's will constitutes a progressive transformation of one's life that results in fewer commonalities with the sinful tendencies of the world's culture and values (Rom 12:1–2).

In praying for the Colossians to know the will of God, Paul and Timothy thus want the readers to focus on the Lord Jesus Christ as the center point of God's plan of redemption and to grow in a deeper understanding of what it means to live in accordance with what God has revealed both in Scripture and through Christ. This is the main point of his prayer. Paul and Timothy likely felt the pressing need to pray incessantly for this because of the threat posed by the competing teaching of "the philosophy." This teaching demeaned the person and work of Christ as well as shifted the focus of the Colossian believers onto rituals and practices that deterred their focus from what was really important.

The term that Paul uses for "knowledge" is the compound form (ἐπίγνωσις, "knowledge") instead of the simple form (γνῶσις, "knowledge"). Although in the past, some commentators have seen a slight distinction between the two terms,[22]

22 See, e.g., Eadie, 20–21, who contends that ἐπίγνωσις, "knowledge," means full and exhaustive knowledge that goes beyond the partial knowledge implicit with γνῶσις, "knowledge"; so also Lightfoot, 138.

this distinction does not hold up to a careful examination of the usage. It can hardly be said that an inferior knowledge is implied in passages such as Rom 11:33 ("Oh, the depth of the riches of the wisdom and knowledge [γνῶσις] of God!"), 2 Cor 2:14, 4:6, and others. BDAG suggests that the compound form is limited to "transcendant and moral matters" in the NT.[23] While this may be true, the same could also be said to be true of the simple form, especially since this was the only kind of knowledge that the NT writers had occasion to discuss. It is best to regard both nouns as interchangeable in Paul's writings and not to find a nuance of exegetical difference between them. It can be said that Paul slightly prefers the simple form—using it twenty-three times to fifteen for the compound form, yet the compound form is slightly favored in the later letters even though both forms persist.

In praying that they would be "filled" (πληρωθῆτε) with knowledge, a word group (πληρόω/πλήρωμα) is here introduced that has special significance throughout Colossians as well as Ephesians. There is no technical significance to the verb in this context (see also Rom 15:14), but it does imply the work of the Holy Spirit in imparting this knowledge. This reading depends on understanding the background of the term as temple imagery and that part of the function of the Spirit under the new covenant is to fill the temple with his presence, power, knowledge, and insight (see the discussion of πλήρωμα, "fullness," at 1:19).

ἐν πάσῃ σοφίᾳ καὶ συνέσει πνευματικῇ, "with a full measure of wisdom and insight that comes from the Spirit." This prepositional phrase indicates the manner by which a knowledge of God's will is apprehended. The indwelling Spirit of God imparts wisdom and insight and thereby enables believers to discern the proper decisions to make regarding what to believe and how to live. Thus the prepositional phrase does not go with the infinitive clause that follows in 1:10 (thus reading "walk with all wisdom and insight"), nor does it go with the main verb (thus "be filled through all wisdom and insight"). Rather, it is most naturally connected with the closest antecedent, "knowledge" (ἐπίγνωσις), which yields the best sense in this context.

The two nouns σοφία, "wisdom," and σύνεσις, "insight," are sometimes used to describe what the Spirit produces in the lives of certain people in the OT. This can be seen in the way God endowed the craftsmen for their work on the tabernacle: "the LORD said to Moses, 'See, I have chosen Bezalel . . . and I have filled him with the Spirit of God, with skill, ability [ἐνέπλησα αὐτὸν πνεῦμα θεῖον σοφίας καὶ συνέσεως], and knowledge in all kinds of crafts" (Exod 31:1–3; see also 35:31, 35). Similarly, Daniel was filled with the Spirit of God and possessed these traits, as King Nebuchadnezzar observed: "I have heard about you that the Spirit of God is in you, and alertness and understanding and abundant wisdom [σύνεσις καὶ σοφία περισσή] were found in you" (Dan [Theod.] 5:14). Perhaps most importantly is the conjunction of these three terms in a messianic

23 BDAG, s.v. ἐπίγνωσις.

text: "the Spirit of the LORD will rest on him—the Spirit of wisdom and of understanding [πνεῦμα σοφίας καὶ συνέσεως]" (Isa 11:2). This rich OT tradition regarding the work of the Spirit in producing wisdom and insight probably influenced Paul's understanding of an important aspect of the ministry of the Spirit under the new covenant. He thus uses the term πνευματικός, "having to do with the divine spirit,"[24] to make this connection explicit. It is likely that the entire phrase is a deliberate echo of Isa 11:2, reflecting Paul's understanding that the text was fulfilled in Jesus's arrival.[25] But Paul builds upon it to describe the work of the Spirit in filling the world with a knowledge of God.

Although a number of commentators and versions interpret πνευματικός as "spiritual" in contrast to the physical realm or as connected to the human spirit (e.g., NRSV; KJV), the fact that Paul is praying for "wisdom and insight" on their behalf makes it more likely that he understands these as gifts bestowed by the Spirit, just as God provided them under the old covenant. This is consistent with Paul's usage elsewhere, especially in 1 Corinthians, where the term is often used to speak of a manifestation of the Spirit (e.g., 1 Cor 2:12–13; 12:1; 14:1–2). Paul utters a similar prayer in Eph 1:17–18, where he asks God to impart his Spirit to these believers to give them wisdom and revelation in knowing God better (although the word σύνεσις, "insight," does not appear).[26] Here, however, the prayer is more specifically directed to practical insights for knowing what to believe and how to live.

The adjective πάσῃ, "all," which modifies both nouns (σοφία and σύνεσις), would suggest the abundance of divine wisdom and insight available under the new covenant, in which the presence of God's Spirit with believers is the hallmark trait of this new age. Since the Spirit is historically involved in providing both wisdom and insight, it is therefore preferable to interpret πνευματικός, "spiritual," as modifying both nouns (so most commentators).

The "wisdom and insight" Paul wants for them is the ability to know practically the true desires of God for them as they face the pressures and enticements of the errant "philosophy" and as they continue to bring their lifestyles into conformity with his call to holiness and purity. The competing teachers at Colossae offered their own brand of σοφία, "wisdom," and no doubt made disparaging remarks about the inadequacy of the gospel as the Colossians heard it from Epaphras and as present in the apostolic traditions passed on to them. But 1:10 makes it clear that Paul also wants them to grow in their discernment of what it means to live in accordance with God's will in their day-to-day lives. For the old-covenant people of God, this involved discerning how to live out the injunctions of Torah (Deut 4:6). This was David's prayer for Solomon during his preparation

24 See BDAG, s.v. πνευματικός 2.

25 Beetham, *Echoes of Scripture*, 78–79.

26 So also Fee, *Empowering Presence*, 643, who observes that it is an "understanding that the Spirit endues."

to become king: "may the LORD give you discretion and understanding [σοφίαν καὶ σύνεσιν] when he puts you in command over Israel, so that you may keep the law of the LORD your God" (1 Chr 22:12 NIV). The book of Proverbs frequently commends this practical "wisdom and insight" to the people of God (e.g., Prov 2:3, 6; 9:10; 24:3). Consistent with Proverbs, the psalmist declares that "the fear of the Lord is the beginning of wisdom [σοφίας]; all who follow his precepts have good understanding [σύνεσις]" (Ps 111:10 [110:10 LXX]).

**10** περιπατῆσαι ἀξίως τοῦ κυρίου εἰς πᾶσαν ἀρεσκείαν, "so that you walk worthily of the Lord, pleasing him in every way." The overall purpose and direction of the prayer is to seek God's help for the Colossians so they would order their lives in a way that would please the Lord in every respect. The aorist infinitive should be taken as introducing a purpose clause and not as result.[27] The goal of being filled with a knowledge of his will is directed toward proper Christian conduct.

"Walking worthily" (περιπατέω with ἀξίως) is a Pauline expression (see 1 Thess 2:12, where Paul exhorts the Thessalonians to "walk worthily of God" [εἰς τὸ περιπατεῖν ὑμᾶς ἀξίως τοῦ θεοῦ]). Paul frequently uses the image of "walking" as a metaphor for Christian conduct (see, e.g., Rom 6:4; 8:4; 13:13; 14:15; 1 Cor 3:3; 7:17; 2 Cor 5:7; 10:2; Gal 5:16). The metaphor appears only once in the Gospels and, in that instance, on the lips of the Pharisees and scribes who inquire of Jesus, "Why do your disciples not walk [περιπατοῦσιν] according to the tradition of the elders, but eat with defiled hands?" (Mark 7:5 ESV). This is not surprising since the image was used extensively within the Judaism at that time, especially as evidenced at Qumran. The term "walk" (הָלַךְ) as a metaphor for behavior appears numerous times, for instance, in the Community Rule. The members of the community are frequently enjoined to "walk in perfection" in the sight of God (e.g., 1QS 1.8; 3.9; 11.19), "walk on paths of light" (1QS 3.20), "walk according to his will" (1QS 5.10), and to "walk unblemished in all his paths" (1QS 2.2). Conversely, they must not "walk in the stubbornness of a guilty heart" (1QS 1.6; see also 2.26) or to "walk on paths of darkness" (1QS 3.21; 4.11).

The metaphor of "walking" for conduct and behavior is not a Greek concept. The root of this usage can be found in the Hebrew Scriptures. The one who is wise will "walk [הָלַךְ; LXX = περιπατέω] in the way of righteousness, along the paths of justice" (Prov 8:20). The book of Proverbs makes extensive use of the image of "walking" (הָלַךְ) as a metaphor for life conduct (see, e.g., Prov 1:15; 2:7, 13, 20; 10:9; 13:20; 14:2; 15:21; 19:1; 20:7; 28:6, 18, 26). The image can be found as early as 2 Kgs 20:3, where Hezekiah prays, "Remember, LORD, how I have walked [περιεπάτησα] before you faithfully and with wholehearted devotion and have done what is good in your eyes" (NIV). In Isaiah, the house of Jacob is enjoined, "Let us walk in the light of the Lord" (Isa 2:5). The importance

27 So, rightly, Gnilka, 41, and Hübner, 50.

of this metaphor for expressing life conduct not only continued into Second Temple Judaism and into the thought of the apostle Paul but persisted into later Judaism where *halakah* became a technical term for rabbinical interpretations of the Torah on matters regarding daily life.[28]

The former rabbi's appeal to the Colossians was "to walk worthily of the Lord" (so also Eph 4:1). "Worthily" (ἀξίως) would suggest that they bring their lives into conformity with the ethical and lifestyle claims made upon them by the Lord and that their lives would be a suitable demonstration of their new identity in him. Paul will repeat this in different words later in the letter when he says, "Therefore, as you received Christ Jesus the Lord, so walk in him" (2:6). Paul makes a similar appeal to the Philippians when he instructs them to "conduct yourselves in a manner worthy of the gospel of Christ [ἀξίως τοῦ εὐαγγελίου τοῦ Χριστοῦ πολιτεύεσθε]" (Phil 1:27). The κύριος, "Lord," that Paul speaks of here and throughout Colossians is the Lord Jesus Christ (see 1:3; 2:6; 3:17, 24). He earnestly desires and prays for them to orient their lives completely around Christ—the one with whom they are now identified through union with him in his death, resurrection, and new life (2:12–13; 3:1). Later he will tell them that they need to put their focus on Christ (3:1–4) as the basis for eliminating sinful behaviors from their lives (3:5–11) and to appropriate the virtues that are consistent with their new life in Christ (3:12–17). The fundamental problem with the leaders of "the philosophy" is that their lives are not sufficiently centered on Christ (2:19).

The motivation that Paul wants to see exhibited in the lives of the Colossians is an earnest desire to please Christ in every respect. Once again, this is a thoroughly Pauline concept. He sums up the duty of Christians as a matter of excelling in "how you ought to walk and to please God [περιπατεῖν καὶ ἀρέσκειν θεῷ]" (1 Thess 4:1). Although Paul never elsewhere uses the noun (ἀρεσκεία, "pleasing"), he uses the verb (ἀρέσκω, "please") to describe the motive that should inspire Christians (e.g., Rom 8:8; 1 Cor 7:32; 1 Thess 2:4). The danger for believers is to take their focus off Christ and put it on pleasing people (Gal 1:10; 1 Thess 2:4) or pleasing themselves (Rom 15:1, 3). The language is probably drawn from an OT and Jewish background. Under the old covenant, offerings were pleasing to the Lord (Mal 3:4), but ultimately praise will please God (ἀρέσει τῷ θεῷ, "will please God") more than sacrifice (Ps 69:30–31 [68:31–32 LXX]). Josephus reports that Hyrcanus and the Pharisees sought to live in a way that was pleasing to God (Josephus, *Ant.* 13.289). Philo commends those "who seek to live in accordance with the will of God, in a manner pleasing [ἀρεσκείαν] to the true and living God" by despising the pleasures of the flesh (Philo, *Spec. Laws* 1.176). Similarly, he elsewhere applauds those who have a zeal to please God (ἡ πρὸς θεὸν ἀρεσκεία, "pleasing to God") and to say and do everything consistent with piety (Philo, *Spec. Laws* 1.317).

28 See *HJP* 2:339–46; G. G. Porton, "Halakah," *ABD* 3:26–27.

ἐν παντὶ ἔργῳ ἀγαθῷ καρποφοροῦντες καὶ αὐξανόμενοι τῇ ἐπιγνώσει τοῦ θεοῦ, "by bearing fruit and increasing in every good work through the knowledge of God." The Colossians will walk worthily of the Lord if their lifestyle is now characterized by a growing tendency to display good deeds (and not evil behavior) and by getting to know the one living and true God and his will for their lives. The remainder of the prayer is structured around a series of four adverbial participles dependent upon the aorist infinitive περιπατῆσαι, "so that you walk . . ." Normally one would expect the participles to be in the accusative case in agreement with the implied accusative of reference (ὑμᾶς, "you") that functions as the subject of the infinitive. Barth and Blanke take this as an indication that they should be understood as imperatival participles,[29] although they do not produce any examples of a similar grammatical construction in support of their contention. Wilson, however, citing Peake, claims that an infinitive followed by nominative participles was common in classical Greek and can be seen in a similar construction in Eph 4:1–3 (περιπατῆσαι . . . ἀνεχόμενοι . . . σπουδάζοντες, "to walk . . . bearing with . . . endeavoring").[30] A search of the construction in the LXX produces additional examples (e.g., Isa 13:3: πληρῶσαι τὸν θυμόν μου χαίροντες ἅμα καὶ ὑβρίζοντες, "to fulfill my wrath, at the same time rejoicing and reviling," NETS; see also, e.g., Jer 13:23; 44:3 [51:3 LXX]). In Colossians, each of the four participles are best interpreted as expressive of the means by which the Colossians should walk worthily of the Lord and please him.[31] The present tense of all four participles should be understood as imperfective in aspect and seen as regular and ongoing characteristics of the Christian life.

The first two participles were already used in this letter at 1:6 where they described the impact of the gospel: it was leading to conversions (αὐξανόμενον, "increasing") and producing Christian growth (καρποφορούμενον, "bearing fruit"). Here the authors vary the usage by applying the two participles to the Colossians themselves, "you are bearing fruit and increasing." At issue is whether the participles should be seen as closely linked so that each prepositional phrase preceding and following the participles should be interpreted as modifying both,[32] or whether the first prepositional phrase (ἐν παντὶ ἔργῳ ἀγαθῷ, "in every good work") only modifies the first participle (καρποφοροῦντες, "bearing fruit") and the second prepositional phrase (τῇ ἐπιγνώσει τοῦ θεοῦ, "in the knowledge of God") only modifies the latter participle (αὐξανόμενοι, "increasing"). This second option is advocated by a handful of scholars who see the presence of an A B B′ A′ chiastic structure here.[33] This is rather unlikely, however. The first two participles should be seen as closely connected to each

29 Barth and Blanke, 178–79.

30 Wilson, 106; Peake, 499.

31 So also Moo, 100; Sumney, 48.

32 E.g., Lohse, 29.

33 E.g., Wilson, 106, and Wolter, 62.

other as a unit and not as coordinate. This is supported by the fact that these two participles are connected by καί, "and," while the other two participles lack the conjunction. The two prepositional phrases, then, modify both participles, with the first indicating the sphere or area of growth ("in every good work"), and the second expressing the means of the growth ("through the knowledge of God").

The biggest change from the previous usage is that the "increase" (αὐξάνω) no longer refers to evangelistic growth of the church in terms of numbers, but here refers to the Colossians' spiritual growth. This is consistent with the later usage of the term in this letter (Col 2:19; see also 2 Cor 10:15; Eph 4:15). "Bearing fruit" (καρποφορέω) continues to carry the same idea of spiritual growth, but here it is specified as taking place "in every good work" (ἐν παντὶ ἔργῳ ἀγαθῷ). The passage clearly shows that the apostle Paul is concerned that believers display good works as an outcome of their salvation (see also Eph 2:10; 1 Thess 1:3). Realizing this collapses the supposed distance between Paul and James on the role of works in the life of a believer (see Jas 2:17, 26). Paul's language and teaching about "bearing fruit" and "increasing" here may be dependent on the teaching of Jesus in his parable of the four soils, especially as reflected in the Markan form (Mark 4:1–9, 13–20; cf. Matt 13:1–9, 18–23; Luke 8:4–8, 11–15). Mark's version says that the seed that fell into good soil "brought forth grain, growing up and increasing and yielding [εδίδου καρπὸν ... αὐξανόμενα] thirty and sixty and a hundredfold" (Mark 4:8 NRSV). In his explanation of the parable, Jesus says that some people, like the seed sown on good soil, "hear the word and accept it and bear fruit [καρποφοροῦσιν], thirty and sixty and a hundredfold" (Mark 4:20 NRSV). Paul does not mention what kinds of good works he sees as important, but there is an implied contrast with the "evil works" (ἐν τοῖς ἔργοις τοῖς πονηροῖς) that once kept them alienated from God (Col 1:21). Presumably, these works would be defined in large measure by Paul's later appeal to "put to death" various kinds of evil behaviors (3:5–11) and to practice a range of good works (3:12–17).

The means available to the Colossians for their fruitbearing and growth in good works is their "knowledge of God" (τῇ ἐπιγνώσει τοῦ θεοῦ). Knowing God entails acquiring a knowledge of his will for their lives and being guided and energized by the Spirit for living out his demands (1:9). Lightfoot remarked that the knowledge of God "is the dew or the rain which nurtures the growth of the plant" (Deut 32:2; Hos 14:5).[34] Most commentators take it as an instrumental dative,[35] but, surprisingly, none of the versions take it this way; they almost uniformly translate it as "increasing *in* the knowledge of God." Thus, it could be taken as a dative of reference and translated "in," or, as Moo suggests, a dative of sphere.[36] Dunn rightly critiques this view by saying that in this case, "the author

34 Lightfoot, 139.

35 E.g., Sumney, 49; Barth and Blanke, 180; Dunn, 72; Lohse, 29.

36 Moo, 97.

could hardly have failed to complete the balance of the sentence by inserting ἐν."[37] Also, if we see the prepositional phrase as modifying both participles, the interpretations of it as a dative of sphere or reference are immediately ruled out since "in the knowledge of God" does not fit with "bearing fruit." Believers bear fruit on the basis of or by means of their knowledge of God.

**11** ἐν πάσῃ δυνάμει δυναμούμενοι κατὰ τὸ κράτος τῆς δόξης αὐτοῦ εἰς πᾶσαν ὑπομονὴν καὶ μακροθυμίαν, "by being strengthened with all power in accordance with the might of his glory so that you might have great endurance and patience." The Colossians will be able to live in a way worthy of the Lord only if they are empowered to do so by God himself. This is due to the fact that Paul portrays the Christian life as difficult to live because there is powerful supernatural opposition. At a number of intervals in this letter, Paul speaks of hostile spirits—principalities, powers, thrones, dominions, elemental spirits—that oppose Christ and his people (1:16; 2:8, 10, 15, 20). These powers stand behind "the philosophy" and, presumably, are one of the reasons that the Colossians find it difficult to resist.

The style of this clause is repetitive and full for rhetorical impact—"be empowered in all power by power." The threefold emphasis on God's enabling power stresses the magnitude of his power as well as its availability for believers. The prepositional phrase ἐν πάσῃ δυνάμει, "with all power," is used by Paul on only one other occasion—to describe the power of the antichrist figure in 2 Thess 2:9, who operates in accord with Satan. That passage underlines the fact that Paul did not minimize or trivialize the power of the realm of darkness. This is also the only place in the NT where the verb δυναμόω, "to be strengthened," appears in conjunction with the term δύναμις, "power." The two terms appear together once in the LXX in a psalm that celebrates God as the divine warrior who fights for and empowers his people: "command your power [δυνάμει], O God; make powerful [δυνάμωσον], O God, that which you wrought for us" (Ps 68:28 [67:29 LXX] NETS). Nowhere else does Paul use the verb, but he does use the compound form (ἐνδυναμόω, "empower") on other occasions to describe God's infusion of strength into his life (Phil 4:13; see also 1 Tim 1:12; 2 Tim 4:17). Eph 6:10 is most relevant to this context because it is directed to the community of believers and has the supernatural opponents in view: "finally, be strong in the Lord and in his mighty power [ἐνδυναμοῦσθε ἐν κυρίῳ καὶ ἐν τῷ κράτει τῆς ἰσχύος αὐτοῦ]" (NIV).

The rhetorical emphasis on divine power is paralleled in a variety of Qumran texts, but typically with two power-denoting terms, not three (e.g., 1QH 12.32, "the strength of his power" [כוח גבור]; 5.4; 12.32; 20.35; 23.8; 1QM 10.5; 1QS 11.19). This stylistic trait is apparently drawn from the OT (e.g., 1 Chr 29:12, "in your hands are strength and power" [כוח וגבורה]; 2 Chr 20:6; Ps 71:18; Isa 40:26; Jer 16:21). Here, Paul heightens the rhetorical emphasis on the power of God even more by (1) adding the adjective πάσῃ, "all," to modify δυνάμει, "power,"

37 Dunn, 72.

(2) utilizing redundancy to heighten the impact—namely, by modifying the verb with its cognate noun (δύναμις, δυναμόω, "power," "empower"), and (3) using a prepositional phrase immediately preceding and following the participle: "*with* all power being empowered *in accordance with* power."

The noun κράτος, "might," often appears in doxological contexts in the NT (e.g., 1 Tim 6:16; 1 Pet 5:11), many times with δόξα, "glory" (see 1 Pet 4:11; Jude 25; Rev 1:6; 5:13), to magnify and praise the power of God. This does not mean that Paul is citing liturgical language at this point in the letter, since he appears to be multiplying words for power for rhetorical effect and since he does use the term outside of doxologies elsewhere (e.g., Eph 1:19; 6:10). The term κράτος, "might," appears extensively in Second Temple Jewish texts with reference to the great power of God (e.g., "the Jews called upon the Sovereign who with power [μετὰ κράτους] shatters the might of his enemies," 2 Macc 12:28; see also 3:34; 7:17; 9:17; 11:4; 3 Macc. 1.27; 2.6; 3.11; 5.13; 6.5; Jdt 9:14; 11:22; 13:11; Wis 11:21; 15:2–3; Sir 18:5; 47:5). Rather than rooting the source of the power directly in θεός, "God," Paul says that it comes from "his glory" (τῆς δόξης αὐτοῦ). The glory of God is often linked with his power in the OT. Celebrating God's sovereignty over the heavens, Isaiah declares that God reigns over the stars "because of abundant glory and might of strength [ἀπὸ πολλῆς δόξης καὶ ἐν κράτει ἰσχύος]" (Isa 40:26 NETS). The psalmist exclaims, "I have seen you in the sanctuary and beheld your power [δύναμιν] and your glory [δόξαν]" (Ps 63:2 [62:3 LXX]; see also 1 Chr 16:28; Isa 2:10, 19, 21). Paul can use the terms "power" and "glory" interchangeably. On the one hand, he can attribute the resurrection to the power of God (1 Cor 6:14), while on the other he can present it as a manifestation of the "glory" of God" (Rom 6:4). Schreiner notes, "'Glory' refers to the power of God that accomplished the resurrection of Christ."[38] Paul may have chosen to speak of the power of God in this way to the Colossians to evoke the imagery of God as the divine king, seated on his throne, radiating the splendor of his majesty. The image thereby stresses both the sovereignty of God over heaven and earth as well as his extrordinary power, to which he gives believers direct access.

Paul's comments here may thus subtly prepare the way for his polemic against "the philosophy." In contrast to its teaching, Paul affirms in his prayer that there is abundant divine power available for the needs of the Christian life, that this power is available directly from God, and that prayer is one of the key means for acquiring God's power. Negatively put, one does not need to invoke the aid of angelic intermediaries, engage in ascetic practices to curry favor with God or angels, or use any ritual means for obtaining divine power. Yet Paul's declaration of God's power for them would also provide encouragement to these believers by reassuring them of the superiority of his power over and against the competing claims of the local territorial gods and goddesses. Leto, the mother

38 Schreiner, *Romans*, 311.

of Apollo, for instance, is extolled in an inscription at the sanctuary of Apollo Lairbenos (thirty miles north of Colossae) with the epithet, Δυνατὴ θεός, "powerful goddess."[39] Another Phrygian inscription discovered at Dionysopolis (near the sanctuary of Apollo Lairbenos) praises Mother Leto because "she makes possible the impossible" (ἐξ ἀδυνάτων δυνατὰ πυεῖ).[40]

Paul thus sees divine power as essential to "walking worthily of the Lord" and "pleasing him in every way." But more specifically in this context, he and Timothy are praying that God would strengthen the Colossians for "endurance" (ὑπομονή) and "patience" (μακροθυμία). Although these terms appear together on occasion as virtues Christians are called to pursue (see 2 Tim 3:10; Jas 5:7–11; 1 Clem 64.1; Ign. *Eph.* 3.1), they should not be regarded as synonyms or as forming a hendiadys.[41] In general terms, "endurance" is needed in light of the difficulties the Colossians face from the leaders of the faction, and "patience" is a virtue that is especially important for relating to one another in the Christian community.

One cannot underestimate the disruption and pressure put on the community of believers at Colossae by the advocates of "the philosophy." Paul uses strong language and imagery to describe their activity. He warns the Colossians against those who would take them captive (2:8), judge them (2:16), disqualify them from the prize (2:18), and deceive them through clever argumentation (2:4). In Paul's eyes, the community was under siege and needed God's power to help them endure and resist the verbal attacks of these aggressors. Lohse notes that the word "endurance" (ὑπομονή) "signifies the kind of perseverance which is to be proven in battle by holding the position one has taken against all enemy attacks."[42] He points to the equivalent Hebrew word in the Qumran texts that speaks of the perseverance of the faithful as illustrated in the following hymn: "I give you thanks, Lord, because you . . . have protected me from all the traps of the pit, for vicious men have ambushed my soul when I relied on your covenant. They are a council of futility, a devilish assembly. They do not know that through you I subsist [מעמד] and in your compassion you have saved my life" (1QH 10.20–23). "Endurance" (ὑπομονή) is a major theme in 4 Maccabees and was displayed by Eleazar and the seven brothers in facing the attacks of the gentile persecutors. The writer goes so far as to say that "by their endurance [ὑπομονή], they conquered the tyrant" (4 Macc. 1.11) and even represents the enemy as impressed by this virtue: "for the tyrant Antiochus, when he saw the courage of their virtue and their endurance [ὑπομονήν] under the tortures, proclaimed them to his soldiers as an example for their own endurance [ὑπομονή]" (4 Macc. 17.23). Although there is nothing in the larger context of Colossians

39 *TAM* V.1.250. See the discussion in Mitchell, *Anatolia*, 1:192.

40 Ramsay, *Cities and Bishoprics of Phrygia*, 1.1.153 (no. 53).

41 Contra Sumney, 50–51.

42 Lohse, 30.

that would suggest that Paul is preparing the congregation for persecution,[43] they are a community facing attack and have ample need for divine assistance to endure. Paul wants for them what the believers in Ephesus would later display when faced with dangerous teaching. The Lord declares to them: "I know your works, your toil and your patient endurance [ὑπομονήν], and how you cannot bear with those who are evil, but have tested those who call themselves apostles and are not, and found them to be false. I know you are enduring patiently [ὑπομονήν] and bearing up for my name's sake, and you have not grown weary" (Rev 2:2–3 ESV).

In the parable of the soils, which we have already noted may have had some influence on the shaping of this prayer, the people represented by the seed planted in the good soil are the ones who "when they hear the word, hold it fast in an honest and good heart, and bear fruit with patient endurance [ἐν ὑπομονῇ]" (Luke 8:15 NRSV). In Paul's larger thought, "endurance" (ὑπομονή) is necessary because believers have not fully entered the kingdom and live in an age characterized by trials and difficulties prior to the return of Christ (Rom 5:3–4; 8:25; 1 Thess 1:3; 2 Thess 1:4; see also Jas 1:3). This has very much been his own experience (2 Cor 6:4).

But the endurance that God gives not only sustains individual Christians but helps them live harmoniously in community: "may the God who gives endurance [ὑπομονῆς] and encouragement give you a spirit of unity among yourselves as you follow Christ Jesus" (Rom 15:5). This leads to the connection with the second word of the pair, μακροθυμία, "patience." The situation at Colossae was ripe for the springing up of tensions and interpersonal conflict as the believers debated among themselves about the competing teaching and its advocates. No doubt there was a range of responses to it at this stage, with some very tempted to embrace it and others admantly opposed to it. Paul and Timothy thus pray for the community to have patience with one another through this difficult time of tension. Patience is clearly a virtue that Christians should always embrace regardless of the circumstances (Col 3:12; cf. 1 Cor 13:4; Gal 5:22). It is also especially needed as the community awaits the parousia of the Lord (Jas 5:7–8). But it is particularly important for the Colossians as they attempt to preserve the unity of the community during a time of turmoil provoked by the aggressive teachers of "the philosophy." Paul expresses it well in his letter to the Ephesians: "be patient, bearing with one another in love" (Eph 4:2 NIV).

**12** μετὰ χαρᾶς εὐχαριστοῦντες τῷ πατρὶ, "by giving thanks with joy to the Father." This is now the fourth participle in the series and is coordinate with the previous three, both in form (present tense, nominative case) and in function (adverbial expressing means). Because of this, we would be in error to interpret it as an independent imperatival participle and as introducing a new section

43 Contra Gnilka, 43.

in the letter.[44] Some interpreters have argued that 1:12–14 is no longer part of the intercessory prayer but forms a brief introduction to the hymn that follows (1:15–20).[45] This argument is based largely on the amount of traditional words and phrases ostensibly drawn from the liturgy of the early church. Deichgräber argued that the section constituted a literary unit that could properly be categorized as a "hymn to God" or a "eulogy."[46] Käsemann contended that the Christ-hymn itself actually began at 1:12.[47] Although few scholars have followed Deichgräber and Käsemann in their conclusions regarding the hymnic character of this section, many continue to argue that the author of Colossians incorporates a great deal of traditional material into a segment that introduces the Christ-hymn. The number of terms and phrases in this brief section that are unique or rare in Paul's writings could very well be suggestive of pre-Pauline tradition. This would include terms such as ἱκανόω, "qualify," μερίς, "portion," κλῆρος, "lot," ἅγιοι ἐν τῷ φωτί, "saints in the light," and βασιλεία τοῦ υἱοῦ τῆς ἀγάπης αὐτοῦ, "kingdom of his beloved son." The use of the relative pronouns in 1:13a (ὃς ἐρρύσατο ἡμᾶς, "he rescued us") and 1:14a (ἐν ᾧ ἔχομεν τὴν ἀπολύτρωσιν, "in him we have redemption") may also point to confessional or liturgical material. It is precarious, however, to infer from the use of traditional words and phrases that the entire section is a single liturgical unit, especially since the first verbal element (εὐχαριστοῦντες, "giving thanks") fits so well into the flow of thought from 1:9 through 1:12.

Interpreters have been fairly evenly divided over whether μετὰ χαρᾶς, "with joy," goes with what precedes ("for all endurance and patience with joy," RSV; so also ESV; KJV)[48] or with what follows ("while joyfully giving thanks to the Father," NRSV; so also UBS[5]; NIV; NASB; NLT).[49] Although the idea of rejoicing amid trials is a solid Pauline and early Christian notion, the evidence here supports the second view—namely, that thanksgiving is expressed with joy. There is a certain symmetry to the text that can be observed in noticing that each of the participles in the series is modified by a preceding prepositional phrase (under the assumption that we take καρποφοροῦντες καὶ αὐξανόμενοι, "bearing fruit and increasing," as a unit). This enhances the likelihood that "with joy" modifies the following participle, "giving thanks." Although the precise words, "give thanks . . . with joy," are not found elsewhere in Paul, the idea of offering prayer to God with a grateful heart that is full of joy for his salvation is entirely fitting for the people of God at all times; see, for example, Ps 100:1, "A psalm. For giving thanks. Shout for joy to the LORD, all the earth," or Ps 28:7, "The LORD is my strength and my shield;

44 As Hübner, 51; Lohse, 32–34; and Käsemann, "Baptismal Liturgy," 154.

45 E.g., Hübner, 51; Pokorný, 50–51; Gnilka, 44; Lohse, 32.

46 Deichgräber, *Gotteshymnus*, 78–79.

47 Käsemann, "Baptismal Liturgy," 152–54.

48 E.g., Barth and Blanke, 183; Pokorný, 50.

49 E.g., Moo, 100; Hübner, 51.

my heart trusts in him, and I am helped. My heart leaps for joy, and I will give thanks to him in song."

It is not surprising for Paul and Timothy to pray regularly that thanksgiving would be an important part of how the Colossians "walk worthily" before the Lord. Paul understood thanksgiving and gratitude to God as a characterizing feature of the Christian life (on the verb εὐχαριστέω, "give thanks," see *Comment* on 1:3). He will later tell the Colossians that they should give thanks to God the Father in everything they do (Col 3:17). The fact that Paul mentions "giving thanks" as last in the series has nothing to do with its relative importance to the content of the other participles, but it may be his way of providing a transition to the next section—the hymn of praise to the exalted Christ.

Yet here it is not Christ who is to be praised, but "the Father." He is worthy of praise because he is the one who authorizes people to be his heirs (1:12b, c). He is the Father of the Lord Jesus Christ (1:3) who effected his plan of redemption (1:13) and through it extended "forgiveness of sins" (1:14). Peake aptly notes, "The word [Father] is selected to emphasize God's Fatherly love as the source of their redemption."[50]

τῷ ἱκανώσαντι ὑμᾶς εἰς τὴν μερίδα τοῦ κλήρου τῶν ἁγίων ἐν τῷ φωτί, "who qualified you [to receive] a portion of the inheritance of the saints in the [realm of] light." Through his great plan of redemption, God has made it possible for the Colossian believers to enter into an entirely new mode of existence. They have been freed from satanic bondage, come under the reign of the Lord Jesus Christ, experienced forgiveness of sin, and now live in a realm characterized by life, purity, and righteousness. The adjectival participle ἱκανώσαντι, "qualified," which modifies τῷ πατρί, "the Father," indicates that he has "qualified" or "authorized" (so BDAG, s.v.) the readers to obtain an inheritance. This sense of the verb, however, is not attested in the LXX, where it is used to indicate "it is enough" or "it is sufficient." The sense here of "authorize" is well-illustrated in a second-century BC papyrus document that says "if accounts are demanded, consider that you have full powers [ἱκανωθῆναι] until my arrival" (*P.Tebt.* 1.20).[51] Paul uses the verb only one other time, but with a meaning similar to this passage: "he has made us competent [ἱκάνωσεν] as ministers of a new covenant—not of the letter but of the Spirit; for the letter kills, but the Spirit gives life" (2 Cor 3:6 NIV). Although the sense of "authorize" is prominent in both passages, here the context is salvation, whereas in the Corinthian passage it is for ministry as διάκανοι, "servants." There is a conceptual similarity with the prologue of John that speaks of those who exercise faith as receiving the ἐξουσία, "right," to become children of God (John 1:12).

If our analysis of the variant readings is correct (see the discussion in *Notes* [h.]), Paul has here shifted the pronouns from ὑμᾶς, "you," to ἡμᾶς, "us."

50 Peake, 500.

51 As cited in MM 302.

This could be the result of drawing on confessional material from the early church, but more likely here it reflects a slight change of focus wherein he is now including himself and all Christians as people whom God has qualified to share in the inheritance.

In Paul's portrayal of God qualifying believers to receive a portion of the inheritance, he draws on language straight from the OT. Both μερίς, "portion," and κλῆρος, "lot, share," were used together repeatedly in LXX Deuteronomy to refer to the allotments given to the various tribes of Israel in the land, with the exception of the Levites, however, who "have no share or inheritance [μερὶς καὶ κλῆρος] among their brothers" because "the Lord is their inheritance [κλῆρος]" (Deut 10:9; see also 12:12; 14:27, 29; 18:1). Here and elsewhere in the LXX, the two nouns appear to be used interchangeably. This is also true of the coordinate usage of the two terms in Acts 8:21, where Simon the magician is told, "You have no part or share [μερὶς οὐδὲ κλῆρος] in this ministry" (NIV). The nature of the genitive relationship (τὴν μερίδα τοῦ κλήρου, "the portion of the lot") has been widely debated in the commentaries. Some commentators have argued that it is a partitive genitive, "a portion of the lot."[52] This is predicated on understanding μερίς, "portion," to refer to a part, and κλῆρος, "lot," to the whole—a meaning that cannot be substantiated in the LXX or the NT. It is best, with Lightfoot, to take the genitive as one of apposition, "the portion, which is the lot/share."[53] The expression refers to the inheritance believers receive from God.

Many interpreters have pointed to similar language that appears in the Qumran texts, especially in the Community Rule: "to those whom God has selected he has given them an everlasting possession; until they inherit them in the lot of the holy ones" (1QS 11.7). Yet this language itself is derived from the OT, and the conceptuality here is substantially different from what we find in Paul and Colossians.[54]

The possessive genitive τῶν ἁγίων, "the saints," are those to whom the inheritance belongs. If we read this text through the lens of the Qumran literature and certain Jewish apocalyptic texts, this could be a reference to angels. Many have tried to make the case that the angelic interpretation best fits the context here.[55] This view would be out of sync with Paul's consistent use of the term to refer to believers. Furthermore, Paul has already used the term twice in this letter (1:2, 4) to speak of people at Colossae who are Christians. Since the invocation of angels factors prominently in the teaching of "the philosophy," to say here that believers have gained an inheritance "together with the angels" would not advance Paul's concern to diminish their dependence on angelic mediation. What Paul says is that God has qualified believers to receive an inheritance that belongs to the saints.

52 E.g., Harris, 31; Peake, 500.

53 Lightfoot, 141. So also Barth and Blanke, 187.

54 So also Shogren, "Presently Entering the Kingdom," 173–76.

55 E.g., MacDonald, 50; Pokorný, 52; Lohse, 36.

This inheritance is in the realm of the light (ἐν τῷ φωτί, "in the light"; dative of sphere). The prepositional phrase thus qualifies the inheritance (ἡ μερὶς τοῦ κλήρου, "the portion, which is the lot"), as most commentators assert,[56] and not "the saints" (NLT). By affirming that this inheritance is in the realm of the light, Paul contrasts it with the realm from which they have been rescued, the domain "of darkness" (τοῦ σκότους; 1:13). The language is reflective of a dualism, but not an ultimate cosmic dualism that espouses two competing powers of nearly equal status and strength. As the Christ-hymn will make clear, Christ is sovereign over all supernatural powers by virtue of his work as creator and by his work in redemption, whereby he has already defeated the hostile powers (see 2:15). This sole occurrence of φῶς, "light," in Colossians is consistent with the usage of the image elsewhere in Paul. Perhaps most significant is the fact that Paul has elsewhere characterized the new identity of believers as "light" (1 Thess 5:5). He tells the Ephesians, "You were once darkness, but now you are light in the Lord. Live as children of light" (Eph 5:8 NIV). This realm is characterized by "goodness, righteousness, and truth" (Eph 5:9). Similarly, he tells the Romans that living consistently with the light involves laying aside a multiplicity of sinful behaviors (Rom 13:12–13).

**13** ὃς ἐρρύσατο ἡμᾶς ἐκ τῆς ἐξουσίας τοῦ σκότους, "he rescued us from the powerful realm of darkness." In the next two clauses, both of which are introduced with aorist indicative verbs, Paul explains the basis on which God authorized the Colossian believers to receive their divine inheritance. The masculine relative pronoun ὅς, "who," refers to God as the subject of the rescue and transference. Rather than coordinating these next two clauses and putting them in the same grammatical form as the previous verb by making them adjectival participles in the dative case (i.e., τῷ ῥυσαμένῳ . . . τῷ μεταστάντῳ, "[giving thanks to the Father who qualified us], rescued us . . . and transferred us"), Paul shifts to the relative pronoun in the nominative case followed by two finite verbs. This could be for stylistic variation (such a change can be observed in 2 Cor 1:9–10), but it may also point to the citation of confessional material here. If so, this might explain the change of pronouns from ὑμᾶς, "you," to ἡμᾶς, "us,"[57] if this were the most compelling reading from the manuscript tradition. But, as I have argued in *Notes* [h.], it is more likely that Paul already shifted to the first-person plural in the previous verse. Nevertheless, because of the unique vocabulary and the introduction of it by a nominative relative pronoun, it is still probably reflecting the use of traditional material.

God's powerful act of rescue was not from Roman imperial might or any other human agency but from the invisible, powerful realm of evil. The term he chooses for rescue would evoke recollection of God's celebrated prior act of deliverance on behalf of his people when he rescued them from their bondage

56 E.g., Moo, 102; Harris, 31.

57 So also Hübner, 52; Lindemann, 22–23.

in Egypt. The verb ῥύομαι, "rescue, deliver," was used repeatedly throughout the LXX to refer to this mighty divine act of deliverance. See especially the following texts:

- "Say therefore to the people of Israel, 'I am the LORD, and I will bring you out from under the burdens of the Egyptians, and I will deliver [ῥύσομαι] you from slavery to them, and I will redeem you with an outstretched arm and with great acts of judgment. I will take you to be my people, and I will be your God, and you shall know that I am the LORD your God, who has brought you out from under the burdens of the Egyptians. I will bring you into the land that I swore to give to Abraham, to Isaac, and to Jacob. I will give it to you for a possession. I am the LORD.'" (Exod 6:6–8 ESV)
- "Thus the LORD saved [ἐρρύσατο] Israel that day from the hand of the Egyptians, and Israel saw the Egyptians dead on the seashore." (Exod 14:30 ESV)
- "And I delivered you [ἐρρυσάμην] from the hand of the Egyptians and from the hand of all who oppressed you, and drove them out before you and gave you their land." (Judg 6:9 ESV)

Because of the verbal and conceptual correspondence, many interpreters have suggested that Paul is here developing a "second exodus" motif, which serves as the antitype and fulfillment of God's prior intervention.[58] Some interpreters have missed this altogether and simply describe the author's language as more generally coming from God's deliverance of individuals from the danger of death.[59] While agreeing that Paul may be highlighting the new exodus here, Moo has cautioned that commentators have often overemphasized that motif in explaining the passage and have missed the possible simultaneous allusion to deliverance from exile that is found in Isaiah (see Isa 42:7, 16; 49:9; see also Ps 107).[60] Although the term ῥύομαι, "rescue," is never used in the verses he cites, it is used of the freed exiles in Isa 48:20 and 49:25. They are also called the company of "the redeemed" (Isa 51:10; 52:9). In addition to this, it is important to note that throughout the Greek Bible the term was used for a variety of acts of divine deliverance from enemies, such as the people of Israel from the Canaanites (Judg 8:34), David from Saul (2 Sam 12:7) and from all his enemies (2 Sam 22:18, 49; Pss 18:1, 17, 19 [17:1, 18, 20 LXX]; 54:7 [53:9]), Daniel from the lions (1 Macc 2:60), and the people of Israel from various enemies throughout their history (Ezra 8:31; Neh 9:28; Pss 22:4 [21:5 LXX]; 34:4 [33:5]; 106:43 [105:43]; 107:6 [106:6]; 124:7 [123:7]; 1 Macc 12:15; 3 Macc. 6.39). Because of his mighty acts of deliverance, God is called Israel's "redeemer" (ὁ ῥυσάμενος; Isa

58 E.g., Beetham, *Echoes of Scripture*, 81–95; Barth and Blanke, 188; Wright, 62.
59 E.g., Bormann, 74–75; Maisch, 70–71.
60 See Moo, 103–4.

44:6; 47:4; 48:17; 49:7, 26; 54:5, 8; also 59:20 [ὁ ῥυόμενος]). Nevertheless, because the exodus stands out in biblical history as God's paradigmatic act of deliverance (see also Josephus, *Ant.* 6.89; Philo, *Worse* 1.93; *Spec. Laws* 2.218), the subsequent reference to "transferral" that corresponds with receiving the promised land, and the reference to "redemption" (ἀπολύτρωσις) in 1:14, it is probably best to interpret this as "second exodus" imagery.[61]

In sharp contrast to the exodus and every other divine act of deliverance from enemies under the old covenant, Paul here affirms that God's new act of deliverance is from the compelling sway of an invisible, evil realm. He characterizes this domain as an ἐξουσία, "authority"—that is, a "sphere in which power is exercised."[62] Because the term is contrasted with βασιλεία, "kingdom," in the next line, it is best to understand it as a realm and not as a personification of evil (such as Satan or an evil angel) or in the more abstract idea of "tyranny" or "lawlessness."[63] Yet, by using the expression "authority of darkness," Paul refers to the realm over which the principalities and powers rule.[64] God's powerful act of redemption is later described in the letter with the image of a Roman triumphal procession in which the principalities and powers are the vanquished foes (2:15). It is significant that one of Paul's most common expressions for demonic powers is ἐξουσία, "authorities" (1:16; 2:10; see also 1 Cor 15:24; Eph 1:21; 3:10; 6:12). Although the term ἐξουσία, "authority," often denotes the right to rule or command, the idea of the domain or realm over which someone rules is also well-attested (e.g., Luke 4:6; 23:7).

"Darkness" (σκότος), however, is the characterizing feature of this realm. This term is probably chosen because it contrasts with "light" (φῶς)—the defining feature of the inheritance believers receive (Col 1:12). The language is particularly reminiscent of Qumran, where this imagery is used extensively to distinguish the faithful covenant people of God from all others. Most notably, 1QM describes an eschatological battle in which the forces of God are aligned against the angelic armies of Belial (e.g., 1QM 1.1, 5, 11; 4.2; 13.4–5, 10, 11).

The precise expression ἐξουσία τοῦ σκότους, "authority of darkness," does appear one other time in the NT (Luke 22:53), where it refers to the motivating force behind the arrest of Jesus. The personification of evil in that passage gives it a slightly different sense than here. Similarly, Luke describes the commission Paul received from the Lord at his Damascus Christophany to go to the gentiles as a call "to open their eyes and turn them from darkness to light, and from the power of Satan [τῆς ἐξουσίας τοῦ σατανᾶ] to God, so that they may receive forgiveness of sins" (Acts 26:18 NIV). Satan is here depicted as the archenemy of God who possesses authority over a realm. But once again, in Colossians the

61 So also Shogren, "Presently Entering," 176–77.

62 BDAG, s.v. ἐξουσία.

63 Contra Lightfoot, 141.

64 See Dibelius and Greeven, 9.

emphasis is more on the domain itself than on the figure who holds the power. Both the possessor of power and the domain are brought together in Eph 2:2, where one of the three forms of bondage that held believers in captivity prior to their redemption in Christ is "the ruler of the kingdom of the air [τὸν ἄρχοντα τῆς ἐξουσίας τοῦ ἀέρος], the spirit who is now at work in those who are disobedient" (NIV). Here the term ἐξουσία, "authority" is clearly used for the domain, but Satan is also identified as the one who holds sway over this realm. A similar concept is probably in Paul's mind as he writes Col 1:13.

καὶ μετέστησεν εἰς τὴν βασιλείαν τοῦ υἱοῦ τῆς ἀγάπης αὐτοῦ, "and transferred us into the kingdom of his beloved Son." The believing community has not only been delivered from this evil domain, but they have been incorporated into a new dominion. Paul uses the colorful word μεθίστημι, "transfer," to describe God's gracious and powerful act of installing them under his own rule. He has used this term on one other occasion to speak of a faith that can "move" mountains (1 Cor 13:2). Josephus used the term on a few occasions to speak of a group of people who were relocated by a ruler from one geographical place to another. For instance, in his narration of the Assyrian king Tiglath-Pileser's conquest of Israel in the eighth century BC, Josephus says that the king "made the inhabitants prisoners, and transplanted them into his own kingdom [μετέστησεν εἰς τὴν αὐτοῦ βασιλείαν]" (Josephus, *Ant.* 9.235). He used the same word to describe the Jewish exile to Babylon after the destruction of the city of Jerusalem: "and now it was that the king of Babylon sent Nebuzaradan, the general of his army, to Jerusalem, to pillage the temple; who was ordered to burn it and the royal palace, and to lay the city even with the ground, and to transplant the people into Babylon [καὶ τὸν λαὸν εἰς τὴν Βαβυλωνίαν ματαστῆσαι]" (Josephus, *Ant.* 10.144). This terminology may have reminded the readers of a time in the second century BC when the Syrian king Antiochus transferred several thousand Jews from Mesopotamia and Babylon to the territories of Lydia and Phrygia (Josephus, *Ant.* 12.149).

The transferral Paul speaks of is not into a geographical location but into a new realm of existence—a realm (βασιλεία) governed by the Son of God who reigns as Lord over heaven and earth. This term clearly evokes a recollection of Jesus's proclamation and teaching about the kingdom of God, and this is one of the fourteen occurrences of that term in Paul's writings. This stands out as unique because it is one of the few times that the kingdom is described as the kingdom of Christ (the Son) and not the kingdom of God. In Eph 5:5, however, Paul does explicitly refer to it as "the kingdom of Christ and God." On one occasion, Jesus did refer to the kingdom as his own: "I tell you the truth, some who are standing here will not taste death before they see the Son of Man coming in his kingdom [ἐν τῇ βασιλείᾳ αὐτοῦ]" (Matt 16:28). It is possible, then, that Paul viewed the "kingdom of God" and the "kingdom of the Son" as one and the same entity, with the terminology capable of interchangeable usage. Hübner rightly warns that any distinction should not be overemphasized since the Son of God wields no other dominion than that of his Father: "when Christ rules, the Father rules."[65]

Most commentators, however, have affirmed a slight distinction while maintaining that the two references are largely coterminous. By using the expression, "kingdom of the Son," it is quite possible that Paul had in mind the period between Jesus's resurrection/exaltation and his second coming to restore all things and inaugurate the kingdom of God in its full and complete sense.[66] This would fit with Paul's teaching in 1 Cor 15:23–28, where he declares that Jesus must reign until he puts all his enemies under his feet. After this, "the end will come, when he hands over the kingdom to God the Father after he has destroyed all dominion, authority and power" (1 Cor 15:24 NIV).

It is likely that Paul's stress on the kingdom of Christ here has to do with the strong emphasis in this letter on Christ's lordship and reign over all of the hostile principalities and powers. The Christ-hymn celebrates his lordship over all the powers in heaven (1:15–20), Paul represents Christ as achieving a massive victory over them by his death on the cross (2:15), and Christ currently functions as "head" over every power and authority (2:10). This was important for the Colossians to hear since they were being enticed to embrace a teaching that was inspired by spirits from the realm of darkness (2:8). As members of the kingdom of Christ, they are now aligned with a Lord who can enable them to resist such teaching and everything else that the powers of darkness would endeavor to do in an effort to reassert their reign.

The genitive case in the construction, ὁ υἱὸς τῆς ἀγάπης αὐτοῦ, "the son of his love," should be interpreted as an attributive genitive, thus giving the sense, "his beloved Son" (so RSV; NRSV; ESV; NLT).[67] The language would evoke recollection of Jesus's baptism as recorded in the Synoptic Gospels, but which may have been known among the Colossians through oral tradition. After the Spirit descends upon Jesus in the form of a dove, a voice from heaven declares, "This is my beloved Son [οὗτός ἐστιν ὁ υἱός μου ὁ ἀγαπητός], with whom I am well pleased" (Matt 3:17 ESV; see also Mark 1:11; Luke 3:22). Subsequently, during Jesus's transfiguration, the heavenly voice makes the same declaration (Matt 17:5; Mark 9:7). The reference to Jesus as God's beloved Son has clear messianic overtones (see 2 Sam 7:12–16; Ps 2:2; 4QFlor 1.10–13). In Paul's thought, although Jesus already possessed the status of divine sonship, he was appointed as son of God *in power* after his resurrection and exaltation (Rom 1:4; cf. Rom 8:34; Col 3:1).

Since 2 Sam 7:12–14, 18 is the fountainhead of tradition within Judaism (see, e.g., Pss. Sol. 17; 4QFlor 1.1–12; 4Q252 5.1–4; 4 Ezra 7.28–29) and early Christianity that the Messiah, as a descendent of David beloved by God, would

65 Hübner, 53.

66 So, e.g., Sumney, 57; Dunn, 79; Pokorný, 54; Lightfoot, 142; Eadie, 36.

67 See BDF §165.

rule as king, the terminology that Paul has chosen here is a deliberate echo of that important OT messianic text.[68] Beetham notes that Paul thus declares that "God's dominion had been given an eschatological, worldwide escalation in the coming of Jesus his messiah, the son of David, the son of God."[69]

**14** ἐν ᾧ ἔχομεν τὴν ἀπολύτρωσιν, τὴν ἄφεσιν τῶν ἁμαρτιῶν, "in whom we have redemption, the forgiveness of sins." Paul brings his intercessory prayer report to a conclusion by affirming the new status and identity of the Colossian believers as those who are redeemed and forgiven based on their union with the Lord Jesus Christ. The prepositional phrase that begins this clause, ἐν ᾧ, "in whom," is part of the participationist Christology that pervades Colossians and is typical of Paul's thought in general. The antecedent to the masculine relative pronoun is "the Son" and thus restricts the blessings of redemption and forgiveness to those who are members of his kingdom.

The present indicative verb (ἔχομεν) stresses the present status of the Colossian believers. This new status is directly based on the actions expressed in the two indicative verbs that occur in the immediately preceding verse (1:13). This declaration of present experience is part of the overall emphasis of the apostle in this letter on realized eschatology. As Peake notes, the present tense also suggests that redemption and forgiveness are "an abiding possession."[70]

The concept of redemption was an important salvation metaphor in Paul. He uses the term ἀπολύτρωσις, "redemption," in his definition of the gospel in Rom 3:24: "justified freely by his grace through the redemption [ἀπολυτρώσεως] that came by Christ Jesus" (NIV). The context for this statement is his indictment of all humanity as stained by the guilt of sin (3:9–20) and his summarizing remark, "for all have sinned" (3:23). This passage provides a clear connection between the sinfulness of humanity and God's merciful work of procuring redemption through the Lord Jesus Christ. The notion of present redemption based on the work of Christ can also be found in 1 Cor 1:30, where Paul announces that Christ is "our righteousness, holiness, and redemption." Paul also presents redemption as having a future aspect when he speaks of the redemption of the body (from the corrupting influence of sin; Rom 8:23) as well as redemption on the day of judgment (which implies the forgiveness of sins; Eph 1:14; 4:30). There is thus no contradiction between the present and future aspects of redemption; both involve freedom from the guilt of sins.[71]

In a society where slavery flourished, metaphors stemming from this institution would have been understood by all. Given Paul's later address to slave owners and slaves in this letter (3:22–4:1) and in Philemon (which was addressed to the same locale), the metaphor of redemption would have had

---

68 Beetham, *Echoes of Scripture*, 97–112.

69 Beetham, *Echoes of Scripture*, 112.

70 Peake, 501.

71 So also F. Büchsel, "ἀπολύτρωσις," *TDNT* 4:353; C. Brown, "Redemption," *NIDNTT* 3:199.

special significance for the readers. The term "redemption" (ἀπολύτρωσις and the uncompounded form λύτρωσις) was widely used for the payment of a price to free an individual from slavery.[72] Nevertheless, it was the exodus event in Israel's history that was the principal informing background to Paul's use of redemption language.[73] The verb λυτρόω, "redeem," pervades the LXX of Exodus, Deuteronomy, and the Psalms as the key Greek term to describe God's mighty act of deliverance. In Exod 6:6 LXX, the Lord instructs Moses to tell the Israelites: "I am the Lord, and I will bring you out from the domination of the Egyptians, and I will deliver [ῥύσομαι] you from slavery to them, and I will redeem [λυτρώσομαι] you with an outstretched arm and with great acts of judgment" (NETS; see also Exod 15:13; Deut 7:8; 9:26; 13:6; 15:15; 21:8; 24:18; Ps 77:15 [76:16 LXX]). The fact that this passage has both "rescue" and "redemption" in common with Col 1:13–14 may provide partial confirmation to the supposition that Paul is developing a second-exodus theme in Colossians.

The exodus was the extraordinary event that became the foundation for understanding the identity of the people of Israel and the touchstone of assurance that God would redeem his people in the future. Isaiah thus reminds the exiled Israelites in Babylon that God would redeem them (e.g., Isa 51:11; 52:3) and thereby reaffirms his identity as "the redeemer" (e.g., Isa 41:14; 43:14; 44:6, 24). Because the exile resulted from the sinfulness of God's people, forgiveness of sin would be a feature of the return: "I have swept away your offenses like a cloud, your sins like the morning mist. Return to me, for I have redeemed you" (Isa 44:22 NIV). The psalmist often calls the people of God to remember their past deliverance (most notably, the exodus) as a means of bolstering their assurance that their God was powerful enough and concerned enough to deliver them from present enemies (see Pss 77:15, 78:42; 119:154).

The compound term ἀπολύτρωσις, "redemption," only appears once in the LXX (Dan 4:34) and the compound verbal form twice (Exod 21:8; Zeph 3:1). The LXX translators preferred the uncompounded forms λυτρόω, "redeem," λύτρωσις, "redemption," and λύτρον, "ransom." Paul, however, shows a clear stylistic preference for the compounded form, using it consistently for the noun, but then switching to the uncompounded verbal form in the one place he uses the verb "redeem" (Titus 2:14). The addition of a preposition to noun and verbal forms is a clear stylistic proclivity of Paul.

Paul never explicitly mentions the price of redemption (λύτρον, "ransom") in this letter or in any of his earlier letters. In 1 Tim 2:6 he does use the compound word ἀντίλυτρον, "ransom," and defines it as the sacrificial death of Jesus on the cross. Because the death of Christ is so foundational to the new life presented in our letter (Col 1:20, 22; 2:12, 15, 20; 3:1), we can assume that this was the price that was paid. What is left unexpressed—here and elsewhere in

---

72 See BDAG, s.v. ἀπολύτρωσις.

73 So also Barth and Blanke, 190–91; Dunn, *Theology*, 227–28.

Paul—is an indication to whom the price was paid. He gives no indication that the price was paid to the devil (contra the *Christus Victor* view of the atonement). In fact, if this were Paul's conviction, we might have expected him to make this explicit in Colossians since the theme of the hostile powers is so prominent and significant to the readers. The idea of a ransom price was suggested by Jesus himself during his earthly ministry when, pointing to the cross, he remarked that "the Son of Man did not come to be served, but to serve, and to give his life a ransom [λύτρον] for many" (Mark 10:45//Matt 20:28). Paul appears to pick up on this earlier when he told the Corinthians that they had been bought with a price (1 Cor 7:21–23). That price was Christ's blood that he shed on the cross (διὰ τοῦ αἵματος τοῦ σταυροῦ αὐτοῦ) as the means of securing the redemption (Col 1:24; cf. Acts 20:28; Eph 1:7). He did this by taking their place in receiving the condemnation and punishment due to them because of their transgressions (2 Cor 5:21; see also 1 Tim 2:6; 1 Pet 2:24).

The slavery from which Jesus freed his people is expressed here as a twofold form of bondage. First, they have been delivered from a realm that was characterized by darkness and that trapped them in a life of sinful behaviors and alienation from God (1:13; cf. 1:21). Second, they have been redeemed from the guilt of their sinful acts that made them liable to the judgment and wrath of God. The redemption that God provides through the cross of Christ thus brings "forgiveness of sins" (τὴν ἄφεσιν τῶν ἁμαρτιῶν). This accusative expression is in apposition to τὴν ἀπολύτρωσιν, "redemption," and is thus expexegetical (or explanatory).

Some scholars have observed that the term ἄφεσις, "forgiveness," is not Paul's normal way of describing salvation and that its appearance here (and at Eph 1:7) could be taken as a sign of a different author.[74] Yet one cannot simply dismiss the use of the verbal form (ἀφέθησαν, "forgiven") in Rom 4:7 (as an example of Paul's familiarity and usage of "forgiveness") since it is in an OT quotation; it appears at an important juncture in his explanation of the gospel. But more importantly, the *concept* of forgiveness is pervasive and foundational to Paul's thought. In the creedal tradition that he passes on to the Corinthians (and presumably many others), Christ's death "for our sins" is central (1 Cor 15:3). He tells the Galatians that Christ gave himself "for our sins" (Gal 1:4). The idea of forgiveness of sins is present in Rom 3:21–26 with the nexus of concepts he presents there as the solution to the universal sinfulness of humanity. Furthermore, "the gift of righteousness" bestowed upon believers (Rom 5:17) answers the problem of the trespass and disobedience of Adam, which set the pattern for all of humanity to follow after him. This gift, which is a manifestation of God's grace, is a functional equivalent of the expression, "forgiveness of sins" (see also 1 Cor 1:30; Phil 3:9). Similarly, some have also contended that the plural ἁμαρτίαι, "sins," is un-Pauline and that Paul conceives of sin as a cosmic power against which

74 E.g., Kiley, *Colossians as Pseudepigraphy*, 65.

believers struggle.[75] But once again this kind of distinction is false and ignores some of the evidence of the letters. While it is true that Paul can conceive of sin as a cosmic power (Rom 5:12–21; 7:7–25), he also cites Ps 32:1–2 approvingly: "blessed are they whose transgressions are forgiven, whose sins [ἁμαρτίαι] are covered" (Rom 4:7). Such a position also ignores the interchangeability of ἁμαρτίαι, "sins," with παραπτώματα, "transgressions," in Paul's thought (see Rom 4:25; 5:15, 16, 17, 18, 20; 11:11, 12; 2 Cor 5:19).

If the language that Paul uses in Col 1:13–14 comes from widely used traditional material in the early church, the discussion of whether it sounds "Pauline" may be somewhat moot. The important observation to make is that the convictions represented by it are thoroughly consistent with Paul's thought on the nature of salvation. The context of the original usage of this material is beyond recovery. So the common assumption that it is reflective of baptism is possible,[76] but only speculative. It could just as easily have come from an early Christian confession concerning the heart of the gospel.

It is quite possible that Paul has selected traditional material and shaped 1:13–14 to build a theological foundation for his polemic against the teaching of "the philosophy." Many of the older commentators saw the word ἀπολύτρωσις, "redemption," as key and suggested that the leaders of the faction were presenting an alternative system of redemption. Lightfoot, for instance, cited statements about Marcosian and Valentinian forms of Gnosticism as illustrations of how a false idea about redemption "would naturally be associated with an esoteric doctrine of angelic powers."[77] Others have looked at passages in the Nag Hammadi codices for understandings of alternative forms of redemption in antiquity. Wilson is correct, however, in asserting that these gnostic teachings are "still in the remote future so far as the author of Colossians is concerned; there is no sign that the 'false teachers' had gone to such lengths as the later Gnostics were to do."[78]

Based on all of the indicators of the nature of the teaching of the Colossian "philosophy," there is nothing that demonstrates they were presenting a system of redemption—that is, another way of salvation. But this does not mean that Paul's teaching about "deliverance," "redemption," and "transfer" of kingdoms was not directly relevant. These truths would have communicated to the Colossian believers their new freedom from the tyranny of demonic powers by virtue of their union with the exalted Christ. Therefore, the alternative ways of dealing with the powers suggested by the adherents of "the philosophy" would be unnecessary. To further substantiate this, Paul will next turn his attention to giving them a grand view of the power and greatness of the Lord whom they now serve in his poetic praise of Christ.

75 E.g., Lindemann, 23–24.
76 E.g., Lohse, 40; Schweizer, 53–54.
77 Lightfoot, 143.
78 Wilson, 121.

## *Explanation*

This passage is an extension of the prayer report that Paul began in 1:3, but now he moves from an expression of his constant gratitude to God for the Colossian believers to a summary of how he and Timothy pray for them constantly. The depth of concern displayed by Paul and Timothy for the Colossians is somewhat remarkable, given the distance that separated them and, more importantly, the fact that the authors of the letter lacked personal and direct familiarity with this Lycus Valley community of believers. Because of this, the passage is as much a statement about Paul and Timothy as it is about the Colossians. Many in Paul's situation as a prisoner would have become self-absorbed with worry and mental preparation for the impending trial. Yet Paul remains concerned about the churches—not just those he has been directly involved in planting, but others as well. He clearly felt some level of responsibility for the Colossian church since it was founded by someone who came to know Christ through his own proclamation and ministry, presumably while he was in Ephesus in AD 52–55. Paul did not entertain occasional fleeting thoughts about the Colossians but exhibited a regular concern that resulted in him and Timothy engaging in intercessory prayer for them every single day (this frequency is the minimum required by the governing verbal expression, "we do not stop praying and interceding," 1:9).

The heart of Paul's prayer is that the Colossian believers would gain a much better understanding of God's will for their lives, so that they would conduct their lives in a manner both worthy of the Lord and pleasing to him. He wants them to do this by flourishing in a life devoted to good works, by depending on God's power for dealing with their circumstances and living their daily lives, and by developing a heart of gratitude in their new status of belonging to God.

The prayer as a whole could be expressed to God for any group of Christians at any time. It is not so situational that it relates only to the particular circumstances the readers are facing in Colossae. Yet many of the elements of the prayer seem particularly well-suited for the situation the readers face.

The primary request of the prayer is for the Colossians to gain an expanded and clear knowledge of God's will for their lives (1:9). It is striking, however, that Paul modifies knowledge with two prepositional phrases. He wants their knowledge to be tempered and informed by wisdom and for their insight to be guided and inspired by the Holy Spirit. It is clear elsewhere in this letter that the opponents were offering the congregation a teaching that had a reputation as wisdom (2:23), but the clear implication is that Paul did not regard it as such. For Paul, the principal source of wisdom and knowledge is Christ (2:3). One of the major difficulties he has with the teaching of "the philosophy" is that the advocates are not properly connected to Christ and drawing on his wisdom (2:19). Therefore, the ringleaders of the opposition are not within the will of God and conducting their lives in a way that is honorable to the Lord or pleasing to him.

Paul's prayerful goal that the Colossians demonstrate growth in performing good works based on a proper knowledge of God and his desires for them is an aim that is important for all Christians. What he means by good works is unpacked later in the letter when he appeals to them to get rid of sinful behaviors in their lives (3:5–11), by displaying virtuous behavior (3:12–17), and by living appropriately within their spheres of responsibilities as members of households (3:18–4:1). Failure to do this would presumably result in evil deeds, but living according to these revealed standards of God's will would issue in good deeds. On this topic, there is an important convergence with the concerns expressed in the letter by James when he asks the rhetorical question, "What good is it, my brothers and sisters, if someone claims to have faith but has no deeds?" (Jas 2:14 NIV). Paul clearly looked for good deeds in evaluating whether someone was genuinely a Christian (see, e.g., 1 Thess 1:3), but he also expects true believers to exhibit these good deeds in increasing measure throughout their lives (see also Eph 2:10).

Another significant element of the prayer is that they would grow in dependence on God's power—the magnitude of which he emphasizes in two prepositional phrases (1:11). The readers will need divine enablement to resist the opposing teachers and their message, as well as for dealing with the disruptive influence this teaching has already had on the community of believers at Colossae. Thus "endurance" for bearing up under this trial and "patience" with fellow believers who have variously responded to "the philosophy" are quite relevant for the situation. But the Colossians will also need God's regular empowering for their continuing struggle with the principalities and powers. If the enticement of the teaching, rituals, and practices of "the philosophy" has something to do with their sense of vulnerability to the hostile powers, then Paul's prayer for them to be strengthened by the vast spiritual power available to them from God is crucially important. This is also a major theme and concern reflected in the letter to the Ephesians (see esp. Eph 1:19–23; 3:14–19, 20–21; 6:10–20).

The final aspect of the prayer is for the Colossians to give joyous thanks to God for their new situation in life, as a people chosen by God who now possess a new status expressed by the metaphor of "light" (1:12–14). Paul began his prayer by informing them that he and Timothy regularly give thanks that they show evidence of belonging to God by their faith in Christ and the love they show in the Christian community (1:3–5). He now concludes the prayer by enjoining them to give thanks for the fact that they belong based on God's work for them in and through his Son. In some fashion, the opponents were using the language of disqualification in their efforts to gain adherents to their specific teaching and practices (2:18). Paul's prayer that the believers would understand and deeply embrace the fact that God has qualified them to belong to himself and the kingdom of his Son is vitally important for them to have the fortitude and ability to resist the competing and dangerous teaching. Helping them to understand and exult in their new identity as saints, participants in the light, and united to Christ is a major part of Paul's strategy in this letter, especially in 1:21–23, 26–29, 2:1–15, and 3:1–4.

The final portion of the prayer (1:13–14), which also provides a transition to the hymnic praise of Christ (1:15–20), provides an explanation of how God has made it possible for the Colossian believers to belong and thus functions to give further reasons for the joyous thanksgiving that should characterize the lives of Christians. Ultimately, the forgiveness of sins has made it possible for people to have a relationship with God, and this forms part of the definition of redemption (see 1:14). Yet Paul also defines redemption here both as an act of rescue that God has performed to deliver humanity from the realm of the hostile principalities and powers, as well as a transfer and membership in the realm over which the resurrected Christ is Lord (1:13). This emphasis furthers the special concern that Paul has in this letter about the adversarial role of the principalities and powers. The implication of this portion of the passage is that the readers should therefore no longer fear the dark spiritual powers, that they have been dramatically delivered from this realm in their conversion, and that they no longer belong to that realm. Their identity is now defined by belonging to an altogether new realm characterized by "light" and ruled over by Jesus Christ, the Son of God, who is full of love.

This teaching provides an assurance that neither astral fate nor spirits of any kind can make any legitimate claim on the life of a Christian. That realm stands in opposition to Christ, just as light is in opposition to darkness. Believers can therefore rejoice and give thanks for the assurance of belonging and by all that is entailed in membership in this new realm. But this belonging also gives access to spiritual power from God (1:11), which enables his people to bear fruit in good deeds (1:10).

# Hymnic Praise to Christ (1:15–20)

## *Bibliography*

**Aletti, J.-N.** *Colossiens 1,15–20.* **Arnold, C. E.** *Colossian Syncretism*, 246–70. ———. "'Head' of the Church," 346–66. **Balchin, J. F.** "Colossians 1:15–20," 65–94. **Bammel, E.** "Versuch," 88–95. **Bandstra, A. J.** "Plērōma as Pneuma," 96–102. **Bauckham, R.** "Where Is Wisdom to Be Found?," 129–38. **Baugh, S.** "Col 1:15–20," 227–44. **Baur, F. C.** *Paul the Apostle.* **Beasley-Murray, P.** "Colossians 1:15–20," 169–83. **Beetham, C. A.** *Echoes of Scripture.* 113–56. **Benoit, P.** "L'hymne christologique," 226–63. ———. "Plèroma," 136–58. **Botha, J.** "Stylistic Analysis," 238–51. **Bruce, F. F.** "Colossians 1:15–20," 99–111. **Brucker, R.** *Christushymnen.* **Buresch, K.** *Klaros.* **Bürger, C.** *Schöpfung und Versöhnung.* **Burney, C. F.** "Christ as the ARXH," 160–77. **Cannon, G.** *Traditional Material*, 19–37. **Capes, D. B.** *Old Testament Yahweh Texts.* **Carr, W.** *Angels and Principalities.* **Chiai, G. F.** "Allmächtiger Götter," 61–106. **Collins, C. J.** "Colossians 1,17," 64–87. **Copenhaver, A.** "Echoes of a Hymn," 235–55. **Cosgrove, C. H.** "Early Christian Hymns," 158–80. **D'Andria, F.** *Hierapolis of Phrygia.* **Deichgräber, R.** *Gotteshymnus.* **Dübbers, M.** *Christologie und Existenz*, 84–177; **Dunne, J.** "Regal Status," 3–18. **Edsall, B.,** and **J. R. Strawbridge.** "The Songs We Used to Sing?," 290–311. **Ellis, E. E.** "Colossians 1:12–20," 415–28. **Fee, G.** *Pauline Christology*, 289–338. **Fischer, K. M.** *Tendenz und Absicht.* **Fossum, J.** "Colossians 1:15–18," 183–201. ———. "Image of the Invisible God," 13–39. **Fowl, S.** *Story of Christ*, 103–54. **Gabathuler, H. J.** *Haupt.* **Gese, H.** "Weisheit," 218–48. **Gloer, W. H.** "Homologies and Hymns," 115–32. **Gordley, M. E.** *Colossian Hymn.* **Graf, F.** *Magic in the Ancient World.* **Harrison, J. R.** "Confession Inscriptions," 337–87. **Hartmann, L.** "Universal Reconciliation," 109–21. **Hegermann, H.** *Schöpfungsmittler*, 138–57. **Heil, J. P.** *Colossians*, 63–81. **Helyer, L.** "Arius Revisited," 59–67. ———. "Colossians 1:15–20," 167–79. ———. "Cosmic Christology," 235–46. ———. "Recent Research," 51–67. **Hengel, M.** "Chrustuslied," 357–404. ———. "Hymns and Christology," 78–96. **Hofius, O.** "Erstgeborener," 185–203. **Hölscher, A.** "Bild Gottes," 114–33. **Holtzmann, H. J.** *Kritik.* **Hooker, M. D.** "Where Is Wisdom to Be Found?," 116–28. **Hurtado, L.** *Lord Jesus Christ.* ———. *One God, One Lord.* **Huttner, U.** *Early Christianity in the Lycus Valley.* **Jobes, K.** "Sophia Christology," 79–103. **Käsemann, E.** "Baptismal Liturgy," 149–68. ———. *Leib und Leib Christi.* **Kehl, N.** *Christushymnus.* **Laks, A.,** and **G. W. Most,** eds. *Studies on the Derveni Papyrus.* **Lamp, J. S.** "Wisdom in Col 1:15–20," 45–53. **Lee, M. V.** *Body of Christ.* **Löhr, H.** "Christian Hymnody," 157–74. **Loke, A. T. E.** *Divine Christology.* **Magie, D.** *Roman Rule.* 2 vols. **Maier, H. O.** "Colossians and Empire," 323–49. **Maurer, C.** "Begründung," 79–93. **Merkelbach, R.** *Philologica.* **Merkelbach, R.,** and **J. Stauber.** "Orakel des Apollon," 1–54. **Michaelis, W.** *Versöhnung des Alls.* **Miller, C.** "Imperial Cult," 314–32. **Müller, P.** *Anfänge der Paulusschule.* **Münderlein, G.** "Erwählung," 264–76. **Murphy-O'Connor, J.** *Paul.* ———. "Tradition and Redaction," 231–41. **Norden, E.** *Agnostos Theos.* **Overfield, P. D.** "Pleroma," 384–96. **Papanikolaou, D.** "Aretalogy of Isis," 59–70. **Peppard, M.** "Poetry," 319–42. **Percy, E.** *Probleme.* **Pizzuto, V. A.** *Cosmic Leap of Faith.* **Porter, S. E.** *Καταλλάσσω.* **Ricl, M.** "Cults of Phrygia Epiktetos, 133–48. **Robinson, J. M.** "Formal Analysis," 270–87. **Robinson, T. L.** "Oracles and Their Society," 59–77. **Rollins, W. G.** "Christological *Tendenz*," 123–38. **Roose, H.** "Leib-Metapher," 117–41. **Sappington, T. J.** *Revelation and Redemption.* **Schenke, H.-M.** *Der Gott "Mensch."* **Schille, G.** *Hymnen.* **Schleiermacher, F.** "Ueber Koloss. 1, 15–20," 497–537. **Schnelle, U.** *Theology*, 539–57. **Schnabel, E. J.** *Law and Wisdom.* **Schottroff, L.** "Ist Allein in Christus Heil?," 79–89. **Schweizer, E.** "Colossians 1:15–20," 97–104. ———. "Versöhnung des Alls," 487–501. **Standhartinger, A.** "Kolosserhymnus," 69–91. **Stettler, C.** *Kolosserhymnus.* **Strawbridge, J. R.** *Pauline Effect*, 135–73. **Vollenweider, S.** "Hymnus," 208–31. **Walter, N.** "Geschichte und Mythos," 224–34. **Wedderburn, A. J. M.** "Theology of Colossians," 1–71.

**Weiss, J.** *Christ.* **Wengst, K.** *Christologische Formeln und Lieder.* **West, M. L.** *Greek Meter.* **Wink, W.** *Engaging the Powers.* **Wright, N. T.** "Poetry and Theology," 99–119. **Zeilinger, F.** *Erstgeborene.*

## *Translation*

*15He is the image of the invisible God,*
*Firstborn over all creation,*
*16For in him all things were created,*
*in[a] the heavens and upon[a] the earth,*
*the invisible and the visible,*
*whether thrones or dominions,*
*whether principalities or authorities*
*All things have been created through him and for him.*

*17And he is before all things,*
*and all things hold together in him.*
*18And he is the head of the body, the church.*

*He is the beginning,*
*Firstborn from the dead,*
*that he would be preeminent in all things,*
*19for in him all the fullness was pleased to dwell*
*20and through him to reconcile all things to him*
*by making peace through the blood of his cross,*
*through him,[b] whether things on earth or things in heaven.*

## *Notes*

a. [1:16] The Majority text and some other witnesses insert the neuter plural article τά before ἐν τοῖς οὐρανοῖς and before ἐπὶ τῆς γῆς. This is likely due to scribal assimilation to the same expressions in 1:20.

b. [1:20] The prepositional phrase δι' αὐτοῦ is missing in Codex Vaticanus (B) and many Western witnesses (D F G it vg Jerome and Augustine). It is present, however, in 𝔓[46], Codex Sinaiticus (א), and many Alexandrian witnesses (A C P Ψ 33 cop[bo] et al.), along with the Majority text. Although the textual witnesses are fairly evenly split, the internal evidence would tip the balance in favor of the inclusion of the phrase. It is the more difficult reading from the vantage point of the scribe because it appears repetitive (note the use of δι' αὐτοῦ in 1:20a) and unnecessary. Nevertheless, it could represent the hymn writer's rhetorical emphasis on Christ as the agent of reconciliation. The absence of the phrase in some manuscripts may be explained by homoeoteleuton. Although some commentators favor the inclusion,[1] most commentators and the majority of English versions omit the phrase; the exceptions include NASB; NKJV.

1 See, e.g., Pao, 105; Foster, 200; Wilson, 155.

## *Form/Structure/Setting*

### *Form (and Literary Context)*

This beautiful ascription of praise to Christ extols his universal sovereignty and preeminence, especially against a backdrop of evil spiritual forces. His exalted position is rooted in the fact that he himself created the universe and continues to sustain what he has made. But this extraordinary paragraph also lauds Christ for establishing a new order of humanity based on his death on the cross and resurrection from the dead. These two ideas—sovereignty and redemption—are brought together in the final line that points to a time when Christ will ultimately pacify all his enemies, and all of creation will be characterized by a universal shalom.

### Literary Context

The content of this passage fits with what the apostle has said previously in the introduction of the letter and lays an important foundation for his engagement with the assumptions and explicit teaching of the oppositional group within the Colossian church. In his introductory expression of thanksgiving to God, Paul recognizes the special relationship of Christ to the Father when he calls God "the Father of our Lord Jesus Christ" (1:3). He then describes Christ as the appropriate object of the saving faith of the Colossians and thus as the basis of their hope (1:4–5). They heard this good news from one of their own, Epaphras, whom Paul describes as a "servant of Christ" (1:7). More immediately, he describes Christ as the Son of God and as the ruler of a new order of humanity into which the Colossians have been installed, after being rescued from a dominion controlled by a supernatural evil ruler (1:13). The readers have thus been prepared for a passage that proclaims that Christ is sovereign over all the powers of darkness, that he is Lord over a new domain (the church), and that he will subjugate all opposition in the future, establishing a universal peace.

The passage also forms the basis for much of his subsequent teaching in the letter. Following his praise of Christ, Paul immediately picks up the theme of reconciliation and applies it specifically to the Colossian believers (1:21–23). Jesus's death and resurrection serve as the theological heart of the letter and explain how the new humanity came into existence by their solidarity with Christ in these foundational actions (2:9–13). Paul reiterates the theme of "fullness" by affirming its ecclesiological relevance: "all the fullness of deity lives in him bodily, and you have been filled in your union with him" (2:9–10). But it is Christ's sovereignty over the supernatural forces of evil that Paul puts in bold relief. They have been gloriously defeated by this death and resurrection (2:15), and Christ now reigns supreme over them (2:10). Thus, the church should not be deceived and led astray by the influence of these forces (2:8), because believers have died to the compelling pull of their power (2:20).

## History and Traditions

There is a massive amount of literature written about this remarkable passage. Not only have the series of extraordinary statements made about Jesus Christ attracted comment and explanation through the centuries but the literary form, the style of writing, and the religious-historical background of the content have been the focus of numerous academic monographs and journal articles, especially over the past century. The year 1913 marked a decisive turning point in the study of Col 1:15–20. In that year, Eduard Norden published the results of his research on forms of religious discourse under the title, *Agnostos Theos*. His treatment of Col 1:15–20, however, was very brief—only five pages—but it served as the catalyst for numerous form-critical studies that would later conclude that this elegant and poetic passage was a portion of an early Christian hymn. In Norden's study, he observed a handful of formal characteristics, such as the use of relative clauses in making doctrinal predications, as indicative of a solemn, formulaic style that is appropriate for prayer. Norden stopped short of concluding that the author cited a hymn, but he suggested that the passage was a doxology that stemmed from Hellenistic-Jewish circles.[2] For Norden, the author of this passage depended heavily on liturgical phraseology and shaped it into a doxological praise of Christ. Although Norden exercised the most influence on the subsequent course of scholarship, he was not the first to conclude that this passage was traditional. A few years earlier in 1909, J. Weiss had suggested that Col 1:15–20 represented "a kind of dogmatic hymn" that could be "divided into two exactly corresponding strophes (vv. 15–17 and 18–20)."[3] Weiss contended that the background of the hymn was rooted in Stoic teaching about the Logos as well as Philo of Alexandria.

Prior to Weiss and Norden, scholars had long noted the elevated style of the passage. As early as 1832, Schleiermacher commented on the parallelism present in the structure of the passage.[4] In 1856, Eadie described these six verses as a lofty paragraph characterized by "marvelous terseness and harmony . . . in rich and glowing accumulation of sentences," in which the apostle "can scarcely find language of sufficient energy and lustre to tell in it the honour and majesty of the Redeemer. . . . How he exults in the precious theme, and how his soul swells into impassioned panagyric!"[5] But the focus for most commentators remained strictly on the interpretation of the christological statements made in these six verses, with a few exceptions. In 1872, Holtzmann made observations on the doublets, the parallelism, and the relative clauses in the style of the text, but these he attributed to a later interpolator who substantially expanded the original text of Colossians.[6]

---

2 Norden, *Agnostos Theos*, 250–54.

3 Weiss, *Christ*, 84–85. Norden, *Agnostos Theos*, 253n2, acknowledges the contribution by Weiss.

4 Schleiermacher, "Ueber Koloss. 1, 15–20," 497–537, esp. 501–3.

5 Eadie, 41.

6 Holtzmann, *Kritik*, 124, 149–50.

Following the seminal work of Weiss and Norden, the entire course of scholarship shifted to include detailed investigations into the form and style of the passage while simultaneously attempting to discern its history-of-religions background.[7] In his 1927 commentary on Colossians, M. Dibelius characterized 1:15–20 as a "christologische Exkurs" in two parts with substantial parallelism between the two, although he hesitated calling it a hymn at that time. He argued that the author was indebted to the Logos teaching of Hellenistic Judaism and the gnostic *Urmensch* myth for much of the content and conceptuality.[8] This observation pointed the direction for future scholarship on this passage.

E. Lohmeyer, in his important 1930 commentary on Colossians,[9] recognized certain formal characteristics that he described as hymnic (with each line following a strict rhetorical pattern), but he contended that the beginning of this passage is in v. 13.[10] He argued that the passage was formulated by Paul himself for the purpose of confronting the situation in the Colossian church. He went in an entirely different direction than Dibelius, however, in rooting the content of the hymn squarely within Judaism. He argued that although many elements of the hymn come from Jewish Wisdom and Greek popular philosophy, the entire hymn was shaped against the backdrop of the Jewish Day of Atonement ritual (Lev 16). His analysis of the formal features of the hymn have not proven compelling to contemporary interpreters, nor has his connecting it to Jewish conceptions of the Day of Atonement. Lohse, for instance, has noted that the term "to reconcile" (ἀποκαταλλάξαι) "does not allude, even remotely, to a connection with Jewish conceptions of sacrifices and of the great Day of Atonement."[11] Nevertheless, a more recent stream of scholarship has given a positive appraisal of this background and regards it as a direction that is worth building on today.[12]

In a highly influential essay published in 1949 in a Festschrift for R. Bultmann, E. Käsemann built on the earlier work of Dibelius and argued that the concrete religious background of the hymn reflects "the contours of the gnostic myth of the Archetypal Man who is the Redeemer."[13] This myth, according to Käsemann, had penetrated Hellenistic Judaism to the point that

---

7 Helpful summaries of the research on the exegesis of 1:15–20 are contained in Gabathuler, *Jesus Christus*, 11–124, and in Benoit, "L'hymne christologique," 226–63. Gabathuler summarizes the work of eighteen scholars, beginning with Schleiermacher and ending with Conzelmann (1962). Benoit summarizes treatments from Schliermacher to Pöhlmann (1973). Helyer, "Recent Research," 51–67, has provided a summary and critique of studies appearing in the 1980s.

8 Dibelius (1927), 6–7, 14–15.

9 Lohmeyer's 1930 commentary was the first edition of his commentary on Colossians, but the eighth edition in the Kritisch-exegetischer Kommentar series. His was preceded by commentaries written by H. A. W. Meyer, A. H. Franke, and E. Haupt.

10 Lohmeyer, 40–45.

11 Lohse, 46.

12 Stettler, *Christushymnus*, 9–10. See also Stuhlmacher, *Biblical Theology*, 439–40; Gese, "Weisheit," 242–43.

13 Käsemann, "Baptismal Liturgy," 155. So also, Bultmann, *Theology*, 1:176, 178–79.

it was combined with the conceptions of Sophia and Logos. The Christian community had taken this religious hymn celebrating the enthronement of the gnostic redeemer and edited it for its own purposes. This Christianized hymn was known and used in the Colossian community prior to the writing of this letter.[14] The writer of Colossians then appropriated the hymn for his own purposes, which had to do primarily with polemicizing against a false teaching that was threatening the Colossian community. In particular, the opponents ("the Colossian syncretists") "felt that they were in the hands of cosmic powers and authorities" and that the soteriological act of forgiveness of sins proclaimed to them was insufficient for protecting them from the menace of the cosmos. They needed assurance that the *Kyrios* "is mightier than the cosmic powers and holds sway over them."[15] In the words of Wagenführer, "Only a cosmic Christ, who is at once the soul of the world and its Creator, could satisfy and overcome the religious concern of the Colossian syncretism."[16] For Käsemann, the original form of the hymn celebrated the *Urmensch* as Lord of the universe who would one day reconcile the universe to himself. The references to "the church" (τῆς ἐκκλησίας; 1:18a) and "through the blood of his cross" (διὰ τοῦ αἵματος τοῦ σταυροῦ αὐτοῦ; 1:20b) do not fit with this conceptuality. Käsemann thus reasoned that these must be additions to the hymn by Christian hands before the author of the letter received it.[17] In terms of the hymnic form, Käsemann assumed far more than he proved. He relied on Norden ("a critic with so expert a knowledge") and pointed to the relative clauses that for him "bear a liturgical stamp" and are "characteristic of hymnal texts," the various lines of verse "clearly stylized in liturgical fashion," as well as the unique theological concepts.[18]

Käsemann's contribution represented the high point of the *religionsgeschichtliche Schule* and its emphasis on gnosis as a major contributing factor to much of NT theology and terminology. His influence can be seen in much of the subsequent scholarship on the Colossian hymn. Yet in recent decades, NT scholarship has rightly cast significant doubt on the postulation of a pre-Christian gnosis. Few scholars today see gnosis as a religious system forming the background to anything in Colossians, and especially in seeing the original form of the Colossian hymn as "the supra-historical and metaphysical drama of the Gnostic Redeemer."[19] It is highly unlikely that the original hymn can be understood as a pre-Christian composition since it contains clear references to the Christian kerygma.[20] However, Käsemann's conclusions regarding the hymnic form of

14 Käsemann, "Baptismal Liturgy," 152.

15 Käsemann, "Baptismal Liturgy," 167. In this understanding, Käsemann is in full agreement with Dibelius (15).

16 Wagenführer, *Die Bedeutung Christi*, 19 (as cited in Käsemann, "Baptismal Liturgy," 167).

17 Käsemann, "Baptismal Liturgy," 151–53.

18 Käsemann, "Baptismal Liturgy," 151–53.

19 Käsemann, "Baptismal Liturgy," 155.

20 See Strecker, *Theology*, 552.

the passage and editorial insertions to the original form of the hymn have been widely accepted and developed. Nevertheless, he was right to see the Wisdom tradition as relevant to understanding the hymn and also in pointing to the concern the readers would have had about cosmic powers and evil spiritual forces.

In the last few decades, there does appear to be a semblance of a consensus reached that the essential framework and much of the terminology of the hymn is rooted in the Wisdom tradition (especially as seen in Proverbs, Wisdom, Sirach, and Philo). Some of the predications made about Christ, such as "image of God," "firstborn," and "the beginning" have been seen by many interpreters as rooted in the characterizations of divine Wisdom. Lohse observes that "with these designations the hymn relates to the characterizations which Hellenistic synagogues gave to Wisdom."[21] Similarly, Dunn has argued for seeing the language of the hymn as terminology that is "used commonly in Hellenistic Judaism in reference to divine Wisdom," while observing that "the Wisdom character of the hymn is a matter of broad consensus."[22] Bormann likewise concludes that, "the biblical-Jewish Wisdom tradition is the most important source of the hymn in Colossians 1:15–20."[23]

Proverbs 8 is the fountainhead for the personification of wisdom in biblical and Jewish tradition. The writer assigns wisdom a place alongside God in the beginning and attributes to wisdom a role in creating the universe:

> The LORD created [ἔκτισεν] me at the beginning [ἀρχήν] of his work, the first of his acts of long ago. Ages ago I was set up, at the first, before the beginning of the earth. When there were no depths I was brought forth, . . . before the mountains had been shaped, before the hills, I was brought forth [γεννᾷ]. . . . When he established the heavens, I was there, . . . when he marked out the foundations of the earth, then I was beside him, like a master worker; and I was daily his delight, rejoicing before him always, rejoicing in his inhabited world and delighting in the human race. (Prov 8:22–31 NRSV)

This conceptuality was developed in subsequent Jewish literature—especially the wisdom tradition and Philo. The seventh chapter of the Wisdom of Solomon contains noteworthy statements about Wisdom that bear similarity to the Colossian hymn:

> For wisdom, the fashioner [τεχνῖτις] of all things, taught me. There is in her a spirit that is intelligent, holy, . . . all-powerful, overseeing all, and penetrating

21 Lohse, 46. See Schweizer, 63–88.

22 Dunn, 86.

23 Bormann, 87. See also, e.g., Beetham, *Echoes of Scripture*, 113–41; Stettler, *Christushymnus*, 339; Strecker, *Theology*, 553; Schnelle, *Theology*, 552; Sappington, *Revelation and Redemption*, 172–74; Schnabel, *Law and Wisdom*, 258.

> through all spirits that are intelligent, pure, and altogether subtle. For wisdom is more mobile than any motion; because of her pureness she pervades and penetrates all things [διὰ πάντων]. For she is a breath of the power of God [τῆς τοῦ θεοῦ δυνάμεως], and a pure emanation of the glory of the Almighty; therefore nothing defiled gains entrance into her. For she is a reflection of eternal light [φωτὸς ἀϊδίου], a spotless mirror of the working of God, and an image [εἰκών] of his goodness. Although she is but one, she can do all things [οὖσα πάντα δύναται]. . . . Compared with the light she is found to be superior, for it is succeeded by the night, but against wisdom evil does not prevail. (Wis 7:22–30 NRSV; see also 1:7; 9:9)

Similar exalted statements about personified Wisdom are made by Sirach. The voice of Wisdom declares, "Before the ages, in the beginning [ἀπ' ἀρχῆς], he created me, and for all the ages I shall not cease to be" (Sir 24:9). Throughout this entire section of Sirach, Wisdom is portrayed as the divine Shekinah that dwelt in Zion (Sir 24:7–12).[24]

Philo of Alexandria continues the tradition of reflecting on Wisdom as a personfied attribute of God, using some of the language to describe Wisdom that we find in the Colossian hymn:

> "And God planted a pleasaunce in Eden toward the sun-rising, and placed there the man whom He had formed" (Gen. ii. 8). By using many words for it Moses has already made it manifest that the sublime and heavenly wisdom [οὐράνιον σοφίαν] is of many names; for he calls it "beginning" [ἀρχήν] and "image" [εἰκόνα] and "vision of God." (Philo, *Alleg. Interp.* 1.43 LCL)

Throughout his writings, Philo's comments about the personified Word of God overlap with what he says about personified Wisdom. His descriptions about the Word also bear terminological and conceptual similarities to Col 1:15–20. For instance, he observes, "The image of God is the Word through whom the whole universe was framed" (Philo, *Spec. Laws* 1.81 LCL).[25]

Although it seems clear that many of the functions of personified Wisdom are transferred to Christ by the hymn writer and thus appropriated by the author of the letter, there are significant limitations to this perspective. It should first be observed that whereas Wisdom exists prior to the material creation, the texts regularly characterize Wisdom as "the *first* of God's 'creations,' and thus, though preexistent, *personified* Wisdom is never visualized as eternal," as Fee aptly observes.[26] Christ is not portrayed as a created being in the hymn. The fact that he is "before all things" (1:17a) suggests his eternality.

---

24 Stettler, *Christushymnus*, 116.

25 See Beetham, *Echoes of Scripture*, 120–30.

26 Fee, *Christology*, 300n31.

Some statements made about Christ in the hymn go beyond anything present in the Wisdom traditions. This would include the claim that Jesus is the goal of creation (εἰς αὐτόν; 1:16f), that he "holds all things together" (συνέστηκεν; 1:17b), that he is the head of the body (1:18), that he is preeminent (πρωτεύων; 1:18d), that "all the fullness" dwells in him (πᾶν τὸ πλήρωμα; 1:19), and that he reconciles all of creation to God and brings universal peace (1:20). It is also important to note that Wisdom is never represented as a redeemer. Other traditions need to be considered for their contribution to the hymn. I will provide a brief explanation here, but the full details will be unpacked in the commentary. These traditions would include the following.

(1) *Atonement (Versöhnung) Tradition in the OT.* H. Gese, C. Stettler, and P. Stuhlmacher have made a strong case for understanding the background of the hymn not only in Wisdom theology but in the atonement (*Versöhnung*) tradition of the OT.[27] It is important to observe that the hymn is introduced by the redemption effected by Christ and the resultant forgiveness of sins (1:14). In the section immediately following the hymn (1:21–23), reconciliation of believers to God is based on a bloody sacrifice that has been made on their behalf. This atonement finds its roots in the OT sacrificial system and the Day of Atonement ritual. This view is given full expression in Stettler's monograph on the Christ-hymn.[28]

(2) *Royal Davidic Messiah.* This is especially seen in the allusion to a Davidic, messianic psalm in the hymn writer's declaration that Jesus is "firstborn of all creation" (1:15b; see Ps 89:27).[29] It should also be noted that the language of "ruling," although expressed by the term κεφαλή, which is dependent on a common Koine metaphor, likewise is descriptive of the work of the Messiah who is establishing his own reign and kingdom (1:13). The role of Christ in bringing universal shalom (1:20b) should also be seen as reflecting OT messianic texts.

(3) *Jewish Apocalyptic and Folk Magic.* The enumeration of the powers (1:16) is dependent on the language of Jewish apocalyptic, with the terms also appearing in Jewish folk-magic texts. Whether this listing goes back to the original hymn writer or should be seen as an editorial addition has been a matter of debate.

(4) *The Oral Gospel Tradition.* When the hymn writer speaks of the fullness being "well pleased" (εὐδόκησεν) to dwell in Christ (1:19), there may be an allusion to the baptismal tradition of Jesus recorded by the Synoptic writers.

(5) *Common Koine Usage.* The head-body imagery (1:18) is a metaphor derived from common physiological understandings of the period attested in medical writers, some philosophers, and Philo. The term "preeminent" (1:18d; πρωτεύων) is found in many of the documentary inscriptions from Asia Minor.

---

27 Gese, "Weisheit," 218–48; Stuhlmacher, *Biblical Theology*, 436–41.

28 Although I agree with the substance and much of the details of this thesis, there are a number of places where I will contend for a different background in the commentary.

29 See also Dunne, "Regal Status," 13–14.

And there are other terms for which there are no direct Hebrew or Aramaic equivalents.[30]

(6) *Other OT Texts.* Beyond the messianic texts, the hymn writer may have depended directly on other OT texts.[31] Although "beginning" (ἀρχή) is used to describe personified Wisdom, it is difficult to escape the fact that anyone familiar with the LXX would have immediately connected it to Gen 1:1. It is possible that the hymn writer was also thinking of the first verse of Torah in describing Christ as the beginning of the new creation.[32] Another important term in the hymn that is best explained on the basis of the OT is "fullness" (1:19; πλήρωμα). In the commentary I will explain how OT texts describing the glory of the Lord filling the temple set the conceptual framework for this language.

It is possible that the passage also contains some liturgical statements that had been used in other contexts. This was actually Norden's conclusion. But any effort to identify these has proven to be futile.

The Wisdom tradition was a help to early Christians in their effort to understand the being and work of Christ in a framework of monotheism by providing an important analogy in personified divine Wisdom. This tradition gave Christians some of the language to describe Christ's preexistence, his role in creation, and his exalted nature. Although the language and imagery of Wisdom takes us far down the road of interpreting many formulations in the Christ-hymn, it falls short in explaining all of the unique statements in the hymn. It is therefore best to interpret the hymn in light of a "combination of backgrounds," especially representing OT and Jewish traditions.[33] Similarly, Gordley concludes that the passage is a Christian hymn employing a variety of Jewish and Hellenistic traditions, but he minimizes the importance of the Wisdom tradition (as well as the other traditions I have mentioned) in favor of emphasizing that "the phraseology has a Stoic, or Middle Platonist, or more generally, a 'philosophical' feel to it."[34]

---

30 Even Stettler, *Christushymnus*, 346, acknowledges this and points to the lexemes ἀόρατος, ὁρατός, συνίστημι, and πρωτεύω in particular as having a Greek origin.

31 Contra Strecker, *Theology*, 553, who says that "the influence of the *Old Testament* is minimal" (emphasis original).

32 This is argued by Burney, "Christ as the ARXH," 160–77, and further developed by Wright, "Poetry and Theology," 455–58. Burney contended that "Paul is giving an elaborate exposition of the first word in Genesis, *Berêshîth*, and interpreting *rêshîth* as referring to Christ" (160). He further argued that Paul was making this connection through the prism of personified Wisdom as found in Prov 8:22. But, as Barth and Blanke, 239, correctly observe, "a weakness of Burney's argument is the fact that in the first stanza of the hymn the designation of Christ as *archē* (beginning), which one would expect within the framework of this theory, is missing and is replaced by *eikōn* (image)." Wright senses this difficulty (456) and modifies Burney's scheme, by putting the emphasis back on the Wisdom tradition and by suggesting a chiastic pattern that makes the *archē* of v. 18b parallel with the *eikōn* of v. 15a (457). This latter arrangement is not compelling. For a further critique of Burney's thesis, see Pizzuto, *Cosmic Leap*, 238–41.

33 So Moo, 114.

34 Gordley, *Colossian Hymn*, 218.

## The Hymnic Form

Since the early 1900s and the work of Weiss and Lohmeyer, a strong consensus emerged understanding Col 1:15–20 (in some cases, 1:13–20) as an early Christian hymn. The consensus was sufficiently strong that it could be assumed rather than argued in many of the commentaries and scholarly literature. Consequently, most of the discussion has focused on attempts to determine the wording of the original hymn, the nature of the insertions made by the author of Colossians, and the *religionsgeschichtliche* source of each statement. It is not possible to review all of the proposals that have been put forth about the extent of the original hymn in the space constraints of a commentary; other works have done this.

Some of the approaches have argued that the exemplar hymn was quite short. C. Burger, for instance, suggested that it simply consisted of two four-line strophes:[35]

I. ὅς ἐστιν εἰκών,
πρωτότοκος πάσης κτίσεως,
ὅτι ἐν αὐτῷ ἐκτίσθη τὰ πάντα,
τὰ ὁρατὰ καὶ τὰ ἀόρατα.
II. ὅς ἐστιν ἀρχή,
πρωτότοκος ἐκ τῶν νεκρῶν,
ὅτι ἐν αὐτῷ κατῴκησεν εὐδόκησεν πᾶν τὸ πλήρωμα,
εἴτε τὰ ἐπὶ τῆς γῆς, εἴτε τὰ ἐπὶ τοῖς οὐρανοῖς.

J. Murphy-O'Connor argued for a similar arrangement of two four-line strophes. He observed that "the elements in the existent text which disturb the balance must have been added by a later hand."[36] Such approaches, however, assume a certain view of the formal characteristics of hymns in the ancient world that should be questioned. Gordley rightly observes that the major weakness of this kind of arrangement "is that it is not clear from comparison with other ancient texts that such a high degree of verbal and syntactical correspondence would be necessary from a first to a second strophe in a composition of this nature."[37]

There has been a tendency in more recent scholarship, however, to question whether Col 1:15–20 contains, in whole or in part, a preexisting hymn that the writer of the letter cites and edits. N. T. Wright has argued that the passage is a carefully constructed piece of poetry composed by the apostle Paul himself.[38] Many others have seen it as a Pauline composition but differ on whether it is

---

35 Burger, *Schöpfung und Versöhnung*, 38.
36 Murphy-O'Connor, *Paul*, 240–41.
37 Gordley, *Colossian Hymn*, 11.
38 Wright, "Poetry and Theology," 99–119.

hymnic, poetic, or exalted prose.[39] The issue of whether Paul wrote the hymn is intimately connected to whether the apostle wrote the Colossian letter as a whole. A conclusion on the authorship of the hymn has to be decided on whether Paul was capable of writing in this style and whether the terminology and theology of the passage are consistent with his thought.

The definition of what constitutes a "hymn" in ancient literature has been widely debated. In Greek literary circles, a hymn would have been constructed in a metrical pattern based on long and short syllables. These syllables would have been arranged in a sequence that usually contained no more than twelve syllables.[40] The arrangement could be composed in trimeter, tetrameter, pentameter, or hexameter in different styles (such as Ionic, Aeolic, or iambic), which gave the text a measured sense of rhythm. The Colossian text fails to meet any of these standards, especially due to the varied line lengths and syllable patterns. Thus, some scholars have attempted to postulate a ground form of the hymn that would fit a Greek standard. But to do this, they have had to argue for multiple editorial insertions or even compositional changes (e.g., changing an infinitive to a finite verb) to achieve a meter that would work.

But this is an overly restrictive understanding of "hymn," especially when we consider that the hymn may very well have had its origins in a Jewish context. Even within a purely Hellenistic context, there was a far less restrictive use of the term "hymn."[41] The main feature of many of the Greek hymns in the Roman period is that they were songs written in honor of a god.[42] They were all "comparatively restricted in length, simple in structure, and devoted to praise of the god."[43] Inscriptions from Asia Minor attest to guilds of choral singers (ὑμνῳδοί), who would sing hymns of praise in honor of Zeus, Apollo, Artemis, and other gods. Standhartinger notes that these hymns were often sung by choral processions and were even accompanied at times with dance.[44] Typical features of these kinds of hymns included "lists of the god's powers and interests and tastes and favourite places . . . accumulations of the god's epithets; portrayals of the god engaged in characteristic activities . . . and accounts of how the god was born and acquired his or her 'honours' and functions."[45] But the precise form of these hymns remains varied. On the one hand, a fourth-century BC inscription in Erythrae (in ancient Boeotia, central Greece) records a paean of praise to Apollo and his son, Asclepius, that was written with a complex

39 E.g., Maurer, "Begründung," 71–93, esp. 85, sees it as hymnic, but as a Pauline composition.

40 For an extensive discussion of meter, see M. L. West, *Greek Meter* (Oxford: Clarendon, 1982).

41 See Vollenweider, "Hymnus," 212–14. He notes that the semantic range of the Greek lexeme ὕμνος is broad and imprecise.

42 See Edsall and Strawbridge, "Songs We Used to Sing," 296–97. They rightly observe that "the term 'hymn' could be used to designate any song of praise to a god, including those without meter" (296).

43 R. C. T. Parker, "Hymns (Greek)," *OCD*³ 736.

44 Standhartinger, "Kolosserhymnus," 87.

45 Parker, "Hymns (Greek)," 736.

metrical structure.[46] Standhartinger notes that although "meter is the language of the gods," not all of the gods preferred metrical hymns. She cites a first-century BC inscription containing an Isis aretalogy from Cyme in Asia Minor (midway between Pergamum and Smyrna) as an example of a nonmetrical type of hymn:[47]

> (3) Isis I am. The ruler of every land. I was educated by Hermes and I invented with Hermes sacred and public writing in order that everything might not be written in the same script. (4) I laid down laws for men and legislated what no one could alter. (5) I am the eldest daughter of Kronos. (6) I am the wife and sister of King Osiris. (7) I am the one who discovered fruit for men. (8) I am the mother of King Horos. (9) I am the one who rises in the constellation of the Dog. (10) I am the one who is called goddess among women. . . . (12) I separated earth from sky. (13) I pointed out the routes of the stars. (14) I arranged the course of the sun and moon . . . (55) I conquer fate. (56) It is to me that fate listens.[48]

What is significant to note in this "prose hymn," is that many of the features NT scholars often point to in discerning hymnic material is absent. There are no relative clauses, no participles, the line lengths vary considerably, and there are very few parallel lines (until lines 55 and 56). The distinctive feature of this prose hymn is the abundant use of the first person, "I am" (ἐγώ).

Standhartinger cites an additional prose hymn (or prose encomium) in honor of Isis recorded on a first-century BC inscription found in Maroneia (Thrace).[49] This one however contains many poetic devices, such as strongly rhythmical clauses, equal line lengths (isocolon), parallelism, anaphora, homoeoteleuton, repetition, assonance, rhetorical questions, as well as the use of rare vocabulary.[50] In contrast to the previous Isis aretalogy, the writer never uses the first person, but only the second person and third person. What these two texts teach us is that there was substantial variety that could be used in composing hymns of praise to the gods. What they have in common with each other and with the Colossian hymn is a "creedal quality" in what they affirm.[51] They would function to bring coherence to the belief structure of the adherents to this religious movement.

M. Peppard is correct in observing that NT scholarship has not yet delineated a method for identifying poetry or hymns in the NT that is scientific, "a type of inquiry whose results are repeatable when applied by different people

---

46 *IErythr* 205, cited and discussed by Standhartinger, "Kolosserhymnus," 80–82.

47 *IKyme* 41, cited and discussed by Standhartinger, "Kolosserhymnus," 84–85.

48 Translation by Horsley, *NewDocs* 1:19–20 (§2).

49 *SEG* 26.821, cited and discussed by Standhartinger, "Kolosserhymnus," 85–86.

50 Papanikolaou, "Aretalogy of Isis," 60–61.

51 *NewDocs* 1:18 (§2).

on the same texts."[52] He correctly observes that some of the rationales are too vague and applicable to too many texts to be regarded as legitimate criteria, such as parallelism, a series of threes, unusual vocabulary, figurative language, and theological or christological terms and concepts.[53] Other corroborating criteria, in his view, have more merit, such as beginning the hymn with a relative pronoun, a rhythmical style, or a setting of worship.[54] He also notes that ancient Greek rhetoricians commonly agreed that meter distinguishes poetry from prose.[55] This would thus call into question N. T. Wright's classification of Col 1:15–20 as poetry. Peppard points to the categories of "prose hymn" or "prose encomium" as potentially a more accurate identification.[56] R. Brucker suggests the category of "praise" (*epainos*) as a more apt category for classifying the so-called Christian hymns of the NT.[57] He sees this as a subset of epideictic rhetoric and not necessarily a genre of texts. But given the prevalence of the term "hymn" in relationship to the praise of the gods, one wonders if Brucker's suggestion advances the discussion materially. "Hymnic praise" (*Christuslob*) may very well be the best way to characterize Col 1:15–20.[58]

The matter of diversity of form with respect to "hymns" takes on even greater significance as we move into a Jewish cultural context. The predominance of OT and Jewish traditions contained in the Colossian hymn would suggest that the author is a Jewish Christian, or a gentile Christian who had substantial familiarity with Jewish tradition. When we consider the definition and usage of the term "hymn" in the first century, it is important to observe that Philo and Josephus could describe the Psalms (and other OT songs) as "hymns."[59] Philo even called the authors of the Psalms ὑμνογράφοι ("hymn writers") and ὑμνῳδοί ("hymn singers").[60] Another first-century Jewish text similarly claims that in the songs he wrote, David was a ὑμνογράφος (4 Macc. 18.15).[61]

In Second Temple Judaism, we encounter an "incredible diversity" of hymns.[62] In his important study of the Colossian hymn, Stettler concludes that the style of praise we find in the OT book of Psalms is sufficient for understanding the Christ-hymn.[63] He argues that Col 1:15–20 represents a mixed form

52 Peppard, "Poetry," 323.
53 Peppard, "Poetry," 324.
54 Peppard, "Poetry," 324.
55 Peppard, "Poetry," 327.
56 Peppard, "Poetry," 328.
57 Brucker, *Christushymnen*, 319 (see his overall conclusions on pp. 347–54). He suggests that Phil 2:5–11, for instance, should be understood as *laus Christi* ("praise of Christ") in contrast to *carmen Christi* ("hymn of Christ"). His research is focused principally on Philippians.
58 So also Vollenweider, "Hymnus," 226.
59 Standhartinger, "Kolosserhymnus," 78.
60 Standhartinger, "Kolosserhymnus," 78.
61 See also Vollenweider, "Hymnus," 213, who notes that Greek-speaking Judaism also referred to its Psalms as "hymns" and placed them in the context of the Hellenistic praise of divine beings.
62 Gordley, *Colossian Hymn*, 110.
63 Stettler, *Christushymnus*, 84.

based on the *Berakah* ("blessing") and an OT "hymn."[64] He finds that many of the specific stylistic traits of the Colossian hymn can also be found in the OT book of Psalms, such as the frequency of causal clauses beginning with ὅτι.[65] As is widely known, parallelism of lines is a regular feature of the Psalms. But the praise of God for who he is (including his role as creator), his mighty works, and especially for his acts of redemption is central to the Psalms.

By understanding Col 1:15–20 with a broader definition of hymn and by opening up the possibility that the style may reflect OT precedents, especially as found in the book of Psalms (and other OT songs), interpreters are freed from the necessity of having to reconstruct the Colossian hymn under the parameters of Greek meter.[66] One of the immediate implications of this is that the final form of the hymn as present in the Colossian letter may very well be the original. In other words, phrases that were originally deemed to be insertions into the original hymn may have been part of the original composition and should not necessarily be dismissed because they extend the line lengths. Of course, arguments have also been made regarding their inappropriateness to the original hymn on other grounds, such as conveying a theology seen as lacking coherence with the postulated original.[67] But this latter way of arguing is highly speculative. The three phrases most commonly understood to be editorial insertions into the hymn are the following:

(1) εἴτε θρόνοι, εἴτε κυριότητες, εἴτε ἀρχαί, εἴτε ἐξουσίαι, "whether thrones or dominions, whether principalities or authorities" (1:16). The list of principalities and powers is often taken to be an explication of the "invisible" that was added to the hymn by the author of the letter.[68] For them, this represents an attempt by the author of the letter to make the hymn more relevant to the polemic against opposing teaching at Colossae. On the other hand, this enumeration of the powers over whom Christ is sovereign may be one of the reasons the Colossian author chose this hymn for inclusion in the letter.

(2) τῆς ἐκκλησίας, "the church" (1:18). Lohmeyer had argued that this appositional genitive led to what he perceived to be an awkward construction, "he is the head of the body, the church."[69] But it was Käsemann who exerted the most influence on subsequent scholarship by asserting that in the original hymn, "the body" in view was not the Christian community but a cosmological entity in creation.[70] Lohse concurs: "originally, then, the reference was to Christ as the

64 Stettler, *Christushymnus*, 86.

65 Stettler, *Christushymnus*, 81.

66 Contra Kehl, *Christushymnus*, 28–51, for whom a reconstruction based on syllable counts is foundational to his approach.

67 See the comment by Schweizer, 56: "above all, one cannot help but notice the theological difference between the hymn itself and the commentary which the author of the Epistle provides."

68 See, e.g., Robinson, "Formal Analysis," 283; Martin, 288 (although he includes the "visible and invisible" as part of the addition).

69 Lohmeyer, 61n2.

70 Käsemann, "Baptismal Liturgy," 150–53, esp. 151.

head of the body, i.e. of the cosmos."[71] Whereas seeing Christ as "head" of a cosmic body would fit with the first strophe of the hymn, seeing Christ as "head" of the church fits well with the second strophe. If 1:17–18a is a transitional or bridge strophe, the inclusion of "the church" would be appropriate to the hymn. Furthermore, the letter writer does not use "body" elsewhere in a cosmic sense; he only uses it with reference to the church.[72]

(3) διὰ τοῦ αἵματος τοῦ σταυροῦ αὐτου, "through the blood of his cross" (1:20). Käsemann also rejected this phrase as part of the original and argued that one is compelled to see it as "a Christian interpolation into the earlier hymn."[73] He reasoned that the original hymn focused on Christ as mediator in creation and as the risen and exalted one. The reference to the event of the cross does not fit with this pattern. But this reasoning fails to take into account that the cross is the foundational event for the creation of the church, the basis for the beginning of the new creation, and the means by which alienated humanity can be reconciled to God. If there is no stylistic reason for seeing this as an alien intrusion into the text, it is best to see it as integral to the original hymn. There is not a sufficient reason for denying that the author of the original hymn may have had a soteriological (redemption) focus in the second strophe that also has cosmic implications.

Rather than interpreting Col 1:15–20 as a hymn that has been reworked either by an early Christian hand or by the author of the letter, it is best to take it as a citation in its original form that remains unedited (apart from the possibility that there was an introductory line that has potentially been omitted, such as, "Blessed be Jesus Christ . . ."). The exercise of speculating about possible insertions into the hymn is precarious, especially if the content fits well with the body of the letter.[74]

It is also difficult to say with any certainty that the hymn is not a Pauline construction. It must be admitted, however, that there are terms and concepts in the hymn that are without parallel in Paul's other writings, such as Christ as "before all things" (1:17), Christ as the one who sustains creation (1:17b), "thrones" as a term for spirit powers (1:16), Christ as "preeminent" (1:18), "all the fullness" dwelling in Christ (1:19), and Christ reconciling the universe to himself

71 Lohse, 43. Whereas Käsemann saw this addition originating from a Christian redaction of the original gnostic-redeemer hymn, Lohse attributes the addition to the author of Colossians. Others who regard τῆς ἐκκλησίας as an addition to the original hymn include, e.g., Schnelle, *Theology*, 545; Hübner, 56; Gnilka, 57–59; Martin, 56.

72 There are a growing number of scholars who see it as part of the original hymn. See, e.g., Bormann, 98.

73 Käsemann, "Baptismal Liturgy," 152. Similarly, Pokorný, 60, writes that "the sentence becomes smoother if we omit 'by the blood of his cross.'" See also, e.g., Schnelle, *Theology*, 545; Hübner, 56; Gnilka, 57–59; Schweizer, 59; Martin, 56–57.

74 Bormann, 85, notes that the number of exegetes who take the hymn as it stands is increasing. See also Barth and Blanke, 231.

(not just alienated humanity, 1:20).[75] Yet all of these ideas are demonstrably consistent with Paul's thought, otherwise the hymn would not have been included in this letter. But is this uniqueness sufficient to affirm that it came from another hand? Paul is clearly capable of writing in an elevated style and making use of parallelism to convey his thought in a moving and artistic manner (see, e.g., 1 Cor 13). There are elements to this hymn that may bear a Pauline fingerprint, however. I will mention three of these: (1) the pair ἀρχαί and ἐξουσίαι (1:16) is Paul's most common expression for referring to hostile spiritual powers; (2) the church as "the body" of Christ (1:18) is a uniquely Pauline expression; and (3), Paul has a stylistic penchant for creating compound verbs with the addition of prefixed prepositions as a way of intensifying the meaning of the verb. The hymn represents the first instance in the Greek language that the verb ἀποκαταλλάσσω ("reconcile") appears (1:20), although there are instances of the simpler form, καταλλάσσω, in common usage. All of this, however, may simply point to the fact that the original author of the hymn may have been influenced by Pauline oral tradition that made its way back to the Lycus Valley through the teaching of Epaphras. Or it could mean that Paul himself composed the hymn, as an increasing number of scholars are arguing.[76] Because of this Pauline stamp on the hymn, the origin of the hymn itself likely does not go back to the earliest days of the Jesus movement in Jerusalem. Yet, as Stettler points out, most of the christological statements go back to the earliest period in Jerusalem when the Greek and Aramaic-speaking church formulated its wisdom Christology.[77] These elements were likely then given shape by the later composer of the hymn (who was influenced by Paul) or by Paul himself. The existence of a high Christology should not be taken as an indication of a late date (such as late 1st cent.) for the hymn. There are a growing number of NT scholars defending the origin of a high Christology in the immediate post-Easter church of Jerusalem.[78]

Since Paul admonishes the Colossians to "let the word of Christ [i.e., about Christ] dwell in you richly by teaching and admonishing one another in all wisdom with spiritual psalms, hymns, and songs and with gratitude, singing in your hearts to God" (3:16), I am inclined to see 1:15–20 as one of those hymns that were circulated and sung in the community worship of the Lycus Valley and with which the readers were already familiar.[79] That this passage represents

75 Martin, 65, writes that "the chief argument against Paul's authorship [of the hymn] is the evidence of the unusual terms and constructions."

76 This conclusion is reached, e.g., by Beale, 78–79; Garland, 82; Helyer, "Colossians 1:15–20," 167–79, esp. 172.

77 Stettler, *Christushymnus*, 347.

78 Thiselton, 33. This is one of the major contributions of the work of L. Hurtado in his works *Lord Jesus Christ* and *One God, One Lord*.

79 In this, I agree with Lohse, 46. He notes, "Certainly the hymn was known and sung by more than one community—not by the Colossians alone. It was doubtless the common property of communities in Asia Minor."

a hymn (or at least psalm-like poetry,[80] the Jewish *Berakah* style, or "exalted prose") is confirmed by the parallelism and repetition exhibited in the passage (see below), along with the shift to the third person. The overall effect is a style that differs markedly from anything else in the letter. This conclusion is also suggested by the intensely christological focus, with short clauses affirming the identity and work of Christ. Yet even this conclusion must be held somewhat lightly because there is no direct evidence of Col 1:15–20 ever being sung or recited in a community setting in the churches of subsequent generations after the composition of Colossians.[81] Edsall and Strawbridge have observed that although Col 1:15–20 is referred to more than any other passage from Paul's letters in pre-Nicene Christian writings, it is never treated as a hymn or placed in a liturgical setting.[82] An argument from silence such as this does not defeat the whole notion that this passage was a hymn, especially since the passage was so often cited in theological argumentation to affirm a high Christology, but it does temper the strength of the conclusion.

### *Structure*

Attempts at discerning the structure of this text can be summarized into two approaches, with a host of variations on these two descriptions.

The first approach divides the passage into two strophes: 1:15–17 and 1:18–20. The content of the first lauds Christ as Lord over the entire creation, whereas the second praises him as Lord of redemption. Dibelius, for example, emphasized the *Stichworte* πρωτότοκος πάσης κτίσεως in 1:15 and πρωτότοκος ἐκ τῶν νεκρῶν in 1:18, resulting in the following overall structure:[83]

I. 15 ὅς ἐστιν εἰκὼν ... *πρωτότοκος πάσης κτίσεως*·
16 ὅτι ἐν αὐτῷ ἐκτίσθη τὰ πάντα ... τὰ πάντα δι᾽ αὐτοῦ καὶ εἰς αὐτὸν ἔκτισται
17 καὶ αὐτός ἐστιν πρὸ πάντων ...
II. 18a καὶ αὐτός ἐστιν ἡ κεφαλή ...
18b ὅς ἐστιν ἀρχή, *πρωτότοκος ἐκ τῶν νεκρῶν* ...
19–20 ὅτι ἐν αὐτῷ εὐδόκησεν πᾶν τὸ πλήρωμα ... δι᾽ αὐτοῦ ἀποκαταλλάξαι τὰ πάντα ...

This division turns, in part, on how one understands ἡ κεφαλὴ τοῦ σώματος τῆς ἐκκλησίας in 1:18a. For Dibelius, as for many others, τῆς ἐκκλησίας is interpreted as a redactional addition to the original hymn, and ἡ κεφαλὴ τοῦ σώματος is understood to have cosmic significance. This, however, makes that clause more

80 Stettler, *Christushymnus*, 79, asserts that it is "ganz vom alttestamentlichen Psalmenstil."

81 Löhr, "Christian Hymnody," 171.

82 Edsall and Strawbridge, "Songs We Used to Sing," 301–3.

83 Dibelius and Greeven, 10. See also Käsemann, "Baptismal Liturgy," 150–51.

appropriate to the previous strophe since it continues the theme of Christ's sovereignty over the universe.

Stettler also contends for a two-strophe arrangement of the passage but argues that τῆς ἐκκλησίας is an original part of the hymn.[84] He conjectures that the first line of the original hymn was left out and would have been a declaration of blessing. He sees the posited first line as parallel with 1:18a. Stettler's overall reconstruction is as follows:

I. [Εὐλογητὸς Ἰησοῦς Χριστός]
15a ὅς ἐστιν εἰκὼν τοῦ θεοῦ τοῦ ἀοράτου,
b πρωτότοκος πάσης κτίσεως,
16a ὅτι ἐν αὐτῷ ἐκτίσθη τὰ πάντα
b ἐν τοῖς οὐρανοῖς καὶ ἐπὶ τῆς γῆς,
c τὰ ὁρατὰ καὶ τὰ ἀόρατα,
d εἴτε θρόνοι εἴτε κυριότητες
e εἴτε ἀρχαὶ εἴτε ἐξουσίαι.
f τὰ πάντα δι' αὐτοῦ καὶ εἰς αὐτὸν ἔκτισται,
17a καὶ αὐτός ἐστιν πρὸ πάντων,
b καὶ τὰ πάντα ἐν αὐτῷ συνέστηκεν.

II. 18a καὶ αὐτός ἐστιν ἡ κεφαλὴ τοῦ σώματος τῆς ἐκκλησίας,
b ὅς ἐστιν ἀρχή, πρωτότοκος ἐκ τῶν νεκρῶν,
c ἵνα γένηται ἐν πᾶσιν αὐτὸς πρωτεύων
19 ὅτι ἐν αὐτῷ εὐδόκησεν πᾶν τὸ πλήρωμα κατοικῆσαι
20a καὶ δι' αὐτοῦ ἀποκαταλλάξαι τὰ πάντα εἰς αὐτόν,
b εἰρηνοποιήσας διὰ τοῦ αἵματος τοῦ σταυροῦ αὐτοῦ,
c δι' αὐτοῦ εἴτε τὰ ἐπὶ τῆς γῆς
d εἴτε τὰ ἐν τοῖς οὐρανοῖς.

His display is based largely on a Hebrew translation supplied by H. Gese that ostensibly shows the continuity of the Colossian hymn with the psalms of the Hebrew Bible and its comparability to Hebrew meter.[85] But this arrangement misses some of the obvious parallelism in the Greek text (e.g., the πρωτότοκος statements; the καὶ αὐτός ἐστιν lines). It would also suggest that the hymn had its origins at the beginning of the Jesus movement in Jerusalem, which is possible, but not likely given some of the distinctively Greek terms and concepts in the hymn.

In his extensive study of the hymn, Gordley also presents a two-strophe structure for the hymn, but he also finds a concluding summary (an epode).[86]

84 See Stettler, *Christushymnus*, 92.
85 See Stettler, *Christiushymnus*, 93.
86 Gordley, *Colossian Hymn*, 190–96.

He contends that each strophe consists of eight lines that are fairly evenly balanced (the first contains 83 syllables and the second has 78). His interpretation can be depicted as follows:

**Strophe**

I. 15 ὅς ἐστιν εἰκὼν τοῦ θεοῦ τοῦ ἀοράτου,
πρωτότοκος πάσης κτίσεως,
16 ὅτι ἐν αὐτῷ ἐκτίσθη τὰ πάντα
τὰ πάντα δι᾽ αὐτοῦ καὶ εἰς αὐτὸν ἔκτισται·
17 καὶ αὐτός ἐστιν πρὸ πάντων
καὶ τὰ πάντα ἐν αὐτῷ συνέστηκεν,
18 καὶ αὐτός ἐστιν ἡ κεφαλὴ τοῦ
σώματος τῆς ἐκκλησίας·

**Anti-Strophe**

II. ὅς ἐστιν ἀρχή, πρωτότοκος ἐκ τῶν νεκρῶν,
ἵνα γένηται ἐν πᾶσιν αὐτὸς πρωτεύων,
19 ὅτι ἐν αὐτῷ εὐδόκησεν
πᾶν τὸ πλήρωμα κατοικῆσαι
20 καὶ δι᾽ αὐτοῦ ἀποκαταλλάξαι
τὰ πάντα εἰς αὐτόν,
εἰρηνοποιήσας διὰ τοῦ
αἵματος τοῦ σταυροῦ αὐτοῦ,

**Epode**

[δι᾽ αὐτοῦ] εἴτε τὰ ἐπὶ τῆς γῆς
εἴτε τὰ ἐν τοῖς οὐρανοῖς.

In order to achieve this arrangement, however, Gordley minimizes some of the structural parallelism that many other interpreters have rightly noticed. He also needs to split some clauses—even to the extent of separating the article from the nouns they modify (as in 1:18 with τοῦ σώματος and in 1:20 with τοῦ αἵματος). To obtain a balance between strophes, he also needs to eliminate twenty words in 1:16 (ἐν τοῖς οὐρανοῖς καὶ ἐπὶ τῆς γῆς, τὰ ὁρατὰ καὶ τὰ ἀόρατα, εἴτε θρόνοι εἴτε κυριότητες εἴτε ἀρχαὶ εἴτε ἐξουσίαι). Although it is possible that the author of Colossians was making redactional additions for his unique purposes, it is also possible that the writer was not at all concerned with meter and similar line lengths. Finally, it seems unlikely that the author of the hymn would compose an epode without a verbal element. In this case, the epode is dependent on the participle εἰρηνοποιήσας in the second strophe.

Another approach to the structure of the hymn also contends that there are two strophes but argues that there is a three-line bridge (a *Zwischenstrophe* or *strophe intermédiaire*) between the two. This description takes into account the extensive parallelism in the way it was structured. The skeletal structure of the hymn could be depicted in the following way that displays the precise verbal parallels:

I. 15a ὅς ἐστιν . . .
15b πρωτότοκος . . .
16a ὅτι ἐν αὐτῷ
16f δι᾽ αὐτοῦ καὶ εἰς αὐτὸν

17a καὶ αὐτός ἐστιν
18a καὶ αὐτός ἐστιν

II. 18b ὅς ἐστιν . . .
18c πρωτότοκος . . .
19a ὅτι ἐν αὐτῷ
20a δι᾽ αὐτοῦ . . . εἰς αὐτὸν

The basic idea of two strophes beginning with ὅς ἐστιν and connected by a transitional link or refrain with the parallel καὶ αὐτός ἐστιν is widely accepted, but with many variations on some of the details.[87] This is the approach to the overall structure that is most convincing. While the skeletal structure is parallel, the hymn writer used a degree of freedom in expanding on the various lines and did not feel compelled to conform to Greek meter or even similar line lengths.

### *Setting*

If the passage circulated as a hymn prior to its use in this letter, is it possible to discern the specific setting for its use? Käsemann sought to build a case for understanding it as part of a primitive Christian baptismal liturgy.[88] But he can only do this by including 1:12–13 as a central part of his case, which contrasts the before and after of the believers' experience—darkness/light, rescue and incorporation, and the authority of darkness/the kingdom of the Son. The hymn itself does not emphasize baptismal motifs but extols the person of Christ in the most exalted terms, especially emphasizing the absolute supremacy of Christ over all of creation. Consequently, it is better to see 1:15–20 as a hymn of praise to Christ that would have been used in the course of the normal worship of the Christian communities in the Lycus Valley.

While the vast majority of scholarly treatments of this passage focus on the form and structure of the text, very little has been said about the setting of the passage in its Phrygian and Lycus Valley context. Many scholars have rightly pointed to the important role this hymn plays in laying a theological foundation for the author's polemic against "the philosophy" threatening the church at

87 See, e.g., Moo, 115–16; Wilson, 126–27; Benoit, "L'hymne christologique," 229; Pokorný, 58–58; Beasley-Murray, "Colossians 1:15–20," 169–70; Martin, 55. See also Wright, "Poetry and Theology," 446, who takes a similar approach. Pao, 87, affirms this overall structure but sees 1:17a–18a as the center of a chiasm (with 17b as the midpoint).

88 Käsemann, "Baptismal Liturgy," 44–45. Martin, 65, furthered this viewpoint, asserting that "it may well have been part of their baptismal liturgy."

Colossae, but virtually no one places this passage in the larger context of the claims about Christ set against the backdrop of the rival claims of the principal deities worshiped in this area. Yet this represents some of the most important observations that can be made about the passage. The declaration of Christ's preeminence and sovereignty over all other powers—heavenly or earthly—is directly counter to the claims of Zeus, Apollo, Mēn, the Great Mother, and the divine power of the emperor.

The Christian community of Colossae would have consisted of many people who, like the Thessalonians, "turned to God from idols to serve the living and true God" (1 Thess 1:9). Most of their relatives, friends, neighbors, coworkers, and fellow citizens continued to worship these deities. What is said about Christ in this hymn would have elicited a strong reaction from adherents to any of these local gods and goddesses. For the Christians in the Colossian community who formerly gave their allegiance to these deities, the words of this hymn would have provided a powerful reassurance that their new allegiance to Christ was rightly placed. A big part of the message of the hymn is that Christ has no rival—despite claims to the contrary.

Although Colossae has never been excavated, we still have a good idea of many of the principal deities worshiped there through numismatic evidence and also because they would have shared a commitment to many of the deities worshiped elsewhere in the Lycus Valley. We also know that Paul intends for his letter to be read by the Christian community in Laodicea. Furthermore, if Col 1:15–20 represents a hymn that was known and sung by Christians throughout the Lycus Valley, then the religious environment of the surrounding region to Colossae becomes particularly relevant for interpreting the statements of the hymn and how it would have been understood contextually.

The region had a particularly close affiliation with Apollo in a variety of his local manifestations. He was worshiped in Hierapolis as Apollo Archegetes (Ἀρχηγέτις), protector and leader of the city. It is noteworthy that Christ is proclaimed as sovereign over all rival ἀρχαί (1:16) and that he is the ἀρχή (1:18). Apollo was honored by an elaborate frieze in the second century on the back of the stage in the theater at Hierapolis depicting scenes from his life and his works. Among other things, he is depicted as a healing god who could protect the city from pestilence.[89] But Apollo was also worshiped as an oracle god, and one could consult him by going to his temple near the Plutonium, an entrance to the underworld. Approximately eighteen miles northwest of Colossae was an important sanctuary for the Phrygian deity Mēn Karou.[90] Numismatic evidence points to the worship of Mēn at Colossae.[91] Mēn was worshiped as a

89 See D'Andria, *Hierapolis of Phrygia*, 168–70.

90 See the discussion in Huttner, *Early Christianity in the Lycus Valley*, 52–53.

91 See von Aulock, *Münzen und Städte Phrygiens*, nos. 453, 591 (a bust of Mēn in a Phrygian cap with a moon sickle); Head, *Greek Coins of Phrygia*, 157 (no. 16).

lunar god and was popular at his sanctuary as a god of healing. An inscription from Saittai lauds Mēn in grand terms: "there is one god in the heavens, the great heavenly Mēn, great power of the immortal god" (εἷς θεὸς ἐν οὐρανοῖς, μέγας Μὴν Οὐράνιος, μεγάλη δύναμις τοῦ ἀθανάτου θεοῦ).[92] The Great Mother (Μεγάλη Μήτηρ) was likely also worshiped at Colossae and was certainly popular throughout the region. As the "mother of the gods" (Μήτηρ Θεῶν) she claimed a primacy of place among the Anatolian deities. Zeus was also worshiped in Laodicea, Hierapolis, and presumably at Colossae. As the highest god of the Greek pantheon, he would claim sovereignty and supremacy. Another deity worshiped throughout Phrygia, Caria, and Lydia was a pagan god called Theos Hypsistos (Διὸς/θεὸς ὕψιστος, "God Most High"). The adjective ὕψιστος emphasizes his preeminent position among the gods. Many more deities could be mentioned here, along with the exalted claims that are made of them. But this is sufficient to illustrate how the Colossian hymn was composed and regularly sung in a context where there were many rivals to the claims of the supremacy, sovereignty, and preeminence of Jesus Christ.

Another characteristic of the local, popular religious environment were inscriptions attesting to people publicly confessing their sin to many of the same deities as part of a process of propitiating the anger of these powerful territorial gods.[93] These texts are commonly referred to as the "Lydian-Phrygian confession inscriptions" (*Beichtinschriften*). They have been collected and published by G. Petzl[94] and supplemented with the publication of additional discoveries bringing the total to about 175.[95] These texts follow a similar pattern of (1) indicating a transgression that has taken place against the deity, (2) mentioning how the person was punished ("struck") by the god, (3) stating that the anger of the deity has been propitiated, and (4) concluding with praise for the deity, often including an ascription of the power of the deity. These crude and simple monuments put the power of these deities to punish transgressors on public display so that all could see.[96] Nineteen of these inscriptions were found at the sanctuary of Apollo Lairbenos, less than thirty miles due north of Colossae and about twenty miles north of Hierapolis.[97] In one of these texts, a certain Sosandros from Hierapolis admits that he did not keep an oath that he made to Apollo Lairbenos and entered the sanctuary in an impure condition. He was afflicted by a punishment from Apollo and then had this stele erected as

92 *TAM* V,1.1–8. Cited also in MM 171.

93 See my more extensive discussion of these texts in "Paul and Folk Belief," 429–49. See also Chiai, "Allmächtige Götter," 61–106.

94 G. Petzl, *Die Beichtinschriften Westkleinasiens*, Epigraphica Anatolica 22 (Bonn: Habelt, 1994). Abbreviated below and henceforth as *BWK*.

95 G. Petzl, "Neue Inscriften aus Lydien (II): Addenda und Corrigenda zu 'Die Beichtinschiften Westkleinasiens,'" *Epigraphica Anatolica* 28 (1997): 69–79.

96 As Chiai, "Allmächtiger Götter," 105, summarizes it, "These gods have the power (*dynamis*) to acknowledge and punish sins and criminals by giving terrible diseases."

97 These represent nos. 106–24 (pp. 122–144) in *BWK*.

his confession and as a warning to others.[98] The implication is clear. Apollo is a powerful god who should be feared. He will strike down those who violate his moral code or neglect his cultic requirements. Yet the supplicant could be "reconciled" to the deity by propitiating his wrath through confession and public proclamation of his power. This system of divine territorial justice is attested for many of the local Phrygian and Lydian deities, but especially of Apollo, Zeus, Mēn, and the Great Mother. The power of the Great Mother is praised in one of these propitiation texts: "I, Aurelius Trophimus, son of Artemisios, inquired of the goddess and set up this monument for the Mother of the gods praising [εὐλογῶν] your power [δυνάμις]."[99] Another unique feature of these texts is that these deities were served by divine messengers ("angels"), who would sometimes reveal to the offender the nature of the offense or the required response. The god, Mēn, for instance, "commanded through an angel [δι' ἀγγέλου] to purchase the [stolen] shirt and to write the manifestations of his power [τὰς δυνάμεις] on a monument."[100] This and many other reliefs of Mēn depict him wielding a scepter—a symbol of his judicial power and sovereignty. These texts demonstrate that those who turned to Christ from a background of worshiping these territorial deities of Phrygia would have brought with them a great fear about the implications of turning their backs to these powerful gods they once worshiped. It would have been important for them to know the power and sovereignty of Christ over these rivals. The fear of being struck down by their former gods for their infidelity would have been very real. They would also need to know that there is a different basis for being reconciled to the God that they now serve; that basis is found in the death of Jesus on the cross (Col 1:20).

It is in the magical texts, however, where one finds profuse praise of the power of various gods and goddesses, exclamations of their sovereignty over the heavenly realm, the earth, and the underworld, and numerous epithets extolling their supernatural attributes. This is not surprising because practitioners of magic were primarily concerned with supernatural power and how to solicit the assistance of divine beings. Many of these texts use some of the same terminology and conceptuality as the Colossian hymn. I am not making a case for a genetic relationship of the source of statements in the Colossian hymn as my predecessors in the history of religions school did, but rather suggesting that interpreters must consider the contextual relevance of the praise of Christ in the hymn against the backdrop of rival claims to sovereignty.

A first-century silver lamella found in northern Asia Minor (Amisos, Pontus) begins with a series of divine epithets to describe the god called upon for protection: "I am the Great One who sits in heaven ['Εγώ εἰμι ὁ μέγας ὁ ἐν οὐρανῷ καθήμενος] upon the moving vault of the whole cosmos, Arsenophris . . . the one

98 *BWK* 120.1–8 (pp. 139–40).
99 *BWK* 97.1–6 (pp. 114–15).
100 *BWK* 3.8–11 (pp. 3–5).

who rules over kings. . . . Let no more harm appear! Drive away, drive away the lawsuit from Rufina! . . . And may no poison [φάρμακον] harm me. . . . [I am] king of kings."[101] The Greek magical papyri are replete with ascriptions of power and sovereignty to the particular deity being called upon to grant the request of the suppliant. One of these texts invokes Helios in the most exalted terms as lord of heaven and earth: "Hail, O lord, Great Power, Great Might, King, Greatest of gods, Helios, the lord of heaven and earth, God of gods: mighty is your breath, mighty is your strength, O lord" (*PGM* IV.640–43). Another text invokes Helios as creator of τὰ πάντα—even of angelic powers:

> Listen, Helios, father of the world; I call upon you with your name . . . [28 magical names are listed] . . . You are the holy and powerful name considered sacred by all the angels; protect me, so-and-so, from every excess of power [ἐξουσίας] and from every violent act. Yes, do this, lord, god of gods . . . [18 magical names are listed] . . . creator of the world, creator of the universe [κόσμου κτίστα, τὰ πάντα κτίστα], lord, god of gods, MARMARIŌ IAŌ. I have spoken of your unsurpassable glory, you who created gods, archangels, and decans [ὁ κτίσας θεοὺς καὶ ἀρχαγγέλους καὶ δεκανούς]. The ten thousands of angels stood by [you] and exalted the heaven, and the lord witnessed to your Wisdom [σοφίᾳ], which is Aion . . . and said that you are as strong as he is. (*PGM* IV.1180–209)

In another text, Eros is called upon in an invocation and is extolled as creator of "all things" (τὰ πάντα) and is also ascribed the epithet, "firstborn": "I call upon you, author of all creation, who spread your own wings over the whole world . . . who fitted all things [τὰ πάντα] together by your power, firstborn (πρωτόγονε), founder of the universe . . ." (*PGM* IV.1749–58). The Great Mother is invoked as "the beginning," eternal, the source of all things, and as sovereign: "[come to me] . . . Mother of all things . . . Beginning [ἀρχή] and end are you, and you alone rule all. For all things are from you, and in you do all things [πάντα], Eternal one, come to their end" (*PGM* IV.2834–39).

It is also important to note that in the magical tradition, part of the invocation could involve singing and declaring the power and epithets of the deity in hymnic form. In a magical text, possibly to Sarapis, the petitioner seeks protection from astrological fate and describes how he "hymns" the names, attributes, and power of the god:

> I call on you, lord, holy, much hymned [πολυύμνητε], greatly honored, ruler of the cosmos [κοσμοκράτωρ], [Sarapis]; . . . I call on you, lord; I hymn your holy power in a musical hymn [ᾠδικῷ ὕμνῳ ὑμνῶ σου τὸ ἅγιον κράτος], AEĒIOYŌŌŌ. . . . Protect me from all my own astrological destiny; destroy my foul fate; and [may I enjoy] many good things, for I am your slave and petitioner and have

101 Kotansky, *Greek Magical Amulets*, 181–201 (no. 36).

> hymned [ὕμνησά] your valid and holy name, lord, glorious one, ruler of the cosmos [κοσμοκράτωρ], of then thousand names, greatest, nourisher, apportioner, [Sarapis]. (*PGM* IV.619–40)

The performative act of singing a hymn to the deity invoked in the ritual was common in the magical texts.[102] The known corpus of Greek magical papyri contains a handful of hexametric hymns as part of the prescribed rituals.[103]

In the Colossian hymn, Christ alone is praised as sovereign over every being. This claim is based on the fact that he is not only creator of the world but is the creator of all the visible and unseen powers. He existed prior to every god, goddess, angel, or spirit. He is preeminent over *all things*.

While the Colossian hymn strongly emphasizes Christ's supremacy over supernatural powers, it also asserts his sovereignty over all things "on the earth" (1:16, 20). This not only includes chthonic, terrestrial, and underworld spirits and deities, but earthly rulers. The lordship of Christ extends to "all things" (τὰ πάντα), which encompasses the full extent of Roman imperial might. The authority of Rome had permeated the entirety of the political and civic life of Roman Asia. The imperial reliefs from the Sebasteion of Aphrodisias dramatically depict Rome's extensive subjugation of distant lands throughout the Mediterranean world and beyond. The successive princepes of Rome had brought about the global *pax Romana* through their overwhelming military might. Yet these Caesars were not considered mere men. They were regarded as gods. Nero himself was lauded as an incarnate deity who ruled the earth.[104] When it comes to the Roman Imperium, the distinction between humanity and deity becomes somewhat blurred. Reflecting on the life of Nero, Titus Calpurnius Siculus exclaimed:

> Caesar, whether you are Jupiter himself on earth in altered guise, or one other of the powers above concealed under an assumed moral semblance (for you are very god [*es enim deus*])—rule, I pray, this world, rule its peoples for ever! Let love of heaven count naught with thee; abandon not, O father, the peace you have begun![105]

Even some of the Roman coinage from Hierapolis and Laodicea depict Nero with the local gods, such as Zeus Laodiceus and Apollo.[106] Coins from the Claudian period also attest to the establishment of a temple in Hierapolis dedicated "to the imperial race."[107] The Colossian hymn thus celebrates the

---

102 See, e.g., *PGM* III.233ff.; 389; XIII.444–45. These were often referred to as an ἐπαοιδή or ἐπῳδή.

103 See the discussion in Graf, *Magic in the Ancient World*, 215–16.

104 For references, see Maier, "Colossians and Empire," 338–39.

105 Calpurnius Siculus, *Ecl.* 4.142–46 (LCL), as cited in Maier, "Colossians and Empire," 337.

106 See Maier, "Colossians and Empire," 337.

107 Miller, "Imperial Cult," 325.

universality of Jesus's sovereignty—in heaven and on earth, over spirits and gods, over local provincial rulers and even the Roman Imperium with its Caesar attributed with divine power and authority.[108] Absolutely nothing in existence falls outside of Christ's dominion.

If the Colossian hymn was known and sung in house-church gatherings throughout the Lycus Valley, it certainly provided many believers with a magnificent perspective on the God to whom they had given their allegiance. Despite the grandiose claims of Zeus, Apollo, Mēn, the Great Mother, or even the Roman emperor, they could be assured that they were worshiping a deity who is truly Lord of all. And despite the fact that they continued to suffer under the influence of malevolent powers as well as at the hands of Roman imperial might, they could be confident that one day Jesus would pacify all rival powers and usher in an era of universal peace.

Part of the function of the hymn within this letter would have been to provide the Colossian (and Laodicean) believers with this kind of reassurance.[109] But the more direct and immediate role it played was in laying a foundation for dealing with the harmful teaching of "the philosophy."[110] Much of the terminology and themes of the hymn is taken up and developed in the letter, especially in the polemical section. Paul thus cites (or composes) an emotionally moving and magnificent hymn extolling the unsurpassed supremacy of Christ over all of creation, especially the entirety of the supernatural realm. The hymn eliminates any reason that the Colossian community would have for succumbing to the influence of the factional teachers in the community. Most importantly, it answers the root question in the minds of some: Where does Christ stand in relationship to the gods, goddesses, spirits, and powers that they once worshiped and who need to be appeased or obeyed?

## *Comment*

**15** ὅς ἐστιν εἰκὼν τοῦ θεοῦ τοῦ ἀοράτου, "He is the image of the invisible God." The style of the passage shifts markedly here to a series of short, staccato-like ascriptions of praise to Christ characterizing him in the most exalted of

108 Sumney, 68, writes that "the claim of Christ's superiority also sets the church against the claims of the empire."

109 Schnelle, *Theology*, 540, observes that "the church in Colossae was obviously in danger of reactivating central elements of their previous religious practice—such as the veneration of stars and intermediary divine beings (angels), reverence and fear of demons, belief in fate, and practice of ascetic disciplines—in combination with their Christian faith."

110 So also Vollenweider, "Hymnus," 227, who concludes that praise to Christ has a decisive function in the argumentation of the letter. In contrast to the attactiveness of the cosmic powers, which the Colossian "philosophy" apparently invoked, the hymn emphasized the all-pervading reality and rule of Christ, the mediator of creation. Schnelle, *Theology*, 543, notes that this text is "the foundational text that provides the basis for the debate with the rival teaching." See also, e.g., Dübbers, *Christologie und Existenz*, 17; Fowl, *Story of Christ*, 154.

terms—as Lord of all creation and as Lord of redemption. This passage is likely a hymn of praise to Christ already known to the Colossian church that Paul cites as a theological foundation to many of the important themes he will address in this letter.

The relative pronoun (ὅς) refers to Christ. The immediate antecedent is the ἐν ᾧ of 1:14a. The focal point of the prayer in 1:9–14 was the Father until 1:13b, where the focus shifts to the Son. It is part of Paul's report that he is praying that the lives of the Colossian believers would be characterized by a heart of thanksgiving to the Father who rescued them from the kingdom of darkness and transferred them "into the kingdom of his beloved Son." The hymn that follows elaborates on the marvelous qualities and attributes of the Son of God. Many interpreters have seen the ὅς as a stylistic indicator that the author is now citing traditional material. This is typical of other passages in the NT identified as hymns of praise to Christ (e.g., see Phil 2:6–11; 1 Tim 3:16; Heb 1:3; 1 Pet 2:22). Because of the shift from the prayer report to the poetic praise of Christ, it would have been natural to begin the new section with a specific designation of the subject. But the beginning of this passage is abrupt and even lacks a conjunction (such as δέ or γάρ). The original form of the hymn may have had an opening line that began something like Εὐλογητὸς ὁ κύριος Ἰησοῦς Χριστός ὅς, "blessed be the Lord Jesus Christ who . . ."[111]

In describing Jesus as the εἰκὼν τοῦ θεοῦ, the readers familiar with the LXX would have immediately thought of the creation of Adam and Eve in the image of God as recorded in Gen 1:26–27:

> Then God said, "Let us make man in our image [εἰκόνα], after our likeness. And let them rule over the fish of the sea and the birds of the heavens and the livestock and all the earth and all the creeping things that creep on the earth." So God created man in his own image, in the image of God [εἰκόνα θεοῦ] he created him; male and female he created them.

Paul speaks of Adam as being created and existing in the image of God elsewhere (1 Cor 11:7). He also elsewhere refers to Christ as "the image of God," using the same langauge as here: "he is the image of God" (ὅς ἐστιν εἰκὼν τοῦ θεοῦ; 2 Cor 4:4). It is possible that the author of the hymn is referring directly to the creation account in Genesis and applying it to Christ.[112] But if the hymn was originally composed in a Jewish context, and possibly in Jerusalem in the circle associated with Stephen, it may reflect a well-known Jewish interpretive tradition of Gen 1—namely, the language of Jewish Wisdom, which was first developed in Prov 8:22–31. Subsequently, the "image of God" language was applied to the figure of personified Wisdom in a handful of Jewish texts. This is

111 Stettler, *Christushymnus*, 92–93.

112 As Beale, 280–86, argues.

significant because Wisdom is represented as being with God in the beginning and participating with him in the creation of the heavens and the earth. For the earliest Christians, the language of personified Wisdom helped to explain the preexistence of Christ and his role in creating the world.

In the first-century BC Wisdom of Solomon, personified Wisdom is described as "an image of his goodness" (εἰκὼν τῆς ἀγαθότητος αὐτοῦ; Wis 7:26) just after being called "all powerful" (παντοδύναμον; 7:23) and as "a breath of the power of God and an emanation of the pure glory of the Almighty" (7:25 NETS). Ben Sira speaks of Wisdom in equally exalted terms: "I came forth from the mouth of the Most High, and covered the earth like a mist. I dwelt in the highest heavens, and my throne was in a pillar of cloud" (Sir 24:3–4 NRSV).[113]

Philo of Alexandria also uses the term "image" (εἰκών) as a title for personified Wisdom. He declares, "By using many words for it Moses has already made it manifest that the sublime and heavenly wisdom is of many names; for he calls it 'beginning' [ἀρχήν] and 'image' [εἰκόνα] and 'vision of God'" (Philo, *Alleg. Interp.* 1.43 LCL). Philo often connects Wisdom with the Word (λόγος) in his writings (see also Wis 9:1–2), and "image" (εἰκών) is an important title for the Word in Philo.[114] For instance, he notes, "the image of God [εἰκὼν θεοῦ] is the Word through whom the whole universe was framed" (Philo, *Spec. Laws* 1.81 LCL).[115] God becomes knowable through his Word and by his Wisdom. In Jewish thought, these were personifications of his attributes and not to be understand as ontologically independent entities such as hypostases or intermediaries. But then a new development takes place in the Enochic tradition whereby preexistent Wisdom is identified with the messianic "Son of Man," "the Chosen One" (1 En. 48.1–7).[116]

The author of the hymn, and by extension, Paul, has thus appropriated the language of Wisdom and the Word to give expression to the work and identity of Christ in his preexistent state. This happens at multiple intervals throughout this hymn.[117] But this identification of Wisdom and Messiah had apparently already happened within Judaism (according to the Enochic tradition).

113 Numerous interpreters point to the foundational importance of personified Wisdom in the Jewish wisdom tradition as foundational to this passage. Among them is Hengel, "Hymns and Christology," 95, who emphasizes the role of Prov 8 and Sir 24 in the early Christian transference of the characteristics of personified Wisdom to Christ. See also Stuhlmacher, *Biblical Theology*, 438; Schnabel, *Law and Wisdom*, 258; Kehl, *Christushymnus*, 61–67.

114 Beetham, *Echoes of Scripture*, 125.

115 See also, Philo, *Confusion* 146–47; *Dreams* 1.239; 2.245; *Flight* 101.

116 See Stettler, *Kolosserhymnus*, 140–41.

117 Stuhlmacher, *Biblical Theology*, 438, notes that Col 1:15–20 is "a paradigmatic example of the early Christian effort to understand the being and work of the preexistent and exalted Christ by analogy to the reign of wisdom (cf. similarly 1 Cor. 1:30; 8:6; and John 1:1–18)." Fee, *Christology*, 289–338, denies the presence of Wisdom Christology in the hymn. Part of his reason for this is that the Son is portrayed as eternal, whereas Wisdom is said to be created (e.g., Sir 1:4, 9). But this does not preclude the possibility that the hymn writer, and Paul, goes *beyond* the depiction of Wisdom. In other words, Wisdom provides an analogy, not an equation.

The hymn writer also adds the adjective "invisible" (ἀόρατος) to describe God. This is a surprisingly rare term to characterize God in biblical literature.[118] It appears in 1 Tim 1:17 in the ascription of praise "to the King eternal, immortal, invisible [ἀοράτῳ], the only God" (see also Rom 1:20; Heb 11:27), but it never appears in the LXX to describe God. The idea, however, is clearly present in the Torah. Moses could only see God's glory since the Lord revealed to him, "you cannot see my face; for no one shall see me and live" (Exod 33:20 NRSV). The conviction that God was invisible was deeply entrenched within Judaism. Josephus compares the invisibility of the soul to God, saying that it is "like God himself, invisible [ἀόρατος] to human eyes" (Josephus, *J.W.* 7.346–47 LCL). One Jewish text declares that "there is one God, who rules alone, exceedingly great, unbegotten, universal ruler [παντοκράτωρ], invisible [ἀόρατος], who himself sees all things" (Sib. Or., frag. 1.7–8; see also Sib. Or. 3.11). Other texts speak of "the invisible God" (ὁ ἀόρατος θεός; T. Ab. A 16.4) and "the invisible Father" (Apoc. Mos. 35.3).

In affirming that Jesus "is" (ἐστιν) the image of the invisible God, the hymn is referring to Jesus in his present exalted state. But because the next few lines of the context speak of his role in creating the world and the second part of the hymn speaks of his incarnate role in shedding his blood on the cross to secure reconciliation, the verb should also be understood as making a timeless assertion.[119] Thus, Jesus is the image of God in his preexistence, incarnation, and exaltation.[120] The language of Wisdom would have helped Jewish-background believers understand the unique identity of Jesus in relationship to the Father in a way that did not threaten their commitment to monotheism.

For gentiles in the Colossian church who had a background in the local traditional religions and magical practices, this perspective on Jesus Christ as the image of the invisible God would have been encouraging and challenging as they continued to adjust their understanding of him in light of all the other gods and spirits they once worshiped. For one thing, the article modifying God (τοῦ θεοῦ) would have served as a subtle but definite reminder that they had given their allegiance to *one* God who is the creator of heaven and earth. This monotheistic confession has had and will continue to have significant implications for how they relate to their past religious convictions and practices.

A significant part of the past experience of the Colossian believers was an understanding that statues, figures, and images represented the gods that they worshiped. Philo says they look upon the figures they have made and the pictures they have painted of them as gods (Philo, *Decalogue* 70). But for Christians (and Jews), the one God cannot be represented in graven images or painted

---

118 Stettler, *Kolosserhymnus*, 129, sees this as a typical Hellenistic expression and as the first indication that the hymn was composed in Greek and did not have a Hebrew or Aramaic original.

119 So also Beale, 82.

120 See also Stettler, *Christushymnus*, 337.

depictions; he is invisible. In fact, the Torah explicitly prohibits God's people from making "a carved image [εἴδωλον], or any likeness of anything that is in heaven above, or that is in the earth beneath" (Exod 20:4 ESV). But the authentic bearer of the image and likeness of the one true God is a person, the Lord Jesus Christ. It is not his physical appearance that bears the image of God, especially since he bore this image in his preexistent state before his incarnation, but that image is reflected in all that he is as a person and through the works that he does that only God can do. In the context of magic, some gods were occasionally described as "invisible," such as Aion (*PGM* XIII.71) or the Headless One (*PGM* V.123), but even these deities could also be represented with figures.

πρωτότοκος πάσης κτίσεως, "firstborn over all creation." Although on the surface this expression could be interpreted as a reference to Christ as the first of all beings to be created, this is not how it is functioning here. This statement is a metaphor that manifestly emphasizes the sovereignty of Christ over all of creation. The term πρωτότοκος typically refers to the first son to be born within a household. Thus, the LXX uses this term with reference to Esau as the firstborn son of Isaac (Gen 25:25) and Reuben as the firstborn of Jacob (Gen 35:23; 49:3; Exod 6:14), as does the NT in referring to Jesus as Mary's firstborn (Luke 2:7). But the term could also be used in a metaphorical sense. Consequently, the nation of Israel was regarded as God's firstborn (Exod 4:22) as a way of expressing the closeness of their relationship to the Lord.[121] The genitive case that follows is normally used of the father (or mother) of this firstborn son, but since "creation" and not a person is indicated by the genitive in our passage, this points to a metaphorical meaning for πρωτότοκος. This could suggest that Christ possess a close filial relationship with the Father, as in the reference to Israel as God's firstborn, but this probably does not capture the full extent of its meaning.

Some have thought that this is yet another allusion to the personified Word or Wisdom. Yet the passages in Philo used to support this view use πρωτόγονος and not πρωτότοκος, and they refer to the Word (λόγος) and not personified Wisdom, such as the following: "This hallowed flock He leads in accordance with right and law, setting over it His true Word [λόγον] and Firstborn Son [πρωτόγονον υἱόν] Who shall take upon Him its government like some viceroy of a great king" (Philo, *Agriculture* 51 LCL).[122] With this and other passage passages in Philo, the metaphorical sense expressed is the idea of "primacy in rank" and "authority to rule."[123]

While the Philonic background to the term has merit by maintaining the allusions to personified Wisdom (if we are correct to assume that Wisdom is usually present in every reference to Word in Philo), it is better to see the hymn

121 See LEH, s.v. πρωτότοκος.

122 See also Philo, *Confusion* 146–47, and *Dreams* 1.215.

123 Beetham, *Echoes of Scripture*, 126–27.

writer here using the language of a royal psalm.[124] The Lord declares in Ps 89:27 [88:28 LXX]: "I will make him the firstborn [πρωτότοκον], the highest of the kings of the earth." The text is making explicit reference to the Davidic king. Earlier the psalmist says, "I have made a covenant with my chosen one, I have sworn to my servant David: I will establish your descendants forever, and build your throne for all generations" (Ps 89:3–4 NRSV), and "I have found David my servant; with my sacred oil I have anointed [LXX ἔχρισα] him" (Ps 29:20 NRSV). The messianic overtones of this passage are explicit. As with the previous interpretation, the emphasis here is on the sovereignty of this ruler. He is appointed to the role of a firstborn. In this case, he possesses the rights of the firstborn of God himself. The title thus belongs to Christ as the Son of David. This interpretation thus suggests that the hymn writer is not only drawing on the Wisdom tradition but also on the Davidic messianic tradition in the complex of ideas used to extol the supremacy of Christ's lordship. The genitive, πάσης κτίσεως, is therefore not a genitive of relationship or source, but an objective genitive: Christ rules all of creation.

This understanding of the phrase completely rules out an Arian interpretation that regards Christ as part of creation. As we have seen, the language does not have to do with physical descent, but priority in rank.[125] It is the language of sovereignty. It is similar to the use of the term in Heb 1:6 where God enjoins all of the angels to worship his firstborn.

**16** ὅτι ἐν αὐτῷ ἐκτίσθη τὰ πάντα ἐν τοῖς οὐρανοῖς καὶ ἐπὶ τῆς γῆς, "for in him all things were created in the heavens and upon the earth." Christ surpasses divine Wisdom in that he was the Father's personal agent in creating the entire universe. The conjunction ὅτι, "for," provides support to the claim that Christ is sovereign over all creation precisely because he was the creator. It also clarifies that the writer is not making the assertion that Christ was the first created being. Rather, he existed before the creation and is responsible for the created order. Although it is possible to take the ἐν αὐτῷ as instrumental ("by him"; KJV; NIV1984; NET; CSB),[126] it is better to take it as a a dative of sphere and as indicating that the creation takes place "in him."[127] He will use διά to express instrumentality at the end of this verse; the significance of the ἐν probably encompasses some sense of instrumentality but goes beyond it. The phrase occurs three times in this hymn and once in the introduction to it: believers have redemption "in him" (1:14), the universe was created "in him," it holds together "in him" (1:17), and all the fullness dwells "in him" (1:19). The sense of the expression here is that all of creation came into existence "under

124 So also Fee, *Pauline Christology*, 301.

125 Thiselton, 34, rightly observes that "if firstborn literally means first created it seems odd to support that claim with an argument that all created things were created through him (for he would be one of the 'all things' that were created)."

126 So Sumney, 66.

127 Moo, 121.

the control of" or "under the influence of" Christ.[128] In close association with "the invisible God," Christ exerted his power and wise design in originating all of creation. Prov 8 declares that Wisdom was with the Father "at the beginning of his work" and "before the beginning of the earth," serving "beside him, like a master workman" (Prov 8:22–23, 30). In a similar way, the Jewish Wisdom tradition attributes a creative role to personified Wisdom: "God of the fathers and Lord of mercy, who made all things [τὰ πάντα] by your word and by your wisdom [τῇ σοφίᾳ] formed human beings to rule over the creatures that were made by you" (Wis 9:1–2 NETS). In the same way, Christ, in close association with the Father, displayed his creative work in fashioning heaven and earth, providing them with structure and order.

The hymn writer stresses that Christ created τὰ πάντα, "all things." He leaves nothing outside the scope of Christ's powerful creative hand by clarifying that he is referring to everything "in heaven and upon the earth." This echoes the language of the creation account in LXX Genesis where it is said that "God saw all things [τὰ πάντα] that he had made, and they were very good. And heaven and earth [ὁ οὐρανὸς καὶ ἡ γῆ] and all the *kosmos* [κόσμος] were finished" (Gen 1:31–2:1). The prologue of John contains the same announcement: "through him all things [πάντα] were made; without him nothing was made that has been made" (John 1:3 NIV). The idea of Christ acting alongside the Father in creating the world is not a new idea, however, in Paul's thought. Paul told the Corinthians, "For us there is one God, the Father, from whom are all things [τὰ πάντα] and for whom we exist, and one Lord, Jesus Christ, through whom are all things and through whom we exist" (1 Cor 8:6). In his mind, Paul can ascribe the role of creator to Christ without surrendering his monotheism. What emerges here and in 1 Cor 8:6 is a "christological monotheism" in which Paul includes Jesus the Messiah in the Shema (Deut 6:4).[129] Paul could believe and declare, "Hear, O Israel, the LORD our God, the LORD is one," and yet now understand Jesus Christ to be an integral part of God's essential oneness.

Although the verb ποιέω is used throughout the creation account in LXX Genesis (e.g., "in the beginning, God made [ἐποίησεν] the heaven and the earth"; Gen 1:1), the verb κτίζω does appear in Genesis and is used throughout the LXX for God's act of creation (e.g., "God Most High, who created [ἔκτισεν] the heaven and the earth"; Gen 14:19, 22). The psalmist declares, "Let them praise the name of the Lord, for he commanded, and they were created [ἐκτίσθησαν]" (Ps 148:5 LXX [NETS]). Paul refers to God as "the creator" (ὁ κτίσας) in Rom 1:25 and later in Colossians (3:10). The aorist tense of the verb here, ἐκτίσθη, should be understood in its perfective aspect—as a comprehensive summary of the act of creation.[130]

128 BDAG, s.v. ἐν 4.
129 Wright, "Poetry and Theology," 460.
130 See Campbell, 11.

In Ps 89, God is represented as sovereign precisely because he is the creator. The psalmist extols God's might because "the world and all that is in it, you have founded them. The north and the south, you have created them" (Ps 89:11–12 ESV). He then exclaims, "You have a mighty arm; strong is your hand, high your right hand" (Ps 89:13 ESV). Of course, in this royal psalm, he appoints David his "firstborn, the highest of the kings of the earth" (Ps 89:27), who will reign with his delegated power, authority, and might. This intermixing of royal Davidic language with the functions of personified Wisdom blends into a portrayal of Christ who is unique in his preexistent divine qualities and combined with Davidic sonship and authority.

For the gentile readers of Colossians, these words would have brought reassurance about the place of Christ in relation to the other gods and goddesses they once worshiped. But there were competing claims. The Derveni Papyrus (4th c. BC), found near Thessaloniki, extols Zeus in the following words: "Zeus the head, Zeus the middle, and from Zeus all things were made."[131] Such claims about the gods are found also in the realm of magic and folk belief. In a recipe for an amulet invoking Helios for protection, Helios is invoked as "creator of the world, creator of the universe [κόσμου κτίστα, τὰ πάντα κτίστα], lord, god of gods," and as "you who created gods, archangels, and decans" (*PGM* IV.1200–1205). In yet another invocation of Helios for revelatory magic, he is extolled as the one "who creates all things" and as the one "from whom, indeed, all elements [στοιχεῖα] have been arranged" (*PGM* IV.439–40). Because of his role as creator, he is invoked as "you who rule Heaven and earth, Chaos and Hades, where men's daimons dwell . . . the master of the world [δέσποτα κόσμου]" (*PGM* IV.443–44; see also IV.1709; XIII.63 and 571 that invoke Helios as τὰ πάντα κτίσαντα). But the Colossian hymn challenges all such rival claims. As the next line of the text reveals, Christ is superior because he created the spiritual realm, of which Helios and all other so-called gods were a part. As Stettler rightly notes, "Jesus is the one to whom even the angelic beings, good and Satanic, owe their being and continued existence."[132]

τὰ ὁρατὰ καὶ τὰ ἀόρατα, εἴτε θρόνοι εἴτε κυριότητες εἴτε ἀρχαὶ εἴτε ἐξουσίαι, "the invisible and the visible, whether thrones or dominions, whether principalities or authorities." The hymn expands on the "all things" by defining them in the most comprehensive way possible—both the visible and the invisible. The term, ὁρατός, is not a common biblical expression, only occurring here in the NT and in four other locations in the LXX and never elsewhere in contrast to ἀόρατος. The combination of the two terms is common, however, in the philosophers. Plato uses ὁρατός to describe the world of sense perception, while using

131 Translation by A. Laks and G. W. Most, *Derveni Papyrus*, 17 (column SVII); Greek text in R. Janko, "Derveni Papyrus," 34.

132 Stettler, *Christushymnus*, 338.

ἀόρατος to refer to the realm of the archetypes.[133] He is followed in this usage by Philo. For instance, in one passage Philo speaks about the one who "judges the visible world of sense [τὰ ὁρατὰ καὶ αἰσθητά] to be not holy but profane, compared with the pure and undefiled nature of the invisible world [τῶν ἀοράτων] of mind" (Philo, *Prelim. Studies* 1.25 LCL). It is doubtful that the hymn writer (or Paul) is using the contrasting terms in this philosophical sense. He is more likely using τὰ ὁρατά to refer to the entire realm of physical creation—people, plants, animals, land, ocean, as well as the sun, moon, and stars. By contrast, he is using τὰ ἀόρατα to speak of the invisible realm of spirits and angels. This interpretation is confirmed by the list of four different categories of spiritual beings that follows and more clearly specifies what he means by τὰ ἀόρατα.

Many interpreters have seen this list of powers as a redactional insertion into the original hymn.[134] This is because it destroys some of the balance between the length of the two strophes of the hymn and has the appearance of an elaboration (or intrusion) as an editorial explanation of the "invisible." Because of the prominence of the powers in the rest of the letter and in relationship to the teaching of "the philosophy," it has thus appeared to some as the letter writer's own commentary. But if we do not measure the strophes of the hymn by the standard of Greek meter and see them more in the style of Hebrew poetry, then the notion that they are a redactional addition is more difficult to support. Although we have no way of determining the answer to this question with any certainty, it does not matter for the interpretation of the text and for how Paul uses it in relation to his engagement with "the philosophy." The purpose of this delineation of the powers here in the larger context of the letter is to extol Christ's supremacy and lordship over against the powers. This would have served to encourage the Colossian believers to hold on tight to Christ (2:19), who was sovereign over the spiritual powers that were a focal point of their concerns.

There is also a question of whether the hymn is referring to human rulers or supernatural spirit powers.[135] While it is true that Paul can use the expression ἐξουσίαι as a way of referring to earthly rulers (see Rom 13:1; see also Luke 12:11 where the terms are used to refer to the rulers and authorities of the synagogues), he consistently uses the tandem ἀρχαὶ καὶ ἐξουσίαι to refer to angelic powers, and more specifically, to evil spiritual powers (see 1 Cor 15:24; Col 2:10, 15; Eph 1:21; 3:10; 6:12). The later context of Colossians confirms that this is his usage in this letter when he speaks of these principalities and authorities

133 See the texts in W. Michaelis, "ὁρατός, ἀόρατος," *TDNT* 5:368.

134 See, e.g., Wedderburn, "Theology of Colossians," 15–16; Kehl, *Christushymnus*, 46; Gnilka, 57, 65; Martin, 56.

135 Bammel, "Versuch," 88–95, posits a chiastic structure in which the visible world consists of θρόνοι and ἐξουσίαι and the invisible world consists of κυριότητες and ἀρχαί. But this arrangement should be rejected because it splits the one phrase that Paul normally keeps together, i.e., the ἀρχαί and ἐξουσίαι.

defeated by Christ's work on the cross (Col 2:15). While it may be possible to see these powers influencing human governments and earthly structures, that is not the primary concern here. Although there is no doubt that the hymn's explicit teaching that Christ is sovereign over all things has implications for the claims of the Roman Empire, the emphasis here is upon his sovereignty over the invisible realm of spirits.[136] That is the explicit teaching of the letter in its polemic with "the philosophy."

The first term, θρόνοι, "thrones," appears nowhere else in Paul and, indeed, nowhere else in the NT as a reference to rulers (either earthly or heavenly).[137] The term itself is common in Revelation, for instance, but only with reference to the throne of God or the thrones of the twenty-four elders, but never to actual beings. It is known, however, both in Judaism and in folk magical texts as a category of spirit beings. In 2 (Slavonic) Enoch, the term "thrones" appears in connection with an array of different kinds of angelic beings: "I saw . . . all the fiery armies of the great archangels, and the incorporeal forces and the dominions and the origins and the authorities, the cherubim and the seraphim and the many-eyed thrones" (2 En. 20.1). Similarly, the term appears in the Testament of Levi for good angels: "there with him are thrones and authorities [θρόνοι, ἐξουσίαι]; there praises to God are offered eternally" (T. Levi 3.8). The Testament of Abraham (shorter recension), which is likely a first-century document, enumerates "thrones" along with "principalities and authorities" in a list of angelic powers: "and Death said to Abraham, 'I tell you, in all the creation which God created, there is not to be found one like you. For he searched among the angels and archangels, and principalities and powers, as well as thrones [ἐν τοῖς ἀγγέλοις καὶ ἀρχαγγέλοις καὶ ἀρχαῖς καὶ ἐξουσίας θρόνοις]'" (T. Ab 13.10).[138] Although not common in magical texts, "thrones" are invoked in a pagan magical text: "I conjure you by the one who is in charge of the air. And again I conjure you by the seven thrones [θρόνων]." The text then provides the names of the seven thrones (*PGM* CI.39–41).[139] A compound form of the noun σύνθρονοι appears in two *defixiones* for underworld spirits. A lead curse tablet found in North Africa begins with this adjuration: "I invoke you, whoever you are, spirit of the untimely dead, by the seven associated thrones [συνθρόνων] of the king of

136 Sumney's comment (68) that "the claim of Christ's superiority also sets the church against the claims of the empire," while true, is not the uppermost concern of the letter.

137 D. Sanger, "θρόνος," *EDNT* 2:156, describes this usage in Colosians as "a peculiar feature in the use of θρόνος, not found elsewhere in the NT."

138 The best critical edition of the text is by F. Schmidt, *Le testament grec d'Abraham*, 78–79. The relevant portion of the text cited here comes from manuscript E, which Schmidt contends is the best Greek text for the shorter recension. The majority of scholars date this text to the first century BC or first century AD. See J. R. Mueller, "Abraham, Testament of," *ABD* 1:44; Schmidt, "Two Recensions," 80, who dates the composition to the second half of the first century AD.

139 The Greek text is found in Wortmann, "Neue magische Texte," 88. It is discussed by Gager, *Curse Tablets*, 101–6 (no. 30).

the underworld [this is followed by seven names]."[140] Similarly, a *defixio* found in a grave in Cyprus includes not only an invocation of the gods in Hades but also the associated beings seated on thrones (σύνθρονοι).[141]

The second term, κυριότητες, is equally rare, but it also appears in a list of powers in Eph 1:21. As with "thrones," this term was known in some Jewish apocalyptic texts and in the context of magic. The basic sense of the term evokes "the majestic power that the κύριος wields, ruling power, lordship, dominion" (see 2 Pet 2:10; Jude 8).[142] It came to represent a "special class of angelic powers."[143] In addition to 2 En. 20.1, it also appears in a list of angelic powers in 1 Enoch: "he will summon all the forces of the heavens, and all the holy ones above, and the forces of the Lord—the cherubim, seraphim, ophanim, all the angels of governance, the Elect One, and the other forces on earth (and) over the water" (1 En. 61.10).[144] Although much later than the NT, the Syriac *Cave of Treasures* 1.3 is often cited as attesting this use of κυριότητες for angelic beings:[145] "the Lord made . . . the invisible powers, that is, the angels, archangels, thrones, authorities, powers, rulers, cherubs and seraphs, and all the ranks and spiritual armies."[146] There is one Jewish magical text that uses this term in conjunction with "thrones" (manuscript D of T. Sol. 8.6: καὶ οἱ θρόνοι καὶ αἱ κυριότητες), but this, too, is quite late, though likely based on much earlier traditions. The term is found in a Christian magical text (c. AD 300)—"I invoke you, O god almighty, who is above every ruler and authority and lordship [κυριότητος]"—yet it is possible that it reflects dependence on Colossians or Ephesians (*PGM* 21.2–3).[147]

The third and fourth terms, ἀρχαί and ἐξουσίαι, "principalities" and "authorities," are the terms Paul commonly uses for evil supernatural powers. They are often linked together when they appear in the letters (1 Cor 15:24; Eph 1:21; 3:10; 6:12). He uses these terms twice later in this letter (2:10, 15). The term ἀρχαί appears without ἐξουσίαι in only one other place with reference to spirit powers in Paul (Rom 8:38), but there it occurs with δυνάμεις and ἄγγελοι. The term ἐξουσίαι, on the other hand, is never used by itself with reference to demonic powers, but the singular is used to refer to the realm of Satan (Col 1:13; see also Eph 2:2). It does, however, appear in 1 Peter in conjunction with

140 Audollent, *Defixionum Tablellae*, 320 (no. 240.1–2).

141 Audollent, *Defixionum Tablellae*, 65 (no. 35.37).

142 BDAG, s.v. κυριότης 2.

143 BDAG, s.v. κυριότης 3.

144 There is no Greek fragment of Enoch extant for this portion of the book. One can only infer the Greek original based on the Ethiopic text.

145 See, e.g., W. Foerster, "κυριότης," *TDNT* 3:1096–97.

146 Translation by A. Toepel, "The Cave of Treasures," in Bauckham, Davila, and Panayotov, *Old Testament Pseudepigrapha*, 540. The original text was likely composed in Syriac, and there are no extant Greek versions, so one can only infer equivalent forms on the basis of cognate terms. The *History of the Rechabites* 16.1 refers to "thrones and dominions," but this appears in a section that was likely a Christian interpolation.

147 Translation by Meyer, *Ancient Christian Magic*, 55 (no. 36).

ἄγγελοι and δυνάμεις to speak of Christ's subjection of the powers (1 Pet 3:22). This reference possibly relies on a traditional formulation. "Principalities" and "authorities" (ἀρχαί and ἐξουσίαι) are used in a number of the Jewish texts already cited (see 1 En. 61.10; 2 En. 20.1; T. Levi 3.8; T. Ab. 13.10; see also 1 En. 6.7–8 [ἀρχαί] and 3 Bar. 12.3 [ἐξουσίαι]). The terms also appear in a Jewish folk magical text where the demon, Ornias, is compelled to reveal how demons access heaven: "for the principalities and authorities and powers [ἀρχαὶ καὶ ἐξουσία καὶ δυνάμεις] above fly around and are considered worthy of entering heaven" (T. Sol. 20.15). These terms, however, are quite rare in the magical papyri (but see *PGM* I.215 and IV.1193; see also the Christian magical text, *PGM* P13.15–16). One magical text invokes the ἀρχαί of fire in a charm for gaining a direct vision (*PGM* IV.939).

All of these terms were part of a reservoir of terminology widely known within Judaism and folk magical practice for angelic powers—either good or evil. It is also possible that the readers of this letter would see this as a statement about Christ's superiority over their local gods (which Paul would have seen as animated by the demonic realm; see 1 Cor 10:20–21). The principal deity at Hierapolis, Apollo, is called Apollo Archegetes (ἀρχηγέτις). The term means, generally, the "leader" or "chief."[148] This title was engraved on the architrave of the theater as part of a longer inscription commemorating the construction of the edifice.[149]

The context of Paul's usage of these terms is wholly determinative of whether they should be interpreted as good or evil spirit beings. At this point in the hymn, when seen in isolation from the context of the letter, there is nothing to suggest which of the two moral categories these angelic beings would fall into. In fact, in this first strophe of the hymn, there is an emphasis on the universality of Christ's sovereignty, which would suggest that both good and evil angels are in view. The second strophe of the hymn, however, implies a rupture in the invisible realm that requires pacification and would thus suggest that the emphasis may be more upon the domain of evil spirits.[150] This is confirmed by the introduction of the hymn that speaks of God rescuing his people from "the authority of darkness" (ἐκ τῆς ἐξουσίας τοῦ σκότους; 1:13) and then later in the letter when Paul speaks of the dramatic victory of God over the ἀρχαί and ἐξουσίαι (2:15). It is also important to note that the ἀρχαί and ἐξουσίαι are consistently portrayed as evil beings in Paul's writings.

Why the author of the hymn (or Paul) has chosen these terms for the angelic powers and not others is impossible to discern. This is particularly true of θρόνοι since it appears nowhere else in the NT or LXX for demonic spirits or angels. Nevertheless, these terms were known and readily understandable by Jews and

148 LSJ, s.v. ἀρχηγέτις.

149 *CIG* 3905.1. See also the text and translation in D'Andria, *Hierapolis of Phrygia*, 147–49.

150 Contra Carr, *Angels and Principalities*, 48–52.

gentiles alike. Stettler may be correct in concluding that they represent the *summa* of the invisible realm.[151] They signify the entirety of the spiritual domain.

The hymnic elaboration on the invisible realm of evil principalities and powers was highly relevant to the Colossian Christian community. There are three reasons for this: (1) the people of Colossae (and indeed much of the ancient world) feared the supernatural realm of spirits because of the threat they posed to the stability of daily life. These powers are responsible for various kinds of ills both on an individual and at a community and societal level. They cause "natural" disasters, famine, disease, plagues, and earthquakes. They are also behind sickness, disease, fevers, strife, and even astral fate; (2) the Colossian "philosophy" claimed to have an answer for averting the harmful workings of these hostile powers through the shamanic wisdom of its teachers and the rituals of power and invocation of angelic helpers; (3) as the letter unfolds, it becomes clear that Paul believes that the teaching and practices of "the philosophy" have, ironically, been inspired by the hostile powers themselves.

τὰ πάντα δι᾽ αὐτοῦ καὶ εἰς αὐτὸν ἔκτισται, "all things have been created through him and for him." The second strophe is brought to completion through a reaffirmation of the sovereignty of Christ by repeating the fact that he is creator of all things.

Once again we should understand τὰ πάντα as universal in scope, but with special reference to the invisible realm—the domain of principalities, powers, thrones, and dominions. Instead of using the aorist tense of the verb, the hymn writer has chosen to use the perfect tense (ἔκτισται). Through this means, the author emphasizes a stative *Aktionsart*,[152] and thereby stresses Christ's exalted status as creator. Thus, the writer begins and ends his justification for affirming the universal sovereignty of Christ (as "firstborn over all creation") by emphasizing his role as creator of all things. In the words of the Davidic psalm, this means that as "firstborn," Christ is "the highest of the kings of the earth" (Ps 89:27 NRSV). Because he is creator of all things, he is truly παντοκράτωρ. Christ is the same God revealed in Isaiah as "the Creator of the ends of the earth" (Isa 40:28 NRSV). His sovereignty as creator extends over the heavens and earth: "He sits enthroned above the circle of the earth, and its people are like grasshoppers. He stretches out the heavens like a canopy, and spreads them out like a tent to live in. . . . He . . . brings out the starry host one by one and calls forth each of them by name. Because of his great power and mighty strength, not one of them is missing" (Isa 40:22, 26 NIV). He is the same God extolled in the prayer of Israel at the beginning of the Second Temple era: "You are the LORD, you alone. You have made heaven, the heaven of heavens, with all their host, the earth and all that is on it . . . and you preserve all of them [τὰ πάντα]; and the host of heaven [στρατιαὶ τῶν οὐρανῶν] worships you" (Neh 9:6 ESV).

151 Stettler, *Christushymnus*, 338.

152 So Campbell, 12.

Whereas in 16b, all things were created "in him," now the hymn writer says that they are created "through him" and "for him." The δι' αὐτοῦ, "through him," indicates that Christ is the agent of creation. The passive verb probably implies that the Father is the final or ultimate source of creation, which is what we would expect from the OT and Jewish tradition. The divine passive of this verb "also presupposes the OT idea of creation as background to the declarations of 1:16."[153] Paul told the Corinthians that Christ is the one "through whom are all things" (δι' οὗ τὰ πάντα; 1 Cor 8:6). The εἰς αὐτόν, "for him," indicates that Christ is the goal of creation. Such an affirmation is unprecedented for anything predicated of divine Wisdom in Jewish tradition. An eschatological goal now emerges. Christ is the one who will restore creation to what it was originally intended to be, thus anticipating the final lines of the hymn where it is said that Christ will reconcile all things to himself (Col 1:20). Christ as the goal of creation is also without parallel in Paul's writings, where creation is seen as "for" God (see Rom 11:36 [εἰς αὐτὸν τὰ πάντα]; see also 1 Cor 8:6), but Christ's involvement in the eschatological consummation is prominent in his letters (see esp. 1 Cor 15:20–28; 1 Thess 4:13–5:11). There is one strand of Jewish tradition, however, that affirms that the world was created "for the Messiah" (b. Sanh. 98b [I.10.8.A Neusner]).

Some interpreters have attempted to explain the three prepositions describing Christ's role in creation as dependent upon Aristotle's discussion of three causes—efficient ("in him"), instrumental ("through him"), and final causation ("for him"),[154] or as a Platonic/Stoic theory of causation.[155] For instance, the second-century emperor and philosopher, Marcus Aurelius, praises the harmony of nature: "All that thy seasons bring, O Nature [ὦ φύσις], is fruit for me! All things come from thee, subsist in thee, go back to thee [ἐκ σοῦ πάντα, ἐν σοὶ πάντα, εἰς σὲ πάντα]" (*Meditations* 4.23; see also Seneca, *Ep.* 65.8).[156] While the coincidence of language is striking with the same three prepositions, Marcus Aurelius's worldview regarding nature was probably not widely held or even known in the rural community of Colossae. Similarly, positing an allusion to Aristotle overly interprets the language and does so on the basis of a school tradition with which the readers were probably not familiar. As noted above, it is also likely that the "through him" and "for him" help explain the "in him" of 1:16b,[157] and should thus not be seen as three distinct modes of causation. This approach also ignores the role of the Father in the divine passives, who would properly be seen as the final cause.

153 Barth and Blanke, 198.

154 Aristotle, *Phys.* 2.3–9 (194b–200b).

155 Norden, *Agnostos Theos*, 240–50, which he terms the Stoic *Allmachtsformel*. See also the discussion in Hay, 57.

156 See Barth and Blanke, 197, who argue for a dependence on the Stoic language.

157 So also Pao, 96.

The emphasis on Christ as creator of all things precludes finding the origin of the Christology in this passage in an Adam Christology.[158] Similarly, it rules out an angel Christology since angels are never portrayed as being involved in creating the world.[159]

**17** καὶ αὐτός ἐστιν πρὸ πάντων, "and he is before all things." Because of his preexistence before the creation of the world, Christ possesses sovereignty over all of his creation. The καὶ αὐτός, "and he," introduces a refrain or interlude (a *Zwischenstrophe*) in this poem of praise to Christ. It is complemented by a second καὶ αὐτός two lines later (1:18a) that concludes this three-line middle section of the hymn. The intensive pronoun αὐτός is a rhetorical variation from the relative pronoun ὅς that begins the first and second strophes of the hymn. It emphatically refers to Christ who has been the subject of the first strophe.

The prepositional phrase πρὸ πάντων, "before all things," could be taken as a temporal expression.[160] Although Paul has never used this precise phrase elsewhere, the other eleven uses of the preposition πρό in his writings consistently have a temporal sense (e.g., 1 Cor 2:7; 4:5; 2 Cor 12:2). The temporal interpretation would also fit with the previous context, where it was affirmed that Christ existed at the time of creation. But the first strophe also represents Christ as sovereign over creation, and his preexistence as creator serves to support the claim of sovereignty (as the ὅτι in 1:16a suggests). Thus, by existing temporally prior to all of creation, Christ is superior in rank and status to the creation in its entirety. This would include not only every sociopolitical structure and the entire range of rulers from the local official to the emperor himself. But more importantly, in light of the problem and concerns facing the Colossians, it would extend to the realm of all gods, goddesses, and supernatural powers—astral, aerial, or chthonic. Consequently, the phrase is an expression of temporal priority, but this serves to buttress the claim that Christ is Lord of all.[161] Barth and Blanke translate the expression as "it is he who reigns over all things."[162] The present tense of ἐστιν highlights the status of Christ. Otherwise, one would have expected the imperfect ἦν, "he was before all things" (as in John 1:1: "in the beginning was the Word"), if this were strictly a descriptive temporal expression.

καὶ τὰ πάντα ἐν αὐτῷ συνέστηκεν, "and all things hold together in him." In this second line of this intermediate strophe, the hymn extols Christ's present role of sustaining all of creation. The hymn writer once again uses τὰ πάντα to speak of the entirety of creation.

158 Loke, *Divine Christology*, 64.

159 Loke, *Divine Christology*, 68.

160 The temporal view is supported by, e.g., Moo, 125; Schweizer, 71; Lightfoot, 156.

161 Most commentators support the interpretation of the phrase as both temporal and status. These include, e.g., Beale, 95–96; Pao, 98; Foster, 190; Sumney, 70; Hay, 58; MacDonald, 61; Wilson, 143; Barth and Blanke, 203; Gnilka, 66; Dunn, 93; Lohse, 52.

162 Barth and Blanke, 203.

In the earlier English translation history of συνέστηκεν, the verb was regularly translated "consist": "by him all things consist" (KJV; see also ERV; ASV). This intransitive and now obsolete use of "consist" was employed to express the idea, "to have a settled existence, subsist, hold together."[163] Nearly all English versions now translate it as "hold together." The basic semantic sense of the verb συνίστημι is "coherence" or "being in a state of close relationship."[164] It is common in Paul's writings as a transitive verb, occuring fourteen times, but is normally used in contexts where it refers to commending a person to someone else (e.g., Rom 16:1) or with the extended sense of "demonstrating" something (e.g., Rom 3:5). But this is the only intransitive use of the verb in Paul's writings. Second Peter uses the aorist form of the verb intransitively, but with reference to the initial creation of the heavens: "the earth was formed [συνεστῶσα] out of water" (2 Pet 3:5). The perfect tense in Colossians should be understood as a stative, with an emphasis on the present work of Christ in maintaining his creation. It is possible that the use of the perfect tense here lends prominence to the clause.[165]

The use of this particular verb for sustaining creation is unique to this hymn, but the idea of God (or Wisdom, Word, or the Spirit) holding together the creation occurs in the wisdom literature and more broadly in Hellenistic Judaism. In Wis 1:7 we read, "Because the spirit of the Lord has filled the world, and that which holds all things together [τὸ συνέχον τὰ πάντα] knows what is said" (NRSV). Similarly, Sir 43:26 says that "by his word all things hold together [ἐν λόγῳ αὐτοῦ σύγκειται τὰ πάντα]." Philo speaks of God as "creator of the universe, the Father of the world, who holds together [συνέχων] earth and heaven" (Philo, *Moses* 2.238 Yonge; see also *Heir* 23). He can also speak of "reason" (τὸ λογεῖον) as that which "holds together [συνέχοντος] and regulates the universe" (Philo, *Moses* 2.133). In yet another passage, he refers to the role of the Logos in holding together all things: "the word [λόγος] of the living God being the bond of every thing, as has been said before, holds all things together [συνέχει τὰ μέρη πάντα], and binds all the parts, and prevents them from being loosened or separated" (Philo, *Flight* 112 Yonge). In all of these instances, however, the authors use different verbs to express the same concept, but συνίστημι can be found in the Hellenistic philosophical and popular religious traditions for the act of creation and for sustaining the creation.

This usage occurs as early as Plato. He uses the verb συνίστημι to speak of the act of creation: "the creator of the heavens" (τῷ τοῦ οὐρανοῦ δημιουργῷ) worked "to make them [συνεστάναι] and all that is in them" (Plato, *Republic* 530A). A text that most closely resembles the idea found in the Colossian hymn is found in a first-century AD philosopher of the Peripatetic school writing in the Aristotelian

163 OED, s.v. "consist" 1.a.

164 BDAG, s.v. συνίστημι.

165 Campbell, 14.

tradition, who closely parallels the language of our hymn (Ps.-Aristotle, *On the Cosmos* 6 [397b] LCL):[166]

> It remains now to discuss summarily, as the rest has been discussed, the cause that holds the world together [συνεκτικῆς]; for in describing the cosmos, if not in detail, at least sufficiently to convey an outline, it would be wrong for us to omit altogether that which is supreme in the cosmos. It is indeed an ancient idea, traditional among all mankind, that all things are from God and are constituted for us by God, and nothing is self-sufficient if deprived of his preserving influence [ἐκ θεοῦ πάντα καὶ διὰ θεοῦ συνέστηκεν]. . . . For God is indeed the preserver of all things and the creator of everything in this cosmos however it is brought to fruition; but he does not take upon himself the toil of a creature that works and labours for itself, but uses an indefatigable power, by means of which he controls even things that seem a great way off.

The concept of a deity sustaining creation also penetrated popular religion, as seen in the famous aretology to Isis where she is extolled as a goddess who "holds all things together" (ἅπαντα συνέστηκεν; *P.Oxy.* 1380.185). This includes the basic components of the creation order, including wet and dry as well as hot and cold. But Isis is also revered as one to whom "the spirits become her subjects" (δαίμονες ὑπήκοοι σοὶ γίνονται; *P.Oxy.* 1380.164–65).

In a pagan magical text, Eros is invoked as the "author of all creation" (τὸν ἀρχηγέτην πάσης γενέσεως), "the founder of the universe," "firstborn" (πρωτόγονε), and—in precisely the same language as the Colossian hymn—as the one by whom "all things hold together" (τὰ πάντα συνέστηκεν) (*PGM* IV.1750–771, esp. 1770–71). The intent of all these epithets is to extol the power of the deity who is being called upon to perform the request of the suppliant. Yet the text also warns that this deity can bring pain, is sometimes irrational, is a generator of frenzy, and whose light becomes darkness (*PGM* IV.1771–74).

The term also appears in a syncretistic magical text that has a mix of Jewish and pagan traditions for ritual power. Called the Eighth Book of Moses, the text contains an invocation to a god who "holds together the vault of heaven and the earth" (διὰ σὲ συνέστηκεν ὁ πόλος καὶ ἡ γῆ; *PGM* XIII.76). The same epithet is cited later in the text (*PGM* XIII.586).

In contrast to all of the competing claims of deities who declare they have created the world and hold it together, the Colossian hymn praises Jesus Christ as the one and only God who fulfills this role. He served as the agent of the one, true invisible God in creating the universe, and now upholds that creation.

166 D. J. Furley, *Aristotle III* (LCL 400), 335, observes that "the theology and cosmology of the *De Mundo* is, in general, Peripatetic, but the author borrows his details from many schools." The work itself did not derive from the hand of Aristotle but was likely written by a first-century eclectic philosopher (pp. 337–41).

Similar to the Colossian hymn, the poetic praise to Christ at the beginning of the book of Hebrews exalts Christ as the agent through whom God created the world (Heb 1:2) and as the one who "upholds [φέρων] the universe by the word of his power" (Heb 1:3). This becomes part of the basis for his argument that Christ is superior to the angels (Heb 1:4).

There is surprisingly little that is said in the OT about God sustaining or "holding together" his creation. This was likely assumed based on his role as creator and his universal sovereignty over his creation. The Colossian hymn makes it explicit, however, that Christ was not only God's agent in the creation of the universe but has the ongoing role of maintaining it by his power. This claim buttresses his status as sovereign over all the created order, including the invisible world of spirits and the so-called gods and goddesses.

**18 καὶ αὐτός ἐστιν ἡ κεφαλὴ τοῦ σώματος τῆς ἐκκλησίας**, "and he is the head of the body, the church." The hymn writer reaffirms Christ's sovereignty by employing a new metaphor—the image of a head in relationship to the body. But the focus is no longer on the universe (τὰ πάντα), but now on the church. The introductory **καὶ αὐτός ἐστιν** stands parallel to the same expression in 1:17a, where the author extols Christ's universal sovereignty. The two expressions form an *inclusio* that marks the middle strophe, or refrain, of the hymn. The pronoun **αὐτός** is emphatic and "resumes with emphasis a subject which has already been named."[167] The person of the preexistent, incarnate, and now resurrected and exalted Christ is brought into bold relief as sovereign over the entire universe and in a special relationship to his church.

The characterization of the church as the body of Christ is thoroughly Pauline. He declares to the Corinthians, "Now you are the body of Christ [ὑμεῖς δέ ἐστε σῶμα Χριστοῦ] and individually members of it" (1 Cor 12:27 NRSV; see also 12:12–14). Similarly, to the Roman believers he asserts, "So we, who are many, are one body in Christ, and individually we are members one of another" (Rom 12:5 NRSV). The use of the metaphorical "body" with reference to a group of people was widespread in the ancient world, but it was particularly at home within Stoicism. Seneca and Cicero, along with Marcus Aurelius and Epictetus, frequently drew the analogy of a human body to universal humanity.[168] Seneca even represents Nero as the "head" of the Roman Empire, with his health flowing through the *corpus imperii* (the "body" of the empire):

> We are pleased to hope and trust, Caesar [Nero], that in large measure this will happen. That kindness of your heart will be recounted, will be diffused little by little throughout the whole body of the empire [*per omne imperii corpus*], and all things will be moulded into your likeness. It is from the head [*capite*] that comes the health of the body; it is through it that all the parts are lively and alert or

167 W. Radl, "αὐτός," *EDNT* 1:179.

168 Lee, *Body of Christ*, 46, 101–2.

languid and drooping according as their animating spirit has life or withers. (Seneca, *De clementia* 2.2.1)

Whereas Paul may have been influenced by the widely known Stoic use of the imagery and some of its entailments, his understanding of the body was profoundly shaped by his theological convictions. His conception of the work of the Holy Spirit in "baptizing" or incorporating diverse individuals into one unified community of Christ followers was central to his understanding (1 Cor 12:13).[169] The Spirit is the life-giving principle of this new community. This was made possible by the substitutionary death of Christ on behalf of the community as the means of securing forgiveness of sins, redemption, and reconciliation to God (see 1 Cor 11:23–26). The hymn will make specific mention of "the blood of his cross" near the conclusion (Col 1:20b). The objective unity of this new community with Christ in his sacrificial act is stressed by Paul when he says, "One died for all; therefore all have died" (2 Cor 5:14b). The author of Ephesians extends the image of the body even further when he characterizes the church as the bride of Christ (Eph 5:22–33).[170]

Here, for the first time in Paul's writings, the hymn writer introduces the idea that Christ is the κεφαλή ("head") of the body. The meaning of the image as conveying lordship and sovereignty is clear because it is parallel with the affirmation that Christ is πρὸ πάντων ("before all things") in 1:17a. This is consistent with the widespread usage of κεφαλή as a metaphor for a leader or one who has a superior rank.[171] It also corresponds to the OT usage of ראשׁ, "head," where "it has stood for the chief and leader of a social group since ancient times."[172] In many of these instances, κεφαλή is the preferred translation in the LXX, as in Judges 11:11 NRSV, "So Jephthah went with the elders of Gilead, and the people made him head and commander [εἰς κεφαλὴν καὶ εἰς ἀρχηγόν] over them" (see also Deut 28:13, 44; 2 Sam 22:44; Ps 18:43 [Ps 17:44 LXX]; Isa 7:8–9; 9:13–14; 19:15; Jer 31:7 [38:7 LXX]). A similar usage can be found in Josephus (e.g., *J.W.* 4.261, where Jerusalem is referred to as the "head" of the whole nation), Philo (e.g., *Moses* 2.30, where Philadelphus is referred to as the "head" of all the kings), and other ancient writers. Paul himself uses the term in this sense later in the letter at 2:10 and earlier in 1 Cor 11:3.

Although it would have been easy for the hymn writer to say more simply and directly that Christ is κύριος τῆς ἐκκλησίας, "lord of the church," he expands the

169 See Stettler, *Kolosserhymnus*, 207–10.

170 Stettler, *Kolosserhymnus*, 219, overstates his case by concluding that Paul derived his image of the body of Christ from the church as the bride of Christ. The image of the body of Christ is prior and more extensively used in Paul. The two ideas are related but are not coextensive.

171 See BDAG, s.v. κεφαλή.

172 Stettler, *Kolosserhymnus*, 225. See HALOT, s.v. ראשׁ 9.a–h, which suggests the glosses "leader" or "chief" when it is used to refer to a tribal leader, clan elder, chief of the people, the king, or a military commander.

metaphor of the body by naming Christ as its "head." This image will become even more important to Paul as he elaborates on it later in the letter (2:19). The "head-body" imagery has occasioned much discussion and debate among scholars, especially regarding the source of the imagery as well as the implications of this background for understanding the original form of the hymn.

The heart of the controversy centers on whether the hymn writer was originally representing Christ as head of a cosmic body (i.e., the universe) and the genitive τῆς ἐκκλησίας was a later redactional addition to the hymn by the author of the letter. E. Käsemann was the most prominent advocate of the view that the "head-body" concept in the hymn was derived from the gnostic primitive-man myth.[173] But as we have noted earlier, the gnostic system Käsemann presented post-dated the NT. It is also unlikely that the idea of a collective body of the redeemer sprang from gnosis. K.-M. Fischer rightly concluded that "the use of the concepts, 'head, body, and members' in gnostic texts is inconsistent. Thus, the idea that these terms had their origin in a Gnostic myth is excluded."[174] Almost all scholars have now jettisoned the gnostic view. Fischer himself, along with a host of other scholars, concluded that the original hymn reflects more broadly a Hellenistic conception of the universe as a cosmic body (or, *Makroanthropos*) over which sat a universal god (*Allgott*) as ruling head who wisely guided and controlled the body.[175] This can be seen in texts such as an Orphic fragment (frag. 168), where Zeus is depicted as head of the cosmos that he permeates with his divine power, or in Plato's *Timaeus*, which portrays the universe as a living body that is directed by a divine soul (Plato, *Tim.* 31b; 32a, c; 39e; 47c–48b).[176] Most interpreters advocating this conceptual background, however, argue that this idea was mediated to the author of the hymn through Hellenistic Judaism as seen, for instance, in the thought of Philo.[177] Yet, it must be noted that Philo never explicitly refers to the Logos as κεφαλή.[178]

It is clear, however, that (1) Paul himself had nowhere else applied this imagery to Christ as head of the universe, (2) he does not do so in this letter (thus, 2:19), and (3) the only way that this passage could be interpreted in this fashion is if we assume that τῆς ἐκκλησίας was not an original part of the hymn.[179] It is difficult to see why Paul would have cited a hymn that included content that did not fit what he was trying to say and that he would need to amend.

173 Käsemann, *Leib und Leib Christi*, 37–48.

174 Fischer, *Tendenz und Absicht*, 68.

175 Fischer, *Tendenz und Absicht*, 68–74. According to Fischer, this *Allgott* appeared in various manifestations, including Marduk, Zeus, the Syrian sun-god, Aion, Isis, Sophia, and Logos. See also, e.g., Lincoln, 598–99; Pokorný, 82; Lindemann, 27; Lohse, 54–55; Schweizer, 58–59, 82–83; Schenke, *Der Gott "Mensch,"* 153–56; Hegermann, *Schöpfungsmittler*, 138–57.

176 E.g., Lohse, 53; E. Schweizer, "σῶμα," *TDNT* 7:1029–30, 1032, 1074–77.

177 See, e.g., Hegermann, *Schöpfungsmittler*, 47–67.

178 See my "Jesus Christ: 'Head' of the Church," 347–50, for additional critique of this view.

179 Sumney, 71, aptly comments (citing Hay, 60): "such hypotheses about additions to the original poem at this point, in any case, are 'unnecessarily complicated and improbable.'"

These observations should at least give us pause to ask if there is an alternative way of understanding the background of the "head-body" imagery that would better explain its use here.

I have argued elsewhere that the best background for interpreting the "head-body" imagery here and in its further development in Col 2:19 is the physiological understandings of the head in relationship to the body as exhibited in the medical writers, some philosophers, and Philo.[180] These writers also used the coordinated imagery in a metaphorical sense. In this view, the head functions not only as the ruling part of the body but also as the supply center of the body since it is the source of sensation, movement, and will. The implication for our passage would be that as the head of the church, Christ provides leadership and direction for his people, while at the same time serving as the source of the church's life energy for its growth to maturity. Lightfoot, too, argued for the relevance of this background. He concluded that Christ as "head of the church" means that he is "the inspiring, ruling, guiding, combining, sustaining power, the mainspring of its activity, the centre of its unity, and the seat of its life."[181]

This conception can be seen in Hippocrates, who contended that the κεφαλή (containing the brain) is the coordinating and controlling center for the various parts of the body. He notes:

> In these ways I hold the brain [ἐγκέφαλος] is the most powerful organ of the human body, for when it is healthy it is an interpreter to us of the phenomena caused by the air, as it is the air that gives it intelligence. Eyes, ears, tongue, hands and feet act in accordance with the discernment of the brain [ἐγκέφαλος]; in fact the whole body [σώματι] participates in intelligence in proportion to its participation in air. To consciousness the brain is the messenger.[182]

In dependence on the Hippocratic tradition, Plato also ascribes a leading function to the head in relationship to the body: "The divine revolutions, which are two, they bound within a sphere-shaped body [σῶμα], in imitation of the spherical form of the All, which body we now call the 'head' [κεφαλήν], it being the most divine part and reigning [δεσποτοῦν] over all the parts within us. To it the gods delivered over the whole body they had assembled to be its servant" (*Tim.* 44d). Through the sinews (νεῦρα), veins, and limbs (τὰ μέλη), the head is able to communicate sense impressions. For these reasons, Plato can describe the κεφαλή in terms of the acropolis of a country (*Leg.* 969b–c). Against Aristotle and some Stoic writers (esp. Zeno and Chrysippus), Galen defended the position of Hippocrates and Plato that the κεφαλή, containing the brain, was the ruling part of the body. He notes: "nor is it necessary that because

---

180 "Jesus Christ: 'Head' of the Church," 346–66. See also my *Colossian Syncretism*, 259–60.

181 Lightfoot, 157. So also Barth, *Ephesians*, 1:190.

182 Hippocrates, *Morb. sacr.* 19.1–10 (W. H. S. Jones, LCL).

the brain, like the Great King, dwells in the head [κεφαλήν] as in an acropolis, for that reason the ruling part of the soul is in the brain, or because the brain has the senses stationed around it like bodyguards, or even if one should go so far as to say that as heaven is to the whole universe, so the head is to man, and that therefore as the former is the home of the gods, so the brain is the home of the rational faculty."[183]

In dependence on Hippocrates and especially Plato, Philo reflects this common physiological understanding of the head in relationship to the body in his writings. He uses some of the same language to describe the role of the head. He asserts, "The head, like the citadel of a king, has as its occupant the sovereign mind" (*QG* 2.5). Philo frequently uses the word "leader" (ἡγεμονικός) to characterize the head (e.g., *Creation* 119; *Flight* 110, 182; *Dreams* 2.207; *Moses* 2.30, 82; *Spec. Laws* 3.184; *QG* 1.3, 10; 2.5; *QE* 2.124). He can also refer to it as "the master limb of the members" (ὁ κυριώτατος τῶν μελῶν; *Spec. Laws* 1.147). The head is "the first, highest and principal part"; it is the "chief" (*QE* 1.17).

In this line of the Colossian hymn, the author transitions from extolling Christ as Lord of all creation to Christ as Lord of the church. Christ is the inaugurator of this new humanity; he establishes it on the basis of his blood shed on the cross and his resurrection from the dead; and the church becomes his instrument for reaching the world and making peace. While Paul is intimately concerned with the health and well-being of localized congregations of believers, which he commonly refers to as "churches," he simultaneously has a grand vision of these individual communities as a corporate entity that he can also speak of as "the church." The entire collection of individual believers understood as one unified group is how ἐκκλησία is used in the hymn. This usage is consistent with how he employs the term for the universal church in 1 Cor 12:28.[184] He will use it again in this sense in Col 1:24 but will shift to his localized usage of the term in 4:15–16. The "body" is thus not the world, but the church. The new community that Christ has created will eventually become a worldwide phenomenon and will have a worldwide impact, but the focal point of the hymn is on the church as the body. There is thus no need to posit an earlier form of the hymn that does not include the genitive expression, τῆς ἐκκλησίας.

The imagery of "head-body" would be particularly meaningful to the Colossians and appropriate to their situation. They would readily understand the sense of it because it was a simple metaphor, widely used, and conveying the dual notion that Christ provides leadership and direction for his people as well as the idea that Christ supplies the church with its life energy for its growth to maturity, which he develops in 2:19. The hymn thus buttresses Paul's claim that the Colossians should be looking to Christ for protection, help, and

183 Phillip de Lacy, *Galen: On the Doctrines of Hippocrates and Plato*, Corpus Medicorum Graecorum 4.1.2, Part 1 (Berlin: Akademie, 1978), 120.1–10.

184 So also Stettler, *Christushymnus*, 202.

direction rather than angelic beings and the teaching of "the philosophy" that was effectively diverting their focus away from Christ himself.

ὅς ἐστιν ἀρχή, πρωτότοκος ἐκ τῶν νεκρῶν, "he is the beginning, firstborn from the dead." This clause marks the beginning of the second strophe and stands parallel with ὅς ἐστιν εἰκών in 1:15.[185] The verse division here is unfortunate, as this would have been the better place to mark a new section of thought. The second clause of the strophe, πρωτότοκος ἐκ τῶν νεκρῶν, "firstborn from the dead," helps to interpret the first as referring to the resurrection as the basis and beginning of the new humanity that Christ has created. For readers of the LXX, the term ἀρχή evokes Gen 1:1 and the beginning of all things (see also Hab 1:12 NETS, "are you not from the beginning [ἀπ' ἀρχῆς], O Lord, my holy God"; see also Pss. Sol. 8.31). The Apocalypse directly applies the title to Christ in referring to him as "the Alpha and the Omega, the first and the last, the beginning [ἡ ἀρχή] and the end" (Rev 21:6; 22:13). Yet the hymn writer is not here referring to the primordial beginning but the beginning of the new order that Christ has inaugurated through his resurrection, as the next clause makes clear.[186] Some interpreters have seen in this term a reference to Christ as personified Wisdom. The writer of Proverbs declares of personified Wisdom, "the Lord possessed me at the beginning [ἀρχήν] of his work, the first of his acts of old. Ages ago I was set up, at the first, before the beginning [ἀρχῆ] of the earth" (Prov 8:22–23 ESV; see also Wis 6:22; Sir 24:9).[187] But once again, the following clause makes it clear that the author of the hymn is not referring to the absolute beginning, when Wisdom helped craft the creation of the world, but the beginning of the new creation. As such, ἀρχή here corresponds with ἀπαρχή in 1 Cor 15:20, where Paul declares, "But Christ has indeed been raised from the dead, the firstfruits [ἀπαρχή] of those who have fallen asleep" (NIV; see also 1 Cor 15:23). As the first to be raised from the dead, Christ establishes a new order and a new beginning.

Whereas in the first strophe Christ is lauded as πρωτότοκος πάσης κτίσεως, "firstborn of all creation," he is here extolled as πρωτότοκος ἐκ τῶν νεκρῶν, "firstborn from the dead." In the first instance, the hymn writer highlights Christ's sovereignty over all of creation; in this case, he points to Christ as the first to be resurrected from the dead and thereby the pioneer and leader of a new humanity. The expression implies that Christ is the first to be raised by the power of God from among those who have died. In Luke's conversion account of Paul in Acts, he says that "the Messiah would suffer and, as the first [πρῶτος] to rise from the dead, would bring the message of light to his own people and to the Gentiles" (Acts 26:23 NIV). Both of these ideas from the first and second strophes come together in Rev 1:5 where it speaks of Jesus Christ as

185 So also Bormann, 99.

186 So also Hübner, 62.

187 E.g., Pao, 100; Dunn, 97.

"the firstborn from the dead [ὁ πρωτότοκος τῶν νεκρῶν], and the ruler of the kings of the earth" (ESV). He is both the inaugurator of the new creation and sovereign over all the earth.

As both "the beginning" and "the firstborn from the dead," he reigns as Lord over the church. As the forerunner of the new order, he is the leader and ruler of this new humanity—just as his temporal priority over creation entails his sovereignty over it.[188] Although ἀρχή is properly translated "beginning" here, the secondary notion of "ruler" or "authority" is also present.[189] Similarly, because he is the first to be raised from the dead by the Father and is "the beginning" of this new order of existence, he also functions as the "head" or "leader" of this new humanity. It is noteworthy that Apollo makes a rival claim. He was worshiped in Hierapolis as Apollo Ἀρχηγέτης, the leader and protector of the city.[190]

ἵνα γένηται ἐν πᾶσιν αὐτὸς πρωτεύων, "that he would be preeminent in all things." Christ's sovereignty over the church—indeed over all of creation—is now explicitly stressed in this clause. Because he is the beginning of the new creation and the firstborn from the dead, he wields supremacy over the church and will ultimately manifest his complete sovereignty over all of his rebellious creation. As the first strophe reveals, he already wields sovereignty over all of creation. Thus, ἐν πᾶσιν should not be limited to a masculine interpretation ("among all people," i.e., all members of the church), but as a neuter with reference to all of creation.[191] This is consistent with the neuter τὰ πάντα that is used throughout the hymn (see 1:16, 17, 20). The presence of the pronoun αὐτός, which does not need to be expressed, thus places a strong emphasis on the person of Christ as fulfilling this role. It picks up the ὅς of 1:18b and reiterates the double αὐτός in the intermediary strophe (1:17a and 18a).

The hymn writer could have expressed this clause as an indicative statement parallel with the first two: Christ is not only the beginning and the firstborn from the dead, but he is also preeminent over all things. But he expresses it as a dependent result clause.[192] The writer sees his resurrection from the dead as issuing in a new state of affairs. He has become the Lord of a new humanity, the church. This was an entity that did not exist prior to his incarnation, death, and resurrection. But he is not only preeminent in this new community of believers but will become preeminent over all the universe. This is not a contradiction

188 So also Beale, 104. See also Barth and Blanke, 207, who note that this expression indicates that "he is ruler."

189 BDAG s.v. ἀρχή 6, characterizes this usage as "an authority figure who initiates activity or process."

190 See Humann et al., *Alt. v. Hierapolis* 2, 4, 153.

191 So also Lightfoot, 158.

192 The conjunction ἵνα is perhaps best understood in this context as a marker denoting result. However, BDAG s.v. ἵνα 3 notes that "in many cases purpose and result cannot be clearly differentiated, and hence ἵνα is used for the result that follows according to the purose of the subj. or of God. As in Semitic and Gr-Rom. thought, purpose and result are identical in declarations of the divine will."

with the assertion of his sovereignty in the first strophe, but it reflects the manifestation of his dominion over and against the reality of a massive revolt. Thus, he currently holds first place within the church, but the realization of his supremacy over all creation is yet future. The Philippian hymn likewise points to this future time of the imposition of Christ's full sovereignty: "that at the name of Jesus every knee should bow, in heaven and on earth and under the earth" (Phil 2:10 NIV). Lightfoot points out that syntactially, the γένηται answers to the ἐστιν of v. 17 in terms of "the absolute being" and "the historical manifestation."[193]

The verb πρωτεύων, here in a participial form, is a hapax legomenon in the NT and is most frequently translated "preeminent/preeminence" (ESV; ASV; RSV; NKJV; KJV; NAB). Others have rendered it as "first place" (CEB; CSB; NRSV; NASB), "first" (NLT; NET), "supreme" (REB; NEB; NJB), "supremacy" (NIV), or "above all others" (CEV). It was used in the LXX to describe how the Persian king had made Haman "to be first [πρωτεύειν] and to be leader of the kingdom" (Esth 5:11 NETS). Josephus uses it of Antipater, father of Herod the Great, who was an Idumean and "preeminent" (πρωτεύων) in that nation (*J.W.* 1.123). Although the term is not very common, it does appear in a number of honorific inscriptions in Asia Minor. For instance, in Miletus, a certain Gaius Julius Eukrates is honored for being "preeminent [πρωτεύων] over his fatherland and over all of Asia."[194] Another inscription, from Cyaneae (Lycia), extols a man named Jason, son of Nikostratus, as "a remarkable man, preeminent [πρωτεύων] among the people of our city, who served as high priest of the ruler cult and as *grammateus* of Lycia."[195] In nearby Aphrodisias, Zenon Aeneas is honored as "preeminent in his fatherland" (πρωτεύοντος ἐν τῇ πατρίδι) for being victorious in many athletic games.[196] The term also appears in some magical papyri. In one text it is used with reference to the "chief" (πρωτεῦον) name of the god, Typhon (*PGM* IV.244). Perhaps most significant, however, is that it is used on one occasion to refer to an angelic mediator:

> O lord Apollo, come with Paian
> Give answer to my questions, lord, O master
> Leave Mount Parnassos and the Delphic Pytho
> Whenever my priestly lips voice secret words,
> Preeminent [ἄγγελε πρωτεύων][197] angel of the great Zeus, Iao,
> And you Michael, who rule heaven's realm,
> I call, and you, archangel Gabriel. (*PGM* I.298–303)

193 Lightfoot, 158.

194 *IMilet* I.2,7a.9–10.

195 *IGRR* 3.704.II.A.5 (Cyaneae, Lycia). See also, *IKios* 39.3 (Kios, Bithynia); *TAM* II.905.63.50 (Rhodiapolis, Lycia).

196 *MAMA* 8.513.5–6.

197 The reading here is disputed. Buresch, *Klaros*, 52, reads πρωτεύων. Preisendanz, *Papyri*, 1.16, suggests πρῶτε <θε>οῦ.

If this reading is correct, this papyrus text gives evidence of a use of the term in reference to an angel. This is highly relevant to this context because the situation at Colossae likely involved the invocation of angels to the neglect of a dependence upon Christ. This text also shows the tendency to syncretize Jewish angels with messengers of Zeus, including Apollo, which may help to explain some of the syncretistic tendencies among those advocating "the philosophy."

The Colossian hymn, in contrast to any other claim, asserts the preeminence of Christ over all rivals. This includes thrones, dominions, principalities, authorities, angels, messengers of Zeus, Apollo, or any other potential rival. In no uncertain terms, the hymn declares Christ to be supreme over all things.

**19** ὅτι ἐν αὐτῷ εὐδόκησεν πᾶν τὸ πλήρωμα κατοικῆσαι, "for in him all the fullness was pleased to dwell." This clause provides the ground[198] for the claim in the previous line that Christ is preeminent in everything. His preeminence is rooted precisely in the fact that God himself is present in the person of Christ.

We are immediately confronted with the issue of determining what is the subject of this sentence. Lightfoot contends that God is implied as the subject and πᾶν τὸ πλήρωμα understood as the direct object.[199] But God has not been the subject of any of the preceding clauses or of any verb in the hymn. And since πᾶν τὸ πλήρωμα is best understood as the subject of κατοικεῖ in 2:9, we should take it as the subject here.[200]

The term πλήρωμα is used by Paul in his earlier letters (e.g, Rom 11:12, 25; 13:10; 15:29; 1 Cor 10:26; Gal 4:4), but he never uses it with the kind of technical theological significance that it bears here. The source and meaning of the expression πᾶν τὸ πλήρωμα, "all the fullness," has rightly been the focal point of voluminous discussion in the literature on this hymn. There have been four major viewpoints expressed on the derivation of the term (with some variations in each): (1) it comes directly from Gnosticism; (2) it is derived more generally from Hellenistic thought in the Roman period; (3) it is from the Jewish Wisdom tradition, or (4) it reflects OT and Jewish origins, especially associated with God's presence in the temple. What immediately follows is further discussion on each of these four scholarly viewpoints.

(1) Some older commentaries and German scholarship associated with the history of religions school of thought have contended that the hymn writer took up the term and its associated conceptual framework directly from *Gnosticism.* The fountainhead for much of this subsequent scholarship can be seen in the work of F. C. Baur. Baur argued that the use of πλήρωμα here (and in Ephesians) "suggests to us the Pleroma of the Gnostics."[201] He highlighted Irenaeus's

---

198 The conjunction ὅτι here functions as the ground or basis for the previous assertion; see Harris, 45.

199 Lightfoot, 158. So also Eadie, 68, and many of the older commentaries.

200 See also Beale, 107, 125–28.

201 Baur, *Paul the Apostle*, 2.9.

description of the Valentinian school, which spoke of the πλήρωμα as the sum of the aeons. In particular, Baur cited *Adversus Haereses*, where Irenaeus states, "These thirty aeons, as the Valentinian doctrine of aeons represents them, are τὸ ἀόρατον καὶ πνευματικὸν κατ᾽ αὐτοὺς πλήρωμα, which is divided into an Ogdoas, a Dekas, and a Dodekas."[202] The gnostic view was taken up further and popularized by the widely influential commentary of M. Dibelius. He contended that πλήρωμα was a technical term from the advocates of the Colossian "philosophy," which he interpreted to be a form of Gnosticism.[203] They had applied the term not to Christ, but to the στοιχεῖα. For them, πλήρωμα was the name for the divine realm of the spiritual powers (the αἰῶνες) that populated the heavenly spheres. Dibelius depended heavily upon the second- to third-century *Corpus Hermeticum* for support. In this world of thought, God is encompassed within the entire divine realm, and the collective is viewed as one: "god [is] the master, maker, father, and container of the whole universe, the all who is one and the one who is all. For the plenitude [πλήρωμα] of all things is one and is in one, not because the one duplicates itself but because both are one" (*Corp. herm.* 16.3; see also 6.4; 12.15). Käsemann saw this line of the hymn along with the term πλήρωμα as one of the clearest expressions of its gnostic, mythological character. He went so far as to say that it "is only properly comprehensible in a gnostic setting."[204]

Lightfoot contended that there was a convergence between the gnostic and Colossian uses of πλήρωμα, but he did not argue for a derivation of the Colossian use from Gnosticism. He argued that the gnostic use was mediated to them from Cerinthus, whose thought, he suggested, "was a development of the Colossian heresy."[205] He concluded that Paul's use of the term in Colossians corresponds precisely with the use of the term by his opponents (whom he characterizes as Essene Judaizers) and that it had a Palestinian origin. Despite having a lengthy essay on this term and its ongoing history of usage, he does not provide us with a discussion of the Palestinian usage he has in mind. Lightfoot argues that the difference between Paul and the Essene Judaizers is that they postulated "a doctrine of a plurality of mediators" ("thrones, dominions, principalities, and powers"), whereas Christ is the synthesis of all the various divine attributes, virtues, and energies in a single person.[206]

Almost all interpreters today reject the gnostic hypothesis for understanding the usage of πλήρωμα in the hymn.[207] One of the principal arguments is that in

202 *Haer.* 1.1.3 (as cited in Baur, *Paul the Apostle*, 2.10).

203 Dibelius, 18.

204 Käsemann, "Baptismal Liturgy," 158.

205 Lightfoot, 265.

206 Lightfoot, 262.

207 Wilson, 153, concludes, "Certainly there is no need to attempt to interpret it in terms of second-century Valentinianism: it was the Gnostics who took over the term, and adapted it to their own purposes."

Valentinian gnosis, God himself does not belong to the πλήρωμα, whereas in Colossians the "fullness" is related to God himself.[208] The Valentinian system as a whole originated in the second century and is therefore too late to have influenced the hymn writer. It is also important to add that there is no sense within the hymn of the radical, anti-cosmic dualism that characterizes gnosis. The nature of the alienation between the creator and the creation is not a material/immaterial divide but a rupture that is caused by sin and that can only be overcome by a blood offering.

(2) E. Lohse rejected the gnostic derivation of the term for understanding its usage in Colossians and suggested that it was taken up from the broader *Hellenistic* milieu.[209] Yet he does not cite relevant Hellenistic texts as representative of what the author of the hymn had in mind in speaking of the "fullness," and he does not consider the possibility that this usage may have derived from the OT and Judaism. He correlates this line of the hymn with 2:9 to reach the conclusion that it is the fullness of deity that dwells in Christ.[210]

(3) Others have pointed to the *Jewish Wisdom* tradition that had been influenced by Hellenism. J. D. G. Dunn, for instance, observes that the Stoics used the term to refer to "the divine rationality that permeates the world."[211] He traces a trajectory from Stoicism to Hellenistic Judaism and its conception of divine Wisdom, especially as seen in Wis 1:6–7: "for wisdom is a kindly spirit . . . because the spirit of the Lord fills [πεπλήρωκεν] the world, and that which holds all things together knows what is said" (NETS). But even this usage, Dunn thinks, could have come from the OT (see Ps 139:7; Jer 23:24). When combined with the theme of divine indwelling, which was present in Jewish thought (e.g., T. Benj. 6.4; T. Zeb. 8.2; 1 En. 49.3), Dunn concludes that the theme of the fullness of God dwelling in individuals "is traditionally Jewish and is wholly a piece with the Wisdom tradition."[212] He then sees the author of Colossians as responsible for the development of the use of the noun πλήρωμα. E. Schweizer also points to the Jewish Wisdom tradition but combines it with the kind of Logos speculation that we find in Philo (*Dreams* 1.62, 75) wherein God "has filled" (ἐκπεπλήρωκεν) the Logos with divine powers.[213]

(4) The most compelling explanation for the background of the term in this context is the *Old Testament* use of the language of filling, especially with respect to the temple—the place where God dwelt and mediated his presence to his people. Although the LXX never uses the exact noun πλήρωμα to refer to God and his presence, the adjective πλήρης as well as the cognate term πίμπλημι

208 Hübner, 197. See also his essay, "πλήρωμα," *EDNT* 3:108.

209 Lohse, 58. See also G. Delling, "πλήρωμα," *TDNT* 6:303–4.

210 Lohse, 58.

211 Dunn, 99.

212 Dunn, 100.

213 Schweizer, 78.

frequently appear in connection with God's glory filling the temple (or the tabernacle). This can be seen, for instance, in the following passages (all NETS):

- "and the cloud covered the tent of witness, and the tent was filled with the glory of the Lord [δόξης κυρίου ἐπλήσθη ἡ σκηνή]" (Exod 40:28 LXX [40:34 MT]; see also 40:29 LXX [40:35 MT])
- "the glory of the Lord filled the house [ἔπλησεν δόξα κυρίου τὸν οἶκον]" (1 Kgs 8:11)
- "the Lord's glory filled the house [δόξα κυρίου ἔπλησεν τὸν οἶκον]" (2 Chr 7:1; see also 7:2)
- "the house was full of his glory [πλήρης ὁ οἶκος τῆς δόξης αὐτοῦ]" (Isa 6:1)
- "And the glory of the Lord arose from the cheroubin into the atrium of the house, and the cloud filled the house [ἔπλησεν], and the court was filled [ἐπλήσθη] with the radiance of the glory of the Lord" (Ezek 10:4)
- "a spirit took me up and brought me into the inner court, and behold, the house was full of the glory of the Lord [πλήρης δόξης κυρίου ὁ οἶκος]" (Ezek 43:5)
- "the house of the Lord was full of glory [πλήρης δόξης ὁ οἶκος κυρίου]" (Ezek 44:4)
- "I will fill this house with splendor [δόξα, glory; πλήσω τὸν οἶκον τοῦτον δόξης], says the Lord Almighty" (Hag 2:7)

The "glory of the Lord" (כְּבוֹד יְהוָה; δόξα κυρίου) in these passages is a way of expressing the visible manifestation of God's presence. In rabbinic terms, it is the Shekinah that fills the temple and reflects the reality of God's brilliant presence.[214] His divine radiance is associated with his theophanic appearances in the OT. It is also an expression of the divine Wisdom, as we see in Wis 7:25: "she is a breath of the power of God, and a pure emanation of the glory of the Almighty [ἀπόρροια τῆς τοῦ παντοκράτορος δόξης]" (NRSV).[215] The author of the Colossian hymn therefore employs the expression "all the fullness" (πᾶν τὸ πλήρωμα) as a way of referring to God himself in his manifested presence.[216] This idea is confirmed by the way Paul elaborates on the expression in 2:9 in saying that "all the fullness *of deity*" lives in the person of Christ in his bodily existence. This suggests that just as God mediated his presence through the temple (and, earlier, the tabernacle) under the old covenant, he now reveals himself in a person—the Lord Jesus Christ. His revealed presence has shifted from a place to a person.

---

214 Stuhlmacher, *Biblical Theology*, 439. See also Stettler, *Christushymnus*, 21.

215 Stettler, *Christusmhymnus*, 29, 116.

216 Beetham, *Echoes of Scripture*, 153, notes that it "appears to be a circumlocution for the divine presence."

This understanding is corroborated by the accompanying words in this passage. The only other time that the combination of εὐδοκέω and κατοικέω appear together in Scripture is in Ps 68:16 (67:17 LXX), which refers to Zion (i.e., Jerusalem) as the place where God was pleased to dwell (τὸ ὄρος ὃ εὐδόκησεν ὁ θεὸς κατοικεῖν). The reference to the sanctuary ("the holy place": ἐν τῷ ἁγίῳ) in the subsequent verse and in v. 24 (v. 25 LXX) shows that the temple was particularly in view as God's dwelling place.[217] Whereas θεός is the explicit subject in the psalm, the writer of the Colossian hymn uses πᾶν τὸ πλήρωμα to speak of the divine presence with overtones of the many references to God's glory filling the temple.[218] The noun τὸ πλήρωμα alone would have been sufficient to convey this thought, but the addition of the adjective πᾶν serves to emphasize the divine presence in Jesus Christ.

It is appropriate to ask the question of *when* the divine presence took up residence in Christ. Certainly the first half of the hymn functionally describes Jesus as divine in lauding him as creator, sustainer, and sovereign of the universe. But Col 1:20b speaks of his work on the cross (and thus his incarnation), and thus the hymn writer may be pointing to a time when the divine fullness came to dwell in Christ. It is significant that all four Gospels include the account of the Holy Spirit coming upon Jesus at his baptism at the outset of his ministry (Matt 3:13–17; Mark 1:9–11; Luke 3:21–22; John 1:32–34). All three Synoptic accounts use the verb εὐδοκέω in God's response to this event: "this is my beloved son, with whom I am well pleased [εὐδόκησα]" (Matt 3:17; Mark 1:11; Luke 3:22). Although the Gospel writers do not use the term κατοικέω to portray the Spirit taking residence in Jesus, they speak of the Spirit "coming upon him" (ἐρχόμενον ἐπ' αὐτόν, Matt 3:16), "descending on him" (καταβαῖνον εἰς αὐτόν, Mark 1:10; καταβῆναι, Luke 3:22), and "coming down . . . and remaining on him" (καταβαῖνον . . . καὶ ἔμεινεν ἐπ' αὐτόν, John 1:32). John's language, in particular, is evocative of taking up residence. The coming of the Spirit upon Jesus was the one event where the divine presence was visibly manifest upon him and stayed with him throughout his three-year ministry. Much of the work of his ministry was explicitly done in dependence on the divine Spirit dwelling in him (e.g., Matt 12:28; see also Matt 4:1; Luke 4:1, 14). In Luke's programmatic statement of how Jesus would conduct his ministry, he cites Isa 61:1–2 to declare how Jesus would do his works in the power of the Spirit: "the Spirit of the Lord is upon me [πνεῦμα κυρίου ἐπ' ἐμέ], because he has anointed me [ἔχρισέν με] to proclaim good news to the poor. He has sent me to proclaim liberty to the captives and recovering of sight to the blind, to set at liberty those who are oppressed" (Luke 4:18 ESV). The language of "taking up residence" (κατοικῆσαι) suggests that the Colossian hymn writer is referring to the Holy Spirit as God's empowering

217 So also Beetham, *Echoes of Scripture*, 147.

218 Beetham, *Echoes of Scripture*, 153, suggests that this phrase may have been chosen by the hymn writer "for poetic heightening," which is appropriate in a hymn.

presence coming upon Jesus through the duration of his ministry. The term πλήρωμα thus serves as a circumlocution for the Spirit.[219] For Paul, the Holy Spirit is active through Christ in the new creation by functioning as the "life-giving Spirit" (1 Cor 15:45).[220]

In light of this understanding of πλήρωμα as a positive christological affirmation in the hymn, it is doubtful that the term was a catchword of "the philosophy."[221] This is corroborated by the fact that it never reappears in the polemical sections of the letter (2:5, 8, 16–23). The Valentinian gnostic uses of the term are therefore irrelevant for this discussion. Furthermore, it also never appears in the pagan Greek magical papyri,[222] and although it appears in a handful of Christian inscriptions in Asia Minor, it is very rare in the pagan inscriptions and never appears in a religious context. The hymn thus affirms that Jesus was divine as attested by his preexistent sovereign work in creation, but that the divine presence specially manifested in his incarnate life by the Holy Spirit to effect the work of redemption and reconciliation. As God manifested his glorious presence through the temple under the old covenant, he manifests his saving presence now through the Spirit in the Lord Jesus Christ. The ministry of the Spirit in this new-covenant age has even more glory (2 Cor 3:8).

**20 καὶ δι᾽ αὐτοῦ ἀποκαταλλάξαι τὰ πάντα εἰς αὐτόν**, "and through him to reconcile all things to him." Whereas the previous clause, "all the fullness was pleased to dwell in him," provides the basis for the declaration that Christ is preeminent in everything, this clause asserts the aim or goal of Christ's sovereign preeminence. He will effect a reconciliation that has comprehensive and universal significance.

Christ's agency in achieving this reconciliation is expressed by the phrase δι᾽ αὐτοῦ. The hymn writer used this expression in the first strophe to describe Christ's agency in creating the universe (1:16). He uses it twice in the latter part of this second strophe to stress Christ's role in creating a universal *shalom* (1:20a, c).

The hymn writer articulates the goal of reconciliation with an aorist infinitive that is parallel with the previous aorist infinitive, with both functioning in a complementary relationship to εὐδόκησεν. "Reconcile" is a double compound with two prepositions: ἀπό+κατά+ἀλλάσσω. The base verb indicates "change" and, with the addition of κατά, came to be used of a changed relationship,

219 See also Bandstra, "Plērōma as Pneuma," 96–102. He finds linguistic support for this interpretation in the unamended text of 2 Bar. 21.4, where the parallelism suggests an identification of the Spirit with fullness: "the one who fixed the firmament by his *fullness* and fastened the height of heaven by the *Spirit*." Münderlein, "Erwählung," 272, concludes that the term is "a striking paraphrase of the Holy Spirit." See also Kehl, *Christushymnus*, 120–25 (section: "Der Geist Gottes als Pleroma"); Pokorný, 85.

220 See Kehl, *Christushymnus*, 124.

221 So also Pokorný, 121; Bürger, *Schöpfung und Versöhnung*, 112–13; Percy, *Probleme*, 77.

222 It does appear in a fourth-century Christian magical text (*PGM* 13.1), but it reflects influence from NT vocabulary.

a "reconciliation." Paul used the verb καταλλάσσω six times to convey the notion of people being reconciled to God (Rom 5:10; 2 Cor 5:18–20) or people being reconciled to each other (1 Cor 7:11). He also used the noun form καταλλαγή to describe reconciliation to God (Rom 5:11; 11:15; 2 Cor 5:18–19). This is the first appearance of the compound ἀποκαταλλάσσω in Greek literature, with it used only one other time in Colossians (1:22) and then in Eph 2:16. This suggests that the term was coined by the original author of the hymn. Since Paul himself was fond of creating compound verbs to intensify their meaning, this could suggest that he was the author of the hymn or may point to his editorial activity. It is important to observe that none of these terms for reconciliation played a role in Greek and Roman religions, either with respect to the relation between humanity and the deity or with reference to the cosmos as a whole.[223]

The meaning of reconciliation in this context has strong continuity with Paul's two major passages on reconciliation (Rom 5:8–11; 2 Cor 5:18–21). Reconciliation is accomplished by the death of Christ and the shedding of his blood, and it produces a new situation of peace with God. It is likely that the ἀπό- prefix was added to the common Pauline term to intensify the verb by accenting two distinctive features of the concept of reconciliation in this passage: (1) to include the entire universe in the scope of reconciliation, and (2) to make Christ the agent of reconciliation (see also 1:22). As Porter notes, "These are new senses of reconciliation previously unattested even in Pauline usage, and fittingly spoken of using a new, emphatic form of the lexical item."[224]

In this context, the extent of the reconciliation is the entire universe, as indicated by the use of τὰ πάντα. It is important to observe that the referent here is not just to "all people" but to all of creation. In the first strophe of the hymn, Christ is lauded as the creator of τὰ πάντα (1:16a, f), and in the intermediate strophe he is declared to be the sustainer of τὰ πάντα (1:17b). The need for reconciliation implies that there has been a significant rupture in the relationship between people and their creator that has resulted in estrangement and enmity (see 1:21) but that this has had implications that extend throughout the universe.[225] This notion is consistent with Paul's thought, who declares that the entire creation has been adversely affected and awaits the moment it will be "set free from its bondage to corruption and obtain the freedom of the glory of the children of God" (Rom 8:21 ESV; see Rom 8:18–23).

Whereas in Paul's teaching elsewhere on reconciliation God is the one who is reconciled (Rom 5:10; 2 Cor 5:20), here Jesus is the one who is the focal point of the reconciliation. He is lauded as both the agent of reconciliation (δι' αὐτοῦ, "through him") and as the object of reconciliation—that is, all of creation is reconciled εἰς αὐτόν, "to him." Some interpreters, however, take this as a contracted

223 See F. Büchsel, "καταλλάσσω," *TDNT* 1:254.

224 Porter, *Καταλλάσσω*, 184–85.

225 See also Stettler, *Christushymnus*, 341.

reflexive form with a rough breather—αὑτόν—translating it as "himself" and seeing the reference to God.[226] But Porter has observed that "there is far less evidence that the dative and genitive forms could be so used in hellenistic Greek."[227] It is also best to take the twelve references to the various forms of αὐτός in the hymn as all referring to Christ. The overt christological emphasis of the hymn is apparent even here. If πᾶν τὸ πλήρωμα is a reference to the Holy Spirit, as we have suggested, the Spirit would thus be the subject of the act of reconciliation, which would be a unique occurrence in Paul's writings.

εἰρηνοποιήσας διὰ τοῦ αἵματος τοῦ σταυροῦ αὐτοῦ, δι' αὐτοῦ εἴτε τὰ ἐπὶ τῆς γῆς εἴτε τὰ ἐν τοῖς οὐρανοῖς, "by making peace through the blood of his cross, through him, whether things on earth or things in heaven." The means of effecting this widespread reconciliation and resultant universal peace is Christ's death on the cross. The impact of his shed blood transcends the personal forgiveness of sins to include an ultimate *shalom* for all of creation.

This dependent adverbial participle should be taken as one of means. It not only introduces how the reconciliation is accomplished but further defines it in this context as making peace. The anticipation of a Messiah who would usher in an era of *shalom* was a prominent theme in the OT prophets (see, e.g., Isa 9:1–7; 11:6–9; Zech 9:9–10; Mic 5:2–6). The Colossian hymn points to a time of universal peace that would come with redemption (Isa 52:3, 9) and salvation (Isa 52:7, 10). This is consonant with the role of the Messiah as "prince of peace" (שַׂר־שָׁלוֹם), "the guarantor and guardian of peace in the coming Messianic kingdom."[228] It is significant to note that peace is one of the outcomes of the suffering of the Servant of Yahweh in Isa 53 (see esp. Isa 53:5). Peace is correlated with wounds that are healed (see also Isa 38:17; 57:18–19; Jer 6:14; 8:15; 33:6) and the forgiveness of sins.[229]

The language of "making peace" in this passage would no doubt have evoked notions of the Roman imperial claims of the empire-wide *Pax Romana* and the peace that came as a result of the pacification of many nations through numerous military victories.[230] This was celebrated in the various reliefs of the Sebasteion in nearby Aphrodisias, which we can assume would have been familiar to some of the readers of this letter.[231] The various people groups represented include Judeans, Egyptians, and peoples from territories in the far reaches of the empire. A variety of texts also celebrate this peace brought by victorious Roman rulers. Julius Caesar is lauded as εἰρηνοποιός (Dio Cassius, *Hist. rom.* 44.49.2). Augustus is called εἰρηνοφύλαξ after subduing "unsociable, hostile, and brutal" nations (Philo, *Embassy* 147 [Yonge]). An inscription from western Asia Minor (Priene)

226 See, e.g., Wilson, 154.
227 Porter, *Καταλλάσσω*, 172.
228 W. Foerster, "εἰρήνη," *TDNT* 2:405–6.
229 See T. S. Hadjiev, "Peace, Rest," *DOTP* 576.
230 So, e.g., Sumney, 77.
231 See also Maier, "Colossians and Empire," 336–37.

praises the emperor as one "who has made war to cease and ordered the world with peace [κοσμήσοντα (δὲ εἰρήνην)]" (*IPriene* 105.36).[232]

Many interpreters have described the widespread feeling of fear and angst throughout the Mediterranean region about the instability of the world. This angst was generated by a sense that the physical elements and heavenly bodies (regarded as animated by angelic beings) were in conflict and that this could lead to a catastrophic collapse.[233] Aware of this concern, Philo presents God as the one who is the peacemaker and peacekeeper (εἰρηνοποιός καὶ εἰρηνοφύλαξ) who destroys the factious hostilities in the various parts of the universe (ἐν τοῖς μέρεσι τοῦ παντός) (Philo, *Spec. Laws* 2.190–92).[234]

The author of the Colossian hymn also assumes a massive disruption in the order and harmony of the world that requires divine pacification. The last line of the hymn stresses that the need for reconciliation extends not only throughout the world but also into the heavens. He had earlier elaborated on the heavenly realm as the place where "thrones, dominions, principalities, and authorities" existed (Col 1:16). The writer of Colossians interprets these supernatural beings as evil and as the objects of Christ's conquest (2:15), over whom he now sovereignly reigns (2:10). In the eschatological future, Christ will fully and completely pacify everything upon the earth (τὰ ἐπὶ τῆς γῆς). This will include all geopolitical entities—not excluding the might of Roman imperial power. The hymn does make ultimate political claims that relativize the powers of the world and put Nero and all of his successors in a subservient light. But as the letter makes clear, this political subjugation will not take place until Christ appears in glory (3:4).

Nevertheless, Christ's pacification has already encompassed and will extend to everything in the heavens (τὰ ἐν τοῖς οὐρανοῖς). The emphasis here is on the demonic powers who exert their influence over life in the earthly sphere. Although still operative, they have been defeated, and believers share in Christ's authority over this realm by virtue of their union with him (2:9–10). Yet, these forces, too, will be completely subjugated when Christ returns in glory.

The *Weltangst* experienced in day-to-day life by people living in the Lycus Valley was closely associated with these supernatural powers. This is what prompted individuals to turn to local shamans, magical practices, mystery cult ritual, and other mechanisms for protection and help.[235] But on a societal level, too, people were concerned about the impact these powers could have. In a

232 These and additional texts are found in Maier, "Colossians and Empire," 333–34.

233 See, e.g., Schweizer, 80–81.

234 L. Hartmann, "Universal Reconciliation," 109–21, regards the idea of reconciliation at the end of the Colossian hymn as similar to the Philonic way of thinking of the Logos—both Philo and the author of Colossians share the same basic perspective on the universe.

235 See Wolter, 87, who remarks, "The people of that time found the possibility of protection from the ongoing threats to their own existence and thereby the possibility of overcoming their own tremendous fears (*Weltangst*) above all in the various forms of magic, the mysteries, asceticism, and the cultic veneration of the world-governing powers."

few decades after this letter was written, the people of nearby Hierapolis would face a deadly plague that they would attribute to the wrathful displeasure of the gods. The devastation caused by this plague would prompt them to send an embassy to Claros to consult the Clarian Apollo for instructions on how these forces could be appeased or overcome. The plague may be associated with the epidemic that struck portions of the empire after the Parthian campaign of Lucius Verus in AD 162–166.[236] The disease may have been brought back to the region by the returning soldiers.[237] An inscription set up to honor the Clarian Apollo afterward directly attributes the plague to the wrathful displeasure of various gods and evil powers and gives instructions on how they could be appeased. These powers included Earth (Γαῖα), Aither (Αἰθέρ), "the gods of the heavens" (ἐπουρανίοις θεοῖς), Demeter, "the gods of the underworld" (ἐνερτερίοις τε θεοῖσιν), and the evil powers (Κῆρες).[238]

Whereas the advocates of "the philosophy" advocated invoking angels, the practice of rituals and taboos, and the observance of certain festivals for overcoming the influence of evil powers, the hymn declares that they have already been overcome through an event that took place in Jerusalem roughly thirty years earlier. The bloody death of Jesus of Nazareth on a Roman cross (διὰ τοῦ αἵματος τοῦ σταυροῦ αὐτου), ironically, has had an impact that extends from earth to heaven and from the geopolitical sphere to the heavenly realm.[239] The blood that Jesus shed on the cross is significant to Paul because of its atoning significance. It is the means by which God is propitiated (Rom 3:25), by which sinful people are justified (Rom 5:9), and through which redemption is secured (Eph 1:7). It represents the basis for the new covenant (1 Cor 11:25). It is by the blood of Jesus that believers are reconciled to God and brought near to him (Eph 2:13). Yet the hymn writer here takes it a massive step further by saying that the blood of Jesus is the basis for universal and cosmic peace. This is consistent with what Paul says later in the letter about the cross of Christ as representing a decisive defeat of the hostile supernatural powers (Col 2:15). Because of the readers' overt concern about the personal and cosmic threat posed by evil spiritual forces, this letter becomes the occasion for the hymn writer and Paul to draw out the implications of the cross on a much broader scale.

The δι' αὐτοῦ, "through him," that begins the last line of the hymn once again stresses the agency in this universe-wide act of creating peace. Although this phrase is textually suspect (see the notes), it is likely authentic and represents part of the writer's strategy of extolling Jesus Christ as Lord of heaven and earth.

---

236 Robinson, "Oracles and Their Society," 71.

237 Magie, *Roman Rule*, 1:663.

238 For the inscription, see R. Merkelbach and J. Stauber, "Die Orakel des Apollon von Klaros," *EA* 27 (1996): 11–14 (no. 4). See also Merkelbach, *Philologica*, 167–70.

239 Although it is possible that this phrase is the letter writer's redactional addition to the hymn he received, the statement fits the overall context well (1:22; 2:14), is consonant with Pauline theology, and "could have become part of a hymn in the Pauline circle" (Strecker, *Theology*, 551–52).

The repetition of this prepositional phrase may be explained as a stylistic device called *anadiplosis*, the repetition of a phrase from the preceding line at the start of the next.[240] The purpose in this context may have been designed to emphasize the role of Christ in creating the atonement and making peace.[241]

The universal reconciliation and cosmic peace that the hymn celebrates is anticipated as a future event. Nero is still reigning supreme over the Roman Imperium and is increasingly leading the empire away from any semblance of peace—especially for Christians in the years ahead. And in the supernatural realm, evil spirits continue to wreak all forms of terror and harm both to individuals and on far larger scales. Nevertheless, for followers of Christ, this messianic peace and reconciliation has already become part of their present experience. Paul thus begins the letter with his typical greeting invoking the messianic *shalom*: "grace and peace to you from God our Father" (1:2). Later in the letter, he urges the Colossians to let the messianic peace reign in their hearts (3:15). They also experience a present reconciliation with God that will ultimately lead to Christ presenting them to God in the eschatological future as people who have experienced atonement through Christ's death (1:22). The ultimate and final experience of universal *shalom*, however, according to this letter, remains in the future and will take place when Christ appears in glory (3:4). At that time, all hostile political forces and evil supernatural powers will be pacified and will no longer be able to incite trouble, destruction, and death. Paul's dramatic language of victory over enemies to describe Christ's defeat of the evil supernatural powers on the cross (2:15) indicates that they will be finally vanquished as foes and not redeemed as friends.[242] This passage thus provides no hint that these defiant and harmful powers will be redeemed and reconciled to God. The passage does not teach a universal salvation.[243]

## *Explanation*

These six verses represent the most significant christological passage in the entirety of Scripture. This densely packed set of declarations about the Lord Jesus Christ laud his sole supremacy over the entire universe. Yet these astonishing

240 Stuhlmacher, *Biblical Theology*, 437 (who cites O. Hofius, *Christushymnus*, 10–12, as providing supporting examples).

241 See also, Stettler, *Christushymnus*, 270. He calls it an "eine inhaltliche Steigerung und Präzisierung."

242 Contra Wink, *Engaging the Powers*, 73–85 (in a section titled, "The Powers Will be Redeemed"). See also Michaelis, *Versöhnung des Alls*, 24–25 (cited in Gnilka, 76). See my extended discussion of this issue in *Colossian Syncretism*, 267–68. Most interpreters thus rightly describe the "reconciliation" of the principalities and powers as a "subjugation" or "pacification." See, e.g., Aletti, 112–13; Sappington, *Revelation and Redemption*, 175 ("a peace imposed on them by a superior force"); Dibelius and Greeven, 19; Percy, *Probleme*, 105 ("unterworfen"); Gabathuler, *Jesus Christus*, 143 ("Unterwerfung").

243 So also, e.g., Beale, 111; Sumney, 76, 79.

pronouncements are said about someone who was put to death by mere human beings just thirty years earlier.

The primary aim of this text is to praise the sovereignty of Christ over all of creation. No one could be regarded in more exalted terms than Christ in what is said about him in this 112-word hymn. He is identified with the one living and true God, the God of Israel. He is praised as an eternal being; there was never a time when he did not exist. He is fully and completely God. The high Christology of this passage was not written as a romanticized portrayal of Christ a few generations after he walked the earth but was likely composed while many of the original Jesus followers were still alive.

But despite the lofty and glorious descriptions of Christ, this text speaks of blood—Jesus's own human blood. He bled out through cuts, gashes, and lacerations sustained in the process of a judicial execution until his human life expired. He died a humiliating death on a Roman cross, but he regained his life through resurrection and became the center point of God's plan of salvation for alienated humanity.

There is much that is declared in the hymn without explanation. That Jesus is divine and equal with the monotheistic God of Israel is affirmed without clarification. Yet the language of divine Wisdom that is used for some of the formulations may help point forward toward a resolution. That Jesus is simultaneously the eternal God, the source of all creation, and sustainer of the universe and yet is a flesh-and-blood human capable of dying is likewise declared without explanation.

Leading up to these six verses of praise to Christ in the context of the letter, Paul informs the Colossian Christians of how he regularly prays for them. Much of what he says anticipates the contents of the hymn. First, he tells them that he prays for them to grow in knowledge of God (1:10). But this would mean growing in knowledge of the Son—the one in whom all of God's fullness dwells, his agent in creating the universe, the one who eternally existed with him, and the one who is the center point of his plan of redemption. Second, Paul expresses his thanksgiving to the Father for his plan of salvation (1:12). But the means by which the Father has qualified believers to share in the inheritance of the saints in the light is by securing forgiveness of sins through Jesus's atoning death on the cross, thus making reconciliation possible. Finally, the hymn will show how Christ's "rescue" that Paul speaks of was possible (1:13). He reveals that people experience a bondage to a dominion ruled by an evil supernatural being. This prepares the readers for noticing how the hymn extols Christ's sovereignty over all evil spiritual powers—thrones, dominions, principalities, and authorities. Both Paul and the hymn assume that a rebellion has taken place in creation, resulting in a captivity from which people need to be rescued.

For Paul, the best way to express the magnificent things he wants to say about Christ is through the language of worship and praise. He thus adopts a form that was familiar to Jews for centuries—the style of psalm-like praise to the one living and true God. Whether this was a preexisting song of praise known and sung in the Lycus Valley or whether Paul composed it for this occasion, the lyrics of hymnic praise were for him the most appropriate way to communicate these lofty truths. The hymn writer has adopted language from personified divine Wisdom to assist in expressing the excellencies of Christ. But the composer writes in a style and with language that could be broadly understood by a gentile audience. Yet gentiles with some familiarity with the Scriptures of Israel as represented by the LXX would have the deepest appreciation for and catch the nuances of what is communicated.

The overall effect would have touched the emotions of the community in a profound way. The hymn would buoy their spirits, strengthen the weak, build confidence, heighten resolve, increase their fidelity, dispel doubts, and flood them with joy. The God they now serve is unlike any other. He has no rival.

Although the hymn is often described as a hymn of praise to Christ for his role in creation and redemption, this does not quite capture the essence of it. The passage should be seen as *a hymn of praise to Christ for his absolute sovereignty.* He is sovereign over all of creation, extending to all known gods, goddesses, and spirits, as well to the Roman imperium and every human ruler.

Even the second strophe of the hymn (1:18b–20) extols Christ's preeminence and points to the future when he will subjugate his enemies and bring universal peace. In the first strophe of the hymn (1:15–16), the declarations about his role in creation are made in support of the claim of his sovereignty over all of creation. Similarly, in the bridging strophe (1:17–18a), the statement about the church begins with an affirmation of his sovereignty over his people—he is "head" of the body.

Christ's sovereignty is rooted in the fact that he is identified with the monotheistic God of Israel. The hymn declares that all the fullness of God dwells in him, that he is the creator God, that he existed prior to the creation, that he sustains and maintains the creation, that he is "the beginning" (Gen 1:1), that he is the goal of creation and will lead it to its predetermined end of universal reconciliation and peace, that there are no other gods who rival him, and that as the "image of God" he is an expression of divine Wisdom (a personified attribute of the one God).

But as the God of Israel, he is fulfilling his promise to Abraham and his descendants that the salvation of God would extend to all the peoples of the earth. The hymn thus extols the role of Christ as the beginning of a new creation by virtue of his death and resurrection (he is the "firstborn from the dead").

The hymn puts a strong emphasis on the opposition—the invisible realm of evil spiritual powers here referred to as "thrones, dominions, principalities, and authorities." This is not surprising given the way the hymn is introduced, acclaiming Christ's redemptive work of rescuing his people "from the authority of darkness" and transferring them into the kingdom of the Son (1:13). This supernatural drama could only be accomplished by someone who is sovereign over all things, especially powerful opposition. Why is this relevant to the Colossians and all Christians living in the region? There are three reasons for this overt emphasis in the hymn.

First, believers in the Lycus Valley needed to know that Christ is sovereign over all rivals.[244] One cannot underestimate how difficult it would have been for many to turn their backs on Zeus as an all-powerful god who providentially cared for every area of their lives, especially as seen in all of the epithets ascribed to him in local inscriptions. M. Ricl notes that "the functional epithets appended to the name of Zeus paint an image of the supreme deity in his local manifestations that presents no surprise: they define him as a rural protector and provider of crops and cattle par excellence."[245] He was worshiped locally as *anadotēs* ("causing the plants to sprout"), *aristos* ("the best"), *basilikos* ("kingly"), *hekatoistitēs* ("who makes crops bear a hundredfold"), *koiranos kosmou* ("king of the world"), *ktēsios* ("protector of house and property"), *megas/megistos* ("great/greatest"), *sōtēr* ("savior"), and many more.[246] The Colossian hymn to Christ thus presents a direct and strong challege to the claims of Zeus and many other deities. The believers needed reassurance that Christ was more powerful than all of the mighty territorial gods who threatened punishment for infidelity. The hymn would have helped to dispel their fears of being struck down by Zeus, Mēn, Apollo, the Great Mother, or any other territorial god because Jesus Christ is supreme over all.[247] They could fully trust in him to protect them and keep them secure. As he says later in the letter, "your life has been hidden with Christ in God" (3:3). They also needed to know that Christ was sufficiently strong to protect them from all supernatural spirits coming to harm them as a result of a curse, a ritual of power, the evil eye, or any other malicious design. And, finally, they would be comforted to know that Christ is ultimately sovereign over Roman imperial power and the vicissitudes and difficulties of life under Roman rule.

Second, they needed to know that they owe Christ their sole allegiance and are called to obey him first and foremost. Although they were raised in a religious environment where dual or multiple allegiances were common, Christ

244 Many interpreters have seen this as the primary emphasis. Martin, 66, for instance, says that the theme of the hymn is "the sole supremacy of Christ and his present victory over all spiritual powers." Müller, *Anfänge der Paulusschule*, 79, notes: "the hymn celebrates the installation of Christ as Lord (*die Herrscherstellung*) over all the principalities and powers." See also, e.g., Fowl, *Story of Christ*, 152; Pokorný, 74. Contra Dübbers, *Christologie und Existenz*, 176, who concludes that the hymn does not praise Christ as cosmic ruler and as Lord over the church, but as the exclusive mediator of creation and salvation in which all existence and new existence has its basis. What he affirms is true, but it does not do justice to the many affirmations wherein Christ should be seen as Lord over all things.

245 Ricl, "Cults of Phrygia Epiktetos," 139.

246 Ricl, "Cults of Phrygia Epiktetos," 139–40.

247 As Harrison, "Confession Inscriptions," 342, notes, "the temperament of [these] deities was unpredictable and especially vindictive towards the ritually disobedient."

seeks undivided loyalty. There is no room for polytheism or syncretism in Christianity. It is the will of God expressed through his Son that is of paramount importance to believers.

Finally, the most immediate need was for the Colossians to demonstrate their allegiance and obedience to Christ by denying the demands of "the philosophy" that was gaining influence among them. According to Paul, the teaching and practices of this faction were not κατὰ Χριστόν ("according to Christ"; 2:8), and these opposing teachers were not holding tight to Christ, the head of the church (2:19). The theological affirmations of the hymn effectively subvert the claims and assumptions of "the philosophy," thereby eliminating the need for the Colossians to give heed to their teachings.

The Colossian hymn thus celebrates Christ as Lord of all. Although the title κύριος does not occur in the hymn (although the functional equivalent, κεφαλή, appears in 1:18a), almost every line of the passage exalts the supremacy of Christ over all things.[248] Building on this foundation, Paul employs κύριος thirteen times throughout the letter to further elaborate on Christ's lordship. The extraordinary assertions are based on Jesus's role as creator of the universe and his identification with the one God. But the hymn also hails Jesus more specifically as Lord of the church based on his death and resurrection. This gives him a claim over the people he has gathered to be members of his corporate body, and it gives Paul the right, as a commissioned servant (διάκονος) of the Lord, to teach the Colossians and admonish them in ways that would bring them to maturity in Christ (1:24–29). In the end, Christ will bring all of history to a conclusion and usher in a universal peace by subjugating all opposition and reconciling his people to himself.

This passage has much in common with Phil 2:5–11—another passage that has been identified as a christological hymn in the Pauline corpus. Aside from similarities of form, both passages evince a similar threefold emphasis on the preexistence, incarnation, and exaltation of Jesus Christ. Both passages speak of Christ in such exalted terms that he is virtually identified with the one God. The Philippian passage goes so far as describing him as ἴσα θεῷ ("equal with God"; Phil 2:6). Both passages likewise speak of Jesus's humanity as expressed by his death on the cross (Phil 2:8). And both passages speak of a future when all rebellion will be overcome, and Jesus will be recognized as Lord (Phil 2:9–11). And similar to the Colossian hymn, the Philippian hymn celebrates Christ's supremacy over supernatural powers by declaring that every knee will bow and confess that Jesus is Lord and that this includes all heavenly beings, all terrestrial beings, and all underworld spirits. Yet each of the hymns shows a unique

248 Capes, *Old Testament Yahweh Texts*, 60, notes that "although this passage does not contain the title 'Lord,' it affirms ideas which are consistent with Paul's κύριος Christology." See also idem, *Divine Christ*, 49.

contextual relevance for the primary specific concerns Paul was addressing in the respective letters.

Although Colossians is not cited as frequently as other Pauline letters in early Christian writings, the Colossian hymn is one of the most highly cited Pauline passages in all the pre-Nicene Christian literature.[249] J. R. Strawbridge observes that it was used "over 670 times by more than 50 different pre-Nicene authors."[250] This is due largely to the important role the passage played in the Arian controversy and in providing crucial statements for the formation of the church's doctrine about Christ. In the early fourth century, Arius emerged as an influential teacher within the church and advanced the thesis that Christ was a being begotten from God, created in time, and was not God in the flesh. He effectively denied the full deity of Christ. Among the passages that Arius appealed to in support of his position was Col 1:15 (Jesus was "firstborn of all creation").[251] Of course, seen in the context of Ps 89, the hymn writer of the Colossian hymn was not asserting that Jesus was a created being but was making a statement about his sovereignty. Most pre-Nicene writers pointed to other statements within the hymn to demonstrate that Jesus was fully divine and fully human.

Elements of this passage were not only cited in the Arian controversy but were taken up and used by gnostics. Although the existence of pre-Christian gnosis as a coherent system of redemption and religious belief is highly doubtful, gnostics made ample use of terminology and statements from the Colossian hymn.[252] This can be seen especially with the *plērōma* or "fullness" language in 1:19 (and also 2:9),[253] but also with the language of "the all," "the invisible god," and "the head."[254]

It is difficult to overestimate the significance of this important text through two thousand years of church history. It has been crucially formative in Christian doctrine for the shaping of Christology, and its majestic assertions have been inspirational through the ages for Christian worship.

---

249 Strawbridge, *Pauline Effect*, 135.

250 Strawbridge, *Pauline Effect*, 135.

251 See the discussion in Strawbridge, *Pauline Effect*, 170–75.

252 See Wilson, 158.

253 See Overfield, "Pleroma," 384–96, who effectively argues that the hymn writer did not derive his usage of the term *plērōma* from gnostic sects, but rather that later gnosis depended on Colossians for its use of the term.

254 See, e.g., the ample use of Colossians in the Gospel of Truth (NHC I 3 and XII 2).

# Reconciliation of the Colossians to God (1:21–23)

## *Bibliography*

**Bing, C. C.** "Colossians 1:21–23," 74–88. **Campbell, C. R.** *Hope of Glory*. **Caneday, A. B.** "If You Continue in the Faith," 20–33. **Heil, J. P.** *Colossians*. **Jones, C. P.** "Hellenistic Cult-Association," 195–204. **Parker, R.** *Greek Gods Abroad*. **Porter, S. E.** *Καταλλάσσω*. **Tachau, P.** *"Einst" und "Jetzt."*

## *Translation*

21 *And once you were estranged (from God) and enemies in your thinking through your evil deeds.* 22 *But now he reconciled*[a] *you in the body of his flesh through death*[b] *to present you holy and blameless and innocent before him* 23 *if you remain in the faith, established and firm, not shifting from the hope of the gospel, which you have heard, which has been preached in all creation under heaven, of which I, Paul, became a servant.*[c]

## *Notes*

a. [1:22] The testimonies of Sinaiticus (א) and Vaticanus (B) are split on the precise form of the Greek term for "reconciled," and the reading of 𝔓[46] is partially missing. Sinaiticus is joined by the Majority text, other Alexandrian witnesses (A C P Ψ 81 cop[bo, sa]), and much of the Western tradition (many Old Latin manuscripts and the Vulgate) in supporting the aorist active third-singular form, ἀποκατήλλαξεν ("he reconciled"). Vaticanus is alone in having the aorist passive second-plural form, ἀποκατηλλάγητε ("you were reconciled"). It is likely, however, that 𝔓[46] supports this reading. The term occurs at the end of a line where the papyrus is broken away at that point. It appears to read: αποκαταλ[ ], with the next line beginning with γητε. A third reading is present in some Western witnesses (D F G it[b, d, g] vg[ms])—the perfect passive participle nominative masculine plural, ἀποκαταλλαγέντες ("having been reconciled"). The weight of the external evidence tips fairly strongly in favor of the first reading ("he reconciled you"), but as many have noted, the second reading is the more difficult reading because it does not fit well in the context: "you were reconciled . . . to present you" is confusing and grammatically inappropriate. This reading could explain the first as a scribal smoothing of this awkward wording.[1] Moo represents most commentators when he notes, "This may be one of those occasions when a reading is too difficult to be accepted."[2] But, as Metzger and others have noted, if the first reading is original, "it is exceedingly difficult to explain why the other readings should have arisen."[3] It is

1 So Sumney, 81, who adopts the second-person plural reading as original. So also Lightfoot, 161–62.

2 Moo, 141.

3 Metzger, *Textual Commentary*, 554–55.

not satisfying simply to assume that the passive variant arose "in some accidental way early in the transmission of the text."[4] Long ago, Lohse suggested that the second-person passive reading likely arose as "an ancient alteration by which the direct address to the community was strengthened" by a scribe.[5] This is certainly possible, and when combined with the external evidence supporting the first reading, ἀποκατήλλαξεν should be the preferred reading. The third reading lacks sufficient external support and would leave this paragraph without a main verb.

b. [1:22] Sinaiticus (א) and Vaticanus (B) are are once again split over the inclusion of the pronoun αὐτοῦ after διὰ τοῦ θανάτου ("through the death"). Sinaiticus is joined by a few other witnesses (A P 81 326 614 syr[p, h]) in supporting the inclusion of αὐτοῦ ("through *his* death"). This reading should be regarded as a scribal addition to bring clarity, but whose death is in view is easily inferred by the use of the pronoun from the previous prepositional phrase, ἐν τῷ σώματι τῆς σαρκὸς αὐτοῦ ("in the body of his flesh") and by the reference to τοῦ σταυροῦ αὐτου ("his cross") in 1:20.

c. [1:23] It should be noted that other textual witnesses expand on Paul's role as διάκονος, "servant," with additional epithets: some texts add καὶ ἀπόστολος, "and apostle," while Sinaiticus (א) and P add, κῆρυξ καὶ ἀπόστολος, "herald and apostle" (while Codex Alexandrinus inserts these two titles before διάκονος). These are likely scribal expansions for theological reasons or to align the text more closely with 1 Tim 2:7 or 2 Tim 1:11, the latter which reads ἐγὼ κῆρυξ καὶ ἀπόστολος καὶ διδάσκαλος, "I am a herald and an apostle and a teacher."

## *Form/Structure/Setting*

### *Form (and Literary Context)*

Following the beautiful and moving hymn of praise to Christ celebrating his sovereignty over all things and his death and resurrection that inaugurated a new people of God, Paul applies the message of the hymn directly to the Colossians. He thus begins this section with, "and you," with the "you" referring specifically to the Colossian believers (and not to "you gentiles" and assuming a Jew-gentile distinction with the language).

Paul focuses on the theme of reconciliation, which he picks up from the final portion of the hymn. He repeats the term "reconcile" and makes it the main verb of this new section of the letter. Whereas in the hymn he used it in a comprehensive sense of bringing all of creation into a unified whole (similar to the idea of Eph 1:10 where he speaks of bringing everything under the headship of Christ) and ushering in an era of universal peace, here he develops reconciliation in his more usual sense of people being reconciled to God. The first few lines of this section explain the need for the reconciliation. Apart from the work of Christ, people are alienated from God and are estranged from him both in disposition and in actions.

Paul employs an early Christian literary form that highlights the before and after of conversion. This "once-now" form was widely used by Paul and other

4 Beale, 129.

5 Lohse, 64n16.

Christian authors to contrast the plight of pre-Christian existence with the blessings of new life in Christ.[6] This contrast of life situations takes the reader back to the introduction to the hymn (1:12–13) that speaks of believers being rescued from the dominion of darkness and transferred into the kingdom of the Son.

Verses 21–23 form a coherent section[7] focused on the theme of the reconciliation of the Colossians to God. The section concludes with the mention of Paul's role as a servant of the gospel, which provides a bridge to the theme of the next section.

### *Structure*

This section consists of one sentence of sixty-seven words. There is a degree of complexity to the structure of this sentence, witnessed in part by its length, syntax, participial constructions, and relative clauses, and a conditional statement.

Since it is one sentence, there is one main verb, ἀποκατήλλαξεν, "he reconciled." The subject is not explicitly stated and is carried over from the preceding section (the hymn) and should be understood to be Christ. The direct object is fronted to the beginning of the section and is the accusative, ὑμᾶς "you." Paul expands on this with three accusative modifiers (ὄντας ἀπηλλοτριωμένους καὶ ἐχθρούς) that describe the plight of believers before receiving Christ. The simple sentence rearranged into English word order would be:

"Christ reconciled you *(now)*
who were estranged and enemies." *(once)*

This passage is also structured around a "once-now" (ποτέ-νυνί) literary form that contrasts the nature of their lives before and after Christ. To lead with the "once," Paul must start the sentence with the accusatives.

The infinitive clause (παραστῆσαι ὑμᾶς, "to present you") expresses the goal of the reconciliation. It also serves as the apodosis (the "then" clause) of the conditional sentence for which the protasis (the "if" clause") follows in v. 23. Simply put, it could be expressed as follows:

"If you remain in the faith . . . he will present you blameless before him."

The eschatological presentation before the divine tribunal is logically future to the main verb and to the protasis.

---

6 Tachau, *"Einst" und "Jetzt,"* 96–112, identifies what he calls "the ποτέ-νῦν schema" as a literary form in the NT that contrasts one's sinful past (*die sündige Vergangenheit*) with the presence of salvation (*die Gegenwart des Heils*).

7 Heil, *Colossians*, 75–80, sees vv. 21 and 22 as B′ and v. 23 as A′ of a macro-chiasm that extends from 1:15–23. It is unlikely, however, that v. 23 should be split from the other two verses since all three verses constitute one sentence and a coherent unit of thought.

The protasis ("if you remain in the faith") is a first-class condition and is qualified by a series of three modifiers. The first, a perfect participle, should be interpreted as a causal clause providing the basis for remaining in the faith—that is, "because you have been established." The next two describe the intended result: "you will be firm and will not shift away from the hope of the gospel." Paul then concludes the passage with a series of three genitive descriptions of the gospel itself.

### *Setting*

Paul wants the Colossians to know that they live in the reality of being reconciled to Jesus Christ—the one who is sovereign over all other gods and every political power. In contrast to the territorial deities of the region, Jesus will not strike the Colossians down with some kind of affliction for neglecting ritual obligations or for their moral infractions. In fact, Christ takes the initiative to reconcile them to himself despite their moral terpitude and hostility to him. The warning about "shifting away from the hope of the gospel" (1:23) may very well make allusion to the dangers inherent in the teaching of "the philosophy," which Paul will later say is not "according to Christ" (2:8).

## *Comment*

**21** Καὶ ὑμᾶς ποτε ὄντας ἀπηλλοτριωμένους καὶ ἐχθροὺς τῇ διανοίᾳ ἐν τοῖς ἔργοις τοῖς πονηροῖς, "And once you were estranged (from God) and enemies in your thinking through your evil deeds." After concluding the hymn with its message of reconciliation applied to all things in heaven and on earth, Paul unpacks what this means specifically for the Colossian believers. Before he does that, he explains the nature of their condition that causes them to be in need of reconciliation to God.

The introductory καὶ ὑμᾶς, "and you," transitions the discourse from its universal scope to its specific focus on the Colossian believers. The pronoun ὑμᾶς never appeared in the hymn and was last used in 1:9 where Paul begins his prayer report detailing how he is praying for "you" Colossians. There is no basis for seeing Paul's remarks here as limited just to gentile Christians at Colossae. His comments apply equally to both groups.

The adverb ποτέ ("once") contrasts with the νυνί ("now") of 1:22a and describes their spiritual condition prior to giving their allegiance to Jesus Christ. This way of contrasting the plight of those who are not believers with those who have experienced salvation in Christ occurs elsewhere in Paul's writings (see Rom 11:30: "for just as you were at one time [ποτε] disobedient to God but now [νῦν] have received mercy"; see also Eph 5:8; Phlm 11). Sometimes he varies the form with the use of τότε ("then") in place of ποτέ (Gal 4:8–9). Other times the ποτέ ("once") is implicit (Rom 6:17–22; 7:5–6), and yet in other passages the νῦν ("now") is implied (Rom 6:17; Eph 2:1–10, 11–22).[8] The radical disjuncture between the past and the present was Paul's own experience despite the fact that he was an observant and zealous Jew in his life before Christ. Those who saw this change in him noted that "the man who formerly persecuted us is now [ποτε νῦν] preaching the faith he once tried to destroy" (Gal 1:23 NIV).

The first thing he says about the pre-Christian condition of the Colossians is that they were alienated from God. Rather than using the aorist passive indicative second-person finite verb form (ἀπηλλοτριώθητε, "you were estranged") to express this, he uses a perfect participle in the accusative case preceded by the accusative participle of εἰμί. The accusative form of both participles makes them the grammatical direct objects of the main verb of the section, ἀποκατήλλαξεν, "he reconciled," that will appear in v. 22. The participle ὄντας forms a periphrastic construction with ἀπηλλοτριωμένους "to express still more forcibly the persistence of the new state of things."[9] In other words, "they existed in a persistent state of alienation from God."[10] The verb itself only appears elsewhere in Paul's writings in Ephesians, both times as perfect participles. In the first, he speaks of unbelieving gentiles as "alienated from Christ" (Eph 2:12) and in the second, the audience is described as "alienated from the life of God" (Eph 4:18). The conceptuality, however, is thoroughly Pauline. Those who are not in Christ are under condemnation (Rom 3:9; 5:18; 8:1), destined for God's wrath (Rom 5:9), experiencing death (Rom 5:12), and falling short of the glory of God (Rom 3:23). The verb is used twice in the LXX of Ezekiel to speak of Israel's estrangement from God resulting from their idolatrous practices (Ezek 14:5, 7). One Second Temple Jewish text refers to those who fell into fornication and idolatry and "were alienated from God" (ἀπηλλοτριώθησαν θεοῦ; T. Benj. 10.10).

The alienation spoken of here is not between Jews and gentiles (or between humans generally), but a separation from God (and his Son). Although God is not explicitly stated as the one from whom they are alienated, this is certainly implict. The parallel passages make this clear, as does the full context of the passage. God is the recipient of the thanksgiving (1:3–8), the focal point of the prayer (1:9–14), and the one with whom Christ is identified in the hymn (1:15–20). The reconciliation expressed in 1:21–23 is strictly and explicitly directed at the relationship between humans and God.[11]

The second characteristic of their lives before Christ is that they were

8 Tachau, *"Einst" und "Jetzt,"* 86, contends that the two adverbs often characterize the "then-now" schema, but are not essential to it and that there are exceptions. He argues that the form of the schema is not found in the OT, but first appears in Jos. Asen. (pp. 52–58, 68–70).

9 BDF §352 (p. 179). It is possible to understand the participles as expressing the idea of concession ("although you were alienated"; see, e.g., Pao, 106), but this may be overinterpreting them. It is perhaps best to see them simply as expressing "he reconciled . . . you who once were estranged" and allow the ποτέ to express the temporal idea without adding another adverbial thought.

10 Lohse, 62.

11 Contra Dunn, 106, who sees a dual reference, with the secondary being a reconciliation between Jews and gentiles.

enemies (ἐχθροί) of God. Paul expresses the same idea in Romans where he says that in their pre-Christian state the believers were enemies of God, but they had since been "reconciled to God through the death of his Son" (Rom 5:10). Paul specifies in Colossians that they were enemies in the "mind" (τῇ διανοίᾳ). This, too, is a word that only appears elsewhere in Paul's letters in Ephesians, where it is used in a similar way. Paul says that in their former lives, believers were carrying out the desires of the body "and of their minds" (τῶν διανοιῶν; Eph 2:3). He also says that they were "darkened in their mind" (τῇ διανοίᾳ; Eph 4:18). The term has the basic sense of their disposition toward God.[12] It should not be construed simply as "the mind" and reduced to the intellectual and reasoning faculty, as integral as this is to the word. This term often was used to translate the Hebrew word לֵב, "heart," which also refers to one's affections. The terms καρδία ("heart") and διανοία appear together in the Gospel tradition regarding the love that is owed to God: "you shall love the Lord your God with all your heart [καρδία] and with all your soul and with all your mind [διάνοια] and with all your strength" (Mark 12:30; see also Matt 22:37; Luke 10:27). Enemies "in the mind" or "thinking" thus refers to an overall orientation and disposition of one's life that is opposed to God, his plans, and his will.

This life-tendency was evident in their deeds, which Paul describes here as evil. Some have taken the preposition ἐν either in a causal sense ("because of your evil behavior"; NIV; cf. CSB) or in an instrumental sense ("by wicked works"; KJV; NKJV; cf. NLT). The latter sense is preferable and could also be rendered, "as expressed through your evil deeds" (NET). The evil deeds are thus the means by which the hostility of the mind is seen.[13]

**22** νυνὶ δὲ ἀποκατήλλαξεν ἐν τῷ σώματι τῆς σαρκὸς αὐτοῦ διὰ τοῦ θανάτου, "but now he reconciled you in the body of his flesh through death." The horrible plight of separation from the one living and true God has been resolved through the sacrificial death of Christ on the cross. The νυνί ("now") forms the counterpart to the previously expressed ποτέ ("once") and introduces the presentation of the wonderful state of reconciliation with God that the Colossians will enjoy. Because of this contrast, the conjunction δέ probably has an adversative sense and should be rendered, "but now."

At the end of the Colossian hymn, a future universal "reconciliation" is declared that will result in a profound *shalom* in all of creation. Because of the sinful rebellion that has taken place, the reconciliation spoken of in 1:20 will necessarily entail a subjugation and pacification of all the hostile "principalities and authorities" as well as rebellious humanity who refuse to recognize Jesus as Lord. Paul now takes up the theme of reconciliation and applies it directly to the Colossian believers. But in this instance, he uses the term in the more common sense of reconciliation as friends and precisely in the same way that he

12 See BDAG s.v. διάνοια 2.

13 So also Moo, 140.

uses the term in his two great passages on reconciliation (Rom 5:10–11; 2 Cor 5:18–20), although in these two passages he uses the simpler term, καταλλάσσω. The subject of the verb is not expressed, which has resulted in some dispute over whether it should be understood as God[14] or Christ.[15] Although God is the subject of "reconciled" in both the Romans and Corinthians passages, there are good reasons for seeing Christ as the subject here. First, Christ was the subject throughout the hymn, which is the immediately preceding context. Second, the referent to the personal pronoun (αὐτοῦ) in the following prepositional phrase is Christ, and that phrase fits more naturally into the context if Christ is the subject of the verb (i.e., "Christ reconciled you . . . in the body of his flesh").

Christ accomplishes this reconciliation through the crucifixion of his human body on the cross. Paul expresses Jesus's humanity here in a unique way: ἐν τῷ σώματι τῆς σαρκὸς αὐτοῦ, "in the body of his flesh." This pleonastic expression helps to distinguish Christ's physical body from his "body" referred to in the hymn—that is, the corporate community, the church (1:18a). This precise expression does occur once in the LXX as a way of referring to the physicality of one's existence: "a person who is sexually promiscuous with the body of his flesh [ἐν σώματι σαρκὸς αὐτοῦ] will never cease until a fire burns out" (Sir 23:16 NETS; see also 1 En. 102.5; Philo, *Dreams* 2.232). The term σῶμα is used frequently by Paul to refer to one's physical body in its weakness, mortality, and ultimate corruption (e.g., Rom 1:24; 4:19; 6:12; 7:24). It would have been adequate for Paul to simply say, "Christ reconciled us in his body." But Paul uses the attributive genitive expression τῆς σαρκός to strongly emphasize Christ's humanity. The noun σάρξ is an important anthropological term in Paul, and he often uses it to express the theological idea of the evil inclination in individuals (as its use in Col 2:13, 18), which is not the usage here. But on a number of occasions, Paul can use the word to simply indicate the physical material of the body that is weak and subject to death (e.g., Rom 6:19; 7:18).[16] The "body of flesh" or "fleshly body" merely indicates his "physical body," as it is translated by some of the versions (e.g., NIV; CEB; NET; NLT). The preposition ἐν is here best understood as means,[17] and could be rendered "by" his human body (as the NIV; NET; NJB; CSB; CEB).

Some have suggested that the emphasis on Christ's physical body here may be a polemical move on Paul's part to counteract the teaching of "the philosophy," which may have had docetic leanings and was questioning the idea of Jesus suffering in the flesh.[18] But it is highly doubtful that the factional teaching had gnostic or docetic (or even Platonic) tendencies. The emphasis of this passage

14 So, e.g., Lohse, 64n17.
15 So, e.g., Pao, 107; Barth and Blanke, 221; Dunn, 107.
16 See the discussion in Dunn, *Theology of Paul*, 62–69.
17 So also Sumney, 85.
18 E.g., Moule, 72.

has more to do with distinguishing the physical body of Christ from the church as the body of Christ (Col 1:18a).

Christ reconciled the Colossian believers to God διὰ τοῦ θανάτου ("through death"). The force of the αὐτοῦ from the previous phrase continues here ("through *his* death"). This is another way of expressing "through the blood of his cross" (1:20b) as the basis presented in the hymn for reconciliation. Once again, this is the same idea expressed by Paul in Romans: "we were reconciled to God by the death of his Son" (Rom 5:10).

παραστῆσαι ὑμᾶς ἁγίους καὶ ἀμώμους καὶ ἀνεγκλήτους κατενώπιον αὐτοῦ, "to present you holy and blameless and innocent before him." Christ's ultimate goal in reconciling sinful people to himself is to present them to himself at the final tribunal as a people who are entirely pure without blame. But just as the experience of reconciliation is brought forward and enjoyed by all who are presently in Christ, so also is the purifying work of Christ to prepare a people who are without blame.

Although the language of "presenting" is common in OT sacrificial contexts (e.g., Lev 16:11: "Aaron shall present [προσάξει] the bull as a sin offering" [ESV]), the term from our passage (παρίστημι) never appears in the LXX of Leviticus and is rare in other OT sacrificial contexts (although see Paul's use in Rom 12:1). The common word used for sacrifice is προσάγω (usually translating the *hiphil* of קָרַב). The more relevant imagery standing behind this passage is the legal technical language of presenting someone before a judge.[19] The immediate background is the divine tribunal at the end of time. Paul says to the Romans, "We will all stand [παραστησόμεθα] before the judgment seat of God" (Rom 14:10). And we discover in the Corinthian correspondence that Christ will be the agent of God's judgment at that time: "for we must all appear before the judgment seat of Christ" (2 Cor 5:10). But as Lohse aptly points out, "it is the aim of God's work of reconciliation that those who have been reconciled by Christ's death will be irreproachable when they stand before him."[20] This end-time presentation is beautifully expressed in Ephesians using the imagery of the church as a bride: "that he might present [παραστήσῃ] the church to himself in splendor, without spot or wrinkle or any such thing, that she might be holy and without blemish" (Eph 5:27 ESV).

But just as the end-time verdict of believers before the judgment seat of God is brought forward into the present experience of believers through justification, so also there are dimensions of this presentation to God that are presently experienced by the people of God. This can be seen especially in Paul's use of

19 BDAG, s.v. παρίστημι 1.e., documents this verb as a legal technical term meaning "bring before (a judge)."

20 Lohse, 65 (although Lohse sees the primary referent to the present lives of Christians lived in God's presence). Moo, 143, sees the final judgment as the primary referent in this context. See also Campbell, *Hope of Glory*, 308.

the term ἅγιοι, "holy ones." While the principal focus of this passage is upon the future,[21] there is simultaneously a present sense. Thus, Paul calls believers in all of his churches ἅγιοι, "holy ones" (e.g., Rom 1:7; 8:27; 12:13; 15:25, 26, 31; 16:2, 15; 1 Cor 1:2; 6:1, 2; 14:33; 16:1, 15). Yet believers are currently in the process of becoming "holy," and Paul is praying for this to happen (1 Thess 5:23). Nevertheless, by virtue of their union with Christ, they are already sanctified (1 Cor 1:2; 6:11). Consequently, the end-time presentation of believers at the divine tribunal as holy is possible because of the work of Christ on the cross, but this status is something they presently experience because they are "in Christ." Paul's own present ministry is tied to this end-time presentation insofar as he is striving to teach and help believers to bring their lives into alignment with their status before God (Col 1:28).

The second word that Paul uses to describe the state of believers at the time of their presentation is ἄμωμος, "blameless." This term is used extensively in the LXX of the Torah to characterize the kind of animal offering that the Lord required (e.g., Lev 1:3: "he shall offer a male without blemish [ἄμωμον];" see also, e.g., Lev 1:10; 3:1, 6, 9; 4:3, 14, 23, 28, 32; Num 6:14). Here in Col 1:22 the reference is not to the absence of physical defect but to moral purity. The metaphorical use is also found in the OT. The psalmist declares that it is the person "who walks blamelessly [πορευόμενος ἄμωμος]" who will dwell with God on his holy hill (Ps 15:2 [14:2 LXX]). Proverbs affirms that "all who are blameless [ἄμωμοι] in their ways" are acceptable to God (Prov 11:20). Paul himself appealed to the Philippian believers to be "blameless [ἄμεμπτοι] and innocent, children of God without blemish [ἄμωμα] in the midst of a crooked and perverse generation" (Phil 2:15 NRSV). He tells the Ephesian believers that God's purpose for choosing them was that they should be "holy and blameless before him [ἁγίους καὶ ἀμώμους κατενώπιον αὐτοῦ]" (Eph 1:4).

The third term that Paul uses to characterize the way that they will appear before the Lord at the end is ἀνέγκλητος, "blameless, irreproachable." Paul has used this earlier in his correspondence with the Corinthinans to assure them that the Lord Jesus would sustain them to the end, "blameless [ἀνέγκλητος] on the day of our Lord Jesus Christ" (1 Cor 1:8). The eschatological orientation of this statement is clear. This term is far less common than the previous two, only appearing once in the LXX (3 Macc. 5.31) and not at all in Philo. Josephus uses it to describe the Samaritans, who were "blameless" (ἀνέγκλητον) because they did not join a sedition in Judea after the death of Herod the Great (Josephus, *Ant.* 17.289). The term was also known and used in Asia Minor where it appears in a number of inscriptions. In an inscription from northwest of Colossae at Koloe (Lydia) dating to the mid-second century BC, an association of "hero worshipers" (ἡρωισταί) honor a recently deceased priestess named Stratonike.

21 Contra Pao, 108–9, who contends that "a future reference is not necessary."

Among the virtues for which she is honored is that "she was irreproachable [ἀνέγκλητος]."[22]

The three terms that Paul has chosen to describe the eschatological status of believers in their appearance at the divine tribunal display assonance, with each beginning with the vowel α-. This rhetorical flair underlines the absolute purity of believers as they will stand before the judgment seat at the end. All three of these terms have substantial overlap in meaning and highlight the gracious and effective work of Christ in redeeming them and completely forgiving them for all of their sins. This powerful combination of terms for moral rectitude may also imply the transfer of Christ's righteousness to them as an entailment of their union with him.

The final prepositional phrase, κατενώπιον αὐτοῦ, "before him," has in view this end-time presentation for divine judgment. The only other time this expression appears in the Pauline literature is in Ephesians 1:4 where it says, "he chose us in him before the foundation of the world, that we should be holy and blameless before him (κατενώπιον αὐτοῦ)." There it also refers primarily to the future when all believers will stand before God.[23] The preposition also appears in Jude where it unmistakably is used in doxological praise with reference to the divine judgment: "Now to him who is able to keep you from stumbling and to present you blameless before (κατενώπιον) the presence of his glory with great joy . . ." (Jude 24). The pronoun, αὐτοῦ, "his," most likely refers to Christ who is the subject of the main verb of the sentence.[24] In Paul's thought, the impending day of the Lord as a time of divine judgment has become "the day of our Lord Jesus Christ" when all will appear before the judgment seat of Christ (1 Cor 1:8; 2 Cor 5:10; see also 2 Tim 4:1).

**23** εἴ γε ἐπιμένετε τῇ πίστει, "if you remain in the faith." The positive declarations of the previous verse that the Colossians have been reconciled to God and that they will be presented at the end of time before the divine magistrate as completely blameless is now tempered by a warning. This notice serves as an exhortation for them to align their daily lives with the core Christian convictions that they have received.

The εἴ γε introduces a first-class condition. The protasis (the "if" statement) is expressed by the indicative verb ἐπιμένετε, and the apodosis (the "then" statement) is most likely the immediately preceding infinitival purpose clause παραστῆσαι ὑμᾶς, "to present you," which is logically future in relationship to its aorist main verb, ἀποκατήλλαξεν, "he reconciled you." Expressed simply, "if you abide in the faith, then he will present you blameless." Although some have seen the apodosis as "he reconciled," this does not make sense in the context since they are already experiencing the benefits of reconciliation to Christ

22 *SEG* 57:1188.1–31, esp. line 15. See Jones, "Hellenistic Cult-Association," 195–204.

23 See my *Ephesians*, 81.

24 So also Pao, 108, et al.

(and the Father). Neither would that construction make logical sense: "if you abide in the faith, then he has reconciled you." The concern here is to encourage final perseverance.

The verb Paul has chosen, ἐπιμένω, means to "continue in a pursuit."[25] It can be used literally of remaining in a particular location (e.g., Paul "remained" with Cephas for fifteen days; Gal 1:18) or metaphorically to remain or continue "in an activity or state."[26] Paul asks the Romans rhetorically, "Are we to continue [ἐπιμένωμεν] in sin that grace may abound?" (Rom 6:1 ESV) and answers with an emphatic, "by no means." Although this is the only time that Paul uses the verb in a first-class condition, he twice uses it with the particle ἐάν in a third-class condition (Rom 11:22–23).

Paul's intent is for the Colossians to persist in τῇ πίστει, "the faith." He is likely referring to an active trust in the resurrected Christ and continued belief in the tenets of the gospel message they had received.[27] This is the way that he has used the term in its earlier occurrence in Colossians (1:4). His critique of the leaders of the factional teaching implies a lack of faith on their part when he states that they are not "holding tight to the head" (2:19). While it is possible that the reference is to "the faith" in the sense of maintaining the core doctrines they have received (as in 2:7; Eph 4:5, 13; see also 1 Tim 4:6),[28] this is not the primary meaning here. Nevertheless, trusting in the elements of the apostolic faith that they have received through Epaphras would also be entailed in this. Trust in Jesus as a person would simultaneously involve trusting "the teaching about Christ" (Col 3:16) and not giving heed to anything taught about him that was inconsistent with what they had received.

The overall effect of this conditional clause is to function as an admonition and appeal to the Colossians. Caneday aptly describes it as "an urgent appeal to persevere in the gospel of Christ in order that we might be presented holy, blameless, and irreproachable before God in the day of judgment."[29] It is probably going too far and overinterprets the conditional clause in this context to understand the protasis under the assumption that it will be fulfilled in the lives of the Colossians as though it were a causal clause, "*since* you remain in the faith." The first-class condition "makes an assertion for the sake of an argument" and not necessarily as corresponding to reality.[30] Thus, as Caneday notes, "Paul assumes for the sake of his argument that the Colossians will remain steadfast in the Christian faith. Whether they would remain steadfast required them to

25 LSJ, s.v. ἐπιμένω 3.

26 BDAG, s.v. ἐπιμένω 2.

27 So also Beale, 116; Pao, 109; Moo, 144–45; Wilson, 165.

28 See McKnight, 178. Caneday, "If You Continue in the Faith," 22, sees "the faith" as a metonymy for the gospel.

29 Caneday, "If You Continue in the Faith," 21.

30 Porter, *Idioms*, 256.

heed the apostle's exhortation."[31] The statement has the semantic function of a strong exhortation to persevere in their faith in Christ. They must persevere to be presented holy, blameless, and irreproachable on the final day. Yet the very fact that Paul chooses the first-class condition and not the third-class condition may reveal something of the confidence he has that those who have been rescued from the dominion of darkness and have become members of the kingdom of the Son of God will remain in the faith. Lightfoot is not without justification in asserting that the indicative mood of the verb "converts the hypothesis into a hope."[32] Moo is correct, however, in describing this conditional sentence as "a real warning" and putting it into the context of Paul's central concern in the letter—namely, "to encourage the Colossian Christians to resist the blandishments of the false teachers and to continue to grow in their knowledge of Christ."[33]

τεθεμελιωμένοι καὶ ἑδραῖοι καὶ μὴ μετακινούμενοι ἀπὸ τῆς ἐλπίδος τοῦ εὐαγγελίου, "established and firm, not shifting from the hope of the gospel." The first of the three expressions that follow provides the basis for persevering. The second two express the result. The perfect participle, τεθεμελιωμένοι, should be interpreted as causal. Because the Colossians have a firm foundation on the basis of the gospel and their union with Christ, they will be able to persevere in the faith. Paul tells the Corinthians that "no one can lay any foundation [θεμέλιον] other than the one already laid, which is Jesus Christ" (1 Cor 3:11 NIV; cf. Eph 2:20). Paul describes his ministry to the Corinthians as building on that foundation (1 Cor 3:10). In a similar way, through receiving the gospel that was preached and by their union with Christ, the Colossians have been established on a strong foundation. This is the reason that Paul can be confident for their future. Paul's use of the language likely reflects OT and Jewish usage, and particularly as it relates to the founding of God's eschatological temple (see Isa 28:16; also Isa 54:11). The Qumran community saw themselves as God's eschatological temple or city and made use of the imagery of its foundations (see 1QS 8.5–11; 9.3).[34]

"Firm and not shifting" are the intended results toward which Paul is aiming. The first is stated positively and the second negatively. "Firm" (ἑδραῖος) is a term that only appears in the Pauline writings and nowhere else in the NT or LXX. Paul urges the Corinthians to be "steadfast and not shifting [ἑδραῖοι γίνεσθε, ἀμετακίνητοι]" (1 Cor 15:58), the term ἀμετακίνητος being an adjectival cognate of the participle that appears here in our verse. The combination of these two terms is a uniquely Pauline idiom. Josephus uses ἑδραῖος a handful of times in a

31 Caneday, "If You Continue in the Faith," 29.

32 Lightfoot, 163. Most commentators contend that the construction denotes some level of confidence in the outcome; see, e.g., Beale, 116; Sumney, 86; Dunn, 110; Eadie, 82; Peake, 513.

33 Moo, 143–44.

34 See *NIDNTTE* 2:431. See also MacDonald, 73; Lohse, 66.

nonfigurative way. For instance, he employs it to describe the steep precipices of the upper part of the city of Gamala where the Jewish soldiers could find "nothing that was stable [ἑδραῖον] to stand upon" (Josephus, *J.W.* 4.77). He also speaks of a tower that was built "firm" (ἑδραῖος; Josephus, *J.W.* 3.284). Another Jewish text uses the adjective metaphorically to speak of the prayers of Jeremiah and Baruch "as a firm pillar [στῦλος ἑδραῖος]" in the midst of Jerusalem (4 Bar. 1.2). The term is also attested in the inscriptions of Asia Minor.[35] It appears, for instance, as an epithet to two different deities on an altar dedication discovered in Patara (Lycia), south of Colossae. The text reads, "Theos Soter Hedraios [ἑδραίου] Asphales and Poseidon Hedraios [ἑδραίου] and Helios Apollo."[36] The epithet "Asphales" emphasizes the role of the god as providing safety and security.[37] Ignatius picks up on the metaphorical use of the term and exhorts the Ephesians to "be firm in the faith [ἑδραῖοι τῇ πίστει]" (Ign. *Eph.* 10.2) and likewise urges Polycarp to "stand firm [στῆθι ἑδραῖος]" (Ign. *Pol.* 3.1). Many English versions use the term "steadfast" to translate it in Colossians (e.g., CSB; ESV; NRSV; RSV; NASB; ASV), while others opt for "firm" (NIV; NET).[38]

In contrast to being firmly established is the danger of moving away from their convictions stemming from the gospel. Paul now warns them to avoid this departure. This is the only time that he uses the verb μετακινέω in his writings, but he is familiar with the adjective ἀμετακίνητος, "immovable," which he uses in 1 Cor 15:58. The middle voice of the verb was commonly employed to express the idea of "going from one place to another."[39] It appears in the LXX of Isaiah as part of an illustration to underline the faithfulness of God in extending mercy to his people: "nor as a threat to you would I remove the mountains, nor would the hills be shifted [μετακινηθήσονται], so neither shall the mercy that comes from me to you fail" (Isa 54:9b–10 NETS). Josephus used the term to refer to the moving of the tabernacle (*Ant.* 3.293), to moving a vessel out of its place (*J.W.* 2.147), and to the undesirability of changing anything that is in the law (*Ag. Ap.* 2.184). Paul here uses it as a metaphor for shifting away from the hope that has come to the Colossians believers through the gospel. It is best to understand the genitive τοῦ εὐαγγελίου as a genitive of source.[40] As in 1:5, "hope" should here be seen as eschatologically oriented, but also as something that is partially experienced in the present. Yet the immediate context here, the apodosis of the conditional clause, is future oriented. The Colossians will be

---

35 It appears in a funerary inscription from Nacrason (Mysia) with reference to a house that is firmly established (οἶκος ἑδραῖος); see Hermann and Polatkan, *Testament des Epikrates*, 7,1.B.101 (pp. 8–17 no. 1).

36 *TAM* II.403. See also *TAM* IV.404 (Διὸς Σωτῆρος ἑδραίου).

37 Parker, *Greek Gods Abroad*, 25, suggests that the epithets refer to protection from earthquakes, but it is probably to be understood more broadly than this.

38 The CEB inexplicably shifts to a botanical metaphor and renders it "rooted."

39 LSJ, s.v. μετακινέω 1.

40 So also Pao, 110; Sumney, 87; Barth and Blanke, 224. Lightfoot, 163, takes a similar view by regarding it as a subjective genitive, "the hope held out by the Gospel."

presented holy, blameless, and irreproachable before the Lord at his throne in the future judgment.

**οὗ ἠκούσατε, τοῦ κηρυχθέντος ἐν πάσῃ κτίσει τῇ ὑπὸ τὸν οὐρανόν, οὗ ἐγενόμην ἐγὼ Παῦλος διάκονος,** "which you have heard, which has been preached in all creation under heaven, of which I, Paul, became a servant." The paragraph concludes with an expansion on the gospel by means of three consecutive genitival expressions. The first is οὗ ἠκούσατε, "which you have heard." This picks up and repeats what he said in 1:6 when he refers to "the day you heard it [the gospel] and came to know the grace of God in truth."

The second genitive expression characterizes the manner in which they heard it: τοῦ κηρυχθέντος, "which has been preached." For the Colossians, this took place when Epaphras communicated to them the content of the *kērygma*. The verb κηρύσσω is Paul's preferred term for the proclamation of the key elements of the gospel message, which he refers to as τὸ κήρυγμα Ἰησοῦ Χριστοῦ, "the *kērygma* of Jesus Christ" (Rom 16:25). The Christ hymn, especially if it is traditional, shows that a significant part of the early Christian proclamation was centered on the person of Christ, especially an understanding of his identity as the preexistent Son of God, his incarnation and atoning death on the cross, his resurrection from the dead, his creation of the church as his visible presence on earth, and his return in power to bring universal peace. The proclamation of the message of the gospel is foundational to Paul's apostolic ministry and to the work of every church that he has established. He tells the Roman church, "How, then, can they call on the one they have not believed in? And how can they believe in the one of whom they have not heard? And how can they hear without someone preaching [κηρύσσοντος] to them?" (Rom 10:14 NIV).

He then revels in how much of the work of proclaiming the gospel has already been accomplished in the thirty-plus years since the church began on Pentecost. When he says that it has been proclaimed "in all creation under heaven," we of course need to see this as hyperbole. The gospel has only spread throughout the Mediterranean region—including Israel, Syria, Nabataea, Anatolia, Greece, Macedonia, Italy, and possibly to Egypt and North Africa. But it obviously had not spread to all of the continents and islands of the entire globe. One cannot underestimate, however, how this movement spread so rapidly to such a broad geographical region that encompassed many different people and cultural groups. From a first-century perspective, this represents much of the full extent of the Roman Empire and the known world.

Some have taken the πᾶς κτίσις as a personal reference (i.e., limited to humanity) rather than a geographical reference and understand it as "every creature" (e.g., NIV; RSV; NAB; NJB; NKJV; KJV; Geneva; Tyndale).[41] Yet the expression was used in the hymn to speak of the entirety of creation (1:15). Paul also uses it in Romans to refer comprehensively to creation: "we know

41 E.g., Lohse, 66.

that the whole creation [πᾶσα ἡ κτίσις] has been groaning as in the pains of childbirth right up to the present time" (Rom 8:22 NIV). It is best to take it in a geographical sense, as we have noted, but to see it as hyperbole to underscore the extensive spread of the gospel in one generation. The comprehensive scope is emphasized by the addition of the phrase ὑπὸ τὸν οὐρανόν, "under heaven." The phrase (with or without the article) is especially common in the LXX of the Wisdom literature to speak of the entirety of creation (e.g., Prov 8:26, 28; Eccl 1:13; 3:1; Job 1:7; 2:2). Luke uses the expression to speak of "devout men from every nation under heaven [ἀπὸ παντὸς ἔθνους τῶν ὑπὸ τὸν οὐρανόν]" staying in Jerusalem (Acts 2:5 ESV). This passage is particularly instructive because it employs similar hyperbole to speak of Jews coming from many different provinces of the Roman Empire to visit Jerusalem. It also demonstrates that a writer could choose to use the term ἔθνη to refer to diverse groups of peoples. The geographical interpretation of the phrase in Col 1:23 also coheres with Paul's statement in 1:6 that "the gospel is bearing fruit and increasing throughout the whole world [ἐν παντὶ τῷ κόσμῳ]." Foster may be correct in observing that part of Paul's point to the Colossians may be to help them see that "they should not regard themselves as part of some precarious and marginal movement."[42]

The third genitive expression, οὗ ἐγενόμην ἐγὼ Παῦλος διάκονος, "of which I, Paul, became a servant," describes his own personal involvement in the spread of the gospel. It also functions as a transition to the next section where Paul will expand on his stewardship of the gospel. The genitive relative pronoun οὗ directly modifies the much earlier τοῦ εὐαγγελίου. The ἐγὼ Παῦλος reminds us of the beginning of the letter where Paul names himself as the author of the letter along with Timothy (1:1). It also points forward to the conclusion of the letter where Paul vouches for the authenticity of the letter with his own signature: "this greeting is with my own hand—from Paul" (4:18). Although it is possible that the letter was not written by Paul and was composed by one of his followers in his name, the letter seeks to give the impression that it was written by Paul himself. This statement is no exception.

Paul has used this emphatic self reference, ἐγὼ Παῦλος, three other times in letters that are generally thought to be authentic. In the first instance, he uses it in an emotional and rhetorically powerful way to argue against the ritual of circumcision to the Galatians ("Listen! I, Paul [ἐγὼ Παῦλος], am telling you that if you let yourselves be circumcised, Christ will be of no benefit to you"; Gal 5:2 NRSV). As deSilva notes, Paul "wants to have their full attention and to bring the full weight of his personal experience and authority" to bear on what he is about to say.[43] In the second instance, he adds the emphatic "I, Paul [ἐγὼ Παῦλος]" to bring gravity to the strength of his appeal to the Corinthians

42 Foster, 210.

43 DeSilva, *Galatians*, 414.

to resist the false apostles (2 Cor 10:1; see also 2 Cor 12:13, αὐτὸς ἐγώ).[44] The third use of the expression is employed as an emphatic way to convey sincerity in a promise he makes to Philemon (Phlm 19): "I, Paul, write this with my own hand: I will repay it." The function of the expression in Colossians has nothing to do with vouching for the authenticity of his comments, but it does focus the readers' attention on the seriousness of Paul's call from God to be a διάκονος, "servant," of the gospel, which he will expand upon in the sentences that follow. He "became" (ἐγενόμην) a servant of the gospel when he received his call from God on the road to Damascus nearly thirty years prior (Acts 9:1–25; 22:1–21; 26:1–23).

Although Luke does not describe Paul's Damascus road encounter with the risen Christ as a commission to become a διάκονος of the gospel, Paul himself characterizes his ministry in these terms. He tells the Corinthians that he and Apollos are "servants [διάκονοι] through whom you believed" according to the assignment of the Lord (1 Cor 3:5). He later says that God has made him and his coworkers sufficient to be "servants [διακόνους] of the new covenant" (2 Cor 3:6) and that they are "servants of God [θεοῦ διάκονοι]" (2 Cor 6:4) and "servants of Christ [διάκονοι Χριστοῦ]" (2 Cor 11:23). Although the related verb διακονέω originally referred to table service (see Acts 6:2), it was frequently used in the wider sense of service in general. It overlapped in meaning with δουλεύω insofar as both could be used for the rendering of service. But whereas διακονέω referred simply to rendering service for someone, δουλεύω stressed the relationship of subordination under which the service was rendered.[45] Paul used both διάκονος (Col 1:7, 25; see also Rom 16:1; Eph 3:7; 6:21) and δοῦλος (Col 4:12; see also, e.g., Rom 1:1; Gal 1:10; Phil 1:1) and their verbal cognates to refer to the manner of service that he and other believers performed for the Lord.

## *Explanation*

In this brief paragraph, Paul returns to a description of the radical contrast between the lives of the Colossans before they came to know Christ and after. He portrays the contrast using the disjunctive literary schema of "once" and "now." In the introduction to the hymn, he referred to their former and present existence in terms of darkness and light and also with the language of being rescued from bondage to one domain and transferred into the kingdom of Christ. At the beginning of this section the seriousness of the plight is highlighted, as Paul characterizes them as being alienated from God and in a state of hostility to him.

Now, however, Christ has reconciled them. No mention is made of any initiative on their part to search for God or solicit his favor. They simply heard the

44 Martin, *2 Corinthians*, 484, notes that "it gives an air of authority to what follows."

45 A. Weiser, "διακονέω," *EDNT* 1:302.

gospel and exercised faith. The hymn celebrated a future reconciliation, but there it was broader than how it is used here. Whereas at the conclusion of the hymn reconciliation is presented as Christ ushering in an era of universal peace that entails the subjugation of rebellious heavenly and earthly powers, here it involves a reconciliation that results in Christ living in the believers (1:27) and in their being united to him (2:9–15).

This reconciliation will lead to their end-time presentation before the divine tribunal in a state of utter purity and blamelessness because of what Christ did for them "in the body of his flesh through death" (1:22). Nevertheless, Paul issues the Colossians a warning about the indispensability of remaining in the faith. Perseverance to the end is Paul's expectation and the condition for their presentation as holy, blameless, and irreproachable before the eschatological judgment. Yet Paul displays a confidence that they will persevere, expressed both in the grammar of the passage (a first-class condition with the indicative mood) as well as in the statement that they have already been well-established in the faith.

The Colossians will need to demonstrate their fidelity to the faith by not shifting away from the gospel they have received. As the next chapter of the letter will show, one of the ways this should be done is by recognizing that the teaching of "philosophy" is not in accordance with the teaching about Christ and thus not acceding to this new teaching or the demands of its advocates. Paul thus calls them to remember the gospel that they heard and that was preached to them. This is the essential teaching about Christ that Paul has been preaching throughout the Mediterranean world. This is the faith that they should trust and to which they should adhere.

# The Apostle Paul's Labor for the Gospel (1:24–2:5)

## *Bibliography*

**Arnold, C. E.** *Ephesians: Power and Magic.* **Bauckham, R.** "Colossians 1:24," 168–70. **Beale, G. K.,** and **B. L. Gladd.** *Hidden But Now Revealed,* 198–214. **Bockmuehl, M. N. A.** *Revelation and Mystery.* **Bornkamm, G.** "Hoffnung," 56–64. **Brown, R. E.** *Semitic Background.* **Burkert, W.** *Ancient Mystery Cults.* **Cahill, M.** "Neglected Parallelism," 142–47. **Campbell, C. R.** *Hope of Glory.* **Caragounis, C. C.** *The Ephesian Mysterion.* **Clark, B.** *Completing Christ's Afflictions.* **D'Andria, F.** *Hierapolis of Phrygia.* **Fee, G. D.** *Empowering Presence.* **Gladd, B. L.** *Revealing the Mysterion.* **Goodrich, J.** *Paul as an Administrator of God.* **Grundmann, W.** *Begriff der Kraft.* **Heil, J. P.** *Colossians.* **Huttner, U.** *Early Christianity in the Lycus Valley.* **Immendörfer, M.** *Ephesians and Artemis.* **Kremer, J.** *Leiden Christi.* **Lang, T. J.** "Disbursing the Account of God," 116–36. **———.** *Mystery.* **Leppä, O.** *Making of Colossians.* **Meyer, M. W.** *Ancient Mysteries.* **Mitchell, S.** *Anatolia.* 2 vols. **Perriman, A.** "Pattern," 62–79. **Piper, J.** *Filling Up.* **Reitzenstein, R.** *Mystery Religions.* **Reumann, J.** "Stewards of God," 339–49. **Riesner, R.** *Paul's Early Period.* **Rojas, J. M. G.** "Word of God," 63–79. **Standhartinger, A.** "Pauline School," 572–93. **Stettler, H.** "Colossians 1:24," 185–208. **Stuhlmann, R.** *Das eschatologische Maß.* **Sumney, J. L.** "Vicarious Suffering," 664–80. **Tanriver, C.** "Three New Inscriptions from Tripolis," 81–96. **Trudinger, L.** "Colossians 1:24," 36–38. **White, J.** "Paul Completes the Servant's Sufferings," 181–98. **Windisch, H.** *Paulus und Christus.* **Yates, R.** "Colossians 1:24," 88–92.

## *Translation*

24 *Now I rejoice in my*[a] *suffering for you, and I fill up in my flesh what is lacking in the afflictions
of Christ for his body, which is the church,* 25 *of which I became a servant in accordance with the
stewardship from God that was given to me for you to fulfill the word of God,* 26 *which is the mystery
hidden from the ages and the generations but is now revealed to his saints.* 27 *God willed to disclose to
them what is the wealth of the glory*[b] *of this mystery*[c] *among the gentiles, which*[d] *is Christ in you, the
hope of glory.* 28 *We proclaim him, admonishing every person and teaching every person in all wisdom
that we might present every person mature in Christ.* 29 *To this end I labor, striving in accordance with
his empowering, which mightily works in me in power.* 2:1 *For I want you to know how great a struggle
I have for*[e] *you and those in Laodicea*[f] *and all who have not seen my face in the flesh,* 2 *that their hearts
may be encouraged, united*[g] *in love in all the riches of the full assurance of insight into knowing the
mystery of God, which is Christ.*[h] 3 *In him are all the treasures of wisdom and knowledge concealed.*
4 *I say this so that no one deceives you with persuasive teachings.* 5 *For even though I am away from
you in the flesh, yet I am with you in the Spirit, rejoicing and seeing your order and the firmness of
your faith in Christ.*

## *Notes*

a. [1:24] The pronoun μου is inserted here by a handful of manuscripts (א$^{2}$ 075 81 323 vg$^{mss}$ et al.). It is likely a scribal addition to increase the clarity of the sentence by specifying who is suffering. Because it is implicitly understood, I have included "my" in the translation.

b. [1:27] 𝔓⁴⁶ omits τῆς δόξης, "of the glory."

c. [1:27] Some Western witnesses (D F G vg$^{mss}$) replace τούτου, "*this* mystery," with τοῦ θεοῦ, "the mystery *of God*." This is due to a scribal harmonization with 2:2.

d. [1:27] The external evidence is split on whether the pronoun is a neuter singular (ὅ, "which") or a masculine singular (ὅς, "who"). The masculine pronoun has the support of Sinaiticus (ℵ), some additional Alexandrian witnesses (C H I Ψ 81 104), codex D, and the Majority text (along with codices K and L). This reading was adopted in the editions by Stephanus, Scrivener, Griesbach, and Tischendorf. The neuter pronoun is attested in 𝔓⁴⁶, Codex Vaticanus (B), Codex Alexandrinus (A), most of the Western tradition, and a few other witnesses. The neuter pronoun is the more difficult reading from the vantage point of a scribe—i.e., it is more natural to think of Christ indwelling believers than a mystery (the antecedent of ὅ) living in them. The neuter is thus the more likely reading.

e. [2:1] Codex D and the Majority text have the preposition περί instead of the better attested ὑπέρ. This may be due to harmonization with περὶ ὑμῶν in 1:3 and its frequent usage throughout Paul (see Rom 15:14; 1 Cor 1:4, 11; Phil 1:27; 2:19, 20; 1 Thess 3:9; 2 Thess 1:3, 11; 2:13). Yet Paul is likewise fond of the construction ὑπὲρ ὑμῶν, especially in this letter (see 1:7, 9, 24; 4:12, 13).

f. [2:1] Some manuscripts (104, 424, vg$^{ms}$, syr$^{har}$) insert καὶ τῶν ἐν Ἱεραπόλει, "and those in Hierapolis," which makes explicit what is implicit in the context and to harmonize with 4:13.

g. [2:2] The Majority text and some additional witnesses (e.g., Ψ 81 104) use the genitive case for the participle (συμβιβασθέντων) instead of the nominative (συμβιβασθέντες). This can be explained as a scribal alteration to conform the participle to the case of the previous pronoun (αὐτῶν).

h. [2:2] There are a variety of manuscript variations at the end of the verse, with many manuscripts inserting καὶ πατρός, "and the Father" after "the mystery of God." Lightfoot has provided a convenient listing of eleven different variations.[1] The two most commonly attested readings are: (1) τοῦ μυστηρίου τοῦ θεοῦ, Χριστοῦ, "the mystery of God, which is Christ." (2) τοῦ μυστηρίου τοῦ θεοῦ καὶ πατρὸς καὶ τοῦ Χριστοῦ, "the mystery of God, both of the Father and of Christ" (NKJV). The former is supported by 𝔓⁴⁶ and Vaticanus (B; along with the Latin father, Hilary of Poitiers [4th c.]), but hardly any other witnesses. The latter is attested by the Majority text (along with K L 075 0208 0278 104 630 and the Harclean Syriac).[2] Between these two, the shorter reading should be preferred here as the original for the reason cited by Metzger: "it alone provides an adequate explanation of the other readings as various attempts to ameliorate the syntactical ambiguity of τοῦ θεοῦ, Χριστοῦ."[3] The other principal variants include the following, but all of them should be understood as scribal attempts to add clarity or amplification:

- τοῦ μυστηρίου τοῦ θεοῦ πατρὸς τοῦ Χριστοῦ, "the mystery of God, the Father of Christ." This is the reading of Codex Sinaiticus (ℵ [minus the article τοῦ] along with A C 1175, some manuscripts of the Vulgate, the Coptic Bohairic and some manuscripts in the Sahidic). This reading has been adopted in the

1 Lightfoot, 252–53.

2 It is also found in the texts of Scrivener and Stephanus.

3 Metzger, *Textual Commentary*, 555. This is the reading adopted by the vast majority of commentators. It was adopted in the editions of Tischendorf, Tregelles, Griesbach, and Westcott-Hort. It is also the preferred reading of UBS⁵ and NA²⁸. Lightfoot, 253, advocated for this shorter reading and noted, "This passage is altogether an instructive lesson in textual criticism."

THGNT. A similar variant, which is different only in the addition of a καί, reads: τοῦ μυστηρίου τοῦ θεοῦ καὶ πατρὸς τοῦ Χριστοῦ, "the mystery of the God and Father of Christ." It is supported by a handful of manuscripts (Ψ 365 945 1505, some manuscripts of the Vulgate, and some Bohairic manuscripts). But this phraseology was likely influenced by the well-known beginnings of some of the epistles: "Blessed be the God and Father of our Lord Jesus Christ" (2 Cor 1:3; Eph 1:3; 1 Pet 1:3; see also Rom 15:6; 2 Cor 11:31).

- τοῦ μυστηρίου τοῦ θεοῦ, ὅ ἐστιν Χριστὸς, "the mystery of God, which is Christ." This reading is found in Codex Clarmontanus (D), some manuscripts of the Vulgate, and Augustine.
- τοῦ μυστηρίου τοῦ Χριστοῦ, "the mystery of Christ." This reading appears in 81 and 1241. It is an attractive reading because it is shorter, but it is poorly attested and may be an attempt to harmonize with 4:3 (τὸ μυστήριον τοῦ Χριστοῦ).
- τοῦ μυστηρίου τοῦ θεοῦ ἐν Χριστῷ, "the mystery of God in Christ." This reading is slimly attested (33 and Ambrosiaster). It is a further attempt at clarity and may be influenced by the expression, "God in Christ," elsewhere in Paul's letters (see Rom 6:11; 8:39; Eph 4:32; Phil 3:14; 1 Thess 2:14; 5:18).

## *Form/Structure/Setting*

### *Form (and Literary Context)*

This section is notable for its extensive use of the first-person singular. Bormann has observed that "in this section, the 'I' statements dominate."[4] Nine verbs in this section are in the first-person singular, and the first-person personal pronoun occurs five times. If the authenticity of the letter is accepted, the first-person reflects the apostle Paul's self-understanding of his commission to proclaim the gospel, his suffering in fulfilling his mission, his service on behalf of the Colossians, and his concern for their community. Wilson has summed up the significance of the use of the first person in this section by stating, "This very personal passage would therefore be entirely in keeping with authentic Pauline authorship. Indeed, it may be that this passage is one of the strongest arguments against any theory of pseudepigraphy."[5] Others, however, have seen the first-person statements as part of the literary device of pseudonymity. Lincoln, for instance, concludes that this section is "probably better interpreted as that of a follower looking back in admiration over the apostle's career."[6] He describes the intent of the author in the following terms: "the writer, by taking on the persona of the imprisoned apostle, establishes his credentials in the Pauline tradition and strengthens his bond with the readers so that they will be ready to accept the extensive exhortations that follow."[7] Of course, the decision about authorship rests on more than this passage, and I have already concluded that the preponderance of evidence weighs more strongly on the side of authenticity (see *Introduction*, sec. 4).

4 Bormann, 108.
5 Wilson, 190.
6 Lincoln, 613.
7 Lincoln, 613.

This section represents an expansion on the final words of the previous paragraph where Paul summarizes his ministry: "I, Paul, became a servant of this gospel" (1:23 NRSV). In the first part of this section, he describes his service with respect to the church as a whole (1:24–29), and in the second part he summarizes his ministry specifically for the Colossians and believers in the Lycus Valley (2:1–5).

Paul understands his service to be a divinely bestowed stewardship (1:25). He describes it in terms that suggests that he sees his work as a continuation of the ministry of the Servant as found in Isaiah. Christ has fulfilled the atoning work of the Servant, but Paul continues the role of the Servant to be "a light for the gentiles" (Isa 42:6; 49:6; see also Acts 13:47; 26:23). This service involves first and foremost the proclamation and teaching of the word of God (Col 1:25), which he has described earlier as "the word of truth" (1:5), "the grace of God in truth" (1:6), and "the gospel" (1:23). The center point of this gospel is Christ—the heart of God's redemptive plan for the world—who is the fulfillment of the Danielic "mystery" (Dan 2). Paul situates the Colossians in this redemptive plan, which they have heard from Epaphras (Col 1:7) and have responded to in faith (1:4).

This section is thus a prose description of the Paul's role as a servant of the gospel, with elaborations on the nature of the gospel itself (1:26–27; 2:2–3)—especially as "the mystery." The heart of the gospel is Christ himself, whom Paul explicitly identifies as the mystery. Thus, Christology continues to be of paramount importance in this letter. The final two verses of this section form a bridge to the next part of the letter, where Paul will begin his polemic against the teaching that is threatening the health and stability of the church.

Paul's joy is a theme that begins and ends this section, thus forming an *inclusio*. In the first instance, he speaks of his joy in fulfilling his apostolic service despite the suffering he experiences (1:24). In his concluding remarks, he tells of his anticipated joy in seeing God's work among the Colossians as they grow in their faith and as the church gains stability (2:5). The main theme of this entire section could be summed up by the aim expressed in the final clause: *the firmness of your faith in Christ*. This is the goal for which Paul strives and willingly suffers. He pursues this goal ardently in his ministry with all of his churches.

Many of the themes in this section bear similarity to and even employ some of the same terminology and phraseology as Eph 3:1–13. This could be accounted for by postulating that the composition of Ephesians was done on the basis of literary dependence on Colossians. Yet one can also make the case that the letters were written at the same time to the same general area and that the differences represent different pastoral concerns. The common themes include the following:

- Paul is suffering for the Colossians and experiencing affliction (θλῖψις; Col 1:24); in Ephesians he is a prisoner "for you gentiles" (Eph 3:1) and suffering affliction (θλῖψις; Eph 3:13).

- Paul has a stewardship (οἰκονομία) given to him by God (Col 1:25; Eph 3:2, 9).
- Paul has a role in making known (γνωρίζω) the mystery (μυστήριον) (Col 1:26–27; Eph 3:3–5, 10).
- The mystery had been hidden from the ages (ἀποκεκρυμμένον ἀπὸ τῶν αἰώνων) (Col 1:26; Eph 3:9).
- Christ is the content of the mystery (Col 2:2; Eph 3:4).
- The mystery is a blessing to the gentiles and, in fact, represents great "wealth" (πλοῦτος) to them (Col 1:27; 2:2; Eph 3:6, 8).
- Paul is a servant (διάκονος) of the gospel (Col 1:25; Eph 3:7).
- Paul conducts his ministry by the power (ἐνέργεια and δύναμις) of God (Col 1:29; Eph 3:7).
- The mystery (Christ) represents wisdom (σοφία; Col 2:3; Eph 3:10).
- Faith (πίστις) gives people access to Christ (Col 2:5; Eph 3:12).
- Paul wants to encourage the hearts of the Colossians (Col 2:2); in Ephesians he does not want them to lose heart (Eph 3:13).

The most substantial difference has to do with the emphasis in Ephesians on the inclusion of the gentiles—that is, they are fellow heirs, fellow members of the body, and fellow sharers with the Jews in the promise of Jesus Christ through the gospel (Eph 3:6). This emphasis is consistent with Eph 2:11–22, which stresses Christ as the basis for Jew-gentile unity in the church. It is likely that there is a much larger Jewish presence in the churches addressed in that letter. It is also quite possible that the author of Ephesians is addressing a problem of disunity within the church between Jews and gentiles.[8] Josephus attests to the presence of anti-Semitism in western Asia Minor when he says that the gentiles of that area "feel a hatred for our religion which is undeserved and unauthorized" (Josephus, *Ant.* 16.45).

In a section such as this, it is important to keep the comments of Dunn in mind: "Paul treated matters of structure and format as completely adaptable to what he wanted to say."[9] Of course, he has certain stylistic proclivities, but he writes with a great deal of flexibility in his manner of expression.

### *Structure*

The passage divides into two major sections that can be described as (1) Paul's service for the church (1:24–29), and (2) Paul's service for Christians in Colossae and the Lycus Valley (2:1–5). These two sections cohere and should be seen as an integral unit of thought.[10]

---

8 See my *Ephesians*, 174–75.

9 Dunn, 113.

10 Some commentators, however, make a stronger distinction between 1:24–29 and 2:1–5 and present them as two distinct paragraphs. See, e.g., Foster, 211–12, 232; Sumney, 96–97, 112–13.

The first section (1:24–29) is essentially one very long sentence in the Greek text consisting of 123 words. Paul is able to expand this sentence through the use of six relative clauses, prepositional phrases, participial clauses, and appositional modifiers. This is typical Pauline style.

This first section can be subdivided into three main subdivisions of thought:

1. Paul's role as a servant of the gospel along with its attendant afflictions (1:24–25)
2. The revelation of the mystery (1:26–27)
3. The proclamation of the gospel (1:28–29)

The concluding thought of the first two subdivisions leads to the content of the segments that follow. Specifically, Paul ends the first segment with "to fulfill the word of God" (1:25). He modifies this with the appositional expression "the mystery," which he then unpacks in the second segment. He ends that segment with the statement that the mystery is "Christ in you, the hope of glory" (1:27) and then begins the third and final division with a relative pronoun (ὅν) that refers to Christ and introduces his comments on proclaiming Christ (1:28–29).

The second section (2:1–5) consists of two long sentences (56 and 24 words respectively). These sentences contain two distinct thoughts:

1. Paul's efforts to encourage their hearts (2:1–3)
2. A warning about being deceived by persuasive teachings (2:4–5)

In neither of the two main sections of thought (1:24–29; 2:1–5) do we find expressions that have been regarded as traditional material.

Some have posited various chiastic arrangements for 1:24–2:5:

Alletti proposed chiastic arrangements for each of the two sections:[11]

| | | | |
|---|---|---|---|
| A | | | Paul's suffering performance for the church (1:24) |
| | B | | Paul's ecclesial competence (1:25) |
| | | C | His goal: the mystery and its recipients (1:26) |
| | | C′ | His goal: the glorious dimension of the mystery and the recipients (1:27) |
| | B′ | | The universal performance and its finality (1:28) |
| A′ | | | Paul's suffering performance (1:29) |

| | | | |
|---|---|---|---|
| A | | | Paul struggles for the Colossians and the church (2:1) |
| | B | | For their encouragement and their knowledge (2:2ab) |
| | | C | The mystery to know (2:2c–3) |
| | B′ | | For resisting specious teaching (2:4) |
| A′ | | | Paul's vigilance over the solidity of the Colossians faith (2:5) |

11 Alletti, 134.

Heil advanced the following chiastic structure:[12]

A Paul is rejoicing in the suffering of his flesh (1:24–25)
  B The richness of the glory of the mystery in all wisdom (1:26–28)
    C In this labor Paul is struggling (1:29a)
      D According to the working of Christ (1:29b)
      D′ That is working in Paul in power (1:29c)
    C′ The great struggle of Paul is on behalf of his audiences (2:1)
  B′ All the richness of the mystery of Christ in whom is all wisdom (2:2–3)
A′ Though absent in the flesh Paul is rejoicing over their faith (2:5)

Dunn suggests the following arrangement:[13]

A χαίρω (1:24)
  B γνωρίσαι (1:27)
    C πλοῦτος . . . μυστηρίου (1:27)
      D ἀγωνιζόμενος (1:29)
      D′ ἀγῶνα (2:1)
    C′ πλοῦτος . . . μυστηρίου (2:2)
  B′ ἐπίγνωσιν (2:2)
A′ χαίρω (2:5)

Moo puts forward yet another possibility:[14]

A Rejoice, flesh (1:24)
  B Make known, riches, mystery (1:27)
    C Contend (1:29)
    C′ Contending (2:1)
  B′ Knowledge, riches, mystery (2:2)
A′ Delight, body (2:5)

While there is merit to seeing the repetition of certain themes, it is much more difficult to demonstrate an intentional chiastic arrangement by the author of the letter. The majority of commentators see no such structuring present. While the various arrangements have points in common (especially Dunn and Moo), it is better to see these recurring themes as movement from general (Paul's ministry to the church at large, 1:24–29) to the specific (Paul's ministry to the Colossians, 2:1–5). Beyond the repetition, there are few additional formal characteristics to

12 Heil, *Colossians*, 83–99.
13 Dunn, 12.
14 Moo, 148.

suggest a chiastic arrangement. The lack of agreed upon formal criteria leads to substantially varying line lengths among the various proposals.

### *Setting*

The Colossian Christians and believers throughout the Lycus Valley were part of a much larger movement that was spreading rapidly throughout the Mediterranean world. The one living and true God had revealed a redemptive plan through the apostle that had reconciled people alienated from God to him. At the heart of this reconciling work is the person of Jesus Christ who, through his death and resurrection, had made an atoning sacrifice and now was living to gather people to himself in one body, the church. This redemptive plan was in fulfillment of OT expectation, although the precise nature of it was hard to discern and understand—it was a mystery. This divine mystery superseded all other mysteries as espoused and practiced by so many of the local religions. In Paul's view, there was only one mystery, and it centered on Christ.

Paul was uniquely commissioned by the one God as a servant of this mystery. This is why Paul was writing to them and was wielding an authority in what he writes to them. Paul's apostolic concern extended to all believers in the Lycus Valley, especially Colossae, Laodicea, and Hierapolis. What Paul said to them in this section of the letter was a prelude to the serious warnings he would deliver to them in the rest of the letter. In short, they were in danger of being led astray by a set of deceitful teachings and practices that the apostle referred to as "the philosophy."

Paul's absence and suffering reflected the fact that he was in Roman custody and did not have the freedom to travel and be with them. Indeed, he was "in chains" (4:3, 18). This letter, and the presence of his emissaries that carry the letter, were his only means of communicating with them at this time.

## *Comment*

**24** Νῦν χαίρω ἐν τοῖς παθήμασιν ὑπὲρ ὑμῶν, "now I rejoice in my suffering for you." As Paul begins the next section of his letter to the Colossians, he not only reveals that he has been suffering but that he is doing so on their behalf and that he is pleased to do so. The adverb νῦν that stands at the head of this discourse is a temporal marker indicating that what he is about to describe is his present experience at the time of writing.[15]

When the risen Christ appeared to Ananias after Paul's encounter on the Damascus road, the Lord revealed that Paul would suffer much for the sake of his name as he fulfilled his commission as God's "chosen instrument" (σκεῦος ἐκλογῆς) to take the gospel to the gentiles (Acts 9:15–16). Yet in the midst of his many forms of suffering, Paul has found not only comfort from the presence

15 See BDAG, s.v. νῦν 1.

of the Lord but even a sense of delight. With a strong degree of irony, he here claims in Col 1:24 that he is "rejoicing" (χαίρω) in the sufferings he is presently experiencing during his Roman custody. He had previously spoken of joy in connection with the divine redemption of the Colossians (1:11–12) and will again speak of joy in his confidence that the Colossians will gain firmness in their faith in Christ and that the church will be stabilized (2:5). But this is the only time in this letter that he reflects on his own joy amid suffering. Yet this is a significant theme in his other letters. He tells the Corinthians, "In all our affliction, I am overflowing with joy" (2 Cor 7:4) and that in all his suffering as a servant of God he experiences sorrow, yet is "always rejoicing" (2 Cor 6:10). He understands himself to be representing the suffering of Jesus to believers in his churches to the extent that "we who live are always being given over to death for Jesus' sake, so that the life of Jesus also may be manifested in our mortal flesh" (2 Cor 4:11 ESV). To the Philippians, he compared his suffering to being "poured out like a drink offering." Yet despite this suffering, he declares, "I rejoice and rejoice with all of you" (Phil 2:17). Ultimately his joy derives from his union with the resurrected and living Christ (Phil 4:4), but the circumstantial basis for his joy comes from fulfilling his role as a servant (διάκονος) of God on behalf of the churches and assisting them in their progress in the faith. Paul's understanding of his apostolic role along with its associated suffering extends not only to the churches he has directly planted but also to those for whom he bears an indirect responsibility. This includes the churches of the Lycus Valley, which were established by the evangelistic work of Epaphras during Paul's Ephesian ministry.

καὶ ἀνταναπληρῶ τὰ ὑστερήματα τῶν θλίψεων τοῦ Χριστοῦ ἐν τῇ σαρκί μου ὑπὲρ τοῦ σώματος αὐτοῦ, ὅ ἐστιν ἡ ἐκκλησία, "and I fill up in my flesh what is lacking in the afflictions of Christ for his body, which is the church." Paul not only rejoices in his sufferings, but he contends that they fulfill an important role in extending and fulfilling the mission of the Suffering Servant as he takes the gospel to the gentiles (see below).

# Excursus: Filling Up What Is Lacking in the Afflictions of Christ

In the next line of the section, Paul states, "I fill up in my flesh what is lacking in the afflictions of Christ for his body, which is the church." He appears to be saying that his own sufferings have efficacy in completing some kind of deficiency in the afflictions of Christ. Since it is not readily apparent what this deficiency is and how Paul supplements it, this verse has occasioned extensive discussion in the literature, with numerous articles and entire monographs dedicated to resolving the issue. There have been a wide variety of views expressed regarding the meaning of the verse, with no clear consensus that has emerged. Even in recent years, new solutions have been proposed to account for the difficulties and nuances of this verse. I will summarize the principal views (below),[16] and then provide a discussion of the solution that I think best explains the preponderance of the evidence. I have grouped some of the views together, while recognizing that there are nuanced differences among the authors of each particular view.

1. *Paul contributes to a divinely appointed amount of suffering that must be endured before Christ returns.* According to this view, Paul has appropriated apocalyptic language to describe his role in the context of the eschatological woes of the Messiah or the messianic birth pangs. He understands himself to be contributing to an alloted measure of suffering prior to the end of the age. These are afflictions that the people of God must face as followers of Messiah and implies no lack to the sufficiency of his atoning suffering and sacrifice upon the cross. The majority of contemporary interpreters hold this view.[17]
2. *By virtue of his union with Christ, Paul (and the people of God) continue to suffer with Christ through the experience of opposition to the gospel in the outreach and ministry of the church.* This view emphasizes that Jesus is closely identified with his corporate body and continues to suffer as his people suffer. This view is consistent with the overt emphasis in the letter on identification with Christ. In the earlier history of the church, this was the majority view.[18]

16 For a similar mapping of the views, see Maisch, 134–36. For a full history of the interpretation of this text prior to 1956, see Kremer, *Leiden Christi*, 10–154.

17 Pao, 123–26; H. Stettler, "Colossians 1:24," 185–208; Bird, 65–66; Moo, 151–52; M. Silva, "ὕστερος," *NIDNTTE* 4:578; Harris, 60; Witherington, 144–45; Thompson, 45; Dunn, 115–17; Wright, 87–90; Stuhlmann, *Das eschatologische Maß*, 99–101; Bauckham, "Colossians 1:24," 168–70; Martin, NCB, 70; Bruce, 83; Lohse, 70; Moule, 76; Bengel, 165.

18 Wilson, 171; MacDonald, 79; Hay, 71–74; Cahill, "Neglected Parallelism," 142–49; Yates,

3. *Paul understands himself to be participating in the afflictions of the Suffering Servant (of Isa 52:13–53:12) as he fulfills the task of being a light to the gentiles through taking the gospel to all the nations.* Paul identifies with and continues the role of the Suffering Servant and fulfills the expected suffering that would come through the proclamation of the gospel. This view appreciates the contextual emphasis on Paul's role as a "servant" (διάκονος) of the gospel (1:23, 25).[19]
4. *Paul sees Christ's suffering as insufficient for the full reconciliation of believers. He therefore labors to present every person mature in Christ.* This is a more recent interpretation that endeavors to put this statement in the larger context of Paul's remarks regarding reconciliation. It emphasizes that whereas the suffering of Christ on the cross was sufficient for the forgiveness of sins and bringing people into a relationship with God, the complete reconciliation of believers has not yet been attained. It is to this end that Paul labors and suffers.[20]
5. *Paul's sufferings resemble those of Christ's, which serve as a type or example for his followers.* Paul's "filling up" of the sufferings is essentially imitative of what Christ has already suffered. Believers continue the work that Christ began.[21]
6. *Paul's suffering was for the sake of Christ, and he exhibits the suffering of Christ to those he is endeavoring to save by proclaiming the gospel.* Christ's afflictions are deficient in the sense that they have not been represented to the nations. Piper notes, "God intends for the afflictions of Christ to be presented to the world through the afflictions of his people."[22] There is thus a missionary purpose behind this suffering.
7. *Paul, along with subsequent saints and martyrs, earned a treasury of merit through his sufferings that can be drawn upon by believers.*[23] Paul's sufferings supplement this treasury of merit.
8. *The language of this verse is a financial metaphor that speaks of the evangelistic distribution of the assets accrued by Christ's afflictions.* This view thus sees a missionary purpose behind the passage but finds Paul construing it in financial terms consistent with his perception that he has been entrusted

---

"Col 1.24," 91–92; Schweizer, 101–5; Scott, 31; Peake, 514–15; Ellicott, 140; Eadie, 87–89; Melanchthon, 44; Calvin, 318; Aquinas, 36–37. Earlier interpreters who held this view include Chrysostom, Theophylact, Augustine, and Anselm.

19 White, "Paul Completes the Servant's Sufferings," 181–98; McKnight, 189–91; Lincoln, 614. H. Stettler, "Colossians 1:24," 194–96, also sees this as part of the picture Paul is presenting.

20 Clark, *Completing Christ's Afflictions*, 158–63; Beale, 139–43; Foster, 219–20.

21 Perriman, "Pattern," 62–79; Abbott, 232; Lightfoot, 166. Sumney, "Vicarious Suffering," 664–80 (and in his commentary, pp. 100–101), holds to a form of this view but finds the background in the accounts of noble death in Greco-Roman literature. In these instances, it is vicarious suffering, but not expiatory.

22 Piper, *Filling Up*, 24.

23 Abbott, 230, cites Cajetan, Bellarmine, and Bisping as holding this view.

with the stewardship (οἰκονομία) of God's account (ὁ λόγος τοῦ θεοῦ). The shortage, or deficiency, is the transfer of the credit that has not been disbursed.[24]

9. *The passage is an attempt to interpret the death of Paul theologically as representative suffering and a death of one for many.* This view assumes the pseudepigraphical nature of the letter and seeks to understand the author's intent in making this statement.[25]

There are many additional views that could be mentioned, but these are not treated here because they are unlikely explanations of the text. One that can be immediately dispensed with is the view that Christ's vicarious suffering on the cross was inadequate for the remission of sins and to secure salvation for his people. One interpreter has gone so far as to say that Paul carried away the sufferings "which Christ could not carry away completely."[26] Such a view is completely at odds with what Paul has said earlier in the letter about the efficacy of Christ's work on the cross and what he will say later in the letter about it (1:12–14; 20; 2:11–15; 3:1–4). Of course, it is also contrary to the heart of his gospel as he presents it throughout his other letters (e.g., Rom 3:21–26).

The most popular view for taking into account the language and details of this text has been the apocalyptic view (view 1 above). It fits with the additional eschatological and apocalyptic language of the context. In the previous passage, Paul spoke of an eschatological presentation of believers before the divine tribunal (1:22). In this section he describes the gospel as a hidden mystery (τὸ μυστήριον τὸ ἀποκεκρυμμένον) that needed to be revealed (φανερόω) and disclosed (γνωρίζω). The idea that the people of God would experience θλίψεις, "afflictions," before the end is attested elsewhere in the NT. It is often said by advocates of this view that Second Temple Jewish texts and Christian apocalyptic texts spoke of a divinely apportioned amount of suffering that must be endured by God's people before the end of the present age.[27] But a reconsideration of these texts calls that assumption into question. The most commonly cited text is from 4 Ezra: "for he [God] has weighed the age in the balance, and measured the times by measure, and numbered the times by number; and he will not move or arouse them until that measure is fulfilled" (4 Ezra 4.36–37). Although this passage is consistent with the apocalyptic notion of the measuring of times, it says nothing about suffering or completing a divinely apportioned

24 Lang, "Disbursing the Account of God," 116–36.

25 Standhartinger, "Pauline School," 579–80. Leppä, *Making of Colossians*, 105, notes that the author of Colossians is endeavoring to protect Paul's uniqueness after his martyrdom and thus portrays the death of Paul as completing the afflictions of Christ.

26 Windisch, *Paulus und Christus*, 244 (as cited in Lohse, 69).

27 Thus, Dunn, 116, observes, "Foreshadowed is the apocalyptic thought that there is an appointed sum of suffering that must be endured in order to trigger (as it were) the final events of history (Rev 6:9–11; 4 Ezra 4.33–34)."

amount of suffering before the end. It is focused on the measuring of time itself and the completion of a set number of days until the end of the age.[28] The following context does mention the travail of a woman about to give birth and "the pangs of birth" as a metaphor for the suffering of the people of God (4 Ezra 4.40–43), but this is a signal of what God's people will experience immediately before the end of the age. It is consistent with what Jesus says in Matthew's account of the Olivet Discourse when he spoke of "the tribulation of those days" (τὴν θλῖψιν τῶν ἡμερῶν ἐκείνων; Matt 24:29) as part of a "great tribulation" (θλῖψις μεγάλη; Matt 24:21; see also Mark 13:19, 24). The onset of these afflictions is referred to as the "beginning of the birth pains" (ἀρχὴ ὠδίνων) of the Messiah just prior to his parousia (Matt 24:8; Mark 13:8).[29] But it is important to note that Paul saw these messianic woes not as a characteristic of the age[30] or what he was presently experiencing, but as an intensification of suffering that would take place just prior to Jesus's return. He associates it with the day of the Lord and the coming of Jesus like a thief in the night: "while people are saying, 'peace and safety,' destruction will come on them suddenly, as labor pains on a pregnant woman [ὥσπερ ἡ ὠδὶν τῇ ἐν γαστρὶ ἐχούσῃ], and they will not escape" (1 Thess 5:1–3 NIV).[31] One cannot miss the "sudden" (αἰφνίδιος, 1 Thess 5:3) nature of these pains. They are not typical of the age but important signposts of the impending day of the Lord.

Another text often cited in support of the apocalyptic view is Rev 6:9–11, where, after the opening of the fifth seal, the souls of the martyrs under the altar ask the Lord how long he will delay before coming in judgment. They are told "to wait a little longer, until the full number of their fellow servants, their brothers and sisters, were killed just as they had been" (Rev 6:11 NIV). But once again, the context has to do with the period of time immediately before the judgment of God upon the persecutors. The passage is thus not describing the circumstances of the entire period of time between the cross/resurrection event and the second coming of Christ.[32]

The idea that there is a divinely fixed amount of suffering is inferred without

---

28 Talbert, 201, also levels this criticism. He notes, "The limit that God has set on the final suffering is a time limit . . . not a numerical limit."

29 H. Stettler, "Colossians 1:24," 206, appeals to Stuhlmann, *Das eschatologische Maß*, 100, as demonstrating "that the concept of a preordained quota of sufferings existed in Jewish eschatology, on which Paul extensively draws." But Stuhlmann only appeals to the rabbinic texts cited in Strack-Billerbeck's comments on the messianic woes mentioned in Matt 24:8 (Strack-Billerbeck, *Kommentar*, 1:950). Some of these texts describe the circumstances just prior to the day of the Lord, including the battle of Gog and Magog, and then the judgment. None of them attest to a "quota" that must be fulfilled. Paul, however, sees the messianic woes as yet future (1 Thess 5:1–3).

30 Contra Stuhlmann, *Das eschatologische Maß*, 100.

31 Lohse, 70, cites an array of rabbinic texts that speak of "the travail of the Messiah," but fails to note that Paul understood the messianic woes to take place immediately before Christ's return in judgment.

32 Contra Dunn, 116, who speaks of the death of Christ as "the first trigger" to this apocalyptic notion of suffering for God's people.

explicit textual warrant.[33] Bauckham observes, "The suffering required is that which the task of witness demands."[34] Yet as Stettler notes, the notion of a set amount of suffering follows from the observation that the parousia will not take place until the full number of gentiles is filled up through the gentile mission (Rom 11:25).[35] But a fixed amount of suffering that must be filled up is not explicitly stated in any of these texts. Nor is it adequate to appeal to Mark 13:20 ("if the Lord had not cut short those days, no one would be saved; but for the sake of the elect, whom he chose, he has cut short those days"; NRSV) since this refers to the intensity of the suffering and not a predetermined amount.

In short, the idea of a well-known apocalyptic perspective that God has ordained a set amount of suffering for his people prior to the return of the Messiah appears to be a chimera. Furthermore, if it were not a widely known assumption within Judaism, it would have been unreasonable for Paul to have expected his readers at Colossae to grasp this nuance here. Thus, we need to look to another solution to the difficulties presented by this text.

A significant clue for interpreting this difficult passage lies in recognizing the literary parallel that frames this brief section of text:

1:24: ἀνταναπληρῶ τὰ ὑστερήματα τῶν θλίψεων τοῦ Χριστοῦ
1:25: πληρῶσαι τὸν λόγον τοῦ θεοῦ

M. Cahill has written an important article on this parallel and observes how it has seldom factored into the discussion about the passage.[36] He observes that the two verbs are cognates and that there is an inextricable connection between affliction and the proclamation of the gospel. He notes that the primary concern of the passage is not the afflictions but the spread of the gospel, with suffering accompanying the task of evangelization. He comments, "The text is not dealing with suffering as such, but precisely and concretely with the sufferings which Paul experienced as part and parcel of his work as a traveling missionary."[37] Thus, the focal point is on spreading ("fulfilling") the word of God, the missionary task of the apostolic service, and less on the suffering. Cahill's approach to this passage is insightful, and I will build on it by providing some additional evidence and by taking into account more of the context than he did.

The two parallel verbal elements—ἀνταναπληρῶ and πληρῶσαι—are obviously not the same verbs; one is a double compound verb built on the same stem

33 Other passages sometimes cited in support of this view fall short of actually demonstrating that a predetermined amount of suffering needs to be completed before the coming of the Messiah (e.g., 2 Bar. 23.4; b. Yebam. 62a; 63b). These passages actually refer to a fixed number of people to be born.

34 Bauckham, "Colossians 1:24," 169.

35 Stettler, "Colossians 1:24," 205.

36 Cahill, "Neglected Parallelism," 142–47.

37 Cahill, "Neglected Parellelism," 144.

as the other. But "fulfilling the word of God" (πληρῶσαι τὸν λόγον τοῦ θεου) is so unusual that it suggests that Paul has a rhetorical aim in employing it. That purpose may very well be to draw attention to the intrinsic connection between spreading the gospel and the experience of suffering affliction. More will be said below about the meaning of ἀνταναπληρόω. Ephesians also uses the language of filling and fullness with reference to the mission of the church. The body of Christ is filled with the fullness of God so that the members can fill the world with the gospel of Christ (Eph 1:23; see also Eph 3:19; 4:10).[38] After explaining to them his apostolic role as a "servant" (διάκονος) of the gospel, Paul encourages the readers of Ephesians "not to lose heart in my suffering for you [ἐν ταῖς θλίψεσίν μου ὑπὲρ ὑμῶν]" (Eph 3:1–13, esp. 3:13).

What is "lacking" with respect to the afflictions of Christ is therefore related to suffering associated with the spread of the gospel. Cahill notes, "As there is yet more preaching of the word to be done, so there is yet more suffering."[39] They are "the afflictions of Christ" insofar as they are done in imitation of Christ in the suffering he experienced in his earthly ministry. But they are also Christ's afflictions in that they are experienced by his body—the church. Because the resurrected Christ is intimately connected to his people, he is not only aware of their suffering but to some extent inevitably suffers with them because he lives in and through them. Paul will assure the Colossians just a few lines later that Christ is "in you" (Col 1:27). A major theme of this letter is their identity with Christ expressed, in particular, by the "in Christ" and "with Christ" language.

The interpretation of the text that I am presenting here is thus a form of view 2 summarized above, which I would articulate this way: *by virtue of his union with Christ as head of the body, the church, Paul's suffering is tantamount to Christ suffering as the apostle fulfills his stewardship of making the gospel known.* But Paul's understanding of his ministry needs to be seen in light of his commission to be a "servant" (διάκονος) of the gospel. A handful of recent studies have rightly emphasized that Paul sees himself continuing the ministry of Christ as the Servant in functioning as a light to the gentiles (view 3). Thus, I would supplement the above summary by adding that *as a servant of the gospel, Paul continues the ministry of the Isaianic servant in being a light to the gentiles.*[40]

H. Stettler has observed that "Paul considered himself to be more than just *a* messenger of Christ. Paul was convinced that his very mission was to fulfill that of the Servant of the Lord—an indication of the unique significance he

---

38 See my *Ephesians*, 116–20, for a full explanation of the nuances of this passage.

39 Cahill, "Neglected Parallelism," 143. Sumney, "Vicarious Suffering," 667, who shows no awareness of Cahill's work, contends that this view (as articulated by others), ultimately "leaves the difficult phrase 'the things lacking in Christ's afflictions' unexplained. But his concern is completely resolved if one sees the afflictions as integrally related to the spread of the gospel, which has not yet been completed.

40 This overall conclusion represents a change in my own view on this interpretational issue from the apocalyptic view, which I formerly held. See my "Colossians," *ZIBBC* 3:381–82.

ascribed to his own mission."[41] Paul makes a number of allusions to the Servant passages of Isaiah (see Isa 52:7 and 53:1 in Rom 10:15–16; Isa 65:1 in Rom 10:20; Isa 52:15 in Rom 15:21; Isa 49:8 in 2 Cor 6:2; Isa 49:1 in Gal 1:15–16).[42] J. White has also argued for this view, stating that "Paul understood his mission to the Gentiles as the fulfillment of the Isaianic servant's commission to be a light to the Gentiles."[43] What was still "lacking" in the Suffering Servant's task was the fulfillment of bringing this good news to the nations—that is, taking the gospel to the ends of the earth (Isa 49:6). Christ had completely fulfilled the vicarious suffering of the Servant by his death on the cross: "he was pierced for our transgressions" and "crushed for our iniquities" (Isa 53:5), "the LORD has laid on him the iniquity of us all" (Isa 53:6), he was "stricken for the transgression of my people" (Isa 53:8), his soul was made an offering for guilt (Isa 53:10), and "he bore the sin of many" (Isa 53:12). But the work of the Servant of the Lord was still not complete. The nations still needed to receive the light (Isa 42:6; 49:6; 60:3). The call of Isa 52:7 still needed to be fulfilled: "how beautiful upon the mountains are the feet of him who brings good news, who publishes peace, who brings good news of happiness, who publishes salvation, who says to Zion, 'Your God reigns'" (ESV). Yet, just as Jesus was "despised and rejected" (Isa 53:3), suffering would accompany the spread of the gospel.[44] This was consistently the experience of Paul as he fulfilled his commission as apostle to the gentiles (see, e.g., 1 Cor 4:9–13; 2 Cor 4:8–12; 6:4–10; 11:23–27; Eph 3:13), and it would be the experience of other disciples as they took the message to the world.

In conclusion, any deficiency or lack in the afflictions of Christ that Paul is completing has no reference to the inadequacy of his atoning sacrifice, an apocalyptically understood predetermined measure of suffering to be completed, or to his work of complete reconciliation. Rather, it has to do with completing the mission of the Servant of the Lord to take the gospel to the nations and endure the afflictions that would accompany this service. I will provide further support for this position in the treatment of the details of the text that follows.

---

41 H. Stettler, "Colossians 1:24," 194.

42 H. Stettler, "Colossians 1:24," 194.

43 White, "Paul Completes the Servant's Sufferings," 196.

44 H. Stettler, "Colossians 1:24," 194, denies that any of the language of Isa 53 applies to Paul, whereas White, "Paul Completes the Servant's Sufferings," 197–98, finds the suffering language applicable to Paul as he completes the task of bringing the gospel to the gentiles.

The verb ἀνταναπληρόω is yet another double compound verb formed with two prepositions (ἀντί + ἀνά) and the verb πληρόω. We have seen Paul employ a similar construction at the end of the hymn with his term for reconciliation (ἀπό+κατά+ἀλλάσσω). As I noted in connection with that verb, Paul has a stylistic penchant for creating compound verbs with the addition of prefixed prepositions as a way of intensifying the meaning of the verb. It is still possible, however, that he is attaching a nuance of meaning to the prepositional prefix, but this would need to be confirmed by the context. In his monograph on Col 1:24, B. Clark has undertaken a comprehensive survey of all occurrences of ἀνταναπληρόω in the Greek language.[45] He has concluded that the single-prefixed form, ἀναπληρόω, is an intensification of the unprefixed form. But the addition of the second prefix, ἀντί, does exert a semantic influence. In the thirteen occurrences of this double-compound verb (from the 4th c. BC to the 4th c. AD), he concludes:

> Assumed in the action is a previous and inadequate contribution from a source that (for whatever reason) is subsequently unable to accomplish "fullness" (however it is conceived); then in the action of the verb is a subsequent and sufficient (i.e., truly completing) contribution that, it follows, is *necessarily* from another source.[46]

One of these occurrences is particularly significant for Colossians because it uses ἀνταναπληρόω in conjunction with ὑστερέω. It is found in Eusebius's commentary on Isaiah and borrows Paul's image of an olive tree from Rom 11:

> But now instead of the severed branches being restored, the (branches) from the wild olive tree filled up the lacking part [ἀντανεπλήρωσαν τὸ ὑστεροῦν], [namely], the place of the discarded (branches); and in this way by the power of the Savior the fullness [πλήρωμα] of those who are being saved was established.[47]

The new branches are added in place of the branches that have been cut off and thereby restore what was missing. In summary, the verb means "to bring to completion in place of another."[48] This understanding of the compound verb fits well with the overall conclusion that I am suggesting—namely, that by continuing the work of the messianic servant of the Lord, Paul fills up what is lacking in the afflictions of Christ in his mission to be a light to the gentiles.

The noun ὑστέρημα refers to "the lack of what is needed."[49] As such, it can be

45 Clark, *Completing Christ's Afflictions*, 13–50.

46 Clark, *Completing Christ's Afflictions*, 49.

47 Eusebius, *Commentary on Isaiah* 2.250, as cited in Clark, *Completing Christ's Afflictions*, 32–33.

48 Clark, *Completing Christ's Afflictions*, 158.

49 BDAG, s.v. ὑστέρημα 1.

used of the lack of material resources for sustenance (e.g., Luke 21:4; 2 Cor 8:14). The psalmist declares that for those who fear the Lord, "there is no want [ὑστέρημα]" (Ps 34:9 [33:10 LXX]). Elsewhere, Paul uses the noun twice with the verb ἀναπληρόω, where "the ὑστέρημα of one person means to make up for the person's absence" or "represent the person in the person's absence" (1 Cor 16:17; Phil 2:30).[50]

The noun is modified by the genitive τῶν θλίψεων, "the afflictions." Paul employs θλῖψις about two dozen times, but never uses it to describe the suffering of Christ on the cross. In Luke's account of Paul's farewell address to the Ephesian elders, Paul claims that the Holy Spirit was testifying to him in every city that "afflictions" (θλίψεις) await him (Acts 20:23). This indeed turned out to be the case as he fulfilled his apostolic call of taking the gospel throughout the Mediterranean world. He told the Corinthians that the "affliction" (θλῖψις) he experienced in Asia caused him to despair of life (2 Cor 1:8). "Afflictions" were part of the hardships he experienced in fulfilling his ministry (2 Cor 6:4). Yet, in the midst of that, he could experience joy because he knew that "affliction produces endurance" (Rom 5:3). Our passage is the only time, however, that Paul spoke of "the afflictions of Christ" (τῶν θλίψεων τοῦ Χριστοῦ). It is unlikely that this is a reference to the passion of Christ in his crucifixion.[51] The genitive here could be taken as a possessive genitive ("Christ's afflictions"),[52] an attributive genitive (messianic afflications),[53] a subjective genitive ("the sufferings that Christ experiences"—when the members suffer, Christ also suffers),[54] a partitive genitive indicating the whole of which the τὰ ὑστερήματα are a part,[55] or as a genitive of reference ("afflictions endured for Christ's sake" or "afflictions like those of Christ").[56] The possessive interpretation is the simplest and most likely way of taking it. In this context, it refers to the afflictions that Christ continues to experience in his body, the church, as it undertakes the mission he has entrusted to it.

The afflictions Paul experiences are ἐν τῇ σαρκί μου, "in my flesh," which is a way of expressing the actual physical and painful effects of the opposition he was experiencing as he proclaimed the gospel. He also uses it in his letter to the Galatians where he describes a physical affirmity he was experiencing as he

50 BDAG, s.v. ὑστέρημα 1. Because of this common usage and the fact that Paul uses the term in his earlier writings, it is unlikely that "the philosophy" at Colossae was using it in a technical sense and that Paul was deliberately drawing on that usage of their word, as Moule, 79, contends. The Marcosian gnostics existed much later than the writing of this letter.

51 G. Delling, "ἀνταναπληρόω," *TDNT* 6:307n3, observes that "θλῖψις is never used in the NT for Jesus' own sufferings; it always refers to afflictions which result from union with Him."

52 The ESV, NRSV, RSV, NASB, NIV, and CSB all translate it, "Christ's afflictions."

53 Pao, 125.

54 This was a common interpretation in the earlier history of interpretation; so Chrysostom, Theophylact, and Augustine, as cited in Abbott, 231.

55 Campbell, 22.

56 See Harris, 59.

proclaimed the gospel to them (Gal 4:13–14; see also Rom 7:18 where he uses it to express the moral weakness of his physical body). The phrase in our verse modifies the verb (ἀνταναπληρόω) and not the noun (θλῖψις). Paul is thus "filling up" in his flesh the remaining afflictions accruing as he proclaims the gospel. As Campbell puts it, "He literally embodies the task of global gospel proclamation and the sufferings it brings."[57]

Paul's suffering is in the service of Christ's body, the church. His afflictions were not for the purpose of reducing the amount of suffering that the Colossian believers would endure, nor were they intended to shorten the time of the messianic woes. The church as a whole had been given the task of taking the gospel to the world, but the apostle had a special commission to take the gospel to the gentiles and thus to fulfill the prophecy of Isaiah that the mission of the Servant was to be a light to the gentiles.

**25** ἧς ἐγενόμην ἐγὼ διάκονος κατὰ τὴν οἰκονομίαν τοῦ θεοῦ τὴν δοθεῖσάν μοι εἰς ὑμᾶς πληρῶσαι τὸν λόγον τοῦ θεοῦ, "of which I became a servant in accordance with the stewardship from God that was given to me for you to fulfill the word of God." Paul here reiterates his divinely appointed role as a διάκονος, "servant," but expands on the focus from being a servant of the gospel (1:23) to a servant of the church. The feminine singular relative pronoun ἧς refers to ἡ ἐκκλησία, "the church," mentioned in the previous line; he also uses much of the same language that he did in 1:23 (οὗ ἐγενόμην ἐγὼ Παῦλος διάκονος).[58] The shift of focus from the gospel to the church is natural for Paul, since building the church is the necessary entailment of proclaiming the gospel. His entire course of ministry had been equally devoted to these two interrelated and complementary goals. He told the Philippians that if he were to survive his imprisonment, he would continue to devote his life to "the progress [προκοπή] of the gospel" and to their "progress [προκοπή] in the faith" (Phil 1:12, 25). He saw the creation of church communities as the necessary means by which believers would grow in the faith. Throughout the course of his ministry, he never proclaimed the gospel without working to immediately establish a church among those who had responded. As the apostle to the gentiles (Rom 11:13; Gal 2:8), Paul understood himself to have a responsibility to more than one local church and to more churches than he had personally established. As Moo observes, this can be seen most clearly in the way that he claims authority over the Roman church, a group he has never met, based on his apostolic commission (Rom 1:5; 11:13; see also Rom 1:13–14; 15:16).[59] He is here appealing to that same commission (and consequent authority) to set the stage for the appeals he is about to make to the Colossians to resist the teaching and practices of "the philosophy."

Paul grounds his unique role in the commission he received from God.

---

57 Campbell, 23.

58 On διάκονος, see my comments on 1:23.

59 Moo, 153.

The preposition (κατά) serves "to introduce the norm which governs something."[60] In this case, the stewardship that Paul received from God has determined the course of his life and ministry. Luke narrates Paul's divine call on three separate occasions in the book of Acts (Acts 9:1–30; 22:1–21; 26:1–23), which emphasizes its importance not only for Paul but for the spread of the gospel and the establishment of the church. Paul refers to the stewardship that he received from God as an οἰκονομία. This term was used frequently in papyri, inscriptions, and Greek literature for the management of a household, estate, or even the administration of a city.[61] Paul used the term when writing to the Corinthians to describe his apostolic role as "entrusted with a stewardship" (οἰκονομίαν πεπίστευμαι; 1 Cor 9:17). This should be correlated with two earlier references to the related noun οἰκονόμος: he and his ministry companions are "stewards of the mysteries of God" (οἰκονόμους μυστηρίων θεοῦ; 1 Cor 4:1), and "it is required of stewards [οἰκονόμοις] that they be found faithful" (1 Cor 4:2). J. Goodrich has made a strong case that the most relevant background to this language is to be found in the context of private commercial administration.[62] This would include supervising such things as a rural estate, a factory, an urban shop (*taberna*), a mine, a bath, a granary, and an array of other businesses.[63] The οἰκονόμος was most commonly a slave or freedman and thus bore a responsibility of compulsory obedience to the master or patron.[64] Nevertheless, the οἰκονόμος held a significant level of responsibility and wielded a great deal of authority in making investments and managing business affairs. In many instances, the manager oversaw a team of subordinates. Because of this high level of responsibility, the chief ethical virtue sought in the manager was loyalty (πίστις / *fides*).[65] The terms οἰκονομία and οἰκονόμος appear numerous times in the inscriptions of Asia Minor and would have been readily understood by the readers of Colossians. For instance, in nearby Aphrodisias, a person named Menandros is mentioned as the οἰκονόμος of the city.[66]

---

60 BDAG, s.v. κατά 5a.

61 See BDAG, s.v. οἰκονομία; LSJ s.v. οἰκονομία.

62 Goodrich, *Paul as an Administrator of God*, 200 (see ch. 4 of his monograph for the evidence).

63 Goodrich, *Paul as an Administrator of God*, 81.

64 Goodrich, *Paul as an Administrator of God*, 73, 78.

65 Goodrich, *Paul as an Administrator of God*, 96. Goodrich concludes that one of the reasons Paul chose this metaphor to use in the Corinthian correspondence was that "Paul sought simultaneously to emphasize the servility and authority of apostles in order to eliminate partisanship and to defend himself against critics" (202). Although this study brings a substantial amount of insight into the role of the οἰκονόμος, I am not convinced that it needs to exclude the municipal οἰκονόμος as informing Paul's use of the metaphor. There are many overlapping characteristics and responsibilities. It would be somewhat surprising for the private sphere to be the only pertinent background to this language, especially when Paul specifically mentions a man named Erastus who served as the οἰκονόμος τῆς πόλεως at Corinth (Rom 16:13) and because οἰκονόμος was a common civic title in Asia Minor. Erastus likely served as either a *quaestor* or an *aedilis* for the city. He would thus have had high social status and significant responsibility for managing the financial affairs of the city.

66 *CIG* 2811.3–4.

In Ephesians, Paul uses οἰκονομία to refer both to the comprehensive plan that God has designed for the redemption of the world (Eph 1:10; 3:9) and to his responsibility to serve as a steward (οἰκονομία) of that plan (Eph 3:2). It is the latter usage of the term that overlaps with its occurrence here in Colossians. In fact, the language of both texts corresponds significantly:

Col 1:25: τὴν οἰκονομίαν τοῦ θεοῦ τὴν δοθεῖσάν μοι εἰς ὑμᾶς
Eph 3:2: τὴν οἰκονομίαν τῆς χάριτος τοῦ θεοῦ τῆς δοθείσης μοι εἰς ὑμᾶς

In Ephesians, he refers to his call as a stewardship of the grace of God. But the gospel itself could be referred to as "the gospel of God's grace" (τὸ εὐαγγέλιον τῆς χάριτος τοῦ θεοῦ; Acts 20:24), and Paul had referred to the gospel earlier in Colossians as "the grace of God in truth" (1:6). He regularly associated his experience of God's grace with his apostleship (see Rom 1:5; 12:3; 15:15; 1 Cor 3:10; 15:10; Gal 2:9). This responsibility for the stewardship of the gospel was bestowed upon Paul when he received his call from the risen Lord on the Damascus road. He elaborates on this to the Galatians when he says that God "set me apart from birth and called me by his grace, [and] was pleased to reveal his Son in me so that I might preach him among the gentiles" (Gal 1:15–16). He tells the Colossians at Col 1:25 that his stewardship came directly from God (τοῦ θεοῦ should be interpreted as a genitive of source).

He says more explicitly that the duty of his stewardship was "to fulfill the word of God" (πληρῶσαι τὸν λόγον τοῦ θεου). The verb πληρόω refers to bringing something to completion that has already begun.[67] Here Paul speaks of his divine calling to devote his life to making the gospel known. Earlier he had told the Roman church, "So from Jerusalem all the way around to Illyricum, I have fully proclaimed the gospel of Christ [πεπληρωκέναι τὸ εὐαγγέλιον τοῦ Χριστου]" (Rom 15:19 NIV). This does not mean that he had completed his stewardship of the gospel but that he had accomplished a significant portion of that call (see Acts 14:26 where Luke reports that Paul and his companions had "fulfilled" [ἐπλήρωσαν] a portion of the work).[68] The usage of this word in the sense of fulfilling a responsibility may also be seen at the end of this letter when Paul admonishes Archippus, "see that you fulfill [πληροῖς] the ministry that you have received in the Lord" (Col 4:17).

As I noted earlier, Paul's divine vocation to fulfill the proclamation of the word of God formally corresponds to his comments at the outset of this section that he is filling up the afflictions of Christ. The verbs are the same (with the

67 BDAG, s.v. πληρόω 3.

68 Riesner, *Paul's Early Period*, 241–53, contends that Paul interpreted his calling in light of Isa 66:18–21 and that he completed proclaiming the gospel and establishing churches along an arc that extended from Tarsus to Cilicia, Lydia, Mysia, Bithynia, Macedonia, and to the far west (see Isa 66:19).

verb in 1:27 being a compounded form), and both statements mutually interpret each other. The idea is that as Paul fulfills his task of taking the gospel to the gentiles, he would experience suffering. These afflictions were a necessary entailment of his proclamation of the word of God.[69] Luke records that the Lord said to Paul when he called him, "I will show him how much he must suffer for the sake of my name" (Acts 9:16).

**26** τὸ μυστήριον τὸ ἀποκεκρυμμένον ἀπὸ τῶν αἰώνων καὶ ἀπὸ τῶν γενεῶν - νῦν δὲ ἐφανερώθη τοῖς ἁγίοις αὐτοῦ, "which is the mystery hidden from the ages and the generations, but is now revealed to his saints." Paul elaborates on the word of God by calling it a mystery that was long concealed but that has now been revealed. The expression τὸ μυστήριον, "the mystery," is in apposition to τὸν λόγον τοῦ θεοῦ, "the word of God," and thus shows that there is a close connection between the mystery and the gospel. His reference to the mystery triggers an expanded discussion on the nature and content of the message that he proclaims as a servant of the gospel and as a steward of God. This is his second expansion on the gospel (see 1:5–8).

Why Paul would choose the term μυστήριον to describe the gospel and what precisely he means by it requires further discussion. As a Jew, trained as a rabbi, fully conversant with the Hebrew Bible, and raised in a context where the impending apocalyptic triumph of God was expected to break into human existence, Paul would have been intimately familiar with the book of Daniel. As the fountainhead of the prevailing apocalyptic worldview within Judaism, Daniel contributed much to the structure and content of Paul's thinking—including the idea of history as summed up in two ages (this present evil age and the age to come), the language of the kingdom, God's plan of redemption, as well as an understanding of life under the influence of evil spiritual powers. The second chapter of Daniel narrates a dream that was given to the Babylonian king, Nebuchadnezzar II. The troubling dream required interpretation through divine revelation, and Daniel was the only one in the royal court who was able to provide this to the king. In his interpretation of the dream, Daniel speaks of it as a mystery that required divine revelation: "there is a God in heaven who reveals mysteries [רָזִין; μυστήρια], and he has made known to King Nebuchadnezzar what will be in the latter days" (Dan 2:28 ESV). After Daniel has explained the meaning of the various elements of the dream, Nebuchadnezzar proclaims, "Truly, your God is God of gods and Lord of kings, and a revealer of mysteries [רָזִין; μυστήρια], for you have been able to reveal this mystery [רָזָה; τὸ μυστήριον]" (Dan 2:47 ESV). The content of the dream/mystery had to do with God's plan for the ages and disclosed that there would be a succession of

69 Pao, 128, notes that "to suffer is part of the proclamation of the word of God." He rightly advises that "the significance of the parallels between Paul's need to 'fill up' that which is lacking in the afflictions of Christ in v. 24 and his commitment to fulfill the word of God in this verse should not be downplayed."

kingdoms but in the end, "the God of heaven will set up a kingdom that shall never be destroyed" (Dan 2:44 ESV). It would be a kingdom that would extend to the entire earth (Dan 2:35). This passage provides the essential backdrop for understanding Paul's use of the word "mystery." Yet the book of Daniel was the source of the usage of the term in other Jewish literature (1 En. 9.6; 16.3; 52.1–9; 4 Ezra 4.36–38; 1QS 9.18; et al). A commentary on Habakkuk from Qumran speaks of how "God has disclosed all the mysteries [כול רזי דברי עבדיו] of the words of his servants, the prophets" to the Teacher of Righteousness in the context of God revealing all that would happen at the end of the age (1QpHab 7.1–16, esp. line 5). Paul's Jewish readers of Colossians would no doubt think immediately of the Jewish apocalyptic context and the book of Daniel.

But in the vastly gentile context of the Lycus Valley in Roman Asia, Paul's non-Jewish readers would have their own understandings of the usage of the term "mystery" based on the widespread use of the term in the local cults that boasted of ritual initiations termed "mysteries." The term appears numerous times in the inscriptions of Asia Minor. Below is a brief survey of some of those occurrences:

- At the famous Apollo temple at Claros (just north of Ephesus), an envoy of Lappa (Crete) is mentioned who consulted the oracle. As part of his procedure, he went through ritual mystery initiation: παραλαβὼν τὰ μυστήρια ἐνεβάτευσεν, "he received the mysteries and then he entered."[70] This text will also be discussed later because it contains a rare word (ἐμβατεύω) that appears in Col 2:18.
- At Dionysopolis (Phrygia), thirty miles north of Colossae, an inscription describes how a certain Gaius Antonius Apellas was struck by the local god many times because he would not come and celebrate the mystery rite (τῷ μυστηρίῳ), although he was summoned to do so.[71] The god is not explicitly mentioned but is likely Apollo Lairbenos, since the inscription was discovered close to his sanctuary.
- In Lagina (Caria), about eighty miles southwest of Colossae, an inscription honors Phanias Aristeou for overseeing "the mysteries" (τῶν μυστηρίων) many times.[72] No deity is mentioned in this inscription, but the most likely candidate would be the goddess Hekate, whose cult center was in Lagina.
- An inscription from Panamara (just south of Lagina) mentions the ritual performance of mysteries (μυστηρίοις θρησκεύεσθαι; [ἐ]πιτελεσθῆναι μυστήρια).[73] No specific deity is mentioned.

---

70 Macridy, "Antiquités," 46. Other texts from Claros also mention performance of mysteries: ἐπετέλε[σε] καὶ μυστήρια; see Macridy, "Antiquités," 50 (no. 15), 51 (no. 16), and 52 (no. 20).

71 *MAMA* 4.104–5 (no. 281). The text is discussed in Petzl, "Beichtinschriften," 126 (no. 108). See also Burkert, *Ancient Mystery Cults*, 138n55.

72 *IStrat* 658.5–10, esp. line 8. See also, *IStrat* 676.8; 705.17.

73 *IStrat* 14.4, 8.

- Another inscription found at Panamara records a letter of a priest of Zeus inviting people to a festival of the god that will involve his "mystery" (μυστήριον).[74]
- In Sardis, an inscription mentions the mysteries of Sabazios (μυστηρίων Σαβαζίου).[75] Another mentions the mysteries of the moon god, Mēn (τὰ τοῦ Μηνὸς μυστήρια).[76] Yet another refers to a mystery for Attis (μυστηρίῳ Ἄττει).[77]
- At Cremna (Pisidia), about eighty-five miles east-southeast of Colossae, a priest and priestess are mentioned in connection with a mystery rite (μυστήρια τῆς θ<ε>οῦ) in honor of the Ephesian Artemis.[78]
- The inscriptions of Ephesus demonstrate the frequent use of "mystery" (μυστήριον) with reference to the cult of the Ephesian Artemis.[79] In one of these, a priestess of Artemis named Aurelia is honored for reviving "all the mysteries of the goddess" according to the ancient custom.[80] But mysteries were celebrated in other cults in Ephesus, as in the cult of Demeter Karpophoros (τὰ μυστήρια ἐπιτελεῖν).[81]

Anyone living in Roman Asia would be very familiar with this term because of its extensive use in cults that had ritual initiations. Of course, the term was used extensively outside of Asia Minor for initiation into the mysteries of a deity. It is widely known that "the most influential and popular of the Greek mysteries were those of Demeter and Kore at Eleusis" (thirteen miles northwest of Athens).[82] Many ancient cults had ritual inititiation practices termed "mysteries." Among them were Dionysus (the Bacchic mysteries), Orpheus, Isis, Osiris, Mithras, and many more. Mystery rituals of initiation were also prominent within magical practices and often served as the basis for the adept gaining knowledge of spiritual and divine matters and becoming endued with spiritual power. But within Anatolia, and Phrygia in particular, the most well-known cult where mystery rituals were practiced was the cult of Cybele (the Great Mother) and her consort, Attis. Many ancient authors, including Arnobius, Livy, Catullus, Prudentius, Lucian, and Apuleius, describe these rites.[83] The term "mystery" was used in connection with all of these cults because of the emphasis

74 *IStrat* 23.1–4, esp. line 4. See also *IStrat* 30.1–5, esp. line 3.

75 *SEG* 29.1205.9–13. This text is discussed by Horsley in *NewDocs* 1:21–23 (§3).

76 *SEG* 49.1676[1].28.

77 *SEG* 43.866.6.

78 *SEG* 42.1223.

79 *IEph* 26.3; 667A.10; 702.13; 987.11; etc. See Immendorfer, *Ephesians and Artemis*, 271n648, for a full listing.

80 *IEph* 3059.3–6.

81 *IEph* 213.1–15, esp. line 14.

82 Meyer, *Ancient Mysteries*, 17. See his collection of the most important ancient texts describing the mysteries as they were celebrated at Eleusis (16–45).

83 The texts are conveniently assembled in Meyer, *Ancient Mysteries*, 111–54.

on maintaining secrecy regarding the nature of the rituals and the associated visions and revelations.

Because of the prominence of "mysteries" in the religions of the Roman world, it has been tempting for some scholars to contend for this being the direct source for the term as it is used in Colossians (and Ephesians). Lightfoot, for instance, asserted that Paul had borrowed this term from the ancient mysteries (along with a handful of other terms), which he filled with new content.[84] Some within the history of religions school of thought also made the claim that Paul drew directly on mystery-cult usage.[85] Bultmann, in particular, argued that Paul described the death of Christ "in analogy with the death of a divinity of the mystery religions."[86] For him, the language of the mysteries thus pervaded Paul's conceptual world and vocabulary (including dying and rising with Christ, baptism, and the Lord's Supper).

Paul used the term "mystery" in his other letters to describe various aspects of the gospel that he proclaims (e.g., Rom 16:25–26; 1 Cor 2:7; 15:51). In each of these, he is not describing secret rites known and performed only by those who were members of the community. Rather, he is using the term to characterize the nature of God's plan of salvation as something that was previously unknown in its manner of execution and could only be understood by divine revelation. In this regard, his use of the term reflects the Danielic and Jewish apocalyptic use of the expression. In an important monograph, B. Gladd concludes that "mystery in Daniel and Second Temple Judaism is a rich technical term, denoting an eschatological revelation of God's wisdom."[87] This is seen especially in 1 Cor 2:7: "We declare God's wisdom, a mystery that has been hidden and that God destined for our glory before time began" (NIV). The language of the "hiddenness" and "disclosure" of the mystery corroborates this background to the term and its usage here.[88]

The question naturally arises as to what exactly was hidden that required divine disclosure? Gladd aptly concludes that, in this text, "the mystery is the exalted, kingly Messiah affixed to the cross."[89] No one could have conceived

---

84 Lightfoot, 167–68. See also Scott, 32.

85 This idea comes to its most complete expression in Windisch, *Paulus und Christus*, 215–18. He contended that Paul represented Christianity as a mystery religion and that he served as a mystagogue. See also Reitzenstein, *Mystery Religions*, 389–90, 458; Reumann, "Stewards of God," 349.

86 Bultmann, *Theology*, 1:298–300, esp. 298.

87 Gladd, *Revealing the Mysterion*, 108.

88 The Danielic and Jewish apocalyptic background to the usage of the term "mystery" in Paul's writings in general and Colossians in particular continues to be the consensus view in NT scholarship. See also Beale and Gladd, *Hidden but Now Revealed*, 202–4; Bockmuehl, *Revelation and Mystery*, 221–30; Caragounis, *Ephesian Mysterion*, 143–46; Brown, *Semitic Background*, 1–30, 56–66; K. Prümm, "Mystères," *DBSup* 6:1–225, esp. 173–225; Bornkamm, "μυστήριον," *TDNT* 4:824; and most commentaries.

89 Gladd, *Revealing the Mysterion*, 156.

that the messianic Lord of glory would suffer and die as a prelude to his eschatological reign.[90]

Nevertheless, given the widespread usage of the term in the context of the secret rituals of the various local religions, it is surprising that Paul does not avoid using the term altogether.[91] Many believers at Colossae would have turned to Christ from a background in the cults of the local deities and brought with them an understanding of the term "mystery." It is also likely that the advocates of "the philosophy" learned from their experience of illumination through mystery-cult initiation and may possibly have even been using the term "mystery" to describe the source of their understanding of spiritual insight and power. Yet Paul shows no reticence in using the term and, in fact, uses it four times in this letter (see also 1:27; 2:2; and 4:3). But he does not leave the term devoid of explanation. He points to Christ as *the* mystery (2:2) and elaborates on the role of Christ as the central figure to the one living and true God's plan of redemption. In a powerful rhetorical strategy, he effectively subverts his readers' prior understanding of "mystery" and replaces it with his own definition rooted in the OT and expressed in the gospel.[92] Part of the implicit message of this text would be that the Colossians made the right decision in turning to Christ from their prior experience with mystery cults, and now they once again need to turn away from a dangerous and pseudo-mystery in "the philosophy" and reaffirm their allegiance to Christ alone.

The fact that the mystery was previously hidden (ἀποκεκρυμμένον) is consistent with its usage in Daniel where the text affirms that God alone "reveals deep and hidden [ἀπόκρυφα] things" (Dan 2:22 Theodotian).[93] The term can be used generally of hiding or concealing something (e.g., a person hidden [ἀποκεκρυμμένον] in a cistern [2 Macc 10:37] or "no unrighteous deed of yours will be hidden" [οὐκ ἔσται ὑμῖν ἔργον ἀποκεκρυμμένον; 1 En. 98.6]), but because of the collocation here with "mystery," "revelation," and "disclosure," the apocalyptic overtones come to the foreground.

More specifically, Paul says the mystery was hidden ἀπὸ τῶν αἰώνων καὶ ἀπὸ τῶν γενεῶν, "from the ages and generations." Although αἰῶνες was a term that could be used of spiritual powers, and the singular form of the word could be used for the god, Aion, there is no sufficient reason to interpret it in that

90 Beale, 145–46, clarifies that the content was not completely unknown, but that the term in this context indicates "a notion of making much clearer something in the OT that was to some small degree partially understood in the OT itself."

91 Some have objected to seeing any allusion to mystery cults here by contending that the readers would have made no connection because Paul uses the singular (e.g., Pao, 128; Lohse, 74), but the inscriptional evidence shows that the singular could, in fact, be used to refer to the mystery of a local deity (see above).

92 Contra Wright, 91, who notes, "It is unlikely that the word contains a veiled allusion, or an implicit challenge, to pagan mystery-cults," who merely asserts this opinion without argumentation.

93 The LXX uses the term σκοτεινός, "dark" or "obscure" things.

sense here.[94] The adverb νῦν, "now," that begins the following line suggests that the phrase should be taken in a temporal sense. Furthermore, Paul never uses the term with reference to spiritual powers. The combination of the two terms is found in the LXX to refer to extended periods of time (Exod 40:15; Lev 3:17). It also appears in the doxology of Eph 3:21, εἰς πάσας τὰς γενεὰς τοῦ αἰῶνος τῶν αἰώνων, as a way of expressing "forever."

The time of revelation has now come, and God has disclosed the mystery through the proclamation of the word. The term φανερόω is used synonymously with ἀποκαλύπτω and can thus be translated, "reveal."[95] The revelation of Jesus as the Messiah and as the center point of God's plan of redemption is given to all "the saints."[96]

**27** οἷς ἠθέλησεν ὁ θεὸς γνωρίσαι τί τὸ πλοῦτος τῆς δόξης τοῦ μυστηρίου τούτου ἐν τοῖς ἔθνεσιν, "God willed to disclose to them what is the wealth of the glory of this mystery among the gentiles." Paul continues his discourse about the mystery by specifying to whom it has now been revealed and by elaborating on the content of the mystery. The plural relative pronoun (οἷς) refers to "the saints" in the previous line as the recipients of this revelation. Rather than simply saying that "God revealed it," he inserts the verb ἠθέλησεν to underline that this overall plan of salvation was not simply an ad hoc reaction but a constituent part of the divine will. Paul has used the noun form (θέλημα) on three other occasions in this letter to speak of God's plan (1:1, 9; 4:12). Paul tells the Galatians that Christ "gave himself for our sins to deliver us from the present evil age, according to the will [τὸ θέλημα] of our God and Father" (Gal 1:4). Ephesians speaks of "the mystery of his will" (Eph 1:9) whereby God "predestined us for adoption to himself as sons through Jesus Christ, according to the purpose of his will [τοῦ θελήματος αὐτοῦ]" (Eph 1:5 ESV).

The verb γνωρίζω, "to disclose," continues Paul's use of apocalyptic language. Here it may allude more specifically to Daniel's revelation of the dream about God's plan for the ages to King Nebuchadnezzar. The verb appears eleven times in that chapter in Theodotion's version of Daniel (Dan [Th.] 2:5, 6, 10, 15, 17, 23 [2x], 28, 29, 30, 45). Daniel tells the king that "there is a God in heaven who reveals mysteries, and he has made known [ἐγνώρισεν] to King Nebuchadnezzar what will be in the latter days" (Dan [Th.] 2:28). The object of that revelation is introduced in Col 1:27 by the interrogative pronoun (τί).[97] Although one would expect "the mystery" to be the object, the focal point is on the noun πλοῦτος, "wealth," which is modified by the attributive genitive δόξης,

94 Those who take it as a reference to cosmic powers here include Lindemann, 34; Dibelius, 24–25 (he contends that both expressions, αἰῶνες and γενεαί, are coextensive with the οἱ ἄρχοντες τοῦ αἰῶνος τούτου in 1 Cor 2:6–8); Scott, 33.

95 R. Bultmann and D. Lührmann, "φανερόω," *TDNT* 9:4.

96 See the discussion of ἁγίοι at 1:2.

97 Although it could be seen as introducing an indirect question (so, Harris, 63), it is better to interpret its use here as an object marker (Pao, 130).

"glory." "Mystery" finally appears in the third position in the genitive case, also modifying "wealth," and it should probably be taken as a genitive of reference.[98] The mystery is what is revealed, but the buildup is lavish. The combination of πλοῦτος and δόξα is found many times in the LXX. It is often found in contexts extolling the "wealth and honor" of kings (1 Chr 29:28; 2 Chr 17:5; 18:1; 32:27; Esth 1:4). David proclaims that "riches and honor" come from God (1 Chr 29:12; see also 1 Kgs 3:13; 2 Chr 1:12). Here it is applied in a metaphorical sense to the mystery. Ephesians uses the same language to extol "the wealth of his glorious [ὁ πλοῦτος τῆς δόξης] inheritance in the saints" (Eph 1:18) where the beneficiary is God himself, who is presented as treasuring his people (now consisting of gentiles as well as Jews) as his own inheritance.

The beneficiaries of this glorious wealth are the gentiles. They have now been included in God's plan of salvation through Jesus the Messiah. No longer are they enemies of God and estranged from him (Col 1:21), but through Christ they are reconciled to God (1:22), redeemed (1:14), and share in the inheritance with the Jews (1:12). Ephesians elaborates on the inclusion of the gentiles as part of the mystery by calling them συγκληρονόμα, σύσσωμα, συμμέτοχα, "fellow heirs," "fellow members of the body," and "fellow sharers (of the promise)" (Eph 3:6). This follows the eloquent declaration that Christ has destroyed the division separating Jews and gentiles and has reconciled them both in one body to God through the cross (Eph 2:14–16).

The gentile readers of Colossians would have received this message with joy and gratitude for the opportunity to be included in the one true and living God's plan of salvation through Christ. The emphasis on it as "glorious wealth" to them highlights its extraordinary value and would reinforce their decision to forsake their former gods and embrace the God of Israel. It also prepares the way for Paul's polemic to resist the teaching of "the philosophy," which is not according to Christ (Col 2:8).

ὅ ἐστιν Χριστὸς ἐν ὑμῖν, ἡ ἐλπὶς τῆς δόξης, "which is Christ in you, the hope of glory." One of the remarkable features of God's plan of salvation through Christ is that the resurrected and glorified Messiah would pneumatically indwell his people. The neuter relative pronoun (ὅ) refers to the "mystery" (μυστήριον) and enables Paul to predicate this unique feature of new life in Christ. Although almost all English versions render ἐν ὑμῖν as "in you,"[99] some interpreters suggest that it should be understood as "among you."[100] On its own, the expression could be understood either way. The argument for taking it as "among" points to the immediately preceding phrase, ἐν τοῖς ἔθνεσιν, "among the gentiles," as a

---

98 Moo, 157, takes it as an expexegetical genitive, but the result is equivalent. Both ways of taking the genitive specify the content of the riches.

99 The NJB is one of the only exceptions ("among you").

100 E.g., Barth and Blanke, 265; Bockmuehl, *Revelation and Mystery*, 182; Wolter, 105; Pokorný, 103; Aletti, 143; Lohse, 76.

contextual reason for understanding it in the same way here. The idea would thus be that the mystery consists of Christ "preached among the nations" and is now "the Lord proclaimed in the community's midst."[101] The majority of interpreters, however, have rightly interpreted the expression to refer to the indwelling of Christ in every believer. Most of the time, Paul speaks of believers being "in Christ," but he sometimes also refers to Christ indwelling believers (2 Cor 13:5; Gal 2:20; 4:19). What Paul says here is similar to what he told the Romans (Χριστὸς ἐν ὑμῖν) in a passage characterizing the new life of the believer (Rom 8:10). In that passage, the indwelling of Christ is made coextensive with possession of the Spirit (Rom 8:9, 11) and serves as the basis of future hope as well as an empowering presence to overcome evil practices (8:11, 13).[102] In Colossians, the empowering presence of Christ in every individual (note the triple reference to πάντα ἄνθρωπον in Col 1:28) is the basis for presenting every person "mature" before God at the divine tribunal. Paul will subsequently tell the Colossians that they have been "filled" in him (2:10). Their union with Christ and solidarity with him is a distinctive emphasis in Colossians as expressed by the many "in him" and "with him" statements. This present and dynamic connection with Christ is central to Paul's understanding of the Christian life in Colossians. It will also serve the Colossians as the basis for how they can resist the influence of "the philosophy."

The present indwelling of Christ also provides them with the assurance that they will be with him at his future coming in glory (see also 3:4).[103] The hope of a glorious future with Christ has already been expressed in the final line of the hymn, which speaks of Christ's reconciling work and ushering in an era of universal peace (1:20), as well as in Paul's reference to Christ presenting them as holy, blameless, and innocent before God at the final judgment (1:22; see also 1:28). Paul has used the expression ἐλπὶς τῆς δόξης, "the hope of glory," previously when he declared that through Jesus "we have also obtained access by faith into this grace in which we stand, and we rejoice in hope of the glory of God" (Rom 5:2 ESV). The genitive case should be taken as an objective genitive—that is, the hope of sharing in the glory.[104] Throughout Paul's letters, hope is grounded in Christ and points forward to the return of Christ and the glorious future that believers will share with him. In Titus, this eschatological future is memorably expressed as "waiting for our blessed hope, the appearing of the glory of our great God and Savior Jesus Christ" (Titus 2:13).[105]

---

101 So Lohse, 76.

102 See also 2 Cor 13:3, 5; Gal 2:20; 4:19; Eph 3:17.

103 Campbell, *Hope of Glory*, 278, comments, "Christ represents the source and means through which glory may be accessed. . . . The glory that Christ facilitates for gentiles (and Jews) stands as the endpoint and *telos* of the mystery that was hidden for ages and generations but now revealed to God's people."

104 See Harris, 65.

105 Bornkamm, "Hoffnung," 56–64, contends that the author of Colossians has completely recast

In summary, the mystery that Paul proclaims is multifaceted, but it is centered on Jesus Christ as the Messiah. Paul states this succinctly in Col 2:2: "the mystery of God is Christ" (see also Eph 3:4).[106] Christ is central to the divine plan of salvation. But no previous generation of God's people could have anticipated the full extent of what God would accomplish through his Messiah (see Eph 3:5). This pertains especially to Messiah's suffering, death, and resurrection as the means for making full and final atonement for his people, the full inclusion of the gentiles in the people of God, and the pneumatic indwelling of the resurrected Christ in every believer. There is thus one mystery, Christ, with many applications.

**28** ὃν ἡμεῖς καταγγέλλομεν νουθετοῦντες πάντα ἄνθρωπον καὶ διδάσκοντες πάντα ἄνθρωπον ἐν πάσῃ σοφίᾳ, "we proclaim him, admonishing every person and teaching every person in all wisdom." Here Paul further unpacks the meaning of his stewardship of the mystery. It involves first and foremost the proclamation of the gospel, but it also entails faciliating the growth of believers in the Christian communities.

The masculine relative pronoun (ὅν) refers to Christ in the previous line. Christ himself is the object of Paul's proclamation. He is also the content of the mystery. For Paul to proclaim Christ is tantamount to proclaiming the mystery or preaching the word of God.

Throughout Col 1:23–27, the subject has been the first-person singular with reference to Paul and his commission from God (e.g., οὗ ἐγενόμην ἐγὼ Παῦλος διάκονος [1:23; see also 1:25]). Now he shifts the subject to the first-person plural (ἡμεῖς) to include not only his missionary associate, Timothy (see 1:1), and the person who brought the gospel to the Colossians, Epaphras (see 1:7), but possibly all who have a leadership function within the Christian communities. Paul is uniquely called as a servant of God to take the gospel to the gentiles, but the role of ministering the gospel extends to all leaders of every Christian community.

The governing verb of the following section is καταγγέλλομεν, "proclaim," which is then modified by two adverbial participles—νουθετοῦντες and διδάσκοντες, "admonishing and teaching." These are most naturally interpreted as participles of means to clarify how the proclamation is carried out.[107] This could mean that the evangelistic message will often involve admonishing and teaching as Paul does, for instance, in the synagogue at Thessalonica when

Paul's future hope into a strictly spatial understanding of above and below in a way that is expressive of cosmic spheres of power. For him, hope has thus become an object that already lies in heaven prepared for believers. But it is unlikely that there was gnostic influence on the author of the letter or on the Colossian community. As I have noted, there are also a handful of references to the future return of Christ, the divine judgment, and the future eschatological era of peace in the letter.

106 It is best to interpret the genitive in Eph 3:4 (τῷ μυστηρίῳ τοῦ χριστοῦ) as a genitive of apposition, "the mystery, which is Christ." See Arnold, *Ephesians*, 188.

107 So also Campbell, 25.

Luke reports that he "reasoned" (διελέξατο) with them from the Scriptures, "explaining and proving" (διανοίγων καὶ παρατιθέμενος) that it was necessary for the Christ to suffer and to rise from the dead (Acts 17:2–3). But it more likely demonstrates that Paul understood the proclamation of the word to include not only a presentation of the gospel leading to people putting their faith in Christ but also the ongoing ministry of the word in helping them to grow in their faith in the context of the Christian communities. Paul did not separate these two facets of ministering the gospel. His initial proclamation was always followed by the creation of communities where the word of God could continue to be taught.

The term καταγγέλλω was used extensively by Luke throughout the book of Acts to describe the announcement of the gospel of Jesus Christ throughout the Mediterranean world, resulting in the establishment of many churches (Acts 4:2; 13:5, 38; 15:36; 16:17; 17:3, 13, 23; 26:23). Paul himself used the term in a number of his letters to refer to this proclamation of the gospel (1 Cor 2:1; 9:14; Phil 1:17, 18). In Philippians, it is set parallel to "preaching Christ" (τὸν Χριστὸν κηρύσσουσιν; Phil 1:15–17). Lohse observes that the term has "practically become a technical term for missionary preaching" and that the gospel was "explained and developed in admonition and instruction."[108]

Part of the responsibility for leaders within the churches is to provide "admonishment" (νουθετέω) to fellow believers. Paul expresses this as a duty of those who "have charge over you [προϊσταμένους ὑμῶν] in the Lord" (1 Thess 5:12 NRSV). In that context, it involved providing warnings to those who were disorderly or disruptive in the community (1 Thess 5:14; 2 Thess 3:15). The biblical use of the word may retain some of its original etymological sense (built on νοῦς and τίθημι, meaning "to put in mind").[109] It is noteworthy that Philo often pairs νουθετέω (or the noun form, νουθεσία) with παιδεύω, "instruct."[110] The same pairing occurs in Ephesians, where fathers are exhorted to raise their children "in the discipline and instruction [ἐν παιδείᾳ καὶ νουθεσίᾳ] of the Lord" (Eph 6:4). The NT usage of the term thus refers to "counsel about avoidance or cessation of an improper course of conduct."[111] Luke uses the term in reporting Paul's description of his three-year ministry in Ephesus: "therefore be alert, remembering that for three years I did not cease night or day to admonish [νουθετῶν] every one with tears" (Acts 20:31 ESV). Although Paul sees it as a duty of the leaders, he also presents it as a responsibility that believers have for one another (Col 3:16; also Rom 15:14). But this kind of "warning" or "admonition" should be done in an attitude of love (1 Cor 4:14).

Paul also says that it is his responsibility, and by extension, the responsibility of all church leaders, to teach (διδάσκοντες) every person as part of the ministry

108 Lohse, 76–77.

109 See Silva, "νουθετέω," *NIDNTTE* 3:423.

110 See Silva, "νουθετέω," 3:424.

111 BDAG, s.v. νουθετέω.

of proclamation. Moses served as an important exemplar in this respect. He declared, "Now, O Israel, listen to the statutes and the rules that I am teaching [διδάσκω] you, and do them, that you may live" (Deut 4:1 ESV). This was a solemn obligation given to him by the Lord himself: "the LORD commanded me at that time to teach [διδάξαι] you statutes and rules, that you might do them in the land that you are going over to possess" (Deut 4:14). The scribe Ezra devoted himself to the study of the Scripture, practicing it, and "teaching [διδάσκειν] its decrees and laws in Israel" (Ezra 7:10 NIV). According to the Gospel writers, Jesus himself engaged in an extensive teaching ministry throughout Israel. Matthew records that Jesus "went throughout all Galilee, teaching [διδάσκων] in their synagogues and proclaiming [κηρύσσων] the gospel of the kingdom" (Matt 4:23). His teaching activity extended also to Jerusalem and the temple courts (John 7:14). The apostles continued this teaching ministry. Luke records that the earliest Jerusalem Christians "devoted themselves to the apostles' teaching" (Acts 2:42). The heart of their teaching focused on Jesus and the gospel (including his resurrection from the dead) (Acts 4:2). Paul affirms that "teacher" (διδάσκαλος) was one of the most important spiritual gifts that the exalted Christ bestowed on his churches (1 Cor 12:28; Eph 4:11).

Admonishment is closely tied to teaching here in Col 1:28 and in Col 3:16. It is imperative for church leaders not only to instruct believers in the essence of the Christian faith and the content of Scripture but also in the moral dimensions of their new lives in Christ. Paul exemplified this latter aspect in what he told the Thessalonians: "you received from us how you ought to walk and to please God" (1 Thess 4:1). Accordingly, he admonishes the Colossians, "as you have received Christ Jesus the Lord, so walk in him" (Col 2:6; see also 1:10).

The expression πάντα ἄνθρωπον, "every person," appears three times in this verse—admonishing "every person," teaching "every person," and presenting "every person" perfect. The repetition signals a strong emphasis, but what is the precise nature of that emphasis? Dunn connects it to the "all things" (τὰ πάντα) of 1:20 and contends that "every person . . . will in the end be found 'in Christ.'"[112] But this explanation approaches universalism and does not take into account that the reconciliation of 1:20 involves a pacification of those who rebel against God. McKnight rejects this view as well and argues that "all" simply refers to the inclusion of the gentiles in the salvation of God, "both Jew and gentile."[113] But interpreting "all" to mean "both" would be unprecedented in Greek and is without parallel in Paul's writings. Lightfoot suggested that the expression referred to "the universality of the Gospel."[114] But that fails to explain how "every person" is presented perfect in Christ at the judgment day. The best way to interpret the threefold "every person" is to understand it as referring to

112 Dunn, 125.

113 McKnight, 201.

114 Lightfoot, 170.

every person who responds in faith to the gospel and becomes a member of the Christian community. In a high group context such as this, "every person" is a way of stressing *every individual member*. Each person who comes to Christ will need to be taught the essence of the Christian faith and admonished according to their own struggles, weaknesses, proclivities, and sinful tendencies. Paul will state this in different terms in the next section of the letter when he says, "as you received Christ Jesus the Lord, walk in him" (2:6).

The admonishment and teaching that Paul refers to is carried out ἐν πάσῃ σοφίᾳ, "in all wisdom," in dependence upon Christ (in whom are "all the treasures of wisdom and knowledge," 2:3) and his teaching, and in continuity with the wisdom of God revealed by the Spirit and in line with God's will as revealed in Scripture (see 1:9). This form of wisdom runs counter to the teaching and admonishment of the advocates of "the philosophy," whose teaching only has "the reputation for wisdom" (2:23) but is inconsistent with Christ.

ἵνα παραστήσωμεν πάντα ἄνθρωπον τέλειον ἐν Χριστῷ, "that we might present every person mature in Christ." The goal of Paul and his companions was not simply to register conversions or to resocialize people in a new community but to facilitate substantive change in their lives to the degree that they could be presented to God as "perfect" at the final judgment. He has already mentioned this as the goal of their reconciliation to God (1:22), but there he spoke of it as presenting them "holy and blameless and innocent" before God. Once again, Paul brings an eschatological orientation by focusing on the status of the Colossian believers at the time when they would appear before the divine tribunal. Although Paul is concerned about the community as a whole, he emphasizes the lifestyle and conduct of every individual believer by now using for the third time in this statement the expression, πάντα ἄνθρωπον, "every person."

The ultimate goal is for every single believer in Christ to be τέλειον, "perfect" (KJV; ASV; NJB; NAB; the Vulgate translates as *perfectum*), "mature" (CEB; NIV; ESV; NRSV), or "complete" (NASB). Under the law, Israel was expected to bring sacrificial animals that were "perfect" (τέλειος)—that is, without spot or blemish of any kind (Exod 12:5).[115] The LXX also uses the noun with reference to people who were righteous in moral character. Thus, Noah was described as both τέλειος and δίκαιος (Gen 6:9). It was the will of God for every Israelite to be blameless before God: "you shall be perfect [τέλειος] before the Lord your God" (Deut 18:13 NETS). The same goal is found in the Dead Sea Scrolls (e.g., 1QS 3.9–10: "may he, then, steady his steps in order to walk with perfection on all the paths of God").[116] This objective is reiterated by Jesus in the Matthean Sermon on the Mount: "be perfect [τέλειοι], therefore, as your heavenly Father is perfect [τέλειος]" (Matt 5:48 NRSV). In his letter to the Ephesians, Paul aspires for the community to grow into "a perfect man" (ἀνὴρ τέλειος) (Eph 4:13).

115 See LSJ, s.v. τέλειος.

116 See also 1QS 1.8; 2.2; 4.22; CD 2.15–16; 7.5.

Since his contrast there is with children (νήπιοι, Eph 4:14), it suggests the notion of movement from immaturity to maturity. Paul is thus not saying in Colossians that every individual believer will reach a state in which there is an utter and complete absence of sin (thus there is the need for ongoing admonitions), but that there should be substantial movement in that direction. Nevertheless, by virtue of their union with Christ, the implication is that all believers share in Christ's righteousness and are thereby "perfect." The focal point in Colossians, however, is on their daily walk and that they should be actualizing in their lives the righteous character of their new identity in Christ.

Lohse suggests that it is conceivable that the leaders of "the philosophy" regarded themselves as τέλειοι in the sense that they were filled with supernatural wisdom and divine power as a result of special experiences with the divine or by initiation into the mysteries.[117] While this description would aptly characterize the leaders of the faction at Colossae, it cannot be known with certainty whether this was a catchword of "the philosophy" since it does not occur in the polemical section of the letter and because of its usage in the LXX, the Gospels, and elsewhere in Paul. The term is also not used in the magical texts of the adept.

**29** εἰς ὃ καὶ κοπιῶ ἀγωνιζόμενος κατὰ τὴν ἐνέργειαν αὐτοῦ τὴν ἐνεργουμένην ἐν ἐμοὶ ἐν δυνάμει, "to this end I labor, striving in accordance with his empowering, which mightily works in me in power." Paul ends the paragraph by once again calling attention to the strenuous labor that he exerts on behalf of the Colossians and, indeed, all of his churches. Yet he clarifies that he is able to do this because of the infusion of divine power that he experiences.

The neuter singular relative pronoun (ὅ) refers to the full extent of the gospel ministry he has just described in the previous verse.[118] This includes not only the evangelistic proclamation of the gospel in the synagogues and the marketplaces but also the task of forming communities where these groups of Christ-followers are instructed and facilitated in their growth. Paul has shifted his focus from the first-person plural (he, his companions, and all Christian leaders) to the first-person singular (with only himself in view), which ties his remarks here more closely to the beginning of the paragraph (1:24) where he describes his personal suffering in carrying out his apostolic ministry and service. The preposition (εἰς) refers to the goal of his labor as presenting every person mature in Christ.

The verb and participle combination (κοπιῶ ἀγωνιζόμενος) underline the strenuousness of his apostolic labor. Paul uses the verb κοπιάω, "I labor" (as well as the noun, κόπος), to refer to physical work for sustenance and payment (e.g., 1 Cor 3:8; 4:12; Eph 4:28; 1 Thess 2:9; 2 Thess 3:8; 2 Tim 2:6), but more

117 He cites Iamblichus, *Mysteries* 3.7, and *Corp. herm.* 4.4 in support of this. See Lohse, 78. See also Lightfoot, 170–71.

118 So also Campbell, 26, who notes that "the antecedent to the relative pronoun is the entire idea of the previous verse."

frequently in the metaphorical sense of exertion for the service of the gospel (Rom 16:6, 12; 1 Cor 15:10, 58; 16:16; 2 Cor 11:23, 27; Phil 2:16; 1 Thess 1:3; 3:5; 5:12; see also 1 Tim 4:10; 5:17). The following participle (ἀγωνιζόμενος) should be interpreted as one of means describing how he carries out his labor.[119] The verb (and the noun ἀγών, "struggle") would have been well-known to the Colossians because of its widespread use in athletic games in Asia Minor and beyond. An ἀγών (*agōn*) was an athletic contest held in honor of a god or a local hero. They most commonly involved athletic events, but also extended to competion in music, poetry, and equestrian events and were usually held within the framework of religious festivals.[120] Although common in the classical era (especially the Panhellenic *agōn*, the Olympic Games), they were revived in the late Hellenistic and Roman era.[121] Various kinds of games were held periodically in most of the cities of Asia Minor. The games were organized and funded by an ἀγωνοθέτης, a position that is attested in hundreds of inscriptions from Asia Minor.

In Laodicea, annual games were held in honor of the city's founder, Antiochus II, and in honor of the patron deity of the city, Zeus.[122] Hierapolis established games in honor of the emperor from the time of Augustus. The city also held Pythian games in honor of the god, Apollo.[123] A frieze on the theater at Hierapolis included the figure of an ἀγωνοθέτης.[124] Two steles were discovered in the village of Thiounta (in the territory of Hierapolis), mentioning a phratry (a group of citizens) whose members took turns serving as an ἀγωνοθέτης and officiating at an eight-day festival.[125] Each stele depicts the gods who were honored during these games and include Zeus, Demeter, Hermes, and Helios. In the nearby city of Tripolis, excavations uncovered an inscription honoring a certain Marcus Aurelius Epaphroditus and Marcus Aurelius Iulianus who were both boxers and "struggled gloriously" (ἀγωνισαμένους) and fought to a draw "in the contest [τὸν ἀγῶνα] of the great Attalianeia Olympia, which was first held in our city."[126]

Paul was familiar with this extensive use of the term in athletic contexts and appropriated it as a metaphor for intense struggle in his service of the gospel. There is no doubt that people living in the Lycus Valley would understand this metaphor. He tells the Corinthians, "Every athlete [ὁ ἀγωνιζόμενος] exercises self-control in all things. They do it to receive a perishable wreath, but we an imperishable" (1 Cor 9:25 ESV). He uses both the noun and the verb

---

119 The participle could be taken as attendant circumstance (as Harris, 66–67, notes), but Wallace, *Grammar*, 640–43, rightly limits this category to participles in the aorist tense that precede an aorist main verb.

120 Mitchell, *Anatolia*, 1:198, 219.

121 See S. D. Lambert and A J. S. Spawforth, "Agōnes," *OCD*[3] 41–42.

122 Huttner, *Early Christianity in the Lycus Valley*, 58, 64.

123 Huttner, *Early Christianity in the Lycus Valley*, 45, 62.

124 D'Andria, *Hierapolis of Phrygia*, 222.

125 See Mitchell, *Anatolia*, 1:187.

126 Tanriver, "Three New Inscriptions from Tripolis," 84–85.

as metaphors of his strenuous labor in the service of the churches (Phil 1:30; 1 Thess 2:2; see also 1 Tim 6:12; 2 Tim 4:7). In a similar way to this passage, both terms appear in connection with each other in 1 Tim 4:10: "that is why we labor and strive [κοπιῶμεν καὶ ἀγωνιζόμεθα], because we have put our hope in the living God, who is the Savior of all people" (NIV).

This labor and striving certainly includes intercessory prayer, for which Paul commends Epaphras (Col 4:12).[127] But it likely also extends to the continuous evangelistic proclamation of the gospel in a variety of venues, countless hours of intense teaching and passing on of tradition, engaging dangerous teachings, dealing with problems, establishing leadership, and caring for, encouraging, and admonishing the believers. This is on top of the literal wage-earning work for sustenance that Paul regularly did.

Paul now concludes this paragraph with an overt emphasis on the power of God that enables him to carry out his apostolic service. He uses a collocation of three power-denoting terms to stress that he is able to accomplish all that he does because God is so powerfully working in and through him. The preposition κατά governs both accusative expressions (τὴν ἐνέργειαν and τὴν ἐνεργουμένην) and indicates not just the governing norm ("in accordance with")[128] but probably expresses the means by which Paul conducts his ministry ("in reliance on").[129] Thus, some versions translate the phrase, "*with* all the [or his] energy" (see NRSV; ESV; RSV; NIV; cf. NJB; CSB; CEB). The NLT captures the idea well by rendering it, "depending on Christ's mighty power."

The noun ἐνέργεια can simply mean "working" or "action," but when it occurs in connection with God (or a divine being), it connotes the operation of supernatural power. In the prayer of Eph 1:19, it occurs in conjunction with other terms for power, including δύναμις, ἰσχύς, and κράτος. It is distinguished from the common word for power (δύναμις) by the fact that δύναμις normally occurs in contexts where it expresses potentiality, whereas ἐνέργεια is typically used for the realization of power.[130] Paul is thus emphasizing that the power of God is the driving energy and force behind his ability to carry out the extraordinary demands of his apostolic service. When he writes to the Ephesians, he associates this enabling power with the grace of God: "I became a servant according to the gift of the grace of God that was given to me according to the mighty working of his power [κατὰ τὴν ἐνέργειαν τῆς δυνάμεως αὐτου]" (Eph 3:7; see also 1 Cor 15:10). At this point in his career, Paul has had many years of experiencing God's empowering hand upon his life and ministry—often experiencing it in the most trying and difficult of circumstances. During an

127 Lightfoot, 171–72, says that wrestling in prayer "is the predominant idea," but the previous verse would suggest that it is the entire ministry of the gospel.

128 See BDAG, s.v. κατά 5.

129 Harris, 67.

130 Grundmann, *Begriff der Kraft*, 58.

especially hard period when he was struggling with some kind of debilitating afflication, the Lord revealed to him: "my grace is sufficient for you, for my power is made perfect in weakness" (2 Cor 12:9; see also Rom 15:19; 1 Cor 2:4–5; 2 Cor 4:7; 6:7).

It would have been sufficient for Paul to end the paragraph here, but he adds an additional line that puts the enabling power of God into bold relief. The adjectival participle τὴν ἐνεργουμένην modifies the cognate noun τὴν ἐνέργειαν and expresses a redundancy for rhetorical emphasis: "the power that powerfully works in me." To underline divine enablement even more, he adds the prepositional phrase ἐν δυνάμει, "in power." Paul wants the Colossians to know in no uncertain terms that the one true and living God whom he serves is directly involved in helping him fulfill his mission. Paul thus becomes an example to the Colossian believers as they fulfill their own calling.[131] God is not aloof and unavailable, nor does he need to be accessed through ritual means. Christ lives in them and directly empowers them. Through reflecting on his own experience, Paul effectively undermines their felt need to access spiritual power through ritual or shamanistic means.

**2:1** θέλω γὰρ ὑμᾶς εἰδέναι ἡλίκον ἀγῶνα ἔχω ὑπὲρ ὑμῶν καὶ τῶν ἐν Λαοδικείᾳ καὶ ὅσοι οὐχ ἑόρακαν τὸ πρόσωπόν μου ἐν σαρκί, "for I want you to know how great a struggle I have for you and those in Laodicea and all who have not seen my face in the flesh." What Paul says of his struggle and suffering for all Christians, he now particularizes and applies to the Christians in the Lycus Valley. The chapter division here is thus unfortunate since this subsection (2:1–5) is intimately connected to the previous paragraph (1:24–29).

The introductory, postpositive γάρ, "for," does not provide a basis or explanation for the previous section; it simply functions to introduce a new paragraph that represents an application of what he has just said to the Colossian believers and their neighbors.[132] The beginning words θέλω . . . ὑμᾶς εἰδέναι, "I want you to know," is a rhetorical way of stressing what Paul is about to say in the lines that follow. He has used this construction on an earlier occasion when he wrote to the Corinthians (1 Cor 11:3). He emphasizes to the Colossians the magnitude of the suffering and effort he faces on their behalf. The adjective ἡλίκος, "how great," is rare in the NT (and never in the LXX), only occurring here and in Jas 3:5 where it refers to how great a fire can be ignited by the tongue. The term was used by Jewish authors of the time. Josephus employs it ten times, including a reference to the great size of the wall surrounding Jerusalem (Josephus, *J.W.* 2.218) as well as of the formidable enemies of Israel that God subdued before them (Josephus, *J.W.* 5.377). Philo uses the term to speak of "how great an evil [ἡλίκον ἐστὶ κακόν] it is" to conceal the offenses of the mind (Philo, *Flight* 193;

131 See my discussion of Paul as a model for believers in *Ephesians: Power and Magic*, 161–62.

132 This represents the use of γάρ "as a narrative marker to express continuation or connection"; see BDAG, s.v. γάρ 2.

see also *Dreams* 2.179) as well as "how great a good [ἡλίκον ἐστὶν ἀγαθόν] it is" for the mind to find rest (Philo, *Dreams* 2.228). Paul uses the adjective here to describe the intensity of the struggle (ἀγών) he is having for the believers in the Lycus Valley. This picks up and continues his use of the metaphor from 1:29 where he used the verbal form (see there for the usage of the noun and verb in the Lycus Valley). The idea is that he not only feels responsibility for these believers but that he is emotionally invested in them and has expended himself in praying for them and contending for their faith, especially in light of the threat he sees to the stability of their faith because of the influence of "the philosophy."

Paul specifies that his struggle is on behalf of the Colossians (ὑπὲρ ὑμῶν) and the believers in Laodicea. The final clause does not introduce a third group of people but characterizes the Colossians and Laodiceans as people who do not know Paul personally. Lightfoot has accurately observed that the καὶ ὅσοι, "all who,"[133] "introduces the whole class to which the persons previously enumerated belong."[134] This construction can be seen elsewhere in the NT such as at Acts 4:6: "Annas the high priest, Caiaphas, John, and Alexander, and all who [καὶ ὅσοι] were of the high-priestly family" (Acts 4:6 NRSV; see also Rev 18:17). It represents a general statement after the particular—that is, Paul engages in his intense apostolic service for the benefit of all those who do not know him personally, especially the Colossian and Laodicean believers. The καί, "and," that begins the clause should thus be taken epexegetically.[135]

Paul's lack of personal presence to believers in the Lycus Valley could have been adequately expressed by ὅσοι οὐχ ἑόρακαν τὸ πρόσωπόν μου, "all who have not seen my face." He has used the combination of ὁράω and πρόσωπον elsewhere to characterize physical presence (see 1 Thess 2:17; 3:10; see also Acts 20:25; Rev 22:4). But the addition of ἐν σαρκί, "in the flesh," strongly emphasizes that these believers do not know Paul personally. The entire clause suggests that Paul had never visited the Lycus Valley.

The fact that Paul is in a great struggle for the Laodiceans as well as the Colossians not only emphasizes his sense of apostolic responsibility for believers in Laodicea,[136] but also means that they are likely facing the same threat as the Colossians from "the philosophy."[137] One can only wonder how much overlap in content there would have been between the letter Paul wrote to the Laodiceans (Col 4:16) and the letter to the Colossians on this matter. The other prominent city in the Lycus Valley that has close connections to Laodicea and Colossae was

133 The expression could be rendered "as many as." But see BDAG, s.v. ὅσος 2, where it is noted, "Even without πάντες/πάντα, ὅσοι/ὅσα has the mng. *all that*."

134 Lightfoot, 172.

135 So also Pao, 136.

136 For a discussion of Laodicea and Christianity in that city, see the *Introduction*.

137 Lohse, 80, rightly notes, "The acute danger, against which the letter wants to warn the Colossians (2:6–23), clearly threatens not only this community [the Colossian community], but all Christians in the whole area."

Hierapolis. It is clear that there was a church established there since Epaphras was also working hard on their behalf (4:13). They are likely to be included in the group, "all who have not seen my face."

**2** ἵνα παρακληθῶσιν αἱ καρδίαι αὐτῶν συμβιβασθέντες ἐν ἀγάπῃ, "that their hearts may be encouraged, united in love." The Christian community at Colossae (and likely elsewhere in the Lycus Valley) had experienced some level of division as a result of the impact of the teaching and harsh and judgmental rhetoric of the leaders of "the philosophy." With his comments here, Paul strives to unify Christians in this area by grounding them in an accurate knowledge of Christ.

Paul wants to encourage their hearts by pointing them to Christ and the implications of life in union with him. Although the verb παρακαλέω could be understood in the sense of providing consolation (as in comforting someone who has experienced a great loss; see Gen 37:35; Ps 119:50 [118:50 LXX]; 2 Cor 1:4; 7:6), here he uses the term to express the idea of instilling them with encouragement in light of the internal conflict within the community. His goal is for them to be fortified in their knowledge of Christ in order to stand up against the deceitful teaching of "the philosophy" (see the similar use of the verb in 2 Thess 2:17; Titus 1:9) and that the community might emerge through this trial unified. Throughout the OT and in Second Temple texts, καρδία, "heart," was used metaphorically as the place of a person's intellectual and spiritual life. The biblical emphasis is on "the inner life and attitude."[138] As the following phrases will make clear, Paul not only wants to lift them up emotionally but to reinforce their thinking and bolster their decision-making capabilities. He shifts from the second person ("your") to the third person ("their") to reflect the inclusion of the Laodicean believers and other believers in the Lycus Valley within the scope of his comments.

Paul clarifies further how this encouragement would happen by expressing that he wants their hearts to be συμβιβασθέντες ἐν ἀγάπῃ, "united in love." The verb συμβιβάζω is the causative of συμβαίνω, "bring together."[139] Herodotus, for instance, uses it of the joining together of Lydians of Asia Minor with the Medes during the Persian War, thus effecting a reconciliation and unity (Herodotus *Hist.* 1.79; see also Thucydides, *P.W.* 2.29). This adverbial participle should be interpreted as one of manner or means. The masculine gender appears out of sync with the feminine subject, but it is probably a construction according to the sense—that is, Paul is thinking of the people (not just their hearts), in which case the masculine would be appropriate. Rather than "join together," the verb could alternatively be understood in the sense of "instruct." It is tempting to opt for this sense because "instruct" is the sole way that the verb is used throughout the LXX (e.g., "you are to teach [συμβιβῶ] the people of Israel all the statutes that the LORD has spoken to them through Moses," Lev 10:11 NRSV; see also Exod

138 M. Silva, "καρδία," *NIDNTTE* 2:623.

139 LSJ, s.v. συμβιβάζω.

4:12, 15; 18:16; Ps 32:8 [31:8 LXX]). Paul knows this usage and has employed it in this sense in his correspondence with the Corinthians (1 Cor 2:16). It would also fit with the emphasis on acquiring insight, knowledge, and wisdom in the lines of text that follow. But Paul uses this verb one other time later in Colossians, where the idea of being "joined together" is part of a larger physiological metaphor of head and body, with the joints and ligaments holding the body together (2:19). This is also the way the verb is used in Ephesians, where the author makes the declaration that it is from Christ that "the whole body is being joined together and held together [συμβιβαζόμενον] through every joint that brings supply" (Eph 4:16). This usage tips the balance in favor of the verb being understood here as "joining together." The following prepositional phrase, ἐν ἀγάπῃ, "in love," is also more appropriate to the idea of "joining together" than it would be to "instructing." The idea of "instructing in love" would be without parallel in Paul's writings. The same phrase, however, is used in the identical context in Ephesians where Paul speaks of the body "building itself up in love" (Eph 4:16).

Nevertheless, the idea of instructing is not altogether absent from its use here nor is it absent from the contexts of Col 2:19 or Eph 4:16. For Paul, unity is based not just on putting up with one another despite differences (Eph 4:2) and by cultivating important social virtues (Col 3:12–14), but it is also based on—and, indeed, primarily on—a unified understanding of Christ and the implications of being united with him. In a series of prepositional phrases that follow, Paul will stress the importance of acquiring insight (σύνεσις) and knowledge (ἐπίγνωσις and γνῶσις) about Christ. This twofold basis for unity—love for one another and a right understanding of Christ—is seen in the other context where συμβιβάζω occurs in Colossians (2:19). The head (Christ) not only holds the body together but supplies the body with all the resources it needs and causes its growth. This includes empowering the apostolic service of Paul and all the other gifted teachers and leaders in the church to instruct and admonish every member of the community (1:28–29). There is a similar use of the term in Eph 4:16 where the overall context emphasizes unity through a twofold emphasis on love and social virtue, while at the same time stressing the importance of confessing a common faith (Eph 4:4–6, 15), growing in a knowledge of the faith (Eph 4:13), and the role of gifted teachers to pass on the faith (Eph 4:11–13). It is quite possible that Paul has chosen this rare word to convey this double understanding of being "knit together" on the basis of sound instruction. Schweizer expresses the same thought when he notes, "This binding together takes place through the apostle's actual teaching."[140]

**καὶ εἰς πᾶν πλοῦτος τῆς πληροφορίας τῆς συνέσεως, εἰς ἐπίγνωσιν τοῦ μυστηρίου τοῦ θεοῦ, Χριστοῦ,** "in all the riches of the full assurance of insight into knowing the mystery of God, which is Christ." The goal here is to gain insight into Christ and know him, but Paul expresses it in an expansive way

140 Schweizer, 116.

that needs to be carefully probed. The preposition εἰς should be taken as an indication of purpose. It directly modifies συμβιβασθέντες, "joined together," as its immediate verbal antecedent. Others have seen it as indicating the purpose of Paul's struggle (thus ἀγῶνα ἔχω in 2:1),[141] or a purpose of the encouragement (thus παρακληθῶσιν in 2:2).[142] It is best, however, to see the καί as coordinating it with the previous prepositional phrase (ἐν ἀγάπῃ), with both modifying the participle. The flow of thought would be that Paul is exerting himself strenuously to the end that the members of these Christian communities would be encouraged by being (1) united in love and (2) united around the goal of knowing Christ. The focal point in the prepositional phrase is the noun σύνεσις, "insight," which is in the last position in the phrase and in the genitive case. Paul used it earlier in the introductory prayer report to convey to the Colossians how he was praying for them, specifically that they would have a knowledge of God's will "with all wisdom and spiritual insight [σύνεσις]" (1:9). The term refers to a comprehension and understanding—here with reference to God's plan in and through Christ.[143] The noun πλοῦτος, "wealth," that stands at the outset of the clause immediately modifies the following genitive noun πληροφορία, "full assurance." This should be understood as an epexegetical genitive;[144] thus the "wealth" is the full assurance. Paul has used this noun on only one other occasion where it describes the way that the gospel came to the Thessalonian believers providing them with "full assurance" (1 Thess 1:5). The author of Hebrews uses it of the full assurance of hope (Heb 6:11) and of faith (Heb 10:22). The final noun in the clause, σύνεσις, also in the genitive case, is in an attributed-genitive relationship to the head noun, πλοῦτος.[145] This means that "wealth" modifies "insight" in a way similar to an adjective.[146] More precisely, the phrase "wealth of full assurance" modifies "insight." The overall idea is that as the Colossians grow in their knowledge and comprehension of Christ, it will lead to an abundance of assurance or conviction. This is precisely what they need in light of their tendency to be led astray by the teaching of "the philosophy."

The last εἰς phrase also introduces a purpose statement, but this explicates the prior εἰς phrase by providing a specification of the content of the "insight" (σύνεσις) that Paul desires for these believers to attain. He wants them to grow deeply in their knowledge of Christ. Maisch summarizes it well: "the third element designates the most important goal of the apostolic struggle: the addressees should be led to the correct knowledge of Christ."[147] The noun ἐπίγνωσις, which

141 Harris, 73.

142 Pao, 137.

143 See the commentary on 1:9 for additional discussion.

144 So also Harris, 74, and Campbell, 28. In a similar vein, Moule, 86, describes it as "descriptive of πλοῦτος—the wealth consists of conviction."

145 So also Campbell, 29.

146 For a full discussion of this use of the genitive, see Wallace, *Grammar*, 89–91.

147 Maisch, 145.

he has used twice earlier (see 1:9, 10 and the discussion of the term there), is indistinguishable in meaning from γνῶσις, which he will use in the next verse (2:3). More specifically, he wants them to know τὸ μυστήριον τοῦ θεοῦ, Χριστοῦ, "the mystery of God, which is Christ." The genitive case of Χριστοῦ should be understood as a genitive of apposition and thus defining the content of the mystery. Rather than seeing the wording here as "awkward and careless,"[148] we should see it as emphatic. Christ is the definition of the mystery of God; he is the single true mystery that the Colossians should focus on and be devoted to, perhaps especially in contrast to the advocates of "the philosophy," who have depended on spiritual insight from other mysteries and ritual initiation. Paul has just told his readers that the mystery is "Christ in you, the hope of glory" (1:26). The insight and knowledge that Paul wants believers in the Lycus Valley to attain is both personal and factual related to Christ. He wants them to grow in their recognition that Christ now dwells in them personally and that they have been united with him in his death and resurrection, which has led to a new life through the powerful creative work of God (Col 2:11–13; 3:1–4). But he also wants them to know about Christ and to be instructed in all of the details about him (3:16). Paul and his companions are devoted to the proclamation of Christ and teaching about him (1:28–29).

**3** ἐν ᾧ εἰσιν πάντες οἱ θησαυροὶ τῆς σοφίας καὶ γνώσεως ἀπόκρυφοι, "in him are all the treasures of wisdom and knowledge concealed." Paul wants the Colossians to grow in their knowledge of Christ precisely because he is the source of all knowledge related to ultimate reality, salvation, and supernatural matters. Most importantly, he is the executor of God the Father's plan of redemption.

The prepositional phrase with the masculine relative pronoun (ἐν ᾧ) refers directly to Christ, the nearest antecedent, and not further back either to God or to the mystery. Paul has used this expression earlier to refer to Christ ("in him [ἐν ᾧ] we have redemption," 1:14), and he will use it later ("in him [ἐν ᾧ] you were circumcised," 2:11, and "in him [ἐν ᾧ] you were co-resurrected," 2:12).

Paul speaks of wisdom and knowledge as "treasures" (θησαυροί) that are hidden (ἀπόκρυφοι). This combination is natural and is found in the LXX of literal treasures; for example, Antiochus Epiphanes "took the hidden treasures [τοὺς θησαυροὺς τοὺς ἀποκρύφους]" that he found in Jerusalem (1 Macc 1:23; see also Isa 45:3). Paul has used the term treasure (θησαυρός) on one other occasion to speak of the light of the gospel of the glory of Christ that lives within believers as a "treasure in jars of clay" (2 Cor 4:7). One of the parables of the kingdom in Matthew's Gospel compares the kingdom of heaven to a treasure hidden (θησαυρῷ κεκρυμμένῳ) in a field that a man found "and then in his joy went and sold all he had and bought that field" (Matt 13:44 NIV). The fact that ἀπόκρυφοι, "hidden," appears here in our verse in the predicate position at the

148 Hay, 79.

end of the sentence makes it emphatic (vs. the attributive position at the outset of the clause, "hidden treasures").

The hiddenness of σοφία καὶ γνῶσις, "wisdom and knowledge," means that they are not readily accessible by all—they are only found in Christ. In Scripture, the combination of the two terms appears primarily in the Wisdom literature (e.g., Prov 8:12; 30:3; Eccl 1:16, 17, 18; 2:21, 26; 7:12; 9:10; Sir 21:18; Wis 6:22). The two terms also come together in the prophetic anticipation of Messiah: "the Spirit of the LORD shall rest upon him, the Spirit of wisdom [σοφίας] and understanding [συνέσεως], the Spirit of counsel and might, the Spirit of knowledge [γνώσεως] and the fear of the LORD" (Isa 11:2 ESV). But this text also includes a third term from this context in Colossians, σύνεσις, which may indicate that this passage was in Paul's mind as he wrote.

I have already noted that Paul depends on the book of Daniel for his understanding and use of the term μυστήριον, "mystery," in Colossians (Col 1:26, 27; 2:2; 4:3). The terms for wisdom, understanding, and knowledge occur in conjunction with "mystery" in Dan 2, further suggesting Paul's dependence on this tradition:

> Then the mystery [μυστήριον] of the king was disclosed to Daniel. In the night in a vision the matter was clearly brought to light. Then Daniel blessed the Lord Most High and crying out he said, "Let the name of the great Lord be blessed forever, because wisdom [σοφία] and majesty are his. And he changes seasons and times, deposing kings and setting up, giving to the sages wisdom [σοφίαν] and understanding [σύνεσιν] to those who have knowledge [ἐπιστήμη]. (Dan 2:19–21 NETS)

At the outset of the book, the Theodotian text of Daniel speaks of the wisdom and knowledge of Daniel and his three companions, which according to the course of the narrative, came from their dependence on the Lord: "[they were] young men, who had no physical defect in them and were handsome in appearance and versed in all wisdom [σοφίᾳ] and endowed with knowledge [γνῶσιν] and full of discernment and who had strength in them to stand in the king's house" (Dan [Th.] 1:4 NETS).

The book of Proverbs asserts that "the LORD gives wisdom [σοφίαν]; from his mouth come knowledge [γνῶσις] and understanding [σύνεσις]" (Prov 2:6 ESV). But the preceding context also has "hidden treasure," an additional concept from our passage: "if you seek it like silver and search for it has for hidden treasures (מַטְמוֹנִים;[149] Prov 2:4 ESV). The LXX translates the term with θησαυρός, while Symmachus and Theodotion read ἀπόκρυφος. As Beale notes, this fivefold word combination is unique to the OT.[150] The terminology of this section of

149 BDB, s.v. מַטְמוֹן, "hidden treasure."

150 Beale, 156–57.

Colossians thus represents Paul's reflections on Messiah in light of prophetic texts (Isa 11 and Dan 2) and the Wisdom literature (Prov 2).

Yet it is also likely that the advocates of "the philosophy" were using some of this language to entice the Colossian believers. Paul explicitly says that the opposing teaching had a "reputation for wisdom" (λόγον μὲν ἔχοντα σοφίας, Col 2:23). The leader of the faction also depended on insight he had gained through mystery initiation (see the discussion on 2:18). We can also assume that "knowledge" and "insight" may very well have been part of their appeal. And Lightfoot long ago suggested that "in ἀπόκρυφοι the Apostle adopts a favourite term of the Gnostic teachers, only that he may refute a favourite doctrine."[151] Although I have argued that the Colossian philosophy had nothing to do with Gnosticism, the term ἀπόκρυφος was used extensively in magical texts, including Jewish magic. Secrecy was important in magic. At the conclusion of a ritual spell, the adept is given the instruction, "So keep this in a secret place [ἀποκρύφῳ] as a great mystery [μεγαλομυστήριον]. Hide it, hide it!" (*PGM* XII.321). The Jewish and syncretistic Eighth Book of Moses begins with the heading, "The sacred, hidden [ἀπόκρυφος] book of Moses called 'eighth' or 'holy'" (*PGM* XIII.345; see also XIII.731–32).[152] Toward the end of the book is "a secret [ἀπόκρυφος] prayer of Moses to Selene" (*PGM* XIII.1057).

This does not mean that Paul was dependent on the shamanistic and magical tradition in place of the OT background, but he was likely aware of the usage of this language in "the philosophy." He was not willing to surrender the language to their use and find alternative modes of expression. Rather, as he has done with the term "mystery," he redeems the terms and fills them with alternative content based on his understanding of Christology in light of the OT.

**4** Τοῦτο λέγω, ἵνα μηδεὶς ὑμᾶς παραλογίζηται ἐν πιθανολογίᾳ, "I say this so that no one deceives you with persuasive teachings." Paul begins to conclude this section by drawing out the implications of what he has previously said for the threat the Colossians face. As such, he creates a bridge to the next section, where he will polemicize against "the philosophy" in earnest. The referent of τοῦτο λέγω, "I say this," refers in the first instance to the immediately preceding three verses that began with "for I want you to know . . ." (2:1).[153] At the heart of this portion is his desire that they grow into a much deeper understanding

151 Lightfoot, 174.

152 For an introduction and translation of this text, see T. E. Klutz, "The Eighth Book of Moses," in Bauckham, Davila, and Panayotov, *Old Testament Pseudepigrapha*, 189–235.

153 Most commentators regard this expression as pointing back to what Paul has previously said and not forward to what he is about to say. Some (e.g., Wilson, 188; Moule, 88; Bruce, 92) interpret it as prospective. But this requires taking ἵνα in an imperatival (ecbatic) sense and not in its normal usage as introducing a purpose statement. Moule, for instance, sees this verse as beginning a new paragraph and suggests the translation, "What I mean is, nobody is to talk you into error by specious words." While the ecbatic sense is used by Paul (1 Cor 1:12; Gal 3:17) and is possible, it is better to see Paul as reaffirming his christological basis for speaking against the faction at Colossae.

and knowledge of Christ. Of course, this is predicated in large measure on what he has previously said in the letter about Christ, especially in the Christ-hymn. Thus, Paul is saying, "I am affirming the importance of a full and proper understanding of Christ, so that you are not deceived." The ἵνα thus serves its normal function of introducing a purpose clause.

The μηδείς, "no one," is not hypothetical but represents the first reference to those within the Colossian congregation who are teaching things contrary to the sound teaching about Christ that Paul is commending to them. The term παραλογίζομαι, "deceive," would have been readily available to Paul through its usage in the LXX. It occurs in many narrative texts to refer to such things as Laban's deception of Jacob (Gen 29:25), the Gibeonites deception of Joshua and Israel (Josh 9:22), Delilah's deception of Samson (Judg 16:10), Michal's deception of Saul (1 Sam 19:17), and the witch of Endor's accusation that Saul had deceived her (1 Sam 28:12). It appears one other time in the NT in James where he admonishes his readers to "be doers of the word, and not hearers only, deceiving [παραλογιζόμενοι] yourselves" (Jas 1:22 ESV). The accusation of deception is a strong allegation, but Paul will raise it again later when he refers to "the philosophy" as "empty deceit" (κενὴ ἀπάτη, 2:8). The intensity of the rhetoric suggests that Paul has a definite group in mind and is not simply preparing them for the possibility of a problem sometime in the future.

The means (ἐν) by which they were deceiving the Colossians was with πιθανολογία, "persuasive words." The term is quite rare and never appears elsewere in the NT or LXX. Neither does it ever appear in the writings of Josephus or Philo. Many commentators have pointed to its usage in classical writers to illustrate its usage here. For instance, Socrates warns against accepting an argument based on πιθανολογία and not on demonstration (ἀπόδειξις) (Plato, *Theaet.* 162E).[154] Earlier in the same context, he chides his interlocutor by saying, "you are young, my dear boy; so you are quickly moved and swayed by popular oratory [πείθει]." The first-century philosopher Epictetus uses the cognate term πιθανολογική: "great is the power of argumentation and persuasive reasoning [πιθανολογική]" (Epictetus, *Diatr.* 1.7). Dibelius, BDAG, and others point also to a fourth-century usage of the term describing a judicial matter: "they are seeking to keep the plunder through persuasive words [διὰ πειθανολογίας]" (*P.Lips.* 1.40.3.7).[155] The meaning of the term in its usage is closely related to its etymology, which represents a combination of a cognate of πείθω, "persuade" (πιθανός, "persuasive") and λόγια, "words" or "sayings." The adjective πιθανός never appears in the LXX or NT, but it is used extensively by Philo and Josephus. Paul elsewhere uses similar language when he speaks of how he proclaims the gospel: "my message and my preaching were not in persuasive words of wisdom

154 See also Aristotle, *Eth. nic.* 1.3 (1094B).

155 See BDAG, s.v. πιθανολογία, and Dibelius, 26.

[οὐκ ἐν πειθοῖς σοφίας λόγοις], but in demonstration of the Spirit and of power" (1 Cor 2:4). As Paul will subsequently say to the Colossians, the teaching of "the philosophy" is not κατὰ Χριστόν—that is, it is not in accordance with sound teaching concerning Christ. If pressed, he might also say that it lacks the demonstration of the Spirit of God and true spiritual power.

**5** εἰ γὰρ καὶ τῇ σαρκὶ ἄπειμι, ἀλλὰ τῷ πνεύματι σὺν ὑμῖν εἰμι, "for even though I am away from you in the flesh, yet I am with you in the Spirit." There is no doubt that the apostle wishes he were physically present with the Colossians to help them through this challenge. Yet he assures them not only that his thoughts are with them but that, in a very real sense, he is present with them through the indwelling Holy Spirit that they all share.

This is an occasion where the first-class conditional statement introduced with εἰ indicates not just a condition assumed true for the sake of an argument but a reality based on the extaordinary distance separating Paul from the Colossians. The verb ἄπειμι, "I am away from [you]," expresses his physical absence from his readers. The same term appears in the LXX of Job when he says, "Help is far from me [ἀπ᾽ ἐμοῦ ἄπεστιν]" (Job 6:13 NETS). Paul has used this verb on previous occasions to speak of his physical separation from readers (e.g., 1 Cor 5:3; 2 Cor 10:1, 11; 13:2, 10; Phil 1:27). The presence of τῇ σαρκί, "in the flesh," emphasizes the lack of physical presence and sets up the contrast with τῷ πνεύματι, "in the Spirit."

Paul uses the strong adversative ἀλλά, "but," to introduce the apodosis to emphasize that, despite his absence, he truly is present with them. Throughout the OT, God assured his people of his presence when they faced difficulty. For instance, in Isaiah the Lord says, "So do not fear, for I am with you; do not be dismayed, for I am your God. I will strengthen you and help you; I will uphold you with my righteous right hand" (Isa 41:10 NIV; see also Gen 26:24; 28:15; Isa 43:5; Jer 1:8, 19; 15:20; 30:11; 42:11; 46:28; Hag 1:13; 2:4). Jesus assured his disciples at the end of Matthew's Gospel, "Surely I am with you always, to the very end of the age" (Matt 28:20). In each of these occurrences, the LXX and NT use the preposition μετά, "with," but here in Colossians, Paul uses the preposition σύν. It may be that Paul shifts from μετά to σύν as a way of expressing spiritual association and presence—not physical presence. This may provide an important clue for the interpretation of πνεῦμα.

The key debate in this passage is whether Paul uses πνεῦμα with reference to his human spirit or to the Holy Spirit. The majority of commentators and English versions interpret it as a reference to the human spirit with the idea being, "my thoughts are with you" (e.g., "my heart is with you" [NLT]; "I keep thinking about you" [CEV]).[156] A handful of interpreters, however, have argued

156 See, e.g., Foster, 240–41; Pao, 141; Moo, 173; Harris, 78; Lohse, 83; Schweizer, 119–20; Lightfoot, 175.

that this as a reference to the Holy Spirit.[157] Fee associates this passage closely with 1 Cor 5:3, where he understands πνεῦμα to be a reference to the Holy Spirit (so also the NLT): "For though I am away from you in the body [ἀπὼν τῷ σώματι], I am present with you in the Spirit [παρὼν δὲ τῷ πνεύματι]." He notes, "When the Corinthians are assembled, the Spirit is understood to be present among them (see on 3:16); and for Paul that means that he, too, is present among them by that same Spirit."[158] Although in 1 Corinthians the contrast is between σῶμα and πνεῦμα and in Colossians it is σάρξ and πνεῦμα, the difference should not affect our interpretation since both σῶμα and σάρξ can refer to the physicality of a person. Paul's choice of σὺν ὑμῖν and not μεθ' ὑμῶν may be intentional to convey a presence that is spiritual in nature—that is, based on their common possession of the Spirit and their common union with the exalted Christ.[159] Paul has used the preposition σύν repeatedly throughout Colossians to describe the close association of believers with the exalted Christ—who is not physically present with them but is nevertheless closely associated with them and dynamically present through their spiritual union (see Col 2:12, 13, 20; 3:3, 4, 9).[160] What Paul says here is an extension of that idea. It goes beyond Paul's presence by means of the letter.[161] He shares a close bond with them through the mutual indwelling of the Holy Spirit ("Christ in you"; Col 1:27). His presence with them is far more profound than the mere sentiment, "my thoughts are with you." He shares with the Colossians a very real bond in the Spirit-indwelt body of Christ that is tantamount to being present with them.

χαίρων καὶ βλέπων ὑμῶν τὴν τάξιν καὶ τὸ στερέωμα τῆς εἰς Χριστὸν πίστεως ὑμῶν, "rejoicing and seeing your order and the firmness of your faith in Christ." Paul's ultimate goal in writing this letter is to see their faith in Christ become strong and for this to have a positive effect on the health and stability of the Colossian congregation as well as for believers throughout the Lycus Valley.

The participles χαίρων καὶ βλέπων, "rejoicing and seeing," are in the opposite order than we might expect. The logical flow would suggest that Paul would at first see their faith in Christ strengthened and that would lead him to rejoice. But as many scholars note, this is best taken as a hendiadys so that the two participles are seen as a unified expression (with perhaps an emphasis on rejoicing because of its first position).[162] Many versions thus translate it,

157 Bormann, 120; Fee, *Empowering Presence*, 645–66; Dunn, 134; Pokorný, 108; E. Schweizer, "πνεῦμα," *TDNT* 6:436.

158 Fee, *Empowering Presence*, 125.

159 See BDAG, s.v. σύν, where σύν is described as a "marker of accompaniment and association." The entry goes on to describe how it can be used with a "focus on association in activity."

160 Beale, 158, comes close to the same conclusions when he says that "πνεῦμα (pneuma) refers neither specifically to the Holy Spirit nor merely the human spirit in general but to the regenerated human spirit in union with Christ." I would contend, however, that the emphasis lies more on the Holy Spirit in this text.

161 This is the position of Sumney, 120.

162 See Wilson, 189; Lohse, 84; BDF §471.1.

"rejoicing to see" (NET; CSB; NASB; ESV; RSV; NKJV; see also NRSV; cf. NIV), which captures the sense well. The fact that Paul anticipates rejoicing reveals the confidence that he has in the Colossians and that they will respond well to what he has said in the letter. As Paul began this section of the letter on a note of joy (1:24), he concludes it by striking the same note. There is joy in the suffering he is experiencing in his apostolic service precisely because he sees his efforts contributing to the strengthening of their faith in Christ and the stability of the church.

The first of the two objectives that he will rejoice to see is their τάξις, "order." Older commentators have pointed out that the term has a background in a military context, indicating the proper rank, position, and deportment of soldiers (e.g., Xenophon, *Anab.* 1.2.18; Plutarch, *Pyrrh.* 16).[163] But it was also used in the LXX and NT of the priestly divisions (Ps 110:4 [109:4 LXX]; Luke 1:8). Thus, Hebrews uses it six times to refer to "the order of Melchizedek" (Heb 5:6, 10; 6:20; 7:11, 17). It came to be used more broadly as a metaphor for things that are done "in an orderly manner."[164] It is probably this more general sense that Paul has in mind here and in the only other time that he uses it, in his conclusion of 1 Cor 14 to affirm that in the regular times of worship, "all things should be done decently and in order [τάξιν]" (1 Cor 14:40). The opposite of this would be disorder, and this is precisely what Paul is concerned about in writing to the Thessalonian believers. He urges them to "admonish the disorderly" (1 Thess 5:14). This concern is taken up again in 2 Thessalonians where he warns the congregation to "keep away from any brother who is walking disorderly [ἀτάκτως] and not according to the tradition they received from us" (2 Thess 3:6; see also 3:11). The "disorderly" were having an unhealthy impact on the church in Thessalonica in large measure, and like the advocates of "the philosophy" at Colossae who were following τὴν παράδοσιν τῶν ἀνθρώπων (2:8), they were not following the traditions that were passed on to them from the apostle.

The second objective is to see evidence of "the firmness [τὸ στερέωμα] of their faith in Christ." This is the only time that this noun appears in the NT, but it is used extensively in the LXX. The psalmist extols God who is "my rock [στερέωμα], my fortress, and my deliverer" (Ps 18:2 [17:3 LXX]; see also Ps 71:3 [70:3 LXX]). The verbal form (στερεόω) was used in a similar way. The psalmist declares that God "made firm [ἐστερέωσεν] the world, that it shall not be shaken" (Ps 93:1 [92:1 LXX] NETS). Luke uses the verb to speak of the feet and ankles of the lame beggar that "were made strong" (ἐστερεώθησαν) by the healing power of the Lord (Acts 3:7, 16). He also uses it to refer to the churches that "were strengthened in the faith [ἐστερεοῦντο τῇ πίστει]" (Acts 16:5). The adjectival

163 See, e.g., Lightfoot, 176, who describes the term as "a military metaphor." He goes so far as to say that the term was suggested to Paul by his Roman custody and presence of soldiers of the praetorian guard.

164 BDAG, s.v. τάξις 2.

form appears in 2 Timothy to refer to the apostolic teaching as "God's firm foundation [στερεὸς θεμέλιος]" (2 Tim 2:19). Paul has used different terms in his other letters to express the same ideas. To the Roman believers, he holds up Abraham as an example because "he grew strong in his faith [ἐνεδυναμώθη τῇ πίστει]" and gave glory to God (Rom 4:20). He admonishes the Corinthians to "stand firm in the faith [στήκετε ἐν τῇ πίστει], act like men, and be strong" (1 Cor 16:13 ESV).

The goal of Paul's apostolic labor, and specifically now for the Colossians, is to see their faith in[165] Christ become strong. But for this to happen, they need an accurate knowledge of Christ (see 2:2) and to discern the implications of this knowledge of Christ for the various teachings of "the philosophy." He will later indict the advocates of this dangerous teaching for "not holding tight to Christ" (Col 2:19).

## *Explanation*

Following the hymnic praise to Christ earlier in the letter where Christ is extolled as sovereign over the universe, preeminent over all of creation, and the one who will ultimately bring universal peace (1:15–20), Paul here writes about the reconciliation of estranged humanity to the one God through the atoning death of Christ. The good news of God's reconciling work through Christ is at the heart of the gospel that Paul proclaims as God's servant. God has bestowed on Paul a unique stewardship to make known the gospel. As such, Paul is continuing the mission of the Isaianic Servant to be a light to the gentiles and bring good news of peace. But this stewardship comes with affliction. Paul has suffered and is continuing to suffer for the cause of Christ. He is currently languishing in the bonds of Roman custody.

The execution of his mission to fulfill the word of God has resulted in many people living in Colossae and the surrounding territory coming to know Christ (through Epaphras during Paul's minsitry at Ephesus). Paul feels a deep level of responsibility for these believers and reaches out to them through this letter and intercedes for them through his ardent intercessory prayers. But his labor on their behalf comes in a context of suffering. Yet because of the greater good that God will accomplish through him, it brings Paul joy.

The gospel that Paul proclaims and teaches is not a recent innovation. It was planned long ago by God and has only been recently revealed. At the heart of this gospel is the revelation that Jesus of Nazareth is the long-awaited Messiah of Israel and that his atoning death has enormous significance for gentiles who are now included in the people of God. Part of the gospel is the announcement that Jew and gentile alike experience the pneumatic indwelling of the resurrected

165 The preposition εἰς here indicates that Christ is the object of their faith and is the equivalent to an objective genitive; see Harris, 79, and Campbell, 31.

and exalted Christ. The subsequent section of the letter will unpack more of the meaning and significance of this union with Jesus Christ.

Paul declares that he, his missionary companions, and all Christian leaders are dedicated to proclaiming this good news. Indeed, this is the mission of the church. This is indicated by the shift to the first-person plural in 1:28. And God's word continues to be taught in all of the newly established communities of believers so that every single believer would mature into full conformity with God's revealed will. This work is carried out by the infusion of divine energy that God supplies.

Paul wants believers throughout the Lycus Valley to know that he continues to struggle for them both in prayer and in the ministry of the word. He wants to encourage them in two ways: (1) that they would be unified together in love, and (2) that they would know Christ by knowing the full range of truths about who he is, what he has done, and what he has taught, and by growing deeper in their experiential knowledge of Christ personally—especially in what it means to be united with him. He wants them to embrace Christ as the true and ultimate source of wisdom and knowledge.

Paul wants them to become so well-grounded in knowing Christ that they can discern and reject dangerous and deceitful teaching. This is crucially important because they now face a threat from the so-called philosophy, which Paul will discuss in the section that follows. Ultimately, Paul wants to see their faith in Christ grow firm and strong and for the churches in the Lycus Valley to experience stability.

Christology remains the leitmotif in this section. The heart of this passage can be summed up in Paul's passionate efforts to see these believers grow firm in their faith in Christ. He wants them to grow deep in their knowledge, insight, and understanding of Christ. This is the basis for true unity. Paul declares that all the treasures of wisdom and knowledge are in Christ. There is therefore no reason for seeking spiritual wisdom and insight from other sources.

# Living for Christ and Resisting a Dangerous Set of Teachings (2:6–15)

## *Bibliography*

**Arnold, C. E.** *Colossian Syncretism.* ———. "Jesus Christ: 'Head' of the Church," 346–66. **Attridge, H.** "On Becoming an Angel," 481–98. **Beard, M.** *Roman Triumph.* **Bevere, A.** *Sharing in the Inheritance.* **Bornkamm, G.** "Heresy of Colossians," 123–45. **Buls, H. H.** "Colossians 2:12," 13–16. **Bürger, C.** *Schöpfung und Versöhnung.* **Canavan, R.** *Clothing the Body.* **Cannon, G.** *Traditional Material.* **Carr, W.** *Angels and Principalities.* ———. "Two Notes on Colossians," 492–500. **Davies, W. D.** *Paul and Rabbinic Judaism.* **Deichgräber, R.** *Gotteshymnus.* **Deissmann, A.** *Bible Studies.* ———. *Light from the Ancient East.* **Dunn, J. D. G.** "Colossian Philosophy," 153–81. **Egan, R. B.** "Lexical Evidence," 34–62. **Fee, G.** *Pauline Christology,* 289–338. **Ferguson, E.** "Spiritual Circumcision," 485–97. **Frey, J.** "Die paulinische Antithese," 45–77. **Gardner, P. D.** "Circumcised in Baptism," 172–77. **Giem, P.** "*Sabbatōn,*" 195–210. **Goulder, M.** "Colossians and Barbelo," 601–19. **Gräbe, P. J.** "Salvation in Colossians," 287–304. **Grundmann, W.** *Begriff der Kraft.* **Hatina, T. R.** "Perfect Tense-Form," 224–52. **Hay, D. M.** "All the Fullness of God," 163–80. **Hayes, H. D.** "Colossians 2:6–19," 285–88. **Heil, J. P.** *Colossians.* 101–33. **Hoppe, R.** *Der Triumph.* **Hunt, J. P. T.** "Colossians 2:11–12," 227–44. **Lightfoot, J. B.** "Colossian Heresy," 13–59. **Lohse, E.** "Ein hymnische Bekenntnis," 427–35. **Luttenberger, J.** "Der gekreuzigte Schuldschein," 80–95. **Marshall, P.** "ΘΡΙΑΜΒΕΥΕΙΝ," 302–17. **Meeks, W. A.** "Moral Formation," 37–58. **Merk, O.** "Erwägungen zu Kol 2,6f," 407–16. **Peterson, J.** "Baptism in Colossians," 65–77. **Robinson, J. A. T.** *Body.* **Sappington, T. J.** *Revelation and Redemption.* **Schille, G.** *Hymnen.* **Schweizer, E.** "Elementen der Welt," 111–18. ———. "Slaves of the Elements," 455–68. **Smith, I. K.** *Heavenly Perspective.* **Smith, R. R. R.** "Imperial Reliefs from the Sebasteion," 88–138. **Son, S.-W.** "σῶμα," 222–38. **Standhartinger, A.** *Entstehungsgeschichte.* **Stettler, C.** "Opponents," 169–200. **Sumney, J.** "Opponents," 366–88. **Tripp, D.** "Colossians 1:19, 2:9," 78–79. **Van Kooten, G. H.** *Cosmic Christology.* **Walsh, B. J.** "Contextual Reading," 1–17. **Wedderburn, A. J. M.** *Baptism and Resurrection.* **Weiss, H.** "Law," 294–314. **Wengst, K.** *Formeln.* **Williamson, L.** "Led in Triumph," 317–32. **Wood, K. H.** "Sabbath Days," 338–42. **Yates, R.** "Colossians 2:15," 573–91. ———. "Metaphor of Forgiveness," 248–59.

## *Translation*

[6]*Therefore, as you received Christ Jesus the Lord, walk in him,* [7]*being rooted and built up in him and established in the faith,*[a] *just as you were taught, and abounding in thanksgiving.*[b] [8]*Watch out that someone will not lead you away as a captive through the philosophy, which is empty deceit, on the basis of human traditions, inspired by demonic spirits of the world and not inspired by Christ.* [9]*For in him all the fullness of deity dwells in bodily form.* [10]*And you are filled in him, who*[c] *is the head of every ruler and authority.* [11]*In him you were also circumcised with a circumcision not done physically but in the removal of the body—that is, the flesh, in the circumcision done by Christ* [12]*when you were buried with him in baptism.*[d] *In him also you were raised through faith in the power of God, who raised him from the dead.* [13]*And you, being dead in your transgressions and in the uncircumcision of your flesh, he made you alive with him, when he forgave us all our wrongdoings.* [14]*He cancelled the promissory note*

*with its terms that were against us and condemned us; he took it away by nailing it to the cross.* [15]*He disarmed the rulers and the authorities and*[e] *he exposed them publicly, leading them in a triumphal procession in him.*

## Notes

a. [2:7] The Majority text has the preposition ἐν, "in," before the article/noun (τῇ πίστει). This is most likely a clarifying addition prompted by the prevalence of this preposition in the near context. The simple τῇ πίστει, "in the faith," is original and corresponds to Pauline usage (see, e.g., Rom 4:19, 20; 11:20; 14:1; 2 Cor 1:24; Phil 1:27).

b. [2:7] Codex Vaticanus (B) along with the Majority text and a few other witnesses have the more expansive περισσεύοντες *ἐν αὐτῇ* ἐν εὐχαριστίᾳ, "abounding *in it [faith]* with thanksgiving." Nearly all commentators rightly regard this addition as a scribal assimilation to Col 4:2, γρηγοροῦντες ἐν αὐτῇ ἐν εὐχαριστίᾳ, "watching in it with thanksgiving." The other difficulty with this reading is that it requires πίστις, "faith," to be interpreted in the active sense of belief or trust (so Lightfoot, 177) rather than "that which is believed," i.e., the content of the faith passed on to the Colossians (see the *Comment* on 1:7).

c. [2:10] Some fairly important witnesses (𝔓[46] B D F G) read ὅ ἐστιν, "which is," instead of ὅς ἐστιν, "who is." The neuter relative would then refer to τὸ πλήρωμα, "the fullness," instead of to Christ. No recent commentators or versions accept the alternative with the neuter. The most likely explanation is that it arose as an assimilation to the recurring ὅ ἐστιν, "which is," that is found elsewhere in the letter (see 1:24, 27; 3:14).

d. [2:12] Codices Sinaiticus (א) and Alexandrinus (A) agree with the Majority text in supporting the reading βαπτίσματι, "in baptism," which reflects the neuter βάπτισμα. 𝔓[46], Codex Vaticanus (B), D, F, G, and a few other witnesses read βαπτισμῷ, "in baptism," which reflects the masculine noun (βαπτισμός). This is a clear case of scribal assimilation to the far more common βάπτισμα (which appears nineteen times in the NT) and, more importantly, is the term that Paul uses in Rom 6:4 (see also Eph 4:5).

e. [2:15] Two early and very important witnesses (𝔓[46] B) include a καί, "and," here. This fits the context well since it precisely parallels the structure of 2:14:

> ἐξαλείψας τὸ . . . χειρόγραφον . . . καὶ αὐτὸ ἦρκεν . . . προσηλώσας αὐτό
> ἀπεκδυσάμενος τὰς ἀρχὰς . . . *καὶ* ἐδειγμάτισεν . . . θριαμβεύσας αὐτούς

Although none of the major critical editions of the Greek NT (NA[28]/UBS[5], SBLGNT, WH, Tisch[8]) read the text with καί, "and," some English versions supply "and" in translation; e.g., "he disarmed the rulers and authorities and made a public example of them" (NRSV; see also RSV; ESV; CSB; Tyndale; Geneva). Both the external and internal evidence favor the inclusion of καί, "and" (so also Lohse, 112n38).

## Form/Structure/Setting

### *Form (and Literary Context)*

Colossians 2:6–15 forms the theological heart of the letter. Following a summons to conduct their lives in a way that is consistent with their confession of Jesus Christ as their Lord and a stern warning about a teaching that threatens their commitment to Christ, the apostle Paul grounds these Colossian believers in a deeper understanding of what it means to be in a relationship with him. The expression "in him" appears six times in this section, and "with him" occurs three times. In this text, Paul reveals and develops the meaning of this crucial concept.

Part of the way he does this is through affirming the identification of believers with Christ in the key events of salvation: his burial, resurrection, and coming to life. He points to baptism as the Christian rite that illustrates this identification with Jesus in his death and resurrection. This has significant continuity with his earlier teaching on this topic in Rom 6 (see the *Excursus: Participation in the Death and Resurrection of Christ*). He also does this through developing a set of metaphors that are unique to this passage: (1) God filling his people just as he filled the tabernacle or the temple with his presence under the old covenant; (2) Jesus performing a spiritual circumcision on his new-covenant people as a way of conveying how he has dealt with their sinful inclination; (3) God cancelling a promissory note that contained deadly stipulations for defaulting on one's obligation to God; this image is elaborated even to the point of God taking this document away from them and nailing it to the cross; and (4) God disarming, publicly exposing, and leading the demonic powers in a triumphal procession. The first two images come from Paul's OT and Jewish background, but the latter two are drawn from his Greco-Roman context.

In terms of rhetorical analysis, Witherington suggests that Paul is employing Asiatic rhetoric here because of the rhythm and meter exhibited in this passage, which he says would "sound" more impressive to the first-century hearer than it would have read.[1] He claims that such rhetoric was "highly emotive and grandiose," in which "the sentences tend to flow fast and furious with the piling up of phrases, clauses, synonyms, and the like." Yet, as Aletti notes, the style of this section is typical of Pauline exhortation.[2] It is difficult to see how the description that Witherington gives of Asiatic rhetoric could not equally apply to Rom 6–8. In terms of rhetorical function, Witherington characterizes this section as the second *probatio* ("proof") within a document that he regards as a piece of deliberative rhetoric.[3] He contends that Paul's purpose here is to show how a particular course of conduct is preferable to another.[4] Bird, on the other hand, while agreeing that this is a deliberative discourse, asserts that this section is crafted as a *refutatio*.[5]

A number of scholars have contended that the author was appropriating and editing hymnic material in this section of Colossians. Schille postulated that that author has cited a "song of redemption" (*Erlöserlied*), but heavily edited and

1 Witherington, 151–52.
2 Aletti, 159.
3 Witherington, 151.
4 So also Lincoln, 619.
5 Bird, 73.

supplemented it to assist his engagement with the teaching of "the philosophy."[6] His reconstruction of the hymn was based on remnants that he finds embedded in 2:9, 10b, 11b, and 13b–15. Schille's thesis has not found support in the subsequent course of scholarship, since much of 2:9–13a can better be explained as the author drawing upon and applying thoughts from the hymn of 1:15–20 as well as from Rom 6. Nevertheless, a substantial group of scholars have contended that a hymnic text can be discerned as laying behind 2:13b–15 or 2:14–15.[7] The principal arguments for this include the switch to the first-person plural (which is consistent with a confession), the change of verbal subject from the second-person plural to God, the abundant use of participles, short clauses, parallel lines, and the concentration of words used only here.

Gnilka has observed, however, that the extraordinarily divergent results on the reconstruction of the original "cross-triumph song" makes one feel rather skeptical about accepting the conclusion that the author is drawing on a fixed and coherent hymn (or even a fragment of a hymn).[8] Many other scholars have reached a similar conclusion and contend that it is inferring too much to postulate an actual hymn,[9] but that it is better to see the author of Colossians employing traditional imagery throughout this section.[10] But even discerning what is traditional imagery is rather difficult without external sources with which to compare it. Moreover, the style of this section—especially the abundant use of aorist participles, the alternation of pronouns from second person to first person, and the creative employment of imagery—is consistent with the style of the author of this letter and, indeed, with the apostle Paul himself.

### *Structure*

In this section, Paul delivers an admonition, issues a warning, and then provides an extensive theological argument explaining how it is possible for the Colossians to carry it out. The admonition (2:6–7) is given with a present imperative (περιπατεῖτε, "walk"), which is followed by a series of four present participles that give expression to the means by which the primary action is to be accomplished. The warning (2:8) is also delivered with a present imperative (βλέπετε μή, "watch out"), but then followed by a series of four prepositional phrases.

At the beginning of 2:9, Paul uses a ὅτι, "because," to signal his explanation

---

6 Schille, *Hymnen*, 31–37.

7 E.g., Lohse, "Hymnisches Bekenntnis," 427–35; Wengst, *Formeln*, 186–94; Burger, *Schöpfung und Versöhnung*, 79–114; Cannon, *Traditional Material*, 44–49; Lindemann, 43–45; Hoppe, *Triumph*, 252–59; Standhartinger, *Entstehungsgeschichte*, 213.

8 Gnilka, 120.

9 See Barth and Blanke, 390, who conclude that "the thesis of a literally cited hymn fragment is hardly defensible"; see also Deichgräber, *Gotteshymnus*, 168–69.

10 E.g., Schweizer, 136, notes, "What we have here is traditional imagery used in abundant measure"; see also Gnilka, 121.

for the basis of adhering to the admonition and warning. Most immediately, this conjunction refers to the two indicative assertions of 2:9–10, but its causal force effectively reaches to the end of the section (2:11–15). This is confirmed, in part, by the fact that the two ἐν ᾧ καί, "in him also," phrases in 2:11–12 refer to and explain the two ἐν αὐτῷ, "in him," phrases of 2:9–10. In simpler terms, Paul is unpacking the meaning for the Colossians of what it means to be "filled in him" (2:10).

The verses of 2:11–13 are structured around the three aorist finite verbs that are the primary assertions of this section:

περιετμήθητε, "you were circumcised"
συνηγέρθητε, "you were raised with him"
συνεζωοποίησεν, "he made you alive with him"

This is more accurate grammatically than structuring the passage around the three σύν-compund verbs. The aorist participle συνταφέντες, "buried together with," should be seen as dependent on the first verb, περιετμήθητε, "you were circumcised," and thereby explanatory of its meaning. This circumcision is not compounded with the preposition σύν, "with," precisely because this form of spiritual circumcision is not something Christ himself experienced but rather is a procedure he performs (see *Comment* on 2:11). This rite is experienced by believers through their identification with Jesus in his burial (συνταφέντες).

The final two sentences of the section (2:14–15) lack any formal grammatical connection to 2:13 (such as any form of conjunction). Grammatically, 2:13–15 comprise three coordinate clauses, which all share the same subject (God):

συνεζωοποίησεν, "he made you alive with him"
ἦρκεν, "he has taken [it] away"
ἐδειγμάτισεν, "he exposed them"

Rather than taking the final two clauses (2:14–15) as independent assertions, it is better to interpret their semantic values as explanatory to 2:13: συνεζωοποίησεν ὑμᾶς σὺν αὐτῷ, "he made you alive with him," despite the absence of a conjunction such as γάρ, "for," or ὅτι, "because."

This results in a certain balance and symmetry in the flow of thought from 2:9–15. The two principal assertions that form the core thought of the passage would then be "you have been filled in him" (2:9) and "he made you alive with him" (2:13). These statements overlap significantly in meaning. The skeletal structure of the passage could then be diagrammed in the following way:

ἐστὲ ἐν αὐτῷ πεπληρωμένοι, "you have been filled in him" (2:10)
  περιετμήθητε, "(in him) you were (also) circumcised" (2:11)
  συνηγέρθητε, "(in him) you were (also) raised together with him" (2:12)

συνεζωοποίησεν, "he made you alive with him" (2:13)
ἦρκεν, "he has taken (it) away (from you)" (2:14)
ἐδειγμάτισεν, "he exposed (them)" (2:15)

The statements of 2:11–12, while supporting the assertion of 2:10, also support the assertion of 2:13. This makes spiritual circumcision (dying with Christ) and being raised with Christ explanations of what it means to be made alive with Christ. This interpretation thereby results in a greater continuity with the content of Rom 6.

Finally, it is important to observe that 2:14 and 2:15 share an identical grammatical structure—aorist participle . . . finite verb . . . aorist participle:

ἐξαλείψας τὸ . . . καὶ αὐτὸ ἦρκεν . . . προσηλώσας αὐτό
ἀπεκδυσάμενος τὰς . . . ἐδειγμάτισεν . . . θριαμβεύσας αὐτούς.

Noting this helps in assessing their significance (see *Comment* on 2:14—15).

The symmetry noted here is missed by Heil, who makes 2:11–12 and then 2:13–15 the C and C′ members of a macrochiasm spanning the entirety of 2:6–23.[11]

## *Setting*

Although the passage begins as a general ethical exhortation ("as you received Christ Jesus the Lord, walk in him," 2:6), it quickly shifts into a dire warning ("watch out that someone will not lead you away as a captive," 2:8). In the remainder of the passage, Paul lays a firm theological basis for how the Colossians can resist the impulses of the dangerous teaching and live in a way that honors and pleases their Lord.

It is in this passage that we learn that there is a threatening teaching that Paul refers to as "the philosophy" (which is likely the faction's self-designation) and just how dangerous Paul understands it to be. He not only sees the teaching as inconsistent with a confession of faith in Christ, but he goes so far as to assail the teaching as "empty deceit" and "inspired by demonic spirits." In fact, Paul sees the Colossians as facing the threat of being swept up by this teaching into a form of bondage (like booty that is taken by a victorious army in a war).

Spiritual powers figure prominently in this passage. The section begins and ends with reference to them, but with a dramatic reversal. At the outset, Paul unveils the fact that demonic spirits are behind this captive-taking "philosophy," but at the end, the rulers and authorities are spectacularly defeated by God through the work of Christ in his cross and resurrection. These principalities and powers seem to function at two levels. On the surface, the Colossians appear to be aware of the danger of spirits and are searching for mechanisms to ward

11 Heil, *Colossians*, 101–33.

off their influence in day-to-day life. On a deeper level, the demonic spirits are cleverly inspiring the very rituals and practices that create bondage. In other words, the ostensible solution is the actual poison.

This passage does not suggest that "the philosophy" was propounding an alternate system of salvation. At issue is the Colossians' potential relinquishing of the lordship of Jesus Christ over every area of their lives. Their concern about matters of daily life in this rural, agricultural, pastoral, and mining area extended to common issues such as dealing with curses, the evil eye, plagues, disease, sickness, and a host of other problems often perceived as stemming from spirits. This made the Colossians susceptible to traditional ways of handling these problems and, particularly, by trusting the advice of a shaman figure who would have solutions for the community because of his esoteric wisdom and knowledge.

Paul's burden in this text is to reshape the thinking of the Colossian believers so that they could finally understand that in Christ they have all they need. He wants them to know that they are so closely united with the resurrected Christ that they share in his power and authority over the demonic realm.

## *Comment*

Some interpreters highlight 2:6–7 and characterize it as the author's statement of the theme of the letter.[12] Formally, however, it is the beginning of the first section of the body of the letter in which Paul begins his polemic. The lack of a conjunction (asyndeton) with v. 8 ties that verse closely to vv. 6–7. Paul's warning to "watch out" for those advocating the competing teaching is thus seen as an instance of how the Colossians should "walk in him" (2:6b)—that is, by discerning and resisting teaching that is not part of "the faith" in which they are being confirmed (2:6).

**6** Ὡς οὖν παρελάβετε τὸν Χριστὸν Ἰησοῦν τὸν κύριον, "therefore, as you received Christ Jesus the Lord." Paul is anxious for these Colossian believers to conduct their lives in a manner that is consistent with their confession of faith in the Lord Jesus Christ. This will involve the Colossians gaining increased stability in the core teachings of the Christian faith that they received and in living a life of gratitude to God for his grace. The conjunction οὖν, "therefore," is a major structural signal that Paul uses throughout the letter to mark a transition to a new topic (see 2:6, 16; 3:1, 5, 12). It also retains some inferential force and would here function to call the readers to reflect on what has already been said thus far in the letter about Christ Jesus the Lord, whom they have received. This would most immediately refer to their faith in Christ (2:5; see also 1:4), which corresponds to "receiving" Christ (2:6) but also to knowing Christ (2:2–3), experiencing "Christ in you" (1:27), being reconciled to God through the death

12 See Moo, 177; Dunn, 136–43.

of Christ (1:22), growing in their understanding of Christ as Lord of creation and Lord of redemption (1:15–20), knowing the redemption and forgiveness of sins he provides (1:14), and experiencing life in the new dominion of the Son of God (1:13).

The language Paul chooses for receiving (παρελάβετε) Christ comes from Paul's Jewish heritage. It is a technical expression for receiving oral tradition and corresponds to the Hebrew קִבֵּל *qibbēl*, "receive," that was often coordinated with מָסַר *masar*, "deliver." These are the expressions used in Mishnah *'Abot* 1:1: "Moses *received* Torah at Sinai and *handed it on* to Joshua" (translation by Neusner). Paul has used the term in this sense elsewhere in his letters for receiving the creedal statement about the death, burial, and resurrection of Christ (1 Cor 15:1, 3), the tradition of the Lord's Supper (1 Cor 11:23), the gospel itself (Gal 1:9, 12), the word of God (1 Thess 2:13), and the ethical tradition of how believers should walk and please God (Phil 4:9; 1 Thess 4:1).

The content of the tradition the Colossians have received is probably best interpreted in the most expansive sense as both the person of Christ and the confessional traditions about him. The preceding verse spoke of the readers as having put their faith in Christ as a person (2:5). The following verse refers to them being confirmed in the faith that they were taught (2:6). Consequently, it would be inappropriate to limit the referent either to the kerygmatic traditions[13] or to receiving the person of Christ into their lives.[14] The Colossians learned these traditions through Epaphras (1:7) and on that basis put their faith in Jesus and "received" him personally into their lives.

The Jesus whom the Colossians received is both "Messiah" (Χριστός) and "Lord" (κύριος). In light of Paul's emphasis on the revelation of the mystery as "Christ in you" (1:27; 2:2), it is likely that he is using Χριστός, "Messiah," in its full significance as a title[15] and not as a proper name.[16] Paul's earlier explanation of Jesus as the mystery stresses the closeness and intimacy that new-covenant believers would have with God in and through the Messiah. "Receiving" Christ thus results in being "in Christ" and experiencing "Christ in you." Their reception of Christ also entails their need to acknowledge him as Lord of all creation (1:15–17) and Lord over the church (1:18; see also 1:3, 10). As Paul will soon relate, he is concerned that they are running the risk of relinquishing their allegiance to Christ as Lord by giving heed to the rival teaching.

ἐν αὐτῷ περιπατεῖτε, "walk in him." Having prayed that they would conduct their lives in a manner that is worthy of the Lord (1:10; see *Comment* there on the word), Paul now enjoins them to live their lives ἐν αὐτῷ, "in him." The simplicity of expression can mask the depth of meaning that he intends. The preposition

---

13 So Sumney, 126.
14 Barth and Blanke, 300.
15 So also Wilson, 192.
16 Contra Lohse, 93.

(ἐν) should be interpreted as having local significance and refers to the sphere in which they live their lives. It is a strongly relational concept that predicates their daily life on the union and solidarity they experience with the risen Christ. As their Lord, Christ establishes the norms and standards for their new life. He provides them with both perspective and motivation through the traditions they have received. Jesus is also a dynamic presence in their lives who enables them to fulfill his ethical imperatives and to live out the values and mission of his kingdom. The thought here corresponds with his exhortation to the Galatians to "walk in/by the Spirit" (πνεύματι περιπατεῖτε; Gal 5:16). It is appropriate to understand the writer's choice of the present tense of the verb as indicating that this should be the Colossians' regular manner of life.

**7 ἐρριζωμένοι καὶ ἐποικοδομούμενοι . . . καὶ βεβαιούμενοι . . . , περισσεύοντες ἐν εὐχαριστίᾳ**, "being rooted and built up . . . and established . . . , and abounding in thanksgiving." The four participles that follow the main verb περιπατεῖτε, "walk," explain how the action is to be carried out and are thus participles of means.[17] They are probably not to be interpreted as attendant-circumstance participles since neither the main verb nor the participles are aorist and since the participles do not precede the main verb.[18] Participles of means are common after present imperative and present hortatory-subjunctive verbs (e.g., 1 Cor 4:12; Gal 5:26; Eph 5:18–20; 6:9; Jude 23).

ἐρριζωμένοι, "being rooted," varies from the other three participles in that the author uses the perfect tense whereas the others are present. Paul is thereby suggesting that they have already taken root in Christ, and this serves as the basis for further growth. Jeremiah uses the image with reference to God's providential care of people: "you plant them, and they take root [ἐρριζώθησαν]; they grow and produce fruit" (Jer 12:2 ESV). Isaiah speaks of the danger people face who are not well-rooted: "scarcely are they planted, scarcely sown, scarcely has their stem [ἡ ῥίζα] taken root in the earth, when he blows on them, and they wither" (Isa 40:24 ESV). Of course, in the parable of the sower, Jesus also warned about those who had no root and were scorched when the sun rose (Matt 13:6). The use of the imagery here is certainly appropriate in a context where Paul is concerned about the stability of this group of believers in light of the challenge presented by "the philosophy."

ἐποικοδομούμενοι, "built up." Paul rapidly shifts metaphors from botany to buildings with the second participle. He uses a similar combination of metaphors in 1 Cor 3:5–14 where he moves from planting, watering, and growth in 3:5–8 to building imagery in 3:9–14. He uses the same compound verb (ἐπ-οικοδομέω) in that context as well where the architectural imagery indicated that Paul was thinking of the new-covenant people of God as a temple ("Do you not know that you are God's temple and that God's Spirit dwells in you?," 1 Cor 3:16 NRSV;

---

17 Sumney, 128, refers to them as expressing "manner."

18 See Wallace, *Grammar*, 642.

see also Eph 2:20). This combination of metaphors is also found in the Rule of the Community at Qumran: "when such men as these come to be in Israel, then shall the party of the *Yahad* truly be established, an 'eternal planting,' a temple for Israel" (1QS 8.4–5).[19]

The passive voice of the participle here is consistent with the emphasis on their union with Christ (ἐν αὐτῷ) as the source of their growth. But this growth is also stimulated by acquiring a deeper knowledge and understanding of the traditions they have received, as the following line emphasizes. Jude employs the same image to stress the importance of learning the core teaching of the faith ("you, beloved, build yourselves up [ἐποικοδομοῦντες] on your most holy faith," Jude 20 NRSV).

καὶ βεβαιούμενοι τῇ πίστει καθὼς ἐδιδάχθητε, "established in the faith, just as you were taught." The third participle continues the thought of the first two by commending an additional way the Colossians believers should conduct their lives in relationship to Christ. The emphasis here is on gaining a complete understanding of the apostolic teaching that results in a firmness and stability in their lives. This is precisely what they need in light of the threat presented by the deviant teaching. At the turn of the century, Deissmann argued that βεβαιόω and its cognates was consistently used by Paul and his circle in a technical sense—that is, in the legal sense of "guarantee," "surety," or "confirmation." He claimed that there was an extensive use of the term with this legal sense in the documentary papyri.[20] Although some commentators have followed him in this conclusion,[21] the word was not always used in a technical sense in the literature of the day and could have the meaning "establish" in a way similar to the use of στηρίζω, "establish," in 1 Thess 3:2, 13; 2 Thess 2:17; 3:3.[22] The general notion of "establish" is also the way that Paul uses the term in 1 Cor 1:8 and 2 Cor 1:21.

The idea of being established thus interprets the two previous metaphors of being rooted and firmly built but extends the focus beyond participation in Christ to a firmness that comes from knowing and appropriating apostolic doctrine. It is thus best to interpret τῇ πίστει, "in the faith," as a reference to teaching (*fides quae creditur*) and not to the act of believing.[23] This is confirmed by the reference to the received traditions in 2:6a and by the explanatory καθὼς ἐδιδάχθητε, "just as you were taught," that immediately follows. The dative case should thus be taken as a dative of reference.[24]

The Colossians received (or ἐδιδάχθητε, "were taught") the doctrines that comprised the gospel from Epaphras (1:7), who presumably received these teachings from the apostle Paul during his ministry in Ephesus (AD 55–57) where the

19 Translation from Wise, Abegg, and Cook, *Dead Sea Scrolls*, 129.
20 Deissmann, *Bible Studies*, 104–9, esp. 109.
21 E.g., Martin, NCB, 78.
22 M. Silva, "στηρίζω," *NIDNTTE* 1:498–99; see also BDAG, s.v. στηρίζω 2.
23 So Lohse, 94, and most commentators; contra Lightfoot, 177.
24 Harris, 182.

book of Acts claims that "all the residents of Asia heard the word of the Lord" (Acts 19:10 ESV). The language that Paul uses in our passage—"the faith" (ἡ πίστις)—is suggestive of a widely agreed upon set of teachings that Christians throughout Asia Minor (and perhaps the Mediterranean world; see 1:6) would have recognized as the basis for their confession. It is important to see that the theological appeal that Paul makes to the Colossians in light of the competing teaching of "the philosophy" was not based on his own idiosyncratic belief structure but on a common core of beliefs that he shared with other followers of Christ in Jerusalem, Antioch, Ephesus, Corinth, Rome, and elsewhere.

περισσεύοντες ἐν εὐχαριστίᾳ, "abounding in thanksgiving." The fourth participial clause conveys a characteristic trait of any believer who understands the substance of the truths of the gospel and knows the dynamic experience of life in relationship to the risen Christ. All who have truly experienced redemption, forgiveness of sins, union with Christ, and everything that the gospel entails have a constant and profound sense of gratitude to God for his goodness. Although this clause is technically fourth in a series of parallel expressions, the first three are semantically linked in meaning since all convey the notion of gaining a firmer foundation. The fourth then conveys a second characteristic of the Christian life that flows out of the previous three. In other words, as one acquires a more extensive understanding of the cardinal truths of the faith and as one grows deeper in a knowledge of Christ personally, a profound gratitude will well up within the person and will be expressed to God.

Grammatically, the first three participles are linked by the coordinating conjunction καί, "and," which ties them closely together. The καί, "and," is missing before the fourth participle, but it should still be seen as dependent on περιπατεῖτε, "walk," and not on the immediately preceding ἐδιδάχθητε, "you were taught," or βεβαιούμενοι, "being established."

περισσεύω, "to abound," is a favorite term for Paul and is often used to describe both the lavishness of God's gifts to his people (e.g., the unsparing gift of Christ's sacrifice resulting in justification [Rom 5:15]; God's grace abounding to his people [2 Cor 9:8; Eph 1:6–8]) and their overflowing response to him (e.g., overflowing in hope [Rom 15:13]; excelling in building up the church [1 Cor 14:12]; abounding in the work of the Lord [1 Cor 15:58]; extravagant in their love [1 Thess 4:9–10]). The pairing with εὐχαριστία, "thanksgiving," also occurs in 2 Cor 4:15 and 9:12. Thanksgiving to God is a major theme in this letter and in Paul's writings as a whole (see *Comment* on 1:3 and 1:12).

**8** Βλέπετε μή τις ὑμᾶς ἔσται ὁ συλαγωγῶν, "Watch out that someone will not lead you away as a captive." The second major imperative of this section is a serious warning and explains one way in which the Colossian believers are to conduct their lives in Christ.

Βλέπετε μή, "watch out," is a form of warning that Paul uses elsewhere in his writings (1 Cor 8:9; Gal 5:15). It appears also in the Olivet Discourse where Jesus warns his disciples, "Watch out that no one deceives you" (βλέπετε μή τις ὑμᾶς πλανήσῃ; Mark 13:5 NIV; see also Matt 24:4; Luke 21:8). Paul finds the Colossian believers facing a dangerous situation in which they could be led astray.

τις ὑμᾶς ἔσται ὁ συλαγωγῶν, "that someone will not lead you away as a captive." Paul refuses to name the person or persons respresenting the threat to the Colossian Christians, but simply uses the indefinite pronoun τις, "someone," to identify them. Some have thought that this language means that there is no identifiable and specific threat and that the author simply wants to make the church resistent to potential threats.[25] But it is clear enough that Paul can use the indefinite pronoun to refer to opponents that he would rather not name, as in Galatians (see Gal 1:7: τινές εἰσιν οἱ ταράσσοντες ὑμᾶς, "some who trouble you"). It is also reading too much into the singular form of the pronoun to conclude that there was only one individual teacher who posed the trouble. The τις, "someone," could refer to the principal spokesperson for a faction.

The grammatical construction of τις ἔσται, "someone will be," with the articular participle is somewhat unusual, but is equivalent to a relative clause,[26] "watch out for someone *who will* lead you away captive." Normally in such a warning, one would expect the use of the subjunctive. Lightfoot, however, suggested that the switch to the indicative "shows that the danger is real."[27] Because of the exceptional nature of this construction, this is a valid observation. The language concretizes the reality of the threat.

Paul further underlines the threat to the church by utilizing the rare word συλαγωγέω, "to lead captive." In fact, this is the first documented occurrence of the word in the history of the Greek language. If Paul himself coined the word, his meaning would have been clear enough to the original readers. The neuter plural noun τὰ σῦλα, "plunder," was used to refer to booty or plunder that was seized (often with reference to the cargo of a ship).[28] The second part of the word, -αγωγέω (a cognate of ἄγω, "to lead"), was commonly appended to nouns and indicated the action of leading or carrying away; for example, λιθαγωγέω ("to transport stones"), σιταγωγέω ("to convey corn"), φορταγωγέω ("to carry loads"), and δουλαγωγέω ("to carry away as a slave"). Perhaps the most comparable example would be λαφυραγωγέω, "to carry off as booty," which occurs in Josephus (λαφυραγωγήσαντες δὲ τὰ ἐν τῇ χώρᾳ, "they took a great many of spoils in that country"; Josephus, *Ant.* 13.385). The term σῦλα, "plunder," was not unfamiliar to Paul since he uses the verbal form of it (συλάω, "to rob") in 2 Cor 11:8. In like manner, he is also familiar with the -αγωγέω ("lead away") termination since he uses it in connection to δουλαγωγέω, "slave," in 1 Cor 9:27 ("I punish my body and subdue it as a slave [δουλαγωγῶ]"). This information

25 E.g., Wolter, 120.
26 BDF §412.
27 Lightfoot, 178.
28 See LSJ, s.v. συλάω II.

suggests that Paul could easily have coined συλαγωγέω, "to lead captive," and that this term should not necessarily be counted as another example of a hapax legomenon pointing to pseudonymity.

Because of the serious threat presented by the factional teaching, which Paul characterizes as "empty deception" and as inspired by τὰ στοιχεῖα τοῦ κόσμου, "demonic spirits," he creates this colorful term to shock the Colossians into reflecting on the gravity of the danger facing them. His appeal is quite similar to what he delivered to the Galatians when he warned them that they were facing the imminent threat of being reenslaved to the dominion of τὰ στοιχεῖα τοῦ κόσμου, "demonic spirits" (Gal 4:3). Now he once again uses the language of captivity and slavery to speak of the substantial danger posed by the purveyors of the Colossian "philosophy." Whereas in Galatians the readers were in danger of being victimized by the powers through embracing Torah and nomistic obervances, in Colossae the danger is presented as being reenslaved to the powers through acceding to the ritualistic observances advocated by a shaman figure. The imaginative proposal by Wright that Paul is making a contemptuous pun on the term συναγωγή, "synagogue," by using συλαγωγέω, "to lead captive,"[29] should be dismissed. Such a rhetorical device is quite without precedent in Paul's writings, and the threat to the church Paul is concerned about was not posed by the local synagogue(s).

διὰ τῆς φιλοσοφίας καὶ κενῆς ἀπάτης κατὰ τὴν παράδοσιν τῶν ἀνθρώπων, "through the philosophy, which is empty deceit, on the basis of human traditions." The danger that Paul sees for the Colossians is posed by something that he calls "the philosophy." This may have been the opponents' self-designation for their teaching and practice. Although it is possible to interpret the article as generic and thus denoting a class—that is, philosophy in general—the context strongly argues against this. Paul is concerned about a very specific threat with a unique set of beliefs and practices and is not firing a general broadside against philosophy as a whole. Neither does the appearance of the word φιλοσοφία, "philosophy," render it necessary for us to narrow our focus to one of the well-known school philosophies of the time, such as Platonism, Pythagoreanism, or Stoicism. The word itself was used much more broadly than it is in contemporary English usage. Philo used the term to refer to the Jewish religion (τῆς Ἰουδαϊκῆς φιλοσοφίας, "the Jewish philosophy," *Embassy* 245; see also 156) and also spoke of the Therapeutae as practicing philosophy (*Contempl. Life* 89). Josephus describes the three major sects of Judaism as "philosophies" (Ἰουδαίοις φιλοσοφίαι τρεῖς ἦσαν, "the Jews had three philosophies," Josephus, *Ant.* 18.11; see also *J.W.* 2.119). Theon of Smyrna even used the term to refer to the core practices of local religions that had mystery initiation rituals: "one might say that philosophy [φιλοσοφία] is the rite of genuine initiation and the handing of those mysteries which are genuine mysteries" (*Expositio rerum mathematicarum* 14).[30]

29 Wright, 100.

30 Cited in Lohse, 95.

It is also significant to note that esoteric knowledge expressed in texts and formulas of ritual power were termed "philosophy." In an anthology of excerpts from much earlier works, Stobaeus speaks of how a prophet imbued with esoteric knowledge works "in order that philosophy and magic [φιλοσοφία μὲν καὶ μαγεία] might nourish the soul" (*Anthologium* 1.407).[31] The book of Daniel understands "philosophy" in this sense when the LXX translates הַחַרְטֻמִּים הָאַשָּׁפִים, "magicians and enchanters" (NRSV), as σοφιστὰς καὶ τοὺς φιλοσόφους, "wise men and philosophers" (Dan 1:20). It is noteworthy that instead of φιλοσόφους, "philosophers," the Theodotion version translates the same expression as μάγους, "magicians." This understanding of philosophy also became characteristic of the Solomonic magical tradition, which employed the term to describe the rituals and formulas that were passed on. In his description of this tradition and its effectiveness in performing exorcisms, Josephus claims that Solomon studied this phenomenon "philosophically" (ἀλλ' ἐν πάσαις ἐφιλοσόφησε; *Ant.* 8.44). The use of the term "philosophy" here in Col 2:8 is thoroughly consistent with a Christian shaman figure who served the community through the practical wisdom he attained through the esoteric traditions he received ostensibly coming down from a figure such as Solomon.

The "philosophy" at Colossae is deemed by Paul to be "empty deceit"—a very harsh evaluation of the rival teaching. Grammatically, the genitive expression (κενῆς ἀπάτης) functions epexegetically to characterize the philosophy. Paul could have used either of these terms alone to denounce the teaching, but the combination forms a particularly strong condemnation. These terms do appear together, however, in some Jewish texts that warn against the dangers of idolatry. One text honors the pious in Israel who "do not honor with empty deceits [ἀπάτησι κεναῖς] works of men, either gold or bronze, or silver or ivory, or wooden, stone, or clay idols of dead gods . . . such as mortals honor with empty-minded [κενεόφρονι] counsel (Sib. Or. 3.584–90). The work T. Naph. 3.1 warns Israelites about the dangers of being corrupted "with vain words to beguile your souls" (ἐν λόγοις κενοῖς ἀπατᾶν τὰς ψυχὰς ὑμῶν). Similar to Paul's fear, this author is concerned about demonic influence ("the will of Beliar" [3.1] and "spirits of deceit" [3.3]) that would lead them to forsake God's will by making a compromise with idolatry. It is not surprising that the term ἀπάτη, "deceit," can be found in a Jewish text that condemns magical practices (Sib. Or. 3.224–27). It had become proverbial in certain segments of Judaism to speak of magic as deceit, especially as seen in the expression γοητεία καὶ ἀπάτη, "magic and deceit" (see Josephus, *Life* 40; Philo, *Creation* 165; *Decalogue* 125).

Paul then uses a series of three κατά, "according to," phrases to characterize the deceitful teaching still further. With the accusative case that follows, this preposition functions as a "marker of norm of similarity" and can be translated

---

31 Cited in Lohse, 95.

"in accordance with."[32] But the usage of the preposition here appears to go beyond this to convey the actual *source* of the deceitful teaching.[33] This interpretation is brought out well by the NLT ("that come from") or the NIV ("which depends on").

In the first instance, Paul indicates that "the philosophy" had its source in "human tradition" (κατὰ τὴν παράδοσιν τῶν ἀνθρώπων). This is precisely the same language used in Mark's Gospel to refer to Pharisaic tradition (Mark 7:8). This convergence has led some scholars to suggest that the deceitful teaching in Colossae "was essentially a form of Jewish thought being presented as a 'philosophy' by Jewish apologists."[34] Yet the Pharisees were not the only group in antiquity who passed on venerable traditions. The transmission of tradition was central to many Greco-Roman religions. Lohse has presented some of the most important texts illustrating the role of tradition in local religions that offered mystery rituals.[35] In most of these, there were no written liturgies or sacred texts that conveyed the tradition; it was passed on orally and through observation of the key events. Ritual enactment of the informing myth—the "sacred tale"—was often central to the practice of the religion.

The passing on of "tradition" held a prominent place in the practice of magic. In fact, most magical texts purport to be effective traditions that go back hundreds of years. Rituals, names, and conjurations have been collected and passed on as valuable παράδοσις, "tradition" (*PGM* I.54; IV.476). A Jewish-influenced magical text, for instance, gives insight into this process: "I am Moses your prophet to whom you transmitted your mysteries [παρέδωκας τὰ μυσηρία] celebrated by Israel" (*PGM* V.109–10). The content of the material passed on here had as its ultimate aim for the person to gain power over all kinds of demonic spirits. The rituals of power within Judaism that allegedly stemmed from Solomon were a set of traditions that had been passed on for years and were the basis for the spiritual knowledge used by Jewish shamans (like Sceva, Acts 19:14) to serve the community.

The perpetrators of the deceitful teaching at Colossae may very well have claimed that they were relying on valuable traditions (indeed, even *Jewish* traditions, but of the Solomonic magical tradition). The accompanying genitive expression, τῶν ἀνθρώπων, "of/from men," could be either possessive or a genitive of source. Either way, this was probably Paul's comment added to demean the claim of the rival teachers that their tradition was based ultimately on divine revelation.

κατὰ τὰ στοιχεῖα τοῦ κόσμου καὶ οὐ κατὰ Χριστόν, "inspired by demonic spirits of the world and not inspired by Christ." Paul now takes his polemic

32 See BDAG, s.v. κατά 5.a.

33 So Harris, 84.

34 Dunn, 148.

35 Lohse, 95–96.

an enormous step further by asserting that their traditions were actually demonically inspired. The second κατά, "according to," once again should be interpreted as indicating the source of the teaching. Because of the ultimately demonic origin of the teaching, it would therefore be appropriate to translate it as "inspired by."

The precise meaning of the expression τὰ στοιχεῖα τοῦ κόσμου has been a matter of extensive debate and is one of the key interpretive issues in Colossians. The issue therefore calls for a more extended treatment in an excursus (see below).

Opposed to this teaching that was mediated as human tradition but ultimately derived from the influence of demonic spirits, Paul reveals his firm conviction that it is οὐ κατὰ Χριστόν, "not inspired by Christ." For Paul, this is the biggest problem of all with "the philosophy." The exalted Christ who presently reigns as head of the church has neither revealed nor commended this set of beliefs and practices for his people. Paul thus sums up his main contention against the advocates of this deceitful teaching by claiming that they are "not holding tightly to the head" (2:19). Proper Christology is then the leitmotif of the letter. Paul's concern is well-expressed by the summary exhortation standing at the head of this section, "as you received Christ Jesus the Lord, walk in him" (2:6). He wants the Colossian believers both to know the exalted Christ personally but also to bring their convictions into conformity with the commonly received tradition about Jesus Christ, the Messiah.

# Excursus: The τὰ στοιχεῖα τοῦ κόσμου as Demonic Spirits

## *Bibliography*

**Arnold, C. E.** *Colossian Syncretism.* 158–94. ———. "*Stoicheia* as Evil Spirits in Gal 4:3–9," 55–76. **Bevere, A.** *Sharing in the Inheritance.* **Blinzler, J.** "Lexikalisches," 429–43. **Böttrich, C.** *Weltweisheit.* **Bousset, W.,** and **H. Gressmann.** *Religion des Judentums.* **Carr, W.** *Angels and Principalities.* **Cumont, F.** *Astrology and Religion.* **DeMaris, R. E.** *Colossian Controversy.* **Gundel, H. G.** *Weltbild und Astrologie.* **Gundel, W.** *Dekane und Dekansternbilder.* **Jordan, D.,** and **R. Kotansky.** "Two Phylacteries from Xanthos," 167–74. **Lincoln, A.** *Paradise Now and Not Yet.* **Nickelsburg, G. W. E.** *Jewish Literature.* **Nilsson, M. P.** *Geschichte der griechischen Religion.* 2 vols. **Olbricht, T. H.** "*Stoicheia*," 308–28. **Pfister, F.** "Die στοιχεῖα," 411–27. **Rusam, D.** "Neue Belege," 119–25. **Sappington, T. J.** *Revelation and Redemption.* **Scheu, L. E.** *"Weltelemente" beim Apostel Paulus.* **Schweizer, E.** "Elementen der Welt," 111–18. ———. "Slaves of the Elements," 455–68. **Scott, J. M.** *Adoption.* **Standhartinger, A.** *Entstehungsgeschichte.* **Wedderburn, A. J. M.** "Theology of Colossians," 1–71. **Wink, W.** *Naming the Powers.*

One scholar has aptly said, "What is meant by the '*stoicheia* of the world' belongs to the most disputed questions of the research on Colossians."[36] In the last forty years still no consensus has been achieved, yet it appears that a majority of scholars interpret the expression as a reference to spirits. There is good reason for this since contextually this view makes better sense of Col 2:8 and 20 and because there is adequate precedent for this usage in the mid-first century AD.

The term στοιχεῖα itself has a broad range of usage in Greek literature of the period. In a very helpful article, Josef Blinzler has provided a useful summary of the semantic range of the term:[37]

1. Letters, characters
2. The alphabet, ABCs
3. The foundation or principles of a science or institution
4. The rudiments or initial basis for something
5. The physical elements (usually earth, air, fire, and water, and sometimes ether)
6. Fundamentals
7. The planets and stars
8. Spirits of the physical elements (i.e., spirits governing the elements), star-spirits

36 Standhartinger, *Entstehungsgeschichte*, 19.

37 Blinzler, "Lexikalisches," 429–43.

9. Demons, spirits

Not all of these possibilities would fit the context in Col 2:8 or 20, so meanings such as "letters," "the alphabet," and "stars" can be immediately ruled out. Nevertheless, a wide variety of views continue to be expressed in recent scholarship. Below is a brief survey of the options:

1. *Basic Instruction.* Many of the older commentators argued that the term referred to the elementary principles of religion—that is, a basic stage of religious understanding. Lightfoot, for instance, argued that the term spoke of "rudimentary instruction."[38] Sappington has revived this view by terming it "the religious ABCs."[39] Demaris reaches a similar view, contending that they should be thought of as "guiding principles in the world" functioning in the same way the Jewish law functioned in engendering human bondage.[40]
2. *Non-Christian Religions.* In his important entry in *TDNT* on the term, Delling argued that the term στοιχεῖα refers to pre-Christian religion as a whole. Yet Paul's addition of τοῦ κόσμου, "of the world," provides a negative evaluation of the στοιχεῖα. Thus, he contends that the expression was "a comprehensive judgment on all pre-Christian religion."[41]
3. *The Domain of Flesh, Sin, and Death.* Blinzler rightly understood the negative role that the στοιχεῖα play in Galatians and Colossians and interpreted them in the Pauline categories of evil influence expressed by the terms "flesh," "sin," and "death."[42]
4. *Created Things.* Barth and Blanke argue that since the most common use of the term refers to the four physical elements, the phrase should be translated, "components of the world" and understood to be "created things."[43] The idea would be conceptually similar to Rom 1:21 where Paul says of the gentiles that they venerate created things rather than the creator.

5a. *Spirits (Those Governing the Physical Elements or Stars).* Finally, a substantial group of scholars contends that the term refers to spirits or angelic powers. Wedderburn has noted that certain selected physical elements or "constituent parts" of the world may have been coupled with a Jewish linking of these elements with angelic powers.[44] Moo takes a similar view, arguing that στοιχεῖα most commonly refers to physical elements but that it also includes reference to "those deities or spirits who were so

38 Lightfoot, 180.
39 Sappington, *Revelation and Redemption*, 169–70.
40 DeMaris, *Colossian Controversy*, 54–55.
41 G. Delling, "στοιχεῖον," *TDNT* 4:1075.
42 Blinzler, "Lexikalisches," 442.
43 Barth and Blanke, 378.
44 Wedderburn, "Theology of Colossians," 8.

closely related to those elements."[45] Because of the association of these spirits with the elements or stars, some scholars see them as spirit beings that are very powerful, as reported in BDAG: "transcendent powers that are in control over events in this world, *elements, elemental spirits*."[46]

5b. *Spirits (Demonic Powers)*. A slight variation of the previous view would be that the expression is simply an equivalent to the Pauline expression, ἀρχαὶ καὶ ἐξουσίαι, "principalities and powers."[47] Martin suggests the translation "demonic powers."[48] This is essentially the same view as the previous, but it stresses that the term is part of the reservoir of terminology for demonic spirits and not necessarily closely associated with physical elements or stars in the way it is used in Colossians or Galatians.

The combined strength of the evidence favors this latter view (5b)—that is, the expression is another way of referring to the demonic powers. Accordingly, the best translation for the term would be "demonic spirits."

This view has probably not commanded the consensus of scholarship because there are no ancient texts indisputibly dating to the first-century AD or earlier attesting this usage. Furthermore, Blinzler and Delling have profoundly influenced the course of scholarship by their cavalier dismissal of the spirit interpretation on the basis of the late date of the texts. Many commentators have simply parroted their conclusions.[49]

This approach to the dating is much too simplistic and does not adequately deal with the age of *the traditions* lying behind the ancient texts using στοιχεῖα in the sense of "spirits." Before presenting four texts that may suggest a pre-Christian date for this usage of the term, it is important to point out that the concept of the four elements and the stars as divine cosmic powers unequivocally existed before the time of the NT.[50] Dio Chrysostom (from Prusa, Bithynia) demonstrates that this thinking found its way into Asia Minor when he refers to the four physical elements as the four immortal and divine horses of Zeus, a concept that he explicitly adapted from the teaching of the magi (Dio Chrysostom, *Or.* 36.39–54). But this divinization of the elements was present in Greek thought as early as Empedocles (5th c. BC), who equated Zeus with fire, Hera with air, Hades with earth, and Nestis with water (Empedocles, frag. 6).[51]

At issue, however, is when the term στοιχεῖα first began to be applied to the

45 Moo, 191.

46 BDAG, s.v. στοιχεῖον 2. See also Gnilka, 127.

47 E.g., Harris, 85; Bevere, *Sharing in the Inheritance*, 98; Garland, 142; Hübner, 76–79; Lindemann, 40.

48 Martin, NCB, 78.

49 E.g., Wolter, 124, after citing Blinzler's and Delling's conclusions regarding the dating of the texts, states, "it is therefore hardly possible to identify the 'principalities and powers' [or, to be precise, 'angels'] mentioned in Col 2:15, 18 with the *stoicheia*."

50 See Cumont, *Astrology and Religion*, 1–35; Nilsson, *Geschichte der griechischen Religion*, 2:497; A. Lumpe, "Elementum," *RAC* 4:1081–82.

51 See A. Lumpe, "Elementum," *RAC* 4:1081.

divinized elements or the spirits standing behind them. I will discuss five texts that likely contain traditions dating to the first century AD or earlier.

(1) *Alexander Romance* (Pseudo-Callisthenes) 1.1.1–4; 1.12.4; 1.13.3. This well-known novel about the life of Alexander the Great contains a number of references to στοιχεῖα where it refers to angelic or spirit powers. The first passage (1.1.1–4) refers to the third and last pharaoh of Egypt, Nectanebo II, who ruled 360–342 BC, and says of him that "he prevailed over all by magic power [τῇ μαγικῇ δυνάμει]" and that "he subjected to himself all the cosmic powers [κοσμικὰ στοιχεῖα] by a word." The immediate context clarifies that he was able to do this by invoking angels (ἐπεκαλεῖτο τοὺς ἀγγέλους) and by calling on the Libyan god Amon (1.1.3–4). This text not only illustrates the use of στοιχεῖα for spiritual powers, but it does so in a context where there is reference to ritual (magical) power and the invocation of angels. The dating of the *Alexander Romance* is complex because a number of recensions are attested in a variety of manuscripts ranging in date from the third century AD to the Latin translation of the tenth century. The text cited here comes from the earliest recension (recension α) that is regarded as the hypothetical original form of the text. Recent scholarship has tended to date the original form of the composition of the document quite early. Stoneman contends that "most of the component elements of the *Romance* were already in existence in the third century BC."[52] This includes, he argues, "most notably, the part of Nectanebo in the story."[53] He concludes that "all this suggests that the main outlines of the narrative could have been fully formed as early as 50–100 years after Alexander's death."[54] Additional references to the cosmic powers (κοσμικὰ στοιχεῖα) occur in recension α (1.12.4) and recension β (1.13.3).

(2) Testament of Solomon 18.1–2. In this portion of the Testament, Solomon commands thirty-six demons to appear before him so that he can interrogate them and force them to divulge how they can be defeated: "I commanded another demon [δαίμονα] to appear to me. And there came to me thirty-six elements [στοιχεῖα]" (18.1). Following this, they all respond to Solomon's question, "Who are you?" by affirming, "We are the thirty-six elements [στοιχεῖα], the world rulers of this age of darkness" (18.2). Each of these demons are then identified as spirits who are decans of the zodiac (18.4). These spirits are not transcendent to the extent that they are detached and uninvolved in human experience; they are very much involved by inflicting all kinds of physical illnesses and various other kinds of maladies upon people. The term στοιχεῖα is also used in this way at 8.2, but the eighteenth chapter is the one portion of the Testament that can be positively dated to as early as the first century BC (see the *Introduction* of the present work for a discussion about the dating of this text).

52 Stoneman, *Alexander Romance*, 9.
53 Stoneman, *Alexander Romance*, 10.
54 Stoneman, *Alexander Romance*, 11.

The Egyptian astrological decan tradition is a well-attested teaching in the Ptolemaic era.

(3) 2 Enoch 16.7. The longer recension of 2 Enoch uses the term "elements" in connection with "spirits" and "angels": "Thus she [the sun] goes, day and night, in accordance with the heavenly cycles, lower than all the cycles, swifter than the heavenly winds, and spirits and elements and flying angels, with 6 wings to each angel."[55] Although the text is written in Slavonic, the Greek text standing behind this portion would likely have read: πνεύματα, στοιχεῖα, ἄγγελοι.[56] Recent scholarship is leaning toward an early date (as early as the first century AD) for the original form of 2 Enoch.[57] Böttrich has suggested that the primitive form of the text stood in the shadow of the more popular 1 Enoch prior to AD 70 and afterward became widely used in the esoteric circles of Jewish mysticism.[58]

(4) *PGM* XXXIX.18–19. This brief papyrus text contains a recipe for love magic, a crude drawing of the god Bes, and many *nomina barbara*. The conjuration of the text is simply: "I adjure you by the twelve elements of heaven [στοιχείων τοῦ οὐρανοῦ] and the twenty-four elements of the world [στοιχείων τοῦ κόσμου], that you attract Herakles whom Taaipis bore, to me, to Allous, whom Alexandria bore, immediately, immediately, quickly, quickly."[59] Although this papyrus dates to the fourth century AD, the tradition it contains is much earlier. In particular, this text reflects the astrological decan tradition that was characteristic of the astronomy and cosmology of the Ptolemaic era in Egypt.[60] The concept of astrological "decans"—spirits associated with the zodiac or certain segments of the 360° of the heavenly sphere—is in the oldest astrological handbooks. Outside of Egypt, it was known in a Greek inscription of the third century BC and was also used of astral gods in Rome during the first century BC (see Manilius, *Astronomica* 4.298, 372). These decans could also be referred to as "angels" or "demons." The application of στοιχεῖον to an astrological spirit or god appears elsewhere in the Greek magical papyri, such as in *PGM* IV.1303, where it is applied to the constellation of the Bear: "Bear, greatest goddess, ruling heaven, reigning over the pole of the stars, highest, beautiful-shining goddess, incorruptible element [στοιχεῖον] . . ." (see also *PGM* IV.1126).

(5) An exorcistic phylactery from Xanthos in Lycia (a hundred miles south of Colossae).[61] Although this amulet dates to the third or fourth century AD, it shows no sign of Christian influence. The magical names, magical characters, and the Ouroboros serpent all reflect traditions of magic that date much earlier.

55 Translation by F. I. Anderson in *OTP* 1:130.
56 Bousset and Gressman, *Religion des Judentums*, 323.
57 See Nickelsburg, *Jewish Literature*, 225.
58 Böttrich, *Weltweisheit*, 54.
59 Translation by E. R. O'Neil in *Greek Magical Papyri in Translation*, 279.
60 Gundel, *Weltbild und Astrologie*, 77–81.
61 Jordan and Kotansky, "Two Phylacteries from Xanthos," 161–74.

Jewish influence is present through the mention of *Adonaē* and *Sabaoth* as well as the enigmatic inclusion of the Aramaic *talitha*. The text of this phylactery reads:

> Holy elements [οἰστυχία (editors read, στοιχεῖα)], holy *charactēres* [magical characters] powerful and strong, drive away every wicked demon [δέμονα], occurrence or happening or encounter or evil eye, drive and chase them away from Ioannes, whom Theoktista bore, now, now, quickly, quickly! [Bibi]ou, Bibaōth, Babouth, Iaōth, Enou Talitha, Ōmōkōth, Eōth, Kallōthōth, Iaōth, Idouaōth, Thiōyōth, Iabrēaēaōth, Laloudēth, Marmaraiōth, Mamaōth, Aaataara, Ōai ii Iaō I aaaaa y ēēē eeee.[62]

The crucial element for us to observe here is that, if the editors of the text are correct in reading στοιχεῖα in place of οἰστυχία, this would be the first epigraphically attested occurrence of στοιχεῖα in western Asia Minor. Such garbled spellings are common in the magical texts (such as the spelling of δαίμων as δέμονα) in this text. In this text, the στοιχεῖα are seen as supernaturally powerful beings who can come to the rescue of the person afflicted.

Although additional texts could be discussed, these should be adequate to demonstrate that there is a distinct possibility the term στοιχεῖα was used with reference to spirits in the first century AD and earlier. The final text may also suggest that it was current in Asia Minor and was known and used of powerful supernatural beings in the context of magic. This evidence is at least sufficient to warn interpreters against an a priori dismissal of the spirit interpretation only on the basis of the date of the evidence.[63] The possibility, then, that Paul could have used στοιχεῖα as part of his vocabulary for spirits should at least be considered in the evaluation of the respective contexts where the term occurs in his writings.

The term only appears four times in Paul's writings, the earliest of which is in Gal 4:3, 9. The use of the term there would suggest that it was part of Paul's vocabulary for the powers and not derived from the teaching of "the philosophy" at Colossae. Nevertheless, it may be significant that the only occurrences of τὰ στοιχεῖα τοῦ κόσμου are in letters to churches in Asia Minor. Both of the occurrences in Gal 4 are best interpreted as references to evil spirit beings, warranting the translation, "demonic spirits."

In Gal 4:3, Paul explains to his readers (both Jews and gentiles) that "while we were minors, we were enslaved by the demonic spirits of the world" (ὑπὸ τὰ στοιχεῖα τοῦ κόσμου). Determinative for a proper interpretation of this passage is the Jewish two-age framework. He compares the period prior to the coming of Christ to a time of minority when a child is under guardians and trustees. But Paul's evaluation of this time is quite severe. He uses the language of slavery (ἤμεθα δεδουλωμένοι, "we were enslaved"; Gal 4:3) to describe the plight. Even

62 Translation by Jordan and Kotansky, "Two Phylacteries from Xanthos," 164.

63 As is done, for instance, by Moule, 91–92.

the language he uses for "guardians and trustees" in Gal 4:2 (ἐπιτρόποι and οἰκονόμοι) may evoke the memory of Israel's bondage in Egypt under severe taskmasters.[64] But the genitive predication τοῦ κόσμου, "of the world," places the στοιχεῖα firmly into Paul's Jewish two-age understanding of life. The most likely explanation for Paul's use of στοιχεῖα here is that it derives from his apocalyptic worldview, which envisions the present evil age as dominated by hostile principalities and powers. The advent of Christ and his work on the cross, however, has redeemed believers from the present evil age (Gal 1:4) and from the slavery experienced under the realm of demonic spirits.

In Gal 4:9, the second occurrence, Paul continues his negative evaluation of the στοιχεῖα by characterizing them as "weak and worthless" (τὰ ἀσθενῆ καὶ πτωχά). This type of language was typical in OT and Jewish thought for referring to idols and the gods of this age as weak and worthless (see Deut 4:28; Ps 115:4–8; Isa 44:9–20; Wis 15:15–19; Ep Jer 6:3–72). Epistle of Jeremiah 6:17–18 (6:15–16 LXX) says, "For just as someone's dish is useless when it is broken, so are their gods when they have been set up in the temples" (NRSV). Paul can likewise speak of idols as demons (1 Cor 10:20). But the stronger argument for interpreting the στοιχεῖα here as demonic comes in Paul's comment that his readers, in their pre-Christian experience, "served those who were by nature not gods" (ἐδουλεύσατε τοῖς φύσει μὴ οὖσιν θεοῖς; Gal 4:8b). This is similar to the language that Paul uses in 1 Cor 10:20 when he refers to the beings that the Corinthians formerly worshiped as so-called gods and subsequently says that when pagans make their sacrifices, they are actually offering them to demons (δαιμονίοις καὶ οὐ θεῷ; 1 Cor 10:20). By the Galatians giving their allegiance to Jesus Christ, they had effectively turned away from the domain of the στοιχεῖα and the slavery experienced under their sway. The idea is quite similar to Col 1:13, where Paul describes conversion as a deliverance from the domain of darkness (ἐκ τῆς ἐξουσίας τοῦ σκότους) and transferral into the kingdom of his Son.

The overall thrust of Paul's appeal in Galatians is to the gentile believers not to embrace the form of Torah observance advocated by the Judaizing opponents (especially circumcision and the keeping of purity laws and ritual observances). To orient one's life around the law in this fashion is tantamount to returning to the domain of the demonic powers.

The contexts of both occurences of the term στοιχεῖα in Colossians argues strongly in favor of the interpretation of the term as spirits. Moule, who thinks the issue of the date is determinative against the spirit interpretation, has noted, "there is no reason to deny that a belief in demonic powers is natural in this context."[65] In Col 2:8, Paul sounds a strong note of warning against the opponents by characterizing their "philosophy" as empty deceit. He further demeans their teaching with a series of three κατά, "according to/stemming from," statements:

64 Scott, *Adoption*, 81–86.

65 C. Moule, 91–92.

| | |
|---|---|
| κατὰ τὴν παράδοσιν τῶν ἀνθρώπων | ("on the basis of human traditions") |
| κατὰ τὰ στοιχεῖα τοῦ κόσμου | ("inspired by demonic spirits of the world") |
| καὶ οὐ κατὰ Χριστόν | ("not inspired by Christ") |

The first phrase indicates the intermediate source of the teaching that the opponents are disseminating at Colossae. It is passed on as human tradition in ways similar to how the Pharisees pass down their traditions. The second and third phrases describe the ultimate source of the teaching from both a positive and negative point of view. In the final analysis, the teaching is from demons and not from the Lord Jesus Christ. Because of the presence of καί, "and," linking the final two phrases, it is clear that they are more closely associated with each other than with the first phrase ("on the basis of human traditions"), which lacks a conjunction. In addition, by inserting the negative particle οὐ, "not," before the preposition of the third phrase, the author establishes a direct contrast with the immediately preceding phrase.[66] This results in two contrasting statements about the origin of the teaching ("from this . . . and not from this"). Since the latter of these two is a personal being, it is reasonable to infer that the contrasting member is a personal being (in this case a plurality of beings).

It is consistent with Paul's thought to ascribe the ultimate source of dangerous teaching to angels and spirits. He warned the Galatians, "Even if we or an angel from heaven should preach to you a gospel contrary to the one we preached to you, let him be accursed" (Gal 1:8). He told the Corinthians that the "god of this age" blinds the minds of unbelievers so they cannot apprehend the gospel of Christ (2 Cor 4:4). One of the ways that Satan accomplishes this blinding is through teaching that is counter to the gospel. Paul revealed that the recently arriving "super apostles" at Corinth were in fact masquerading as servants of Christ while they were actually inspired by Satan (2 Cor 10:13–15). The notion of demonically inspired false teaching becomes particularly acute in the Pastorals, where the readers are warned that "now the Spirit expressly says that in later times some will depart from the faith by devoting themselves to deceitful spirits and teachings of demons" (1 Tim 4:1; see also 2 Tim 2:25–26). Among the church leaders of the second and third centuries, this became a prominent explanation for the source of deviant teachings (see, e.g., Barn. 2.10; Herm. Mand. 11.3–4; Ign. *Trall.* 6–8; Justin, *1 Apol.* 26; 58; Irenaeus, *Haer.* 1.13.1, 3, 4; 5.26.2; Tertullian, *Praescr.* 40).

Paul's use of the term in Galatians demonstrates that it was part of his own vocabulary, but this does not mean that it was unknown to the advocates of "the philosophy," especially if they were drawing on Jewish terminology for the realm of spirits (as Paul does). The fact that the term appears in Jewish folk tradition (e.g., T. Sol. 18.1–2) may indicate that Paul's opponents as well as his readers at

66 Lohse, 99, speaks of a "sharply formulated antithesis."

Colossae were already familiar with the term as part of the language used for demonic spirits.

Paul's polemic against "the philosophy" in this text would have startled his readers as they began to realize that he was actually asserting that these competing teachers were inspired by the same malicious powers from which they were seeking protection. The genitive expression τοῦ κόσμου, "of the world," was likely Paul's own addition, as in Galatians, to make it clear that these spirits belong to the present evil age and were demonic. The biggest problem of all for the Colossian Christians is that the teaching of "the philosophy" stands diametrically opposed to their faith in Christ (see also Col 2:19).

In the second occurrence of στοιχεῖα in Colossians, Paul declares that "you have died with Christ from the demonic spirits of the world" (ἀπεθάνετε σὺν Χριστῷ ἀπὸ τῶν στοιχείων τοῦ κόσμου; 2:20). This entailment of Christ's death for his people flows out of his dramatic statements regarding Christ's victory over the principalities and powers (ἀρχαὶ καὶ ἐξουσίαι) through his death on the cross in the previous paragraph (Col 2:15). He referred to the significant spiritual implications of this death with reference to the powers at the outset of the letter when he describes the Colossians' conversion in terms of God rescuing them "from the authority of darkness" (ἐκ τῆς ἐξουσίας τοῦ σκότους) and transferring them into the kingdom of his beloved Son (Col 1:13). In Col 2:20, Paul uses the preposition ἀπό, "away from," to emphasize their decisive separation from the compelling influence of the powers of darkness.

It is unlikely, as some commentators have surmised, that the teachers of "the philosophy" were asserting that the στοιχεῖα were controlling the heavenly realm and thus blocking a person's access to the presence of God, either in their quest to gain a visionary experience of the divine throne[67] or on the day of death when the soul would ascend to heaven.[68] The concern of the readers was probably much more mundane and directed toward their hostile influence on matters relating to daily life—causing sickness, effecting a curse, harming crops or livestock, causing plagues, earthquakes, floods, and all kinds of other forms of evil. The rival teachers presented a solution to this concern that focused on rituals of power and calling on angels (Col 2:18) to avert their influence. The apostle Paul now says that not only are the teachers of "the philosophy" themselves unduly influenced by the powers but that the readers' participation with Christ in his death has monumental significance for the powers. They now can discern and resist the influence of demonic spirits—in whatever way that they manifest their influence. Most immediately, Paul calls on the Colossians to resist the "regulations" imposed on them by the advocates of "the philosophy" (Col 2:20b–23). Their focus should rather be on Christ, the living head of the church (Col 2:19; 3:1).

67 Lincoln, *Paradise Now and Not Yet*, 115.
68 Schweizer, 166.

**9** ὅτι ἐν αὐτῷ κατοικεῖ πᾶν τὸ πλήρωμα τῆς θεότητος σωματικῶς, "for in him all the fullness of deity dwells in bodily form." The reason that the Colossians need to resist the teaching of "the philosophy" and can resist it is because they are in a dynamic personal relationship with Jesus Christ who is God in the flesh. This renders superfluous any dependence on other spiritual beings or other forms of accessing ritual power.

The subordinating conjunction ὅτι, "because," that begins this section signals that Paul is now giving the basis for their refusal of the dictates of the rival teachers. The force of the ὅτι continues through 2:12 and likely to the end of this section (2:15). In other words, all of the positive theological content expressed throughout this section combines to form a powerful set of reasons that the Colossians need to resist the persuasive efforts and judgmental indictments by the advocates of "the philosophy." Barth and Blanke rightly reject the notion that the conjunction marks the beginning of a citation of a hymn or other piece of tradition here that extends throughout this section.[69] As many scholars have noted, this section may very well contain traditional statements but is not itself a coherent piece of tradition.

In this line of text, Paul elaborates on an important christological affirmation made in the hymn. The similarity of wording is striking (as seen below where the common words are underlined):

<u>*ὅτι ἐν αὐτῷ*</u> εὐδόκησεν <u>*πᾶν τὸ πλήρωμα*</u> <u>*κατοικῆσαι*</u> (1:19)
"for in him all the fullness was pleased to live"

<u>*ὅτι ἐν αὐτῷ*</u> <u>*κατοικεῖ*</u> <u>*πᾶν τὸ πλήρωμα*</u> τῆς θεότητος σωματικῶς (2:9)
"for in him all the fullness of deity lives in bodily form"

This comparison shows that the two principal explanatory comments that Paul makes are (1) his characterization of the fullness as "deity" (θεότης) and (2) his qualification of its dwelling in Christ "in bodily form" (σωματικῶς). These two terms would normally signify a sharp contrast, but here they are joined in a unity to describe Christ.

The ἐν αὐτῷ, "in him," that begins this clause is used in a slightly different way than the subsequent use of the same phrase in 2:10 and the resumptive ἐν ᾧ, "in him," of 2:11 and 12. These latter three phrases continue the participationist-Christology theme that pervades this letter, whereas the "in him" at the beginning of 2:9 pertains to Christ himself.

In repeating the hymnic declaration that πᾶν τὸ πλήρωμα, "all the fullness," dwells in Christ (see the discussion of πλήρωμα in the comments on 1:19), Paul switches from the aorist tense (1:19) to the present tense here (2:9). The natural way to interpret this shift is to see an emphasis on incarnation in the earlier

69 Barth and Blanke, 311.

reference and an indication of permanence in this passage. In other words, what began in the incarnation now continues in Christ's exalted state.

The genitive expression τῆς θεότητος, "of the deity," should be interpreted as an epexegetical genitive and thereby functions to clarify the meaning of "all the fullness."[70] The term θεότης, "deity," is quite rare, occuring nowhere else in the NT or LXX (nor even in Josephus or Philo), yet it becomes exceedingly common in the Greek-speaking church in reference to Christ.[71] This passage probably exerted a decisive influence on that development. In terms of Jewish literature, the term never appears except in the Apocalypse of Sedrach (2.5; 7.10; 14.8; 15.1), but the final form of this text dates into the late Byzantine era. Although it may have been written as early as the mid-second century, it shows substantial signs of Christian editing and cannot be used to illustrate its usage here. Paul has probably chosen this term because it was known and used by Greek writers around the time of the first century (e.g., Plutarch, Comarius, Lucian) who used it in the sense of "deity" or "divine nature."[72] Plutarch uses it, for instance, to speak of some humans who become heroes (εἰς ἥρωας), then lesser gods (εἰς δαίμονας), and then become sharers in the divine nature (θεότητος μετέσχον; see Plutarch, *Def. orac.* 415; see also *Is. Os.* 359d). The transformation Plutarch speaks of has reference to a change in the essence or substance of the individual. Colossians 2:9 thus comes close to the later "substance" theology of the church. Barth and Blanke affirm this and say that it designates "the substance of the divine," which is correct at a basic level, yet one must be cautious not to read back into this text the fully articulated construct of substance (οὐσία; *substantia*) as the underlying being of the Trinitarian God that was worked out by the time of Nicaea (AD 325).[73] One must also be careful to differentiate θεότης, "deity," from θειότης, "divinity." The latter refers to a "quality or characteristic(s) pertaining to deity"[74] and not properly to the divine nature itself. Fee regards the term as a "periphrasis for 'God,'"[75] but this does not explain why Paul did not simply use θεός, "God," especially since he uses it in Eph 3:19 (τὸ πλήρωμα τοῦ θεοῦ, "the fullness of God"). The most likely explanation for his use of θεότης, "deity," here is that Paul wanted to put stress on Christ's quality or state of being as God, which this term would effectively communicate.

The switch to the present tense of the verb "live/dwell" (κατοικεῖ) conveys that the fullness of deity continues to dwell in Christ, especially in his role as the resurrected head of the church.[76] But the overriding emphasis of the text is

---

70 So also Pokorný, 121; G. Schneider, "θεότης," *EDNT* 2:142.

71 See Lampe, *Patristic Greek Lexicon*, 637–39.

72 BDAG, s.v. θεότης.

73 Barth and Blanke, 312.

74 See BDAG, s.v. θειότης.

75 Fee, *Pauline Christology*, 308.

76 So also Schweizer, 138.

that deity resides in Jesus Christ's human body (σωματικῶς)—that is, deity and humanity come together in an inextricable union in Christ.

The vast majority of interpreters have understood σωματικῶς, "bodily," to refer to the literal physical body of Christ; that is, it speaks of Jesus's incarnation, life on earth, and continuing existence in a resurrected and glorified body.[77] This view is thoroughly consistent with the hymn of 1:15–20 that presents Christ as the preeminent Lord of all creation yet also declares that it was his human blood shed on the cross that is the basis for the reconciliation of his people. Paul connects this directly with the human body of Jesus in his initial comments on the hymn when he says that "God reconciled you in the *body* of his flesh" (ἀποκατήλλαξεν ἐν τῷ σώματι τῆς σαρκὸς αὐτοῦ; 1:22a). Of course, the whole notion of resurrection (2:12) is predicated on the assumption that Jesus possessed a human body so that he could become "firstborn from among the dead" (1:18b).

A number of interpreters, however, have argued that the σκιά-σῶμα, "shadow-substance/reality," contrast of 2:17 is decisive for interpreting the use of σωματικῶς in 2:9. If this is correct, σωματικῶς thus means "essentially," "really," "actually." Thus Pokorný writes, "In Christ one encounters the true, authentic fulness of God, over against which all other conceptions of God, speculations, and experiences are secondary."[78] This view has a long history of adherents extending back to many of the Greek Fathers and some of the Reformers.[79] Hübner has rightly objected that such a use of σωματικῶς is difficult to verify lexicographically.[80] Furthermore, the earlier usage of σῶμα, "body," in the letter would lead the readers to think that Paul is referring either to the physical body of Jesus or the corporate body, the church.

The idea that σωματικῶς does, in fact, refer to the church is a view that has been expressed by a handful of interpreters. The idea would be that "all the fullness of deity" expresses itself through the body—that is, in the church. From this perspective, σωματικῶς thus becomes a metaphor for the church. Gnilka thus claims that this is a dynamic ecclesiological conception as opposed to an ontological statement about Christ.[81] One of the problems with this view is that it renders the ἐστέ, "you are," of 2:10 unnecessary. It is better to see the beginning of 2:10 as marking the ecclesiological relevance of what is said about Christ in 2:9.

Van Kooten has argued for a cosmological interpretation of σωματικῶς. He contends that Christ is "the space which is filled with the cosmic body (σῶμα), a body which comprises the principles (ἀρχαί), powers (ἐξουσίαι), and other celestial forces. The cosmos is viewed as coextensive with Christ."[82] But this is to confuse

77 See, e.g., Harris, 89; Wilson, 199; Moo, 194; Sumney, 133; Hübner, 179–80; Dunn, 152.
78 Pokorný, 122.
79 See, e.g., Calvin, 331, and Melanchthon, 59.
80 Hübner, 80.
81 Gnilka, 129.
82 Van Kooten, *Cosmic Christology*, 23–27.

ontology with function. Paul is certainly concerned to explain the relationship of Christ to the cosmic powers to the Colossians, but he is not arguing that they are coextensive but rather that Christ is their creator (Col 1:16), has broken their enslaving grip on believers (2:15), and exerts his authority over their domain (Col 2:10). Lohse is therefore correct in explaining one of the implications of this text by asserting that "whoever has been transferred into the domain of his kingdom is free from the powers which rule in the cosmos and which want to force their enslaving yoke upon men."[83]

In summary, this statement in Col 2:9 is purely christological and affirms the full deity of Christ in his bodily existence—a mode of existence that he assumed in his incarnation and now retains in a resurrected and glorified body. The statement summarizes and builds upon the high Christology of the hymn, but Paul explicitly and emphatically avoids any hint of Platonic disdain of matter. He thus avoids the dualism that other Christians later fell into as they attempted to explain the divine nature of Christ in a direction that led to a docetic Christology (see, e.g., 2 John 7).

**10 καὶ ἐστὲ ἐν αὐτῷ πεπληρωμένοι**, "and you have been filled in him." Paul now draws out the implications of his high view of Christ for the Colossian church in a way that stresses their participation with Christ in his authority over the demonic realm. Whereas 2:9 is an explicitly christological statement, the καὶ ἐστέ . . ., "and you are . . . ," immediately shifts the focus back to the church. The focus will remain on the church throughout this section, but as here, Paul will draw out the implications of different facets of the work of Christ for the current benefit and life of the church.

Before Paul expresses the predicate in this perfect periphrastic construction, he interjects between the verb and its participial complement the prepositional phrase, ἐν αὐτῷ, "in him." This places a significant stress on the inextricable connection between Christ and his people and simultaneously points to their need to draw on this connection for the challenges they face. Participation with Christ is the theme of this section as expressed in the repetition of "in him" and "with him" in 2:11, 12, 13, and 15. Paul is convinced that by virtue of this close connection with the living head of the church, the Colossians have all of the resources they need to remain in the faith (1:23) and to conduct their lives in a manner that is pleasing to Christ (2:6).

Paul asserts that they "have been filled" (ἐστέ . . . πεπληρωμένοι) and thus live in the state of being filled ("you are filled"). He does not specify the content of the filling here as he does in Rom 15:14 where he says that believers are "filled with knowledge" (πεπληρωμένοι πάσης τῆς γνώσεως). The idea here may overlap partly with the language of the Johannine prologue: "from his fullness [πλήρωμα] we have all received, grace upon grace" (John 1:16). More immediately, this statement picks up on the poetic declaration made about Christ in the

83 Lohse, 101.

hymn (1:19) and shows how it is relevant to the life of the church. It is remarkable that "all the fullness" (πᾶν τὸ πλήρωμα) dwells in Christ, but Paul's purpose here is not to prompt reflection on who Christ is for a doxological purpose but to show that there is profound meaning and real-life relevance for the readers. Paul's use of this terminology in the letter has its background in the Jewish temple and the notion of God filling the temple with his presence and glory (see the discussion of πλήρωμα on 1:19). The language overlaps significantly with his understanding of the new-covenant blessing of the Holy Spirit as the empowering presence of God for his people.

The application that Paul has in mind here is revealed in the following relative clause, ὅς ἐστιν ἡ κεφαλὴ πάσης ἀρχῆς καὶ ἐξουσίας, "who is the head of every ruler and authority." The "fullness" that the Colossians possess is specified by the fact that they share in Christ's power and authority over the realm of the demonic by virtue of their union with him. Paul has already affirmed that Christ is κεφαλή, "head," in 1:18, but there he is head of his body, which is the church. Here he is saying something substantially different since the genitive τοῦ σώματος, "of the body," is missing. He is not declaring Christ to be the sovereign or leader over his church, but that he is κεφαλή, "head," absolutely, particularly with respect to the demonic powers. Paul is drawing on the metaphorical use of the term to indicate "authority over" or "ruler." This usage can be seen, for instance, in Judg 11:8–9, 11 LXX where Jephthah is made "head and commander" (εἰς κεφαλὴν εἰς ἡγούμενον) over all the inhabitants of Gilead. In Hellenistic Judaism, Philo frequently uses the term ἡγεμονικός, "governing part" or "leader," and its cognates, to characterize the head (e.g., *Creation* 119; *Flight* 110, 182; *Dreams* 2.207; *Moses* 2.30, 82; *Spec. Laws* 3.184; *QG* 1.3, 10; 2.5; *QE* 2.124).

The objects over which Christ exerts his reigning power as Lord are expressed in the genitive case, πάσης ἀρχῆς καὶ ἐξουσίας, "every ruler and authority," with the case best interpreted as objective genitive. The terminology Paul uses for the angelic powers are the same terms that appeared in the hymn (1:16) and that he will use again in 2:15. By themselves, the words could refer to good angels or demonic spirits, but the subsequent context of 2:15 points unequivocally toward seeing them as evil powers. These are spirits that Christ has defeated and exposed through his work on the cross. The adjective πάσης, "every," stresses the comprehensive nature of Christ's lordship over this realm; there is not one evil power who stands outside of his sovereignty.

The fact that Paul defines the "filling" of the Colossians in this way by adding the second clause ("who is the head of every ruler and authority") suggests that the powers were a major issue for the Colossians. Paul has just indicated that demonic spirits were ultimately behind the dangerous teaching that they were facing (2:8). But they were probably also struggling with profound concern about the ongoing impact of the powers on daily life. This concern made them vulnerable to the teachings, knowledge, and rituals of the shamanistic leader of the faction. Part of Paul's solution is to help these believers comprehend the full significance of what it means for them to be "in Christ." Because they are "filled" in Christ, they share in his authority over the demonic powers. This realization would take them a long way in overcoming their fear of spirits, which for them take the form of terrestrial/chthonic spirits, astral powers, spirits in wildlife and nature, underworld spirits, and a host of other threatening demonic powers. The statements Paul makes in 2:10 thus function as the lead argument for the rest of the section by stressing the power and sufficiency of Christ for believers, who are in a dynamic union with him. Therefore, they do not need to call upon angels or perform any of the rituals of power prescribed by "the philosophy."

**11** ἐν ᾧ καὶ περιετμήθητε περιτομῇ ἀχειροποιήτῳ, "in him you were also circumcised with a circumcision not done physically." Paul now describes a second feature about their new lives in Christ. The death of Christ has delivered an enormous setback to the indwelling power of evil that bends them toward acts of sin and disobedience.

Paul assures the Colossians that based on their union with Christ (ἐν ᾧ), they have been spiritually circumcised (περιετμήθητε). He will subsequently show that this new-covenant form of circumcision has a close connection with what God accomplished in the nexus of events associated with their water baptism (2:12). The circumcision that Paul speaks of here is of course metaphorical, since the actual physical rite of circumcision came to an end as a defining mark of the people of God in the inauguration of the new-covenant age and the beginning of God's new creation (see Gal 6:15). Circumcision, however, was the sign of the covenant that God made with the patriarch, Abraham: "you shall be circumcised in the flesh of your foreskins, and it shall be a sign of the covenant between me and you" (Gen 17:11 ESV). It then became part of the Mosaic code (Lev 12:3; see also John 7:22: "Moses gave you circumcision"), and its importance was reaffirmed by the Lord to Joshua as the Israelites took possession of the land (Josh 5:2–8). The Hasmoneans demonstrated a passion for enforcing circumcision as a defining mark of what it meant to be Jewish and to have zeal for the Torah (see 1 Macc 1:60–61; 2:46, 50; Josephus, *Ant.* 12.278).

Although Paul himself was physically circumcised on the eighth day (Phil 3:5) according to the requirement of the law, his perspective on the role and function of this rite changed dramatically as a result of his experience with the risen Christ and his new understanding of the realities of the new age that had dawned. He told the Roman church that for the new people of God, circumcision was not something "external and physical" (ἡ ἐν τῷ φανερῷ ἐν σαρκὶ περιτομή), but that "circumcision is a matter of the heart, by the Spirit, not by the letter" (καὶ περιτομὴ καρδίας ἐν πνεύματι οὐ γράμματι; Rom 2:28–29 NRSV). This accords well with the spiritual circumcision that was anticipated in the OT. The law itself even commended this when it enjoined the people of Israel to "circumcise, then, the foreskin of your heart, and do not be stubborn any longer"

(Deut 10:16 NRSV; see also Jer 4:4) and later spoke of God himself performing this work on his people (Deut 30:6).

For Paul, this divine operation of spiritual circumcision has taken place in the work of Christ. By describing it as happening ἀχειροποιήτῳ, literally "not done by hand," he emphasizes that it is not the physical rite that he is referring to but the unique work of God. This term is used only one other time by Paul and appears in a context where he is speaking of the eternal home that God has prepared—"a house not made with hands [ἀχειροποίητον], eternal in the heavens" (2 Cor 5:1). Mark uses it in a similar way to speak of the new-covenant temple where he reports Jesus as saying, "I will build another, not made with hands" (ἀχειροποίητον; Mark 14:58 NRSV). The same idea appears in Daniel's description of the dream of Nebuchadnezzar where "a stone was cut out, not by human hands [ἄνευ χειρῶν]" that destroyed the statue representing four successive kingdoms and then became a kingdom that filled the world (Dan 2:34, 45).

The positive counterpart χειροποίητος, "made with hands," often occurs in anti-idolatry contexts in the LXX where the word is used to demean the idols as not having a divine origin, but as simply human creations (see, e.g., Lev 26:1, 30; Isa 2:18; 10:11; 16:12; Dan 5:4, 23). But Paul's intent in Colossians is not to insinuate that the old-covenant rite of circumcision was on par with idolatry; it was a divine institution and mandated by God. He is stressing that God has replaced this rite with something that is not a physical procedure done by human hands on the eighth day of the life of every male but is a divine work that takes place at the time of spiritual rebirth.

ἐν τῇ ἀπεκδύσει τοῦ σώματος τῆς σαρκός, "but in the removal of the body, that is, the flesh." Literal physical circumcision involved the removal of a portion of skin. In his development of spiritual circumcision, Paul says that it, too, involves the removal of what he terms "the body of the flesh." Interpreting precisely what he means by this has proven difficult to interpreters. There are three principal views.

(1) *Stripping off the literal physical body to free the believer for ascent to heaven.* A number of interpreters have seen in this reference to the stripping off of an allusion to a gnostic worldview and its disdain for material existence. In this view the Colossian philosophers would have contended that the body is the foremost obstacle that binds one to the earth and prevents the ascent to the heavenly homeland.[84] The σῶμα τῆς σαρκός, "the body of flesh," is understood simply as the human body in its limitations. Whereas in the mystery cults, a person underwent a ritual initiation in which the soul experienced rebirth and transformation, the author of this letter claims that a spiritual rebirth has taken place through union with Christ in his burial and resurrection. The believer in Christ experiences this through the ritual of baptism. Lindemann argues that the Colossian "philosophy" was a Jewish-influenced Christian gnosis that actually

84 See, e.g., Lohse, 102; Lindemann, 42; Bornkamm, "Heresy of Colossians," 128.

practiced physical circumcision as a visible act that signified the removal of one's deep connection to the material world.[85] He argues for the plausibility of the practice of this ritual in gnostic circles on the basis of a passage in the Gospel of Philip where the writer says that Abraham's circumcision teaches that "it is proper to destroy the flesh" (Gos. Phil. 82).

In addition to the problematic assumption that some form of gnostic religious system of redemption was in existence at this time in Asia Minor, this view falters in not providing a compelling explanation of the phrase in context. Lindemann does the best job of dealing with the precise wording of the text, but there is no explicit evidence that any gnostic group practiced circumcision as a symbolic act of assuring its adherents that they would be free of their bodies in the future.[86] Furthermore, it is not at all clear that the opponents at Colossae actually practiced circumcision since this discussion is not a part of the polemic against "the philosophy."

(2) *A reference to the death of Christ.* Moule has argued that the phrase refers to Christ stripping off his physical body in death.[87] The expression thereby corresponds to the participation of believers with Christ in his burial/death as signified by baptism. This view necessitates understanding τῇ περιτομῇ τοῦ Χριστοῦ, "the circumcision of Christ," as an objective genitive.[88] This view claims the advantage of providing a better contextual fit with 2:15 where the cognate term ἀπεκδυσάμενος, "stripping off," is used with reference to the death of Christ. It also corresponds precisely with Paul's earlier use of the phrase, σῶμα τῆς σαρκός, "the body of flesh," in 1:22 where it clearly refers to Christ's physical body put to death.

A number of commentators have rightly objected to this view since one would have expected the author to include an αὐτοῦ, "his," at the end of the phrase so that the text would essentially read: "in the removal of *his* body." As the text currently stands, it would be natural to assume that the subject of the verb ("you") would be the implicit reference for the phrase—that is, "in the removal of *your* flesh." Dunn protests against this objection by observing that each reference to flesh thus far in Colossians (1:22, 24; 2:1, 5) has denoted physical flesh. But this is to ignore the fact that two of the subsequent references to flesh (2:18, 23) are used in the Pauline ethical sense.[89]

(3) *Stripping off the sinful tendency.* The consensus view has been to understand the expression as referring to the implications of the work of Christ for the sinful propensity within individuals, the phenomenon that Paul refers to as "flesh."[90] Moo aptly describes the phrase as "a metaphor for the conquering of the power

85 Lindemann, 42.
86 Lindemann, 42.
87 C. Moule, 95–96.
88 Also holding to this view: Dunn, 157–58, and Lincoln, 624.
89 Dunn, 157.
90 See, e.g., Moo, 200; Sumney, 137; MacDonald, 99; Bruce, 104.

of sin that takes place when a person comes to Christ."[91] This view is seen in a number of English versions: "your whole self ruled by the flesh was put off" (NIV); "the cutting away of your sinful nature" (NLT); "by the stripping away of the old nature" (NEB); and "by the complete stripping of your natural self" (NJB). It is likely that the variant reading in which τῶν ἁμαρτιῶν, "of the sins," was inserted between "body" and "flesh" originated as an early interpretive understanding of the expression and was then reflected in the Authorized Version: "putting off the body of the sins of the flesh" (so also in the Geneva Bible, Bishops' Bible, and Tyndale). This view would correspond well with Paul's ethical use of "flesh" and provides consistency with this use of the term in 2:18 and 23. It also would prove to be a strong conceptual parallel with Gal 5:24 where Paul declares that "those who belong to Christ Jesus have crucified the flesh with its passions and desires."

This latter view provides the best explanation of all the evidence. The content of the verse bears a striking similarity to the ideas and terminology of Rom 6:6: "we know that our old self was crucified with him in order that the body of sin might be brought to nothing, so that we would no longer be enslaved to sin" (ESV). In common between the two passages is the experience of co-crucifixion or co-burial with Christ signified by the ritual of baptism and the impact that this has on the body. The σῶμα τῆς ἁμαρτίας, "body of sin," in Romans refers to the body as determined by the power of sin. The difference in the Colossian passage is that Paul here uses the term σάρξ, "flesh," in its ethical sense yet carrying the same idea: the body as it is determined by the power of this evil inclination.

This explanation of the phrase also coheres well with Col 3:9 where Paul uses the aorist participle ἀπεκδυσάμενοι τὸν παλαιὸν ἄνθρωπον, "having stripped off the old self." This verse looks back to the conversion event as a time when "the old self," which is coextensive with the flesh, was dealt a decisive blow that is foundational to the ability of believers to eradicate vices and appropriate Christian virtues. In an anticipatory way, this is precisely what Paul is saying in Col 2:11–12. Spiritual circumcision has to do with the victory that Christ has gained over the power of sin in the lives of believers that will enable them to conduct themselves in a manner that is pleasing to him.

This is the first attested use of the terms ἀπέκδυσις, "stripping off," and ἀπεκδύομαι, "to strip off," in the Greek language. Although some interpreters include these in lists of hapax legomena to count against the Pauline authorship of the letter,[92] the authentic Pauline letters show a familiarity with cognate compounds (see ἐκδύομαι, "take off," in 2 Cor 5:3–4; ἐνδύομαι, "put on" in Rom 13:12, 14; 1 Cor 15:53, 54; Gal 3:27; 1 Thess 5:8; ἐπενδύομαι, "put on" in 2 Cor 5:2, 4). This is consistent with Paul's penchant for using compound forms with

91 Moo, 200.
92 E.g., Lohse, 85.

prepositions that are unique or seldom used elsewhere, especially with ἀπό, "from" (e.g., ἀπολύτρωσις, ἀπεκδέχομαι, ἀποτολμάω, ἀποστυγέω, ἀπελεύθερος, ἀπόκριμα, ἐξαπορέομαι, ἀποκαραδοκία, ἀπορφανίζω).

The noun σάρξ, "flesh," is best explained in terms of the Pauline ethical use of the term (as, e.g., in Rom 8:3–13; Gal 5:13, 16, 17, 19, 24). The genitive case should be taken as expexegetical and thus explanatory of σῶμα, "body," that is, the body determined by the power of the flesh. In an influential study, Davies argued that behind this use of "flesh" is the Jewish concept of the evil and good "inclination" (יֵצֶר, *yēṣer*).[93] Every person struggles with a tendency to do evil based upon a strong inner bent or inclination. The nonsectarian wisdom texts from Qumran have revealed a similar ethical use of "flesh" to what is found in Paul that also corresponds with the later rabbinic idea of the evil impulse (e.g., 4Q416 frag. 1.10–16; 4QInstruction[c] [= 4Q417] frag. 2.16–18; 4Q418 frag. 81.1–2). In 4Q416 frag. 1.10–16 there is an ethical and eschatological contrast between two groups: one designated "flesh" and characterized by evil and impurity, and the other designated "sons of truth." Frey suggests that this view would have been prominent in Jerusalem at the time that the young Saul was receiving his rabbinic training.[94]

The idea here is that by union with Christ in his death, believers have been freed from the compelling power and bondage of this inner bent toward evil. This does not mean that believers are entirely free from its influence. Otherwise, the ethical admonitions of Col 3 would be superfluous. It does mean, however, that identification with Christ has profound implications for one's ability to resist evil influence and to appropriate virtue.

ἐν τῇ περιτομῇ τοῦ Χριστοῦ, "in the circumcision done by Christ." This is an interpretive translation of an ambiguous genitive expression here best understood as a subjective genitive. The thought Paul is expressing is that Christ is the one who has performed the circumcision—a spiritual circumcision involving the excision of the sinful compulsion in the lives of believers. Not all would agree with this interpretation, however, and a variety of views have been expressed regarding the nature of the relationship of the genitive to the head noun:

1. *Objective genitive: the circumcision performed on Christ, namely, his death on the cross.* This view asserts that Christ is the recipient of the circumcision, but not the literal circumcision on the eighth day of his life on earth (Luke 2:21), but to a circumcision that should be interpreted as the removal of his fleshly body—that is, a reference to his death.[95]

93 Davies, *Paul and Rabbinic Judaism*, 17–35.

94 Frey, "Die paulinische Antithese," 45–77.

95 See, e.g., Wilson, 204; Talbert, 214; Bevere, *Sharing in the Inheritance*, 69; Beetham, *Echoes of Scripture*, 176–77; Lincoln, 624; Dunn, 158; Barth and Blanke, 367–68.

2. *Subjective genitive: the circumcision performed by Christ.* This view, which is adopted here, is also reflected in the NIV, NLT, NET, and CEB.[96] It asserts that Christ is the one who performs this spiritual circumcision by uniting believers with him and enabling them to participate in his death on the cross.
3. *Attributive genitive: Christian circumcision.* Some have contended that the genitive τοῦ Χριστοῦ, "of Christ," simply functions to characterize and describe the circumcision. It could also be referred to as a "genitive of quality."[97] Thus, it could also be termed a "Christ-circumcision" or a "Christian circumcision."[98]
4. *Possessive genitive: the circumcision belonging to Christ, brought about through union with him.* Closely related to the preceding view is one that contends that spiritual circumcision belongs to Christ and is experienced by people who are brought into a union with him. This view also overlaps significantly with the second view (subjective genitive) because it implies that Christ is the one who performs this act on believers.[99]

The latter three views have much in common since they agree that the σῶμα τῆς σαρκός, "the body of flesh," refers to the sinful tendency and not to the physical body of Christ. Furthermore, they would all agree that the circumcision is not performed on Christ but on believers. It has already been observed that seeing a reference to Christ's death is unlikely because of the absence of the possessive αὐτοῦ, "his," after σῶμα τῆς σαρκός, "the body of flesh." Another argument against this view is that it creates an awkward inconsistency between the two references to circumcision in 2:11—namely, "you were circumcised" (2:11a) refers to some form of spiritual circumcision experienced by believers, whereas "in the circumcision of Christ" (2:11c) would refer to his physical death. It is more likely that 2:11c would explain the meaning of circumcision in 2:11a than offer an entirely different referent. Finally, it seems likely that Paul would have used the compound form of the verb with σύν, "with" (thus συνπεριετμήθητε, "you were circumcised together with") if he had intended to express the idea that believers participate in Christ's circumcision. As it is, he avoided using the compound form precisely to keep his readers from associating it with the other three compounds (συνταφέντες, "you were buried with," συνηγέρθητε, "you were raised with," and συνεζωοποίησεν, "he made you alive with") that communicate their solidarity with Christ in what he experienced.

It has been argued that the aorist participial clause of 2:12a, συνταφέντες

96 So also Hübner, 82; Scott, 44.

97 See BDF §165.

98 See Wolter, 128–29; Pokorný, 125; Gnilka, 132–33.

99 Advocating this view are Harris, 91; Moo, 200; Aletti, 172; Schweizer, 143; Eadie, 147; Abbott, 251.

αὐτῷ ἐν τῷ βαπτισμῷ, "when you were buried with him in baptism," modifies and explains "the circumcision of Christ" (2:11c), but it is more natural to take it with the main verb of the sentence, περιετμήθητε, "you were circumcised," and thereby clarifies the when and how of this spiritual circumcision.

Deciding among the latter three views is much more difficult since there is only a slightly nuanced difference of meaning between the three. The subjective-genitive view (no. 2) makes it much more explicit that Christ is the one who performs the circumcision. The possessive genitive view (no. 4) has the advantage of being the more common usage of the genitive when used with Christ in Colossians (e.g., 1:1, 7; 2:17; 4:12), but this is nullified by the fact that Paul does use the subjective genitive on occasion (e.g., 1 Cor 16:17; 2 Cor 7:6, 15; 8:24; 1 Thess 1:3). Furthermore, if we take the genitive as possessive or attributive, it results in a measure of redundancy with 2:11a: "you were circumcised in him . . . with a circumcision belonging to him." It is better to understand the author as advancing the discussion by asserting that "you were circumcised in him . . . with a circumcision that he performs." This results in a corporate/participational emphasis in the first clause and a more precise indication of Christ's work in the second.

In conclusion, Paul is affirming that Christ has performed a spiritual circumcision that consists of the removal of the compulsion to sin ("the flesh") for all who are incorporated into him.

**12** συνταφέντες αὐτῷ ἐν τῷ βαπτισμῷ, "when you were buried with him in baptism." The circumcision that Christ performs on believers takes place in the events associated with their baptism.

Jesus's death, expressed as his burial (θάπτω), is part of the primitive Christian confession of faith recorded in 1 Cor 15:3–4. The same compound form of the word (with the preposition σύν, "with") is used by Paul in Rom 6:4 to describe the identification of believers with Christ in his death. Nowhere else in the NT is θάπτω, "buried," used to describe the death of Jesus. The similarity of the two passages is best seen when the texts are compared:

> συνετάφημεν οὖν αὐτῷ διὰ τοῦ βαπτίσματος (Rom 6:4)
> 
>     συνταφέντες αὐτῷ ἐν τῷ βαπτισμῷ (Col 2:12)

> "therefore we were buried with him through baptism"
> 
>     "when you were buried with him in baptism"

The similarity between the two texts also extends to baptism as the rite through which believers are said to participate in Christ's death. A key part of Paul's concern in Rom 6 is to convey to believers that by virtue of their participation in Christ, the power of sin has been broken and no longer exerts a compelling reign over their lives. They have been set free from the overwhelming power of sin (Rom 6:7) and no longer have to serve it as an irresistable despot over their lives

(Rom 6:6). They are, in fact, liberated from its dominating curse and are now able to live for God (Rom 6:10–11). The issue of the formal relationship between Col 2:12 and Rom 6 will be handled in the *Excursus* (see below, "Participation in the Death and Resurrection of Christ as the Basis for a New Life—Now and in the Future").

The parallelism of the principal verbs of this section is broken by the fact that the co-burial is expressed as an aorist participle instead of an aorist finite verb. One may have expected the succession of περιετμήθητε – συνταφῆτε – συνηγέρθητε ("you were circumcised"–"you were buried with him"–"you were raised with him"). Yet the burial with Christ is grammatically dependent on περιετμήθητε, "you were circumcised," and thereby explains when and how the spiritual circumcision takes place.[100] It is not to be interpreted as dependent on the verb that follows (συνηγέρθητε, "you were raised") because the ἐν ᾧ καί, "in him also," introduces a new thought. The time of this participle is coincident with the main verb. In other words, the circumcision takes places precisely in the events associated with conversion-initiation (expressed by "baptism"). There is nothing in this context or in Paul's theology as a whole that would suggest that there is an event following conversion that constitutes God's work in delivering his people from the compelling influence of sin.

Paul further specifies that this takes place ἐν τῷ βαπτισμῷ, "in baptism." From the very beginning of the Christian movement, baptism was the ritual of initiation into the new community established by Jesus Christ. Peter declared the importance of this rite at the end of his Pentecost sermon (Acts 2:38), and the three thousand who responded to his message were baptized (Acts 2:41). The practice of baptism continued as the gospel spread to various regions and among those who were not Jews; for example, the Samaritans (Acts 8:12), the Ethiopian (Acts 8:38), the first group of gentiles (Acts 10:47–48), and in the gentile mission (Acts 16:15, 33; 18:8).

It is important to note[101] that water baptism is a metaphor for the action of the Spirit. In Paul's thought, it is the work of the Spirit that incorporates believers into the body of Christ. This action of the Spirit can itself be termed a "baptism" (1 Cor 12:13; see also Acts 1:5). Although there is little explicit emphasis on the Spirit in Colossians, the work of the Spirit is implicit in the filling and fullness language. It must be remembered that Paul began this section with the summarizing declaration "you have been filled in him" (Col 2:10). The typical Pauline (and early Christian) pattern of hearing the gospel and responding to it in faith is also presumed here. Earlier he expressed his thanksgiving to God for how the Colossians had heard the word of truth, the gospel (1:5), and put their faith in Jesus Christ (1:4). Paul is thus not establishing baptism here as the essence of conversion-initiation apart from the other essential elements (hearing

100 So also Hübner, 83.

101 Along with Dunn, 160.

the gospel, responding in faith, and the coming of the Spirit). Moo aptly notes that the rite of baptism functions here "in a kind of metonomy" where it stands as a "shorthand for the whole experience."[102]

Because of the importance of water baptism in early Christianity and because of the symbolic significance that Paul ascribes to it in Rom 6, it is doubtful that Paul mentions it here to counter an aberrant baptismal practice or understanding in the Colossian "philosophy." For Paul, this ritual powerfully symbolizes the participation of believers in the death and resurrection of Christ. Yet certainly it can be said that the readers at Colossae needed to internalize and think through the implications of what it meant for them to be in this relationship of solidarity with Christ. Their participation in Christ's death clearly entailed not only their deliverance from the power of sin as it came to expression through the evil influence of the flesh (2:11b), but also deliverance from the domain of the principalities and powers (1:13; 2:15). Paul affirms later in the letter that they have died with Christ (ἀπεθάνετε σὺν Χριστῷ) from the demonic spirits of the world (2:20). This is something the Colossian believers needed to hear because they were being unduly influenced by these demonic spirits (2:8).

Paul's use of συνταφέντες, "you were buried with," is the first of a succession of three verbs compounded with the prepositional prefix σύν, "with" (συνταφέντες, συνηγέρθητε, συνεζωοποίησεν: "you were buried with," "you were raised with," and "he made you alive with"). As Hübner notes, these verbs function to make more precise what it means to be ἐν Χριστῷ, "in Christ."[103] The "in Christ" theme has been dominant in this section (2:6, 7, 9, 10, 11, and 12) and is prominent throughout the letter. The σὺν Χριστῷ, "with Christ," statements highlight an objective dimension to this relationship with Christ by stressing a profound identification with Christ in the key salvational events.

ἐν ᾧ καὶ συνηγέρθητε, "in him also you were raised." Believers are not only identified with Christ in his death but also in his resurrection. The dative relative pronoun in the phrase ἐν ᾧ καί, "in him also," could refer to baptism since this is the immediate antecedent (NIV; NASB; RSV),[104] but in light of the prominence of the "in Christ" motif in this section and the formal parallelism with the previous ἐν ᾧ καί, "in him also," that clearly refers to Christ (2:11), it is better to see the referent as "him" (Christ) (so Geneva; Bishops'; Tyndale).[105] Most of the versions leave this expression untranslated and thus miss a very important emphasis of the author.

The theme of co-resurrection is a development of what Paul says in Rom 6:4, 5, 8, and 10. It should be noted, however, that whereas Paul explicitly uses the compound term συνετάφημεν, "we were buried with him," in Rom 6:4, he does

102 Moo, 202.
103 Hübner, 82.
104 Moo, 203; Wilson, 205; Lightfoot, 185.
105 Dunn, 160.

not there use συνηγέρθημεν, "we were raised with him," to describe the solidarity with believers in his resurrection. At issue, of course, is whether the authentic Paul maintained an eschatological reserve and intentionally avoided using such an expression precisely to avoid an enthusiasm that would assert that "the resurrection has already happened" (2 Tim 2:18). This issue will be discussed more extensively in the *Excursus* below (see "Participation in the Death and Resurrection of Christ as the Basis for a New Life—Now and in the Future").

It is the conclusion of this writer that the author of Colossians is here making explicit what was already implicit in Rom 6:4–10—that believers participate with Christ in his resurrection. This is something believers experience by virtue of their union with him and is qualitatively and substantially different from the actual experience of bodily resurrection, which they still await (Col 3:4). Paul can emphasize a participation in the resurrection of Christ as a way of expressing how believers are empowered now to live in a manner pleasing to God—to "walk in newness of life" (Rom 6:4), "to live for God" (Rom 6:10), "to be alive to God" (Rom 6:11), and to be able "to present yourselves to God as those who are alive from the dead" (Rom 6:13).

The emphasis here on co-resurrection is partly explained by the writer's need to affirm to the readers that they "have been filled" to such an extent in Christ that they share in his power and authority over the demonic powers (Col 2:10). By portraying believers as standing with Christ in his present exalted state, the Colossians would be assured that they can resist the insidious influence of these evil spirits. It is unlikely that "the philosophy" was teaching that these powers blocked their access to heaven. Rather, the Colossians already were concerned about the influence of evil spirits on day-to-day life. Paul here provided the Colossians with a theological foundation for directly standing against these spirits and not being enticed by the shamanistic rituals of "the philosophy" as a means for dealing with them.

διὰ τῆς πίστεως τῆς ἐνεργείας τοῦ θεοῦ τοῦ ἐγείραντος αὐτὸν ἐκ νεκρῶν, "through faith in the power of God, who raised him from the dead." Faith is the necessary human response that brings people into a relationship with Christ and enables them to experience his circumcising work, as well as to be objectively identified with Christ in his death and resurrection. Throughout Paul's writings, the object of faith is normally expressed as Christ himself, just as he expresses at the beginning of this letter when he speaks of hearing about τὴν πίστιν ὑμῶν ἐν Χριστῷ Ἰησοῦ, "your faith in Christ Jesus" (1:4; see, e.g., Rom 3:22, 26; Gal 2:16, 20; 3:22; Phil 3:9). But this faith in Christ cannot be seen apart from what Christ has accomplished through his death and resurrection and the involvement of the Father in raising Christ. Thus, Paul says that righteousness is reckoned to those "who believe in him who raised from the dead Jesus our Lord" (Rom 4:24). He also proclaims that it is essential to "believe in your heart that God raised him from the dead" to be saved (Rom 10:9). The emphasis on putting one's faith in the resurrecting power of God is a natural extension of these two passages.

Some interpreters understand the article (τῆς) before πίστις, "faith," as a possessive and translate, "through your faith" (e.g., NIV; NET; NJB).[106] Although this is possible, it is not necessary since there are instances of this articular construction in Paul where the article does not function in a possessive sense (see Gal 3:14, 26; Eph 3:17). It is better to leave it at the level of principle here: "you were co-resurrected through faith," as in Eph 2:8, "you were saved through faith."

The explicit object of the faith is τῆς ἐνεργείας τοῦ θεοῦ, "the power of God." The genitive case should be understood as an objective genitive—an interpretation with which all modern interpreters would agree. Another interpretive tradition can be seen in the KJV and Geneva versions that render it "through the faith of the operation of God." The interpretive note in the Geneva Bible clarifies, "through faith which comes from God" (so also Luther, "[faith] *den Gott wirket*"). This is an expression that would be without precedent in Paul. It is more natural to see God as the object of faith in correspondence with the similar idea expressed in Rom 4:24 and 10:9. The term ἐνεργεία, "power," in contrast to other power-denoting terms that speak of capacity or ability (e.g., δύναμις, ἰσχύς, or κράτος), is most often used in contexts where it refers to the actual exercise of power.[107] Grundmann captures this distinction well when he notes, "'Ενεργεία is actuality in contrast to δύναμις which expresses potentiality. 'Ενεργεία designates the realization of δύναμις."[108] In this passage, the power of God is not seen in its potential but in its actualization through the incredible act of raising a person from the dead.

As many interpreters have noted, τοῦ ἐγείραντος αὐτὸν ἐκ νεκρῶν, "who raised him from the dead," may be traditional language that is regularly found in Paul (Rom 4:24; 8:11; 10:9; 1 Cor 15:15; Gal 1:1; 1 Thess 1:10).[109] On the other hand, the author may simply be describing the fact without making a conscious allusion to traditional formulations.

Why Paul would here stress the Colossians faith in the power (ἐνεργεία) of God—an idea that he nowhere else asserts—is a worthy question to raise. It may very well have to do with the need of the Colossian believers to be reassured of the effective reality of the power of the one living and true God whom they now serve. If they are at all struggling with a concern about demonic spirits and are tempted to accede to the demands of a shaman figure, Paul has effectively demonstrated that they are serving a God who is sufficiently powerful to raise the dead.

**13** καὶ ὑμᾶς νεκροὺς ὄντας ἐν τοῖς παραπτώμασιν καὶ τῇ ἀκροβυστίᾳ τῆς σαρκὸς ὑμῶν συνεζωοποίησεν ὑμᾶς σὺν αὐτῷ, "and you, being dead in your transgressions and in the uncircumcision of your flesh, he made you alive with

106 Harris, 94; Moo, 204.
107 See BDAG, s.v. ἐνεργεία.
108 Grundmann, *Begriff der Kraft*, 58.
109 See Dunn, 162.

him." As a prelude to his assertion of their new life in Christ, which includes the forgiveness of their sins, Paul reminds the Colossians of their plight before God. His claim that they were spiritually dead provides a dramatic backdrop and contrast to God making them alive.

The καὶ ὑμᾶς, "and you," does not single out the gentile readers, as some interpreters assume.[110] If this were true, then nothing Paul has said about dying and rising with Christ, being filled in him, and having the sinful inclination removed would then apply to the Jewish portion of the readers since Paul has used the second-person plural throughout this section. The usage here corresponds with his universal application of the hymn in 1:21, which he similarly addresses to καὶ ὑμᾶς, "and you." Paul is here addressing the entire community,[111] including the Jewish members of the group. The accusative case of the three terms ὑμᾶς νεκροὺς ὄντας, "you, being dead," is necessary because it serves as the direct object of the main verb συνεζωοποίησεν, "he made you alive with him." This clause is fronted to the beginning of the sentence to stress the hopeless condition of being dead that will contrast with God's merciful work of making them alive. As the third member of a three-term accusative direct object, ὄντας is an adjectival participle modifying ὑμᾶς (along with νεκρούς). The verbal sense of the participle could be interpreted as either temporal or concessive,[112] but clearly expresses their hopeless state. The nature of their condition as "dead" is obviously not physically dead (as the term is used in 2:12 where Jesus is raised bodily from among those who are physically dead), but refers to a spiritual condition. This is the same construction and use of the terms as in Eph 2:1, 5, but the idea is found elsewhere in Paul's writings. In Rom 4:17, Paul describes the God in whom Abraham placed his faith as the one "who gives life to the dead [τοῦ ζῳοποιοῦντος τοὺς νεκρούς] and calls into existence the things that do not exist" (NRSV). For both Jews and gentiles, God is able to create new life out of their sinful and empty mode of existence (see also John 5:21). Such an idea has a precedent in Judaism, especially as seen in a text that describes conversion as a change from death into life (e.g., Jos. Asen. 8.9). Paul can also use the adjective "dead" metaphorically to refer to the resultant state of believers with respect to sin (Rom 6:11; cf. Col 2:20 for the same idea, but different terminology).

The παραπτώματα, "transgressions," are offenses against the revealed law of the one God. It is precisely this problem that resulted in the dead state and necessitated the suffering and death of Christ as a substitution (Rom 4:25). The term itself is quite common in Paul, especially in Romans where it occurs nine times. The LXX of Ezekiel attributed the exile to the transgressions (παραπτώματι) of Israel (Ezek 15:8), and God, speaking through the prophet, longs for the day that

110 E.g., Pao, 169; Campbell, 39; Harris, 94; Dunn, 163.

111 So also Lohse, 107.

112 Harris, 94, leaves open both possibilities. Beale, 195, opts for the concessive: "and *though* you were dead . . . nevertheless he made you alive with him."

the house of Israel would no longer go astray "nor defile themselves anymore with all their transgressions [παραπτώμασιν]" (Ezek 14:11).

It is tempting to take τῇ ἀκροβυστίᾳ τῆς σαρκὸς ὑμῶν, "in the uncircumcision of your flesh," in a literal sense and to infer from this that the vast majority of the readers were gentile. Most interpreters take it this way but then also see a symbolic significance to the expression—that is, that uncircumcision is a symbol of the gentiles' alienation from God (as in Eph 2:11). In favor of this view is the fact that Paul will later use the term ἀκροβυστία, "uncircumcision," to refer to gentiles as distinct from Jews (Col 3:11). Some would also point to the way he begins this sentence with καὶ ὑμᾶς, "and you," that serves to single out gentile Christians as Paul's intended hearers at this interval in the letter. But I have already argued that the second-person plural address is directed to all readers of the letter, Jew and gentile alike. It is therefore preferable to take this expression in a purely symbolic sense that is equally applicable to Jews and gentiles. It refers to the state of spiritual "uncircumcision" that made it necessary for Christ to perform a spiritual circumcision on all who would receive him by faith (see 2:11). Certainly, Paul's words here may have prompted Paul's gentile readers to remember their pre-conversion state of alienation from God under the old covenant. But this is not Paul's point. The universal sinfulness of humanity—both Jews and gentiles—is part of the message. All require a spiritual circumcision—even Jews who, ironically, are περιτομή, "circumcision," in the literal sense. Yet even as "the circumcision," their hearts were uncircumcised (Deut 10:16; 30:6; see Rom 2:29). The σάρξ, "flesh," is also here understood in the same sense in which it is used in 2:11, in the moral sense of the evil inclination or sinful impulse (see the more extensive discussion there on σάρξ).[113] In light of this explanation, it is therefore inappropriate to use this verse as a piece of evidence supporting the notion that the readers were exclusively or even primarily gentiles. It is likely that there were some Jews within the Christian community of Colossae and the Lycus Valley (see the *Introduction*).

The subject of the verb next shifts from the second-person plural to the third person singular. The assumed subject is God, although this is not made explicit (so almost all commentators). God will remain the subject of all seven verbs and participles in 2:13–15. This change was essential because although the second-person plural would have worked here ("you were made alive with him"), it would not work with some of the participles that follow (e.g., ἐξαλείψας, "he cancelled"; προσηλώσας, "he nailed"; ἀπεκδυσάμενος, "he disarmed." The view that the change in person was precipitated by the inclusion of a hymnic or confessional piece in 2:13–15 is unpersuasive (see *Form, Structure, Setting*). Paul's declaration that God συνεζωοποίησεν ὑμᾶς σὺν αὐτῷ, "made you alive with him," serves as a summary statement of 2:9–12, especially the co-resurrection (συνηγέρθητε) of 2:12b. This is the first time that the compound verb συζωοποιέω,

113 So also Moo, 207.

"make alive with," appears in the Pauline corpus (see also Eph 2:5), but that is not significant in terms of the authorship question since Paul often uses the simple ζῳοποιέω, "make alive" (e.g., Rom 4:17; 8:11; 1 Cor 15:22, 36, 45; 2 Cor 3:6; Gal 3:21). The rhetorical stress of this passage on participation with Christ that is accented by the repetition of the preposition σύν, "with," prompted this formulation. What is distinctive here is the emphasis on this new life as a present experience, since most of the Pauline references speak of the future bodily resurrection; for example, "he who raised Christ from the dead will give life [ζῳοποιήσει] to your mortal bodies" (Rom 8:11). But the theme of a present experience of new-creation life is indeed present in Paul's writings (e.g., 2 Cor 3:6; 5:17; see below the *Excursus*, "Participation in the Death and Resurrection of Christ as the Basis for a New Life—Now and in the Future"). The stress on the present reality of resurrection life in union with Christ is best accounted for by the situation at Colossae. The readers needed to know the incredibly profound implications of being connected to the risen Christ. They possess spiritual power and resources that render completely unnecessary what "the philosophy" was offering to them.

χαρισάμενος ἡμῖν πάντα τὰ παραπτώματα, "when he forgave us all our wrongdoings." The very παραπτώματα, "wrongdoings," that resulted in a state of being dead (2:13a) have been forgiven by God. This forgiveness took place as part of the conversion experience—that is, in being made alive with Christ. The action of the aorist participle χαρισάμενος, "forgave," occurs coincidental to the action of the main verb συζωοποιέω, "make alive with," on which it depends.[114] There is no grammatical necessity for this action to precede the main verb,[115] nor is there any logical necessity.[116] Forgiveness is one element in a complex of actions that take place in the conversion event when a person is brought into a dynamic relationship with Christ. The apostle Paul uses the verb χαρίζομαι, "forgive," on a number of occasions to speak of one person forgiving another (e.g., 2 Cor 2:7, 10; 12:13; see also Col 3:13; Eph 4:32). This is the only occasion in the Pauline letters where it is used of God extending forgiveness to people. The use of the term here may have been prompted by the image of the cancellation of debt that immediately follows (Col 2:14). The verb χαρίζομαι, "forgive," could also mean "to cancel a sum of money that is owed,"[117] as in Luke 7:42–43: "he cancelled [ἐχαρίσατο] the debt of both."[118] The more common verb for "forgive" in the NT is ἀφίημι (see, e.g., Rom 4:7; the noun form is ἄφεσις, which Paul has already used of God's forgiveness of his people in Col 1:14; see also Eph 1:7). The verb χαρίζομαι is a distinctly Pauline term and is a cognate of χάρις, "grace." It likely

114 Porter, *Verbal Aspect*, 384.
115 Contra Eadie, 157.
116 Contra Abbott, 254.
117 BDAG, s.v. χαρίζομαι 2.
118 So also Lightfoot, 186.

carries with it his theology of the grace of God (cf. Col 1:2, 6). Forgiveness is something that is an undeserved divine gift—freely offered and freely bestowed.

In this clause, Paul switches to the first-person plural (ἡμῖν, "us") for the first time in this section. The easiest explanation is that Paul is now associating himself more directly with the experience of the readers. He, too, is a sinner who has committed παραπτώματα, "wrongdoings" (cf. 1 Tim 1:15–16). This use of the first-person plural extends through 2:14. Once again, it is unlikely that this is an unedited indicator that the author is citing a traditional piece in 2:13–15 or that he is continuing a Jew-gentile contrast ("we"-"you"). The inclusion of the adjective πάντα, "all," indicates that there are no sins outside of the scope of God's forgiveness. This will be strongly underlined in the set of images that follow in 2:14.

The emphasis on forgiveness in these two verses does not necessarily indicate that "the philosophy" was an alternate religious system offering another means of forgiveness involving ascetic practices and other religious rituals.[119] This is probably to go too far in mirror reading the text. There is no other indication in the polemical portions of the letter that the means of forgiveness was an issue.

**14** ἐξαλείψας τὸ καθ' ἡμῶν χειρόγραφον τοῖς δόγμασιν ὃ ἦν ὑπεναντίον ἡμῖν, "he cancelled the promissory note with its terms that were against us and condemned us." Paul here creates an elaborate metaphor that expresses what took place on the cross that secured the pardon of all believers from their indebtedness to God. He develops this as a way of elaborating on the forgiveness that Christ has secured for his people.

The aorist participle ἐξαλείψας, "cancelled," is not connected to the preceding clause with a conjunction (e.g., καί) and should be interpreted as subordinate to the previous participle χαρισάμενος, "forgave," upon which it is grammatically dependent. The action is coincident with this verb and may also be understood as expressing the means by which the forgiveness is achieved; so, rightly, the ESV translates, "by canceling the record of debt." The verb (ἐξαλείφω) can be used to speak of "wiping away" something (such as tears, Rev 7:17; 21:4), erasing something (such as a name from the book of life, Rev 3:5), or in the stronger sense of "destroy" or "cancel." This latter sense is more appropriate to the context since the object is a document.

What God cancels is a χειρόγραφον, here translated as a "promissory note." The term is widely known in the documentary papyri to refer to an instrument of indebtedness but is used here as a metaphor in connection with forgiveness. Deissmann was the first to reveal how this term was used in the documentary papyri.[120] He described papyri that functioned as official contracts acknowledging the debt of one party to another. These documents, effectively functioning as certificates of indebtedness, typically contained the promise, "I will

119 Contra Wolter, 135.

120 Deissmann, *Light from the Ancient East*, 330–35.

repay" (ἀποδώσω). An example of such a document can be seen in *P.Oxy.* 2.269, pp. 250–52 (AD 57):

> Dioscorus, son of Zenodorus, Persians of the Epigone, to Tryphon, son of Dionysius, greeting. I acknowledge the receipt from you at the Serapeum at Oxyrhynchos through the bank of Archibus, son of Archibus, of the sum of 52 silver drachmae of the Imperial coinage, which is the total amount of my debt. I will repay [ἀποδώσω] you on the 30th of the month Caesareus of the current 3rd year of Nero Claudius Caesar Augustus Germanicus Imperator, without any delay. If I do not repay you in accordance with this agreement [ἐὰν δὲ μ[ὴ ἀπ] οδ[ῶ]ι καθὰ γέγραπται], I will forfeit to you the aforesaid sum with the addition of one half, with proper interest for the overtime, for which you are to have the right of execution upon me and upon all my property, as if in accordance with a legal decision. This note of hand is valid wherever produced and whosoever produces it. Date, copy of the signature of the borrower, and copy of the docket of the bank through which the payment was made.

This certificate, called a χειρόγραφον in column 2 ("exact from him his bond" [χειρόγραφον]; lines 6–7), is more than an IOU (I owe you) because it contains a specific promise to repay, indicates when it will be repaid, and includes penalties for late payment or default on the loan. Luttenberger built on the work of Deissmann and confirmed many of the elements of his study, concluding that the term χειρόγραφον is a technical term from the sphere of ancient banking practices.[121] He reproduces a photograph of a first-century χειρόγραφον (*BGU* 664) that first appeared in Deissmann's work, illustrating the presence of a signature at the bottom of the document,[122] a practice that may explain why these documents were given the name "hand writing" (χειρόγραφον).

Dozens of such documents have now been discovered and published in the various corpora of papyri. An overview of these "promissory notes" demonstrates that although the form of the documents may vary, many adhere to the following scheme:

> Name of debtor
> Name of creditor
> Declaration of indebtedness (ὁμολογῶ ἔχειν παρά σου, "I agree to obtain from you")
> Indication of the amount of money
> Promise to repay (ἃς καὶ ἀποδώσω σοι, "which also I will repay to you")
> Penalty for defaulting on the obligation (ἐὰν δὲ μὴ ἀποδῶ καθὰ γέγραπται, "but if I do not repay as it is written . . .")

121 Luttenberger, "Schuldschein," 80–95, esp. 83.
122 Luttenberger, "Schuldschein," 84.

These texts range in date from the first century BC to late in the Roman era, with many dating to the first century AD (some first-century AD examples would include *BGU* 3.981; *P.Genova* 2.262; *P.Gen.* 2.95; *P.Mil.Congr.XIV.* 78; *P.Oxy.* 4.745; 49.3466; 49.3487; *P.Stras.* 4.290; *P.Turner* 17; *SB* 6.9569; *Stud.Pal.* 20.1). An agreement to repay a loan dated to AD 86/87 and published in 2010 provides the record of a debt owed to the late father of a girl named Thermuthis that was secured with a χειρόγραφον (*P.Oxy.* 75.5052). The penalty for defaulting on the loan was rather heavy: "if I do not repay her in accordance with what is written, I will pay . . . with the addition of one half and the appropriate interest for the excess time, and you and Thermuthium are to have the right of execution upon me and all my property, as if in consequence of a lawsuit" (lines 22–27). Another document (second century BC) notes, "I have his [χειρόγραφον] . . . Wherefore I ask, if it seems (right) to order his arrest until he makes repayment to me" (*P.Monac.* 3.52.10–17).[123]

Examples of receipts for the repayment of a loan have also been discovered; for example, ἀπέχω παρὰ σοῦ ἃς ὀφε[ι-]λες μοι κατὰ χειρ[ό]γραφον, "I receive from you what you owe to me in accordance with the *cheirographon*" (*P.Oxy.* 38.2834 [AD 42]; see also *P.Yale* 1.63). A χειρόγραφον could also serve for other types of agreements, such as a contract for the lease of land (*P.Corn.* 8 [AD 193]) or a document recording the conveyance of a vineyard (*P.Mich.* 5.266 [AD 38]). The record office where these documents was prepared was called a γραφεῖον (see *P.Mich.* 2.123 for an entire *grapheion* register that records all documents drawn up day-by-day during the seventh year of Claudius [AD 45–46] in Tebtunis). The cognate term χειρογραφία was used as the Greek equivalent of an affidavit and appears to have been used more broadly than the term χειρόγραφον, which tended to be used for loan agreements.

This usage of the term χειρόγραφον as derived from legal practice about debts is also amply attested in Greek literature (e.g., Polybius, *Hist.* 30.8.4; Plutarch, *Moralia* 829A [= *Vit. aere al.* 4). It was transliterated into Latin as *chirographum* and became a Roman legal term (e.g., Cicero, *Fam.* 7.18; Juvenal, *Sat.* 16.41). This legal usage also penetrated Judaism and is attested in a few texts, such as the book of Tobit: "then Tobit gave him the receipt [τὸ χειρόγραφον], and said to him, 'Find a man to go with you and I will pay him wages as long as I live; and go and get the money" (Tob 5:3 RSV; see also 9:5). This common usage is also found in the Testament of Job: "And I, without delay, would bring forth their note [τὸ χειρόγραφον] and read it, crowning the transaction as cancelled" (T. Job 11.11).

Despite the widespread Greco-Roman usage of the term (which also penetrated Judaism), some interpreters have argued for a more specific background in Jewish apocalyptic.[124] They point to the second-century AD Apocalypse of

123 As translated by Llewelyn in *NewDocs* 9:58 (§20).

124 E.g., Sumney, 144; Lincoln, 625; Dunn, 164; Sappington, *Revelation and Redemption*, 212–20.

Zephaniah that speaks of two different "manuscripts" upon which good and evil angels have written down all the good deeds of the righteous and all the sins of humanity, which are then used for and against humanity at the final judgment (see Apoc. Zeph. 3.6–9; 7.1–8; this tradition is taken up in the ca. fourth-century Apocalypse of Paul 17 and possibly also in the Anonymous Apocalypse 3.13ff. and 4.3ff.). In his vision of the judgment scene, Zephaniah falls on his face before the Lord and says, "May your mercy reach me, and may you wipe out my manuscript because your mercy has come to be in every place" (Apoc. Zeph. 7.8). Although this text is not preserved in Greek, the word translated "manuscript" reflects a Coptic transliteration of the Greek χειρόγραφον, rendering it likely that this was the term in the Greek original. It is also striking that the verb "wipe out" (although we do not know what the Greek original would have been) occurs in conjunction with the manuscript.

There are a number of good reasons, however, to reject this identification as the most relevant background to the metaphor in Col 2:14. It first needs to be observed that it is only attested in one apocalyptic text and is not a widely attested tradition within Judaism (or even apocalyptic Judaism). This reading of the term also assumes too much on the part of the predominantly gentile readers of Colossians; it is unreasonable to expect that they would be familiar with a relatively obscure Jewish apocalyptic concept such as this, especially when virtually all the readers would be well aware of its common legal usage in everyday loan agreements. There are also some crucial differences between the two contexts. In Apocalypse of Zephaniah there are *two* manuscripts, not just one (as in Colossians). One of these angelic documents records all the good deeds of the person facing judgment—a feature missing in the way the image is expressed in Colossians. And finally, there are no "decrees of judgment" (δόγματα) in the angelic documents of the apocalypse; the certificates are simply records of deeds. Wilson is probably correct in finding the apocalyptic association of the term as irrelevant for Colossians and contending that it is "an adaptation [of the term] to a different (and possibly later) set of associations."[125]

The dative expression τοῖς δόγμασιν, "with its terms," is most naturally connected to the immediate antecedent, χειρόγραφον, "promissory note" (as most commentators assert) and not with the preceding καθ' ἡμῶν, "inimical" (NAB),[126] or the following ὑπεναντίον ἡμῖν, "against us."[127] The dative case should be interpreted as one of association/accompaniment, "the promissory note *with* its terms."[128] It is unnecesary to posit an implied γεγραμμένον, "written," to explain the dative.[129]

---

125 Wilson, 208.

126 Moo, 211.

127 Barth and Blanke, 329–30; Lohse, 109–10.

128 Harris, 97; Wilson, 209.

129 As Lightfoot, 187, and Eadie, 160, assert.

The hopeless plight of humanity to find favor before a righteous and holy God is doubly underlined with the assertion that "the promissory note with its terms" was ὑπεναντίον ἡμῖν, "against us" and ultimately "condemned us" (καθ' ἡμῶν). The latter phrase was fronted by the author to stand at the beginning of the clause, also interrupting the article from the noun (τὸ *καθ' ἡμῶν* χειρόγραφον, "the promissory note . . . condemning us") as a way of emphasizing how the document condemns people before God. The adjective ὑπεναντίον, "against," is quite rare, only occurring here in Paul's writings. The writer to the Hebrews uses a substantive form of it in the plural to refer to God's enemies (Heb 10:27), a usage quite common in the LXX (e.g., Gen 22:17; Exod 1:10; 15:7; Isa 63:18). The term was used numerous times in tomb inscriptions at nearby Hierapolis; for example, "This tomb and the place around it belong to Marcus Aurelius Nikephoros Tertulleinos, in which he and his wife, Aurelia Zotike, and their children Nikephoros and Dionysos, are buried. It is not lawful for anyone else to be buried here. If someone shall act contrary to [ὑπεναντίον] these things, he shall have to pay the most holy treasury . . ."[130]

In the metaphor in Colossians, the decrees that are "against us" would correspond to the penalties for defaulting on the obligation to repay (ἐὰν δὲ μὴ ἀποδῶ καθὰ γέγραπται, "but if I do not repay as it is written . . .") that was typically part of a χειρόγραφον, "a promissory note." The context indicates that this penalty was death, as seen in Col 2:13a: ὑμᾶς νεκροὺς ὄντας ἐν τοῖς παραπτώμασιν, "you were dead in your transgressions." The term παραπτώματα, "transgressions," which is mentioned twice in the passage, would explain the manner of default: a life with no transgressions is expected by God, but humanity has failed in this obligation before God.

Paul develops this extended metaphor to help the Colossians better understand the nature of their obligation to God, the dire penalty for reneging on their obligation, and the extent of God's mercy in devising a way to take care of this penalty. The solution is found in the cross of Jesus Christ. What Paul expresses here is the heart of the gospel in a way that is colorful and unique.

What remains to be asked is whether the overall metaphor of the written code "with its terms against us" can be more narrowly interpreted as the writer's reference to the Jewish law? There does seem to be sufficient evidence to warrant this conclusion, a view that has many adherents.[131] If so, this passage would correspond significantly to Eph 2:15 and would provide an alternative and creative way of saying that the cross of Jesus Christ has ended the era of Torah. In other words, the Mosaic law specified the obligation of humanity to exhibit holiness (e.g., Lev 11:44), all have defaulted on this obligation before God, and now the terms of covenant failure apply, rendering all liable to the penalty of death. This passage also has another point of contact with Ephesians

130 Humann et al., *Alt. v. Hierapolis* 147; see also 76; 88; 105; 116; 186; 204; et al.

131 Harris, 96; Wright, 102; Abbott, 256; Lightfoot, 187; Peake, 527; Eadie, 164–65; et al.

in that both make use of new-creation language: "that he might create [κτίσῃ] the two into one new man in him" (Eph 2:15) and "God made you alive with him" (Col 2:13). The biggest difference is the emphasis in Ephesians on Jew and gentile being brought together into the new humanity—an emphasis consonant with the writer's overall purpose.

This view also provides the best explanation for the presence of the term δόγματα, "terms," here. Josephus, for instance, uses this noun to refer to the doctrines and laws of the Torah: "it becomes natural to all Jews, immediately and from their very birth, to esteem these books to contain divine doctrines [δόγματα], and to persist in them, and, if occasion be, willingly to die for them" (Josephus, *Ag. Ap.* 1.42; see also 3 Macc. 1.3; Sib. Or. 3.656). This is the same use of δόγματα that is found in Eph 2:15 where the Torah is described as τὸν νόμον τῶν ἐντολῶν ἐν δόγμασιν, "the law consisting of commandments in regulations." In that passage, the author of Ephesians claims that the law was abolished (καταργήσας) through the work of Christ on the cross. The author means that the Torah has now been superseded in terms of its covenant-regulating function. The principal alternative explanation is to interpret δόγματα, "terms/regulations," as referring to the observances and rules imposed by the opponents at Colossae.[132] Support for this can be found in the fact that the verbal cognate (δογματίζεσθε) is used by the author in Col 2:20 to refer to the commandments and teachings of the advocates of the Colossian "philosophy." The problem with this view is that the opponents were advocating many practices that were not found in the OT. Paul is not saying in Col 2:14 that God cancels any kind of human teaching or law that people may try to impose on believers by nailing them to the cross. The metaphor of the χειρόγραφον (*cheirographon*, "promissory note") has to do with the legitimate obligation that all people have before God to live in accordance with the way the creator has designed them to live. This means a life free from "transgressions" (παραπτώματα). In other words, this section is part of the positive theological teaching of the letter and not a part of Paul's direct polemic against the teaching of the opponents.

Abbott thus rightly comments that "here the χειρόγραφον is the Mosaic Law, which being unfulfilled is analogous to an unpaid 'note of hand.'"[133] As many scholars have noted, the Jewish people are culpable before God because they had agreed to obey the law (Deut 27:14–26; 30:15–20). Gentiles were guilty for disobedience to the law of God written on their hearts, which their consciences accuse them of violating (Rom 2:14–15). The image of "the promissory note with its terms" is perfectly suited to express the idea of defaulting on the obligation to obey the creator's ordinances and fits well the resultant state of guilt because of παραπτώματα, "transgressions."

Some have objected to pressing the metaphor this far by arguing that it

132 E.g., Yates, "Metaphor," 257; Weiss, "Law," 304.
133 Abbott, 255.

hardly seems Pauline to represent God as crucifying the Mosaic law. But this is simply an elaboration of the image of erasure or cancelling (ἐξαλείψας) and would correspond with other statements that Paul makes about Christ being an end (τέλος) to the law for righteousness to everyone who believes (see Rom 10:4). In other words, Christ has abolished (καταργήσας) the law as a covenantal system for all who are identified with him in his death and resurrection (Eph 2:15). Transgressions are no longer atoned for through the sacrifice of animals. Rather, the one sacrifice of Christ results in the forgiveness of transgressions and effectively renders the Sinai covenant, with all of its regulations and consequences for disobedience, null and void. The cross represents the end of the law.

καὶ αὐτὸ ἦρκεν ἐκ τοῦ μέσου προσηλώσας αὐτὸ τῷ σταυρῷ, "he took it away by nailing it to the cross." This line extends the metaphor even further by envisioning God as taking the promissory note away from his people and nailing it to the cross. Of course, nothing literal of this sort has happened; the metaphorical language is a very creative way of helping the Colossians internalize the reality of the forgiveness that results from Christ's death on the cross. But if the χειρόγραφον (*cheirographon*) also refers to the Sinai covenant, as we have argued, the expression is also a picturesque way of referring to the end of an era.

The placement of the neuter pronoun (αὐτό) before the verb may be emphatic.[134] The perfect tense of the verb points both to the completion of the act and the resultant condition of freedom that ensues. The prepositional phrase ἐκ τοῦ μέσου, literally "away from among the midst [of you]," expresses the location from which an object has been removed, such as the stones the Israelites removed from the middle of the Jordan River (ἐκ μέσου τοῦ Ιορδάνου; Josh 4:3, 8). It is a rhetorical way of stressing how the χειρόγραφον was indissolubly bound to them until Christ was able to remove it by his work on the cross.

Although the precise expression "nailed to the cross" (προσηλώσας τῷ σταυρῷ) never appears anywhere else in the NT, it was the common language for referring to this action. Josephus, for example, speaks of the Roman procurator of Palestine, Gessius Florus, having certain Jews of the equestrian order whipped and nailed to a cross (σταυρῷ προσηλῶσαι) before his tribunal (*J.W.* 2.308; see also 5.451; Philo, *Dreams* 2.213). This extension of the image to include its nailing to the cross may be reflective of the Roman practice of attaching an indictment of the crucified man to the cross, as we see in Mark 15:26.[135]

**15** ἀπεκδυσάμενος τὰς ἀρχὰς καὶ τὰς ἐξουσίας, "he disarmed the rulers and the authorities." In this final verse of the section, Paul elaborates on the implications of the death, resurrection, and exaltation of Christ for the demonic powers. In fact, more is said here about Jesus's defeat of the powers than anywhere else in the NT. The three verbs in the text colorfully depict this decisive and powerful act of Christ for the benefit of his people.

---

134 So Abbott, 256.

135 Smith, *Heavenly Perspective*, 104.

The structure of this verse precisely parallels the sequence of thought in 2:14. Semantically, both 2:14 and 2:15 provide two different but interrelated sets of actions that explain how God has made the Colossians alive with Christ and also how he has forgiven all of their trespasses. The aorist participle ἀπεκδυσάμενος, "disarmed," is technically dependent on the main verb ἐδειγμάτισεν, "he exposed," but should be interpreted as an attendant-circumstance participle, thereby indicating the first in the twofold sequence: "he disarmed them and he exposed them." The coordinating καί, "and," would reinforce this interpretation of the grammar (see *Notes* for a discussion of the textual variant).

There has been substantial disagreement among interpreters over the centuries regarding how the first assertion should be interpreted. The conflict stems over whether God or Christ is the subject, whether the participle should be interpreted as active or reflexive in significance, and what is the object of the participle. For clarity, the various views could be set out as follows:

1. The participle is active in significance. God is the subject, and the rulers and the authorities are the objects. The idea is that God has stripped the evil spirits of their power and authority with respect to Christ and all those who are incorporated into him.[136] This view is represented by most of the English versions, with many of them leaving the clothing image aside and translating it as a military metaphor: "he disarmed the rulers and authorities" (see, e.g., ESV; cf. NIV; NASB; NKJV; CSB; NRSV; NLT; CEB; REB). The NJB retains the clothing metaphor, "he has stripped the sovereignties and ruling forces."
2. This view is essentially the same as the first but interprets the verb to mean "unclothe." The resultant metaphorical idea is that God has unclothed the rulers and authorities—that is, he has exposed them.[137]
3. The participle is understood as a true middle and as having reflexive significance. Christ is the subject, and the rulers and the authorities are the object. The sense is that Christ has stripped off from himself the hostile powers that clung to him.[138] The NEB brings out this sense by translating the clause "he discarded the cosmic powers and authorities like a garment."
4. The participle is reflexive in significance. Christ is the subject, and the implied object is Christ's physical body, his flesh (the rulers and authorities are seen as the direct object of the verb that follows [ἐδειγμάτισεν]). The resulting idea is that Christ has stripped off his body through death.[139]

136 E.g., Moo, 214; Sumney, 146; Lincoln, 626; Garland, 152; Pokorný, 140–41; Schweizer, 151; Lohse, 111–12; Scott, 48; A. Oepke, "ἀπεκδύω," *TDNT* 2:319; Calvin, 336.

137 Barth and Blanke, 333.

138 This is the view of the majority of the Greek Fathers, including Chrysostom, Severian, Theodore of Mopsuestia, and Theodoret; see also Dunn, 167–68; Lightfoot, 189–91.

139 This is the view of the majority of the Latin Fathers, including Augustine, Hilary, and Ambrose;

5. The participle is reflexive in significance. Christ is the subject, and the object would be implied clothing. The idea Paul expresses is a metaphor of Christ undressing himself prior to donning a victor's garment.[140]
6. The participle should be understood as a middle of personal interest. God is the subject, and the angelic powers associated with the law are the objects. The idea is that God has "stripped for himself" the angels of the law—that is, God has ended their dominion and the era of the law is now over.[141]

The first view—that God has disarmed the hostile powers—best explains all of the available evidence. It has also emerged as the clear majority view among contemporary interpreters.

There is a major difficulty with each of the views that presents Christ as the subject of the participle (views 3, 4, and 5). That is, there is no explicit indication in the text that the subject has changed from God to Christ. Since God is the indisputable subject of the controlling verb of the section (συνεζωοποίησεν) in 2:13 and throughout 2:14, the natural way to read the text is by understanding that he continues to be the subject in 2:15. There is certainly nothing about the content of the three clauses that would require the assumption that there has been a change of subject to Christ.

Although the form of the participle ἀπεκδυσάμενος, "disarmed," is in the middle voice, "the middle is occasionally used, however where an active is expected."[142] The active sense fits this context particularly well. God is not stripping anything from himself; rather, he is doing the stripping. This is the first attested usage of the double compound ἀπ + εκ + δύω, "strip off/disarm," in the Greek language. As we have noted before (see the *Comment* on 2:11), Paul is fond of the stylistic convention of adding a preposition to a word (esp. ἀπό and ἐκ) for emphasis or rhetorical variety. He twice uses the simpler form ἐκδύω, "strip off" (2 Cor 5:3, 4), showing his familiarity with the far more common term, a verb that is used frequently in the LXX and appears four times in the Gospels (e.g., Luke 10:30: "he fell among robbers, who stripped him [οἳ καὶ ἐκδύσαντες αὐτόν] and beat him"). Nevertheless, Paul does use ἀπεκδυσάμενος, "stripping," in Col 3:9 with a reflexive sense: ἀπεκδυσάμενοι τὸν παλαιὸν ἄνθρωπον, "stripping off (from yourselves) the old self." This reflexive idea makes it understandable how some interpreters could interpret 2:15 as "Christ stripped the rulers and authorities (from himself)" (as view 3), but apart from the doubtful assumption that there has been a change of subject, it would result in a very peculiar idea that

---

see also Yates, 51–53; idem, "Colossians 2:15," 590; Robinson, *Body*, 41. Martin (NCB, 87) advocates a variation of this view, i.e., that by stripping off his frail humanity, he also stripped off the principalities and powers that clung to him.

140 Carr, *Angels and Principalities*, 61.

141 See Peake, 528–29; Abbott, 258–61.

142 BDF §316.1; BDAG, s.v. ἀπεκδύομαι; this verb is cited as an example of both.

is without parallel in the NT. While it is clear that Satan sought to tempt Jesus (Matt 4:1–11; Luke 4:1–13) and to incite his crucifixion (Luke 22:3–4; John 13:27; 1 Cor 2:6–8), there is no sense in which demonic powers "clung like a Nessus robe about His humanity."[143] In Greek mythology, this robe was a garment poisoned with the blood of the centaur Nessus. When it was given to Hercules and he donned it, the garment burned him, made him go mad, and drove him to death. Although this image does not seem appropriate to explaining the way that the demonic powers worked in relationship to Jesus, it might have been fitting for illustrating the way Christ bore the sin of humanity on the cross. This would also fit better with Lightfoot's comparison to the removal of the filthy garments from Joshua the high priest as he stood before the Lord (Zech 3:1–5). Of course, the problem is that Paul is not creating a metaphor about sin as a dirty and poisonous garment that needed to be removed, but he is making a statement about evil spirits. If there is a connection with 2:14 and the forgiveness of sin, it may be located in the fact that the devil and his spirits function as accusers before God (Zech 3:1; Rev 12:10). This underlines the importance of the removal of the "promissory note" that God "has taken from us" (2:14). This served as the basis for all accusations that Satan and his cohorts could have brought before God. By taking this away, God has "stripped the rulers and authorities" of any condemning accusations that they could possibly bring before God as judge. God has thereby effectively disarmed them.

The "rulers and authorities" (τὰς ἀρχὰς καὶ τὰς ἐξουσίας) are therefore to be seen as the direct object of ἀπεκδυσάμενος, "disarmed." This, in fact, must be the case if the conjunction καί, "and," is part of the original text at the end of the clause (see *Notes*). It is also unlikely that Paul used the participle ἀπεκδυσάμενος in the absolute sense of "disrobed" (contra view 5) or that an implied object (such as "flesh" or "body" should be supplied), since there is an accusative expression immediately following the verb (contra view 4). In every instance of the cognate verb ἐκδύω, "strip off," the accusative that follows the verb is always to be understood as the direct object (e.g., Lev 6:11 [6:4 LXX]: ἐκδύσεται τὴν στολὴν αὐτοῦ, "he shall strip off his robe"; see also Lev 16:23; Num 20:26, 28; etc.).

These "rulers and authorities" are the hostile powers, the enemies of God and his people. They are not the givers and guardians of the law (contra view 6). The following two clauses make this clear. They are publicly exposed, and they are led as defeated captives in a triumphal procession. Furthermore, they are to be associated with the demonic spirits who inspired the empty and deceitful teaching facing the Colossian church (2:8), and they are the ones to whose evil influence believers have died by virtue of their union with Jesus Christ (2:20).

Most of the major English versions are correct, then, in translating ἀπεκδυσάμενος as "disarmed" and regarding the "rulers and authorities" as the direct object (see again ESV; NRSV; RSV; NIV; CEB; CSB; NASB; NLT;

143 Lightfoot, 190.

REB). At this juncture, it is important to clarify what Paul is saying and what he is not saying. From the larger context of this letter and from Paul's theology as a whole, it is clear that these evil spirits have not been completely disarmed. They are obviously still active in the Colossian church by inspiring the competing teaching. They continue to tempt believers (1 Thess 3:5), to deceive (2 Cor 11:14), to reenslave them in a pattern of life that is apart from the freedom in Christ (Gal 4:3, 9), to gain a foothold in the lives of believers as a way of promoting vices (Eph 4:27), and to oppose and hurt the people of God in every conceivable way (Eph 6:10–20). On top of this, they continue to keep unbelievers blind to the truth of the gospel (2 Cor 4:4) and to work powerfully in non-Christians to keep them enslaved in lifestyles of sinful behaviors (Eph 2:2). In fact, 1 Cor 15:24 teaches that Jesus must reign until he has subdued all of these demonic enemies under his feet.

So, in what sense have they been "disarmed"? This passage needs to be seen in close connection to 2:13–14. God has forgiven all of the Colossians' sins (2:13) and he has cancelled and removed "the promissory note with its terms that were against us and condemned us" (2:14). By doing this, God has utterly and completely removed the ability of the rulers and authorities to bring a just accusation before the heavenly tribunal. Yet there is also the sense that they have been proven to be totally ineffectual to thwart God's redemptive activity in and through Jesus Christ. Furthermore, Christ has already been shown to be superior to all of the demonic powers because he is their creator (1:16) and will ultimately bring universal peace (1:20). Because all of the fullness of the deity dwells in him, he reigns supreme over them (2:10). Now, through his work on the cross, he has demonstrated this supremacy (2:15b–c). The "rulers and authorities" are thus totally powerless against Christ. Throughout this section, it has been Paul's burden and passion to reaffirm that believers are united with Christ in a relationship of solidarity. He has expressed this through the fivefold assertion that believers are ἐν αὐτῷ, "in him," and the fourfold emphasis on participation with him (expressed by the preposition σύν, "with"). The clear message is that by virtue of this union with Christ, "the rulers and authorities" have been effectively disarmed. Insofar as believers hold on tight to Christ (2:19) and appropriate his power and authority (2:10), they will find that these hostile powers are defeated and defeatable enemies.

καὶ ἐδειγμάτισεν ἐν παρρησίᾳ, "he exposed them publicly." Paul continues his portrayal of God's victory over the demonic rulers and authorities in Christ by declaring that they have been publicly exposed. The only other time that this verb appears in biblical literature is in Matthew's account of Joseph's plan not to "expose" (δειγματίσαι) Mary's pregnancy and thereby bring public shame upon her (Matt 1:19). The word is quite rare in the Greek language prior to and around the time of Paul. One important passage illustrating its use is from the Ascension of Isaiah where it appears in connection with a demonic ruler, Sammael: "for Beliar was very angry with Isaiah because of the vision, and because of the exposure ([δει]γματισμοῦ) with which he had exposed ([ἐ] δειγμάτισεν) Sammael" (Ascen. Isa. 3.13). It also appears in the Acts of Peter in connection with Peter's "exposure" of Simon Magus in Rome (Acts Pet. 32[2]). Each of these occurrences illustrate the tendency for the word to be used in the sense of an exposure that leads to public disgrace. This verb is also closely related to its cognate παραδειγματίζω, "expose," which is more common and does occur a few times in the LXX. It is used, for instance, in the lamentation over the king of Tyre—an account behind which many of the early church fathers saw the casting down of Satan from heaven: "Your heart was proud because of your beauty; you corrupted your wisdom for the sake of your splendor. I cast you to the ground; I exposed [παραδειγματισθῆναι] you before kings, to feast their eyes on you" (Ezek 28:17 ESV).

The prepositional phrase ἐν παρρησίᾳ should be taken as "publicly" (so most English versions and interpreters) and not as "boldly."[144] This expression was commonly used to convey the simple idea of "in public" in contrast to the thought of doing something "in secret" (see John 7:4; 18:20). Although "boldness" is part of the semantic range of the term and is used this way by Paul in other contexts (e.g., 2 Cor 3:12), it is the public shame of the rulers and authorities that Paul is stressing here rather than a bold act on the part of God.

The cross (2:11, 14) and resurrection (2:12–13) of Christ remain in view here as the event in which the powers were not only disarmed but were publicly exposed. In what sense were they exposed? Although they may claim to rival God in power and feel it is their due to be worshiped as gods, the cross and resurrection reveal their inflated notions to be empty and baseless. This is seen most brilliantly in what happened on Good Friday and Easter. The efforts of the demonic rulers to put to death God's Messiah reached a dramatic conclusion when Jesus was crucified on the cross. Yet, as Paul tells us elsewhere, they drastically underestimated the wisdom and power of God (1 Cor 2:6–8). Thinking they had effectively put a stop to God's redemptive plan, God turned their evil deed into a dramatic good by raising Jesus from the dead. And ironically, it was precisely by this cross and the blood that Jesus shed that atonement could be provided for the sins of humanity and forgiveness offered to all who are united to Jesus by faith. The cross and resurrection was therefore a public exposure of the demonic powers and their inability to thwart the redemptive plan of God. Their authority to compel service and worship from humanity was likewise shown to be baseless. Paul therefore had adequate reason for referring to the στοιχεῖα, "demonic spirits," as "weak" and "worthless" in Gal 4:9.

θριαμβεύσας αὐτοὺς ἐν αὐτῷ, "leading them in a triumphal procession in him." In the final line of this section, Paul further explains the public exposure of the demonic rulers by comparing their defeat and disgrace to the vanquished foes in a Roman triumph. In other words, God has not only conquered these

144 Lightfoot, 191.

powerful supernatural foes in and through the person of Christ, but he has in some fashion put them on display and paraded them as defeated enemies.

The aorist participial form (θριαμβεύσας) depends on the main verb (ἐδειγμάτισεν) and is perhaps best interpreted as a participle of means: "God exposed them by leading them in a triumphal procession." Thus the time is coincident between the participle and the main verb. Beginning with Romulus's founding triumph in 753 BC, the spectacle of a triumph became well-known in the empire. Beard notes: "To be awarded a triumph was the most outstanding honor a Roman general could hope for. He would be drawn in a chariot—accompanied by the booty he had won, the prisoners he had taken captive, and his no doubt rowdy and raucous troops in their battle gear—through the streets of the city to the Temple of Jupiter on the Capitoline hill, where he would offer a sacrifice to the god. The ceremony became a by-word for extravagant display."[145]

One of the most celebrated and well-narrated triumphs is Plutarch's account of the honor accorded to Lucius Aemilius Paulus (229 BC–160 BC). He was the Roman general who won the Battle of Pydna in 168 BC against the Macedonians. Included in this three-day triumphal parade (θρίαμβος) was the defeated King Perseus, "clad in a dark robe and wearing the high boots of his country, but the magnitude of his evils made him resemble one who is utterly dumbfounded and bewildered. He, too, was followed by a company of friends and intimates, whose faces were heavy with grief" (Plutarch, *Aem.* 34.1). The primary focus, however, was on the victorious Aemilius: "the whole army also carried sprays of laurel, following the chariot of their general by companies and divisions, and singing, some of them divers songs intermingled with jesting, as the ancient custom was, and others paeans of victory and hymns in praise of the achievements of Aemilius, who was gazed upon and admired by all, and envied by no one that was good" (Plutarch, *Aem.* 34.4; see also Dio Cassius, *Hist. rom.* 20.9.24). Dionysius of Halicarnassus notes: "he [the victorious general] accordingly drove into the city with the spoils, the prisoners [τοὺς αἰχμαλώτους], and the army that had fought under him, he himself riding in a chariot drawn by horses with golden bridles and being arrayed in the royal robes, as is the custom in the greater triumphs [θριάμβους]" (*Ant. rom.* 8.67.9–10).

The images of Roman victory over various enemies were lavishly depicted in two hundred panels of life-size statues on three levels of the Sebasteion at nearby Aphrodisias. Although none of the panels depict a Roman triumphal procession, each depicts Roman conquest and the full force of Roman imperial power. The conquered foes are represented in positions of subjugation and humiliation. R. Canavan observes that "in the top tier Roman emperors from Augustus to Nero were portrayed as Olympian gods trouncing nations that appear as cowering and distraught barbarian naked women."[146] One of those conquered

145 Beard, *Roman Triumph*, 1.

146 Canavan, *Clothing the Body*, 82.

foes (Armenia) wore a Phrygian cap.[147] This no doubt indicated that the local Phrygian people should regard themselves as subject to Roman imperial might. Although Paul's remarks here are not a direct attack on Roman power, there is no mistaking the message he wants to convey—namely, that the spiritual forces of evil were soundly and utterly defeated by Christ's work on the cross. And these supernatural powers stand behind a great deal of evil in the experience of the Colossians.

The victories of numerous Roman generals and emperors were celebrated through the streets of Rome from the time of Pompey to Domitian. They were exceedingly popular and widely talked about throughout the empire. The captives were paraded in abject humiliation before the throngs of Romans gathered for the occasion. Some rode on biers or floats, some in wagons, carts, or horse-drawn chariots, and many padded along on foot through the streets bound in chains. There were also many attendants who carried the valuable booty plundered after the battle. The spectacle brought great honor to the victorious general and public shame upon the defeated rulers, their families, and the vanquished warriors.

It is to this well-known imperial spectacle that Paul compares the victory of Christ over the demonic rulers belonging to the authority of darkness. The suggestion that Paul drew the image from festal processions held in honor of the god Dionysus and not the Roman triumph[148] cannot be sustained. That understanding of the image highlights the inspiring deity leading his exultant worshipers in a festal or choral procession. Egan therefore describes the "rulers and authorities" of Col 2:15 as "intimates of Christ" rather than as enemies. This interpretation, however, does severe injustice to the immediate context, which includes the thought of public humiliation as well as the notion of disarming them. P. Marshall has provided additional support for rooting the background of the usage of the term precisely in the context of the Roman triumphal procession.[149]

Some interpreters who rightly interpret the image to be from a Roman triumphal procession have argued that the "rulers and authorities" should not be understood as demonic powers and thus defeated foes but rather as the good angels from the throne of God who are now adoring Christ in the celebration of his splendor.[150] While these interpreters are correct in affirming the joyous celebration accompanying the Roman general in the parade, they are wrong in downplaying and neglecting the fact that the Roman general receives his honor at the expense of the defeated and shamed enemies that formed a substantial part of this parade. The significance of the imagery of a Roman triumph is lost

147 Smith, "Imperial Reliefs from the Sebasteion," 18.

148 Egan, "Lexical Evidence," 34–62.

149 Marshall, "ΘΡΙΑΜΒΕΥΕΙΝ," 302–17.

150 Yates, "Colossians 2:15," 573–91; Carr, *Angels and Principalities*, 47–85.

without the spectacle of the procession of captives and the trophies of victory. As I have noted above, the concurrent images of disarming and public exposure also fit well with the notion of the "rulers and authorities" as the defeated forces in the triumphal procession. This is also consistent with the fact that the combination of terms ἀρχαὶ καὶ ἐξουσίαι, "rulers and authorities," is consistently employed by Paul to refer to hostile angelic powers.

Paul employs the image of triumph on one other occasion. In 2 Cor 2:14 he exclaims, "But thanks be to God, who always leads us in triumphal procession [θριαμβεύοντι] in Christ and through us spreads everywhere the fragrance of the knowledge of him." In this context, it is not the evil rulers and authorities who are the defeated foes but Paul himself and his missionary companions. Once an enemy of God's purposes in Christ, Paul has now been reconciled to God and celebrates God's victorious work in his life. He now serves God as a "slave of Christ" and as an apostle who spreads the knowledge of the Savior everywhere as a fragrance. The defeated "rulers and authorities" of Colossians, however, have not joined with the risen Christ to further his purposes but remain inimical to God and his redemptive work.

The image of triumph over the powers through the cross, resurrection, and ascension also comes to expression in Eph 4:8 where the author cites Ps 68:18 (Ps 67:19 LXX; MT 68:19). The psalm passage refers to God as divine warrior achieving a great victory and ascending his holy mountain. In a christological interpretation of the psalm, the author of Ephesians depicts Christ as the one who has vanquished his enemies (presumably through the cross and resurrection) and has ascended to heaven, where he can distribute divine gifts for service to every member of his body. Just as the Divine Warrior has scattered his enemies and struck their heads (Ps 68:1, 21) and leads "a host of captives in your train" (Ps 68:18), so also Christ has "captured a host of captives" (ᾐχμαλώτευσεν αἰχμαλωσίαν)—that is, the demonic principalities, powers, and authorities.

The final two words of the section—ἐν αὐτῷ—should be interpreted as a reference to Christ and thus translated "in him" (as the ESV; RSV; NASB),[151] and not as a referring to the cross (as the NLT; NIV; NRSV; KJV).[152] This forms a literary *inclusio* with 2:9 where Paul puts before the Colossians the theological basis for resisting the teaching of "the philosophy" (ὅτι ἐν αὐτῷ . . . ἐν αὐτῷ, "for in him . . . in him"). Participation with Christ and union with him are at the heart of what Paul has to say as seen, in part, by the fact that he mentions "in him" five times and "with him" three times. The immediate context also goes beyond Christ's death to focus on his resurrection and the consequent "making alive" of all those who are united with Christ in his resurrection (2:12–13). As we have just noted, Eph 4:8 associates the defeat and procession more closely with the resurrection and ascension of Christ than with the cross. Of course, those

151 So also Moo, 215; Sumney, 148; and most commentators.

152 So also Dunn, 169; Yates, 52; Lightfoot, 192.

who see Christ as the subject of the verbs in 2:15 and interpret the participle ἀπεκδυσάμενος, "stripped," as a reference to Christ's death—that is, "stripping off his body," must take the ἐν αὐτῷ as referring to the cross to avoid the redundancy, "Christ led them in triumph in him." But I have already shown that this interpretation of the subject and the participle is unlikely.

The appropriateness of the metaphor of "triumphal procession" in association with God's work through Christ in the cross, resurrection, and ascension needs to be questioned, especially when the demonic rulers and authorities continue to be powerfully at work against God and his purposes. On the surface, it appears that the metaphor would be better suited to describe God's work in his apocalyptic triumph at the end of the age. It is at that time that Christ will hand the kingdom over to the Father "after he has destroyed every ruler and every authority and power" (1 Cor 15:24 NRSV). The image of a triumphal procession over the powers here seems to be a dramatic instance of realized eschatology.

Yet, the application of this powerful imagery to the impact of the cross and resurrection (and the implied ascension) is consistent with Paul's thought and, in particular, his understanding of the divine drama regarding the demonic rulers and authorities. In Paul's view, the war has been won, and the final eschatological outcome is certain on the basis of the cross and resurrection. This happens in two ways. First, *they have been defeated in their concerted attempt to thwart God's redemptive plan through Christ.* In their limited wisdom and knowledge, they thought they could put an end to God's merciful saving purposes by instigating the death of Christ on the cross (1 Cor 2:6–8). But they underestimated the wisdom of God by not perceiving that it was precisely through the death of Jesus on the cross that God would provide an atoning sacrifice for the sins of the world. As Scott observes, "They imagined that they had won a victory over God, but in the death of Christ he had vanquished them."[153] The death of Jesus thus supplied the means for God to provide forgiveness to all who put their faith in Christ. It also takes away from the rulers and authorities their ability to justly accuse Christians before God; the cross utterly removes any basis for condemnation.

Second, *as vanquished enemies, they will be defeated in their attempts to thwart the unfolding of God's redemptive plan in and through the resurrected Christ, who is head of the church.* The final "in him" (2:15) draws the readers' thoughts back to the "in him" that begins this section (2:9–10), where Paul asserts that "you have been filled in him who is the head over every ruler and authority." By virtue of his death and resurrection, Christ now wields an authority over the demonic rulers that he also extends to his people. Because of this, the enemies have not been able to stop the progress of the gospel. It is "bearing fruit and growing in the entire world" (1:6). Furthermore, all the attempts of the demonic spirits to hurt the health and stability of the church through "the philosophy" or any other means can be stopped as long as believers understand that they have died to the

153 Scott, 49.

compelling influence of the powers (2:20), "hold on tight to Christ" (2:19), "seek the things that are above, where Christ is, seated at the right hand of God" (3:1), and actualize their identity in him.

The cross and resurrection of Christ thus exposes the demonic rulers as defeated enemies who are unable to stop the redemptive work of God. They are effectively "disarmed," but not in an ultimate or absolute sense. Paul's burden here is to show that they are ineffective against people who have given their allegiance to Jesus Christ, participated with him in his death and resurrection, and live on the basis of the power and authority that they now possess over this realm in relationship to Christ. Paul thus effectively takes away any sense of need the Colossian believers may have for calling upon angels, engaging in rituals of power, or seeking any other means of accessing spiritual power. They have all they need in Jesus Christ. Scott recognized this as the heart of the message in this section years ago when he wrote, "His [the Colossian's] safety was to be found in the conciliation of the friendly powers by means of offerings, sacred rites, spells, and talismans, so that they would protect him against the opposing demons. . . . But he [Paul] insists always that this protection is offered by Christ and that all else is useless. . . . We have a power on our side which can overcome everything that is against us."[154]

154 Scott, 287.

# Excursus: Participation in the Death and Resurrection of Christ as the Basis for a New Life—Now and in the Future

### *Bibliography*

**Agersnap, S.** *Baptism and the New Life.* **Burns, J. P.** "Baptism as Dying and Rising with Christ," 407–38. **Callan, T.** *Dying and Rising with Christ.* **Campbell, C. R.** *Paul and Union with Christ.* **Campbell, D. A.** *Framing Paul.* **Cranfield, C. E. B.** "Romans 6:1–14 Revisited," 40–43. **Eckstein, H.-J.** "Auferstehung und gegenwärtiges Leben," 8–23. **Frank, N.** *Kolosserbrief im Kontext*, 172–92. **Hartman, L.** *Die Taufe.* **Lona, H. E.** *Die Eschatologie.* **Macaskill, G.** *Union with Christ.* **Merklein, H.** "Paulinische Theologie," 25–69. **Müller, P.** *Anfänge der Paulusschule.* **Pelser, G. M. M.** "Dying and Rising with Christ," 115–34. **Schlarb, R.** *Wir sind mit Christus Begraben.* **Schnelle, U.** *Gerechtigkeit und Christusgegenwart.* **Schrage, W.** *Ethik des neuen Testaments.* **Shkul, M.** "New Identity and Cultural Baggage," 367–87. **Siber, P.** *Mit Christus Leben.* **Still, T. D.** "Eschatology in Colossians," 125–38. **Tannehill, R. C.** *Dying and Rising with Christ.* **Wedderburn, A. J. M.** *Baptism and Resurrection.* **Witulski, T.** "Gegenwart und Zukunft," 211–42. **Wright, N. T.** *Resurrection*, 236–41. **Zeller, D.** "Die Mysterienkulte und die paulinische Soteriologie," 42–61.

In Col 2:12 and 3:1 (cf. Eph 2:6), Paul uses the past tense (aorist indicative) to assert that believers have not only died with Christ (συνηγέρθητε), but also have been raised with him. This is the first time in any of his writings where he has declared that believers are co-resurrected. He stops short of this in Rom 6. In that passage, he uses the past tense to affirm that believers have died with Christ ("we were buried [συνετάφημεν] with him," Rom 6:4), but he does not take the next step of asserting that believers have already experienced resurrection with Christ. When he does speak of the resurrection of believers, he uses the future tense ("we will be united with him in the likeness of his resurrection" [ἀλλὰ καὶ τῆς ἀναστάσεως ἐσόμεθα]; Rom 6:5). This is often referred to by scholars as Paul's eschatological reserve (*eschatologische Vorbehalt*), in which he intentionally avoids speaking of the resurrection of believers as happening in the past in any sense and explicitly reserves resurrection for the future. His reason for this is ostensibly to avoid the triumphalism that some in the Corinthian community were apparently proclaiming as evidenced by Paul's sarcastic comments to them: "Already you have all you want! Already you have become rich! You have begun to reign—and that without us! How I wish that you really had begun to reign so that we also might reign with you!" (1 Cor 4:8 NIV).

Some interpreters have consequently viewed the assertions of co-resurrection in Colossians as telltale evidence that the letter was not written by Paul (and presumably could not have been approved by Paul if it were written by one of his coworkers). Thus, P. Müller observes that "the resurrection saying deviates plainly from Paul."[155] Similarly, H. Merklein describes the co-resurrection statements as the elimination (*Aufhebung*) of the eschatological reserve and, consequently, inconsistent with the accepted Pauline letters.[156] R. Yates states unequivocally that "the fading hope of an imminent parousia, the shift in terminology, and the hint that resurrection is already realized in baptism are important reasons why Colossians cannot be Pauline."[157]

The notion of the co-resurrection of believers is actually more than "a hint" in Colossians and reflects a clear and explicit linguistic development on Rom 6. At issue, however, is whether Paul himself could have done this and what the motivation may have been for this theological development.

G. Strecker contends that the notion of "rising with Christ" is actually a pre-Pauline description "of the experience of new life that happens in the present as an anticipation of the future."[158] Although it has not been possible to formally identify a pre-Pauline hymn or confession in this section of the letter, he claims that the language and conceptuality may be pre-Pauline (see also 1 Cor 15:29 and 1 Pet 3:18–22). Thus, he contends that Paul modified the language on the basis of his "eschatological reservation" when he incorporated these ideas into his discussion of baptism in Rom 6, whereas the author of Colossians chose to retain the idea of co-resurrection. U. Schnelle takes a similar view, contending that a disciple of Paul has modified this tradition in a similar way as the faction in Corinth in Col 2:12 and that it in no way represents a development of Rom 6 since it deviates from the Pauline interpretation of Rom 6:4.[159] But as I will contend below, I think this overstates the case and makes a distinction that is unnecessary.

T. Witulski argues that while the author of Colossians does think in terms of both temporal and spatial categories, he interprets the soteriological component of the eschatology in terms of the spatial conceptualization of "above" and "below."[160] In contrast to the apostle Paul, the author of Colossians conceives of resurrection as an event of the past and thus uses the aorist indicative in Col 2:12 (συνηγέρθητε), nullifying the eschatological reserve of Paul.[161] For Witulski, Paul's futurist eschatology has been changed to a temporal concept of "concealed" and "revealed" (Col 3:4).[162]

155 Müller, *Anfänge der Paulusschule*, 122.
156 Merklein, "Paulinische Theologie," 40–45.
157 Yates, xxiii–xxiv.
158 Strecker, *New Testament Theology*, 562.
159 Schnelle, *Gerechtigkeit und Christusgegenwart*, 80.
160 Witulski, "Gegenwart und Zukunft," 217–18.
161 Witulski, "Gegenwart und Zukunft," 219–20.
162 Witulski, "Gegenwart und Zukunft," 224–27.

Yet, as I will endeavor to show below (see the commentary on 3:1–4), Paul already knows and uses spatial language in his earlier writings when he speaks of "Jerusalem above" (Gal 4:26) and "the upward call of God" (Phil 3:14). He does this while simultaneously maintaining his future-oriented eschatology.[163] This language is deeply rooted in the OT (such as in the expression, "heaven above"; Exod 20:4; Deut 4:39; 5:8; 30:12; etc.) and does not necessarily depend on Hellenistic conceptions. If Paul can hold in tension this kind of spatial language with his temporal understanding of the kingdom, then it becomes a matter of emphasis. And there is no doubt that in Colossians he emphasizes the presence of salvation through the use of spatial language—"above" and "below." There are a variety of reasons Paul stresses the presence of salvation in Colossians. Perhaps foremost is his perception that the Colossian believers needed to better understand their entrance into the kingdom (1:13) and the supernatural power available to them for resisting "the philosophy" and living the Christian life. Yet he may also have chosen to stress "above" and "below" because of how it would have communicated to believers in the Lycus Valley. The extensive necropolis at Hierapolis (as well as Colossae's own necropolis) would have been a constant reminder to people living in that region of the common conception that the dead journeyed "below" to the underworld and a gloomy existence. His language would have assured the readers that not only was Jesus alive and in the world "above," but that believers presently experienced a connection to him and benefitted from supernatural resources that he could impart to them (2:19). Yet at the same time, the author of Colossians assured them of an eschatological future life with Christ in glory (3:4). Thus, the Pauline future eschatology and the spatial conceptuality are held together in Colossians.

In a largely overlooked and important essay, C. E. B. Cranfield expands on the comments in his ICC commentary on Rom 6:1–14 by clarifying four different senses in which believers can be said to be raised with Christ.[164] (1) The first is a *juridical* sense and relates to the status of believers before God. He explains that "God wills to see them as having died in Christ's death and having been raised in his resurrection."[165] Although in Rom 6 Paul does not expressly state that believers have been raised with Christ, Cranfield finds vv. 11 ("consider yourselves alive to God in Christ Jesus") and 13 ("present yourselves to God as those who have been brought from death to life") to point strongly in this direction. He concludes, and I think rightly, "I cannot accept the contention (though it is quite often stated very confidently) that there is a substantial disagreement between this passage and Col 3:1."[166] (2) The second is *baptismal.*

163 Wedderburn, *Theology*, 52, rightly observes that the temporal and spatial categories should not be separated too far.

164 Cranfield, "Romans 6:1–14 Revisited," 40–43. See also Cranfield, *Romans*, 1:296–320.

165 Cranfield, "Romans 6:1–14 Revisited," 41.

166 Cranfield, "Romans 6:1–14 Revisited," 41.

Cranfield contends that "it is surely implied" that believers have been raised with Christ in baptism, especially since Christ's death would have "no saving efficacy apart from its sequel in his resurrection."[167] (3) The third is the *moral* or ethical sense. Paul's injunction to "walk in newness of life" at Rom 6:4, as well as at the end of the passage where he exhorts them to "present yourselves to God as those who have been brought from death to life, and your members to God as instruments for righteousness" (Rom 6:13), suggests a form of inner reflection on the implications of the Christ event that naturally leads to ethical living.[168] (4) The final sense is the *eschatological*, and in particular that believers will be physically raised in the final resurrection. Cranfield notes that this is present as a secondary reference in Rom 6:8b ("we believe that we will also live with him") and probably also in v. 5b ("we shall certainly be united with him in a resurrection like his").[169] But Cranfield asserts that this is also present in Col 3:4. He concludes his essay by declaring that "the fact that Christ himself has already been raised from the dead has a significant bearing on our present life."[170]

While it is true that Paul never uses the aorist indicative to refer to the resurrection of believers as a past event, neither does the author of Colossians. He uses the past tense of *co*-resurrection (συν + ηγέρθητε), and this is an important distinction. Believers are so closely identified with Christ that they participate with him not only in his death but also in his resurrection. Believers have not yet experienced the resurrection of their bodies; that is still future (Col 3:4). Since they have been incorporated into the body of Christ as represented in the ritual of baptism, they are the beneficiaries of the implications of Christ's death on the cross *and* his resurrection to the right hand of God.[171] Schnelle himself comes very close to this understanding when he says that "those who believe and have been baptized are not yet risen, but they still participate in a real way in the powers of Jesus's resurrection."[172] And, again, he later says, "Jesus Christ has died and been raised from the dead, and believers have been made by their baptism to share completely in this saving event."[173]

G. Macaskill has rightly stressed the connection between baptism and the death/resurrection of Christ with the clothing metaphor in Paul.[174] In Gal 3:27, those who are baptized into Christ have been clothed with him, indicating that believers share in the identity of Christ as sons of God. He notes the continuity between Col 3:9–10 (with the clothing imagery of "putting off" and "putting

167 Cranfield, "Romans 6:1–14 Revisited," 40.

168 Cranfield, "Romans 6:1–14 Revisited," 42–43.

169 Cranfield, "Romans 6:1–14 Revisited," 43.

170 Cranfield, "Romans 6:1–14 Revisited," 43.

171 Murphy-O'Connor, *Paul*, 247, contends that the co-resurrection statements in Colossians "are simply an alternative, and more vivid, expression of the body theme" and thus should not be seen as discontinuous with Paul.

172 Schnelle, *Paul*, 330.

173 Schnelle, *Paul*, 331.

174 Macaskill, *Union with Christ*, 196–97.

on") and Col 2:11–15 "where baptism entails death to the flesh and the written code, and resurrection into the new reality that is 'in Christ.'"[175] Cranfield also shows the continuity of the clothing metaphor in Colossians with Rom 13:12, 14 ("put on the armor of light" and "put on the Lord Jesus Christ").[176]

Throughout the centuries, church leaders and scholars saw no conflict between Romans and Colossians on the matter of co-resurrection. Identification with Christ in his resurrection was seen as the logical and necessary counterpart to dying with Christ. In his comments on Col 2:12, Chrysostom exclaims, "You believed that God is capable of raising, and so you were raised."[177] Augustine saw co-resurrection as the basis for new life in Christ. Summarizing Augustine's teaching on this theme, J. Burns comments that "this identification of the Christian with Christ, in death and resurrection, was explicitly connected to Augustine's understanding of the union of the head and members in the body of Christ."[178] Augustine saw participation with Christ in his resurrection and ascension as principally a moral one, but also as foreshadowing the future bodily resurrection. Burns also noted that "Augustine insisted that the ritual or symbolic death and resurrection of the Christians accomplished the real destruction of sin and introduced a new life in their minds and will; it also gave the promise of immortal bodily life."[179] Likewise, many modern interpreters have seen the language of co-resurrection in Colossians as fully consistent with Paul's theology.[180] J. D. G. Dunn has said that Paul was quite capable of making this kind of statement and that "the shift in emphasis does not amount to much."[181] N. T. Wright regards the co-resurrection statements in Colossians as thoroughly Pauline, but with a distinctive emphasis.[182] Both Sumney and Lincoln, who regard the letter as pseudonymous, contend that the difference between Colossians and Romans on the notion of rising with Christ is a matter of emphasis and not of substance.[183]

Why did Paul not use the aorist indicative verb (συνηγέρθητε) in Rom 6 or elsewhere in his earlier writings? Even Cranfield believes that Paul may have resisted using this linguistic formulation to avoid being misinterpreted along the triumphalistic lines that we see evidenced at Corinth (1 Cor 4:8). This may

175 Macaskill, *Union with Christ*, 197.

176 Cranfield, "Romans 6:1–14 Revisited," 43.

177 Chrysostom, *Hom. Col.* 6.236 (P. Allen).

178 Burns, "Baptism as Dying and Rising with Christ," 426. See his footnotes 74–78 for the key texts in Augustine's writings.

179 Burns, "Baptism as Dying and Rising with Christ," 427.

180 See C. Campbell, *Paul and Union with Christ*, 375–79. See also D. A. Campbell, *Framing Paul*, 297–99.

181 Dunn, 161.

182 Wright, *Resurrection*, 236–41. Similarly, Lincoln, 624, contends that it is a "shift in emphasis rather than a major change of thought."

183 Sumney, 139, notes, "Colossians and Romans do not differ as radically as some have thought." Lincoln, 624, says that because of this continuity of thought, "it should not be made a decisive factor in the issue of authorship."

very well be the case, but the context at Colossae was very different than that at Corinth. At Colossae, Paul needed to emphasize the presence of salvation and the supernatural resources available to believers through the resurrected Christ.

The concern about the hostile role of the principalities, powers, authorities, thrones, and elemental spirits prompted Paul to stress the full implications of the union of believers with Christ. This connection is made explicit in Col 2:9–10 where Paul says, "For in him all the fullness of deity dwells in bodily form. And you are filled in him, who is the head of every ruler and authority." The believers at Colossae needed to know that they have supernatural resources available through their union with Christ that would enable them to resist the principalities and powers. Another way of expressing this is through emphasizing that they have been raised with Christ. What was implicit in Rom 6 is now made explicit for a pastoral reason.

In assessing this issue, one needs to make a sharp distinction between the beliefs of the Colossian Christians and those held and advocated by the purveyors of "the philosophy." It is quite possible that the opposing teachers may have held a set of convictions that approached a "theology of glory" or an overrealized eschatology. This would have especially been true if they had been initiated into one or more of the mystery cults and were drawing on the knowledge to inform their teaching and practice. If Paul were writing directly to them, he may have maintained his "eschatological reserve" to dampen their enthusiasm.

Yet the indicators of this letter suggest that the Colossians themselves needed reassurance about the power and authority available to them through their union with Christ in light of their struggle with the principalities and powers. Paul goes out of his way to assure the Colossians that the powers have been defeated by Christ's work on the cross (2:15), that Christ is preeminent over the powers by virtue of the fact that he created them (1:16–18), that in Christ the Colossians have died to the compelling force of their influence and power (2:20), and that they are united with Christ and "filled" in him who rules over these hostile forces (2:10). The notion of being united with Christ in his resurrection is a way of stressing the power and authority available to them through Christ and his Spirit to stand up against these powers and their influence. Calvin made this connection many years ago when, in commenting on Col 2:12, he connected it to the divine power available to them: "because it is impossible for believers to be severed from their head, the same power of God which showed itself in Christ is diffused to them all in common."[184]

The author of Colossians is thus not advocating a theology of glory or overrealized eschatology,[185] but a theology of power—power to overcome all the work of the enemy. Paul stated this in different terms to the Philippians when he said, "I want to know Christ and the power of his resurrection, to share in his

184 Calvin, 333.

185 In fact, the author of Colossians associates glory with the future return of Christ (3:4).

sufferings, and to be like him in his death" (Phil 3:10). The author of Colossians is not proclaiming power apart from suffering; Paul's own example of writing this letter while in chains dispels that notion (Col 4:18), as does his reflections on the suffering he has experienced for the gospel (1:24–25; 2:1). Paul wants the Colossians to know and experience the power of Christ working in and through them as they learn to hold onto Christ tightly as their living head (2:19). They need Christ's power to resist the teaching and practices of "the philosophy," which Paul sees as demonically inspired (2:8). But they also need the resurrection power of Christ to put to death their sinful behaviors (3:5–11), to appropriate the virtues of Christ (3:12–17), to live as Christians in the household (3:18–4:1), for endurance and patience (1:11), and to serve and minister to one another in the body of Christ (1:28–29).

## *Explanation*

For all converts everywhere, Paul deeply desires and strives for them to become firm, secure, and well-grounded in what they have believed and to know Jesus Christ as their Lord—the one who is alive, having been raised from the dead, and is presently and actively functioning as their Lord. Paul wants them to know the tradition of beliefs that they have received and that are commonly held by Christians all over the Mediterranean world. This is "the faith" that Paul has received, that he is passing on through his apostolic ministry, and that he deems crucial to their ongoing vitality as a community. This tradition not only encompasses a set of beliefs about the one living and true God and the identity and work of Jesus Christ, but it extends to a set of ethical and lifestyle obligations that should characterize the conduct of every member of this new community (see, e.g., 1 Thess 4:1, "you received from us [the tradition] of how it is necessary for you to walk and please God"). Paul will emphasize certain aspects of both the creedal and ethical parts of this tradition in this letter, particularly those portions that he deems relevant to what the Colossian believers are currently facing.

This letter is not just a positive encouragement to the Colossian believers at a time when they are progressing and doing well in trouble-free times. They face a major threat and are possibly unaware of just how serious a danger this poses to their community. The seriousness of the problem is of such an order that Paul has deemed it essential to write to them and to use rather strong language in conveying the severity of the threat. In essence, there is a faction within the church—likely with a respected, vocal, and influential leader who is looked upon as wise in spiritual matters—that is advocating a set of beliefs, rituals, and practices that Paul sees as dangerous. In fact, he characterizes the faction's teaching as "empty deceit" that is inspired by demonic spirits and is out of sync with what they have been taught about Christ. The danger is so acute that Paul compares their vulnerability to property and servants that are seized and taken away by a victorious army after a war. It is difficult to know if the ringleader of the faction has these kinds of devious designs on the congregation of believers at Colossae or whether he has simply been the pawn of evil spirits who are using him to accomplish their designs as they ardently oppose the unfolding of the redemptive plan of Christ in the world. I suspect it is the latter. The factional leader probably thinks he is serving the community well through his knowledge of esoteric traditions that can supplement their new faith in Christ.

There is no indication that the advocates of "the philosophy" are opposing the gospel by offering another way to be saved. They are functionally challenging the lordship of Jesus Christ over daily life by promoting beliefs, rituals, and practices that render Christ irrelevant to matters of daily concern. Everyone living in this region had a deep concern about the impact of spirits on everyday life. Their livelihood depended on averting plagues that could wipe out their livestock and ensuring the fertility of their crops and animals. They were also concerned about their personal well-being and often needed the wisdom and skills of a person who knew the spiritual world to break the power of a curse, to expel an evil spirit from a family member or a dwelling, to cure a fever or a serious sickness, or even to alter the seemingly inexorable pull of fate (as charted in a horoscope).

In this section of the letter, Paul makes a case for the relevance of Christ for all of life. The unspoken but implicit message is that there is no need to seek out a "spirit person" or accede to the demands of a shaman figure who brings traditional remedies to every manner of problem. Paul's recurring theme in this section is: consider what it means to be "in Christ." By knowing and drawing on the connection that believers have to Christ, the allure of "the philosophy" would disappear. Furthermore, as Paul will show in Col 3 and 4, this dynamic relationship with Christ also serves as the basis for getting rid of sinful patterns of behavior (3:1–11), appropriating the virtues essential for all Christians (3:12–17), for living properly in a Christian household (3:18–4:1), as well as for prayer and mission (4:2–6).

There are two main reasons that the Colossians can conduct their lives in a way that is pleasing to Christ and also will be able to resist the pull of "the philosophy." First, they are completely "filled" in Christ (2:10). The language of filling and fullness in Colossians is imagery drawn from the OT temple and is coextensive with Paul's understanding of the work of the Holy Spirit. Just as Christ was filled with the divine Spirit and conducted his earthly ministry by the Spirit's power and now continues to live in the closest association with the Spirit, so believers are similarly filled by virtue of their union with Christ. One of the key points of the relevance of this truth for the Colossians is that they are in solidarity with one who has sovereignty over the demonic powers. This means that they share in Christ's power and authority over this realm. This truth functions to alleviate their fear of evil spirits and to eliminate the enticing qualities about the shamanistic teaching. Through dependence upon Christ and appropriation of their authority in him—not by a myriad of esoteric folk rituals—believers can defeat the influence of the authorities of darkness and walk in a manner worthy of the Lord (1:10; 2:6).

Second, God has made them alive with Christ (2:13). This is coextensive with the "newness of life" (Rom 6:4) and the "new life of the Spirit" (Rom 7:6) that he speaks of in Romans. This is the language of new creation (2 Cor 5:17) and speaks of the renewing work of God in the life of believers that enables them to live in a way that is pleasing to the Lord. In Ephesians, he speaks of the renewal that is accomplished by the Spirit (Eph 4:23).

This new life together with Christ is the result of dying and rising with Christ. Similarly, this identification with Christ in his death and resurrection also serves as the basis for their experience of "fullness" in him. The one rite that Paul does affirm and build upon is the Christian ritual of baptism, which serves as a vivid portrayal of being buried with Jesus in his death and then being raised with him from the dead to an entirely new life.

In a unique development, Paul describes the identification of believers with Christ in his death as a spiritual circumcision. Although the precise interpretation of this passage has been widely disputed, it is best interpreted as a procedure performed by Christ that results in a critical blunting of the impact of the sinful appetite (a phenomenon Paul calls the "flesh") in every believer. In Romans, Paul describes unredeemed humanity as slaves to sin or as "slaves to impurity" (Rom 6:16, 19), but because of the identification of believers with the death and resurrection of Christ, there is freedom. Paul declared, "for freedom Christ has set us free; stand firm therefore, and do not submit again to a yoke of slavery" (Gal 5:1 ESV). This freedom does not entail the absence of evil influence in day-to-day life; rather, it means that believers are now free to yield themselves to Christ and to righteousness so that they can become increasingly pure in their conduct. Believers now have the opportunity to "present yourselves to God as those who have been brought from death to life" (Rom 6:13). They are no longer trapped in a life of sinful behavior.

The basis of this new life in union with Christ is the forgiveness that God has bestowed on his people because of the death of Jesus on the cross. In a unique development, Paul employs a legal metaphor to describe the certainty of the forgiveness that God has extended. Drawing from the field of business and commerce, Paul creatively seizes on a term that was commonly used as a technical expression for a loan document or promissory note. He implies that humanity has defaulted on the loan and that devastating legal consequences now obtain (which he says in 2:13a is "death"). In developing this image, Paul says that God has cancelled this document, taken it away from his people, and nailed it to the cross (2:14). This last statement precisely clarifies the means by which forgiveness has been achieved—that is, through the death of Jesus on the cross. This metaphor of the cancelled and crucified promissory note bears some overlap in meaning with another legal metaphor that Paul employs—the concept of "justification" by faith. Although both are legal metaphors, one comes from the sphere of the courtroom and the other from the realm of business. Both, however, are closely related to the notion of forgiveness of sins and both result in freedom from condemnation.

The final basis Paul gives for the new life in Christ is that God has won an extraordinary and decisive victory over the evil rulers and authorities by the work of Christ in his cross and resurrection (Col 2:15). Nowhere else in Paul's writings is there such an elaborate and glorious depiction of the implications of Christ's work with respect to the powers of darkness. Paul declares that God has disarmed, exposed, and publicly humiliated them. Paul once again creates a vivid metaphor to convey the certainty and decisiveness of this defeat of the powers. He compares their defeat to the defeated armies of an enemy king that are paraded through the streets of Rome in a parade of triumph. This victory won by Christ through his cross and resurrection was the most important victory over the powers; the final eschatological victory simply represents the ultimate pacification of these forces that remain hostile in the present age. This victory is so important to believers because it means that all who are in Christ and appropriate the power and authority available through him can resist their influence and live the virtuous and mission-centered lives God has called them to live. Because of their union with Christ, they have died to the compelling influence of these demonic spirits (2:20). The Colossians are therefore free to walk in a manner pleasing to God and to refuse to accept the dictates coming from the advocates of "the philosophy."

# Warnings against "the Philosophy" (2:16–23)

## *Bibliography*

**Alexander, P. S.** "Incantations and Books of Magic," 342–79. **Arbesmann, P. R.** *Fasten.* **Argall, R. A.** "Religious Error," 6–20. **Arnold, C. E.** *Colossian Syncretism.* ———. "'Head' of the Church," 346–66. ———. "Sceva, Solomon, and Shamanism," 7–26. **Attridge, H.** "On Becoming an Angel," 481–98. **Aune, N. A.** "Heresiproblemet i Kolossæ," 97–105. **Bandstra, A. J.** "Mediator?," 329–43. **Beetham, C. A.** *Echoes of Scripture.* 193–218. **Betz, H. D.** *Mithras Liturgy.* **Bevere, A.** *Sharing in the Inheritance.* **Bonner, C.** *Studies in Magical Amulets.* **Bornkamm, G.** "Heresy of Colossians," 123–45. **Bruce, F. F.** "Colossian Heresy," 195–208. **Burkert, W.** *Ancient Mystery Cults.* ———. "ΓΟΗΣ," 36–55. **Canavan, R.** *Clothing the Body.* **Carr, W.** *Angels and Principalities.* ———. "Two Notes on Colossians," 492–500. **Cole, H. R.** "Time-Keeping," 273–82. **Demaris, R. E.** *Colossian Controversy.* **Dibelius, M.** "Isis Initiation," 61–121. **Eitrem, S. E.** "'ΕΜΒΑΤΕΥΩ," 90–94. **Evans, C. A.** "Colossian Mystics," 188–205. **Foerster, W.** "Irrlehrer," 71–80. **Fowl, S.** *Story of Christ.* **Francis, F. O.** "EMBATEUEIN," 197–207. ———. "Humility and Angelic Worship," 163–95. **Frankfurter, D.** *Roman Egypt.* **Gerlitz, P.** "Fasten als Reinigungsritus," 212–22. **Goodenough, E. R.** *Jewish Symbols.* **Goulder, M.** "Colossians and Barbelo," 601–19. **Griffiths, J. G.** *The Isis-Book.* **Guichard, C.** "Oracular Temples at Klaros and Didyma." **Hayes, H. D.** "Colossians 2:6–19," 285–88. **Hemberg, B.** "Die idaiischen Daktylen," 41–59. **Hengel, M.** *Judaism and Hellenism.* **Holbrook, F. B.** "Sabbath," 64–72. **Hollenbach, B.** "Col. II.23," 254–61. **Hooker, M. D.** "False Teachers," 315–31. **Hopfner, T.** "Hekate-Selene-Artemis," 125–45. **Hurtado, L.** *One God, One Lord.* **Kraft, R.** "Multiform Jewish Heritage," 174–205. **Kraus, T.** *Hekate.* **Lähnemann, J.** *Kolosserbrief,* 134–52. **Lane, E.** *Corpus Monumentorum.* ———. "Men," 2161–74. **Lane Fox, R.** *Pagans and Christians.* **Lesses, R.** *Ritual Practices to Gain Power.* **Lightfoot, J. B.** "Colossian Heresy," 13–59. **Lincoln, A. T.** *Paradise Now and Not Yet.* **Lyonnet, S.** "Adversaries," 147–61. ———. "Mystères d'Apollon Clarien," 417–35. **Macridy, T.** "Altertümer," 155–73. ———. "Antiquités," 36–67. **Martin, T. W.** *By Philosophy and Empty Deceit.* ———. "Discern the Body of Christ," 249–55. ———. "Time-Keeping," 105–19. **Merisch, N.** "Kolossai," 309–11. **Moir, I. A.** "Col 2,17–18," 363–65. **Müller, P.** "Verehrung der Engel," 123–46. **Nilsson, M. P.** "Religion in den grieichischen Zauberpapyri," 59–93. **Parke, H. W.** *Oracles of Apollo.* **Percy, E.** *Probleme.* **Preisendanz, K.** "Salomon," 660–704. **Ramsay, W. M.** "Mysteries," 198–209. ———. *Teaching of Paul.* **Reicke, B.** "Zum sprachlichen Verständnis, 39–53. **Reitzenstein, R.** *Mystery Religions.* **Roberts, J. H.** "Jewish Mystical Experience," 161–89. **Robinson, J. A. T.** *Body.* **Rowland, C.** "Apocalyptic Visions," 220–31. **Royalty, R. M.** "Dwelling on Visions," 329–57. **Sappington, T. J.** *Revelation and Redemption.* **Schenke, H.-M.** "Widerstreit," 391–403. **Schweizer, E.** "Slaves of the Elements," 455–68. **Smith, I. K.** *Heavenly Perspective.* **Sokupa, M. M.** "Calendrical Elements," 172–89. **Son, S.-W.** "σῶμα," 222–38. **Stettler, C.** *Christushymnus.* ———. "Opponents," 169–200. **Sumney, J.** "Opponents," 366–88. **Thornton, T. C. G.** "New Moon Festivals," 97–100. **Torijano, P.** *Solomon the Esoteric King.* **Trebilco, P.** *Jewish Communities.* **Vergeer, W. C.** "Σκιά and Σῶμα," 379–93. **Walker-Ramisch, S.** "Voluntary Associations," 128–45. **Wedderburn, A. J. M.** *Baptism and Resurrection.* **Weiss, H.-F.** "Antignostische Polemik," 311–24. **Williams, A. L.** "Cult of the Angels," 413–38. **Yates, R.** "Worship of Angels," 12–15. **Yinger, K.** "Translating καταβραβευέτω," 138–45.

## Translation

*[16]Therefore, let no one judge you in regard to food and drink or in regard to the matter of a festival or new moon[a] or Sabbath; [17]these[b] are a shadow of what is coming, and the body belongs to Christ. [18]Let no one condemn you by wanting [you to engage in] ascetic practices and the worship of angels,[c] which he has[d] seen upon entering. [This person is] puffed up in vanity by his fleshly mind [19]and is not holding tight to the head from whom the whole body—through the joints and ligaments being nourished and united—grows the growth from God. [20]If you died with Christ from the demonic spirits of the world, why do you comply with their dictates as though you were living in the world? [21][They say:] "Do not handle! Do not taste! Do not touch!" [22]These things all lead to corruption with use according to the commandments and teachings of men. [23]These things amount to a gratification of the flesh although they have a reputation for wisdom in freely chosen worship and asceticism and[e] severe treatment of the body, but do not have any honor.*

## Notes

a. [2:16] Codices Sinaiticus (א) and Alexandrinus (A; 𝔓[46] is illegible) here read the contracted form, νουμηνία (so also the THGNT), whereas NA[28] and UBS[5] follow the bulk of the manuscript tradition, which has νεομηνία. The difficulty with the latter reading is that νεομηνία is not attested in Koine before the second century from when it prevails.[1] It is likely, then, that νεομηνία reflects a scribal modification to confom it to contemporary usage.

b. [2:17] Instead of the plural relative pronoun ἅ, Codex Vaticanus (B, along with F G 614) read the singular ὅ. This is likely a scribal assimilation to the ὅ ἐστιν of 1:24, 27, and 3:14.

c. [2:18] Codex Sinaiticus (א) makes the curious insertion of μελλόντων, "the coming angels." This was likely influenced by the presence of the participle in the previous verse, σκιὰ τῶν μελλόντων.

d. [2:18] The Majority text, along with many Western witnesses (א[2] C D[c] K L P Ψ 075 0150 Vg it[ar, f, g, mon, o] Jerome Augustine), insert a negative: ἃ μὴ ἑόρακεν ἐμβατεύων, "entering what he has *not* seen" (F and G insert οὐκ). There would have been a strong scribal motive to strengthen the polemic by asserting that the opponents had not experienced authentic visions. Westcott and Hort rightly note that "the insertion of the negative glosses over without removing the manifest difficulty of the phrase."[2]

e. [2:23] A few important manuscripts (𝔓[46] and B along with 1739) omit the second καί. This puts ἀφειδίᾳ σώματος in apposition to ταπεινοφροσύνῃ, thus defining the nature of the "humility," rather than coordinating it as the third member of the series of descriptors of the reputed wisdom of "the philosophy." Many commentators concur with the omission as the original reading, arguing that a scribe would be more likely to add the καί. Thus, Wilson notes, "In any case, having written two datives linked by a *kai* a scribe would almost inevitably think that a third should also be linked."[3] There would be a stronger motivation, however, for a scribe to omit the καί since "humility" is normally used as a positive virtue in Paul, and here it is a characterization of the false teaching.[4] Therefore, the καί should be retained as the original reading in accord with the testimony of nearly the entire manuscript tradition.

---

1 See MM, s.v. νεομηνία, and *NewDocs* 3:76–77 (§50).

2 Westcott and Hort, *Original Greek*, 127.

3 Wilson, 229; see also Sumney, 160.

4 So also Barth and Blanke, 361n96.

## *Form/Structure/Setting*

### *Form (and Literary Context)*

Colossians 2:16–23 forms the polemical core of the letter. The polemic began as early as 2:4 when Paul issued his first warning, "I am saying this so that no one may deceive you with persuasive teachings." This was then taken up in far more serious tones in 2:8, when he warned, "Watch out that someone will not lead you away as a captive through the philosophy, which is empty deceit, on the basis of human traditions, inspired by demonic spirits of the world and not inspired by Christ." Now he takes up the polemic in earnest, warning the Colossians repeatedly of the dangers of the teaching and practices of the so-called philosophy. His polemic involves issuing three warnings. Each are followed by a description of certain practices of the rival teaching (sometimes citing actual maxims or catchwords from the opponents) and then delivering brief, incisive critiques. Lohse rightly notes that the author here uses a "pointed polemical style" that is "filled with catchwords."[5]

In the previous section (2:6–15), Paul layed the theological foundation as the basis for his appeal to the Colossians to resist the judgments, condemnatory statements, and dictates of the factional teaching. The heart of his argument is that they can resist the rival teaching because they are "in Christ" and "have been filled in him" (see 2:9–10 and the repeated use of "in him" throughout the passage). In other words, if the Colossians would think deeply about the implications of their relationship with Christ and draw on the resources that they have in him, they would no longer have any reasons for acceding to the demands and judgments of the advocates of the philosophy. A crucially important part of the Colossians being "in Christ" is recognizing that they have participated with Christ in his death (2:12a), resurrection (2:12b), and newness of life (2:13d). Their sins are not only forgiven, but they have participated with Christ in his resurrection above all the hostile spiritual forces.

The theme of hostile supernatural powers is woven throughout 2:6–15 and looms in the background of 2:16–23. Paul, in fact, attributes the ultimate source and inspiration of the dangerous teaching at Colossae to "demonic spirits of the world" (2:8). He assures the Colossians that a significant part of what it means for them to be in Christ and "filled in him" is that they participate in his headship over every "rule and authority" (2:10). And the section concludes with an eloquent affirmation of Christ's divestiture of the demonic powers, his public exposure of them, and his extraordinary triumph over them (2:15). This leads immediately into the next section, which begins the direct polemic. The hostile powers are not mentioned in 2:16–23, but their prominent role, influence, and threat is what drives this section. They are behind the taboos, they motivate the ritual initiation (and all of the preparatory practices), and they prompt the

5 Lohse, 114.

invocation of angels. It is precisely because of their influence that shamanic wisdom and power is needed.

The introductory οὖν, "therefore," should therefore be taken as a full inferential conjunction and not simply as a discourse marker noting a transition to the next topic of discussion. The theological ground that Paul lays in 2:6–15 is foundational to his polemic of 2:16–23.

The sentences throughout this section are difficult. The unusual syntax and abbreviated phrases and clipped clauses make it a challenge for the interpreter to discern the meaning. The various hapax legomena and unusual expressions should not be taken as the telltale fingerprints of a pseudepigrapher but of a polemical style that weaves together catchwords and catchphrases from the rival teaching. Although the modern reader can find this section nearly inscrutable in places, the Colossian readers and hearers would have picked up on the language immediately and associated it with precisely what they were hearing from the rival teacher.[6] The problem we face in the interpretive task is in discerning what those catchphrases are and in determining what they mean in the context of the rival teaching. Some are relatively easy to identify, such as μὴ ἅψῃ μηδὲ γεύσῃ μηδὲ θίγῃς, "do not handle, do not taste, do not touch" (2:21), which is commonly agreed to represent actual statements from the philosophy. Others are much more difficult to identify with any kind of certainty, such as ἐθελοθρησκία, "freely chosen worship" (2:23). In the final analysis, it may not make much difference in how we interpret the nature of the practices of the rival teaching to discern which are catchwords and which are descriptive statements from the author of the letter. The more important task is gaining a sense of what the expressions mean in the overall meaning structure of "the philosophy."

There is no doubt that passion and emotion come through in the three warnings that Paul gives to the Colossians and in the critique of the philosophy in this section. But it is going too far to say that the author "loses something of his composure."[7] The apostle's warnings are direct and reflect his concern about the threat the philosophy presents to the health and stability of the Colossian community of believers. Paul's descriptions of the rituals and regulations of the group are measured and concise. And there is no doubt that his critiques are sharp and hard-hitting. He directly indicts the character of the leader of the faction, calling him arrogant (2:18) and influenced by his flesh. But in Paul's view, this is a very serious matter. This ringleader is hurting the Colossian church by judging and condemning them and by foisting a variety of rules and regulations upon them that are completely extraneous to their new life in Christ. In light of this polemic and the gravity of what is at stake, it is surprising that M. Hooker could make the statement that "if false teaching exists, then it cannot be serious,

6 So, rightly, Sumney, 148.
7 Hay, 101.

either in character or magnitude."[8] It is equally perplexing to understand Dunn's comment that the author is here using "a more relaxed style of polemic."[9]

There is a great deal of rhetoric in this passage insofar as Paul is seeking to persuade the Colossians not to yield to the dictates and criticisms of the rival teacher. Yet few scholars have sought to assess this passage in terms of the rhetorical handbooks for oral discourse. Bird notes that for an audience listening to the passage read aloud, the passage would sound "like the *refutatio* of a deliberative discourse by striking up arguments against the opposing viewpoint."[10]

### *Structure*

This section is structured around three distinct warnings. The first two are delivered as third-person singular imperatives, and the third is a question that is the apodosis of a first-class conditional sentence:

1. μὴ . . . τις ὑμᾶς κρινέτω, "let no one judge you" (2:16)
2. μηδεὶς ὑμᾶς καταβραβευέτω, "let no one condemn you" (2:18)
3. τί ὡς ζῶντες ἐν κόσμῳ δογματίζεσθε; "Why do you comply with their dictates as though you were living in the world?" (2:20)

The first warning section (2:16–17) focuses on the judgmental attitude of the opponents around matters pertaining to food, drink, and calendar observances. These areas of concern are flagged with the threefold use of the preposition ἐν. Paul then gathers these up with the neuter relative pronoun (ἅ) and makes a two-pronged theological critique, stressing the transitory nature of the observances and undermining the opponents' right to judge the Colossian believers because they belong to Christ and answer to him (2:17).

The second warning section (2:18–19) calls into question the rival teacher's right to condemn the Colossians. The imperatival verb is followed by four present participles that form the structure of the rest of the section:

μηδεὶς ὑμᾶς καταβραβευέτω, "let no one condemn you"

1. θέλων ἐν, "wanting you to . . ." (2:18b)
2. ἐμβατεύων, "entering" (2:18d)
3. φυσιούμενος, "puffed up" (2:18e)
4. οὐ κρατῶν, "not holding tight" (2:19a)

The first two are descriptive of the activity of the rival teacher, and the second two are indictments against him. The first is best interpreted as means (θέλων

8 Hooker, "False Teachers," 316.
9 Dunn, 34.
10 Bird, 73.

ἐν, "*by* wanting you to") and is expressive of the kinds of preparatory observances and ritual activities he is pressing on the Colossians. The second clause (ἐμβατεύων)—one of the most difficult to interpret in the entire letter—is perhaps best taken as causal and forms the grounds for the rival teacher's spiritual knowledge based on his actual words: "*because* he has entered what he has seen." In other words, he has experienced a ritual initiation ceremony, which gives him a basis for his knowledge and judgments. The third and fourth participial clauses are best understood as adjectival clauses (modifying μηδείς) and represent sharp and serious critiques of the character of the factional leader by asserting that he is at once arrogant (φυσιούμενος, he is "puffed up") and out of touch with the Lord Jesus Christ (οὐ κρατῶν, "not holding tight"). The section is brought to conclusion with a brief christological excursus, begun with ἐξ οὗ, that extols the present work of Christ in directly supplying every member of his body and by instructing them, resulting in the growth of the body.

The third and final section (2:20–23) is introduced by a conditional sentence that forms a question. It is not a rhetorical question but a real question, which Paul intends for them to ponder deeply. In this question, the protasis of the sentence is the theological basis for rejecting the dictates of the rival teaching: "if you died with Christ from the demonic spirits of the world," as indeed they had through identification with Jesus's death on the cross (2:15), then they can deny the demands that are being placed upon them. Following the pattern of the previous two warnings, Paul provides description of the dangerous practices, followed by the critique. In 2:21, he cites some of the taboos that the rival teacher was advocating, then gathers these together with a neuter relative pronoun at 2:22a (ἅ), as he had done in 2:17a, and delivers a pointed critique. He does this once again with a neuter pronoun (ἅτινά; 2:23a) and, once again, provides a sharp critique (2:23g).

The syntax of the last sentence (2:23) is notoriously difficult to interpret, and there have been a variety of approaches (see *Comment* for a full discussion of the grammatical complexities of this verse). I will argue that the best way to understand it is to take the final prepositional phrase (πρὸς πλησμονὴν τῆς σαρκός) as the predicate of ἅτινά ἐστιν. This means that for rhetorical purposes, the predicate is held in abeyance to the end, with an intervening concessive clause (λόγον μὲν ἔχοντα σοφίας, "although having a reputation for wisdom") and four prepositional phrases. The structure could be depicted this way (the main clause is in bold):

**ἅτινά ἐστιν–**
  λόγον μὲν ἔχοντα σοφίας
    ἐν ἐθελοθρησκίᾳ καὶ
    ταπεινοφροσύνῃ καὶ
    ἀφειδίᾳ σώματος,
    οὐκ ἐν τιμῇ τινι
**–πρὸς πλησμονὴν τῆς σαρκός.**

**These things amount to–**

although they have a reputation for wisdom

in freely chosen worship and

asceticism and

severe treatment of the body,

but do not have any honor

**–a gratification of the flesh.**

The particle μέν and its attendant clause, although normally completed by δέ, is here completed by the οὐκ clause: "although it has a reputation for wisdom . . . it is without honor."

## *Setting*

In the limited confines of his Roman custody, the apostle Paul received word that a serious problem was affecting the Colossian community of believers. This information likely came from Tychicus (and perhaps also even Onesimus), who provided him with a detailed account—no doubt with a series of stories about how it was impacting particular individuals within the church. Having access to both of these people from the Colossian congregation also gave the apostle an opportunity to ask specific questions about the precise nature of the teaching, the persons involved in advocating it, and the effect that it was having. Because of his strong sense of pastoral and apostolic responsibility for this group—since they had come to know Christ through the agency of Epaphras (who learned the gospel directly from Paul)—the apostle wrote to them not only to build them up in their knowledge of Christ but to expose the danger of the teaching that had emerged and to persuade them to resist it.

The overall identification and reconstruction of the nature of this rival teaching has long been disputed (see the *Introduction* for a more detailed account of the interpretive options). Was it a Jewish faction in the church who advocated a form of Jewish mysticism, replete with rituals and practices that led to heavenly-ascent experiences? Or did the opponents create a new form of mystery cult devoted to the *stoicheia* that combined within it some elements of Judaism and Christianity?

Neither of these popular explanations accounts for all of the evidence from the letter. The category that brings the most coherence to the widely disparate elements of the teaching and practices of the group is shamanism. A figure in the church at Colossae emerged who functioned as a healer, exorcist, and wise man. He was reputed for his knowledge about spirits and how to deal effectively with them. Likely a local Jew who became a Christian, he followed Christ but syncretized his faith with beliefs and practices from local pagan cults and practices, folk Judaism, and rituals of power from the pervasive magical practices that were empire wide. He sought to serve the community by doing the work of a traditional healer and exorcist.

## *Comment*

**16** Μὴ οὖν τις ὑμᾶς κρινέτω, "therefore, let no one judge you." The conjunction (οὖν) is not simply a discourse marker indicating a transition to a new topic. It has the full force of an inferential conjunction[11] and thereby roots the believers' ability to resist the dictates of the opposing teaching in all of the benefits they receive from being united with Christ (2:6–15).

The indefinite pronoun τις, "anyone," could indicate that there is no specific person(s) that Paul has in mind as he writes these warnings.[12] However, because of the unique and concrete details he uses to describe the nature of the threat to the Colossian believers, it is far better to see the use of the pronoun here as a reluctance to name the particular individuals involved. This usage of the pronoun is consistent with the way Paul uses it in Gal 1:9 ("if anyone [τις] is preaching to you a gospel contrary to the one you received") where Paul has specific opponents in mind that he could name.

Paul's concern that the Colossian believers not allow themselves to be judged provides us with insight into how the factional teachers operated. This warning needs to be seen as parallel to the two subsequent warnings (2:18a; 2:20b), which help to interpret the meaning of judging here. The judgment rendered by the opponents in Colossae was far more severe than the kind of interpersonal tensions that erupted in the Roman church over the observance of particular days and customs regarding food and drink (Rom 14–15). The advocates of "the philosophy" went so far as to render some type of authoritative "disqualification" of any believers who did not comply with their many and varied dictates (Col 2:18a) that included extreme asceticism, rituals involving angels, and taboos. In Rome, the judging was nothing more than one group of believers showing disdain for another group (Rom 14:3). Paul's goal in Rome was to help both sides (the "strong" and the "weak") mature in their perspectives toward one another, while his goal in Colossians is for the believing community to resist and reject any pronouncements made by the factional leaders.

This is the only time in the NT where believers are instructed not to permit someone to judge them. All other imperatives of this verb are injunctions to believers not to judge one another. The most important of these is Jesus's instruction in the Sermon on the Mount: "judge not, that you be not judged" (Matt 7:1 ESV; see also Luke 6:37). Admonition of a brother or sister may be necessary, but it needs to be done with love (Matt 5:43–44), mercy (Matt 5:7), and a humble introspection that recognizes one's own need to receive admonition (Matt 7:3–5). This kind of loving correction was entirely absent from the approach of the leaders of "the philosophy." Theirs was a set of harsh, authoritative judgments that needed to be resisted. Consequently, Paul tells the Colossians to quit listening

---

11 So also BDAG, s.v. οὖν.

12 So Hooker, "False Teachers," 326.

to them and to cease putting up with their condemning judgments. The precise nature of their authoritative judgment is difficult to discern. There is no indication that they held official leadership positions in the church, but they certainly commanded some level of respect and wielded significant influence.

ἐν βρώσει καὶ ἐν πόσει, "in regard to food and drink." Part of what they were insisting on was a set of regulations that pertained to what the Colossians would choose to eat and drink, or perhaps more to the point, what they should refuse to eat and drink. These regulations probably had less to do with the establishment of their new identity as followers of Christ and much more to do with taboos associated with rituals for acquiring spiritual power.

The combination of the two nouns is not very common in the LXX or NT, but it does appear in connection with Daniel's refusal to consume the food and drink prescribed by the king (Dan 1:10) as well as in the controversy in the Roman church between the groups that Paul referred to as "the weak" and "the strong" (Rom 14:17). This evidence, combined with the OT dietary laws as a whole, has led some interpreters to conclude that these food regulations at Colossae were somehow connected to Jewish identity and faithfulness to the covenant.[13] Others have simply connected these dietary restrictions to some form of Jewish ascetic tradition.[14] But one cannot interpret the food and drink regulations apart from the other features of the teaching of "the philosophy," which include visionary practices. Thus Pao may be closer to the mark when he asserts that the regulations pertain both to the identity of Jewish Christians and to the preparatory rites for visionary experiences.[15]

But seeing these food and drink regulations as an identity marker of sorts is problematic. Throughout this letter, there is little or no indication that the factional leaders are imposing the Jewish law on the Colossian gentile Christian community as the means of clarifying their identity as the true people of God. Furthermore, drink regulations were not a part of the Mosaic legislation. As Smith observes, "It seems likely that the Colossian philosophers went beyond the Mosaic regulations as can be seen by the reference to drink."[16] The only possible Jewish explanations would be that the drink laws related to a Nazirite vow (Num 6:3) or to the convictions of certain scrupulous Jews who declined to drink wine because it may have served as a libation to pagan gods (e.g., Add Esth 14:17: "I have not honored the king's feast or drunk the wine of libations"). Although it is difficult to conceive of the philosophers promoting the value of undertaking a Nazirite vow for the entire gentile Christian group, it is plausible that they would want to insist on complete separation from drink (and food) that may have idolatrous connections. Yet this type of rigorous mentality would not

13 Dunn, 172.

14 E.g., Sumney, 150.

15 Pao, 185.

16 Smith, *Heavenly Perspective*, 116.

be consistent with a group that has valued some form of ritual initiation practice (Col 2:18) and possibly other forms of pagan or folk rituals.

An explanation that does fit with the overall set of distinguishing marks of this teaching is that the food and drink regulations have something to do with ascetic practices associated with visionary experience and rituals connected to the warding off of evil spirits. Much of the evidence for this will be discussed below in the comments on 2:18 and 2:20–23. Plutarch speaks about a variety of practices in common with what we have here that are part of the rites of mysteries. These practices include fasting, eating of raw flesh, festivals, harsh treatment of the body, the observance of days ("ill-omened and gloomy days"). He notes: "I should say that these acts are not performed for any god, but are soothing and appeasing rites for the averting of evil spirits" (*Obsolescence of Oracles* 417c).

ἢ ἐν μέρει ἑορτῆς ἢ νεομηνίας ἢ σαββάτων, "or in regard to the matter of a festival or new moon or Sabbath." The advocates of "the philosophy" not only sought to impose strict requirements regarding diet but also insisted on certain weekly, monthly, and annual observances. The phrase ἐν μέρει ("in the matter of") is common for making reference to a particular case or affair;[17] for example, "I am sending the brothers so that our boasting about you may not prove empty in this matter [ἐν τῷ μέρει τούτῳ]" (2 Cor 9:3 ESV; see also 3:10).

The combination of the three terms is a conventional description of the Jewish festival calendar.[18] They appear together in 1 Chr 23:31 ("whenever burnt offerings were offered to the LORD on Sabbaths, new moons, and feast days" [ESV]) and in 1QM II, 4 ("and the chiefs of the divisions with their enlisted shall have charge of their feasts, their new moons and their Sabbaths and all the days of the year"). A Jewish provenance for the collocation of the three terms, however, does not necessarily imply that the "philosophers" were motivated by a desire to advocate Torah observance to maintain fidelity to covenant obligations. The meaning of these calendar observances could be altered in a different cultural context where Jews are the minority and where gentiles have similar festivals. Although "Sabbaths" is distinctively Jewish, "new moon" celebrations were prominent in the local religious culture, as were also various kinds of "festivals." Wilson is correct in observing that "this verse offers proof that there was a Jewish element in the false teaching, but it would be a mistake to conclude from this that it was purely Jewish and then go on to assume that the situation in Colossae as the same as in Galatia."[19] There is the distinct possibility that these observances may have undergone a fundamental reinterpretation along mystical, magical, and even local religious lines.

The term ἑορτή ("festival") is quite common in the LXX and Jewish writings to refer to the main festival celebrations of Judaism, such as Passover

17 See BDAG, s.v., 1.b. θ.
18 Wolter, 157.
19 Wilson, 219.

(Exod 12:14), Pentecost (Exod 23:15–16), and Tabernacles (Lev 23:34), but it is not a distinctively Jewish term and was broadly used for any kind of religious festival. Various kinds of festivals were popular and important to all religions of the Roman era. Regular religious festivals were characteristic of an array of local Carian, Phrygian, and Lydian religions, such as the monthly festivals of the underworld goddess Hekate,[20] or the festivals in honor of the Ephesian Artemis ("throughout the year, festivals [ἑορτάς] and the sacred assembly of the Artemisia are to be celebrated"; *IvE* 24b.30).

Celebrations associated with the "new moon" (νεομηνία; νουμηνία is the contracted form and the best reading here; see *Notes* above) were typical of Judaism, but so also in the various religions of Asia Minor. Simply put, the new moon is the dark phase of the moon when it lies between the sun and the earth. This unilluminated portion of the moon faces directly toward the earth and is invisible until it appears as a thin crescent at sunset. The moon then becomes increasingly visible until it is fully illuminated as the full moon fifteen days later. In the lunar calendar of Judaism, the new moon established the first day of the month. The Torah specified appointed feasts (ἑορταί; Num 10:10; cf. 1 Sam 20:5, 18) and burnt offerings (Num 28:11; 29:6; cf. 1 Chr 23:31; 2 Chr 31:3; Ezek 46:6; Josephus, *Ant.* 3.238) at the beginning of every month, which makes the conjunction of "new moons" and "festivals" here quite natural in a Jewish context.

New-moon celebrations, however, did not hold a significant place in the Qumran community, presumably due to their adherence to a solar calendar. This observation should temper the assumption of some kind of connection between Qumran Essenism and the Colossian "philosophy."

Once again, it is also possible that the manner of celebrating a "new moon" and its significance may have been interpreted quite differently in rural Colossae—far away from Israel and in a church with many gentiles converted from the local religions. In folk belief, the "new moon" was a crucial time for the performance of certain magical rites (*PGM* IV.787, 2389; XIII.30, 387). Preparations for certain mystery initiation rituals were also conducted on a "new moon" (see Lucian, *Men.* 4.72–109). In Phrygia, one of the most popular deities was the moon-god Mēn (Μήν).[21] Numismatic evidence confirms that this deity was worshiped at Colossae.[22] Although inscriptional evidence reveals very little about the nature of the worship of this deity, certainly the phases of the moon would have had significance to the devotees of this heavenly god. The moon goddess Selene was also worshiped in Colossae according to the numismatic evidence. In the folk magical texts, Selene was closely associated with Artemis and Hekate. These three deities were frequently called upon to

20 See Kraus, *Hekate*, 50–51.

21 See Lane, "Men," 2164–74; idem, *Corpus Monumentorum*.

22 Merisch, "Kolossai," 309–11.

protect their worshipers from hostile spirits populating the heavens, the earth, and the underworld.[23] One text claims that "Selene, when she goes through the underworld, breaks whatever [spell] she finds" (*PGM* VII.455–56).

The term "Sabbath" is distinctively Jewish. As such it underlines an unequivocal Jewish contribution to this controversial teaching. What is less clear is the role that Sabbath observance has in the beliefs and practices of "the philosophy." Despite the genitive-plural termination (-ων), it should be understood as a singular and thus consistent with the singular "festival" and "new moon."[24] The Torah enjoined strict Sabbath observance (Exod 20:8: "Remember the Sabbath day, and keep it holy"; Exod 20:10–11; 31:14–16; 35:2–3; Lev 16:31; 23:2, 32; Deut 5:12–15), and the Prophets reiterated its importance (Isa 58:13; Jer 17:21–24, 27). Sabbath observance became one of the defining marks of Judaism during the Maccabean revolt, to the extent that the Jews would not defend themselves by fighting on the Sabbath (1 Macc 2:32–38). There is evidence in Josephus that Sabbath observance was very important to the Jews of Asia Minor, including those of the Lycus Valley, as seen in a civic decree made in Laodicea during the reign of Julius Caesar supporting their distinctive practices (Josephus, *Ant.* 14.241–42):

> The magistrates of the Laodiceans to Gaius Rubilius, the son of Gaius, the consul sends greeting. Sopater, the ambassador of Hyrcanus the high priest, has delivered to us a letter from you, whereby he lets us know that certain ambassadors were come from Hyrcanus, the high priest of the Jews, and brought a letter written concerning their nation, wherein they desire that the Jews may be allowed to observe their Sabbaths and other sacred rites, according to the laws of their forefathers, and that they may be under no command, because they are our friends and confederates: and that no one may harm them in our provinces.

The Ephesian Jews petitioned the civic authorities for permission to observe their weekly Sabbath without hindrance or fines, and the petition was granted (Josephus, *Ant.* 14.262–64). Similar decrees were made on behalf of Jews in Halicarnassus (Josephus, *Ant.* 14.256–58) and Sardis (Josephus, *Ant.* 14.259–61). In his important study of Judaism in Asia Minor, Trebilco concludes, "Although our evidence does not enable us to be specific about exactly how they observed the Sabbath, we can be certain that the Sabbath was important for Jews of Asia Minor in this period."[25]

It is important to remember that Jewish observances like the Sabbath could have received a different interpretation and assigned a different reason for dutiful

23 See Hopfner, "Hekate-Selene-Artemis," 125–45.

24 So also BDAG, s.v. 1.b.β., where it is demonstrated that τὰ σάββατα can be used for a single Sabbath day. This probably reflects the influence of the Aramaic שַׁבְּתָא.

25 Trebilco, *Jewish Communities*, 18.

observance than in mainstream Judaism. The example of Elchasai is instructive here. In his teaching, followers were instructed to keep the Sabbath for astrological reasons: "but, moreover, honour the day of the Sabbath, since that day is one of those during which prevails (the power) of these *stars*" (Hippolytus of Rome, *Haer.* 9.11). Given the varied mix of observances that comprised the teaching of the philosophy, a unique motivation for Sabbath observance would not be surprising.

**17** ἅ ἐστιν σκιὰ τῶν μελλόντων, τὸ δὲ σῶμα τοῦ Χριστοῦ, "these are a shadow compared to what is coming, and the body belongs to Christ." These two clauses have been notoriously difficult to interpret because of the multivalence of the imagery and the grammar of the second clause. Counter to the prevailing interpretation, I will contend that this verse provides two reasons for the Colossians to stand up against the judgments of the ringleader(s) of the factional teaching: (1) the practices they advocate are ephemeral and in no way to be compared with the future life in Christ, and (2) the Colossian believers belong to Christ, are answerable only to him as their master, and should not come under the judgments of others.

The scholarship on this verse has long been dominated by the view that the author is drawing on a Platonic σκία-σῶμα ("shadow"-"substance/reality") contrast that has come to the author (or the opponents) through the intermediary influence of Hellenistic Judaism as seen by the presence of this imagery in Philo. For both authors, εἰκών ("image/form") was the more common counterpart to σκία, but σῶμα could be used to emphasize the true reality or substance. For instance, in discussing his allegorical method of interpretation, Philo notes: "proceed onward to look at the passage in a figurative way, considering that the mere words of the scriptures are, as it were, but shadows of bodies [σκιάς τινας ὡσανεὶ σωμάτων εἶναι], and that the meanings which are apparent to investigation beneath them, are the real things to be pondered upon" (Philo, *Confusion* 190). Similarly, Philo asserts that "it is absurd for a shadow [σκιάν] to be looked upon as of more importance than the bodies [σωμάτων] themselves" in referring to certain kinds of Mosaic archetypes (*Migration* 12). Even Josephus employed this imagery to distinguish the substance (the σῶμα) of the reign of Archelaus, which he had already assumed, from Herod the Great's conferral of the reign upon him (the σκία) (Josephus, *J.W.* 2.28).

This σκία-σῶμα contrast is found nowhere else in the Pauline corpus or in the NT. The author of Hebrews, however, appropriates the σκία-εἰκών contrast to distinguish the law from the new realities in Christ: "the law is only a shadow of the good things that are coming [σκιὰν . . . τῶν μελλόντων ἀγαθῶν]—not the realities [τὴν εἰκόνα] themselves" (Heb 10:1 NIV). Most interpreters have assumed that this "shadow-substance" contrast is the best explanation for Col 2:17, but this should be called into question. In the first instance, we need to ask why the author chose not to use the more well-known σκία-εἰκών contrast (as in Hebrews) to avoid potential confusion regarding σῶμα. He repeatedly uses σῶμα throughout the letter to refer to the body of Christ, the church (see 1:18, 24; 2:19; 3:15) or to the physical body (2:11, 23). But in the very next sentence, the nearest context, he uses σῶμα to refer once again to the body of Christ (2:19). Furthermore, throughout the Pauline corpus, σῶμα Χριστοῦ refers to the literal body of Christ (Rom 7:4; 1 Cor 10:16) or to the church as his body (1 Cor 12:27; Eph 4:12). The author of Hebrews avoids this confusion by using εἰκών instead of σῶμα since he, too, will speak of the σῶμα Ἰησοῦ Χριστοῦ a few lines after employing the σκία-εἰκών contrast (cf. Heb 10:1 with 10:10). This should raise the possibility that the author of Colossians did not intend for σῶμα to be seen in contrast to σκία and that σῶμα Χριστοῦ should be taken as referring to the body of Christ, the church.[26]

An additional problem for the consensus view is the genitive case, Χριστοῦ. The contrast would be more apt if Christ were in the nominative case so that it is unequivocally in an appositional relationship: thus, τὸ δὲ σῶμα [ἐστιν] ὁ Χριστός ("the substance/reality is Christ"). Schweizer goes so far as to suggest an emendation to the nominative,[27] but there is no manuscript evidence of an alternative tradition, and such an emendation should only be suggested as a last resort. Some English versions ignore the genitive case and translate it as a nominative; for example, "Christ himself is that reality" (NLT); "the reality is Christ" (NET); "the substance is the Messiah" (CSB); "the reality, however, is found in Christ (NIV). Some versions take the genitive as a possessive and translate it with "belong," which is correct, but because they continue to see it as part of the σκία-σῶμα contrast, the resulting translation is confusing: "but the substance belongs to Christ" (RSV; NRSV; ESV; NASB).

T. Martin has sought to solve the problem by arguing that 17b (τὸ δὲ σῶμα τοῦ Χριστοῦ) is coordinate with 16a (μὴ οὖν τις ὑμᾶς κρινέτω), with κρινέτω as the implied verb of the antithetical clause: "don't let anyone critique you . . . but let everyone critique (discern) the body of Christ."[28] He thus understands the verb in its implied second use in the positive sense of "discerning" and interprets it in light of 1 Cor 11:29, "for the person who eats and drinks while not discerning the body eats and drinks judgment to himself." But it is more natural to interpret the conjunction δέ as coordinating the two clauses of v. 17 than to supply κρινέτω, which is now far removed from this clause. The grammatical objection he raises about the prevailing interpretation would be alleviated if the second clause is interpreted as continuative and not contrastive. Furthermore, he limits the eating and drinking to the eucharistic meal,[29] but this conclusion

26 Some commentators have argued that there are two levels of meaning present with σῶμα in this passage (e.g., C. Moule, 103), but this is unnecessary if the writer is not using the Hellenistic σκία-σῶμα contrast. Gupta, 100, even argues for a triple-layering by suggesting that the personal, human body of Christ is also in view.

27 Schweizer, 157–58.

28 Martin, "Discern the Body of Christ," 254.

29 See Martin, *By Philosophy and Empty Deceit*, 116–17.

is not clearly inferred from the context (especially if no typology is involved). As in Rom 14:17, the terms could refer simply to scruples or taboos regarding what one eats and drinks (see also Dan 1:10).

I would contend that the overall solution to the interpretational difficulties presented by this verse are best solved by (1) not reading it in light of a Hellenistic σκία-σῶμα contrast, and (2) not finding a salvation-historical or "law-gospel" contrast in this verse, but rather (3) viewing σκία in its common sense of conveying something that is less or inferior, and (4) interpreting τὸ σῶμα τοῦ Χριστοῦ as the body (the church) belonging to Christ. The resultant interpretive translation would be: "*don't let anyone judge you regarding food and drink rules or calendar observances; these are fleeting compared to the blessings of the coming age, which has dawned in Christ. Furthermore, the body belongs to Christ and is answerable only to him.*"

In much of the OT, a "shadow" is something that is fleeting and is only present for a brief duration. Thus, one of Job's friends declares, "Our days on earth are a shadow" (Job 8:9 ESV). Job himself says, "He comes out like a flower and withers; he flees like a shadow and continues not" (Job 14:2 ESV). The psalmist laments, "Man is like a breath; his days are like a passing shadow" (Ps 144:4 ESV; see also Ps 109:23; cf. 1 Chr 29:15; Wis 2:5; 5:9). The fact that a shadow is transitory, lasting only for a moment, fits well with the temporal expression τῶν μελλόντων that modifies it here in our verse. The genitive here may best be interpreted as comparative and thus giving the sense, "these things are a fleeting shadow *compared to* what is coming."

The eschatological coordinate οἱ μέλλοντες further distances this discussion from the Platonic (and Philonic) "shadow/substance" contrast.[30] Paul often used this expression, usually in the singular, to speak of the age to come (Rom 5:14; 8:18, 38; 1 Cor 3:22; see also Eph 1:21; 1 Tim 4:8; 6:19; 2 Tim 4:1). Paul can use the present participle of μέλλω to refer to the present blessings of the dawning new age in Christ (as he does in Gal 3:23: "now before faith came, we were held captive under the law, imprisoned until the coming faith was revealed"). The practices of the Colossian faction are not so much a foreshadowing of what is to come (as Heb 10:1) but are viewed as transitory and inconsequential in light of the realities of the age to come. The best commentary on ἅ ἐστιν σκιὰ τῶν μελλόντων is the parallel critique that Paul gives of other practices of the faction in 2:22a: the various prohibitions that the rival teachers advocate receive Paul's condemnation: ἅ ἐστιν πάντα εἰς φθορὰν τῇ ἀποχρήσει, "these things all lead to corruption with use." The ritual practices and observances mentioned in 2:16 as well as those in 2:21 are not strictly Torah observances or "works of the law" (τὰ ἔργα τοῦ νόμου) as in Romans and Galatians.[31] These are rituals

30 Hay, 105, calls it a "non-Philonic futurist eschatology."

31 So also Seitz, 136n13, who states that "the references Paul uses also are flexible enough to apply to any rite or calendar requirement and not just rites within his own specific Jewish frame of reference."

and observances unique to the Colossian situation. This is borne out, in part, by the fact that the Torah contains no prohibitions regarding drinks, yet this was an issue here (as seen with ἐν πόσει). So, once again, this is unlikely to be an "old order"-"new order" contrast but rather a diminution of various kinds of ritual observances (including Jewish practices, such as Sabbath) in light of the new realities in Christ. Since the new age in Christ has already dawned, the Colossians now have the opportunity, indeed the obligation, to give their full allegiance and devotion to him.

The next clause is not contrastive but provides a second indictment of the rituals and observances insisted upon by the rival teachers. The conjunction δέ need not be taken as introducing a contrast; it may serve as a simple continuative.[32] This clause thus provides the second reason for denying the demands of the factional leaders.[33] The verb ἐστιν is thus assumed from the previous clause by ellipsis, and the genitive τοῦ Χριστοῦ should be taken as a possessive genitive: "and the body is of Christ" (or "the body is the possession of Christ," i.e., belongs to Christ). This genitive, then, is in accord with every other occurrence of σῶμα Χριστοῦ in Paul's writings.

Thus, Paul reminds them that the body (the totality of Christians in Colossae and the Lycus Valley) belongs to Christ. Since they belong to Christ, they are accountable only to him and should feel no sense of obligation to align themselves with the dictates of the rival teachers and thus not subject themselves to the harsh judgments of these teachers. In fact, Paul's comments to the Romans regarding the judgments of other people are equally appropriate here: "Who are you to pass judgment on [ὁ κρίνων] the servant of another? It is before his own master that he stands or falls" (Rom 14:4 ESV). The advocates of the philosophy have no right to judge the Colossian believers; they are answerable only to their own master, Christ. The body belongs to Christ.

In light of this analysis, it is then unlikely that Paul has appropriated a Hellenistic philosophical argument from the opponents and turned it against them. He has simply used biblical and Jewish ideas to construct an eschatological and christological argument opposing the ritual practices of the faction.

**18** μηδεὶς ὑμᾶς καταβραβευέτω, "let no one condemn you." This is the second in a series of imperatival warnings (the first is in 2:16, μὴ οὖν τις ὑμᾶς κρινέτω) that Paul gives to the Colossian Christians, urging them not to allow themselves to come under the judgment and condemnation of the factional teachers. The compound verb καταβραβεύω is often interpreted as a metaphor from the context of athletic events and is thought to reflect the decision of a judge (βραβεύς), who could disqualify a competitor and deprive them of the reward or prize. Many of the versions reflect this interpretation: "let no one keep defrauding you of

32 So BDAG, s.v. δέ notes that it can express "simple continuation." So also Barth and Blanke, 341.

33 Barth and Blanke, 341, also take this view and note that "v. 17b can be viewed as an independent statement that justifies the prohibition expressed in v. 16 of judging the recipients of the epistle."

your prize" (NASB); "let no one cheat you of your reward" (NKJV); "don't let anyone . . . rob you of your prize" (CEB). But this may overinterpret a word that can be used more simply as an alternative to κατακρίνω, "condemn."[34] In a careful study of the term, K. L. Yinger has attempted to make the case that καταβραβεύω should not be read here as retaining a connection with athletic competition and thus has no implicit reference to a "prize" (βραβεῖον) or an umpire (βραβεύς).[35] Although it is true that one is hard-pressed to find any reference to καταβραβεύω in first-century texts within an athletic context, one also needs to admit that the compound term is quite rare, that the cognate terms are common in athletic contexts, that Paul has a penchant to use athletic imagery, and that he was probably looking for a term to add rhetorical variety to his polemic against the opponents (following his use of the term, μή . . . κρινέτω in 2:16).

The compound term never occurs elsewhere in the NT or in the LXX or Jewish literature. The uncompounded form βραβεύω appears later in Colossians (3:15), but with no contextual indicator that a prize should be understood as part of the metaphor. It can, in fact, be used without any explicit connection to athletic events, as for instance, of Gideon who judged Israel for forty years (ἔτη τεσσαράκοντα βραβεύων αὐτοῖς; Josephus, *Ant.* 5.232). For the use of the term in athletic contests in Asia Minor, see below on 3:15. The prepositional prefix κατά- should be seen as functioning in a way similar to its use as a compound with κρίνω, so that the meaning is altered negatively from "judge" to "condemn." In this context, καταβραβεύω functions as an equivalent to κατακρίνω and should be translated as "condemn." It is probably overinterpreting the word to conclude that it implies a disqualification from receiving a prize and then to interpret what that prize might be.

θέλων ἐν ταπεινοφροσύνῃ, "wanting [you to engage in] ascetic practices." This is the first in a series of four present participles (θέλων, ἐμβατεύων, φυσιούμενος, κρατῶν) that are grammatically dependent on καταβραβευέτω. The first two convey the means and the basis for the judgment; the latter two provide the author's critique of the inappropriate and unfounded indictments of the opponents. The translation, "insisting on," is reflected in a number of modern versions (RSV; NRSV; ESV; CSB; NLT) and is accepted by some interpreters.[36] Most commentators, however, reject this interpretation, arguing that it is a Septuagintal construction reflecting the Hebrew חָפֵץ בְּ and that it should be translated "delighting in" (NIV; NASB; NAB; see 1 Sam 18:22; 2 Sam 15:26; 1 Kgs 10:9; 2 Chr 7:11).[37] Although this translation is possible, it does not fit the context nor is it found elsewhere in the NT. "Delighting in" may aptly describe

34 Barth and Blanke, 342.

35 Yinger, "Translating καταβραβευέτω," 138–45.

36 Pao, 188; Harris (1991), 120–21; Martin, 93.

37 E.g., Harris (2010), 107; Barth and Blanke, 342–43; Lightfoot, 193.

the mindset of the opponents toward their practices, but Paul is here explaining the means by which they are condemning the Colossians. This translation would only be appropriate if it were understood that the "delighting in" grew beyond the bounds of personal enjoyment to a situation where others were being implored, "you must experience this too!" And that is precisely the case here. These are ritual practices that are being thrust upon the Colossian community through the powerful influence of a shamanistic teacher. This is confirmed in the following section where Paul says that the opponents are "dictating" (δογματίζεσθε) certain practices and then cites a few examples (2:20–21). Those in the congregation who refuse to engage in the practices are facing some sort of scorn or condemnation. The verb θέλω should therefore be understood to refer to the set of practices that the opponents "want" or "purpose" for the Colossians to do. The language is similar to Gal 6:13: "they want you to be circumcised" (θέλουσιν ὑμᾶς περιτέμνεσθαι). The preposition ἐν here in Col 2:18 specifies the particular practices that the opponents are advocating, just as it does in 2:16b (ἐν βρώσει καὶ ἐν πόσει), 2:16c (ἐν μέρει ἑορτῆς . . . ), and in 2:23 (ἐν ἐθελοθρησκίᾳ . . . οὐκ ἐν τιμῇ). The translation "insisting on" fits the context and expresses the strong desire the teacher has for getting the Colossians to engage in these ritual behaviors.[38] One could also translate the expression more simply as "wanting [you to engage in] ascetic practices." Failure to engage in these practices leads to some kind of implicit judgment, condemnation, or scorn from the spiritually wise and knowing leaders of the philosophy.

One of the practices that the opponents enjoin is "humility" (ταπεινοφροσύνη). Because Paul commends "humility" as a virtue in the next chapter (3:12) and elsewhere in his writings (Phil 2:3; Eph 4:2), and yet warns against it here, the term likely carries a different sense for the opponents. This has led some of the versions to qualify it here and at Col 2:23 with the adjective "false" in translation (see NIV; NKJV). The term may very well be a self-description of one of the practices of the philosophy. The question would then be what kind of practice it refers to.

Most commentators rightly conclude that it refers to fasting. Although νηστεία is the common term for fasting, "humility" and fasting are associated in the LXX and in Judaism, perhaps because it gives evidence of a contrite heart and submissive spirit before God. Thus, the psalmist says, "I would put on sackcloth and would humble my soul with fasting" (NETS; ἐταπείνουν ἐν νηστείᾳ; Ps 35:13 [34:13 LXX]; see also Isa 58:3; Pss. Sol. 3.8; T. Jos. 10.1). This association continued in early Christian texts (see Herm., Vis. 3.10.6; Sim. 5.3.7).

In Jewish apocalyptic texts, fasting was often a prerequisite for gaining a vision.[39] In the Greek Apocalypse of Ezra, Ezra is told by an angel to fast, which

38 Nevertheless, Martin, 93, is correct in saying that "'insisting on' . . . indicates the desire on the part of the errorists to impose their views on the Colossian church."

39 See the discussion of the key texts in Francis, "Humility and Angelic Worship," 167–71.

he dutifully carries out over an extended period of time. As a result, he "saw the mysteries of God and his angels" (Gk. Apoc. Ezra 1.3–5). F. O. Francis interprets the destitute condition of Isaiah and the band with him as "a rigorous life of fasting and lamentation" that led to the visionary experience of chs. 7–11 in the Martyrdom and Ascension of Isaiah.[40] He also claims that the two dominant themes of the Testament of Isaac are Isaac's fasting and his entrance to heaven.[41] Even Philo seems to evince an association between fasting and visionary experience (Philo, *Dreams* 1.33–37; *Moses* 2.67–70).

But it is also important to see that Jewish apocalyptic texts ascribe a healing and exorcistic function to fasting. This is well-illustrated in the Apocalypse of Elijah: "But a pure fast is what I created, with a pure heart and pure hands. It releases sin. It heals diseases. It casts out demons" (1.20–21). This type of thinking influenced some segments of early Christianity. Thus, fasting can be prescribed as a way to deliver someone from the affliction of demons, as seen, for instance, in Pseudo-Clement: "hence, in order to the putting of demons to flight, the most useful help is abstinence, and fasting, and suffering of affliction" (*Homily* 9.10). J. Behm observes, "The original and most powerful motive for fasting in antiquity is to be found in fear of demons who gained power over men through eating. Fasting was also an effective means of preparing for intercourse with the deity and for the reception of ecstatic or magical powers."[42] He also notes that "in magic fasting is often a pre-condition of success in the magical arts. The texts always demand sobriety, if not extended fasting, to strengthen the magical force."[43] A number of the spells in the magical papyri demand fasting for success (e.g., *PGM* I.235; III.334, 412, 427). In some instances, a certain kind of food may be prohibited, as in this ostensibly Jewish charm: "And I adjure you, the one who receives this conjuration, not to eat pork, and every spirit and daimon, whatever sort it may be, will be subject to you. . . . Keep yourself pure, for this charm is Hebraic and is preserved among pure men" (*PGM* IV.380–86).

For the oracles of Apollo at Claros and Didyma, which we will argue have special significance for our understanding of the Colossian philosophy, fasting was an essential preliminary practice, both for the divining priest (mantis) and for those undergoing the ritual mystery initiation and receiving the oracular pronouncements.[44] Parke explains:

---

40 Francis, "Humility and Angelic Worship," 169. Gerlitz, "Fasten als Reinigungsritus," 212–22, goes so far as to say that "originally all fasting practices of religious history can be traced back to an apotropaic-cathartic reason and they were magically based." Still the most thorough study of this motive for fasting is Arbesmann, *Fasten*, esp. ch. 2, §6, "Das apotropäische Fasten," 21–63.

41 Francis, "Humility and Angelic Worship," 169.

42 J. Behm, "νῆστις," *TDNT* 4:926.

43 J. Behm, "νῆστις," *TDNT* 4:927.

44 Lane Fox, *Pagans and Christians*, 386; Guichard, "Oracular Temples at Klaros and Didyma," 139–41. See Iamblichus, *Mysteries* 3.11.

> A date or dates in the month, perhaps the seventh or the twentieth—those numbers particularly associated with Apollo—was declared the Holy Night for the purpose of consultation, and the procedure was described as a Mystery. The enquirers would be required to satisfy the priest that they were not ritually impure and may have been expected to undergo some mild requirements—to abstain from certain food or drink and from sexual intercourse, to submit to lustration with holy water, and to repeat certain liturgic formulae after the priest.[45]

But fasting and self-deprivation were not limited to the Apollo cult. Initiation into the mysteries of Isis was preceded by a ten-day period of purification that included fasting (Apuleius, *Metam.* 11.23 [= 284–85]).[46]

The reference to ταπεινοφροσύνη here and in 2:23 should not necessarily be limited to fasting. Although this may be the primary thought conveyed by this catchword of the contrary teaching, it could extend to various other kinds of prohibitions (e.g., encompassed by "Do not handle! Do not taste! Do not touch!," 2:21) or bodily deprivations (ἀφειδία σώματος, 2:23).

καὶ θρησκείᾳ τῶν ἀγγέλων, "the worship of angels." The ringleaders of "the philosophy" were also strenuously advocating a significant role for angels in their ritual and practice. This expression has stood at the center of much of the debate about the identity of the opponents—and rightly so. This and the following clause (ἃ ἑόρακεν ἐμβατεύων) are two of the most specific clues about the precise nature of the contrary teaching.

Over the long history of interpretation of this phrase, it has been commonly understood to be an objective-genitive construction, with the angels taken as the objects of veneration. Going back as far as the fourth century, Chrysostom understood the opponents as teaching that Christians needed the intervention of angelic mediators because of the transcendence of God. Thus Chrysostom says, "There are some who maintain that we must be brought near by angels, not by Christ; for Christ to do so would seem too great an act on our behalf."[47] Calvin, likewise, saw the faction as teaching the need for angels to mediate the relationship people have with God, a view that entered the church through Platonism. He comments, "But as they imagined that God is approached by the assistance of the angels, and that, consequently, some worship must be shown to them, so they placed angels in the seat of Christ, and adorned them with Christ's office."[48] Given his context, it is not surprising to find that he saw this practice as parallel to the worship of saints in the Roman Catholic church of his day. This angelic-mediation view was popular with commentators in the 1800s and early 1900s.[49]

---

45 Parke, *Oracles of Apollo*, 222–23.

46 See Griffiths, *Isis-Book*, 290–91.

47 Chrysostom, "Homilies on Colossians," in ACCS, 39.

48 Calvin, 339.

49 E.g., Eadie, 180–82; Peake, 482–84.

With the rise of the history of religions school, the interpretation of the "worship of angels" as reflecting the angels serving as mediators continued, but the source of the influence was now seen as gnosis or Gnosticism. The teaching of Colossians was often described as a form of anti-gnostic polemic.[50] Variations of this emerged with scholars who wanted to take the Jewish elements of the philosophy seriously. Thus, Lightfoot argued that it was a Jewish Gnosticism of an Essene-type.[51] Others have downplayed the potential gnostic connections and have argued that the competing teaching was syncretistic, amalgamating local mysteries, Judaism, and even magical practices.[52] Nevertheless, the factional leaders were imploring the Colossians "to pay homage to angels or powers intermediate between God and man."[53]

Yet another variation of this view is advocated by those who find the tradition that angels were involved in the giving of the law on Sinai as relevant for understanding Col 2:18 (Acts 7:38, 53; Gal 3:19; Josephus, *Ant.* 15.136). The idea behind this view was that since angels mediated the law to Israel, they would be offended or angered if it were not obeyed. Angels were thus honored by obedience to the law, including all of the calendar observances and purity regulations. Theodore of Mopsuestia was one of the early advocates of this view. For him, the Colossian opposition contended that "the angels were angered if the law were not being kept."[54] Aquinas thus concluded that the opponents "maintained that the worship mandated in the law had to be kept, because it had been given through angels."[55] Similarly, Theodoret notes, "Those who defend the law lead persons to worship angels, since they say that the law was given through them."[56] This view has been taken up in more recent years by S. Lyonnet.[57] This view, however, struggles to take into account the non-Jewish elements of the teaching. Furthermore, the term νόμος is entirely absent from Colossians.

In 1973, F. O. Francis published a seminal article that challenged the long-standing consensus view and has resulted in a situation in which the scholarly world is now split on how to interpret "the worship of angels."[58] Francis argued that the angels were not the object of veneration, but God himself was the unexpressed object of worship by the angels before his heavenly throne.[59] Francis contended that the genitive τῶν ἀγγέλων should be interpreted as a *subjective*

---

50 See, e.g., Schenke, "Widerstreit," 393, and Weiss, "Antignostische Polemik," 311–24. Lohse, 129, contends that it is "pre-Gnostic."

51 Lightfoot, "Colossian Heresy," 29.

52 Ramsay, "Mysteries," 198–209. See also Hübner, 86–89, 94–97, although he shows no sign of seeing how similar his views are to those of Ramsay.

53 Ramsay, "Mysteries," 206.

54 Theodore of Mopsuestia, "Commentary on Colossians," in ACCS, 39.

55 Aquinas, 68.

56 Theodoret of Cyrrhus, "Interpretation of the Letter to the Colossians," in ACCS, 39.

57 Lyonnet, "Adversaries," 149–50; so also Percy, *Probleme*, 168.

58 Francis, "Humility and Angelic Worship," 163–95.

59 Francis, "Humility and Angelic Worship," 177.

*genitive*—that is, the angels were performing the worship, not receiving it. This explanation of the phrase was part of a larger interpretation of the factional teaching at Colossae as a Jewish mysticism, in which the earthly congregation sought to participate in the heavenly angelic liturgy by *worshiping with the angels*.[60]

Building on the work of Francis, others have sought to strengthen his view in various ways, but especially by developing a better understanding of the ascetic-mystical piety that comes to expression particularly in Jewish apocalypticism.[61] They point to the desire in these Jewish circles to join with the angels in worshiping God at his heavenly throne (see, e.g., T. Job 48–50; Apoc. Ab. 17; Ascen. Isa. 7.13–9.33; Apoc. Zeph. 8.3–4).[62] Others have also pointed to Qumran as a community that saw itself worshiping with the angels at the heavenly temple on each Sabbath. This can be seen especially prominent in the Songs of the Sabbath Sacrifice (4Q400–407), but also in other texts (e.g., 1QH 3.21–22; 1QSb 4.25–26).[63]

This interpretation, however, falls short on grammatical grounds in its failure to account for all facets of the Colossian philosophy, in not taking into account the inscriptional and local evidence pertaining to angels, and in overlooking another relevant branch of Judaism, namely, folk Judaism and Jewish magic. But as P. Müller has noted, there is no positive evidence of Jewish mystical movements, especially as we see in Qumran and the later *merkabah* mysticism, in the Lycus Valley.[64]

Although there is no evidence of Jewish mysticism in western Asia Minor, there is ample evidence of a form of Judaism in which angels figured quite prominently. It is precisely in the domain of Jewish magic and folk belief where rituals involving angels are very significant. This is also the place where a great deal of syncretism takes place—Jews borrowing from their pagan neighbors and vice versa—because the overriding interest is in spiritual power and learning what is effective in averting demonic attack, curses, and the evil eye. This is the kind of Judaism reflected in the beliefs and practices of a figure like Sceva in Ephesus (Acts 19:13) or Eleazar, who cast an evil spirit out of a man in the presence of Titus and Domitian (Josephus, *Ant.* 8.46–49). It is also the Judaism of magical amulets and various kinds of protective magic and healing charms. Those who have this kind of esoteric knowledge in the community would wield great influence and authority by virtue of their wisdom in spiritual matters.

60 This view has attracted many contemporary adherents, e.g., Sumney, 154–55; idem, "Opponents," 377–78; Dunn, 179–82; Royalty, "Dwelling on Visions," 350; Sappington, *Revelation and Redemption*, 158–64; Hurtado, *One God*, 32–33; Yates, "Worship of Angels," 12–15; Rowland, "Apocalyptic Visions," 73–83; Evans, "Colossian Mystics," 188–205; Carr, *Angels and Principalities*, 69–72; Lincoln, *Paradise Now and Not Yet*, 111–12.

61 See esp. Sappington, *Revelation and Redemption*, 19–137.

62 See, e.g., Dunn, 180–81.

63 As, e.g., Stettler, *Christushymnus*, 66–67.

64 Müller, "Verehrung der Engel," 128.

Consequently, I would contend that "the worship of angels" in Colossians refers to *rituals and invocations involving angels for protection, healing, and averting evil.* For the advocates of the philosophy, the angels are not mediators of salvation or for a relationship with God. They are God's assistants who can be called upon for help in time of trouble. The case for this view was first presented in 1995[65] and subsequently reaffirmed with new evidence in 2012.[66] It has proven persuasive to a handful of interpreters.[67]

This is not an entirely new view in the history of the interpretation of this passage. Others have hinted at it in the past. A. L. Williams argued at the turn of the century that "the worship of angels" referred to a type of angelic veneration that had its roots in the fringes of Judaism.[68] He observed that "there is almost no evidence for the worship of them [angels] being recognized in early times by thoughtful Jews, save indeed in connexion with exorcism and magic."[69] Local religious influences, he believed, would have reinforced this attitude toward angels that had been adopted by some of the Colossian Christians. For Williams, the essence of the problem at Colossae had its origin in Judaism, albeit a syncretistic form. His overall view of this phrase comes closest to what I am presenting here, but others have also seen magic and folk-belief influences on the Colossian teaching.[70]

It is not an accident that Paul has used θρησκεία here and not a form of προσκυνέω or λατρεύω. The terms θρησκεία and θρησκεύω tend to be used by ancient authors when rituals and observances are more the focus, rather than the attitude of the heart, prayer, praise, thanksgiving, and singing. Thus LSJ includes the glosses "cult" and "ritual" as glosses in their entry on the noun.[71] For the verb, they suggest the gloss "perform religious observances."[72] Josephus thus uses the noun regularly to refer to the rituals, ceremonies, and observances at the Jerusalem temple (see, e.g., Josephus, *J.W.* 1.148). The term was also used, for instance, in the famous Delphi inscription in connection with the rituals that were performed in consulting the oracle god Apollo.[73] In another instance it was used in connection with the ritual services provided by priests of Isis in shrines in the Fayyum of Egypt.[74] Plutarch discusses the origin of the term and connects it to "extravagant and superstitious ceremonies" along with "enthusiastic" practices associated with Orphic and Dionysiac rituals:

65 See Arnold, *Colossian Syncretism*, 8–102.

66 See Arnold, "Sceva, Solomon, and Shamanism," 7–26.

67 See Moo, 226–27; Wilson, 222–23; Hay, 104–5; MacDonald, 112–13; Lincoln, "Colossians," 563–64.

68 Williams, "Cult of Angels," 413–38.

69 Williams, "Cult of Angels," 432.

70 See Ramsay, "Mysteries," 208; Hübner, 87.

71 LSJ, s.v. θρησκεία.

72 LSJ, s.v. θρησκεύω.

73 *SIG* §801d, line 4 (p. 494): (τήν θρησεκίαν τοῦ Απόλλωνος τοῦ Πυθίου).

74 *BGU* XIII.2215, iii, 1–4. See the discussion in Frankfurter, *Roman Egypt*, 100.

> The word "threskeuein" [θρησκεύειν] came to be applied to the celebration of extravagant and superstitious ceremonies [ταῖς κατακόροις καὶ περιέργοις ἱερουργίαις]. Now Olympias, who affected these divine possessions [τὰς κατοχάς) more zealously than other women, and carried out these divine inspirations [τοὺς ἐνθουσιασμούς] in wilder fashion . . . (Plutarch, *Vit. Alex.* 2)

This derivation and use of θρησκεύειν was apparently widely known, as evidenced by Gregory of Nazianzus referring to it much later: "these Thracian orgies, from which the word Worship [θρησκεία] is said to be derived" (Gregory of Nazianzus, *Oration on the Holy Lights* 5). It is significant to note that Celsus, in his accusation that certain Jews practiced magic, incantations, and sorcery, employs the term θρησκεύειν to describe these rituals and practices (ἐκ γοητείας θρησκεύοντες) (see Origen, *Cels.* 5.9).

Although Paul has never before used this term, he likely employs it here to call attention to the ritual performances related to the angels.[75] The "worship" that the faction is foisting on believers at Colosse is the performance of rituals with angels as their focus and object. In other words, it encompasses the invocation and adjuration of angels for help and protection.

The subjective-genitive interpretation of the expression is also ruled out on linguistic grounds. In my own analysis of θρησκεία followed by a genitive modifier, whenever the noun is followed by a divine being in the genitive case, that being is always the object of veneration.[76] This evidence corroborates the statement made in BDAG that "the being who is worshiped is given in the obj. gen."[77] Many recent interpreters have found this evidence compelling.[78]

---

75 Stettler, *Kolosserhymnus*, 66–67n202, misses the emphasis on ritual associated with the term θρησκεία when he contends that it is a broad word for worship.

76 Arnold, *Colossian Syncretism*, 90–95.

77 BDAG, s.v. θρησκεία. See also W. Radl, "θρησκεία," *EDNT* 2:154, who notes that the term in Col 2:18 "does not refer to a heavenly service of worship by angels (subj. gen.), but to human activity (obj. gen.).

78 E.g., Bevere, *Sharing in the Inheritance*, 102, who writes that "I think it is no longer possible for scholarship to maintain the notion that θρησκείᾳ τῶν ἀγγέλων in Col. 2.18 is simply a subjective genitive. It is here I believe Arnold's argument to be of most value. He clearly demonstrates that the lexical evidence and the usage of θρησκεία in connection with genitives of objects of worship strongly suggest that it is extemely difficult to understand 2.18 in a purely subjective-genitive sense." See also Müller, "Verehrung der Engel," 127–28, 146.

# Excursus: Ancient Texts Illustrating the "Worship" of Angels

### *Bibliography*

**Arnold, C. E.** *Colossian Syncretism*, 11–89. ———. "Sceva, Solomon, and Shamanism," 7–26. **Aydaş, M.** "New Inscriptions," 124–25. **Bohak, G.** *Ancient Jewish Magic*. **Bonner, C.** *Studies in Magical Amulets*. **Cline, R.** *Ancient Angels*, 146–51. **Daniel, R.** "Testament of Solomon XVIII 27–28, 33–40," 294–303. **Davila, J. R.** *Descenders to the Chariot*. **Dorigny, A. S.** "Phylactère alexandrin," 287–96. **DuBois, T. A.** *Shamanism*. **Gager, J. G.** *Curse Tablets*. ———. *Moses*. **Goodenough, E. R.** *Jewish Symbols*. **Gordon, R.** "Divination Kit," 189–98. **Gundel, H.** *Dekane und Dekansternbilder*. **Horsley, G. H. R.**, and **J. M. Luxford.** "Pagan Angels in Roman Asia Minor," 141–83. **Jordan, D. R.**, and **R. Kotansky.** "Two Phylacteries from Xanthos," 167–74. **Klutz, T.** *Rewriting the Testament of Solomon*. **Kotansky, R.** "Graeco-Egyptian Magic *Lamellae*," 349–70. ———. *Greek Magical Amulets*. **Lesses, R.** *Ritual Practices to Gain Power*. **Mastrocinque, A.** "Divinatory Kit," 173–87. **Morgan, M.** *Sepher Ha-Razim*. **Müller, P.** "Verehrung der Engel," 123–46. **Preisendanz, K.** "Ein Wiener Papyrus," 161–67. **Schäfer, P.** *Jewish Mysticism*. ———. *Synopse zur Hekhalot-Literatur*. ———. *Übersetzung der Hekhalot Literatur*. **Schwarz, S. L.** "Reconsidering the *Testament of Solomon*," 203–37. **Torijano, P. A.** *Solomon the Esoteric King*. **Wünsch, R.** *Antikes Zaubergerät*, 1–50.

Rituals related to angels involve a host of practices. This would extend to invocations, "calling upon" angels, adjurations, incantations, wearing amulets, and engaging in various behaviors that would incline angels to hear and respond to the requests or commands of the supplicants. There are numerous texts that could be used to illustrate this approach to angels in Asia Minor and in Judaism. These are chosen to provide an illustrative overview of this kind of practice that was widespread in the ancient world.

### *Amulets*

The naming and invocation of angels was a significant part of numerous amulets from the Roman era. The amulets usually served an apotropaic function—that is, to ward off the attacks of evil spirits. Calling on angels held a particularly important role in Jewish folk rituals of power and in the Jewish amulet tradition.

In 2004, M. Aydaş published an inscription found in front of the so-called Jewish tomb at the necropolis of Hierapolis, just a few miles northwest of Colossae.[79] The writing was inscribed on a thin piece of silver rolled up as a scroll and placed in a silver tube. It dates to "the early Christian period."

79 Aydaş, "New Inscriptions," 124.

The text reads: "I adjure [ἐνορκίζομαι] you by God who founded the earth and the heavens. I adjure you by the angels [τοὺς ἀγγέλους], cherubim, (the) harmony (above?), Michael, Raphael, Abrasax—to be averted from injury." This amulet provides one of the closest local pieces of evidence to the kind of invocation of angels that I am contending was taking place at Colossae. This text illustrates an adjuration of angels for protection—a common folk practice. It is difficult to know if this text was used by a Jew, a pagan, or a Christian. Because it was found in close proximity to a Jewish tomb, it is possible that it was owned and used by a Jewish person for protection. Angels from Judaism are explicitly invoked, but both pagans and Christians are known to call on these angels. Abrasax is a pagan deity who was popular in magic, yet he was invoked by Jews as well. There are no explicitly Christian symbols on this text.

An amulet discovered northwest of Colossae in the region of Mysia (in the city of Cyzicus) invokes Jewish angels and features other Jewish elements.[80] The amulet was made from bronze and fashioned into a disk roughly 4.5 cm in diameter. It was found in a Roman necropolis and dated to the third century. The inscription reads: "Michael, Gabriel, Ouriel, Raphael. Protect the one who wears this. Holy, holy, holy. ΠΙΠΙ RPSS. Angel, Araaph, flee, O hated one; Solomon pursues you." All four of the named angels figure prominently in the Testament of Solomon, especially in ch. 18. For instance, Ouriel is invoked in T. Sol. 18.7: "The third [demon] said, 'I am called Artosael. I do much damage to the eyes. Should I hear, "Ouriel, imprison Artosael," I retreat immediately.'" The expression ΠΙΠΙ is probably an attempt to represent יהוה in Greek characters, which is probably also suggested by the preceding Trisagion of Isa 6:3.[81] The reference to Solomon demonstrates a dependence on the Solomonic magical tradition known in Asia Minor (see below). The figure of a Solomon as a horseman carring a spear is a common motif among these types of amulets.[82] It is possible to take the evil angel Araaph (Ἀρααφ) as an alternative spelling for the lion-form spirit, "Araps" (Ἀραψ), in T. Sol. 11.4. Despite the many Jewish elements on this amulet, the reverse side includes pagan motifs, Helios, Selene, and the Horus eye, illustrating the syncretistic nature of the amulet.

Three polished black stones that functioned as amulets were part of a magical apparatus discovered at Pergamum.[83] These amulets invoke the angels Michael, Gabriel, Ragouel, and Raphael along with a reference to Ἰαεω (possibly understood to be Yahweh; cf. *PGM* IV.396, 3069) and even two pagan deities, Stheno and Mercury. There are also numerous *nomina barbara* on the amulets. The various components of the apparatus include a triangular-shaped bronze table, a bronze disk, a bronze spike, two bronze rings, two bronze plates, and the three

80 Dorigny, "Phylactère alexandrin," 287–96.

81 Dorigny, "Phylactère alexandrin," 287–96.

82 See Goodenough, *Symbols*, 2:227–35; Bonner, *Studies in Magical Amulets*, 208–21.

83 Wünsch, *Antikes Zaubergerät*.

amulets. Hekate, the goddess of witchcraft and sorcery, figures prominently on the triangular table, which may have served for theurgic divination[84] or curse function.[85] Wünsch dates the entire apparatus to AD 200–250. If the apparatus belonged to a pagan shaman, which seems likely based on the predominance of the pagan motifs, the invocation of the Jewish angels suggests that this tradition was sufficiently well-known to catch the attention of non-Jewish shamans.

Numerous amulets have been discovered throughout Asia Minor, including a horde of nineteen silver lamellae found in gravesites in the region of Lydia.[86] Most of these contain various magical symbolism, *characteres*, and magical figurines. Amulets are notoriously difficult to date. R. Kotansky has, however, dated one Greek amulet from Asia Minor to as early as the first century BC. This silver tablet was discovered in Pontus (in the city of Amisos; northwest of Colossae on the south shore of the Black Sea).[87] The amulet is likely Jewish and invokes "the ruler of the kingdoms of the gods" and a series of magical names (ABRIAÔTH ALARPHÔTHO SETH) to drive away a curse from a woman named Rouphina. The final line of the text states, "I am the one ruling the place in Moses's name."[88]

Additional amulets invoking angels could be cited and described, but this is sufficient for illustrating the type. The fact that Christians adopted this practice can be seen in the discovery of various Christian amulets. For instance, archaeologists recently discovered a phylactery lamella near a tomb in the city of Xanthos in the territory of Lycia (about 110 miles south of Colossae). This amulet belonged to an otherwise unknown Christian named Epiphanius. The text of the inscription reads: "Lord, help the bearer [of this tablet] Epiphanius, whom Anastasia bore. I adjure you Solomon, the great angel Michael, Gabriel, Ouriel, Raphael. I adjure you Abrasax. I adjure you in Hebrew: thaobarao Sabaoth, Epiphanius . . . Iaw . . . Iao . . . noeitho . . ."[89] The amulet reveals the impulse to syncretize by gathering names of power irrespective of religious tradition.

## *The Solomon Magic Tradition in Judaism*

In the first-century BC work titled the Wisdom of Solomon, the author claims that God gave Solomon "unerring knowledge of what exists" (Wis 7:17 NRSV). This knowledge extended to the spiritual domain and included wisdom about "the powers of spirits" (πνευμάτων βίας; Wis 7:20 NRSV), the constellations of

84 This is the view of Mastrocinque, "Divinatory Kit," 180.

85 Gordon, "Divination Kit," 193, thinks that the amulets protect the practitioner from the goddess Hekate herself when she makes an appearance.

86 Kotansky, "Graeco-Egyptian Magic *Lamellae*," 349–70.

87 Kotansky, *Greek Magical Amulets*, 181–82.

88 For further discussion, see Gager, *Curse Tablets*, 225–26 (no. 120); idem, *Moses*, 157–59.

89 Jordan and Kotansky, "Two Phylacteries from Xanthos," 167–74. See the discussion in Cline, *Ancient Angels*, 146–51.

the stars (ἄστρων θέσεις; Wis 7:19), and the powerful workings of the *stoicheia* (ἐνέργειαν στοιχείων; Wis 7:17).

The theme of Solomon's esoteric knowledge and abilities is also developed by Josephus in the eighth book of his *Antiquities*. Josephus describes how Solomon's extensive wisdom included insight on how to get rid of evil spirits. He says, "God also enabled him to learn that skill which expels demons . . . he left behind him the manner of using exorcisms, by which they drive away demons, so that they never return" (Josephus, *Ant.* 8.45). In Josephus's view, this powerful, secret wisdom was then passed down for generations. He then describes a dramatic situation in which a Jewish man named Eleazar cast an evil spirit out of a man in front of a distinguished Roman audience that included the emperor Vespasian and his sons, Titus and Domitian (who also would, in turn, serve as Roman emperors). Also present for the event were a number of Roman officers and soldiers (Josephus, *Ant.* 8.46–49). As Bohak notes, Josephus presents Eleazar as "an experienced, and we might even say professional, exorcist, who had the special implements and texts needed for this kind of ritual."[90] This Eleazar has much in common with the Sceva of Acts 19.

Many of the traditions associated with Solomon for healing, performing exorcisms, and dealing with demonic powers have been compiled into a Jewish magical handbook called the Testament of Solomon. The final form of the document postdates the NT era,[91] but it likely contains many traditions, terminology, and invocations that were current during the time of Jesus and Paul. One portion of this compilation, the eighteenth chapter, may date as early as the first-century BC.[92] Part of the basis for this was the discovery of a fifth-century papyrus fragment of this chapter as well as the astrological "decan" tradition.[93] This document may have had an independent existence in written and/or oral tradition. G. Bohak has argued that Jewish magical traditions were generally passed on orally throughout the Second Temple period and only came to be written down in the third century and beyond.[94]

---

90 Bohak, *Ancient Jewish Magic*, 103.

91 Klutz, *Rewriting the Testament of Solomon*, 35, argued that the Testament reached its full form some time between the last quarter of the second century and the middle of the third. Schwarz, "Reconsidering the *Testament of Solomon*," 208, argues that the final form of the testament came together later than Klutz posits. Nevertheless, she recognizes that "the individual spells were ancient elements, gathered over time into a spellbook collection" (208).

92 Klutz, *Rewriting the Testament of Solomon*, 35. See also Gundel, *Dekane und Dekansternbilder*, 45, 92.

93 Preisendanz, "Wiener Papyrus," 161–67, and Daniel, "Testament of Solomon XVIII 27–28, 33–40," 294–303. Schwarz, "Reconsidering the *Testament of Solomon*," 219, notes, "Such decan lists [as contained in T. Sol. 18] are known from earlier Egyptian sources, and, based simply on its form and content, this version could easily once have been an independent document. It is quite plausible that this chapter was one of the oldest portions of the story, and that it circulated independently of the rest until it was agglomerated with other Solomonic incantation materials at some later point."

94 Bohak, *Ancient Jewish Magic*, 138. He notes, "It thus seems quite clear that most of Second Temple Jewish magic was transmitted orally, and even when it was trasmitted in writing, as in the case

The framework of this text is Solomon's interrogation of thirty-six demons and compelling them to divulge the nature of their evil work and how they can be defeated. These demons correspond to every ten degrees of the heavenly sphere and can be called στοιχεῖα (T. Sol. 18.1, 2). One by one these evil spirits appear before Solomon and give up the information that he seeks. When Solomon summons the first spirit, he says to him, "Who are you?" (18.4). The spirit replies, "I am the first decan of the zodiac and I am called Ruax. I cause heads of men to suffer pain and I cause their temples to throb. Should I hear only, 'Michael, imprison Ruax,' I retreat immediately."

And so it goes on, one after the other, with each spirit revealing its name, a particular evil it accomplishes, and how it can be thwarted. Many of the spirits cause physical ills (such as damage to the eyes or ears, tumors, problems with the internal organs, fevers, convulsions, hysteria, and paralysis). Others incite relational problems in the home and the community (such as conflicts between husbands and wives, jealousies, strife, dissension, and perversions).

What is of special interest to us here is that the demon is driven out by invoking an angel to perform the deliverance. But it cannot be just any angel. The Jewish healer needs to know the precise angel who has power to defeat the particular afflicting spirit. It does no good, for instance, to call on Gabriel if the person has a tumor. The angel who is effective for this is one named Sabael (T. Sol. 18.10).

In sum, the eighteenth chapter of the Testament of Solomon is essentially a Jewish shaman's diagnostic and treatment manual. By looking at the presenting symptom, the holy man can identify the name of the demon causing the problem and then invoke the appropriate angel to alleviate the demonic attack and thus bring healing to the person.

As I have suggested previously, this is likely the kind of Jewish folk tradition that informed the methodology of a Jewish shaman figure like Sceva (Acts 19:11–20).[95] It it this kind of Jewish folk tradition that may have stood behind the objectionable teaching at Colossae.

## *Qumran Magical Handbooks*

A number of magical handbooks have been identified among the sectarian documents discovered at Qumran. These texts include 11QApocryphal Psalms (11Q11; 11QPsAp[a]), 4QExorcism (4Q560), and 4QSongs of the Sage (4Q510 and 511; 4QShir[a, b]).

of some exorcistic hymns, its 'performance' normally included an oral recitation but no writing." Torijano, *Solomon the Esoteric King*, 86, notes, "It is most probable that the traditions that contained information about Solomon and the demons were quite common as early as the second century BCE."

95 Arnold, "Sceva, Solomon, and Shamanism," 7–26.

11QApocryphal Psalms, a document dating to the middle of the first century AD, bears substantial similarities to the eighteenth chapter of the Testament of Solomon. The overall function of this fragmentary text is apotropaic—that is, to drive away evil spirits, indicated in part by the words "exorcising" and "the demon" in the first column. In the beginning of column one, Solomon is mentioned, followed by the statement, "He will invoke," before it breaks away. The text goes on to speak of spirits and demons. In column two, the text begins with the same question of interrogation of the demons—"Who are you?"—that we find in the Testament of Solomon.[96] Column three speaks of a powerful angel who fights against an evil spirit and then once again uses the same interrogation formula ("Who are you?"). Column four refers to "those possessed" and then mentions that the angel Raphael will heal them. The text ends with a recitation of Ps 91—a biblical text often cited in connection with exorcism and protection from demons. P. Torijano rightly points to a fourfold structure that this text has in common with the Testament of Solomon: (1) an identifying formula ("Who are you?"); (2) a description of the demon; (3) the threat of binding at the hands of YHWH; and (4) the rhetorical invocation of an angel.[97] These commonalities suggest that the date of this Solomonic exorcism tradition is certainly earlier than the mid-first century AD when this text was copied. It also corroborates our observation that the Jewish exorcism formulae encapsulated in T. Sol. 18 predates the NT.

## *Later Jewish Traditions*

This tradition involving knowledge of angelic names, the adjuration of angels, and various magical techniques allegedly stemming from Solomon can be traced in a trajectory that can be seen in a variety of Jewish documents that extend to the Middle Ages and beyond. It can be seen especially in the Sepher ha-Razim and in the Hekhalot literature.

The Sepher ha-Razim—that is, the "Book of Mysteries," is a manual of Jewish magic consisting of roughly eight hundred lines that may date to the late third or early fourth century AD.[98] M. Morgan notes, "It is crucial to recognize what fascinates us most about this text, the magic, is part of a folk tradition which dates from an earlier time."[99] The volume begins by attributing the source of its esoteric content to Solomon: "the Books of the Mysteries were disclosed

96 Torijano, *Solomon the Esoteric King*, 51–52, contends that this interrogation technique and the name of Solomon were linked in a popular exorcistic tradition that was probably widespread in Judaism from the first century BC.

97 Torijano, *Solomon the Esoteric King*, 52.

98 See the English translation in Morgan, *Sepher Ha-Razim*. Regarding the date of the document, he writes that "the consensus of those scholars who have worked with the text is to support Margalioth's dating of SHR to the early fourth or late third century CE" (8).

99 Morgan, *Sepher Ha-Razim*, 9.

to him [Solomon], and he became very learned in books of understanding, and (so) ruled over everything he desired, over all the spirits and demons that wander in the world, and from the wisdom of this book he imprisoned and released, and sent out and brought in, and built and prospered" (lines 26–28 of the preface [p. 19]). Among the various spells in the document are some for warding off demons, and central to dealing with these demons is calling on angels. The names of nearly seven hundred angels are mentioned in this book. For instance, in one portion of the document, sixteen different angels are named and described. The reader is told that "in a place where their name is invoked an evil spirit cannot appear" (2.123 [p. 54]). The reader is then told how to make a gold lamella with the names of these angels inscribed upon it "if you wish to drive off an evil spirit so it will not come to a woman when she is in childbirth and so it will not kill her child" (2.124–25 [p. 54]).

The Hekhalot writings are a collection of Jewish esoteric and revelatory texts produced in late antiquity or the early Middle Ages.[100] They describe the ascent-to-heaven experiences of a number of Jewish rabbis and provide details of what they have seen, heard, and learned in the heavenly palaces (the *hekhalot*) in their visionary experience. Bohak has noted that "it is quite possible that the lore contained within them was passed orally for many generations before being first committed to writing."[101] These texts have often been described as reflecting Jewish mysticism. In a recent monograph titled *Ancient Jewish Mysticism*, P. Schäfer raises serious questions about this categorization since they do not reflect a mystical union (*unio mystica*) with the deity that is central to the common understanding of mysticism.[102] Rather, he speaks of them as representing a "liturgical communion" of the suppliant with the angels in heaven.

Although the Hekhalot writings are often mined for their contribution to an understanding of *merkabah* mysticism, what has been missed is their contribution to understanding Jewish magic. The texts are filled with esoteric knowledge about the names of the angels, magical formulas and charms, and techniques for adjuring the angels. These adjurations were the subject of a study by R. Lesses in a Harvard Theological Studies monograph. She noted that "one best understands the adjurations of the Hekhalot literature within the overarching category of ritual practices involving the use of divine or angelic names in order to gain power of various kinds."[103] She argued that these texts functioned as "instructions for performances" rather than merely literary accounts.[104] As such, they

100 These Hebrew and Aramaic texts have been compiled and edited by P. Schäfer (with the assistance of M. Schlüter and H. G. von Mutius) in a large folio volume titled, *Synopse zur Hekhalot-Literatur*. A German translation is available in the four-volume set edited by P. Schäfer, *Übersetzung der Hekhalot Literatur*.

101 Bohak, *Ancient Jewish Magic*, 330.

102 Schäfer, *Jewish Mysticism*, 354–55.

103 Lesses, *Ritual Practices to Gain Power*, 367.

104 Lesses, *Ritual Practices to Gain Power*, 378.

enable the holy man to serve the Jewish community to fulfill a variety of human needs. In an important monograph dealing with the function of the Hekhalot literature within the Jewish communities, J. Davila contends that "a central element of the Hekhalot texts themselves is the quest for ritual power."[105] He has argued convincingly that the religious functionaries described in the Hekhalot literature correspond to the anthropological model of shamanism.[106]

In summary, there is a strong tradition within Judaism of invoking angels in rituals of power that extended to Asia Minor. This tradition was so well-known that non-Jews appropriated the names of angels and other Jewish symbolism into their own rituals. This can be seen, for instance, in the use of the names Michael, Gabriel, Raphael, and other angel names in pagan amulets. Christians, too, used these ritual techniques and names in the creation of amulets for protection.

---

105 Davila, *Descenders to the Chariot*, 42.

106 Davila, *Descenders to the Chariot*, 49, 306. On the topic of shamanism, see now DuBois, *Shamanism*.

ἃ ἑόρακεν ἐμβατεύων, "entering the things he has seen." This clause continues to be one of the most perplexing exegetical problems of the letter. Although there is no consensus on how it should be interpreted, the relevant evidence does suggest a plausible solution. If the participle refers to ritual initiation in the local mysteries (and I am convinced that the evidence points to this), then the clause refers to visionary experience that occurred in ritual initiation. The experience and content of this vison served as a basis for the authority and arcane knowledge of the rival teacher(s) at Colossae. Each part of this clause will now be examined in detail.

The referent of the neuter relative pronoun (ἅ) could be taken to refer to the two preceding nouns and their modifiers (ταπεινοφροσύνη καὶ θρησκεία τῶν ἀγγέλων) as Francis and others who hold to a Jewish-mysticism interpretation understand it. On this view, "humility" and "worship with the angels" are the objects of the visionary experience. But this view faces the insuperable difficulty of having to explain "humility" (or ascetic behaviors) as an object of visionary experience. Whereas it makes sense to contend that angels are the objects of vision, it is not intelligible to hold that the abstract idea of "humility" is also an object of the visionary experience. Francis tries to escape this difficulty by arguing that ταπεινοφροσύνη should be understood as "instruction in humility for the purpose of obtaining visions"—that is, angelic instruction is the object of the vision.[107] Others have sought to address this problem by suggesting that the visionaries saw angels performing worship and exhibiting humility.[108] Both of these views strain credulity in seeing humility as an object of vision and are quite without parallel. Stettler has sensed this problem and has argued that this is a *constructio ad sensum* that refers only to the angels worshiping God.[109] But this raises the grammatical question of why the author did not simply use the feminine singular relative pronoun (ἥν) to refer to the antecedent feminine noun (θρησκεία) as he does in 1:4 (τὴν ἀγάπην ἣν ἔχετε) and 4:17 (τὴν διακονίαν ἣν παρέλαβες) if he wanted to limit the referent to the worship? It is true, as Beetham observes, that the author of the letter uses the neuter plural relative pronoun to refer back to the totality of a plural antecedent several times in Colossians (he mentions ἅ in 2:17, 22 among others),[110] but there are two important differences: (1) in the two other cases, Paul makes a polemical comment about some facet of the rival teaching by summing up the teaching and issuing a judgment with the construction, ἅ ἐστιν . . . . In 2:18 the ἐστιν is missing, and the comment is simply descriptive of the teaching. And (2), the entire phrase may be a quotation (or catchword) of the factional teacher(s), and because of

107 Francis, "Humility and Angelic Worship," 180.

108 Rowland, "Apocalyptic Visions," 75; Sappington, *Revelation and Redemption*, 160. Moo, 229, also rightly questions this view: "it is difficult to see how the ascetic practices preceding a vision could be the object of the vision itself."

109 Stettler, *Kolosserhymnus*, 68.

110 Beetham, *Echoes of Scripture*, 204.

this, the relative pronoun may not conform to the syntactical patterns of the rest of the book.

A preferable explanation would be to interpret the relative pronoun as the direct object of the participle ἐμβατεύων. The overall meaning then depends on how one interprets the participle. Should it be taken metaphorically as "go into detail about" (ESV)?[111] Or should it be understood as referring to some aspect of ritual mystery initiation? The evidence points to the latter (see the extended discussion below). In both of these views, the precise content of the relative pronoun is not stated explicitly and must be inferred. But this is not a difficulty since there are many examples of Paul using the neuter plural relative pronoun to refer to something not explicitly stated in the context. See, for example, 1 Cor 4:6 (ἃ γέγραπται), 10:20 (ἃ θύουσιν), and 2 Cor 5:10 (ἃ ἔπραξεν). Presumably, the content is what the opposing teachers claim to see in their visionary experience.

Essentially all interpreters are agreed that the verb ἑόρακεν refers to some kind of visionary experience. The heart of the debate centers on whether to interpret the visions as Jewish ascent-to-heaven experiences or as visions associated with ritual initiation in the Apollo cult or another of the local mysteries. Heavenly visions were clearly an important feature in the mystical texts from Qumran (4Q400–405), but also in many Jewish apocalypses and in the later *merkabah* traditions. But visionary experience also played an important role in mystery initiation rituals,[112] including the local mysteries. In fact, one of the major reasons for seeking initiation was to receive a vision from a deity. Pausanias reports that the underworld gods (θεοὶ καταχθόνοι) near the Maeander River in western Asia Minor would send visions (ἀποστέλλουσιν αὐτοῖς ὀνειράτων ὄψεις) to all whom they wished to enter their adytum (the inner sanctum of a temple) (Pausanias, *Descr.* 10.32.13). Visionary experience was also significant in rituals of power. The term ὁράω occurs frequently in magical texts. The magical papyri contain many recipes for conjuring a "god," with the goal of having an appearance and eliciting the spirit power to fulfill a request or provide protection from other evil spiritual beings.[113] The content of the vision may be seen, in part, by a possible liturgical tradition from the mystery cult of the Idaean Dactyls, which likely originated in Phrygia (see Strabo, *Geogr.* 10.3.22).[114] The text reads: "I have been initiated [τετέλεσμαι], and I went down (κατέβην) into the [underground] chamber of the Dactyls, and I saw the other things down below [τὰ ἄλλα εἶδον], virgin, dog, and all the rest" (*PGM* LXX.4–25 [= *P.Mich.* III, 154). This text is relevant for our purposes for four reasons: (1) it may be illustrative of local cult practices in Asia Minor; (2) the vision is associated with a two-stage ritual of initiation (which I will argue, below, is the best interpretation of the context of

111 So also, Moo, 228–29.

112 See Burkert, *Ancient Mystery Cults*, 92–93.

113 See, e.g., *PGM* IV.2479ff.; VII.335ff.; XII.145ff.; XII.154ff.

114 On the Idaean Dactyls, see Hemberg, "Idaiischen Daktylen," 41–59.

ἐμβατεύω); (3) the vision is connected to descent to an underground chamber at the sanctuary, which is also true of ἐμβατεύω at Claros; and (4) the visionary experience is described by "seeing things" using the verb ὁράω (τὰ ἄλλα εἶδον). Visionary experience was also central to the ritual initiation in the so-called Mithras Liturgy (*PGM* IV.475–829).[115] The term ὁράω appears repeatedly throughout the text to introduce what the initiate sees in the rite. Entry into the adyton is never mentioned, but it is probably assumed as the climax of the ritual. In this text, the initiate ascends to heaven and has a powerful vision of hostile gods, angels, planets, and stars. However, because of the adept's spiritual transformation and knowledge of magical formulae, these beings change from a posture of hostility to favor. The initiation serves to provide protection from these malignant forces and certainly enhances the initiates' spiritual knowledge and wisdom.

Dibelius observed long ago the important role that visionary experience played in the Isis initiation as reported by Apuleius. Lucius, the initiate, is instructed to perform a number of purification rites and observe a set of carefully delineated prohibitions as preparation for initiation into the mystery of Isis. As the time for his initiation approaches, Lucius goes to the sacred temple in a procession of devotees. He is then dressed in a linen garment and is taken by the priest into the temple where he is led into the adyton and is consecrated into the mystery of Isis. Apuleius describes the sacred act of initiation:

> Listen then, but believe, for my account is true. I approached [*accessi*] the boundary of death and treading on Proserpine's threshold, I was carried through all the elements [*per omnia vectus elementa*] after which I returned [*remeavi*]. At dead of night I saw the sun flashing with bright effulgence. I approached close to the gods above and the gods below and worshiped them face to face. (Apuleius, *Metam.* 11.23)

He aptly summarizes the content of this section as an entry into the realm of the dead, a vision of the underworld gods, a joyous return connected with a journey through all the elements, and an epiphany of light with a vision of the gods above.[116]

W. Burkert has noted that "one of the main characteristics of mysteries is the *makarismos*, the praise of the blessed status of those who have 'seen' the mysteries."[117] This blessed status involves the appeasement of hostile forces leading to the possibility of a safer and happier existence in this world.

Ἐμβατεύω is a term that has attracted more attention than any other word in

115 On this text, see Betz, *Mithras Liturgy*.

116 Dibelius, "Isis Initiation," 64. Griffiths, *Isis-Book*, 295, contends that the passage is indeed descriptive of the initiate's movements and what he has seen, albeit in a heightened symbolic sense.

117 Burkert, *Ancient Mystery Cults*, 93.

the letter. And rightly so. It is a hapax legomenon in the NT and stands at the center of the debate regarding the precise nature of the teaching of the Colossian philosophy. If the term reflects a mystery cult initiation ritual, then the opposing teaching is unequivocally syncretistic. But not all interpreters agree with this, and the debate continues.

The difficulty of interpreting ἃ ἑόρακεν ἐμβατεύων can be seen in the textual tradition (with the scribal insertion of μή or οὐκ), as well as in the proposed emendations to the text. Lightfoot, for instance, suggested emending the text to ἃ ἑώρα [or αἰώρα] κενεμβατεύων, "to indulge in vain speculations."[118] Similarly, Hort had conjectured ἀέρα κενεμβατεύων, "idly treading upon air."[119] But the assumption of a corrupt text and these conjectural emendations are unnecessary. The text can be explained through seeing ἐμβατεύω as a catchword of "the philosophy."

The basic sense of ἐμβατεύω is clear; it represents a compound of ἐν + βαίνω, resulting in the meaning "to enter." But the term was rarely used in Greek literature. When it was used, it could retain this literal sense, such as to ascend a mountain (Josephus, *Ant.* 2.265) or to enter a place aggressively, "to invade" (1 Macc 12:25; 13:20; 14:31; 15:40). It was also used metaphorically for entering into possession of something (Josh 19:49, 51) or entering into an investigation of a matter (2 Macc 2:30). Each of these meanings has been suggested for Col 2:18.

One of the more common interpretations of the term in Colossians is that it has something to do with entering into an examination or explanation of the visionary experience. Thus, some versions translate the expression by "dwelling on visions" (NRSV; cf. ASV). Others strengthen the manner of investigation by rendering it as "intruding into" (NKJV; KJV). Calvin noted, "Such people in reality break through and intrude into secrets which God does not wish to reveal to us yet . . . reproving the rashness of those who inquire farther than is allowable."[120] Others shift the focus from personal investigation to explanation. Accordingly, the NIV translates it as "goes into great detail about what they have seen" (with similar language, so also ESV; CEB; NET). Some modern commentators still find this to be the most compelling solution.[121] Yet others shift the nuance to conviction about the content of their visionary experience and render it, "taking his stand on visions" (RSV; NASB; NAB).

In an influential article on this term, Francis made the case that "entry into possession of property" (as in Josh 19:49, 51 and in many legal papyri) provides the best explanation of the use of the term in Colossians.[122] He contends that "it is *not* a plot of ground, but it *is* a portion in the Lord" and that the "Colossians

118 Lightfoot, 197.

119 Westcott and Hort, *Original Greek*, 127.

120 Calvin, 340. So also Eadie, 182.

121 Moo, 229; Harris, 108; Bird, 86; Garland, 181; Barth and Blanke, 348.

122 Francis, "EMBATEUEIN," 197–207.

sought to enter heaven in order to possess themselves of salvation, a portion in the Lord."[123] He tied his interpretation of this term to his overall view that the problematic teaching at Colossae was a form of Jewish mysticism in which people sought the experience of visionary ascent to heaven to worship God around his heavenly throne, together with the angels. Many have followed him in this view.[124]

Yet the interpretation that best fits this context and coheres well with the other elements of "the philosophy" is that the term retains its basic sense of "entering," but has become a technical term associated with cultic ritual initiation in the local mysteries. This view was first suggested by W. M. Ramsay in 1913 and by M. Dibelius in 1917, independently from one another.[125] It followed closely after the discovery and publication of a series of inscriptions from the temple of Apollo at Claros (about 15 miles northwest of Ephesus and 1.5 miles north of Notion), in which ἐμβατεύω appeared as an expression for the second, higher stage of initiation into the mysteries of Apollo.[126] An expanded paraphrase of the resulting interpretation would be "what he had seen when he entered the adyton [the inner sanctuary of the temple] and experienced the visions of the higher, climactic stage of his initiation." This visionary experience in the context of ritual initiation became a basis for the claims of the rival teacher's authority, spiritual power, and esoteric wisdom within the Colossian congregation. This experience is what qualified him to serve as a community healer and wise man, a role that anthropologists refer to as a shaman.

---

123 Francis, "EMBATEUEIN," 199.

124 E.g., Sumney, 156; Stettler, *Christushymnus*, 68; Bevere, *Sharing in the Inheritance*, 106–7; Dunn, 183; Sappington, *Revelation and Redemption*, 155–56. Yet Fowl, *Story of Christ*, 127, rightly observes that "unfortunately, for Francis, none of these texts [the Jewish mystical texts] uses ἐμβατεύειν."

125 Ramsay, *Teaching of Paul*, 283–305; Dibelius, "Isis Initiation," 61–121.

126 The inscriptions were published by Macridy in two stages: (1) "Altertümer," 155–73, in 1905, and (2) "Antiquités," 36–67, in 1912.

# Excursus: Ἐμβατεύω as a Technical Term of Ritual Initiation

## *Bibliography*

**Arnold, C. E.** *Colossian Syncretism*, 104–57. ———. "Initiation, Vision, and Spiritual Power," 173–86. **Burkert, W.** *Ancient Mystery Cults*. **Dibelius, M.** "Isis Initiation," 61–121. **Francis, F. O.** "EMBATEUEIN," 197–207. **Graf, F.** *Apollo*. **Guichard, C.** "Oracular Temples at Klaros and Didyma." **Macridy, T.** "Altertümer," 155–73. ———. "Antiquités," 36–67. **Merkelbach, R.** *Philologica*, 162–53. **Parke, H. W.** *Oracles of Apollo*. **Picard, C.** *Éphèse et Claros*. ———. "Oracle d'Apollon Clarios," 190–97. **Ramsay, W. M.** *Teaching of Paul*, 283–305. **Robert, L.** *Inscriptions*. ———. "Les fouilles de Claros," 3–29. **Robert, L.**, and **J. Robert.** *Claros I*. **Rutherford, I.** "Interpreting an Oracle," 449–57. **Varhelyi, Z.** "Syncretism at the Oracle of Claros," 13–31.

The oracle of Apollo at Claros was famous throughout Hellenistic and Roman times. The temple dates to the fourth century BC, but the oracle itself was founded in the eighth century on the site of a sacred spring and grove. Embassies came from all over Asia Minor and the Mediterranean world to consult the oracle.

Of the twenty-seven epigraphic oracles extant from Claros dating between the first and third centuries, nineteen were delivered to cities, and two of these cities included Laodicea and Hierapolis. Cities of the Lycus Valley were not only familiar with the oracle but sometimes sent embassies to seek a response from the god. Hierapolis was, in fact, one of five cities where Clarian epigraphic oracles survive outside of Claros.[127] Hierapolis was also home to two local forms of the god Apollo: Apollo Kareios (the epithet could mean "Carian") and Apollo Archegetes. The most well-known embassy from Hierapolis took place in AD 160 to seek the god's advice about the ravages of a plague, commonly interpreted as the Antonine Plague, that gripped portions of the empire after the Parthian campaign of Lucius Verus (see Dio Cassius, *Hist. rom.* 71.2.4; Aelius Aristides, *Hieroi Logoi* 2.37–45; Galen, *Methodus Medendi* 5.12.6; *Ad Thrasibulum* 34.[128] Laodicea also consulted the Clarian Apollo annually.[129] The nearby cities of Herakleia Salbake (eighteen miles southwest of Colossae) and Tabai (twenty-four miles south-southwest of Colossae) also regularly consulted the

127 Varhelyi, "Oracle at Claros," 15.

128 Varhelyi, "Oracle at Claros," 15; Text is translated by Rutherford, "Interpreting an Oracle," 450–51.

129 Robert and Robert, *Claros I*, 5. Robert, *Inscriptions*, 305.

oracle.[130] Thus, there was a direct connection between the Lycus Valley (as well as neighboring towns) and Claros, which can explain how the vocabulary of the cult would be familiar to people living in Colossae.

Four inscriptions contain the term ἐμβατεύω and use it as a technical expression for the second stage of the mystery initiation ritual. The relevant portions are cited below:

1. οἵτινες μυηθέντες **ἐνεβάτευσεν**, "these men were initiated and then they entered."[131] This text speaks of two men who came from Amisus (Pontus) to consult the oracle in AD 132.
2. παραλαβὼν τὰ μυστήρια **ἐνεβάτευσεν**, "he received the mysteries and then he entered."[132] Inscribed on one of the columns of the Apollo temple, this text refers to Alexander, an envoy from Lappa (Crete), who came to Claros to consult the oracle in the second century. The text also names the versifier of the oracles, the priest, the choral singers, and the cithara player.
3. μυηθέντες καὶ **ἐνβατεύσαντες** ἐχρήσαντο, "after they were initiated and they entered, they consulted the oracle."[133] In this text, two men named Antonius and Flabulaeus represent their city, Neocaesarea (Pontus) in consulting the Clarian Apollo.
4. μυηθέντες καὶ **ἐμβατεύσαντες**, "they were initiated and then they entered."[134] This inscription records the visit of a delegation from Pergamum.

Four additional inscriptions provide supplemental evidence about the mystery initiation rituals that were practiced at the Clarian temple. Four use the expression ἐπετέλεσε καὶ μυστήρια, "he also performed the mysteries," and one uses the term μυεῖν, "to initiate into the mysteries."[135]

There has been widespread agreement among scholars who have worked on these inscriptions that ἐμβατεύω should be understood as the second stage of a two-part ritual of initiation.[136] A two-part ritual would be similar to the mysteries of Demeter and Kore at Eleusis where the initial action was described as μύεσθαι, "to be initiated," and the second part as ἐποπτύειν, the highest grade of initiation (that also included visionary experience). The ἐμβατεύειν at Claros

130 Robert, *Inscriptions*, 205.

131 Macridy, "Altertümer," 170 [= §V.4] (1905); *OGIS* 530 (pp. 192–97); *IGRR* 4.1586 (p. 521).

132 Macridy, "Antiquités," 46 [= série I.1] (1912).

133 Macridy, "Altertümer," 165 [= §II.2] (1905).

134 Merkelbach, *Philologica*, 162–67 (= no. 2); Picard, "Oracle," 190–97; *CIG* II.3538; Robert, *Inscriptions*, 305.

135 Macridy, "Antiquités," 50 (no. 15), 51 (no. 16), and 52 (no. 20). The fourth is an unpublished inscription (= inv. no. 94) cited in Picard, *Éphèse et Claros*, 303–4.

136 Parke, *Oracles of Apollo*, 219–24; Robert, "Les fouilles de Claros," 548–49; Picard, *Éphèse et Claros*, 303–8; idem, "Oracle d'Apollon Clarios," 193; Ramsay, *Teaching of Paul*, 291–96.

would correspond to the ἐποπτύειν at Eleusis, and the entire ritual could be summarized as ἐπιτέλειν καὶ μυστήρια, "performing the mysteries."

The precise details of what this ritual looked like is difficult to reconstruct because we have limited written testimony of what took place at Claros, although there are three writers who provide written testimony to how the oracle operated (Tacitus, *Ann.* 2.54; Pliny the Elder, *Nat.* 2.232; Iamblichus, *Mysteries* 3.11). Iamblichus gives us the most detail:

> It is agreed by everyone that the oracle at Colophon [the Clarian Apollo] prophesies by means of water. There is a spring in a subterranean chamber, and from it the prophet drinks on certain appointed nights, after performing many preliminary ceremonies, and after drinking, he delivers his oracles, no longer seen by the spectators present. . . . Still, not every inspiration that the water gives is from the god, but this only bestows the receptivity and purification of the luminous spirit in us through which we are able to receive the god. But the presence of the god is different from and prior to this, and flashes like lightning from above. This holds aloof from no one who, through a kindred nature, is in union with it; but it is immediately present and uses the prophet as an instrument while he is neither himself nor has any consciousness of what he says or where on the earth he is, so that even after prophesying, he sometimes scarcely gets control of himself. Even before drinking, he fasts the whole day and night, and after becoming divinely inspired, he withdraws by himself to sacred, inaccessible places, and by this withdrawal and separation from human affairs, he purifies himself for receiving the god; and through these means, he has the inspiration of god illuminating the pure sanctuary of his own soul, and providing for it an unhindered divine possession, and a perfect and unimpeded presence. (Iamblichus, *Mysteries* 3.11)

Although Iamblichus writes later than the first century, he likely conveys an accurate framework for how the oracle at Claros operated in the first century and before. Now because of the excavation of the Apollo temple at Claros, we are able to put together a more detailed picture than either Ramsay or Dibelius could reconstruct. Although the temple was discovered in 1907, Louis Robert was the first to direct a systematic excavation of the structure from 1950 to 1960. Over the past couple of decades, the site was further excavated by a French delegation led by Juliette de Genière and now under the direction of Professor Nuran Sahin.

It is relevant to our inquiry to note that there was a labyrinth-like subterranean level underneath the temple structure.[137] This was built around the sacred spring—the source of the water from which the priest would drink for prophetic inspiration. We can conclude that the term ἐμβατεύω gave expression to the action of going down the steps of the sanctuary leading to this underground area and entering the room where vision and revelation would take place.

137 Graf, *Apollo*, 72.

Archaeological evidence and comparison with what happened at the Apollo sanctuary at Didyma and Delphi can bring further clarification. In his important monograph on the Apollo oracles in Asia Minor, H. W. Parke explains ἐμβατεύω as entering the holy place, but notes that this is the same place where the oracles were given. He observes, "The 'entrance' was presumably the formal approach to the hall of consultation by means of the basement passages."[138] Describing the labyrinth under the temple, he says that a series of underground passages led to a subterranean chamber of inquiry, the adyton.[139] It was here, on a "holy night," that the temple officials would lead individual inquirers or official embassies to consult the oracle. The prophet would then go to the farthest part of the adyton to seek inspiration from Apollo and return with his message from the god. Parke gives a vivid description of the process:

> The ceremony itself in its reformed style[140] must have been very impressive. Meeting in the temple in the dark and escorted by *mystagogoi* in batches down the steps and along the passages to the lamp-lit room, where they presented their enquiries and waited while the prophet went beyond them into the chamber containing the spring. His voice may have been heard indistinctly from within, and was taken up by the *thespiodos*, who chanted the response in verse. . . . After the enquirers had emerged they must have been supplied with a copy of the *thespiodos*'s poem, which had been taken down in shorthand by the secretaries.[141]

He contends that this whole procedure was described as a "mystery."[142] To be more precise, however, it is important to distinguish the delegations who came to consult the oracle from those who consulted the oracle *and* undertook the mystery initiation rites. The inscriptions make clear this distinction.

Celeste Guichard describes it in this way:

> The cult officials accompanied the *mantis* in his descent. The entire group first walked through a small doorway at the back of the porch and the left of the large, central door. After crossing the threshold, the officials turned right, descended the staircase and followed a corridor to the first of two subterranean rooms—all

138 Parke, *Oracles of Apollo*, 146.

139 Parke, *Oracles of Apollo*, 219–24, provides a full reconstruction of how he believes the oracle of Apollo at Claros functioned.

140 In trying to reconcile Tacitus's description of the procedure of the events at Claros (*Ann.* 2.54) with the account by Iamblichus (*Mysteries* 3.11), Parke proposes that the Clarian oracle underwent something of a revival during the reign of Hadrian. See Parke, *Oracles of Apollo*, 219–24. This is certainly not to deny the popularity of the oracle during the Hellenistic era. Parke speculates that it may have faced somewhat of a decline during the first century AD, but our lack of information about the oracle during the first century may imply nothing more than the fact that we have an inadequate amount of source material.

141 Parke, *Oracles of Apollo*, 223.

142 Parke, *Oracles of Apollo*, 222.

> of the cult officials, except the *mantis*, remained in the first room. The *mantis* continued alone into the next, hypaethral chamber and drank from the sacred spring which enabled him to communicate with Apollo.[143]

As Guichard contends, because the *mantis* received inspiration in the hypaethral chamber, the oracular inspiration took place in a portion of the temple open to the sky, thus lending an astrological flavor to the entire experience. "The hypaethral spaces at Didyma and at Klaros enabled the *mantis* to be in contact with the cosmos as it exists above, below, and all around."[144] This would also fit with the experience of Apuleius, who witnessed the cosmic powers in his initiation in the Isis sanctuary at Cenchrae (Apuleius, *Metam.* 11.23).

It thus appears that ἐμβατεύω referred to the initiate's descent to the subterranean level of the temple and entry into the most sacred part of the sanctuary, the adyton. This was not only the place of consultation but was also the place of visionary experience. Thus, as Robert notes, "The consultants had been 'initiated,' and they had performed the act which is called *embateuein*, that is to say, 'to enter.' . . . It refers to entering into the *adyton*. Certain consultants were the object of the performance of special ceremonies and secrets, of mysteries according to the usage of the time."[145]

It is difficult to know why the uncommon term ἐμβατεύω came to be used in this specialized sense of entering the adyton of Apollo's temple in the second and sacred part of ritual initiation. The most that we can say at this point is that the term was associated with entry into the temple centuries earlier. Euripides speaks of Apollo himself as the one who "enters" the temple in Lycia (Λυκίας ναὸν ἐμβατεύων Ἄπολλον; Euripides, *Rhes.* 224–26). In this passage, he is implored to come by night to the temple to be a saving guide to a traveler.

Various elements of the context of Col 2 that are descriptive of the rival teaching suggest that we should understand ἐμβατεύω to retain its technical significance of ritual initiation in Col 2:18. This includes the connection to visionary experience, the concern with fasting and taboos, the role of the "elements" (στοιχεῖα or *elementa*) in 2:8 and 20, the spiritual wisdom acquired by the adept (2:23), and the concern about deliverance from supernatural enemies. There is no other compelling reason to explain why the author of Colossians would have used this very rare term to speak of "entering." Furthermore, the advocates of the Jewish mystical view cannot produce a single example of ἐμβατεύω in Jewish mystical or apocalyptic literature to refer to entry into heaven.[146]

---

143 Guichard, "Oracular Temples at Klaros and Didyma," 89.

144 Guichard, "Oracular Temples at Klaros and Didyma," 102.

145 Robert, "Les fouilles de Claros," 548–49.

146 Bird, 86, mistakenly assumes that there are examples of this usage in Jewish literature when he says, "The word was frequent in Jewish apocalyptic literature in reference to visionary ascents."

εἰκῇ φυσιούμενος ὑπὸ τοῦ νοὸς τῆς σαρκὸς αὐτοῦ, "[this person is] puffed up in vanity by his fleshly mind." The third participle in the series levels a biting indictment of the character of the shamanistic teacher. He is profoundly arrogant. His unique spiritual experiences have caused him to see himself as superior to the Colossian believers and possessing knowledge that they do not have. Consequently, he arrogates to himself the right to judge them, disqualify them, and dictate to them how they should live.

The term φυσιόω is a distinctively Pauline term that he used six times in 1 Corinthians and nowhere else in the NT. It conveys the simple image of something that is inflated with air, such as a bellows (thus "puffed up"), and it was naturally applied to someone who was arrogant or conceited. Paul saw it as the opposite of love (1 Cor 13:4). He worried that an accurate knowledge about the dangers of food offered to idols could lead some of the Corinthian believers to be arrogant toward their brothers and sisters because "knowledge puffs up [φυσιοῖ], but love builds up" (1 Cor 8:1). He even goes so far as to identify a certain group within the Corinthian congregation that were already acting arrogantly as in 1 Cor 4:18: "some are arrogant [ἐφυσιώθησαν], as though I were not coming to you." The term itself is rare in literature predating Paul, but it does occur in Jewish moral literature (T. Levi 14.7–8).

He characterizes the arrogance that the teacher is exhibiting with the adverb εἰκῇ, "without cause," the preferred translation of many versions (NRSV; ESV; NASB).[147] Paul uses this term four times elsewhere with more of the nuance "in vain," which puts the emphasis on the failure to obtain results (see Rom 13:4; 1 Cor 15:2; Gal 3:4; 4:11). Here the accent is more on the absence of any warrant for the arrogance. The factional leader is conceited and yet has no reason for his excessive pride.

Paul knew that there was a great temptation to pride that stemmed from extraordinary supernatural experiences. After he narrates his experience of visionary ascent to heaven, he reveals to the Corinthians that the Lord took unique steps to ensure his humility. He writes, "So to keep me from becoming conceited because of the surpassing greatness of the revelations, a thorn was given me in the flesh, a messenger of Satan to harass me, to keep me from becoming conceited" (2 Cor 12:7 ESV). Whereas Paul may have had reason for boasting in his experience, the Colossian teacher had none since his spiritual experience was rooted in experience that was not from the Lord.

Opposition to pride and arrogance is a prominent theme in the wisdom literature. "All those who are arrogant are an abomination to the LORD; be assured, they will not go unpunished" (Prov 16:5 NRSV). Sirach warns, "Mockery and abuse issue from the proud, but vengeance lies in wait for them like a lion" (Sir 27:28 NRSV). True wisdom is "far from arrogance" (Sir 15:8 NRSV). Ezekiel associates arrogance with the proud prince of Tyre who,

147 BDAG, s.v. εἰκῇ, suggests the gloss "without cause" for Col 2:18.

in Jewish tradition, became symbolic of a ruler who oppresses God's people (Ezek 28:2, 17).

In Paul's view, this arrogance flows directly from this leader's "flesh" (σάρξ). As in Col 2:11, σάρξ is best understood here in the moral sense of "evil inclination" and not simply as human weakness.[148] Flesh is here personified with the ability to think and act by possessing a mind (νοῦς), "the mind of the flesh." The thought is similar to what Paul expresses in Rom 8:7 (NIV): "the mind governed by the flesh" (τὸ φρόνημα τῆς σαρκός). Paul will conclude his polemic against the rival teaching by claiming that all the teaching and efforts of the rival teacher represent the gratification of his own flesh (Col 2:23).

It is not just the content of the factional teaching that is in error, it is the character of the teacher himself. Paul thus invites the Colossians to discern the inconsistency between this teacher's approach to them and what should be foremost in a servant of God. Hubris, a judgmental attitude, and pride are inconsistent with a life oriented around Christ and his purposes, regardless of the incredible visionary experiences and spiritual wisdom someone purports to have.

**19** καὶ οὐ κρατῶν τὴν κεφαλήν, ἐξ οὗ πᾶν τὸ σῶμα, "[this person is] not holding tight to the head from whom the whole body . . ." This fourth participial clause in the series expresses Paul's most serious charge against the rival teacher. He was not receiving his inspiration and direction from the risen Christ, nor was he adhering tightly to the apostolic teaching. In this context, the verb κρατέω means to "adhere strongly" to someone or something.[149] The context points to the lack of immediate and direct connection to Christ in his role as head of the church in his resurrected and heavenly position. But the term may also be suggestive of the teaching of Christ and his apostles that had been passed on to the churches. In a Jewish setting, the term could be used for holding on tight to the traditions of the elders (Mark 7:3). In the early church, it was applied to the Pauline doctrinal convictions that were passed on in the churches (2 Thess 2:15). The writer of Hebrews also uses it to refer to the common confession of the church: κρατῶμεν τῆς ὁμολογίας (Heb 4:14). What Paul says here was signaled by his earlier condemnation of the rival teaching when he said that it was οὐ κατὰ Χριστόν, "not according to Christ," and κατὰ τὴν παράδοσιν τῶν ἀνθρώπων, "in accord with human traditions" (i.e., not Pauline tradition).

Instead of simply saying that the opposing teacher was "not holding tightly *to Christ*," Paul uses the functional title κεφαλή, "head," which he introduced in the central refrain of the hymn: αὐτός ἐστιν ἡ κεφαλὴ τοῦ σώματος τῆς ἐκκλησίας, "he is the head of the body, the church" (1:17c). He does this so he can elaborate on the dynamic and present role that Christ has in relationship to his church—a

---

148 Contra Dunn, 185. For support for this view, see the discussion at 2:11.

149 BDAG, s.v. κρατέω.

role ever so important at a time of controversy and conflict.[150] One of the central ideas is that the resurrected Christ is not aloof from his church but is presently and actively involved in resourcing his people and giving them leadership and direction. Paul wants the Colossians to recognize that the factional leader is not receiving his directions and inspiration from the risen Christ.

The source of the head-body imagery has been much disputed (see the full discussion at 1:18). Paul's use of it here is likely rooted in popular understandings of head in relation to body that had its origins in the discussions of the medical writers Hippocrates, Galen, and Rufus of Ephesus. These were influential on Hellenistic Judaism (e.g., Philo) and other Jewish texts. This understanding is corroborated by the use of other physiological terms in this context (such as ἁφαί and σύνδεσμοι). It is unlikely that head-body should be understood here in a Hellenistic or gnostic cosmic sense—that is, as the ruling principle of the universe conceived as directing a cosmic body (e.g., a macroanthropos).

Paul claims that it is from the head that the whole body is supplied and instructed. The prepositional phrase (ἐξ οὗ) is a *constructio ad sensum* referring to Christ, since one would expect a feminine relative pronoun (ἐξ ἧς) in reference to the preceding feminine noun (τὴν κεφαλήν).

**διὰ τῶν ἁφῶν καὶ συνδέσμων ἐπιχορηγούμενον καὶ συμβιβαζόμενον**, "through the joints and ligaments being nourished and instructed." The entire body receives help that is mediated διὰ τῶν ἁφῶν καὶ συνδέσμων, "through the joints and ligaments." Lightfoot has demonstrated that ἁφαί is virtually synonymous with ἄρθρα, "joints."[151] The term σύνδεσμοι was the common word in the medical writers to refer to "ligaments" (the bands of connective tissue that hold together a joint).[152] Some have seen these terms as referring to church officers, as those who mediate Christ's presence, provision, and direction.[153] But there is nothing in the context to suggest that the author is limiting his focus to these leaders as the source of supply to the body, nor do we find these terms used elsewhere for church officers.[154] It is best to view them as referring to the various members of the body and thus as an alternative to τὰ μέλη, "the parts [of the body]," as in 1 Cor 12:27: "now you are the body of Christ and individually members of it" (NRSV).

Paul explains that the body of believers is being regularly supplied (ἐπιχορηγούμενον) from the head through the intermediate agency of the various members. The term is part of Paul's vocabulary, using it twice elsewhere.

150 See the more extensive development of the background and meaning of the head-body imagery in Arnold, "'Head' of the Church," 346–66.

151 Lightfoot, 198–99. See his commentary for the relevant references.

152 See, e.g., Galen, *Usefulness of the Parts of the Body* 1.442.22; 2.202; *Doctrines of Hippocrates and Plato* 94.11–19; Rufus of Ephesus, *On Names* 142.11–12; 157.6.

153 Theodoret was the first to assert this view, stating that the terms refer to apostles, prophets, and teachers (as cited in Lohmeyer, 179n6). See also Gnilka, 220, and Schnackenburg, *Ephesians*, 189.

154 Schweizer, 164–65, also denies that the reference is to church officers.

In 2 Cor 9:10, he begins by speaking of God's providential sovereignty as the one "who supplies [ἐπιχορηγῶν] seed to the sower and bread for food," but then switches to the uncompounded form when he draws a metaphorical application: "[he] will also supply [χορηγήσει] and increase your store of seed and will enlarge the harvest of your righteousness" (see also Gal 3:5). The uncompounded form is much more common and is frequently used for the supply of food to people (1 Kgs 4:7 [2x], 27 [5:1 LXX]; 1 Macc 14:10; 3 Macc. 6.30), but it is also used in the LXX for God's provision of nonmaterial benefits, such as wisdom (Sir 1:26). Neither form is a medical term, so he is not formally continuing the medical analogy. Paul has a penchant for creating compounded forms, but ἐπιχορηγέω was common in the papyri[155] and is found in local inscriptions.[156]

The head also unites (συμβιβαζόμενον) the members of the body as they depend on him. Nearly all the English versions render συμβιβάζω as "knit together" (KJV; NKJV; RSV; ESV; NET) or "held together" (NRSV; NIV; NJB; NAB; CSB), thereby continuing the physiological analogy. As noted at Col 2:2, however, the verb could be interpreted as "instruct." This is how Paul uses the term elsewhere (1 Cor 2:16) and how it is always used throughout the LXX. Although "unite" better fits the context here, there still may be overtones of "instruct" present in the use of the verb. The unity of the body of believers in the Lycus Valley is being disrupted by an influential and powerful teacher, who is instructing them in ways that Paul sees as deceitful and injurious to the health of the church. His strong appeal to them is to resist this teaching. By pointing them to Christ as head of the church, he affirms Jesus's present and continuing role, especially through caring and providing for the church, as well as unifying the church in love. Yet the head of the church is also continuing to instruct them "through the joints and ligaments"—that is, through other members of the body. This is consistent with the role he ascribes to the various members in the next chapter when he says, "Let the word of Christ dwell in you richly, teaching and admonishing one another" (Col 3:16 ESV). Presumably this would also include receiving instruction from those who have been gifted as teachers (1 Cor 12:28–29; Eph 4:11; 1 Tim 1:7). When we consider the response to false teaching in the second century and the appeal to the authority of the church officers, especially the bishop (see, e.g., Ign. *Eph.* 6.1; 20.2; *Magn.* 6.1; *Trall.* 7.3), it comes as somewhat of a surprise that Paul does not take that approach here. Yet the charismatic function of the body comes to the fore in this context, including the roles of teaching and admonishing. The basis of the teaching he invokes, however, is the widely received tradition about the person and work of Christ, "the teaching [λόγος] about Christ" (Col 3:16). Concentrating on this instruction is part of what is entailed in seeking "the things above where Christ is seated at

155 The word appears often in marriage and divorce contracts with the meaning "to provide for," "to support." For examples, see Lohse, 122n62, and MM, s.v. ἐπιχορηγέω.

156 As, e.g., in Miletus and Lydia: *IMilet* I 9.360 (*SEG* 4.425); *TAM* V.2.1196.

the right hand of God" (Col 3:1). Christ unifies his body through the common confession of Christ as Lord.

The end result is a picture of the resurrected Christ who is very involved in the affairs of his church, even in a rural community populated with miners, wool growers, and farmers. The relationship the Colossians have, expressed in the σύν-compounds of 2:11–13, is the basis for resisting the dangerous teaching and the way forward so that they can grow.

αὔξει τὴν αὔξησιν τοῦ θεοῦ, "grows the growth from God." For the subject of this verb, we have to go back to πᾶν τὸ σῶμα, "the whole body." The image of "growth" is a Pauline thought: "I planted, Apollos watered, but God gave the growth" (1 Cor 3:6 NRSV; see also 2 Cor 9:10). This growth involves not only grasping the true teaching about Christ but also increasing in their trust in their living head (see also 2 Cor 10:15). It also extends to a growth in their personal righteousness before God (2 Cor 9:10), a topic that Paul will take up in Col 3.

Once again, Paul emphasizes direct and immediate divine involvement in the lives of the Colossians by expressing that the growth is a "growth from God." Christ, as head, is the immediate source of the growth, but ultimately God (the Father) causes the growth. The genitive is best interpreted as a genitive of source. This growth "is wholly distinct from the mere swelling of the visionaries' heads (v. 18: they are 'puffed up')."[157]

The function of the head in relationship to the body is developed in similar terms in Eph 4:15–16, but with some unique twists. The setting of Ephesians is not polemical, so the head-body teaching is not expressed as an indictment of the deficiencies of a rival teacher—that is, "he is not holding tight to the head," as in Colossians. Nevertheless, the comments are made in the context of a warning about "the trickery of people by craftiness in a strategy of deception" (Eph 4:14). In Ephesians, there is a more overt emphasis on the unity of the body through the addition of the adjectival participle συναρμολογούμενον, "being joined together" (4:16)—an emphasis consistent with the theme of unity in the letter. Ephesians also stresses the unique contribution of each individual member of the community to the whole (κατ' ἐνέργειαν ἐν μέτρῳ ἑνὸς ἑκάστου μέρους, 4:16)—an emphasis consistent with the overall concern of the chapter, which speaks of the grace given to each member of the body (4:7) to contribute to its growth. The differences with Colossians thus have more to do with emphasis than with a substantively new development.

**20** Εἰ ἀπεθάνετε σὺν Χριστῷ ἀπὸ τῶν στοιχείων τοῦ κόσμου, "if you died with Christ from the demonic spirits of the world." As an additional basis for the Colossians to resist the teaching of the opponents, Paul draws out the implications of their identification with the death of Christ, especially with respect to the hostile powers. For rhetorical impact, he structures his appeal using a first-class

157 Sumney, 158–59.

conditional sentence, "if you died with Christ," as indeed they had according to 2:12 as signified by their baptism (συνταφέντες αὐτῷ ἐν τῷ βαπτισμῷ).

The idea of "dying to the powers" is a natural extension of Paul's thought on the implications of being united with Christ (see esp. Rom 6:3–11).[158] He has previously declared that, by virtue of their connection with Christ, believers have died to sin (Rom 6:2, 7, 10), to the world (Gal 6:14), and to the law (Rom 7:6; Gal 2:19). They have entered into a new existence in which these forces, though still existing and exerting their influence, no longer have governing jurisdiction over their lives. Paul now interprets death with Christ as also including death to another category of powers associated with the present evil age: they have died to the influence of evil angelic powers. This implication of identification with the death of Christ flows out of Paul's dramatic statements regarding Christ's victory over the principalities and authorities that he described earlier (Col 2:15). He also spoke of this deliverance from the powers in his prelude to the Colossian hymn (Col 2:13) when he described their conversion as God rescuing them "from the authority of darkness" and transferring them into the kingdom of his beloved Son. It is unusual for Paul to use the preposition ἀπό following ἀποθνήσκω, since he usually expresses the results of "dying with Christ" as a "dying to" something with the dative. By using ἀπό, however, separation is stressed—believers have experienced a decisive separation from the governing and compelling influence of the powers.

The concept here corresponds substantially to what he expressed to the Galatians. In that context he explains that even Jewish believers were at one time enslaved to demonic powers (ὑπὸ τὰ στοιχεῖα τοῦ κόσμου ἦμεν δεδουλωμένοι; Gal 4:3). But now Christ has brought "redemption" (ἐξαγοράζω) for those under law (Gal 4:5). The implication for the Galatian gentiles is that to embrace the practices of Torah would be tantamount to regressing to a life in the old age where evil powers held sway in a way that was similar to what they experienced in their idolatrous pagan past (Gal 4:8–10). Although Torah observance is not at issue for the Colossians in the same way that it was for the Galatians, there is a very real danger for the Colossians that in accepting the practices of "the philosophy," they would actually come under the influence of the demonic powers once again.

As noted earlier (see the *Excursus*, "The τὰ στοιχεῖα τοῦ κόσμου as Demonic Spirits," above), the best interpretation of στοιχεῖα in Colossians is that the expression serves as yet another term referring to demonic spirits (in addition to θρόνοι, κυριότητες, ἀρχαί, ἐξουσίαι, and τὰ ἀόρατα). That meaning fits this context better than trying to envision believers dying to "rudimentary teaching" or the four elements (earth, water, air, fire). It is also doubtful in this context

158 Fowl, *Story of Christ*, 148, observes that "Paul uses the metaphor of dying to something as a means of speaking of the transfer of allegiance that a Christian undergoes upon entering union with Christ."

that the στοιχεῖα were blocking a person's access to the heavenly realm on the day of death when the soul would ascend.[159] It is far more likely that advocates of the philosophy were teaching that the στοιχεῖα were pervasively influential, dangerous, and harmful and needed to be managed through ritual acts of power. The Colossian believers and the rival teachers were concerned about the impact of the στοιχεῖα on matters of daily life—causing sickness, effecting a curse, bringing poor crops, plagues, earthquakes, and "natural" disasters. By calling on good angels (Col 2:18) and following a variety of ritual practices and taboos, the advocates of the philosophy contended, the work of these evil spirits could be averted. Paul takes a fundamentally different perspective. Something has happened in the death and resurrection of Christ that has had a profound impact on the status of the powers in relationship to believers. The Colossians are not automatically immune to the powers in and of themselves, but in Christ they are "dead" to their influence and are filled with his resources for resisting (Col 2:10).

τί ὡς ζῶντες ἐν κόσμῳ δογματίζεσθε, "Why do you comply with their dictates as though you were living in the world?" Paul's immediate and pressing concern is the tendency of the Colossian believers to subject themselves to the demands of the shaman-like teacher. The taboos ("Do not handle! Do not taste! Do not touch!," 2:21), the ascetic practices (2:18, 23), the food regulations (2:16), the calendar observances (2:16), and the ritual practices (2:18) are all unnecessary and counter to their new life in union with Christ. Through this rhetorical question, Paul seeks to jar them into realizing that their perspective is misaligned. Although they believe that the practices that the rival teacher is advocating will help them in matters of daily life, Paul wants them to see that they are not God-honoring or even neutral. Ultimately, they bear the fingerprints of demonic inspiration (2:8), but here he links them with life in the present evil age. He uses κόσμος in the theological sense of a pattern of life determined by the present evil age (cf. Gal 1:4). He has already used the term to qualify the στοιχεῖα and connect them to this age (2:8, 20a). Paul will therefore call the Colossians to seek the "things above" where Christ is, to whom they belong (τὰ ἄνω, Col 3:1, 2; cf. Phil 3:20). By accepting the teaching of the opponents, the Colossians would be reverting into a slavery that they once experienced in their pagan past (see Gal 4:3, 8–10), when they lived under the dominion of the present evil age.[160] "Why . . . as though you were living in the world" is tantamount to Paul saying, "Why . . . as though you were living in slavery."

Paul characterizes the demands that the opponents are making on the Colossians as δόγματα by using the verbal form of this term (δογματίζω). The word group is not itself negative; for example, the noun can be used for regulations that are healthy for the church (as with the Jerusalem "decrees"; Acts 16:4).

159 Schweizer, 166.
160 So also Lohse, 123.

It takes on a negative evaluation here through its connection with "the world." The passive voice points to the rival teacher as the one who is imposing rules and regulations upon the Colossians. Some have suggested that this is a "permissive passive" and that Paul is asking them why they are *allowing* themselves to be placed under these dictates.[161] There is no doubt that the rival teacher is doing his best to make the demands, as Paul's previous polemic confirms when he warns against this teacher taking them captive by his teaching (2:8), judging and disqualifying them (2:16, 18). But Paul's appeal to them here is that they do not need to accede to these demands and that there are good reasons for not doing so.

**21** μὴ ἅψῃ μηδὲ γεύσῃ μηδὲ θίγῃς, "Do not handle! Do not taste! Do not touch!" Paul cites three examples of the kinds of rules that the opponents were foisting on the Colossians. Nearly all interpreters have correctly regarded this verse as either a direct quotation from the philosophy or the author's stereotyping of their taboo-oriented regulations. Since the collocation of these three prohibitions have not been found in any ancient literature, it is impossible to verify that they come verbatim from the opponents. But two of the terms (θιγγάνω and γεύομαι) are not part of Paul's vocabulary either.

Dunn has noted that "here again the echo of characteristically Jewish concerns is strong, and particularly purity concerns, though that is missed by almost all commentators."[162] He points to the fundamental importance of distinguishing clean and unclean foods within Judaism as well the emphasis on maintaining purity by not "touching" anything that is ritually unclean, such as a corpse (Num 19:11–13), someone with a bodily discharge (Lev 15), or a leper (Lev 13:45–46). These concerns were maintained by various Jewish groups in the Second Temple period, including the Qumran community. More specifically, in Jewish apocalyptic texts, purity was a prerequisite for heavenly visions.[163] Part of the reason for this is that no one can enter the heavenly temple in an impure state (4Q400 1 I, 14: "They do not tolerate anyone whose path is de[praved.] There is n[o] impurity in their holy offerings").

But there was also a different stream of Judaism that was concerned about purity and advocated strict laws of avoidance. This was the folk Judaism that was interested in ritual practices to gain power for protection, divination, healing, and to help in matters of daily life. Sepher ha-Razim provides numerous examples of prohibitions linked to the invocation of angels and rituals of power. In the instructions for a divination ritual that would provide supernatural insight into the day of one's death and also result in the production of oil with great healing power, the suppliant was instructed to take some aged oil and invoke

161 See BDAG, s.v. δογματίζω; Moo, 234n186.

162 Dunn, 191.

163 See Sappington, *Revelation and Redemption*, 150–53. See also his summary of "qualifications for heavenly revelations" on pp. 63–70.

angels ("I adjure you, O angels of wisdom and understanding"; Sepher ha-Razim 5.23). Prior to the adjuration, however, the person was required to purify himself in the following way:

> But before you perform this rite, purify yourself from all impurity for three weeks of days, and guard yourself from all (meat of) small animals and from all that yields blood (when slaughtered) even fish, and do not drink wine, and do not come near a woman, and do not touch a grave, be wary of nocturnal pollution, and walk in humility and prayer, and make your prayers and supplications long, and devote your heart to the fear of heaven, and you will succeed. (Sepher ha-Razim 5.34–37 [Morgan])

The purpose of this purity is to gain power over the angels one is invoking so that they are obligated to reveal information or do one's bidding. Earlier in the book, it is revealed that "these angels tell everyone who, in purity, gains power over them, what will happen on the earth . . ." (Sepher ha-Razim 1.90). The book is replete with avoidance instructions for this purpose:

- "do it in (a state of purity) and you will succeed" (1.84);
- "do this on the twenty-ninth of the month when the moon has waned completely. Take care to keep yourself from intercourse, from wine, and from all (kinds of meat for three days" (2.36–37);
- "purify yourself from all impurity, and do not eat *nevelah* [meat from an animal that has died from natural causes] and do not touch a woman's bed, for seven days" (2.163–64);
- "(in order to succeed) abstain from meat, from wine, from (contact with) the dead, from menstruating women, and from every unclean thing" (2.184–86); and
- "guard yourself, take care, and keep pure for seven days from all (impure) food, from all (impure) drink, and from every unclean thing" (2.26–27).

Similar instructions are given in other Jewish documents that contain shamanistic instructions, such as in the Hekhalot literature. Lesses devotes an entire chapter to "ascetic preparations for Hekhalot adjurations" in her monograph titled *Ritual Practices to Gain Power.*[164] Among these preparations are the avoidance of sexual activity and food restrictions.

In the Greek magical papyri, there is a similar emphasis on avoidance of foods and sexual activity in preparation for ritual adjurations.[165] For instance,

164 Lesses, *Ritual Practices to Gain Power*, 117–60.

165 Lesses, *Ritual Practices to Gain Power*, 121, says that by contrast, the *PGM* adjurations "mandate only the avoidance of sexual activity." But there are many examples of food restrictions in preparation for a ritual of power.

one text instructs the participant in a divination rite to "abstain from meat and the bath" (*PGM* IV.735). Another says, "Keep yourself pure for 7 days before the moon becomes full by abstaining from meat and uncooked food . . . and by abstaining from wine" (*PGM* IV.53–58). Yet another instructs the adept to "refrain from all unclean things and from all eating of fish and from all sexual intercourse, so that you may bring the god into the greatest desire toward you" (*PGM* I.290–93). Sometimes there is just the simple instruction to "keep yourself pure" (*PGM* IV.28, 304). There is also evidence of dependence upon Jewish traditions in the Greco-Egyptian texts to help ensure the success of the rituals: "I adjure you, the one who receives this conjuration, not to eat pork, and every spirit and daimon, whatever sort it may be, will be subject to you" (*PGM* IV.3080–81). The instructions for this spell conclude with, "Keep yourself pure, for this charm is Hebraic and is preserved among pure men" (*PGM* IV.3085–86). There was clearly two-way borrowing of traditions—pagan to Jewish and Jewish to pagan—in the realm of folk practice and ritual power.

Paul's summary of the prohibitions includes three aorist verbs in a prohibitive subjunctive construction. The first expression, μὴ ἅψῃ (ἅπτω), is a very common word throughout the LXX and NT, but it can be used to convey sexual relations. This is the sense in Gen 20:4 where it says that "Abimelech had not touched [ἥψατο]" Abraham's wife Sarah when she was at Gerar. Paul uses the verb with this meaning in mind in 1 Cor 7:1 when he advises that "it is good for a man not to have sexual relations [μὴ ἅπτεσθαι] with a woman." But the term is quite commonly used in the LXX for avoiding contact with anything that is impure (e.g., Lev 5:2–3; 6:27 [6:20 LXX]; 7:21; 11:8, 24, 26, 27, 31).

The second, μηδὲ γεύσῃ (γεύομαι), is clearly limited to food and is consistently translated "do not taste" in the English translations. This is the only time it appears in Paul's writings, but it is found in the Gospels, Acts, and Hebrews. It is commonly used not simply of experiencing a taste of a food or drink in the mouth (Matt 27:34; John 2:9) but for eating and consuming. Thus, Peter "became hungry and wanted something to eat [γεύσασθαι]" (Acts 10:10), and Paul ate a meal (γευσάμενος) with the believers at Troas (Acts 20:11).

The final prohibition, μηδὲ θίγῃς (θιγγάνω), overlaps significantly in meaning with the first and is often translated "handle" or "touch." The verb is rare, only appearing once in the LXX, but twice in Hebrews. In its single occurrence in the LXX, it is used interchangeably with ἅπτω: "Any who touch [θιγεῖν] the mountain shall be put to death. No hand shall touch [ἅψεται] it (Exod 19:12–13). According to LSJ, it can also be used of having sexual relations with someone.[166]

In summary, this is either Paul's caricatured summary or actual citation of a series of prohibitions advocated by the rival teacher. They are a set of regulations

166 LSJ, s.v. θιγγάνω I.2.

that include food prohibitions, but also extend to the realm of sexual activity.[167] The various regulations have parallels in the Mosaic law and in Second Temple Jewish texts, but there are also parallels in the pagan and Jewish magical tradition.[168] The reason for the prohibitions and their purpose is the key issue. The appropriate context is not in Jewish apocalyptic mysticism as many have argued, but in the context of Jewish and pagan shamanism. Various kinds of taboos were prerequisite to success in rituals of power. Acceding to these prohibitions has nothing to do with eternal salvation[169] but with protection, healing, divination, and matters of daily life. But Paul is not impressed. "By repeating these key words, Paul expresses his vexation and anger over these regulations."[170]

**22** ἅ ἐστιν πάντα εἰς φθορὰν τῇ ἀποχρήσει, "all these [practices] lead to corruption with use." Paul now summarizes his response to the rules and practices advocated by the rival teacher with two polemical comments. In the first instance, he claims that these ritual practices lead to moral corruption (2:22). Then, second, he warns that they are simply a gratification of the evil inclination (2:23). These comments complete his direct attack on the teaching of the philosophy and provide yet a further basis for the Colossians to resist the dangerous practices they are presenting.

The neuter plural relative pronoun (ἅ) refers to the practices of the previous verse and all that is implied in δογματίζεσθε (2:20). It gathers together all of the ritual practices, the rigorous ascetic preparations with all of the taboos, and any theological grounding or justification that the rival teacher has given, and condemns the entire package (πάντα) as leading to corruption. Many interpreters contend, however, that the pronoun refers only to the material things standing behind the regulations, such as food and drink.[171] Part of their reasoning for this is that rules and regulations do not perish with use, only consumable goods. But the more explicit antecedents for the pronoun are the regulations themselves ("Do not handle! Do not taste! Do not touch!"). Furthermore, these regulations likely also refer to sexual taboos as well. More importantly, however, is the likelihood (see below) that "perish" is not the correct way to understand φθορά in this context.

The foundational syntactical structure of the clause is parallel to that of 2:23:

2:22: ἅ ἐστιν . . . εἰς φθοράν ("these things . . . [lead] to corruption")
2:23: ἅτινά ἐστιν . . . πρὸς πλησμονήν ("these things . . . [lead] to gratification")

167 Bormann, 149, is too restrictive in contending that they are sexual taboos in connection to calender regulations.

168 See the comments of Wilson, 227–28, who warns against limiting the background of these expressions to Judaism.

169 Contra Hübner, 90, who describes them from the perspective of their advocates as *heilsnotwendig*.

170 Barth and Blanke, 356.

171 E.g., Dunn, 193; Wilson, 228; C. Moule, 108.

The two main structural differences are stylistic: (1) there is a different form of the relative pronoun in 2:23,[172] and (2) a different preposition that can bear the same meaning is used in 2:23. Of course, the two nouns predicate different reasons for denying the rules and teachings of the opponents, although they are closely related reasons.

Most commentators and versions have interpreted φθορά as "perish" (KJV; RSV; NRSV; ESV; NJB; NAB) in the sense of final destruction ("what is destroyed," CSB; or "cease to exist," CEB) or as items that "deteriorate" (NLT).[173] This accords well with a common usage of the word to refer to anything that is perishable, including the physical body (1 Cor 15:42, 50). But φθορά may also have an ethical sense whereby it expresses the notion of a "corruption" that is tantamount to an "inner depravity."[174] Thus, 2 Pet 1:4 speaks of "the corruption that is in the world because of lust [ἐν ἐπιθυμίᾳ φθορᾶς]" (NRSV). Similarly, the same book warns against those who promise freedom, "but they themselves are slaves of corruption [φθορᾶς]; for people are slaves to whatever masters them" (2 Pet 2:19). The idea of moral corruption better fits the context in Col 2:22 than ultimate destruction or as a reference to food that perishes.

Paul's comments here have much in common with Jewish anti-idolatry polemic, especially as seen in the wisdom literature. Wisdom 14:12 declares that "idea of making idols was the beginning of fornication, and the invention of them was the corruption [φθορά] of life." The larger context warns of practices that the Colossians are in danger of appropriating as part of the philosophy's syncretistic approach to life. These include "secret rites and initiations," "frenzied revels with strange customs," and "works of sorcery and unholy rites" (Wis 12:4; 14:15, 23 NRSV). God's judgment will come upon the pagan idols "because, though part of what God created, they became an abomination, snares for human souls and a trap for the feet of the foolish" (Wis 14:11 NRSV). There is no sign that the Colossians are in danger of forsaking their Christian faith and turning to a worship of other gods, but the kinds of practices they are being pushed to engage in is a step in that direction. Even in folk Judaism, the rituals of power are unconcerned with fidelity to the one living and true God; their sole concern is with spiritual power and what works to thwart an evil spirit or to bring healing. The realm of magic and folk belief is the one place within Judaism where we can see a strong impulse to syncretism that even extended to naming other gods and spirits. It appears that Paul has no trouble employing elements of traditional Jewish anti-idolatry polemic to warn the Colossian Christians of these dangers. Paul could have easily said along with the author of Wisdom, "The worship of idols [εἰδώλων θρησκεία] not to be named is the beginning and cause and end of every evil" (Wis 14:27 NRSV).

172 BDAG, s.v. ὅστις, notes that "quite oft. ὅστις takes the place of the simple rel. ὅς, ἥ, ὅ."

173 E.g., Pao, 196; Dunn, 193.

174 BDAG, s.v. φθορά 4, "inward depravity, depravity."

It is now necessary to circle back to the beginning of the clause and consider the interpretation of ἐστιν . . . εἰς. The Authorized Version translated it literally according to the form: "which are all to perish." More recent versions have added words to help clarify the force of the preposition; thus, "things that are all *destined to* perish" (NIV; similarly NASB; NET; NAB). This is consistent with the use of εἰς as a marker to express the goal or result of an action.[175] If moral corruption is the preferred way of interpreting φθορά in this context, then a term such as "lead" would be a better way of communicating the force of the preposition to convey result. Thus, "these things *lead to* corruption."

These rituals and practices lead to corruption "with use" (τῇ ἀποχρήσει). The compound form is quite rare in Greek, never occurring elsewhere in the NT or in the LXX or even in Jewish authors such as Josephus and Philo. But it is consistent with Paul's stylistic preference to prefer composite forms and is thus probably coextensive in meaning with the simple forms χρῆσις and χράομαι, which are far more common. As such, it simply refers to the state of being used. Thus, by following the commands and teachings of the philosophy, the Colossians would be led into a moral corruption. Many commentators have overinterpreted ἀπόχρησις here by suggesting that the preposition intensifies its meaning from "use" to "consumption"[176] or by supposing that "the unusual word was chosen for its expressiveness."[177] Lohse has rightly noted that the term simply speaks of "normal use."[178]

κατὰ τὰ ἐντάλματα καὶ διδασκαλίας τῶν ἀνθρώπων, "according to the commandments and teachings of men." This prepositional phrase modifies the preceding ἅ ἐστιν πάντα, "all these practices are . . . ," which, in turn, refers to the three examples of taboos that the rival teacher is trying to enforce on the Colossian believers. The phrase is an echo of Isa 29:13: "The Lord said: These people draw near me; they honor me with their lips, while their heart is far from me, and in vain do they worship me, teaching human precepts and teachings [ἐντάλματα ἀνθρώπων καὶ διδασκαλίας]" (NETS). In that context, as Assyria threatens Jerusalem, the hearts of the people of Israel are not focused on God and in accord with his revelation, but with their idols and with a worship that is rooted more in the vain imaginations of their leaders. This passage is also quoted in the Synoptic tradition (Mark 7:6–7 // Matt 15:8–9) in Jesus's denunciation of the Pharisees as hypocrites for elevating their own rules above the explicit commands of the Mosaic law.[179] Beetham notes that in the Synoptic passages, "Jesus was of the opinion that at least some of the Jewish leaders

175 BDAG, s.v. εἰς 4.d., e.

176 Dunn, 193.

177 Lightfoot, 204.

178 Lohse, 124.

179 Moo, 238, suggests that Paul here is depending directly on the Synoptic tradition rather than independently citing Isaiah. But this cannot be determined with certainty, given Paul's frequent citations of and allusions to Isaiah.

had made an idol out of their man-made religion, and he denounces them in the prophetic spirit of Isaiah."[180] Paul now appropriates the same anti-idolatry polemic to brand the opposing teaching as a set of idolatrous "commandments and teachings" that has its origin not in revelation from the one living and true God, but *from men* (τῶν ἀνθρώπων). Paul's grave concern about the philosophy is that it is an idolatry that will lead the Colossian believers away from the worship of God.[181] This indictment is particularly appropriate to the Colossian opponents, who were likely basing their teaching and practices on wisdom and insight gained from spiritual experience, including revelatory experience in ritual initiation.

**23** ἅτινά ἐστιν . . . πρὸς πλησμονὴν τῆς σαρκός, "these things . . . lead to the gratification of the flesh." This final sentence, which represents the culmination of the polemic, is quite complex and is fraught with a variety of interpretational difficulties. This has led interpreters to regard it as "virtually impenetrable"[182] and "one of the most difficult to translate in the NT,"[183] with one concluding that "the sentence can hardly be translated with certainty."[184] Nevertheless, a reasonable solution can be achieved for each of the individual issues that yields an overall understanding of the verse that is compelling. In summary, Paul concludes that the various practices of the opponents that he cites are simply a manifestation of the works of the flesh (Gal 5:19). Although many interpreters have seen the overall message of the verse as claiming that the regulations proffered by the philosophy are impotent in combating the desires of the flesh (e.g., "they lack any value in restraining sensual indulgence," NIV),[185] there has been no indication in the letter that the rival teacher is wanting to help the Colossians defeat the impulses of the flesh. Rather, the teacher is advocating certain rituals and practices that will help the Colossians deal with issues of daily life that are perceived to be connected to spirit influences. Just as φαρμακεία, "witchcraft" or "sorcery," is a manifestation of the flesh (Gal 5:20), so these practices are simply a gratification of the flesh. They not only lack value, but they diminish the dependence of the Colossian believers upon Christ, who is present with them to empower them and help them.

Discerning the overall structure of the verse has led to a variety of different views since the predicate of ἅτινά ἐστιν could be variously construed:

1. It is a periphrastic construction (ἅτινά ἐστιν . . . ἔχοντα): "such rules indeed appear wise . . ."[186]

180 Beetham, *Echoes of Scripture*, 217.
181 Beetham, *Echoes of Scripture*, 216, 218.
182 Hay, 111.
183 MacDonald, 116.
184 Bornkamm, "Heresy of Colossians," 134.
185 E.g., Pao, 196.
186 Translation by Harris, 189 (see also 115). See also Abbott, 275; BDF §353.4.

2. The predicate consists of the last two prepositional phrases (ἅτινά ἐστιν ... οὐκ ἐν τιμῇ τινι πρὸς πλησμονὴν τῆς σαρκός). This is the interpretation of many modern English versions as, for instance, the NRSV, "these have indeed an appearance of wisdom . . . but they are of no value in checking self-indulgence," or the NLT, "these rules may seem wise. . . . But they provide no help in conquering a person's evil desires" (see also KJV; NASB; RSV; NIV; NJB; NAB; CEB).[187]
3. The predicate is the final prepositional phrase (ἅτινά ἐστιν ... πρὸς πλησμονὴν τῆς σαρκός). This view is reflected in the NET translation, "Even though they have the appearance of wisdom . . . they in reality result in fleshly indulgence."[188]

The third view is the most compelling since λόγον μὲν ἔχοντα σοφίας ... οὐκ ἐν τιμῇ τινι, "having a reputation for wisdom . . . , but do not have any honor," forms a separate unit. It also reflects a parallel construction with the previous verse: "these things lead to corruption" (2:22) // "these things lead to the gratification of the flesh" (2:23). Paul is thus predicating the dangers of acceding to the demands of the rival teaching. The predicate, "leads to the gratification of the flesh" is held in abeyance to the end of the verse and rhetorically emphatic. One of the chief problems with the opposing teaching is that it is a manifestation of the realm of the flesh and not of Christ and the Spirit.

The intervening unit of thought has posed its own set of difficulties for interpreters. The complicating factor is that the particle μέν is usually answered by the conjunction δέ when it functions as a correlative (quite often, "on the one hand . . . on the other"; or "some . . . others"). The problem here is that there is no corresponding δέ. Consequently, some have seen μέν functioning as an emphatic ("indeed").[189] In this context, however, it is best to interpret it as a marker of contrast. In this instance, the "contrast can be supplied fr. the context, and therefore can be omitted as obvious: . . . *they have the reputation of being wise* (but are foolish)."[190] The negative οὐκ thus marks the contrasting member, "[the various rules] lack any honor." Hollenbach is correct in affirming that the particle μέν follows "immediately after the first word of the grammatical unit to which the μέν pertains."[191] Thus, it modifies λόγον and introduces a subordinate clause within the relative clause begun by ἅτινά ἐστιν.[192]

187 See also Moo, 239; Lightfoot, 205.

188 See also Sumney, 164; Hollenbach, "Col. II.23," 254; Lähnemann, *Kolosserbrief*, 146; Reicke, "Zum sprachlichen Verständnis," 39–53; Dibelius, 37; Bengel, 178.

189 So Lähnemann, *Kolosserbrief*, 147n148 ("Das hat zwar den Logos der Weisheit"); Reicke, "Zum sprachlichen Verständnis," 42–43, which he refers to as μέν *solitarium*.

190 BDAG, s.v. μέν 2.a.

191 Hollenbach, "Col. II.23," 254–61.

192 I follow Hollenbach's analysis in the main but disagree with his conclusion that because the clause λόγον μὲν ἔχοντα ... σώματος is a subordinate clause, it "rules out the possibility that μέν is functioning here as μέν ... δέ to indicate contrast" (Hollenbach, "Col. II.23," 259). By contending

The participial subordinate clause—λόγον μὲν ἔχοντα σοφίας—should be interpreted as concessive: "although [the regulations] have a reputation for wisdom." The participle is neuter plural (not masculine singular) and has the same referent as ἅτινα—all of the rules, regulations, and rituals advocated by the opponents. In this context, λόγος has the more narrow sense of "appearance"[193] (NIV; NRSV; ESV; NASB; NKJV; NET) or "reputation" (CSB). The latter is slightly more appropriate to the context. According to LSJ, λόγος can be used to convey the "*esteem, consideration, value* put on a person or thing,"[194] which provides a more apt contrast with the final clause, οὐκ ἐν τιμῇ τινι, "without any value."

Paul's claim that the practices and teaching of the philosophy had a reputation for wisdom forces us to ask about the nature of the wisdom giving it honor and status in the community. When we consider all of the disparate elements that comprised their system, it is doubtful that Paul was referring to the traditional Greek wisdom of one of the major philosophical schools of thought (Platonism, Stoicism, Cynicism, or any of the rest); nor was he speaking of traditional Jewish wisdom (as reflected in the wisdom literature: Proverbs, Ecclesiastes, Wisdom of Solomon, or Wisdom of Jesus ben Sirach). Rather, he was speaking of the esoteric and arcane wisdom that circulated in Jewish folk belief as well as in Greek and Roman folk belief. This wisdom was knowledge about the spiritual realm—the operations of spirits and how to thwart them through invocations and rituals. This was the wisdom of a shaman figure who served the community as a healer and exorcist. This practical knowledge is why a magician (γοής) could be referred to as a "wise man" (σοφιστής) in Greek literature.[195]

Within the Judaism of the Hellenistic and Roman era, there was a species of wisdom purportedly going back to Solomon that looked to this patriarch as the fountainhead of esoteric knowledge pertaining to dealing with evil spirits through ritual power and incantations.[196] The tradition has its roots in 1 Kgs 3:5–12 and 4:29–34, where Solomon requests wisdom from the Lord. The Wisdom of Solomon interprets this as, among other things, a knowledge of astral powers, the realm of spirits, and magic: "for it is he [God] who gave me unerring knowledge of what exists, to know the structure of the world and the activity of

that "the remaining οὐκ ἐν τιμῇ τινι must also, then, be a subordinate clause, subordinate to the preceding subordinate clause but possibly to the main clause," he makes the sentence unnecessarily complicated. He does not provide a compelling reason to deny that οὐκ is sufficient contextual grounds for marking the contrastive element (as BDAG notes). Also following Hollenbach is, e.g., Fowl, *Story of Christ*, 149.

193 BDAG, s.v. λόγος 1.a.β.

194 LSJ, s.v. λόγος I.4.

195 For the references, see Burkert, "ΓΟΗΣ," 55.

196 For additional texts and discussion of this theme, see Arnold, *Colossian Syncretism*, 201–4, and idem, "Sceva, Solomon, and Shamanism," 7–26. See also Torijano, *Solomon the Esoteric King*; Alexander, "Incantations and Books of Magic," 3.375–79 (= "Appendix: Solomon and Magic"); Hengel, *Judaism and Hellenism*, 1:130; see also 2:88n175–77; Preisendanz, "Salomon," 660–704; E. Lohse, "Σολομών," *TDNT* 7:462–63; Kraft, "Multiform Jewish Heritage," 196–97; Nilsson, "Religion in den griechischen Zauberpapyri," 64–65.

the elements [ἐνέργειαν στοιχείων] . . . the constellations of the stars . . . *the powers of spirits* [πνευμάτων βίας] . . . and the virtues of roots [δυνάμεις ῥιζῶν]" (Wis 7:17–20 NRSV [emphases mine]). The Solomonic magical tradition appears in the Great Paris Magical papyrus[197] as well as many other magical papyri and amulets.[198] The tradition of Solomon's great "wisdom" in dealing with evil spirits is perhaps best illustrated by Josephus:

> Now so great was the prudence and wisdom [σοφίαν] which God granted Solomon that he surpassed the ancients, and even the Egyptians, who are said to excel all men in understanding, were not only, when compared with him, a little inferior but proved to fall far short of the king in sagacity. . . . And God granted him knowledge of the art used against demons [τὴν κατὰ τῶν δαιμόνων τέχνην] for the benefit and healing of men. He also composed incantations [ἐπῳδάς] by which illnesses are relieved, and left behind forms of exorcisms [ἐξορκώσεω] with which those possessed by demons drive them out, never to return. And this kind of cure is of very great power among us to this day, for I have seen a certain Eleazar, a countryman of mine, in the presence of Vespasian, his sons, tribunes and a number of other soldiers, free men possessed by demons, and this was the manner of the cure. . . . And when this was done, the understanding and wisdom [σοφία] of Solomon were clearly revealed. (*Ant.* 8.41–49 LCL [Thackeray and Marcus])

The first-century Jewish exorcist Eleazar drew on this wisdom tradition to perform exorcisms. One could presume that this Eleazar had much in common with Luke's Sceva figure of Acts 19.

This arcane wisdom associated with Solomon can now be seen in a mid-first-century document from Qumran known as 11Q11 (11QApocryphal Psalms[a] or 11PsAp[a]). This five-column Hebrew text had an apotropaic function—that is, to drive away evil spirits, indicated in part by the words "exorcising" and "the demon" in the first column. In the beginning of column one, Solomon is mentioned, followed by the statement, "he will invoke," before it breaks away. The text goes on to speak of spirits and demons. The text has many structural and content similarities with the T. Sol. 18, a passage that has great significance for understanding the invocation of angels at Colossae. 4Q510 and 4Q511, also known as 4QSongs of the Sage, represent hymns that were probably recited to ward off the influence of demons. The identity of the sage in this text is likely Solomon. In the spirit of Ps 91, this song emphasizes trust in God as the principal means of protection. The text begins, "And I, the Sage, declare the grandeur of

197 See *PGM* IV.850–929. The charm is introduced as Solomonic magic (Σολομῶνος κατάπτωσις [line 850]; ἡ Σολομῶνος πραγματεία [line 853]) and has a parallel in T. Sol. 1.3 in lines 899ff.

198 See Alexander, "Incantations and Books of Magic," 376–77, and Preisendanz, "Salomon," 662–84.

his radiance in order to frighten and terr[ify] all the spirits of the ravaging angels and the bastard spirits, demons, Liliths, owls, and [jackals . . . ] and those who strike unexpectedly" (4Q510 1.4–6).

Finally, there are numerous Jewish, pagan, and Christian amulets that depict or mention Solomon. One example is a small limonite stone amulet that on one side depicts Solomon as a mystagogue, haloed, and holding a scroll.[199] A snake is depicted beside him, perhaps a symbol of the demonic over which Solomon has power. The inscription reads, "Help." On the reverse side is the inscription, "Ouriel, Sabao, help!" a clear invocation of two angels widely known in Judaism.

This Solomonic magical wisdom is epitomized, however, in the Testament of Solomon, where σοφία can be defined in terms of the ability to command and manipulate demons.[200] In the superscription at the head of the various versions of the Testament of Solomon, the king is given the epithet σοφός or σοφώτατος.[201] Thus, Solomon is represented as saying, "When I saw the Prince of Demons approaching, I glorified God and said, 'Blessed are you, Lord God Almighty, who has granted to your servant Solomon wisdom [σοφίαν], the attendant of your thrones, and who has placed in subjection all the power of the demons [πᾶσαν τὴν τῶν δαιμόνων δύναμιν]" (T. Sol. 3.5).

This arcane wisdom tradition within Judaism, often overlooked, best explains the reputation of wisdom possessed by the rival teacher at Colossae. He had significant influence on the community because of that reputation. The appropriation of this wisdom tradition at Colossae marks the first time that Christians adapted this tradition for their purposes, yet it becomes common in the amulets and Christian texts of ritual power.[202] The Christian preservation, use, and editing of the Testament of Solomon is an additional case in point of their interest in this tradition.

ἐν ἐθελοθρησκίᾳ καὶ ταπεινοφροσύνῃ καὶ ἀφειδίᾳ σώματος, "in freely chosen worship and asceticism and severe treatment of the body." These three expressions further specify some of the practices that contribute to the wisdom reputation of the rival teaching. The preposition ἐν here functions as a marker of specification and could be translated "consisting in."[203] The first of the three, ἐθελοθρησκία, "freely chosen worship," is a hapax legomenon and never appears in Greek literature prior to Colossians.[204] It is difficult to know with certainty if it is a catchword of the opponents or a polemical comment that Paul has

199 See the discussion of this amulet in Goodenough, *Symbols*, 2:232. See also C. Bonner, *Studies in Magical Amulets*, 310 (§339).

200 McCown, *Testament of Solomon*, 48, comments: "in the *Test* he is already the wise man and magician *par excellence*, the favorite of God, endowed by him with divine σοφία, which includes insight into the crafty wiles of his demonic captives."

201 Preisendanz, "Salomon," 662.

202 See, e.g., Meyer and Smith, 20.29–30 (= *PGM* P10.29–30); 21.9–10 (= *PGM* P17.9–10): "exorcism of Solomon against every unclean spirit."

203 BDAG, s.v. ἐν 12.

204 Hübner, 93.

constructed. The term is built on θρησκία, "religious observances,"[205] and not θρησκεία (Col 2:18), although the words are cognate. The ἐθελο- prefix denotes something that is "freely chosen" or "voluntary," as in ἐθελοδουλεία, "voluntary subjection" (one who voluntarily puts himself into slavery). The term may indicate that the leaders of the faction were creating a voluntary society of sorts within the church at Colossae. Voluntary societies of all kinds were common in Asia Minor. Walker-Ramisch notes, "As did the mystery cults, some associations prided themselves on closely guarded secret knowledge to which only the fully initiated members of the society could be privy. The secrecy was particularly characteristic of medical or healing societies."[206] Dibelius suggested this when he observed that the term probably finds its explanation in the nature of the mystery religions: "insofar as the mysteries do not cultivate their religion in national or municipal societies but in the voluntary union of a free association, they are really 'voluntary cults.'"[207] But it is highly unlikely that the teachers of the faction were attempting to create a rival community to the church. They were advocating a set of practices and rituals of power that they were attempting to foist upon the entire church. There is a certain irony in the characterization of their rituals and practices as "freely chosen," since they were "taking captive" (2:8), "judging" (2:16), and "condemning" (2:18) certain members of the Colossian community who were not following their practices. The term is most likely a catchword of the opponents that the factional leader may have brought with him from his own previous initiatory experience and cultic involvement. As such, for him, it is a positive term suggesting the alignment of some of the practices and experience with the local mysteries.

The second characteristic feature of the reputed wisdom of "the philosophy" is ταπεινοφροσύνη, "humility," which is best understood in this context as fasting and possibly extending to other ascetic practices and bodily deprivations. As noted in our discussion of the first time it was mentioned as a practice that the rival teacher commended (see the comments on 2:18), fasting was often seen as necessary preparation for the reception of a vision, both in Judaism and in paganism. It was also frequently a prerequisite for receiving an oracle. But fasting and the observance of other taboos were also essential for success in rituals of power, including expulsion of spirits and healing.

Closely related to fasting and taboos is the third feature Paul mentions—ἀφειδίᾳ σώματος, "severe treatment of the body." Most commentators interpret

---

205 LSJ, s.v. θρησκία. Since the term is built upon θρησκία and not σκία, it is inappropriate to speculate that the author has created a polemical term echoing σκία (Col 2:17) as, for instance, Hay, 111, does when he writes that "the Greek term ends in '-skia,' which suggests a punning allusion to the charge in verse 17 that the Error's regulations are mere 'shadow' or illusion" (similarly, Sumney, 165). Of course, this is also impossible if it is a catchword of the opponents.

206 Walker-Ramisch, "Voluntary Associations," 133.

207 Dibelius, "Isis Initiation," 89. Similarly, Bornkamm, "Heresy of Colossians," 134, notes that they "voluntarily accepted initiation into the mysteries of the στοιχεῖα."

this as an extreme asceticism, which accompanies the practices of the rival teaching at Colossae.[208] The term itself is not common in pre-Christian Greek literature, only occurring a handful of times (e.g., Lucian, *Athletics* 24, where it is used to describe the result of intensive training on an athlete preparing for boxing or for the pancratium so that they are "unsparing with their bodies" [τῶν σωμάτων ἀφειδεῖν] when they face tough competition or danger). The verb (φείδομαι, "spare") without the negative (ἀ-), however, is quite common and appears seven times in Paul's writings (e.g., Rom 11:21: "for if God did not spare [οὐκ ἐφείσατο] the natural branches, neither will he spare you [οὐδὲ σοῦ φείσεται]"). This would suggest that despite the fact that ἀφειδία is a hapax legomenon in Paul, it should not be interpreted as the fingerprint of a pseudepigrapher. In light of the rules and regulations mentioned in Col 2:16, 20, 21, and 22 that characterized what the rival teacher was pushing on the Colossians, it is best to interpret this "unsparing" treatment of the physical body as the various forms of self-denial that the teacher regarded as essential for the rituals to be effective. Fasting, the observance of an array of taboos, avoidance of sexual contact, and possibly other practices were being foisted upon the Colossian believers by the advocates of the philosophy.

οὐκ ἐν τιμῇ τινι, "[but] do not have any honor." Although the rival teaching, along with all of its attendant practices, has a reputation for wisdom, it lacks honor. This prepositional phrase thus functions as the contrasting member to the concessive clause beginning at v. 23a (ἅτινά ἐστιν λόγον μὲν ἔχοντα σοφίας . . . ). The negative οὐκ is sufficient to mark the contrast at a point where we would also normally expect to find the conjunction δέ.

Many interpreters and English versions, however, connect this phrase with the following prepositional phrase and render it as "they are of no value in stopping the indulgence of the flesh" (ESV; cf. NRSV; NASB; NIV; NLT). This view also understands πρός as "against" and interprets τιμή as "value."[209] Yet as I have argued above, it is best to see the final prepositional phrase as the predicate of ἅτινά ἐστιν, thus, "these things lead . . . to the indulgence of the flesh." The view also relies on the less common meaning of "against" for the preposition πρός.

MacDonald is right to point us to importance of "honor" in Mediterranean society.[210] This is particularly apt in a context where reputation is an explicit concern—the philosophy has a "reputation" (λόγον) for wisdom. In an honor-shame culture, the development and maintenance of a good reputation would have been considered highly important. Unlike cult groups in modern Western contexts that are often unconcerned about public perception, the rival teacher at Colossae and those associated with him would have been concerned about

---

208 So Hübner, 93; Lindemann, 51–52; Lohse, 126–27.

209 See, e.g., Moo, 241; Wilson, 231; Martin, 99; C. Moule, 108; Lightfoot, 206–8.

210 MacDonald, 123.

stature, reputation, and praise within the Christian community. That reputation may have been tied to the correspondence of its rituals and practices with those from other local religious traditions that had long been deemed honorable and wise.

One of the ways that the Colossian teacher may have been claiming honor is by touting the divine honor conferred upon him through visionary experience and the honor of having a visionary dream appearance from a divine being. Pausanias speaks of a temple of Asclepius just northeast of Delphi that no one may enter "except those whom Isis herself has honoured [προτιμήσασα] by inviting them in dreams" (Pausanias, *Descr.* 10.32.13). Pausanias goes on to observe that this practice was typical in western Asia Minor: "the same rule is observed in the cities above the Maeander by the gods of the lower world; for to all whom they wish to enter their shrines they send visions seen in dreams." Phrygian inscriptions speak of the underworld goddess Hekate honoring various people with visionary appearances.[211] This association of "honor" with visionary experience in the local religious traditions may suggest that the leader of the Colossian faction was claiming this kind of honor for the rituals and experience that he was advocating.

Many previous interpreters have rightly seen this connection between "honor" and the mystery cults, such as Schneider, who notes that "τιμή is probably a current term in the vocabulary of the mysteries to denote election and deification. The false teachers plainly espouse the view that from the cult of the στοιχεῖα and observance of the precepts imposed on them there develops for participants in the cult an honour which consists in the vision of God."[212] But this infers too much by reconstructing an entire "cult of the στοιχεῖα" at Colossae. It is more in line with the available evidence to suggest simply that the Colossian teacher was affirming there was honor in the visionary experience that he himself experienced and that he was advocating for the Colossians. This visionary experience set him apart from other individuals, bestowing him with special knowledge, especially for performing rituals of power for protection, healing, and thwarting the demonic.

It is also important to note that honor can also be seen in the context of Jewish folk belief and rituals of power. The Sepher ha-Razim contains a ritual in which the suppliant invokes angels and appeals to an angelic presence to grant the kind of favor that would result in honor before people:

> Say the name(s) of the angels in the presence of the moon and the stars and continue thus: I adjure you that you will give favor, kindness, and affection that

211 See *SEG* 40.1241; 43.943b. See additional texts and the discussion in Reitzenstein, *Mystery Religions*, 320–21.

212 J. Schneider, "τιμή," *TDNT* 8:177. See also Bornkamm, "Heresy of Colossians," 134.

> radiate from your countenance. (Give them to) me, N son of N, so that I will find favor, kindness, affection, and honor in the eyes of every man.[213]

Requests for honor through ritual invocation are attested in the Greek magical papyri (see *PGM* IV.1616, 1653–55, 2168–69, 2175).

In contrast to any honor that the purveyors of the philosophy may claim due to their vaulted visionary experiences, Paul states unequivocally that their teaching and practices are without honor. The presence of the indefinite pronoun τινι, here best interpreted as feminine modifying τιμῇ (and not as masculine, "to anyone"), stresses that the teaching is devoid of *any* honor.

[ἅτινά ἐστιν] . . . πρὸς πλησμονὴν τῆς σαρκός, "[these things] . . . amount to a gratification of the flesh." The predicate of ἅτινά ἐστιν is held in abeyance until this point and is completed with the final prepositional phrase. The various practices of the Colossian philosophy only lead to satisfying one's own carnal thoughts and desires and do not represent rituals and behaviors that are pleasing to God. As Paul said earlier, they are κατὰ τὰ στοιχεῖα τοῦ κόσμου and not κατὰ Χριστόν (2:8). Because they stem not from "above" (3:1–2) but from a mind influenced by the flesh (2:18), they only satisfy the flesh and not Christ. The construction ἔστιν + πρός is also found in John 11:4 where John reports Jesus as saying concerning Lazarus, "This illness does not lead to death [οὐκ ἔστιν πρὸς θάνατον]" (see also 1 John 5:16, 17). As Eadie notes, πρός after ἔστιν in these cases denotes result.[214]

The complexity of the syntax of this verse has led to a variety of alternate interpretations. The most common view (discussed above) connects this phrase with the immediately preceding prepositional phrase and renders it, "but they are of no value in stopping the indulgence of the flesh" (ESV). But this view does not recognize the ἔστιν + πρός construction, overlooks the use of τιμή as "honor" in this context, and misses seeing οὐκ ἐν τιμῇ τινι as the counterpart to the λόγον μὲν ἔχοντα σοφίας clause. The most significant problem, however, is that the resultant meaning does not fit the context well. These interpreters assume that one of the primary motivations of the teaching of the philosophy is to deal with the problem of conquering the flesh. Yet there is no indication elsewhere in the letter that the rival teachers are concerned about helping believers defeat the influence of the flesh and lead virtuous lives that are pleasing to God. Their concern is wrapped up in numinous spiritual experience. The observances, taboos, and various ritual practices are not for conquering the flesh but are preparations for visions.

Calvin, in line with many of the Greek and Latin fathers, interpreted σάρξ in this context in a positive sense and as coextensive with σῶμα. Thus he explains, "They gave no honour to the body for satisfying the flesh, that is, according to

213 Sepher ha-Razim 1.172–74.

214 Eadie, 203.

the measure of necessity."[215] Similarly, Melanchthon, depending on Jerome's opinion, explains, "Paul's command is that the body should be granted what is sufficient for it."[216] But this view is far afield from the polemical nature of this context. Although Paul can use σάρξ in a non-pejorative sense and does so in Colossians (e.g., 2:1, 5), throughout the polemical section of this letter he has used the term in its theological sense of the evil impulse in every individual that influences thought and action in ways that are displeasing to God (see 2:11, 13, 18). Thus, with most interpreters, it is best to understand it here in the Pauline moral sense.[217]

The noun πλησμονή, "gratification, satiety," is a hapax legomenon in the NT, although it occurs regularly throughout the LXX and would be familiar to its readers. It was often used for the kind of satisfaction experienced through eating or drinking one's fill (e.g., Ezek 39:19; Hag 1:6; see also Josephus, *Ant.* 11.34; Philo, *Contempl. Life* 37). Here Paul speaks of the appetite of the flesh as the controlling influence behind the Colossian philosophy. It is an instantiation of the warning that he gave to the Galatians when he wrote, "Walk by the Spirit, and you will not gratify the desires of the flesh" (Gal 5:16 NIV). The advocates of the philosophy have effectively "set their minds on the things of the flesh" (Rom 8:5) and thereby exhibit a hostility to God (Rom 8:7) and are not pleasing to God in what they are teaching (Rom 8:8). In Paul's view, the opponents have not removed the flesh (Col 2:11) and are living in accord with their old nature (Col 3:9); they are only satisfying the desires of their flesh. This sharp comment concludes Paul's explicit polemic directed at this rival teaching. He clearly does not evaluate it as a matter of indifference or as an acceptable but not preferred set of practices. He regards it as dangerous to the health of the church and as an expression of the evil impulse.

## *Explanation*

In this section of the letter, Paul warns the Colossian community about their potential victimization by a specific set of teachings and practices that have emerged from within the church that he regards as dangerous to their health and stability. Paul therefore urges them to resist this teaching and to do so based upon their relationship to the Lord Jesus Christ.

The dangerous teaching is not gnosis or a school philosophy (such as Cynicism, Platonism, or neo-Pythagoreanism). Neither is it a Christianized mystical form of Judaism or even the powerful influence from a nearby Jewish

---

215 Calvin, 344.

216 Melanchthon, 72.

217 So also Moo, 242n216; Sumney, 168; Martin, 99; et al. Contra Dunn, 197, who takes σάρξ as referring to the ethnic identification of the Colossian Jews. This, of course, overlooks that many of the Colossian believers were gentiles.

synagogue. Nor is it an emerging mystery cult baptized with a modicum of Christian thought and practices. Rather, the problem at hand reflects the inroads of folk belief and local traditional practices into the congregation at Colossae. More specifically, it appears that a shaman-like figure has surfaced within the church who claims to have estoteric wisdom and has spiritual knowledge for dealing with spirits and functioning as a healer within the community. This person may have come from a Jewish background and could have performed this function within the Jewish community before becoming a Christian. Such people were known to have ministered within Jewish communities and are represented by figures such as Eleazar in Josephus's *Antiquities* and Sceva in Acts 19. It is precisely in the realm of Jewish magic and folk belief where the greatest amount of syncretism is attested in ancient Judaism. What matters most to these practitioners is what works. What names of angels work with which maladies? What rituals of power are most effective? There is frequent borrowing from pagan magic and pagan religious traditions in Jewish folk belief.

This section consists of three distinct and pointed warnings to the Colossian believers. Each of the three warnings is followed by a brief description of some of the questionable and contested practices. This is then followed by a concise critique that flows from Paul's theological convictions rooted in the nature of new life in Christ. This section therefore functions as the heart of the polemic of the letter. It is where we find the most details about the nature of the competing teaching. It is also where we get a sense of how dangerous Paul perceives this teaching to be and a few reasons as to why he deems it problematic.

The foundational problem is that the Colossian believers are yielding to the beliefs and practices of the rival teacher ("Why do you comply with their dictates?"; 2:20). We do not know exactly how pervasive these teachings and practices have become in the Colossian church, but apparently some have accepted their premises and practices, and likely others are tempted to do so. The second two warnings provide some insight into the mode of the rival teacher's approach among the Colossian believers. He is "judging" and "condemning" them (2:16, 18). Someone could only do this if he was accorded a great deal of respect and regarded as a spiritual authority. This would fit with a shaman-like figure in the community. He is the one whom the community looks to for understanding spiritual matters, for healing and exorcism, and conceivably also for divinatory guidance. The rituals of power and invocations that he prescribes must be followed scrupulously both in the preparation and in execution. Failure to do so could invoke his ire and result in the ritual not working.

We learn a great deal about the nature of the competing teaching in Paul's descriptive comments (2:16, 18, 22–23). The two most unique and distinctive elements of the teaching are translated as "the worship of angels" and "entering what he has seen" (2:18). The first should be understood as rituals involving angels or even as invoking angels or calling upon angels. This defining characteristic of the factional teaching places it firmly in the context of Jewish folk belief. Calling upon angels for help and deliverance was fundamental to the practice of Jewish magic and shamanistic practice. This can be seen in Jewish amulets, Qumran exorcistic texts, the traditions contained in the Testament of Solomon, Sepher ha-Razim, the Hekhalot literature, and more. Knowing the right angel to invoke and performing associated rituals were important to its proper functioning. Jews frequently invoked angels for protection from evil spirits, for healing, for success in matters of daily life, and for a variety of other reasons.

The second unique and defining feature of the teaching, "entering what he has seen," is an abbreviated clause likely reflecting a key component of an initiation ritual ceremony. Paul has cited enough that the Colossians would have known precisely what he was referring to. It would have probably evoked in their minds the whole ritual initiation that the ringleader of the faction claimed as the basis for his esoteric spiritual knowledge. The precise term that is used here—ἐμβατεύω—can be seen in three inscriptions from the Apollo temple at Claros (just north of Ephesus) where it was used in a technical sense of the second, higher stage of initiation in the rites of Apollo at that sanctuary. It is likely that the primary teacher of the faction at Colossae had undergone a similar ritual of initiation with its attendant visionary experience, resulting in spiritual insight that he was using for the benefit of the community.

In his other descriptive comments, Paul notes that the teaching had a reputation for "wisdom" (2:23). Although this characterization could be applied to many different religious traditions and philosophical schools, it would also be consonant with the well-known Solomonic "wisdom" tradition pertaining to exorcism and the invocation of angels. "Freely chosen worship" (2:23) may have been a self-description that aligned the factional teaching at Colossae with similar teaching in voluntary cult associations. No doubt it would have enhanced the reputation of the group with the gentile members of the congregation. The group also characterized itself as having "honor" (2:23)—a significant claim in a Mediterranean honor-shame culture. But it may go deeper than that in alluding to the honor accorded to the primary teacher by a divine being, angel, or spirit who appeared to him through visionary experience.

Extreme asceticism and the observance of various kinds of taboos were also a foundational part of the practices of this group. Paul twice uses the term ταπεινοφροσύνη, "humility," to characterize the faction (2:18, 23). But in the context of their practice, this probably did not refer to an attitude of humility, especially since Paul accuses the leader of arrogance, but of fasting and other ascetic practices. Some of the practices were undoubtedly extreme since Paul could speak of them as "unsparing treatment of the body" (2:23). Apparently the opponents were imposing all kinds of rules and regulations upon the Colossians (2:20–22). Paul could summarize these as "commandments and teachings of men" (2:22). He alludes to these dictates and taboos by citing a series of their frequently uttered commands: "do not handle! do not taste! do not touch!" (2:21).

Some of these pertained to dietary restrictions and taboos ("in regard to food and drink"; 2:16). Others pertained to calendar observances ("in regard to the matter of a festival or new moon or Sabbath"; 2:16). Asceticism and the observance of taboos were prerequisite and essential in the performance of rituals of power. Calendar observances factored into these as well since some rituals were most effective on certain days, and one would not want to be displeasing to a god or any spiritual being by neglecting a prescribed observance.

The heart of Paul's critique of this group is essentially christological. They are not "holding tight to the head" (2:19). He takes up "head-body" imagery (2:17, 19), which he introduced in the hymn (1:18), not only to portray Christ in his position as the resurrected and exalted Lord but also as intimately connected to and involved with his people. He depicts Christ as directly supplying resources to his people to sustain them and to facilitate their growth and development. Paul also instructs his people—presumably providing them with positive grounding in "the faith" (1:23; 2:7), but also in warning them against unhealthy teachings and practices, such as they are currently facing. The key is that the Colossians cannot listen to just anyone who sets out to instruct them; they need to discern who is properly connected to the living Christ. Hay is thus correct in noting that the author's "fundamental objection is that it [the opposing teaching] does not focus on Christ."[218] By faulting the ringleader of the rival teaching for "not holding tight to the head," Paul implicitly commends the paramount importance for every Colossian believer to focus on Christ, an exhortation that he will take up in earnest in 3:1–4. Paul's critique thus reinforces what he has said in 2:9–15 regarding their new identity in Christ and their present connection to him who has "filled" them (2:10).

Paul specifically appeals to their identification with the death of Christ as a fundamental basis for resisting the dictates of the opponents (2:23). But whereas in 2:11–12 he associates dying with Christ to the circumcision Christ performs on his people—namely, dealing with the evil propensity in every individual ("the flesh")—here he links dying with Christ with dying to the influence of demonic spirits (2:20). This is vital to his polemic because Paul not only sees the opposing teacher as not properly connected to Christ, but he regards the teaching as ultimately inspired by demonic spirits (2:8), thus resulting in it becoming empty and deceitful. But the theme of the demonic is not only relevant to an understanding of the source of the rival teaching, but it is foundational to understanding why the teaching was gaining a foothold in the Colossian community in the first place.

Shamanism presupposes an animistic worldview. The cultural context of the Lycus Valley and western Asia Minor reveals a lively belief in spirits, angels, territorial gods and goddesses, curses, the evil eye, and a variety of other beliefs and practices that could be called animistic. Concern about evil spirits and the impact that they could have on one's family, livestock, crops, and community

218 Hay, 113.

was a live issue—not only among gentiles but among Jews as well. This is why a Jewish shaman like Sceva and his seven sons could have a prominent role as itinerant exorcists (Acts 19:13–14).

Therefore, by drawing out the implications of Christ's death to demonic spirits (2:20; see also 2:15), Paul not only removes the reason for resisting the practices of the philosophy but also deals with the reason they would be inclined to listen to a traditional community healer. Their union with Christ, which includes dying with Christ to the demonic powers, means that by understanding and appropriating their new identity in him, they have a full and adequate basis for battling demonic powers themselves. In other words, they do not need the various rituals of power along with the preparatory fasting, observances, and taboos; they have a direct and immediate relationship with Christ that renders these practices unnecessary. Because they are connected to the resurrected, living, and exalted "head," they share in Christ's power and authority over the realm of demonic forces (2:10).

Colossians does not reflect the kind of institutionalization of the church that we find in Ignatius and the postapostolic era. There is a strong emphasis in this section on the individual members of the body and their connection to Christ as head. It is through "the joints and ligaments"—the empowered members of the body—that the church is nourished and instructed (2:19). Paul makes no appeal to bishops, elders, overseers, or deacons in this context to remove the influence of this dangerous teaching. A time will come when a problem like this would be solved with a plea to "obey the bishop and the presbytery" (Ign. *Eph.* 20.2; see also *Trall.* 7.1–2). Although there were most probably leaders within the Colossian church, Paul's stress here is upon the responsibility of each individual member of the congregation to resist this rival teaching and to help others. There is an emphasis in this letter on the mutuality of the members of the body that is in continuity with the main letters of Paul. Ultimately, Paul asserts, "the body belongs to Christ" (2:17) and is directly answerable to him. But he has not left them as orphans. He is in direct connection with every member, resourcing and instructing them so that they, in turn, can minister to one another and the body can grow.

Yet the opponents are formidable and not to be underestimated. In the process of exposing and polemicizing against this faction known as "the philosophy," Paul unveils the true and ultimate opponents. These are the world, the flesh, and the devil. We have already discussed the prominence of the theme of the demonic that underlies the situation at Colossae and is mentioned explicitly in this passage as the στοιχεῖα, which I have translated "demonic spirits." These spirits belong to the κόσμος, "the world"—an expression that Paul uses coextensively with the Jewish notion of the present evil age. And the very last word of the passage is σάρξ, "the flesh" (2:23), which Paul contends is at the root of the rituals and practices of this dangerous teaching. This threefold nexus of evil influence is in continuity with the dangers Paul warns about in his main letters.

Finally, although it has often been overlooked, there is a futurist eschatological motivation that Paul provides to the Colossians for resisting the rival teaching. He asserts that some of the practices and observances are fleeting (they are a "shadow") compared to the marvels of the age to come (2:17). The overt emphasis in Colossians is widely recognized to be on realized eschatology, but future eschatology is not altogether absent (see also 3:4).

Because of the complexities of this passage and the abundance of expressions that can be variously interpreted, it may be helpful to conclude with an interpretive paraphrase of the text.

### *First Warning (2:8)*

*Warning:* In light of your new life in Christ, especially in view of your participation with Christ in his death and resurrection, do not permit yourselves to be judged by members of the group within the church calling themselves "the philosophy."

*Description:* Don't let their judgments affect you when you choose not to follow their demands when it comes to matters pertaining to food and drink or in matters regarding calendar observances such as festivals, new-moon celebrations, and Sabbath observances.

*Critique:* Their practices and observances are fleeting, ephemeral, and do not really matter. What matters far more is the age to come in Christ. Furthermore, you are all a part of the body of Christ and are accountable only to him and not to those who have set themselves up as your judges.

### *Second Warning (2:16–17)*

*Warning:* Do not allow yourselves to be condemned by these teachers within the church.

*Description:* Do not give in when they push you to practice their forms of extreme asceticism, including their insistence on fasting. Furthermore, do not agree to participate in their rituals of power that involve invoking and calling upon angels. Despite the fact that the lead teacher of this faction claims a vast and superior spiritual knowledge because of his experience of ritual initiation and visions of spiritual beings, do not listen to him, accede to his demands, or allow your heart to be condemned by him.

*Critique:* This person is driven by his arrogance and is controlled by his evil inclination. He is not basing his teaching and practices on a vital connection with Jesus Christ, who leads, nourishes, and instructs his church. Learn to draw on the other members of your community who live in a close relationship with Christ. This would include the leaders and teachers in your community. It is through them that you will be resourced, encouraged, and instructed. When all of the members of the body live in this mutual interchange, the church will grow and flourish, and God will be present, facilitating this growth.

### *Third Warning (2:18–19)*

*Warning:* Because you have participated with Christ in his death and now have the resources in Christ to resist demonic spirits, do not agree to follow the dictates of these new teachers.

*Description:* Don't allow yourselves to become convinced that you need to obey the various taboos that they have set up, whether they involve food and drink, ritual observances, or avoiding sexual contact—even if the rival teacher says they are essential to effect a healing, exorcism, or the breaking of a curse. Their practices have acquired a reputation for esoteric wisdom and are purported to be honorable. They claim that these rituals are freely chosen and have a long history of continuity with traditional religious practice. They argue that the extreme asceticism they practice, which amounts to an unsparing treatment of the body, is essential.

*Critique:* But their connection is actually worldly and is more closely aligned with the influence of demonic spirits. They are passed on through human commandments and teachings. In God's eyes, these practices are not honorable. They are manifestations of the evil inclination and lead only to satisfying the desires of the flesh.

# Focusing Thoughts and Affections on Christ (3:1–4)

## *Bibliography*

**Barram, M.** "Colossians 3:1–17," 188–90. **Beetham, C. A.** *Echoes of Scripture*, 219–30. **Bevere, A.** *Sharing in the Inheritance*. **Grässer, E.** "Kol 3,14," 139–68. **Hay, D.** *Glory at the Right Hand*. **Heil, J. P.** *Colossians*, 135–44. **Keener, C.** "Heavenly Mindedness," 175–90. **Kreitzer, L. J.** "Plutonium of Hierapolis," 381–93. **Levison, J. R.** "Apocalyptic Dimension," 93–108. **Lincoln, A. T.** *Paradise Now and Not Yet*. **Still, T.** "Eschatology in Colossians," 125–38. **Swart, G.** "Eschatological Vision," 169–77. **Wright, N. T.** *Resurrection of the Son of God*, 236–40.

## *Translation*

1 *Therefore if you were raised with Christ, seek the things above where Christ is, seated at the right hand of God.* 2 *Set your minds on the things above, not the things upon the earth.* 3 *For you died, and your life is hidden with Christ in God.* 4 *When Christ, your*[a] *life, is revealed, then you also will be revealed with him*[b] *in glory.*

## *Notes*

a. [3:4] As in three previous passages (1:7, 12; 2:13), the manuscript tradition is divided over whether the pronoun should be second-person plural (ὑμῶν) or first-person plural (ἡμῶν). In favor of ἡμῶν is Codex Vaticanus (B), the Majority Text, and some important versions (cop$^{sa}$; syr$^{p, h}$). The origin of this reading could be explained by a scribe changing the pronoun to the second person to bring it into conformity with the second-person verbs and pronouns used throughout this section (3:1a, b, 2a, 3, 4b). This reading has proven compelling to an array of modern interpreters[1] and has also appeared in a number of versions (e.g., NASB; RSV; ASV; NKJV; KJV). Nevertheless, the external evidence strongly favors the second-person plural (ὑμῶν). This reading has the support of 𝔓$^{46}$ and Codex Sinaiticus (א), as well as the Western text (including the Old Latin and the Vulgate) and other important Alexandrian witnesses. It is important to note that despite the critical apparatuses listing Codex Vaticanus (B) in support of ἡμῶν, it is not clear that B actually supports that reading. The main text of B reads ΗΖΩΗΜΩΝ (η ζωη μων), with neither vowel present. The vowel η was added as a superscript letter between and above the η and the μ. At issue is whether this was done by the original hand of B or by a corrector. At minimum, this casts doubt on the support of B for the first-person plural reading. As Moo has noted, it is also possible to attribute a scribal motivation for the alteration from the original second person to the first, i.e., "a scribe sought to 'universalize' the text."[2] Thus, it is best to agree with the editors of the UBS$^{5}$ and NA$^{28}$ and read ὑμῶν (CSB; CEB; ESV; NRSV; NIV; NLT; NET; NJB; NAB).[3]

b. [3:4] "With him" (σὺν αὐτῷ) is absent from Codex Alexandrinus.

---

1 E.g., Wilson, 240; Dunn, 202; Lohse, 134; Lightfoot, 210.

2 Moo, 251n20.

3 So also Metzger, *Textual Commentary*, 557; Foster, 315; Moo, 250n20; Sumney, 174; Barth and Blanke, 398; Pokorný, 162.

## *Form/Structure/Setting*

### *Form (and Literary Context)*

This brief section of four verses serves as a pivot point in the letter by recapitulating some of the main theological ideas presented in the first two chapters and by providing an introductory basis for the ethical teaching that will follow. Paul informed the Colossians at the outset of the letter that he had been praying that they would "walk in a manner worthy of the Lord, fully pleasing to him" (1:10 ESV). Paul now gives them more specific instruction on what he means by the prayer and by the subsequent exhortation he delivered to them, "as you received Christ Jesus the Lord, so walk in him" (2:6 ESV). Most of the second chapter makes it clear that they need to resist the admonitions, judgments, and teachings of "the philosophy" (2:6–23). But they must also align their lives with the lifestyle expectations of followers of Christ generally, especially as it pertains to eliminating sinful affections and behavior (3:5–11), appropriating Christian virtues (3:12–17), and ordering their lives according to the standards of a Christian household (3:18–4:1).

In 3:1–4, Paul reiterates a handful of key theological ideas that center on their union with Christ in his death and resurrection, new life in him, and their hope. The passage is framed by the preposition σύν, "with," forming an *inclusio*: they have been raised *with* Christ (συνηγέρθητε; 3:1a) and they will appear *with* him (σὺν αὐτῷ) in glory (3:4b). The emphasis on their relationship and solidarity with Christ is consistent with the repetition of σύν in the heart of the theological core of the letter: συνταφέντες (2:12), συνηγέρθητε (2:12), and συνεζωοποίησεν ὑμᾶς σὺν αὐτῷ (2:13).

He first reaffirms their identification with Christ in his resurrection by repeating the compound verb, συνηγέρθητε (2:12; 3:1). He then speaks of their identification with Jesus's death on the cross by baldly asserting that "you died" (3:3a). This draws on ἀπεθάνετε σὺν Χριστῷ, "you died with Christ" (2:20), as well as συνταφέντες αὐτῷ ἐν τῷ βαπτισμῷ, "you were buried with him in baptism" (2:12). The latter makes it clear that the Colossians have not experienced physical death but rather a real unity with Christ in his death, especially as expressed in their baptism. The resultant new life in Christ finds expression in the twice-mentioned ἡ ζωὴ ὑμῶν (3:3, 4a). This draws on Paul's earlier affirmation that God has "made you alive with Christ [συνεζωοποίησεν ὑμᾶς σὺν αὐτῷ]" (2:13). Finally, he reiterates their eschatological hope: Christ will return, and they will appear with him in glory (3:4). This repeats and elaborates on his early statement that Christ in them is the "hope of glory [ἡ ἐλπὶς τῆς δόξης]" (1:27). The nexus of these crucial truths serves as the foundation for how they can live out and actualize the instructions that Paul gives to them.

The emphasis on union with Christ, identification with his death, and the resultant newness of life are thoroughly Pauline and are prominent especially in Rom 6:1–14. The statement about co-resurrection in Colossians goes beyond what Paul has explicitly said in his earlier letters, but it is implicit in his thought about the meaning of living "in Christ" and in his statement about "newness of life" for believers that issues from the implications of Jesus's resurrection (Rom 6:4).

There has been debate about the source of some of the other statements in this section, especially the language of "above" (τὰ ἄνω; 3:2a), "hidden" (κέκρυπται; 3:3a), and "revealed" (φανερωθῇ, φανερωθήσεσθε; 3:4a, b). A previous generation of scholars has argued that this terminology was reflective of a Hellenistic or gnostic set of worldview assumptions.[4] More recent research has demonstrated that this language is part and parcel of Jewish apocalyptic thought, which the author shared with some of his readers.[5] This extends even to the language of spatial dualism, which is found in a variety of apocalyptic writings.[6] Both Bevere and Levison have placed a special emphasis on the Syriac Apocalypse of Baruch as an important source that reflects the "shared apocalyptic perspective" between that document and Col 3:1–4.[7] Both writers have stressed that the readers would already be familiar with the terminology and eschatological perspective reflected in 2 Baruch, but this assumes that the readers of Colossians would be predominantly Jewish (or gentile sympathizers well-versed in an apocalyptic worldview). Such an assumption is flawed. It is better to see the author as expressing his own convictions that reflect some of the convictions found in Jewish apocalypses and to acknowledge that there may be some degree of contextualization of the language to gentile readers in the Lycus Valley. Keener has demonstrated how this language would communicate to readers who are familiar with Platonism or Stoicism.[8] Yet the author of the letter may also be mindful of some of the prominent religious and worldview assumptions of people living in the Lycus Valley. This will be brought out in the *Comment* section below.

### *Structure*

This section is structured around the two parallel exhortations that form the heart of the passage:

τὰ ἄνω ζητεῖτε, "seek the things above" (3:1b)
τὰ ἄνω φρονεῖτε, "set your mind on the things above" (3:2a)

Every other clause modifies one of these two injunctions.

The initial clause, formally a first-class condition, functions as the basis for the first imperative. "If you were raised with Christ" (3:1a), which the Colossian

4 This found its most detailed expression in an important essay by E. Grässer, "Kol 3, 1–4," 139–68.

5 See Bevere, *Sharing in the Inheritance*, 148–81, and Levison, "Apocalyptic Dimension," 93–108.

6 See the texts cited in Bevere, *Sharing in the Inheritance*, 152.

7 Bevere, *Sharing in the Inheritance*, 150, argues that there is no evidence of a direct literary connection between the two.

8 Keener, "Heavenly Mindedness," 175–90.

believers indeed have experienced by virtue of their union with Christ (2:12), is the foundational truth that enables them to live in obedience to the command. The third clause—"where Christ is" (3:1c)—is a local clause explicating "the things above."

Following the second exhortation (τὰ ἄνω φρονεῖτε; 3:2a) is a parallel exhortation that is worded in the negative and lacks the verb (μὴ τὰ ἐπὶ τῆς γῆς; 3:2b), which is implicit from the previous clause. This, in turn, is followed by a series of three clauses (3:3–4) that provide an explanation for how the Colossians will be able to fulfill these instructions. The conjunction, γάρ (3:3a), is the formal marker that indicates that the clauses that follow establish this basis.

The first reason is rooted in their death with Christ and being hidden with him (3:3). The second reason has to do with their participation with Christ in his future coming (3:4). This is expressed with two coordinate clauses using a ὅταν . . . τότε, "when . . . then" construction, which is used in the Synoptic tradition and Paul of events associated with the return of Christ (e.g., Matt 25:31; Mark 13:14; Luke 21:20; see also 1 Cor 15:28; 1 Thess 5:3).

J. P. Heil has discerned an ABB'A' chiastic structure that spans 3:1–7.[9] The major problem with this is that it does not take into account the conjunction οὖν, "therefore," at 3:5, which functions to introduce a new hortatory section of the letter that is based on the theological summary of 3:1–4. Nearly every commentator rightly recognizes a break between 3:1–4 and 3:5–11.

### *Setting*

Having concluded his direct polemic against the teaching and practices of the opponents, Paul now transitions to the more general ethical teaching of the letter. Yet he has not lost sight of "the philosophy."[10] Eadie goes too far when he says that "the apostle leaves his scornful flagellation of the false teachers, and comes to a more congenial occupation."[11] What Paul says in this passage reminds the readers why they need to resist the leaders of the rival faction and to focus on Christ. The fact that he repeats the core theological truths of Col 2—dying and rising with Christ and new life in union with him, which formed the basis for denying the injunctions of the opponents—would naturally remind the Colossians to resist the dangers of "the philosophy." But there is nothing in Col 3:1–4 that appears to be tailored as a specific response to some feature of the factional teaching.

Wilson has noted that the passage reveals that the readers have "an inadequate appreciation of the significance of Christ and his work" and that they are

9 Heil, *Colossians*, 135–44.

10 So also, Pao, 204, who notes that it is "incorrect, however, to consider . . . that Paul does not have the false teachers in mind in the remaining sections."

11 Eadie, 207. Barth and Blanke, 391–92, likewise see Paul leaving behind the concerns of "the philosophy."

burdened with anxiety about the implications of what Christianity means for them in their environment, especially in view of their concerns about cosmic powers.[12] Seen in the context of the letter as a whole, this is true. The emphasis on co-resurrection and identification with the risen Christ who is at the right hand of the Father stresses the Colossians' access to the power and authority of Christ in their struggle with supernatural enemies. The fact that their lives are hidden with Christ in God assures them of their security and safety from the evil designs of hostile powers. Their future hope and their present access to that heavenly hope in the realm "above" address local concerns about the dangers and terrors of the world "below." So although the passage does not continue the polemic against the opponents, it does address some of the theological themes relevant to the readers that make them susceptible to falling prey to the teaching of "the philosophy."

This passage also has a transitional function that prepares the readers for the ethical teaching of the letter. New life in Christ that is rooted in the objective identification and participation of believers with Christ in his death and resurrection lays a strong foundation for the injunctions to put away sinful behavior, to appropriate Christian virtue, and to reorder their lives around the new values of what it means to live in a Christian household.

## *Comment*

**1** Εἰ οὖν συνηγέρθητε τῷ Χριστῷ, "Therefore, if you were raised with Christ." The conjunction οὖν, "therefore," functions as a discourse marker to indicate a major division in the letter. It retains some of its inferential force because the contents of 3:1–4 summarize many of the key theological themes of Col 1 and 2. Understanding the implications of their identification with Christ in his resurrection is not only crucial to the Colossians for resisting the teachings and practices of "the philosophy," but is also foundational to the process of eliminating sinful behavior and appropriating Christian virtues. Paul introduces the idea of being raised with Christ in 2:12 where it is included among a trio of σύν-compounds that unpack the meaning of relationship with Christ: συνταφέντες, συνηγέρθητε, συνεζῳοποίησεν—a co-burial, co-resurrection, and co-coming to life. He now reiterates this concept and uses it as the principal basis for the ethical section of the letter.

He uses a similar construction in 2:20 for dying with Christ: εἰ ἀπεθάνετε σὺν Χριστῷ, "if you died with Christ." Because of the reality of their experience of both dying and rising with Christ (2:12–13), the first-class conditional construction with εἰ + the indicative verb functions rhetorically to emphasize this new status on which their lives are now based. The burial with Christ is not mentioned here but is assumed as a prerequisite to co-resurrection.

12 Wilson, 235.

Some interpreters have argued that the language of resurrection applied to the present experience of believers goes beyond what the apostle Paul would have said since he maintained an eschatological "reservation" (*Vorbehalt*) by which he always stopped short of speaking of a present experience of resurrection.[13] One must remember, however, that the author is not speaking of any sort of actual resurrection (like the opponents in 2 Tim 2:18, "the resurrection has already happened"), but an identification with Christ in *his resurrection*. Recognizing the force of the σύν-compound is crucial in this regard. Still correctly notes, "Colossians employs resurrection language to speak of a believer's conversion to, union with, and transformation through Christ."[14] Furthermore, this passage maintains a future eschatology for believers that they have not already experienced ("you will be revealed with him in glory," 3:4). See the *Excursus*, "Participation in the Death and Resurrection of Christ as the Basis for a New Life—Now and in the Future."

τὰ ἄνω ζητεῖτε, "seek the things above." Paul urges the Colossians to orient their lives around values that are important to God and what he has revealed. This expression picks up and expresses in different terms the injunction of 2:6, "as you have received Christ Jesus the Lord, walk in him." The verb (ζητεῖτε) evokes a recollection of the teaching of Jesus when he calls his followers to "seek first [ζητεῖτε] the kingdom of God and his righteousness" (Matt 6:33).

Because of the language of "above" (ἄνω), some interpreters have suggested that the orientation of the author of Colossians has shifted from a Jewish temporal understanding to a Hellenistic spatial perspective ("above" and "below"), as seen, for instance in gnostic texts.[15] The Teachings of Silvanus (NHC VII 4) 103.1–9 says something similar to this passage:

> My son, do not allow your mind to stare downward, but rather let it look by means of the light at things above. For the light will always come from above. Even if it (the mind) is upon the earth, let it seek to pursue the things above.

The immediate context of this text, however, betrays substantial Christian influence and may very well have been influenced by Colossians.[16] And whereas this text reveals a hidden God from above (Teach. Silv. 116.12–15) and counsels readers to "prepare yourself to escape from the world rulers of darkness and of this kind of air which is full of powers" (117.14–16), Colossians speaks of a battle with spiritual powers in life here and now and a future revelation of Christ to his people (Col 3:4). "Above" in Col 3:1 should not be interpreted in a gnostic or

13 See, e.g., Lindemann, 53.
14 Still, "Eschatology in Colossians," 133.
15 See Grässer, "Kol 3, 1–4," 154–59.
16 A few lines later the author says, "strip off the old garment of fornication, and put on the garment which is clean and shining," which may draw on the language of Col 3:5, 8, 9, 10.

Platonic sense of an invisible and unknown world that is inaccessible until the day of death when the soul is freed from the body and begins a heavenly journey.

The language is probably derived from the OT where in the LXX, ἐν τῷ οὐρανῷ ἄνω, "in heaven above," is a common expression (see Exod 20:4; Deut 4:39; 5:8; 30:12; 1 Kgs 8:23; Ps 113:11). The God of the Bible is a heavenly God. He is "the LORD, the God of heaven" (Gen 24:7 ESV). He looks "down" from his "holy habitation, from heaven" (Deut 26:15). Thus, in the Johannine tradition, Jesus lifts his eyes above (ἄνω) to speak to his Father (John 11:41). Paul himself has used the language in his earlier writings to speak of "Jerusalem above" (ἄνω Ἰερουσαλήμ; Gal 4:26) and the "upward call of God in Christ Jesus" (τῆς ἄνω κλήσεως τοῦ θεοῦ ἐν Χριστῷ Ἰησου; Phil 3:14). The latter expression is conceptually close to our passage.

This injunction would have resonated with people who were well-versed in Platonic or Stoic philosophy, as Keener has demonstrated.[17] He shows how this was a familiar philosophical idiom for contemplating divine, heavenly reality. Yet, for the author of Colossians, "the object of heavenly contemplation is no transcendent abstraction . . . but Christ."[18] Those living in the Lycus Valley who heard this admonition ("seek the things above") would inevitably see a contrast with the prevailing Greek and local belief that the dead journeyed "below" to the underworld where they lived in a shadowy existence and not to somewhere "above." This belief was deeply entrenched in this region because Hierapolis was the location of a famed Plutonium—an entrance to the underworld. This Plutonium is mentioned by a number of ancient writers including Strabo, Dio Cassius, and Pliny the Elder.[19] Archaeological remains from Hierapolis also reveal that the myth of the abduction of Persephone by Hades to abscond with her to the underworld had a prominent place in this city. A large statue of Hades seated on a throne was found in the theater and is now displayed in the Hierapolis Museum. Also, an inscribed artistic depiction of the abduction scene was discovered on the second story of the theater. The scene portrays Hades embracing the kidnapped Persephone in his chariot pulled by four horses, while Athena and Aphrodite witness their departure to the underworld. Coinage from Hierapolis also depict this famous scene.[20] The association of Hierapolis with this legend originated and persisted because of the gateway to Hades (the Plutonium) located at the temple of Apollo in the city. The presence of the Plutonium at Hierapolis may also be the reason for the extensive necropolis there with over twelve hundred tombs. This is the largest ancient necropolis found anywhere in Anatolia. It served not only Hierapolis but those who would bring their dead from a distance to entomb them near this portal to the world below.

---

17 Keener, "Heavenly Mindedness," 175–90.

18 Keener, "Heavenly Mindedness," 183.

19 Strabo, *Geogr.* 13.4.14; Pliny the Elder, *Nat.* 2.208; Dio Cassius, *Hist. rom.* 68.27.3.

20 Head, *Greek Coins of Phrygia*, 233 (#38, plate XXIX, 12) and 242 (#87, plate XXX, 10).

Christ has not only been raised from the dead, but he is currently in heaven ("above"). He is not in the underworld, nor are his people destined to live a shadowy existence in the world below. Believers are already identified with Christ in his heavenly exaltation. They do not need to fear the underworld or the underworld gods and spirits, who were frequently invoked in curse rituals. They are joined with someone who is superior to these beings, exalted above them, functions as head over every "ruler and authority" (2:10), and is Lord over all (1:15–20).[21] Paul urges the Colossians now to orient their lives around the purposes, ethics, and priorities of their exalted Lord.

οὗ ὁ Χριστός ἐστιν ἐν δεξιᾷ τοῦ θεοῦ καθήμενος, "where Christ is, seated at the right hand of God." The resurrected Christ has been exalted and is currently in heaven ("above") and is at the right hand of the Father. The genitive singular relative pronoun (οὗ) has become an adverb of place, "where," and functions similar to ὅπου.[22]

Although it is possible to construe ἐστιν . . . καθήμενος as a periphrastic construction and see Paul as making one assertion, "where Christ is seated at the right hand of God" (CEB; NLT; NIV [1984]; NAB; KJV), it is better to interpret this as two assertions: (1) Christ has been exalted to heaven, and (2) he is seated at the right hand of the Father. Thus, most versions punctuate it with a comma following the copula, "where Christ is, seated at the right hand of God" (NIV [2011]; ESV; NRSV; RSV; CSB; NJB; NASB). The placement of the prepositional phrase between the copula and the participle suggests the distinction.[23]

The first assertion ("where Christ is") affirms Christ's exaltation; he now lives "above." He has been resurrected not to a transformed earthly life but to a heavenly existence. He is with the Father.

The second assertion, "seated at the right hand of God," echoes the language of Ps 110:1 (109:1 LXX).[24] In this royal psalm, "Melchizedek is viewed as the ideal model of what God's vicegerent over Jerusalem should look like, and thus Melchizedek provides the pattern for his future Davidic heir."[25] The psalm portrays a time when the Davidic king will have a universal reign. Many NT writers saw the beginning of the fulfillment of this psalm in Jesus, the son of David (see, e.g., Matt 22:44; Mark 12:36; Luke 20:42–43). In fact, D. Hay has

---

21 Kreitzer, "Plutonium of Hierapolis," 381–93, points to the relevance of the Plutonium for interpreting Eph 4:8–10. In his view, the comments about Christ's descent to the "lower parts" of the earth is a veiled reference to the Plutonium. Christ's ascent following the descent is "a powerful expression of his conquering the forces of death" (382). Although he is correct in pointing out the relevance of the Greek underworld tradition for reading Eph 4:8–10, his conclusion that Ephesians was written by an unnamed disciple of Paul from Colossae for the church at Hierapolis is not compelling.

22 Harris, 120; Campbell, 48. See BDAG, s.v. οὗ.

23 Pao, 211.

24 For a full discussion of this echo of the psalm in Colossians, see Beetham, *Echoes of Scripture*, 219–30.

25 Beetham, *Echoes of Scripture*, 223.

counted twenty-three quotations or allusions to Ps 110:1 in the NT, making it the most referenced OT text in the entire NT.[26] In the inaugurated eschatology of Colossians (and Paul), Jesus has risen to this exalted position and has begun his reign; thus, he is "head over every rule and authority" (2:10; see also Eph 1:21 where Jesus is "head over all things for the church"). Nevertheless, his reign has not been fully realized because he has not been fully revealed (Col 3:4). The enemies that Christ is contending with now are not human opponents but spiritual beings who are attempting to thwart God's redemptive mission and disrupt the life of the church. This includes the "demonic powers of the world," whom Paul sees as responsible for inspiring the deceptive and harmful teaching of "the philosophy" (2:8).

**2** τὰ ἄνω φρονεῖτε, μὴ τὰ ἐπὶ τῆς γῆς, "set your minds on the things above, not the things upon the earth." Paul repeats his initial admonition but varies the imperative verb from ζητεῖτε to φρονεῖτε. Some regard the latter verb as an intensification or stonger sense.[27] This may overstate the distinction since we find the two verbs appearing together in Wis 1:1 with φρονέω mentioned first: "think [φρονήσατε] of the Lord in goodness and seek [ζητήσατε] him with sincerity of heart" (NRSV). There is no lessening of emphasis in the second clause. It is better to describe the difference as one of nuance in meaning. The verb φρονέω implies a stronger emphasis on the thought process, which is consistent with its noun cognate φρήν, the "mind," as "the seat of the mental faculties, perception, thought."[28] Thus, for the verb, BDAG explains that it can mean, "develop an attitude based on careful thought."[29] Hence, Paul admonishes the Philippians to "have this attitude [φρονεῖτε] in yourselves which was also in Christ Jesus" (Phil 2:5 NASB) and then points to the life of Christ in his condescension and life of humble and sacrificial service. This verb was quite common in Paul, occurring some twenty-two times in his undisputed letters. The most common translation of the verb in Col 3:1 is "set your mind on" (ESV; NRSV; NIV; RSV; NASB; NKJV). One needs to be careful, however, not to make a firm distinction here between the mind and the emotions. The noun φρήν can also indicate "heart, as seat of the passions."[30] Some of the older versions effectively bring this aspect out in the translation "set your affection on" (KJV; Geneva; Bishops'; Tyndale). The distinction made by some scholars between the mind and emotions here is unjustified, as for instance, Moo's statement, "It may also be a further polemical dig at the false teachers, who are perhaps advocating a spiritual orientation that focused on the emotions at the expense of the mind."[31]

The key contrast that Paul makes here is between "the things above" and

---

26 Hay, *Glory at the Right Hand*, 228.

27 E.g., Wilson, 238.

28 LSJ, s.v. φρήν 3.

29 BDAG, s.v. φρονέω 3.

30 LSJ, s.v. φρήν 1.

31 Moo, 248 (who also cites Wright, 131, and Lincoln, *Paradise Now and Not Yet*, 125).

"the things upon the earth." Although the Colossians may infer a connection with "the things below" (the underworld and its gods and spirits), Paul wants them to consider what he regards as earthly things. This prepares the ground for what he will say in Col 3:5–11 about the need to put to death τὰ μέλη τὰ ἐπὶ τῆς γῆς, "the members, those upon the earth." In most instances, Paul speaks in positive terms about "the earth" (ἡ γῆ) as God's good creation. He cites, for instance, Ps 24:1 in 1 Cor 10:26: "The earth is the Lord's, and everything in it" (NIV). Yet, although Paul acknowledges that God created everything on the earth (Col 1:16), he also recognizes that there has been a rupture in his creation that needs reconciliation through the blood of the cross (Col 1:20). It is precisely the impact of that moral rupture that is in view here. It has had a negative impact on social relationships, human desires and emotions, and sexuality. Thus, he regards his opponents in Philippians as having their minds "set on earthly things" (οἱ τὰ ἐπίγεια φρονοῦντες; Phil 3:19). He can also speak of this bent toward evil as "the flesh" (Col 2:11, 13, 18, 23; see also, e.g., Gal 5:16, 17, 19, 24) and in its larger socially structured manifestation, "the world" (Col 2:8, 20; see also, e.g., 1 Cor 2:12; 3:19; Gal 4:9). Moo may be correct in asserting that "Paul is almost certainly suggesting that it is the false teachers who are occupied with 'earthly things,'"[32] but this is not explicit, and the implications of this passage reach far beyond the ideas and practices of the purveyors of "the philosophy." Paul is dealing here with the broader human tendency to engage in these sorts of unhealthy and unholy practices.

**3** ἀπεθάνετε γὰρ καὶ ἡ ζωὴ ὑμῶν κέκρυπται σὺν τῷ Χριστῷ ἐν τῷ θεῷ, "for you died and your life is hidden with Christ in God." Believers are able to orient their lives around Christ and his values because they have been joined with Christ in his death and in his resurrection life. This profound and real union with Christ is the basis for change. Death to the power of sin and a renewed life empowered by Christ will enable the Colossians to discard evil and unhealthy practices like old clothes and to appropriate virtues consistent with being chosen by God.

The statement, "for you died" (ἀπεθάνετε γάρ) is almost startling in its starkness. Although σὺν Χριστῷ, "with Christ," is implied, it is not explicitly stated. There is an emphasis here on the fundamental reality of the change that has taken place for believers with respect to their identity and former manner of life. Paul wants them to see a radical discontinuity between their preconversion experience and their present lives. For him it is tantamount to saying that a death has taken place. He has already described this in other terms equally as radical—as a transfer of dominions, from the realm of darkness to the kingdom of God's Son (Col 1:13). In the following section, Paul will prompt them to regard their pre-Christian existence as their "old" (παλαιός; 3:9) identity and experience. But the overriding thought here is that it is "dead." They are so closely joined to Christ that what can be affirmed as true for him is also true in their experience (2:12).

32 Moo, 248.

Because they are dead to their former life and its influences, Jesus is their Lord and not the power of sin or the demonic spirits of the world (2:20). They are no longer under a compulsion to follow their former ways and set of influences. This means that they can actualize their new identity into a new way of life, in which they can "walk in a manner worthy of the Lord" (1:10). They can render their old manner of life dead in practice (νεκρώσατε; 3:5). The key is that they need to "walk *in him*"—that is, in union with Christ, actively drawing on his resources as the living head who supplies every member of the body (2:19).

Paul explains it to the Corinthians in this way: "therefore, if anyone is in Christ, the new creation has come: The old has gone, the new is here!" (2 Cor 5:17 NIV; see also Rom 6:4; Gal 6:15). Although the old life may not feel dead and, in fact, may seem alive, powerful, and even overwhelming, there is truly a new reality that has come into existence through union with Christ. Realizing this new reality begins with reordering one's thinking in a comprehensive way.

Not only are believers joined to Christ in his death, but they participate with him in his resurrection life (2:12–13). Although, clearly, this is not fully realized, which Paul clarifies in 3:4, there is a real sense in which believers gain present benefits on the basis of their close association with Christ in his heavenly session. "Your life" (ἡ ζωὴ ὑμῶν) refers to their new post-conversion experience with Christ. Rather than simply stating, "you died *and rose*" with Christ to a new life, Paul highlights an aspect of their new life that stresses their security in Christ when he says, "your life is now hidden [κέκρυπται] with Christ in God." Some have suggested that the hiddenness stresses the secrecy or mysteriousness of this new life in a transcendent realm. Hay notes, "The full reality of the life they have is hidden for the moment, even to the believers themselves."[33] Similarly, Dunn comments that "it is not perceived by those who have not yet been let into the secret and so is meaningless or folly to them."[34] Bevere finds the source of the language in the notion of the hiddenness of wisdom in the heavenly realm, especially as seen in 2 Baruch.[35]

The best explanation is that the writer is here using language from Isaiah and the Psalms that expresses the safety and security of the people of God as they trust in him when they face their enemies. It is said regarding the servant of the Lord in Isa 49:2 that "in the shadow of his hand he hid me [ἔκρυψέν με]; he made me into a polished arrow and concealed me [ἐσκέπασέν με] in his quiver" (NIV). In Ps 27:5–6 (26:5–6 LXX), the psalmist extols the protective intervention of the Lord: "he hid [ἔκρυψεν] me in a tent in the day of troubles, he sheltered me in the secret spot of his tent; high on a rock he set me. And now, look, he set my head high against my enemies (NETS; see also Ps 32:7).

In a similar fashion, Ps 31:19–20 (30:20–21 LXX) declares: "O how abundant

---

33 Hay, 117.

34 Dunn, 207.

35 Bevere, *Sharing in the Inheritance*, 153–54.

is your goodness that you have laid up [ἔκρυψας] for those who fear you, and accomplished for those who take refuge in you, in the sight of everyone! In the shelter of your presence you hide them [κατακρύψεις αὐτοὺς ἐν ἀποκρύφῳ τοῦ προσώπου σου]" (NRSV). The relevance of this psalm to the Colossian situation is all the more striking because the opponents speak with "accusing tongues" (31:20 [30:21 LXX]) and "with pride and contempt they speak arrogantly against the righteous" (31:18 [30:19 LXX]; NIV). Paul repeatedly urges the Colossian believers to resist the arrogant judgments of the advocates of "the philosophy," which has no doubt hurt and bruised them.

Their lives are doubly secure because they are not only with Christ, but with Christ *in God*. The theme of concealment and protection is especially prominent in Ps 91. The psalmist writes that God "will cover you with his pinions, and under his wings you will find refuge" (Ps 91:4 ESV). In this place of refuge, God protects his people from "the terror of the night," "the arrow that flies by day," "the pestilence that stalks in the darkness," and "the destruction that wastes at noon day" (Ps 91:5–6 ESV). The LXX interprets some of these expressions to be spirit forces, especially as seen in the last phrase, δαιμόνιον μεσημβρινόν, "midday demon." The solution for the Colossians when they face demonic attack is not to invoke angels for protection and deliverance, but to call on their God. The psalmist reassures them that "when he calls to me, I will answer him; I will be with him in trouble; I will rescue him and honor him" (Ps 91:15 ESV). The means by which God will rescue them may be through the agency of angels, as the psalmist notes: "for he will command his angels concerning you" (Ps 91:11), but their focus is not to be on the angels but on God himself (see Ps 91:1–2). With the coming of Christ and the revelation of him as the Son of God, believers are to seek Christ and call on him since he is in God. It is quite possible that the words of Ps 91 were in Paul's mind as he wrote the letter to the Colossians.

**4** ὅταν ὁ Χριστὸς φανερωθῇ, ἡ ζωὴ ὑμῶν, "when Christ, your life, is revealed." Despite the strong emphasis in Colossians on identification with Christ in his resurrection and heavenly session, the author has not lost sight of a futurist eschatology. "When Christ is revealed" speaks of his coming parousia.[36] The anticipation of this future life with Christ in glory is consistent with the Pauline understanding of hope and serves as an additional motivating factor for the ethical admonitions that follow.

The use of φανερόω to refer to the second coming of Christ is nowhere else attested in Paul, but it is established in early Christian tradition (see 1 Pet 5:4; 1 John 2:28; 3:2). This verb is expressive of revelation and corresponds to ἀποκαλύπτω. As such, Paul may have chosen to use it here because of the stress on the hiddenness of believers with Christ in God (Col 3:4). There will come a time in the future when believers are no longer hidden but revealed in glory

36 So also Still, "Eschatology in Colossians," 129.

when Christ returns. Paul used the verb earlier to speak of the disclosure of the mystery that had been concealed for generations (1:26).

The surprising turn here is the interjection of ἡ ζωὴ ὑμῶν, "your life," as a descriptive expression of Christ. It states simply and in bold relief the overall theological message of the letter: "Christ is your life." There is an extraordinary emphasis on Christology in Colossians, but it is Christology that is ecclesiologically relevant. Union with Christ in his death, resurrection, heavenly enthronement, and now in future glory is the leitmotif of the letter. The main problem with the advocates of "the philosophy" is that they are not properly grounded in Christ (2:19). Participationist Christology is the lens by which our author views the Christian life. Paul expressed the same thought in different terms in Phil 1:21: "for to me, to live is Christ and to die is gain." To the Corinthians he speaks of the life of Jesus being revealed (φανερωθῇ) in our mortal bodies (2 Cor 4:11). And to the Galatians he declares, "I have been crucified with Christ. It is no longer I who live, but Christ who lives in me" (Gal 2:20 ESV). Paul's understanding of this union is consistent with what is expressed in Colossians.[37] It goes far beyond a symbolic representation that might suggest a mere affinity with Christ, or Christ as an illustrious exemplar. It extends rather to a real, spiritual, dynamic, and empowering present relationship built on a profound identification with the key salvation events of his death and resurrection.

τότε καὶ ὑμεῖς σὺν αὐτῷ φανερωθήσεσθε ἐν δόξῃ, "then you also will be revealed with him in glory." Paul assures the Colossians that a fixed time has been set in the future when Christ will return and believers will experience a glorious future with the Lord. This constitutes the future hope that he referred to in 1:27 when he spoke of "Christ in you, the hope of glory." Earlier in the Pauline corpus, he speaks of "the coming glory" that is to be revealed (Rom 8:18). At the time that the Savior returns, he will "transform the body of our humiliation that it may be conformed to the body of his glory" (Phil 3:20–21 NRSV).[38] Paul tells the Corinthians that "the trumpet will sound, and the dead will be raised imperishable, and we shall be changed" (1 Cor 15:52 ESV). This is the nature of the glory that awaits believers. Despite the strong emphasis on realized eschatology in Colossians, there is much that is yet to be fulfilled. The present is not the time of glory for the Colossians. They hope for this.

In contrast, Lindemann argues for discontinuity with the accepted Pauline letters (esp. 1 Thess 4:13–18 and 1 Cor 15), contending that in Col 3:4 future bodily resurrection is not in view, only a future glorification.[39] But this is an unwarranted distinction in a context where the language is overtly apocalyptic and accords well with what Paul has said previously. In the accepted Paulines,

---

37 Contra Grässer, "Kol 3, 1–4," 163–64.

38 Wright, *Resurrection*, 238, notes, "The 'appearing' of the Messiah and the 'appearing' of believers with him, is a fresh way of referring to the same event that Paul described in Philippians 3:20–21."

39 Lindemann, 54.

the glorification of the bodies of believers and participation with Christ in his glory at the return are elements of the same overall event.

## *Explanation*

In the Sermon on the Mount, Jesus called on his disciples to "seek first the kingdom of God and his righteousness" (Matt 6:33 ESV). In language reminiscent of that important injunction, Paul urges the Colossians to "seek the things above" and "set your mind on the things above" (Col 3:1–2). He wants them to focus their thoughts and affections on the meaning of their new life in Christ and the ethical values that characterize the reign of Christ.

Paul has just finished a firm and direct attack on a rival teaching at Colossae that he regards as dangerous to the well-being of this emerging and growing Christian congregation there (2:16–23). One of the main concerns that he has about the leader(s) of this factional group is that this person is not depending on the resurrected Lord and the accepted traditions associated with him (2:19; see also 2:8). As a basis for this polemic, Paul affirms to the Colossians the meaning and significance of their relationship to Christ: they have been buried with him in his death, they have been raised with him, and they now experience a new life in union with him (2:9–15). In this passage, he reaffirms these important themes and briefly elaborates on them. This establishes their importance as the basis for resisting the teaching of "the philosophy" and as the essential foundation for how they will be able to live out Jesus's call to righteousness by putting away sinful behavior (3:5–11), appropriating the virtues consistent with God's righteousness (3:12–17), and living in a transformed household that is now profoundly aligned with Christian values (3:18–4:1).

Although Paul has finished his direct polemic against the teachings and practices of the rival teachers, there are five theological emphases in this brief passage that are particularly relevant to the kinds of worries and concerns the Colossians faced that would have rendered them susceptible to what "the philosophy" had to offer.

(1) *Being Raised with Christ.* Paul introduces this section with an emphasis on their experience of co-resurrection with Christ (3:1a). This reaffirms what he has already said in 2:12. The purpose of the co-resurrection theme is not only to emphasize Jesus's power over death and his resultant new life (3:4a; cf. Rom 6:4) but his victory over the principalities, powers, and authorities (2:15). Since believers participate in Christ's resurrection through their union with him, they share in his power and authority over the demonic realm. This receives further emphasis in our passage by Paul's use of the language of Ps 110:1 to speak of Christ's enthronement at the right hand of God. The enemies who become the footstool for the Lord's feet are not the Romans or any other human opponents; they are the demonic powers whom Christ defeated by his death and resurrection. These are the real opponents who stand behind the political powers and

every form of teaching and practice that is counter to the redemptive purposes of God in Christ. Because of their identification with Christ, believers now have access to the power and authority of Christ over this realm (2:10).

(2) *Dying with Christ.* Paul also reiterates that the Colossians have died with Christ (3:3). He had earlier asserted that they have been buried with Christ (death with Christ is implicit) as represented in their baptism (2:12a). When he repeats this theme in 2:20, he explicitly brings out the relevance for the supernatural opponents: they have died with Christ "from the demonic spirits of the world" (2:20a). By participating in Christ's death, they not only experience deliverance from the power of sin as it comes to expression in the evil influence of the flesh (2:11b) but also deliverance from the realm of the demonic powers (1:13; 2:15). This is important for the Colossians to know because Paul regards the teaching of "the philosophy" as being ultimately derived from demonic influence (2:8). This declaration that the power of evil influence—whether felt through the flesh or from the demonic—is now broken because of the work of Christ helps prepare the way for the Colossians to rid themselves of unholy practices and to put on Christian virtues. As Barram notes, "Since believers have participated in Christ's resurrection, the behaviors that characterized their former lives must die even as they themselves have died."[40]

(3) *Christ is "above" and not "below."* People living in the Lycus Valley were accustomed to thinking of the dead as descending to the world below. The realm of Hades and of various underworld gods and spirits was "below." By contrast, Christ has been exalted "above" and sits at the Father's right hand. He is superior to all of the powers below. Believers are called to focus their thoughts and affections on heavenly matters. This includes living by God's standards of holiness and righteousness.

(4) *Believers are safe and secure.* Because Christians are "with Christ in God," they are safe because of their union with him (3:3). They are joined with a person who has defeated the power of sin, the flesh, death, and all supernatural opposition. "Hidden with Christ" is a way of expressing their security in him. As an eagle protects her young under her wings, so the Lord hides his children away under his protective care. The Lord is their shelter, rock, and refuge. This assurance alleviates fear.

(5) *The future of believers is determined and is glorious.* Paul repeats the eschatological hope of Christ's return (3:4; see 1:27), but emphasizes how this will result in a glorious future for believers. There is no political power, astral spirit, horoscope, or ritual curse that can alter the future that Christ has prepared for those who are in him. God is sovereign, and his purposes cannot be thwarted by any power.

The fear of demonic spirits, cosmic powers, and underworld spirits made the Colossians susceptible to the teachings, rituals, and practices of the shamanistic

40 Barram, "Colossians 3:1–17," 190.

teacher. In this passage—and throughout Colossians—Paul addresses these underlying concerns by exploring with them the full set of implications for what it means to be in a relationship with Jesus Christ. With regard to "the philosophy" at Colossae, it means that these believers do not need to accede to the impulse to rely on ritual power and traditions that come from local religions and spiritual practices. Because they are in Christ, they can draw deeply on what this means for their lives not only for resisting "the philosophy" but for cultivating the distinctively righteous and holy lifestyles that are necessary in being joined to a holy God.

# Dealing with the Sins of the Past (3:5–11)

## *Bibliography*

**Beetham, C. A.** *Echoes of Scripture*, 231–44. **Bevere, A.** *Sharing in the Inheritance*, 182–224. **Bock, D. L.** "'The New Man' as Community," 157–67. **Cadwallader, A.** "Honouring the Repairer of the Baths," 150–83. **Campbell, D. A.** "Scythian Perspective," 81–84. ———. "Unravelling Colossians 3.11b," 120–32. **Canavan, R.** *Clothing the Body*. **Charlesworth, J. H.** "Dualism in 1QS III–IV," 389–418. **Cohen, S. J. D.** *Beginnings of Jewishness*. **Dunbabin, K. M. D.** "*Baiarum Grata Voluptas*," 6–46. **Easton, B.** "New Testament Ethical Lists," 1–12. **Elliot, S.** *Cutting Too Close*, 159–229. **Ferguson, E.** *Baptism*. **Graillot, H.** *Cybele*, 287–319. **Hansen, B.** *"All of You Are One,"* 358–78. **Harper, K.** "Porneia," 363–83. **Harrisville, R. A.** "Concept of Newness," 69–79. **Heil, J. P.** *Colossians*. **Huffman, D. S.** *Prohibitions*. **Huttner, U.** *Early Christianity in the Lycus Valley*. **Kim, J. H.** *Clothing Imagery*. **Maier, H. O.** "Barbarians, Scythians and Imperial Iconography," 385–406. **Malherbe, A. J.** *Moral Exhortation*, 138–41. **Martin, T. W.** "Scythian Perspective in Col 3:11," 249–61. ———. "Scythian Perspective or Elusive Chiasm," 256–64. **Meeks, W.** "In One Body," 209–21. ———. "Moral Formation," 37–58. **Porter, S.** "P.Oxy. 744.4," 565–67. **Reitzenstein, R.** *Mystery Religions*, 338–51. **Rolle, R.** *World of the Scythians*. **Roller, S.** *God the Mother*. **Rosner, B.** *Greed as Idolatry*. **Shkul, M.** "New Identity," 267–87. **Smith, R. R. R.** "*Ethne* from the Sebasteion at Aphrodisias," 50–77. **Strelan, R.** "Languages of the Lycus Valley," 77–103. **Thomson, I. H.** *Chiasmus*. **Vögtle, A.** *Die Tugend- und Lasterkataloge*. **Walsh, B. J.**, and **S. C. Keesmaat.** *Colossians Remixed*. **Wibbing, S.** *Tugend- und Lasterkataloge*. **Yamauchi, E.** *Persia and the Bible*. ———. "Scythians," 13–18.

## *Translation*

[5]*Therefore, put to death [your*[a]*] earthly members: sexual immorality, impurity, inappropriate passion, evil desire, and greed, which is idolatry.* [6]*Because of these practices, the wrath of God is coming upon the sons of disobedience*[b]. [7]*Among them you also once walked when you lived in accordance with these vices.* [8]*But now you need to take off all these things: anger, wrath, malice, slander, and filthy talk from your mouths.* [9]*Don't lie*[c] *to one another since you have taken off the old self with its practices* [10]*and have put on the new self, which is being renewed in knowledge in accordance with the image of the one who created it,* [11]*where there is no*[d] *Greek or Jew, circumcision or uncircumcision, barbarian, Scythian, slave, or free. But Christ is all*[e] *and in all.*

## *Notes*

a. [3:5] The Majority text and a few other witnesses include ὑμῶν here. But this is likely a scribal addition to enhance clarity.

b. [3:6] The two earliest and most important witnesses of the text of Colossians, 𝔓[46] and B, both omit the phrase, ἐπὶ τοὺς υἱοὺς τῆς ἀπειθείας, "upon the sons of disobedience." The reading of Codex D is uncertain (it contains ἐπὶ τούς, but with insufficient space for the rest of the phrase; it appears that a corrector has written υἱοὺς τῆς ἀπειθείας in the margin in extremely small and faint script). A few other versions (syr^pal cop^sa eth^ro) and church fathers (e.g., Cyprian and Ambrosiaster) also omit the phrase. Since Eph 5:6 contains a nearly identical phrase, διὰ ταῦτα γὰρ ἔρχεται ἡ ὀργὴ τοῦ θεοῦ ἐπὶ τοὺς υἱοὺς τῆς ἀπειθείας, and it is not textually suspect, it is natural to assume a strong scribal motive of harmonization. Thus, many commentators[1] and many modern versions (e.g., ESV; RSV; NIV; NLT) conclude that the shorter reading is authentic. Although this is a very difficult issue (UBS⁵ supports the longer reading only with a "C" rating) and the evidence is almost evenly divided, this is one instance where it is best to part company with the united testimony of 𝔓⁴⁶ and B and support the Majority text and Western tradition (along with a number of other Alexandrian text witnesses). In addition to the geographical diversity of manuscripts supporting the inclusion are two internal arguments: (1) without the phrase, it is difficult to account for the subsequent ἐν οἷς, "among whom," at the beginning of 3:7; (2) similarly, the inclusion provides a more natural explanation for the presence of the καὶ ὑμεῖς, "you also," of 3:7 as referring to fellow gentiles immersed in a sinful pattern of life as those among whom the Colossians once walked prior to their conversion.[2] The evidence thus supports the inclusion of the phrase (see NRSV; KJV; NASB; CSB; CEB; Geneva; Tyndale).[3]

c. [3:9] While the vast majority of witnesses have the imperative (μὴ ψεύδεσθε), two codexes (A and G) have the infinitive (μὴ ψεύδεσθαι), and 𝔓⁴⁶ has the subjunctive (μὴ ψεύδησθε). Neither NA²⁸ nor UBS⁵ include these variants in their apparatuses. S. E. Porter, however, argues for the subjunctive as the original reading.[4] He adduces one example (*P.Oxy.* 744.4; 1st c. BC) to demonstrate that the use of the negated present subjunctive in a prohibition was not a "mistake" in Hellenistic Greek and suggests that the original reading with the subjunctive may have been eradicated by copyists attentive to Attic practice. Yet one example does not establish an "Attic practice." It is also unlikely that the original subjunctive would have been lost in the entirety of the manuscript tradition.

d. [3:11] A handful of manuscripts (D, F, G) add the phrase ἄρσεν καὶ θῆλυ, "male and female." This can easily be dismissed as assimilation to Gal 3:28.

e. [3:11] The Majority text along with B, D, Ψ, and many others include the neuter plural article τά before πάντα. But it is easier to explain the origin of the reading as a scribal insertion to bring it into conformity with τὰ πάντα (1:16, 17, 20). Codex Sinaiticus (א), along with A C 33 1241, omit the article. The difference in meaning is negligible.

## *Form/Structure/Setting*

### *Form (and Literary Context)*

The christological focus of Colossians continues in this section and concludes with the exclamation, "Christ is everything" (3:11). This corresponds with the assertion in the previous section that "Christ is your life" (3:4) and forms an *inclusio* encompassing the entirety of 3:1–11. The Colossian believers are thus called to orient the entirety of their lives around the risen Christ—his

1 See, e.g., Foster, 324; Beetham, *Echoes of Scripture*, 240n53; Pao, 221; Moo, 260; Lohse, 139n30; Lightfoot, 213.

2 For both arguments, see Metzger, *Textual Commentary*, 557.

3 So also Wilson, 246, 248; Sumney, 186; Leppä, *Making of Colossians*, 163; Dunn, 210; Lindemann, 55.

4 Porter, "P. Oxy. 744.4," 565–67.

kingdom, his priorities, and his ethics. The following two sections thus unfold specific ways that they should align themselves with his ethical mandates. The present section focuses on behaviors that they need to avoid or quit practicing (3:5–11). The following section (3:12–17) commends virtues and practices that they should develop.

The conjunction, οὖν ("therefore"), at 3:5 signals that this section is closely tied to the previous paragraph. The realization that the readers have died with Christ (3:3), that they have been raised with Christ (3:1), that their lives are secure in Christ (3:3), and that they have a glorious future in Christ (3:4) should both motivate and empower them to live according to Christ's ethical demands. This theological basis—especially participation in the death and resurrection of Christ as well as the new life in Christ—is something that Paul has developed in 2:9–15.

The metaphor of "putting to death" or "mortifying" (νεκρώσατε; 3:5) sinful behaviors should be seen as closely tied to the assertion that they have died with Christ (3:3; see also 2:12, 20). Similarly, "putting on the new" develops the notion that they have been raised with Christ (3:1; see also 2:12). Both of these ideas bear a close correspondence with Paul's appeal to the Romans to walk in newness of life based on their participation in Christ's death and resurrection (Rom 6:4).

# Excursus: Virtue and Vice Lists

One can find groupings of ethical values into lists of vices and virtues in many religious and philosophical traditions in the Greco-Roman world, including Persian religion. The history of religions school contended that the Colossian lists had their roots in Iranian concepts. E. Lohse, for instance, depends on R. Reitzenstein's contention that the Colossian virtue and vice lists were derived directly from Iranian anthropology, in which a person's members are his good or bad deeds and are enumerated according to a schema of fives.[5] But the theological framework and thought world behind these two traditions and their respective lists are profoundly different. The most that could be said is that there was an indirect influence through Persian influence on Judaism during the Second Temple period that is reflected in certain texts, such as 1QS 3.14–4.26. But even this much has been called into question by more recent scholarship.[6]

B. Easton contended that the background to the lists that we find in the NT can be traced directly to Stoicism.[7] He writes that "we may consequently take for granted that the New Testament lists of virtues have a direct relation to corresponding catalogs current among contemporary Stoic teachers."[8] Part of his argument was based on how many of the words that appear in the NT lists are not found in the Greek OT, but are discoverable in the Greek ethical literature of Stoicism and Hellenistic Judaism (influenced by Stoicism), such as in 3–4 Maccabees. But of the ten words that appear in the two lists of Col 3:5, 8, only two do not appear in the OT (πάθος and αἰσχρολογία).

Diogenes Laertius, for instance, cites the founder of Stoic philosophy, Zeno (333–264 BC), discoursing about a variety of vices that were unhealthy, including some that are mentioned by Paul: "desire [ἐπιθυμία] or craving is irrational appetency, and under it are ranged the following states: want, hatred, contentiousness, anger [ὀργή], love, wrath [θυμός], resentment" (Diogenes Laertius, *Lives* 7.113). Similar lists of vices (and virtures) appear in a variety of Stoic writers including Chrysippus, Andronicus, Epictetus, Musonius Rufus, Dio Chrysostom, and others. These lists were not comprehensive, nor were they organized into a heirarchy of values.

This literary form extended into the literature of Hellenistic Judaism. Philo spoke out against committing oneself to a lifestyle pursuit of pleasure and

---

5 Lohse, 137. See Reitzenstein, *Mystery Religions*, ch. 13 ("Virtues and Vices as Members"), 338–51.

6 See Yamauchi, *Persia and the Bible*, 458–66. Thus Bevere, *Sharing in the Inheritance*, 183, rightly concludes that "the connection between the vice and virtue lists in Colossians and Iranian mythology is remote at best."

7 Easton, "New Testament Ethical Lists," 1–12.

8 Easton, "New Testament Ethical Lists," 11.

warned how this lifestyle would result in becoming characterized by a range of over 150 different vices, concluding that it leads to a "mass of misery and misfortune without relief" (*Sacrifices* 5.32). Included in this list are some vices related to the passions, speech ethics, and greed (πλεονέκτης), but none having to do with sexual purity.

The Wisdom of Solomon (14:23–27) enumerates an extensive list of vices and concludes by attributing all evil to the worship of idols:

> For whether they kill children in their initiations, or celebrate secret mysteries, or hold frenzied revels with strange customs, they no longer keep either their lives or their marriages pure [καθαρούς], but they either treacherously kill one another, or grieve one another by adultery, and all is a raging riot of blood and murder, theft and deceit, corruption, faithlessness, tumult, perjury, confusion over what is good, forgetfulness of favors, defiling of souls, sexual perversion, disorder in marriages, adultery, and debauchery. For the worship of idols not to be named is the beginning and cause and end of every evil. (NRSV)

None of these vices, however, are mentioned in Colossians where Paul also takes idolatry in a metaphorical sense.

Some have seen the overall shape and content of the virtue and vice lists of Colossians as "particularly similar to the external shape of the paraenetic wisdom tradition of hellenistic Judaism (esp. Pseudo-Phocylides)."[9] There are a handful of similarities in Pseudo-Phocylides with the Colossian passage, as seen in the following lines:

> Do not tell lies, but always speak the truth. (line 7)

> Anger that steals over one causes destructive madness. (line 63)

> Rage is a desire, but wrath surpasses it. (line 64)

Nevertheless, the form of the sentences of Pseudo-Phocylides is more in the form of aphorisms made to appear as Greek hexametric poetry, whereas Colossians gives two simple lists of virtues and vices.

There is insufficient evidence to suggest that the author of Colossians was directly dependent on Stoic or Stoic-influenced sources. The content of the lists varies too greatly to find any form of direct lineage, and the virtue of self-sacrificial love is entirely absent in Stoicism. Bevere also notes that "the four cardinal virtues of Stoicism (σωφροσύνη, φρόνησις, δικαιοσύνη, ἀνδρεία) and their corresponding vices are not present in any of the New Testament catalogs."[10]

---

9 E.g., Pokorný, 164.

10 Bevere, *Sharing in the Inheritance*, 185.

More fundamentally, Paul's reasons for commending the specific ethical values he names differs considerably. Stoicism did not root its appeals for virtuous conduct in a new identity bestowed by the divine, nor did it speak of an eschatological judgment.

A much more promising framework for interpreting the background of the virtue and vice lists in Colossians (and elsewhere in the NT) is the Jewish "Two Ways" tradition echoing "the basic theme of the Holiness Code: 'You will be holy, for I the Lord am holy,' and perhaps more importantly, 'You shall not be like the Gentiles' (Lev 18:2–3; 19:21; 20:22–26)."[11] This tradition is deeply embedded in Second Temple Jewish tradition (such as passages in 1 and 2 Enoch; Testaments of the Twelve Patriarchs; Jubilees; and the Dead Sea Scrolls) and in early Christian texts (Barn 18–20 and Did. 1–6).

This "Two Ways" tradition is prominently expressed in the Community Rule of Qumran (1QS 3.14–4.26). This representative text expresses the heart of the moral struggle experienced by every member of the community.[12] Similar to Colossians, it represents the nature of the struggle in overtly spiritual (or cosmic) terms and speaks of the wrath of God coming upon those who are dominated by a lifestyle given over to the practice of the vices. The language and thought world of this tradition have many points of commonality with Colossians. There is an extensive list of vices enumerated:

> To the spirit of deceit belong greed, frailty of hands in the service of justice, irreverence, deceit, pride and haughtiness of heart, dishonesty, trickery, cruelty, much insincerity, impatience, much insanity, impudent enthusiasm, appalling acts performed in a lustful passion, filthy paths for indecent purposes, blasphemous tongue, blindness of eyes, hardness of hearing, stiffness of neck, hardness of heart in order to walk in all the paths of darkness and evil cunning. (1QS 4.9–11)

Not only are some of the same vices named in this passage—greed, lustful passion, and filthy paths for indecent purposes (references to sexual sins), and blasphemy—but the writer speaks of "the scorching wrath of God" coming upon those who walk in these ways (1QS 4.12). It is significant that both writers share the notion that the covenant people of God struggle against the influence of an evil dominion with a powerful, supernatural, spirit-wielding authority.[13] In the case of Qumran it is "Belial's dominion" (1QS 2.19), and in Colossians it is the "dominion of darkness" (Col 1:13). Both texts envision a range of evil

---

11 See Bevere, *Sharing in the Inheritance*, 190; see also, McKnight, 300–301.

12 Wibbing, *Tugend- und Lasterkataloge*, 45–61, who also sees this text as the most important background for the NT virtue and vice lists, provides a detailed study of the virtues and vices listed in this passage as well as a discussion of their OT background.

13 Charlesworth, "Dualism in 1QS III–IV," 398, rightly notes that this text does not teach a psychological dualism, "since for post-exilic Jews angels . . . were unquestionably cosmic beings and not merely psychological projections."

spirits exerting influence over the lives of God's people. However, Colossians stresses a decisive defeat of this realm by the work of Christ on the cross (2:15), a rescue and redemption of the new-covenant people from the realm of darkness (1:13–14), and a dying to the compelling nature of their influence (2:20). Furthermore, Colossians stops short of the extreme dualism of the Community Rule that envisions two spirits struggling for influence in the soul of every individual ("until now the spirits of truth and injustice feud in the heart of man"; 1QS 4.24) and claims that God apportions two spirits in varying measure in each person's life.[14] An additional decisive difference in Colossians is the notion that every individual within the new community (which includes an abundance of gentiles) has been fundamentally changed by a creative act of God who clothes them with an entirely new identity and the divine resources that go along with it (Col 3:9–11).

The immediate antecedent for Paul's virtue and vice lists in Colossians is found in his letter to the Galatians (5:17–24). In that text, Paul frames the vices list as "the deeds of the flesh" (probably to be understood as the *yetzer hara*) and the virtues list as "the fruit of the Spirit." Although he does not explicitly attribute the vices to the flesh in Colossians, the role of the flesh in prompting evil is significant in the preceding theological foundation he lays (2:11, 13, 18, 23). But Paul also provides vice lists in his other letters, including Rom 1:29–31; 13:13; 1 Cor 5:10–11; 6:9–10; 2 Cor 12:20–21; see also Eph 4:31; 5:3–5; 1 Tim 1:9–10; 2 Tim 3:2–5; and Titus 3:3.

Virtue and vice lists were not a fixed literary form in antiquity. There was substantial variety in how ancient writers expressed lists of deeds that were deemed unhealthy and harmful and those that should be commended for the good of each community.[15] Similarly, there were a variety of motivations for living in accord with certain virtues and avoiding particular vices. Paul has most in common with Jewish moral exhortation and especially the "Two Ways" tradition of Qumran and other Second Temple Jewish texts.

---

14 This determinism is reflected most strongly in 4Q186, an astrological text that speaks of how the stars (or zodiacal spirits) are responsible for which parts of each individual are apportioned into the realms of darkness and light.

15 Malherbe, *Moral Exhortation*, 138, notes that not only are the forms of the lists varied, but the functions that they perform are similarly diverse.

### *Structure*

This section consists of two sentences governed respectively by two aorist imperative verbs: νεκρώσατε (3:5) and ἀπόθεσθε (3:8). Each section is evenly balanced by a list of five vices that the Colossians are implored to eliminate from their lives. The first group of five (3:5) are primarily related to the importance of developing sexual purity in their thoughts and in their behavior. The final term in the group of five extends to the eradication of forms of greed that pertain not only to their sexual desires but also more generally to wealth and material gain. The second group of five (3:8) are vices that pertain to social relationships within the community. If these practices were left unchecked, they would destroy the cohesiveness and unity of this fledgling Christian community.

There is a sixth vice that Paul names in the second group, lying, but he does so by altering the grammatical form from a noun to a present imperative with a negative: μὴ ψεύδεσθε (3:9). Semantically, this vice is parallel to the preceding five. The change of form, however, preserves the symmetry to the preceding group of five.

Paul gives additional theological reasons for eliminating these vices at the conclusion of each list. He underlines the severity of the first list of vices by asserting that these practices result in the manifestation of God's wrath at the end of time (3:6–7). For the second list of vices, he appeals to their new identity in union with Christ, stressing the implications of their participation in the death and resurrection of Christ (3:9–10). He does so with two aorist participles (ἀπεκδυσάμενοι and ἐνδυσάμενοι) that form the basis for the action of taking off these vices. Grammatically, they ground the previous imperative (ἀπόθεσθε; 3:8), but semantically their force extends also to the leading imperative of the passage (νεκρώσατε; 3:5). They also form a transitional basis in providing a theological ground for the next section—putting on virtues (3:12–17).

Paul modifies "the new self" with an adjectival participle expressing that the new self they have put on is itself in the process of renewal (3:10). The Colossians have entered an altogether new existence that involves participation in a new community where there are no racial, cultural, religious, or economic distinctions among the members (3:11).

He concludes the section with the resounding acclamation that "Christ is everything" to this new community (3:11). Christ also indwells every member of the community regardless of their background. The adversative conjunction ἀλλά in Col 3:11 suggests that there is a sharp contrast between the new community and their former communal ties and forms of solidarity.

Sumney has argued that there is a micro-chiastic structure in 3:7: (a) among whom (b) you walked (c) then (c′) when (b′) you lived (a′) among them. This is plausible and stresses the character of the readers' former lives.[16] Once again, Heil has tried to make the case for a larger-scale chiastic structure that spans

16 Sumney, 193.

3:1–7: (a) 3:1–2 (b) 3:3 (b′) 3:4 (a′) 3:5–7.[17] But his proposal ignores the symmetry between 3:5–7 and 3:8–10.

## *Setting*

The kind of vices that are enumerated in this section would be those that gentile converts would struggle with after becoming Christians. This is particularly the case with the first grouping (3:5) that stresses sinful sexual behaviors and thoughts. This is another line of evidence suggestive of a predominantly gentile-Christian readership of this letter. It may have come across as particularly jarring to these gentile-Christian readers, who have struggled with the extent to which they were to renounce their former idolatries, to discover that sexual and monetary greed was tantamount to idolatry.

There is nothing in this section that is explicitly tied to "the philosophy." In other words, there is no evidence that the opponents were antinomians throwing off the sexual mores of the Christian community. Nevertheless, some of the vices may have at least an indirect connection to the factional teachers and the social impact they were having on the community. When we consider Paul's warnings, "let no one judge you" (2:16), "let no one condemn you" (2:18), and when he asks, "Why do you comply with their dictates?" (2:20) and then observes, "this person is puffed up in vanity by his fleshly mind" (2:19), it is reasonable to infer the relevance of 3:9–10. Their judgments amounted to "slander" and may very well have been delivered with "anger" and "wrath." And Paul has previously warned the Colossians that the opponents' teaching is "empty deceit"—which amounts to "lying" (3:9). Of course, the naming of these various vices and the appeal to eradicate them would apply to every way they may be manifested in the community life—not just with reference to the impact of the dangerous teaching.

The theological affirmations of this section would do double duty. Although they are principally given to ground the ethical and Christian behavior of the Colossian believers, they would also reinforce the earlier theological teaching of the letter and thus prompt the Colossians to grow deeper in their understanding of their relationship to Christ and thereby further enable them to resist the dictates and demands of the opposing teachers.

## ***Comment***

**5** Νεκρώσατε οὖν τὰ μέλη τὰ ἐπὶ τῆς γῆς, "Therefore, put to death your earthly members." Based upon their participation in Christ, Paul appeals to the Colossians to eradicate sinful attitudes and behaviors in their lives. The conjunction οὖν roots the imperative in the indicative expressions of 3:1–4. In particular, he calls them to draw on the full significance of their new life in Christ,

17 Heil, *Colossians*, 135–44.

especially their participation in his death and resurrection. The co-resurrection with Christ, who is sitting at the right hand of God, is "an implied assurance of power"[18] to fulfill the ethical demands that Paul will delineate. Paul also grounds their transformation process in the eschatological hope—not only in the fact that Jesus will return, but that they can anticipate a glorious future together with him. It is inconsistent with this future existence in glory to continue to allow sinful thoughts and actions to have a part in daily life here and now.

The metaphor of putting to death—νεκρώσατε—is a strong way of expressing the seriousness of effectively dealing with the problem of persistent sins. The verb only appears two other times in the NT, and both to refer to Abraham's body at the time God made the promise to him that he would become a father in his advanced years—that is, his body was "as good as dead" (Rom 4:19; Heb 11:12). The aging process had rendered his body impotent. But the metaphor of killing vice, or sins, is expressed in other terms in Romans. Paul says, "If you live according to the flesh, you will die; but if by the Spirit you put to death [θανατοῦτε] the deeds of the body, you will live" (Rom 8:13 NRSV). This is an extension of his previous comments when he implored the Romans, "You also must consider yourselves dead to sin and alive to God in Christ Jesus. Let not sin therefore reign in your mortal body, to make you obey its passions. Do not present your members to sin as instruments for unrighteousness, but present yourselves to God as those who have been brought from death to life, and your members to God as instruments for righteousness" (Rom 6:11–13 ESV). By participating with Christ in his death as represented in baptism, believers have "crucified the flesh with its passions and desires" (Gal 5:24). The crucifixion of the flesh now needs to be actualized in their daily lives. This notion of mortifying sinful passions and desires is thoroughly Pauline. Although Colossians does not explicitly mention the role of the Spirit in this process, it is an implicit aspect of the new life stemming from the co-resurrection.

It is overinterpreting the tense to assert that "the verb is in the aorist tense; decisive and critical action is in view."[19] The decisive and critical action comes from the metaphor of killing, not the aorist tense. Neither would it be correct to interpret νεκρώσατε as a one-time event, such as a crisis moment of full surrender. As in the present tense of θανατοῦτε in Rom 8:13, the action of mortifying is ongoing. It is best to see no emphasis in the aorist tense of the imperative here but to understand it as simply commanding the action.

Rather than specifying "the flesh" as the object of killing, the author identifies τὰ μέλη τὰ ἐπὶ τῆς γῆς, literally, "the members, those upon the earth." Although Paul frequently used μέλη to refer to people as the variously gifted members of the body of Christ (e.g., Rom 12:5; 1 Cor 12:12, 18, 20, 22, 25–27; Eph 4:25; 5:30), he could employ the same term to speak of an individual's body

18 H. Moule, 120.
19 H. Moule, 120.

parts complicit in sin, such as making the members of one's body the "members of a prostitute" (πόρνης μέλη; 1 Cor 6:15). In Rom 6, he portrays the parts of the body as instruments that align with the will of the one who controls them, and thus as "slaves" of sin or righteousness. Thus, he implores them to "present your members to God as instruments of rightesousness" (Rom 6:13 NRSV) and to "present your members [τὰ μέλη ὑμῶν] as slaves to righteousness for sanctification" (Rom 6:19 NRSV). Putting to death the earthly members means that they will "not present" their "members to sin as instruments for unrighteousness" (Rom 6:13 ESV) nor will they present their members "as slaves to impurity and to lawlessness leading to more lawlessness" (Rom 6:19 ESV). The identification of the body parts with vices in which evil exerts its influence on the individual "members" is found in Judaism (see, e.g., 2 Bar. 49.3: "Will they put on the chained members which are in evil and by which evils are accomplished?").[20] This concept is found on the lips of Jesus in Matthew's Sermon on the Mount when Jesus advises tearing out one's eye or cutting off a hand as a remedy to the sinful practices that those members of the body commit (Matt 5:29–30). In a similar vein, James speaks of sinful passions "that wage war in your members" (Jas 4:1 NASB). In our verse, these members are characterized as "belonging to the earth" (Col 3:5), which takes us back to 3:2 and the contrast between focusing on the things above or the "things upon the earth."

Paul then identifies five vices that need to be exposed as sin and eradicated from the lives of the Colossian believers. It is doubtful that these five are chosen because "the philosophy" has stimulated their practice or has failed to deal with them. These are standard lifestyle concerns, especially for gentiles, in the early stages of the Christian growth. The first four all have to do with sexual purity.[21]

[νεκρώσατε] . . . πορνείαν ἀκαθαρσίαν, "[put to death] sexual immorality, impurity." The five accusative nouns are in apposition to τὰ μέλη, "the members," and thus explain the identity of the members and that they function as the direct objects of "put to death."[22] The noun πορνεία, "sexual immorality," appears ten times in Paul and functions as a broad term to cover any type of sexual activity deviating from the design that God has established in creation.[23] In the Genesis account, God created the original couple as "male and female" (ἄρσεν καὶ θῆλυ, Gen 1:27) and instituted marriage as the context for sexual relations: "a man leaves his father and mother and is united to his wife, and they become one flesh" (Gen 2:24 NIV). The unfolding of the biblical narrative assumes this as the standard, as does the entirety of Jewish tradition.

20 See R. Dabelstein, "νεκρόω," *EDNT* 2:461.

21 So also Dunn, 213–15; Moo, 256–58. Contra Hay, 124, who notes that "the vices identified by 'impurity,' 'passion,' and 'evil desire' would easily suggest sexual associations, but there seems no strong reason to limit their sense here in that fashion."

22 Contra Lightfoot, 211, who posited an implicit verb at the head of the list, such as ἀπόθεσθε, "take off."

23 See Harper, "*Porneia*," 363–83.

Thus, sexual contact outside of marriage is prohibited, especially as seen in the injunctions against adultery (Exod 20:14; Lev 20:10; Deut 5:18). Since marriage symbolized the intimate connection between God and his people, the unfaithfulness of Israel when they pursued other gods was often classified as a spiritual adultery (see, e.g., Jer 3:1–25; 5:7; Ezek 16:38; Hos 4:13–14). Wisdom 14:12 thus states, "The idea of making idols was the beginning of fornication [πορνείας]" (NRSV).

Exhortations to avoid various forms of πορνεία are found in many Second Temple Jewish texts, but it is a major theme of the Testaments of the Twelve Patriarchs. Harper observes that in the Testaments, "πορνεία has become an inclusive sexual category denoting illicit sexual activity, including incest, prostitution, exogamy, and unchastity."[24] Thus, T. Jud. 18.2 warns, "Therefore, guard yourself, my children from πορνεία," and T. Sim. 5.3 counsels, "Guard yourselves from sexual promiscuity [τοῦ μὴ πορνεύειν] because fornication [πορνεία] is the mother of all wicked deeds; it separates from God and leads men to Beliar." Building on the biblical account of Reuben's sin with Bilhah (Gen 35:22), the Testament of Reuben elaborates in detail on the dangers of sexual immorality. The Damascus Document regards fornication as the first of three nets that Belial uses to snare Israel (CD 4.15–17).

Jesus elevated sexual immorality to a matter that goes beyond the individual acts to one's thought life and affections. He declared that "out of the heart come evil thoughts—murder, adultery [μοιχεῖαι], sexual immorality [πορνεῖαι], theft, false testimony, slander" (Matt 15:19 NIV). And, more pointedly, he warned in the Sermon on the Mount that fantasizing about a sexual act with another person is tantamount to committing it: "I say to you that everyone who looks at a woman with lust has already committed adultery with her in his heart" (Matt 5:28 NRSV; see T. Reu. 4.8 for a description of Joseph not only resisting Potiphar's wife but "purg[ing] his thoughts from all fornication [πορνείας]."). Behind this warning is the biblical assumption that God is aware of one's thoughts: "you have set our iniquities before you, our secret sins in the light of your presence" (Ps 90:8 NIV; see also Ps 44:21; Matt 6:6, 18). In the first century BC, a similar warning can be found in Jewish wisdom literature when Sirach warned against "looking at a prostitute," against "gazing at another man's wife," and against "meddling with his servant girl" (Sir 41:20–22 NRSV).[25]

Warning gentile Christians throughout the Mediterranean world to avoid πορνεία was one of the primary concerns of the so-called Jerusalem Council (Acts 15:20, 29; 21:25). This was likely due to the Jewish perception of rampant sexual immorality among the gentiles. Although Stoicism did maintain a sexual ethic, the term πορνεία never appears in writers such as Plutarch and Epictetus.[26]

---

24 Harper, "*Porneia*," 372. See also Hauck and Schulz, "πόρνη, κτλ," *TDNT* 6:587.

25 See the discussion in Harper, "*Porneia*," 371–72.

26 M. Silva, "πορνεία," *NIDNTTE* 4:110.

In general, sexual contact outside of marriage was not only tolerated but seen as acceptable in Roman society except with a married woman, where μοιχεία, "adultery," was viewed as a crime against another man.[27] Paul's instructions here would have forced them to consider their participation even in some of the pleasures of life that they took for granted, such as going to the baths, where there would have been a constant temptation to fall in this regard. There is a reason why Aphrodite/Venus was most frequently found at the bath. K. Dunbabin explains that Venus "signifies just that world of beauty and luxury which lay at the heart of the bath-aesthetic. Straightforward erotic appeal—the baths as a potential centre for amorous encounters—doubtless played a part in this aesthetic."[28]

The apostle Paul had much to say about πορνεία. He reaffirms marriage as the proper context for sexual expression (1 Cor 7:2; see Eph 5:22–33, esp. 5:31; cf. Heb 13:4) and regards as πορνεία any sexual activity taking place outside of that relationship.[29] To the Thessalonians, he goes so far as to define sanctification as abstaining from πορνεία (1 Thess 4:3), possibly because various kinds of sexual immorality were a significant problem in that community. He characterized the issue of incest at Corinth as a kind of sexual immorality that is not even tolerated among the gentiles (1 Cor 5:1) and should thus not be countenanced at all within the church. And he viewed various forms of sexual immorality as entirely inconsistent with life in the kingdom of God (1 Cor 6:9).

Paul's command to put to death ἀκαθαρσία, "impurity," also likely pertains to sexual immorality and should be seen in this context as an admonition to sexual purity.[30] This is the sense in which he uses the term in two other passages where sexual integrity is prominent. In Rom 1:24 he declares that God gave sinful humanity up "in the lusts of their hearts to impurity [εἰς ἀκαθαρσίαν], to the dishonoring of their bodies among themselves" (ESV). The emphasis in Rom 1:25–28 is on homosexual practices. Paul concludes his extended discussion of πορνεία in 1 Thess 4:3–8 by asserting that "God did not call us to be impure [ἐπὶ ἀκαθαρσίᾳ], but to live a holy life" (1 Thess 4:7 NIV). The two vices of πορνεία and ἀκαθαρσία are also found together elsewhere in Paul (2 Cor 12:21; Gal 5:19; Eph 5:3). Understanding impurity in terms of sexual sin is also found in Second Temple Jewish texts (see CD 7.1–3; 1QS 4.10; 11QTemple Scroll[b] 66.13; 4QAramaic Levi[a] 1.7–18). It is highly doubtful that Paul would have in mind here any concerns related to traditional Jewish understandings of impurity regarding food laws. It is possible that he has a more general sense of impurity in mind (see 1 Thess 2:3), but that is rather unlikely here because of the close proximity of πορνεία.

---

27 Harper, "*Porneia*," 367.

28 Dunbabin, "*Baiarum Grata Voluptas*," 24–25.

29 So Harper, "*Porneia*," 379.

30 Contra Lightfoot, 211, who regards the reference to ἀκαθαρσία here as "uncleanness in any form."

[νεκρώσατε] . . . πάθος ἐπιθυμίαν κακήν, "[put to death] inappropriate passion, evil desire." The next two vices he instructs the Colossians to eradicate are likely also associated with sexual propriety in the Christian community. Although "passion" could refer to an intense desire for an array of objects or activities, or to sins such as gluttony or anger, it is used by the apostle Paul on two occasions to refer to intense sexual desire. This involves heated and unbridled desire (πάθει ἐπιθυμίας) for various kinds of illicit sexual relations—a sinful tendency that Paul sees as characteristic of gentiles who have not had their appetites informed by a knowledge of the one living, true, and holy God (1 Thess 4:5). But it also extends to what Paul would regard as a dishonorable passion (πάθη ἀτιμίας) for same-sex relations (Rom 1:26).

In 4 Maccabees, where the term πάθος appears over sixty times, the author appeals to the readers to learn how to make godly reason (ὁ εὐσεβὴς λογισμός) the master of the emotions, including sexual desire (4 Macc. 1.1). Joseph is held up as an example of a person who, although he was at the prime of his sexual desire as a young man when he was tempted by Potiphar's wife, "gained mastery over his sensuality" and "quenched the burning ardor of his passions [παθῶν]" by the exercise of reason (4 Macc. 2.1–6). Paul may have been able to agree to a certain extent with the philosophical approach of the author of this Hellenistic Jewish discourse, but he would have viewed this approach as profoundly inadequate in light of Christ. For Paul, victory over sexual passion can be achieved—and, indeed, should be achieved by Christians—by drawing on the full significance of participation with Christ in his death to sin and the passions and the power available through union with Christ in his resurrection.

The term ἐπιθυμία, often translated "lust," has a long history in OT, Jewish, and early Christian literature to express inappropriate sexual desire. In and of itself, the term does not have negative connotations; it simply expresses "desire," "yearning," or "longing" for something (see, e.g., Phil 1:23 where Paul uses it of a desire to depart and be with Christ; see also 1 Thess 2:17).[31] It becomes negative only when the object of desire is forbidden. By adding the adjective κακός, "bad" or "evil," Paul makes it clear that he is thinking of an evil desire prompted by the evil inclination. Part of walking in a manner that is pleasing to God and becoming like him in his holiness is to "not let sin reign in your mortal body so that you obey its lusts [ἐπιθυμίαις]" (Rom 6:12 NASB). The way to do this is to "walk by the Spirit, and you will not gratify the desires of the flesh" (Gal 5:16 NIV). This begins with recognizing that those who are in Christ Jesus "have crucified the flesh with its passions and desires [τοῖς παθήμασιν καὶ ταῖς ἐπιθυμίαις]" (Gal 5:24 NIV). Paul could be referring to a wide variety of sinful desires in Col 3:5, but since the previous three words refer to illicit sexual desires and conduct, this expression likely refers to sexual lust. This is consistent with

31 BDAG, s.v. ἐπιθυμία.

how Paul uses the term on other occasions (Rom 1:24; 1 Thess 4:5; see also Prov 6:25 LXX).

[νεκρώσατε] . . . καὶ τὴν πλεονεξίαν, ἥτις ἐστὶν εἰδωλολατρία, "[put to death] . . . greed, which is idolatry." The final vice that Paul calls them to mortify in this list is πλεονεξία, "greed." The meaning is consistent with the etymology; it is the selfish and excessive desire to have more of something (πλέον, "more" + ἔχειν, "to have"). Most modern versions translate it as "greed," but there is also a long history of rendering it as "covetousness" (ESV; NKJV; RSV; ASV; KJV; Tyndale; Geneva). Since the first four vices have to do with sexual desire and expression, it is natural for us to consider whether our author was interpreting greed in this narrower sense—that is, as an inordinate desire for more sex. This would fit with the command in the law not to covet a neighbor's wife (Exod 20:17; Deut 5:21). But the law also prohibits coveting a neighbor's house, and the reference to greed or covetousness in Col 3:5 probably extends beyond sexual desire to avarice (the insatiable desire for wealth) and to other objects. This is supported by the grammar of the passage in that the flow of the list is slightly disrupted by the insertion of καί, "and," the inclusion of an article (τήν) before πλεονεξίαν, and the addition of a descriptive relative clause that modifies it. This may indicate that the first four terms belong together in a series as a coherent group, but that the final term should be differently interpreted. Paul only uses πλεονεξία on five other occasions—none of which have an exclusively sexual reference. He uses it to refer to financial greed in 1 Thess 2:5 (see also Eph 4:19) and more broadly of the insatiable desire to acquire more and more in Rom 1:29 and Eph 5:3. Avarice is clearly the more common usage of the term and is the best way to take it here.[32] As such, it is relevant to note Jesus's comments about greed as represented in the parable of the rich fool in Luke's Gospel. Jesus warns, "Be on your guard against all kinds of greed [πλεονεξίας]; life does not consist in an abundance of possessions" (Luke 12:15 NIV).

Paul underlines the severity of greed by stating that it is tantamount to idolatry. The singular feminine relative pronoun ἥτις makes it clear that Paul is referring to the immediately preceding noun (feminine singular) and not to the entire list. When Paul refers to a series of nouns in Colossians, he tends to use the plural of the neuter pronoun (ἅ ἐστιν; see 2:17, 22). The accusation of idolatry is very serious in a biblical perspective. The first two commands of the Decalogue were prohibitions of idolatry (Exod 20:3–6; Deut 5:7–8). Biblical history is replete with examples of the people of God violating this prohibition, worshiping false gods, and incurring God's wrath. The prophets repeatedly call on Israel to repudiate their idols, as in Ezek 14:6: "Therefore say to the people of Israel, 'This is what the Sovereign LORD says: Repent! Turn from your idols and renounce all your detestable practices!'" (NIV).

Throughout the OT, an idol (גִּלּוּל; εἴδωλον) is a carved, cast, or sculpted image

32 See Rosner, *Greed as Idolatry*, 103–11.

of another god or goddess, such as Baal, Asherah, or a myriad of others known to Israel in the ancient Near East. For a Jew writing to the people of God living in the Lycus Valley, an idol would be any of the local deities they may be tempted to worship and serve, such as Apollo, Zeus, Artemis, Aphrodite, Demeter, Kore, and others. Paul was certainly concerned about this and spoke out against idolatry elsewhere (see, e.g., 1 Cor 10:14; 12:2; 1 Thess 1:9). Yet he is not specifically denouncing the worship of literal idols here, but is using εἰδωλολατρία, "idolatry," in a metaphorical way to speak of idols of the heart. As Rosner puts it, "Idolatry involves trusting, loving, and serving gold and silver objects rather than the true and living God. So does greed."[33] Thus, there is a pattern in the OT of warning against the danger of trusting wealth rather than God as the source of one's security (see Pss 49:7–8; 52:7; 62:10; Prov 10:15; Jer 48:7).

There is no precise parallel in OT and Jewish tradition for the metaphorical use of the term identifying greed with idolatry. Some have pointed to T. Jud. 19.1: "my children, love of money leads to idolatry [πρὸς εἴδωλα ὁδηγει], because once they are led astray by money, they designate as gods those who are not gods." But this passage only asserts a relationship—one leads to the other. Ezekiel 14:3 speaks of certain Israelites who "have taken their idols into their hearts"—an idea that is taken up in the Dead Sea Scrolls (CD 20.9–12; 1QS 2.11–18). Philo compared "money lovers" to idolaters when he said of them that they "procure gold and silver coins from every side and treasure their hoard like a divine image in a sanctuary, believing it to be a source of blessing and happiness of every kind" (Philo, *Spec. Laws* 1.23). None of these texts, however, corresponds to the metaphorical usage that we have in Col 3:5. The closest conceptual similarity is from the Synoptic tradition and Jesus's statement about God and mammon: "No one can serve two masters; for either he will hate the one and love the other, or he will be devoted to the one and despise the other. You cannot serve God and mammon" (Matt 6:24 RSV). Nevertheless, as Rosner points out, the innovation here may be more in form than in content since "the way for the expression seems to have been paved by the comprehensive scope of the first commandment, by the characterization of idolatry in terms of evil desire, and above all by the association of wealth with apostasy."[34] Paul seems to have picked up on this in his criticisms of those who have made their stomach—that is, their carnal desires, into a god (Rom 16:18; Phil 3:19). As early as the time of Hosea, sexual immorality began to be understood as a form of idolatry (Hos 1:2; 4:12–13). This association becomes prominent in Second Temple Judaism. In Jubilees, "fornication is a leitmotiv, and it includes idolatry and sexual transgression."[35] Testament of Benjamin 10.1 speaks of Israel falling into fornication and idolatry and becoming alienated from God.

33 Rosner, *Greed as Idolatry*, 174.

34 Rosner, *Greed as Idolatry*, 99.

35 Harper, "*Porneia*," 373.

Paul's overriding concern here is to jar the Colossians into considering what kinds of things persist in their lives that command their love, service, and trust. This is the role reserved for God alone; anything that fills that role is idolatry and should thus be renounced and eradicated from one's life. The pursuit of money (see 1 Tim 6:10), the pursuit of sex, or the passioned pursuit of anything else could displace the proper role of God in one's life and should therefore be resisted as idolatry. Ephesians likewise sounds this warning in similar terms (Eph 5:5). And, finally, the author of Hebrews summarizes the concern well by advocating trust in God over wealth when he says, "Keep your lives free from the love of money, and be content with what you have; for he has said, 'I will never leave you or forsake you'" (Heb 13:5 NIV).

**6** **δι' ἃ ἔρχεται ἡ ὀργὴ τοῦ θεοῦ ἐπὶ τοὺς υἱοὺς τῆς ἀπειθείας**, "because of these practices, the wrath of God is coming upon the sons of disobedience." The neuter plural relative pronoun (ἅ) gathers all five of the vices listed in 3:5 and asserts that God will hold humanity accountable for the practice of these sins. This concluding declaration of the certainty of God's judgment on these practices is consistent with the other vice lists present in the NT (see 1 Cor 6:10–11; Gal 5:19–21; Eph 5:3–6). Those in the community familiar with the history of Israel would know that God has previously poured out his wrath upon his people because of their idolatry. The prophet Ezekiel recounts how God poured out his wrath on Israel because they had defiled the land with their idols (Ezek 36:18; see also 2 Chr 24:18; Ezek 20:8).

The precise expression ἡ ὀργὴ τοῦ θεοῦ is a reference to the eschatological wrath of God coming at the end of the age when he judges the world (see Rom 2:5, 8; 3:5; 5:9; 9:22; 1 Thess 5:9; Eph 2:3). One should not interpret it through the lens of common human emotion but through the objective standard of God's holiness and justice by which he holds the world accountable. In his Olivet Discourse, Jesus warned of this future time of wrath "in which there will be great distress and wrath [ὀργή] against this people" (Luke 21:23). John the Baptist, too, warned of "the wrath to come" (Matt 3:7 // Luke 3:7). But this theme comes to full expression in Revelation as it unfolds the meaning and extent of "the wrath of the Lamb" (ἡ ὀργή τοῦ ἀρνίου; Rev 6:16–17; see also Rev 11:18; 14:10; 16:19; 19:15).

The verb ἔρχεται, "is coming," in Col 3:6 should thus be understood as a futuristic present referring to this upcoming time of eschatological judgment. The eschatological reference in 3:4 to the revelation of Christ in glory corroborates this assumption. Nevertheless, Paul does speak of a present manifestation of God's wrath against sin at the beginning of Romans (Rom 1:18). An instantiation of this is evident in 1 Thess 2:16 in God's wrath coming upon those who conspired together to put Jesus to death on the cross. Perhaps most salient to our passage is the warning Paul gives to the Thessalonians as part of his concluding appeal to them to abstain from πορνεία. He informs them that "the Lord is an avenger [ἔκδικος] in all these things, just as we have already told you beforehand

and solemnly warned you" (1 Thess 4:6 NRSV). In the horizon of Paul's thought, believers have been saved from the future day of wrath (Rom 5:9), but they cannot take this as a license to indulge their sexual appetites and greed. If those practices warrant the outpouring of God's wrath in the future, they cannot expect to escape God's discipline in the present. But recognizing the seriousness with which God takes these offenses should be sufficient reason for the Colossian believers to eradicate them from their lives.

The coming manifestation of God's wrath will be directed upon people who have resisted and disobeyed God. "Sons of" is a common Semitic manner of expression that characterizes people by the descriptive term in the genitive case that follows, which should be interpreted as an attributive genitive. Thus, a "son of injustice" (υἱὸς ἀδικίας; 2 Sam 7:10) is an unjust person, and a "son of power" (υἱὸς δυνάμεως; 2 Sam 17:10) is a strong warrior (see also "sons of the covenant," Ezek 30:5; "sons of this age," Luke 16:8; 20:34). The precise phrase, υἱοὶ τῆς ἀπειθείας, "sons of disobedience," is unique, appearing here for the first time. It is also found in Eph 2:2 and 5:6 to characterize those who do not know Christ and live in ways that are displeasing to God. According to Rom 11:32, this typifies all of humanity—Jew and gentile alike—putting them in need of Christ's redemption: "God has imprisoned all in disobedience [εἰς ἀπείθειαν] so that he may be merciful to all" (NRSV). But in our passage, the emphasis falls on sexual sin and greed as particularly egregious to God, warranting his retributive wrath.

**7** ἐν οἷς καὶ ὑμεῖς περιεπατήσατέ ποτε, ὅτε ἐζῆτε ἐν τούτοις, "among them you also once walked when you lived in accordance with these vices." The interpretation of the pronouns (οἷς and τούτοις) in these two clauses is dependent on whether the preceding phrase, ἐπὶ τοὺς υἱοὺς τῆς ἀπειθείας, is judged to be original. If the phrase is not part of the original text, then the two pronouns would need to be regarded as neuter and as referring to the neuter pronoun of 3:6 (ἅ), which, in turn, refers to the list of five vices. If the phrase is original, then οἷς could be interpreted as masculine and as referring to the immediately preceding υἱοί, "sons." This is not grammatically necessary, however, and it could still refer further back to the five vices. The subsequent τούτοις could refer then either to people ("when you lived among the sons of disobedience") or to the five vices ("when you lived in these ways"). The versions are widely divided on the textual issue and the interpretation of the pronouns. The various composite views could be summarized as follows:

1. "the sons of disobedience" is original; οἷς refers to people; τούτοις refers to the vices: "among whom you also once walked when you lived in accordance with these vices").[36]
2. "the sons of disobedience" is original; οἷς refers to the vices; τούτοις refers to the vices: "These are the ways you also once followed, when you

36 See Sumney, 192–95; Wilson, 241, 248; Dunn, 217–18.

were living that life," NRSV; see also CEB; CSB; NKJV; TEV; NASB; ASV; KJV; Tyndale).[37]

3. "the sons of disobedience" is original; οἷς refers to vices; τούτοις refers to people: "all these things made up your way of life when you were living among such people," NJB; see also NET).
4. "the sons of disobedience" is not original; οἷς refers to the vices; τούτοις refers to the vices: "you used to walk in these ways, in the life you once lived," NIV; see also RSV; NAB; NLT).[38]

The view that best explains the evidence is the first. I argued in the *Notes* that the evidence tilts in favor of seeing ἐπὶ τοὺς υἱοὺς τῆς ἀπειθείας as original. If that is the case, the nearest antecedent of οἷς is υἱοί, and this fits the context well. The principal argument against this is that περιπατέω ἐν is most commonly used by Paul not with reference to people but to things, such as "walking in wisdom" (Col 4:5) or "walking in love" (Eph 5:2).[39] But the alternative is clearly possible and is reflected in biblical usage. God "walks among" his people (ἐμπεριπατέω ἐν; Lev 26:12; 2 Cor 6:16). The language of Eph 2:2–3 is very close to the wording in Col 3:7: ἐν τοῖς υἱοῖς τῆς ἀπειθείας· ἐν οἷς καὶ ἡμεῖς πάντες ἀνεστράφημέν ποτε ἐν ταῖς ἐπιθυμίαις. This text supports the personal interpretation of the pronoun, whether stemming from the same author or whether it is seen as an early use of Col 3:7 interpreted and redacted for its use in Ephesians. The versions and commentaries agree that the ἐν οἷς in the Ephesian passage refers to the "sons of disobedience."

καὶ ὑμεῖς, "you also," is a reference to the readers and "represents an implied distinction from the ungodly among whom you no longer are."[40] It is written with the assumption that most of them are gentiles. This also fits with the characterization of those who typically practice the five vices listed in 3:5 as gentiles. Jews saw the gentile world as practicing every manner of sexual sin. In saying that the Colossians formerly "walked" (περιπατέω) among the gentiles, Paul asserts that they did so in practicing all of the same vices. That was "once" (ποτε)—that is, prior to their conversion when they learned Christ (Col 1:7). The gospel (1:5, 23) has changed everything for the Colossian believers. They have now been brought into a relationship with Christ and are called to "walk" (περιπατέω) in a manner that is worthy of the Lord (1:10). They can only do this by virtue of their relationship to him, so Paul urges them to "walk in him" (ἐν αὐτῷ περιπατεῖτε; 2:6)—that is, drawing on their new life in him and the full significance of being united with Christ in his death and resurrection (3:1–4). In him, they can—and, indeed, must—overcome sexual sin and greed.

---

37 See Eadie, 219; Calvin, 348.

38 See Foster, 324–26; Moo, 260–62; Lohse, 139–40; Lightfoot, 213.

39 E.g., Lightfoot, 213.

40 Williams, 127.

In a clause that is somewhat redundant, Paul affirms that in the period before they received Christ, they were living their lives in accordance with the vices of sexual impurity and passion as well as greed. It is noteworthy that Paul shifts from the aorist tense to the imperfect to express "when you lived" (ἐζῆτε). The imperfective aspect here emphasizes a progressive action.[41] In this case, it could be interpreted to mean that this was the pattern of their lives—their lifestyle. The demonstrative pronoun (τούτοις) is most likely neuter and refers back to the ἅ of 3:6, which summarizes the five vices. Living in "these things" consisted of a lifestyle characterized by sexual sin and avarice (see 1 Cor 6:9–11). Grammatically the pronoun could refer to the masculine noun at the end of 3:6 (υἱοί), which would give the clause the sense "when you lived among them." This interpretation is possible and would not vary much in overall significance from the alternative. In this case it would be "when you lived among people who practiced these vices." The use of the demonstrative (τούτοις) instead of the personal pronoun (αὐτοῖς) tips the balance in favor of seeing the referent as the vices, since Paul seldom used the demonstrative for people (see also Col 3:14). Because of their new identity in Christ, especially the fact that they have died to sin (2:20; 3:3), the Colossians are obligated to no longer live in sin (see Rom 6:2: "How can we who died to sin still live in it?"). Their resurrection with Christ (Col 2:12; 3:1) puts them under the obligation to live for God (Rom 6:11: "alive to God in Christ Jesus").

**8 νυνὶ δὲ ἀπόθεσθε καὶ ὑμεῖς τὰ πάντα**, "but now you need to take off all these things." Paul introduces a new list of five vices for the Colossian believers to eliminate from their lives as a consequence of their conversion. Paul shifts the metaphor from "putting to death" to "taking off" as clothing.

"Now" (νυνί) corresponds with "once" (ποτέ) from the previous verse and is used to signal the decisive change of life that has occurred now that they have received Christ. The pattern of life in the pre-Christian era for every individual believer should contrast sharply with the new lifestyle expectations for followers of Christ. Paul uses this language elsewhere to describe conversion (Rom 11:30). Onlookers used the "once-now" contrast to describe the massive change to Saul after his Damascus road experience (Gal 1:23). The terms are used twice in Ephesians to characterize conversion. The author states in very stark terms in Eph 5:8 that "once you were darkness, but now you are light in the Lord" (see also Eph 2:2). The contrastive language also appears in 1 Peter: "once you were not a people, but now you are God's people" (1 Pet 2:10 NRSV).

Paul introduces the metaphor of taking off clothing (ἀπόθεσθε) to introduce the next list of five vices that he wants them to deal with in their lives. The verb can be found in the literal sense in the LXX and NT, such as in the description of Aaron entering the tent of meeting and taking off his linen garments (Lev 16:23; see also Acts 7:58). The metaphor of the change of clothing in Colossians

---

41 Campbell, 53.

may be an allusion to the ritual clothing of priests (Lev 6:11; Ezek 42:14; 44:19).[42] The priests were to don special robes when they went into the temple to fulfill their priestly duties (Exod 28:4–5). Paul has appropriated the image of "taking off" and "putting on" to describe the duty of believers to eliminate vices and practice virtues. The clothing metaphor simultaneously serves to define their new identity as the people of God.[43] Just as the priestly robes and turban identifed the priest as "holy to the Lord," the "clothing" of believers will also mark them out as a holy people.

Paul uses the language of "taking off" (ἀποτίθημι) in addressing the Roman Christians when he admonishes them, "Let us lay aside [ἀποθώμεθα] the works of darkness" (Rom 13:12). In Ephesians, the verb appears in conjunction with eliminating lies and falsehood (Eph 4:25) and in taking off the former manner of life (Eph 4:22). The aorist tense in our passage corresponds to the aorist tense of the previous imperative (νεκρώσατε; 3:5) and represents no special emphasis. Paul has already used the cognate verb ἀπεκδύομαι, "take off," in Col 2:15 and 3:9 to speak of the work of God in divesting the principalities and powers and in taking off the old self of those who come to faith in Christ. Perhaps the shift of verbs is motivated by the shift of subjects. Here the emphasis is clearly on the role of the believing community to participate with God in the transformational process by attending to the vices that are rooted in their lives and discarding them like old clothing.

The inclusion of καὶ ὑμεῖς, "you also," is somewhat surprising since it is unnecessary and is missing from the imperative clause that introduces 3:5–11. But the first subsection does conclude with it (ἐν οἷς καὶ ὑμεῖς περιεπατήσατέ ποτε; 3:7a) and the inclusion of the expression here provides a link of continuity. Since this passage does not assert a "we" (Jewish Christian)-"you" (gentile Christian) distinction,[44] the expression is probably best interpreted here as emphatic, "you, in particular."[45] This is also preferable to finding a distinction between "you" and "other Christians."[46] The emphatic expression puts the spotlight on the Colossian Christians to distance themselves from the kind of people they once were when they practiced the vices mentioned here. The vices listed in this second list of five are relevant to Jew and gentile Christian alike.

"All these things" (τὰ πάντα) serves as a heading for the group of five vices Paul lists in what follows. Since he is introducing a new section with five vices, it is doubtful that the τὰ πάντα is retrospective as well[47] or used in a general sense of "all of whatever kind."[48] The five vices that follow are all related to social

---

42 See the discussion in Canavan, *Clothing the Body*, 151–52.
43 Canavan, *Clothing the Body*, 153.
44 Contra Barth and Blanke, 406.
45 So also Moo, 262.
46 Contra Abbott, 262.
47 Contra Ellicott, 182.
48 Contra Lightfoot, 214.

relationships within the community. The first three have to do with emotions that can result in speech and actions that are harmful to others. The final two are actions that are destructive to the social life and unity of the community.

ὀργή, "anger," is a term that we encountered in 3:6 to refer to the eschatological judgment of God upon the world. Both OT and NT writers frequently used it to characterize God's righteous indignation at sin and the action he would take against it. Here, however, it is cast in a negative light as an emotion that is inconsistent with one's new life in Christ. For the Greeks, "anger as the expression of unrestrained passion stands in contradiction to sound judgment and reason."[49] Anger (ὀργή) is roundly condemned in the Jewish wisdom literature. Sirach declares, "Anger and wrath [ὀργή], these also are abominations, yet a sinner holds on to them" (Sir 27:30; see also 28:3). The Testament of Dan warns that there is an evil spirit associated with anger (T. Dan 1.7–8; 2.4; see also Eph 4:27).

The second of the five vices, θυμός, "wrath," is virtually synonymous to ὀργή, "anger," and is similarly condemned as an emotion that ruptures relationships and leads to violent acts. In his final words to Simeon and Levi, Jacob said, "Cursed be their anger [θυμός], for it is fierce, and their wrath [μῆνις], for it is cruel!" (Gen 49:7 ESV). It is a lifestyle characteristic of the godless in heart in that they cherish anger (θυμός; Job 36:13). Second Temple Jewish literature reaffirms the biblical warnings against wrath. It is an emotion that can cause one to commit murder (Wis 10:3). It is regarded as an evil thing (πονηρὸς ὁ θυμός) that "troubles the soul itself" (T. Dan 3.1). The people of God should therefore "avoid wrath, and hate lying, in order that the Lord may dwell among you, and Beliar may flee from you" (T. Dan 5.1). Paul lists it as a vice elsewhere (2 Cor 12:20; Gal 5:20; see also Eph 4:31).

Throughout the LXX, both terms are often coupled together and used to express the kind of emotion that is dangerous to the life of the community. The psalmist therefore pleads with the people of God to "refrain from anger [ὀργῆς], and forsake wrath [θυμόν] . . . but those who wait for the LORD shall inherit the land" (Ps 37:8–9 ESV [36:8–9 LXX]). The writer of Proverbs notes that "wrath is cruel [θυμός]" and "anger [ὀργή] is overwhelming" (Prov 27:4 NRSV). Therefore, "the wise turn away anger [ὀργήν]," but "fools give full vent to their rage [θυμόν]" (Prov 29:8, 11 NIV). Sirach notes that God did not create his people for fierce anger (ὀργὴ θυμοῦ; Sir 10:18).

The third term that Paul lists in Col 3:8 is κακία ("badness" or "evil"), most often translated here as "malice" (influenced by the Vulgate's *malitia*). It refers to a "mean-spirited" attitude or disposition.[50] It issues in a desire to cause pain or injury to a person. According to Wis 16:14, "a person kills in his wickedness [κακίᾳ]" (NETS). In Greek literature, it seems to function as the opposite of

49 M. Silva, "ὀργή," *NIDNTTE* 3:532.

50 BDAG, s.v. κακία 2.

ἀρετή, "virtue."[51] It is "a force which destroys fellowship."[52] Paul includes κακία in his various lists of vices (Rom 1:29; Eph 4:31; see also Titus 3:3). In other NT letters, believers are urged to "take off" this vice (ἀποθέμενοι . . . περισσείαν κακίας in Jas 1:21 and ἀποθέμενοι . . . πᾶσαν κακίαν in 1 Pet 2:1). The eradication of "malice" is thus part of standard Christian moral exhortation.

The fourth vice, βλασφημία, "blasphemy" (or "slander" as in most English versions), refers to speech that is insulting, denigrating, defaming, and harmful to another person. The Gospel tradition includes it in a list of vices that proceed from the heart of an individual (Matt 15:19; Mark 7:22). It appears in the parallel list of vices in Eph 4:31 and as a characteristic of the speech of the opponents in 1 Tim 6:4. It is also found in early Christian vice lists (Herm. Mand. 8.1.3; Did. 3.6). It is commonly translated "blasphemy" when the slander is directed against God (Rev 13:5–6), but here it is more likely used of defaming and hurtful speech of believers toward one another in the Christian community.

The final vice mentioned in this list is αἰσχρολογία, "shameful speech." This is a very rare term that only appears here in the NT and is never used in the LXX, Philo, or Josephus. It does appear in Did. 5.1 in a list of behaviors that represent "the way of death." In later Christian history, Clement of Alexandria uses it it a way that "might properly be defined as storytelling involving such unseemly deeds as adultery or pederasty" (*Paed.* 2.6.52).[53] Paul uses the noun αἰσχρός, "obscene," in Eph 5:12 in reference to those who engage in sexual sin to say that "it is shameful even to speak of the things they do in secret." The "shameful speech" that Paul speaks of here then most likely has to do with talk about sexual themes done in a derisive way. Thus "obscene talk" (ESV) and "dirty language" (NLT) would be appropriate translations, whereas "abusive language" (NRSV) or "abusive speech" (NASB) focus on the impact of such speech.

The prepositional phrase that concludes the verse, ἐκ τοῦ στόματος ὑμῶν, "from your mouth," modifies the final noun, αἰσχρολογία, "take off . . . filthy talk from your mouths." Some have argued that it modifies the main verb and thereby goes with all five nouns, as the REB, "banish them all from your lips."[54] But this would mean that the first three vices—anger, wrath, and malice—are restricted only to verbal expressions and not more generally to one's attitude or other expressions of these vices.[55] Others have claimed that the phrase goes with the last two terms, slander and filthy talk (as the GNV, "no insults or obscene talk must ever come from your lips").[56] This reading fits with βλασφημία as a verbal sin, but there is nothing in the grammar to suggest this interpretation.

51 M. Silva, "κακός," *NIDNTTE* 2:597.
52 W. Grundmann, "κακός, κτλ.," *TDNT* 3:484.
53 BDAG, s.v. αἰσχρολογία.
54 Pao, 223.
55 So, rightly, Harris, 130.
56 Moo, 263; Barth and Blanke, 407; Pokorný, 168.

The most natural reading is to tie it strictly to the final noun. Paul makes a similar statement, but in different words, in Eph 4:29, where he uses λόγος σαπρός, "filthy word," instead of αἰσχρολογία, "filthy talk," and speaks of it coming ἐκ τοῦ στόματος ὑμῶν.

There is no indication that these five vices are related in any direct way to the opponents. They could stem from Paul's awareness from Epaphras of ways the Colossian believers needed to grow. Yet many of the expressions are found in traditional lists of early Christian moral exhortation. As Schweizer notes, "Clearly the vices mentioned are those which affect relations between people and which endanger the community."[57]

**9** μὴ ψεύδεσθε εἰς ἀλλήλους, "don't lie to one another." Although Paul has switched his manner of expression to a finite verb, this injunction conceptually functions as a sixth vice that one should put away. It is closely associated with βλασφημία of Col 3:8 in that the intent or result of a lie is often harm to someone else. Understanding this as parallel to the previous five vices also helps to explain the asyndeton construction in a place where Paul would normally use the conjunction δέ or καί to transition to a new exhortation.

The present imperative with μή has been interpreted by some in a cessative-ingressive sense, "*stop* lying to one another" (CEV; NAB). Contextually this would assume that there was widespread lying within the community that needs to be stopped, but this certainly cannot be demonstrated. It is better to take it as a more general command not to lie,[58] or at least to see it in the same way as the commands to put away slander and filthy talk.

Telling lies to fellow members of the body is exceedingly harmful to the cohesiveness and well-being of the community. A lie injures another party and undermines trust. The prohibition against bearing false witness was the ninth of the Ten Commandments (Exod 20:16; Deut 5:20). Truthfulness is of the very character of God, and every word he speaks is true (Prov 30:5). He expects his people to reflect this virtue in their community life. Speaking truth and avoiding falsehood was an expectation of the people of God throughout their history. Testament of Dan 5.1 sums it up well: "Observe the Lord's commandments, then, my children, and keep his Law. Avoid wrath [θυμός], and hate lying [μισήσατε τὸ ψεῦδος], in order that the Lord may dwell among you, and Beliar may flee from you."

Paul urges the readers of Ephesians to "put away falsehood" (ἀποθέμενοι τὸ ψεῦδος) and to "let each one of you speak the truth with his neighbor, for we are members of one another" (Eph 4:25 ESV). He regards untoward anger, lying, and other vices as providing an opportunity for the devil to gain a foothold (Eph 4:27).

57 Schweizer, 193.

58 Moo, 265. Huffman, *Prohibitions*, 31–58, has argued forcefully against interpreting any present imperative negative commands as cessative-ingressive without adequate contextual warrant. In this passage, he sees a progressive sense and suggests the gloss, "do not be lying to one another."

While this is a general command with relevance to the entire community of believers, it has particular relevance to those in the community who are spreading the dangerous teaching. At the outset of his polemic against "the philosophy," Paul castigated it as "empty deceit" and "inspired by demonic spirits of the world" (2:8). This is tantamount to saying that these teachers are spreading lies to fellow members of the community. These rival teachers appealed to visions as the source of their inspiration (2:18). This bears a striking similarity to the prophet Zechariah's denunciation of false prophets who spoke on the basis of their visions (Zech 13:1–4). The prophet points to a day when God would remove these prophets from the land together with "the spirit of uncleanness [τὸ πνεῦμα τὸ ἀκάθαρτον]" (13:2). On that day, "the prophets will be ashamed, each of his vision when he prophesies . . . because they lied [ἀνθ' ὧν ἐψεύσαντο]" (13:4 NETS).

ἀπεκδυσάμενοι τὸν παλαιὸν ἄνθρωπον σὺν ταῖς πράξεσιν αὐτοῦ, "since you have taken off the old self with its practices." Although grammatically this adverbial clause forms the basis for desisting from lying, semantically it serves as the reason for laying aside all of the sinful practices listed in 3:9 as well as those delineated in 3:5.[59] The participle should be interpreted as causal, "*because* you have taken off the old self."[60] Some interpreters, however, have argued that it should be understood as an imperative, "take off the old self."[61] Yet the grammatical arguments for the imperative are far from decisive. Lightfoot argues that "though both ideas are found in St. Paul, the imperative is the more usual."[62] Yet this is the only instance of a second-person plural imperative in the present tense followed by an aorist participle in Paul. There is one occurrence of an aorist imperative followed by an aorist participle (στῆτε . . . περιζωσάμενοι; Eph 6:14), which is probably best interpreted as a participle of means. The other examples he adduces are hortatory subjunctives followed by a participle. Both Lightfoot and Lohse cite the parallel passage in Eph 4:21–24 as support for an imperatival interpretation here, but the infinitive construction in that passage is best described as epexegetical (ἐδιδάχθητε . . . ἀποθέσθαι, "you were taught . . . to take off") and should not be interpreted as an imperatival infinitive. And the fact that imperatives precede (Col 3:5, 8, 11) and follow (3:12) the two aorist participles in Colossians does not necessitate an imperatival interpretation. Paul often interlaces his exhortations with statements of identity (as he does in 3:3, "for you died and your life is hidden with Christ in God").

The essential idea is that Paul is here making an identity statement and thereby rooting the process of change in the reality of their new life in union with Christ. Believers should resist lying because it is inconsistent with their

59 Moo, 265; Aletti, 229.
60 So also, e.g., Campbell, 54; Pao, 226; Sumney, 198–99; Wilson, 250; Eadie, 222.
61 Barth and Blanke, 410; Lightfoot, 214–15.
62 Lightfoot, 214–15.

new identity in relationship to a holy God who never lies or deceives. This is supported by the use of the clothing imagery.

The imagery of taking off and putting on clothing was common in the ancient world and thus readily accessible to Paul and his readers. It appears in mystery-religion texts (Apuleius, *Metam.* 11.24), gnostic texts, and in the OT and Second Temple Jewish texts.[63] R. Canavan has made a strong case, however, for interpreting this text in accordance with the "social-political visual landscape in which the text was crafted and heard"—a process she calls "visual exegesis."[64] She examines the visual replicas of the emperors clothed with the virtues of Rome and contends that "they set the model for the identity of citizens and subject people."[65] Local representations of the emperor were accessible through coins, funerary monuments, stelae, and statuary discovered in Colossae, Hierapolis, Laodicea, and Aphrodisias. In sum, the metaphor of a change in clothing denotes a change in identity, just as donning a toga or stola symbolized the assumption of a Roman identity.[66] Augustus, she contends, "modelled the values essential to being a Roman citizen symbolised through the wearing of the toga. . . . The Romans in the act of clothing put on the virtues of Rome."[67] These virtues included "*dignitas*, *humanitas*, *gravitas*, and *pietas*."[68]

Given the all-pervasive influence of Roman culture at this time, Canavan's emphasis on the visual landscape is important. Clothing did differentiate people and conveyed a particular identity. This was a visible and daily part of life.

Yet it was not only the Roman imperial context that is relevant. Clothing as a recognizable marker of identity characterized the local religious context and should supplement Canavan's case. Perhaps most striking in this regard is the clothing that identified a priest of the Great Mother goddess, Cybele. These male priests, known as the *galli*, attired themselves in clothing that made them sharply distinguishable from anyone else. The *gallus* wore a long yellow stola (normally the dress of a female) of fine linen or silk and pulled together in the middle by a belt. The sleeves covered the full length of the arms and were tight around the wrists. The shoes were often simple sandals made of yellow leather. The priest also wore medallions that hung as necklaces and depicted various deities (such as Cybele, Zeus, or Attis). They also wore an inscribed plate that had the appearance of a miniature temple. They grew their hair long and marked their bodies with tatoos.[69] Lucian provides a detailed description of the rigorous and frenzied initiation ritual for these priests that included self-castration and culminated

63 J. H. Kim (*Clothing Imagery*) has written the most comprehensive assessment of clothing imagery and its significance in the Pauline corpus.

64 Canavan, *Clothing the Body*, 192.

65 Canavan, *Clothing the Body*, 67.

66 Canavan, *Clothing the Body*, 5, 107, 191–92.

67 Canavan, *Clothing the Body*, 113.

68 Canavan, *Clothing the Body*, 68.

69 Graillot, *Cybele*, 298.

with the change of clothing that would now identify them as priests of Cybele.[70] People living in Colossae (or anywhere in the Mediterranean world) would infer identity and status based on the clothing that they wore. Not only that, but they would expect a certain set of behaviors to correspond to the identity.[71]

Yet to some extent we are left without sufficient evidence on understanding the nuances of clothing and what it signified, in that there are no surviving textiles from this area during this time. So we do not know if Lycus Valley Jews, for instance, wore distinctive clothing. Nor do we know if slaves wore clothing that identified them as slaves.

Nevertheless, it is also important to acknowledge Paul's indebtedness to biblical tradition and how it influenced his use of the imagery here. The reference to the creator and image of God in 3:10 along with the Adam typology suggests that the creation narrative may be relevant. Beale points to the account of God providing garments of skin to Adam and Eve after their fall and clothing them (Gen 3:7, 21).[72] He discerns a typology present here and explains it this way: "Believers have laid aside the clothes of the first Adam (the 'old man') in which they could not come into God's presence, and have 'clothed themselves' with the last Adam ('the new' man), in whom they have been 'renewed.'"[73]

Kim finds the scene in Zechariah involving Joshua the high priest as particularly relevant for this passage (Zech 3:3–5).[74] As Joshua stood before the angel of the Lord clothed with filthy garments, the angel said, "Remove [ἀφέλετε] the filthy clothes from him . . . and clothe [ἐνδύσατε] him with a full-length robe" (Zech 3:4 NETS). This text not only points to the work of God in changing their status ("I have taken your iniquity away from you," Zech 3:4 ESV), but to their ethical renewal.

It is doubtful that there is one specific background to the change-of-clothing metaphor that Paul uses in Col 3:5, 9–10, and 12.[75] He employs it as a metaphor readily understandable by people living the Lycus Valley, but deeply enriches it by drawing on OT imagery—especially the creation narrative and the priestly scene involving Joshua the high priest—as well as by his own convictions about the new creation and dying and rising with Christ. A prominent part of the meaning of the clothing imagery is the way it conveys identity. And associated

---

70 Lucian, *De syria dea* 50–51. See the section titled, "Change of Clothes," in Elliott, *Cutting Too Close*, 163–66.

71 Based on the descriptions in *Anthologia Graeca*, 6.217–234, Roller, *God the Mother*, 230, summarizes the behavior of the *galli* in the course of their rituals: "they shrieked . . . waved their hair wildly . . . and banged on various noisy instruments." Of course, this contrasts sharply with the *dignitas*, *pietas*, and *gravitas* of the toga-wearing Roman male.

72 Beale, "Colossians," 866–67.

73 Beale, "Colossians," 866.

74 Kim, *Clothing Imagery*, 166, 174–75.

75 This is Kim's conclusion at the end of his detailed study of clothing imagery. He sees a mixture of Roman (*toga virilis*), OT, and Jewish traditions coming together in Paul's use of this imagery. See Kim, *Clothing Imagery*, 224–33.

with one's identity is a concomitant set of behaviors that flow from it and characterize it.

Many scholars associate the change of clothing metaphor with the ritual of baptism.[76] This is natural since this is the initiation ritual for Christians that signifies the change in identity and marks one as a follower of Jesus Christ. The letter also explicitly mentions baptism at Col 2:12 where the author draws a contrast between the old life and the new. Furthermore, the author in Col 2:11 uses the noun form (ἀπέκδυσις) of the verb used here (ἀπεκδύομαι) in Col 3:9, albeit with reference to spiritual circumcision as a removal of the flesh (not a removal of clothing). Foster, however, has rightly observed that "there is no evidence at this stage of the history of the church of a baptismal liturgy that required the divesture of clothing."[77] That development did come later, but it is not evident in any of the baptismal accounts in Acts. A change of clothing as part of the baptismal ritual is attested in some early-church traditions. Chrysostom says that the one who was baptized put on a white robe after emerging from the font and wore the garment for seven days. He notes that the baptized person "has put off the old garment of sin and has put on the royal robe" (Chrysostom, *Baptismal Instructions* 2.25).[78] Certain gnostic circles also used the imagery of taking off and putting on clothing in the baptismal ritual: "It is necessary that we put on the living man. Therefore, when he is about to go down into the water, he unclothes himself, in order that he may put on the living man" (e.g., Gospel of Philip, NHC II 3 75.22–24). But this evidence is much later than the first century. Because there is no early evidence for the change of clothing in baptism, Barth and Blanke rule out any allusion to baptism at all in this passage, insisting that "above all, Col gives no indication of attributing such significance to baptism, and it does not justify the assumption that the reference here is to baptism."[79] Yet as noted above, there is a reference to baptism in 2:12, and the causal interpretation of the aorist participles (ἀπεκδυσάμενοι . . . ἐνδυσάμενοι) would suggest a reference to conversion. From the beginning stages of the church, baptism was the Christian ritual signifying conversion. Perhaps it is this passage that stimulated the later change of clothing in the practice of this ritual.

Paul asserts that the reason that the Colossians can eliminate from their lives the sinful practices enumerated in 3:5–9 is because they have taken off τὸν παλαιὸν ἄνθρωπον. This expression corresponds in an antithetical way to τὸν νέον in the next clause. Many English versions have translated the phrases the "the old self . . . the new self" (ESV; NRSV; NASB; NIV; NAB; CSB; TEV) or "the old nature . . . the new nature" (RSV; NEB; or "the old human nature . . .

76 E.g., Canavan, *Clothing the Body*, 26, 46–47, 193; Kim, *Clothing Imagery*, 155–70; Moo, 266–67; MacDonald, 137; Wilson, 250; Still, 329; Wright, 138; Hay, 126.

77 Foster, 333.

78 The text is from P. W. Harkins, ed. and trans., *St. John Chrysostom: Baptismal Instructions*, ACW 31 (New York: Newman Press, 1963): 52. See the discussion in Ferguson, *Baptism*, 543.

79 Barth and Blanke, 409.

the new nature" as in CEB; REB; or "your old sinful nature . . . your new nature" as in NLT). These translations rightly bring out the individual sense of the language Paul uses, but they miss the broader corporate dimension. Moule aptly comments, "These phrases do not merely mean 'one's old, bad character' and 'the new, Christian character' respectively, as an *individual's* condition: they carry deeper, wider, and more *corporate* associations, inasmuch as they are part of the presentation of the gospel in terms of two 'Adams,' the two creations."[80] Most commentators join Moule in seeing a reference here to two orders of humanity represented by Adam and Christ.[81] The reference to creation and the image of God in 3:10 reinforces this view. But the expressions should be understood in *both* an individual and corporate sense. Kim puts it well in saying that they refer to "individuals in accordance with the old or new order of existence."[82] Wright is unreasonably critical of the NIV when he says that "'self' in NIV is misleadingly individualistic."[83] No one English term can capture the dual sense expressed by παλαιὸν ἄνθρωπον.

Paul uses the same expression (ὁ παλαιὸς ἄνθρωπος) in Rom 6:6 where he declares that it was crucified with Christ. Our passage begins with the injunction to reflect on the believers' participation in the death of Christ (3:3), building on the assertion of 2:12 that believers have been buried with Christ in baptism. Both here and Rom 6 stress the ethical implications of this identification with Christ in his death ("do not let sin reign in your mortal body," Rom 6:12; "put to death your earthly members," Col 3:5). The same thoughts are developed in Eph 4:22 where Paul says that the readers were taught to take off τὸν παλαιὸν ἄνθρωπον.

The final prepositional phrase, σὺν ταῖς πράξεσιν αὐτοῦ, "with its practices," puts the focus on the behaviors associated with the former manner of life. The old identity in solidarity with Adam is associated with conduct that reflects the implications of Adam's fallen state. These are the practices that typified their lives prior to coming to faith in Christ and deserve the wrath of God (3:6).

**10** καὶ ἐνδυσάμενοι τὸν νέον, "and have put on the new self." This participial clause should also be interpreted as causal and thereby serves as a second and related basis for eliminating sinful practices. Believers can change their behavior because there has been a fundamental change in who they are. In fact, there is an obligation before God to change their conduct to bring it into consistency with their new identity.

The parallel passage in Eph 4:24 uses the synonym καινός (versus νέος) to characterize the new self. Older commentators sometimes suggested that there

80 C. Moule, 119.

81 E.g., Kim, *Clothing*, 182; Pao, 226; Moo, 268; Barth and Blanke, 410–12; Still, 328–29; Wright, 138; Eadie, 222. Contra Foster, 336, who observes, "Nowhere in the letter does the author make reference to Adam."

82 Kim, *Clothing*, 182.

83 Wright, 138.

was a nuance of difference in meaning between these two passages as a result of the word choice.[84] The wordbook by R. C. Trench, which maintained a rigid distinction between the words, exerted a significant influence on older scholarship.[85] He suggested that νέος contemplated the new from a temporal perspective, whereas καινός stressed quality—that is, the new as set over against that which is worn out through use or age.[86] As such, Ephesians emphasizes the time that has transpired from Adam until the new man was born; Colossians emphasizes the condition of the old man who has cast off his former way of life "as the snake its shrivelled skin, coming forth a new creature."[87] But this distinction cannot be maintained in post-classical Greek, when the terms began to be used interchangeably, as evidenced by their usage in the LXX.[88]

Barth and Blanke contend that "the new man" should be understood to be Christ himself.[89] They claim that this fits best with Paul's thinking elsewhere when he declares that believers have "put on" Christ (Rom 13:14; Gal 3:27). But this interpretation would appear to suggest that the risen Christ would be in constant need of renewal. It also makes Christ a created being (τοῦ κτίσαντος αὐτόν, "the one who created him") if the Father is the subject of the action of the participle and αὐτόν refers to Christ. Rather, the "new self" is the person who has put their faith in Christ and now belongs to the new order of humanity in Christ. This is the new identity of the person who has been united with Christ and of whom it can be said, Christ is now "your life" (Col 3:4).

τὸν ἀνακαινούμενον εἰς ἐπίγνωσιν κατ᾽ εἰκόνα τοῦ κτίσαντος αὐτόν, "which is being renewed in knowledge in accordance with the image of the one who created it." In a touch of irony, Paul states that it is not the old that is renewed, but the new. The new self, he claims, is in the process of a constant renewal. The verb is unique to Paul—only occuring elsewhere in the LXX or NT at 2 Cor 4:16 where it refers to the inner self being renewed day by day. The imperfective aspect of the verb points to the process, and the passive voice suggests the divine agency in the renewal.[90] The specific divine agent is likely the Holy Spirit, as the parallel passage in Eph 4:23 makes explicit (ἀνανεοῦσθαι δὲ τῷ πνεύματι, "to be renewed by the Spirit").[91] Furthermore, the noun form of this verb, ἀνακαίνωσις, appears in Titus 3:5 where the Holy Spirit is named the agent of the renewal

84 E.g., Lightfoot, 281; Ellicott, 183. Of modern commentators, Wilson, 251, follows Lightfoot in maintaining this distinction.

85 See Trench, *Synonyms*, 211–17 (§60).

86 Trench, *Synonyms*, 212 (§60).

87 Trench, *Synonyms*, 216 (§60).

88 Harrisville, "Concept of Newness," 69–79. He claims that in the NT the terms are used synonymously and both imply a qualitative as well as a temporal significance (79).

89 Barth and Blanke, 412–13.

90 Barth and Blanke, 413, claim that "the passive voice points to God as the one who performs the action."

91 I have argued elsewhere (*Ephesians*, 288–89) that the πνεῦμα should here be interpreted as the Holy Spirit and not the human spirit.

(ἀνακαινώσεως πνεύματος ἁγίου). There is likely no intended difference in meaning between the νέος [ἄνθρωπος] . . . ἀνακαινόω that Paul uses here and the καινός ἄνθρωπος . . . ἀνανεόω that he uses in Eph 4:23–24, other than of the rhetorical variety. The somewhat surprising idea of the "new being renewed" is suggestive of the complexity of the concept he is introducing here. The new Adam, Christ, is in no need of renewal, but all those who have been incorporated into him need to align their lives completely with Christ and their new identity in him. They need to divest themselves of every vice and appropriate all the virtues of their new life. As Paul explains it, this needs to be done on the basis of recognizing that a fundamental change has already occurred in who they are. As followers of Christ, symbolized by the ritual of baptism, they have taken off their old identity and have put on a new identity. No longer are they to live in ways consistent with their old identity, but they are to "walk in newness of life" (Rom 6:4 NRSV).[92] They are called to "become what they are already."[93] Yet this is done in cooperation with the divine agent—the Holy Spirit—who is effecting the renewal.

The one other place where Paul uses the noun for renewal (ἀνακαίνωσις), he urges believers to "be transformed by the renewal of your mind" (Rom 12:2 ESV). Here at Col 3:10 he speaks of the involvement of the mind in the process of renewal by saying that it is "in knowledge" (εἰς ἐπίγνωσιν). The preposition (εἰς) denotes the goal or purpose of the transforming work of God. There is a progressive change in thinking that leads to more extensive knowledge about God, his plan, his purposes, and, especially here, his lifestyle expectations and ethics. This entails the development of a distinctively Christ-oriented worldview. Paul began the letter by relating how he regularly prays for the Colossians that they would "be filled with the knowledge [ἐπίγνωσιν] of his will, with a full measure of wisdom and insight that comes from the Spirit so that you walk worthily of the Lord, pleasing him in every way by bearing fruit and increasing in every good work through the knowledge [ἐπιγνώσει] of God" (Col 1:9–10). He here picks up this theme and urges its realization in their lives. This can only be accomplished through deepening their knowledge of who Christ is and who they are in relationship to him since in Christ "are hidden all the treasures of wisdom and knowledge" (Col 2:3). Part of what this means for them is that they will need to quit listening to the teaching and demands of the advocates of "the philosophy," which is leading them into deceitful teachings and unhealthy practices. As the Pastoral Epistles teach, they need to come "into a knowledge of the truth" (εἰς ἐπίγνωσιν ἀληθείας, 1 Tim 2:4; 2 Tim 2:25; 3:7). This involves thinking deeply about and setting their minds on the things above (Col 3:2).

This process of renewal takes place in conformity to a standard that God himself has established since the beginning of creation. That standard is the image of God (εἰκών τοῦ θεοῦ, the *imago dei*). Paul here alludes to the creation

92 So also Still, 329.
93 Pao, 227.

of Adam in his image in Gen 1:26–27: "Then God said, 'Let us make man in our image [ἄνθρωπον κατ᾽ εἰκόνα], after our likeness' . . . So God created man in his own image [καὶ ἐποίησεν ὁ θεὸς τὸν ἄνθρωπον κατ᾽ εἰκόνα θεοῦ], in the image of God he created him."[94] But this is not solely an allusion to Gen 1 since Paul declared in the hymn that he cites at the outset of this letter that Christ himself is "the image of the invisible God" (1:15). Adam is thus the prototype for Christ, the last Adam.[95] Christ is the image of God *par excellence* and serves as the pattern for the new creation incorporated into him. This corresponds with Paul's teaching in Romans where he says that God has predestined believers "to be conformed to the image of his Son [συμμόρφους τῆς εἰκόνος τοῦ υἱοῦ αὐτου]" (Rom 8:29).

Accordingly, the Father should be understood as the subject of the participle (τοῦ κτίσαντος)[96] and is both the author of the original creation and the author of the new creation. The pronoun αὐτόν refers to "the new self" (the νέος [ἄνθρωπος]) that God has created in his redemptive work. Christ, as the supreme image of God, thus functions as the model and pattern for the new humanity. The goal of the Christian community is to be transformed into the image of Christ. This is not only a restoration to the pre-fall condition of Adam, but something that transcends it, since the model is Christ himself.[97] Pao aptly comments, "The christocentric emphasis is retained here, where Paul is urging believers to conform to Christ, who is the perfect image of the Creator."[98] Jesus thus serves as "the head and prototype of the new humanity of the new creation."[99] This passage gives more meaning and texture to Paul's statement that "if anyone is in Christ, he is a new creation. The old has passed away; behold, the new has come" (2 Cor 5:17 ESV; see also Gal 6:15).

In summary, the new self is in the process of being renewed through the work of the Holy Spirit. That renewal process involves developing a substantially new way of thinking about life in all respects—especially about one's new identity and the implications of that for daily life. The supreme model for this new life is Christ himself, who perfectly embodies God's design from the original creation.

**11 ὅπου οὐκ ἔνι Ἕλλην καὶ Ἰουδαῖος, περιτομὴ καὶ ἀκροβυστία, βάρβαρος, Σκύθης, δοῦλος, ἐλεύθερος,** "where there is no Greek or Jew, circumcision or uncircumcision, barbarian, Scythian, slave, or free." Prior to their conversion, the Colossian believers thought of themselves through the lens of their ethnic,

94 See Beetham, *Echoes of Scripture*, 231–45; Beale, 865.

95 Beetham, *Echoes of Scripture*, 244.

96 This is the view of most commentators. Chrysostom and some early church fathers argued that Christ should be interpreted as the subject and the author of creation.

97 See Eadie, 229–30, who notes that "the image conferred in renovation, though generically the same, cannot be in all points identical with that given in creation. It is fuller and lovlier . . . a higher form of life, having its type in the . . . second Adam."

98 Pao, 227.

99 Beetham, *Echoes of Scripture*, 244.

religious, cultural, and social backgrounds. Paul here declares that Christ has relativized those former categories of belonging. What matters above all is that they belong to Christ and should understand their identity in relation to him.

The adverb of place, ὅπου, "where," refers to ὁ νέος, "the new self." Although not properly a location, it is the new reality that God has created in Christ. One needs to see this in terms of both the individual and the corporate entity. An individual enters the community, for instance, as a Jew, a Scythian, a slave, or as a freed slave. But these distinctions, while persisting, do not retain the same level of significance in the new society that God is creating. Paul summarily negates them in saying, οὐκ ἔνι, "there is not . . ." The ἔνι (here not to be misunderstood as ἑνί, the dative of εἷς) is an abbreviated form of the preposition ἐν and the verb ἐστιν, always with the negative in the NT and with the meaning, "there is not."[100] The fact that these distinctions are not entirely negated becomes clear in his discussion of the duties of the various members of the Christian household in 3:18–4:1.

Two of the four pairings delineated in this text—Jew/Greek and slave/free—are included in Gal 3:28: "there is neither Jew nor Greek, there is neither slave nor free, there is no male and female, for you are all one in Christ Jesus" (ESV). Why Paul here omits the gender pairing is not clear. It is too speculative to posit that ethnic and class distinctions played a part in the Colossian "philosophy," but gender did not.[101] It is also too speculative to assume that our passage reflects a pre-Pauline tradition here,[102] possibly from a baptismal context that is reflected also in 1 Cor 12:13 and Gal 3:28.[103] Baptism is not explicitly in view in this section, and this assumption would not explain the omissions (male/female) and the unique pairing (barbarian/Scythian).

The first pairing—Jews and Greeks—reflects a Jewish way of viewing the world. Ἰουδαῖος is an ethnogeographic term and can be translated "Judean" after the southern portion of Palestine that encompasses the city of Jerusalem.[104] In the NT era, it took on ethnic significance and was commonly used to refer to the Jewish people. Josephus uses the term hundreds of times to refer to his people, regardless of whether they lived in Judea, Ephesus, or Rome. Of particular significance is the fact that he uses it to refer to the Jews who lived in the Lycus Valley (Josephus, *Ant.* 14.241–42). This was the common way of referring to the Jewish people throughout the NT, where it appears 195 times. The term was also known locally. The inscription ἔθνους Ἰουδαίων appears on a statuary base found at Aphrodisias identifying various peoples subject to Roman rule.[105]

100 BDF §98.
101 Pao, 229.
102 Bevere, *Sharing in the Inheritance*, 120.
103 Moo, 271–72.
104 See the discussion in Cohen, *Beginnings of Jewishness*, 69–106, esp. 72.
105 Smith, "*Ethne* from the Sebasteion at Aphrodisias," 55 (no. 9).

The contrasting member of this pair is Ἕλλην, "Hellene" or "Greek." It is not simply a geographical term and limited to Achaia or Macedonia but is simultaneously a term expressive of Greek language and culture and could be applied to a wide variety of ethnicities, including Jews. When it is used by a Jewish writer in conjunction with Ἰουδαῖος to form a contrasting pair, it refers to all other people in distinction from Jews. Josephus uses this pairing frequently (e.g., Josephus, *Ant.* 13.378; 16.160; 18:257) as do Luke (e.g., Acts 14:1; 16:3; 18:4; 19:10, 17; 20:21) and Paul (Rom 1:16; 2:9, 10; 3:9; 10:12; 1 Cor 1:22, 24; 10:32; 12:13).

The second pair—περιτομὴ καὶ ἀκροβυστία, "circumcision and uncircumcision"—overlaps significantly with "Jews and Greeks" but focuses more on the religious distinctiveness between the two groups. Circumcision was the single most important marker of Jewish identity and expressed loyalty to the Torah. God gave it to Abraham as a sign of the covenant: "This is my covenant, which you shall keep, between me and you and your offspring after you: every male among you shall be circumcised [περιτμηθήσεται]. You shall be circumcised [περιτμηθήσεσθε] in the flesh of your foreskins [ἀκροβυστίας], and it shall be a sign of the covenant between me and you" (Gen 17:10–11 ESV). Failure to keep this ritual put one outside of the covenant (Gen 17:14). During the Maccabean era, some Jews "removed the marks of circumcision," which the author of 1 Maccabees regards as tantamount to abandoning the covenant (1 Macc 1:15). Mattathias expressed zeal for the law when he "forcibly circumcised all the uncircumcised boys that they found within the borders of Israel" (1 Macc 2:46 NRSV). The book of Jubilees strongly reinforces this distinctive practice of the Jewish people as an eternal commandment handed down from Abraham that identifies the covenant people of God (Jub. 16.25–32). The writer declares: "This law is for all the eternal generations . . . it is an eternal ordinance ordained and written in the heavenly tablets. And anyone who is born whose own flesh is not circumcised on the eighth day is not from the sons of the covenant" (Jub. 16.25–26). During the reign of the Hasmonean leader, John Hyrcanus, circumcision was foisted upon defeated gentiles (the Idumeans) as a condition for them to stay in their land (Josephus, *Ant.* 13.257). The law had made a provision for a foreigner who wished to celebrate the Passover as long as he was willing to submit to circumcision (Exod 12:48–49). Philo speaks of gentiles who have become προσήλυτοι by virtue of "the fact of their having come over [προσεληλυθέναι] to a new and God-fearing constitution, learning to disregard the fabulous inventions of other nations, and clinging to unalloyed truth" (Philo, *Spec. Laws* 1.51). Becoming a proselyte involved submitting to circumcision, as Izates from the royal house of Adiabene, discovered. He knew "that he could not be thoroughly a Jew [βεβαίως Ἰουδαῖος] unless he were circumcised" (Josephus, *Ant.* 20.38). Circumcision was thus a religious identity marker associated with the Jewish people and fidelity to the Torah. "Uncircumcision" (ἀκροβυστία) was a Jewish (and, later, a Christian) way of referring to anyone who had not submitted to the rite of circumcision. The term was never used in pagan literature.

The third pair—βάρβαρος, Σκύθης, "barbarian, Scythian,"—has proven much more difficult to identify. There has been ongoing debate over the precise meaning of the terms, whether they are meant to refer to contrasting groups as the first two pairs (Jews and non-Jews; circumcised and uncircumcised), and why the author did not coordinate this pair with καί.

The more natural contrast with βάρβαρος would have been Ἕλλην, as Paul does in Rom 1:14: "I am a debtor both to Greeks and to barbarians" (NRSV). The term "barbarian" properly refers to a non-Greek speaker and has linguistic overtones.[106] Paul thus says in 1 Cor 14:11: "if I do not know the meaning of the language, I will be a foreigner [βάρβαρος] to the speaker and the speaker a foreigner [βάρβαρος] to me" (ESV). The term is onomatopoeic and suggests the way non-Greek speakers sound to Greeks. Strabo explains:

> When all who pronounced words thickly were being called barbarians [βαρβάρων] onomatopoetically, it appeared that the pronunciations of all alien races were likewise thick, I mean of those that were not Greek [Ἑλλήνων]. Those, therefore, they called barbarians [βαρβάρους] in the special sense of the term, at first derisively, meaning that they pronounced words thickly or harshly; and then we misused the word as a general ethnic term, thus making a logical distinction between the Greeks [Ἕλληνας] and all other races. (Strabo, *Geogr.* 14.2.28)

Strabo then refers to the fact that "barbarians" also do not live according to the Greek fashion (Ἑλληνικῶς ζῆν). Thus, barbarians are both linguistically and culturally different than Greeks. The widespread usage of this term for those who did not speak Greek, or speak it properly, is evidence against those who would interpret the term as referring to those who live in the southern regions of the known world at the time, such as Ethiopia.[107] But perhaps most significantly for our text is the fact that Tatian, in his *Oratio ad Graecos*, classifies Phrygians and Carians as barbarians (Tatian, *Or. Graec.* 1).[108] This corresponds with a resurgence of Phrygian identity within the Hellenization and Romanization that was taking place in Phrygia and the Lycus Valley.

Why Paul would have referred to Scythians in this group of pairings has been puzzling to interpreters. There is no evidence of Scythian presence in the Lycus Valley, either in the first century or in previous centuries. And the readers' knowledge of Scythians would be limited. Originally a nomadic tribe from what is today the Russian steppes, many Scythians eventually settled in the territory north of the Black Sea that today is part of southern Ukraine

106 See BDAG, s.v. βάρβαρος.

107 Contra Sumney, 206, 208–9.

108 See the discussion in Huttner, *Early Christianity in the Lycus Valley*, 29.

and southern Russia, including the Crimean Peninsula. Important cities of Scythia were Chersonesos (near modern Sevastopol), Olbia, and Nikonion. From Strabo's vantage point, the northern part of the inhabited world extended "to the remote confines of Scythia [Σκυθίας] and Celtica" and the south "to the remote confines of Ethiopia [Αἰθιόπων]" (Strabo, *Geogr.* 1.1.13). This suggests that if Paul were envisioning a geographical contrast of north and south, he would have paired Scythian and Ethiopian, especially since Ethiopian people were known to Greeks and Jews. Virgil speaks of "the tribes of Scythia by the waters of Maeotis, where the turbid Danube tosses his yellow sands" (Virgil, *Georg.* 3.349–50). Ovid describes the place as "icy Scythia, a gloomy and barren soil, a land without corn, without trees" (Ovid, *Metam.* 8.785–89).

Greek authors often engaged in a cultural stereotyping of Scythians, regarding them as unrefined, savage, and uncouth.[109] Jewish writers joined this chorus by speaking of their "savage cruelty" (3 Macc. 7.5), as "brute beasts" who "take a pleasure in killing men" (Josephus, *Ag. Ap.* 2.269), and as "barbarous" (ἐξηγρίωται) and "uncivilized" (Philo, *Embassy* 10). This led many interpreters to describe "Scythian" in Col 3:11 as a subcategory of "barbarian." Lightfoot went so far as to say that they were "the lowest kind of barbarian."[110] Others have referred to them as "the quintessential barbarian."[111] Yamauchi asserts that "their reputation for ferocity, their scalping of captives, and their other barbarous customs made their name synonymous with savagery down into the Christian era."[112] For him, the term "Scythian" would have aroused a strong emotional response from the Colossians and served Paul's purpose well by demonstrating that "even those cruel, barbaric Scythians—the epitome of savagery in the ancient world—were capable of redemption through the grace of Christ."[113] But not all Greek writers spoke of the Scythians in such negative terms. Apollonius characterized the Scythians as wise (Apollonius of Tyana, *Letters* 61). A Scythian philosopher, Anacharsis, was widely known and highly regarded by the Greeks (e.g., Herodotus, *Hist.* 4.76–77; Diogenes Laertius, *Lives* 1.101–5; Plutarch, *Sol.* 5). Lucian says that Anacharsis came out of Scythia to Athens "out of a longing for Greek culture" (Lucian, *Scyth.* 1.1). While in Athens, he aspired to know "their finest laws, their greatest men, their customs, assemblies, their way of life, their constitution" (Lucian, *Scyth.* 1.4). For Greeks, the Scythian prince Anacharsis "came to exemplify the wise barbarian."[114]

Other interpreters have argued that it is important to see "barbarian" and "Scythian" as a contrasting pair since the first, second, and fourth pairs are

109 See BDAG, s.v. Σκύθης.

110 Lightfoot, 218.

111 "Σκύθης," *EDNT* 3:256.

112 Yamauchi, "Scythians," 98. He cites 2 Macc 4:47; 3 Macc. 7.5; 4 Macc. 10.7; Josephus. *Ag. Ap.* 2.269; Tertullian, *Apol.* 9.9.

113 Yamauchi, "Scythians," 98.

114 M. Gagarin, "Anacharsis," *OCD*[3] 79.

opposites—that is, mutually exclusive categories. T. Martin, for instance, has attempted to make the case that one should view the pairing of barbarian and Scythian "from a Scythian perspective rather than a Greek perspective."[115] For him, the Cynics identified closely with the Scythians to distinguish themselves from the rest of humanity. But this explanation only works if one accepts his reconstruction of the Colossian philosophy as a form of Cynic philosophy; otherwise, there is no reason to interpret the terms from a Cynic perspective. I have already cast doubt on this reconstruction in the *Introduction*, and few interpreters have found his Cynic background to "the philosophy" compelling.

D. A. Campbell has sought to bring an entirely new perspective to the debate by proposing a double chiastic structure for the four pairs:[116]

| **First Two Pairs** | | **Second Two Pairs** | |
|---|---|---|---|
| Greek | a | barbarian | c |
| Jew | b | Scythian | d |
| circumcision | b′ | slave | d′ |
| uncircumcision | a′ | free | c′ |

He contends that the chiasm results in the opposition of barbarian to Scythian through the social categories of slave and free. The antithesis is no longer barbarian and Scythian, but between "free barbarian and Scythian slave." But he is hard pressed to find compelling evidence to support the contention that Scythian should correspond to slave, despite his assertion that the term "Scythian" "denoted slaves procured from the north of the Black Sea."[117] He also faces difficulty in asserting a correspondence between barbarian and free. Foreign non-Greek speakers ("barbarians") could just as easily be slaves, and they often were.

It is thus highly unlikely that barbarian and Scythian reflects an antithetical pair or that Scythian should be interpreted as either denoting or connoting a slave. The fact that Paul does not use the connective καί may be a signal that he is breaking his pattern of using antithetical pairs in this instance.

Why Paul chose to use "Scythian" in this third pairing in association with barbarian remains unsolved. He mentions Scythians nowhere else in his

115 Martin, "Scythian Perspective in Col 3:11," 249–61, esp. 256. Campbell, "Scythian Perspective," 81–84, provides an apt critique of this view.

116 Campbell, "Unravelling Colossians 3:11b," 120–32. He is followed in his case by Pao, 228–29.

117 Campbell, "Unravelling Colossians 3:11b," 120–32. Martin, "Scythian Perspective or Elusive Chiasm," 261, has responded by assessing his evidence and rightly concluding that "neither the primary literature nor the secondary literature cited by Campbell substantiates such a claim. Thomson, *Chiasmus*, 33–34, also finds Campbell's proposal unconvincing.

letters, nor is the term used anywhere else in the NT. He had an extensive array of other choices available to him. He could have mentioned Britannian (if he were referring to the northernmost regions), Bactrian, Persian, or Indian (eastern), Ethiopian (southern), or Iberian (western). Or, for local people, he could have referred to local territorial-tribal groupings, such as Carian, Lydian, or Phrygian.

Some have strained to find some local connection with Scythians. A. Cadwallader has suggested that one of the names in a list of sixty-six on a recently discovered column from Colossae may have been Thracian or "even specifically Scythian."[118] But this depends on a reconstruction, is highly speculative, and would still be very slim evidence for a Scythian connection with Colossae. U. Huttner suggests the possibility that a memory of the Cimmerian expulsion by the Scythians had survived in the area.[119] They were a people group who were driven out of the territory north of the Black Sea in the seventh century BC and then overthrew Phrygia. Yet this was hundreds of years earlier, and there is no local evidence of an ongoing memory of this event.

There is, however, an archaeological discovery that may have some relevance for interpreting this text—the statuary, reliefs, and inscriptions from the Sebasteion at Aphrodisias, about forty miles east of Colossae (see the discussion in the *Introduction*). The graphic and selective depictions of the various subjugated peoples were not a comprehensive list of conquered peoples, but an impressive and representative selection of the different peoples spanning every direction to the extremes of the empire. The reliefs depicted the diverse *ethnē* that comprised the extent of the Roman world rule. Although no Scythians are named in the inscriptions or depicted in the reliefs, it could be that they were represented but that the inscription was among those lost from the structure. Yet more importantly, these were representatives of extremely diverse groupings of people—geographically, ethnically, and culturally—who were part of the impressive Roman imperium.

"Barbarian, Scythian" may therefore be a way of referring to anyone who is not Greek and to every people group throughout the Roman empire, including the most obscure and distant peoples. This would be consistent with Paul's comment at the outset of the letter that the gospel has gone out to the "whole world" (ἐν παντὶ τῷ κόσμῳ, Col 1:6).

δοῦλος, ἐλεύθερος, "slave, free," the fourth pair, represents a socioeconomic classification. As with the previous three pairings, Paul endeavors to communicate to the Colossians that these categories of identity are now irrelevant for members of the body of Christ. Paul expresses a similar conviction to the Corinthians when he explains, "For in one Spirit we were all baptized into one body—Jews or Greeks, slaves or free" (1 Cor 12:13 ESV). Social status was

118 Cadwallader, "Honouring the Repairer of the Baths," 111, 113.

119 Huttner, *Early Christianity in the Lycus Valley*, 136.

irrelevant for belonging to the church. Slaves were welcome on the same footing as free individuals. Paul tells the slaves in the Corinthian church, "Were you a slave when called? Do not be concerned about it" (1 Cor 7:21 NRSV). He then advises them to gain their freedom if they have the opportunity.

The overall message of our text is clear. The new corporate entity that Christ has created possesses an inherent unity that transcends every status indicator and boundary marker that previously informed their identity. As a new community created to reflect the image of God, ethnic, religious, cultural, and socioeconomic distinctions are all relativized and subsumed under the all-encompassing importance of their new identity in Christ.[120] The former identity markers remain and continue to be important, but they do not matter as much as the new. Christ and his body have priority over all other markers.

ἀλλὰ πάντα καὶ ἐν πᾶσιν Χριστός, "but Christ is all and in all." As Paul began this section with a focus on Christ and the relationship of believers to him (3:1–4), he now concludes it with a short, emphatic spotlight on Christ and his defining importance to the new community. In fact, Χριστός occurs as the final word of the entire section, where it stands in an emphatic position.

Paul makes two assertions about Christ. In the first he declares that Christ is πάντα. This is materially different than the many statements about Christ's relationship to τὰ πάντα in the hymn of praise to Christ at the outset of the letter (1:15–20). Within the hymn, τὰ πάντα refers to all of creation—everything in heaven and on earth—including the invisible powers. Christ created τὰ πάντα, he sustains τὰ πάντα, he will reconcile τὰ πάντα to himself, and he is πρὸ πάντων, but he is not to be identified with τὰ πάντα. Paul is careful to maintain a distinction between the creator and the created order. In the second strophe of the hymn, however, Paul speaks of Christ in relationship to the church and declares him to be the head of this new community. The aspiration of the hymn writer is that for this new community, Christ may become "preeminent" (πρωτεύων) among all its members (ἐν πᾶσιν, 1:18)—that is, "that he might come to have first place in everything."[121] Paul takes up this theme here by affirming that "Christ is everything" in the sense that he is all important.[122] There is nothing in all of creation that should supplant the place that Christ has in the affections and priorities of every believer and every believing community. The NLT is thus correct in translating, "Christ is all that matters" (so also the NJB: "there is only Christ: he is everything"). Meyer explains it: "Christ is the sum total of all desires and strivings,"[123] and as Moule puts it, "Christ is all that matters."[124]

---

120 So also Bormann, 168; Walsh and Keesmat, *Colossians Remixed*, 113.

121 This is the translation offered by BDAG, s.v. πρωτεύω.

122 So also Harris, 134; Williams, 133.

123 Meyer, 356; cited also by Beale, 286.

124 C. Moule, 121.

The second assertion, linked to the first by the presence of the conjunction καί, declares that Christ is "in all" believers. It is grammatically possible to take πᾶσιν as neuter,[125] but it is more likely here that Paul is affirming the closeness, solidarity, and presence of Christ with all of his people. This would be consistent with the threefold emphasis on "with him" (σύν) at the outset of this section (3:1–4). It also fits with Paul's revelation of "the mystery" as "Christ in you" (Χριστὸς ἐν ὑμῖν; 1:27). Once again, Paul is not making a pantheistic statement ("Christ is in all things") but an ecclesiologial statement ("Christ is in all believers"). This is vitally important for the Colossians to know. They have direct and immediate access to Christ and all the resources that are in him (2:10). Their relationship to him and access to spiritual power does not need to be mediated through a shaman figure. Christ is also the basis for their unity as a new community since he is in all believers—regardless of their social, cultural, ethnic, or even religious background.

These two statements are similar to what Paul says in 1 Cor 15:28 where Paul concludes his discussion of the end of time when all of creation will be made subject to the Son and ultimately the Father, "that God may be all in all" (ἵνα ᾖ ὁ θεὸς πάντα ἐν πᾶσιν). There is a shift of emphasis, however, from the future to the present in Colossians, and the focus is put solely on Christ. He is both "everything" to them and their primary bond of unity—"for you are all one in Christ Jesus" (Gal 3:28) and constitute "one body" (Col 3:15).

## *Explanation*

"Christ is everything." He is preeminent over all of creation and should hold first place in the lives of all the Colossian believers. There is nothing that is more important than Christ and his purposes, plans, and will. Because of that, the Colossians should be motivated to bring every area of their lives under his lordship. This includes not only how they respond to the teaching of the opponents but all of their behavior and lifestyle choices. What they believe and how they live should be ordered around the Lord Jesus Christ. As Paul told the Colossians in the previous section, Christ is "your life" (3:3).

Developing sexual purity in one's thought life and behavior is extremely important, especially for a group of gentile believers in a highly sexualized culture. For gentile believers living in Colossae (or anywhere in the Roman world), adopting the sexual ethic Paul prescribes would have been difficult since it ran counter to the prevailing cultural norms. Sex with slaves, sex before marriage, having a mistress, homosexual behavior, and even entertaining thoughts of these things are now deemed inconsistent with life in Christ. Paul stresses the need to eradicate sexual impurity in his first grouping of five vices (3:5). Even the fifth vice mentioned, greed, not only refers to the desire for more money but likely

125 As Lightfoot, 219, does.

also speaks of an insatiable desire for sex. Paul reserves his harshest critique for these twin passions—more money and more sex. They are tantamount to idolatry and thus displace the position that Christ should have in the life of these believers. The Hebrew Bible is replete with references to God's hatred of idolatry and accounts for how he pours out his wrath on those who practice idolatry. It comes as no surprise, then, to see Paul speak of the assuredness of God's wrath coming upon those who orient their lives around these things.

Paul also focuses on their need to attend to certain negative emotions and their consequent behavior, which can disrupt and harm the social cohesion of the community. Unchecked emotions such as anger are inconsistent with new life in Christ and can manifest in ways that hurt others, such as in slandering fellow believers. But Paul here names a variety of behaviors that will injure others in the Christian community—such as lying to one's brothers and sisters, speaking obscene and shameful talk, and having a mean-spirited disposition. Such behavior cannot be ignored; they must be brought under control.

The danger Paul sees in many of these vices is expressed in the metaphor he chooses for how to deal with them: they must be "killed" (3:5). He applies this to sexual matters and greed, but it could be extended to all the vices. No doubt this would have jarred the Colossian believers as they heard the letter read for the first time. Paul was very serious about how important it was for the Colossian community—indeed, every individual—to deal with these issues in their lives. These sinful practices need to be completely eradicated. "Killing" implies taking the most drastic measures to do so. This text (along with Rom 8:13) and the metaphor of killing were the impetus to John Owen in writing his highly influential volume, *Of the Mortification of Sin in Believers*, which was published in 1656.

The second metaphor—"take off"—is less startling, but just as decisive (3:8). The "taking off" metaphor prepares the reader for the next section that will speak of "putting on" virtues. It implies the complete removal of these vices from one's life.

Paul is not insisting here on a program of moral improvement to be undertaken simply through rigorous exertion of the will. He roots the possibility, and indeed the necessity, of moral change in the supernatural renewal of the person that has already taken place in becoming a Christian. When the Colossians put their faith in Christ (1:4; 2:12), they entered a relationship with Christ that was objectively experienced as a participation with Christ in his death and resurrection. Paul here describes the implications of this participation in terms of a change of identity: they have taken off the old self and have put on the new. This new identity is both individual and corporate, and it has significant implications for the life of the corporate community.

Although participation with Christ in his death results in a decisive change that Paul refers to as "having taken off the old self" (3:9b), this does not mean that believers no longer experience an inner impulse to sin. Schweizer expresses it memorably: "in baptism the old Adam is indeed drowned; but the scoundrel can still swim!"[126] The full and compelling force of the influence of the old self has beeen dealt a decisive blow. Believers have died to the influence of the "demonic forces of this world" (2:20). This means that they now have the opportunity and obligation to resist or, as Paul puts it here, to kill these influences in their lives. The indicative of the dying with Christ and rising with him now issues in the imperative to live by a new standard. And, as Lohse has observed, "the fact that the imperative in Col's exhortation is based on and developed out of the indicative agrees completely with Pauline theology."[127]

God himself is powerfully at work in the lives of believers, renewing them in accordance with his own image. The passive voice of the verb ἀνακαινούμενον, "being renewed" (3:10), is a divine passive. Elsewhere, Paul talks about the Holy Spirit as the agent of renewal in the life of a believer (e.g., Rom 8:13; Gal 5:16, 18, 25; Eph 4:23; 2 Thess 2:13; Titus 3:5), but the divine work is certainly not absent in Colossians. It comes to its most prominent expression in Colossians through the stress on being "in Christ" (see esp. Col 2:10), with the implication that Christ himself empowers and resources believers to change. He is "in all" believers and is powerfully at work in their lives (3:11).

The standard for the ethical and moral change is the image of God (Col 3:10). Believers are called to be like God in his holiness and purity (Lev 11:44–45). The ultimate bearer of this image is Christ himself (Col 1:15). Thus, Paul calls these believers to put their focus on Christ and to conform their lives to his example, his purpose, and his will (3:1).

The reference to God's coming wrath in Col 3:6–7 is not intended to scare the Colossian believers into changing their behavior or else face the consequences of God's wrath. Paul makes it clear that this wrath is reserved for those who have not entered the Christian community (i.e., it is for "the sons of disobedience"), and he clarifies that this is not them ("among whom you *once* walked"). But the mention of God's eschatological wrath against evil is a reminder of how seriously God takes the practice of these vices. They are not to be trifled with, ignored, or minimized. They need to be put to death.

But the overall basis for ethical change in the lives of these Colossian believers is Christ himself. As Paul exclaims at the end of this section, "Christ is everything." Yet Christ should be everything to them in every respect. His kingdom priorities should have first place in all of their thinking and aspirations. This was, in fact, how Paul lived and what he modeled to his churches, as he so eloquently explains to the Philippians: "Indeed, I count everything as loss because of the surpassing worth of knowing Christ Jesus my Lord. For his sake I have suffered the loss of all things and count them as rubbish, in order that I may gain Christ" (Phil 3:8 ESV).

126 Schweizer, 202.

127 Lohse, 145.

# Putting on the Virtues of God's Chosen People (3:12–17)

## *Bibliography*

**Barclay, J. M. G.** *Paul and the Gift.* **Bevere, A.** *Sharing in the Inheritance.* **Canavan, R.** *Clothing the Body.* **Cavin, R. L.** *New Existence*, 126–83. **Daniell, D.** *Bible in English.* **Detwiler, D. F.** "Church Music," 347–69. **Fee, G.** *Empowering Presence.* **Gordley, M. E.** *Colossian Hymn.* ———. *Teaching through Song.* **Hengel, M.** "Hymns and Christology," 78–96. **Kim, J. H.** *Clothing Imagery.* **Malan, F. S.** "Church Singing," 509–24. **McClure, J.,** and **R. Collins.** *Bede.* **Mitchell, S.** *Anatolia.* 2 vols. **Pao, D. W.** *Thanksgiving.* **Reynolds, J.,** and **R. Tannenbaum.** *Jews and God-Fearers at Aphrodisias.* **Smith, J. A.** "First-Century Christian Singing," 1–15. **Waelkens, M.** *Die kleinasiatischen Türsteine.* **Witherington, B.,** and **G. F. Wessels.** "In the Name of the Lord," 303–33.

## *Translation*

12 *Therefore, as God's*[a] *chosen people, holy and beloved, clothe yourselves with a heart of compassion,*
*kindness, humility, gentleness, and patience.* 13 *Bear with one another and forgive each other. If someone*
*has a complaint*[b] *against someone else, just as the Lord*[c] *forgave all of you, so all of you [should forgive]*
*others.* 14 *Upon all these [virtues, clothe yourselves with] love, which*[d] *is the bond of perfection.* 15 *Let*
*the peace of Christ control your hearts, since you were called to it in one*[e] *body. And be thankful.* 16 *Let*
*the word of Christ*[f] *dwell in you richly by teaching and admonishing one another in all wisdom with*
*spiritual psalms, hymns, and songs and with gratitude*[g] *singing in your hearts to God.* 17 *And whatever*
*you do in word or in work, do everything in the name of the Lord Jesus, giving thanks to God the Father*
*through him.*

## *Notes*

a. [3:12] Most manuscripts include the article before "God" (ὡς ἐκλεκτοὶ τοῦ θεοῦ), but a handful omit it (A D F G 1505 1881). The impact on interpretation is negligible.

b. [3:13] Codex D has μέμψις, "reason for complaint," instead of μομφή, "blame," and codex G has ὀργή, "wrath." Both represent scribal attempts to correct the use of μομφή, a hapax both in the NT and LXX as well as being quite rare in Greek literature.

c. [3:13] The Byzantine tradition, along with a few other witnesses (the Alexandrian C Ψ $\text{cop}^{\text{bo}}$ $\text{cop}^{\text{sa}}$), reads "Christ" (Χριστός) here. This reading was adopted by Tischendorf and appears in many of the early English versions, such as Tyndale, Geneva, Bishops, and KJV (and now, the NKJV). Metzger attributes the Byzantine reading to scribal assimilation to Eph 4:32, "forgiving one another, as God in Christ forgave you."[1] This is the best explanation, especially since θεός is also a variant (ℵ and some manuscripts of the Vulgate). These two variants would also serve as interpretations of the more ambiguous κύριος.

---

1 Metzger, *Textual Commentary*, 557–58.

d. [3:14] The neuter relative pronoun ὅ does not agree with its antecedent, ἀγάπην, in gender. This likely motivated a scribe to alter the wording to ἥτις. This correction became preserved in the Byzantine tradition along with K L Ψ and a handful of other witnesses. Both Sinaiticus (א) and Codex D read the masculine nominative ὅς. This was probably motivated by agreement with the gender and number of σύνδεσμος.

e. [3:15] 𝔓[46] B 6 and 1739 omit ἑνί, which results in the translation, "you were called in body (or, in [the] body)." This is likely an accidental error.

f. [3:16] Codex Sinaiticus (א) has "the word of the Lord," while A and C have "the word of God." Since ὁ λόγος τοῦ Χριστοῦ is unique in the letters of Paul, it is not surprising to find scribes bringing this expression into conformity with the more common "the word of the Lord" (1 Thess 1:8; 2 Thess 3:1; see also Acts 8:25; 13:44, 48, 49; 15:35, 36; 16:32; 19:10, 20) and "the word of God" (Col 1:25; see also Rom 9:6; 1 Cor 14:36; Eph 6:17; 1 Thess 2:13; 1 Tim 4:5; 2 Tim 2:9; Titus 2:5).

g. [3:16] At issue is whether the article should be included or omitted with the noun—that is, should the text read ἐν τῇ χάριτι or simply ἐν χάριτι. If the article is original, then the noun should likely be interpreted as "grace" in the normal Pauline sense. Without the article, it is possible to read the phrase as "with gratitude." The textual witnesses are evenly split. In support of the inclusion of the article are some very important Alexandrian (𝔓[46] B Ψ) and Western witnesses (D F G). But there are also some important Alexandrian witnesses (א A C 33 81 104) in support of the omission, along with the entire Byzantine text. The difficulty of making this decision is evident in the NA[28] and UBS[5], which include the article but place it in brackets to indicate the uncertainty. With the THGNT, I lean toward the omission as original, with the assumption that a scribe may have been motivated to insert an article to clarify that the term should be read as a reference to God's grace and not simply as "with gratitude," a less common usage of χάρις in Paul's letters.

## *Form/Structure/Setting*

### *Form (and Literary Context)*

This is a distinct and coherent section of the letter, but it is closely linked to 3:5–11 as the heart of the moral exhortation of Colossians. Both of these passages, however, are deeply rooted in the theological convictions Paul expressed in 3:1–4, which is a summary and slight expansion on the key themes of 2:9–15. At the heart of this teaching is the essence of new life in Christ flowing out of the participation of believers in the death and resurrection of Christ. This real participation with Christ enables believers to think differently and behave differently and is thus crucial to Paul's understanding of how Christians can rid themselves of vices and appropriate virtues. Whereas the previous section focused on the negative (vices), this section commends the positive (virtues).

This passage also continues the clothing metaphor that Paul introduced in 3:8 with the admonition to "take off" certain vices as one would take off a set of clothes and then to "put on" the new self (3:9–10). Paul begins this new section with the admontion to "put on" a collection of virtues (3:12) and to "put on" (the verb is implied) love (3:14). The metaphor is extended also by the use of term "bond" (3:14), which functions like a belt in holding all of the garments in place. The clothing metaphor was a common image that probably reflects a combination of the local visual landscape (as Canavan has suggested), but that is also infused with meaning from the OT and Judaism (see the extended discussion at 3:9). Consequently, there is no allusion here to the practice of putting on a baptismal garment.[2] This was a custom developed much later than the composition of this letter. The clothing metaphor comes to an end in 3:14 since the next verse simply delivers an exhortation with no image attached ("be thankful"), and Paul introduces the new image of "indwelling" in 3:16.

The virtues that Paul commends in this section are deeply rooted in the OT and Judaism, as well as in the teaching and example of Jesus as represented in the Gospel traditions. Some of the virtues overlap with the same or similar ones in Stoic moral exhortation. Yet some of the virtues Paul mentions are entirely absent in Stoic ethics (most notably, love). The explicit theological basis for these virtues in the teaching and example of Jesus and in the OT also differentiates Paul's moral exhortation here sharply from Stoicism.

Paul continues the explicit and overt christological emphasis in this section that is characteristic of the letter as a whole. He provides it with a new accent by highlighting the importance of the teaching about Christ (along with the teaching of Christ himself) as a crucial foundation for taking off vice and appropriating virtue (3:16). Despite its important role, Paul actually frames this passage not with Christology but with a focus on God the Father. Paul says that he is the one who has chosen the Colossian believers as a people for himself, set them apart as his own, and poured out his love upon them (3:12). The passage ends with Paul's appeal to the Colossians to respond to the Father by rendering their gratitude to him (3:17). This concentration on the Father forms an *inclusio* bracketing the passage. Yet the very last words of the passage are "through him"—that is, through Christ (3:17). Christ is the agent of the Father's redemptive plan.

There is significant overlap between this passage and Paul's other lists of virtues, especially Galatians 5:22–23—a list he terms "the fruit of the Spirit." Common to the lists are love, peace, patience, kindness, and gentleness. Although not typically classified as a virtue list, 1 Thess 5:12–18 contains many of the same virtues worded as exhortations. These include love, peace, patience, and gratitude.

## *Structure*

The overall structure of the passage is best described in terms of three divisions. The first section consists of the principal imperative followed by ten virtues that Paul is encouraging the readers to "put on" (3:12–15). The second section expresses the foundation or basis for the development of these virtues, which is "the word of Christ" (3:16). The final section is a summary admonition to do everything "in the name of the Lord Jesus" (3:17).

The introductory admonition "put on" corresponds to the previous

---

2 Contra, e.g., MacDonald, 145–47.

admonition to "take off" (3:8)—both an expression of the clothing metaphor that Paul uses throughout these two sections (3:8–11 and 3:12–15). Before he enumerates the virtues, however, he briefly reminds the readers of their new situation in life based on God's redemptive work. They have been chosen by God and are thus holy and beloved (3:12b). This reminder serves to motivate and call them to an alignment with their new identity bestowed on them by God.

This is followed by two groupings of five virtues that Paul wants them to develop in their lives. The first group are all nouns in the accusative case functioning as the direct objects of "put on." This set corresponds in form to the previous set of vices, the group of five nouns in the accusative case serving as the direct objects of "take off" (3:8). The grammatical form of the second group of five virtues (3:13–15) varies considerably from the first. Two are expressed with present participles, one with an implied verb (picking up the ἐνδύσασθε of 3:12a), and the final two with present imperative verbs. Although some interpreters have seen this second group of five as a series of independent admonitions, it is best to regard it as a second group of five virtues semantically dependent on the main verb ἐνδύσασθε of 3:12a. This is explicitly the case with the third virtue mentioned, love, which is formally dependent on the main verb. The middle three of this group (forgiveness, love, and peace) also have explanatory glosses attached to each of them, further differentiating them in form from the previous group of five.

The precise function of the second section of the passage (3:16) has been more difficult to determine, in large measure because of the asyndeton, which makes the nature of its connection to the preceding more ambiguous. The content of this section, however, would suggest that it is not simply an independent exhortation with no connection to the virtue and vice lists, but that it is part of the basis or means by which vices can be eradicated and virtues can be cultivated. Perhaps one of the most significant clues is the presence of the term "admonish" (νουθετοῦντες), which has to do with aligning one's behavior with a standard. By focusing on the teaching of and about Christ, expressed especially through the lyrics of the musical worship of the church, the Colossian believers will be able to live out the attitudinal and behavioral standards of their new life in Christ as the chosen and holy people of God. This verse thus provides the basis not only for this section (3:12–15), but the previous section as well (3:5–11).

The final section of this passage (3:17) serves as the conclusion to the entirety of this portion of the letter dealing with vices and virtues (3:5–15). Believers are called to live the entirety of their lives as representatives of the Lord Jesus and to do so by his power. This will include how they relate to one another in the Christian household (3:18–4:1). Thus 3:17 both summarizes the previous moral exhortation and introduces the household code that follows.[3] It thus functions as a hinge between the two passages.

3 So also Schweizer, 211.

## *Setting*

Paul regularly gives general moral exhortation to the Christian communities to which he writes, and this letter is no exception. This is part of his overall approach to facilitate their development "to walk in a manner worthy of the Lord, fully pleasing to him" (Col 1:10; see also Eph 4:1; Phil 1:27; 1 Thess 2:12; 4:1). Yet it would be a mistake to see this passage as completely disconnected from his concerns and teaching about "the philosophy" that he views as harmful to the health of their community. Although many elements of this passage overlap with the general moral exhortation of his other letters, there are portions of this set of moral exhortations that appear to be particularly relevant to the Colossian congregation.

Most importantly is the ongoing christological focus (see esp. 3:16–17), which is intentionally counter to the teaching of the opponents who, Paul claims, are not holding tightly to Christ (2:19). In this passage, Paul calls the Colossians to be profoundly influenced by the teaching of Christ and in everything they do and say to represent him well. Paul's summons to do everything "in the name of the Lord Jesus" may also counter the methods of the factional teachers who, in their rituals of power, may be calling on the names of other gods, goddesses, angels, and spirits to accomplish their goals.

It is striking to note that "humility" (ταπεινοφροσύνη) was advocated by the teachers of "the philosophy" (2:18) as well as by Paul (3:12). Yet they use the term in substantially different ways. For the factional teachers, "humility" was asceticism—fasting and taboos of various sorts—probably associated with their quest to gain ritual power. For Paul it was an attitude that was displayed in the life of the community. It referred to a disposition that was the opposite of arrogance. The judgmental attitude of the opponents was anything but a display of humility.

Finally, it should be observed that Paul has contextualized his approach to musical worship to this diverse group of Christians living in the Lycus Valley. The threefold expression, "psalms, hymns, and spiritual songs," is meant to reflect the rich variety of musical forms and styles that should be reflected in the community as it expresses itself to God in musical worship (see the commentary on 3:16). Paul did not insist on one musical form, such as the Jewish practice of singing the book of Psalms, but rather encouraged an approach that was appreciative of other forms as long as they magnified Christ and were Spirit-inspired.

## *Comment*

**12** Ἐνδύσασθε οὖν, "therefore, clothe yourselves." Building still further on the theological heart of the letter stressing participation with Christ in his death and resurrection, Paul here shifts his appeal from vices to be eliminated to virtues that should be embodied. The conjunction (οὖν) retains its inferential force as did the previous two occurences of the same conjunction (3:1, 5). The immediate reference is to 3:1–4, the theological basis for the moral exhortation of 3:5–17. Ultimately, however, the entire chapter is grounded in the theological center of the letter, 2:9–15.

Ἐνδύσασθε, "put on," is the counterpart to ἀπόθεσθε, "take off," in 3:8 and continues the clothing metaphor. Paul has already used this verb (in participial form) in 3:10 to describe the work of God in endowing them with a new identity ("the new self") that God is working to renew. Here the subject shifts from God to the believing community, and Paul thereby stresses the responsibility of the Colossians to participate with God in the renewal process, which means that they will appropriate a series of virtues that Paul is about to commend to them.

ὡς ἐκλεκτοὶ τοῦ θεοῦ ἅγιοι καὶ ἠγαπημένοι, "as God's chosen people, holy and beloved." Rather than moving straight to the moral exhortation as he did in 3:5 and 8, Paul inserts this clause that speaks to their new status and serves as a powerful motivation to comply with Paul's appeal. The language here is not from the Hellenistic or Roman environment but comes straight from Paul's Jewish background and reflects his convictions about the nature of the people in this new Christian movement. The gentile believers of Colossae now share in the heritage of Israel. Together with Jewish believers, they have become ἐκλεκτοὶ τοῦ θεοῦ, "God's chosen people." This expression was commonly used in the OT and Second Temple Jewish literature to refer to the Jewish people as God's covenant community. The psalmist exclaims, "O offspring of his servant Abraham, children of Jacob, his chosen ones [ἐκλεκτοὶ αὐτοῦ]" (Ps 105:6 NRSV [104:6 LXX]; see also Pss 105:43; 106:5; Isa 65:9). The Wisdom of Solomon declares that "God's grace and mercy are with his elect [ἐν τοῖς ἐκλεκτοῖς αὐτοῦ]" (Wis 4:15; see also Wis 3:9; Sir 46:1). Paul here appropriates the language of the old-covenant people of God and applies it to those who have put their faith in the Jewish Messiah. Bormann and others infer too much when they assert that "here the church is seen as the true Israel."[4] There is a substantial difference between sharing in the blessings and displacing ethnic Israel. Paul is not adopting a supercessionist theology of the church replacing ethnic Israel. Rather, he has previously asserted that he regards gentile believers in Jesus the Messiah as branches that are grafted into the Jewish stock (Rom 11:17, 24). He also holds out the belief that at the end of time, Israel as a people would turn en masse to Jesus as their Messiah (Rom 11:25–26) to the extent that he could say, "all Israel will be saved" (Rom 11:26). Dunn rightly observes that the appropriation of this covenantal language as descriptive of the uncircumcised gentile Christians of this city was likely "a bone of contention with or provocation to the more traditional Jewish synagogues in Colossae."[5] But Paul could see a divine purpose even

---

4 Bormann, 168. Wright, 141, notes that "as God's new humanity (3:10) the church is God's true Israel, to whom have been transferred the epithets which formerly belonged to Israel according to the flesh."

5 Dunn, 228.

in this when he notes to the Romans, "I glorify my ministry in order to make my own people jealous, and thus save some of them" (Rom 11:13–14 NRSV). The notion of believing gentiles and Jews in one eschatological people of God is thoroughly consonant with Paul's thought. He speaks of the ethnically mixed congregation at Rome in similar terms—not only referring to them as chosen by God (κλητοῖς), but also as "loved by God" (ἀγαπητοῖς θεοῦ) and "holy ones" (ἁγίοις) (Rom 1:7).

"Holy and beloved" are epithets describing God's elect—the Colossian believers. Paul has spoken of them five times previously as God's holy ones (1:2, 4, 12, 22, 26; see the comments on 1:2). They are called out as a people who are consecrated to God and belong to him. As such they are called to be like him in holiness, purity, and integrity (Lev 11:44–45; 19:2; 20:26).

But it is particularly meaningful that God calls these new people belonging to him as deeply loved (ἠγαπημένοι). The Lord told his old-covenant people through the prophet Jeremiah that "I have loved you with an everlasting love" (Jer 31:3 ESV). This same love he has bestowed on gentiles who have entered a relationship with him through the new covenant. Thus, Paul can assure the various communities he has founded of God's deep love for them. He affirms to the Thessalonians that God has chosen them and that they are now "loved [ἠγαπημένοι] by God" (1 Thess 1:4). And, similarly, in his second letter to the Thessalonians, Paul speaks of how he always thanks God for them as "brothers and sisters loved [ἠγαπημένοι] by the Lord" because "God has chosen you" (2 Thess 2:13).

Paul wants the Colossian believers to know that the attitudes and behavior that he is appealing to them to develop are motivated by and rooted in the knowledge that God has chosen them as his own, that he has bestowed on them his righteousness, and that he has a profound love for them. This awareness should not only prompt within them a heart of gratitude (3:15c) but should serve as a powerful impetus to align their lives with the expectations of their Lord.

σπλάγχνα οἰκτιρμοῦ, "a heart of compassion." This is the first of a list of ten virtues that Paul wants the Colossians to put on. Many of the older English versions rendered this expression, "bowels of mercy" (KJV; Geneva; Douay-Rheims). The noun σπλάγχνον could refer to the bowels as physical organs, but it was commonly used in Greek literature more broadly of the various inward parts of the human body, such as the heart, lungs, liver, and kidneys.[6] Philo illustrates this literal usage well when he notes that "the internal parts, or the entrails [σπλάγχνα], as they are called, are the stomach, the heart, the lungs, the spleen, the liver, and the two kidneys" (Philo, *Creation* 118; see also *Alleg. Interp.* 1.12). The term came to be used metaphorically as the seat of feelings and affections. In English, the term "heart" is a common way to express this metaphorical sense and thus came to be the preferred rendering of σπλάγχνον in this passage

6 See LSJ, s.v. σπλάγχνον.

(see, e.g., NASB; ESV; ASV; cf. NET; CSB; NJB; the NIV and NRSV omit the metaphor entirely and simply translate, "clothe yourselves with compassion"). The two terms appear in conjunction with each other in only one other place in Paul's writings, Phil 2:1 ("affection and compassion," σπλάγχνα καὶ οἰκτιρμοί), but as two coordinate terms and not with "compassion" modifying "affection."

χρηστότητα, "kindness." Almost all English translations render the term by "kindness," but it can be understood as "goodness."[7] Kindness is a characteristic of the God that the Colossians now serve. The psalmist exclaims, "O how much is the abundance of your kindness [χρηστότητος]" (Ps 31:19 NETS [30:20 LXX]; see also Pss 25:7; 68:10; 145:7; Rom 2:4; 11:22). The first-century BC Psalms of Solomon saw God's kindness manifested in his response to sinners: "your kindness is upon sinners in repentance" (T. Sol. 9.7). But Paul points to a kindness of God to people that precedes repentance when he says that it is the kindness of God that actually leads people to repentance (Rom 2:4). Titus 3:4 roots God's gracious act of salvation to gentiles and Jews in his kindness toward them. Elsewhere Paul says that in the eschatological future, the redeemed people of God will display "the immeasurable riches of his grace in kindness" (Eph 2:7). Kindness, however, was not a virtue that can be attested for any of the local gods and goddesses. It was certainly not a defining virtue of Zeus, Apollo, Artemis, or Hades. It was an important virtue in Stoicism as seen, for instance, in Arius Didymus, who lists it along with piety, good fellowship, and fair dealing yet subordinate to justice (Arius Didymus, *Epitome* 2.7.5b2; see also Epictetus, *Diatr.* 2.22.36). It is also listed as a praiseworthy virtue in honorific inscriptions in Asia Minor, such as a first-century inscription honoring the proconsul Marcus Aefulanus (*ISmyrna* 591.13; see also *SEG* 35.1330.8 [Amastris, Paphlagonia]; 53.1357 [Silandos, Lydia]). Paul wants the community of believers in Colossae to embrace and practice in their own lives this virtue that characterizes their Father. He has already named it as a product of the presence of the Spirit in his letter to the Galatians (Gal 5:22). Kindness is a virtue that Paul himself displays as a servant of God (2 Cor 6:6). But according to the biblical testimony, people who do not know God typically do not practice the kind of kindness reflected in the life of God (Rom 3:12; see also Ps 14:3).

ταπεινοφροσύνην, "humility." Paul regarded this as a very important virtue in the life of the Christian community. It was an attitude strongly commended in the OT. The Lord declares through the prophet Isaiah, "This is the one I esteem: he who is humble and contrite in spirit, and trembles at my word" (Isa 66:2). Paul saw this virtue perfectly embodied in Jesus, who "humbled [ἐταπείνωσεν] himself by becoming obedient to death—even death on a cross!" (Phil 2:8 NIV; see also Matt 11:29). Like kindness, this was a virtue that Paul embodied in his service to the churches: "I served the Lord with all humility

---

7 BDAG, s.v. χρηστότης, gives "goodness" and "generosity" as possible alternative translations. The overriding idea is "the quality of being helpful or beneficial."

and with tears" (Acts 20:19). Throughout the OT, an arrogant spirit is actively opposed and chastised by God, but the one who is humble is commended (see, e.g., Ps 138:6; Prov 11:2; Isa 2:11; Ezek 17:24; 21:26; see also Luke 1:52). In writing to Christians in Asia Minor, Peter cites the psalmist as declaring, "God opposes the proud but gives grace to the humble" (1 Pet 5:5 NRSV, quoting Prov 3:34). Paul commends this virtue to the Ephesian believers along with gentleness and patience (Eph 4:2).

Humility is not a virtue commended by the Stoics, nor is it found in the typical lists of virtues in the honorific inscriptions of Asia Minor. The term does appear in the Stoic writer Epictetus, but in a context where it "denotes weakness and pusillanimity" (Epictetus, *Diatr.* 3.24.56).[8]

But ταπεινοφροσύνη was clearly something that the opposing teachers at Colossae valued, but in a quite different sense than Paul is using it here. For the advocates of "the philosophy," ταπεινοφροσύνη was coextensive with ascetic behavior—that is, a humility expressed in fasting and the observance of taboos (see the commentary on 2:18 and 23; in this latter passage, it is associated with severe treatment of the body). In this context, Paul commends "humility" as a social virtue that is the antonym of arrogance.

πραΰτητα, "gentleness." The fourth virtue that Paul commends has often been translated as "meekness," especially by older English versions (Tyndale; Geneva; KJV; ASV; RSV; yet cf. NRSV; ESV; NKJV), but also as "gentleness" (NASB; NIV; REB; CEB; CSB; NLT). Bauer's lexicon describes the usage of the word as pertaining to "not being overly impressed by a sense of one's self-importance" and suggests the translations, "gentle," "humble," "considerate," and "meek."[9] The NT consistently uses both the noun (πραΰτης) and the adjective (πραΰς) as a positive virtue, with no overtones of weakness, servility, or inappropriate submissiveness. Yet the English word "meek" can sometimes be understood as "deficient in spirit and courage"[10] or "easily imposed on."[11] To avoid this misunderstanding, the English "gentleness" is preferable. But in its positive use, "meekness" conveys "gentleness," "humility," and "obedience."[12] Lightfoot notes that it is helpful to distinguish it from its opposites, which would include "rudeness" and "harshness" (ἀγριοτής, χαλεπότης).[13]

Jesus himself commended this virtue in the Sermon on the Mount when he said, "Blessed are the meek, for they shall inherit the earth" (Matt 5:5 ESV). This was the example he left as he told his disciples, "I am gentle [πραΰς] and humble [ταπεινός] in heart" (Matt 11:29 NIV; see also Matt 21:25). Moses, too, was regarded as "very meek [πραΰς σφόδρα], more than all people who were on

8 W. Grundmann, "ταπεινός, κτλ.," *TDNT* 8:5.
9 BDAG, s.v. πραΰτης.
10 Merriam-Webster, s.v. "meek."
11 American Heritage College Dictionary, 863.
12 OED, s.v. "meekness," 1.
13 Lightfoot, 221.

the face of the earth" (Num 12:3 ESV). This virtue is repeatedly extolled in the Psalms ("he leads the humble [πραεῖς] in what is right, and teaches the humble [πραεῖς] in his way," Ps 25:9 ESV [24:9 LXX]; see also Pss 34:2; 37:11; 76:9; 147:6; 149:4).

This virtue is not common in Greek moral exhortation, especially in Stoicism. Neither is it common in Hellenistic Judaism as evidenced, in part, by its absence in Philo. Yet it is found in some honorific inscriptions from Asia Minor in public praise of certain public officials. An inscription from nearby Aphrodisias lauds a certain Aelius Aurelius Ammianus Paulinus for, among other things, the way he conducts himself in "meekness and gentleness" (πραΰτητι καὶ ἐπεικείᾳ) (*CIG* 2788.20–21; see also *SEG* 57.1198 [from Lydia]).

The virtue is commended in Second Temple Jewish texts, especially in Sirach. The sage advises, "Child, in gentleness [πραΰτητι] conduct your affairs" (Sir 3:17 NETS; see also Sir 4:8; 10:28). It is also in a list of virtues prescribed for the community at Qumran (1QS 2.24). The apostle Paul—in line with his Jewish tradition and the example of Christ—engaged the Corinthians with "the meekness and gentleness [πραΰτητος καὶ ἐπιεικείας] of Christ" (2 Cor 10:1). He also listed meekness/gentleness as one of the fruits of the Spirit (Gal 5:23) and as indispensible for the unity among believers at Ephesus (Eph 4:2). Even in difficult situations requiring the need for correction and discipline, he advises meekness (Gal 6:1; 2 Tim 2:25).

μακροθυμίαν, "patience." Once again, Paul puts forward a virtue that is characteristic of God and is exemplified in the Lord Jesus. The OT frequently describes God as patient. In his self-revelation to Moses, the Lord passes before him and says, "the Lord, the Lord God is compassionate and merciful, patient (μακρόθυμος) and very merciful and truthful" (Exod 34:6 NETS; see also Num 14:18; Neh 9:17; Pss 86:15; 103:8; 145:8). Paul and other NT writers also characterized God as patient (e.g., Rom 2:4; 9:22; 1 Pet 3:20; 2 Pet 3:15). One of the ways patience is exhibited is by being slow to anger (Prov 14:29; 15:18; 16:32). This corresponds with the previous sections where the Colossians are exhorted to take off "anger and wrath" (Col 3:8).

In describing how he conducted his ministry to the Corinthians, Paul says that he exhibited patience (2 Cor 6:6). Part of the reason for this is the patience he himself experienced from the Lord Jesus: "I was shown mercy so that in me, the worst of sinners, Christ Jesus might display his immense patience as an example for those who would believe in him and receive eternal life" (1 Tim 1:16 NIV).

As with some of the other virtues Paul commends, patience was not significant in Greco-Roman moral exhortation. But it was significant in Jewish literature in this era. Appeals to patience appear, for instance, in the Testaments of the Twelve Patriarchs. The Testament of Dan advises, "Keep yourselves from every evil work, my children, and cast aside anger and every lie; love truth and patience [μακροθυμίαν]" (T. Dan 6.8; see also T. Dan 2.1; T. Jos. 2.7; 17.2).

Injunctions to patience can also found in the Qumran literature (e.g., 1QS 4.3; 4Q420 2 II, 4; 4Q435 1 I, 4).

For Paul, patience is a fruit of the Spirit (Gal 5:22) and essential to the life of the Christian community (Eph 4:2). He has already spoken of it, along with endurance and joy, as an outcome of God's strengthening power that is at work within them (Col 1:11). The leaders of the Colossian church will need patience as they deal with the advocates of the unhealthy teaching infecting the community.

Given the terms Paul uses to describe the leaders of "the philosophy" toward the Colossian believers—taking them captive (2:8), judging them (2:16), and disqualifying them (2:18)—it is evident that they did not embrace and practice the virtues that Paul here commends. Their social interactions with the Colossians were tantamount to spiritual abuse.

**13** Paul continues his exhortation by introducing a list of five additional virtues for the Christian community at Colossae to "put on" as clothing. Whereas the previous list was structured as a group of five nouns in the accusative case as direct objects of ἐνδύσασθε, he here in 3:13–15 varies the form by using two participles, two imperative verbs, and assuming the force of ἐνδύσασθε to introduce the third and central virtue, love. He also provides additional comments about the middle three virtues—forgiveness, love, and peace. Some have thought that this next group of virtues provides concrete examples of how the first group of five can be worked out and lived in the life of the community.[14] It is better, however, to see them as an additional group of ethical imperatives—although conceptually overlapping with some of the previous virtues—but not simply the means by which the first set are expressed.[15]

ἀνεχόμενοι ἀλλήλων, "bear with one another." Developing the ability to overlook minor offenses aids in enhancing the cohesiveness of community. Older translations rendered this verb "forbearing" (Geneva; KJV; ERV; ASV; RSV). It is used with the sense of regarding others with tolerance[16] and exhibiting patience with others—even to the extent of "enduring possible difficulty."[17] There is thus a degree of overlap with the final virtue (patience) of the previous group. Paul uses precisely the same construction in Eph 4:2, where he has the identical objective of fostering a unified community on a foundation of humility, gentleness, patience, and love.

Once again, the example of Jesus informs Paul since Jesus had to "bear with" the weaknesses and failings of his disciples. Concerned about their lack of faith and inability to help a demonized boy, Jesus exclaimed, "How long am I to bear [ἀνέξομαι] with you?" (Mark 9:19). In writing to Polycarp, Ignatius pointed to

14 Moo, 278, for instance, sees the first group as conveying attitudes and the second group actions. He notes that Paul "intends to present these actions as the natural outgrowth of the general attitude conveyed by all five virtues together." Similarly Wolter, 185.

15 So also Foster, 349.

16 BDAG, s.v. ἀνέχω.

17 Louw-Nida, §25.171.

the example of Jesus and advised, "Bear with all people, even as the Lord bears with you; endure [ἀνέχου] all in love, just as you now do" (Ign. *Pol.* 1.2).

There has been some dispute among interpreters about whether to take the present participles (ἀνεχόμενοι and χαριζόμενοι) as independent imperatives[18] or as dependent (circumstantial) participles of means[19] or even as participles of attendant circumstance.[20] It is clear that the imperative ἐνδύσασθε extends its force over this second group of five virtues, as evident by the fact that it is assumed as the main verb for τὴν ἀγάπην (Col 3:14). It would thus be natural to assume that the two participles are in a dependent relationship on this imperative. However, the final two virtues (3:15) are introduced by imperative verbs, and they are semantically coordinate with the previous three commended virtues (3:13–14), forming a coherent unit of five. Grammatically, then, it is most appropriate to regard the two participles as dependent on ἐνδύσασθε, but we cannot deny them an imperatival force in this section. Therefore, they are best regarded as participles of means (or manner), but simultaneously with an imperatival flavor.[21]

It would be wrong for the Colossian believers to conclude from this admonition that they should "bear with" the teaching and judgments of the advocates of "the philosophy." Lohse rightly observes that "chapter 2 shows that the false teaching should be rejected, not patiently endured."[22] Paul chides the Corinthians for "putting up with" (ἀνέχομαι) the opponents adversely impacting their community (2 Cor 11:4, 19–20). Here he is encouraging the Colossians to be tolerant of one another and not to let small things get under their skin. But they also need to be vigilant not to allow the tensions they are facing because of the influence of the teachers of "the philosophy" to disrupt their unity and harmony. Eadie says it well: "the sense is, having patience with one another—waiting with composure under injury or provocation, till those who so offend may come to a better mind."[23] It must be remembered that the Christian gatherings at Colossae would include people who formerly would not have associated intimately in a tightly-woven community. People of various ethnicities sharing different cultural heritages and political opinions, slaves along with slave owners, wealthy and peasants—all would be endeavoring to live together on the basis of

---

18 Foster, 349; Sumney, 216; Bevere, *Sharing in the Inheritance*, 218; Lohse, 147. Porter, *Idioms*, 186, finds the independent use of the participle functioning as a command to be a legitimate category, especially in light of papyri examples of this usage.

19 Pao, 243; Wallace, *Grammar*, 652, includes the participles of Col 3:13 as among a handful that have been regarded as imperatival, but that designation, he argues, "should be seriously questioned."

20 Moo, 278. Attendant circumstance for these two participles does not fit Wallace's criteria for determining this interpretation. Wallace stipulates that the tense of the main verb and the participle are usually aorist, the participle will precede the main verb, and they are usually found in narrative literature (see Wallace, *Grammar*, 642).

21 Beale, 296n8, reaches a similar conclusion.

22 Lohse, 148n111.

23 Eadie, 237.

their common bond of being in Christ. Surely mundane, but important, matters like food preferences, music styles, dress, décor, and so much more would have given rise to disagreements.

χαριζόμενοι ἑαυτοῖς, "forgive each other." Looking again to the example of Christ as a basis for their behavior in the Christian community, Paul appeals to the Colossians to forgive each other for their offenses. This is the same verb that he used earlier to describe God's forgiveness of all the sins of his people in Christ (2:13; see the commentary on that passage). By using this term, the emphasis falls on the pardoning of a debt, just as one would pardon a financial debt (Luke 7:42). In this context, the debt could be anything that injures or hurts another person within the community. The pronoun (ἑαυτοῖς) is here functioning not as a reflexive pronoun ("forgive yourselves") but as a reciprocal pronoun ("forgive each other") and is thus parallel with the reciprocal pronoun (ἀλλήλων) in the previous clause.[24]

ἐάν τις πρός τινα ἔχῃ μομφήν, "if someone has a complaint against someone else." In order to be explicit, Paul gives an example of an occasion when forgiveness would need to be extended to someone else in the community. The term Paul uses here for "complaint" (μομφή) is somewhat surprising since the word appears nowhere else in the NT or even in the LXX. Although the noun is rare in Greek literature, the verbal form (μέμφομαι) is quite common, and Paul himself uses it on one occasion (Rom 9:19), which demonstrates his familiarity with it. Consequently, this should not be used as an argument against Pauline authorship of the letter.

καθὼς καὶ ὁ κύριος ἐχαρίσατο ὑμῖν, οὕτως καὶ ὑμεῖς, "just as the Lord forgave all of you, so all of you [should forgive] others." Paul's point is that if someone in the community has been hurt and has a just complaint against the offender, the gracious act of Christ in extending forgiveness to the undeserving should motivate and inspire a similar response. Fostering a grudge, harboring bitterness, seeking revenge, keeping accounts of wrongs suffered, and fuming inside over how one was wronged are no longer acceptable responses within the Christian community. Although the Father is the one who forgives in Col 2:13, here "the Lord" is likely a reference to the exalted Christ.[25] Colossians consistently uses this title for Christ, although "God in Christ" is the subject of forgiveness in Eph 4:32.

As Paul penned this passage and the parallel passage in Ephesians, he may have had in mind Jesus's teaching in the Sermon on the Mount, "forgive us our debts, as we forgive our debtors" (Matt 6:12 KJV).[26] The change in terminology

24 See BDAG, s.v. ἑαυτοῦ 2., where it is classified as a "marker of reciprocal relationship, for the reciprocal pron[oun]."

25 Lohse, 148.

26 Scott, 72–73, notes, "It has sometimes been pointed out as remarkable that Paul never makes an allusion to the Lord's Prayer, but we can hardly doubt, with a verse like this before us, that it was familiar to him." See also Bruce, 155.

from ἀφίημι to χαρίζομαι would stem from the latter's use in Col 2:13 and Paul's overall theology of grace.

In the teaching of Jesus, full and complete forgiveness is predicated on repentance (Luke 17:3–4). It would be a mistake for the Colossians to pardon the offenses of the leaders of "the philosophy" apart from them changing their convictions and system of belief, renouncing what they have been teaching, and ending their hurtful judgments against the Colossian believers. But as one could infer from the following comment on the supremacy of love, the Colossians can and should extend the offer of forgiveness to their erring brothers and pray that they would change their hearts and repent of their ways that have been harmful to the Colossian church. Only then could true forgiveness occur. As Paul says to the Roman church regarding unbelieving Israel (citing Deut 28:32), "All day long I have held out my hands to a disobedient and contrary people" (Rom 10:21 ESV), so should the Colossian believers be prepared to forgive the opposing teachers. Out of love, forgiveness is graciously offered; yet it is not completed until it is received and the offender has repented from disobedience and obstinacy.

**14** ἐπὶ πᾶσιν δὲ τούτοις τὴν ἀγάπην, ὅ ἐστιν σύνδεσμος τῆς τελειότητος, "upon all these [virtues, clothe yourselves with] love, which is the bond of perfection." Love is the summative and most important virtue of all for Christians. As the eighth virtue in a list of ten, it appears to be buried in the middle of the list. But Paul's language makes it clear that it is foundational to all the rest.

The clause is missing a verb, but this is best supplied from the leading verb of this section and should be understood as ἐνδύσασθε . . . τὴν ἀγάπην, "put on . . . love." It thereby continues the clothing imagery to this point. This is furthered by the use of ἐπὶ πᾶσιν, "upon all these," and σύνδεσμος, "bond," in this context. Precisely how to interpret ἐπὶ πᾶσιν has occasioned much discussion among interpreters. Should it be understood as "in addition to these"—that is, one more virtue coordinate to the previous seven (e.g., NET: "to all these virtues add love")?[27] Should it be taken as "above all," as many English versions render it (e.g., KJV; RSV; NRSV; ESV; CSB; NLT) and then seen as the most important of all virtues? Or should it be translated "upon all of these" and regarded as an extension of the clothing metaphor, with love represented as a kind of outer garment worn upon all of the other articles of clothing (e.g., NJB: "over all these clothes, put on love"; NIV; NAB; REB; CEB)? In support of this last view, there are a handful of reasons for seeing Paul continue his use of the clothing metaphor here. First, as already noted, Paul explicitly depends on ἐνδύσασθε from 3:12 as the assumed main verb of the clause. This would have served to immediately reengage the minds of the readers with the image of putting on clothing. Second, the preposition ἐπί is often used with reference to the putting on of clothing, especially a ἱμάτιον, a "robe" or "cloak" (e.g., Gen 9:23) or simply ἱματισμός,

27 BDAG, s.v. ἐπί 7.: "marker of addition to what is already in existence, 'to,' 'in,' 'in addition to.'"

"clothing" (e.g., Exod 3:22; Ruth 3:3). It should be noted that the translation "above," in the sense of "above all," is not an option in the standard lexica for ἐπί. The common way of expressing "above all" in Greek would have been πρὸ πάντων (e.g., Jas 5:12; 1 Pet 4:8). Third, the term σύνδεσμος, "bond," was also used in ancient literature in connection with clothing—as something that fastens a garment.[28] Consequently, it would have been natural for the readers to envision a continuation of the metaphor and to think of love as comparable to an outer garment, such as a robe or a cloak, that was put on over all of the rest. Lightfoot observes that "love is the outer garment which holds the others in their places."[29] Beale suggests that there may be an allusion to priestly clothing since the priest wore a linen tunic over his undergarments.[30] Even the same language of ἐνδύω . . . ἐπί is used in Lev 16:4 to describe what the priest is to put on.

The elaboration of this metaphor with an application to the virtue of love, combined with Paul's comment that it is the "bond of perfection," not only puts a significant stress on the importance of love in the community but emphasizes the role of love in relationship to the previous seven virtues. Moo says they are "empowered by love."[31] The kind of other-centered and self-sacrificial love that Jesus modeled should serve to deepen one's compassion for fellow believers in the community. For each of the virtues, love provides motivation, encouragement, and capacity to appropriate them in the care and service of others.

Although the preferred translation of ἐπὶ πᾶσιν is "upon all," like a cloak worn over and upon all the other clothing, the rendering "above all" is partially justified based on the foundational role that love plays in Paul's theology and ethics. It begins with a knowledge of God's great love for his people, as Paul affirmed to the Colossians at the outset of this section (3:12) and is so important throughout his writings (see, e.g., Rom 5:5, 8; 8:39; 2 Cor 13:11, 13; Eph 2:4; 5:2; 1 Thess 1:4; 2 Thess 2:13, 16). Yet for Paul, everyone who has come to know and experience God's love is now called to actively express that love to others in the day-to-day life of the Christian community. He thus begins his letter to the Colossians by commending them for the love they have for all God's people (1:4) and by affirming that it is God's will and design for them to be a unified community that is "knit together in love" (2:2).

Paul characterizes this "bond," which represents love, with the genitive qualifier, τῆς τελειότητος. This could be interpreted as an attributive genitive and thus seen as an adjectival expression modifying σύνδεσμος in the sense of a "perfect bond" (e.g., NET; NJB; NAB). Some offer a more expansive and interpretive rendering by adding the term "unity" (e.g., NIV: "binds them all together in

28 See LSJ, s.v. σύνδεσμος.

29 Lightfoot, 222. Canavan, *Clothing the Body*, 143, notes that "this progression has been aligned to the layers of clothes usually worn in the first century CE, namely the underwear of the tunic as the virtues and the outer garment of the himation or toga as the love that is worn over all.

30 Beale, 298.

31 Moo, 282.

perfect unity"; cf. CSB; CEB; NASB) or "harmony" (e.g., RSV: "binds everything together in perfect harmony"; cf. NRSV; ESV; NLT). In the only other use of the genitive of τελειότης in the NT or LXX, it is used as an attributive genitive (Wis 6:15: φρονήσεως τελειότης, "perfect understanding"). But it should be noted that Paul has twice used the cognate term τέλειος in Colossians. In the first instance, he says that the goal of his ministry is to "present everyone perfect/mature in Christ" (Col 1:28). At the end of the letter, he uses it once more in reporting that Epaphras regularly struggles in prayer for them to the end that they "may stand perfect/mature in the will of God" (Col 4:12). This would lead us to conclude that it would be best to interpret τελειότητος as an objective genitive, a bond that leads to the goal of maturity.[32] As such, it could indicate purpose or result, but it likely encompasses both.[33] Sumney summarizes the meaning well in saying that "love, then, binds together Christian virtues and thus leads to 'perfection' or maturity."[34] Foster says that love is "the bond that results in the formation of a perfect (mature) community."[35] As "the bond of perfection," love is foundational to life in the Christian community and informs, inspires, and guides the practice of all the other virtues. Like a belt that holds all the clothing in place, love gives all the other virtues deeper meaning and greater significance.

Some have suggested that Paul's statement about "perfection" may be in response to a false idea of perfection advocated by the false teachers at Colossae, who sought to achieve a higher spiritual status through asceticism and mysticism.[36] This is unduly speculative, especially since "perfection" is not part of the Jewish mystical texts. If anything, Paul's emphasis on love stands in stark contrast to the methods of the opponents, who stressed power over love and who were quick to judge over displaying compassion, humility, and kindness.

**15** καὶ ἡ εἰρήνη τοῦ Χριστοῦ βραβευέτω ἐν ταῖς καρδίαις ὑμῶν, "let the peace of Christ control your hearts." Paul here expresses his desire that the peace that Christ has achieved and provides would permeate the lives of the Colossians—both in their inner lives as individuals and between one another in their corporate relationships.

Peace is one of the central blessings of the new covenant. The OT anticipated shalom as characteristic of kingdom life in the age to come (e.g., Isa 9:6–7). The christological hymn at the outset of this letter declares that Christ, as Messiah, has accomplished his mission and has ushered in an era of peace (Col 1:20). He did this not by a massive military campaign and victory but, ironically, "through

32 So also, e.g., Moo, 282; Harris, 142. Beale, 299, attempts to be more specific by characterizing it as a genitive of product (the "bond that produces completeness"), but this is a subset of the objective genitive.

33 Dunn, 233; Lohse, 149.

34 Sumney, 219.

35 Foster, 353.

36 Pao, 245; Lincoln, "Colossians," 648.

the blood of his cross." For it was by his work on the cross that he vanquished the ultimate enemies to peace—the power of sin (that separates people from the God of peace) and the principalities, powers, and authorities (that work in concert with the flesh and sin to keep people at enmity with God and with others). Although this peace will ultimately become a universal peace, during this era it is uniquely located in the "one body," the church. Christ himself announced this coming peace when he told his disciples, "Peace I leave with you; my peace I give to you" (John 14:27 NRSV). This peace becomes a central theme for Paul in his writings. He typically begins his letters by invoking God to bestow peace on the community to whom he is writing, as in this letter: "grace to you and peace from God our Father" (Col 1:2; see additional comments on peace there).

The expression, "peace of Christ," is unique in Paul's letters and in the entire NT. It is consistent, however, with the christological focus of the letter and with the poetic declaration of Christ as the one who has achieved this peace (1:20). The genitive τοῦ Χριστοῦ could be classified as a subjective genitive ("peace produced by Christ") or genitive of source ("peace from Christ").

Paul's wish is for this peace to rule in their hearts. It would have been natural for him to use βασιλευέτω, "let it reign," since this was part of his vocabulary (cf. Rom 6:12). Yet he uses a term unique to this letter (and to the entire NT): βραβεύω. He employed a compound form of this term (καταβραβεύω) earlier in Col 2:18 (see the commentary there for discussion of the term). Since καταβραβεύω was part of his polemic against the opposing teachers, it was probably not a word that he took from them to turn against them. In Greek literature, the term βραβεύω often appears in the context of an athletic contest along with its cognates βραβεύς, "umpire" or "judge (at the games)," and βραβεῖον, "prize (in the games)."[37] Paul twice uses the latter term as in 1 Cor 9:24: "Do you not know that in a race all the runners run, but only one receives the prize [βραβεῖον]?" (see also Phil 3:14). The use of the term here would be consistent with Paul's penchant to use athletic imagery (and thus, as a hapax legomenon here, does not necessarily point to a pseudepigraphical author). It may also be significant that the term βραβεύς does appear locally in an inscription from Aphrodisias. It is found in the well-known God-fearers inscription as an epithet to describe a man named Hortasius, who was a stonecutter and a judge in the games (Ὁρτάσιος λατύ(πος?) βραβεύς; *SEG* 36.970, line b.2.49).[38] It is also found in an inscription from Maionia (near Sardis) (*TAM* V.1.515, line 8).[39]

"In your hearts"[40] has both individual and corporate implications. Relief from anxiety needs to come first to the individual before it can permeate the

37 LSJ, s.v. βραβεύς and βραβεῖον.

38 Reynolds and Tannenbaum, *Jews and God-Fearers at Aphrodisias*, 5–7. The text of this inscription also appears in *NewDocs* 9:73 (§25).

39 On the annually elected office of βραβευτής in Asia Minor, see Mitchell, *Anatolia*, 1:182–83.

40 For more information about καρδία, see the commentary on 2:2.

community. In a more expansive way, Paul encouraged the Philippians, "Do not be anxious about anything, but in every situation, by prayer and petition, with thanksgiving, present your requests to God. And the peace of God, which transcends all understanding, will guard your hearts [τὰς καρδίας ὑμῶν] and your minds in Christ Jesus" (Phil 4:6–7 NIV). In his Sermon on the Mount, Jesus taught his followers extensively about gaining a freedom from anxiety (Matt 6:25–34). His peace can enable his disciples to live by his injunction, "let not your hearts be troubled, neither let them be afraid" (John 14:27 ESV).

The affairs of daily life certainly gave the Colossians much to worry about. Extraordinary difficulties sometimes led people in the ancient world to seek help from a shaman figure—a person with reputed spiritual power who could help by providing healing, protection, deliverance, or assistance. A sick child, a failing crop, a flock stricken by some disease, a ritually performed curse from a neighbor, the loss of money at the hands of a thief, public defamation from a former friend's lie, and many other things would not only create anxiety and rob the person of peace but could motivate a person to opt for local traditional spiritual means of help rather than looking to Christ. Paul reassures the Colossians that peace can be found in Christ and can pervade the deepest parts of their souls and emotions. The psalmist exclaims, "In peace I will lie down and sleep, for you alone, LORD, make me dwell in safety" (Ps 4:8 NIV).

Yet Paul also wants this peace to rule within the community in their relationships with one another. All of the preceding virtues he has listed have to do with interpersonal relationships. Peace is no less the case. The presence of an oppositional faction within the church has likely resulted in some level of division and disharmony. This is amplified all the more with the judgmental tone that the advocates of "the philosophy" had taken with the Colossian believers.

**εἰς ἣν καὶ ἐκλήθητε ἐν ἑνὶ σώματι**, "since you were called to it in one body." The feminine singular relative pronoun ἣν refers explicitly to the "peace" Paul is speaking of. The Colossian believers have been called into a relationship with "the Prince of Peace" (Isa 9:6) and entered his kingdom (Col 1:13) that is characterized by "righteousness and peace and joy in the Holy Spirit" (Rom 14:17). Although this is the only occurrence of καλέω, "call," in Colossians, it is extensive throughout Paul's writings, occuring over thirty times. It corresponds with Paul's assurance to the Colossians at the outset of this section that they are ἐκλεκτοί, "elect" (Col 3:12).

God calls individuals into a corporate life, a new community, that Paul often refers to by using the metaphor of a body, as he has done earlier in Colossians (Col 1:18, 24; 2:17, 19). To stress the unity of individual members with one another in this corporate life, Paul describes the body using the adjective εἷς, "one" (so also in Rom 12:4–5; 1 Cor 10:17; 12:12–13, 20; Eph 2:16; 4:4). Although some have wondered whether Paul is here differentiating the one universal body of Christ from the local congregation, there is no need to make this distinction. Paul is speaking simultaneously of both. What he says about the worldwide church should be conceptualized and applied to every local community of believers.[41] Thus, the unity and peace that characterizes the one body of Christ should find concrete and tangible application among the members of the Christian community at Colossae.

καὶ εὐχάριστοι γίνεσθε, "and be thankful." Paul's concluding admonition in this section is for the Colossians to develop hearts of gratitude to God. This call to thankfulness takes the reader back to the beginning of the paragraph where Paul assured them that God has chosen them, that they are deeply loved by him, and that he has set them apart for his purposes and made them holy—all profound reasons for gratitude.

Since the previous items in this list represented social virtues, some older commentators assumed that this final item should be interpreted in like manner. So some suggested εὐχάριστοι should be understood as "be friendly" and that it was functioning similar to χρηστοί in Eph 4:32: γίνεσθε . . . εἰς ἀλλήλους χρηστοί, "be kind to one another."[42] But Paul has already admonished the Colossians to put on kindness (χρηστότης, Col 3:12), and thanksgiving and gratitude are a prominent theme in this letter (1:3, 12; 2:7; 3:17; 4:2), thus reinforcing the likelihood that is what he is referring to here. The term is actually quite rare and only occurs here in the NT. But it is cognate to εὐχαριστέω ("give thanks") and εὐχαριστία ("thanksgiving"), which Paul uses frequently. It is therefore doubtful that Paul used εὐχάριστοι as "beneficence"[43] here, since he consistently and often uses the cognate terms always with the sense of "thanksgiving."

Paul wants the Colossians to reflect on and express gratitude to God for his favor toward them and for including them in his great plan of salvation (Col 1:12). They have been delivered from the domain of darkness and have entered the kingdom of his beloved Son. Their sins have been forgiven, and they have been joined to Christ and identified with him in his death and resurrection, and so much more. All of this should elicit heartfelt gratitude to God. Yet the imperative verb realistically reflects the need for this to be an intentional and regular act. In the midst of pressure, difficulty, and crisis, it is natural to myopically focus on the troubles and not to reflect on the blessings.

Throughout his ministry—and to the Colossians—Paul modeled a thankfulness for people within the Christian communities. He begins this letter by thanking God for them (Col 1:3), which is typical of his letters (e.g., 1 Thess 1:2: "we give thanks to God always for all of you"). Part of the thanksgiving he wants them to express is for the fellow members of the body and God's gracious work in each of their lives. This attitude will help them live out the social virtues.

---

41 So also Barth and Blanke, 425.

42 Calvin, 352, for instance, says that he takes the term as a reference to "sweetness of manners" and prefers the translation, "be lovable." Yet he also admits that gratitude would positively affect relationships within the community.

43 "Beneficent" is part of the range of usage for this term. See LSJ, s.v. εὐχάριστος III.

Although thanksgiving is inward and personal, it also finds a corporate expression. This clause thus bridges the gap into the next verse that speaks of corporate worship with singing (Col 3:16). This heartfelt worship of God with thanksgiving would thus influence the attitudes of the Colossian believers toward one another and both motivate and direct the way they would implement all of the virtues Paul has just commended to them. For instance, as Paul has already said, reflecting on the fact that the Lord has forgiven them will motivate and inform their readiness to forgive others in the body (3:13).

**16** With this verse, Paul returns to the christological focus of the letter and wants believers in Colossae to become deeply rooted in teaching about Christ. The musical worship of the church is an important means for how this should take place in the community at Colossae.

ὁ λόγος τοῦ Χριστοῦ ἐνοικείτω ἐν ὑμῖν πλουσίως, "let the word of Christ dwell in you richly." The precise connection of this clause with the preceding in the flow of thought is difficult to ascertain because of the asyndeton. It may be that the thread of connection is thankfulness since Paul ends the previous section with "be thankful" (3:15c), here mentions "singing with thankfulness" (3:16c), and concludes the entire section with "giving thanks to God" (3:17c). The absence of a conjunction may also cause the reader to see a close tie with the previous two main imperatives governing the previous two sections—"put on" (3:9–11) and "take off" (3:12–15)—and infer that "the word of Christ" is the basis for those actions. In other words, all that is entailed in the gospel of Christ (especially dying and rising with him as well as being united with him in his exaltation; 3:1–4) is essential for eradicating vices, appropriating virtues, and living life in community with other believers. Letting the word of Christ "dwell in you richly" is not merely an additional injunction, it is foundational.

This is the only occurrence of "the word of Christ" in Paul's letters (although ῥῆμα Χριστου appears in Rom 10:17). In general, λόγος has a broad range of usage and may refer to a word, a statement, a question, a command, an oral presentation, a narrative, or a written discourse.[44] Here it needs to be understood in the more expansive sense and regarded as the oral and written teaching about Christ. Paul has already spoken of "the word *of God*" earlier in Colossians (1:25), where it refers to the gospel that God has called him to make fully known, and he uses this expression elsewhere in his writings (Rom 9:6; 1 Cor 14:36; Eph 6:17; 1 Thess 2:13; 1 Tim 4:5; 2 Tim 2:9; Titus 2:5). There is a distinctive emphasis on the word in Colossians. Hübner notes, "The church is the church of the word for the author of Colossians because God is effectively present in the word."[45] This word is coextensive with the gospel since Paul earlier speaks of the gospel as the ὁ λόγος τῆς ἀληθειάς, "the word of truth" (Col 1:5).

44 See BDAG, s.v. λόγος; LSJ, s.v. λόγος.

45 Hübner, 107.

The genitive τοῦ Χριστοῦ leaves some ambiguity about how it relates to ὁ λόγος, so commentators have been split on whether to take it as a subjective genitive (the word spoken by Christ)[46] or an objective genitive (the word about Christ).[47] Interpreters on both sides of this debate can interpret it to be the gospel, so the issue is one of emphasis.[48] Since the subjective-genitive interpretation makes Christ the active speaker,[49] it would appear to limit the application to Christ's spoken words in his earthly ministry and prophetic words spoken by Christ (i.e., by the Spirit of Christ) in the assembly of believers. It is more appropriate to broaden the reference to include traditional summaries of the gospel message (e.g., 1 Cor 15:3–4), christological hymns (e.g., Col 1:15–20), and apostolic reflection on the gospel, including Paul's own summary and interpretation of the work of Christ, such as we have in Col 1 and 2. "The message about Christ" (CEV; CSB; NLT) is the best interpretive translation. Gordley is certainly correct in seeing a direct reference to the hymn of Col 1:15–20 referenced here ("let the hymnic account of Christ dwell in your richly"),[50] but there is no reason to exclude other Spirit-inspired christologically focused psalms, hymns, and songs. These varied terms would suggest that there is more than one hymn that is in view. And while there is an emphasis in this passage on the teaching function of music in the worship of the early church, psalms, hymns, and songs are not the only way that teaching about Christ can be communicated. In reflecting on the Christ-hymn, however, the Colossians would be reminded that Christ is acclaimed to be "the image of the invisible God" (1:15). As such, he himself is the personal revelation of the one living and true God.[51] He is the one in whom dwells all the fullness of the godhead in bodily form (2:9).

Paul wants Jesus's words and the teaching about his work to be on their thoughts continually and for their significance to penetrate deep into their souls. The metaphor of "taking up residence" (ἐνοικέω) reinforces the importance of deeply meditating and aligning one's life with the words of Christ and teaching about him. Paul uses the same language in Romans to refer to the indwelling of the Spirit (Rom 8:11; see also v. 9). But the Spirit is also involved here through inspiring the psalms, hymns, and songs that magnify and teach about Christ (see the discussion of πνευματικός, below). This association is seen in Ephesians where he encourages the believers to take up "the sword of the Spirit, which is the word of God" (Eph 6:17).

---

46 E.g., Beale, 302; C. Moule, 125; Lightfoot, 224.

47 E.g., Pao, 247; Moo, 286; Sumney, 223. Wolter, 189, refers to it as a "Genitive des Inhalts."

48 E.g., C. Moule, 125, can say that it is "the Gospel, the 'Word' uttered by Christ in his life and ministry and through his person, and repeated by each Christian as he proclaims the Gospel by life and witness." And, similarly, Pao, 247, who takes it as an objective genitive, says that the expression refers to "the gospel about and centered on Christ."

49 Lightfoot, 224, notes that "Christ is the speaker."

50 Gordley, *Colossian Hymn*, 268.

51 So also Hübner, 107, who notes, "Als Ikone Gottes, ist Christus die *personhafte Offenbarung Gottes*."

The adverb πλουσίως, a cognate of πλούσιος ("rich," "wealthy"), is a metaphor for abundance. It is used in Titus 3:6 of the abundance of the Spirit poured out on believers. Paul is here encouraging the Colossian believers to devote themselves to learning more about Christ, to meditate on who he is and what he has done, and to allow every aspect of their lives to be profoundly influenced by him. By contrast, the advocates of "the philosophy" are failing to look to Christ and be determined by his teaching (Col 2:19). The various forms of the music will help to facilitate making the teaching about Christ (especially through the christological lyrics of the songs) both memorable and moving.

ἐν πάσῃ σοφίᾳ διδάσκοντες καὶ νουθετοῦντες ἑαυτούς, ψαλμοῖς ὕμνοις ᾠδαῖς πνευματικαῖς, "by teaching and admonishing one another in all wisdom with spiritual psalms, hymns, and songs." Paul highlights how important the lyrics of the music in the corporate worship of the gathered community are in grounding believers in the teaching about Christ. He also affirms the role of wisdom and the Spirit in this process.

Paul's comment here would remind the readers of what he wrote earlier in describing the goal of his ministry as proclaiming Christ, "admonishing and teaching everyone with all wisdom [ἐν πάσῃ σοφίᾳ], that we may present everyone mature in Christ" (1:28). For Paul, Christ is the fountainhead of wisdom. In him "are hidden all the treasures of wisdom and knowledge" (2:3). This is underlined by the Colossian hymn where the language of personified Wisdom is used to describe Christ. The wisdom language here reinforces the christological focus of this section and counteracts the teaching of "the philosophy" that merely has "the reputation for wisdom" (2:23), but falls short because of the way it diminishes the person and work of Christ.

This clause consists of two present-tense participles that are dependent on the main verb, ἐνοικείτω. Most English versions retain ambiguity in expressing that relationship, such as the ESV's "let the word of Christ dwell in you richly, teaching and admonishing one another" (see also CSB; NET; NASB; ASV; KJV; NKJV). Yet there are three possible ways of interpreting the syntactical relationship of the participles to the main verb more specifically.

1. They can be taken as *temporal* participles and as related actions that are happening contemporaneously with the main verb. This view is represented in the NIV translation: "let the message of Christ dwell among you richly *as* you teach and admonish one another" (see also NAB; the CEV translates, "*while* . . . you teach and instruct each other").[52]
2. Many versions have interpreted them as *imperatival* participles and thus conceptually less connected to the main verb. Some of the versions put a period after the first clause and treat the next clause as an independent admonition as, for example, the CEB: "The word of Christ must live

52 Sumney, 224; Moo, 288.

in you richly. Teach and warn each other . . ." (see also NLT; NJB; the NRSV and REB use a semicolon).[53]

3. The final, and preferred, way of taking these participles is to interpret them as expressive of *means*. Although no English versions render it this way, this is the view of a growing number of interpreters.[54] This interpretation would stress *how* the word of Christ should dwell within the Colossian believers: "let the word of Christ dwell in you richly *by* teaching and admonishing each other."

This grammatical construction—a present imperative verb followed by a present participle interpreted as expressing means—is common in Paul's writings (e.g., 1 Cor 10:25, 27; 16:2; Eph 6:9).[55] This construction occurs on two other occasions in Colossians (καταβραβευέτω θέλων [2:18]; προσκαρτερεῖτε γρηγοροῦντες [4:2]). I have argued elsewhere that this is also the best way to interpret the parallel passage in Eph 5:18–19: πληροῦσθε ἐν πνεύματι λαλοῦντες ἑαυτοῖς ἐν ψαλμοῖς καὶ ὕμνοις καὶ ᾠδαῖς πνευματικαῖς, "be filled with the Spirit *by* speaking to one another with spiritual psalms and hymns and songs."[56] In the Ephesian passage, corporate worship is not the only way to be filled with the Spirit; it is rather one important way of experiencing the Spirit that the author wanted to emphasize. Similarly here, learning about Christ through the lyrics of the church's songs does not exhaust how the Colossians are to grow in their knowledge of Christ, yet for a largely nonliterate culture, this becomes a very important means for learning theology. Because the main verb is imperative, there is an imperatival tone that accrues to the present participles that follow despite interpreting them as means. But contrary to the second view, we need to see the participles more closely connected to the main verb and resist seeing them as a second, independent command. The temporal interpretation is possible and is correct in that the action of the participles are coincident with the main verb; however, Paul's usage and the context would suggest a more specific interpretation specifying how the action of the main verb is to be carried out.

The musical worship of the early church would have had both a didactic and admonitory function in the gathered assembly. As the Colossians hear and sing truths about Christ, both their minds and hearts would be engaged in absorbing this content. But Paul takes it a step further by appealing to the admonitory (νουθετοῦντες) role that it should play. As noted in the standard lexicon, this term has to do with "counsel about avoidance or cessation of an improper course of

53 Barth and Blanke, 427; Lohse, 150; Lightfoot, 224.

54 Beale, 303; Pao, 248; Detwiler, "Church Music," 356–57. Meyer, 364, prefers defining it as "a modal definition." Lincoln, "Colossians," 649, writes that "the use of psalms, hymns, and songs, therefore, is a primary means by which mutual teaching and admonition take place."

55 Wallace, *Grammar*, 639, notes that "the participle of means is often used in the present tense *after* a present imperative.

56 See my *Ephesians*, 351–52.

conduct."[57] In the immediate context, this would involve the Colossians aligning their lives with a set of ethical values that are consistent with the God they now serve and "killing" (3:5) those practices that are inconsistent with life in Christ. But it would also involve realigning their convictions with the full range of truth expressed in the life and teaching of the Lord Jesus Christ. Since Paul judges the advocates of "the philosophy" to be out of sync with Christ (2:19), the Colossians need to take a very careful assessment of how they are being influenced by this teaching and to resist it.

The reflexive pronoun (ἑαυτούς) should here be interpreted as having a reciprocal function—that is, "one another."[58] It serves as a reminder that the musical worship of the church is not only vertically focused on God who receives the worship as a sacrifice of praise, but it is also horizontally focused to the benefit of each of the members of the gathered congregation.

Paul conveys the specific form of the musical worship through the use of three different terms—ψαλμοῖς, ὕμνοις, and ᾠδαῖς, "with psalms, hymns, and songs." The dative case has an instrumental sense here. There has been a great deal of discussion about whether these terms are essentially synonymous or whether they can be differentiated and represent three distinct forms of musical expression. Most modern interpreters contend that no distinctions can be drawn.[59] One of the arguments for this view is that all of the terms, including ὕμνος, can be found in the LXX as another way of referring to various psalms. The three terms actually appear in close conjunction with each other two times in the LXX—in the superscriptions of Psalms 66 and 75 (= Psalms 67 and 76 in BHS and the English versions). Beale has even suggested that Paul may have had these psalms specifically in mind as he penned Col 3:16. Psalm 76:1 (75:1 LXX) reads, "Regarding completion. Among hymns [ὕμνοις]. A Psalm [ψαλμός]. Pertaining to Asaph. An Ode (ᾠδή)" (NETS). He concludes that Col 3:16 refers "to actual OT psalms or songs/hymns composed on the basis of such psalms, which would now be related to the new revelation of Christ."[60]

It is certainly easy to conceive of Jewish believers in Christ living in the Lycus Valley moved by the Spirit to compose psalms of praise to Messiah and to do so based upon the content and inspiration of the OT Psalter. But what about gentile followers of Christ who were raised with their own distinctive musical styles and earnestly desired to praise Christ with forms that were uniquely Anatolian, Greek, or Roman (or possibly even unique to the folk style of the Lycus Valley)? At the minimum, I would contend that the three different terms that Paul uses here are a rhetorical way of expressing musical variety in the worship of the

57 BDAG, s.v. νουθετέω.

58 See BDAG, s.v. ἑαυτοῦ 2.: "marker of reciprocal relationship."

59 See, e.g., Moo, 289; McKnight, 332; Foster, 362; Barth and Blanke, 427–28; Still, "Colossians," 334; Garland, 212; Dunn, 238; Detwiler, "Church Music," 359–63; Smith, "First-Century Christian Singing," 10, 14; Malan, "Church Singing," 516.

60 Beale, 305.

Colossian church. But there may be some discernible distinctions of musical forms represented with these terms.[61]

The term ὕμνος was commonly used by Greeks for their form of musical praise to the numerous gods and goddesses throughout the Greco-Roman world. Hymns written in honor of Demeter, Apollo, Hermes, Aphrodite, and other deities dating from the seventh to fifth centuries BC have been preserved. These "Homeric hymns" contain a strong didactic element and reveal epithets and attributes of the gods, key events associated with their ascent to Olympus, as well as "the strengths, abilities, and special areas of influence with which each god or goddess is concerned."[62] The composition of hymns in honor of the gods was widespread in the religious traditions of the Hellenistic and Roman era. These were often sung in praise to the various deities in their temples. Of particular concern for our purposes is the inscriptional evidence from western Asia Minor. There are numerous occurrences of the word ὕμνος as well as the related terms ὑμνῳδός (hymn singing), ὑμνῳδοί (choral singers), ὑμνῳδία (singing of a hymn), ὑμνωδάρχης (choirmaster), ὑμνογράφος (composer of hymns), ὑμνοδιδάσκαλος (teacher of hymns), ὑμνολογέω (to sing a hymn), and ὑμνολόγος (sing a hymn). Two inscriptions give the names of a choral procession (οἱ ὑμνῳδήσαντες κοῦροι) who traveled from Laodicea on the Lycus to the temple of Apollo at Claros to consult the oracle and to sing praise in honor of the god.[63] Numerous inscriptions from Claros mention hymn singers (ὑμνῳδοί) coming with various delegations. An inscription from Stratonikeia preserves a decree from the council of that city for the appointment and training of hymn singers (ὑμνῳδοί) for the worship of Zeus Panamaros and Hekate.[64] References to hymn singers (ὑμνῳδοί) are also found in honorific inscriptions discovered in nearby Akmonia[65] and Aphrodisias.[66] An entire guild of hymn writers who composed hymns in honor of "the most holy goddess Artemis" is referred to in an inscription from Ephesus.[67] This evidence would strongly suggest that for gentiles living in the Lycus Valley, the term ὕμνος and its cognates would be associated with the musical worship associated with the traditional gods and goddesses.

On the other hand, the term ψαλμός is quite rare in the inscriptions of Asia Minor. It does, however, appear in an inscription from nearby Aphrodisias, but

---

61 Wilson, 268; Scott, 75; Williams, 142; Lightfoot, 224–25; Calvin, 353. Sumney, 225, recognizes that the author "may intend clear distinctions among these musical types" but "the specifics are lost to current readers."

62 Gordley, *Teaching through Song*, 33. See his extensive discussion of these hymns on pp. 28–55. For the text of these hymns, see Rayor, *Homeric Hymns*.

63 *SEG* 37.962.1–22; 37.966.1–23.

64 *IStratonikeia* 1101 (= *SEG* 15.655).

65 *MAMA* VI list 149.171, line A.3.13; Waelkens, *Türsteine*, 423.13 (from the city of Akmonia).

66 McCabe, *Aphrodisias*, no. 18.16.

67 *IEph* 645.

this is a Jewish inscription that refers to a certain Benjamin as a ψαλμολόγος.[68] The verbal form, ψάλλω (to pluck or play strings on a musical instrument) is also rare in the inscriptions from western Asia Minor. It is found on an inscription discovered in the city of Teos (northwest of Ephesus) that refers to the teaching of children through music (διδάξει τούς τε παῖδας . . . μουσικά), which includes κιθαρίζειν ἢ ψάλλειν, playing on a *kithara* or plucking strings.[69] But, in general, ψαλμός was a term used frequently in Jewish contexts. It is especially prominent in the LXX, particularly in the titles of numerous psalms (ψαλμὸς τῷ Δαυιδ, "a psalm of David" [Ps 3:1]; see also the titles of Pss 4–14, 18–24, etc.), and from it the entire Psalter was named. It may be of significance to note that the deeply Hellenized Philo of Alexandria never uses ψαλμός in his writings, but he does employ ὕμνος on many occasions. Because the verb ψάλλω often refers to the plucking of strings, some commentators have thought that Paul's use of the term in this context may be differentiated from the others by referring to musical accompaniment.[70] Yet the verb can also be used of singing without instrumental accompaniment (see, e.g., Rom 15:9; 1 Cor 14:15; Eph 5:19),[71] so a distinction of this nature is strained.

Given the extensive usage of the terms ψαλμός in a Jewish context and ὕμνος in Greek culture, it seems best to take these two terms as reflecting a variety of musical form in worship, particularly as it relates to Jews and Greeks.[72] The one, but diverse, manifestation of the body of Christ in Colossae consisted of both Jews and Greeks. Despite their oneness (Col 3:11), their cultural distinctiveness and backgrounds persisted. What Paul is communicating here is a warrant for diversity of cultural forms in the worship styles of the gathered community.

The final word of the trio—ᾠδαί, "songs"—is a more general word for songs and is not the unique domain of any cultural group. It is used throughout the LXX and many times in the book of Psalms. It is in the title of the "Songs of Ascent" (ᾠδὴ τῶν ἀναβαθμῶν, "a song of the steps"; see the titles of the LXX Pss 119–133). But it was also used extensively in Greek literature, beginning as early as the Homeric hymns. The term does appear in the inscriptions of Asia Minor but is not common. It is found, for instance, in a funerary inscription from Ephesus referring to a group of mourners who honored the deceased "with tears and songs [ᾠδαῖς]."[73]

68 Reynolds and Tannenbaum, *Jews and God-Fearers at Aphrodisias*, 5–7. The text of this inscription also appears in *NewDocs* 9:73 (§25).

69 *SEG* 14.751, esp. lines 17–19.

70 So Lightfoot, 225.

71 BDAG, s.v. ψάλλω.

72 Contra Hengel, "Hymns and Christology," 80, who asserts that "the author is merely using the three most important Septuagint terms for the religious song." At the beginning of the article, however, he strongly differentiates ψαλμός and ὕμνος according to their Jewish and Greek backgrounds.

73 *IEph* 2103.7.

It seems best to conclude that the apostle is using these three terms not in an undifferentiated, synonymous manner but as a rhetorical way of commending diversity of forms and musical styles in the house churches of Colossae and the Lycus Valley. In addition to the common content of the lyrics of the music focusing on the person and work of Christ, the adjective "spiritual" (πνευματικαί) expresses another element of commonality between the various forms of psalms, hymns, and songs. Despite the agreement of the gender and number of the adjective with the final term, "spiritual" should be interpreted as modifying all three words.[74] Barth and Blanke suggest that it is placed after all three for emphasis.[75] Regarding this term, Fee rightly concludes that "for Paul it is an adjective that primarily refers to the Spirit of God."[76] The songs are "spiritual" in the sense that the Holy Spirit is active in encouraging, moving, prompting, and inspiring the composition of these songs—in a variety of cultural forms—to the praise of Christ. As Hengel notes, "They were not regarded as purely human creations, but as works of the Holy Spirit."[77] But the Spirit is also involved in the community when they assemble to sing these songs of praise to God; as Martin notes, "It is the Spirit who stirs the worshipper and directs his thought and emotion in lyrical praise whatever be the precise musical form."[78]

ἐν τῇ χάριτι ᾄδοντες ἐν ταῖς καρδίαις ὑμῶν τῷ θεῷ, "with gratitude singing in your hearts to God." Gratitude is a significant motivation for Christians everywhere to sing praise to God. The word translated "gratitude" here is Paul's oft-recurring term for "grace" (χάρις). This has led some interpreters to argue that Paul is using it in that sense here. Fee, for instance, suggests that it refers to "our standing in grace that makes such singing come from the heart."[79] Nevertheless, "thanks" or "gratitude" as a "response to generosity or beneficence"[80] is a common meaning for χάρις. Paul himself uses it elsewhere in this sense. He exclaims to the Corinthians, "Thanks [χάρις] be to God for his indescribable gift!" (2 Cor 9:15), and "thanks [χάρις] be to God who gives us the victory through our Lord Jesus Christ" (1 Cor 15:57; see also Rom 6:17; 7:25; 2 Cor 2:14; 8:16). Contextually, Paul concluded the previous section with an admonition to "be thankful" (Col 3:15), and in the next verse he draws the entire section (3:12–17) to a close by, once again, encouraging the readers to give thanks to God (3:17). One of the ways of expressing this gratitude to God is by singing songs of praise. It is therefore best to conclude, with almost all English versions, that χάρις should

74 So also Wolter, 190; Lincoln, "Colossians," 649; Martin, 116; Lohse, 151.

75 Barth and Blanke, 428.

76 Fee, *Empowering Presence*, 32 (see the larger discussion of the term on pp. 28–32).

77 Hengel, "Hymns and Christology," 81.

78 Martin, 116.

79 Fee, *Empowering Presence*, 655. Lightfoot, 225, also takes it as "grace," but connects it with the preceding clause.

80 BDAG, s.v. χάρις 5.

here be interpreted as gratitude and that the prepositional phrase should be seen as modifying the participle "singing" (ᾄδοντες).

This participle is the verbal form (ᾄδω) of the previously occuring word for "song" (ᾠδή). It is a general word for singing, without any particular connotations. The only other time it appears in Paul is in the parallel passage in Eph 5:19. Both the noun and verb appear together in Rev 5:9 where it speaks of the twenty-four elders who "sang a new song" (ᾄδουσιν ᾠδὴν καινήν) before the Lamb (see also Rev 14:3; 15:3; see also Pss 96:1 [95:1 LXX]: "oh sing to the LORD a new song"]; 137:3–4; 144:9). Syntactically, the participle is parallel with διδάσκοντες καὶ νουθετοῦντες and dependent on ἐνοικείτω.[81] It provides an additional perspective on the role of musical worship in the church. The psalms, hymns, and songs have a dual audience: the first is "one another" (ἑαυτούς), to whom the songs fulfill both a teaching and admonitory function; the second is God (τῷ θεῷ), to whom it is an expression of worship and gratitude. This musical worship engages each individual deeply—both in their thinking and in their emotions, which is entailed by the expression, "in your hearts" (ἐν ταῖς καρδίαις ὑμῶν), as they sing these lyrics of praise to God and to one another.

In the parallel passage, believers sing their praise "to the Lord" (τῷ κυρίῳ), which, in that context, is a reference to Christ (Eph 5:19). This raises the possibility that Paul's reference to "God" here might speak of Christ. This would be consistent with the christological emphasis of the entire letter and the high Christology of the Christ-hymn (1:15–20).

One interpreter has suggested that Paul's exhortation to sing hymns of praise in honor of Christ may have been partly motivated to counter an emphasis on singing for apotropaic purposes (i.e., warding off evil spirits) within "the philosophy."[82] He cites evidence within early Jewish literature illustrating how some Jews would recite songs, chants, and hymns to neutralize attacks from evil spirits. For example, in 4QSongs of the Sage$^{a}$, the author declares, "And I, a Sage, declare the splendour of his radiance in order to frighten and terr[ify] all the spirits of the ravaging angels and the bastard spirits, demons, . . ." (4Q510 1.4–5; see also 11Q5 XIX).[83] Paul may have had a complex of motives for including this exhortation to musical worship and praise, and this could be one of those motivations. It is entirely plausible that the teachers of "the philosophy" were using psalms, hymns, and songs to bring relief from demonic attack (much like David did for Saul; see 1 Sam 16:23). But this was not the primary reason for the inclusion of this exhortation. The musical worship had a teaching function through the lyrics to ground believers more deeply in their knowledge of the Lord Jesus Christ.

---

81 Moo, 288, however, takes it as subordinate to the previous participles and describing the attitude that accompanies "teaching and admonishing."

82 Cavin, *New Existence*, 177–79.

83 As cited in Cavin, *New Existence*, 178.

**17** This verse both summarizes and concludes the entire set of exhortations in this central portion of the letter (3:5–16). Everything that the Colossian believers do and say should be done as an expression of their new life in Christ. This means that not only should their speech and conduct align with the teaching of Christ and his kingdom purposes, but Christ himself serves as the basis and empowerment for living day-to-day. This final admonition thus takes us back to the transitional section of the letter that also served as the foundation for the ethical admonitions, where Paul stressed their participation with Christ in his death, resurrection, and exaltation (3:1–4). It also ties in directly with the admonition that Paul gave in 2:6–7: "therefore, as you received Christ Jesus the Lord, walk in him, being rooted and built up in him and established in the faith, just as you were taught, and abounding in thanksgiving." Living under the lordship of Jesus Christ is all important for Christians.

καὶ πᾶν ὅ τι ἐὰν ποιῆτε ἐν λόγῳ ἢ ἐν ἔργῳ, "whatever you do in word or in work." The neuter singular relative pronoun (ὅ), with the neuter indefinite pronoun (τι), combine to form the idea of "something" (see 1 Cor 16:2). When the indefinite particle (ἄν) is added to these two, the three terms convey the sense of "whatever" (see the ὅ τι ἄν construction in Luke 10:35; John 2:5; 14:13; 15:16). Here we have the two pronouns combined with another form of the indefinite particle (ἐάν) to express the idea of "whatever." This precise construction is found in the LXX (see 1 Sam 19:3) and in the NT (Mark 6:23: ὅ τι ἐάν με αἰτήσῃς, "whatever you ask me"). In our passage, this three-word combination is also modified by the neuter singular adjective (πᾶν), thus yielding the sense of "everything, whatever you do."[84] Paul then repeats the adjective in the second clause, "do everying [πάντα]," thereby placing a strong emphasis on every single word and action that believers carry out 24 hours per day, seven days a week, throughout their lives. This combination of three terms in the nominative case functions as a "pendent" nominative ("the logical rather than the syntactical subject"[85] of the main verb) since the main verb is second-person plural.[86] It introduces and amplifies the πάντα of the second clause.

The combination of λόγος and ἔργον to convey speech and behavior in the broadest possible sense is found elsewhere in Paul (Rom 15:18; 2 Thess 2:17; see also 2 Cor 10:11), as well as in the NT (see, e.g., Acts 7:22; 1 John 3:18) and the LXX (Sir 3:8; 9:17). The present tense of the main verb (ποιῆτε) should be

---

84 Almost all English versions do not translate the adjective (πᾶν) to avoid redundancy. One exception, however, is the Douay-Rheims version: "all whatsoever you do in word or in work . . ." The Tyndale version of 1534 also brings this out: "and all thynges (whatsoever ye do in worde or dede) . . ." The Vulgate also retained the literal sense: "omne quodcumque facitis in verbo aut in opere omnia."

85 Wallace, *Grammar*, 51. Others refer to it as a "left dislocation"—i.e., "information that is syntactically outside the main clause (i.e., it is dislocated), which is then reiterated somewhere in the main clause using a pronoun" (Campbell, 60–61, citing Runge, *Lexham Discourse Greek NT*, loc. cit.).

86 So also Harris, 148.

understood in its imperfective aspect, which is consistent with the comprehensive focus on every conceivable word or action carried out by believers throughout the course of their lives.

πάντα ἐν ὀνόματι κυρίου Ἰησοῦ, "everything in the name of the Lord Jesus." The second clause, which functions as the main clause of the sentence, is missing a verb. The main verb of the previous clause (ποιῆτε), which is a dependent relative clause, carries its force to the second clause and should be understood: [ποιεῖτε] πάντα ἐν ὀνόματι κυρίου Ἰησοῦ. The emphasis thus falls on the πάντα. All of life is to be carried out under the lordship of Jesus Christ.

The phrase ἐν ὀνόματι κυρίου is the LXX translation of בְּשֵׁם־יְהוָה, "in the name of the Lord," and appears throughout the OT. It sometimes contrasts the words and actions done in the name of other gods with those done in the name of Yahweh. For instance, Deut 18 contrasts the prophet "who speaks in the name of other gods" with the prophet who "speaks in the name of the LORD" (Deut 18:20, 22 ESV; see also 1 Sam 17:45). It generally refers to actions undertaken with the authorization and empowerment of Yahweh. For instance, the Levites ministered "in the name of the Lord" (Deut 18:5, 7), prophets were called to speak "in the name of the LORD" (2 Chr 18:15; cf. Ezra 5:1; Jer 26:20; 44:16), blessings were to be imparted "in the name of the LORD" (Deut 21:5; cf. 2 Sam 6:18), and enemies were defeated "in the name of the LORD" (Ps 118:10–12). Indeed, for the people of God, all of life was to be lived "in the name of the LORD" as the prophet Micah states: "all the peoples walk each in the name of its god, but we will walk in the name of the LORD our God forever and ever" (Mic 4:5 NRSV). In Colossians and consistent with his use of the term "Lord" throughout his writings, Paul is thinking principally of the sovereign lordship of Jesus Christ. Paul thus appropriates the title of Yahweh and applies it to Christ—the one who is the image of the invisible God, the creator of the world, and preeminent in all things (Col 1:15–18). With this phrase, "in the name of the Lord," Paul is telling the Colossians that every moment of their lives should be lived in the service of the Lord Jesus Christ and by his empowerment. They represent Christ as they tend their sheep, farm their crops, work in the mines and quarries, do business in the marketplace, interact with their neighbors, and care for their families. Indeed, they speak and act on behalf of Christ in every sphere of life and should depend on his grace and power to represent him well. Their baptism signifies that they have identified with Jesus in his death and resurrection (2:11–13); this is tantamount to the fact that they have been baptized in the name of the Lord (Matt 28:19; Acts 10:48). So Paul thus concludes this section by reiterating the theological basis for how he began this series of exhortations: because the Colossians have died with Christ and have been raised with him, they can now "seek the things above" (Col 3:1–4). This involves eradicating vices and putting on virtues.

Yet this passage also speaks to some of the ritual methods of the shamanistic practitioners and teachers among them. Magic and shamanism were primarily concerned about accessing spiritual power for healing, protection, deliverance from spirits, and other practical concerns. Calling on the names of gods, goddesses, angels, spirits, and mighty assistants was a central part of how rituals of power were accomplished. Invoking the right name (ὀνομάζειν . . . τὸ ὄνομα) was how Sceva and his sons performed exorcisms in Ephesus (Acts 19:13). There are numerous references in ancient magical texts to invoking names. One magical text reads: "I conjure you by the 'great names' [ὀνομάτων]. . . . You, these holy names [ὀνομάτα] and these powers [δυνάμεις], confirm and carry out this perfect enchantment; immediately; immediately; quickly; quickly!"[87] Deliverance from the varied attacks of evil spirits in the eighteenth chapter of the Testament of Solomon—an independent shamanistic handbook that may have circulated as early as the first century BC—is predicated on knowing the name of the right angel who could effectively thwart the work of the harmful spirit. Paul's message to the shamanistic teachers (and all of the Colossian believers who may have been tempted to follow them) is to depend on Christ alone. They belong to him, they represent him, they are united with him in his death and resurrection, and they share in his power and authority over hostile spirits (see 2:9–10, 19). They have no need to revert to traditional spiritual means, and especially calling on the names of other angelic and spirit powers, for dealing with the issues of life.

εὐχαριστοῦντες τῷ θεῷ πατρὶ δι᾿ αὐτοῦ, "giving thanks to God the Father through him." As they live their day-to-day lives, their disposition should be one of constant gratitude to the Father. Thanksgiving pervades this section. Paul concluded his list of virtues with the appeal to "be thankful" (3:15). He then asserted that gratitude should motivate their singing of praise to God (3:16). Now he ends the entire section by encouraging them to let thanksgiving to God pervade everything they do in their day-to-day lives. The participle is best interpreted as one of manner, and not as an independent imperative.[88] It conveys the emotion or attitude that should characterize how believers should live their daily lives, with constant awareness of God's gracious work on their behalf.[89]

This gratitude should be directed to the Father, but "through"[90] the Lord Jesus Christ (δι᾿ αὐτοῦ). It is the Father who has "qualified us to receive a portion of the inheritance of the saints in the realm of light" by transferring us "into the kingdom of his beloved Son" (1:12–13). It is this new status and resultant new life in Christ that should occupy the minds of believers and prompt them to have a constant attitude of thanksgiving to God (1:12). Paul expresses a similar thought to the Romans: "thanks be to God through Jesus Christ our Lord!"

87 *PGM* CI.52.

88 Contra Barth and Blanke, 431, who take it as an imperatival participle. The REB translates it as an imperative, "and give thanks through him to God the Father" (see also CEB).

89 Wallace, *Grammar*, 627, describes a participle of manner as referring to "the *emotion* (or sometimes *attitude*) that accompanies the main verb."

90 The phrase should be read "through him" and not "because of him," which would require the pronoun to be in the accusative case.

(Rom 7:25). The contrast to thanksgiving is grumbling and complaining—acts of ingratitude. Thus, Paul can say to the Philippians, "Do everything without complaining" (Phil 2:14 NLT).[91] But as he reaffirms in the parallel to this Colossian passage, everything should be done with a heart of thanksgiving to God (cf. Eph 5:20).

## *Explanation*

The christological focus of the letter continues in this passage with the role that Christ plays as the agent in the Father's overall plan of redemption. The passage begins by stressing the action of the Father in choosing a people for himself and ends with Paul summoning the church to give thanks to God the Father, but all of this is accomplished "through him"—that is, through the Lord Jesus Christ.

God has not only chosen the Colossian believers, but he has poured out his love on them and set them apart to be his own (3:12). They belong to him not only as individuals but as one unified body that he has created (3:15). Now Paul appeals to them to live their lives in a way that is consistent with their calling and their new status as ἅγιοι, "holy ones." In continuity with his self-revelation to Israel, God expects his people to "be holy, for I am holy" (Lev 11:44–45; 19:2).

The set of ten virtues that Paul specifically names here are crucial for the Colossians to integrate into their lives because they reflect the very character of the God whom they now serve and are consistent with the example that Jesus himself set in his time on earth. These virtues will also enhance their life in community together as God's people.

Central to these virtues is love. Paul presents it here as foundational to the practice of all the other virtues. As "the bond of perfection," it is like a belt that holds all of the other garments in place (3:14). Chrysostom likens it to the ropes used by the sailors of cargo vessels: "though its rigging be large, yet if it lacks girding ropes, it is of no service."[92] The capacity to follow the example of Christ, deny oneself, and put the interests of others first will help drive such virtues as compassion, kindness, gentleness, and humility. God's deep love for his people (3:12) should motivate and inspire their love for one another. Paul put it beautifully in Eph 5:1–2: "therefore be imitators of God, as beloved children. And walk in love, as Christ loved us and gave himself up for us, a fragrant offering and sacrifice to God" (ESV).

Yet each of the virtues is reflected both in the heart and actions of the Father as well as in the life and example of the Lord Jesus Christ. For instance, the Psalms repeatedly extol the compassion of the Lord, and Paul can elsewhere refer to God as "the Father of compassion" (ὁ πατὴρ τῶν οἰκτιρμῶν; 2 Cor 1:3). More than once in his earthly ministry, Jesus was "moved with compassion"

91 See Pao, 251, and his *Thanksgiving*, 153–59.

92 Chrysostom as cited by Gorday, "Colossians," 49.

(e.g., Matt 15:32; 20:34; Mark 1:41; 6:34), which caused him to act by providing healing, supplying food, or in other tangible ways.

All the virtues that Paul lists in this passage are attitudes and dispositions that are cultivated, fostered, and developed in believers individually, but they come to expression in the social relations between members of the community. For instance, the "bowels of mercies" (Col 3:12 KJV) that Paul commends begins with each individual developing a heart that is warm, sensitive, empathetic, tender, and full of love. Yet this disposition then needs to be expressed in the context of Christian community. It is empty to profess a compassionate heart when the reality is that it is largely devoid of the tangible expressions of this compassion toward fellow believers.

The theme of thankfulness is woven throughout this passage. Paul ends his list of virtues by insisting that thankfulness should be a regular part of their daily lives (3:15). He continues by saying that a heart of gratitude should motivate their musical worship of God and be a part of their expressions of praise (3:16). And he draws the section to a close by once again entreating them to constantly give thanks to the Father through Jesus Christ (3:17). Paul models this kind of thankfulness to God throughout his letters.

Paul sees teaching about Christ as foundational to life change. This would also include Christ's own teaching from his earthly ministry. The apostle sees christological grounding as essential for being able to eradicate vices from one's life and to appropriate virtue. Central to this teaching about Christ is an understanding of how believers participate with him in his death and resurrection. This new life with Christ (2:12–13; 3:1–4) empowers believers to fulfill the behavioral demands of living in a way that is pleasing to God. One of the ways that this rich christological teaching was delivered in the largely nonliterate culture of the Lycus Valley was through the medium of music. The lyrics of the songs that they were singing to God were intensively focused on the person and work of Christ and were inspired by the Spirit (3:16). The language of this passage stresses the involvement of all three persons of the Godhead in the life of the community to further their growth to obedience. These songs were not only instructive, but were admonitory—nudging them to change old and deeply rooted patterns of behavior to bring them into alignment with the ethical demands of the one true God whom they now serve. This musical worship was also expressed in a rich variety of musical forms as expressed in the words, "psalms, hymns, and spiritual songs." It is likely that this language reflects both Jewish and Greek cultural forms, especially through the terms "psalms" and "hymns."

The Venerable Bede tells of a seventh-century herdsman from the Yorkshire coast in England named Caedmon, who took portions of the Bible and crafted them into songs for the benefit of the common people. Bede writes, "Whatever he learned from the holy Scriptures by means of interpreters, he quickly turned into extremely delightful and moving poetry, in English, which was his own tongue. By his songs the minds of many were often inspired to despise the world and to long for the heavenly life."[93] Bede later notes that among the scriptural portions that he turned into verse were the accounts of the incarnation, passion, and resurrection of the Lord, as well as the coming of the Holy Spirit and the teaching of the apostles.[94] Music is a powerful medium for communicating doctrinal truth, and the abbess Hild of the Abbey of Whitby in Northumbria certainly "recognised the value of Caedmon's gift in teaching about the Christian faith."[95] It is especially noteworthy that Caedmon's Scripture-saturated lyrics not only grounded the illiterate common people in the gospel but moved them to despise the practice of vice and to pursue virtue.

Many of the passages of the NT that have been identified on form-critical grounds as hymnic are intensely christological, including the Christ-hymn of this letter (Col 1:15–20; see also Phil 2:6–11; 1 Tim 3:16; although not in a Pauline letter, Heb 1:3 should also be mentioned). These hymns cover the central themes of Christology: the preexistence, incarnation (including the atoning death of Christ), and exaltation. A rich tradition of christologically oriented "psalms, hymns, and spiritual songs" has no doubt been lost to us. One of these hymns is mentioned by the younger Pliny in a letter to Emperor Trajan regarding his observations of Christians meeting in northern Asia Minor (Bithynia and Pontus) in the early second century: "they had met regularly before dawn on a fixed day to chant verses alternately among themselves in honour of Christ as if to a god [*carmenque Christo quasi deo dicere*]."[96]

Paul concludes his moral exhortation of Col 3:5–17 that everything believers do—both in speech and in conduct—should be done in the recognition that they now represent the Lord Jesus Christ himself and that all should be done through his empowerment. No longer should they call on the names of angels or any other powerful supernatural assistant; everything they do should be done solely by depending on Christ alone.

93 Bede, *Ecclesiastical History*, 215.

94 Bede, *Ecclesiastical History*, 216–17.

95 Daniell, *Bible in English*, 41.

96 Pliny the Younger, *Letters* 10.96.7 (Radice, LCL).

# Living in the Christian Household (3:18–4:1)

## *Bibliography*

**Arzt-Grabner, P.** "Everyday Life in a Roman Town." **Aune, D. E.** *Literary Environment.* **Balch, D. L.** *Let Wives Be Submissive.* ———. "Household Codes," 25–50. **Barclay, J. M. G.** "Ordinary but Different," 237–50. **Bevere, A. R.** *Sharing in the Inheritance*, 225–54. **Bornkamm, G.** "Hoffnung," 56–64. **Bradley, K.** *Slavery and Society.* **Clark, S. B.** *Man and Woman in Christ.* **Crouch, J. E.** *Colossian Haustafel.* **Gehring, R. W.** *House Church and Mission.* **Gielen, M.** *Haustafelethik.* **Glancy, J. A.** *Slavery in Early Christianity.* **Hartman, L.** "Code and Context," 237–47. **Hering, J. P.** *Colossian and Ephesian Haustafeln.* **Hopkins, K.** *Conquerors and Slaves.* **Huttner, U.** *Early Christianity in the Lycus Valley.* **Joshel, R.** *Slavery in the Roman World.* **Lee-Barnewall, M.** "Turning Κεφαλή on Its Head," 599–614. **Leppä, O.** *Making of Colossians*, 174–77. **Lincoln, A. T.** "Household Code," 93–112. **Lips, H. von.** "Haustafel," 261–80. **Lührmann, D.** "Neutestamentliche Haustafeln," 83–97. **MacDonald, M. Y.** "Household Codes," 65–90. ———. "Slavery, Sexuality, and House Churches," 94–113. **Munro, W.** "Colossians III.18–IV.1," 434–47. **Osiek, C.,** and **D. L. Balch.** *Families.* **Schüssler Fiorenza, E.** *In Memory of Her.* **Standhartinger, A.** "Household Code," 117–30. **Still, T. D.** "Eschatology in Colossians," 125–38. **Thompson, J. W.** *Moral Formation.* **Tidball, D.** *In Christ, in Colossae*, 118–34. **Vasser, M.** "Grant Slaves Equality," 59–71. **Verner, D. C.** *Household of God.* **Webb, W. J.** *Slaves, Women, and Homosexuals.* **Weidinger, K.** *Die Haustafeln.* **Wold, B. G.** "*4QInstruction*," 286–300. ———. *Women, Men and Angels.*

## *Translation*

18 *Wives,*

*submit yourselves to your*[a] *husbands as is fitting in the Lord.*

19 *Husbands,*

*love your wives and do not be be embittered toward them.*

20 *Children,*

*obey your parents in everything, for this is pleasing in the Lord.*

21 *Fathers,*

*do not provoke*[b] *your children so they do not become discouraged.*

22 *Slaves,*

*obey your earthly masters in every respect*[c]*—not serving to be seen*[d] *as people pleasers but in*
*sincerity of heart, fearing the Lord.*[e] 23 *Whatever*[f] *you do, do your work wholeheartedly, as*
*for the Lord and not for people,* 24 *since you know that you will receive your reward—your*
*inheritance—from the Lord. Serve*[g] *the Lord Christ,* 25 *for the one who does wrong will be*
*repaid for what he has done wrong and there is no partiality [with the Lord].*

4:1 *Masters,*

*grant to your slaves justice and equality, since you know that you have a master in heaven.*

## *Notes*

a. [3:18] The Byzantine text inserts τοῖς ἰδίοις ("your own") here (so also L 6 365 614 630 et al.), which is reflected in the TR (and thus in the KJV and NKJV). The reading makes explicit the thought that is already present in the text since it is describing family relationships. The addition can be attributed to scribal assimilation to Eph 5:22 (and 1 Pet 3:1). Other witnesses (D F G 075 it vg^mss^) add ὑμῶν to the same effect.

b. [3:21] Instead of ἐρεθίζετε (B K Ψ 630 1739 vg 𝔐 [𝔓46 has ἐρεθ before the text breaks away]), some witnesses have παροργίζετε (ℵ A C D F G L 075 vg^mss^). Although there is an impressive array of MSS from the Alexandrian and Western test types, it is likely secondary, due to scribal assimilation to Eph 6:4 (μὴ παροργίζετε τὰ τέκνα). This is the conclusion of most commentators and Metzger, *Textual Commentary*, 558, which gives ἐρεθίζετε a "B" rating.

c. [3:22] 𝔓46 and a few other MSS omit κατὰ πάντα.

d. [3:22] A significant grouping of manuscripts (ℵ C Ψ 𝔐 et al.) has the plural, ὀφθαλμοδουλείαις, but the difference in meaning is negligible. The translators of the KJV, who accept the plural reading, make no distinction in translation ("not with eyeservice").

e. [3:22] The Byzantine text, along with 𝔓46 and a variety of other witnesses (K 104 630 et al.) has θεόν. The Alexandrian (ℵ A B Ψ 33 81) and Western (D F G it vg) traditions read κύριον. "Lord" is more likely here because of Paul's contrast with earthly κύριοι and the emphasis he places on κύριος (as Christ) throughout these household instructions.

f. [3:23] The Majority text inserts "everything" (πᾶν) into this expression, viz. πᾶν ὅ τι ἐὰν ποιῆτε (K L 630 𝔐 et al.), instead of the more simple ὃ ἐὰν ποιῆτε (𝔓46 ℵ A B C D F G 33 81 365 et al.). This was probably motivated by aligning it with the wording of Col 3:17 and perhaps to heighten the emphasis.

g. [3:24] The Majority text and a few other witnesses (K L Ψ 075 104 630 𝔐 et al.) insert γάρ at the outset of the sentence. This reading is reflected in some of the older English versions, "for ye serve the Lord Christ" (KJV; see also Geneva, Tyndale, NKJV). This is a secondary intrusion motivated by the lack of a conjunction and to make explicit an interpretation of the verb as indicative and the clause as explanatory.

## *Form/Structure/Setting*

### *Form (and Literary Context)*

This passage continues the christological focus of the letter by drawing out the implications of the lordship of Christ to the various groups of members in the Christian household. Christ is referred to as "Lord" (κύριος) no less than seven times in the span of nine verses. The heart of this passage could best be expressed in the exhortation of 3:24a: "serve the Lord Christ." But what will service to the Lord look like in the different social contexts in which believers find themselves throughout the week? In the previous two sections, Paul has established their new identity in Christ based on their union with him in his death, resurrection, and exaltation (3:1–4). He has likewise declared that they have been re-created by God—they have been stripped of their "old self" and have put on the "new self" that is being renewed into the image of God (3:9–10). Consequently, they should rid themselves of every kind of vice (3:5–11) and put on the key Christian virtues of love, compassion, kindness, humility, patience, and others (3:12–15). Although in their new community of faith, the old ethnic and social distinctions are relativized, they are still living in the world and need to live out the implications of their faith in these contexts. This diverse group of believers is still composed of Jews, Greeks, Romans, Anatolians, as well as slave holders, peasants, and slaves (3:11). What are the implications of this new identity and the lordship of Jesus Christ for the varied social relationships within the Christian community? Paul addresses six different categories—three different pairs—of social groupings, all of whom also belong to extended households. These include wives and husbands, children and fathers, and slaves and masters.

Paul's remarks begin abruptly and transition abruptly to the next section. No conjunction marks a transition at the beginning or end. He simply begins immediately with a vocative address to one of these social groups and delivers an imperative. The section following his instructions to the household concludes the paraenesis of the letter with three exhortations that address all believers in the community once again (4:2–6). The abruptness of our section, combined with its unique literary form and the ease with which 4:2–6 could follow immediately upon 3:12–17, has led many interpreters to think that 3:18–4:1 may be a distinct literary unit that has been inserted, somewhat awkwardly, into the paraenesis of this letter.[1]

But it is not as awkwardly placed as it may initially appear.[2] In the immediately preceding verse, Paul has just exhorted the Colossians, "Whatever you do in word or in work, do everything in the name of the Lord Jesus, giving thanks to God the Father through him" (3:17). How the Colossian believers should interact with and respond to the various members of their household in light of their relationship to the Lord Jesus Christ and their obligations to him would be a natural elaboration of this injunction.[3]

The specific content of this passage, along with some of the distinctive elements of its form, has led many interpreters to regard it as a literary type that was common in Hellenistic and Hellenistic-Jewish writings. They have suggested that Paul has either borrowed a preexisting unit and slightly Christianized it or that he has modeled his passage on these precedents.

---

1 Munro, "Colossians III.18–IV.1," 434–47, goes too far in arguing that the code has been interpolated into the letter. Cf. Lohmeyer, 153, who wrote that "the insertion at this place in the text reflects no rhyme or reason. If this pericope were eliminated, no trace of its absence would be detected" (as cited by Standhartinger, "Household Code," 123). Wilson, 273, rightly observes that "the fact that a passage could easily be omitted does not mean that it does not belong."

2 Contra Dunn, 242, who says, "it is not closely related to the context."

3 Hartman, "Code and Context," 239, notes that 3:17 "becomes a bridge to the household code; indeed, it might very well be regarded as the introduction."

# Excursus: The Household Code

This passage has much in common with texts in other NT letters that specify the conduct expected of various members within the Christian household. These passages include Eph 5:21–6:9, 1 Tim 2:8–15, 5:1–2, 6:1–2, Titus 2:1–10, and 1 Pet 2:11–3:12. In subsequent Christian tradition, there are similar household rules in 1 Clem. 21.6–9; Ign., *Pol.* 4.1–5.1; Pol. *Phil.* 4.2–3; Did. 4.9–11; and Barn. 19.5–7. They typically address the duties and responsibilities of husbands and wives, slaves, and sometimes children and slave masters. Because of their unique content addressing groups within the extended household, Luther referred to them as *Haustafeln*, "house tables"—an expression that has persisted.[4] English-speaking interpreters have commonly referred to them as the "household codes." Colossians is likely the earliest of these texts and would thereby have the distinction of being the first Christian household code.

Prior to the 1900s, interpreters of Colossians saw 3:18–4:1 as the letter writer's own composition addressing household relationships. Not detecting a literary form held in common with other ancient writers, commentators tended to focus on the specific content of the passage and its role in the larger argument of the letter. One group of ancient interpreters observed that these household texts only appear in letters written to churches in Asia Minor and that the cultural context of this area incited believers to a certain kind of unbridled freedom and antinomianism, sometimes furthered along by deviant teachers within the churches.[5] They then contended that the household codes were a response to this broad situation. Some of the older interpreters focused on the "false teaching" looming in the background of Colossae and saw the writer as countering the presumed asceticism that was having a negative impact on household relationships.[6] Others saw it as the apostle's efforts "to prevent false inferences from the doctrine that natural distinctions are done away in Christ" (Col 3:11; cf. Gal 3:28).[7] Finally, some simply saw these instructions as Paul moving from general Christian admonitions to more specific ones. Among these, Aquinas, in a manner that anticipates the later discussion of the household code, saw the apostle Paul as giving special directions to "three kinds of relationships

4 Barth and Blanke, 462.

5 Eadie, 251–52. He cites Chrysostom and Theophylact as supporting this view.

6 Lightfoot, 104, speaks of these household instructions as stemming from the practical implications of doing everything in the name of the Lord (Col 3:17), but also points to "the speculative tenets of Gnosticism" leading "to rigid asceticism or to unbridled license." Peake, 542, cites Holtzmann, Oltramare, and Weiss as seeing these instructions as a response to the impact of the false teaching.

7 Peake, 542.

the Philosopher [Aristotle] finds in domestic society; that of husband and wife; father and child; and master and slave."[8]

In the early 1900s, M. Dibelius changed the course of scholarship by arguing that the author of Colossians borrowed a household-code schema from the popular moral teaching of the Stoics, especially as seen in writers such as Epictetus and Seneca, and Christianized it with multiple motivating references to "the Lord."[9] It was his student Karl Weidinger, however, who picked up this thesis and developed it into a doctoral dissertation.[10] Weidinger emphasized that this form had already been adopted by Hellenistic Judaism, as seen in Philo, Josephus, and Pseudo-Phocylides.[11] For both Dibelius and Weidinger, the code met a need in early Christianity for special instructions on how believers should conduct themselves in daily life (*Alltagsleben*).[12] In a book-length monograph focused on the origin and intention of the Colossian household code, J. Crouch downplayed the Stoic background of the code and emphasized the Hellenistic-Jewish background as most relevant to Colossians. In particular, he emphasized texts that spoke of social duties in reciprocal terms. He also stressed the role of the code in curbing the license that church members were exhibiting as a result of the emancipatory tendencies stemming from Paul's leveling of social distinctions as expressed in Gal 3:28, combined with the Hellenistic religious influence affecting the churches through cults such as those of Dionysus, Isis, and Cybele.[13]

In recent years a broad consensus has been reached that the Colossian passage and the other NT household codes "are derived from the Hellenistic discussion 'concerning household management' (*peri oikonomias*), especially as outlined by Aristotle."[14] A trio of scholars—D. Lührman, K. Thraede, and D. Balch—independently reached this conclusion, and it has proved compelling to most interpreters since.[15] They find that this discussion continued from Aristotle down to the first century and beyond and influenced Hellenistic Judaism. Rather than seeing the codes as setting forth Christian duties for daily life, they contended that these texts were more outward looking and had political, social, and economic implications relating to the relationship of the *oikos* to the state.[16]

It is informative to sample some of the key ancient texts that have featured prominently in this discussion. The fountainhead of the presentation on "household management" is Aristotle:

---

8 Aquinas, 93.

9 See Balch, "Household Codes," 25.

10 Weidinger, *Die Haustafeln*.

11 Dibelius accepted the conclusions of his student, as seen in his excursus on *Haustafeln* in his HNT commentary (Dibelius, 48–50).

12 Dibelius, 48.

13 See Crouch, *Colossian Haustafel*.

14 Balch, "Household Codes," 26. Dunn, 243, declared that the debate regarding the origin of this material "should probably now be regarded as settled."

15 Balch, "Household Codes," *ABD* 3:318.

16 Lührmann, "Neutestamentliche Haustafeln," 86–88.

> And now that it is clear what are the component parts of the state, we have first of all to discuss household management [περὶ οἰκονομίας]; for every state is composed of households [οἰκιῶν]. Household management falls into departments corresponding to the parts of which the household in its turn is composed; and the household in its perfect form consists of slaves and freemen. The investigation of everything should begin with its smallest parts, and the primary and smallest parts of the household are *master and slave, husband and wife, father and children* [δεσπότης καὶ δοῦλος, καὶ πόσις καὶ ἄλοχος, καὶ πατὴρ καὶ τέκνα]: we ought therefore to examine the proper constitution and character of each of these three relationships, I mean that of mastership [δεσποτική], that of marriage (there is no exact term denoting the relation uniting wife and husband), and thirdly the progenitive relationship (this too has not been designated by a special name). Let us then accept these three relationships that we have mentioned. There is also a department which some people consider the same as household management and others the most important part of it, and the true position of which we shall have to consider: I mean what is called the art of getting wealth. (Aristotle, *Pol.* 1.1253b.1–14; emphases mine)

This passage names the same three pairs of household members as the Colossian passage, without describing their duties. In his continued discussion, Aristotle makes it clear that he regards slaves as property and so need to be governed. He also argues that women, "by nature," are inferior to men and should be ruled: "the male is by nature [φύσει] superior and the female inferior, the male ruler [ἄρχον] and the female subject [ἀρχόμενον]" (Aristotle, *Pol.* 1.1254.14–16). Here he is specifying the gender roles within the state and not simply the marriage relationship. Nowhere in his works does he address the three pairs of household groupings as Paul does here.

The three pairs of household relationships are also discussed by Seneca in one of his epistles, as Lührmann, Dibelius, and others have noted:[17]

> That department of philosophy which supplies precepts appropriate to the individual case, instead of framing them for mankind at large—which, for instance, advises *how a husband should conduct himself towards his wife, or how a father should bring up his children, or how a master should rule his slaves*—this department of philosophy, I say, is accepted by some as the only significant part, while the other departments are rejected on the ground that they stray beyond the sphere of practical needs—as if any man could give advice concerning a portion of life without having first gained a knowledge of the sum of life as a whole! (Seneca, *Ep.* 94.1–2; emphases mine)

17 Dibelius, 48; Lührmann, "Neutestamentliche Haustafeln," 85.

The epistle continues by discussing the importance of this form of practical wisdom, but it never provides specific instruction for each of the household members. He merely defends the usefulness of this wisdom and how it leads—from the man's perspective—to "the proper way of living with wife and children" (94.3) and how it can "produce a good man" (94.4).

Another important ancient author discussing the Aristotelian theme of "household management" is Arius Didymus (first century BC). He was a Stoic philosopher and friend of Octavian (Caesar Augustus), serving as his advisor. D. Balch has emphasized the importance of this author in his discussions of the household codes.[18] He compares household management to the functioning of a small city and regards it as the foundation for the state:

> Having sufficiently defined "virtues" and, more or less, the many crowded headings of the topos on "ethics," it is necessary successively to go through in detail both "household management" and "politics," since the human being is by nature a political animal. . . . A primary kind of association [*politeia*] is the legal union of a man and a woman for begetting children and for sharing life. This is called a household and is the source for a city, concerning which it is necessary to speak. For the household is like any small city, if, at least as is intended, the marriage flourishes, and the children mature. . . . The relationship of parents to children is monarchic, of husbands to wives aristocratic, of children to one another democratic. . . . When they come together and take for themselves a helper of the partnership—either a slave by nature (strong in body for service, but stupid and unable to live by himself, for whom slavery is beneficial) or a slave by law—a household is organized by the union of the ones added together and by the forethought of all for one thing that is profitable. The man has the rule of this household by nature. For the deliberative faculty in a woman is inferior, in children it does not yet exist, and in the case of slaves it is completely absent. (Arius Didymus, *Epitome of Stoic Ethics* 147.26–149.8)[19]

The text discusses some of the duties of the various members of the household along with their role responsibilities. It also reflects some of the commonly held Greek and Roman assumptions about the nature and limitations of women, children, and slaves. But as with the rest of the ancient texts, there is no direct address to each of the household members. The discussion is intended strictly for the male heads of the home and how they should manage their households.

One of the key Hellenistic-Jewish texts often cited as reflecting this literary topos is Philo's treatment of the fifth commandment:

---

18 Balch, *Let Wives Be Submissive*, 40–45; idem, "Household Codes," 40–45.

19 The translation is from Balch, "Household Codes, 41–42. He has translated from the portion of Arius Didymus cited in Stobaeus, *Anthologicum*, book II, chapter 7, excerpt 26. This portion is not included in the Pomeroy translation.

> In the fifth commandment on honouring parents we have a suggestion of many necessary laws drawn up to deal with the relations of old to young, rulers to subjects, benefactors to benefited, slaves to masters. For parents belong to the superior class of the above-mentioned pairs, that which comprises seniors, rulers, benefactors and masters, while children occupy the lower position with juniors, subjects, receivers of benefits and slaves. And there are many other instructions given, to the young on courtesy to the old, to the old on taking care of the young, to subjects on obeying their rulers, to rulers on promoting the welfare of their subjects, to recipients of benefits on requiting them with gratitude, to those who have given of their own initiative on not seeking to get repayment as though it were a debt, to servants on rendering an affectionate loyalty to their masters, to masters on showing the gentleness and kindness by which inequality is equalized. (Philo, *Decalogue* 165–67)

Although this text makes a few comments about masters and slaves, children and parents, it does not mention the pair of husband and wife. It is also quite brief and contains no instructions or exhortations to the various members of these groupings.

The final text I will mention that is commonly cited in discussions of the household code is a passage in Josephus that makes a few comments about regulations in the Torah pertaining to marriage and honoring one's parents:

> What are our marriage laws? The Law recognizes no sexual connexions, except the natural union of man and wife, and that only for the procreation of children. . . . The woman, says the Law, is in all things inferior to the man. Let her accordingly be submissive [ὑπακουέτω], not for her humiliation, but that she may be directed [ἄρχηται]; for the authority [τὸ κράτος] has been given by God to the man. . . . Again the Law does not allow the birth of our children to be made occasions for festivity and an excuse for drinking to excess. It enjoins sobriety in their upbringing from the very first. It orders that they shall be taught to read, and shall learn both the laws and the deeds of their forefathers, in order that they may imitate the latter, and, being grounded in the former, may neither transgress nor have any excuse for being ignorant of them. . . . Honour to parents the Law ranks second only to honour to God, and if a son does not respond to the benefits received from them—for the slightest failure in his duty towards them—it hands him over to be stoned. It requires respect to be paid by the young to all their elders, because God is the most Ancient of all. (Josephus, *Ag. Ap.* 2.199–207)

Yet as with all of the preceding passages, this text makes no direct address to the household members. In commenting on the Torah, it goes beyond the Torah in some of its assumptions and instructions, as in what it says regarding the husband "ruling" (ἄρχω) and the wife "obeying" (ὑπακούω).

There are certainly additional texts that could be presented in this overview,[20] but these are sufficient to reaffirm the presence of a topos on household management beginning with Aristotle and extending through Hellenistic literature, influencing Hellenistic Judaism and ultimately Christian texts. What is lacking is evidence to demonstrate that there was a *Gattung* or schema that resembled the central features of what we have in Col 3:18–4:1.[21] Four conspicuous differences can be observed: (1) these texts do not begin with a direct address to each member of the household; (2) they do not contain a second-person plural command with instructions on behavior that is appropriate to each role; (3) they do not include a subsequent comment that grounds the command—either by the use of an explanatory or causal conjunction or by employing a causal participle; and (4) they are not structured in terms of reciprocal duties. Most of them are descriptive of the manner of conduct that is expected and present it from the vantage point of the *paterfamilias*. D. Verner has also observed this discontinuity and argued that the household-code form we encounter in Colossians is exclusively Christian (although "shaped by the *topos* 'concerning household management'").[22] He correctly asserts that the NT texts "employ this topos in a way essentially unparalleled in pagan philosophical or apologetic literature."[23] Balch has countered by citing a handful of ancient texts where he says that some of these characteristics are present (Epictetus, *Diatr.* 3.12.10; Tob 4:3–21; Philo, *Cherubim* 48–49; *Spec. Laws* 2.67–68),[24] but none of these texts address a series of members within the household, and they do not demonstrate the other distinctive traits as he claims.

The selection of texts we have examined, as well as an array of other Hellenistic and Hellenistic-Jewish texts, demonstrate that there was a traditional *motif* in ancient literature of discussing household relationships and specific duties attached to each member of the household. There was, however, *no literary convention* or formula on how this topic was addressed.[25]

It should also be observed that there is no evidence that the Colossian

20 Standhartinger, "Household Code, 120–21, has called attention to Ps.-Charondas 61.16–22 and Ps.-Zaleukos 228.13–14. These texts are preserved in Stobaeus, *Anthologicum* 4.2.19, 24, and may reflect "street-philosophy" from the Hellenistic period. Because of their obscurity, one wonders how widely known these traditions would have been.

21 Contra Lohse, 154, who contended there was a "fixed schema." Hering, *Haustafeln*, 11, observed that "nearly all scholars, irrespective of their disagreements, would agee that the HT [*Haustafel*] form is an identifiable unit, which can be investigated under the assumptions of the *Formgeschichte* school, and have operated, since Dibelius, under these presuppositional guidelines." More recently, Foster, 370, has said that "the schema of the household code is known to have existed more widely prior to the composition of Colossians."

22 Verner, *Household of God*, 90–91.

23 Verner, *Household of God*, 90.

24 Balch, "Household Codes," *ABD* 3:318–19.

25 Hering, *Haustafeln*, 11, likewise concludes that the efforts to identify this as as a distinctive *Gattung* have "remained an unrealised goal." See his conclusions on pp. 58–60. See also Gielen, *Haustafelethik*, 26, and von Lips, "Haustafel," 261–80.

household code had an existence prior to its incorporation into the letter to the Colossians.[26] The fact that there was no literary form identifiable as a household code prior to the Colossian text undermines the viability of this scholarly construct.

It still remains for us to discuss the origin of the content of the code as we find it in Colossians. Does it originate in the tradition of discussions about the role of the household in relationship to the state that began with Aristotle and continued into the Roman era? At the heart of this tradition is the contention that the male head of the household—the *paterfamilias*—rules over every sphere, including his wife, his children, and his slaves. It assumes that any breakdown of this heirarchical arrangment would be detrimental to the state. Or is it possible that this text has its roots in Hellenistic (especially Stoic) discussions about proper citizenship and are focused primarily on the conduct of the individual, without concern about the new community's relationship to the state? Or is the author of Colossians doing something unique here by drawing out the implications of the lordship of Christ for the various members of the household, while rooting his discussion in biblical thought? The evidence points to this latter option.

From the very beginning of the letter, Paul has demonstrated a particular attentiveness to wisdom and Torah. He reports to the Colossians that he is praying regularly that they may be filled with a knowledge of the Lord's will "in all spiritual wisdom [σοφίᾳ] and understanding" (1:9). This wisdom pertains to how they conduct themselves in their daily lives, that they might "walk in a manner worthy of the Lord" (1:10). He portrays the Lord Jesus Christ as the source of this wisdom, claiming that it is in him the Colossians will find "all the treasures of wisdom [σοφίας] and knowledge" (2:3). He uses the language of the Jewish personified Wisdom tradition (see my comments on 1:15–20) to describe the Lord Jesus in the most exalted of terms, pointing to his role in creation and redemption (1:15–20). And in the immediate context of our passage, Paul urges the members of the community at Colossae to "let the word of Christ dwell in you richly by teaching and admonishing one another with all wisdom" (3:16).

In an important essay on the household code in Colossians, A. Lincoln has argued that the Jewish wisdom tradition is foundational for understanding the origin of this code.[27] "Wise living in the household" was a prominent theme in Jewish wisdom, especially as seen in Proverbs and Sirach. Numerous instructions regulate the conduct of husbands and wives (Prov 5:18, 19; 12:4; 18:22; 19:13–14; 31:10–31; Sir 9:1; 26:1–4, 13–18), parents and children (Prov 1:8; 6:20; 10:1; 13:24; 15:20; 19:13, 18, 26; 23:13–14; Sir 3:1–16; 30:1–13), and masters and slaves (Prov 14:35; 17:2; 19:10; 27:27; 29:19, 21; Sir 33:25–33). All three pairings are discussed in the same passage in Sir 7:19–28. In addition to

26 Contra Crouch, *Colossian Haustafel*, 33, who concludes that although Colossians lacks the characteristics of the Stoic schema, the *Haustafel* of 3:18–4:1 did exist prior to its inclusion in Colossians.

27 Lincoln, "Household Code," 93–12, esp. 104–111.

these texts may now be added a series of texts from 4QInstruction (4Q415–418; 4Q423; also known as 4QSapiential Work or *musar le-mebin*; see also 1Q26) that likely constitutes pre-Essene Jewish wisdom teaching.[28] They were published about the same time that Lincoln's article appeared. These texts also include instructions pertaining to husbands and wives (4Q415 2 ii; 4Q416 2 iii 20–21; 4Q416 2 iv 1–13), parents and children (4Q416 2 iii 15–19), and masters and slaves (4Q416 ii 7–17). B. G. Wold has correctly noted that although NT scholars almost universally contend that Hellenistic influences lie behind the form and content of the household codes of the NT, "this position should be re-evaluated" in light of the Jewish wisdom tradition within the Qumran literature.[29] Since this document was not available until 1999, it was not consulted by many previous monographs written on the household codes (including Dibelius, Weidinger, Crouch, Lührmann, Balch, and others).

Lincoln observes that central to the author of Colossians understanding of Christian wisdom is the conviction that "the fear of the Lord that is the beginning and sum of wisdom is now the acknowledgment of Christ as cosmic Lord."[30] Lincoln, however, sees this wisdom teaching combined with the Aristotelian tradition on household management, but this is entirely unnecessary since neither the form of the Colossian code nor the specific content require this. Part of his argument is based on the admonition to "walk in wisdom [σοφίᾳ] toward outsiders" (4:5a), which he interprets as "an eye to outsiders' accusations about the religion's potential social threat."[31] In other words, conformity to Roman social norms in the Christian household would serve as an apologetic to society that the new Christian community would not disrupt the established social order. Yet the immediately following line defines this as "making the best use of the time" (4:5b), and the larger context has to do with communicating the gospel of Christ (4:3). It is inferring too much to interpret this as maintaining a Roman social order.

In addition to the Jewish wisdom tradition, the author of Colossians shows a keen interest in the creation narrative—especially in his portrayal of Christ as creator in his eloquent hymn of praise at the outset of the letter (1:15–20)—as well as in his allusions to the ethical tradition (the halakah) of the Torah. J. Gnilka has emphasized the writer's dependence on the Decalogue in creating the two vice catalogs of Col 3:5, 8.[32] L. Hartman finds within the Colossian code "echoes of and interpretative applications of the Decalogue" and argues that the code functions as the application of "the Decalogue to God's elected and beloved people."[33] While the echoes of the Decalogue in the household code

28 Wold, "*4QInstruction*," 286–300. For a critical edition of this text, see M. J. Goff, *4QInstruction*.
29 Wold, "*4QInstruction*," 286.
30 Lincoln, "Household Code," 104–5.
31 Lincoln, "Household Code," 104.
32 Gnilka, 185.
33 Hartman, "Code and Context," 242.

could be attributed to the author's own reflections on the significance of these commandments for the Christian household, it is possible that they could have been mediated through the Jewish wisdom tradition. For instance, the fifth commandment, "honor your father and your mother" (Exod 20:12; Deut 5:16), is also found in 4QInstruction, but with additional teaching on how this should be accomplished (4Q416 2 iii 15–17). At its core, wisdom has to do with a right comprehension of life that results in right conduct rooted in God's revelation of himself and his ways in the Torah.

Yet the foremost indicator of the origin and function of the Colossian household code is the multiple references to "the Lord" (κύριος) throughout this passage. This is far from a Christian veneer appended to these instructions; Christ as the Lord of every member of the household is foundational to the whole. It is summed up well with the command that applies to all: "serve the Lord Christ" (Col 3:24b). The Colossian code is therefore a set of instructions that portray what living under the lordship of Christ looks like in every household relationship. The sevenfold reference to Christ as Lord in this passage makes this explicit. Wives are called to submit to their husbands not simply "as is fitting," but "as is fitting *in the Lord*" (3:18). Children are instructed to obey their parents because this is "pleasing *in the Lord*" (3:20). Slaves are called to obey their masters "in sincerity of heart, *fearing the Lord*" (3:22). They are admonished to do their work "wholeheartedly, *as for the Lord*" (3:23). They are reminded that in doing so, they will receive an inheritance "*from the Lord*" (3:24). And finally, masters are summoned to impart justice and equality to their slaves, because they have "*a Lord in heaven*" (4:1). There should be no doubt that the writer of this passage was concerned to root all of these household relationships in his understanding of what it means to live under the lordship of Jesus Christ. This is a further expression of what it means that Jesus is "head of the body, the church" (1:18).

As to the purpose of these discussions in the literature, there was a significant difference between the Stoic tradition that focused on personal and individual responsibility and the Aristotelian philosophical tradition that emphasized the role of the household (the *oikos*) in relation to the state. As we turn to Jewish texts, the focus shifts again to how members of a household can live faithfully in obedience to the Torah, such as the commandment to honor one's parents (Exod 20:12; Deut 5:16). As to the specific function of the Colossian household code, this will be discussed below (in the section on "Setting").

## *Structure*

This passage is simply structured around the direct address of six different groupings of members within the Christian household. Paul uses the vocative case to signal the beginning of his comments to each group. It is easy to imagine that when this letter was read aloud in the respective house churches, each group would have paid particular attention to what was about to be said to them. The six groups form naturally into three related pairs—wives and husbands, children and fathers, and slaves and masters. Some of these groups are overlapping, and one individual may be addressed more than once depending on their role in the household. Most notably, the head of the household would be addressed in the first instance as a husband, then as a father, and possibly then as the master of his slaves. A female slave may have been addressed both as a slave and as a wife. It is conspicuous that the first household grouping addressed is wives. In the Hellenistic texts dealing with household management, the main and often only person addressed is the *paterfamilias*, who was viewed as the one responsible for the entire household, to the extent of ensuring that all other members comply with his directives. In this passage, Paul treats each of the household members as responsible moral agents and appeals directly to them. Many interpreters have correctly observed that Paul addresses the so-called weaker members of each of the three pairs first, thus emphasizing their individual responsibility.

The lack of a conjunction (such as δέ) to mark a transition to a new topic may have functioned as the author's way of tying this section closely to 3:17 (and to the entirety of 3:1–17). As such, the respective duties of each member of the household would have been seen as some of the specific implications of how to "do everything in the name of the Lord Jesus Christ" (3:17).[34]

Most of Paul's comments to each group are rather brief, ranging from seven to sixteen words. His remarks to slaves that extend to fifty-four words are the conspicuous exception. The reason for that may stem from the situation he has just dealt with regarding the offense of Onesimus, a slave from this area, and its implications for the community (see Paul's letter to Philemon). But it may also have been prompted by his desire to remind not only slaves, but all believers at Colossae, that they too are slaves and that they are called to "serve the Lord Christ" (3:25b; see my comments on this verse).

Four of the groupings of household members (wives, children, fathers, and masters) are admonished with only one imperative. Two of these imperatives are followed by a causal or grounding clause ("because" or "for"), one is followed by a manner clause, and the other is followed by a purpose clause indicating the

34 Lincoln, "Household Code," 95, aptly comments, "There is nothing awkward about the flow of the paraenesis. . . . Indeed there are some close connections between the ideas and wording of 3.17 and what follows, with 3.17 now serving as the general heading for the specific applications of the code, as doing all in the name of the Lord Jesus is elaborated for each group within the household."

consequences of not fulfilling the injunction. The instructions to husbands are expressed with two imperatives, and the injunctions to slaves with three.

## *Setting*

The domestic structure of households in the Lycus Valley reflected the patterns found in the Roman world.[35] The head of the household was the *paterfamilias*, to whom the wife owed her obedience. Children were expected to obey both of their parents. The slaves, likewise, needed to obey their masters.

At issue in the interpretation of the Colossian household code is its purpose. Dibelius and Weidinger argued that its purpose was to ground the young Christians in the duties of everyday life.[36] This conclusion was widely accepted in German-speaking scholarship until the 1970s.[37] More recently, Balch, along with Lührmann and Thraede, have contended for an apologetic function to the household codes in the NT. In Balch's terms, the household codes represent "a Christian apology to Greco-Roman society."[38] In particular, he asserted that the codes met the need of a Christian response to outsiders who were accusing the new movement of violating the social standards of Greco-Roman society and thereby presenting a threat to the state. Aune asserts that "the household code is used as an apologetic defense in the face of potential persecution, demonstrating that Christianity is not subversive."[39] This explanation of the function of the codes has proven compelling to many interpreters.

For some of these interpreters, the codes stand in discontinuity with Paul's more egalitarian approach in the commonly accepted epistles. M. MacDonald observes that "there is no doubt that the Colossian household code functions to sustain the patriarchal order of society . . . [and] was part of a strategy for survival for Pauline Christians in a hostile environment."[40] This is often tied to an understanding of the codes, and the Colossian code in particular, as representing a post-Pauline, second-generation development designed to help the church prepare for living harmoniously in Roman society for the long term after the delay of the parousia of Christ.[41] E. Schüssler Fiorenza notes, "In taking over the Greco-Roman ethic of the patriarchal household code, Colossians not only 'spiritualizes' and moralizes the baptismal community understanding expressed in Gal 3.28 but also makes this Greco-Roman household ethic a part of 'Christian' social ethic. However, it is important to keep in mind that such a reinterpretation of the Christian baptismal vision is late—it did not happen before the last third

35 Huttner, *Early Christianity in the Lycus Valley*, 144–45.
36 Dibelius, 48.
37 Lührmann, "Neutestamentliche Haustafeln," 83–84.
38 Balch, *Let Wives Be Submissive*, 81–116, esp. 82.
39 Aune, *Literary Environment*, 196.
40 MacDonald, 166.
41 Lührmann, "Neutestamentliche Haustafeln," 91–97.

of the century."[42] She and others have assumed that accommodation to the patriarchal vision for the household, as exhibited in the household codes, was necessary for the movement to survive in Roman society.

If Colossians is authentic, however, then a different explanation is needed for the function of the codes and their relationship to Paul's earlier letters. As I have argued throughout the commentary, the eschatological hope is still present in this letter.[43] I would also insist that the content of the code is not at variance with Paul's earlier letters.

Yet even if one concludes that the letter is authentic, there is still not an adequate basis for seeing an apologetic motive behind the household code of Colossians. The text is inward focused and not outward facing. As an application of Col 3:17, the author's concern is in helping the community live under the lordship of Christ in their daily lives and household relationships. When Paul speaks of walking in wisdom toward outsiders (4:5), his emphasis is on believers taking advantage of opportunities to "declare the mystery of Christ" (4:3). This is why their speech needs to be "seasoned with salt" (4:6). It has nothing to do with structuring the community in a way that would not prove offensive to non-Christian Roman political and civic leaders. The author shows no concern to accommodate himself to this group when he includes the Christ-hymn in his letter (1:15–20) and speaks of an alternative kingdom (1:13)—a set of statements that could be seen as far more subversive and threatening to the Roman political order than the household codes.

Quite apart from conforming to prevailing Roman cultural norms, there are many elements of the content of the code that are actually countercultural and could be construed as a threat. Most notable in this regard are: (1) the repeated notion that Christ is Lord and that all members of the household should serve him first and foremost. For any of the citizenry who have taken an oath of loyalty to the emperor, this would be highly problematic; (2) the instruction to slave masters to provide their slaves with "justice and equality" (4:1) bordered on revolutionary and could be seen as potentially fomenting a severe threat to the social order. Telling the slave masters that they are actually slaves of a slave master in heaven would have been shocking; (3) informing the slaves that they can expect an inheritance runs counter to Roman tradition and law;[44] (4) addressing wives, children, and slaves directly and as responsible moral agents could be interpreted as presenting a threat to the authority of the *paterfamilias*. Furthermore, addressing each of these groups first in each of the pairings conspicuously gives a precedence to the least powerful. This also undermines the Roman social order; (5) the lack of reaffirmation of the authority of the head of the household would be seen by many as surprising, especially when seen in the context of the kinds

---

42 Schüssler Fiorenza, *In Memory of Her*, 253; also cited in MacDonald, "Household Management," 75.

43 See also Still, "Eschatology in Colossians," 125–38.

44 Standhartinger, "Household Code," 127.

of "soft" virtues that the code stresses—love, gentleness ("do not embitter" and "do not provoke"), and providing "justice and equality" for slaves; and (6) it is striking and unusual that wives are not called to "obey" (ὑπακούω) but to "order themselves" (ὑποτάσσω) under the leadership of their husbands. This, too, could be seen as upsetting the structure of the household by potentially downplaying the overall authority of the *paterfamilias*. There are too many discontinuities with typical Graeco-Roman *oikos* standards for these household instructions to have come wholesale from that tradition, and too many features that could potentially be disruptive to those cultural patterns. All of these things point to the Colossian code as being uniquely Christian and as a set of instructions that flow from Paul's understanding of "how to walk and please God" (1:10) in a Christian household.[45]

It now needs to be asked whether the Colossian household code is in any way a response to the negative impact that the opposing teaching had on the conduct of the various members of the Christian households in Colossae. Most interpreters posit no connection with "the philosophy," but some do. J. Crouch, for instance, saw the Colossian problem as part of a larger trend in early Christianity posed by enthusiastic excesses and asserted that the *Haustafel* emerged as a way of countering this threat.[46] MacDonald has argued for a more direct connection. She sees the code as "fundamental to the response to the problem of false teaching."[47] She focuses particularly on the asceticism, taboos, and ritual practices of the opposing teaching and argues that these "physical-social boundary markers of religion seem to be eliminated."[48] The household code helps believers become secretly integrated into the household quarters where they live as part of the spiritual body of Christ.

It is doubtful, however, that there is any direct connection with lifestyle concerns stemming from the oppositional teaching. There is nothing in the content of the household instructions that ties explicitly to any of the polemic that Paul levels against that group. Even ascetic behaviors would not necessarily violate any of the ethical mandates that he puts forward in this passage. If "the philosophy" consists of some form of folk belief and shamanism, there is nothing about those practices that would constitute a disruption to household structures as they are envisioned here.

What, then, is the purpose of this passage if it is neither an apologetic nor a response to the factional teaching? It is the author's vision of what it means to

45 So also Stuhlmacher, *Biblical Theology*, 479. He concludes: "one can no longer say that in forming its household code tradition early Christianity only took over the ethics of its 'environment.' Rather this tradition represents an *independent Christian formation*, which is just as indebted to the complex early Jewish interpretation of the commandment to honor one's parents and to the Christian event understood as an act of love as it is to the social reality of ancient households."

46 Crouch, *Colossian Haustafel*, 151, notes that the *Haustafel* was "created to serve emerging orthodoxy as a weapon against enthusiastic and heretical threats to the stability of both the church and the social order" (see also p. 157).

47 MacDonald, 167.

48 MacDonald, 167.

live the entirety of life "in the name of the Lord Jesus" (3:17).[49] It is a natural extension of his discussion on what it means to "put on the new self, which is being renewed in knowledge in accordance with the image of the one who created it" (3:10). He has given them specific instructions on what sinful behaviors to eradicate (3:5–9) and what virtues to cultivate (3:12–17). Now he instructs them on the implications of the gospel for their household relationships. He wants them to know what it means to live under the lordship of Christ in their existing social relationships within the household.[50] And for him, the lordship of Christ leads to some fairly radical disjunctions from traditional household relationships.[51]

## *Comment*

**18** Αἱ γυναῖκες, ὑποτάσσεσθε τοῖς ἀνδράσιν ὡς ἀνῆκεν ἐν κυρίῳ, "wives, submit yourselves to your husbands as is fitting in the Lord." Paul begins this section by commending his view of the appropriate response of wives to their husbands within a Christian marriage. The concluding clause, "as is fitting in the Lord," is crucial to interpreting the entire sentence and points to the fact that this exhortation is not simply a concession to Roman (or Jewish) patriarchal culture. Paul is establishing a new vision for family life in the new creation under Christ. There are indeed lines of continuity between his view and the Roman cultural context, but one cannot underestimate the new and, to some degree, countercultural vision for household ethics that he presents.

Rather than directing his initial remarks to the men, as one might expect in a Roman context, he begins with the women. He addresses them by using the vocative to single out the wives as the group he will address. He has only one appeal, and that is for them to submit to their husbands. By form, the verb ὑποτάσσεσθε could be understood as either passive ("be subject to . . ."; thus RSV, NRSV, NASB, NJB) or middle ("submit yourselves"; thus KJV, Geneva, NIV). In the latter case, which is the preferred interpretation, the stress would be on the wife's voluntary submission to her husband. It should be noted that Paul does not instruct husbands to force or demand their wives' submission, as might be expected in Roman culture. He simply urges the wives to align themselves with their husband's leadership.

---

49 Similarly Hering, *Haustafel*, 61–105, endeavors to show the importance of the theological motivation of the Colossian household code rooted in the central role of Christ as *kyrios* transforming the household relationships.

50 Barth and Blanke, 474, observe: "the context of the *Haustafel* in Col describes an ethic that is totally oriented toward the Messiah, and it gives expression to this through the imagery of putting on the 'new self.'"

51 Because of the transformative and countercultural impact of Paul's understanding of the implications of the lordship of Christ on family relationships, Standhartinger is inaccurate in her assessment that "this text has justified and continues to justify oppressive structures in the family" (Standhartinger, "Household Code," 117).

The verb Paul chooses is not ὑπακούω, "obey," as he uses with children and slaves, but ὑποτάσσω.[52] Obedience is what would be expected in a Roman context, as exemplified in the instructions given to a wife "to abide by, and show obedience to, her husband" in a marital contract.[53] Neither does he use terms expressing servitude or compliance with orders, as Philo commends: "wives must be in servitude [δουλεύειν] to their husbands, a servitude not imposed by violent ill-treatement but promoting obedience [εὐπείθειαν ('comply with an order'; 'ready obedience'[54]] in all things" (Philo, *Hypothetica* 7.3).

The verb ὑποτάσσεσθε is commonly translated "submit" or "be subject," but Paul may have chosen this word to emphasize an ordered relationship. Earlier in the letter, Paul spoke of the importance of maintaining "good order" (τάξις) within the Christian community (Col 2:5; see also 1 Cor 14:40).[55] That order is now extended to the husband-wife relationship. The verb, ὑπο + τάσσω, does not stray far from its etymology since it refers to respecting and supporting an order that has been established (τάσσω is the verbal form of τάξις, "order"). For Paul, it is not Roman society that establishes this order, but the Lord. This notion of an ordered relationship can be seen in the usage of ὑποτάσσω in the LXX where it was used, for instance, to express the commitment made by Israel's rulers, the mighty men, and all the sons of King David to Solomon's leadership when he assumed the throne (ὑπετάγησαν αὐτῷ, 1 Chr 29:24).[56] Paul similarly uses the verb (ὑποτασσέσθω) to describe the posture that individual Christians should take with reference to the governing authorities, especially since these authorities have been established by God (Rom 13:1).[57] In both of these instances, there is an order divinely instituted that the people of God are called on to respect. This was true of Jesus himself, as indicated in Luke's Gospel, when he willfully

52 Josephus, *Ag. Ap.* 2.201, speaks of the duty of wives to "obey" and incorrectly regards the Hebrew Scripture as teaching that wives are inferior to their husbands: "For, says the Scripture, 'A woman is inferior to her husband in all things.' Let her, therefore, be obedient [ὑπακουέτω] to him; not so that he should abuse her, but that she may acknowledge her duty to her husband; for God has given the authority [τὸ κράτος] to the husband."

53 See the discussion in Arzt-Grabner, "Everyday Life in a Roman Town," 208–9 (citing Yiftach-Firanko, *Marriage and Marital Arrangements*, 191).

54 LSJ, s.v. εὐπείθεια.

55 Goppelt, *Theology of the New Testament*, 2:168, notes, "This key word of New Testament social ethics quickly alienates readers today and appears to them as an expression of a bygone social order. . . . This reservation, however, misses the point of the statement. We hear the word automatically in terms of the prefix 'sub' (under). In the New Testament, however, the accent did not fall on the prefix but on the root *taxis* (order), or *tassesthai* (to order itself or oneself)."

56 There are some instances in the LXX of ὑποτάσσω used in a much stronger sense of subjugation, such as opposing armies or defeated peoples made subject to a victorious king (e.g., Pss 18:47 [17:48]; 47:3 [46:4]; 60:8 [59:10]; 108:9 [107:10]; 144:2 [143:2]; Wis 8:14). This usage is inappropriate for interpreting the Colossian passage since an entirely different relationship is in view.

57 See also Josephus, *Ant.* 17.314, where the Jewish people request that they might be put under the authority [ὑποτάσσεσθαι] of the Syrian (Roman) governor, which carried with it the responsibility not to be seditious and to live in an orderly manner.

submitted (ἦν ὑποτασσόμενος) to his parents' authority after the incident in Jerusalem in his adolescence when they searched frantically for him (Luke 2:51).[58]

The crucial question here is whether Paul is basing his admonition to wives principally upon the prevailing cultural norms (as reflected in Stoic and popular ethics),[59] or whether he is rooting his understanding in biblical revelation. There are good reasons for opting for the latter.[60] There is indeed a line of continuity between the husband-wife τάξις established by God in the original creation and what it should look like in the new creation.[61] As a Jewish man trained as a rabbi in Jerusalem, Paul would have thought deeply about the creation narrative and its implications for relationships within the household. He would also have been familiar with Palestinian-Jewish exegetical and wisdom traditions that reflected on this, such as the pre-Essene traditions expressed in 4QInstruction that addresses household relationships—including husbands and wives—and contains numerous allusions to Gen 1–3.[62] In this document, the order of creation and the biblical teaching of Gen 2:18 where the woman is described as the husband's helper are significant in establishing a distinction in roles where the husband has a leadership role (see 4Q416 2 iii 20–21; 4Q416 2 iv 1–13; see also Philo, *Spec. Laws* 2.224–27).[63] In Colossians, the theme of creation and new creation is prominent, with Christ presented as Lord of both. Following Paul's presentation of Christ's role in the original creation in Col 1, he then speaks of the central and active role that Christ plays in his new creation (Col 3:10–11). It is not a surprise that Paul would then reflect on Gen 1–2 in light of Christ in presenting the role of husbands and wives in this new creation. The order established by the creation account of Gen 1–3 remains important since Christ was Lord over the original creation (Col 1:15–17), but it has been redefined and enriched by Christ in his role as Lord of redemption and the nature of the new humanity he has created (3:10–11).[64] Accordingly, wives are called to give their allegiance first and foremost to the resurrected Christ, who sits at the right hand

---

58 "We should not understand that he was forced into obedience against his will, as it were. Rather, the Son of God was voluntarily submissive to his earthly parents" (M. Silva, "τάσσω," *NIDNTTE* 4:462).

59 MacDonald, 153, states, "Its use reflects common cultural values about the authority of the head of the household, the *paterfamilias*." Similarly, Lohse, 158, observes that "this directive . . . presupposes the social order of antiquity."

60 So also Beale, 315.

61 Moo, 300, comments that "the wife 'puts herself under' her husband in recognizing and living out an 'order' established by God himself within the marriage relationship (and by extension, in the family of God, the church)."

62 See the discussion in Wold, "*4QInstruction*," 286–300.

63 In contrast to Balch, *Let Wives Be Submissive*, 53–54, who concluded that Philo's specific comments on the fifth commandment of the Decalogue were made "in light of Platonic and Aristotelian political ethics," Wold, "*4QInstruction*," 286–90, esp. 290, argues convincingly that Philo's interpretation of the commandment may "reflect a Jewish interpretive tradition such as attested in *4QInstruction*."

64 Beale, 316, has similarly stressed this as a "new-creational lifestyle."

of God (2:6; 3:2), but then also to align themselves under the leadership that their husbands provide.

What Paul commends may slightly resemble the social structure of Roman society insofar as males were to assume the leadership role within a marriage. But it is the christological interpretation of Gen 1 and 2 that is decisive for interpreting Paul's instructions here. The Roman vision for the marriage relationship, understanding the role of the husband as *patria potestas*, when combined with our awareness of the actual practices of the men in this relationship, stand in stark contrast to the virtues that should characterize a Christian husband. The Christian vision that Paul advocates here is not one of male dominance.

Paul enjoins wives to submit to their husbands ὡς ἀνῆκεν ἐν κυρίῳ, "as is fitting in the Lord." The expression "as is fitting" has led some interpreters to contend that Paul is here indebted to Stoic (or Hellenistic) ethics and that the household instructions reflect a lightly Christianized version of prevailing Roman cultural practices.[65] But there are three observations that call this conclusion into question. First, this particular verb, ἀνήκω,[66] was not common in Stoicism nor was it widely used in the ethics of Hellenistic Judaism. The verb never appears, for instance, in Philo's writings. The typical term for "fitting" and "proper" in Stoicism was καθήκω (and especially the participial form, καθῆκον), and it referred to behavior that was in accord with nature.[67] The only occurrence of καθήκω in Paul's writings is in Rom 1:28, where the term is not used in its specific philosophical sense.[68] The fact that Paul chooses to use ἀνῆκεν and not καθῆκον may suggest that he does not want his remarks to be confused with pagan popular philosophy. Second, ἀνῆκεν was used in the local vernacular Koine in a general sense of appropriateness. For instance, ἀνῆκεν appears on a funerary inscription found in Smyrna to speak of the "fitting" place chosen for the burial of Gaius Julius Krito (*ISmyrna* 363.1–9, esp. line 8). And, third, "in the Lord" is more than a veneer of light Christianizing of Roman household ethics. The lordship of Jesus Christ is the primary theme of the entire letter. The phrase points to the fact that Paul is establishing the contours here of a uniquely christological perspective on what it means to live as a Christian in the household as an implication of putting on the "new self" (Col 3:11).

The comparative particle ὡς marks the manner of what is appropriate or proper in the Lord. The phrase significantly qualifies the nature of appropriate

65 Hay, 143, observes, for instance, that the phrase is "a Christian modification of the Stoic ethical idea of duty as what is 'fitting.'"

66 Although ἀνῆκεν is in the imperfect tense, it should be treated as a present in time with an imperfective aspect.

67 H. Schlier, "καθήκω (τὸ καθῆκον)," *TDNT* 3:438, remarks regarding this usage as found in the vocabulary of philosophy that "in general one may say that τὸ καθῆκον (or τὰ καθήκοντα) denotes that which is fitting or suitable for man, namely, the demands and actions which arise out of the claims of environment and which critical reason sees to be in harmony with his nature."

68 H. Schlier, "καθήκω (τὸ καθῆκον)," *TDNT* 3:439.

submission. Christ himself thereby becomes the pattern for their behavior.[69] As Christ models an ordered relationship to the Father who is "the head of Christ" (1 Cor 11:3), so wives are called to respect the leadership of their husbands.

The ὡς clause likely also marks out a limitation on the scope of the submission.[70] Because Christian wives belong first and foremost to the Lord, they cannot align themselves with or condone practices that are disobedient to the Lord or dishonoring to him. This would certainly include resisting involvement in any form of worship and devotion to other gods but should extend to participating in the practice of any of the vices that Paul has insisted that all believers should "kill" and "take off" (Col 3:5–11). This would, of course, lead to complexity for women to know how to respond in situations where there is a mixed marriage, and the wife is married to an unbelieving husband. But such a situation is not qualitatively different than what Christians face, in general, in their obligation to respect the governing authorities (Rom 13:1, 5), yet knowing there may be a time to refuse compliance (Acts 5:29).

In the parallel passage of Eph 5:21–22, Paul calls all believers to an attitude of submission ("submit to one another in the fear of Christ") before he enjoins the wives to submit to their husbands. Although some interpreters have seen this as simply a heading for the next section of the letter,[71] it is best to understand Paul as advocating a principle of mutual submission.[72] This tempers one's understanding of submission in a way that distances it from the Roman ideal of male heavy-handed dominance and forces us to look more deeply at the meaning of submission through a christologically centered and defined approach.[73] In the Ephesian passage, the motivation for mutual submission is "the fear of Christ"—most likely referring to a deep respect for his example of sacrificial love, self-abasement, and service to others (see esp. Eph 5:1–2).

The nature of the submission of wives to husbands in our text is qualified by the larger context of what it means to be "in the Lord" and the defining characteristics of this new-creation community that he has set forth in Col 3:1–17. As in Ephesians, self-denying love is paramount for all believers (Col 3:14; see Eph 5:1–2). In addition to this, the virtues of humility, gentleness, and patience are set forth (Col 3:12–13; see Eph 4:2–3). Living in the sphere of the Lord entails appropriating all of these virtues as part of what it means to submit, yet all of these virtues are what Paul commends to all believers (including husbands) when he speaks of mutual submission in Eph 5:21. What this means is that

69 So also Pao, 267, who notes that "this clause points to Christ as the pattern of humility and submission."

70 Beale, 317.

71 Clark, *Man and Woman in Christ*, 74–76, and Robinson, *Ephesians*, 123.

72 See, e.g., Arnold, *Ephesians*, 356–57; Best, *Ephesians*, 516; MacDonald, 325–26.

73 So also Lee-Barnewall, "Turning Κεφαλή on Its Head," 599–614. She concludes that although "κεφαλή functions as a metaphor connoting authority and leadership as understood in the ancient Mediterranean culture . . . Paul radically reorients it through his application of Christian values."

Christ should make a qualitative difference in the marriage relationship when compared to the Roman practice and ideal.

Nevertheless, Paul maintains a role differentiation between husbands and wives that assumes a distinctively Christian form of male leadership and a response from the wife that he terms submission. Because he stops short of using the term "obey," he envisions something different than what is typical in Roman households and in some traditional Jewish households (as reflected, for instance, by Josephus who uses the term "obey"). Paul's vision is deeply informed by the creation account, the servant-leadership example of Jesus himself, and the virtues of the new life in Christ. Paul's appeal to the wives in this Christian community could be summed up as "*respect the leadership of your husband*." His concern would be that the wives do not attempt to usurp the husband's leadership or chafe against it.

What Paul does not imply in this appeal is that a wife should give blind obedience to her husband; that she should surrender herself to him; that she loses her unique identity as an individual member of the body of Christ; that she should subject herself to physical or emotional abuse; that she should permit her husband to control her; or, that she no longer has a voice. Although these conditions could take place in a Roman household, they should not be part of the Christian household.

This verse should not be seen as in tension with Gal 3:28 and Paul's declaration that "there is no male and female, for you are all one in Christ Jesus." Col 3:11 says something similar with respect to the gentile-and-Jew as well as the slave-and-free pairings. Christ has relativized these various markers of identity and belonging—including male and female. What matters first and foremost is that they now belong to Christ and gain their value and identity in relation to him. Nevertheless, Christ has not obliterated these categories; they persist and remain in the present age. Sexual identity, ethnic identity, and cultural identity continue to be affirmed and celebrated, along with all of their differences. Men and women continue to have different functions in the home.

**19** οἱ ἄνδρες, ἀγαπᾶτε τὰς γυναῖκας, "husbands, love your wives." The cardinal virtue and center of Paul's ethics is love, and he here urges husbands to love their wives. Of course, this virtue is applicable to every member of the Christian household, including wives, but Paul singles out the husbands, in particular, to concentrate on cultivating and practicing this virtue toward their wives.

The vocative expression, οἱ ἄνδρες, without an attached conjunction, quickly changes the focus from the wives to the husbands. Leading into this passage, Paul has just described love as the first and foremost of all the virtues that functions like a bond that holds all of them together (3:14). This new-creation community has been chosen by God and deeply loved by him (3:2), which motivates and models how believers should love one another. Paul elaborates on this in addressing the husbands in Ephesians where he explicitly says that they should love their wives as Christ has loved the church and has given himself for her (Eph 5:25).

Why were the men singled out in these household instructions for a very strong nudge to love their wives? There are at least three reasons. First, in the Roman context, the male head of the home was regarded as wielding the *patria potestas*—that is, the power of the male head of the household.[74] In Roman marriage, the focus was put upon the wife coming under her husband's *manus*, his hand of authority over his wife.[75] According to some Roman historians, "the powers contained in the *patria potestas* were those of an autocratic ruler."[76] This is well-illustrated in a comment made by Dionysius of Halicarnassus that Roman law (from the time of Romulus) obliged wives "to conform themselves entirely to the temper of their husbands, and the husbands to rule their wives as necessary and inseparable possessions" and to be "obedient [πειθομένη] to her husband" (*Ant. rom.* 2.25.4–5). This kind of authority could incline the husband to harsh expectations, heavy-handedness, and self-interest. Second, none of the Hellenistic and Roman household codes mentioned a responsibility for the husband to love his wife. The focus was more on the rights of the male head of the household. And third, traditional status conventions in Roman society would have led the husbands to regard themselves as the objects of love from their wives.[77]

Counter to this influential and strong Roman tradition, Paul stresses the husband's responsibility, especially to love his wife. In the larger stream of Paul's thought—and indeed in the early Christian tradition as a whole—the primary exemplar of that love is Christ himself, who sacrificed himself for the well-being of others (see Eph 5:1–2). One of the ways that this love shows itself is by doing "nothing from selfish ambition" but considering one's wife as more significant than oneself (Phil 2:3). It involves a regular pattern of denying oneself to attend to the needs of the other (Matt 16:24; Mark 8:34; Luke 9:23). And it involves a form of leadership that does not "lord it over" (κατακυριεύω) or that "asserts authority over" (κατεξουσιάζω) one's wife, but takes the posture of a servant (Matt 20:25; Mark 10:42). This kind of love of a husband for his wife is overwhelmingly countercultural. It demolishes Roman patriarchy and establishes a new form of household leadership.

καὶ μὴ πικραίνεσθε πρὸς αὐτάς, "and do not be embittered toward them." Paul warns husbands about developing an attitude of bitterness toward their wives that could lead toward a harshness in the way they treat them. Bitterness

---

74 See B. Nicholas and S. M. Treggiari, "Patria Potestas," *OCD*[3] 1122–23.

75 B. Nicholas and S. M. Treggiari, "Manus," *OCD*[3] 920. Formally, the *manus* of the husband was reduced by the first century AD, especially with respect to property rights and the wife's right to initiate a divorce. Nevertheless, extensive authority of the husband over his wife persisted. Yet see also D. Medicus, "Manus," *Kleine-Pauly: Lexikon der Antike in fünf Bänden* (München: Deutschen Taschenbuch, 1979), 3:983–84, who contends that the *manus*-marriage was still frequent at the beginning of the principate.

76 H. Volkmann, "Patria Potestas," *Kleine-Pauly: Lexikon der Antike in fünf Bänden* (München: Deutschen Taschenbuch, 1979), 4:552.

77 Lee-Barnewall, "Turning Κεφαλή on Its Head," 610.

is an unresolved anger toward someone that has been allowed to fester and grow. In Ephesians, Paul cautions all believers to "get rid of all bitterness [πικρία], rage and anger" (Eph 4:31 NIV). The author of Hebrews likewise counsels, "See to it . . . that no 'root of bitterness [πικρίας]' springs up and causes trouble" (Heb 12:15 ESV). This kind of "root" may be symptomatic of a heart that is turning away from God (Deut 29:18).

This is the only time that Paul uses the verb πικραίνω. The term appears three times elsewhere in the NT, all in Revelation, to refer to a literal bitterness of taste (Rev 8:11; 10:9–10). It appears multiple times in the LXX in the passive voice with the same metaphorical sense that it has here, "to be embittered" (see Exod 16:20; Ruth 1:20; 1 Esd 4:31; etc.).[78] The Shepherd of Hermas also uses the passive voice in the same way: "when an angry temper holds fast to a man over some matter and he becomes very embittered [πικρανθῇ], again grief enters the heart of the angry-tempered man, and he is grieved by what he has done, and he repents because he has done evil" (Herm. Mand. 10.2.3). Plutarch criticized men who "rage bitterly [διαπικραίνονται] against women," which to him reflected a demeanor of anger and a character that is little and weak (Plutarch, *On the Control of Anger* 457A).

Many English versions translate πικραίνεσθε here with "be harsh" (e.g., RSV; ESV; NIV; CEB) or "treat them harshly" (NRSV; NLT). But this translation fails to capture the attitudinal problem that could potentially drive the destructive behavior. Because of this, it is better to translate it with "do not be embittered," but to understand that this could lead to expressions of unkindness, insensitivity, anger, harshness, severity, or provocation.

It is difficult to discern why Paul would have chosen to address the possibility of bitterness as one of the two things about which he would admonish husbands. It is unlikely that Paul's soft-pedaling of the husband's authority is the source of the problem, as one interpreter has asserted: "the husband's surrender of authority inherent in this new way of life could easily engender bitterness on his part since he was accustomed to a relationship that gave him superiority."[79] Paul's vision for marriage does not involve a complete surrender of the husband's leadership, but it is a redefined form of leadership qualified by love and the example of Christ. As Moo notes, "The leadership that husbands rightly exhibit in marriage is not to be carried out harshly or selfishly, but lovingly."[80] It also assumes that the husband is not unaffected by all that is entailed in Paul's teaching about love and the virtues he commends in Col 3:1–17 based on union with Christ and the transformation of the self. One can only speculate as to why Paul mentions becoming bitter or resentful out of the full range of things he could have said. It is possible that resentment may occur for a variety of mundane

78 See LEH, s.v. πικραίνω.
79 So Sumney, 244.
80 Moo, 304.

reasons, such as the nature and intensity of verbal arguments, feeling that he is not respected, withholding sex, and more. Whatever the reason, bitterness is an ulcer that is corrosive to a marriage.

In conclusion, it is important to note what Paul does not say. He does not admonish the husbands to assert their authority in the marriage or to maintain "an upper hand." Paul's concern is that the marriage would be best served by the husband exhibiting a pattern of selfless love to his wife and not allowing mundane irritations to create bitterness and resentment.

**20** τὰ τέκνα, ὑπακούετε τοῖς γονεῦσιν κατὰ πάντα, "children, obey your parents in everything." The third group that Paul addresses are children in the household. It is significant that he addresses them directly as independent agents and does not address them indirectly through the parents. This not only suggests that they were present in the assembly when the letter was read, but that they are respected as individuals who are capable of making moral decisions. He uses the term τέκνα instead of παιδία since the latter would refer to very young children.[81] Although some have suggested that the reference here includes adult children,[82] this is doubtful. While it is true that the Roman law of *patria potestas* "made adult children liable to the authority and financial control of their father as long as he was alive,"[83] obedience "in everything" would likely only pertain to younger, unmarried children who were still part of the household. The parallel passage in Ephesians (6:4) would also suggest this since the children are still receiving instruction and admonition (παιδεία καὶ νουθεσία) from their fathers.

Rather than using the term "submit" (ὑποτάσσω), Paul uses the much stronger term "obey" (ὑπακούω), which carries with it the expectation of unquestioned compliance with any orders or instructions the parents give. For children, obedience is the expected expression of honoring their parents as given in the fifth commandment (Exod 20:12; Deut 5:16). Philo provides an extensive exposition of this commandment and concludes that children "should obey [ὑπακούειν] the injunctions which are laid upon them, and that they should be obedient to all just and beneficial commands" (Philo, *Spec. Laws* 2.225–36, esp. 236). In Greco-Roman society, the obedience of children was universally expected. The Torah warns parents about "a stubborn and rebellious son who will not obey [ὑπακούων] the voice of his father or the voice of his mother" despite their discipline (Deut 21:18 ESV). In such a case, the child shall be brought out to the elders of the city (Deut 21:19–21; see also 4Q524 [4QTemple Scroll] 14, 5). God holds parents responsible for teaching their children, setting the appropriate boundaries, and holding them accountable to obey. The parents who do not take their duty seriously may find themselves with children who rebel against them

81 BDAG, s.v. παιδίον notes that the word refers to a child that is "normally below the age of puberty."

82 E.g., Barth and Blanke, 439; Sumney, 244, who notes that "children were expected to remain obedient to parents throughout their lifetime."

83 Osiek and Balch, *Families*, 165.

and against the Lord, as the priest Eli discovered. The prophet Samuel revealed that God would judge Eli's family because "his sons blasphemed God, and he failed to restrain them" (1 Sam 3:13 NIV).

Obedience "in everything" (κατὰ πάντα) assumes, as Philo noted (see above), that all of the commands from the parents are just and beneficial. In the rare situations of abuse, the child would presumably have recourse to the leadership of the Christian community.

**τοῦτο γὰρ εὐάρεστόν ἐστιν ἐν κυρίῳ**, "for this is pleasing in the Lord." Earlier in the letter, Paul said that one of the primary goals of the Christian life is that "you walk worthily of the Lord, pleasing [ἀρέσκειαν] him in every way" (1:10). The children in the Colossian community are here told that the foremost way that they can please God is by obeying their parents in every respect. Philo spoke of honoring one's parents as pleasing to the Lord: "if you honor your parents . . . you most certainly are pleasing to those with whom you associate, and you are also acceptable in the sight of God [θεοῦ δ' ἐνώπιον εὐαρεστήσεις]" (Philo, *Names* 40).

Paul used the adjective εὐάρεστος a number of times to describe actions that were "pleasing" or "acceptable" to the Lord. He told the Corinthians that "we make it our goal to please [εὐάρεστοι] him, whether we are at home in the body or away from it" (2 Cor 5:9 NIV). Above all, offering one's life as a living sacrifice of service to the Lord is the kind of sacrifice that is pleasing (εὐάρεστον) to God (Rom 12:1). He urges the Ephesians to discern how to live in a way that is "pleasing" (εὐάρεστον) to the Lord (Eph 5:10).

Some of the versions take the final phrase ἐν κυρίῳ as if it were a dative and translate it "to the Lord" (NKJV; NASB; NAB) or "unto the Lord" (Geneva; KJV). Others reword the final clause to give the simple rendering, "this pleases the Lord" (NIV; ESV; RSV; CSB; CEB; NLT). All of these translations miss the nuances of meaning expressed in this final clause. Wilson and Dunn have rightly suggested that the overall idea is "pleasing (to God) in the Lord (Jesus Christ)."[84] This fits with the notion that God is often the expressed object, the one who is pleased (e.g., Rom 12:1; 14:18; Heb 13:21; cf. Wis 4:10). This leaves open the possibilty that Paul has assumed that God is the implied object, and ἐν κυρίῳ can then be understood as "in the Lord" (and not in the unlikely sense as a dative). It is not necessary, however, to see εὐάρεστος as a Christianizing of a traditional Greco-Roman value, given the writer's indebtedness to the OT here.[85] "The Lord" here and throughout the household instructions is the Lord Jesus Christ (see Col 2:6–7).

The parallel passage in Ephesians bases the motivation for obedience on what is "right" (δίκαιος) and on the twofold promise associated with the fifth

84 Wilson, 280; Dunn, 251.

85 Contra Dunn, 250–51, and Gnilka, 219–20.

commandment of prosperity and a long life (Eph 6:1–3; see Exod 20:12). Obedience is right because it is what the Lord expects and is therefore pleasing to him.

**21** οἱ πατέρες, μὴ ἐρεθίζετε τὰ τέκνα ὑμῶν, ἵνα μὴ ἀθυμῶσιν, "fathers, do not provoke your children, so they do not become discouraged." Although CEV and NJB translate πατέρες as "parents" (see Heb 11:23 for an example of this usage), it is best to understand it here as referring to the fathers, the male heads of the households. This is consistent with his address of the *paterfamilias* in his threefold role as husband, father, and master. Paul has only one thing to say, and that is a warning to the fathers about aggravating their children, because such behavior will prove counterproductive and discourage them.

In this context, the verb ἐρεθίζω means "to make resentful" or "to make someone bitter."[86] This is the only time that Paul uses it in this negative sense. The one other time he uses it is in the positive sense of provoking the Corinthian community to contribute to the collection he is gathering (2 Cor 9:2). It appears a handful of times in the LXX in the same sense as here. Proverbs 19:7 cautions that "he who uses provoking words [ἐρεθίζει λόγους] will not be saved" (NETS). And Deut 21:20 reveals that it is not just fathers that can provoke, but a disobedient son provokes (ἐρεθίζει) his parents.

The outcome that Paul wants fathers to avoid is for the children to become discouraged and to lose heart. A hapax legomenon in the NT, ἀθυμέω means "to become disheartened to the extent of losing motivation."[87] The noun ἀθυμία is never used in the NT. A cluster of occurrences of ἀθυμέω/ἀθυμία appear in the LXX of 1 Samuel to describe Hannah's discouragement about not having a child: "Since the Lord did not give her a child according to her affliction and according to the despondency [ἀθυμίαν] of her affliction, she was also becoming despondent [ἠθύμει] because of this, that the Lord had closed the area of her womb so as not to give her a child. Thus she used to do year by year, when she would go up to the house of the Lord, and she would be despondent [ἠθύμει] and would weep and not eat" (1 Sam 1:6–7 NETS). Paul wants fathers to avoid creating despondency in their children.

This warning to fathers, along with the previous warning to husbands about embittering their wives, presupposes the authority that they exercise in the household. These two warnings also show the very real and ever-present possibility of that authority being misapplied and having it result in negative consequences to members of the household. The fact that Paul twice warns about creating resentment may suggest that this was a problem in many households. A heavy-handed application of authority is not only counter to Paul's ethic of love motivated by and inspired by Christ, but it ignores the virtues of the new self that he has commended to them—especially the virtues of compassion, kindness, humility, and patience (Col 3:12–14).

86 Louw-Nida, §88.168.

87 BDAG, s.v. ἀθυμέω.

It is somewhat surprising that this is the only instruction that Paul gives to the fathers. No doubt it underlies its importance and may point to Paul's concern about the prevailing Roman cultural context of the *paterfamilias* and the damaging repercussions of the heavy hand of authority (his *manus*) accorded to him. While Paul does not here dispute the authority of the father over his children, he "sets the bounds for its use."[88] Dionysius of Halicarnassus describes the nature of authority that Romulus, the legendary founder and lawgiver of Rome, extended to fathers over their children: "the lawgiver of the Romans gave virtually full power to the father over his son, even during his whole life, whether he thought proper to imprison him, to scourge him, to put him in chains and keep him at work in the fields, or to put him to death" (*Ant. rom.* 2.26.4).[89] Even if this were exaggerated or tempered by the time we reach the principate, there was a long tradition in Roman society of the severe treatment of children by their fathers. Paul's vision for the Christian household is different than how fathers had been socialized in Roman society.[90]

The parallel passage in Ephesians adds the positive command to "bring them up in the discipline and instruction of the Lord" (Eph 6:4 NRSV). Fathers are thus given the ultimate responsibilty for training their children in the essentials of the Christian faith as well as instructing and admonishing them on how to live this out in the challenges of daily life.

**22** οἱ δοῦλοι, ὑπακούετε κατὰ πάντα τοῖς κατὰ σάρκα κυρίοις, "slaves, obey your earthly masters in every respect." Paul's address to the slaves is substantially longer than his remarks to any of the other five groups. In fact, it is longer than all of the rest combined (54 words to 51). Interpreters have offered a variety of reasons to account for the disproportionate length. Some have suggested that it is because there were so many slaves in the church.[91] Indeed, there would have been numerous slaves in the Christian community, but their numbers were likely no greater than the number of women or children. Barth and Blanke argue that the length of the comments is due to the fact that "Paul wanted to emphasize that he viewed the state of slavery precisely as not reconcilable with the servitude of a Christian."[92] Yet much of the content of Paul's remarks is aimed at how to live *within* this socioeconomic structure. The traditional explanation is still, perhaps, the best explanation—that is, Paul is handling the situation with Onesimus at the same time that he is writing to the Colossians, and this

---

88 Lincoln, 656.

89 Also cited in MacDonald, 155; Lincoln, *Ephesians*, 400.

90 Dunn, 252, argues for a situation behind this passage in which a too-strong fatherly reaction to the (older) children could have driven them back to the synagogue or, as gentiles, they may have been embarassed at "belonging to such an ethnic sect as Christian Judaism." His view is highly speculative and depends on his overall reconstruction of the situation at Colossae, which I find doubtful. It is better here to see Paul's comments as positively reflecting his view of the Christian household against the backdrop of Roman household practices that he finds objectionable.

91 Dunn, 253; Sumney, 246.

92 Barth and Blanke, 445.

may explain the reason for his more extensive comments on this topic.[93] This explanation, of course, hinges on the question of the authenticity of Colossians. Wilson notes, "On the traditional view, with both Col. and Philem. written about the same time from Rome, and to the same destination, it was very natural to think that Paul here had the case of Onesimus in mind when he wrote."[94] If the letter is pseudepigraphical and written a decade or two later after the death of the apostle Paul, then an array of other possibilities would necessarily pertain.

The principal definition of a slave in Greek and Roman society is one person that is owned by another and therefore their property. Aristotle sets forth "the nature of the slave and his essential quality" in his essay on *Politics*: "one who is a human being belonging by nature not to himself but to another is by nature a slave, and a person is a human being belonging to another if being a man he is an article of property, and an article of property is an instrument for action separable from its owner" (Aristotle, *Pol.* 1.1254a.15–18). Slavery was not only practiced throughout the Roman empire but was accepted even within Judaism.[95]

The reference to "slaves" should not be limited to domestic or household slaves.[96] There is nothing in the content of 3:22–4:1 that applies only to domestic slaves, and Paul could have specified a domestic servant with the word οἰκέτης, a term that he uses elsewhere (Rom 14:4). The Colossian slaves who served in the nearby mines, worked in agriculture, or tended sheep would still have been part of households. We have no way of knowing the precise number of slaves in the Lycus Valley, but we can assume that the number would have been sizeable and may have approached as much as one-third of the population or even more.[97]

Unquestioned obedience was expected of slaves in the socioeconomic structure of Roman-era slavery.[98] This is because they were the property of the slave owner. They had been purchased to work and to perform their assigned duties and were not afforded the freedom to decline the demands of their masters. Bradley writes that "the slave was at the complete and permanent disposal of the master and except by an act of resistance could never find relief from the necessity of obeying because there were no countervailing rights or powers in the condition of slavery itself to which the slave had recourse."[99] Paul therefore

---

93 Moo, 298, 309, 314–15; Lightfoot, 228.

94 Wilson, 283.

95 See the more extended discussion on the characteristics of slavery in the Roman empire in the upcoming WBC volume on *Philemon*.

96 Barth and Blanke, 445, contend that "the house slaves are the ones addressed here, not the slaves on large estates, in mines, or on galleys."

97 Bradley, *Slavery and Society*, 12, notes that "the servile proportion of the population of Italy in the time of Augustus can fairly be estimated at 35 per cent." The need for labor in the mines, the fields, and tending flocks in the Lycus Valley could have driven this percentage even higher. Huttner, *Early Christianity in the Lycus Valley*, 145, writes that "the fact that slaves are addressed separately may suggest that they constituted a relatively large percentage of the Colossian community."

98 Huttner, *Early Christianity in the Lycus Valley*, 145, states, "In the ancient world, subordination of slaves to their masters was taken for granted."

99 Bradley, *Slavery and Society*, 5.

instructs Christian slaves to "obey" (ὑπακούετε) their masters in every respect. The challenge for Christian slaves would come when their owners would command them to do things that would be in conflict with their newfound Christian convictions and ethics, such as any activities related to the master's pagan idolatry[100] or any form of sexual demand that would violate the commands that Paul has given regarding *porneia* (Col 3:5–7).[101] Obeying their masters "in every respect" (κατὰ πάντα) could at times have led to disobedience to the Lord. There would have undoubtedly been occasions when they were faced with the question of whether they obey their non-Christian masters or, out of obedience to the ethical commands of the Lord, disobey their masters and suffer the consequences. Paul does not address this difficult question in the passage, but surely this would have been a topic of discussion when they gathered in their respective house churches in Colossae. How could they apply this teaching and remain faithful to the Lord? In issuing this command, Paul is primarily concerned about admonishing Christian slaves who were intentionally not working conscientiously but were instead deceitfully giving the appearance of working hard in their mundane duties where there was no moral conflict.

The context makes it rather obvious that Paul is instructing the slaves to obey their *earthly* masters, which renders the addition of κατὰ σάρκα κυρίοις superfluous. The likely reason for the inclusion of this phrase is to set up the intentional contrast with "your Lord/master in heaven" (κύριον ἐν οὐρανῷ, 4:1).

μὴ ἐν ὀφθαλμοδουλίᾳ ὡς ἀνθρωπάρεσκοι, "not serving to be seen as people pleasers." Paul addresses the motives and attitudes of slaves as they serve their human masters. He wants them to discharge their duties with the purest of motives. The noun ὀφθαλμοδουλία represents a combination of "eye" (ὀφθαλμός) and "service" (δουλία) and refers to "service that is performed only to make an impression in the owner's presence."[102] This is the first time that this term appears in Greek literature and likely reflects the apostle Paul's penchant for creating compound words (such as ἀποκαταλλάσσω, ἐθελοθρησκία—a fingerprint of his style). He thus warns slaves against the deceit of appearing to work when they actually are not, or ceasing to work once the master turns his back and leaves. This is simply "eye service" and not true work.

When slaves approach their assigned responsibilities in this way, they are simply acting as "people pleasers" (ἀνθρωπάρεσκοι) and are falling short of pleasing the Lord, whom they ultimately serve. The use of the term here and in

---

100 Some slaves, for instance, were assigned to the temple service of a pagan deity, such as Apollo Lairbenos or the mother-god, Ma. See, e.g., Huttner, *Early Christianity in the Lycus Valley*, 50–51, 105–9, although this was tantamount to their manumission.

101 See the discussion of this issue in MacDonald, "Slavery, Sexuality, and House Churches," 94–113. She observes, "Avoiding physical contact with immorality, impurity, passion and evil desire (Col 3.5), for example, would have been completely beyond the control of the slaves of non-Christian slaveholders."

102 BDAG, s.v. ὀφθαλμοδουλία.

the parallel passage in Ephesians (Eph 6:6) are the only occurences of the term in the NT. It appears only once in the LXX where it is used of those who say, "There is no God," engage in corrupt activities, and are "men pleasers" (NETS; ἀνθρωπάρεσκοι; Ps 53:5 [52:6 LXX; see vv. 1–5]). The entire chapter of Pss. Sol. 4 is an indictment of hypocritical religious leaders of Israel who are termed "men pleasers" (διαλογὴ τοῦ Σαλωμων τοῖς ἀνθρωπαρέσκοις, Pss. Sol. 4.1). They are upbraided for having hearts that are far from the Lord (4.1). They live in hypocrisy (4.6), they are deceitful (4.10–11), and they practice all kinds of evil behavior. The writer prays, "Let God reveal the deeds of the "men-pleasers" (ἀνθρωπαρέσκων, 4.7) and "let the flesh of the men-pleasers [ἀνθρωπαρέσκων] be rent by wild animals" (4.19).

Slaves faced an ongoing temptation to project their compliance and give the impression of working hard because they feared reprisal and punishment from their masters. Joshel notes, "Not only were slaves viewed as liars: their condition of enslavement made any and all servile words suspect to their owners. In their view, the slave, motivated by fear of the slave owner's power to punish, tried to please by word and deed because he or she had to, and every enslaved response smacked of duplicity and was suspected by the slaveholder."[103] Christian slaves have a much higher calling that affects their motivation. They have a new identity established by their union with a new master.

ἀλλ' ἐν ἁπλότητι καρδίας φοβούμενοι τὸν κύριον, "but in sincerity of heart, fearing the Lord." Paul calls on slaves to live their daily lives without hypocrisy and with the utmost of integrity (see also Eph 6:5). The term ἁπλότης is used of "personal integrity expressed in word or action."[104] It is often translated as "sincerity," "simplicity" (in the sense of unmixed motives), or "uprightness." The full expression, ἐν ἁπλότητι καρδίας, appears twice in the LXX. It occurs as part of David's prayer to God where he exclaims, "I knew, Lord, that you are the one who tests hearts, and you love righteousness. In simplicity of heart [ἐν ἁπλότητι καρδίας] I have shown zeal for all these things" (1 Chr 29:17 NETS). It also appears at the outset of the book of Wisdom where it is commended to all the people of God: "love righteousness, you rulers of the earth, think of the Lord in goodness and seek him with sincerity of heart [ἐν ἁπλότητι καρδίας]" (Wis 1:1 NRSV). One strand of Jewish wisdom tradition similarly extols the importance of this attitude: "now, listen to me, children, and live in integrity of heart [ἐν ἁπλότητι καρδίας], for in it I have observed everything that is well-pleasing to the Lord" (T. Iss. 4.1; see also T. Iss. 3.8; 7.7). The same Jewish literature also associates it with the fear of the Lord: "live in integrity of heart in the fear of the Lord [ἐν ἁπλότητι καρδίας, ἐν φόβῳ κυρίου], and weary yourself in good deeds" (T. Reu. 4.1). In contrast to hypocritical "eye service" and "people pleasing,"

103 Joshel, *Slavery in the Roman World*, 122.

104 BDAG, s.v. ἁπλότης.

Paul wants slaves to do their work, conduct themselves without duplicitous motives, and walk with integrity.

He wants them to live in a conscious awareness of God's presence and a profound respect for the God to whom they truly belong. The participle (φοβούμενοι) most likely expresses how they can walk with integrity—that is, "by fearing the Lord."[105] Paul thus once again draws on the deep well of the Jewish wisdom tradition that so frequently urges the people of God to root their lives in the fear of the Lord (see Prov 1:7; 9:10; 10:27; 14:27; 19:23; Job 28:28; Sir 1:11, 12, 18, 27, 28; etc.). Here, as elsewhere in Colossians, the reference to κύριος is to Christ and underlines the goal of these household instructions as life lived under the lordship of Christ.[106]

**23** ὃ ἐὰν ποιῆτε, ἐκ ψυχῆς ἐργάζεσθε, "whatever you do, do your work wholeheartedly." In different words, Paul reiterates what he has said in the previous verse regarding the heart attitude of the Christian slaves. "Whatever you do" (ὃ ἐὰν ποιῆτε) also reminds the reader of 3:17 ("whatever you do in word or in work, do everything in the name of the Lord Jesus") and that these instructions are a specific application of that injunction for the day-to-day life of these members of the household.

Dunn aptly observes that "one of the chief dangers of the slave status was a lack of personal motivation, which made all work a drudgery provided grudgingly, with lack of effort and always with a view to doing as little as one could get away with."[107] Paul tells the Christian slaves that their new life in Christ should transform their motivation for service because they are ultimately serving not a human master but the Lord of the universe. He urges them to do their daily work ἐκ ψυχῆς, literally "out of their soul," which has been variously translated by the different versions as "heartily" (KJV; Geneva; ESV; RSV), "with all your heart" (NIV), "from the heart" (CEB), "enthusiastically" (CSB), and "with enthusiasm" (NET). The soul was considered "the seat and center of human life"[108] and was thus coextensive with the "heart" (καρδία) as the core of the person where motivations, affections, and decision-making occurred. The two terms sometimes occur in close conjunction (e.g., Deut 6:6; Ps 84:2 [83:3 LXX]; Acts 4:32). It is possible that Paul is here alluding to the language of the Shema: "you shall love the LORD your God with all your heart and with all your soul [ἐξ ὅλης τῆς ψυχῆς σου] and with all your might" (Deut 6:5 ESV), which Jesus reaffirms (Matt 22:37;

105 So Pao, 273, and Campbell, 64, rightly understand it as a participle of manner. It is also possible to interpret it as a causal participle, such as the NLT: "*because of* your reverent fear of the Lord" (so also the GNB). Foster, 387, and Harris, 158, affirm this understanding.

106 McKnight, 361–62, contends that κύριος here "refers to the slaves' 'masters.'" But were Paul to do so, he would have used the plural κύριοι, as in 3:22 and 4:1; note as well the plural ἀνθρώποις in 3:23. The singular κύριος refers to the Lord Christ here, as well as in the other six references in the household instructions.

107 Dunn, 255.

108 BDAG, s.v. ψυχή.

Mark 12:30; Luke 10:27). Paul wants the devotion and love that Christian slaves have for Christ to lead to transformed motivations for their regular work.

ὡς τῷ κυρίῳ καὶ οὐκ ἀνθρώποις, "as for the Lord and not for people." The comparative particle (ὡς) functions here as "a marker introducing the perspective from which a person, thing, or activity is viewed or understood as to character, function, or role."[109] Paul believes that a change in motivation regarding their work will occur as they begin to reckon that they are ultimately performing their duties "for the Lord" (τῷ κυρίῳ) and not for their human slave masters (ἀνθρώποις).[110] This perspective is rooted in the inner renewal taking place because of their relationship to the Lord. These changes in motives and behavior are part of what it means to "walk in him" (2:6).

Paul's comments about work in his instructions to the slaves are reflective of the Jewish wisdom tradition. Working hard was a deep value in Judaism. Sirach observes, "Hard work was created for everyone, and a heavy yoke is laid on the children of Adam, from the day they come forth from their mother's womb until the day they return to the mother of all the living" (Sir 40:1 NRSV). Idleness and laziness are repeatedly denounced (see, e.g., Prov 10:26; 18:9; 19:15; 21:25; Sir 22:1, 2; 33:29). Sirach also warns about giving the appearance of working hard: "do not craftily perform your task [τὸ ἔργον σου], and do not extol yourself in your time of difficulty" (Sir 10:26 NRSV). Those who work hard will be satisfied: "do your work in good time, and in his own time God will give you your reward" (Sir 51:30 NRSV).

**24** εἰδότες ὅτι ἀπὸ κυρίου λήψεσθε τὴν ἀνταπόδοσιν τῆς κληρονομίας, "since you know that you will receive your reward—your inheritance—from the Lord." In a unique and socially unexpected twist, Paul assures Christian slaves that they will receive an inheritance from the Lord. This is an unusual statement because Roman law prohibited slaves from receiving an inheritance from their masters. In fact, they themselves were regarded in Roman society like other forms of property, which means that they could be inherited upon the death of their masters.

Paul says that they already know this truth about their future inheritance. The perfect participle of οἶδα should be interpreted as causal, "because you know" (as represented by NET; NIV; NRSV). It thereby provides the basis for the admontion to work wholeheartedly for the Lord. When the readers learned about their future divine inheritance could have taken place early in the establishment of the church as Epaphras taught them (Col 1:7), or it could be a reference to what Paul has said earlier in the letter, affirming the inheritance that Christ has qualified them to receive (1:12).

The future tense of ἀπολαμβάνω needs to be taken seriously as affirming a futurist eschatology. Although there has long been a tendency in the scholarship

109 BDAG, s.v. ὡς.

110 These are datives of advantage; so also Campbell, 65, and Harris, 159.

on Colossians to see a transformation of Paul's futurist eschatology into a Hellenistically informed "above" and "below" schema, this statement does not fit the pattern. Bornkamm avers that the future eschatology is present in this verse only because it is part of a traditional paraenetic piece.[111] Yet if 3:18–4:1 represents a preexisting unit, our author has shown himself capable of significant editing, so it would come as a surprise that he did not alter this statement.

"Reward" (ἀνταπόδοσις) only appears here in the Pauline corpus, but it is frequent in the LXX, where it is often used in the sense of future "retribution" (e.g., Isa 34:8; 59:18; 61:2; 63:4; 66:6). But, as here, it is also used in the positive sense of a future "reward" (see, e.g., Ps 19:11 [18:12 LXX]: "in keeping them [God's precepts] there is great reward [ἀνταπόδοσις πολλή]" NRSV; see also 2 Sam 19:37). The more common term for "reward" in Paul's writings is μισθός (1 Cor 3:8, 14, 9:17–18), which could also be understood as "wages" (Rom 4:4). Although ἀνταπόδοσις is a hapax legomenon in Paul, he does use the verbal form (ἀνταποδίδωμι; see Rom 11:35; 12:19; 1 Thess 3:9; 2 Thess 1:6).

The genitive τῆς κληρονομίας should be understood as a genitive of apposition and thereby functions to explain what the reward is. It would evoke in the hearers of this letter a recollection of what Paul had said earlier, that the Father had "qualified you to share in the inheritance [τοῦ κλήρου] of the saints in light" (Col 1:12). The language of inheritance was appropriated from the promises made to Abraham that all who are in Christ now share in by faith (Exod 32:13; Rom 4; Gal 3–4).[112] Paul speaks repeatedly in his letters of a future period when the saints would "inherit" the kingdom (1 Cor 6:9–10; 15:50; Gal 5:21; Eph 1:14; 5:5). The emphasis in this passage is on the full realization of salvation in Christ.[113] Present participation in the resurrection of Christ through union with him (Col 2:13; 3:1) would be a partial fulfillment and foretaste of what lies ahead.

That this reward of inheritance comes ἀπὸ κυρίου points to Christ as the agent of the Father in meting out final judgment and rewards.[114] This is a natural extension of the high Christology of the letter as we have seen in the hymn (1:15–20) and elsewhere (e.g., 2:9). It is also consistent with Paul's anticipation of the judgment seat of Christ (2 Cor 5:10). This image of Christ places him in an eminently superior position to the earthly masters of the slaves.

τῷ κυρίῳ Χριστῷ δουλεύετε, "serve the Lord Christ." With this admonition, Paul encourages Christian slaves to serve their ultimate master, Christ. Most of the English versions, however, take the verb as an indicative—for example, "it is the Lord Christ you are serving" (NIV; see also ESV; NRSV; RSV; ASV; CEB; CSB; NLT; CEV; NJB; NASB; NKJV; KJV). Yet the majority of commentators

---

111 Bornkamm, "Hoffnung," 63n2.

112 See Dunn, 256–57.

113 Beale's assumption that this is a fulfillment of Israel's land promises goes beyond the evidence within Colossians and the earlier Pauline theme of inheritance; Beale, 325.

114 Gnilka, 222, notes that he is "the *Kyrios* of the eschatological judgment."

contend that it should be interpreted as an imperative, which is the best interpretation.[115] The form of the verb is not decisive, and we are thrust entirely onto the context for a decision. In favor of the imperative are two observations: (1) of the other eight second-person plural verbs in this section (3:18–4:1) that form independent clauses, all are imperatives; and (2) as with δουλεύετε, there is no conjunction attached to any of the other eight imperatives. If the poorly attested variant reading γάρ were original (see my discussion in the *Notes*), then δουλεύετε would clearly function as an indicative. With the use of the imperative, Paul wants to reaffirm to them that despite the fact that he calls them to obey their earthly masters (3:22), they should regard themselves as truly serving the Lord first and foremost. This reiterates what he said in the previous verse when he called them to work wholeheartedly, "as to the Lord and not for people" (3:23). Another way of rendering this clause would be, "serve your master, who is Christ!"

Every believer is "a slave of Christ" (1 Cor 7:22 NRSV). They once were enslaved to sin (Rom 6:6) and to other gods and demonic powers (Gal 4:8–9), but they have been bought with a price (1 Cor 6:20; 7:23) and now belong to Christ. Just as Paul himself is now a slave of Christ (Rom 1:1; Gal 1:10; Phil 1:1; see also Titus 1:1), so he urges the Christian slaves at Colossae to regard themselves as slaves to Christ, who is their true master. Their primary allegiance, service, and obedience is to Christ.

The expression "Lord Christ" (κύριος Χριστός) is probably not to be understood as a christological title here, which would be unique in Paul's writings and in the NT. Rather, Χριστός should be taken as a predicate—that is, "serve the Master, who is Christ." There is an implied contrast with 3:22:

ὑπακούετε . . . τοῖς . . . κυρίοις, "obey . . . your masters"
τῷ κυρίῳ (Χριστῷ) δουλεύετε, "serve your master (Christ)"

The verb δουλεύω should here be understood in its commonly used sense of "to be owned by another" and to "perform the duties of a slave."[116] Although what Paul has said could be seen as complicating the lives of Christian slaves by establishing conflicting loyalties, his remarks also clarify that the commands of Christ should supersede those of their earthly masters.

Moo is correct in asserting that "this command is in some ways the center of 3:18–4:1, enunciating the fundamental reality underlining the entire household code . . . tying this section firmly to the overall Christocentric message of Colossians."[117] "Serve the Lord Christ" could, in fact, be an apt way of describing the message of the entire book.

115 See, e.g., Pao, 275; Sumney, 241, 250–51; Moo, 313; Abbott, 295; Lohse, 161; Martin, 123; Schweizer, 226; Peake, 543.

116 BDAG, s.v. δουλεύω.

117 Moo, 313.

**25** ὁ γὰρ ἀδικῶν κομίσεται ὃ ἠδίκησεν, "but the one who has done wrong will be repaid for what he has done wrong." This explanatory clause delivers both a warning and an assurance to slaves in the Christian community at Colossae. There has been some dispute, however, over whether Paul is addressing the slaves,[118] the masters,[119] or both groups[120] with this remark. Paul is most likely speaking primarily to the slaves at this point, since we are still under the vocative heading οἱ δοῦλοι, and he does not transition to his comments to slave masters until 4:1 with the vocative address οἱ κύριοι. If Paul is indeed the author of this letter and has written Philemon at roughly the same time, the situation with Onesimus may have been at the forefront of his thoughts.[121] It is significant that he uses the same verb, ἀδικέω, to describe the offense of Onesimus (Phlm 18). Slaves sometimes did disobey their masters and cause them financial harm or some other injury. Paul here encourages Christian slaves to obey their masters and do their work with the utmost of integrity, causing no harm to their masters. Nevertheless, despite its primary application to slaves, this statement is worded as a maxim and would also apply to the slave masters, and indeed, to all believers.

The verb ἀδικέω, which appears twice here, can be used of acting in an unjust manner or causing damage or injury to someone.[122] Paul uses it eight other times in his letters. The psalmist declares that God is blessed because he can be counted on for "executing judgment for the wronged" (τοῖς ἀδικουμένοις; Ps 146:7 [145:7 LXX] NETS). Paul expresses the same idea of requital for wrongdoing here in our verse with the verb κομίζω. He used the verb to describe the end-time judgment of the Lord: "For we must all appear before the judgment seat of Christ, so that each one may receive what is due [κομίσηται] for what he has done in the body, whether good or evil" (2 Cor 5:10 ESV). In the household instructions to slaves in Ephesians, he uses it in the positive sense of reward: "knowing that whatever good we do, we will receive [κομίσεται] the same again from the Lord" (Eph 6:8 NRSV). The basic idea of the verb is "to bring" something, but with the middle voice it is regularly used with the sense of "recompense." The future tense of the verb, along with Paul's previous use of it in the context of the divine tribunal, suggests that the requital for disobedient slaves is before the judgment seat of Christ.

καὶ οὐκ ἔστιν προσωπολημψία, "and there is no partiality [with the Lord]." Paul assures the readers that the Lord's end-time judgment will be carried out with absolute fairness and equity because of the character or the Lord. The noun

---

118 This view is held by Beale, 327; Moo, 314; Foster, 393; Sumney, 251–52; MacDonald, 158; Hay, 146.

119 So Aquinas, 96–97; Calvin, 355; Abbott, 295; Martin, 123–24.

120 Pao, 276–77; Barth and Blanke, 449; Gnilka, 223; Schweizer, 226–27; Lightfoot, 229.

121 Lightfoot, 229, remarks that "the recent fault of Onesimus would make the Apostle doubly anxious to emphasize the duties of the slave towards the master, lest in his love for the offender he should seem to condone the offense."

122 BDAG, s.v. ἀδικέω.

προσωποληψία is the Greek translation (λαμβάνειν πρόσωπον, "to lift the face") of a Hebrew idiom (נָשָׂא פָּנִים), and it only appears four times in the NT and never in the LXX. It comes from an ancient Near East custom of respectful greeting, where a visitor would approach an important person by humbly bowing his face to the ground. If the person greeted reached his hand down and lifted his face up, this would be a sign of recognition, respect, and esteem.[123] The idiom came to be used as an expression of inappropriate esteem, or partiality. Paul viewed this as wholly outside the character of God since "God shows no partiality" (πρόσωπον θεὸς ἀνθρώπου οὐ λαμβάνει; Gal 2:6). He uses the noun form when he declared to the Roman church that "God shows no partiality [προσωποληψία]" (Rom 2:11). In the Ephesian household instructions, he warns the slave masters that "there is no partiality [προσωποληψία] with him" as part of his basis for admonishing them to quit threatening their slaves (Eph 6:9). This is consistent with the representation of God in the OT where the Torah declares, "The LORD your God is God of gods and Lord of lords, the great, the mighty, and the awesome God, who is not partial [οὐ θαυμάζει πρόσωπον] and takes no bribe" (Deut 10:17 ESV; see also 2 Chr 19:7). Although slaves were frequently the object of unjust treatment by their masters, they, in turn, could be tempted to act out in unjust and injurious ways toward their masters, perhaps in resentment or bitterness. Paul appeals to them to resist this kind of behavior because they now represent the Lord of heaven and earth, who is perfectly just and who will right all wrongs in the future. Nevertheless, because of the proverbial nature of this verse and its applicability to all Christians, MacDonald is probably correct in noting that the slaves "might well have heard a promise in this statement that the injustice of masters would be called to account on a day when there will be no distinction between masters and slaves."[124]

**4:1** οἱ κύριοι, τὸ δίκαιον καὶ τὴν ἰσότητα τοῖς δούλοις παρέχεσθε, "masters, grant to your slaves justice and equality." It is unfortunate that the verse numbering, which came centuries after Paul wrote this letter, introduces a new chapter here. The next verse would have provided a more appropriate chapter break. With the vocative address οἱ κύριοι, Paul begins his address to the sixth and final grouping of individuals—the slave owners. The economy of Colossae and this region of the Lycus Valley would have included many slave owners among those who owned estates, large herds, farmlands, mining interests, textile manufacturers, and various other business endeavors. It is difficult to know how many of these slaveholders would have become Christians through the work of people like Epaphras and, presumably, Philemon.[125]

He has only one instruction, and that is that Christian slaveholders extend

---

123 E. Lohse, "προσωποληψία, κτλ.," *TDNT* 6:799.

124 MacDonald, 159.

125 Without evidence or justification, Schweizer, 227, wrongly assumes that "there were presumably not many [slave masters] in the community at that time."

to their slaves justice and fairness. The basic idea of παρέχω is to "furnish" or "supply,"[126] while the middle voice, as here, was used in the sense of "to grant something to someone."[127] It is ironic and unexpected, in a Roman context, for Paul not to begin with an assertion of the rights and power of the slaveholder but with the rights of the slaves.

The neuter noun δίκαιον refers to what is regarded as obligatory to slave owners in terms of the Roman legal and social standards of justice with respect to slaves. This would entail not abusing or taking advantage of slaves in any way that would be an affront to societal norms. Yet for the Christian slave owner, there is a new standard of δίκαιος defined by God himself. The Torah states that all God's "works are genuine, and all his ways are justice. A faithful god, and there is no injustice [ἀδικία], a righteous (δίκαιος) and holy Lord" (Deut 32:4 NETS; see also 1 Sam 2:2; Ezra 9:15; Pss 7:11; 116:5). Because of who he is, God demands justice from all his people: "justice, and only justice, you shall follow [δικαίως τὸ δίκαιον διώξῃ]" (Deut 16:20 ESV). In the Greek mind, however, "justice" (δίκαιον) is not possible for a slave in relationship to his master precisely because "the slave is a chattel of his lord" (Aristotle, *Mag. mor.* 1.1194b.18–19). Aristotle even says that this kind of justice "appears to consist in equality [ἰσότητι] and parity [ὁμοιότητι]" (Aristotle, *Mag. mor.* 1.1194b.23–24).

In addition to justice, Paul adds the requirement that masters should treat their slaves with ἰσότης. The common usage and understanding of this term is "equality." Stählin summarizes Aristotle as teaching that "in the Greek states equality is a basic principle of democracy along with freedom."[128] Citizens possess the same rights and thus are "equal" (ἴσος) and "alike" (ὅμοιος) (Xenophon, *Hist. graec.* 7.1.1). Arzt-Grabner observes that "a master might have treated his slaves in a just way, but not all of them equally."[129] He observes that there were great differences among the opportunities afforded slaves, with some working in the most menial and strenuous of tasks and others serving as physicians and stewards. This led to significant variation in the amount of money a slave could earn and save in his or her *peculium* (a fund or property used and managed by a slave).

Treating slaves with equality would have been completely unheard of in the moral exhortation or actual practice of this era. Paul's command here is thus without precedent in ancient literature regarding slaves and accordingly raises many questions about what he intended to communicate with the use of this word. Is there any possibility that he was here contending for the full equality of slaves with their masters and other free individuals? And is he planting the seeds for the elimination of slavery within the Christian communities? In this

126 LSJ, s.v. παρέχω.

127 BDAG, s.v. παρέχω.

128 G. Stählin, "ἴσος, ἰσότης, ἰσότιμος," *TDNT* 3:346.

129 Arzt-Grabner, "Everyday Life in a Roman Town," 224.

regard, it is particularly noteworthy that two first-century Jewish groups argued strenuously against the keeping of slaves precisely because it was opposed to "justice" and "equality." The Therapeutae did not use slaves because they believed that all people were created free (ἐλευθέροι) and regarded slavery as an injustice (ἀδικία) and an inequality (ἀνισότης) that invests the stronger with power over the weaker (Philo, *Contempl. Life* 70). Similarly, the Essenes did not keep slaves and denounced the owners of slaves "for their injustice [ἀδίκων] in outraging the law of equality [ἰσότητα]" (Philo, *Good Person* 79).[130] By using the terms "justice" and "equality" with respect to how slaves should be treated, Paul is coming exceedingly close to the position of the Therapeutae and the Essenes.

Most English translations resist using the translation "equality" for ἰσότης and opt for the less extreme rendering "fairness" (e.g., "fairness": NET; NASB; "fairly": ESV; NRSV; RSV; NAB; "fair": CEB; NLT; NIV; CSB; REB; NKJV; NJB). Many of the older versions, however, did use the translation "equal" (e.g., ASV; Tyndale; Geneva; KJV; Douay-Rheims). "Fairness" and "equality" overlap significantly in meaning. The virtues exhibited in "fairness," such as "honesty, impartiality, equitableness, justness, and fair dealing,"[131] would also be entailed in treating someone with equality. But the term "equality" goes beyond this to denote "the condition of having equal dignity, rank, or privileges with others; the fact of being on an equal footing."[132] Is it possible that Paul is going this far in his admonitions to the slave owners in the Christian community of Colossae?

The vast majority of commentators have said no to this and contend that Paul means something more akin to "fairness" in his use of ἰσότης here.[133] In an important article on this topic, Vasser has contended that the ancient texts normally marshaled in support of the meaning "fairness" are actually better translated as "equality."[134] In other words, the contexts of all these passages suggest that ἰσότης means nothing less than "equality," even when "fairness" is an entailment of the equalty. Paul himself uses this noun in only one other place, where it is best understood as "equality." In making his argument to the Corinthians about setting money aside for his collection for the impoverished believers in Judea, Paul says, "Our desire is not that others might be relieved while you are hard pressed, but that there might be equality [ἰσότης]. At the present time your plenty will supply what they need, so that in turn their plenty will supply what you need. The goal is equality [ἰσότης]" (2 Cor 8:13–14 NIV; the NRSV translates both occurrences as "fair balance"). This does not precisely parallel our text in that it does not address social relationships as much as

130 Standhartinger, "Household Code," 128, notes, "Philo's portrait of the Essenes indicates clearly that the catchword ἰσότης (equality) resonates primarily as a political programme against slavery."

131 See *OED*, s.v. "fairness."

132 *OED*, s.v. "equality."

133 E.g., Hay, 147; Pao, 277; Moo, 316; Lightfoot, 230.

134 Vasser, "Grant Slaves Equality," 62–66.

equal measure of goods. "Fairness" in terms of assigning a reasonable amount of responsibilities, providing appropriate food and shelter, and applying appropriate and reasonable discipline for failures is, without doubt, the minimal way of understanding what is entailed by ἰσότης in our text. Yet does Paul imply something more?

Vasser contends that Paul does and concludes that "the author does appear to envision a community in which Christian masters treat their slaves as equals."[135] He stops short of saying that Christian slave masters should grant their slaves freedom, but he does urge that the text be translated, "Masters, grant slaves justice and equality." He argues that Paul is saying something similar to what Seneca advises in his forty-seventh epistle in calling "for masters to treat slaves as equals without thereby demanding the abolition of slavery."[136] But this is a distinction without a substantive difference from the "fairness" view, since there would be no change in the actual status of the slaves; they still remain the property of the slave owner. Seneca was clearly not building a case for the overthrow of the Roman socioeconomic system of slavery. Nor was he contending that individual slave owners free their slaves and begin paying them a wage. He was simply imploring slave owners to treat their slaves with kindness and respect, while seeing them as potential friends. His epistle reveals his concern that Romans are "excessively haughty, cruel, and insulting" to their slaves (*Ep.* 47.11) and reminds his readers that they should "kindly remember that he whom you call your slave sprang from the same stock, is smiled upon by the same skies, and on equal terms with yourself breathes, lives, and dies" (*aeque spirare, aeque vivere, aeque mori*; 47.10). Vasser is on the right track in affirming that "Colossians contains hints that the 'equality' envisioned in 4:1 is even more radical than the behaviour described by Seneca."[137]

We have already seen that Paul shows a countercultural tendency throughout the household instructions as he draws out the implications of the lordship of Christ for the Christian community. He also never creates a theological argument in support of slavery here or in any of his earlier writings (or in Ephesians). So, what is he asking Christian slave owners to do? It is unlikely here that he is advocating an overturning of the legal status of slaves. If he were to do so, it would take far more than an incidental comment in the household instructions, and he never pursued an agenda of advocating for political and social change in Roman society. His focus is on the health and stability of his churches. And here his concern is for aligning the responsibilities of each member of the household with the implications of the lordship of Jesus Christ. Nevertheless, we cannot underplay the weight of his word choice here in choosing the term "equality," especially when combined with "justice" in a Christian context. Sumney is thus

135 Vasser, "Grant Slaves Equality," 69.
136 Vasser, "Grant Slaves Equality," 70.
137 Vasser, "Grant Slaves Equality," 68.

correct in asserting that "if masters would truly accord justice and equality to slaves, then slaves would no longer be treated as slaves. If masters and slaves are equals, there can be no justification for slavery. Therefore, this command to slaveholders subverts the very system that the previous verses seem to support."[138] Over a century ago, H. A. W. Meyer argued that Paul was not exhorting the Christian slave owners to a moral evenness in their treatment of slaves; this would have been better expressed by δικαιοσύνη; nor was he contending for an abolition of slavery; rather, in the Christian household, "he desires to see their inequality in other respects ethically counterbalanced," especially by "the parity [*égalité*] implied in the Christian ἀδελφότης."[139]

It is difficult to escape the conclusion that Paul views the Roman institution of slavery dimly and that it runs counter to his understanding of humanity as created in the image of God and every member of the Christian community as a new creation (Col 3:10–11). Thus, in the new creation, there is no δοῦλος or ἐλεύθερος. Slavery was not part of the creation order and has no warrant in God's economy.

This leaves Paul and the slave owners at Colossae in an ethical conundrum. Paul does not want to foment a slave rebellion beginning within the Christian community. The well-known revolt of Spartacus a century earlier showed the outcome of that approach. But neither does Paul want to take the isolationist approach of the Therapeutae or the Essenes. His goal is for the Christian communities to be ambassadors of God's grace within the cities, towns, and villages where they exist. Thus, Paul sows the seeds of a different life within those Christian communities, where slaves can not only be treated with fairness but be accorded a new status consonant with their identity in Christ. Consequently, Paul appeals to slave owners within the Christian community to view their slaves differently in accordance with their new status in Christ. Note in his letter to Philemon that Paul commended Onesimus to Philemon to receive Onesimus "no longer as a slave but more than a slave, a beloved brother . . . both in the flesh and in the Lord" (Phlm 16 NRSV). Treating slaves "with justice and equality" will begin with according them the dignity and status that come when both masters and slaves recognize that they are "in Christ," "brothers and sisters," "saints," "chosen of God," and "beloved" by him (Col 1:2; 3:12). Does this mean that Christian slave owners should liberate their slaves? Perhaps, but not necessarily, especially since Paul still commands obedience as the response of the slaves (we must remember that some of these Christian slaves would be owned by non-Christian slaveholders). But for Christian slave owners, it does entail an entirely transformed relationship with their slaves.

In light of the foregoing discussion, it would be inappropriate to limit the interpretation of Col 4:1 as an admonition to Christian slave owners to treat

138 Sumney, 253.

139 Meyer, 378.

their slaves equally with one another—in other words, that they should not show partiality or favoritism to certain slaves.[140] The focus is on how slave owners treat each individual slave and would consequently be meaningless to all the slave owners who possessed only one slave.

εἰδότες ὅτι καὶ ὑμεῖς ἔχετε κύριον ἐν οὐρανοῖς, "since you know that you have a master in heaven." The reason Christian slaveholders should grant their slaves justice and equality is because they, too, are accountable to a Master. The participle εἰδότες should be interpreted as causal, "because you know." Their master is the Lord Jesus Christ. This is the seventh occurrence of κύριος in the household instructions in reference to the Lord. The lordship of Christ over everything, even those whom Roman society would regard as most powerful—wealthy slave masters—is stressed by Paul. Christ's current heavenly (ἐν οὐρανῷ) position emphasizes his association with the Father (he is currently "seated at the right hand of God," 3:1) and reminds us of the double reference to heaven in the Christ-hymn where he is extolled as creator of everything in heaven (1:16) and as the one who will consummate all of creation in a final act of reconciliation (1:20). This sovereign Lord is the master above all earthly masters, the one to whom they currently answer, and their end-time judge. The slave masters addressed here are ironically slaves themselves—slaves of Christ (see 4:12 and the position of Paul himself; Rom 1:1; Phil 1:1). This christological perspective overturns their deeply ingrained Roman social perspective concerning power, privilege, and domination. Their social status in the Christian community is no different than the slaves who work for them.

Despite its brevity, the instructions to masters were the most difficult of all the commands to members of the Christian household. Sumney summarizes it well that "at the very least . . . slaveholders in the church must dramatically reorient their thinking about and valuing of their slaves, and this must lead to new ways of treating them, ways that recognize their equality before God and in the church."[141]

## *Explanation*

In the concluding chapter of the book of Joshua, this eminent leader of Israel gathers all the tribes together at Shechem to present themselves before God and to renew the covenant. Joshua implores them, "Now therefore fear the LORD and serve him in sincerity and in faithfulness" (Josh 24:14). He then declares, "But as for me and my house [οἰκία], we will serve the Lord [κυρίῳ]" (Josh 24:15 ESV). First and foremost for Joshua and for the people of Israel, it meant renouncing any other gods and devoting themselves to serve the one holy God who had

140 As, for instance, Beale, 328, and Foster, 395. Foster notes: "masters are not being commanded to make slaves their social equals, but not to discriminate in the way they treat different slaves."

141 Sumney, 254.

rescued them from slavery (Josh 24:16–24). In Paul's instructions to the Christian households of Colossae, he is calling all members of these households to devote themselves to the lordship of Jesus Christ and then casting a vision for what this would look like in daily life in specific and concrete terms. Seven times in this brief passage he refers to "the Lord," thereby grounding their motivation for adhering to the instructions in this code in service of the Lord.

This passage flows directly from the all-encompassing injunction of Col 3:17, where Paul exhorted them, "Whatever you do in word or in work, do everything in the name of the Lord Jesus." These instructions explain what that should look like in the Christian household. As with the Israelites under Joshua, the Colossian believers constitute the new people of God whom he has chosen and upon whom he has poured out his love (3:12). They now have covenant obligations before him to "lead lives worthy of the Lord, fully pleasing to him" (1:10).

Their duties in the household are an expression of their new identity in Christ. Paul has revealed that these believers have been fundamentally transformed by the renewing work of God and are a new creation in his image (3:10). They have been united with Christ in his death, resurrection, and exaltation (2:11–12; 3:1–3) and live an entirely new existence (2:13). And they are also people who live under the reality of the hope of a future life with Christ in glory (3:3–4, 24). These specific duties are an expression of what this new life under the lordship of Christ should look like in their household relationships. The passage is not a direct response to any of the specific teachings of "the philosophy." But it does remind the Colossians that the lordship of Christ is what matters above all.

Many ancient authors discussed the duties of the various members of the household. Household management became a common topos—perhaps stimulated in large measure by Aristotle's discussion of this topic, which he correlated with the well-being of the state. But this did not give birth to a new literary type or form (i.e., a "household code"). Both in form and in content, the relevant passages in the ancient authors are quite different from one another and from the discussion in Colossians.

The Colossian discussion of household responsibilities is also distinct from its Greco-Roman counterparts in terms of the source of its contents. Rather than drawing on traditional Hellenistic ethics coming down from Aristotle and mediated through Stoicism or Hellenistic Judaism, the author of Colossians shows direct dependence on the creation narrative of Genesis, the Torah, and Jewish wisdom. The latter is especially prominent in the details and phraseology of his instructions. All three of these sources are run through the prism of the lordship of Jesus Christ. The Lord of the wisdom literature is now understood to be Christ himself. He is the Wisdom of God. The author is relentlessly insistent on motivating the readers through their allegiance to the Lord, their union with him, their desire to please him, and their obligation to fear and respect him.

In terms of content, the passage bears similarities to other discussions of household duties and responsibilities in the Greco-Roman world. The passage assumes an authority structure that invests the male husband, father, and slave master with the principal leadership role. Wives are called to respect this order, and children and slaves are expected to obey. Yet the similarities end there. The first-century reader would have been struck by the numerous points of discontinuity with traditional Greco-Roman discussions of the household. Many of these elements would have been seen as countercultural and some of them radically so.

We see some of the discontinuity from the very beginning of the text in observing that "wives" are addressed first. Rather than beginning with the *paterfamilias* and describing his authority and duty to rule his household, the passage begins by addressing the subordinate member first. This pattern continues with the other two pairs of relationships. It is also unusual—and significant—that he addresses each member of the household, especially the wives, children, and slaves, as responsible moral agents and does not address them indirectly through the male head of the household.

Overall, Paul casts a new and unique vision for the household. We see in this passage the beginnings of what a Christian household—under the lordship of Christ—could look like while maintaining an integrated presence in the Roman world. Unlike the Essenes or Therapeutae, Paul did not encourage his churches to flee society and become isolationist communities. But neither did he want his new communities to accommodate themselves to the prevailing characteristics of Roman society. His vision for them was to be truly in the world but not of the world. They were to live in Roman society, but in full obedience to the biblical tradition and to the Lord Jesus Christ. The households of believers would look different than traditional Roman households. And, in particular respects, there would be points of conflict with prevailing Roman custom and structure.

For the first-century reader, one of the most noticeable differences is the apparent deemphasis on the authority of the *paterfamilias* and the redefinitions of his role. First of all, Paul never refers to him with one of the words for "ruler" (ἡγεμών, δεσπότης, or ἄρχων) that appear in some of the other descriptions of his duties in ancient discussions of the household. He definitely bears an authority and wields a leadership role, but this has been significantly qualified. The defining characteristic is now love (3:19), which Paul has described as the virtue that is over all and binds together all the other virtues (3:14). Part of the way that this is manifested is in not embittering their wives and in not provoking and discouraging their children. The overall effect is to dampen and restrict the heavy-handed authority that was typical of the Roman *paterfamilias* and to elevate the new standard of Christlike love.

Instead of obedience, Paul calls wives to "submit," which should be understood as a voluntary respect of the leadership role that the husband has been appointed to by God's design in the creation account. But this, too, is qualified by what is appropriate in the Lord and leaves the door open to potential disregard of leadership initiatives that would be counter to the ethics and virtues of life in Christ.

As with any home in any culture in antiquity, the children are instructed to obey. But in this instance, their obedience should be motivated by the knowledge that the Lord himself will find their compliance pleasing to him.

The final pairing addressed is slaves and their masters. Every culture and society in antiquity maintained this institution, but it was a particularly significant part of the Roman empire, with a substantial portion of the population serving as slaves. Paul's principal concern here was advising believers on how to live within this socioeconomic structure and, to that extent, he is accommodating to the prevailing culture. Yet Paul never—here or elsewhere—attempts to justify this structure on biblical or theological grounds and, as many interpreters have rightly observed, he sows the seeds of deconstructing it. Here he does so quite shockingly by telling the Christian slave masters to provide their slaves "justice and equality" (4:1). When these two words appear in conjunction in other Jewish texts, they entail an antislavery point of view. This, of course, puts the slave owners in a very difficult situation. Paul has not explicitly advocated manumission, but he is urging an entirely different treatment of their slaves and is not only leaving the door open for manumission but hinting in that direction. For the slaves, Paul simply advocates for compliance and for a strong work ethic, which is deeply rooted in Jewish wisdom literature.

"Serve the Lord" could be the banner over this entire section. Although this command is given to the slaves (3:24b), it is appropriate to every member of the household. Christ is the one who has rescued them from their ultimate slavery (1:13) and has given them a place in his own kingdom (1:14). Both slaves and slave masters are answerable to one master of all. Yet this slave master—the Lord of heaven and earth—loves his people dearly and will bestow on them an inheritance of life (1:12). "Christ is your life" (3:4) remains the theme of this section.

# Communicating the Gospel (4:2–6)

## *Bibliography*

**Barclay, J. M. G.** *Paul and the Gift.* **Bockmuehl, M. N.** "Colossians 4:3," 489–94. **Heil, J. P.** *Colossians,* 177–85. **Lövestam, E.** *Spiritual Wakefulness.* **Pao, D.** *Thanksgiving.* **Rapske, B.** *Roman Custody.* **Sweeney, J. P.** "Christian Witness," 449–61.

## *Translation*

[2]*Devote yourselves to prayer, watching in it with thanksgiving,*[a] [3]*at the same time praying also for us, that God would open to us a door for the word—to speak the mystery, which is Christ,*[b] *because of which*[c] *I have been bound in chains.* [4]*[Pray] that I might reveal it as it is necessary for me to speak.* [5]*Walk in wisdom toward those who are outside, redeeming the time.* [6]*Let your speech always be with grace, seasoned with salt, that you may know how it is necessary to reply to each person.*

## *Notes*

a. [4:2] Codex D omits ἐν εὐχαριστίᾳ. Wilson, 290, is probably correct in assuming that this was an accidental omission.

b. [4:3] Codex Vaticanus (B), L, 614, 2495, and a few other witnesses read τοῦ θεοῦ instead of τοῦ Χριστοῦ. This is best explained as a scribal assimilation to Col 2:2: τοῦ μυστηρίου τοῦ θεοῦ, Χριστοῦ.

c. [4:3] Bockmuehl, "Colossians 4:3," 489–94, in dependence on Wettstein, has suggested that the text should here be construed as διό and not δι' ὅ. This construal would, of course, not be possible if the masculine form of the relative pronoun (ὅν) as attested in Vaticanus (B), F, G, and a few Vulgate manuscripts is correct. But if the neuter form of the text is correct, it is a possible interpretation because there were no word divisions, punctuation, accents, or breathing marks in the manuscripts of the first few centuries, and the text could read διό or δι' ὅ. Bockmuehl finds a handful of later minuscule manuscripts (i.e., 1, 3, 4, 7, 14, 19, 20, 21, 37, 72, and 80) that support this transcription and reading. He then also posits a full stop after τοῦ Χριστοῦ with the διό introducing a new clause: *διό* καὶ δέδεμαι, ἵνα φανερώσω αὐτό, ὡς δεῖ με λαλῆσαι, "For it is to this end that I am imprisoned, in order that I might manifest it, as indeed I am obliged to do" (p. 492). Wilson, 289, 292–93, follows him in this interpretation, but he appears to be the only commentator to do so. The only change of meaning is one of emphasis. As Bockmuehl has observed, it creates a more "substantive link between Paul's bonds and his task of preaching the mystery" (p. 492). The parallel passage in Ephesians would seem to suggest that the traditional reading of the passage is preferable because of the way Paul's imprisonment is expressed there (ὑπὲρ οὗ πρεσβεύω ἐν ἁλύσει; Eph 6:20).

## *Form/Structure/Setting*

### *Form (and Literary Context)*

Many interpreters have referred to this brief section as a set of general admonitions prior to the personal greetings that will conclude the letter.[1] A careful look at the content of this section reveals that it is not a series of disconnected instructions but a coherent series of exhortations related to furthering the impact of the gospel.[2] Paul began this letter by elaborating on the gospel (1:5–8), and now he concludes the body of the letter by highlighting the importance of the gospel once again. Specifically, just as the gospel is "bearing fruit and increasing" throughout the Mediterranean world (1:5), Paul wants it to do so in the Lycus Valley through the lives and testimony of the Colossian believers. He also wants it to spread in Rome through his witness and that of his companions despite his imprisonment. In short, the Colossians should diligently pray for an open door for the gospel (4:2–4), their daily conduct should be a witness to the gospel (4:5), and they should be prepared to give verbal testimony to the gospel (4:6).

Although Paul does not use the word "gospel" (εὐαγγέλιον) in this section, he refers to it in a variety of other ways. He speaks of it as "the word" (ὁ λόγος, 4:3; see 1:5, 25; 3:16), "the mystery" (τὸ μυστήριον, 4:3; see 1:26–27; 2:2), and a message that needs to be spoken (λαλέω, 4:3–4; φανερόω, 4:4; ἀποκρίνομαι, 4:6). The theme of the gospel thus serves as a macro *inclusio* over the first and final parts of the body of the letter.

"Walking in wisdom" (4:5) is one point of connection between this section and the household instructions (3:18–4:1). The admonitions to the various members of the household are an expression of how daily conduct should reflect biblical wisdom now interpreted by life in Christ, the ultimate expression of the wisdom of God. Paul is convinced that lives rooted in and exhibiting this kind of wisdom will prove attractive to unbelievers ("those outside").

The more significant line of continuity with the household instructions is the christological focus. Whereas the heart of the household code could be expressed in the command to "serve the Lord Christ" (3:24), this section could be summed up with "spread the good news about Christ." This passage furthers the intensely christological emphasis of the entire letter.

Additional themes link this section to earlier parts of the letter. These include the themes of prayer (1:3, 9), thanksgiving (1:3, 12; 2:7; 3:15, 17), wisdom (1:9, 28; 2:3; 3:16), the proper conduct of believers expressed with "walking" (1:10; 2:6,

---

1 E.g., Sumney, 255, speaks of them as "a collection of somewhat general exhortations" (so also Calvin, 356). Wilson, 289, calls them "final admonitions." Eadie, 267, refers to them as "general admonitions."

2 See the similar emphasis by Pao, 286–87, 298–302. He regards the main point of this unit as: "Being alert in prayer, believers are called to participate in the proclamation of God's redemptive acts. They must pray faithfully for the expansion of the gospel, and their lives must also be a proclamation of the gospel" (287). Moo, 318, notes that "Colossians 4:2–6 . . . looks outward, with a focus on Paul's evangelistic work and the community's relationships with non-Christians."

3:7), Paul's suffering (1:24), and his commission to proclaim the gospel (1:25–29). Paul's sense of urgency for the gospel ("redeeming the time," 4:5) also connects this text with the futurist eschatology present in this letter (see esp. 1:20; 3:4, 6, 24–25). This passage does not recapitulate all the main themes of the letter, but it does take up many of them.

The style of this section is similar to paraenetic sections in Paul's other letters (see, e.g., Gal 5:25–6:10; Phil 4:4–9; 1 Thess 5:12–22). The present imperatives followed by present participles are typical. Also, the use of the conjunction ἵνα to convey the content of the prayers is common Pauline style. The passage is also rich with imagery. The opening of a door, seasoning with salt, and the language of redemption add color to the text.

The main point of the passage is that Paul wants the Colossians to orient their lives completely around the expansion of the gospel. He wants them to pray for the progress of the gospel, he wants their lives to be a demonstration of the gospel, and he wants them to be prepared to explain God's plan of salvation in a clear and attractive way to anyone who asks about it.

### *Structure*

This passage consists of three sentences structured around three present imperative verbs (with the third verb implied):

τῇ προσευχῇ *προσκαρτερεῖτε*, "devote yourselves to prayer" (4:2)
ἐν σοφίᾳ *περιπατεῖτε*, "walk in wisdom" (4:5)
ὁ λόγος ὑμῶν ἐν χάριτι [*ἔστω*], "let your speech be with grace" (4:6)

The first admonition is the longest—thirty-seven words (versus nine and fifteen words respectively)—and is extended by two participial clauses and two ἵνα clauses expressing the content of the twofold prayer request (4:2–4). The first admonition would have been balanced in size with the others (eight words), but Paul adds a twofold prayer request for himself and his companions. The two present participles (γρηγοροῦντες and προσευχόμενοι) are best understood as expressing the means by which the devotion to prayer would be expressed.

The second imperative is also followed by a present participle expressing means (4:5). "Redeeming the time" formally modifies the preceding imperative verb, but likely carries its semantic force into the next admonition. Thus, awareness of eschatological urgency should inform one's conduct as well as one's speech in terms of making the gospel known (4:6).

There is no final imperative, but it is easily inferred from the context, and thus Paul does not write it. Rather than a present participle, the writer uses a perfect participle, implying the present state of the action—the speech is "seasoned with salt" (4:6). The purpose, expressed with an infinitive clause, is that the Colossians would know how to reply in a gracious way to nonbelievers who query them about their faith.

## *Setting*

If this letter is authentic and assuming that Epaphras communicated the gospel to the Colossians during Paul's Ephesian ministry (ca. AD 53–55), it has been roughly seven or eight years since many of the readers had become Christians. Paul is concerned that their evangelistic zeal not wane. The impact of the upheaval in the church precipitated by the advocates of "the philosophy" may have caused many of the Colossian believes to become preoccupied with these internal matters, with a resultant loss of focus on their obligation to make the gospel known. It is possible that some may even have experienced a loss of confidence because of the judgmentalism of the factional teachers. Paul wants them to pray diligently for the spread of the gospel—not only in the Lycus Valley but also in Rome. He also wants them to let their lives bear witness to the validity of the gospel and to share the gospel in winsome ways to every person who may talk to them about their faith. This should all be done with a sense of urgency because of the eschatological nearness of Christ.

## *Comment*

**2** τῇ προσευχῇ προσκαρτερεῖτε, γρηγοροῦντες ἐν αὐτῇ ἐν εὐχαριστίᾳ, "devote yourselves to prayer, watching in it with thanksgiving." Like the beginning of the instructions to the household (3:18), this section also begins without a conjunction (such as δέ or οὖν) to signal a change of topic. The absence of the conjunction may function to tie it more closely to the preceding section as continuing a set of admonitions to the community that flow from the command to "do everything in the name of the Lord Jesus" (3:17).

Paul began this letter on a note of prayer and thanksgiving to God (1:3), and now he draws the body of the letter to a conclusion on the same note. Whereas at the outset of the letter he reports how he and his coworkers are "always" praying for the Colossian believers, here he appeals to them to give themselves to regular times of intercessory prayer. To reinforce this constancy, he uses the verb προσκαρτερέω, which means "to persist obstinately in" some endeavor.[3] Using the same terminology, he urged the Roman believers to the same goal (Rom 12:12). He likewise instructed the Thessalonians to "pray without ceasing" (ἀδιαλείπτως, 1 Thess 5:17; see also Luke 18:1). This, of course, was his own practice, as he prays "always" (πάντοτε) for his converts (1 Cor 1:4; Phil 1:4; 2 Thess 1:11) and tells the Ephesians that "I do not cease" (οὐ παύομαι) praying for them and giving thanks for them (Eph 1:16). This was also the practice of the church in its earliest days in Jerusalem. Luke reports how they "with one accord were devoting themselves to prayer" (προσκαρτεροῦντες ὁμοθυμαδὸν τῇ προσευχῇ, Acts 1:14 ESV; see also 2:42). The apostles set the example by devoting themselves to prayer and to the ministry of the word (Acts 6:4). This emphasis on

3 LSJ, s.v. προσκαρτερέω.

persistence and constancy in prayer moves beyond the practices of traditional Judaism that stressed set times of prayer in the morning, afternoon, and evening along with the recitation of the Shema and the Shemoneh Esreh (the Eighteen Benedictions).[4]

For Paul, persistence in prayer was motivated by the immediate and direct access they had to the resurrected and exalted Lord, who was leading them and resourcing them for the mission to which he had called them (Col 1:17; 2:9–10, 19). It was also motivated by Paul's eschatological orientation, which underlined the urgency of the mission and the supernatural opposition that believers would face as they sought to fulfill it. The term "watching" (γρηγοροῦντες), an adverbial participle of means,[5] is an echo of Jesus's eschatological discourse delivered on the Mount of Olives. This address to the disciples concludes with the admonition, "Therefore keep watch [γρηγορεῖτε], because you do not know on what day your Lord will come" (Matt 24:42 NIV; see also Mark 13:35, 37). This eschatological emphasis is also seen in Paul's first letter to the Thessalonians where he instructs them on how to live in light of the fact that Christ will return like a thief in the night. He admonishes these believers to "be awake" (γρηγορῶμεν, 1 Thess 5:6; see also 1 Cor 16:13). The letter to the Ephesians also includes an injunction to watch (although there using ἀγρυπνέω; see Mark 13:33) in the context of prayer (Eph 6:18). The expectancy that the Lord could return at any moment (Luke 21:36) prompted this vigilance.[6] But the temptations, spiritual opposition, and character of the times also stimulates the need for watchful prayer and closeness to the Lord. Jesus had instructed his disciples to "watch and pray" so that they would not fall into temptation (Matt 26:41; Mark 14:38). Another text warns believers to "watch" because "your adversary the devil prowls around like a roaring lion, seeking someone to devour" (1 Pet 5:8 ESV). By devoting themselves to prayer with an attitude of watchfulness, the Colossians will be able to resist the attractiveness of "the philosophy." This is the path of seeking the things above where Christ is, seated at the right hand of God (Col 3:1). Yet this devotion to prayer will also enable them to resist other forms of temptation and demonic attack and empower them to fulfill the mission God has given to them.

The thanksgiving (εὐχαριστία) that accompanies this prayerful vigilance provides assurance that the God whom they are addressing will not only hear their requests but will respond to them. The theme of expressing gratitude to

---

4 See Mishnah, *Berakhot* 4–5. See the discussion in D. Instone-Brewer, *Traditions of the Rabbis from the Era of the New Testament, Volume I: Prayer and Agriculture* (Grand Rapids: Eerdmans, 2004): 41–119.

5 Lohse, 164, interprets the participle as an imperative and regards it as an independent command. Beale, 334n2, takes it as a temporal participle. It is common, however, for a present imperative to be followed by a participle of means. That fits the context well here as Paul specifies how they should pray.

6 Contra Lindemann, 69, who contends that the futurist eschatological perspective has disappeared in Colossians. But see my comments on 3:4, 23–25 and elsewhere in Colossians where the eschatological expectation is still vibrant.

God pervades this letter (1:3, 12; 2:7) and ties this section to the concluding admonition of 3:5–17: "whatever you do in word or in work, do everything in the name of the Lord Jesus, giving thanks to God the Father through him." Giving thanks to God in the context of intercessory prayer is something that Paul also commends to the Philippians (Phil 4:6).

**3** προσευχόμενοι ἅμα καὶ περὶ ἡμῶν, "at the same time praying also for us." Paul now shifts the focus to himself and his companions by asking the Colossian believers to pray specifically for them. The participle (προσευχόμενοι) is parallel with the preceding (γρηγοροῦντες) and should also be interpreted as a further specification of how they should pray (i.e., as a participle of means). The adverb ἅμα is "a marker of simultaneous occurrence"[7] and suggests that when the Colossians are engaging in intercessory prayer for themselves and for their community, they should also appeal to God on behalf of Paul and his coworkers. Whom Paul has in mind would certainly include himself and Timothy, whom he names as coauthor of the letter, but may also include Epaphras[8] and others he names in his greetings to the Colossian church (4:10–14). These personal references present a problem to interpreters who consider the letter as pseudonymous. It is necessary to see a deeper sense that transcends the surface meaning. Lincoln, for instance, suggests that the writer "has taken on the persona of Paul (and Timothy) as part of the device of pseudonymity."[9] The readers, he contends, should understand that "prayer is asked for the apostolic ministry of proclaiming the mystery of Christ" in a more general sense.[10] It is more natural, however, to see the prayer request as genuine (see, e.g., 1 Thess 5:25: "pray for us"; see also Rom 15:30; 2 Thess 3:1).

ἵνα ὁ θεὸς ἀνοίξῃ ἡμῖν θύραν τοῦ λόγου, "that God would open to us a door for the word." Despite the difficulty of his circumstances, Paul's heart and passion for communicating the gospel continues unabated. He asks the Colossians to pray that he and his companions would have an opportunity to declare the gospel in Rome. He has previously used the metaphor of God "opening a door" of opportunity for him in his ministry at Corinth (1 Cor 16:9) and then later at Troas (2 Cor 2:12). Luke used the image to describe how God "had opened a door of faith to the gentiles" as he reflected on his ministry in Cyprus, Antioch, Iconium, Lystra, and Derbe (Acts 14:27). The "word" (λόγος) that Paul wants to declare is "the word of truth, the gospel" (Col 1:5; see also 1:25). God had previously opened doors for the gospel, which had resulted in the fact that "the gospel is bearing fruit and growing throughout the whole world" (1:6 NIV).

λαλῆσαι τὸ μυστήριον τοῦ Χριστοῦ, "to speak the mystery, which is Christ." He further describes his proclamation of the gospel as "speaking the mystery."

---

7 BDAG, s.v. ἅμα.

8 Lightfoot, 231, thinks it refers specifically to Paul, Timothy, and Epaphras.

9 Lincoln, 661.

10 Lincoln, 661.

The verb λαλέω stresses the need for a verbal proclamation (see 1 Thess 2:2, 4). He has referred to this mystery earlier in the letter when he spoke of the commission given to him by God to make it known (Col 1:25–26; see the commentary there for a full discussion of "mystery"). The language of "the mystery" comes from the book of Daniel and refers to God's redemptive plan for the end of the age. The essence of that mystery is Christ himself and all of God's redemptive plans centered on the work of Christ (Col 2:2). The content of the mystery is Christ. Hence, the genitive τοῦ Χριστοῦ should be interpreted as a genitive of apposition, thus explaining what the mystery entails. Part of the inscrutibility or hiddenness of this plan no doubt involves the death of the Messiah as the means of effecting the forgivness of sins (1:14). The necessity of the death of the Messiah went beyond the scope of Jewish expectation.

δι' ὃ καὶ δέδεμαι, "because of which, I have been bound in chains." It is precisely because of his public declaration of "the mystery" (the neuter relative pronoun ὅ refers to τὸ μυστήριον) that Paul is in Roman custody. He has earlier referred to his suffering on behalf of the gospel (1:24), but this statement now clarifies why he is suffering. The verb δέω suggests that Paul has been restrained with a chain.[11] This fits with the way that Luke describes his Roman imprisonment: "it is because of the hope of Israel that I am bound with this chain" (Acts 28:20 NIV). He refers to himself in Ephesians as "an ambassador in chains" (ἐν ἁλύσει; Eph 6:20). He could have been manacled on one or both wrists or one or both legs. The chain was likely made of iron and weighed between ten to fifteen pounds.[12] It would have restricted his mobility, made it difficult to sleep, and would have been generally uncomfortable. He would have been bound to a guard who was charged with overseeing his custody and ensuring that he did not escape.[13]

**4** ἵνα φανερώσω αὐτὸ ὡς δεῖ με λαλῆσαι, "[pray] that I might reveal it as it is necessary for me to speak." The last clause of this long sentence that began in 4:2 reiterates Paul's strong sense of his need to proclaim the gospel. A precise understanding of the function of this clause, however, requires determining the specific verb that it is modifying. There are three possibilities: (1) δέδεμαι ("I have been bound in chains . . . that I might reveal the mystery"), thus indicating the purpose of the imprisonment;[14] (2) ἀνοίξῃ ("that God would open to us a door for the word . . . that I might reveal the mystery"), and thereby expressing the second purpose for the open door;[15] and (3) προσευχόμενοι ("praying . . . that I might reveal the mystery"), thus giving the second prayer request.[16] Among these three options, the evidence tips in favor of the third view. This way of

11 BDAG, s.v. δέω 1.b. See also F. Staudinger, "δέω," *EDNT* 1:292.

12 See Rapske, *Roman Custody*, 207.

13 See Rapske, *Roman Custody*, 173–91.

14 Barth and Blanke, 454.

15 Moo, 325; Dunn, 264; Lightfoot, 231.

16 Beale, 339; Pao, 294; Harris, 168–69.

construing the syntax takes the two ἵνα clauses as expressing the content of the prayer (and thus not as purpose clauses) and as parallel. This interpretation is supported by a similar use of the two ἵνα clauses in the parallel passage in Eph 6:18–20 ("pray for me that [ἵνα] a word may be given me [and] . . . that [ἵνα] I could make known with boldness the mystery of the gospel"). Many of the more recent English versions also reflect the last option by putting a full stop at the end of v. 3 and repeating "pray" at the beginning of v. 4 ("pray that I may proclaim it clearly," NIV; see also CEB; NET; NLT; NJB). The end result is that Paul is asking the Colossians to pray for him and his companions in two ways: (1) that God would open a door of opportunity for them to proclaim the gospel, and (2) that he would actually take advantage of that opportunity to proclaim it.

Instead of using one of the typical verbs for proclaiming the gospel—such as κηρύσσω (e.g., Rom 10:8, 14–15; 1 Cor 1:23), καταγγέλλω (e.g., Col 1:28; cf. Rom 1:8; Phil 1:17–18), or εὐαγγελίζω (e.g., Rom 1:15; 15:20; Gal 1:8, 9, 11)—he uses φανερόω. Although this term can be used in the simple sense of "to make something known," Paul often uses it in the more specific and technical sense of "revealing" or "disclosing" something that is hidden. This is particularly true when it is connected to the revelation of "the mystery" (see my comments on Col 1:26; see also Rom 16:26). The twofold use of λαλέω in this context underlines the verbal proclamation of this message.

Paul has a strong inner compulsion to preach the gospel. Yet this drive does not originate with himself but with the commission that God has bestowed on him. He tells the Corinthians that he must proclaim the gospel, "for an obligation is laid on me [ἀνάγκη γάρ μοι ἐπίκειται]" and "woe to me if I do not preach the gospel" (1 Cor 9:16 NRSV). He thus uses the term δεῖ, "it is necessary," to convey the sense of divine necessity.[17] He expresses the same idea in the parallel passage in Ephesians (Eph 6:20). In the LXX of Daniel, the term δεῖ is closely tied to the revelation of the mysteries as eschatological events that are *necessary* to happen in the unfolding of God's sovereign plans (ἃ δεῖ γενέσθαι; Dan 2:29). Paul sees the revelation of this mystery as taking place through his preaching (Rom 16:25–26; Eph 3:1–10; see also Rom 11:13–15; 2 Cor 2:14; 4:10). Through this request, Paul is soliciting the involvement of the Colossian believers in the fulfillment of his apostolic commission of proclaiming God's salvific plans in Christ.

**5** Ἐν σοφίᾳ περιπατεῖτε πρὸς τοὺς ἔξω, "walk in wisdom toward those who are outside." Paul now turns his focus to the evangelistic responsibilities of the Colossian believers—first with regard to the witness of their lives (4:5) and then with regard to the witness of their speech (4:6). He wants their conduct to be characterized by biblical wisdom. The theme of wisdom forms an *inclusio* over

17 Foster, 403, downplays this sense of the verb in this context when he says that "it is focused upon the appropriate mode of speech to produce the maximum effect of the proclamation of the mystery."

the first part and final part of the letter.[18] Paul begins the letter by reporting how he regularly prays that God would fill them with a knowledge of his will "in all wisdom [ἐν πάσῃ σοφίᾳ] and insight that comes from the Spirit" (1:9). Now he concludes the body of the letter with a call for them to "walk in wisdom." The wisdom he refers to goes beyond the practical insights gained from the Jewish wisdom tradition that governs the ethical conduct of the people of God and is now wrapped up in the ethical demands of the Lord Jesus Christ "in whom are hidden all the treasures of wisdom and knowledge" (2:3). They are called to teach and admonish one another on this basis (3:16). The verb περιπατέω, "walk," refers to the way that the Colossians would live their lives each day throughout every week and corresponds to the Jewish understanding of halakah (see my comments on 1:10). This involves every aspect of their lives including sexual ethics (3:5), social ethics and attitudes toward people (3:8–9), the way they treat those who are different than them (3:11), the way they appropriate and exemplify all of the key Christian virtues (3:12–15), and the way they respond to all the members of their household (3:18–4:1).

In this passage, Paul is particularly concerned about the impact their behavior will have on non-Christians in the surrounding community. He labels these people as "those who are outside" (τοὺς ἔξω). He uses this language elsewhere to refer to non-Christians and can contrast them with "those who are on the inside" (τοὺς ἔσω; 1 Cor 5:12–13). "The outsiders" was a typical Jewish way of referring to those who were not part of the chosen people of God.[19] Paul here appropriates that language to refer to those who did not belong to the Christian community. This is consistent with his understanding of the radical change that has taken place to believers, leading to their membership in this new community (see 1:12–13; 2:10–15; 3:1–4). Paul shares a similar concern with the Thessalonians when he urges them "to walk properly before outsiders" (ἵνα περιπατῆτε εὐσχημόνως πρὸς τοὺς ἔξω; 1 Thess 4:12). Paul wants the conduct of the Colossian believers toward individuals in the non-Christian community to reflect the virtues he has commended to them. Yet he is also likely aware that both unbelieving gentiles and Jews in the area would be watching Christians closely to see the quality of their lives and to determine if they were living in alignment with what they were professing, especially as these believers made an appeal to them to join their movement. It is unlikely that Paul is using the expression "those who are outside" to refer here to the proponents of "the philosophy." As we have already noted, this was a faction that was within the church.

τὸν καιρὸν ἐξαγοραζόμενοι, "redeeming the time." Evoking his eschatological perspective regarding the imminence of the Lord's return, Paul summons the Colossians to make good use of their time for the sake of the gospel. He uses the language of "buying" or "purchasing," perhaps to underline the value

18 So also Dunn, 265, and Sumney, 260.
19 Strack-Billerbeck, 3:362.

of time, which in his view is a limited commodity. The uncompounded form ἀγοράζω is the common word for purchasing items in the agora. The compound form ἐξαγοράζω is much less common, but is used by Paul elsewhere for Christ's redemption of believers through his work on the cross (Gal 3:13; 4:5). The form may reflect Paul's penchant for using compound forms, but it may signal a dependence on the LXX of Daniel where King Nebuchadnezzar accuses Daniel and his companions of attempting to "buy time" (ὅτι καιρὸν ὑμεῖς ἐξαγοράζετε; Dan 2:8). Although in Daniel, it is used in the more negative sense of causing a delay, it does reflect the metaphorical use of the precise expression that Paul uses here. It is not surprising that Paul would use a metaphor drawn from Dan 2 since some of the language in Colossians (especially μυστήριον, βασιλεία, δηλόω) is rooted there. The participial form of the verb signals its dependence on the previous verb, περιπατεῖτε, and should be understood as expressing how believers should conduct themselves—namely, by being aware of the shortness of the time and using it wisely.[20] The middle voice should not be taken as deponent but as reflexive: "purchase for yourselves."

Paul's use of καιρός, "time," here should probably be seen in his overall eschatological framework. His passion to engage in his mission was motivated in part by the shortness of time before the Lord would return. He told the Corinthians that "the appointed time [καιρός] has grown very short" (1 Cor 7:29). The parallel passage in Ephesians advises redeeming the time "because the days are evil" (Eph 5:16). This was reflective of Paul's eschatological understanding of living in an age characterized by a proliferation of evil and dominated by powerful supernatural forces (Gal 1:4; Eph 2:2).

The passage thus indicates Paul's desire for the Colossians to conduct their lives in a way whereby the non-Christians living in the Lycus Valley would "be attracted to the gospel, not repelled from it. . . . No opportunity of putting the gospel in a true light is to be wasted."[21] It is possible that the phrase also forms a bridge to the next imperative, so that redeeming the time also "describes seeking an opportunity to speak in a gracious manner to those outside the community of faith."[22]

**6** ὁ λόγος ὑμῶν πάντοτε ἐν χάριτι, ἅλατι ἠρτυμένος, "let your speech always be with grace, seasoned with salt." Paul's third admonition of this section is directed to how the Colossian believers interact with their non-Christian family, friends, and acquaintances. The term λόγος should be taken in the broadest possible sense to refer to any form of interaction these believers would have

20 It should be understood as a participle of means, which is common when a present participle follows a present imperative (so also Sweeney, "Christian Witness," 450). Others have taken it as expressing attendant circumstance (e.g., Pao, 296; Moo, 327n33), but the difference in meaning would be negligible.

21 Scott, 84.

22 Foster, 407.

with people in the larger community.[23] Bormann rightly observes that it is not preaching that is meant, but "everyday communication."[24] It should also not be limited strictly to their responses to questions that unbelievers might ask of them but would extend to all forms of discussion.

Paul urges that these interactions always be carried out ἐν χάριτι, "with grace." Because χάρις is most frequently used by Paul as one of the key terms to describe the heart of his theology—even in this letter (see 1:2, 6)—it is appropriate to consider whether he is using it in that technical sense here. A few interpreters have argued that Paul is indeed referring to divine grace. Pao has noted that "this 'grace' represents the powerful act of God among his people."[25] He points to how Stephen was empowered by God's grace and became mighty in words and deeds in response to those who challenge the gospel (Acts 6:8–10). Similarly, Williams suggested that it refers to being "clothed in that Divine gift of spiritual power" that would make them effective in communicating the gospel.[26] The vast majority of commentators and many of the English versions interpret it as "gracious" (for this translation, see ESV; NET; CEB; NLT; NAB; NRSV; RSV; Geneva). This was a very common usage of the term in Greek, especially in older and poetic Greek, and is used this way elsewhere in the NT (see esp. Luke 4:22: "all spoke well of him and were amazed at the gracious words [ἐπὶ τοῖς λόγοις τῆς χάριτος] that came from his mouth" [NRSV]). It is "the quality of charm or agreeableness."[27] BDAG describes it as expressing "a winning quality or attractiveness that invites a favorable reaction" and suggests translating it as "graciousness," "attractiveness," "charm," or "winsomeness."[28] This usage is found in the wisdom literature (see the LXX of Eccl 10:12: "the words of the mouth of the wise are grace [λόγοι στόματος σοφοῦ χάρις], and the lips of the fool will plunge him into the sea"; NETS). Philo, too, uses it of beautiful slave girls who use "the charm of speech" (λόγους χάριτι) to "storm the hearts of their owners" (Philo, *Good Person* 38). The opposite of this kind of speech would be the kind of foul or rotten talk (λόγος σαπρός) that is roundly condemned in Ephesians (Eph 4:29). The speech Paul commends would be consistent with and proceed from the virtues he describes earlier, particularly kindness, humility, gentleness, patience, and above all, love (Col 3:12–14).

The verb in this clause is implicit and should be regarded as ἔστω or its equivalent.[29] The adverb πάντοτε indicates that this kind of gracious interaction should be the pattern for all of their discussions with outsiders. This is not only

23 The basic sense of λόγος is the utterance of thought in speech. See A. Debrunner, "λέγω, λόγος, κτλ.," *TDNT* 4:75.
24 Bormann, 187.
25 Pao, 297.
26 Williams, 158.
27 Barclay, *Paul and the Gift*, 576–77.
28 BDAG, s.v. χάρις 1.
29 Harris, 170; Sweeney, "Christian Witness," 450; Robertson, *Grammar*, 396.

appropriate as an expression of their new identity as followers of Christ but is crucial for the evangelistic efforts of this Christian community. They want to attract others to join this movement.

The participial clause ἅλατι ἠρτυμένος, "seasoned with salt," further underlines and describes the manner of graciousness. The participle should be interpreted as explanatory ("epexegetical") of the preceding ἐν χάριτι.[30] The perfect tense is stative and indicates that the metaphorical seasoning with salt should be characteristic of all these interactions. Salt was a mineral widely used in the ancient world to enhance the flavor and taste of food. Homer called salt "divine" (θεῖον; Homer, *Iliad* 9.214). Plutarch speculates as to why this is the case and concludes that one of the reasons is due to how delicious it makes food taste and that "some even call it *charites* [joys], because it makes needful food enjoyable" (Plutarch, *Mor.* 685A). Job asks, "Can that which is tasteless be eaten without salt?" (Job 6:6 ESV). The Apocalypse of Sedrach compares the absence of love with the absence of salt at a banquet: "How does one benefit, my children, if one gives a great banquet and invites king and nobleman and prepares every sort of expensive fare in order that nothing should be missing; nevertheless, if there is no salt, that banquet cannot be eaten" (Apoc. Sedr. 1.4). In the NT, the metaphorical use of salt can be seen in the teaching of Jesus. He told his disciples that "you are the salt of the earth" (Matt 5:13) to speak of the positive impact they would have on the world. In Mark's Gospel, he uses it as a metaphor for a certain beneficial quality of human disposition: "Salt is good, but if the salt has lost its saltiness, how will you make it salty again? Have salt in yourselves, and be at peace with one another" (Mark 9:50). In Colossians, Paul applies the metaphor to speech. Other ancient authors did so as well. Cicero's comments about what characteristics are essential to good oratory are the most relevant. After describing the importance of extensive preparation in learning voice control, training the memory, reading broadly, and many other things, he notes, "And lastly we have to cull, from all the forms of pleasantry, a certain charm of humour, with which to give a sprinkle of salt [*quo, tanquam sale*], as it were, to all of our discourse" (Cicero, *De or.* 1.34 [§159]). Dio Chrysostom declared that "just as no meat without salt [ἄνευ ἁλῶν] will be gratifying to the taste, so no branch of literature, as it seems to me, could possibly be pleasing to the ear if it lacked the Socratic grace" (Dio Chrysostom, *Dic. exercit.* 18.13). Paul does not specify what the "salt" represents for Christians, but it probably extends to all conventional matters of speaking and dialogue that were commonly regarded as interesting, enjoyable, and informative. He would stop short, however, of any form of speech that would be regarded as "filthy talk" (αἰσχρολογία, Col 3:8) or "rotten speech" (λόγος σαπρός, Eph 4:29), which probably refers to sexual themes spoken of in a derisive way. He also warns against "dirty jokes" (εὐτραπελία) and other forms of "foolish talk" (μωρολογία) (Eph 5:4).

---

30 Harris, 170.

εἰδέναι πῶς δεῖ ὑμᾶς ἑνὶ ἑκάστῳ ἀποκρίνεσθαι, "that you may know how it is necessary to reply to each person." Paul defines the "salt" as the ability to give an apt and interesting reply to unbelievers who raise questions. "Knowing" (οἶδα) how to respond implies giving thought ahead of time to what one might say in response to anticipated questions and how the response would be delivered. This preparation would involve discussions within the community of believers and seeking counsel from the teachers within the church. Similar language is used in the OT: "Then King Rehoboam took counsel with the old men, who had stood before Solomon his father while he was yet alive, saying, 'How do you advise me to answer this people [πῶς ὑμεῖς βουλεύεσθε καὶ ἀποκριθῶ τῷ λαῷ τούτῳ λόγον]?'" (1 Kgs 12:6 ESV). Peter spoke of the need of being prepared to provide responses to unbelievers who inquire about the faith: "Always be prepared to give an answer [ἕτοιμοι ἀεὶ πρὸς ἀπολογίαν] to everyone who asks you to give the reason for the hope that you have. But do this with gentleness and respect" (1 Pet 3:15 NIV).

The ἑνὶ ἑκάστῳ, "to each one," refers to the unbelievers that the Colossian Christians would naturally encounter in their everyday lives. This would include family members in the extended household, neighbors, friends from the area, coworkers, people with whom they did business, and individuals whom they encountered in the marketplace, theater, bath, and civic institutions. For Paul, each of these interactions would represent a door that God could open to speak the mystery of the gospel. Paul's assumption is that the Colossian believers would be asked questions about their faith and their new community. The novelty of this new community of Christ-followers consisting of Jews and gentiles, slaves and slave owners, and rich and poor would have provoked many questions. One can imagine some of the array of questions people would ask, such as: Have you become a Jew? Who is Jesus? Why are you no longer worshiping Apollo (or Cybele, Artemis, Mēn, Zeus, or any of the other local deities)? Why did you destroy all of the *lares* (household gods) in your home? And many more. Meyer observes, "We may conceive reference to be made to questions as to points of faith and doctrine, as to moral principles, topics of constitution and organization, historical matters, and so forth, which, in the intercourse of Christians with non-Christians, might be put, sometimes innocently, sometimes maliciously (comp. 1 Pet. iii.1), to the former and require *answer*."[31]

The willingness of Christians to talk about their experience with God and the nature of their faith would set them apart from those who had been initiated into one of the local religions that had a mystery-initiation ritual. Typically, such people were not permitted to talk about their experiences with the uninitiated.[32] In his account of Lucius's initiation into the mystery ritual of Isis, Apuleius comments, "Perhaps, my zealous reader, you are eager to learn what was said

31 Meyer, 382.
32 Maisch, 263–64.

and done next. I would tell if it were permitted to tell; you would learn if it were permitted to hear. But both ears and tongue would incur equal guilt, the latter from its unholy talkativeness, the former from their unbridled curiosity" (Apuleius, *Metam.* 11.23).

## *Explanation*

This passage further advances Christology as the main theme of the letter. Paul's focus in this section is on appealing to the Colossians to make known the christologically rich message of the gospel to unbelievers. Just as he began the letter by celebrating the response of the Colossians to the gospel (they heard it [1:5] and put their faith in Christ [1:4]) and the progress it was making throughout the world (1:6), he here returns to the theme of the progress of the gospel. Paul's passion is for the Colossian believers to join him in praying for an open door for the gospel and for them to make it known in deed and in word to everyone they encounter.

For Paul, it is difficult to overestimate the importance of the gospel. It is the message of truth (1:5) that discloses the redemptive plan of the one living and true God. As such, it is "the mystery" that has been concealed for generations but is now being revealed (1:26). Paul himself has been commissioned by God as a *diakonos* to steward this great treasure (1:25). At the heart of this message is Jesus Christ (2:2) and how he is the centerpoint of God's plan of salvation for all who would put their faith in him (1:4, 23; 2:5). It is a message that must be preached to every person under heaven (1:23).

Paul calls the Colossians to devote themselves to pray about all manner of things, but especially for the progress of the gospel (4:2–4). Paul wants them to pray specifically for himself and his companions in Rome that an opportunity would present itself for them to share the gospel message despite the constraints and difficulty of their circumstances. Paul's example is an implicit instruction to the Colossians to pray the same things for themselves and for the communication of the gospel to have this necessary priority in their own lives.

Paul's second admonition to them is that they would conduct their lives in a way that would prove attractive to the nonbelievers around them (4:5). They do this through aligning their lives with biblical wisdom and the ethical teaching of Christ himself, who is himself the Wisdom of God.

And finally, Paul wants the Colossians to consider very carefully how they will reply to the questions that unbelieving acquaintainces will ask of them (4:6). When they do respond, they should formulate their response and deliver it in a way that is informative, interesting, and winsome. The time is short because the Lord could return at any moment. Therefore, Paul advises the Colossians to use their time wisely for the sake of the gospel.

# Personal Greetings and Instructions (4:7–18)

## *Bibliography*

**Aasgaard, R.** *Brothers and Sisters.* **Anderson, C. P.** "Epistle from Laodicea," 436–40. ———. "Hebrews," 258–66. **Arzt-Grabner, P.** "How to Deal with Onesimus," 113–42. **Balabanski, V.** "Where Is Philemon?," 131–50. **Blue, B.** "House Church," 119–222. **Cadwallader, A.** *Fragments.* **Campbell, C. R.** *Paul and Union with Christ.* **Cormack, J. M. R.** "Inscriptions from Aphrodisias," 16–29. **Corsten, T.** "Mann oder Frau," 215–19. **Frank, N.** *Kolosserbrief im Kontext.* **Gehring, R. W.** *House Church and Mission.* **Gielen, M.** "ἡ κατ᾽ οἶκον ἐκκλησία," 109–25. **Hofmann, J.** "Christliche Frauen," 283–308. **Humann, C.**, et al. *Alt. v. Hierapolis.* **Huttner, U.** *Early Christianity in the Lycus Valley.* **Klauck, H.-J.** *Ancient Letters.* **Ladd, G. E.** "Paul's Friends," 507–14. **Lampe, P.** "Keine 'Sklavenflucht,'" 135–37. **Leppä, O.** *Making of Colossians.* **Levine, L.** *Ancient Synagogue.* **Lohse, E.** "Die Mitarbeiter," 189–94. **MacDonald, M. Y.** "Can Nympha Rule This House?," 99–120. **Murphy-O'Connor, J.** "Greeters," 416–26. ———. *Paul.* ———. *Paul the Letter-Writer.* **Nordling, J.** "Onesimus Fugitivus," 97–119. ———. "Paul's Travels," 289–305. ———. "Runaway Slave Hypothesis," 85–121. **Ramsay, W. M.** *St. Paul the Traveler.* **Reynolds, J.**, and **R. Tannenbaum.** *Jews and God-Fearers at Aphrodisias.* **Richards, E. R.** *Letter Writing.* ———. *Secretary.* **Robert, L.**, and **J. Robert.** *Carie II.* **Schnabel, E. J.** *Early Christian Mission.* **Standhartinger, A.** "Pauline School," 572–93. **Stirewalt, M. L.** *Letter Writer.* **Stowers, S. K.** *Letter Writing.* **Taatz, I.** *Frühjudische Briefe.* **Thurston, B. B.** "Paul's Associates," 45–53. **Trainor, M.** *Epaphras.* **Weima, J. A. D.** *Neglected Endings.*

## *Translation*

*7 Tychicus will inform you about all the matters related to me. He is a beloved brother, a faithful*
*servant, and fellow slave in the Lord. 8 I sent him to you for this very purpose: that you might know the*
*matters related to us*[a] *and that he might encourage your hearts. 9 I sent him with Onesimus, the faithful*
*and beloved brother; he is one of you. They will inform you about the matters here.*[b] *10 Aristarchus, my*
*fellow prisoner, greets you; so also does Mark, the cousin of Barnabas. You have received instructions*
*about him: "if he comes to you, welcome him." 11 Jesus, who is called Justus [also greets you]. These*
*[three] are from the circumcision, who alone are my fellow workers for the kingdom of God. They have*
*been a comfort to me. 12 Epaphras greets you; he is one of you and a servant of Christ.*[c] *He is always*
*striving in prayer for you that you will stand*[d] *perfect and fully persuaded*[e] *in all the will of God.*
*13 For I testify about him that he experiences the toil of war*[f] *for you, those in Laodicea, and those in*
*Hierapolis. 14 Luke, the beloved physician, greets you, and so also does Demas. 15 Greet the brothers*
*in Laodicea and Nymphas and the church in his*[g] *house. 16 And when this letter is read among you,*
*make sure that it is also read in the church of the Laodiceans, and that you also read the letter from*
*Laodicea. 17 And tell Archippus: "give attention to the ministry that you received from the Lord that*
*you fulfill it." 18 This greeting is with my own hand—from Paul. Remember my chains. Grace be*
*with you.*[h]

## *Notes*

a. [4:8] The translation here reflects the form of the text that reads: γνῶτε . . . ἡμῶν ("that *you* might know the matters related to *us*"). This reading is supported by Codex Vaticanus (B), along with a number of majuscules (A D F G P 81), and some Old Latin and Syriac texts along with Theodoret and Jerome. It is the preferred reading of most modern language versions (e.g., ESV; NLT; NRSV; NASB; NIV). The Textus Receptus and Tischendorf, however, adopt the reading: γνῷ . . . ὑμῶν ("that *he* might know the matters related to *you*"). This reading is supported by 𝔓$^{46}$ along with some of the uncials (C K L Ψ), the Byzantine text, the Vulgate, some of the early versions (syr$^{p, h}$ cop$^{sa, bo}$), and many of the fathers (including Chrysostom and Ambrosiaster). It was the preferred translation of many of the earliest English translations (Tyndale; Geneva; KJV; Douay-Rheims). Bengel, 186, argued in favor of this reading by contending that an early scribe of Colossians was motivated to conform the original Colossian text (γνῷ . . . ὑμῶν) to the parallel text in Eph 6:22 (γνῶτε . . . ἡμῶν). There is merit to this argument, and considering the early papyrus support for this reading, along with most of the Western and Byzantine witnesses, a decision is much more difficult. Bruce, 176, regarded the external evidence as evenly balanced and suggested that the second reading was the more difficult reading and may be original. Nevertheless, the flow of thought in the context tilts the balance in support of the first reading. First, Paul already knows their circumstances, which has motivated him to write this letter to address the threat that "the philosophy" was presenting to the church. Second, if Ephesians and Colossians were written by the same author at the same time, one would expect Tychicus to carry out the same mission to both communities in terms of relaying information about Paul's well-being and the progress of the gospel in Rome. Third, as Lightfoot, 235, and others have observed, the singular statement "for this very purpose" (εἰς αὐτὸ τοῦτο) connects what Paul has just said previously ("Tychicus will inform you about all the matters related to me") with what follows ("that you might know the matters related to us"). The second reading would introduce a different purpose from the first.

b. [4:9] Codex Boernerianus (G) adds the present middle participle πραττόμενα after τὰ ὧδε. This is the Attic form of πράσσω and would be translated, "what has taken place here." The form never appears anywhere else in the NT or LXX, but it is frequent in Josephus. It is likely a scribal addition here and may have been an interpretive carry-over from the Latin text (so, Lohse, 172n16; Abbott, 299). This sense is already implied by the context without the presence of the verb and thus the author likely deemed it unnecessary. The ESV translates the implied sense, "they will tell you of everything *that has taken place* here."

c. [4:12] Some of the major witnesses are split on whether Ἰησοῦ should be omitted or included here. 𝔓$^{46}$ parts company with ℵ B on this reading and supports the omission, whereas the two major uncials include it. The assessment of the external evidence is muddied further, with the Western form of the text divided. Codex D along with some Old Latin and Vulgate manuscripts, together with Jerome, support the omission, whereas other Old Latin and Vulgate manuscripts, along with Augustine, attest the inclusion. The Majority text is firmly on the side of the omission. A decision based strictly on the weight of the external evidence would be difficult to make because the witnesses are so evenly divided. Since scribes tended to add to the text and because Χριστός Ἰησοῦς appears elsewhere in Colossians (see 1:1, 4; 2:6; see also Rom 1:1, which has Παῦλος δοῦλος Χριστοῦ Ἰησοῦ), which might suggest a motive to harmonize, the internal evidence tips the balance in favor of the shorter reading as original.

d. [4:12] Whereas the UBS$^{5}$ and NA$^{28}$ texts have the aorist passive subjunctive form (σταθῆτε), following 𝔓$^{46}$ ℵ B and other major witnesses,[1] the Majority text and a

---

1 The text of 𝔓$^{46}$ is fragmentary here, but the θ is visible, thus rendering σταθῆτε the likely reading.

few other witnesses have the aorist active subjunctive form (στῆτε). The difference in meaning is negligible. Because σταθῆτε never appears anywhere else in the NT, a scribe may have been tempted to alter the text, especially if the scribe was familiar with Eph 6:14 (στῆτε οὖν).

e. [4:12] Instead of πεπληροφορημένοι (א A B C D F G 33 81 104 365 1739 1881 2464), the Majority text, supported by 𝔓[46] and some other witnesses (K L P Ψ 075 0278 630 1175 sy), reads πεπληρωμένοι, "filled." Since Paul uses this precise form (πεπληρωμένοι, 2:10) earlier and uses the verb πληρόω throughout Colossians (1:9, 25; 4:17) and Ephesians (1:23; 3:19; 4:10; 5:18), there would have been a strong scribal motivation to conform to this usage.

f. [4:13] The manuscript tradition contains five different readings here, including πόνον ("labor" or "pain"), κόπον ("labor" or "distress"), πόθον ("longing" or "desire"), ζῆλον ("zeal" or "ardor"), and ἀγῶνα ("struggle"). The evidence strongly favors the first, πόνον, as original. It is supported by Sinaiticus (א), Vaticanus (B), and Alexandrinus (A), along with C P 0278, 81, and 1175. The text of 𝔓[46] is broken away here, so its testimony is lost. The term is a hapax legomenon in Paul and only appears three other times in the NT (Rev 16:10, 11; 21:4). This fact may have provided sufficient motivation for a scribe to align it with Paul's vocabulary.[2] This explanation does not account for πόθον, however, that never appears in the NT or LXX. But this term is so weakly attested (104, 1912) that it is not a serious contender. Some Western witnesses have κόπον (D F G 629), but this term was common in Paul, occuring eleven times. Because ζῆλον is supported by the Byzantine text (including the uncials K and L), it is the preferred translation of the KJV, Geneva, and NKJV. It does have the additional support of a few other witnesses, such as Ψ, 630, 1505, and the Syriac tradition. But it should be regarded as secondary since it is easier to explain a scribal change to ζῆλον than to πόνον.

g. [4:13] The textual witnesses are divided on which pronoun is the original reading here: should it be (1) αὐτῆς, "her house"; (2) αὐτοῦ, "his house"; or (3) αὐτῶν, "their house"? It is not possible to determine the answer to this on the basis of the form Νυμφαν, because accents were not present in the autograph or in most of the early manuscripts. The acute accent on the first syllable (Νύμφαν) would represent the feminine form, and the circumflex on the final syllable (Νυμφᾶν) would represent the masculine form (likely a contracted form of Νυμφοδωρος). The vast majority of commentators have argued that the best reading is αὐτῆς, "her house," a judgment that is made largely because of the support of Codex Vaticanus (B) and the contention that this reading best explains the origin of the others, assuming that scribes would have been more likely to alter the feminine to masculine to avoid the implication that a woman might be leading a house church.[3] But a further examination of the available evidence suggests that this conclusion rests on a rather weak basis, in part, corroborated by the fact that the UBS[5] gives it a "C" rating. A number of factors should incline interpreters toward a reconsideration of αὐτοῦ, "his house": (1) αὐτῆς rests on a thin foundation of manuscript support (B 0278 6 1739 1881). It also has the support of the Harklean Syriac and the Sahidic (Coptic) versions. But it does not claim the support of one full text type. It is only supported by a few Alexandrian witnesses, and that text type is split. (2) αὐτῶν has a slightly stronger basis of manuscript support with codices Sinaiticus and Alexandrinus,

2 So Foster, 432; Lightfoot, 240; and most commentaries that deal with this variant.

3 See, e.g., Huttner, *Early Christianity in the Lycus Valley*, 95–96; Thurston, "Paul's Associates," 52; Bormann, 196–97; Hübner, 120; Beale, 360–61, 365; Moo, 349; Harris, 181; Sumney, 266; Barth and Blanke, 485–86; Dunn, 274; Garland, 280; Metzger, *Textual Commentary*, 560; Lohse, 174; Scott, 92; Peake, 547; Williams, 167. This reading is reflected in the NA[28] and UBS[5] texts as well as in most of the modern English versions, such as the NIV, NRSV, ESV, NASB, NLT.

along with a few other manuscript witnesses (C P 075 33 81 104 326 1175 2464), together with the versional support of the Bohairic (Coptic) and the Slavonic. This reading is now supported by the THGNT and was the preferred reading of Tischendorf. It was also reflected in the ERV and ASV translations.[4] Yet the emergence of this reading could easily be explained by a scribe who assumed that the ἀδελφούς should properly be included in the referent of the pronoun; thus it was altered to the plural.[5] (3) There is a strong array of external evidence in support of the reading αὐτοῦ. Codex Claramontanus (D) along with a number of other majuscules (F G K L Ψ) and important minuscules (150 365 424 436 630 1505 1852 2200) representing all three textual families—Alexandrian, Western, and Byzantine—support this reading. It is also the reading represented in the Majority text as well as in the Palestinian Syriac. Both Chrysostom and Theodoret also affirm this reading in their commentaries. This reading thus has the broader diversity of witnesses supporting it, which gives it a slight advantage over the others in weighing the external evidence. (4) The name Nymphas, as a masculine name, is attested in the inscriptions of Asia Minor, thus lending to the plausibility that it could have been the name of a male residing in Hierapolis (or Laodicea). The following inscriptions represent a few instances of this name from a diversity of locations in Asia Minor:

- an inscription from Ephesus includes the name Νυμφᾶς Τυρρανίωνος in a list of male names[6];
- an inscription from Perge (Pampylia) mentions a certain [Ν]ụμφᾷ [τ]ῷ ṭατρί[7];
- an inscription from Prusa (Bithynia) includes Κλ(αύδιος) Νυμφᾶς in a list of male names[8];
- a burial inscription from Kibyra (Lycia) was erected as a memorial to Νυμφᾷ τῷ πατρί[9];
- Νυμφᾶν appears on a sarcophagus inscription from the necropolis of Seleucia on the Calycadnus (Cilicia).[10]

Thus, although the name Νυμφᾶς was not common, it was an attested masculine name in Asia Minor.[11] (5) Conversely, the female name Νύμφα or Νυμφη is not attested in the inscriptions of Asia Minor. There are numerous references to Nymphs (Νύμφαι; female goddesses) in these inscriptions, but no indisputable use of the term as a female name. (6) Although many interpreters have assumed an intentional scribal motive for theological reasons (i.e., it is unlikely that a woman would have led a church in her home), no one has considered the possibility that a scribe may have altered the text for a *grammatical* reason. It is conceivable that a scribe may have assumed that Νυμφαν was a female name because of the -αν suffix and thus altered the original masculine pronoun αὐτοῦ to the feminine pronoun αὐτῆς, to provide grammatical concord in gender. A scribe would have encountered many female names in the NT with an accusative

4 Few commentators supported this reading, however, with Lightfoot, 240, the most notable exception.

5 So also Peake, 547.

6 *IEph* 974a.2.

7 *IPerge* 392.2–3.

8 *IPrusaOlymp* 52.b.6.

9 *IKibyra* 293.3–4.

10 R. Heberdey and A. Wilhelm, *Reisen in Kilikien*, Denkschrift der Kaiserliches Akademie der Wissenschaften in Wien, Philosophisch-historische Klasse, Denkschriften 44.6 (Vienna: Carl Gerold's Sohn, 1896), 104 (no. 184.7).

11 Although Lightfoot, 242, was not aware of these inscriptions from Asia Minor when he wrote, he still regarded the name as masculine. He suggested it was the contracted form of Nymphodorus but thought it possible that it could be the shortened form of Nymphius, Nymphicus, Nymphidius, or Nymphodotus.

-αν suffix: Λυδίαν (Acts 16:40); Μαρίαν (Matt 1:20; Rom 16:6); Μάρθαν (John 11:5, 19); Πρίσκιλλαν (Acts 18:2) or Πρίσκαν (Rom 16:3; 2 Tim 4:19); Εὐοδίαν (Phil 4:2); Ἰουνίαν (Rom 16:7); Τρύφαιναν (Rom 16:12); Τρυφῶσαν (Rom 16:12); and Ἰουλίαν (Rom 16:15). In summary, a reassessment of the evidence for this textual problem suggests that the masculine pronoun has slightly stronger evidence in favor of it being the original reading in this passage. The text should thus read, "Nymphas and the church that is in his house."[12]

h. [4:15] The Majority text, along with the Western text, inserts ἀμήν, "amen," after the conclusion of the letter. This is a secondary intrusion into the text by a scribe for reasons of piety and possibly to harmonize with the closing of Galatians (6:18). The TR—Stephanus (1550)—also adds πρός Κολασσαεῖς ἐγράφη ἀπό Ῥώμης διά Τυχικοῦ καί Ὀνησίμου, "written to the Colossians from Rome through Tychicus and Onesimus." This is included in the early English Versions (Geneva; Bishops'; KJV). Tyndale has "sent from Rome by Tichicus and Onesimus."

## *Form/Structure/Setting*

### *Form (and Literary Context)*

There is a notable shift in this section from the imperative to the indicative as Paul begins to bring this letter to a conclusion. The second half of the letter began with a recapitulation of some of the key theological themes (3:1–4) that laid the foundation for the ethical teaching and admonitions of the next major section of the letter (3:5–4:6). Here he shifts the focus of the letter to information about the carriers of the letter, personal greetings, final instructions, and the letter closing. All of Paul's letters include these various elements in the closings, but they vary considerably in size and in how much each of the elements is developed (see Rom 16:1–23; 1 Cor 16:5–24; 2 Cor 13:11–14; Gal 6:11–18; Phil 4:21–32; 1 Thess 5:23–28; 2 Thess 3:16–18; Phlm 23–25). One thing Paul does not mention in this letter is his own plans for travel (cf. 1 Cor 16:5–9), but this is understandable given that he is in Roman custody and does not know if or when he would be released. The formal characteristics of this letter closing correspond with those of other letters from the Greco-Roman era.[13]

One way that this letter is distinct from other private papyrus letters from antiquity is the extensive personal comments at the end.[14] Paul mentions ten different people in this concluding section. This is somewhat surprising given the size of the letter and in comparison to his other letters. This number is only exceeded by those mentioned in the conclusion of Romans. He names the two

---

12 So also Corsten, "Mann oder Frau," 219. This was the understanding of many of the early English versions (KJV; Douay-Rheims; Geneva; Tyndale). See also Ellicott, 206; Eadie, 290; H. Moule, 143.

13 Weima, *Neglected Endings*, 154, concludes, "A comparison of the closing conventions in Paul's letters with those found in Hellenistic and Semitic letters reveals that the apostle was heavily indebted to the epistolary practices of his day. The influence of Greco-Roman letters is particularly evident in Paul's closing greetings and in his autographs."

14 Bormann, 189.

people who will carry the letter, six of his coworkers who extend greetings to the Colossians, and two individuals living in the Lycus Valley to whom Paul sends instructions. Seven of the ten names also appear in Philemon (only Tychicus, Jesus Justus, and Nymphas are missing), which has led some scholars to conclude that this points to a literary dependence upon the letter to Philemon.[15] But if the letters were written at the same time, from the same place, to people of the same area, and carried by the same people, one would expect a high degree of convergence. There are also no other literary features of this section that would suggest that the author of Colossians was simply copying this material; the author adds many of his own distinctive comments about each person.

This section presents a significant and often overlooked obstacle for the theory that Colossians is a pseudepigraphical letter. The extensive list of names and the personal information that is shared would have been unnecessary. It becomes very difficult for interpreters to provide a credible explanation for the kind of personal information that appears in this section. Unless the letter was written by a close associate of Paul's and under his guidance, such as a figure like Timothy, as Dunn supposes,[16] all of the names and the remarks about each person would be a literary fiction, with a deeper level of meaning lurking behind all of the comments. The most obvious possibility is that all of the names and personal comments appear in this section to disguise the pseudepigraphy and give Colossians the appearance of being a genuine personal letter so that it is received as authoritative.[17] But this would be an elaborate way of creating verisimilitude to an authentic letter, taking a substantial portion of the entire letter to do so. And the greater amount of specificity of detail that is shared heightens the possibility of detection.

But it is also the nature of the personal comments about each individual that amplifies the difficulty of the pseudepigraphical hypothesis. For instance, why would it be necessary to mention that Mark might be coming to visit them and that they should prepare for his arrival (4:10)? Why the addition of a person like Nymphas, who is named nowhere else in Paul's letters, and the request to greet the church in that home (4:15)? And why the urgent appeal to Archippus to fulfill his ministry (4:17)?[18] These and other personal comments seem pointless if the author is not Paul (or someone writing under his guidance). For some of the other

---

15 E.g., Lohse, 175–77; Standhartinger, "Pauline School," 574.

16 Dunn, 269–70. Lohse, "Mitarbeiter," 193–94, sees Colossians written soon after the apostle's death, and the various greetings and messages are intended to identify Paul's assistants as legitimate messengers of the gospel and to assure the Colossians that they have heard the correct apostolic message from which they should not be dissuaded.

17 See MacDonald, 185. Lincoln, 669, claims that some of the features of the ending "arise from the verisimilitude of a pseudepigraphical letter." So also Leppä, *Making of Colossians*, 208, who notes that the author of Colossians utilizes the style of Paul "to give an apostolic authorization to the letter," which is something he says is "typical to the whole conclusion of Colossians."

18 MacDonald, 184, recognizes this difficulty when she notes that "it is difficult to accept that the rather urgent instruction to Archippus in v. 17 represents pseudonymous fiction!"

personal comments, one might be able to identify a plausible motive—such as bolstering the authority of those who are mentioned (such at Tychicus, Epaphras, and even Onesimus) to enhance the effectiveness of their ministry in the Lycus Valley. But this is only possible if the letter was written in close proximity in time to Paul's active ministry; otherwise, these coworkers, too, would have passed off the scene. And one also needs to consider the rapidly changing situation for Christians after AD 64 and the burning of Rome. Extensive personal comments are also inconsistent with what we know about pseudepigraphical letters. The so-called Epistle to the Laodiceans contains none.

A comparison of the ending of Colossians with that of Ephesians reveals that one portion of their closings bears almost identical correspondence. In the comments regarding Tychicus (Col 4:7–8; Eph 6:21–22) there are thirty-two identical words found in the same sequence, with only three minor differences: the placement of one phrase (κατ' ἐμέ), the addition of "how I am doing" (τί πράσσω) in Ephesians, and the omission of "and fellow servant" (καὶ σύνδουλος) in Ephesians that describes Tychicus in Colossians. Although many scholars think that the Colossian version is original and that the author of Ephesians has appropriated this section,[19] this could also be regarded as the work of a common author writing at the same time about the same person.

### *Structure*

There are six distinct movements in the structure of this concluding division of the letter. Paul begins this new section by explaining that Tychicus and Onesimus will bring them information about Paul's personal circumstances as well as about the situation of believers in Rome (4:7–9). He frames this section with the double use of the verb γνωρίζω (4:7a, 9c), which begins and ends the section forming an *inclusio*. He says the most about Tychicus, who functions as the principal emissary from Paul and the letter carrier. It will come as a surprise for the Colossians to see Onesimus and to hear how he is described by Paul in the letter. They would no doubt be anxious to hear the entire story from the oral report.

In the second section, Paul passes on greetings from six ministry associates who are serving with him in Rome (4:10–14). Three of these individuals are Jewish-background believers (Aristarchus, Mark, and Jesus Justus), and the remaining three are presumably gentiles (Epaphras, Luke, and Demas). There are three main verbs in this section—all ἀσπάζεται (4:10, 12, 14). Paul elaborates the most on Epaphras, especially focusing on his extensive prayer ministry on behalf of the Colossians while he is separated from them (4:12–13).

The focus changes in the third section from passing on greetings to asking the Colossians to greet their fellow believers in Laodicea and possibly Hierapolis

19 E.g., Lincoln, *Ephesians*, 462; Schnackenburg, *Ephesians*, 286–87.

(if that is the location of Nymphas's house church) (4:15). The lead verb in this section, ἀσπάσασθε, represents the fourth consecutive occurrence of this verb.

In the fourth section, Paul asks the Colossians to make arrangements for an exchange of letters with the community of believers at Laodicea (4:16). He wants each community to hear the contents not only of the letter addressed to them but also what Paul wrote to the other group of believers. The fifth section represents instructions to the entire community to encourage one of their leaders, Archippus, to fulfill the ministry that the Lord had bestowed on him (4:17).

The final three lines represent the formal letter closing (4:18). This includes a signature by Paul himself, a request to remember him before the Lord during this time of custody, and a prayer for God's grace to be with the Colossian believers.

### *Setting*

As he writes this letter, Paul is in Roman custody and endeavoring to carry out his mission and ministry despite the constraints of his circumstances. There are at least eight ministry associates who are with him ministering to him and on behalf of him. The letter does not explicitly state that this group is in Rome, but that is the most likely scenario. Regardless, the letter says nothing about the state of the church in Rome at the time of writing. Neither is there any indication of an impending trial or when Paul might be released.

The mention of Onesimus as accompanying Tychicus to the Lycus Valley ties this letter closely to Philemon. As noted above, both letters name many of the same people, including Onesimus. The most plausible explanation is that Paul wrote both letters at roughly the same time and that the letter to Philemon was delivered by Tychicus as he conveyed the letter to the Colossians and a letter to the Laodicean church (which is now lost). The believers at Colossae likely knew Philemon and his family and were familiar with the situation involving Onesimus, as well as Philemon's probable frustration and anger toward his slave. The letter to the Colossians serves, in part, to rehabilitate Onesimus in their eyes and thereby reinforces the aim of the letter to Philemon. Paul publicly displays his trust in Onesimus as a sign of his changed life because of the impact of Christ upon him.

The letter also updates the Colossians on their leader, Epaphras, who is with Paul in Rome. Paul assures them of Epaphras's ongoing care and ministry to them through devoted and intense prayer for them.

Paul also uses the letter as an opportunity to reaffirm the leadership role of Archippus within the community. It is possible that Paul does so, in part, to counteract the influence of the charismatic and influential voices of the advocates of "the philosophy." Perhaps Archippus needed to be encouraged to assert a stronger leadership role, and simultaneously perhaps the Colossian congregation needed to give more attention to Archippus than to the rival teachers.

Finally, the letter also becomes an occasion for Paul to prepare the Colossians for the possible future arrival of Mark. If there was any question about receiving him because of their knowledge of Mark's past ministry failure and their loyalty to Paul, the apostle wants them to know that Mark has reemerged as a faithful coworker and they should, therefore, welcome him in the fullest sense. Perhaps Mark's story of rehabilitation and reconciliation with Paul would provide a helpful illustration of what could happen between Onesimus and Philemon.

## *Comment*

**7** Τὰ κατ᾽ ἐμὲ πάντα γνωρίσει ὑμῖν Τύχικος, "Tychicus will inform you about all the matters related to me." Although the Colossian believers had never met the apostle Paul, they certainly knew about him and likely felt a sense of spiritual indebtedness to him for his service on behalf of Christ. Knowing their concern about him and his circumstances, Paul has made arrangements for his associate Tychicus to personally fill them in on all that has happened.

The contents of 4:7–8 are nearly word for word with Eph 6:21–22. Thirty-two of its thirty-four words are repeated in Ephesians. The only words that do not appear are καὶ σύνδουλος, "and fellow servant," an additional descriptive phrase of Tychicus. Of the thirty-nine words in the Ephesians passage, only seven introductory words are added: ἵνα δὲ εἰδῆτε καὶ ὑμεῖς τὰ κατ᾽ ἐμέ, τί πράσσω, "now, so that you also might know my circumstances, how I am doing." The expression τὰ κατ᾽ ἐμέ is common to both passages. Although some interpreters have taken this repetition as an indication of the hand of a pseudepigraphical author of Ephesians freely copying from the Colossian text,[20] the correspondence could more easily be accounted for as a common author writing both texts at the same time and narrating his plans for communicating to them through this emissary.

τὰ κατ᾽ ἐμέ, "the matters related to me"—that is, "my circumstances," is an expression that Paul has used previously when he wrote to the Philippians. "I want you to know, brothers and sisters, that what has happened to me [τὰ κατ᾽ ἐμέ] has actually served to advance the gospel" (Phil 1:12 NIV). Josephus also uses the expression to describe communicating his own circumstances to a military commander ("when Sulla and his party were informed what happened to me [τὰ κατ᾽ ἐμέ]"; Josephus, *Life* 405). In assuring the Colossian believers that Tychicus will "inform" them about all that has happened, Paul uses γνωρίζω in the more generic sense of "to cause information to become known,"[21] in contrast to the more technical sense of revealing secret knowledge (see 1:27). The Colossians would have had been keenly interested in hearing about the status of Paul's appeal to the emperor, his health and well-being, how the churches in Rome were faring, the progress of the gospel in the principal city of the empire, and, in particular, how their own leader, Epaphras, was doing.

---

20 See, e.g., Lincoln, *Ephesians*, 462, and Schnackenburg, *Ephesians*, 286–87.

21 BDAG, s.v. γνωρίζω 1.

Paul sends his trusted coworker Tychicus with the three letters (Colossians, Philemon, and Ephesians) and to escort Onesimus back to Colossae, where he will presumably help to mediate the potentially volatile situation with Philemon. According to Luke, Tychicus was originally from Asia (Acts 20:4)—perhaps a convert during Paul's Ephesian ministry in the mid-50s. He was part of the group traveling with Paul through Macedonia and then on to Troas and Miletus after a short stay in Corinth when Paul was gathering a relief collection for the impoverished churches in Judea. Lightfoot suggested that Tychicus may have been "the brother who is famous among all the churches for his preaching of the Gospel" (2 Cor 8:18).[22] While this is possible, there are other coworkers of Paul to whom this flattering description could apply (such as Luke, Barnabas, Aristarchus, and Apollo).[23] Whether Tychicus left Ephesus with Paul after the mob scene in the theater with the adherents of the Artemis cult and accompanied him on his journey through Macedonia to Corinth, or met up with him later, is unknown. It is likely that Tychicus accompanied Paul all the way to Jerusalem since Paul was accused of taking his fellow Asian, Trophimus, into the temple precincts—an event leading to Paul's arrest (Acts 21:29). Both Tychicus and Trophimus may have been official delegates appointed by the Asian churches to present the relief offering to the churches in Judea (see 1 Cor 16:3–4).[24] What happened to Tychicus between this time and Paul's custody in Rome is uncertain since he never appears again in Luke's narrative. His presence here as a coworker of Paul in Rome and now as his emissary to Asia implies a journey to Rome at some point, whether in the company of Paul and Luke on the harrowing sea voyage or later on his own. Tychicus is mentioned twice in the Pastoral Epistles where he continues to function as a trusted emissary to Paul. Paul indicates his intent to send him to Crete to help Titus (Titus 3:12), and during his final imprisonment, Paul sends him back to Ephesus presumably to help the churches, but perhaps also to free up Timothy to come to Paul (2 Tim 4:12).

"Tychicus" is a well-attested name in the inscriptions of Asia Minor.[25] The origin of the name is associated with the goddess Tyche.[26] The name Lepidus Tychicus Heierapolitus is inscribed on a tomb in nearby Hierapolis.[27] It also appears on the famous God-fearers inscription in Aphrodisias.[28] In Ephesus, it appears on a burial inscription[29] and on a list of names of the members of an

22 Lightfoot, 234.

23 See Martin, *2 Corinthians*, 453–54.

24 So also Lightfoot, 233.

25 *NewDocs* 2:109 (§86) notes that "the great majority of this not very common name . . . come from Rome."

26 Cadwallader, *Fragments*, 68–69.

27 Humann et al., *Alt. v. Hierapolis*, no. 122: ἡ σορὸς καὶ ὁ περὶ αὐτὴν τόπος Λεπί[δ]ου Τυχικοῦ Εἱεραπολίτου.

28 Reynolds and Tannenbaum, *Jews and God-Fearers at Aphrodisias*, 5–7. The text of this inscription also appears in *NewDocs* 9:75, line 44 (§25).

29 *IEph* 2223.2.

athletic society.[30] The name is also on a list of delegates from Heraclea Salbacea who traveled to Claros to consult the Clarian Apollo.[31] It is also attested in a handful of inscriptions from Magnesia, Smyrna, Tralles, Saittai, Attouda, and Mysia.

ὁ ἀγαπητὸς ἀδελφὸς καὶ πιστὸς διάκονος καὶ σύνδουλος ἐν κυρίῳ, "he is a beloved brother, a faithful servant, and a fellow slave in the Lord." Paul publicly extols Tychicus with a series of three descriptive phrases that characterize his relationship to Paul and his service to the church. The endearing phrase, "beloved brother," expresses Tychicus's identity as a fellow member with Paul of the body of Christ, but also as one for whom Paul has a very fond affection. He uses the same phrase to describe Onesimus (4:9; Phlm 16), who is accompanying Tychicus. He also uses it to characterize Philemon (Phlm 1). Paul uses the plural, "beloved brothers," to describe believers in Corinth (1 Cor 15:58) and Philippi (Phil 4:1). James uses the expression three times in reference to his readers (Jas 1:16, 19; 2:5).

The second descriptive phrase, "faithful servant," characterizes Tychicus's sensitivity to the needs of Paul and the Christian community and his responsiveness to those needs. The adjective "faithful" (πιστός) depicts his reliability in service to others. Faithfulness is an attribute of God himself who fulfills what he promises and in whom his people can have full confidence (see, e.g., 1 Cor 10:13; 2 Cor 1:18; 1 Thess 5:24; 2 Thess 3:3). The only other person to be described as a "faithful servant" in Paul's letters is Epaphras (Col 1:7). He elsewhere characterizes Timothy as his "beloved and faithful child in the Lord" (1 Cor 4:17). He also commends all of the Colossian and Ephesian believers as "faithful" (Col 1:2; Eph 1:1). It is doubtful that Paul is using the term διάκονος here in a technical sense or as an office (as he does, for instance, in Phil 1:1). At most, he may be stressing one particular aspect of Tychicus's service to the apostle as his faithful agent or emissary and who is also performing the duties of courier.[32]

The final expression Paul uses to describe Tychicus is σύνδουλος, "fellow servant." This is a title he also uses of Epaphras (Col 1:7), but these are the only two occurrences of the term in Paul's letters. Given Paul's penchant to create compound words (such as συνεργός, "fellow worker," Col 4:11; also Rom 16:3, 9, 21; 1 Cor 3:9; 2 Cor 1:24; 8:23) and his frequent use of δοῦλος to describe the status and duty of believers in relationship to Christ (see, e.g., Rom 1:1; 6:16–20; 1 Cor 7:23; 2 Cor 4:5; Eph 6:6), this expression is consistent with his theology and style. This description of Tychicus would remind the Colossians of Paul's admonition to them, "Serve [δουλεύετε] the Lord Christ" (Col 3:24). Although "in the Lord" could go with the last phrase alone or the previous two phrases, it likely modifies all three.

**8** ὃν ἔπεμψα πρὸς ὑμᾶς εἰς αὐτὸ τοῦτο, ἵνα γνῶτε τὰ περὶ ἡμῶν καὶ παρακαλέσῃ

30 *IEph* 2498a.

31 Robert, *Carie II*, 209, no. 145.

32 See BDAG, s.v. διάκονος 1: "one who serves as an intermediary in a transaction, agent, intermediary, courier."

τὰς καρδίας ὑμῶν, "I sent him to you for this very purpose: that you might know the matters related to us and that he might encourage your hearts." The decision for Tychicus to make the long journey from Rome to the port of Ephesus and then on to the Lycus Valley rested with Paul himself. He chose to send Tychicus as his ambassador on this important mission, thus denying himself of the services that this trusted servant was providing for him. The aorist indicative verb would normally indicate an action that has already taken place, but it has not yet happened from Paul's vantage point as he writes this. It is a classic example of an epistolary aorist whereby the author writes from the perspective of the receipients as they read or hear the letter (see also 1 Cor 4:17; 2 Cor 9:3; Phil 2:28; Phlm 12).[33] Thus, instead of using the present tense ("I am sending him to you"), he uses the aorist indicative. Some versions do translate it with the English present, "I am sending him" (e.g., NIV; NAB).

The express purpose (εἰς αὐτὸ τοῦτο) for Paul's sending of Tychicus is to convey information about his own well-being and the details of his circumstances in Rome. The pronoun thus points forward to the next two clauses. Paul uses this combination elsewhere in his writings (see Rom 9:17; 13:6; 2 Cor 5:5). The first stated reason is that the Colossians might know Paul's circumstances. The expression τὰ περὶ ἡμῶν, "the matters related to us," is also used in the parallel passage (Eph 6:22) and in Acts 28:15 and is a variation of κατ' ἐμέ, "the matters related to me" (Col 4:7a), and τὰ ὧδε, "the matters here" (Col 4:9c). The second stated reason is so that Tychicus could encourage their hearts, or rather, that the news that Tychicus would relay to them would serve as a great encouragement.[34] This repeats what he has said earlier about wanting the Colossians to know how he is struggling on their behalf so "that their hearts may be encouraged" (ἵνα παρακληθῶσιν αἱ καρδίαι αὐτῶν, 2:2).

**9** σὺν Ὀνησίμῳ τῷ πιστῷ καὶ ἀγαπητῷ ἀδελφῷ, ὅς ἐστιν ἐξ ὑμῶν, "[I sent him] with Onesimus, the faithful and beloved brother; he is one of you." Onesimus will accompany Tychicus on the journey to the Lycus Valley. Together they will relate all the news surrounding Paul's Roman custody and presumably the progress of the gospel in Rome and the state of the church there.

The name Onesimus is frequent in the inscriptions of Asia Minor. It is also a common and widely attested slave name.[35] A person named Onesimus is listed as a civic official (βουλευτής) in the well-known God-fearers inscription found at nearby Aphrodisias.[36] In the same city, an inscription on a sarcophagus mentions

33 See the discussion of this grammatical structure in Porter, *Verbal Aspect*, 228–30, and BDF §334 (p. 172).

34 Pao, 311, overstates the significance of the verb παρακαλέω in this context, claiming that "it points to the comfort brought about by God's eschatological act of salvation (cf. Isa 40:1–2; 2 Cor 1:6)." The context points strictly to the sharing of news as the source of encouragement.

35 See the evidence in Arzt-Grabner, "Everyday Life in a Roman Town," 212.

36 *SEG* 36.970 (b.2.1, line 36). See Reynolds and Tannenbaum, *Jews and God-Fearers at Aphrodisias*, 5–7. The text of this inscription also appears in *NewDocs* 9:75 (§25) (see line 36).

a certain Polydeukes Kamissenos, son of Onesimus.[37] The name appears seven times in the inscriptions from Claros and numerous times in Ephesian inscriptions, as well as in many other inscriptions throughout Lydia, Caria, and Ionia. The Onesimus in Colossians is undoubedly the same individual who is the subject of Paul's letter to Philemon.[38] He was a slave who belonged to Philemon, had wronged him (Phlm 10), and was regarded by Philemon as "useless" (Phlm 11). Onesimus was now separated from Philemon (Phlm 15), although Paul does not specify how or why. There is much discussion about whether he is a fugitive slave (*fugitivus*) who happened to meet Paul[39] or simply a truant slave (*erro*) who has intentionally sought out Paul.[40] He has now become a Christian through Paul's influence and has been serving Paul during his imprisonment (Phlm 13). Paul now regards him as "useful," has developed a strong affection for him, and wants to keep Onesimus with him in Rome (Phlm 11–13). But a higher priority for Paul is for Onesimus to become reconciled with Philemon. Consequently, he sends him back to Colossae with Tychicus.[41]

The first thing that Paul says about Onesimus is that he is "faithful" (πιστός)—an opinion not likely shared by Philemon and possibly by many of the Colossian believers who were familiar with the situation. Yet Paul's reason for saying this is rooted in Onesimus's transformation by the gospel. Onesimus has been a faithful brother to Paul ever since his conversion. There is a further irony in Paul's use of the word πιστός to describe Onesimus because in papyri slave contracts from the Roman era, the term was used to guarantee that the slave was not a truant or a runaway.[42] He now holds Onesimus with the same regard that he holds Epaphras and Tychicus—as "faithful" (see Col 1:7; 4:7).

In Paul's view, Onesimus's identity has fundamentally changed. According to Philemon, Paul "gave birth" (ἐγέννησα) to him quite recently during Paul's incarceration (Phlm 10). He is now a ἀγαπητός ἀδελφός, "beloved brother." This is the same expression of endearment that Paul uses to refer to Tychicus (Col 4:7; Eph 6:21) and Philemon (Phlm 1). Paul also speaks of all believers within his local churches as "beloved brothers" (see 1 Cor 15:58; Phil 4:1).

Although it is possible to take "he is one of you" (ὅς ἐστιν ἐξ ὑμῶν) to refer to

---

37 Cormack, "Inscriptions from Aphrodisias," 27 (no. 41).

38 If Colossians is a pseudepigraphical letter, the information about Onesimus may be derived from literary dependence on Philemon (thus Frank, *Kolosserbrief im Kontext*, 347, 359–61). The content of this section of the letter is more easily explained, however, by understanding the letter as authentic.

39 This has been the common interpretation in most commentaries. See also Nordling, "Runaway Slave Hypothesis," 85–121, and idem, "Onesimus Fugitivus," 97–119.

40 See esp. Lampe, "Keine 'Sklavenflucht,'" 135–37. So also now Arzt-Grabner, "How to Deal with Onesimus," 133–34, who notes that "Paul's description of Onesimus' situation in Phlm 15 does not fit in with the *fugitivus* hypothesis" but also observes, "However, there is also no clear evidence that Onesimus, intentionally and directly, went to Paul to ask him for help."

41 See my more extensive discussion of Onesimus in the WBC volume on Philemon.

42 Arzt-Grabner, "How to Deal with Onesimus, 128–29, 140.

Onesimus's new status as a believer, it is better to understand it as a reference to the fact that he comes from Colossae and is a current member of the assembly of believers in that city.[43] Paul uses a similar expression later (ὁ ἐξ ὑμῶν, 4:12) to speak of Epaphras as one of them—that is, as a Colossian.[44]

Paul assures the Colossians that when Tychicus and Onesimus arrive, they will fully disclose all that is taking place in Rome. The repetition of the words that he used at the outset of this section—πάντα γνωρίσει ὑμῖν (4:7) and πάντα ὑμῖν γνωρίσουσιν (4:9)—form an *inclusio* that establishes the outer members of a simple A B A′ chiasm.[45] There are two key differences between these two parts: in the first, the emphasis is on Tychicus as the bearer of the information; in the latter, both will relate the news. Also, in the first, the focus is on news regarding Paul; in the latter, the scope is broadened to include all that is happening "here" in Rome. The Colossians would expect Tychicus to bring them an oral report of Paul's situation and all that is taking place in Rome. It may come as more of a shock to them for Onesimus to be involved in giving this report. Paul's directions regarding Onesimus's involvement in this report would underline Paul's trust in him as a new, reliable, and beloved brother[46] and would undoubtedly help the Colossians to view Onesimus in a new light. Of course, they would be anxious to hear the full story of Onesimus's conversion and his service on behalf of Paul and the gospel. The central member of the chiasm would be the two clauses introduced by ἵνα: "that you might know the matters related to us" and "that your hearts might be encouraged" (4:8b). There is no doubt that hearing of Onesimus's conversion and changed life would lift the spirits of the Colossians and showcase the transformative power of God. But they would also be encouraged by news of Paul's well-being, his ongoing work on behalf of the gospel, and the state of the church in Rome.

**10** ἀσπάζεται ὑμᾶς Ἀρίσταρχος ὁ συναιχμάλωτός μου, "Aristarchus, my fellow prisoner, greets you." Paul here begins a series of greetings to the Colossian Christians from his associates who are with him in Rome. He uses the common word for extending a greeting (ἀσπάζομαι) four times in the span of the next

---

43 See BDAG, s.v. ἐκ 3.b., "to denote origin as to family, race, city, people, district." So also Arzt-Grabner, "Everyday Life in a Roman Town," 213.

44 Balabanski, "Where Is Philemon?," 139, uses this clause as evidence that Philemon was not a resident of Colossae. She notes, "If Onesimus *had* lived most of his life in Philemon's household, and Philemon's household *was* located at Colossae, it would be redundant to reiterate this to the Colossians." But the logic does not hold since Epaphras is also described by Paul as ὁ ἐξ ὑμῶν (Col 4:12).

45 Beale, 354–55, regards this as "a classic chiasm."

46 Caution needs to be exercised about inferring too much from the fact that Paul does not characterize Onesimus as a "servant" or "fellow slave." Dunn, 273, for instance, makes much of this and says that "presumably Onesimus does not count as one of Paul's team of fellow workers; . . . he carries no responsibility in Paul's missionary and pastoral work." But it must be observed that Mark, Jesus Justus, Luke, and Demas are not given these descriptors either, and in Philemon Paul says that Onesimus has been serving (διακονέω) him (Phlm 13) and, since his conversion, has become "useful"—presumably for more than mundane domestic responsibilities.

six verses. Forwarding greetings from another person or a group of people by using the third-person indicative of the verb is well-attested in papyrus letters of the period.[47] This can be seen, for instance, in the conclusion of a letter from Antonius Maximus to his sister, Sabina: "my wife, Aufidia, greets [ἀσπάζεται] you and so does Maximus, my son."[48]

The first greeting is from a fellow Jewish believer, Aristarchus. Luke refers to Aristarchus as a Macedonian from Thessalonica (Acts 27:2). Whereas the inscipitional evidence demonstrates that the name was commonly used throughout the Mediterranean world, there is a particularly high concentration of occurrences in central Greece as well as in the Greek islands. The name is also attested in at least six inscriptions from Thessalonica. One of these, dated to 39/38 BC, refers to a certain Aristarchus, son of Aristarchus, who served as a politarch of the city.[49] A first-century AD burial inscription reads, "Here lies Aristarchus. He served as a politarch and was a sensible man."[50] The Aristarchus to whom Paul refers was likely a convert from the apostle's brief, but intensive, ministry in Thessalonica in AD 49. According to Luke, this Aristarchus was with Paul in the mid-50s during the abrupt ending of the apostle's ministry in Ephesus. The enraged adherents of the Ephesian Artemis dragged Aristarchus into the theater along with an associate named Gaius (Acts 19:29). The lives of all three were threatened until the "city clerk" quelled the mob (Acts 19:35 NIV). Aristarchus may have possibly accompanied Paul on his journey through Macedonia to Corinth and back, because Luke reports that he is with Paul and a group of additional associates accompanying Paul to Jerusalem with the relief offering collected for the Judean believers (Acts 20:4). It is uncertain, but possible, that Aristarchus was with Paul through the duration of his Caesarean imprisonment, because Luke indicates that he joined Paul at the outset of his voyage to Rome: "we put to sea, accompanied by Aristarchus, a Macedonian from Thessalonica" (Acts 27:2). Luke never mentions Aristarchus again, but he may have been with Paul (and Luke) during the entirety of this harrowing voyage and then during his first few months in Rome. Paul refers to him in Philemon, along with Mark and Luke, as with him during his Roman custody (Phlm 24).

When Paul speaks of Aristarchus as "my fellow prisoner" (ὁ συναιχμάλωτός μου), it is natural to read this as a literal imprisonment since Paul is in Roman custody and Aristarchus is a close associate who accompanied him from Caesarea to Rome. Some interpreters, however, have seen the expression as metaphorical—a prisoner of Christ like the captives in Christ's triumphal procession, who now spread the aroma of a knowledge of Christ everywhere (2 Cor 2:14).[51] The REB

---

47 Klauck, *Ancient Letters*, 24–25.

48 *BGU* II.632.16–18 (as cited in Klauck, *Ancient Letters*, 15).

49 *IG* X.2.1.109; see also *IG* X.2.1.50.

50 *SEG* 30.628.

51 See C. Moule, 136–37; Pao, 312.

interprets it this way and translates the expression, "Aristarchus, Christ's captive like myself." Because αἰχμάλωτος is often used to refer to a prisoner of war, Sumney also takes the expression as figurative here but with an emphasis on "Aristarchus's participation in the battle against the powers of evil" and "his more general willingness to stand for the faith in the midst of opposition."[52] While it is true that Paul can use the verbal form of this term (αἰχμαλωτίζω) in a metaphorical way (see Rom 7:23; 2 Cor 10:5; 2 Tim 3:6), the context of this passage would suggest that he is describing literal imprisonment.[53] Paul is writing from a context of imprisonment as he writes both Colossians (Col 4:18) and the closely related letter to Philemon (Phlm 1, 9, 10, 13). It would thus not be surprising for him to speak of one of his associates as similarly incarcerated—especially one that traveled with him from Caesarea.[54] It is also possible that Paul chose to use a word that was often used of taking a captive in war to describe their joint situation because he is thinking of the war itself in figurative terms—his struggle on behalf of the kingdom of God against the "dominion of darkness" (ἡ ἐξουσία τοῦ σκότους; Col 1:13). Thus, the imprisonment is real, but the struggle is spiritual. When Paul uses this term to describe Andronicus and Junia as his "fellow prisoners" (συναιχμαλώτους; Rom 16:7), here, too, it is best understood as a real imprisonment—not necessarily at the same time as Paul or in the same location, but as associates who had experienced prison on behalf of the gospel.[55]

καὶ Μᾶρκος ὁ ἀνεψιὸς Βαρναβᾶ, "so also does Mark, the cousin of Barnabas." A second close associate, Mark, also sends his greetings to the Colossians. Because of Paul specifying his relationship to Barnabas, we know that this is the same Mark that Luke speaks of in Acts. His given name was John, but he was also called Mark (Acts 12:12). He was one of the earliest believers from Jerusalem, whose mother, Mary, hosted a gathering of the church that the apostle Peter was familiar with and visited after his miraculous escape from prison (Acts 12:12). It is likely, then, that Mark knew Peter from those earliest days of the church. Mark accompanied Paul and Barnabas to assist them on their journey through Cyprus and into Pamphylia, but he left them and returned to Jerusalem (Acts 13:5, 13). Subsequently, he and his cousin, Barnabas, had a tension-filled split with Paul because of his earlier sudden departure, and Mark traveled with Barnabas to encourage the new believers in Cyprus (Acts 15:36–39). We do not hear about Mark until a decade or more later when he is with Paul during his Roman custody (Phlm 24). There is a substantial backstory here that evidently includes reconciliation with Paul. Mark apparently stays in Rome and reconnects with

---

52 Sumney, 270–71.

53 This is the view of the majority of commentators. See, e.g., Beale, 355–56; Foster, 420–21; Moo, 338; Dunn, 275–76.

54 Ramsay, *St. Paul the Traveler*, 316, suggested that Aristarchus and Luke may have accompanied Paul as his slaves "not merely performing the duties of slaves . . . but actually passing as slaves" and thereby shared Paul's captivity voluntarily. Although this is possible, it is highly speculative.

55 See Thielman, *Romans*, 719, and Fitzmyer, *Romans*, 739.

the apostle Peter (1 Pet 5:13). According to Eusebius (quoting Irenaeus), Mark became the disciple and interpreter of Peter and "handed down to us in writing the things which were preached by Peter."[56] Eusebius also reports the tradition that Mark was the first to travel to Egypt to evangelize and plant churches.[57]

Although it is clear that Mark has a close relationship with Barnabas based on Luke's narrative, this is the first time we hear that they were cousins. This is the only occurrence of the term ἀνεψιός in the NT (but see Num 36:11 LXX; Tob 7:2). Barnabas figures prominently in the first half of the book of Acts. He was a Levite from Cyprus who become a follower of Christ in the earliest days (Acts 4:36). His given name was Joseph, but the disciples called him Barnabas because of the way he provided encouragement to his fellow believers. Luke described him as "a good man, full of the Holy Spirit and of faith" (Acts 11:24). He was among the first to recognize the authenticity of Saul's conversion and courageously brought him to meet the apostles (Acts 9:27). He subsequently ministered together with Saul in the church at Antioch (Acts 11:22–26), traveled to Jerusalem with him bearing the first relief offering (11:30), traveled with Paul on his first journey through Cyprus and south Galatia (Acts 13–14), and accompanied Paul to Jerusalem to consult with the elders (Acts 15). The last we hear of him is when he takes Mark to visit and encourage the new believers on Cyprus (Acts 15:39).

περὶ οὗ ἐλάβετε ἐντολάς, ἐὰν ἔλθῃ πρὸς ὑμᾶς, δέξασθε αὐτόν, "you have received instructions about him: 'if he comes to you, welcome him.'" The Colossian believers had apparently received instructions from someone regarding a potential visit to the Lycus Valley by Mark. It is possible that these directives came from Paul himself—either (1) from some form of earlier communication that Paul had with them (written or oral through a messenger),[58] or (2) delivered orally from Paul through Tychicus and Onesimus and the verb is interpreted as an epistolary aorist. The difficulty with either of these views is that one would expect Paul to use the first person, "I gave/am giving you instructions." He used the first person ἔπεμψα, "I sent/am sending," just a few lines earlier (4:8). This has led some interpreters to speculate that someone else sent the instructions, such as Barnabas[59] or Peter.[60] Moule quipped, "There is no telling when or how these instructions had been conveyed,"[61] and this is how we need to leave the issue.

The statement represents Paul's confirmation of the previous instructions and holds out the very real possibility that Mark may journey to Colossae to visit them. The third-class condition (ἐάν with the subjunctive) is a true condition

56 Eusebius, *Hist. eccl.* 5.8 (LCL); see also 6.14.
57 Eusebius, *Hist. eccl.* 2.16.
58 Lightfoot, 238.
59 Moo, 340.
60 Pao, 313, thinks either are possible candidates.
61 C. Moule, 137.

and does not imply any certainty that he will come. Perhaps his visit depends on Paul's need of him and the outcome of Paul's trial or future ministry priorities. The imperative δέξασθε αὐτόν, "welcome him," entails more than a warm greeting. Paul wants the Colossians to open the doors of hospitality to him.[62] This would include providing him with lodging and food for the duration of the time that he is with them. In this instance, it likely includes receiving his teaching and the messages he brings.

Why it was necessary for Paul to repeat these instructions in his letter to the Colossians is an intriguing question. Most commentators have rightly assumed that word had spread among the churches about Mark's earlier defection in Pamphylia, the subsequent tension that had emerged between Paul and Mark (and Barnabas), and Paul's dim view of Mark's value in his apostolic work. If this kind of news had reached them (no doubt with accretions of additional personal opinions), Mark's arrival in Colossae would not be greeted enthusiastically.[63] To ensure a positive reception and to incline the Colossians to receive Mark's ministry to them, Paul includes this parenthetical comment to them. The fact that Paul refers to Mark as one of his "fellow workers" (συνεργοί) speaks volumes about the healing of the rift (Phlm 24). There is no further historical evidence about Mark traveling to Colossae and the Lycus Valley.

**11 καὶ Ἰησοῦς ὁ λεγόμενος Ἰοῦστος**, "Jesus, who is called Justus [also greets you]." A third Jewish believer serving as a ministry associate to Paul, Jesus Justus, extends his greetings to the Colossian church. The Hebrew equivalent for the name Jesus, *Yeshua* (יֵשׁוּעַ), was a shortened form of "Joshua," *Yehoshua* (יְהוֹשׁוּעַ), meaning "Yahweh is salvation (or help)." The name Ἰησοῦς, "Jesus," was common among Jewish men in the first century. Josephus names nineteen individuals who bear this name, and it appears on inscriptions and ossuaries in Judea.[64] In the NT, it is likely the first name of Barabbas, the Zealot, who was released by Pilate in place of Jesus (Matt 27:16–17).[65] The second name of Paul's associate, Ἰοῦστος, "Justus," is shared by two other individuals mentioned in the NT—Joseph called Barsabbas (also known as Justus) in Acts 1:23 and Titius Justus, a God-fearer in Corinth (Acts 18:7). This name was also common among Jews and proselytes.[66] It is also broadly attested in the inscriptional data from the Mediterranean world. For instance, a burial inscription at Rome addressed to the underworld gods names a certain Poplius Plotius Justus (Π[όπλιος] Πλώτιος

62 See BDAG, s.v. δέχομαι 3, "esp. of hospitality . . . welcome someone into one's house." See also G. Petzke, "δέχομαι," *EDNT* 1:292.

63 Others have suggested that the reason may lie in Mark's relationship to the law-observant party in Jerusalem; see, e.g., Williams, 162–63. But his association with Paul and the apostle's strong commendation would speak against this.

64 M. Silva, "Ἰησοῦς," *NIDNTTE* 2:527.

65 This depends on the variant reading supported by Codex Koridethi (Θ), some Caesarean witnesses (esp. *f*[1]), and some of the early versions.

66 See BDAG, s.v. Ἰοῦστος.

Ἰοῦστος),[67] and the name Titus Mebius Justus appears on one of the Claros inscriptions as a prophet (θεοπρόπος) of the god Apollo.[68] This is the only reference to Jesus Justus in the NT, and there is no additional historical information about him.

**οἱ ὄντες ἐκ περιτομῆς, οὗτοι μόνοι συνεργοὶ εἰς τὴν βασιλείαν τοῦ θεοῦ, οἵτινες ἐγενήθησάν μοι παρηγορία**, "these [three] are from the circumcision, who alone are my fellow workers for the kingdom of God. They have been a comfort to me." These are not the only Jewish Christians in Rome, but they are the only ones serving closely with Paul as coworkers in the unique circumstances of his custody as he endeavors to fulfill his divine commission. Paul has used the term περιτομή, "circumcision," earlier as an identity marker to characterize Jewish people and distinguish them from gentiles, the ἀκροβυστία, "uncircumcision" (3:11).[69] He is not using the term here as a reference to the Jewish law-observant party within the Christian movement (as in Gal 2:12, "the circumcision faction," NRSV).

The first clause, then, through the use of the article (οἱ), refers back to the three individuals he has just mentioned—Aristarchus, Mark, and Jesus Justus. One of the implications of asserting that these three are "from the circumcision"—that is, that they are ethnically Jewish believers—is that the remaining three members of his team who extend their greetings—Epaphras, Luke, and Demas—are gentile Christians. This is the key datum suggesting that the Gospel writer, Luke, if this is the same Luke who authored the third Gospel, is a gentile.

The UBS[5] and NA[28] texts add a comma after the conclusion of the first clause (οἱ ὄντες ἐκ περιτομῆς,) whereas the TR punctuates with a colon (οἱ ὄντες ἐκ περιτομῆς·). There is very little difference in meaning since the following clause, through use of the demonstrative pronoun (οὗτοι), continues the reference to the three individuals and predicates additional information about them. He calls all three of them his συνεργοί, "fellow workers." This is a common designation in Paul's writings for his close associates who partner with him in the work of the gospel. Among those he calls "fellow workers" are Priscilla and Aquila (Rom 16:3), Urbanus (Rom 16:9), Timothy (Rom 16:21; 1 Thess 3:2), Titus (2 Cor 8:23), Epaphroditus (Phil 2:25), and Philemon (Phlm 1). He calls Mark and Aristarchus his "fellow workers" again in Phlm 24 and adds to them Demas and Luke.

The most difficult part of interpreting this clause is his use of the term μόνοι, "only," to describe the three. What is clear is that Paul is not making an isolated statement to the effect that "only these three are my fellow workers for the kingdom of God," as if there were no other believers concerned with the proclamation of the kingdom. The immediately following context disproves this,

67 *IGUR* 2.898.1–2.

68 *SEG* 15.715.

69 See the commentary on 3:11 for a full set of remarks on this term.

as does the host of Christians passionate for the gospel in all of Paul's churches. Nevertheless, this ambiguity has led to three different views of how to understand this clause in light of the larger context. They can best be summarized as follows:

1. *The three men were the only Jewish Christians in Rome (or Ephesus) who were proclaiming the gospel.* Calvin appears to hold this view when he remarks, "He means, therefore, that there were few Jews at Rome who showed themselves to be helpers to the Gospel; rather the whole nation was opposed to Christ."[70] This represents a rather dim view of the state of Christianity among the Jewish population of Rome. The evidence suggests a large Jewish-Christian population in Rome by this time, especially in the Trastevere region. The very spread of Christianity in Rome suggests that at least some of the Jewish Christians were actively proclaiming the gospel, especially if Christianity got its start in the Jewish community. The most common way of interpreting Suetonius's statement, "Since the Jews constantly made disturbances at the instigation of Chrestus, he [Claudius] expelled them from Rome" (Suetonius, *Claud.* 25.4; LCL) is to understand it as referring to disputes in the Jewish community occasioned by the preaching of the gospel of Christ (Suetonius's *Chrestus*). It should also be pointed out that in Philippians (assuming it was written from Rome), Paul commends those who proclaim the gospel out of goodwill and love (Phil 1:15–16), which likely includes both Jewish and gentile believers. Based on the assumption that Paul was imprisoned in Ephesus, J. Murphy-O'Connor contends that "only these convert Jews are engaged in proclaiming the gospel. There may be other Jewish believers but these alone are active missionaries."[71] Apart from the dubious conclusion that Colossians was written during a hypothesized imprisonment in the praetorium of Ephesus, Murphy-O'Connor also makes the questionable claim that Aristarchus, Mark, and Jesus Justus were part of a delegation that came to Paul from Colossae. But there is no evidence of any association of these three with Colossae, and some of the details of the text become more difficult to explain, such as the instuctions to the Colossians to welcome Mark if he comes to them (Col 4:10c). One wonders why Paul would have left out Priscilla and Aquila from the list of ethnic Jewish believers who are faithfully proclaiming the gospel, since they were his coworkers in Ephesus (1 Cor 16:19).
2. *The three men were the only Jewish Christians who had remained faithful to Paul and were participating with him in proclaiming the gospel, especially to the gentiles.* This view emphasizes Paul's apostolic commission to be the apostle to

70 Calvin, 360.

71 Murphy-O'Connor, "Greeters," 422.

the gentiles and takes into account the difficulties that many Jews would have had in participating in this gentile-focused ministry.[72] Moo explains the passage in this way: "a reference to the comparatively few Jewish-Christians who are participating with Paul in gospel ministry would serve to remind his readers of the tensions that Paul's gentile-oriented ministry had created."[73] Dunn takes a similar approach: "the reference presumably is intended to assure the Colossians that there were such Jews, or at any rate other Jews apart from himself, who, as Jews, were fully approving of and cooperative in the Gentile mission ('fellow workers'), despite, presumably, the disapproval of most of their compatriots."[74] This, too, represents an overly negative portrayal of the state of Jewish Christianity in Rome. Undoubtedly there were many Jews who remained law-observant and suspicious of the gospel that Paul was preaching and how he was presenting it to the gentiles. But this view would assume that the letter he wrote to the Roman church a few years earlier explaining his understanding of the gospel left minimal to no impact.

3. *The three men were currently Paul's only Jewish-Christian coworkers in Rome at the time he is writing who are working directly with him in proclaiming the gospel.* Paul is thus not commenting on the state of Jewish Christianity in Rome, but only speaking about his immediate circle of associates. He is simply saying that of this circle, only three of them were ethnically Jewish. This view best explains the details of the passage and avoids the extremely negative implications about Jewish believers in the capital city of the empire where Christianity got its start in the Jewish community and has grown considerably despite imperial persecution. Beale advocates this position and notes that it "does not mean that other Jews were not coworkers with him but only that they [Aristarchus, Mark, and Jesus Justus] were the only Jewish Christians among the group *presently* residing with Paul . . . the only ones *gifted* as coworkers with Paul, who are ethnic Jews."[75]

The possible reason Paul made this statement may very well have had to do with Mark himself. If the Colossians harbored suspicions about Mark and entertained questions about his faithfulness to Paul and—even more importantly—to the

72 Wright, 157, advocates a variant of this overall view in which he interprets "the circumcision" (Col 4:11) to be "the circumcision party" of Acts 10:45; 11:2; and Gal 2:12. In other words, these three once belonged to the law-observant circumcision party, but now are convinced of the gospel as Paul proclaims it and freely participate with him in reaching gentiles.

73 Moo, 341.

74 Dunn, 278. See also McKnight, 390; Wilson, 301; MacDonald, 181; Sumney, 272. This appears to be the view of Lohse when he states, "Although many have deserted him, these three Jewish Christians have persevered with him and stand together with him in the same ministry" (Lohse, 172).

75 Beale, 357. See also Foster, 426; Bruce, 180.

work of the gospel, what Paul says here about him rehabilitates his reputation in their eyes. This is particularly important because Mark would apparently be visiting them shortly. Mark is among the very small circle of Jewish-background believers who are currently working with Paul for the kingdom of God. Mark is also one of the three who had provided profound encouragement to Paul during the almost insurmountable difficulties of carrying out his mission while in Roman custody. The μόνοι is thus not a reflection of Paul's melancholy over how few Jewish believers were faithful to him,[76] but a rhetorical way of establishing Mark as an important member of an elite group of coworkers.

As his co-laborers for the ἡ βασιλεία τοῦ θεοῦ, "the kingdom of God," Paul is emphasizing the present dimension of the kingdom and, in particular, the message of the redemptive work of Christ in delivering people from the domain of darkness and transferring them into "the kingdom of his beloved Son" (ἡ βασιλεία τοῦ υἱοῦ τῆς ἀγάπης αὐτοῦ; 1:13). This work is coextensive with the proclamation of the gospel (1:5–7, 23; see also Acts 28:31). As Jewish-background believers, their understanding of the kingdom of God would also naturally have extended to the future manifestation of the kingdom, as it does for Paul. But the emphasis here is on the proclamation of the inaugurated kingdom.

In the third clause of the series, Paul once again refers back to Aristarchus, Mark, and Jesus Justus, this time by using the masculine relative pronoun (οἵτινες), so that he can make one final remark—that they have been an encouragement to him. Although he normally uses the term παράκλησις to express this idea, here he uses the term παρηγορία, a hapax legomenon in Paul (and in the NT as a whole). The term does occur in Hellenistic-Jewish texts, however, appearing in 4 Maccabees, Josephus, and eleven times in Philo. Josephus uses it, for instance, to describe the remorse-filled hearts of the Israelites toward Moses: "They also repented of what they had said to him in the wilderness when they were angry; and were in grief on those accounts, insomuch that the whole body of the people fell into tears with such bitterness, that it was past the power of words to comfort [ἐκ λόγου παρηγορίας] them in their affliction" (Josephus, *Ant.* 4.195). But the term can also be found in a number of inscriptions from Asia Minor. It appears, for instance, on a first-century AD inscription from the city of Temenothyra in the Phrygian territory (north of Colossae). The inscription is an epitaph bemoaning the loss of a four and a half year-old child whose mother, Valeria, had been crying incessantly and sought comfort (παρηγορία) for her loss.[77] Paul's use of the term probably implies a deep level of comfort that the three of them have brought to him in the difficult circumstances he was facing.

**12** ἀσπάζεται ὑμᾶς Ἐπαφρᾶς ὁ ἐξ ὑμῶν, δοῦλος Χριστοῦ, "Epaphras, who is one of you, greets you. He is a servant of Christ Jesus." Epaphras is mentioned

76 See, e.g., McKnight, 390.

77 J. Chamonard and P. Legrand, "Inscriptions de Phrygie," *BCH* 17 (1893): 266–67.

first in the next group of three who extend their greetings to the Colossians. All three of these men are likely gentiles since Paul singled out the previous group as Jewish. Epaphras has already been mentioned earlier in the letter as the one from whom the Colossians had learned the gospel (1:7).[78] Like Onesimus, he is described as ὁ ἐξ ὑμῶν, "one of you"—that is, from Colossae. He is the only person mentioned in Colossians that Paul describes as a δοῦλος, "servant," but Paul uses the near equivalent expression σύνδουλος, "fellow servant," to characterize him earlier (1:7). He also describes Tychicus as a "fellow servant" (4:7).

πάντοτε ἀγωνιζόμενος ὑπὲρ ὑμῶν ἐν ταῖς προσευχαῖς, "he is always striving in prayer for you." Paul uses the attributive participle ἀγωνιζόμενος, "striving," to describe Epaphras's constant and passionate prayers on behalf of his fellow Colossian believers. Since Epaphras is one of them and is responsible for their initial grounding in the faith, he likely feels a strong sense of responsibility and care for their growth to maturity in Christ. Yet he is also aware of the threat they are facing from the influential advocates of "the philosophy." Unable to accompany Tychicus and Onesimus on their trip to Colossae because he is imprisoned with Paul (Phlm 23), Epaphras devotes himself to praying for them. Paul makes it clear that he is not merely uttering simple prayers of blessing and intercession but is "striving" with God in prayer. This term, as noted earlier (see on 1:29 and 2:1), would have been widely familiar to the Colossians because it is a metaphor based on the wrestling event held in all of the athletic games throughout the empire (see also 1 Cor 9:24–27).[79] The NIV captures the sense of the metaphor well in Col 1:29 where it translates it as "strenuously contend." Moule suggests that Paul may also have been alluding to Christ's "agony" (ἐν ἀγωνίᾳ) in the garden as he prayed earnestly just prior to his passion (Luke 22:44).[80] Trainor makes this connection as well and aptly notes, "Agonia is the holy one's wrestling with the forces of evil in what appears to be a final conflict of sorts. Something of this same sort of contest is found in the presentation of Epaphras."[81] The adverb πάντοτε, "always," and the plural προσευχαῖς, "prayers," stress that this was a daily—and probably multiple times throughout the day—occupation for Epaphras.

ἵνα σταθῆτε τέλειοι καὶ πεπληροφορημένοι ἐν παντὶ θελήματι τοῦ θεοῦ, "that you will stand perfect and fully persuaded in all the will of God." Epaphras prays earnestly for their spiritual maturity and their confidence in God's will. The verb that Paul uses here—the aorist of ἵστημι—is one that is used three times in Eph 6 to describe withstanding spiritual attack (Eph 6:11, 13, and 14). In that passage there is an overt emphasis on intense opposition by evil spiritual forces, but a simultaneous assurance that believers are able to draw on the

78 See the commentary at 1:7 for a full discussion.

79 See also Trainor, *Epaphras*, 83.

80 C. Moule, 138. So also Lightfoot, 239.

81 Trainor, *Epaphras*, 83.

power of God himself to resist their insidious efforts and to stand firm. Paul has emphasized the role of the hostile principalities and powers in the first two chapters of Colossians and has explicitly pointed to their ultimate involvement in inspiring the teaching of "the philosophy" that is now threatening the church (Col 2:8). He has also spoken of the divine resources available to them for this conflict by virtue of their union to the exalted Lord Jesus Christ (2:9–10). It is quite possible that Paul has chosen the passive form of the verb here (σταθῆτε) as a way of "suggesting divine enabling."[82]

Epaphras is praying that the Colossians would stand τέλειοι, "perfect" (KJV; NASB) or "mature" (CEB; NIV; ESV; NRSV). Paul has earlier expressed that the goal of his entire ministry is to "present everyone mature [τέλειον] in Christ" (1:28).[83] Epaphras shares that goal and ministers to the Colossians in the only way that he can—by calling on God to strengthen them for this struggle—hindered as he is by the constraints of his own experience of Roman custody. The "maturity" he prays for could be summed up well in how Paul himself reports how he is regularly praying for them: that they "walk in a manner worthy of the Lord, fully pleasing to him: bearing fruit in every good work and increasing in the knowledge of God" (1:10). A more complete and accurate knowledge of God and his will would entail rejecting the teaching and practices of "the philosophy."

Epaphras is also praying that their confidence would grow significantly in God and his revealed will. Most English versions translate the verb πληροφορέω here as "fully assured" (e.g., ESV; NIV; NASB; CSB; NAB; NRSV; RSV). This assurance comes from being "fully convinced"[84] (GNB), or as Lightfoot aptly renders it, "fully persuaded," of something.[85] The early English versions depended on a textual variant here that had πεπληρωμένοι in place of πεπληροφορημένοι. Thus, the Geneva Bible has "full in all the will of God" (see also Douay-Rheims), and the Authorized Version offers "complete in all the will of God" (see also NKJV). This reading, however, does not have the strongest support (see the *Notes* above). Other interpreters have suggested that πληροφορέω is a synonym of πληρόω and "here takes the place of the more frequently used verb 'to be filled.'"[86] But the usage of πληροφορέω supports the idea of being fully convinced of something. The LXX of Eccl 8:11 says that when a sentence for a crime is not executed quickly, "on account of this the heart of humans was fully convinced [ἐπληροφορήθη] in them to do evil" (NETS). Paul uses the verb twice earlier in his letter to the Romans. He speaks of Abraham being "fully persuaded [πληροφορηθείς] that God had power to do what he had

82 Dunn, 280.

83 See the commentary on 1:28 for a full discussion of this term.

84 See Sumney, 274–75, and C. Moule, 138.

85 Lightfoot, 240. BDAG, s.v. πληροφορέω, suggests the translation, "be fully assured," under the second usage, "2. convince fully."

86 Lohse, 173; see also Hübner, 120.

promised" (Rom 4:21 NIV). When he discusses the matter of Roman Christians considering one day better than another, he advises, "Each one should be fully convinced [πληροφορείσθω] in his own mind" (Rom 14:5 ESV). What this verb means in this context is that the Colossians would become fully persuaded of the Pauline gospel as they have been taught it through Epaphras and that this would result in an increased confidence in what the will of God is for their lives.

Epaphras's strenuous prayers for the Colossians to become fully persuaded of God's will corresponds with how Paul himself is praying for them. At the outset of the letter Paul told them, "For this reason we have also not stopped praying and interceding for you from the day we heard. [We pray] that you may be filled with the knowledge of his will [τοῦ θελήματος αὐτου] with a full measure of wisdom and insight that comes from the Spirit" (1:9). The first-person plural makes it likely that Epaphras was laboring together with Paul on behalf of the Colossians. Here the emphasis goes beyond knowing God's will to becoming fully convinced of and fully assured of what it is. At the heart of knowing God's will is apprehending his plan of salvation fulfilled in the work of Christ and in grasping the full implications of what it means to live in union with Christ. He declares earlier, "to them God has chosen [ἠθέλησεν] to make known among the gentiles the glorious riches of this mystery, which is Christ in you, the hope of glory" (1:27). Epaphras is convinced that if the Colossians could grow in their understanding of Christ and all that is entailed by living their lives in union with him, the allure of "the philosophy" would grow dim, and they would move forward to maturity in him.

**13** μαρτυρῶ γὰρ αὐτῷ ὅτι ἔχει πολὺν πόνον ὑπὲρ ὑμῶν καὶ τῶν ἐν Λαοδικείᾳ καὶ τῶν ἐν Ἱεραπόλει, "for I testify about him that he experiences the toil of war for you, those in Laodicea, and those in Hierapolis." Paul vouches for Epaphras that he is engaging in extensive warfare by praying for all of the Christians in the Lycus Valley. The conjunction γάρ, "for," provides further evidence for Paul's claim that Epaphras is always "struggling" (ἀγωνιζόμενος) for the readers in prayer (4:12).[87] The verb μαρτυρῶ, "I testify," adds a note of seriousness or solemnity to the remarks that Paul is making about Epaphras. It most commonly means "to confirm or attest something on the basis of personal knowledge or belief."[88] It often bears even a legal or forensic significance.[89] This language is a rhetorical way of stressing the importance of what he is about to say regarding Epaphras. The αὐτῷ should not be interpreted as a dative of indirect object, "I bear witness *to him*," but as a dative of reference, "*about him*."[90]

Most of the English versions have interpreted πόνος as "work" or "labor." Thus, some versions translate it, "he has worked hard for you" (CEB; ESV;

---

87 Contra Moo, 345, who sees it functioning simply to add a further thought.

88 BDAG, s.v. μαρτυρέω 1.

89 J. Beutler, "μαρτυρέω," *EDNT* 2:389.

90 So also Campbell, 75.

NRSV; RSV; NET) or "he is working/works hard for you" (CSB; NJB; NAB). The term can refer to hard labor and toil, but it is also used of "the experience of great trouble" and can be translated with "pain," "distress," or "affliction."[91] It is a hapax legomenon in Paul and occurs only three other times in the NT (Rev 16:10, 11; 21:4). It does occur frequently in the wisdom literature where it refers to hard work. Wisdom 3:15, for instance, states, "for the fruit of good labors [πόνων] is renowned" (NRSV; see also Wis 5:1; 8:7, 18; 9:16; 10:10; 15:4; Sir 11:21; 14:15; 28:15). But the same literature also uses it to refer to "troubles": "Wisdom rescued from troubles [ἐκ πόνων] those who served her" (Wis 10:9 NRSV; see also Wis 19:16; Sir 3:27; 31:20). Paul could easily have adopted this terminology from the wisdom literature, but it is somewhat surprising that he did not draw from his common stock of terminology for hard work, such as ἔργον, κόπος, or μόχθος, which leads one to wonder if he may be implying a slightly different nuance than simply "hard work."

The answer to the question of why Paul chose this unique word may lie in the fact that Paul has selected a term that has overtones of "the toil of war" and "the toil of battle," especially for his Greek readers.[92] In Homer, when the word appears alone it is the equivalent of μάχη, "battle," as in these two passages: "Zeus drew destructive darkness over the mighty combat so that around his dear son might be waged the destructive toil of war [μάχης ὀλοὸς πόνος εἴη]" (Homer, *Il.* 16.567–68 LCL), and "swift-footed noble Achilles looked on and caught sight of him, for he was standing on the stern of his ship, huge of hull, gazing on the utter toil of battle [πόνον] and the tearful rout" (*Il.* 11.599–601; see also *Il.* 2.420; 16.651; 17.82; 21.524–25; 22.11; *Od.* 12.117). The combination πόνον ἔχειν appears nowhere in the LXX or even in Philo or Josephus, but it is common in Homer's account of the Trojan War. LSJ reports that this combination is used in Homer as an equivalent of the term μάχεσθαι, "to wage war" (see Homer, *Il.* 6.77; 13:2; 15.416).[93] Especially striking is a passage in the *Iliad* that uses πολὺν πόνον ἔχειν—the precise combination that we have in Colossians—of warfare. In this text, Homer describes the grievous toil of war that the Trojans were experiencing (οἳ ἔχουσι πολὺν πόνον) (Homer, *Il.* 6.525).

Because of the sheer frequency of the term πόνος throughout Homer to describe the pain and toil of war, this language may very well have continued in the oral history of retelling the Trojan War at a popular level. Paul may have chosen this word to convey the fact that Epaphras was laboring in the work of spiritual battle for the Colossians through prayer. He thereby underlines the spiritual nature of the struggle they are facing in Colossae and that the controversy with the advocates of "the philosophy" was not a trifling matter but

91 BDAG, s.v. πόνος.

92 See LSJ, s.v. πόνος 1.

93 LSJ, s.v. πόνος 1.

should be taken with the utmost seriousness. If the ultimate inspiration for "the philosophy" is the demonic spirits of the world (τὰ στοιχεῖα τοῦ κόσμου, 2:8), then Epaphras is battling them on the spiritual level through prayer.

Epaphras is engaging in this deep level of intercession not only for the Colossians but also for believers in Laodicea and Hierapolis.[94] This implies that he is well familiar with the churches and believers in these nearby cities. It also may suggest the likelihood that he was responsible for planting these churches and now exercises a pastoral duty over them. But one troubling implication of this passage is the very real possibility that the churches in Laodicea and Hierapolis are in danger of succumbing to the same threat that is facing the Colossian church through the factional teachers.

**14** ἀσπάζεται ὑμᾶς Λουκᾶς ὁ ἰατρὸς ὁ ἀγαπητὸς καὶ Δημᾶς, "Luke, the beloved physician, greets you, and so also does Demas." Together with Epaphras, these three represent Paul's gentile associates during this period of his confinement in Roman custody. They all convey their greetings to the Colossians.

Luke is mentioned by name at only two other places in the NT. He is listed with Mark, Aristarchus, and Demas as Paul's "fellow workers" (συνεργοί) in Philemon (24). He is also mentioned in 2 Tim 4:11 with reference to Paul's final imprisonment where he laments, "Luke alone is with me." The latter passage illustrates Luke's faithfulness to Paul in a very difficult time after a long road of ministry together. Although Luke is never named in the third Gospel or Acts, ancient historians are united in their testimony that he was the author of both works—amounting to roughly 25 percent of the NT. The earliest evidence supporting his authorship comes from a second-century papyrus ($\mathfrak{P}^{75}$) that includes the subscript, "the Gospel according to Luke" at the end of the scroll. One of the most important early testimonies about Luke comes from Irenaeus: "Luke also, the companion of Paul, recorded in a book the Gospel preached by him" (Irenaeus, *Haer.* 3.1.1). He later writes, "But that this Luke was inseparable from Paul, and his fellow-labourer in the Gospel, he himself clearly evinces, not as a matter of boasting, but as bound to do so by the truth itself" (Irenaeus, *Haer.* 3.14.1). Irenaeus also regarded Luke as referring to himself in the so-called "we" sections in the book of Acts: "as Luke was present at all these occurrences, he carefully noted them down in writing, so that he cannot be convicted of falsehood or boastfulness" (Irenaeus, *Haer.* 3.14.1). Another important ancient source, a second-century prologue to the Gospel of Luke, gives additional historical information: "Luke was a Syrian of Antioch, by profession a physician, the disciple of the apostles, and later a follower of Paul until his martyrdom. He served the Lord without distraction, without a wife, and without children. He died at the age of eighty-four in Boeotia [a region in central Greece], full

94 See the introductory essay on Colossae, Laodicea, and Hierapolis for additional information about these cities.

of the Holy Spirit."[95] Eusebius and Jerome contain similar historical traditions about Luke.[96]

If Luke was the author of the "we" sections of Acts,[97] it would provide evidence that he was with Paul beginning in the late 40s during the apostle's second journey beginning at Troas, accompanying him on his voyage to Samothrace and Neapolis and working with him to establish the church at Philippi (Acts 16:10–17). He then rejoined Paul in the mid-50s at Philippi after the apostle's Ephesian ministry and sailed with him to Troas, Miletus, and on to Jerusalem (Acts 20:5–21:18). He then appears to have stayed with Paul during his custody in Caesarea Maritima and then accompanied him on his harrowing voyage to Rome (Acts 27:1–28:16). If Colossians were written during this Roman imprisonment, Luke has remained with Paul and is serving in the cause of the gospel. How Luke became acquainted with the Colossian church is unknown.

Paul describes him here as ὁ ἰατρὸς ὁ ἀγαπητός, "the beloved physician." This is the only place in the NT where Luke is described as a physician and is the source of that well-known tradition. It must be remembered that in the Roman era and earlier, there was no distinction between healing and spirituality. Healing was often integrated with the worship of the gods, as is well-illustrated in the cult of Asclepius. If Luke received his medical training prior to becoming a follower of Christ, he would have had to thoroughly rethink his healing practices in light of the exclusivity of Christ and the need to renounce idolatry. Surely Luke would have used his training and expertise to treat Paul's health needs as well as those of his other ministry associates.

Little is known about Demas. It is possible that his name is a shortened form of Δημήτριος.[98] The name Δημᾶς does appear a few times in the inscriptions of Asia Minor.[99] He is mentioned in the same three NT passages as Luke, but tragically 2 Tim 4:10 says that "Demas, in love with this present world, has deserted me and gone to Thessalonica" (ESV). Because of this, Gnilka asserts that "Demas is probably Macedonian,"[100] which is a possibility, but is certainly speculative. We know nothing more of Demas in subsequent early-church testimony.

---

95 This is also known as an "Anti-Marcionite prologue." Cited from Fitzmyer, *Luke*, 1:38.

96 Eusebius, *Hist. eccl.* 3.4; Jerome, *Vir. ill.* 7. It should be noted that Calvin, 361, commented, "I do not agree with those who understand this as Luke the Evangelist . . . this is another who is called a physician, to distinguish him from the Evangelist."

97 Gnilka, 242, and many others, would contend that the "we" sections are a literary device and should not be understood as a self-reference. This is complicated further by the fact that the authorship of the book of Acts is disputed.

98 See BDF §125 (pp. 67–68); BDAG, s.v. Δημᾶς.

99 For instance, a certain Aurelius Demas is mentioned as a local magistrate in an inscription from Magnesia (*IMagn.* 197.9–10). In a Phrygian inscription, a man named Demas makes a vow (εὐχή) to Hosios and Dikaios (*MAMA* 5.KB.9.1–6). See also the discussion of the name in *NewDocs* 1:88–89 (§51).

100 Gnilka, 241.

**15** Ἀσπάσασθε τοὺς ἐν Λαοδικείᾳ ἀδελφοὺς καὶ Νύμφαν καὶ τὴν κατ' οἶκον αὐτοῦ ἐκκλησίαν, "greet the brothers in Laodicea and Nymphas and the church in his house." Paul adds one final set of greetings as he brings his letter to a close. He asks the believers at Colossae to greet their fellow Christians at Laodicea. If Paul is asking them to greet the Laodiceans on his behalf, this request appears rather odd since he would have greeted them himself in the letter that he wrote to the Laodiceans (see 4:16).[101] But this is probably not a request from Paul to greet them on his behalf; it more likely refers to Paul's intent "to encourage fellowship between believers in Colossae and Laodicea"[102] and "to express their affection and concern to the Laodiceans."[103] Because of the looming threat of "the philosophy," Paul wants the Christians of the Lycus Valley to communicate with one another and stand united.

In addition to the Laodicean believers, he includes Nymphas and the church in *his* house in this sphere of fellowship. There is a difficult text-critical question here, with some manuscripts attesting the reading, "Nympha and the church in *her* house," and yet others that have "Nymphas (or Nympha) and the church in *their* house." See the extensive discussion of this issue in the *Notes*, where it was concluded that the evidence tips in favor of the masculine singular pronoun and the name, Nymphas.

The expression τὴν κατ' οἶκον ἐκκλησίαν, "the church in the house," points to the fact that there were no dedicated church structures in the earliest history of the church. Private homes were the principal gathering places.[104] Paul uses this expression elsewhere to refer to the home groups hosted by Prisca and Aquila, first at Ephesus (τῇ κατ' οἶκον αὐτῶν ἐκκλησίᾳ; 1 Cor 16:19) and then at Rome (κατ' οἶκον αὐτῶν ἐκκλησίαν; Rom 16:5), and the church at the home of Philemon (τῇ κατ' οἶκόν σου ἐκκλησίᾳ; Phlm 2). The preposition κατά here serves as "a marker of spatial aspect"[105] or "place"[106] and in this context may be translated with "in." This use of κατά evokes the description of the church at Jerusalem in its earliest days when the followers of Jesus were breaking bread in their homes (Acts 2:46; κατ' οἶκον) and were meeting in the temple and in houses (Acts 5:42; κατ' οἶκον). One of the houses where the Jerusalem believers met in those days was the home of Mary (Acts 12:12), the mother of Mark, one of Paul's associates at Rome (Col 4:10). It was natural for the church to meet in homes, following the pattern of some diaspora synagogue gatherings that met in a single room of a

101 Lightfoot, 243, senses this problem and suggests that Paul's greetings are for "a family of Colossian Christians established in Laodicea."

102 Moo, 349.

103 Beale, 360.

104 Blue, "House Church," 120, notes that "the gathering of Christian believers in private homes (or homes renovated for the purpose of Christian gatherings) continued to be the norm until the early decades of the fourth century when Constantine began erecting the first Christian basilicas."

105 BDAG, s.v. κατά B.1.c.

106 W. Trilling, "κατά," *EDNT* 2:253 (sec. 3.a).

private home.[107] The size of the gathering in the house church would have been determined by what the structure could accommodate. No doubt this varied greatly depending on the particular home. The largest room of a Roman-style atrium house could accommodate as many as thirty or forty people.[108]

It is unlikely that Nymphas and his house church were in Laodicea since his group would have been included in the mention of the "brothers (and sisters) in Laodicea" (Col 4:15a). The most natural explanation would be to assume that this house church was located somewhere other than Laodicea but within close proximity.[109] Since Paul has already mentioned that Epaphras has worked hard not only for the Colossian and Laodicean believers but also for those in Hierapolis (4:13), it is possible that the house church that Nymphas hosts in his home is located in Hierapolis.[110] This would also explain why Hierapolis is not explicitly mentioned in this call to mutual greetings and fellowship.

The text makes no additional comments about the role that Nymphas plays in the house church other than functioning as its host and, by extension, serving as a benefactor (εὐεργέτης or προστάτις) of the community. Whether Nymphas held some form of leadership in the assembly should remain an open question.[111]

**16** καὶ ὅταν ἀναγνωσθῇ παρ' ὑμῖν ἡ ἐπιστολή, ποιήσατε ἵνα καὶ ἐν τῇ Λαοδικέων ἐκκλησίᾳ ἀναγνωσθῇ, "and when this letter is read among you, make sure that it is also read in the church of the Laodiceans." As Paul reaches the conclusion of the letter, he asks for an exchange of letters between the Colossian and Laodicean believers. He has apparently written two letters that Tychicus and Onesimus would deliver to the Lycus Valley—one to the Colossians and one to the Laodiceans—and he wants both groups of believers to be familiar with what he has written to the other.

Paul terms his communication to the Colossians an ἐπιστολή, "letter." This was the common word for all written personal communication. Papyrus was the typical medium for such letters. Paul himself uses the term sixteen other times in his correspondence and only twice in a metaphorical sense (2 Cor 3:2–3). The authority of the correspondence depends on the specific context of the letter—that is, who wrote the letter and the purpose of the communication. In this instance, Paul is writing as an apostle of Christ Jesus (Col 1:1) and as a servant (διάκονος) of God bestowed with a divine commision (οἰκονομία) "that was given to me for you" (1:25). What he has to say should bear significant weight for their

107 Levine, *Ancient Synagogue*, 185.

108 Schnabel, *Early Christian Mission*, 2:1303–4.

109 Others, such as Barth and Blanke, 486, have assumed that Paul is addressing Nympha and the community in her house "in a special way for some reason which is not known to us," or that the καί is epexegetical and should be translated "and specifically." In either case, the reason for singling out this one house church is lost to us.

110 Gnilka, 244, also locates this house church in Hierapolis.

111 Many commentators assume that the person named here assumed a leadership role. Maisch, 270, for instance, claims that Nympha had an "outstanding position" in the church and functioned as a "Hausherrn (paterfamilias)."

community. When Paul wrote to the Thessalonians, he actually put them under oath before the Lord to have that letter read (ἀναγνωσθῆναι τὴν ἐπιστολήν) to all the members of the community (1 Thess 5:27).

"When this letter is read" assumes that it will be read aloud on an occasion when the entire community is gathered together.[112] This public reading of the letter is further suggested by the fact that only one copy of the letter would have been available to them and that many in the community would not have had the literary skills to read for themselves. The prepositional phrase παρ' ὑμῖν is commonly translated "among you" (so CSB; NASB; ESV; RSV; NJB; KJV; NKJV), which is the best way to understand it in this context (see also Matt 22:25; John 4:40; Rev 2:13).[113]

The combination ποιήσατε ἵνα should be understood as causative and could be rendered, "to cause, effect" something[114] This usage can be seen in John 11:37 where some of the bystanders after the death of Lazarus wonder aloud if Jesus could have prevented him from dying (ποιῆσαι ἵνα καὶ οὗτος μὴ ἀποθάνῃ;). Here the expression means to "cause something to happen" or to "arrange for something to take place." In this instance, Paul's desire is for the Colossians to make all the necessary arrangements for the letter to be taken to the assembled group of believers in Laodicea so that it might be read to them. Certainly, the rich theological contents of Colossians as well as its ethical teaching would be instructive to the Laodiceans. But it is quite possible that Paul is concerned about the potential threat "the philosophy" poses to the Laodicean church. The letter to the Colossians would thus serve both to alert the Laodicean believers to the nature of the threat and implicitly to enlist their support in encouraging and helping the Colossian church.

καὶ τὴν ἐκ Λαοδικείας ἵνα καὶ ὑμεῖς ἀναγνῶτε, "and that you also read the letter from Laodicea." Paul also wants the letter that he has written to the Laodicean church to be read by the believers at Colossae. Some older interpreters have wondered about the significance of Paul's use of the preposition ἐκ here. They have assumed that if he were to have written a letter to the Laodicean church, he would have used the phrase τὴν πρὸς Λαοδικέας or its equivalent. The ἐκ, they contend, indicates that the letter has originated from the church at Laodicea, and they assume that it was the Laodicean church that has written a letter to Paul.[115] But the best way to understand the sense of the preposition in this

112 BDAG, s.v. ἀναγιγνώσκω 1.b.: "read aloud for public hearing."

113 E. H. Riesenfeld, "παρά," *TDNT* 5:732.

114 BDF §392.1.e.

115 Calvin, 361, writes, "It has been wrongly supposed that the other epistle he mentions was written by Paul. They were quite wrong who thought Paul wrote to the Laodiceans. I have no doubt that it was an epistle sent to Paul." This interpretation was quite old. Chrysostom (Homily 12 on Col 4:12–13) reports that some understood it this way during his time ("some say that this is not Paul's to them, but theirs to Paul, for he said not that to the Laodiceans, but that written 'from Laodicea.'"). In the fifth century, Theodoret of Cyrus, 102, held this view.

context is to take it as Paul's reference to his own letter "that will be forwarded to you from Laodicea," or as the NASB translates, "for your part read my letter *that is coming from* Laodicea" (emphases original).[116]

This reference to a letter by Paul to the Laodicean church has occasioned widespread speculation throughout the history of interpretation regarding its identity and what has happened to it, since no genuine letter written by Paul to this church has ever been known (or even cited in early-church writings). It has also given rise to a pseudepigraphical document called "The Epistle to the Laodiceans" (*Epistula Pauli ad Laodicenses*), but all early and contemporary biblical scholarship regards it as spurious.[117] Jerome wrote in the early fifth century that "it is rejected by everyone."[118] Nevertheless, it was transmitted in some manuscripts of the Vulgate from the sixth to the fifteenth centuries. The epistle is twenty verses in length and extant only in Latin, but it was probably written in Greek sometime between the second and fourth centuries.[119] It represents a compilation of sayings from Paul's genuine letters (especially Philippians and Galatians) and contains no real or purported historical information about the state of the Laodicean church.[120] Among some of the other ideas about the identity of this letter is that it was a letter written by the Laodiceans to Paul (see above), a letter written by Paul from Laodicea, a letter written to the Laodiceans by Epaphras,[121] or that it was a letter written by Paul to the Laodiceans but is the canonical letter to Philemon[122] or even Hebrews.[123] Of course, all of these other ideas assume the authenticity of the letter to the Colossians. But if Colossians is a pseudepigraphon itself, all of this speculation is futile since there is another set of motivations at work. Thus, Lincoln contends that the writer of Colossians is drawing on "the practice of exchanging letters as part of the attempt to attain versimilitude."[124] But, as I have already argued, there are many good reasons for seeing Colossians as an authentic letter that make such putative attempts by the letter writer to disguise the pseudepigraphy as unnecessary.

A significant array of scholars have argued that the letter to the Laodiceans is actually the canonical letter to the Ephesians. This conclusion depends on the

116 Harris, 183.

117 For the text, see Schneemelcher, *New Testament Apocrypha*, 1:128–32, and Elliott, *Apocryphal New Testament*, 543–46.

118 Jerome, *Vir. ill.* 5.

119 Elliott, *Apocryphal New Testament*, 544.

120 See C. P. Anderson, "Laodiceans, Epistle to the," *ABD* 4:231–34.

121 Anderson, "Laodiceans, Epistle to the," *ABD* 4:232; idem, "Epistle from Laodicea?," 436–40.

122 Knox, *Philemon*, 69.

123 Anderson, "Hebrews," 258–66. He suggests that Epaphras was the author of the letter to the Hebrews, that this was the letter to the Laodiceans, and that Epaphras's close association with Paul explains how Hebrews became part of the Pauline corpus.

124 Lincoln, 668. Lindemann, 77, and in his essay, "Gemeinde von 'Kolossae,'" 111–34, has an elaborate theory of how the destruction of Colossae in the earthquake gave the pseudepigrapher an opportunity to write in the name of Paul, ostensibly to the church at Colossae, but actually directed to the church in Laodicea during the post-Pauline era.

assumption that Ephesians was an authentic letter by Paul and was intended as a circular letter, with Laodicea as one of its destinations. This suggestion was first made by Marcion in the second century but was subsequently taken up by others in the history of interpretation. Most notably, this opinion was advocated by J. B. Lightfoot in an extensive essay in his celebrated commentary on Colossians.[125] He was followed in this opinion by a handful of subsequent commentators.[126] But Ephesians was probably not a circular letter in the way these writers have conceived of it and was probably written to the various house churches in the large metropolitan city and its nearby environs.[127]

The most compelling option, however, is to see the letter to the Laodiceans as written by Paul to the church at Laodicea and that it is now lost. This is the consensus view among scholars.[128] It is somewhat surpising the letter was lost given the importance attached to it for the churches of the Lycus Valley, but it is not without precedent. Paul had written at least one other letter to the Corinthian church, which he alludes to as "the previous letter," that has also been lost (see 1 Cor 5:9; see also 2 Cor 2:3–4).

Paul's divine commission as apostle to the gentiles and his consequent authority among the early Christian communities, coupled with this instruction from the apostle to exchange his letters among the churches, no doubt served as a stimulus for the initial collections of the Pauline letter corpus.[129]

**17** καὶ εἴπατε Ἀρχίππῳ· βλέπε τὴν διακονίαν ἣν παρέλαβες ἐν κυρίῳ, ἵνα αὐτὴν πληροῖς, "and tell Archippus: 'give attention to the ministry that you received from the Lord that you fulfill it.'" In a rather unusual twist at the end of this letter, Paul solicits the support of the community to encourage Archippus to fulfill his ministry responsibilities among the Colossians. The second-person plural of εἴπατε makes it clear that Paul wants the entire community of believers to participate in this reaffirmation of Archippus and his calling. One wonders about the potential embarassment or shame that Archippus would feel because of this strategy if Archippus has been in some way derelict in his duty. But the intent of this may not be to shame Archippus as much as it was to build him up in his role in the eyes of the community. Apparently there is an important duty that Archippus needs to accomplish, both for the well-being of the community and possibly for Archippus's own conscience before the Lord.

This is probably the same Archippus named in Phlm 2 as one of the recipients of that letter. Some interpreters have suggested that he is the son of

125 Lightfoot, 274–300.

126 E.g., Abbott, 306; Peake, 547; Williams, 168.

127 See Arnold, *Ephesians*, 23–29, 41–46.

128 See, e.g., Huttner, *Early Christianity in the Lycus Valley*, 93; Pao, 320–21; Moo, 351; MacDonald, 183; Schweizer, 242; C. Moule, 138; Scott, 92–93; Eadie, 291–94; Ellicott, 207; Meyer, 389.

129 Beale, 361, also observes, "That the Colossians were *commanded* by Paul to read the letter from the Laodiceans and vice versa suggests that Paul believed his letters, rather than having only passing significance, had wider authority and relevance than merely for the church directly addressed."

Philemon and Apphia.[130] Although this is a possibility, it cannot be determined with any certainty. The name Archippus is widely attested in the inscriptions in Asia Minor, including the cities of Halicarnassus, Didyma, Erythrai, Miletus, Priene, and Smyrna, but not in the Lycus Valley. Paul says two things about him in Philemon that provide additional insight. First, he says that he hosts a church in his house (Phlm 2). This establishes Archippus as one of the wealthier members of the community if he has a home of sufficient size to host a church. Second, Paul calls him a συστρατιώτης, "fellow soldier" (Phlm 2). This has led some to speculate that he was formerly one of Paul's ministry associates.[131] But this expression could simply mean that he is a fellow soldier in the cause of the gospel while living and serving in Colossae. The only other person Paul gives this title to is Epaphroditus, who was in fact a coworker of Paul's in Rome, whom he commends for nearly dying "for the work of Christ" (Phil 2:25–30).

Paul wants Archippus to "direct his attention"[132] (βλέπε) to the ministry that the Lord has given to him. He has used the plural of this verb many times in his letters to encourage his readers to give careful attention to something (e.g., 2 Cor 10:7) or, with the negative (μή), to warn readers of a threat (e.g., Col 2:8; see also Phil 3:2–3).

The precise nature of "the ministry" (ἡ διακονία) that Archippus has received is difficult to determine, and we can only speculate. Paul has used the noun διάκονος, "minister," three times earlier in the letter to characterize the work of Epaphras (1:7), Tychicus (4:7), and himself (1:25; see also Eph 3:7). In all three instances, it has to do with the work of the gospel. Although the term διακονία could be used for a specific form of service, such as the relief collection that Paul took for the impoverished Judean Christians (2 Cor 9:12), here it it likely used for serving as a leader in the Colossian church. It would be anachronistic, however, to assume a threefold form of ministry (ἐπίσκοποι, πρεσβύτεροι, διάκανοι) as in the Ignatian letters and the later church (e.g., Ign. *Phld.* 1.1; 10.2; *Trall.* 3.1; *Magn.* 2.1; 6.1; *Pol.* 6.1). It may be that he is serving in a leadership role similar to the διακόνοι in Philippi (Phil 1:1). Here it is probably to be understood more in the sense of the same kind of leadership that Epaphras exhibited from whom the Colossians learned the gospel (1:7). This would involve not only evangelism but facilitating their growth through teaching and helping them to become grounded in the full set of implications of the word of God for their lives. As Eph 4:12 puts it, "the work of service" (ἔργον διακονίας) is directed at the building up of the body of Christ.

As a ministry he "received from the Lord" (παρέλαβες ἐν κυρίῳ), Lightfoot supposes that Archippus "received the charge immediately from St. Paul,"[133]

130 E.g., Dunn, 288; Scott, 93; Lightfoot, 308.

131 Lightfoot, 333, suggests that Archippus was Paul's coworker during his ministry at Ephesus.

132 See BDAG, s.v. βλέπω 6.

133 Lightfoot, 245.

although it was ultimately from Christ himself. Yet if it were a mediated charge following a practice like that mentioned in the Pastoral Epistles ("Do not neglect the gift you have, which was given you by prophecy when the council of elders laid their hands on you," 1 Tim 4:14 ESV; see also 2 Tim 1:6), it is more likely to have come from either Epaphras or a group of leaders in Colossae, since Paul had never visited the Lycus Valley. The ἐν κυρίῳ should be taken as an expression of agency, "the ministry you received from the Lord."[134] This is the interpretation that corresponds best with the verb. Paul's ultimate aim is that Archippus would "fulfill" (ἵνα αὐτὴν πληροῖς) the ministry he has been given. Of course, it was Paul's own passion that he himself might fulfill (πληρῶσαι) the commission that he had been given by the Lord (Col 1:25).

Why would the apostle issue instructions like this at the conclusion of his letter? If we take the overall purpose of the letter into account, it would seem that Paul wants Archippus to exercise his rightful leadership role and stand up even more strongly against the ringleaders of "the philosophy." It could be that Archippus has for some reason been reticent to oppose them in the way that he should in order to protect the flock.[135] The opponents may have been intimidating with their rhetoric and strong, assertive judgments (note the nature of Paul's admonitions to the Colossians: "let no one judge you," 2:16; "let no one condemn you," 2:18; "Why do you comply with their dictates?," 2:20). It is also possible that Paul is authorizing Archippus in the eyes of the Colossian community to take a strong and active role against the influence of the advocates of "the philosophy" by instructing the church to encourage Archippus to fully exercise his leadership role. For anyone in the community who is tempted to follow an alternative group of leaders, they now have apostolic instruction to align themselves with the leadership that Archippus will provide.

This instruction, along with many of the other personal greetings and details in Col 4, is very difficult to explain on the assumption that this letter is pseudepigraphical. Dunn has sensed this, too, and has remarked, "The character of the request, coming just before the personally written final phrases, makes its invention by a pseudonymous author less plausible and strengthens the impression that Paul himself was standing directly behind the letter."[136]

**18** Ὁ ἀσπασμὸς τῇ ἐμῇ χειρὶ Παύλου. μνημονεύετέ μου τῶν δεσμῶν. ἡ χάρις μεθ' ὑμῶν, "this greeting is with my own hand—from Paul. Remember my chains. Grace be with you." Paul concludes the letter with his own handwritten greeting, a request of the Colossians, and a prayer for them.

The greeting that he includes here is identical to the greeting he uses

---

134 Campbell, *Union with Christ*, 153–54.

135 It is unlikely that Archippus had "become involved with the false teachers" and had left the community, as Murphy-O'Connor, *Paul*, 236–37, supposes. If this were the case, why does Paul not address the false teachers by name and ask the same of them? The wording of this text is more positive toward Archippus.

136 Dunn, 288.

at the conclusion of his first letter to the Corinthians (1 Cor 16:21; see also 2 Thess 3:17). The wording of the greeting suggests that he used an amanuensis in the drafting of the letter and that he physically writes these three lines. Weima notes, "In the vast majority of Greco-Roman letters that betray the presence of an autograph, the author writes all the subsequent material in the closing (i.e. greetings, farewell wish, postcript), giving the pen back to the secretary only to write the address on the outside of the letter."[137] It is likely that Paul used a secretary in the composition of all his letters.[138] Only in Romans is the amanuensis actually named: "I Tertius, who wrote this letter, greet you in the Lord" (Rom 16:22). We have no way of knowing who Paul was using in the drafting of Colossians. Paul's choice of the term ἀσπασμός is consistent with his frequent use of ἀσπάζομαι and ἀσπασμός in his letters for greetings.

The phrase τῇ ἐμῇ χειρί, "with my own hand," is an autograph formula in ancient letters (see 1 Cor 16:21; Gal 6:11; 2 Thess 3:17; Phlm 19).[139] Weima gives two examples of this in Greek letters: (1) "I have written these things to you in my own hand" (ταῦτά σοι γέγραφα τῇ ἐμῇ χειρί), and (2) "I wrote all in my own hand" (ὁλόγραφον χειρὶ ἐμῇ).[140] Some of Cicero's letters also contain this phrase, "in my own hand" (*mea manu*), which indicates the shift to his own autograph (*Att.* 8.1; 13.28).[141] This practice is well-illustrated with Paul's remarks near the end of Galatians: "see what large letters I use as I write to you with my own hand" (Gal 6:11 NIV). Nevertheless, this practice is not widely attested in ancient letters.

The genitive Παύλου, "from Paul," could best be taken as a genitive of source[142] and as an independent expression: "this greeting is with my own hand: '*from Paul.*'" This is preferable to understanding it as dependent on ἀσπασμός either as a possessive genitive ("the greeting of Paul")[143] or as a subjective genitive ("Paul greets you"),[144] because the genitive is too far separated from the noun it modifies.

For Paul, this practice not only provided a personal touch but likely also served to authenticate a letter as genuinely from him.[145] Second Thessalonians cautions the readers not "to be quickly shaken" by "a letter seeming to be from us" (2 Thess 2:2 ESV) and then concludes with a greeting identical to the greeting in Colossians (2 Thess 3:17).[146] There is no indication that the advocates

137 Weima, *Neglected Endings*, 122.

138 Richards, *Secretary*, 169–98.

139 Richards, *Secretary*, 173; Weima, *Neglected Endings*, 119.

140 Weima, *Neglected Endings*, 119.

141 Richards, *Secretary*, 173.

142 So also Campbell, 78.

143 Robertson, *Grammar*, 685, sees it as an instance of the possessive pronoun and the genitive used together (as in 1 Cor 16:18: τὸ ἐμὸν πνεῦμα καὶ τὸ ὑμῶν, "my spirit and your spirit"), with both having a possessive function.

144 Beale, 362–63n40; Harris, 184.

145 So also Beale, 362; Pao, 322; Moo, 353.

146 Weima, *1–2 Thessalonians*, 638, acknowledges the authenticating function of the autograph

of "the philosophy" were writing letters in the name of Paul in an attempt to persuade the Colossians to their point of view, but the autograph would help to preclude that from happening since some of his opponents were not above sending forged letters in his name.[147]

His plea to "remember my chains" (μνημονεύετέ μου τῶν δεσμῶν) is not a call to pity him in the discomfort of his Roman custody. Rather, it is a call for prayer. In his earlier letters, he has used the noun form of the verb (μνεία) a handful of times—always in the context of intercessory prayer. For instance, he assures the Romans that "without ceasing I remember you always in my prayers" (Rom 1:9; see also Phil 1:3; 1 Thess 1:2; 3:6; Eph 1:16; Phlm 4). He also uses the verb in the sense of "remembering [μνημονεύοντες] you (in prayer) before God" (1 Thess 1:3).

The δεσμόι were the "bonds" or "fetters"[148] he wore that prevented him from escaping from his Roman custody as he awaited trial. They were not a source of shame for Paul but a sign that he was suffering for the cause of the gospel. He has already told the Colossians that "I rejoice in my sufferings for your sake" (Col 1:24).

The final line of his letter to the Colossians is a prayer that God would bestow his grace upon them. This is a variation in form from the typical closing of a papyrus letter in Greco-Roman antiquity, which was ἔρρωσο (the perfect passive imperative of ῥώννυμι, usually translated "farewell" or "goodbye"; see its use in the conclusion of the letter to the gentiles reporting the findings of the Jerusalem Council; Acts 15:29).

Paul includes such a prayer for God's grace at the closing of all his letters (Rom 16:20; 1 Cor 16:23; 2 Cor 13:13; Gal 6:18; Phil 4:23; 1 Thess 5:28; Phlm 25; see also Eph 6:24; 2 Thess 3:18; 1 Tim 6:21; 2 Tim 4:22; Titus 3:15). He often uses the fuller expression—"the grace of the Lord Jesus be with you." "Grace" (χάρις) is at the heart of Paul's theology and is a term that encapsulates the incredible gift of salvation through the Lord Jesus Christ and expresses God's ongoing enabling and sustaining power for Christians through the Holy Spirit. This prayer wish for grace ties the conclusion of the letter to the beginning where Paul prays "grace to you and peace from God our Father" (1:2; see the commentary there for a full discussion of χάρις). The Colossians will need a regular infusion of God's grace to help them to discern and resist the influence of "the philosophy," to facilitate their eradication of vice and appropriation of Christian virtue, to live in accordance with their duties in the Christian household, and to grow to full maturity in the Lord Jesus Christ.

---

formula, but indicates that it can also accomplish a variety of additional purposes, such as "to make a letter legally binding, to give a letter a more personal touch" or "to ensure confidentiality." He also notes that it "enhances the letter's *authority*."

147 Richards, *Letter Writing*, 182.

148 BDAG, s.v. δεσμός 1.

## *Explanation*

This extensive concluding section of this letter provides rich insight into Paul's social network of ministry associates and how they served as an extension of Paul's own ministry. The passage begins with his mention of Tychicus, a fellow Asian believer to the Colossians, and how he has faithfully served Paul in his bonds. He will now serve as Paul's emissary to carry the letter to the Colossian believers and share with them all of the relevant news about Paul and the progress of the gospel in Rome.

Tychicus, however, will be accompanied by Onesimus—a slave from Colossae whom many in the community would undoubtedly know because of their relationship with Philemon. For Paul to call Onesimus a "faithful and beloved brother" implies an enormous backstory of redemption, a changed life, and growth into significant Christian service. The presence of Onesimus with Tychicus would have created quite a shock upon their arrival that would have aroused the curiosity of the Colossian community. No doubt the story of Onesimus's conversion and service to Paul and the gospel would have been a significant part of the news that they would share.

Paul extends greetings to the Colossians from three ethnic Jewish believers who also had been serving as his coworkers in Rome. Among these three was Mark, the cousin of Barnabas, and at one time the traveling companion of Paul on his first trip from Antioch to Cyprus and then on to Pamphylia, when Mark abruptly left (Acts 13:13–14). Paul had viewed this desertion unfavorably and subsequently did not want Mark as part of his team. This story may have circulated and would have likewise left the Colossians feeling indisposed for valuing Mark as a potential contributor to the ministry. Yet Paul here instructs the Colossians to welcome Mark fully on a trip that has been tentatively planned for him to come to Colossae. Once again, here is yet another story of reconciliation and the power of the living Christ to change a life. One wonders if part of Paul's strategy in sending Mark to Colossae is to help Philemon and his household overcome resentment and bitterness and to embrace Onesimus as a brother and as a useful servant of the Lord.

The additional greetings to the Colossian church come from three gentile ministry associates. One of these was Epaphras, their prominent leader who was the first to bring the gospel to the Lycus Valley and who helped to ground them in the faith. Paul wants them to know that Epaphras was still serving them—although separated from them by a great distance. Paul stresses how Epaphras is strenuously praying for them as though it were the toil of war, which it was because of the supernatural opposition they faced. Paul also expresses greetings from Luke, whom he terms "the beloved physician." Together with Mark, God would use these two individuals to write over half of the NT (assuming they are the authors of the Gospel of Mark, the Gospel of Luke, and the book of Acts).

Paul asks the Colossian believers to greet their fellow Christians in Laodicea and possibly also in Hierapolis. The latter can only be inferred if Nymphas and the church in his house are located in that city. There are a handful of reasons to conclude this, especially since Paul had just noted that Epaphras was passionately praying not only for the Colossians but also for believers in Laodicea *and Hierapolis*. These greetings would suggest that Paul assumes and perhaps is encouraging the ongoing intercity relationships of believers among these neighboring cities in the Lycus Valley. Many scholars have assumed that Nymphas/Nympha was a woman who hosted the church in her house. But the text-critical evidence for a masculine resumptive pronoun rests on a stronger basis than that for a feminine pronoun. The masculine name is also attested in the inscriptions of Asia Minor, whereas the feminine name is not.

The reference to "the church in his house" reminds us of the house-church context of early Christianity. There were no dedicated church facilities until the time of Constantine. The size of the house church would obviously have depended on the capacity of the respective houses where the church would meet. The "house" may have been a third-story apartment in an *insula* (especially in urban settings), but in a place like Colossae (or Laodicea or Hierapolis), it could have been a villa or a countryside dwelling.

Paul then instructs the Colossians to arrange for an exchange of letters with the Laodicean church, to whom he has apparently written a separate letter. Although there is an extant "Epistle to the Laodiceans," it is universally regarded as apocryphal and was rejected early by the church. This means that the letter Paul wrote to the Laodiceans has been lost. It must have been lost very early in the collection and transmission process since we do not have any citations of the letter by early Christian leaders and writers. It is unlikely that this lost letter is what we know today as the letter to the Ephesians. It would be very instructive to know the contents of this now lost letter and to see how Paul describes the nature of the threat that "the philosophy" presented to the Laodicean church.

Before he concludes the letter, Paul reaffirms Archippus and the leadership role he is to play in the Colossian church. More precisely, he instructs the Colossian Christians to tell Archippus to fulfill his role of service to the community. The most natural explanation for this kind of instruction is that Paul is elevating the importance of Archippus and his leadership in the eyes of all within the community. Paul may be doing this in light of the challenges that "the philosophy" is presenting to the leadership of the Colossian church.

The letter closes with a prayer for God's grace to be with them. Prayer has been a significant theme in this concluding section of the letter—with Paul recounting the way Epaphras is praying for them (4:12–13), with his own request for prayer from them (4:18b), and now with his prayer for grace (4:18c). Just as Paul began this letter with a prayer for grace (1:2), he now concludes with an appeal to God for his grace (4:18c).

# Indices

# Scripture and Other Ancient Literature Index

## *Old Testament*

## Proverbs

## *New Testament*

**Romans**

**1 Corinthians**

**2 Corinthians**

### Galatians



### Ephesians

### Philippians

**Colossians**

## 1 Thessalonians



## 2 Thessalonians



## 1 Timothy

## *Old Testament Apocrypha / Deuterocanonical Works*

### 1 Esdras



### 1 Maccabees



### 2 Maccabees



### Epistle of Jeremiah



### Judith



### Sirach



### Tobit



### Wisdom of Solomon



## *Old Testament Pseudepigrapha*

### 2 Baruch



### 3 Baruch



### 1 Enoch

## Dead Sea Scrolls



## Philo

## *Josephus*



## *Mishnah, Talmud, and Related Literature*



## *Apostolic Fathers*

## *Classical and Ancient Christian Writings*

## *Inscriptions and Papyri*

# Subject Index

# Author Index